LIQUIDITY RATIOS			
Current ratio	$\frac{\text{Current Assets}}{\text{Current Liabilities}}$	Measures short-term debt-paying ability	Chapter 4, LO5
Quick ratio	$\frac{\text{Cash + Marketable Securities + Receivables}}{\text{Current Liabilities}}$	Measures short-term debt-paying ability	Chapter 14, LO3
Receivable turnover	$\frac{\text{Net Sales}}{\text{Average Accounts Receivable}}$	Average number of times receivables are turned into cash during an accounting period	Chapter 7, LO1
Days' sales uncollected	$\frac{\text{Days in Year}}{\text{Receivable Turnover}}$	Average number of days a company must wait to receive payment for credit sales or to collect accounts receivable	Chapter 7, LO 1
Inventory turnover	$\frac{\text{Costs of Goods Sold}}{\text{Average Inventory}}$	Number of times a company's average inventory is sold during an accounting period	Chapter 6, LO1
Days' inventory on hand	$\frac{\text{Days in Year}}{\text{Inventory Turnover}}$	Average number of days taken to sell inventory on hand	Chapter 6, LO1
Payables turnover	$\frac{\text{Costs of Goods Sold +/−Change in Inventory}}{\text{Average Accounts Payable}}$	Average number of times a company pays its accounts payable in an accounting period	Chapter 8, LO1
Days' payable	$\frac{\text{Days in Year}}{\text{Payables Turnover}}$	Average number of days a company takes to pay accounts payable	Chapter 8, LO1
PROFITABILITY RATIOS			
Profit margin	$\frac{\text{Net Income}}{\text{Net Sales}}$	Percentage of each sales dollar that contributes to net income	Chapter 4, LO5
Asset turnover	$\frac{\text{Net Sales}}{\text{Average Total Assets}}$	How efficiently assets are used to produce sales	Chapter 4, LO5
Return on assets	$\frac{\text{Net Income}}{\text{Average Total Assets}}$	How efficiently a company uses its assets to produce income, or the amount earned on each dollar of assets invested	Chapter 4, LO5
Return on equity	$\frac{\text{Net Income}}{\text{Average Stockholders' Equity}}$	Relates the amount earned by a business to each dollar stockholders invested in the business	Chapter 4, LO5
LONG-TERM SOLVENCY RATIOS			
Debt to equity ratio	$\frac{\text{Total Liabilities}}{\text{Stockholders' Equity}}$	Proportion of a company's assets financed by creditors and the proportion financed by stockholders	Chapter 4, LO5
Interest coverage ratio	$\frac{\text{Income Before Income Taxes + Interest Expense}}{\text{Interest Expense}}$	Degree of protection a company has from default on interest payments	Chapter 10, LO1
CASH FLOW ADEQUACY RATIOS			
Cash flow yield	$\frac{\text{Net Cash Flows from Operating Activities}}{\text{Net Income}}$	Measures a company's ability to generate operating cash flows in relation to net income	Chapter 13, LO2
Cash flows to sales	$\frac{\text{Net Cash Flows from Operating Activities}}{\text{Net Sales}}$	Ratio of net cash flows from operating activities to sales	Chapter 13, LO2
Cash flows to assets	$\frac{\text{Net Cash Flows from Operating Activities}}{\text{Average Total Assets}}$	Measures the ability of assets to generate operating cash flows	Chapter 13, LO2
Free cash flow	Net Cash Flows from Operating Activities − Dividends − Purchases of Plant Assets + Sales of Plant Assets	Measures the amount of cash that remains after deducting the funds a company must commit to continue operating at its planned level	Chapter 9, LO1
MARKET STRENGTH RATIOS			
Price/earnings ratio	$\frac{\text{Market Price per Share}}{\text{Earnings per Share}}$	Measures investors' confidence in a company's future; a means of comparing stock values	Chapter 11, LO1
Dividends yield	$\frac{\text{Dividends per Share}}{\text{Market Price per Share}}$	Measures a stock's current return to an investor or stockholder	Chapter 11, LO1

Financial Accounting

TENTH EDITION

Belverd E. Needles, Jr., Ph.D., C.P.A., C.M.A.
DePaul University

Marian Powers, Ph.D.
Northwestern University

Australia • Brazil • Japan • Korea • Mexico • Singapore • Spain • United Kingdom • United States

Financial Accounting: Tenth Edition
Belverd E. Needles, Jr. and Marian Powers

VP/Editorial Director: Jack W. Calhoun
Editor in Chief: Rob Dewey
Executive Editor: Sharon Oblinger
Sr. Developmental Editor: Joanne Dauksewicz
Marketing Manager: Steve Joos
Content Project Manager: Diane Bowdler
Media Editor: Bryan England
Editorial Assistant: Heather McAuliffe
Composition Buyer: Chuck Dutton
Senior Frontlist Buyer: Doug Wilke
Production: Margaret M. Kearney
Compositor: Black Dot Group
Art Director: Jill Haber
Internal Designer: Nesbitt Graphics
Cover Designer: Harold Burch
Cover Image: Richard Edelman
Senior Photo Editor: Jennifer Meyer Dare

CVS Annual Report reprinted courtesy of CVS Caremark Corporation.

Portions of Southwest Airlines Annual Report courtesy of Southwest Airlines Co.

Company Logo Credits: page 7, Reprinted by permission of CVS; page 115, Reprinted by permission of Boeing; page 166, Reproduced by permission of Netflix, Inc., Copyright © 2008 Netflix, Inc. All rights reserved; (*company logo credits continue on page xxiv*)

Photo Credits: page 3, Scott Olson/Getty Images; page 8, AP Images/Kenneth Lambert; page 16, © Jim West/The Image Works; page 20, Reprinted by permission of CVS; page 29, © Frank Trapper/Corbis; (*photo credits continue on page xxiv*)

Library of Congress Control Number: 2008934899

Student Edition ISBN 13: 978-0-547-19328-1
Student Edition ISBN 10: 0-547-19328-9
Instructor's Edition ISBN 13: 978-0-324-83004-0
Instructor's Edition ISBN 10: 0-324-83004-1

South-Western Cengage Learning
5191 Natorp Boulevard
Mason, OH 45040
USA

Cengage Learning is a leading provider of customized learning solutions with office locations around the globe, including Singapore, the United Kingdom, Australia, Mexico, Brazil, and Japan. Locate your local office at:
international.cengage.com/region

Cengage Learning products are represented in Canada by Nelson Education, Ltd.

For your course and learning solutions, visit **academic.cengage.com**.

Purchase any of our products at your local college store or at our preferred online store **www.ichapters.com**.

Printed in the United States of America
1 2 3 4 5 6 7 11 10 09 08

BRIEF CONTENTS

To Annabelle, Abigail, Autumn, Jeffrey, and Tyler Needles

In memory of Mr. and Mrs. Belverd E. Needles, Sr., and Mr. and Mrs. Benjamin E. Needles

To Mr. and Mrs. Thomas R. Powers

CONTENTS

CHAPTER 9 Long-Term Assets 464

CHAPTER 10 Long-Term Liabilities 512

CHAPTER 11 Contributed Capital 564

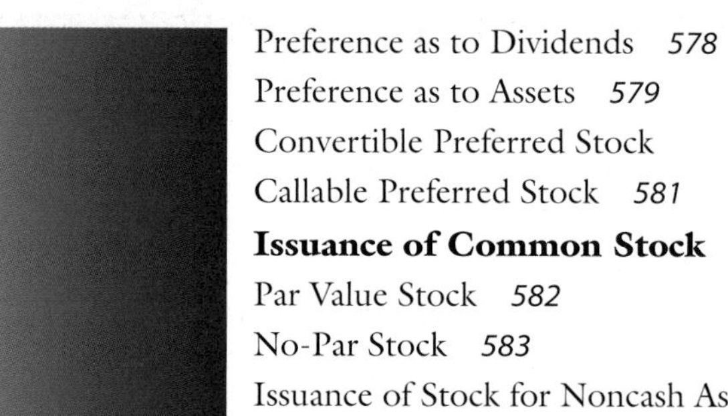

PREFACE

Financial Accounting 10e continues a distinguished tradition of combining academic needs with professional thought to prepare students for a dynamic business world. Through enhanced pedagogy, up-to-date coverage, and integration of real-world data, *Financial Accounting* 10e develops the critical-thinking and decision-making skills that students need to succeed.

This new edition is designed to meet the needs of today's students. Many text and multimedia features are available to help them study more effectively and improve their grades on assignments and tests.

Enhanced Pedagogy for Greater Understanding

Needles/Powers is the most readable comprehensive text on the market. Even poor readers can and do learn from the text. Most importantly, Needles/Powers allows the instructor flexibility in teaching style and material emphasis. Needles works well whether you teach from a preparer or user approach.

—Linda K. Whitten, Sykline College

The fresh, streamlined design of *Financial Accounting* 10e features captioned photos, new line art, concise exhibits, journal entries and T accounts highlighted by screens, and a contemporary color palette that visually unifies the text's elements. These features capture students' interest and foster their understanding. The content has been revised and refocused to make the text accessible to a broad range of interests and levels of reading ability. Detailed information has been made more concise by shortening paragraphs and presenting material in numbered and bulleted lists.

Other important pedagogical features include the following:

- **Focus on Financial Statements** This feature visually reinforces the connection between the financial statements and each chapter's topics. Found at the beginning of each chapter, this quick reference indicates which financial statements are particularly important to the chapter.
- **Decision Points** Each chapter opening includes a Decision Point that briefly introduces a well-known company and poses questions about how the company uses accounting information to make decisions. The company featured in the Decision Point is referenced throughout the chapter and is revisited in **A Look Back At,** a feature at the end of the main text of the chapter that shows how the questions posed in the Decision Point can now be answered. This feature prompts students to hone their critical-thinking skills by examin-

DECISION POINT ▶ A USER'S FOCUS

Netflix, Inc.

Netflix is the world's largest online entertainment subscription service. For a monthly fee, its subscribers have access to more than 90,000 DVD titles, which are shipped free of charge; with certain plans, they also have access to more than 5,000 movies online. At the end of any accounting period, Netflix has many transactions that will affect future periods.[1] Two examples appear in the Financial High-lights below: *prepaid expenses*, which, though paid in the period just ended, will benefit future periods and are therefore recorded as assets; and *accrued expenses*, which the company has incurred but will not pay until a future period. If prepaid and accrued expenses are not accounted for properly at the end of a period, Netflix's income will be misstated. Similar misstatements can occur when a company has received revenue that it has not yet earned or has earned revenue but not yet received it. If misstatements are made, investors will be misled about the company's financial performance.

- What assumptions must Netflix make to account for transactions that span accounting periods?
- How does Netflix assign its revenues and expenses to the proper accounting period so that net income is properly measured?
- Why are the adjustments that these transactions require important to Netflix's financial performance?

A LOOK BACK AT ▶ Netflix, Inc.

In the Decision Point at the beginning of the chapter, we noted that **Netflix** has many transactions that span accounting periods. We asked these questions:

- **What assumptions must Netflix make to account for transactions that span accounting periods?**
- **How does Netflix assign its revenues and expenses to the proper accounting period so that net income is properly measured?**
- **Why are the adjustments that these transactions require important to Netflix's financial performance?**

Two of the assumptions Netflix must make are that it will continue as a going concern for an indefinite time (the continuity assumption) and that it can make useful estimates of its income in terms of accounting periods (the periodicity assumption). These assumptions enable the company to apply the matching rule—that is, revenues are assigned to the accounting period in which goods are sold or services are performed, and expenses are assigned to the accounting period in which they are used to produce revenue.

As you have learned in this chapter, adjusting entries for deferred and accrued expenses and for deferred and accrued revenues have an impact on a company's earnings. By paying close attention to the profit margin ratio, one can assess how well a company is controlling its expenses in relation to its revenues. The **profit margin** shows the percentage of each revenue, or sales dollar, that results in net income. Using data from Netflix's annual report, we can calculate Netflix's profit margin for two successive years as follows (dollars are in thousands):

ing the impact that the concepts presented in the chapter have on the focus company.

- **Learning Objectives** Clearly presented throughout the text and in the end-of-chapter assignments, learning objectives allow instructors to focus on the skills most important to them and their students. Refined over many editions, the learning objectives provide students with a framework of course concepts.

- **Stop, Review, and Apply** These features, which appear at the end of each main section, present questions related to the key concepts discussed in the section; answers to the questions follow the appendixes. Many of the Stop, Review, and Apply boxes also include brief exercises and their solutions.

STOP ▶ REVIEW ▶ APPLY

LO5-1 **What are assets?**

LO5-2 **How are liabilities and stockholders' equity similar, and how do they differ?**

LO5-3 **What three elements affect retained earnings, and what is the effect of each?**

LO5-4 **Give an example of a single transaction that causes both an increase and decrease in assets.**

The Accounting Equation and Net Income Johnson Company had assets of $140,000 and liabilities of $60,000 at the beginning of the year, and assets of $200,000 and liabilities of $70,000 at the end of the year. During the year, $20,000 was invested in the business, and dividends of $24,000 were paid. What amount of net income did the company earn during the year?

Beginning of the year				
Assets	=	Liabilities	+	Stockholders' Equity
$140,000	=	$60,000	+	**$ 80,000**
During year				
		Investment	+	20,000
		Dividends	−	24,000
		Net income		?
End of year				
$200,000	=	$70,000	+	**$130,000**

SOLUTION

Net income = $54,000

Start by finding the stockholders' equity at the beginning of the year. (Check: $140,000 − $60,000 = $80,000)

Then find the stockholders' equity at the end of the year. (Check: $200,000 − $70,000 = $130,000)

Then determine net income by calculating how the transactions during the year led to the stockholders' equity amount at the end of the year. (Check: $80,000 + $20,000 − $24,000 + $54,000 = $130,000)

- **Focus on Business Practice** Updated, redesigned boxes illustrate accounting concepts and practices in the context of the real business world.

FOCUS ON BUSINESS PRACTICE IFRS

How Will Convergence of U.S. GAAP with IFRS Affect Accounting Conventions?

The FASB and the IASB are working toward converging U.S. generally accepted accounting principles (GAAP) with international financial reporting standards (IFRS). Their goal is "to increase the international comparability and the quality of standards used in the United States [which] is consistent with the FASB's obligation to its domestic constituents, who benefit from comparability across national borders."[8] In addition to the comparability convention being affected, other accounting conventions will also be affected by the adoption of IFRS. For instance, conservatism, which has been the bedrock of accounting practice for many decades, would no longer be part of the conceptual framework. The practice of writing up the value of a nonfinancial asset, such as inventory or equipment, that has increased in fair value and recording it as income under IFRS would be considered a violation of the conservatism convention under U.S. GAAP. Such changes will influence the way accountants in the United States analyze financial statements.

The authors have accomplished their goals, the most significant area being to update the information (facts and figures) presented. I would categorize the 10th edition as user-based. There is a strong emphasis on analysis and less on preparation. I am currently using the Needles text and have no plans to change.

—Susan Koepke, Illinois Valley Community College

- **Real-world examples** To illustrate how accounting concepts relate to real-world decision making, the text uses almost 200 publicly held companies, as well as governmental and not-for-profit organizations, as examples. The names of actual companies are highlighted throughout the text and appear in an index at the end of the book.
- **Up-to-date coverage** This edition covers new developments in fair value accounting and international financial reporting standards (IFRS) at appropriate points. IRFS standards are integrated where applicable and are denoted with an IFRS icon.

The Office of the Chief Accountant of the SEC has issued guidance on how to apply fair value accounting.[15] For instance, it says that management's internal assumptions about expected cash flows may be used to measure fair value and that market quotes may be used when they are from an orderly, active market as opposed to a distressed, inactive market. . . .

- **Icons** Positioned in the margins, icons draw students' attention to discussions of important topics and to the usefulness of general ledger software:

  - ♦ The cash flow icon highlights discussions of profitability and liquidity.
  - ♦ The key ration icon highlights discussions of the ratios that are used to measure a company's performance.
  - ♦ The IFRS icon highlights discussions of international financial reporting standards.
  - ♦ The KA icon indicates problems in the end-of-chapter assignments that can be solved using Klooster & Allen's General Ledger Software.
- **Key Terms** Key terms, including key ratios, are highlighted throughout the text and are listed with their definitions in the end-of-chapter review.
- **Study Notes** Study Notes highlight important topics and provide tips on how to avoid common mistakes.

Study Note

A chart of accounts is a table of contents for the ledger. Typically, it lists accounts in the order in which they appear in the ledger, which is usually the order in which they appear on the financial statements. The numbering scheme allows for some flexibility.

- **Accounting equations** Positioned in the margins next to important journal entries, accounting equations reinforce the impact of a transaction on the financial statements.
- **Annual reports** The Supplement to Chapter 1, "How to Read an Annual Report," presents the annual report of CVS Caremark Corporation and the

Comparison Case: CVS Versus Southwest

Financial Analysis

LO5 

C 7. Compare the financial performance of **CVS** and **Southwest Airlines Co.** on the basis of liquidity and profitability for 2007 and 2006. Use the following ratios: working capital, current ratio, debt to equity ratio, profit margin, asset turnover, return on assets, and return on equity. In 2005, total assets and total stockholders' equity for CVS were $15,246.6 million and $8,331.2 million, respectively. Southwest's total assets were $14,003 million, and total stockholders' equity was $6,675 million in 2005. Comment on the relative performance of the two companies. In general, how does Southwest's performance compare to CVS's with respect to liquidity and profitability? What distinguishes Southwest's profitability performance from that of CVS?

financial statements of Southwest Airlines. The assignments at the end of each chapter include a comparison case that refers to the CVS annual report and that requires students to apply the concepts they have learned in the chapter. The Supplement to Chapter 4, "The Annual Report Project," presents a term project devoted to analyzing an annual report. It can be used with the annual report of any company.

Ethical Financial Reporting

Students need to know more about what constitutes ethical financial reporting and good corporate governance. This need has been addressed in a number of ways in this new edition:

- The preview at the start of each chapter points out ethical and governance issues related to the chapter topic.
- Provisions of the Sarbanes-Oxley Act of 2002 are covered in Chapter 1, and their importance is stressed at appropriate points throughout the text.
- In the end-of-chapter material, short cases based on real companies require students to address an ethical dilemma directly related to the chapter content.

Practice, Reinforcement, Mastery

Trusted end-of-chapter exercises, problems, and cases have been updated with current data wherever applicable. "User Insight" requirements of problems develop students' abilities to make sound business decisions based on financial information, and the cases provide many opportunities to engage in making real-world business decisions, solving ethical dilemmas, and applying Excel.

- The end-of-chapter assignments are organized into two main sections;
  - Building Your Basic Knowledge and Skills
  - Enhancing your Knowledge, Skills, and Critical Thinking
- The first two exercises in each chapter contain three or four discussion questions that are useful in generating class discussion about the user aspects of the chapter topics.
- More matching exercises and problems are included than in previous editions.
- Problems have been carefully scrutinized to reduce the number of transactions involved and the time it takes to work the problem.
- Every problem includes one or more User Insight questions.

I would strongly urge [our academic coordinator] to look at this book as having changed significantly and positively since the last time he probably looked at it. I would also suggest it to colleagues at other schools, where the course was appropriate, if they asked for ideas.

—Patricia Doherty, Boston University

- The rich assortment of cases in the Enhancing Your Knowledge, Skills, and Critical Thinking section are grouped as follows:
  - Conceptual Understanding Cases
  - Interpreting Financial Reports
  - Decision Analysis Using Excel
  - Annual Report Case: CVS Caremark Corporation
  - Comparison Case: CVS Versus Southwest Airlines or Walgreens
  - Ethical Dilemma Case
  - Internet Case
  - Group Activity Case
  - Business Communication Case

Chapter-Specific Changes

The following chapter-specific changes have been made in this edition of *Financial Accounting:*

Chapter 1: Uses of Accounting Information and the Financial Statements

- Updated Decision Point on CVS Caremark
- New Annual Reports from 2007 for both CVS and Southwest Airlines
- Revised Focus on Business Practice feature
- Expanded coverage of and revised discussion of performance measures and financial analysis and of how performance measures relate to two major business goals
- Expanded, more detailed coverage on the statement of cash flows relating to business activities and business goals
- IASB now included as a standard setter along with FASB
- Revised to reflect SEC decision to let foreign companies registered in the United States use international financial reporting standards (IFRS)
- Updated discussion of PCAOB
- Table 1, Exchange Rates, replaced with updated information from 2008
- Detailed financial statements rearranged for increased visual clarity

Chapter 2: Analyzing Business Transactions

- Updated Decision Point on the Boeing Company
- New example of recognition violation
- New Focus on Business Practice on the challenge of fair value accounting in an international marketplace
- Cash flow discussion and figure edited for clearer delineation of the sequence of transactions
- Valuation section revised to address fair value and IFRS

Chapter 3: Measuring Business Income

- New Decision Point on Netflix
- Updated example of earnings management (Dell)
- New Focus on Business Practice on revenue recognition principles and rules
- Clarified and simplified coverage of fees receivable

Chapter 4: Financial Reporting and Analysis

- Updated Decision Point on Dell

- Complete revision of learning Objective 1 to reflect proposed changes in the conceptual framework as agreed to by the FASB and IASB
- Coverage of qualitative characteristics revised for clarity and length
- New Focus on Business Practice on convergence of U.S. and international standards and their effect on accounting conventions
- New Focus on Business Practice on how convergence of IAS and IFRS can make financial analysis more difficult
- New Focus on Business Practice on international trends
- New Focus on Business Practice on the use of ratios in determining executive compensation

Chapter 5: The Operating Cycle and Merchandising Operations

- Updated Decision Point on Costco Wholesale Corporation
- Coverage of the operating cycle revised for greater clarity
- Journal entries for merchandising accounting reintroduced into body of the chapter
- New Focus on Business Practice on the Sarbanes-Oxley Act and fraud
- New Focus on Business Practice on the increased use of credit and debit cards
- Clearer differentiation between the cost of goods available for sale and the cost of goods sold
- Expanded coverage of an internal control plan, including key terms

Chapter 6: Inventories

- New Decision Point on Toyota Motor Corporation
- New Focus on Business Practice on market and fair value
- New Focus on Business Practice on LIFO

Chapter 7: Cash and Receivables

- Updated Decision Point on Nike, Inc.
- New Focus on Business Practice on subprime loans
- New Focus on Business Practice on cash collections

Chapter 8: Current Liabilities and the Time Value of Money

- New Decision Point on Microsoft and new in-chapter examples
- Length reduced to allow greater emphasis on necessary content
- Coverage changed to include the addition of fair value and the removal of future value calculations

Chapter 9: Long-Term Assets

- Updated Decision Point on Apple Computer, Inc.
- Coverage of intangibles revised and updated
- Coverage on tax laws revised to address the Economic Stimulus Act of 2008
- Revised Focus on Business Practice on customer lists

Chapter 10: Long-Term Liabilities

- Updated Decision Point on McDonald's Corporation
- New Focus on Business Practice on postretirement liabilities
- Added coverage on leases, debt, and financial risk

Chapter 11: Contributed Capital

- Updated Decision Point on Google, Inc.
- Revised Focus on Business Practice on stock options and politics
- Revised Focus on Business Practice on share buybacks

Chapter 12: The Corporate Income Statement and the Statement of Stockholders' Equity

- Updated Decision Point on Motorola, Inc.
- Revised Focus on Business Practice on evaluating company performance
- Revised Focus on Business Practice on pro-forma earnings
- Revised coverage on nonoperating items
- Reduction of chapter length to increase focus on essential content

Chapter 13: The Statement of Cash Flows

- Revised Decision Point on Amazon.com, which has been moved to this chapter
- Revised Focus on Business Practice on cash flows
- New Focus on Business Practice on the IASB and the direct method of reporting

Chapter 14: Financial Performance Measurement

- Revised Decision point on Starbucks Corporation
- Revised Focus on Business Practice on pro-forma reporting
- Revised Focus on Business Practice on performance measurement

Chapter 15: Investments

- Updated Decision Point on eBay, Inc.
- Expanded coverage of fair value
- New Focus on Business Practice on accounting and the subprime mortgage collapse

Online Solutions for Every Learning Style

South-Western, a division of Cengage Learning, offers a vast array of online solutions to suit your course and your students' learning styles. Choose the product that best meets your classroom needs and course goals. Please check with your Cengage representative for more details or for ordering information.

CengageNOW *Express*™

CengageNOW *Express*™ for Needles/Powers *Financial Accounting* focuses on the textbook homework that is central to success in accounting. This online tool delivers better student outcomes—NOW!—by providing the following:

- **Straightforward assignment creation** Select required exercises and problems, and CengageNOW *Express* automatically applies faculty-approved, Accounting Homework Options.
- **Automatic grading and tracking of student progress** CengageNOW *Express* grades and captures students' scores and makes it easy to monitor their progress. Export the grade book to Excel for easy data management.
- **Instant feedback for students** Students stay on track with instructor-written hints and immediate feedback with every assignment. Links to the

e-book, animated exercise demonstrations, and Excel spreadsheets from specific assignments are ideal for student review.

CengageNOW

CengageNOW for Needles/Powers *Financial Accounting* 10e is a powerful and fully integrated online teaching and learning system that provides you with flexibility and control. This complete digital solution offers a comprehensive set of digital tools to power your course. CengageNOW offers the following:

- Homework, including algorithmic variations
- Integrated e-book
- Personalized study plans, which include a variety of multimedia assets (from exercise demonstrations to video to iPod content) for students as they master the chapter materials
- Assessment options, including the full test bank and algorithmic variations
- Reporting capability based on AACSB, AICPA, and IMA competencies and standards
- Course Management tools, including grade book
- WebCT and Blackboard Integration

WebTutor™

WebTutor™ is available packaged with Needles/Powers *Financial Accounting* 10e or for individual student purchase. Jumpstart your course and customize rich, text-specific content with your Course Management System.

- **Jumpstart** Simply load a WebTutor cartridge into your Course Management System.
- **Customize content** Easily blend, add, edit, reorganize, or delete content. Content includes media assets, quizzing, test bank, weblinks, discussion topics, interactive games and exercises, and more.

Visit *academic.cengage.com* for more information.

Teaching Tools for Instructors

Solutions Manual: The Solutions Manual contains answers to all exercises, problems, and activities that appear in the text. As always, the solutions are author-written and verified multiple times for numerical accuracy and consistency with the core text.

Exam*View*® Pro Testing software: This intuitive software allows you to easily customize exams, practice tests, and tutorials and deliver them over a network, on the Internet, or in printed form. In addition, Exam*View* comes with searching capabilities that make sorting the wealth of questions from the printed test bank easy. The software and files are found on the IRCD.

Lecture PowerPoint: Instructors will have access to PowerPoint slides online and on the IRCD. These slides are conveniently designed around learning objectives for partial chapter teaching and include art for dynamic presentations. There are also lecture outline slides for each chapter for those instructors who prefer them.

Instructor's Companion Website: The instructor website contains a variety of resources for instructors, including the Instructor's Resource Manual (which has

Chapter Planning Matrices, Chapter Resource Materials and Outlines, Chapter Reviews, Difficulty and Time Charts, etc.), PowerPoint Slides, monthly updates of accounting news from newspapers and journals, sample syllabi, and the Accounting Instructors Report newsletter that explores a wide range of contemporary teaching issues.

Klooster & Allen's General Ledger Software: Prepared by Dale Klooster and Warren Allen, this best-selling, educational, general ledger package introduces students to the world of computerized accounting through a more intuitive, user-friendly system than the commercial software they'll use in the future. In addition, students have access to general ledger files with information based on problems from the textbook and practice sets. This context allows them to see the difference between manual and computerized accounting systems firsthand, while alleviating the stress of an empty screen. Also, the program is enhanced with a problem checker that enables students to determine if their entries are correct and emulates commercial general ledger packages more closely than other educational packages. Problems that can be used with Klooster/Allen are highlighted by an icon. The benefits of using Klooster/Allen are that:

- Errors are more easily corrected than in commercial software.
- After the course ends, students are prepared to use a variety of commercial products.
- Inspector is found on the IRCD, and allows instructors to grade students' work completed in Klooster/Allen's General Ledger software.

Klooster & Allen's General Ledger Software, Network Version: A free Network Version is available to schools whose students purchase Klooster/Allen's General Ledger Software.

Instant Access Code CengageNOW™ *Express*: CengageNOW™ *Express* is an online homework solution in accounting that delivers better student outcomes—NOW! CengageNOW™ *Express* encourages practice with the textbook homework that is central to success in accounting with Author-Written Homework from the Textbook, Automatic Grading and Tracking Student Progress, and Course Management Tools, including Gradebook.

Printed Access Code CengageNOW™ *Express*: CengageNOW™ *Express* is an online homework solution in accounting that delivers better student outcomes—NOW! CengageNOW™ *Express* encourages practice with the textbook homework that is central to success in accounting with Author-Written Homework from the Textbook, Automatic Grading and Tracking Student Progress, and Course Management Tools, including Gradebook.

CengageNOW™ Instant Access Code: CengageNOW™ is an online teaching and learning resource that gives you more control in less time and delivers better outcomes—NOW.

CengageNOW™ on Blackboard® Instant Access Code: Combine your course management system with CengageNOW™ through Blackboard®. Your students enjoy seamless access to CengageNOW™ assignments without the need of another login, and student results are posted directly to your course management system gradebook. You get the best of both all in one easy-to-use system.

CengageNOW™ on WebCT® Instant Access Code: Combine your course management system with CengageNOW™ through WebCT®. Your students enjoy seamless access to CengageNOW™ assignments without the need of another login, and student results are posted directly to your course management system gradebook. You get the best of both all in one easy-to-use system.

Learning Resources for Students

Working Papers (Printed): Traditional, printed option for working papers, a set of pre-formatted pages allow students to more easily work end-of-chapter problems and journal entries.

Electronic Working Papers in Excel Passkey Access (for sale online): Students can now work end-of-chapter assignments electronically in Excel with easy-to-follow, preformatted worksheets. This option is available via an online download with a passkey.

Companion Website: The student website contains a variety of educational resources for students, including online quizzing, Crossword Puzzles, Review Problems, the Glossary, Flashcards, and Learning Objectives.

Klooster & Allen's General Ledger Software: This best-selling, educational, general ledger software package introduces you to the world of computerized accounting through a more intuitive, user-friendly system than the commercial software you'll use in the future. Also, the program is enhanced with a problem checker that provides feedback on selected activities and emulates commercial general ledger packages more closely than other educational packages. Problems that can be used with Klooster/Allen are highlighted by an icon.

Instant Access Code CengageNOW™ *Express*: CengageNOW™ *Express* is an online homework solution in accounting that delivers better student outcomes—NOW! CengageNOW™ *Express* encourages practice with the textbook homework that is central to success in accounting with author-written homework from the textbook, Automatic Grading and Tracking Student Progress, and Course Management Tools, including Gradebook.

Printed Access Code CengageNOW™ *Express*: Printed version of Instant Access Code CengageNOW™ *Express.*

CengageNOW™ Instant Access Code: CengageNOW™ is an easy-to-use online resource that helps you study in less time to get the grade you want—NOW.

Student CD-ROM Peachtree: You will have access to Peachtree so you can familiarize yourself with computerized accounting systems used in the real world. You will gain experience from working with actual software, which will make you more desirable as a potential employee.

Acknowledgments

A successful textbook is a collaborative effort. We are grateful to the many professors, other professional colleagues, and students who have taught and studied from our book, and we thank all of them for their constructive comments. In the space available, we cannot possibly mention everyone who has been helpful, but we do want to recognize those who made special contributions to our efforts in preparing the tenth edition of *Financial Accounting*.

We wish to express deep appreciation to colleagues at DePaul University, who have been extremely supportive and encouraging.

Very important to the quality of this book is our project editor, Margaret Kearney, to whom we give special thanks. We also appreciate the support of our Senior Development Editor, Joanne Dauksewicz. The thoughtful and meticulous work of Edward H. Julius (California Lutheran University) is reflected not only in our Study Guide, but also in our Test Bank and CengageNOW Express course. We would also like to thank Jeri Condit for creating the PowerPoint slides, Sue Garr and Linda Burkell for HMAccounting Tutor, and Cathy Larson and James Emig for their accuracy review of the text and solutions.

Others who have had a major impact on this book through their reviews, suggestions, and participation in surveys, interviews, and focus groups are listed below. We cannot begin to say how grateful we are for the feedback from the many instructors who have generously shared their responses and teaching experiences with us.

Pre-Revision Review:
Mary Broyles, *Tulsa Community College-SEC*
Christopher Gilbert, *Glendale Community College*
Marina Grau, *Houston Community College*
Tracey Hawkins, *Clermont College Batavia*
Brian Nagle, *Duquesne University*
Obeua Persons, *Rider University*
Karen Russom, *North Harris College*
Marcia Veit, *University of Central Florida*
Betsy Willis, *Baylor University*
Judith Zander, *Grossmont College*

Advisory Board/Development Reviews:
Bill Allen, *Camden County College*
Ben Bean, *Utah Valley State College-Orem*
Amy Browning, *Ivy Tech Community College-Wabash*
Mary Broyles, *Tulsa Community College*
Robin D'agati, *Palm Beach Community College*
Patricia Doherty, *Boston University*
Christopher Gilbert. *Glendale Community College*
Bob Gutschick, *College of Southern Nevada*
Norma Jacobs, *Austin Community College*
Irwin Jarett, *DePaul University*
Christine Klowezeman, *Glendale Community College*
Susan Koepke, *Illinois Valley Community College*
Linda Miller, *Northeast Community College*
Linda Muren, *Cuyahoga Community College*
Ronald Sabado, *Highline Community College*
Kim Sim, *Roger Williams University*
Warren Smock, *Ivy Tech Community College-Lafayette*
Mary Ann Weldon, *Wayne State University*
Linda Whitten, *Sykline College*

–B.N. *and* M.P.

ABOUT THE AUTHORS

Belverd E. Needles, Jr., Ph.D., C.P.A., C.M.A.
DePaul University

Belverd Needles is an internationally recognized expert in accounting education. He has published in leading journals and is the author or editor of more than 20 books and monographs. His current research relates to international financial reporting, performance measurement, and corporate governance of high-performance companies in the United States, Europe, India, and Australia. His textbooks are used throughout the world and have received many awards, including the 2008 McGuffey Award from the Text and Academic Authors Association.

Dr. Needles was named Educator of the Year by the American Institute of CPAs, Accountant of the Year for Education by the national honorary society Beta Alpha Psi, and Outstanding International Accounting Educator by the American Accounting Association. Among the numerous other awards he has received are the Excellence in Teaching Award from DePaul University and the Illinois CPA Society's Outstanding Educator Award and Life-Time Achievement Award. Active in many academic and professional organizations, he has served as the U.S. representative on several international accounting committees, including the Education Committee of the International Federation of Accountants (IFAC). He is currently Vice-President-Education-Elect of the American Accounting Association.

Marian Powers, Ph.D.
Northwestern University

Internationally recognized as a dynamic teacher in executive education, Marian Powers specializes in teaching managers how to read and understand financial reports, including the impact that international financial reporting standards have on their companies. More than 1,000 executives per year from countries throughout the world, including France, the Czech Republic, Australia, India, China, and Brazil, attend her classes. She has taught at the Allen Center for Executive Education at Northwestern University since 1987 and at the Center for Corporate Financial Leadership since 2002.

Dr. Powers's research on international financial reporting, performance measurement, and corporate governance has been published in leading journals, among them *The Accounting Review; The International Journal of Accounting; Issues in Accounting Education; The Journal of Accountancy; The Journal of Business, Finance and Accounting;* and *Financial Management.* She has also co-authored three interactive multimedia software products: Fingraph Financial Analyst™ (financial analysis software); Financial Analysis and Decision Making, a goal-based learning simulation focused on interpreting financial reports; and Introduction to Financial Accounting, a goal-based simulation that uses the Financial Consequences Model to introduce financial accounting and financial statements to those unfamiliar with accounting.

Dr. Powers is a member of the American Accounting Association, European Accounting Association, International Association of Accounting Education and Research, and Illinois CPA Society. She currently serves on the board of directors of the Illinois CPA Society and the board of the CPA Endowment Fund of Illinois. She has served as vice president of Programs and secretary of the Educational Foundation.

COMPANY LOGO CREDITS (*continued*): page 237, Courtesy of Dell Inc.; page 291, Reprinted by permission of Costco; page 569, Reprinted by permission of Google; page 613, Motorola, Inc.; page 754, These materials have been reproduced with the permission of eBay, Inc. © 2008 Ebay, Inc. All rights reserved.

PHOTO CREDITS (*continued*): page 113, Teh Eng Koon/Getty Images; page 117 © Reuters/Corbis; page 133, Larry W. Smith/Getty Images; page 165, Justin Sullivan/Getty Images; page 173, AP Images/Candice Towell; page 181, Bambu Productions/Getty Images; page 233, Zuma Press/Newscom; page 238, Getty Images; page 260, Getty Images; page 289, AP Images/Don Ryan; page 294, Blend Images/Alamy; page 297, © Macduff Everton/Corbis; page 341, Tom Boyle/Getty Images; page 344, AP Images/Bebeo Matthews; page 347, Reprinted by permission of Autoliv; page 381, Shawn Camp/Getty Images; page 387, AP Images/Steve Helber; page 402, Toshifumi Kitamura/Getty Images; page 423, Stan Honda/Getty Images; page 436, Shawn Thew/Getty Images; page 445, Simon Jauncey/Getty Images; page 465, © Rommel Pecson/The Image Works; page 473, AP Images/Dave Martin; page 485, AP Images/The WIchita Eagle, Brian Com; page 513, AP Images/Greg Baker; page 521, Getty Images; page 527, Mehdi Fedouach/Getty Images; page 565, Chris Hondros/Getty Images; page 576, © Kim Kulish/Corbis; page 587, © Reuters/Corbis; page 609, Patrick Andrade/The New York Times/Redux; page 615, Bernie Nunez/Getty Images; page 630, AP Images/Beloit Daily News, Jim Urquhart; page 655, Scott Eells/Bloomberg News/Landov; page 664, Tony Armour/Jupiterimages; page 678, Pedro Armestre/Getty Images; page 705, AP Images/Lynne Sladky; page 710, The Goodyear Tire & Rubber Company; page 724, © Syracuse Newspapers/Gary Waits/The Image Works; page 753, AP Images/Jae C. Hong; page 757, © E.. Streichan/zefa/Corbis; page 773, Roland Tarcillion/Getty Images.

Financial
Accounting

CHAPTER

1

Uses of Accounting Information and the Financial Statements

Focus on Financial Statements

INCOME STATEMENT
Revenues
– Expenses
= Net Income

STATEMENT OF RETAINED EARNINGS
Opening Balance
+ Net Income
– Dividends
= Retained Earnings

BALANCE SHEET
Assets | Liabilities
Equity
A = L + E

STATEMENT OF CASH FLOWS
Operating activities
+ Investing activities
+ Financing activities
= Change in Cash
+ Starting Balance
= Ending Cash Balance

Although each financial statement gives a unique view of a company's results, all four are interrelated.

Today, more people than ever before recognize the importance of accounting information to a business, its owners, its employees, its lenders, and the financial markets. In this chapter, we discuss the importance of ethical financial reporting, the uses and users of accounting information, and the financial statements that accountants prepare. We end the chapter with a discussion of generally accepted accounting principles.

LEARNING OBJECTIVES

LO1 Define *accounting* and describe its role in making informed decisions, identify business goals and activities, and explain the importance of ethics in accounting. *(pp. 4–9)*

LO2 Identify the users of accounting information. *(pp. 10–13)*

LO3 Explain the importance of business transactions, money measure, and separate entity. *(pp. 13–15)*

LO4 Describe the characteristics of a corporation. *(pp. 15–18)*

LO5 Define *financial position*, and state the accounting equation. *(pp. 18–21)*

LO6 Identify the four basic financial statements. *(pp. 21–26)*

LO7 Explain how generally accepted accounting principles (GAAP) relate to financial statements and the independent CPA's report, and identify the organizations that influence GAAP. *(pp. 26–30)*

DECISION POINT ▶ A USER'S FOCUS

CVS CAREMARK

CVS Caremark operates a chain of more than 6,000 stores. Its pharmacies fill more than 1 billion prescriptions each year. Over the last five years, CVS has opened or purchased 2,100 new stores and more than doubled its sales and profits. This performance places it among the fastest-growing retail companies.

Why is CVS considered successful? Customers give the company high marks because of the quality of the products that it sells and the large selection and good service that its stores offer. Investment firms and others with a stake in CVS evaluate the company's success in financial terms.

Whether a company is large or small, the same financial measures are used to evaluate its management and to compare it with other companies. In this chapter, as you learn more about accounting and the business environment, you will become familiar with these financial measures.

- ▶ Is CVS meeting its goal of profitability?
- ▶ As a manager at CVS, what financial knowledge would you need to measure progress toward the company's goals?
- ▶ As a potential investor or creditor, what financial knowledge would you need to evaluate CVS's financial performance?

Accounting as an Information System

LO1 Define *accounting* and describe its role in making informed decisions, identify business goals and activities, and explain the importance of ethics in accounting.

Accounting is an information system that measures, processes, and communicates financial information about an economic entity.[1] An economic entity is a unit that exists independently, such as a business, a hospital, or a governmental body. Although the central focus of this book is on business entities, we include other economic units at appropriate points in the text and in the end-of-chapter assignments.

Accountants focus on the needs of decision makers who use financial information, whether those decision makers are inside or outside a business or other economic entity. Accountants provide a vital service by supplying the information decision makers need to make "reasoned choices among alternative uses of scarce resources in the conduct of business and economic activities."[2] As shown in Figure 1, accounting is a link between business activities and decision makers.

1. Accounting measures business activities by recording data about them for future use.
2. The data are stored until needed and then processed to become useful information.
3. The information is communicated through reports to decision makers.

In other words, data about business activities are the input to the accounting system, and useful information for decision makers is the output.

Business Goals and Activities

A **business** is an economic unit that aims to sell goods and services to customers at prices that will provide an adequate return to its owners. The list that follows contains the names of some well-known businesses and the principal goods or services that they sell.

FIGURE 1
Accounting as an Information System

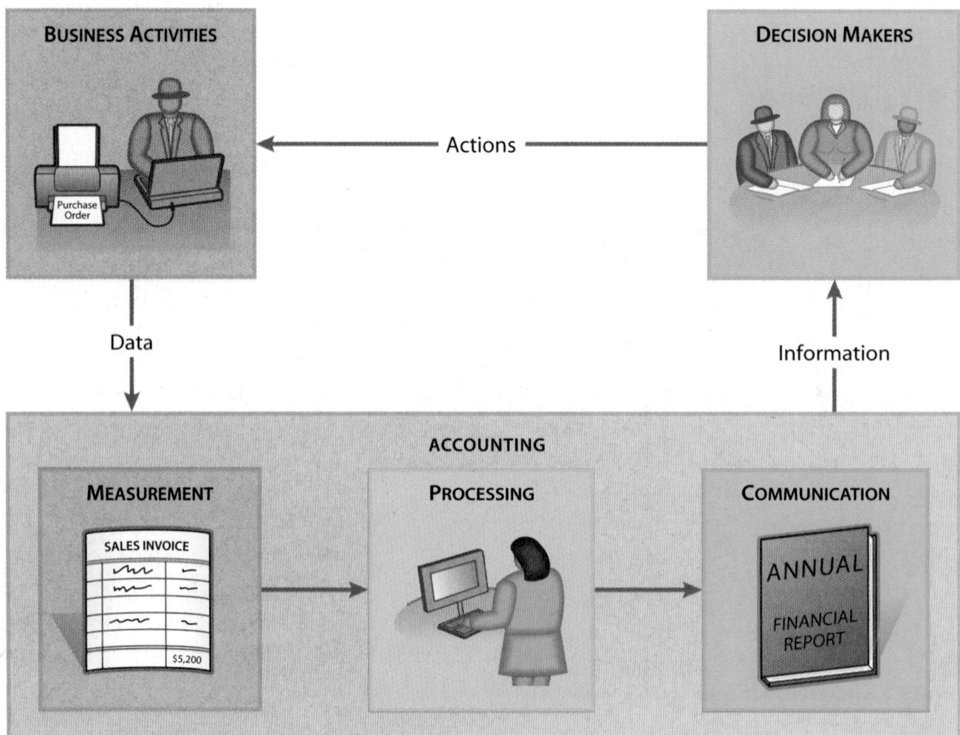

FIGURE 2
Business Goals and Activities

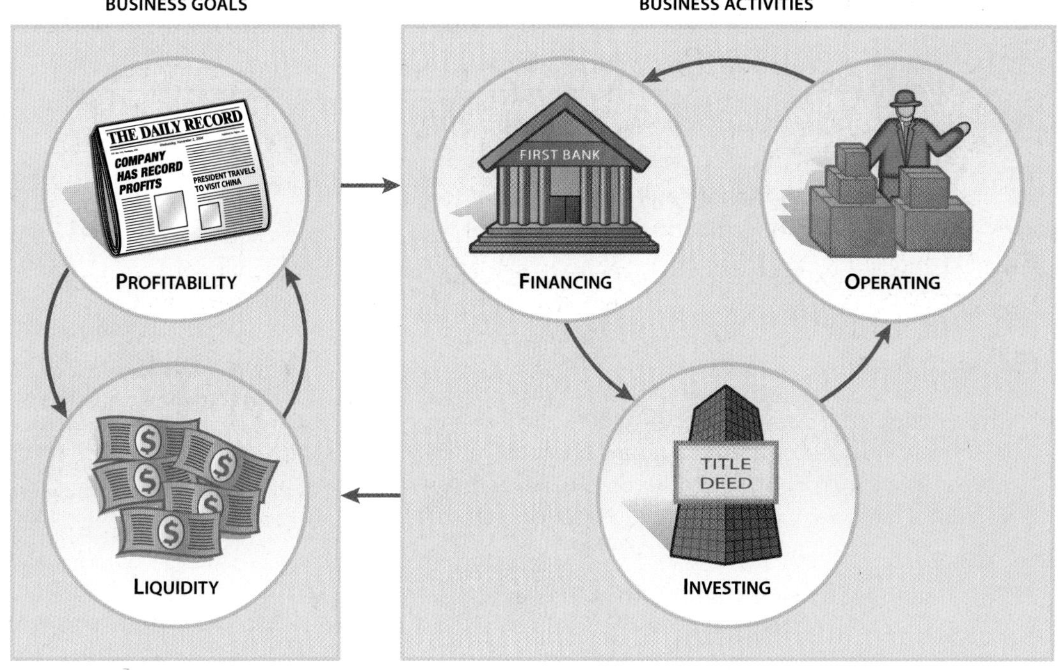

Wal-Mart Corp.	Comprehensive discount store
Reebok International Ltd.	Athletic footwear and clothing
Best Buy Co.	Consumer electronics, personal computers
Wendy's International Inc.	Food service
Starbucks Corp.	Coffee
Southwest Airlines Co.	Passenger airline

Despite their differences, these businesses have similar goals and engage in similar activities, as shown in Figure 2.

The two major goals of all businesses are profitability and liquidity.

- **Profitability** is the ability to earn enough income to attract and hold investment capital.
- **Liquidity** is the ability to have enough cash to pay debts when they are due.

Study Note

Users of accounting information focus on a company's profitability and liquidity. Thus, more than one measure of performance is of interest to them. For example, lenders are concerned primarily with cash flow, and owners are concerned with earnings and dividends.

For example, **Toyota** may meet the goal of profitability by selling many cars at a price that earns a profit, but if its customers do not pay for their cars quickly enough to enable Toyota to pay its suppliers and employees, the company may fail to meet the goal of liquidity. If a company is to survive and be successful, it must meet both goals.

All businesses, whether they are retailers, manufacturers, or service providers, pursue their goals by engaging in operating, investing, and financing activities.

- **Operating activities** include selling goods and services to customers, employing managers and workers, buying and producing goods and services, and paying taxes.
- **Investing activities** involve spending the capital a company receives in productive ways that will help it achieve its objectives. These activities include buying land, buildings, equipment, and other resources that are needed to operate the business and selling them when they are no longer needed.
- **Financing activities** involve obtaining adequate funds, or capital, to begin operations and to continue operating. These activities include obtaining

FOCUS ON BUSINESS PRACTICE

What Does CVS Have to Say About Itself?

In its annual report, **CVS's** management describes the company's goals in meeting the major business objectives:

- Liquidity: "We anticipate that our cash flow from operations, supplemented by commercial paper and long-term borrowings, will continue to fund the growth of our business."
- Profitability: "The profitability of retail and mail-order pharmacy businesses are dependent upon the utilization of prescription drug products. . . . The company evaluates segment performance based on net revenues, gross profit and operating profit."[3]

CVS's main business activities are shown at the right.

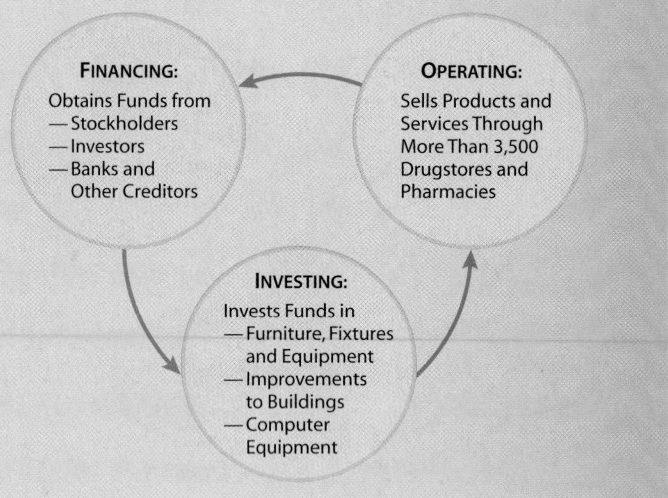

capital from creditors, such as banks and suppliers, and from owners. They also include repaying creditors and paying a return to the owners.

An important function of accounting is to provide **performance measures**, which indicate whether managers are achieving their business goals and whether the business activities are well managed. The evaluation and interpretation of financial statements and related performance measures is called **financial analysis**. For financial analysis to be useful, performance measures must be well aligned with the two major goals of business—profitability and liquidity.

Profitability is commonly measured in terms of earnings or income, and cash flows are a common measure of liquidity. In 2007, **CVS** had earnings or income of $2,637.0 million and cash flows from operating activities of $3,229.7 million. These figures indicate that CVS was achieving both profitability and liquidity. Not all companies were so fortunate in 2007. For instance, **General Motors** reported that it would have to curtail spending on new auto and truck models because its earnings (or profitability) for the first nine months of the year were negative; in fact, its net loss for the period was $3 billion. Even worse, its cash flows (or liquidity) were negative $4.2 billion.[4] Clearly, General Motors was not meeting either its profitability or liquidity goals.

Although it is important to know the amounts of earnings and cash flows in any given period and whether they are rising or falling, ratios of accounting measures are also useful tools of financial analysis. These ratios allow for comparisons from one period to another and from one company to another. For example, to

FOCUS ON BUSINESS PRACTICE

Cash Bonuses Depend on Accounting Numbers!

Nearly all businesses use the amounts reported in their financial statements as a basis for rewarding management. Because managers act to achieve these accounting measures, selecting measures that are not easily manipulated is important. Equally important is maintaining a balance of measures that reflect the goals of profitability and liquidity.[5]

assess **CVS's** profitability, it would be helpful to consider the ratio of its earnings to total assets, and for liquidity, the ratio of its cash flows to total assets.

Financial and Management Accounting

Accounting's role of assisting decision makers by measuring, processing, and communicating financial information is usually divided into the categories of management accounting and financial accounting. Although the functions of management accounting and financial accounting overlap, the two can be distinguished by the principal users of the information that they provide.

Management accounting provides *internal* decision makers who are charged with achieving the goals of profitability and liquidity with information about financing, investing, and operating activities. Managers and employees who conduct the activities of the business need information that tells them how they have done in the past and what they can expect in the future. For example, **The Gap**, a retail clothing business, needs an operating report on each outlet that tells how much was sold at that outlet and what costs were incurred, and it needs a budget for each outlet that projects the sales and costs for the next year.

CVS/pharmacy®

Financial accounting generates reports and communicates them to *external* decision makers so they can evaluate how well the business has achieved its goals. These reports are called **financial statements**. **CVS**, whose stock is traded on the New York Stock Exchange, sends its financial statements to its owners (called *stockholders*), its banks and other creditors, and government regulators. Financial statements report directly on the goals of profitability and liquidity and are used extensively both inside and outside a business to evaluate the business's success. It is important for every person involved with a business to understand financial statements. They are a central feature of accounting and a primary focus of this book.

Processing Accounting Information

It is important to distinguish accounting from the ways in which accounting information is processed by bookkeeping, computers, and management information systems.

Accounting includes the design of an information system that meets users' needs, and its major goals are the analysis, interpretation, and use of information. **Bookkeeping**, on the other hand, is mechanical and repetitive; it is the process of recording financial transactions and keeping financial records. It is a small—but important—part of accounting.

A **computer** is an electronic tool used to collect, organize, and communicate vast amounts of information with great speed. Computers can perform both routine bookkeeping chores and complex calculations. Accountants were among the earliest and most enthusiastic users of computers, and today they use computers in all aspects of their work.

Study Note

Computerized accounting information is only as reliable and useful as the data that go into the system. The accountant must have a thorough understanding of the concepts that underlie accounting to ensure the data's reliability and usefulness.

Computers make it possible to create a management information system to organize a business's many information needs. A **management information system (MIS)** consists of the interconnected subsystems that provide the information needed to run a business. The accounting information system is the most important subsystem because it plays the key role of managing the flow of economic data to all parts of a business and to interested parties outside the business.

Ethical Financial Reporting

Ethics is a code of conduct that applies to everyday life. It addresses the question of whether actions are right or wrong. Actions—whether ethical or unethical, right or wrong—are the product of individual decisions. Thus, when an

FOCUS ON BUSINESS PRACTICE

How Did Accounting Develop?

Accounting is a very old discipline. Forms of it have been essential to commerce for more than five thousand years. Accounting, in a version close to what we know today, gained widespread use in the 1400s, especially in Italy, where it was instrumental in the development of shipping, trade, construction, and other forms of commerce. This system of double-entry bookkeeping was documented by the famous Italian mathematician, scholar, and philosopher Fra Luca Pacioli. In 1494, Pacioli published his most important work, *Summa de Arithmetica, Geometrica, Proportioni et Proportionalita,* which contained a detailed description of accounting as practiced in that age. This book became the most widely read book on mathematics in Italy and firmly established Pacioli as the "Father of Accounting."

organization acts unethically by using false advertising, cheating customers, polluting the environment, or treating employees unfairly, it is not the organization that is responsible—it is the members of management and other employees who have made a conscious decision to act in this manner.

Ethics is especially important in preparing financial reports because users of these reports must depend on the good faith of the people involved in their preparation. Users have no other assurance that the reports are accurate and fully disclose all relevant facts.

The intentional preparation of misleading financial statements is called **fraudulent financial reporting**.[6] It can result from the distortion of records (e.g., the manipulation of inventory records), falsified transactions (e.g., fictitious sales), or the misapplication of various accounting principles. There are a number of motives for fraudulent reporting—for instance, to cover up financial weakness in order to obtain a higher price when a company is sold, to meet the expectations of stockholders and financial analysts, or to obtain a loan. The incentive can also be personal gain, such as additional compensation, promotion, or avoidance of penalties for poor performance.

Whatever the motive for fraudulent financial reporting, it can have dire consequences, as the accounting scandals that erupted at **Enron Corporation** and **WorldCom** attest. Unethical financial reporting and accounting practices at those two major corporations caused thousands of people to lose their jobs, their

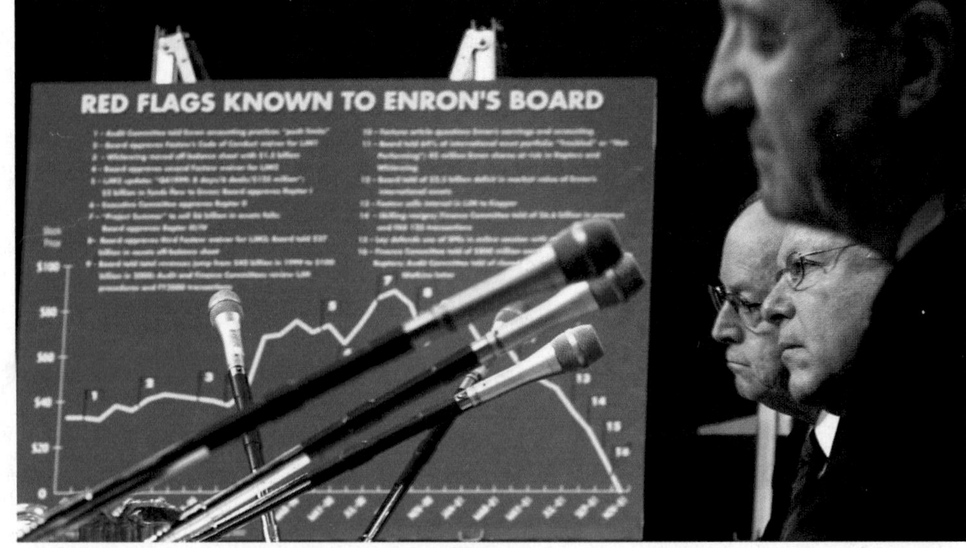

In the wake of one of the largest accounting scandals in history, current and former members of Enron's board of directors John Duncan *(left)*, Herbert Winokur *(center)*, and Norman Blake listen to opening remarks at a hearing of the Senate Permanent Subcommittee on Investigations, May 7, 2002. Unethical accounting practices at Enron led to the collapse of the company and the loss of thousands of jobs and pensions.

investment incomes, and their pensions. They also resulted in prison sentences and fines for the corporate executives who were involved.

In 2002, Congress passed the **Sarbanes-Oxley Act** to regulate financial reporting and the accounting profession among other things. This legislation ordered the Securities and Exchange Commission (SEC) to draw up rules requiring the chief executives and chief financial officers of all publicly traded U.S. companies to swear that, based on their knowledge, the quarterly statements and annual reports that their companies file with the SEC are accurate and complete. Violation can result in criminal penalties.

A company's management expresses its duty to ensure that financial reports are not false or misleading in the management report that appears in the company's annual report. For example, in its management report, **Target Corporation** makes the following statement:

> Management is responsible for the consistency, integrity and presentation of the information in the Annual Report.[7]

However, it is accountants, not management, who physically prepare and audit financial reports. To meet the high ethical standards of the accounting profession, they must apply accounting concepts in such a way as to present a fair view of a company's operations and financial position and to avoid misleading readers of their reports. Like the conduct of a company, the ethical conduct of a profession is a collection of individual actions. As a member of a profession, each accountant has a responsibility—not only to the profession, but also to employers, clients, and society as a whole—to ensure that any report he or she prepares or audits provides accurate, reliable information.

The high regard that the public has historically had for the accounting profession is evidence that an overwhelming number of accountants have upheld the ethics of the profession. Even as the Enron and WorldCom scandals were making headlines, a Gallup Poll showed an increase of 28 percent in the accounting profession's reputation between 2002 and 2005, placing it among the most highly rated professions.[8]

Accountants and top managers are, of course, not the only people responsible for ethical financial reporting. Managers and employees at all levels must be conscious of their responsibility for providing accurate financial information to the people who rely on it.

STOP ▸ REVIEW ▸ APPLY

LO1-1 **Why is accounting considered an information system?**

LO1-2 **What is the role of accounting in the decision-making process, and what broad business goals and activities does it help management achieve and manage?**

LO1-3 **Distinguish between management accounting and financial accounting.**

LO1-4 **Distinguish among these terms: *accounting, bookkeeping,* and *management information systems.***

LO1-5 **What is the difference between misstated financial statements and fraudulent financial reporting?**

Suggested answers to all Stop, Review, and Apply questions follow the appendixes.

Decision Makers: The Users of Accounting Information

LO2 Identify the users of accounting information.

As shown in Figure 3, the people who use accounting information to make decisions fall into three categories:

1. Those who manage a business
2. Those outside a business enterprise who have a direct financial interest in the business
3. Those who have an indirect financial interest in a business

These categories apply to governmental and not-for-profit organizations as well as to profit-oriented ventures.

Management

Study Note

Managers are internal users of accounting information.

Management refers to the people who are responsible for operating a business and meeting its goals of profitability and liquidity. In a small business, management may consist solely of the owners. In a large business, managers must decide what to do, how to do it, and whether the results match their original plans. Successful managers consistently make the right decisions based on timely and valid information.

To make good decisions, managers at **CVS** and other companies need answers to such questions as:

- What were the company's earnings during the past quarter?
- Is the rate of return to the owners adequate?
- Does the company have enough cash?
- Which products or services are most profitable?

Because so many key decisions are based on accounting data, management is one of the most important users of accounting information.

In its decision-making process, management performs functions that are essential to the operation of a business. The same basic functions must be performed in all businesses, and each requires accounting information on which to base decisions.

The basic management functions are:

Financing the business—obtaining funds so that a company can begin and continue operating

FIGURE 3

The Users of Accounting Information

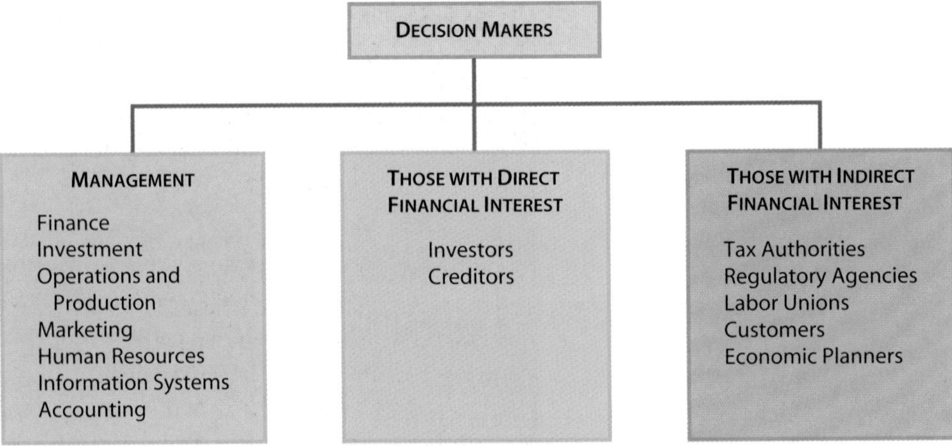

FOCUS ON BUSINESS PRACTICE

What Do CFOs Do?

According to a recent survey, the chief financial officer (CFO) is the "new business partner of the chief executive officer" (CEO). CFOs are increasingly required to take on responsibilities for strategic planning, mergers and acquisitions, and tasks involving international operations, and many of them are becoming CEOs of their companies. Those who do become CEOs are finding that "a financial background is invaluable when they're saddled with the responsibility of making big calls."[9]

Investing resources—investing assets in productive ways that support a company's goals

Producing goods and services—managing the production of goods and services

Marketing goods and services—overseeing how goods or services are advertised, sold, and distributed

Managing employees—overseeing the hiring, evaluation, and compensation of employees

Providing information to decision makers—gathering data about all aspects of a company's operations, organizing the data into usable information, and providing reports to managers and appropriate outside parties. Accounting plays a key role in this function.

Users with a Direct Financial Interest

Most businesses periodically publish a set of general-purpose financial statements with accompanying information that report their success in meeting the goals of profitability and liquidity. These statements show what has happened in the past, and they are important indicators of what will happen in the future. Many people outside the company carefully study these financial reports. The providers of capital in the form of investments in or loans to a business have a direct financial interest in its success and depend on the financial statements to evaluate how the business has performed. These important providers of capital are investors and creditors.

Study Note

The primary external users of accounting information are investors and creditors.

Investors Those, such as **CVS's** stockholders, who invest or may invest in a business and acquire a part ownership in it are interested in its past success and its potential earnings. A thorough study of a company's financial statements helps potential investors judge the prospects for a profitable investment. After investing, they must continually review their commitment, again by examining the company's financial statements.

Creditors Most companies borrow money for both long- and short-term operating needs. Creditors, those who lend money or deliver goods and services before being paid, are interested mainly in whether a company will have the cash to pay interest charges and to repay the debt on time. They study a company's liquidity and cash flow as well as its profitability. Banks, finance companies, mortgage companies, securities firms, insurance firms, suppliers, and other lenders must analyze a company's financial position before they make a loan.

Users with an Indirect Financial Interest

In recent years, society as a whole, through governmental and public groups, has become one of the largest and most important users of accounting information. Users who need accounting information to make decisions on public issues include tax authorities, regulatory agencies, and various other groups.

Tax Authorities Government at every level is financed through the collection of taxes. Companies and individuals pay many kinds of taxes, including federal, state, and city income taxes; social security and other payroll taxes; excise taxes; and sales taxes. Each tax requires special tax returns and often a complex set of records as well.

Proper reporting is generally a matter of law and can be very complicated. The Internal Revenue Code, for instance, contains thousands of rules governing the preparation of the accounting information used in computing federal income taxes.

Regulatory Agencies Most companies must report periodically to one or more regulatory agencies at the federal, state, and local levels. For example, all publicly traded corporations must report periodically to the **Securities and Exchange Commission (SEC)**. This body, set up by Congress to protect the public, regulates the issuing, buying, and selling of stocks in the United States. Companies listed on a stock exchange also must meet the special reporting requirements of their exchange.

Other Groups Labor unions study the financial statements of corporations as part of preparing for contract negotiations; a company's income and costs often play an important role in these negotiations. Those who advise investors and creditors—such as financial analysts, brokers, underwriters, lawyers, economists, and the financial press—also have an indirect interest in the financial performance and prospects of a business. Consumer groups, customers, and the general public have become more concerned about the financing and earnings of corporations as well as about the effects that corporations have on inflation, the environment, social issues, and the quality of life. And economic planners—among them the President's Council of Economic Advisers and the Federal Reserve Board—use aggregated accounting information to set and evaluate economic policies and programs.

Governmental and Not-for-Profit Organizations

More than 30 percent of the U.S. economy is generated by governmental and not-for-profit organizations (hospitals, universities, professional organizations, and charities). The managers of these diverse entities perform the same functions as managers of businesses, and they therefore have the same need for accounting information and a knowledge of how to use it. Their functions include raising funds from investors, creditors, taxpayers, and donors, and deploying scarce resources. They must also plan how to pay for operations and to repay creditors on a timely basis. In addition, they have an obligation to report their financial performance to legislators, boards, and donors, as well as to deal with tax authorities, regulators, and labor unions.

Although most of the examples that we present in this text focus on business enterprises, the same basic principles apply to governmental and not-for-profit organizations.

STOP ▸ REVIEW ▸ APPLY

LO2-1 **Who are the decision makers that use accounting information?**

LO2-2 **A business is an economic unit whose goal is to sell goods or services at prices that will provide an adequate return to its owners. What functions must management perform to achieve this goal?**

LO2-3 **Why are investors and creditors interested in reviewing a company's financial statements?**

LO2-4 **Among the users of accounting information are people and organizations with an indirect interest in business entities. Briefly identify these people and organizations.**

LO2-5 **Why has society as a whole become one of the largest users of accounting information?**

Accounting Measurement

LO3 Explain the importance of business transactions, money measure, and separate entity.

In this section, we begin the study of the measurement aspects of accounting—that is, what accounting actually measures. To make an accounting measurement, the accountant must answer four basic questions:

1. What is measured?
2. When should the measurement be made?
3. What value should be placed on what is measured?
4. How should what is measured be classified?

Accountants in industry, professional associations, public accounting, government, and academic circles debate the answers to these questions constantly, and the answers change as new knowledge and practice require. But the basis of today's accounting practice rests on a number of widely accepted concepts and conventions, which are described in this book. We begin by focusing on the first question: What is measured? We discuss the other three questions (recognition, valuation, and classification) in the next chapter.

Every system must define what it measures, and accounting is no exception. Basically, financial accounting uses money to gauge the impact of business transactions on separate business entities.

Business Transactions

Business transactions are economic events that affect a business's financial position. Businesses can have hundreds or even thousands of transactions every day. These transactions are the raw material of accounting reports.

A transaction can be an exchange of value (a purchase, sale, payment, collection, or loan) between two or more parties. A transaction also can be an economic event that has the same effect as an exchange transaction but that does not involve an exchange. Some examples of "nonexchange" transactions are losses from fire, flood, explosion, and theft; physical wear and tear on machinery and equipment; and the day-by-day accumulation of interest.

To be recorded, a transaction must relate directly to a business entity. Suppose a customer buys toothpaste from **CVS** but has to buy shampoo from a competing store because CVS is out of shampoo. The transaction in which the toothpaste was sold is entered in CVS's records. However, the purchase of the shampoo from the competitor is not entered in CVS's records because even though it indirectly affects CVS economically, it does not involve a direct exchange of value between CVS and the customer.

Money Measure

Study Note

The common unit of measurement used in the United States for financial reporting purposes is the dollar.

All business transactions are recorded in terms of money. This concept is called **money measure**. Of course, nonfinancial information may also be recorded, but it is through the recording of monetary amounts that a business's transactions and activities are measured. Money is the only factor common to all business transactions, and thus it is the only unit of measure capable of producing financial data that can be compared.

The monetary unit a business uses depends on the country in which the business resides. For example, in the United States, the basic unit of money is the dollar. In Japan, it is the yen; in Europe, the euro; and in the United Kingdom, the pound. In international transactions, exchange rates must be used to translate from one currency to another. An **exchange rate** is the value of one currency in terms of another. For example, a British person purchasing goods from a U.S. company like **CVS** and paying in U.S. dollars must exchange British pounds for U.S. dollars before making payment. In effect, currencies are goods that can be bought and sold.

Table 1 illustrates the exchange rates for several currencies in dollars. It shows the exchange rate for British pounds as $1.98 per pound on a particular date. Like the prices of many goods, currency prices change daily according to supply and demand. For example, a year earlier, the exchange rate for British pounds was $1.85. Although our discussion in this book focuses on dollars, some examples and assignments involve foreign currencies.

Separate Entity

Study Note

For accounting purposes, a business is *always* separate and distinct from its owners, creditors, and customers.

For accounting purposes, a business is a **separate entity**, distinct not only from its creditors and customers but also from its owners. It should have its own set of financial records, and its records and reports should refer only to its own affairs.

For example, Just Because Flowers Company should have a bank account separate from the account of Holly Sapp, the owner. Holly Sapp may own a home, a car, and other property, and she may have personal debts, but these are not the resources or debts of Just Because Flowers. Holly Sapp may own another business, say a stationery shop. If she does, she should have a completely separate set of records for each business.

TABLE 1

Examples of Foreign Exchange Rates

Country	Price in $ U.S.	Country	Price in $ U.S.
Australia (dollar)	0.88	Hong Kong (dollar)	0.13
Brazil (real)	0.56	Japan (yen)	0.009
Britain (pound)	1.98	Mexico (peso)	0.09
Canada (dollar)	0.99	Russia (ruble)	0.04
Europe (euro)	1.47	Singapore (dollar)	0.70

Source: ***The Wall Street Journal,*** **January 28, 2008.**

STOP ▸ REVIEW ▸ APPLY

LO3-1 **Use the terms *business transactions, money measure,* and *separate entity* in a single sentence that demonstrates their relevance to financial accounting.**

LO3-2 **Suppose you buy a disposable camera from CVS. From CVS's perspective, how would the terms *business transactions, money measure,* and *separate entity* relate to your purchase?**

The Corporate Form of Business

LO4 **Describe the characteristics of a corporation.**

The three basic forms of business enterprise are the sole proprietorship, the partnership, and the corporation. The characteristics of corporations make them very efficient in amassing capital, which enables them to grow extremely large. As Figure 4 shows, even though corporations are fewer in number than sole proprietorships and partnerships, they contribute much more to the U.S. economy in monetary terms. For example, in 2007, **Exxon Mobil** generated more revenues than all but 30 of the world's countries. Because of the economic significance of corporations, this book emphasizes accounting for the corporate form of business.

Characteristics of Corporations, Sole Proprietorships, and Partnerships

A **sole proprietorship** is a business that is owned by one person. The owner takes all the profits or losses of the business and is liable for all its obligations. Sole proprietorships represent the largest number of businesses in the United States, but typically they are the smallest in size.

FIGURE 4

Number and Receipts of U.S. Proprietorships, Partnerships, and Corporations.

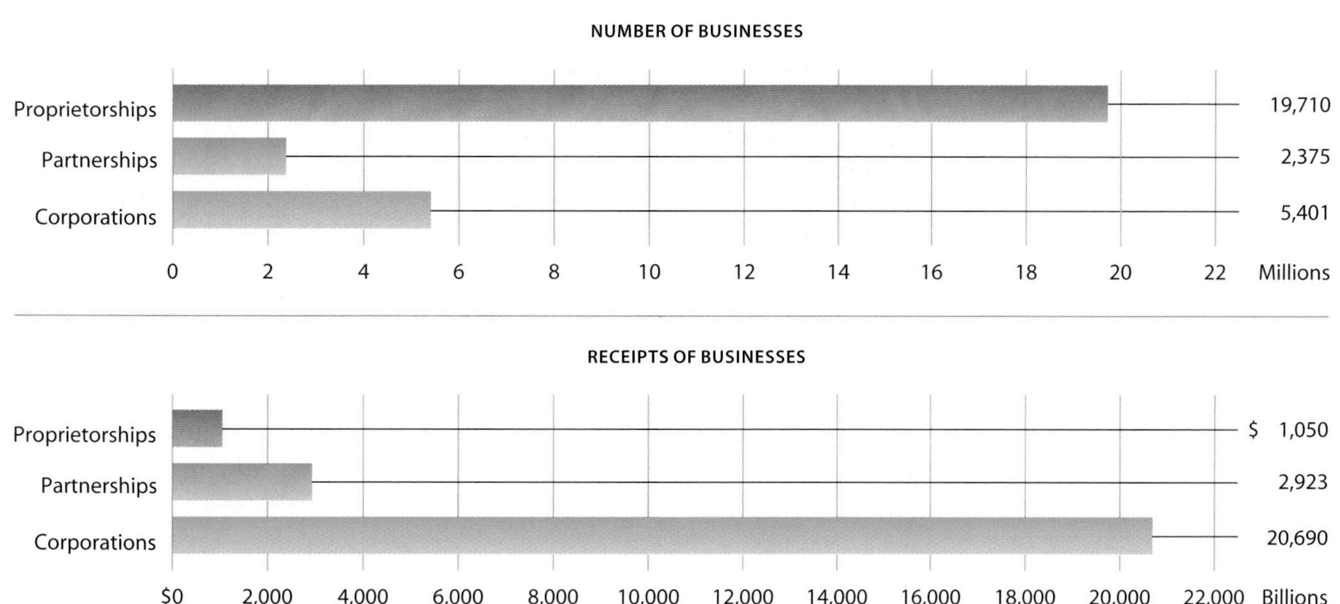

Source: **U.S. Treasury Department, Internal Revenue Service, *Statistics of Income Bulletin,* Winter 2006.**

FOCUS ON BUSINESS PRACTICE

Are Most Corporations Big or Small Businesses?

Most people think of corporations as large national or global companies whose shares of stock are held by thousands of people and institutions. Indeed, corporations can be huge and have many stockholders. However, of the approximately 4 million corporations in the United States, only about 15,000 have stock that is publicly bought and sold. The vast majority of corporations are small businesses privately held by a few stockholders. Illinois alone has more than 250,000 corporations. Thus, the study of corporations is just as relevant to small businesses as it is to large ones.

Study Note

A key disadvantage of a partnership is the unlimited liability of its owners. Unlimited liability can be avoided by organizing the business as a corporation or, in some states, by forming what is known as a limited liability partnership.

A **partnership** is like a sole proprietorship in most ways, but it has two or more owners. The partners share the profits and losses of the business according to a prearranged formula. Generally, any partner can obligate the business to another party, and the personal resources of each partner can be called on to pay the obligations. A partnership must be dissolved if the ownership changes, as when a partner leaves or dies. If the business is to continue as a partnership after this occurs, a new partnership must be formed.

Both the sole proprietorship and the partnership are convenient ways of separating the owners' commercial activities from their personal activities. Legally, however, there is no economic separation between the owners and the businesses.

A **corporation**, on the other hand, is a business unit chartered by the state and legally separate from its owners (the *stockholders*). The stockholders, whose ownership is represented by shares of stock, do not directly control the corporation's operations. Instead, they elect a board of directors to run the corporation for their benefit. In exchange for their limited involvement in the corporation's operations, stockholders enjoy limited liability; that is, their risk of loss is limited to the amount they paid for their shares. Thus, stockholders are often willing to invest in risky, but potentially profitable, activities. Also, because stockholders can sell their shares without dissolving the corporation, the life of a corporation is unlimited and not subject to the whims or health of a proprietor or a partner.

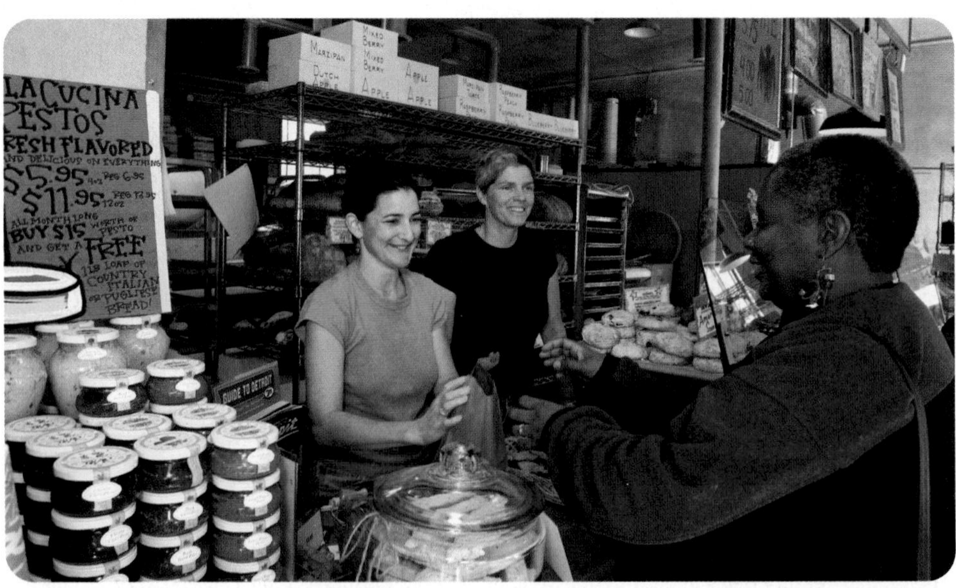

Avalon International Breads in Detroit is a partnership owned by Jackie Victor and Ann Perrault. Because it is a partnership, the owners share the profits and losses of the business, and their personal resources can be called on to pay the obligations of the business.

Formation of a Corporation

To form a corporation, most states require individuals, called incorporators, to sign an application and file it with the proper state official. This application contains the **articles of incorporation**. If approved by the state, these articles, which form the company charter, become a contract between the state and the incorporators. The company is then authorized to do business as a corporation.

Organization of a Corporation

The authority to manage a corporation is delegated by its stockholders to a board of directors and by the board of directors to the corporation's officers (see Figure 5). That is, the stockholders elect a board of directors, which sets corporate policies and chooses the corporation's officers, who in turn carry out the corporate policies in their management of the business.

Stockholders A unit of ownership in a corporation is called a **share of stock**. The articles of incorporation state the maximum number of shares that a corporation is authorized to issue. The number of shares held by stockholders is the outstanding stock; this may be less than the number authorized in the articles of incorporation. To invest in a corporation, a stockholder transfers cash or other resources to the corporation. In return, the stockholder receives shares of stock representing a proportionate share of ownership in the corporation. Afterward, the stockholder may transfer the shares at will. Corporations may have more than one kind of stock, but in the first part of this book, we refer only to **common stock**—the most universal form of stock.

Board of Directors As noted, a corporation's board of directors decides on major business policies. Among the board's specific duties are authorizing contracts, setting executive salaries, and arranging major loans with banks. The declaration of dividends is also an important function of the board of directors. **Dividends** are distributions of resources, generally in the form of cash, to stockholders, and only the board of directors has the authority to declare them. Paying dividends is one way of rewarding stockholders for their investment when the corporation has been successful in earning a profit. (The other way is through a rise in the market value of the stock.) Although there is usually a delay of two or three weeks between the time the board declares a dividend and the date of the actual payment, we assume in the early chapters of this book that declaration and payment are made on the same day.

The composition of the board of directors varies from company to company, but generally it includes several officers of the corporation and several outsiders. The outsiders are called *independent directors* because they do not directly participate in managing the business.

Management Management, appointed by the board of directors to carry out corporate policies and run day-to-day operations, consists of the operating

FIGURE 5
The Corporate Form of Business

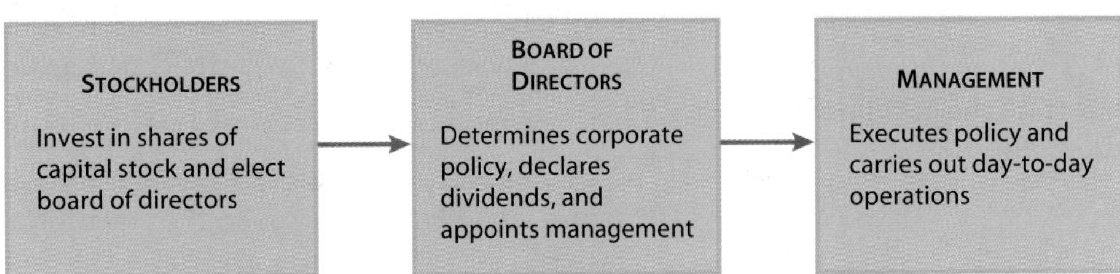
STOCKHOLDERS
Invest in shares of capital stock and elect board of directors
BOARD OF DIRECTORS
Determines corporate policy, declares dividends, and appoints management
MANAGEMENT
Executes policy and carries out day-to-day operations

officers—generally the president, or chief executive officer; vice presidents; chief financial officer; and chief operating officer. Besides being responsible for running the business, management has the duty of reporting the financial results of its administration to the board of directors and the stockholders. Though management must, at a minimum, make a comprehensive annual report, it generally reports more often. The annual reports of large public corporations are available to the public. Excerpts from many of them appear throughout this book.

Corporate Governance

The financial scandals at **Enron, WorldCom**, and other companies highlighted the importance of **corporate governance**, which is the oversight of a corporation's management and ethics by its board of directors. Corporate governance is growing and is clearly in the best interests of a business. A recent survey of 124 corporations in 22 countries found that 78 percent of boards of directors had established ethical standards, a fourfold increase over a 10-year period. In addition, research has shown that, over time, companies with codes of ethics tend to have higher stock prices than those that have not adopted such codes.[10]

To strengthen corporate governance, a provision of the Sarbanes-Oxley Act required boards of directors to establish an **audit committee** made up of independent directors who have financial expertise. This provision was aimed at ensuring that boards of directors would be objective in evaluating management's performance. The audit committee is also responsible for engaging the corporation's independent auditors and reviewing their work. Another of the committee's functions is to ensure that adequate systems exist to safeguard the corporation's resources and that accounting records are reliable. In short, the audit committee is the front line of defense against fraudulent financial reporting.

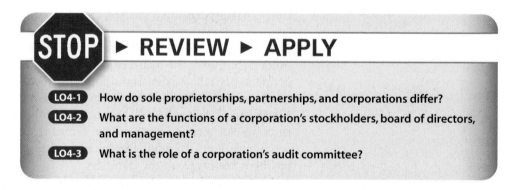

STOP ▸ REVIEW ▸ APPLY

LO4-1 How do sole proprietorships, partnerships, and corporations differ?

LO4-2 What are the functions of a corporation's stockholders, board of directors, and management?

LO4-3 What is the role of a corporation's audit committee?

Financial Position and the Accounting Equation

LO5 Define *financial position*, and state the accounting equation.

Financial position refers to a company's economic resources, such as cash, inventory, and buildings, and the claims against those resources at a particular time. Another term for claims is *equities*.

Every corporation has two types of equities: creditors' equities, such as bank loans, and stockholders' equity. (In the case of sole proprietorships and partnerships, which do not have stockholders, stockholders' equity is called *owners' equity*.) The sum of these equities equals a corporation's resources:

$$\text{Economic Resources} = \text{Creditors' Equities} + \text{Stockholders' Equity}$$

In accounting terminology, economic resources are called *assets* and creditors' equities are called *liabilities*. So the equation can be written like this:

$$\text{Assets} = \text{Liabilities} + \text{Stockholders' Equity}$$

FIGURE 6

The Accounting Equation

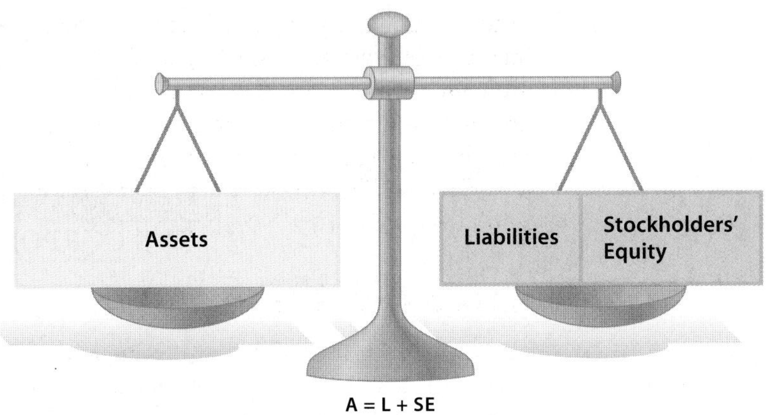

This equation is known as the **accounting equation**. The two sides of the equation must always be equal, or "in balance," as shown in Figure 6. To evaluate the financial effects of business activities, it is important to understand their effects on this equation.

Assets

Assets are the economic resources of a company that are expected to benefit the company's future operations. Certain kinds of assets—for example, cash and money that customers owe to the company (called *accounts receivable*)—are monetary items. Other assets—inventories (goods held for sale), land, buildings, and equipment—are nonmonetary, physical items. Still other assets—the rights granted by patents, trademarks, and copyrights—are nonphysical.

Liabilities

Liabilities a business's present obligations to pay cash, transfer assets, or provide services to other entities in the future. Among these obligations are amounts owed to suppliers for goods or services bought on credit (called *accounts payable*), borrowed money (e.g., money owed on bank loans), salaries and wages owed to employees, taxes owed to the government, and services to be performed.

As debts, liabilities are claims recognized by law. That is, the law gives creditors the right to force the sale of a company's assets if the company fails to pay its debts. Creditors have rights over stockholders and must be paid in full before the stockholders receive anything, even if payment of the debt uses up all the assets of the business.

Stockholders' Equity

Stockholders' equity (also called *shareholders' equity*) represents the claims of the owners of a corporation (the shareholders) to the assets of the business. Theoretically, it is what would be left over if all liabilities were paid, and it is sometimes said to equal **net assets** (also called *net worth*).

By rearranging the accounting equation, we can define stockholders' equity this way:

$$\text{Stockholders' Equity} = \text{Assets} - \text{Liabilities}$$

Stockholders' equity has two parts, contributed capital and retained earnings:

$$\text{Stockholders' Equity} = \text{Contributed Capital} + \text{Retained Earnings}$$

FIGURE 7

CVS Stock Certificate

Contributed capital is the amount that stockholders invest in the business. As noted earlier, their ownership in the business is represented by shares of capital stock. Figure 7 is a **CVS** stock certificate, which represents such ownership.

Typically, contributed capital is divided between par value and additional paid-in capital. **Par value** is an amount per share that when multiplied by the number of common shares becomes the corporation's common stock amount; it is the minimum amount that can be reported as contributed capital. When the value received is greater than par value, the amount over par value is called **additional paid-in capital**.*

Retained earnings represent stockholders' equity that has been generated by the business' income-producing activities and kept for use in the business. As you can see in Figure 8, retained earnings are affected by three kinds of transactions: revenues, expenses, and dividends.

Simply stated, **revenues** and **expenses** are the increases and decreases in stockholders' equity that result from operating a business. For example, the amount a customer pays (or agrees to pay in the future) to **CVS** in return for a product or service is a revenue to CVS. CVS's assets (cash or accounts receivable) increase, as does its stockholders' equity in those assets. On the other hand, the amount CVS must pay out (or agree to pay out) so that it can provide a product or service is an expense. In this case, the assets (cash) decrease or the liabilities (accounts payable) increase, and the stockholders' equity decreases.

FIGURE 8

Three Types of Transactions That Affect Retained Earnings

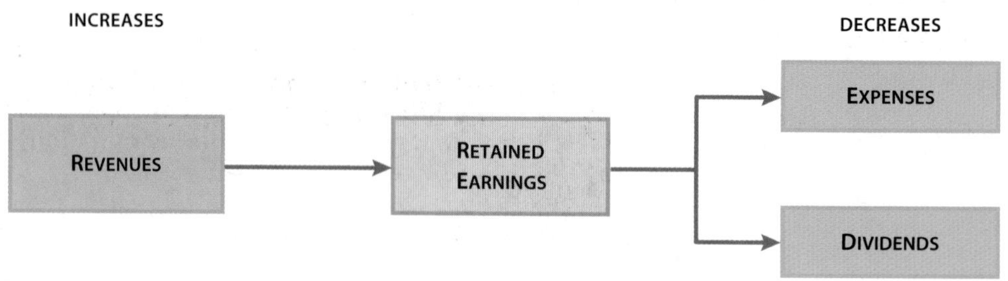

*We assume in the early chapters of this book that common stock is listed at par value.

Generally, a company is successful if its revenues exceed its expenses. When revenues exceed expenses, the difference is called **net income**. When expenses exceed revenues, the difference is called **net loss**. As noted earlier, dividends are distributions to stockholders of assets (usually cash) generated by past earnings. It is important not to confuse expenses and dividends, both of which reduce retained earnings. In summary, retained earnings are the accumulated net income (revenues − expenses) less dividends over the life of the business.

STOP ▶ REVIEW ▶ APPLY

LO5-1 What are assets?

LO5-2 How are liabilities and stockholders' equity similar, and how do they differ?

LO5-3 What three elements affect retained earnings, and what is the effect of each?

LO5-4 Give an example of a single transaction that causes both an increase and decrease in assets.

The Accounting Equation and Net Income
Johnson Company had assets of $140,000 and liabilities of $60,000 at the beginning of the year, and assets of $200,000 and liabilities of $70,000 at the end of the year. During the year, $20,000 was invested in the business, and dividends of $24,000 were paid. What amount of net income did the company earn during the year?

Beginning of the year				
Assets	=	Liabilities	+	Stockholders' Equity
$140,000	=	$60,000	+	**$ 80,000**
During year				
		Investment	+	20,000
		Dividends	−	24,000
		Net income		?
End of year				
$200,000	=	$70,000	+	**$130,000**

SOLUTION
Net income = $54,000

Start by finding the stockholders' equity at the beginning of the year. (Check: $140,000 − $60,000 = $80,000)

Then find the stockholders' equity at the end of the year. (Check: $200,000 − $70,000 = $130,000)

Then determine net income by calculating how the transactions during the year led to the stockholders' equity amount at the end of the year. (Check: $80,000 + $20,000 − $24,000 + $54,000 = $130,000)

Financial Statements

LO6 Identify the four basic financial statements.

Financial statements are the primary means of communicating important accounting information about a business to those who have an interest in the business. These statements are models of the business enterprise in that they show the business in financial terms. As is true of all models, however, financial statements are not perfect pictures of the real thing. Rather, they are the accountant's best effort to represent what is real. Four major financial statements are used to communicate accounting information about a business: the income statement, the statement of retained earnings, the balance sheet, and the statement of cash flows.

Study Note

Businesses use four basic financial statements to communicate financial information to decision makers.

Income Statement

The **income statement** summarizes the revenues earned and expenses incurred by a business over an accounting period (see Exhibit 1). Many people consider it the most important financial report because it shows whether a business

EXHIBIT 1

Income Statement for Weiss Consultancy, Inc.

Weiss Consultancy, Inc.
Income Statement
For the Month Ended December 31, 2010

Revenues		
Consulting fees		$14,000
Expenses		
Equipment rental expense	$2,800	
Wages expense	1,600	
Utilities expense	1,200	
Total expenses		5,600
Income before income taxes		$ 8,400
Income taxes expense		1,200
Net income		$ 7,200

achieved its profitability goal—that is, whether it earned an acceptable income. Exhibit 1 shows that Weiss Consultancy, Inc., had revenues of $14,000 earned from consulting fees. From this amount, total expenses of $5,600 were deducted (equipment rental expense of $2,800, wages expense of $1,600, and utilities expense of $1,200) to arrive at income before income taxes of $8,400. Income taxes of $1,200 were deducted to arrive at net income of $7,200. To show the period to which it applies, the statement is labeled "For the Month Ended December 31, 2010."

Statement of Retained Earnings

The **statement of retained earnings** shows the changes in retained earnings over an accounting period. In Exhibit 2, beginning retained earnings are zero because Weiss began operations in this accounting period. During the month, the company earned an income (as shown on the income statement) of $7,200. Deducted from this amount are the dividends for the month of $2,400, leaving an ending balance of $4,800 of earnings retained in the business.

The Balance Sheet

The purpose of a **balance sheet** is to show the financial position of a business on a certain date, usually the end of the month or year (see Exhibit 3). For this rea-

EXHIBIT 2

Statement of Retained Earnings for Weiss Consultancy, Inc.

Weiss Consultancy, Inc.
Statement of Retained Earnings
For the Month Ended December 31, 2010

Retained earnings, December 1, 2010	$ 0
Net income for the month	7,200
Subtotal	$7,200
Less dividends	2,400
Retained earnings, December 31, 2010	$4,800

EXHIBIT 3 Balance Sheet for Weiss Consultancy, Inc.

Weiss Consultancy, Inc.
Balance Sheet
December 31, 2010

Assets		**Liabilities**		
Cash	$ 61,200	Accounts payable		$ 2,400
Accounts receivable	4,000			
Supplies	2,000	**Stockholders' Equity**		
Land	40,000	Common stock	$200,000	
Building	100,000	Retained earnings	4,800	
		Total stockholders' equity		204,800
Total assets	$207,200	Total liabilities and stockholders' equity		$207,200

Study Note

The date on the balance sheet is a single date, whereas the dates on the other three statements cover a period of time, such as a month, quarter, or year.

son, it often is called the *statement of financial position* and is dated as of a specific date.

The balance sheet presents a view of the business as the holder of resources, or assets, that are equal to the claims against those assets. The claims consist of the company's liabilities and the stockholders' equity in the company. Exhibit 3 shows that Weiss Consultancy has several categories of assets, which total $207,200. These assets equal the total liabilities of $2,400 (accounts payable) plus the ending balance of stockholders' equity of $204,800. Notice that the amount of retained earnings on the balance sheet comes from the ending balance on the statement of retained earnings.

Statement of Cash Flows

Whereas the income statement focuses on a company's profitability, the **statement of cash flows** focuses on its liquidity (see Exhibit 4). **Cash flows** are the inflows and outflows of cash into and out of a business. Net cash flows are the difference between the inflows and outflows.

As you can see in Exhibit 4, the statement of cash flows is organized according to the three major business activities described earlier in the chapter.

Study Note

The statement of cash flows explains the change in cash in terms of operating, investing, and financing activities over an accounting period. It provides valuable information that cannot be determined in an examination of the other financial statements.

- **Cash flows from operating activities:** The first section of Exhibit 4 shows the cash produced by business operations. Weiss's operating activities produced cash flows of $3,600 (liquidity) compared to net income of $7,200 (profitability). The company used cash to increase accounts receivable and supplies. However, by borrowing funds, it increased accounts payable. This is not a good trend, which Weiss should try to reverse in future months.
- **Cash flows from investing activities:** Weiss used cash to expand by purchasing land and a building.
- **Cash flows from financing activities:** Weiss obtained most of its cash from stockholders and paid a small dividend.

Overall, Weiss had a net increase in cash of $61,200, due in large part to the investment by stockholders. In future months, Weiss must generate more cash through operations.

EXHIBIT 4 Statement of Cash Flows for Weiss Consultancy, Inc.

Weiss Consultancy, Inc.
Statement of Cash Flows
For the Month Ended December 31, 2010

Cash flows from operating activities		
Net income		$ 7,200
Adjustments to reconcile net income to net cash flows from operating activities		
(Increase) in accounts receivable	($ 4,000)	
(Increase) in supplies	(2,000)	
Increase in accounts payable	2,400	(3,600)
Net cash flows from operating activities		$ 3,600
Cash flows from investing activities		
Purchase of land	($ 40,000)	
Purchase of building	(100,000)	
Net cash flows from investing activities		(140,000)
Cash flows from financing activities		
Issued common stock	$200,000	
Paid dividends	(2,400)	
Net cash flows from financing activities		197,600
Net increase (decrease) in cash		$61,200
Cash at beginning of month		0
Cash at end of month		$61,200

Note: Parentheses indicate a negative amount.

The statement of cash flows is related directly to the other three financial statements. Notice that net income comes from the income statement and that dividends come from the statement of retained earnings. The other items in the statement represent changes in the balance sheet accounts: accounts receivable, supplies, accounts payable, land, building, and common stock. Here we focus on the importance and overall structure of the statement. Its construction and use are discussed in a later chapter.

Relationships Among the Financial Statements

Exhibit 5 illustrates the relationships among the four financial statements by showing how they would appear for Weiss Consultancy, Inc. The period covered is the month of December 2010.

Notice the similarity of the headings at the top of each statement. Each identifies the company and the kind of statement. The income statement, the statement of retained earnings, and the statement of cash flows indicate the period to which they apply; the balance sheet gives the specific date to which it applies. Much of this book deals with developing, using, and interpreting more complete versions of these statements.

EXHIBIT 5 Income Statement, Statement of Retained Earnings, Balance Sheet, and Statement of Cash Flows for Weiss Consultancy, Inc.

Weiss Consultancy, Inc.
Statement of Cash Flows
For the Month Ended December 31, 2010

Cash flows from operating activities		
Net income		$ 7,200
Adjustments to reconcile net income to net cash flows from operating activities		
(Increase) in accounts receivable	($ 4,000)	
(Increase) in supplies	(2,000)	
Increase in accounts payable	2,400	(3,600)
Net cash flows from operating activities		$ 3,600
Cash flows from investing activities		
Purchase of land	($ 40,000)	
Purchase of building	(100,000)	
Net cash flows from investing activities		(140,000)
Cash flows from financing activities		
Issued common stock	$200,000	
Paid dividends	(2,400)	
Net cash flows from financing activities		197,600
Net increase (decrease) in cash		$61,200
Cash at beginning of month		0
Cash at end of month		$61,200

Weiss Consultancy, Inc.
Income Statement
For the Month Ended December 31, 2010

Revenues		
Consulting fees		$14,000
Expenses		
Equipment rental expense	$2,800	
Wages expense	1,600	
Utilities expense	1,200	
Total expenses		5,600
Income before income taxes		$ 8,400
Income taxes expense		1,200
Net income		$ 7,200

Weiss Consultancy, Inc.
Statement of Retained Earnings
For the Month Ended December 31, 2010

Retained earnings, December 1, 2010	$ 0
Net income for the month	7,200
Subtotal	$ 7,200
Less dividends	2,400
Retained earnings, December 31, 2010	$ 4,800

Weiss Consultancy, Inc.
Balance Sheet
December 31, 2010

Assets		**Liabilities**	
Cash	$ 61,200	Accounts payable	$ 2,400
Accounts receivable	4,000		
Supplies	2,000	**Stockholders' Equity**	
Land	40,000	Common stock	$200,000
Building	100,000	Retained earnings	4,800
		Total stockholders' equity	$204,800
Total assets	$207,200	Total liabilities and stockholders' equity	$207,200

Study Note

Notice the sequence in which these financial statements must be prepared. The statement of retained earnings is a link between the income statement and the balance sheet, and the statement of cash flows is prepared last.

STOP ▶ REVIEW ▶ APPLY

LO6-1 What is the purpose of the statement of retained earnings?

LO6-2 Why is the balance sheet sometimes called the statement of financial position?

LO6-3 Contrast the purposes of the balance sheet and the income statement.

LO6-4 A statement for an accounting period that ends in June can be headed "June 30, 2010" or "For the month ended June 30, 2010." Which heading is appropriate for (a) a balance sheet and (b) an income statement?

LO6-5 How do the income statement and the statement of cash flows differ?

Interrelationship of the Financial Statements Complete the financial statements that appear in the left column below by determining the amounts that correspond to the letters. (Assume no new investments by stockholders.)

Income Statement	
Revenues	$2,775
Expenses	(a)
Net income	$ (b)
Statement of Retained Earnings	
Beginning balance	$7,250
Net income	(c)
Less dividends	500
Ending balance	$7,500
Balance Sheet	
Total assets	$ (d)
Liabilities	$4,000
Stockholders' equity	
Common stock	5,000
Retained earnings	(e)
Total liabilities and stockholders' equity	$ (f)

SOLUTION
Net income links the income statement and the statement of retained earnings. The ending balance of retained earnings links the statement of retained earnings and the balance sheet.

Thus, start with (c), which must equal $750 (check: $7,250 + $750 – $500 = $7,500). Then, (b) equals (c), or $750. Thus, (a) must equal $2,025 (check: $2,775 – $2,025 = $750). Because (e) equals $7,500 (ending balance from the statement of retained earnings), (f) must equal $16,500 (check: $4,000 + $5,000 + $7,500 = $16,500). Now, (d) equals (f), or $16,500.

Generally Accepted Accounting Principles

LO7 Explain how generally accepted accounting principles (GAAP) relate to financial statements and the independent CPA's report, and identify the organizations that influence GAAP.

To ensure that financial statements are understandable to their users, a set of practices, called **generally accepted accounting principles (GAAP)**, has been developed to provide guidelines for financial accounting. "Generally accepted accounting principles encompass the conventions, rules, and procedures necessary to define accepted accounting practice at a particular time."[11] In other words, GAAP arise from wide agreement on the theory and practice of accounting at a particular time. These "principles" are not like the unchangeable laws of nature in chemistry or physics. They evolve to meet the needs of decision makers, and they change as circumstances change or as better methods are developed.

In this book, we present accounting practice, or GAAP, as it is today, and we try to explain the reasons or theory on which the practice is based. Both theory and practice are important to the study of accounting. However, accounting is a discipline that is always growing, changing, and improving. Just as years of

TABLE 2
Large International Certified Public Accounting Firms

Firm	Home Office	Some Major Clients
Deloitte & Touche	New York	General Motors, Procter & Gamble
Ernst & Young	New York	Coca-Cola, McDonald's
KPMG	New York	General Electric, Xerox
PricewaterhouseCoopers	New York	Exxon Mobil, IBM, Ford

research are necessary before a new surgical method or lifesaving drug can be introduced, it may take years for new accounting practices to be implemented.* As a result, you may encounter practices that seem contradictory. In some cases, we point out new directions in accounting. Your instructor also may mention certain weaknesses in current theory or practice.

GAAP and the Independent CPA's Report

Because financial statements are prepared by management and could be falsified for personal gain, all companies that sell shares of their stock to the public and many companies that apply for sizable loans have their financial statements audited by an independent **certified public accountant (CPA)**. *Independent* means that the CPA is not an employee of the company being audited and has no financial or other compromising ties with it. CPAs are licensed by all states for the same reason that lawyers and doctors are—to protect the public by ensuring the quality of professional service. The firms listed in Table 2 employ about 25 percent of all CPAs.

Study Note

The audit lends credibility to a set of financial statements. The auditor does not attest to the absolute accuracy of the published information or to the value of the company as an investment. All he or she renders is an opinion, based on appropriate testing, about the fairness of the presentation of the financial information.

An **audit** is an examination of a company's financial statements and the accounting systems, controls, and records that produced them. The purpose of the audit is to ascertain that the financial statements have been prepared in accordance with generally accepted accounting principles. If the independent CPA is satisfied that this standard has been met, his or her report contains the following language:

> In our opinion, the financial statements . . . present fairly, in all material respects . . . in conformity with generally accepted accounting principles . . .

This wording emphasizes that accounting and auditing are not exact sciences. Because the framework of GAAP provides room for interpretation and the application of GAAP necessitates the making of estimates, the auditor can render only an opinion about whether the financial statements *present fairly* or conform *in all material respects* to GAAP. The auditor's report does not preclude minor or immaterial errors in the financial statements. However, a favorable report from the auditor does imply that on the whole, investors and creditors can rely on the financial statements.

Historically, auditors have enjoyed a strong reputation for competence and independence. The independent audit has been an important factor in the worldwide growth of financial markets.

Study Note

The FASB is the primary source of GAAP, but the IASB is increasing in importance.

Organizations That Issue Accounting Standards

Two organizations issue accounting standards that are used in the United States: the FASB and the IASB. The **Financial Accounting Standards Board (FASB)**

*Established in January 2007, the Private Company Financial Reporting Committee of the AICPA is charged with amending FASB accounting standards so that they better suit the needs of private companies, especially as they relate to the cost or benefit of implementing certain standards. This initiative could ultimately result in two sets of standards, one for private companies and one for public companies.

is the most important body for developing rules on accounting practice. This independent body has been designated by the Securities and Exchange Commission (SEC) to issue the *Statements of Financial Accounting Standards.*

IFRS

With the growth of financial markets throughout the world, global cooperation in the development of accounting principles has become a priority. The **International Accounting Standards Board (IASB)** has approved more than 40 **International Financial Reporting Standards (IFRS)**. Foreign companies may use these standards in the United States rather than having to convert their statements to U.S. GAAP as called for by the FASB standards.

Other Organizations That Influence GAAP

Many other organizations directly or indirectly influence GAAP and so influence much of what is in this book.

Study Note

The PCAOB regulates audits of public companies registered with the Securities and Exchange Commission.

The **Public Company Accounting Oversight Board (PCAOB)**, a governmental body created by the Sarbanes-Oxley Act, regulates the accounting profession and has wide powers to determine the standards that auditors must follow and to discipline them if they do not.

The **American Institute of Certified Public Accountants (AICPA)**, the professional association of certified public accountants, influences accounting practice through the activities of its senior technical committees. In addition to endorsing standards issued by the FASB, the AICPA has determined that standards issued by the IASB are also of high quality.

Study Note

The AICPA is the primary professional organization of certified public accountants.

The **Securities and Exchange Commission (SEC)** is an agency of the federal government that has the legal power to set and enforce accounting practices for companies whose securities are offered for sale to the general public. As such, it has enormous influence on accounting practice.

The **Governmental Accounting Standards Board (GASB)**, which is under the same governing body as the FASB, issues accounting standards for state and local governments.

U.S. tax laws that govern the assessment and collection of revenue for operating the federal government also influence accounting practice. Because a major source of the government's revenue is the income tax, the tax laws specify the rules for determining taxable income. The **Internal Revenue Service (IRS)** interprets and enforces these rules. In some cases, the rules conflict with good accounting practice, but they are nonetheless an important influence on practice. Cases in which the tax laws affect accounting practice are noted throughout this book.

FOCUS ON BUSINESS PRACTICE IFRS

The Arrival of International Financial Reporting Standards in the United States

Over the next few years, international financial reporting standards (IFRS) will become much more important in the United States and globally. The International Accounting Standards Board (IASB) has been working with the Financial Accounting Standards Board (FASB) and similar boards in other nations to achieve identical or nearly identical standards worldwide. IFRS are now required in many parts of the world, including Europe. The Securities and Exchange Commission (SEC) recently voted to allow foreign registrants in the United States. This is a major development because in the past, the SEC required foreign registrants to explain how the standards used in their statements differed from U.S. standards. This change affects approximately 10 percent of all public U.S. companies. In addition, the SEC may in the near future allow U.S. companies to use IFRS.[12]

Accountants from Ernst & Young arrive at the 55th Annual Emmy Awards at the Shrine Auditorium, Los Angeles, September 2003. The independent accounting firm receives and tallies the votes. *Independent* means that the firm has no financial or other compromising ties with the Academy of Television Arts & Sciences, the organization that presents the Emmy Awards.

Professional Conduct

The code of professional ethics of the American Institute of Certified Public Accountants (and adopted, with variations, by each state) governs the conduct of CPAs. Fundamental to this code is responsibility to clients, creditors, investors, and anyone else who relies on the work of a CPA. The code requires CPAs to act with integrity, objectivity, and independence.

- **Integrity** means the accountant is honest and candid and subordinates personal gain to service and the public trust.
- **Objectivity** means the accountant is impartial and intellectually honest.
- **Independence** means the accountant avoids all relationships that impair or even appear to impair his or her objectivity.

The accountant must also exercise **due care** in all activities, carrying out professional responsibilities with competence and diligence. For example, an accountant must not accept a job for which he or she is not qualified, even at the risk of losing a client to another firm, and careless work is unacceptable. These broad principles are supported by more specific rules that public accountants must follow; for instance, with certain exceptions, client information must be kept strictly confidential. Accountants who violate the rules can be disciplined or even suspended from practice.

Study Note

The IMA is the primary professional association of management accountants.

The **Institute of Management Accountants (IMA)** also has a code of professional conduct. It emphasizes that management accountants have a responsibility to be competent in their jobs, to keep information confidential except when authorized or legally required to disclose it, to maintain integrity and avoid conflicts of interest, and to communicate information objectively and without bias.[13]

STOP ▶ REVIEW ▶ APPLY

LO7-1 **What are GAAP? Why are they important to readers of financial statements?**

LO7-2 **As used in an auditor's report, what does *in all material respects* mean?**

LO7-3 **What is the PCAOB, and why is it important?**

LO7-4 **What organization has the most influence on GAAP?**

LO7-5 **Why are international accounting standards becoming more important?**

LO7-6 **Why are codes of ethics important in the accounting profession?**

A LOOK BACK AT ▶ CVS Caremark

The Decision Point at the beginning of this chapter focused on **CVS** Caremark, a successful nationwide chain of more than 6,000 drugstores. It posed these questions:

- **Is CVS meeting its goal of profitability?**
- **As a manager at CVS, what financial knowledge would you need to measure progress toward the company's goals?**
- **As a potential investor or creditor, what financial knowledge would you need to evaluate CVS's financial performance?**

As you've learned in this chapter, managers and others with an interest in a business measure its profitability in financial terms, such as net sales, net income, total assets, and stockholders' equity. Managers report on the progress they have made toward their financial goals in their company's financial statements.

As you can see in the highlights from CVS's financial statements, the company's net sales, net earnings (net income), total assets, and stockholders' equity have increased over the years.[14] But how do we use these data to determine if CVS is meeting its goal of profitability?

Study Note

Most companies list the most recent year of information in the first column, as shown here.

CVS'S FINANCIAL HIGHLIGHTS
(In millions)

	2007	2006	2005
Net sales	**$76,329.5**	$43,821.4	$37,006.7
Net earnings	**2,637.0**	1,368.9	1,224.7
Total assets	**54,721.9**	20,574.1	15,246.6
Stockholders' equity	**31,321.9**	9,917.6	8,331.2

As mentioned earlier in the chapter, one way to measure financial performance is through ratios. Ratios are used to compare a company's financial performance from one year to the next and to make comparisons among companies. The ratio that tells us if CVS is meeting its goal of profitability is the **return on assets** ratio. This ratio shows how efficiently a company is using its assets to produce income.

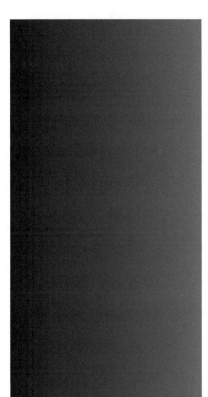

We use two values to calculate return on assets: net income, which is what is left over after expenses are subtracted from revenues (see the income statement in Exhibit 1), and average total assets. Average total assets are the total of this year's assets plus last year's assets divided by two (see the balance sheet in Exhibit 3).

The return on assets ratio for CVS is calculated as follows (amounts are in millions):

	2007	2006
$\frac{\text{Net Income}}{\text{Average Total Assets}}$	$\frac{\$2,637.0}{(\$54,721.9 + \$20,574.1) \div 2}$	$\frac{\$1,368.9}{(\$20,574.1 + \$15,246.6) \div 2}$
K/R	$\frac{\$2,637.0}{\$37,648.0}$	$\frac{\$1,368.9}{\$17,910.4}$
Return on Assets:	$.070 \times 100 = 7.0\%$	$.076 \times 100 = 7.6\%$

We can draw several conclusions from this ratio. First, CVS earned 7.0 to 7.6 cents on each dollar it invested in assets. Second, from 2006 to 2007, its profitability declined from 7.6 to 7.0 percent. Third, CVS is a growing company as demonstrated by the increases in its net sales, net earnings, total assets, and stockholders' equity in every year of the three-year period. These amounts indicate that CVS is a profitable and successful company but faces challenges in maintaining its profitability. You will learn much more about ratios in the chapters that follow.

If you aspire to be a manager of a business, an accountant, an investor, a business owner, or just a good employee, you will need to be familiar with measures like the return on assets ratio. You will also need to master other accounting concepts and terminology and know how financial information is produced, interpreted, and analyzed. The purpose of this book is to help you acquire that knowledge.

CHAPTER REVIEW

REVIEW of Learning Objectives

LO1 Define *accounting* and describe its role in making informed decisions, identify business goals and activities, and explain the importance of ethics in accounting.

Accounting is an information system that measures, processes, and communicates financial information about an economic entity. It provides the information necessary to make reasoned choices among alternative uses of scarce resources in the conduct of business and economic activities. A business is an economic entity that engages in operating, investing, and financing activities to achieve the goals of profitability and liquidity.

Management accounting focuses on the preparation of information primarily for internal use by management. Financial accounting is concerned with the development and use of reports that are communicated to those outside the business as well as to management. Ethical financial reporting is important to the well-being of a company; fraudulent financial reports can have serious consequences for many people.

LO2 Identify the users of accounting information.

Accounting plays a significant role in society by providing information to managers of all institutions and to individuals with a direct financial interest in those institutions, including present or potential investors and creditors. Accounting information is also important to those with an indirect financial interest in the business—for example, tax authorities, regulatory agencies, and economic planners.

LO3 Explain the importance of business transactions, money measure, and separate entity.

To make an accounting measurement, the accountant must determine what is measured, when the measurement should be made, what value should be placed on what is measured, and how to classify what is measured. The objects of accounting measurement are business transactions. Financial accounting uses money measure to gauge the impact of these transactions on a separate business entity.

LO4 Describe the characteristics of a corporation.

Corporations, whose ownership is represented by shares of stock, are separate entities for both legal and accounting purposes. The stockholders own the corporation and elect the board of directors. The board is responsible for determining corporate policies and appointing corporate officers, or top managers, to operate the business in accordance with the policies that it sets. The board is also responsible for corporate governance, the oversight of a corporation's management and ethics. The audit committee, which is appointed by the board and is made up of independent directors, is an important factor in corporate governance.

LO5 Define *financial position*, and state the accounting equation.

Financial position refers to a company's economic resources and the claims against those resources at a particular time. The accounting equation shows financial position as Assets = Liabilities + Stockholders' Equity. (In the case of sole proprietorships and partnerships, stockholders' equity is called *owners' equity.*) Business transactions affect financial position by decreasing or increasing assets, liabilities, and stockholders' (or owners') equity in such a way that the accounting equation is always in balance.

LO6 Identify the four basic financial statements.

The four basic financial statements are the income statement, the statement of retained earnings, the balance sheet, and the statement of cash flows. They are the primary means by which accountants communicate the financial condition and activities of a business to those who have an interest in the business.

LO7 Explain how generally accepted accounting principles (GAAP) relate to financial statements and the independent CPA's report, and identify the organizations that influence GAAP.

Acceptable accounting practice consists of the conventions, rules, and procedures that make up generally accepted accounting principles at a particular time. GAAP are essential to the preparation and interpretation of financial statements and the independent CPA's report. Foreign companies registered in the United States may use international financial reporting standards (IFRS).

Among the organizations that influence the formulation of GAAP are the Public Company Accounting Oversight Board, the Financial Accounting Standards Board, the American Institute of Certified Public Accountants, the Securities and Exchange Commission, and the Internal Revenue Service.

All accountants must follow a code of professional ethics, which is based on responsibility to the public. Accountants must act with integrity, objectivity, and independence, and they must exercise due care in all their activities.

REVIEW of Concepts and Terminology

The following concepts and terms were introduced in this chapter:

Accounting: An information system that measures, processes, and communicates financial information about an economic entity. **(LO1)**

Accounting equation: Assets = Liabilities + Stockholders' (or Owners') Equity. **(LO5)**

Additional paid-in capital: The amount over par value in a corporation's contributed capital. **(LO5)**

American Institute of Certified Public Accountants (AICPA): The professional association of certified public accountants. **(LO7)**

Articles of incorporation: An official document filed with and approved by a state that authorizes the incorporators to do business as a corporation. **(LO4)**

Assets: The economic resources of a company that are expected to benefit future operations. **(LO5)**

Audit: An examination of a company's financial statements in order to render an independent professional opinion about whether they have been presented fairly, in all material respects, in conformity with generally accepted accounting principles. **(LO7)**

Audit committee: A subgroup of a corporation's board of directors that is charged with ensuring that the board will be objective in reviewing management's performance; it engages the company's independent auditors and reviews their work. **(LO4)**

Balance sheet: The financial statement that shows a business's assets, liabilities, and stockholders' equity as of a specific date. Also called the *statement of financial position*. **(LO6)**

Bookkeeping: The process of recording financial transactions and keeping financial records. **(LO1)**

Business: An economic unit that aims to sell goods and services to customers at prices that will provide an adequate return to its owners. **(LO1)**

Business transactions: Economic events that affect a business's financial position. **(LO3)**

Cash flows: The inflows and outflows of cash into and out of a business. **(LO6)**

Certified public accountant (CPA): A public accountant who has met stringent state licensing requirements. **(LO7)**

Common stock: The most common form of stock. **(LO4)**

Computer: An electronic tool for the rapid collection, organization, and communication of large amounts of information. **(LO1)**

Contributed capital: The part of stockholders' equity that represents the amount invested in the business by the owners (stockholders). **(LO5)**

Corporate governance: The oversight of a corporation's management and ethics by the board of directors. **(LO4)**

Corporation: A business unit granted a state charter recognizing it as a separate legal entity having its own rights, privileges, and liabilities distinct from those of its owners. **(LO4)**

Dividends: Distributions to stockholders of assets (usually cash) generated by past earnings. **(LO4)**

Due care: Competence and diligence in carrying out professional responsibilities. **(LO7)**

Ethics: A code of conduct that addresses whether actions are right or wrong. **(LO1)**

Exchange rate: The value of one currency in terms of another. **(LO3)**

Expenses: Decreases in stockholders' equity that result from operating a business. **(LO5)**

Financial accounting: The process of generating and communicating accounting information in the form of financial statements to those outside the organization. **(LO1)**

Financial Accounting Standards Board (FASB): The most important body for developing rules on accounting practice; it issues *Statements of Financial Accounting Standards.* **(LO7)**

Financial analysis: The evaluation and interpretation of financial statements and related performance measures. **(LO1)**

Financial position: The economic resources that belong to a company and the claims (equities) against those resources at a particular time. **(LO5)**

Financial statements: The primary means of communicating important accounting information to users. They include the income statement, statement of retained earnings, balance sheet, and statement of cash flows. **(LO1)**

Financing activities: Activities undertaken by management to obtain adequate funds to begin and to continue operating a business. **(LO1)**

Fraudulent financial reporting: The intentional preparation of misleading financial statements. **(LO1)**

Generally accepted accounting principles (GAAP): The conventions, rules, and procedures that define accepted accounting practice at a particular time. **(LO7)**

Governmental Accounting Standards Board (GASB): The board responsible for issuing accounting standards for state and local governments. **(LO7)**

Income statement: A financial statement that summarizes the revenues earned and expenses incurred by a business over an accounting period. **(LO6)**

Independence: The avoidance of all relationships that impair or appear to impair an accountant's objectivity. **(LO7)**

Institute of Management Accountants (IMA): A professional organization made up primarily of management accountants. **(LO7)**

Integrity: Honesty, candidness, and the subordination of personal gain to service and the public trust. **(LO7)**

Internal Revenue Service (IRS): The agency that interprets and enforces the tax laws governing the assessment and collection of revenue for operating the federal government. **(LO7)**

International Accounting Standards Board (IASB): An organization that encourages worldwide cooperation in the development of accounting principles; it has approved more than 40 international standards of accounting. **(LO7)**

International financial reporting standards (IFRS): Accounting standards set by the IASB that are used in many parts of the world, including Europe, and by foreign companies registered in the United States. **(LO7)**

Investing activities: Activities undertaken by management to spend capital in productive ways that will help a business achieve its objectives. **(LO1)**

Liabilities: A business's present obligations to pay cash, transfer assets, or provide services to other entities in the future. **(LO5)**

Liquidity: Having enough cash available to pay debts when they are due. **(LO1)**

Management: The people who have overall responsibility for operating a business and meeting its goals. **(LO2)**

Management accounting: The process of producing accounting information for internal use by managers. **(LO1)**

Management information system (MIS): The interconnected subsystems that provide the information needed to run a business. **(LO1)**

Money measure: The recording of all business transactions in terms of money. **(LO3)**

Net assets: Assets minus liabilities; stockholders' equity or owners' equity. Also called *net worth.* **(LO5)**

Net income: The difference between revenues and expenses when revenues exceed expenses. **(LO5)**

Net loss: The difference between expenses and revenues when expenses exceed revenues. **(LO5)**

Objectivity: Impartiality and intellectual honesty. **(LO7)**

Operating activities: Activities undertaken by management in the course of running a business. **(LO1)**

Partnership: A business that is owned by two or more people and that is not incorporated. **(LO4)**

Par value: An amount per share that is entered in the corporation's capital stock account; it is the minimum amount that can be reported as contributed capital. **(LO5)**

Performance measures: Indicators of whether managers are achieving business goals and whether business activities are well managed. **(LO1)**

Profitability: The ability to earn enough income to attract and hold investment capital. **(LO1)**

Public Company Accounting Oversight Board (PCAOB): A governmental body created by the Sarbanes-Oxley Act to regulate the accounting profession. **(LO7)**

Retained earnings: Stockholders' equity that has been generated by business operations and kept for use in the business. **(LO5)**

Revenues: Increases in stockholders' equity that result from operating a business. **(LO5)**

Sarbanes-Oxley Act: An act of Congress that regulates financial reporting in public corporations. **(LO1)**

Securities and Exchange Commission (SEC): A governmental agency that regulates the issuing, buying, and selling of stocks. It has the legal power to set and enforce accounting practices for firms whose securities are sold to the general public. **(LO2, LO7)**

Separate entity: A business that is treated as distinct from its creditors, customers, and owners. **(LO3)**

Share of stock: A unit of ownership in a corporation. **(LO4)**

Sole proprietorship: A business that is owned by one person and that is not incorporated. **(LO4)**

Statement of cash flows: A financial statement that shows the inflows and outflows of cash from operating activities, investing activities, and financing activities over an accounting period. **(LO6)**

Statement of retained earnings: A financial statement that shows the changes in retained earnings over an accounting period. **(LO6)**

Stockholders' equity: The claims of the owners of a corporation to the assets of the business; Contributed Capital + Retained Earnings. Also called *shareholders' equity* and *owners' equity*. **(LO5)**

Key Ratio

Return on assets: A ratio that shows how efficiently a company is using its assets to produce income; Net Income ÷ Average Total Assets.

Review Problem

LO6 **Preparation and Interpretation of Financial Statements**

The following accounts and amounts are from the records of Jackson Realty for the year ended April 30, 2010, the company's first year of operations:

Accounts payable	$ 19,000
Accounts receivable	104,000
Cash	90,000
Commissions earned	375,000
Common stock	100,000
Dividends	10,000
Equipment	47,000
Income taxes expense	27,000
Income taxes payable	6,000
Marketing expense	18,000
Office and equipment rent expense	91,000
Salaries and commission expense	172,000
Salaries payable	78,000
Supplies	2,000
Supplies expense	6,000
Utilities expense	11,000

Required

1. Prepare an income statement, statement of retained earnings, and balance sheet for Jackson Realty. For examples, refer to Exhibit 5.

User insight ▶ 2. How are the statements related to each other?

Answer to Review Problem

1.

Jackson Realty Income Statement For the Year Ended April 30, 2010		
Revenues		
Commissions earned		$375,000
Expenses		
Marketing expense	$ 18,000	
Office and equipment rent expense	91,000	
Salaries and commission expense	172,000	
Supplies expense	6,000	
Utilities expense	11,000	
Total expenses		298,000
Income before income taxes		$ 77,000
Income taxes expense		27,000
Net income		$ 50,000

Jackson Realty Statement of Retained Earnings For the Year Ended April 30, 2010	
Retained earnings, April 30, 2009	$ —
Net income for the year	50,000
Subtotal	$50,000
Less dividends	10,000
Retained earnings, April 30, 2010	$40,000

Jackson Realty Balance Sheet April 30, 2010				
Assets		**Liabilities**		
Cash	$ 90,000	Accounts payable	$ 19,000	
Accounts receivable	104,000	Salaries payable	78,000	
Supplies	2,000	Income taxes payable	6,000	
Equipment	47,000	Total liabilities		$103,000
		Stockholders' Equity		
		Common stock	$100,000	
		Retained earnings	40,000	
		Total stockholders' equity		140,000
Total assets	$243,000	Total liabilities and stockholders' equity		$243,000

2. Net income from the income statement appears on the statement of retained earnings. The ending balance (on April 30, 2010) on the statement of retained earnings appears on the balance sheet.

CHAPTER ASSIGNMENTS

BUILDING Your Basic Knowledge and Skills

Short Exercises

LO1 **Accounting and Business Enterprises**

SE 1. Match the terms on the left with the definitions on the right:

	Terms		Definitions
____	1. Accounting	a.	The process of producing accounting information for the internal use of a company's management
____	2. Profitability	b.	Having enough cash available to pay debts when they are due
____	3. Liquidity	c.	Activities management engages in to obtain adequate funds for beginning and continuing to operate a business
____	4. Financing activities	d.	The process of generating and communicating accounting information in the form of financial statements to decision makers outside the organization
____	5. Investing activities	e.	Activities management engages in to spend capital in ways that are productive and will help a business achieve its objectives
____	6. Operating activities	f.	The ability to earn enough income to attract and hold investment capital
____	7. Financial accounting	g.	An information system that measures, processes, and communicates financial information about an identifiable economic entity
____	8. Management accounting	h.	The intentional preparation of misleading financial statements
____	9. Ethics	i.	Activities management engages in to operate the business
____	10. Fraudulent financial reporting	j.	A code of conduct that applies to everyday life

LO3 **Accounting Concepts**

SE 2. Indicate whether each of the following words or phrases relates most closely to (a) a business transaction, (b) a separate entity, or (c) a money measure:

1. Partnership
2. U.S. dollar
3. Payment of an expense
4. Corporation
5. Sale of an asset

LO4 **Forms of Business Enterprises**

SE 3. Match the descriptions on the left with the forms of business enterprise on the right:

____	1. Most numerous	a. Sole proprietorship
____	2. Commands most revenues	b. Partnership
____	3. Two or more co-owners	c. Corporation
____	4. Has stockholders	
____	5. Owned by only one person	
____	6. Has a board of directors	

LO5 **The Accounting Equation**

SE 4. Determine the amount missing from each accounting equation below.

Assets	=	Liabilities	+	Stockholders' Equity
1. ?		$50,000		$ 70,000
2. $156,000		$84,000		?
3. $292,000		?		$192,000

LO5 **The Accounting Equation**

SE 5. Use the accounting equation to answer each question below.

1. The assets of Aaron Co. are $240,000, and the liabilities are $90,000. What is the amount of the stockholders' equity?
2. The liabilities of Oak Company equal one-fifth of the total assets. The stockholders' equity is $40,000. What is the amount of the liabilities?

LO5 **The Accounting Equation**

SE 6. Use the accounting equation to answer each question below.

1. At the beginning of the year, Fazio Company's assets were $45,000, and its stockholders' equity was $25,000. During the year, assets increased by $30,000 and liabilities increased by $5,000. What was the stockholders' equity at the end of the year?
2. At the beginning of the year, Gal Company had liabilities of $50,000 and stockholders' equity of $96,000. If assets increased by $40,000 and liabilities decreased by $30,000, what was the stockholders' equity at the end of the year?

LO5 **The Accounting Equation and Net Income**

SE 7. Carlton Company had assets of $280,000 and liabilities of $120,000 at the beginning of the year, and assets of $400,000 and liabilities of $140,000 at the end of the year. During the year, there was an investment of $40,000 in the business, and the company paid dividends of $48,000. What amount of net income did the company earn during the year?

LO6 **Preparation and Completion of a Balance Sheet**

SE 8. Use the following accounts and balances to prepare a balance sheet with the accounts in proper order for Global Company at June 30, 2009, using Exhibit 3 as a model:

Accounts Receivable	$ 1,600
Wages Payable	700
Retained Earnings	4,700
Common Stock	24,000
Building	22,000
Cash	?

LO6

Preparation of Financial Statements

SE 9. Tarech Corporation engaged in activities during the first year of its operations that resulted in the following: service revenue, $4,800; total expenses, $2,450; and dividends, $410. In addition, the year-end balances of selected accounts were as follows: Cash, $1,890; Other Assets, $1,000; Accounts Payable, $450; and Common Stock, $500. In proper format, prepare the income statement, statement of retained earnings, and balance sheet for Tarech Corporation (assume the year ends on December 31, 2010). (**Hint**: You must solve for the beginning and ending balances of retained earnings for 2010.)

Return on Assets

SE 10. Orbit Machine had net income of $15,000 in 2010. Total assets were $80,000 at the beginning of the year and $140,000 at the end of the year. Calculate return on assets.

Exercises

LO1 LO2 LO3 LO4

Discussion Questions

E 1. Develop a brief answer to each of the following questions.

1. What makes accounting a valuable discipline?
2. Why do managers in governmental and not-for-profit organizations need to understand financial information as much as managers in profit-seeking businesses?
3. Are all economic events business transactions?
4. Sole proprietorships, partnerships, and corporations differ legally; how and why does accounting treat them alike?

LO5 LO6

Discussion Questions

E 2. Develop a brief answer to each of the following questions.

1. How are expenses and dividends similar, and how are they different?
2. In what ways are **CVS** and **Southwest Airlines** comparable? Not comparable?
3. How do generally accepted accounting principles (GAAP) differ from the laws of science?
4. What are some unethical ways in which a business may do its accounting or prepare its financial statements?

LO1 LO2

The Nature of Accounting

E 3. Match the terms below with the descriptions in the list that follows:

____ 1. Bookkeeping
____ 2. Creditors
____ 3. Money measure
____ 4. Financial Accounting Standards Board (FASB)
____ 5. Business transactions
____ 6. Computer
____ 7. Communication
____ 8. Securities and Exchange Commission (SEC)
____ 9. Investors
____ 10. Sarbanes-Oxley Act
____ 11. Management
____ 12. Management information system

a. The recording of all business transactions in terms of money
b. A process by which information is exchanged between individuals through a common system of symbols, signs, or behavior
c. The process of identifying and assigning values to business transactions
d. Legislation ordering CEOs and CFOs to swear that any reports they file with the SEC are accurate and complete

e. An electronic tool for the rapid collection, organization, and communication of large amounts of information
f. Collectively, the people who have overall responsibility for operating a business and meeting its goals
g. People who commit money to earn a financial return
h. The interconnected subsystems that provide the information needed to run a business
i. The most important body for developing and issuing rules on accounting practice, called *Statements of Financial Accounting Standards*
j. An agency set up by Congress to protect the public by regulating the issuing, buying, and selling of stocks
k. Economic events that affect a business's financial position
l. People to whom money is due

LO2 LO4 **Users of Accounting Information and Forms of Business Enterprise**

E 4. Gottlieb Pharmacy has recently been formed to develop a new type of drug treatment for cancer. Previously a partnership, Gottlieb has now become a corporation. Describe the various groups that will have an interest in the financial statements of Gottlieb. What is the difference between a partnership and a corporation? What advantages does the corporate form have over the partnership form of business organization?

LO3 **Business Transactions**

E 5. Velu owns and operates a minimart. Which of Velu's actions described below are business transactions? Explain why any other actions are not considered transactions.

1. Velu reduces the price of a gallon of milk in order to match the price offered by a competitor.
2. Velu pays a high school student cash for cleaning up the driveway behind the market.
3. Velu fills his son's car with gasoline in payment for his son's restocking the vending machines and the snack food shelves.
4. Velu pays interest to himself on a loan he made to the business three years ago.

LO3 LO4 **Accounting Concepts**

E 6. Financial accounting uses money measures to gauge the impact of business transactions on a separate business entity. Tell whether each of the following words or phrases relates most closely to (a) a business transaction, (b) a separate entity, or (c) a money measure:

1. Corporation
2. Euro
3. Sales of products
4. Receipt of cash
5. Sole proprietorship
6. U.S. dollar
7. Partnership
8. Stockholders' investments
9. Japanese yen
10. Purchase of supplies

LO3 **Money Measure**

E 7. You have been asked to compare the sales and assets of four companies that make computer chips to determine which company is the largest in each category. You have gathered the following data, but they cannot be used for direct comparison because each company's sales and assets are in its own currency:

Company (Currency)	Sales	Assets
US.Chip (U.S. dollar)	2,750,000	1,300,000
Nanhai (Hong Kong dollar)	5,000,000	2,800,000
Tova (Japanese yen)	350,000,000	290,000,000
Holstein (Euro)	3,500,000	3,900,000

Assuming that the exchange rates in Table 1 are current and appropriate, convert all the figures to U.S. dollars and determine which company is the largest in sales and which is the largest in assets.

LO5

The Accounting Equation

E 8. Use the accounting equation to answer each question that follows. Show any calculations you make.

1. The assets of Rasche Corporation are $380,000, and the stockholders' equity is $155,000. What is the amount of the liabilities?
2. The liabilities and stockholders' equity of Lee Corporation are $65,000 and $79,500, respectively. What is the amount of the assets?
3. The liabilities of Hurka Corporation equal one-third of the total assets, and stockholders' equity is $180,000. What is the amount of the liabilities?
4. At the beginning of the year, Jahis Corporation's assets were $310,000, and its stockholders' equity was $150,000. During the year, assets increased $45,000 and liabilities decreased $22,500. What is the stockholders' equity at the end of the year?

LO5 LO6

Identification of Accounts

E 9. 1. Indicate whether each of the following accounts is an asset (A), a liability (L), or a part of stockholders' equity (SE):

a. Cash
b. Salaries Payable
c. Accounts Receivable
d. Common Stock
e. Land
f. Accounts Payable
g. Supplies

2. Indicate whether each account below would be shown on the income statement (IS), the statement of retained earnings (RE), or the balance sheet (BS).

a. Repair Revenue
b. Automobile
c. Fuel Expense
d. Cash
e. Rent Expense
f. Accounts Payable
g. Dividends

LO6

Preparation of a Balance Sheet

E 10. Listed in random order are some of the account balances for the Uptime Services Company as of December 31, 2010.

Accounts Payable	$ 25,000	Accounts Receivable	$31,250
Building	56,250	Cash	12,500
Common Stock	62,500	Equipment	25,000
Supplies	6,250	Retained Earnings	43,750

Place the balances in proper order and prepare a balance sheet similar to the one in Exhibit 3.

LO6 **Preparation and Integration of Financial Statements**

E 11. Proviso Corporation engaged in the following activities during the year: Service Revenue, $26,400; Rent Expense, $2,400; Wages Expense, $16,680; Advertising Expense, $2,700; Utilities Expense, $1,800; Income Taxes Expense, $400; and Dividends, $1,400. In addition, the year-end balances of selected accounts were as follows: Cash, $3,100; Accounts Receivable, $1,500; Supplies, $200; Land, $2,000; Accounts Payable, $900; and Common Stock, $2,000.

In proper format, prepare the income statement, statement of retained earnings, and balance sheet for Proviso Corporation (assume the year ends on December 31, 2009). (**Hint**: You must solve for the beginning and ending balances of retained earnings for 2009.)

LO5 **Stockholders' Equity and the Accounting Equation**

E 12. The total assets and liabilities at the beginning and end of the year for Schupan Company are listed below.

	Assets	Liabilities
Beginning of the year	$180,000	$ 68,750
End of the year	275,000	150,500

Determine Schupan Company's net income or loss for the year under each of the following alternatives:

1. The stockholders made no investments in the business, and no dividends were paid during the year.
2. The stockholders made no investments in the business, but dividends of $27,500 were paid during the year.
3. The stockholders invested $16,250 in the business, but no dividends were paid during the year.
4. The stockholders invested $12,500 in the business, and dividends of $29,000 were paid during the year.

LO6 **Statement of Cash Flows**

E 13. Martin Service Corporation began the year 2009 with cash of $55,900. In addition to earning a net income of $38,000 and paying a cash dividend of $19,500, Martin Service borrowed $78,000 from the bank and purchased equipment with $125,000 of cash. Also, Accounts Receivable increased by $7,800, and Accounts Payable increased by $11,700.

Determine the amount of cash on hand at December 31, 2009, by preparing a statement of cash flows similar to the one in Exhibit 4.

LO4 LO5 LO6 **Statement of Retained Earnings**

E 14. Below is information from the statement of retained earnings of Mrs. Kitty's Cookies, Inc. for a recent year.

Dividends	0
Net income	?
Retained earnings, January 31, 2010	$159,490
Retained earnings, January 31, 2009	$105,000

Prepare the statement of retained earnings for Mrs. Kitty's Cookies in good form. You will need to solve for the amount of net income. What are retained earnings? Why would the company's board of directors decide not to pay any dividends to its owners?

LO7 **Accounting Abbreviations**

E 15. Identify the accounting meaning of each of the following abbreviations: AICPA, SEC, PCAOB, GAAP, FASB, IRS, GASB, IASB, IMA, and CPA.

Return on Assets

E 16. Saxon wants to know if its profitability performance has increased from 2009 to 2010. The company had net income of $48,000 in 2009 and $50,000 in 2010. Total assets were $400,000 at the end of 2008, $480,000 at the end of 2009, and $560,000 at the end of 2010. Calculate return on assets for 2009 and 2010 and comment on the results.

Problems

LO6

Preparation and Interpretation of the Financial Statements

P 1. Below is a list of financial statement items.

___	Utilities expense	___	Accounts payable
___	Building	___	Rent expense
___	Common stock	___	Dividends
___	Net income	___	Income taxes expense
___	Land	___	Fees earned
___	Equipment	___	Cash
___	Revenues	___	Supplies
___	Accounts receivable	___	Wages expense

Required

1. Indicate whether each item is found on the income statement (IS), statement of retained earnings (RE), and/or balance sheet (BS).

User insight ▶

2. Which of the financial statements is most closely associated with the goal of profitability?

LO6

Integration of Financial Statements

P 2. The following three independent sets of financial statements have several amounts missing:

	Set A	Set B	Set C
Income Statement			
Revenue	$5,320	$ 8,600	$ m
Expenses	a	g	2,010
Net income	$ 510	$ h	$ n
Statement of Retained Earnings			
Beginning balance	$1,780	$15,400	$ 200
Net income	b	i	450
Less dividends	c	1,000	o
Ending balance	$ d	$16,000	$ p
Balance Sheet			
Total assets	$ e	$ j	$1,900
Liabilities	$ f	$ 2,000	$1,300
Stockholders' equity			
Common stock	200	8,000	50
Retained earnings	2,100	k	q
Total liabilities and stockholders' equity	$2,700	$ l	$ r

Required

1. Complete each set of financial statements by determining the amounts that correspond to the letters.

User insight ▶

2. Why is it necessary to prepare the income statement prior to the balance sheet?

LO1 LO6

Preparation and Interpretation of the Income Statement, Statement of Retained Earnings, and Balance Sheet

P 3. Below are the financial accounts of Special Assets, Inc. The company has just completed its 10th year of operations ended December 31, 2011.

Accounts Receivable	$ 4,500
Accounts Payable	3,600
Cash	57,700
Commissions Expense	225,000
Commissions Payable	22,700
Commission Sales Revenue	400,000
Common Stock	29,000
Dividends	33,000
Equipment	59,900
Income Taxes Expense	27,000
Income Taxes Payable	13,000
Marketing Expense	20,100
Office Rent Expense	36,000
Retained Earnings, December 31, 2010	35,300
Supplies	700
Supplies Expense	2,600
Telephone and Computer Expenses	5,100
Wages Expense	32,000

Required

1. Prepare the income statement, statement of retained earnings, and balance sheet for Special Assets, Inc.

User insight ▶

2. The owners of Special Assets, Inc., are considering expansion. What other statement would be useful to the owners in assessing whether the company's operations are generating sufficient funds to support the expenses? Why would it be useful?

LO1 LO6

Preparation and Interpretation of Financial Statements

P 4. The following are the accounts of Unique Ad, Inc., an agency that develops marketing materials for print, radio, and television. The agency's first year of operations ended on January 31, 2010.

Accounts Receivable	$ 24,900
Accounts Payable	19,400
Cash	1,800
Common Stock	5,000
Dividends	0
Equipment Rental Expense	37,200
Income Taxes Expense	560
Income Taxes Payable	560
Marketing Expense	6,800
Advertising Service Revenue	165,200
Salaries Expense	86,000
Salaries Payable	1,300
Supplies	1,600
Supplies Expense	19,100
Office Rent Expense	13,500

Required

1. Prepare the income statement, statement of retained earnings, and balance sheet for Unique Ad, Inc.

User insight ▶ 2. Review the financial statements and comment on the financial challenges Unique Ad, Inc. faces.

LO1 LO6 LO7

Use and Interpretation of Financial Statements

P 5. The financial statements for the Oros Riding Club follow.

Oros Riding Club, Inc.
Income Statement
For the Month Ended November 30, 2010

Revenues		
Riding lesson revenue	$4,650	
Locker rental revenue	1,450	
Total revenues		$6,100
Expenses		
Salaries expense	$1,125	
Feed expense	750	
Utilities expense	450	
Total expenses		2,325
Income before income taxes		$3,775
Income taxes expense		600
Net income		$3,175

Oros Riding Club, Inc.
Statement of Retained Earnings
For the Month Ended November 30, 2010

Retained earnings, October 31, 2010	$5,475
Net income for the month	3,175
Subtotal	$8,650
Less dividends	2,400
Retained earnings, November 30, 2010	$6,250

Oros Riding Club, Inc.
Balance Sheet
November 30, 2010

Assets		**Liabilities**		
Cash	$ 6,700	Accounts payable		$13,350
Accounts receivable	900			
Supplies	750	**Stockholders' Equity**		
Land	15,750	Common stock	$34,500	
Building	22,500	Retained earnings	6,250	
Horses	7,500	Total stockholders' equity		40,750
		Total liabilities and		
Total assets	$54,100	stockholders' equity		$54,100

Oros Riding Club, Inc.
Statement of Cash Flows
For the Month Ended November 30, 2010

Cash flows from operating activities		
Net income		$3,175
Adjustments to reconcile net income to net cash flows from operating activities		
(Increase) in accounts receivable	($ 400)	
(Increase) in supplies	(550)	
Increase in accounts payable	400	(550)
Net cash flows from operating activities		$2,625
Cash flows from investing activities		
Purchase of horses	($1,000)	
Sale of horses	2,000	
Net cash flows from investing activities		1,000
Cash flows from financing activities		
Issue of common stock	$5,000	
Payment of cash dividends	(2,400)	
Net cash flows from financing activities		2,600
Net increase in cash		$6,225
Cash at beginning of month		475
Cash at end of month		$6,700

Required

User insight ▶ 1. Explain how the four statements for Oros Riding Club, Inc. are related to each other.

User insight ▶ 2. Which statements are most closely associated with the goals of liquidity and profitability? Why?

User insight ▶ 3. If you were the owner of this business, how would you evaluate the company's performance? Give specific examples.

User insight ▶ 4. If you were a banker considering Oros Riding Club for a loan, why might you want the company to get an audit by an independent CPA? What would the audit tell you?

Alternate Problems

LO6 Integration of Financial Statements

P 6. The following are three independent sets of financial statements have several amounts missing.

Income Statement	Set A	Set B	Set C
Revenue	$1,200	$ g	$240
Expenses	a	5,000	m
Net income	$ b	$ h	$148
Statement of Retained Earnings			
Beginning balance	$2,900	$15,400	$132
Net income	c	1,600	n
Less dividends	200	i	o
Ending balance	$3,090	$ j	$ p

Balance Sheet	Set A	Set B	Set C
Total assets	$ d	$30,000	$ q
Liabilities	$1,600	$ 5,000	$ r
Stockholders' equity			
Common stock	2,000	9,000	100
Retained earnings	e	k	280
Total liabilities and stockholders' equity	$ f	$ l	$580

Required

1. Complete each set of financial statements by determining the amounts that correspond to the letters.

User insight ▶ 2. In what order is it necessary to prepare the financial statements? Why is that order necessary?

LO1 LO6 **Preparation and Interpretation of the Income Statement, Statement of Retained Earnings, and Balance Sheet**

P 7. Below are the financial accounts of Metro Labs. The company has just completed its third year of operations ended November 30, 2011.

Accounts Receivable	$ 51,900
Accounts Payable	7,400
Cash	115,750
Common Stock	15,000
Dividends	40,000
Income Taxes Expense	38,850
Income Taxes Payable	13,000
Retained Earnings, November 30, 2010	55,400
Marketing Expense	19,700
Testing Service Revenue	300,000
Office Rent Expense	25,000
Salaries Expense	96,000
Salaries Payable	2,700
Supplies	800
Supplies Expense	5,500

Required

1. Prepare the income statement, statement of retained earnings, and balance sheet for Metro Labs.

User insight ▶ 2. Evaluate the company's ability to meet its bills when they come due.

LO4 LO6 **Preparation and Interpretation of Financial Statements**

P 8. Below are the accounts of Gino's Painting Specialists, Inc. The company has just completed its first year of operations ended September 30, 2010.

Accounts Receivable	$13,200	Income Taxes Payable	$ 3,000
Accounts Payable	10,500	Marketing Expense	1,500
Cash	2,600	Painting Service Revenue	82,000
Common Stock	2,000	Salaries Expense	56,000
Dividends	1,000	Salaries Payable	700
Equipment	6,300	Supplies	400
Equipment Rental Expense	2,900	Supplies Expense	4,100
Income Taxes Expense	3,000	Truck Rent Expense	7,200

Required

1. Prepare the income statement, statement of retained earnings, and balance sheet for Gino's Painting Specialists, Inc.

User insight ▶ 2. Why would the owners of Gino's Painting Specialists, Inc. set their business up as a corporation and not a partnership?

ENHANCING Your Knowledge, Skills, and Critical Thinking

Conceptual Understanding Cases

LO1 LO2

Business Activities and Management Functions

C 1. Costco Wholesale Corporation is America's largest membership retail company. According to its letter to stockholders:

> Our mission is to bring quality goods and services to our members at the lowest possible price in every market where we do business . . . A hallmark of Costco warehouses has been the extraordinary sales volume we achieve.[15]

To achieve its strategy, Costco must organize its management by functions that relate to the principal activities of a business. Discuss the three basic activities Costco will engage in to achieve its goals, and suggest some examples of each. What is the role of Costco's management? What functions must its management perform to carry out these activities?

LO3

Concept of an Asset

C 2. Southwest Airlines Co. is one of the most successful airlines in the United States. Its annual report contains this statement: "We are a company of People, not Planes. That is what distinguishes us from other airlines and other companies. At Southwest Airlines, People are our most important asset."[16] Are employees considered assets in the financial statements? Why or why not? Discuss in what sense Southwest considers its employees to be assets.

LO7

Generally Accepted Accounting Principles

C 3. Fidelity Investments Company is a well-known mutual fund investment company. It makes investments worth billions of dollars in companies listed on the New York Stock Exchange and other stock markets. Generally accepted accounting principles (GAAP) are very important for Fidelity's investment analysts. What are generally accepted accounting principles? Why are financial statements that have been prepared in accordance with GAAP and audited by an independent CPA useful for Fidelity's investment analysts? What organizations influence GAAP? Explain how they do so.

LO1

Operating Cash

C 4. In May 2001, unable to get credit from enough of its lenders, housewares retailer **Lechters, Inc.**, filed for Chapter 11 bankruptcy. It then secured new bank financing in the amount of $86 million. Suppliers, however, remained concerned about Lechters' ability to meet future obligations. Therefore, many suppliers took back their terms of sale specifying the number of days the company had to pay for its merchandise and instead asked for cash in advance or on delivery. Smaller home-furnishing retailers like Lechters struggle against big rivals, such as **Bed Bath & Beyond**, which are more valuable to suppliers and thus can demand better terms and pricing. In spite of these problems and an annual net loss of $101.8 million on sales of $405 million, management believed the company could eventually succeed with its strategy under the bankruptcy.[17] Which is more critical to the short-term survival of a company faced with Lechters' problems: liquidity or profitability? Which is more important in the long term? Explain your answers.

Interpreting Financial Reports

Nature of Cash, Assets, and Net Income

LO6

C 5. Research in Motion Limited (RIM) is not well known, but it produces a well-known product: the Blackberry mobile phone. Information for 2007 and 2006 from the company's annual report appears below.[18] (All numbers are in thousands.) Three students who were looking at RIM's annual report were overheard making the following comments:

Student A: What a great year RIM had in 2007! The company earned income of $774,600,000 because its total assets increased from $2,314,349 to $3,088,949.

Student B: But the company didn't do that well because the change in total assets isn't the same as net income! The company had a net income of only $217,604 because its cash increased from $459,540 to $677,144.

Student C: I see that retained earnings went from negative $100,174 to positive $359,227. Don't you have to take that into consideration when analyzing the company's performance?

RIM Limited
Condensed Balance Sheets
December 31, 2007 and 2006
(In thousands)

	2007	2006
Assets		
Cash	$ 677,144	$ 459,540
Other assets	2,411,805	1,854,809
Total assets	$3,088,949	$2,314,349
Liabilities		
Total liabilities	$ 605,449	$ 318,934
Stockholders' Equity		
Common stock and other	2,124,273	2,095,589
Retained earnings	359,227	(100,174)
Total liabilities and stockholders' equity	$3,088,949	$2,314,349

User insight ▶ 1. Comment on the interpretations of Students A and B, and then answer Student C's questions.

User insight ▶ 2. Estimate RIM's net income for 2007. (Note: RIM did not pay any cash dividends.)

Decision Analysis Using Excel

LO5 LO6

Effect of Transactions on the Balance Sheet

C 6. The summer after finishing her junior year in college, Beth Murphy started a lawn service business in her neighborhood. On June 1, she deposited $2,700 in a new bank account in the name of her corporation. The $2,700 consisted of a $1,000 loan from her father and $1,700 of her own money. In return for her investment, Murphy issued 1,700 shares of $1 par value common stock to herself.

Using the money in this checking account, Murphy rented lawn equipment, purchased supplies, and hired local high school students to mow and trim the lawns of neighbors who had agreed to pay her for the service. At the end of each month, she mailed bills to her customers.

On August 31, Murphy was ready to dissolve her business and go back to school for the fall term. Because she had been so busy, she had not kept any records other than her checkbook and a list of amounts owed by customers.

Her checkbook had a balance of $3,520, and her customers owed her $875. She expected these customers to pay her during September. She planned to return unused supplies to the Lawn Care Center for a full credit of $50. When she brought back the rented lawn equipment, the Lawn Care Center also would return a deposit of $200 she had made in June. She owed the Lawn Care Center $525 for equipment rentals and supplies. In addition, she owed the students who had worked for her $100, and she still owed her father $700. Although Murphy feels she did quite well, she is not sure just how successful she was. You have agreed to help her find out.

1. Prepare one balance sheet dated June 1, 2010 and another dated August 31, 2010 for Murphy Lawn Services, Inc.
2. Using information that can be inferred from comparing the balance sheets, write a memorandum to Murphy commenting on her company's performance in achieving profitability and liquidity. (Assume that she used none of the company's assets for personal purposes.) Also, mention the other two financial statements that would be helpful to her in evaluating these business goals.

Annual Report Case: CVS Caremark Corporation

Analysis of Four Basic Financial Statements

C 7. Refer to the **CVS** annual report in the Supplement to Chapter 1 to answer the questions below. Keep in mind that every company, while following basic principles, adapts financial statements and terminology to its own special needs. Therefore, the complexity of CVS's financial statements and the terminology in them will differ somewhat from the financial statements in the text.

1. What names does CVS give to its four basic financial statements? (Note that the word *consolidated* in the names of the financial statements means that these statements combine those of several companies owned by CVS.)
2. Prove that the accounting equation works for CVS on December 29, 2007, by finding the amounts for the following equation: Assets = Liabilities + Stockholders' Equity.
3. What were the total revenues of CVS for the year ended December 29, 2007?
4. Was CVS profitable in the year ended December 29, 2007? How much was net income (loss) in that year, and did it increase or decrease from the year ended December 30, 2006?

5. Did the company's cash and cash equivalents increase from December 30, 2006 to December 29, 2007? If so, by how much? In what two places in the statements can this number be found or computed?
6. Did cash flows from operating activities, cash flows from investing activities, and cash flows from financing activities increase or decrease from years 2006 to 2007?
7. Who is the auditor for the company? Why is the auditor's report that accompanies the financial statements important?

Comparison Case: CVS Versus Southwest

LO1 LO5 LO7

Performance Measures and Financial Statements

C 8. Refer to the **CVS** annual report and the financial statements of **Southwest Airlines Co.** in the Supplement to Chapter 1 to answer these questions:

K/R

1. Which company is larger in terms of assets and in terms of revenues? What do you think is the best way to measure the size of a company?
2. Which company is more profitable in terms of net income? What is the trend of profitability over the past three years for both companies?
3. Compute the return on assets for each company for 2007. By this measure, which company is more profitable? Is this a better measure than simply comparing the net income of the two companies? Explain your answer.
4. Which company has more cash? Which increased its cash the most in the last year? Which has more liquidity as measured by cash flows from operating activities?

Ethical Dilemma Case

LO7

Professional Ethics

C 9. Discuss the ethical choices in the situations below. In each instance, describe the ethical dilemma, determine the alternative courses of action, and tell what you would do.

1. You are the payroll accountant for a small business. A friend asks you how much another employee is paid per hour.
2. As an accountant for the branch office of a wholesale supplier, you discover that several of the receipts the branch manager has submitted for reimbursement as selling expenses actually stem from nights out with his spouse.
3. You are an accountant in the purchasing department of a construction company. When you arrive home from work on December 22, you find a large ham in a box marked "Happy Holidays—It's a pleasure to work with you." The gift is from a supplier who has bid on a contract your employer plans to award next week.
4. As an auditor with one year's experience at a local CPA firm, you are expected to complete a certain part of an audit in 20 hours. Because of your lack of experience, you know you cannot finish the job within that time. Rather than admit this, you are thinking about working late to finish the job and not telling anyone.
5. You are a tax accountant at a local CPA firm. You help your neighbor fill out her tax return, and she pays you $200 in cash. Because there is no record of this transaction, you are considering not reporting it on your tax return.
6. The accounting firm for which you work as a CPA has just won a new client, a firm in which you own 200 shares of stock that you received as an

inheritance from your grandmother. Because it is only a small number of shares and you think the company will be very successful, you are considering not disclosing the investment.

Internet Case

LO1 LO5

Financial Performance Comparison of Two High-Tech Companies

C 10. **Microsoft** and **Intel** are two very successful high-tech corporations. Access their websites by going to the Needles/Powers Online Study Center at *www.cengage.com/accounting/needles* for a link to their websites. Access each company's annual report and locate the consolidated balance sheet and consolidated statement of income. Find the amount of total assets, revenues, and net income for the most recent year shown. Then compute net income to revenues and net income to total assets for both companies. Which company is larger? Which is more profitable?

Group Activity Case

LO2 LO7

Users of Accounting Information

C 11. Public companies report quarterly and annually on their success or failure in making a net income. The following appeared in *The Wall Street Journal* article cited earlier in the chapter: **"General Motors** expects its cash flow to remain negative this year"; it is "not anywhere near adequate . . . [However,] GM expects earnings to improve."[19]

Your instructor will divide the class into groups representing the following users. Discuss why the user your group is representing needs accounting information. Be prepared to discuss in class.

1. The management of General Motors
2. The stockholders of General Motors
3. The creditors of General Motors
4. Potential stockholders of General Motors
5. The Internal Revenue Service
6. The Securities and Exchange Commission
7. The Teamsters' union
8. A consumers' group called Public Cause
9. An economic adviser to the president of the United States

Business Communication Case

LO1 LO6

Business Goals, Financial Performance, Financial Statements

C 12. Assume you are working part-time for a small business that does not make any use of financial statements. Based on your knowledge after studying Chapter 1, write the owner a brief business memo in good form that identifies the two major goals of a business. In the memo, explain how financial statements can help the owner achieve these goals. Be sure to tell which statements relate to each of the goals.

SUPPLEMENT TO CHAPTER 1

How to Read an Annual Report

More than 4 million corporations are chartered in the United States. Most of them are small, family-owned businesses. They are called *private* or *closely held corporations* because their common stock is held by only a few people and is not for sale to the public. Larger companies usually find it desirable to raise investment funds from many investors by issuing common stock to the public. These companies are called *public companies.* Although they are fewer in number than private companies, their total economic impact is much greater.

Public companies must register their common stock with the Securities and Exchange Commission (SEC), which regulates the issuance and subsequent trading of the stock of public companies. The SEC requires the management of public companies to report each year to stockholders on their companies' financial performance. This report, called an *annual report*, contains the company's annual financial statements and other pertinent data. Annual reports are a primary source of financial information about public companies and are distributed to all of a company's stockholders. They must also be filed with the SEC on a Form 10-K.

The general public may obtain an annual report by calling or writing the company or accessing the report online at the company's website. If a company has filed its 10-K electronically with the SEC, it can be accessed at *www.sec.gov/edgar.shtml.* Many libraries also maintain files of annual reports or have them available on electronic media, such as *Compact Disclosure.*

This supplement describes the major components of the typical annual report. We have included many of these components in the annual report of **CVS Caremark Corporation**, one of the country's most successful retailers. Case assignments in each chapter refer to this annual report. For purposes of comparison, the supplement also includes the financial statements and summary of significant accounting policies of **Southwest Airlines Co.**, one of the largest and most successful airlines in the United States.

The Components of an Annual Report

In addition to listing the corporation's directors and officers, an annual report usually contains a letter to the stockholders (also called *shareholders*), a multiyear summary of financial highlights, a description of the company, management's discussion and analysis of the company's operating results and financial condition, the financial statements, notes to the financial statements, a statement about management's responsibilities, and the auditors' report.

Letter to the Stockholders

Traditionally, an annual report begins with a letter in which the top officers of the corporation tell stockholders about the company's performance and prospects. In CVS's 2007 annual report, the chairman and chief executive officer wrote to the stockholders about the highlights of the past year, the key priorities for the new year, and other aspects of the business. He reported as follows:

> The past year set the stage for a new chapter in our company's history as we completed the transformational merger of CVS Corporation and Caremark Rx, Inc. We are now the largest integrated provider of prescriptions and related health services in the United States, filling or managing more than a quarter of all prescriptions in the nation. Beyond the sheer scale of our operations, CVS Caremark is positioned to improve access for patients, promote better health outcomes, and control payor costs in a way that no pharmacy retailer or PBM could do separately. Our unique model provides us with a significant opportunity to gain share and create new sources of growth going forward.

Financial Highlights

The financial highlights section of an annual report presents key statistics for at least a five-year period but often for a ten-year period. It is often accompanied by graphs. CVS's annual report, for example, gives key figures for sales, operating profits, and other key measures. Note that the financial highlights section often includes nonfinancial data and graphs, such as the number of stores in CVS's case.

Description of the Company

An annual report contains a detailed description of the company's products and divisions. Some analysts tend to scoff at this section of the annual report because it often contains glossy photographs and other image-building material, but it should not be overlooked because it may provide useful information about past results and future plans.

Management's Discussion and Analysis

In this section, management describes the company's financial condition and results of operations and explains the difference in results from one year to the next. For example, CVS's management explains the effects of its strategy to relocate some of its stores:

> Total net revenues continued to benefit from our active relocation program, which moves existing in-line shopping center stores to larger, more convenient, freestanding locations. Historically, we have achieved significant improvements in customer count and net revenue when we do this. As such, our relocation strategy remains an important component of our overall growth strategy. As of December 29, 2007, approximately 64% of our existing stores were freestanding, compared to approximately 61% and 59% at December 30, 2006 and December 31, 2005, respectively.

CVS's management also describes the increase in cash flows from operating activities:

> The increase in net cash provided by operations during 2007 primarily resulted from increased cash receipts from revenues due to the Caremark Merger. The increase in net cash provided by operations during 2006 primarily resulted from an increase in cash receipts from revenues.

Financial Statements

All companies present the same four basic financial statements in their annual reports, but the names they use may vary. As you can see in Exhibits S-1 to S-4, CVS presents statements of operations (income statements), balance sheets, statements of cash flows, and statements of shareholders' equity (includes retained earnings). (Note that the numbers given in the statements are in millions, but the last six digits are omitted. For example, $4,793,300,000 is shown as $4,793.3.)

The headings of CVS's financial statements are preceded by the word *consolidated*. A corporation issues *consolidated* financial statements when it consists of more than one company and has combined the companies' data for reporting purposes.

CVS provides several years of data for each financial statement: two years for the balance sheet and three years for the others. Financial statements presented in this fashion are called *comparative financial statements*. Such statements are in accordance with generally accepted accounting principles and help readers assess the company's performance over several years.

EXHIBIT S-1 CVS's Income Statements

Consolidated means that data from all companies owned by CVS are combined.

CVS Caremark Corporation
Consolidated Statements of Operations

CVS's fiscal year ends on the Saturday closest to December 31.

Fiscal Year Ended

(In millions, except per share amounts)	Dec. 29, 2007 (52 WEEKS)	Dec. 30, 2006 (53 WEEKS)	Dec. 31, 2005 (52 WEEKS)
Net revenues	$76,329.5	$43,821.4	$37,006.7
Cost of revenues	60,221.8	32,079.2	27,312.1
Gross profit	16,107.7	11,742.2	9,694.6
Total operating expenses	11,314.4	9,300.6	7,675.1
Operating profit[1]	4,793.3	2,441.6	2,019.5
Interest expense, net[2]	434.6	215.8	110.5
Earnings before income tax provision	4,358.7	2,225.8	1,909.0
Income tax provision	1,721.7	856.9	684.3
Net earnings[3]	2,637.0	1,368.9	1,224.7
Preference dividends, net of income tax benefit[4]	14.2	13.9	14.1
Net earnings available to common shareholders	$ 2,622.8	$ 1,355.0	$ 1,210.6
BASIC EARNINGS PER COMMON SHARE:[5]			
Net earnings	$ 1.97	$ 1.65	$ 1.49
Weighted average common shares outstanding	1,328.2	820.6	811.4
DILUTED EARNINGS PER COMMON SHARE:			
Net earnings	$ 1.92	$ 1.60	$ 1.45
Weighted average common shares outstanding	1,371.8	853.2	841.6
DIVIDENDS DECLARED PER COMMON SHARE	$ 0.22875	$ 0.15500	$ 0.14500

1. This section shows earnings from ongoing operations.
2. CVS shows interest expense and income taxes separately.
3. The net earnings figure moves to the statements of shareholders' equity.
4. CVS shows the dividends distributed to preferred shareholders. This distribution is not an expense.
5. CVS discloses various breakdowns of earnings per share.

EXHIBIT S-2 CVS's Balance Sheets

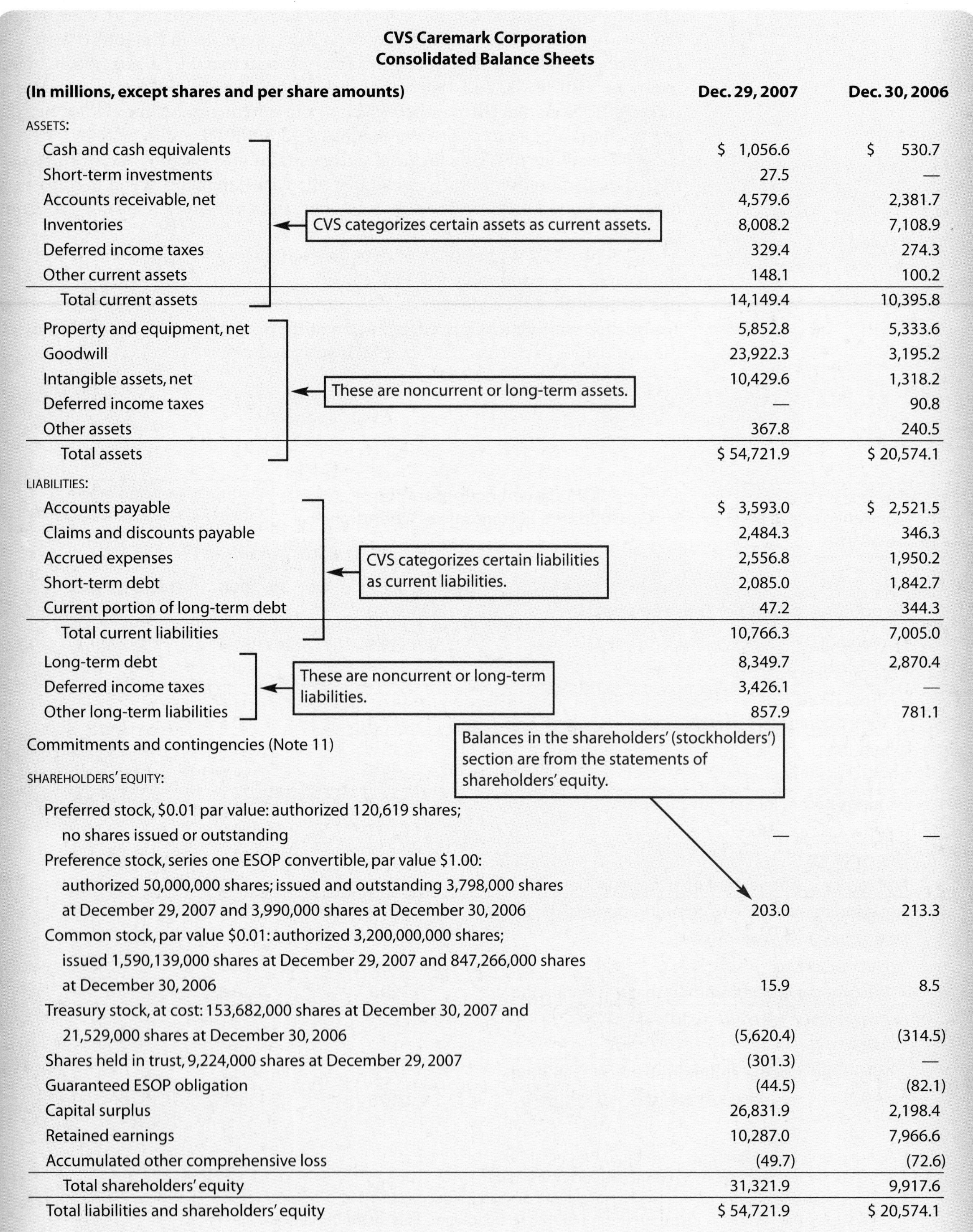
CVS categorizes certain assets as current assets.
These are noncurrent or long-term assets.
CVS categorizes certain liabilities as current liabilities.
These are noncurrent or long-term liabilities.
Balances in the shareholders' (stockholders') section are from the statements of shareholders' equity.

CVS Caremark Corporation
Consolidated Balance Sheets

(In millions, except shares and per share amounts)	Dec. 29, 2007	Dec. 30, 2006
ASSETS:		
Cash and cash equivalents	$ 1,056.6	$ 530.7
Short-term investments	27.5	—
Accounts receivable, net	4,579.6	2,381.7
Inventories	8,008.2	7,108.9
Deferred income taxes	329.4	274.3
Other current assets	148.1	100.2
Total current assets	14,149.4	10,395.8
Property and equipment, net	5,852.8	5,333.6
Goodwill	23,922.3	3,195.2
Intangible assets, net	10,429.6	1,318.2
Deferred income taxes	—	90.8
Other assets	367.8	240.5
Total assets	$ 54,721.9	$ 20,574.1
LIABILITIES:		
Accounts payable	$ 3,593.0	$ 2,521.5
Claims and discounts payable	2,484.3	346.3
Accrued expenses	2,556.8	1,950.2
Short-term debt	2,085.0	1,842.7
Current portion of long-term debt	47.2	344.3
Total current liabilities	10,766.3	7,005.0
Long-term debt	8,349.7	2,870.4
Deferred income taxes	3,426.1	—
Other long-term liabilities	857.9	781.1
Commitments and contingencies (Note 11)		
SHAREHOLDERS' EQUITY:		
Preferred stock, $0.01 par value: authorized 120,619 shares; no shares issued or outstanding	—	—
Preference stock, series one ESOP convertible, par value $1.00: authorized 50,000,000 shares; issued and outstanding 3,798,000 shares at December 29, 2007 and 3,990,000 shares at December 30, 2006	203.0	213.3
Common stock, par value $0.01: authorized 3,200,000,000 shares; issued 1,590,139,000 shares at December 29, 2007 and 847,266,000 shares at December 30, 2006	15.9	8.5
Treasury stock, at cost: 153,682,000 shares at December 30, 2007 and 21,529,000 shares at December 30, 2006	(5,620.4)	(314.5)
Shares held in trust, 9,224,000 shares at December 29, 2007	(301.3)	—
Guaranteed ESOP obligation	(44.5)	(82.1)
Capital surplus	26,831.9	2,198.4
Retained earnings	10,287.0	7,966.6
Accumulated other comprehensive loss	(49.7)	(72.6)
Total shareholders' equity	31,321.9	9,917.6
Total liabilities and shareholders' equity	$ 54,721.9	$ 20,574.1

EXHIBIT S-3 CVS's Statements of Cash Flows

CVS Caremark Corporation
Consolidated Statements of Cash Flows

Cash flows are shown for operating activities, investing activities, and financing activities.

(In millions)	Fiscal Year Ended Dec. 29, 2007 (52 weeks)	Dec. 30, 2006 (53 weeks)	Dec. 31, 2005 (52 weeks)
CASH FLOWS FROM OPERATING ACTIVITIES:			
Cash receipts from revenues	$61,986.3	$43,273.7	$36,923.1
Cash paid for inventory	(45,772.6)	(31,422.1)	(26,403.9)
Cash paid to other suppliers and employees	(10,768.6)	(9,065.3)	(8,186.7)
Interest and dividends received	33.6	15.9	6.5
Interest paid	(468.2)	(228.1)	(135.9)
Income taxes paid	(1,780.8)	(831.7)	(591.0)
NET CASH PROVIDED BY OPERATING ACTIVITIES	3,229.7	1,742.4	1,612.1
CASH FLOWS FROM INVESTING ACTIVITIES:			
Additions to property and equipment	(1,805.3)	(1,768.9)	(1,495.4)
Proceeds from sale-leaseback transactions	601.3	1,375.6	539.9
Acquisitions (net of cash acquired) and other investments	(1,983.3)	(4,224.2)	12.1
Cash outflow from hedging activities	—	(5.3)	—
Proceeds from sale or disposal of assets	105.6	29.6	31.8
NET CASH USED IN INVESTING ACTIVITIES	(3,081.7)	(4,593.2)	(911.6)
CASH FLOWS FROM FINANCING ACTIVITIES:			
Additions to/(reductions in) short-term debt	242.3	1,589.3	(632.2)
Additions to long-term debt	6,000.0	1,500.0	16.5
Reductions in long-term debt	(821.8)	(310.5)	(10.5)
Dividends paid	(322.4)	(140.9)	(131.6)
Proceeds from exercise of stock options	552.4	187.6	178.4
Excess tax benefits from stock based compensation	97.8	42.6	—
Repurchase of common stock	(5,370.4)	—	—
NET CASH PROVIDED BY (USED IN) FINANCING ACTIVITIES	377.9	2,868.1	(579.4)
Net increase in cash and cash equivalents	525.9	17.3	121.1
Cash and cash equivalents at beginning of year	530.7	513.4	392.3
CASH AND CASH EQUIVALENTS AT END OF YEAR	$ 1,056.6	$ 530.7	$ 513.4
RECONCILIATION OF NET EARNINGS TO NET CASH PROVIDED BY OPERATING ACTIVITIES			
Net earnings	$ 2,637.0	$ 1,368.9	$ 1,224.7
Adjustments required to reconcile net earnings to net cash provided by operating activities:			
Depreciation and amortization	1,094.6	733.3	589.1
Stock based compensation	78.0	69.9	—
Deferred income taxes and other non-cash items	40.1	98.2	13.5
Change in operating assets and liabilities providing/(requiring) cash, net of effects from acquisitions:			
Accounts receivable, net	279.7	(540.1)	(83.1)
Inventories	(448.0)	(624.1)	(265.2)
Other current assets	(59.2)	(21.4)	(13.2)
Other assets	(26.4)	(17.2)	(0.1)
Accounts payable	(181.4)	396.7	192.2
Accrued expenses	(168.2)	328.9	(43.8)
Other long-term liabilities	(16.5)	(50.7)	(2.0)
NET CASH PROVIDED BY OPERATING ACTIVITIES	$ 3,229.7	$ 1,742.4	$ 1,612.1

Cash and cash equivalents move to balance sheets.

This section explains the difference between net earnings and net cash provided by operating activities.

EXHIBIT S-4 CVS's Statements of Stockholders' Equity

Each component of stockholders' equity is explained.

CVS Caremark Corporation
Consolidated Statements of Shareholders' Equity

	Shares			*Dollars*		
(In millions)	**Dec. 29, 2007**	**Dec. 30, 2006**	**Dec. 31 2005**	**Dec. 29, 2007**	**Dec. 30, 2006**	**Dec. 31, 2005**
PREFERENCE STOCK:						
Beginning of year	4.0	4.2	4.3	$ 213.3	$ 222.6	$ 228.4
Conversion to common stock	(0.2)	(0.2)	(0.1)	(10.3)	(9.3)	(5.8)
End of year	3.8	4.0	4.2	203.0	213.3	222.6
COMMON STOCK:						
Beginning of year	847.3	838.8	828.6	8.5	8.4	8.3
Common stock issued for Caremark Merger	712.7	—	—	7.1	—	—
Stock options exercised and awards	30.1	8.5	10.2	0.3	0.1	0.1
End of year	1,590.1	847.3	838.8	15.9	8.5	8.4
TREASURY STOCK:						
Beginning of year	(21.5)	(24.5)	(26.6)	(314.5)	(356.5)	(385.9)
Purchase of treasury shares	(135.0)	0.1	—	(5,378.7)	(0.1)	(1.7)
Conversion of preference stock	0.9	0.8	0.5	24.7	11.7	7.3
Employee stock purchase plan issuance	1.9	2.1	1.6	48.1	30.4	23.8
End of year	(153.7)	(21.5)	(24.5)	(5,620.4)	(314.5)	(356.5)
GUARANTEED ESOP OBLIGATION:						
Beginning of year				(82.1)	(114.0)	(140.9)
Reduction of guaranteed ESOP obligation				37.6	31.9	26.9
End of year				(44.5)	(82.1)	(114.0)
SHARES HELD IN TRUST:						
Beginning of year	—	—	—	—	—	—
Shares acquired through Caremark Merger	(9.2)	—	—	(301.3)	—	—
End of year	(9.2)			(301.3)	—	—
CAPITAL SURPLUS:						
Beginning of year				2,198.4	1,922.4	1,687.3
Common stock issued for Caremark Merger, net of issuance costs				23,942.4	—	—
Stock option activity and awards				607.7	235.8	188.8
Tax benefit on stock options and awards				97.8	42.6	47.8
Conversion of preference stock				(14.4)	(2.4)	(1.5)
End of year				26,831.9	2,198.4	1,922.4
ACCUMULATED OTHER COMPREHENSIVE LOSS:						
Beginning of year				(72.6)	(90.3)	(55.5)
Recognition of unrealized gain/(loss) on derivatives, net of income tax				3.4	(0.3)	2.9
Pension liability adjustment				19.5	23.6	(37.7)
Pension liability adjustment to initially apply SFAS No. 158, net of tax benefit				—	(5.6)	—
End of year				(49.7)	(72.6)	(90.3)
RETAINED EARNINGS:						
Beginning of year				7,966.6	6,738.6	5,645.5
Net earnings				2,637.0	1,368.9	1,224.7
Common stock dividends				(308.8)	(127.0)	(117.5)
Preference stock dividends				(14.8)	(15.6)	(16.2)
Tax benefit on preference stock dividends				1.2	1.7	2.1
Adoption of FIN 48				5.8	—	—
End of year				10,287.0	7,966.6	6,738.6
TOTAL SHAREHOLDERS' EQUITY				$31,321.9	$9,917.6	$ 8,331.2
COMPREHENSIVE INCOME:						
Net earnings				$ 2,637.0	$1,368.9	$ 1,224.7
Recognition of unrealized gain/(loss) on derivatives, net of income tax				3.4	(0.3)	2.9
Pension liability, net of income tax				19.5	23.6	(37.7)
COMPREHENSIVE INCOME				$ 2,659.9	$1,392.2	$ 1,189.9

Net earnings are from the income statement.

CVS's fiscal year ends on the Saturday nearest the end of December (December 29, 2007 in the latest year). Retailers commonly end their fiscal years during a slow period, usually the end of January, which is in contrast to CVS's choosing the end of December.

Income Statements CVS uses a multistep form of the income statement in that results are shown in several steps (in contrast to the single-step form illustrated in the chapter). The steps are gross profit, operating profit, earnings before income tax provision, and net earnings (see Exhibit S-1). The company also shows net earnings available to common shareholders, and it discloses the basic earnings per share and diluted earnings per share. Basic earnings per share is used for most analysis. Diluted earnings per share assumes that all rights that could be exchanged for common shares, such as stock options, are in fact exchanged. The weighted average number of shares of common stock, used in calculating the per share figures, are shown at the bottom of the income statement.

Balance Sheets CVS has a typical balance sheet for a retail company (see Exhibit S-2). In the assets and liabilities sections, the company separates out the current assets and the current liabilities. Current assets will become available as cash or will be used up in the next year; current liabilities will have to be paid or satisfied in the next year. These groupings are useful in assessing a company's liquidity.

Several items in the shareholders' equity section of the balance sheet may need explanation. Common stock represents the number of shares outstanding at par value. Capital surplus (additional paid-in capital) represents amounts invested by stockholders in excess of the par value of the common stock. Preferred stock is capital stock that has certain features that distinguish it from common stock. Treasury stock represents shares of common stock the company repurchased.

Statements of Cash Flows Whereas the income statement reflects CVS's profitability, the statement of cash flows reflects its liquidity (see Exhibit S-3). This statement provides information about a company's cash receipts, cash payments, and investing and financing activities during an accounting period.

The first major section of CVS's consolidated statements of cash flows shows cash flows from operating activities. It shows the cash received and paid for various items related to the company's operations. The second major section is cash flows from investing activities. Except for acquisitions in 2006 and 2007, the largest outflow in this category is additions for property and equipment. This figure demonstrates that CVS is a growing company. The third major section is cash flows from financing activities. You can see here that CVS's largest cash inflows are for borrowing of long-term and short-term debt.

At the bottom of the statements of cash flows, you can see a reconciliation of net earnings to net cash provided by operating activities. This disclosure is important to the user because it relates the goal of profitability (net earnings) to liquidity (net cash provided). Most companies substitute this disclosure for the operating activities at the beginning of their statement of cash flows as illustrated in Chapter 1.

Statements of Shareholders' Equity Instead of a simple statement of retained earnings, CVS presents consolidated statements of shareholders' equity (see Exhibit S-4). These statements explain the changes in components of stockholders' equity, including retained earnings.

Notes to the Financial Statements

To meet the requirements of full disclosure, a company must add notes to the financial statements to help users interpret some of the more complex items. The notes are considered an integral part of the financial statements. In recent years, the need for explanation and further details has become so great that the notes often take more space than the statements themselves. The notes to the financial statements include a summary of significant accounting policies and explanatory notes.

Summary of Significant Accounting Policies Generally accepted accounting principles require that the financial statements include a *Summary of Significant Accounting Policies.* In most cases, this summary is presented in the first note to the financial statements or as a separate section just before the notes. In this summary, the company tells which generally accepted accounting principles it has followed in preparing the statements. For example, in CVS's report, the company states the principles followed for revenue recognition:

> The RPS [Retail Pharmacy Segment] recognizes revenue from the sale of merchandise (other than prescription drugs) at the time the merchandise is purchased by the retail customer. Revenue from the sale of prescription drugs is recognized at the time the prescription is filled, which is or approximates when the retail customer picks up the prescription. Customer returns are not material. Revenue generated from the performance of services in the RPS' healthcare clinics is recognized at the time the services are performed. . . . The PSS [Pharmacy Services Segment] recognizes revenues from prescription drugs sold by its mail service pharmacies and under national retail pharmacy network contracts where the PSS is the principal using the gross method at the contract prices negotiated with its customers.

Explanatory Notes Other notes explain some of the items in the financial statements. For example, CVS describes its commitments for future lease payments as follows:

> Following is a summary of the future minimum lease payments under capital and operating leases as of December 29, 2007:

(In millions)	Capital Leases	Operating Leases
2008	$ 16.0	$ 1,584.5
2009	16.0	1,548.3
2010	16.1	1,654.5
2011	16.2	1,418.2
2012	16.5	1,500.5
Thereafter	256.5	14,384.6
	$337.3	$22,090.6

Information like this is very useful in determining the full scope of a company's liabilities and other commitments.

Supplementary Information Notes In recent years, the FASB and the SEC have ruled that certain supplemental information must be presented with financial statements. Examples are the quarterly reports that most companies present to their stockholders and to the SEC. These quarterly reports, called ***interim financial statements***, are in most cases reviewed but not audited by a company's independent CPA firm. In its annual report, CVS presents unaudited quarterly financial data from its 2007 quarterly statements. The quarterly data also includes the high and low price for the company's common stock during each quarter.

Reports of Management's Responsibilities

Separate statements of management's responsibility for the financial statements and for internal control structure accompany the financial statements as required by the Sarbanes-Oxley Act of 2002. In its reports, CVS's management acknowledges its responsibility for the consistency, integrity, and presentation of the financial information and for the system of internal controls.

Reports of Certified Public Accountants

The *registered independent auditors' report* deals with the credibility of the financial statements. This report, prepared by independent certified public accountants, gives the accountants' opinion about how fairly the statements have been presented. Because management is responsible for preparing the financial statements, issuing statements that have not been independently audited would be like having a judge hear a case in which he or she was personally involved. The certified public accountants add the necessary credibility to management's figures for interested third parties. They report to the board of directors and the stockholders rather than to the company's management.

In form and language, most auditors' reports are like the one shown in Figure S-1. Usually, such a report is short, but its language is very important. It normally has four parts, but it can have a fifth part if an explanation is needed.

FIGURE S-1
Auditor's Report for CVS Caremark Corporation

Report of Independent Registered Public Accounting Firm
The Board of Directors and Shareholders
CVS Caremark Corporation

① We have audited the accompanying consolidated balance sheet of CVS Caremark Corporation as of December 29, 2007, and the related consolidated statements of operations, shareholders' equity and cash flows for the fifty-two week period ended December 29, 2007. These consolidated financial statements are the responsibility of the Company's management. Our responsibility is to express an opinion on these consolidated financial statements based on our audit.

② We conducted our audit in accordance with the standards of the Public Company Accounting Oversight Board (United States). Those standards require that we plan and perform the audit to obtain reasonable assurance about whether the financial statements are free of material misstatement. An audit includes examining, on a test basis, evidence supporting the amounts and disclosures in the financial statements. An audit also includes assessing the accounting principles used and significant estimates made by management, as well as evaluating the overall financial statement presentation. We believe that our audit provides a reasonable basis for our opinion.

③ In our opinion, the 2007 consolidated financial statements referred to above present fairly, in all material respects, the consolidated financial position of CVS Caremark Corporation at December 29, 2007, and the consolidated results of its operations and its cash flows for the fifty-two week period ended December 29, 2007, in conformity with U.S. generally accepted accounting principles.

④ As discussed in Note 1 to the consolidated financial statements, effective December 31, 2006, CVS Caremark Corporation adopted Financial Accounting Standards Board (FASB) Interpretation No. 48, *Accounting for Uncertainty in Income Taxes—an interpretation of FASB Statement No. 109.*

⑤ We also have audited, in accordance with the standards of the Public Company Accounting Oversight Board (United States), CVS Caremark Corporation's internal control over financial reporting as of December 29, 2007, based on criteria established in *Internal Control—Integrated Framework* issued by the Committee of Sponsoring Organizations of the Treadway Commission, and our report dated February 25, 2008 expressed an unqualified opinion thereon.

Ernst + Young LLP

Ernst and Young LLP
Boston, Massachusetts

February 25, 2008

1. The first paragraph identifies the financial statements that have been audited. It also identifies responsibilities. The company's management is responsible for the financial statements, and the auditor is responsible for expressing an opinion on the financial statements based on the audit.

2. The second paragraph, or *scope section*, states that the examination was made in accordance with standards of the Public Company Accounting Oversight Board (PCAOB). This paragraph also contains a brief description of the objectives and nature of the audit.

3. The third paragraph, or *opinion section*, states the results of the auditors' examination. The use of the word *opinion* is very important because the auditor does not certify or guarantee that the statements are absolutely correct. To do so would go beyond the truth, because many items, such as depreciation, are based on estimates. Instead, the auditors simply give an opinion about whether, overall, the financial statements "present fairly," in all material respects, the company's financial position, results of operations, and cash flows. This means that the statements are prepared in accordance with generally accepted accounting principles. If, in the auditors' opinion, the statements do not meet accepted standards, the auditors must explain why and to what extent.

4. The fourth paragraph identifies a new accounting standard adopted by the company.

5. The fifth paragraph says the company's internal controls are effective.

CVS
CAREMARK
The Power of One
CVS Caremark Corporation 2007 Annual Report

CVS Caremark Financial Highlights

(in millions, except per share figures)	2007 52 weeks	2006 52 weeks	% change
Revenues	$ 76,329.5	$ 43,821.4	74.2%
Operating profit	4,793.3	2,441.6	96.3%
Net earnings	2,637.0	1,368.9	92.6%
Diluted earnings per common share	1.92	1.60	20.0%
Stock price at calendar year end	39.75	30.91	28.6%
Market capitalization at calendar year end	58,706.42	25,456.49	130.6%

Total Revenues
(dollars in millions)

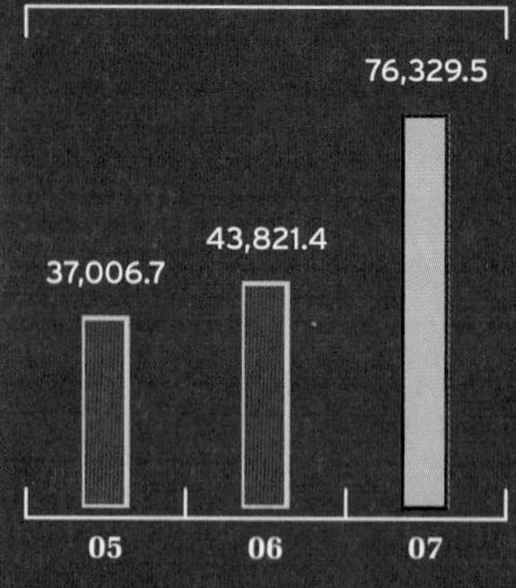

Stock Price at Year End
(at calendar year end in dollars)

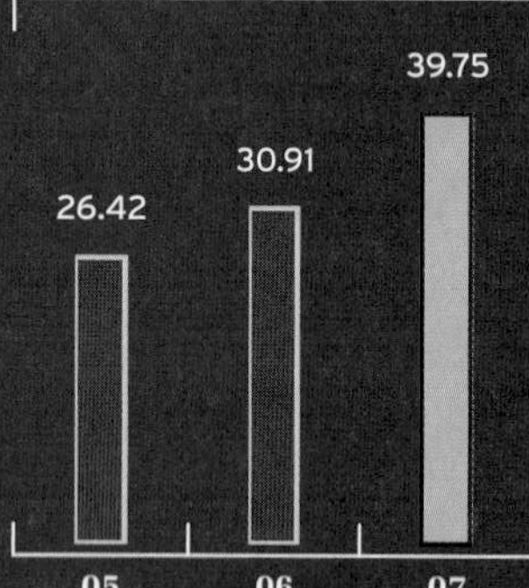

Annual Dividends Declared
(in dollars)

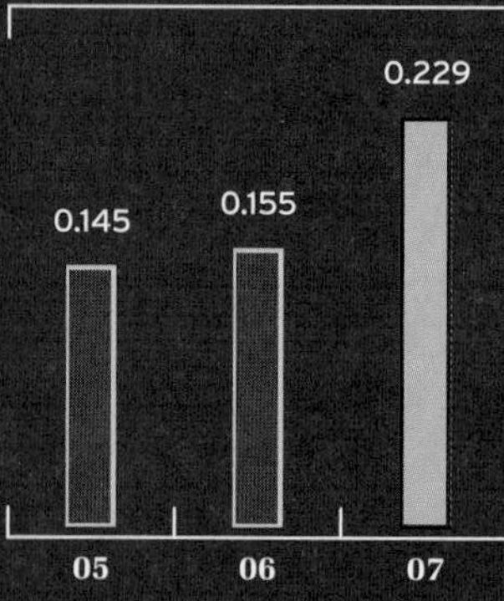

Dear Shareholder:

The past year set the stage for a new chapter in our company's history as we completed the transformational merger of CVS Corporation and Caremark Rx, Inc. We are now the largest integrated provider of prescriptions and related health services in the United States, filling or managing more than a quarter of all prescriptions in the nation. Beyond the sheer scale of our operations, CVS Caremark is positioned to improve access for patients, promote better health outcomes, and control payor costs in a way that no pharmacy retailer or PBM could do separately. Our unique model provides us with a significant opportunity to gain share and create new sources of growth going forward.

It was a very successful year on a number of other fronts as well. Here are some highlights of our key accomplishments:

- CVS Caremark posted record revenue and earnings, driven by solid performance in both the retail and pharmacy services segments.
- We opened 275 new or relocated CVS/pharmacy stores and saw continued improvement in sales and profits in the stores we acquired from Albertson's, Inc., in 2006, and from J.C. Penney in 2004.
- Caremark Pharmacy Services signed up $2.1 billion in new business, a clear sign that payors understand the potential benefits of our combination.
- We opened 316 MinuteClinics, increasing our total at year-end to 462 clinics in 25 states. That's about four times the number operated by our nearest competitor.
- We attained our goal of generating $2 billion in free cash flow, and we launched a $5 billion share repurchase program that we completed in the first quarter of 2008.
- Even in the midst of all this activity, we remained keenly focused on service, execution, and expense control across the company.

Total revenues rose 74.2 percent to a record $76.3 billion. In our CVS/pharmacy segment, same store sales rose 5.3 percent. Gross margins increased in both our retail and PBM businesses, due largely to significant generic drug introductions and purchasing synergies resulting from the merger. Net earnings climbed 92.6 percent to $2.6 billion, or $1.92 per diluted share.

Turning to CVS Caremark's stock performance, the 29.3 percent total return on our shares far surpassed the modest numbers posted by the S&P 500 Index and the Dow Jones Industrial Average (DJIA) in 2007. Our three-year performance is just as impressive. While the S&P 500 and the DJIA returned 21.2 percent and 23.0 percent, respectively, CVS shares returned 78.4 percent.

We're going to offer services that no other competitor can match. In the short time since completing our merger, we've made substantial progress in integrating our two companies. We brought Pharma-Care, CVS' legacy PBM business, under the Caremark umbrella, connected all our back-end systems, and are set to achieve more than

$700 million in cost-saving synergies in 2008. That's over 50 percent higher than our original target at the time we first announced the merger.

We've also made important progress in developing differentiated offerings that we believe will lead to enhanced growth for our company over time. Obviously, we're offering payors and patients all the services they would expect from a world-class PBM; however, we plan to take those services a step further.

For example, let's take the area of compliance. One of the simplest ways for a PBM to control payor costs and improve outcomes is by encouraging patients to take the medicine prescribed to them and to renew their prescriptions promptly. Any PBM has the capability to do this by contacting these patients over the telephone or by mail. However, face-to-face interaction is far more effective, and our CVS/pharmacy stores give us the unique capability to get closer to the consumer. We're developing programs that tap into the combined 23,000 pharmacists and MinuteClinic practitioners in our locations across the country.

We also intend to build upon our No. 1 position in the high-growth specialty pharmacy market, leverage our ExtraCare card and all its unique benefits among our millions of covered lives, enhance our health management programs, and increase use of MinuteClinic by our PBM clients. We'll implement some of our initiatives relatively quickly; others will happen over time.

We're leveraging opportunities for greater profitability in the pharmacy. In both our retail and mail order pharmacies, we are benefiting from the aging population, greater utilization among seniors due to Medicare Part D, and the increasing use of generic drugs. Although their lower prices depress revenue growth and we continue to see pressure on pharmacy reimbursement rates, generics are more profitable than brand name drugs and help drive margin expansion. Moreover, CVS Caremark is now the largest purchaser of generic drugs in the United States, which enables us to drive down costs.

In 2007, the company had a 63 percent generic dispensing rate at retail. With approximately $70 billion in branded drug sales coming off patent in the next five years, we expect that figure to rise to 75 percent by 2012. We should see similar gains for Caremark's PBM business, whose generic dispensing rate is currently at 60 percent.

"In the short time since completing our merger, we've made substantial progress in integrating our two companies. We brought PharmaCare, CVS' legacy PBM business, under the Caremark umbrella, connected all our back-end systems, and are set to achieve more than $700 million in cost-saving synergies in 2008. That's over 50 percent higher than our original target at the time we first announced the merger."

Generic versions of bioengineered drugs represent another opportunity. Currently, the United States has no procedure for approving generic versions of bioengineered drugs when they come off patent. However, we expect to see Congress enact legislation at some point in the future to create a biogeneric approval process at the U.S. Food and Drug Administration. We will be well positioned if or when this occurs.

We continue to open new stores and make the most of recent acquisitions. Despite the past year's merger activity, we continued to execute our organic growth strategy at retail. CVS/pharmacy square footage grew by 3 percent, in line with our annual target. Of the 275 stores we opened, 139 were new locations and 136 were relocations. Factoring in closings, we enjoyed net unit growth of 95 stores. We continued to expand in our newer, high-growth areas such as Los Angeles, San Diego, Phoenix, Las Vegas, and Minneapolis.

The former Eckerd® locations that we acquired in 2004 still enjoyed same store sales growth that outpaced our overall numbers. These stores are benefiting from their locations in high-growth markets – mainly Florida and Texas – and they continue to gain share from competitors as well.

We're also very pleased with the performance of the stand-alone Sav-on® and Osco® stores we purchased from Albertsons. This acquisition strengthened our presence in the Midwest and provided us with an immediate leadership position in Southern California, the country's second-largest drugstore market. In fact, our Southern California CVS/pharmacy stores now lead the entire chain in sales. These new CVS/pharmacy stores are benefiting from an improved merchandise assortment and category focus.

The introduction of the ExtraCare card is encouraging customer loyalty and helping drive an increase in sales and margins.

In the front of the store, we're seeing sales growth across our core categories, especially in beauty, personal care, general merchandise, and digital photo. CVS store brands and proprietary brands have been important drivers of gross margins.

As solid as our front-end business is, it's worth noting that it accounts for 30 percent of our retail sales compared with 70 percent for the pharmacy. The front-end percentage becomes even smaller in the context of CVS Caremark's overall revenues. That's why we expect any impact on CVS/pharmacy from a softer economy to be limited and manageable. After all, our average front-end purchase is a little under $12, and we don't anticipate that consumers will buy less cough medicine, analgesics, or any of the other non-discretionary

"We've done so much more than just combine two very successful businesses. We've literally created a first-of-its-kind company – one with the ability to grow faster than either of its components would have on its own."

items that make up the majority of our front-end sales. We even stand to benefit if consumers turn to our high-quality, lower-cost CVS store brand products to save money.

We're expanding MinuteClinic as part of our broader health care offerings. For many CVS/pharmacy customers, 2007 presented them with their first chance to visit one of our in-store MinuteClinics. Focused on treating a limited number of common ailments at a competitive price, it is helping us lower costs for health plans and self-insured employers.

MinuteClinic has seen more than 1.5 million patients since inception, and customer response has been extremely positive. It is the only retail clinic to meet the rigorous guidelines of The Joint Commission, the nation's chief standards-setting and accrediting body in health care. At least 25 percent of MinuteClinic patients have not previously been CVS/pharmacy customers. That represents a significant opportunity to introduce them to the "CVS easy" shopping experience and reap incremental sales gains in the pharmacy and the front end. As I mentioned earlier, we're also working to incorporate MinuteClinic into our PBM offerings when Caremark sits down at the table with current and potential clients.

Before closing, I want to take this opportunity to thank the outstanding management team we have across our retail and PBM businesses and the more than 190,000 people in our company who helped make the past year's accomplishments possible. I've often said we have the best people in the industry, and they proved me right again. I deeply appreciate their dedication.

I also want to acknowledge the considerable contributions Mac Crawford made at the helm of Caremark for nine years and in his subsequent role as the first chairman of the board of our combined company. Mac chose to step down in November, and I wish him a happy and healthy retirement. We shared the same vision for the future of this industry, and the core team he assembled remains the guiding force at Caremark Pharmacy Services. Former director Roger Headrick provided invaluable guidance during his 11 years on the Caremark board, and I want to thank him for his contributions as well.

We really are at a pivotal moment in our history, with CVS Caremark poised to transform the delivery of pharmacy services in this country. We've done so much more than just combine two very successful businesses. We've literally created a first-of-its-kind company – one with the ability to grow faster than either of its components would have on its own. For us, that's the real "power of one." Thank you for your confidence.

Thomas M. Ryan
Chairman of the Board,
President & CEO
February 27, 2008

CONSOLIDATED STATEMENTS OF OPERATIONS

In millions, except per share amounts	**Fiscal Year Ended Dec. 29, 2007 (52 weeks)**	Fiscal Year Ended Dec. 30, 2006 (52 weeks)	Fiscal Year Ended Dec. 31, 2005 (52 weeks)
Net revenues	**$ 76,329.5**	$ 43,821.4	$ 37,006.7
Cost of revenues	**60,221.8**	32,079.2	27,312.1
Gross profit	**16,107.7**	11,742.2	9,694.6
Total operating expenses	**11,314.4**	9,300.6	7,675.1
Operating profit	**4,793.3**	2,441.6	2,019.5
Interest expense, net	**434.6**	215.8	110.5
Earnings before income tax provision	**4,358.7**	2,225.8	1,909.0
Income tax provision	**1,721.7**	856.9	684.3
Net earnings	**2,637.0**	1,368.9	1,224.7
Preference dividends, net of income tax benefit	**14.2**	13.9	14.1
Net earnings available to common shareholders	**$ 2,622.8**	$ 1,355.0	$ 1,210.6
BASIC EARNINGS PER COMMON SHARE:			
Net earnings	**$ 1.97**	$ 1.65	$ 1.49
Weighted average common shares outstanding	**1,328.2**	820.6	811.4
DILUTED EARNINGS PER COMMON SHARE:			
Net earnings	**$ 1.92**	$ 1.60	$ 1.45
Weighted average common shares outstanding	**1,371.8**	853.2	841.6
Dividends declared per common share	**$ 0.22875**	$ 0.15500	$ 0.14500

See accompanying notes to consolidated financial statements.

CONSOLIDATED BALANCE SHEETS

In millions, except per share amounts	Dec. 29, 2007	Dec. 30, 2006
ASSETS:		
Cash and cash equivalents	$ 1,056.6	$ 530.7
Short-term investments	27.5	–
Accounts receivable, net	4,579.6	2,381.7
Inventories	8,008.2	7,108.9
Deferred income taxes	329.4	274.3
Other current assets	148.1	100.2
Total current assets	14,149.4	10,395.8
Property and equipment, net	5,852.8	5,333.6
Goodwill	23,922.3	3,195.2
Intangible assets, net	10,429.6	1,318.2
Deferred income taxes	–	90.8
Other assets	367.8	240.5
Total assets	$ 54,721.9	$ 20,574.1
LIABILITIES:		
Accounts payable	$ 3,593.0	$ 2,521.5
Claims and discounts payable	2,484.3	346.3
Accrued expenses	2,556.8	1,950.2
Short-term debt	2,085.0	1,842.7
Current portion of long-term debt	47.2	344.3
Total current liabilities	10,766.3	7,005.0
Long-term debt	8,349.7	2,870.4
Deferred income taxes	3,426.1	–
Other long-term liabilities	857.9	781.1
Commitments and contingencies (Note 11)		
SHAREHOLDERS' EQUITY:		
Preferred stock, $0.01 par value: authorized 120,619 shares; no shares issued or outstanding	–	–
Preference stock, series one ESOP convertible, par value $1.00: authorized 50,000,000 shares; issued and outstanding 3,798,000 shares at December 29, 2007 and 3,990,000 shares at December 30, 2006	203.0	213.3
Common stock, par value $0.01: authorized 3,200,000,000 shares; issued 1,590,139,000 shares at December 29, 2007 and 847,266,000 shares at December 30, 2006	15.9	8.5
Treasury stock, at cost: 153,682,000 shares at December 29, 2007 and 21,529,000 shares at December 30, 2006	(5,620.4)	(314.5)
Shares held in trust, 9,224,000 shares at December 29, 2007	(301.3)	–
Guaranteed ESOP obligation	(44.5)	(82.1)
Capital surplus	26,831.9	2,198.4
Retained earnings	10,287.0	7,966.6
Accumulated other comprehensive loss	(49.7)	(72.6)
Total shareholders' equity	31,321.9	9,917.6
Total liabilities and shareholders' equity	$ 54,721.9	$ 20,574.1

See accompanying notes to consolidated financial statements.

40 | CVS Caremark

CONSOLIDATED STATEMENTS OF CASH FLOWS

In millions	**Fiscal Year Ended Dec. 29, 2007 (52 weeks)**	Fiscal Year Ended Dec. 30, 2006 (52 weeks)	Fiscal Year Ended Dec. 31, 2005 (52 weeks)
CASH FLOWS FROM OPERATING ACTIVITIES:			
Cash receipts from revenues	**$ 61,986.3**	$ 43,273.7	$ 36,923.1
Cash paid for inventory	**(45,772.6)**	(31,422.1)	(26,403.9)
Cash paid to other suppliers and employees	**(10,768.6)**	(9,065.3)	(8,186.7)
Interest and dividends received	**33.6**	15.9	6.5
Interest paid	**(468.2)**	(228.1)	(135.9)
Income taxes paid	**(1,780.8)**	(831.7)	(591.0)
Net cash provided by operating activities	**3,229.7**	1,742.4	1,612.1
CASH FLOWS FROM INVESTING ACTIVITIES:			
Additions to property and equipment	**(1,805.3)**	(1,768.9)	(1,495.4)
Proceeds from sale-leaseback transactions	**601.3**	1,375.6	539.9
Acquisitions (net of cash acquired) and other investments	**(1,983.3)**	(4,224.2)	12.1
Cash outflow from hedging activities	**–**	(5.3)	–
Proceeds from sale or disposal of assets	**105.6**	29.6	31.8
Net cash used in investing activities	**(3,081.7)**	(4,593.2)	(911.6)
CASH FLOWS FROM FINANCING ACTIVITIES:			
Additions to/(reductions in) short-term debt	**242.3**	1,589.3	(632.2)
Additions to long-term debt	**6,000.0**	1,500.0	16.5
Reductions in long-term debt	**(821.8)**	(310.5)	(10.5)
Dividends paid	**(322.4)**	(140.9)	(131.6)
Proceeds from exercise of stock options	**552.4**	187.6	178.4
Excess tax benefits from stock based compensation	**97.8**	42.6	–
Repurchase of common stock	**(5,370.4)**	–	–
Net cash provided by (used in) financing activities	**377.9**	2,868.1	(579.4)
Net increase in cash and cash equivalents	**525.9**	17.3	121.1
Cash and cash equivalents at beginning of year	**530.7**	513.4	392.3
Cash and cash equivalents at end of year	**$ 1,056.6**	$ 530.7	$ 513.4
RECONCILIATION OF NET EARNINGS TO NET CASH PROVIDED BY OPERATING ACTIVITIES:			
Net earnings	**$ 2,637.0**	$ 1,368.9	$ 1,224.7
Adjustments required to reconcile net earnings to net cash provided by operating activities:			
Depreciation and amortization	**1,094.6**	733.3	589.1
Stock based compensation	**78.0**	69.9	–
Deferred income taxes and other non-cash items	**40.1**	98.2	13.5
Change in operating assets and liabilities providing/(requiring) cash, net of effects from acquisitions:			
Accounts receivable, net	**279.7**	(540.1)	(83.1)
Inventories	**(448.0)**	(624.1)	(265.2)
Other current assets	**(59.2)**	(21.4)	(13.2)
Other assets	**(26.4)**	(17.2)	(0.1)
Accounts payable	**(181.4)**	396.7	192.2
Accrued expenses	**(168. 2)**	328.9	(43.8)
Other long-term liabilities	**(16.5)**	(50.7)	(2.0)
Net cash provided by operating activities	**$ 3,229.7**	$ 1,742.4	$ 1,612.1

See accompanying notes to consolidated financial statements.

CONSOLIDATED STATEMENTS OF SHAREHOLDERS' EQUITY

	Shares			Dollars		
In millions	**Dec. 29, 2007**	Dec. 30, 2006	Dec. 31, 2005	**Dec. 29, 2007**	Dec. 30, 2006	Dec. 31, 2005
PREFERENCE STOCK:						
Beginning of year	**4.0**	4.2	4.3	**$ 213.3**	$ 222.6	$ 228.4
Conversion to common stock	**(0.2)**	(0.2)	(0.1)	**(10.3)**	(9.3)	(5.8)
End of year	**3.8**	4.0	4.2	**203.0**	213.3	222.6
COMMON STOCK:						
Beginning of year	**847.3**	838.8	828.6	**8.5**	8.4	8.3
Common stock issued for Caremark Merger	**712.7**	–	–	**7.1**	–	–
Stock options exercised and awards	**30.1**	8.5	10.2	**0.3**	0.1	0.1
End of year	**1,590.1**	847.3	838.8	**15.9**	8.5	8.4
TREASURY STOCK:						
Beginning of year	**(21.5)**	(24.5)	(26.6)	**(314.5)**	(356.5)	(385.9)
Purchase of treasury shares	**(135.0)**	0.1	–	**(5,378.7)**	(0.1)	(1.7)
Conversion of preference stock	**0.9**	0.8	0.5	**24.7**	11.7	7.3
Employee stock purchase plan issuance	**1.9**	2.1	1.6	**48.1**	30.4	23.8
End of year	**(153.7)**	(21.5)	(24.5)	**(5,620.4)**	(314.5)	(356.5)
GUARANTEED ESOP OBLIGATION:						
Beginning of year				**(82.1)**	(114.0)	(140.9)
Reduction of guaranteed ESOP obligation				**37.6**	31.9	26.9
End of year				**(44.5)**	(82.1)	(114.0)
SHARES HELD IN TRUST:						
Beginning of year	–	–	–	–	–	–
Shares acquired through Caremark Merger	**(9.2)**	–	–	**(301.3)**	–	–
End of year	**(9.2)**			**(301.3)**	–	–
CAPITAL SURPLUS:						
Beginning of year				**2,198.4**	1,922.4	1,687.3
Common stock issued for Caremark Merger, net of issuance costs				**23,942.4**	–	–
Stock option activity and awards				**607.7**	235.8	188.8
Tax benefit on stock options and awards				**97.8**	42.6	47.8
Conversion of preference stock				**(14.4)**	(2.4)	(1.5)
End of year				**26,831.9**	2,198.4	1,922.4

CONSOLIDATED STATEMENTS OF SHAREHOLDERS' EQUITY

	Shares			Dollars		
In millions	**Dec. 29, 2007**	Dec. 30, 2006	Dec. 31, 2005	**Dec. 29, 2007**	Dec. 30, 2006	Dec. 31, 2005
ACCUMULATED OTHER COMPREHENSIVE LOSS:						
Beginning of year				**(72.6)**	(90.3)	(55.5)
Recognition of unrealized gain/(loss) on derivatives, net of income tax				**3.4**	(0.3)	2.9
Pension liability adjustment				**19.5**	23.6	(37.7)
Pension liability adjustment to initially apply SFAS No.158, net of tax benefit				**–**	(5.6)	–
End of year				**(49.7)**	(72.6)	(90.3)
RETAINED EARNINGS:						
Beginning of year				**7,966.6**	6,738.6	5,645.5
Net earnings				**2,637.0**	1,368.9	1,224.7
Common stock dividends				**(308.8)**	(127.0)	(117.5)
Preference stock dividends				**(14.8)**	(15.6)	(16.2)
Tax benefit on preference stock dividends				**1.2**	1.7	2.1
Adoption of FIN 48				**5.8**	–	–
End of year				**10,287.0**	7,966.6	6,738.6
Total shareholders' equity				**$ 31,321.9**	$ 9,917.6	$ 8,331.2
COMPREHENSIVE INCOME:						
Net earnings				**$ 2,637.0**	$ 1,368.9	$ 1,224.7
Recognition of unrealized gain/(loss) on derivatives, net of income tax				**3.4**	(0.3)	2.9
Pension liability, net of income tax				**19.5**	23.6	(37.7)
Comprehensive income				**$ 2,659.9**	$ 1,392.2	$ 1,189.9

See accompanying notes to consolidated financial statements.

NOTES TO CONSOLIDATED FINANCIAL STATEMENTS

#1 Significant Accounting Policies

Description of Business

CVS Caremark Corporation (the "Company") operates the largest retail pharmacy business (based on store count) and one of the largest pharmacy services businesses in the United States.

The retail pharmacy business sells prescription drugs and a wide assortment of general merchandise, including over-the-counter drugs, beauty products and cosmetics, photo finishing, seasonal merchandise, greeting cards and convenience foods through its CVS/pharmacy® retail stores and online through CVS.com®. The Company also provides healthcare services through its 462 MinuteClinic® healthcare clinics, 437 of which are located in CVS/pharmacy retail stores.

The pharmacy services business provides a full range of pharmacy benefit management services including mail order pharmacy services, specialty pharmacy services, plan design and administration, formulary management and claims processing. Its customers are primarily employers, insurance companies, unions, government employee groups, managed care organizations and other sponsors of health benefit plans and individuals throughout the United States. In addition, through the Company's SilverScript insurance subsidiary, it is a national provider of drug benefits to eligible beneficiaries under the Federal Government's Medicare Part D Program. The Company's specialty pharmacies support individuals that require complex and expensive drug therapies. The pharmacy services business operates a national retail pharmacy network with over 60,000 participating pharmacies (including CVS/pharmacy stores). The Company also provides disease management programs for 27 conditions through our Accordant® disease management offering. Twenty-one of these programs are accredited by the National Committee for Quality Assurance. Currently, the pharmacy services business operates under the Caremark Pharmacy Services®, PharmaCare Management Services® and PharmaCare Pharmacy® names.

As of December 29, 2007, the Company operated 6,301 retail and specialty pharmacy stores, 20 specialty mail order pharmacies, 9 mail service pharmacies and 462 healthcare clinics in 44 states and the District of Columbia.

Basis of Presentation

The consolidated financial statements include the accounts of the Company and its wholly-owned subsidiaries. All material intercompany balances and transactions have been eliminated.

Stock Split

On May 12, 2005, the Company's Board of Directors authorized a two-for-one stock split, which was effected through the issuance of one additional share of common stock for each share of common stock outstanding. These shares were distributed on June 6, 2005 to shareholders of record as of May 23, 2005. All share and per share amounts presented herein have been restated to reflect the effect of the stock split.

Fiscal Year

The Company's fiscal year is a 52 or 53 week period ending on the Saturday nearest to December 31. Fiscal 2007, which ended on December 29, 2007, fiscal 2006, which ended on December 30, 2006 and fiscal 2005, which ended on December 31, 2005, each included 52 weeks. Unless otherwise noted, all references to years relate to these fiscal years.

Reclassifications

Certain reclassifications have been made to the consolidated financial statements of prior years to conform to the current year presentation. These reclassifications include payroll and operating expenses associated with the fulfillment of scripts in the mail order facilities and call center facilities within the Company's pharmacy services business, which have been reclassified from operating expenses to cost of revenues.

Use of Estimates

The preparation of financial statements in conformity with generally accepted accounting principles requires management to make estimates and assumptions that affect the reported amounts in the consolidated financial statements and accompanying notes. Actual results could differ from those estimates.

Cash and Cash Equivalents

Cash and cash equivalents consist of cash and temporary investments with maturities of three months or less when purchased.

Short-Term Investments

The Company's short-term investments consist of auction rate securities with initial maturities greater than three months when purchased. These investments, which are classified as available-for-sale, are carried at historical cost, which approximated fair value at December 29, 2007.

NOTES TO CONSOLIDATED FINANCIAL STATEMENTS

Accounts Receivable

Accounts receivable are stated net of an allowance for uncollectible accounts of $141.4 million and $73.4 million as of December 29, 2007 and December 30, 2006, respectively. The balance primarily includes amounts due from third party providers (e.g., pharmacy benefit managers, insurance companies and governmental agencies) and vendors as well as clients, participants and manufacturers.

Fair Value of Financial Instruments

As of December 29, 2007, the Company's financial instruments include cash and cash equivalents, short-term investments, accounts receivable, accounts payable and short-term debt. Due to the short-term nature of these instruments, the Company's carrying value approximates fair value. The carrying amount and estimated fair value of long-term debt was $8.2 billion as of December 29, 2007. The carrying amount and estimated fair value of long-term debt was $3.1 billion as of December 30, 2006. The fair value of long-term debt was estimated based on rates currently offered to the Company for debt with similar terms and maturities. The Company had outstanding letters of credit, which guaranteed foreign trade purchases, with a fair value of $5.7 million as of December 29, 2007 and $6.8 million as of December 30, 2006. There were no outstanding investments in derivative financial instruments as of December 29, 2007 or December 30, 2006.

Inventories

Inventories are stated at the lower of cost or market on a first-in, first-out basis using the retail method of accounting to determine cost of sales and inventory in our retail pharmacy stores, average cost to determine cost of sales and inventory in our mail service and specialty pharmacies and the cost method of accounting to determine inventory in our distribution centers. Independent physical inventory counts are taken on a regular basis in each store and distribution center location (other than six distribution centers, which perform a continuous cycle count process to validate the inventory balance on hand) to ensure that the amounts reflected in the accompanying consolidated financial statements are properly stated. During the interim period between physical inventory counts, the Company accrues for anticipated physical inventory losses on a location-by-location basis based on historical results and current trends.

Property and Equipment

Property, equipment and improvements to leased premises are depreciated using the straight-line method over the estimated useful lives of the assets or, when applicable, the term of the lease, whichever is shorter. Estimated useful lives generally range from 10 to 40 years for buildings, building improvements and leasehold improvements and 3 to 10 years for fixtures and equipment. Repair and maintenance costs are charged directly to expense as incurred. Major renewals or replacements that substantially extend the useful life of an asset are capitalized and depreciated.

Following are the components of property and equipment:

In millions	**Dec. 29, 2007**	Dec. 30, 2006
Land	**$ 586.4**	$ 601.3
Building and improvements	**896.0**	801.9
Fixtures and equipment	**5,178.1**	4,347.4
Leasehold improvements	**2,133.2**	1,828.5
Capitalized software	**243.9**	219.1
Capital leases	**181.7**	229.3
	9,219.3	8,027.5
Accumulated depreciation and amortization	**(3,366.5)**	(2,693.9)
	$ 5,852.8	$ 5,333.6

The Company capitalizes application development stage costs for significant internally developed software projects. These costs are amortized over the estimated useful lives of the software, which generally range from 3 to 5 years. Unamortized costs were $74.2 million as of December 29, 2007 and $75.5 million as of December 30, 2006.

Goodwill

The Company accounts for goodwill and intangibles under Statement of Financial Accounting Standards ("SFAS") No. 142, "Goodwill and Other Intangible Assets." As such, goodwill and other indefinite-lived assets are not amortized, but are subject to impairment reviews annually, or more frequently if necessary. See Note 3 for further information on goodwill.

Intangible Assets

Purchased customer contracts and relationships are amortized on a straight-line basis over their estimated useful lives of up to 20 years. Purchased customer lists are amortized on a straight-line basis over their estimated useful lives of up to 10 years. Purchased leases are amortized on a straight-line basis over the remaining life of the lease. See Note 3 for further information on intangible assets.

Impairment of Long-Lived Assets

The Company accounts for the impairment of long-lived assets in accordance with SFAS No. 144, "Accounting for Impairment or Disposal of Long-Lived Assets." As such, the Company groups and evaluates fixed and finite-lived intangible assets, excluding goodwill, for impairment at the lowest level at which individual cash flows can be identified. When evaluating assets for potential impairment, the Company first compares the carrying amount of the asset group to the individual store's estimated future cash flows (undiscounted and without interest charges). If the estimated future cash flows used in this analysis are less than the carrying amount of the asset group, an impairment loss calculation is prepared. The impairment loss calculation compares the carrying amount of the asset group to the asset group's estimated future cash flows (discounted and with interest charges). If required, an impairment loss is recorded for the portion of the asset group's carrying value that exceeds the asset group's estimated future cash flows (discounted and with interest charges).

Revenue Recognition

Retail Pharmacy Segment (the "RPS"). The RPS recognizes revenue from the sale of merchandise (other than prescription drugs) at the time the merchandise is purchased by the retail customer. Revenue from the sale of prescription drugs is recognized at the time the prescription is filled, which is or approximates when the retail customer picks up the prescription. Customer returns are not material. Revenue generated from the performance of services in the RPS' healthcare clinics is recognized at the time the services are performed.

Pharmacy Services Segment (the "PSS"). The PSS sells prescription drugs directly through its mail service pharmacies and indirectly through its national retail pharmacy network. The PSS recognizes revenues from prescription drugs sold by its mail service pharmacies and under national retail pharmacy network contracts where the PSS is the principal using the gross method at the contract prices negotiated with its customers. Net revenue from the PSS includes: (i) the portion of the price the customer pays directly to the PSS, net of any volume-related or other discounts paid back to the customer (see "Drug Discounts" below), (ii) the portion of the price paid to the PSS ("Mail Co-Payments") or a third party pharmacy in the PSS' national retail pharmacy network ("Retail Co-Payments") by individuals included in its customers' benefit plans and (iii) administrative fees for national retail pharmacy network contracts where the PSS is not the principal as discussed below.

SEC Staff Accounting Bulletins No. 101, "Revenue Recognition in Financial Statements," and 104, "Revenue Recognition, corrected copy" ("SAB 101" and "SAB 104," respectively) provide the general criteria for the timing aspect of revenue recognition, including consideration of whether: (i) persuasive evidence of an arrangement exists, (ii) delivery has occurred or services have been rendered, (iii) the seller's price to the buyer is fixed or determinable and (iv) collectability is reasonably assured. The Company has established the following revenue recognition policies for the PSS in accordance with SAB 101 and SAB 104:

- Revenues generated from prescription drugs sold by mail service pharmacies are recognized when the prescription is shipped. At the time of shipment, the Company has performed substantially all of its obligations under its customer contracts and does not experience a significant level of reshipments.
- Revenues generated from prescription drugs sold by third party pharmacies in the PSS' national retail pharmacy network and associated administrative fees are recognized at the PSS' point-of-sale, which is when the claim is adjudicated by the PSS' on-line claims processing system.

The PSS determines whether it is the principal or agent for its national retail pharmacy network transactions using the indicators set forth in Emerging Issues Task Force ("EITF") Issue No. 99-19, "Reporting Revenue Gross as a Principal versus Net as an Agent" on a contract by contract basis. In the majority of its contracts, the PSS has determined it is the principal due to it: (i) being the primary obligor in the arrangement, (ii) having latitude in establishing the price, changing the product or performing part of the service, (iii) having discretion in supplier selection, (iv) having involvement in the determination of product or service specifications and (v) having credit risk. The PSS' obligations under its customer contracts for which revenues are reported using the gross method are separate and distinct from its obligations to the third party pharmacies under its national retail pharmacy network contracts. Pursuant to these contracts, the PSS is contractually required to pay the third party pharmacies in its national retail pharmacy network for products sold, regardless of whether the PSS is paid by its customers. The PSS' responsibilities under its customer contracts typically include validating eligibility and coverage levels, communicating the prescription price and the co-payments due to the third party retail pharmacy, identifying possible adverse drug interactions for the pharmacist to address with the physician prior to dispensing, suggesting clinically appropriate generic alternatives where appropriate and approving the prescription for dispensing. Although the PSS does not have credit risk with respect to Retail Co-Payments, management believes that all of the other indicators of gross revenue reporting are present. For contracts under which the PSS acts as an agent, the PSS records revenues using the net method.

Drug Discounts. The PSS deducts from its revenues any discounts paid to its customers as required by Emerging Issues Task Force Issue No. 01-9, "Accounting for Consideration Given by a Vendor to a Customer (Including a Reseller of the Vendor's Products)" ("EITF 01-9"). The PSS pays discounts to its customers in accordance with the terms of its customer contracts, which are normally based on a fixed discount per prescription for specific products dispensed or a percentage of manufacturer discounts received for specific products dispensed. The liability for discounts due to the PSS' customers is included in "Claims and discounts payable" in the accompanying consolidated balance sheets.

Medicare Part D. The PSS began participating in the Federal Government's Medicare Part D program as a Prescription Drug Plan ("PDP") on January 1, 2006. The PSS' net revenues include insurance premiums earned by the PDP, which are determined based on the PSS' annual bid and related contractual arrangements with the Centers for Medicare and Medicaid Services ("CMS"). The insurance premiums include a beneficiary premium, which is the responsibility of the PDP member, but is subsidized by CMS in the case of low-income members, and a direct subsidy paid by CMS. These insurance premiums are recognized in net revenues over the period in which members are entitled to receive benefits. Premiums collected in advance are deferred.

In addition to these premiums, the PSS' net revenues include co-payments, deductibles and coinsurance (collectively referred to as member responsibility amounts) related to PDP members' prescription claims. CMS subsidizes certain components of these member responsibility amounts and pays the PSS an estimated prospective subsidy amount each month. The prospective subsidy amounts received from CMS are recorded in "Accrued expenses" in the accompanying consolidated condensed balance sheets to the extent that they differ from amounts earned based on actual claims experience.

The PSS accounts for CMS obligations and member responsibility amounts using the gross method consistent with its revenue recognition policies, including the application of EITF 99-19. Additionally, the PSS includes actual amounts paid by members of its PDP to the third party pharmacies in its national retail pharmacy network in the total Retail Co-Payments included in net revenues.

Please see Note 13 for further information on revenues of the Company's business segments.

Cost of Revenues

Retail Pharmacy Segment. The RPS' cost of revenues includes: the cost of merchandise sold during the reporting period and the related purchasing costs, warehousing and delivery costs (including depreciation and amortization) and actual and estimated inventory losses.

Pharmacy Services Segment. The PSS' cost of revenues includes: (i) the cost of prescription drugs sold during the reporting period directly through its mail service pharmacies and indirectly through its national retail pharmacy network, (ii) shipping and handling costs and (iii) the operating costs of its mail service pharmacies and customer service operations and related information technology support costs (including depreciation and amortization). The cost of prescription drugs sold component of cost of revenues includes: (i) the cost of the prescription drugs purchased from manufacturers or distributors and shipped to participants in customers' benefit plans from the PSS' mail service pharmacies, net of any volume-related or other discounts (see "Drug Discounts" above) and (ii) the cost of prescription drugs sold (including Retail Co-Payments) through the PSS' national retail pharmacy network under contracts where it is the principal, net of any volume-related or other discounts.

Please see Note 13 for further information related to the cost of revenues of the Company's business segments.

Vendor Allowances and Purchase Discounts

The Company accounts for vendor allowances and purchase discounts under the guidance provided by EITF Issue No. 02-16, "Accounting by a Customer (Including a Reseller) for Certain Consideration Received from a Vendor," and EITF Issue No. 03-10, "Application of EITF Issue No. 02-16 by Resellers to Sales Incentives Offered to Consumers by Manufacturers."

Retail Pharmacy Segment. Vendor allowances the RPS receives reduce the carrying cost of inventory and are recognized in cost of revenues when the related inventory is sold, unless they are specifically identified as a reimbursement of incremental costs for promotional programs and/or other services provided. Funds that are directly linked to advertising commitments are recognized as a reduction of advertising expense (included in operating expenses) when the related advertising commitment is satisfied. Any such allowances received in excess of the actual cost incurred also reduce the carrying cost of inventory. The total value of any upfront payments received from vendors that are linked to purchase commitments is initially deferred. The deferred amounts are then amortized to reduce cost of revenues over the life of the contract based upon purchase volume. The total value of any upfront payments received from vendors that are not linked to purchase commitments is also initially deferred. The deferred amounts are then amortized to reduce cost of revenues on a straight-line basis over the life of the related contract. The total amortization of these upfront payments was not material to the accompanying consolidated financial statements.

Pharmacy Services Segment. The PSS receives purchase discounts on products purchased. The PSS' contractual arrangements with vendors, including manufacturers, wholesalers and retail pharmacies, normally provide for the PSS to receive purchase discounts from established list prices in one, or a combination of, the following forms: (i) a direct discount at the time of purchase, (ii) a discount for the prompt payment of invoices or (iii) when products are purchased indirectly from a manufacturer (e.g., through a wholesaler or retail pharmacy), a discount (or rebate) paid subsequent to dispensing. These rebates are recognized when prescriptions are dispensed and are generally calculated and billed to manufacturers within 30 days of the end of each completed quarter. Historically, the effect of adjustments resulting from the reconciliation of rebates recognized to the amounts billed and collected has not been material to the PSS' results of operations. The PSS accounts for the effect of any such differences as a change in accounting estimate in the period the reconciliation is completed. The PSS also receives additional discounts under its wholesaler contract if it exceeds contractually defined annual purchase volumes.

The PSS earns purchase discounts at various points in its business cycle (e.g., when the product is purchased, when the vendor is paid or when the product is dispensed) for products sold through its mail service pharmacies and third party pharmacies included its national retail pharmacy network. In addition, the PSS receives fees from pharmaceutical manufacturers for administrative services. Purchase discounts and administrative service fees are recorded as a reduction of "Cost of revenues" as required by EITF 02-16.

Shares Held in Trust

As a result of the Caremark Merger, the Company maintains grantor trusts, which held approximately 9.2 million shares of its common stock at December 29, 2007. These shares are designated for use under various employee compensation plans. Since the Company holds these shares, they are excluded from the computation of basic and diluted shares outstanding.

Insurance

The Company is self-insured for certain losses related to general liability, workers' compensation and auto liability. The Company obtains third party insurance coverage to limit exposure from these claims. The Company is also self-insured for certain losses related to health and medical liabilities. The Company's self-insurance accruals, which include reported claims and claims incurred but not reported, are calculated using standard insurance industry actuarial assumptions and the Company's historical claims experience.

Store Opening and Closing Costs

New store opening costs, other than capital expenditures, are charged directly to expense when incurred. When the Company closes a store, the present value of estimated unrecoverable costs, including the remaining lease obligation less estimated sublease income and the book value of abandoned property and equipment, are charged to expense. The long-term portion of the lease obligations associated with store closings was $370.0 million and $418.0 million in 2007 and 2006, respectively.

NOTES TO CONSOLIDATED FINANCIAL STATEMENTS

Advertising Costs

Advertising costs are expensed when the related advertising takes place. Advertising costs, net of vendor funding, (included in operating expenses), were $290.6 million in 2007, $265.3 million in 2006 and $206.6 million in 2005.

Interest Expense, Net

Interest expense was $468.3 million, $231.7 million and $117.0 million, and interest income was $33.7 million, $15.9 million and $6.5 million in 2007, 2006 and 2005, respectively. Capitalized interest totaled $23.7 million in 2007, $20.7 million in 2006 and $12.7 million in 2005.

Accumulated Other Comprehensive Loss

Accumulated other comprehensive loss consists of changes in the net actuarial gains and losses associated with pension and other post retirement benefit plans, unrealized losses on derivatives and adjustment to initially apply SFAS No. 158. In accordance with SFAS No. 158, the amount included in accumulated other comprehensive income related to the Company's pension and post retirement plans was $58.7 million pre-tax ($35.9 million after-tax) as of December 29, 2007 and $87.4 million pre-tax ($55.4 million after-tax) as of December 30, 2006. The unrealized loss on derivatives totaled $21.9 million pre-tax ($13.8 million after-tax) and $27.2 million pre-tax ($17.2 million after-tax) as of December 29, 2007 and December 30, 2006, respectively.

Stock-Based Compensation

On January 1, 2006, the Company adopted SFAS No. 123(R), "Share-Based Payment," using the modified prospective transition method. Under this method, compensation expense is recognized for options granted on or after January 1, 2006 as well as any unvested options on the date of adoption. As allowed under the modified prospective transition method, prior period financial statements have not been restated. Prior to January 1, 2006, the Company accounted for its stock-based compensation plans under the recognition and measurement principles of Accounting Principles Board ("APB") Opinion No. 25, "Accounting for Stock Issued to Employees," and related interpretations. As such, no stock-based employee compensation costs were reflected in net earnings for options granted under those plans since they had an exercise price equal to the fair market value of the underlying common stock on the date of grant. See Note 8 for further information on stock-based compensation.

Income Taxes

The Company provides for federal and state income taxes currently payable, as well as for those deferred because of timing differences between reported income and expenses for financial statement purposes versus tax purposes. Federal and state tax credits are recorded as a reduction of income taxes. Deferred tax assets and liabilities are recognized for the future tax consequences attributable to differences between the carrying amount of assets and liabilities for financial reporting purposes and the amounts used for income tax purposes. Deferred tax assets and liabilities are measured using the enacted tax rates expected to apply to taxable income in the years in which those temporary differences are expected to be recoverable or settled. The effect of a change in tax rates is recognized as income or expense in the period of the change. See Note 12 for further information on income taxes.

Earnings per Common Share

Basic earnings per common share is computed by dividing: (i) net earnings, after deducting the after-tax Employee Stock Ownership Plan ("ESOP") preference dividends, by (ii) the weighted average number of common shares outstanding during the year (the "Basic Shares").

When computing diluted earnings per common share, the Company assumes that the ESOP preference stock is converted into common stock and all dilutive stock awards are exercised. After the assumed ESOP preference stock conversion, the ESOP Trust would hold common stock rather than ESOP preference stock and would receive common stock dividends ($0.22875 per share in 2007, $0.15500 per share in 2006 and $0.14500 per share in 2005) rather than ESOP preference stock dividends (currently $3.90 per share). Since the ESOP Trust uses the dividends it receives to service its debt, the Company would have to increase its contribution to the ESOP Trust to compensate it for the lower dividends. This additional contribution would reduce the Company's net earnings, which in turn, would reduce the amounts that would be accrued under the Company's incentive compensation plans.

Diluted earnings per common share is computed by dividing: (i) net earnings, after accounting for the difference between the dividends on the ESOP preference stock and common stock and after making adjustments for the incentive compensation plans, by (ii) Basic Shares plus the additional shares that would be issued assuming that all dilutive stock awards are exercised and the ESOP preference stock is converted into common stock. Options to purchase 10.7 million, 4.7 million and 6.9 million shares of common stock were outstanding as of December 29, 2007, December 30, 2006 and December 31, 2005, respectively, but were not included in the calculation of diluted earnings per share because the options' exercise prices were greater than the average market price of the common shares and, therefore, the effect would be antidilutive.

New Accounting Pronouncements

The Company adopted Financial Accounting Standards Board Interpretation No. 48, "Accounting for Uncertainty in Income Taxes – an interpretation of FASB Statement No. 109" ("FIN 48") effective December 31, 2006. FIN 48 addresses the uncertainty about how certain income tax positions taken or expected to be taken on an income tax return should be reflected in the financial statements before they are finally resolved. As a result of the implementation, the Company recognized a decrease to reserves for uncertain income tax positions of approximately $4.0 million, which was accounted for as an increase to the December 31, 2006 balance of retained earnings.

The Company adopted SFAS No. 157, "Fair Value Measurement." SFAS No. 157 defines fair value, establishes a framework for measuring fair value in generally accepted accounting principles and expands disclosures regarding fair value measurements. SFAS No. 157 is effective for fiscal years beginning after November 15, 2007 and interim periods within those fiscal years. The adoption of this statement did not have a material impact on its consolidated results of operations, financial position or cash flows.

In June 2006, the Emerging Issues Task Force of the Financial Accounting Standards Board ("FASB") reached a consensus on EITF Issue No. 06-4, "Accounting for Deferred Compensation and Postretirement Benefit Aspects of Endorsement Split-Dollar Life Insurance Arrangements" ("EITF 06-4"), which requires the application of the provisions of SFAS No. 106, "Employers' Accounting for Postretirement Benefits Other Than Pensions" ("SFAS 106") (if, in substance, a postretirement benefit plan exists), or Accounting Principles Board Opinion No. 12 (if the arrangement is, in substance, an individual deferred compensation contract) to endorsement split-dollar life insurance arrangements. SFAS 106 would require the Company to recognize a liability for the discounted value of the future benefits that it will incur through the death of the underlying insureds. EITF 06-4 is currently effective for fiscal years beginning after December 15, 2007. The Company is currently evaluating the potential impact the adoption of EITF 06-4 may have on its consolidated results of operations, financial position and cash flows.

In March 2007, the FASB issued Emerging Issues Task Force Issue No. 06-10 "Accounting for Collateral Assignment Split-Dollar Life Insurance Agreements" ("EITF 06-10"). EITF 06-10 provides guidance for determining a liability for the postretirement benefit obligation as well as recognition and measurement of the associated asset on the basis of the terms of the collateral assignment agreement. EITF 06-10 is effective for fiscal years beginning after December 15, 2007. The Company is currently evaluating the potential impact the adoption of EITF 06-10 may have on its consolidated results of operations, financial position and cash flows.

In December 2007, the FASB issued SFAS No. 141 (revised 2007), "Business Combinations" ("SFAS 141R"), which replaces FASB Statement No. 141. SFAS 141R establishes the principles and requirements for how an acquirer recognizes and measures in its financial statements the identifiable assets acquired, the liabilities assumed, any non controlling interest in the acquiree and the goodwill acquired. The Statement also establishes disclosure requirements which will enable users to evaluate the nature and financial effects of business combinations. SFAS 141R is effective for fiscal years beginning after December 15, 2008. The Company is currently evaluating the potential impact, if any, the adoption of SFAS 141R may have on its consolidated results of operations, financial position and cash flows.

NOTES TO CONSOLIDATED FINANCIAL STATEMENTS

#2 Business Combinations

Caremark Merger

Effective March 22, 2007, pursuant to the Agreement and Plan of Merger dated as of November 1, 2006, as amended (the "Merger Agreement"), Caremark Rx, Inc. ("Caremark") was merged with and into a newly formed subsidiary of CVS Corporation, with the CVS subsidiary continuing as the surviving entity (the "Caremark Merger"). Following the merger, the Company changed its name to CVS Caremark Corporation.

Under the terms of the Merger Agreement, Caremark shareholders received 1.67 shares of common stock, par value $0.01 per share, of the Company for each share of common stock of Caremark, par value $0.001 per share, issued and outstanding immediately prior to the effective time of the merger. In addition, Caremark shareholders of record as of the close of business on the day immediately preceding the closing date of the merger received a special cash dividend of $7.50 per share.

The merger was accounted for using the purchase method of accounting under U.S. Generally Accepted Accounting Principles. Under the purchase method of accounting, CVS Corporation is considered the acquirer of Caremark for accounting purposes and the total purchase price will be allocated to the assets acquired and liabilities assumed from Caremark based on their fair values as of March 22, 2007. Under the purchase method of accounting, the total consideration was approximately $26.9 billion and includes amounts related to Caremark common stock ($23.3 billion), Caremark stock options ($0.6 billion) and the special cash dividend ($3.2 billion), less shares held in trust ($0.3 billion). The consideration associated with the common stock and stock options was based on the average closing price of CVS common stock for the five trading days ending February 14, 2007, which was $32.67 per share. The results of the operations of Caremark have been included in the consolidated statements of operations since March 22, 2007.

Following is a summary of the estimated assets acquired and liabilities assumed as of March 22, 2007. This estimate is preliminary and based on information that was available to management at the time the consolidated financial statements were prepared. Accordingly, the allocation will change and the impact of such changes could be material.

Estimated Assets Acquired and Liabilities Assumed as of March 22, 2007

In millions	
Cash and cash equivalents	$ 1,293.4
Short-term investments	27.5
Accounts receivable	2,472.7
Inventories	442.3
Deferred tax asset	95.4
Other current assets	31.4
Total current assets	4,362.7
Property and equipment	209.7
Goodwill	20,853.0
Intangible assets[(1)]	9,429.5
Other assets	67.1
Total assets acquired	34,922.0
Accounts payable	960.8
Claims and discounts payable	2,430.1
Accrued expenses[(2)]	991.6
Total current liabilities	4,382.5
Deferred tax liability	3,595.7
Other long-term liabilities	93.2
Total liabilities	8,071.4
Net assets acquired	$ 26,850.6

(1) Intangible assets include customer contracts and relationships ($2.9 billion) with an estimated weighted average life of 14.7 years, proprietary technology ($109.8 million) with an estimated weighted average life of 3.5 years, favorable leaseholds ($12.7 million) with an estimated weighted average life of 6.2 years, covenants not to compete ($9.0 million) with an estimated average life of 2 years and trade names ($6.4 billion), which are indefinitely lived.

(2) Accrued expenses currently include $49.5 million for estimated severance, benefits and outplacement costs for approximately 240 Caremark employees that have been or will be terminated. The amount accrued and the number of employees affected may continue to increase as exit plans are finalized and communicated. As of December 29, 2007, $48.1 million of the liability has been settled with cash payments. The remaining liability will require future cash payments through 2008. Accrued expenses also include $1.4 million for the estimated costs associated with the non-cancelable lease obligation of one location. As of December 29, 2007, $0.5 million of the liability has been settled with cash payments. The remaining liability will require future cash payments through 2008.

Standalone Drug Business

On June 2, 2006, CVS acquired certain assets and assumed certain liabilities from Albertson's, Inc. ("Albertson's") for $4.0 billion. The assets acquired and the liabilities assumed included approximately 700 standalone drugstores and a distribution center (collectively the "Standalone Drug Business").

In conjunction with the acquisition of the Standalone Drug Business, during fiscal 2006, the Company recorded a $49.5 million liability for the estimated costs associated with the non-cancelable lease obligations of 94 acquired stores that the Company does not intend to operate. As of December 29, 2007, 81 of these locations have been closed and $3.6 million of this liability has been settled with cash payments. The $47.5 million remaining liability, which includes $3.1 million of interest accretion, will require future cash payments through 2033, unless settled prior thereto. The Company believes the remaining liability is adequate to cover the remaining costs associated with the related activities.

The following unaudited pro forma combined results of operations have been provided for illustrative purposes only and do not purport to be indicative of the actual results that would have been achieved by the combined companies for the periods presented or that will be achieved by the combined companies in the future:

In millions, except per share amounts	**2007**	2006
Pro forma:(1)(2)(3)(4)		
Net revenues	**$ 83,798.6**	$ 78,668.9
Net earnings	**2,906.6**	2,167.5
Basic earnings per share	**$ 1.76**	$ 1.41
Diluted earnings per share	**1.72**	1.37

(1) The pro forma combined results of operations assume that the Caremark Merger and the acquisition of the Standalone Drug Business occurred at the beginning of each period presented. These results have been prepared by adjusting the historical results of the Company to include the historical results of Caremark and the Standalone Drug Business, incremental interest expense and the impact of the preliminary purchase price allocation discussed above. The historical results of Caremark are based on a calendar period end, whereas the historical results of the Pharmacy Services Segment of CVS are based on a 52 week fiscal year ending on the Saturday nearest to December 31.

(2) Inter-company revenues that occur when a Caremark customer uses a CVS/pharmacy retail store to purchase covered products were eliminated. These adjustments had no impact on pro forma net earnings or pro forma earnings per share.

(3) The pro forma combined results of operations do not include any cost savings that may result from the combination of the Company and Caremark or any estimated costs that will be incurred by the Company to integrate the businesses.

(4) The pro forma combined results of operations for fiscal year ended December 29, 2007, exclude $80.3 million pre-tax ($48.6 million after-tax) of stock option expense associated with the accelerated vesting of certain Caremark stock options, which vested upon consummation of the merger due to change in control provisions included in the underlying Caremark stock option plans. The pro forma combined results for the fiscal year ended December 29, 2007 also exclude $42.9 million pre-tax ($25.9 million after-tax) related to change in control payments due upon the consummation of the merger due to change in control provisions in certain Caremark employment agreements. In addition, the pro forma combined results of operations for the fiscal year ended December 29, 2007, exclude merger-related costs of $150.1 million pre-tax ($101.7 million after-tax), which primarily consist of investment banker fees, legal fees, accounting fees and other merger-related costs incurred by Caremark.

#3 Goodwill and Other Intangibles

The Company accounts for goodwill and intangibles under SFAS No. 142, "Goodwill and Other Intangible Assets." Under SFAS No. 142, goodwill and other indefinitely-lived assets are not amortized, but are subject to annual impairment reviews, or more frequent reviews if events or circumstances indicate an impairment may exist.

When evaluating goodwill for potential impairment, the Company first compares the fair value of the reporting unit, based on estimated future discounted cash flows, to its carrying amount. If the estimated fair value of the reporting unit is less than its carrying amount, an impairment loss calculation is prepared. The impairment loss calculation compares the implied fair value of a reporting unit's goodwill with the carrying amount of its goodwill. If the carrying amount of the goodwill exceeds the implied fair value, an impairment loss is recognized in an amount equal to the excess. During the third quarter of 2007, the Company performed its required annual goodwill impairment tests, and concluded there were no goodwill impairments.

Indefinitely-lived intangible assets are tested by comparing the estimated fair value of the asset to its carrying value. If the carrying value of the asset exceeds its estimated fair value, an impairment loss is recognized and the asset is written down to its estimated fair value.

The carrying amount of goodwill was $23.9 billion and $3.2 billion as of December 29, 2007 and December 30, 2006, respectively. During 2007, gross goodwill increased primarily in the Pharmacy Services Segment due to the Caremark Merger. There was no impairment of goodwill during 2007.

The carrying amount of indefinitely-lived assets was $6.4 billion as of December 29, 2007. The Company had no indefinitely-lived assets as of December 30, 2006. The increase in the Company's indefinitely-lived assets during 2007 was due to the recognition of trademarks associated with the Caremark Merger.

Intangible assets with finite useful lives are amortized over their estimated useful lives. The increase in the gross carrying amount of the Company's amortizable intangible assets during 2007 was primarily due to the Caremark Merger and adjustments related to the Standalone Drug Business. The amortization expense for intangible assets totaled $344.1 million in 2007, $161.2 million in 2006 and $128.6 million in 2005. The anticipated annual amortization expense for these intangible assets is $387.2 million in 2008, $373.8 million in 2009, $361.5 million in 2010, $352.7 million in 2011 and $334.5 million in 2012.

Following is a summary of the Company's intangible assets as of the respective balance sheet dates:

	Dec. 29, 2007		Dec. 30, 2006	
In millions	**Gross Carrying Amount**	**Accumulated Amortization**	Gross Carrying Amount	Accumulated Amortization
Trademarks (indefinitely-lived)	**$ 6,398.0**	**$ –**	$ –	$ –
Customer contracts and relationships and Covenants not to compete	**4,444.1**	**(876.9)**	1,457.6	(563.4)
Favorable leases and Other	**623.0**	**(158.6)**	552.2	(128.2)
	$ 11,465.1	**$ (1,035.5)**	$ 2,009.8	$ (691.6)

#4 Share Repurchase Program

In connection with the Caremark Merger, on March 28, 2007, the Company commenced a tender offer to purchase up to 150 million common shares, or about 10%, of its outstanding common stock at a price of $35.00 per share. The tender offer expired on April 24, 2007 and resulted in approximately 10.3 million shares being tendered. The shares were placed into the Company's treasury account.

On May 9, 2007, the Board of Directors of the Company authorized a share repurchase program for up to $5.0 billion of the Company's outstanding common stock.

On May 13, 2007, the Company entered into a $2.5 billion fixed dollar accelerated share repurchase (the "May ASR") agreement with Lehman Brothers, Inc. ("Lehman"). The May ASR agreement contained provisions that established the minimum and maximum number of shares to be repurchased during the term of the May ASR agreement. Pursuant to the terms of the May ASR agreement, on May 14, 2007, the Company paid $2.5 billion to Lehman in exchange for Lehman delivering 45.6 million shares of common stock to the Company, which were placed into its treasury account upon delivery. On June 7, 2007, upon establishment of the minimum number of shares to be repurchased, Lehman delivered an additional 16.1 million shares of common stock to the Company. The May ASR program concluded on October 5, 2007 and resulted in the Company receiving an additional 5.8 million shares of common stock during the fourth quarter of 2007. As of December 29, 2007 the aggregate 67.5 million shares of common stock received pursuant to the $2.5 billion May ASR agreement had been placed into the Company's treasury account.

On October 8, 2007, the Company commenced an open market repurchase program. The program concluded on November 2, 2007 and resulted in 5.3 million shares of common stock being repurchased for $211.9 million. The shares were placed into the Company's treasury account upon delivery.

On November 6, 2007, the Company entered into a $2.3 billion fixed dollar accelerated share repurchase agreement (the "November ASR") with Lehman. The November ASR agreement contained provisions that established the minimum and maximum number of shares to be repurchased during the term of the November

ASR agreement. Pursuant to the terms of the November ASR agreement, on November 7, 2007, the Company paid $2.3 billion to Lehman in exchange for Lehman delivering 37.2 million shares of common stock to the Company, which were placed into its treasury account upon delivery. On November 26, 2007, upon establishment of the minimum number of shares to be repurchased, Lehman delivered an additional 14.4 million shares of common stock to the Company. As of December 29, 2007, the aggregate 51.6 million shares of common stock, received pursuant to the November ASR agreement, had been placed into the Company's treasury account. The Company may receive up to 5.7 million of additional shares of common stock, depending on the market price of the common stock, as determined under the November ASR agreement, over the term of the November ASR agreement, which is currently expected to conclude during the first quarter of 2008.

#5 Borrowing and Credit Agreements

Following is a summary of the Company's borrowings as of the respective balance sheet dates:

In millions	**Dec. 29, 2007**	Dec. 30, 2006
Commercial paper	**$ 2,085.0**	$ 1,842.7
3.875% senior notes due 2007	**–**	300.0
4.0% senior notes due 2009	**650.0**	650.0
Floating rate notes due 2010	**1,750.0**	–
5.75% senior notes due 2011	**800.0**	800.0
4.875% senior notes due 2014	**550.0**	550.0
6.125% senior notes due 2016	**700.0**	700.0
5.75% senior notes due 2017	**1,750.0**	–
6.25% senior notes due 2027	**1,000.0**	–
8.52% ESOP notes due 2008[1]	**44.5**	82.1
6.302% Enhanced Capital Advantage Preferred Securities	**1,000.0**	–
Mortgage notes payable	**7.3**	11.7
Capital lease obligations	**145.1**	120.9
	10,481.9	5,057.4
Less:		
Short-term debt	**(2,085.0)**	(1,842.7)
Current portion of long-term debt	**(47.2)**	(344.3)
	$ 8,349.7	$ 2,870.4

(1) See Note 8 for further information about the Company's ESOP Plan.

In connection with its commercial paper program, the Company maintains a $675 million, five-year unsecured back-up credit facility, which expires on June 11, 2009, a $675 million, five-year unsecured back-up credit facility, which expires on June 2, 2010, a $1.4 billion, five-year unsecured back-up credit facility, which expires on May 12, 2011 and a $1.3 billion, five-year unsecured back-up credit facility, which expires on March 12, 2012. The credit facilities allow for borrowings at various rates depending on the Company's public debt ratings and requires the Company to pay a quarterly facility fee of 0.1%, regardless of usage. As of December 29, 2007, the Company had no outstanding borrowings against the credit facilities. The weighted average interest rate for short-term debt was 5.3% as of December 29, 2007 and December 30, 2006.

On May 22, 2007, the Company issued $1.75 billion of floating rate senior notes due June 1, 2010, $1.75 billion of 5.75% unsecured senior notes due June 1, 2017, and $1.0 billion of 6.25% unsecured senior notes due June 1, 2027 (collectively the "2007 Notes"). Also on May 22, 2007, the Company entered into an underwriting agreement with Lehman Brothers, Inc., Morgan Stanley & Co. Incorporated, Banc of America Securities LLC, BNY Capital Markets, Inc., and Wachovia Capital Markets, LLC, as representatives of the underwriters pursuant to which the Company agreed to issue and sell $1.0 billion of Enhanced Capital Advantaged Preferred Securities ("ECAPS") due June 1, 2062 to the underwriters. The ECAPS bear interest at 6.302% per year until June 1, 2012 at which time they will pay interest based on a floating rate. The 2007 Notes and ECAPS pay interest semi-annually and may be redeemed at any time, in whole or in part at a defined redemption price plus accrued interest. The net proceeds from the 2007 Notes and ECAPS were used to repay the bridge credit facility and commercial paper borrowings.

On August 15, 2006, the Company issued $800 million of 5.75% unsecured senior notes due August 15, 2011 and $700 million of 6.125% unsecured senior notes due August 15, 2016 (collectively the "2006 Notes"). The 2006 Notes pay interest semi-annually and may be redeemed at any time, in whole or in part at a defined redemption price plus accrued interest. Net proceeds from the 2006 Notes were used to repay a portion of the outstanding commercial paper issued to finance the acquisition of the Standalone Drug Business.

To manage a portion of the risk associated with potential changes in market interest rates, during the second quarter of 2006 the Company entered into forward starting pay fixed rate swaps (the "Swaps"), with a notional amount of $750 million. During 2006, the Swaps settled in conjunction with the placement of the long-term financing, at a loss of $5.3 million. The Company accounts for the above derivatives in accordance with SFAS No. 133, "Accounting for Derivative Instruments and Hedging Activities," as modified by SFAS No. 138, "Accounting for Derivative Instruments and Certain Hedging Activities," which requires the resulting loss to be recorded in shareholders' equity as a component of accumulated other comprehensive loss. This unrealized loss will be amortized as a component of interest expense over the life of the related long-term financing. As of December 29, 2007, the Company had no freestanding derivatives in place.

The credit facilities, unsecured senior notes and ECAPS contain customary restrictive financial and operating covenants. The covenants do not materially affect the Company's financial or operating flexibility.

The aggregate maturities of long-term debt for each of the five years subsequent to December 29, 2007 are $47.2 million in 2008, $653.0 million in 2009, $1.8 billion in 2010, $803.9 million in 2011 and $1.0 billion in 2012.

#6 Leases

The Company leases most of its retail and mail locations, nine of its distribution centers and certain corporate offices under non-cancelable operating leases, with initial terms of 15 to 25 years and with options that permit renewals for additional periods. The Company also leases certain equipment and other assets under non-cancelable operating leases, with initial terms of 3 to 10 years. Minimum rent is expensed on a straight-line basis over the term of the lease. In addition to minimum rental payments, certain leases require additional payments based on sales volume, as well as reimbursement for real estate taxes, common area maintenance and insurance, which are expensed when incurred.

Following is a summary of the Company's net rental expense for operating leases for the respective years:

In millions	**2007**	2006	2005
Minimum rentals	**$ 1,557.0**	$ 1,361.2	$ 1,213.2
Contingent rentals	**65.1**	61.5	63.3
	1,622.1	1,422.7	1,276.5
Less: sublease income	**(21.5)**	(26.4)	(18.8)
	$ 1,600.6	$ 1 ,396.3	$ 1,257.7

Following is a summary of the future minimum lease payments under capital and operating leases as of December 29, 2007:

In millions	Capital Leases	Operating Leases
2008	$ 16.0	$ 1,584.5
2009	16.0	1,548.3
2010	16.1	1,654.5
2011	16.2	1,418.2
2012	16.5	1,500.5
Thereafter	256.5	14,384.6
	$ 337.3	$ 22,090.6
Less: imputed interest	(192.2)	
Present value of capital lease obligations	$ 145.1	$ 22,090.6

The Company finances a portion of its store development program through sale-leaseback transactions. The properties are sold and the resulting leases qualify and are accounted for as operating leases. The Company does not have any retained or contingent interests in the stores and does not provide any guarantees, other than a guarantee of lease payments, in connection with the sale-leaseback transactions. Proceeds from sale-leaseback transactions totaled $601.3 million, $1.4 billion, which included approximately $800 million in proceeds associated with the sale and leaseback of properties acquired as part of the acquisition of the Standalone Drug Business, and $539.9 million in 2007, 2006 and 2005, respectively. The operating leases that resulted from these transactions are included in the above table.

#7 Medicare Part D

The Company offers Medicare Part D benefits through its wholly-owned subsidiary SilverScript Insurance Company ("SilverScript") which has been approved by the CMS as a PDP. SilverScript has contracted with CMS to be the Company's PDP and, pursuant to the Medicare Prescription Drug, Improvement and Modernization Act of 2003 ("MMA"), must be a risk-bearing entity regulated under state insurance laws or similar statutes.

SilverScript is licensed through the Tennessee Department of Commerce and Insurance (the "TDCI") as a domestic insurance company under the applicable laws and regulations of the State of Tennessee. Pursuant to these laws and regulations, SilverScript must file quarterly and annual reports with the National Association of Insurance Commissioners ("NAIC"), and the TDCI must maintain certain minimum amounts of capital and surplus under a formula established by the NAIC and must, in certain circumstances, request and receive the approval of the TDCI before making dividend payments or other capital distributions to the Company. The Company does not believe these limitations on dividends and distributions materially impact its financial position. SilverScript is licensed as or has filed expansion applications for licensure as an insurance company in other jurisdictions where it does or may seek to do business. Certain of the expansion insurance licensure applications for states in which SilverScript currently operates were pending as of the date of this filing.

The Company has recorded estimates of various assets and liabilities arising from its participation in the Medicare Part D program based on information in its claims management and enrollment systems. Significant estimates arising from its participation in this program include: (i) estimates of low-income cost subsidy and reinsurance amounts ultimately payable to or receivable from CMS based on a detailed claims reconciliation that will occur in 2008; (ii) estimates of amounts payable to or receivable from other PDPs for claims costs incurred as a result of retroactive enrollment changes, which were communicated by CMS after such claims had been incurred; and (iii) an estimate of amounts receivable from or payable to CMS under a risk-sharing feature of the Medicare Part D program design, referred to as the risk corridor.

#8 Employee Stock Ownership Plan

The Company sponsors a defined contribution Employee Stock Ownership Plan (the "ESOP") that covers full-time employees with at least one year of service.

In 1989, the ESOP Trust issued and sold $357.5 million of 20-year, 8.52% notes due December 31, 2008 (the "ESOP Notes"). The proceeds from the ESOP Notes were used to purchase 6.7 million shares of Series One ESOP Convertible Preference Stock (the "ESOP Preference Stock") from the Company. Since the ESOP Notes are guaranteed by the Company, the outstanding balance is reflected as long-term debt, and a corresponding guaranteed ESOP obligation is reflected in shareholders' equity in the accompanying consolidated balance sheets.

Each share of ESOP Preference Stock has a guaranteed minimum liquidation value of $53.45, is convertible into 4.628 shares of common stock and is entitled to receive an annual dividend of $3.90 per share.

The ESOP Trust uses the dividends received and contributions from the Company to repay the ESOP Notes. As the ESOP Notes are repaid, ESOP Preference Stock is allocated to participants based on (i) the ratio of each year's debt service payment to total current and future debt service payments multiplied by (ii) the number of unallocated shares of ESOP Preference Stock in the plan.

As of December 29, 2007, 3.8 million shares of ESOP Preference Stock were outstanding, of which 3.4 million shares were allocated to participants and the remaining 0.4 million shares were held in the ESOP Trust for future allocations.

Annual ESOP expense recognized is equal to (i) the interest incurred on the ESOP Notes plus (ii) the higher of (a) the principal repayments or (b) the cost of the shares allocated, less (iii) the dividends paid. Similarly, the guaranteed ESOP obligation is reduced by the higher of (i) the principal payments or (ii) the cost of shares allocated.

Following is a summary of the ESOP activity for the respective years:

In millions	**2007**	2006	2005
ESOP expense recognized	**$ 29.8**	$ 26.0	$ 22.7
Dividends paid	**14.8**	15.6	16.2
Cash contributions	**29.8**	26.0	22.7
Interest payments	**7.0**	9.7	12.0
ESOP shares allocated	**0.4**	0.4	0.3

#9 Pension Plans and Other Postretirement Benefits

Defined Contribution Plans

The Company sponsors voluntary 401(k) Savings Plans that cover substantially all employees who meet plan eligibility requirements. The Company makes matching contributions consistent with the provisions of the plans. At the participant's option, account balances, including the Company's matching contribution, can be moved without restriction among various investment options, including the Company's common stock. The Company also maintains a nonqualified, unfunded Deferred Compensation Plan for certain key employees. This plan provides participants the opportunity to defer portions of their compensation and receive matching contributions that they would have otherwise received under the 401(k) Savings Plan if not for certain restrictions and limitations under the Internal Revenue Code. The Company's contributions under the above defined contribution plans totaled $80.6 million in 2007, $63.7 million in 2006 and $64.9 million in 2005. The Company also sponsors an Employee Stock Ownership Plan. See Note 8 for further information about this plan.

Other Postretirement Benefits

The Company provides postretirement healthcare and life insurance benefits to certain retirees who meet eligibility requirements. The Company's funding policy is generally to pay covered expenses as they are incurred. For retiree medical plan accounting, the Company reviews external data and its own historical trends for healthcare costs to determine the healthcare cost trend rates. As of December 31, 2007, the Company's postretirement medical plans have an accumulated postretirement benefit obligation of $18.2 million. Net periodic benefit costs related to these postretirement medical plans were $0.8 million and $0.3 million for 2007 and 2006, respectively. As of December 31, 2006, the Company's postretirement medical plans had an accumulated postretirement benefit obligation of $10.2 million.

Pension Plans

The Company sponsors nine non-contributory defined benefit pension plans that cover certain full-time employees, which were frozen in prior periods. These plans are funded based on actuarial calculations and applicable federal regulations. As of December 31, 2007, the Company's qualified defined benefit plans have a projected benefit obligation of $517.5 million and plan assets of $420.7 million. As of December 31, 2006, the Company's qualified defined benefit plans had a projected benefit obligation of $419.0 million and plan assets of $313.6 million. Net periodic pension costs related to these qualified benefit plans were $13.6 million and $17.2 million in 2007 and 2006, respectively.

The discount rate is determined by examining the current yields observed on the measurement date of fixed-interest, high quality investments expected to be available during the period to maturity of the related benefits on a plan by plan basis. The discount rate for the plans ranged from 5.25% to 6.25% in 2007 and was 6.00% in 2006. The expected long-term rate of return is determined by using the target allocation and historical returns for each asset class on a plan-by-plan basis. The expected long-term rate of return for all plans was 8.5% in 2007 and 2006.

The Company uses an investment strategy, which emphasizes equities in order to produce higher expected returns, and in the long run, lower expected expense and cash contribution requirements. The pension plan assets allocation targets for the Retail Pharmacy Segment are 70% equity and 30% fixed income. The pension plan asset allocation targets for the Pharmacy Services Segment are 77% equity, 19% fixed income and 4% cash equivalents. The Retail Pharmacy Segment's qualified defined benefit pension plans asset allocations as of December 31, 2007 were 72% equity, 27% fixed income and 1% other. The Pharmacy Services Segment qualified defined benefit pension plans asset allocations as of December 31, 2007 were 75% equity, 23% fixed income and 2% other.

The Company utilized a measurement date of December 31 to determine pension and other postretirement benefit measurements. The Company plans to make a $1.5 million contribution to the pension plans during the upcoming year.

Pursuant to various labor agreements, the Company is also required to make contributions to certain union-administered pension and health and welfare plans that totaled $40.0 million in 2007, $37.6 million in 2006 and $15.4 million in 2005. The Company also has nonqualified supplemental executive retirement plans in place for certain key employees.

The Company adopted SFAS No. 158, "Employer's Accounting for Defined Benefit Pension and Other Postretirement Plans-an amendment of FASB Statements No. 87, 88, 106, and 132(R)," effective December 15, 2006. SFAS No. 158 requires an employer to recognize in its statement of financial position an asset for a plan's overfunded status or a liability for a plan's underfunded status, measure a plan's assets and its obligations that determine its funded status as of the end of the employer's fiscal year, and recognize changes in the funded status of a defined benefit postretirement plan in the year in which the changes occur. Those changes are reported in comprehensive income and in a separate component of shareholders' equity. The adoption of this statement did not have a material impact on the Company's consolidated results of operations, financial position or cash flows.

#10 Stock Incentive Plans

On January 1, 2006, the Company adopted SFAS No. 123(R), "Share-Based Payment", using the modified prospective transition method. Under this method, compensation expense is recognized for options granted on or after January 1, 2006 as well as any unvested options on the date of adoption. Compensation expense for unvested stock options outstanding at January 1, 2006 is recognized over the requisite service period based on the grant-date fair value of those options and awards as previously calculated under the SFAS No. 123(R) pro forma disclosure requirements. As allowed under the modified prospective transition method, prior period financial statements have not been restated. Prior to January 1, 2006, the Company accounted for its stock-based compensation plans under the recognition and measurement principles of APB Opinion No. 25, "Accounting for Stock Issued to Employees," and related interpretations. As such, no stock-based employee compensation costs were reflected in net earnings for options granted under those plans since they had an exercise price equal to the fair market value of the underlying common stock on the date of grant.

Compensation expense related to stock options, which includes the 1999 Employee Stock Purchase Plan ("1999 ESPP") and the 2007 Employee Stock Purchase Plan ("2007 ESPP" and collectively the "ESPP") totaled $84.5 million for 2007, compared to $60.7 million for 2006. The recognized tax benefit was $26.9 million and $18.0 million for 2007 and 2006, respectively. Compensation expense related to restricted stock awards totaled $12.1 million for 2007, compared to $9.2 million for 2006. Compensation costs associated with the Company's share-based payments are included in selling, general and administrative expenses.

The following table includes the effect on net earnings and earnings per share if stock compensation costs had been determined consistent with the fair value recognition provisions of SFAS No. 123(R) for 2005:

In millions, except per share amounts		2005
Net earnings, as reported		$ 1,224.7
Add: Stock-based employee compensation expense included in reported net earnings, net of related tax effects[1]		4.8
Deduct: Total stock-based employee compensation expense determined under fair value based method for all awards, net of related tax effects		48.6
Pro forma net earnings		$ 1,180.9
Basic EPS:	As reported	$ 1.49
	Pro forma	1.44
Diluted EPS:	As reported	$ 1.45
	Pro forma	1.40

(1) Amounts represent the after-tax compensation costs for restricted stock grants and expense related to the acceleration of vesting of stock options on certain terminated employees.

The 1999 ESPP provides for the purchase of up to 14.8 million shares of common stock. As a result of the 1999 ESPP not having sufficient shares available for the program to continue beyond 2007, the Board of Directors adopted, and shareholders approved, the 2007 ESPP. Under the 2007 ESPP, eligible employees may purchase common stock at the end of each six-month offering period, at a purchase price equal to 85% of the lower of the fair market value on the first day or the last day of the offering period and provides for the purchase of up to 15.0 million shares of common stock. During 2007, 1.9 million shares of common stock were purchased, under the provisions of the 1999 ESPP, at an average price of $25.10 per share. As of December 29, 2007, 14.1 million shares of common stock have been issued under the 1999 ESPP. As of December 29, 2007, no common stock had been issued under the 2007 ESPP.

The fair value of stock compensation expense associated with the Company's ESPP is estimated on the date of grant (i.e., the beginning of the offering period) using the Black-Scholes Option Pricing Model and is recorded as a liability, which is adjusted to reflect the fair value of the award at the end of each reporting period until settlement date.

Following is a summary of the assumptions used to value the ESPP awards for each of the respective periods:

	2007	2006	2005
Dividend yield[1]	**0.33%**	0.26%	0.26%
Expected volatility[2]	**21.72%**	26.00%	16.40%
Risk-free interest rate[3]	**5.01%**	5.08%	3.35%
Expected life *(in years)*[4]	**0.5**	0.5	0.5

(1) The dividend yield is calculated based on semi-annual dividends paid and the fair market value of the Company's stock at the period end date.

(2) The expected volatility is based on the historical volatility of the Company's daily stock market prices over the previous six-month period.

(3) The risk-free interest rate is based on the Treasury constant maturity interest rate whose term is consistent with the expected term of ESPP options (i.e., 6 months).

(4) The expected life is based on the semi-annual purchase period.

The Company's 1997 Incentive Compensation Plan (the "ICP") provides for the granting of up to 152.8 million shares of common stock in the form of stock options and other awards to selected officers, employees and directors of the Company. The ICP allows for up to 7.2 million restricted shares to be issued.

The Company's restricted awards are considered nonvested share awards as defined under SFAS 123(R). The restricted awards require no payment from the employee. Compensation cost is recorded based on the market price on the grant date and is recognized on a straight-line basis over the requisite service period.

The Company granted 5,000 and 427,000 shares of restricted stock with a weighted average per share grant date fair value of $28.71 and $24.80, in 2006 and 2005, respectively. In addition, the Company granted 1,129,000, 673,000 and 812,000 restricted stock units with a weighted average fair value of $33.75, $29.40 and $26.02 in 2007, 2006 and 2005, respectively. Compensation costs for restricted shares and units totaled $12.1 million in 2007, $9.2 million in 2006 and $5.9 million in 2005.

In 2007, the Board of Directors adopted and shareholders approved the 2007 Incentive Plan. The terms of the 2007 Incentive Plan provide for grants of annual incentive and long-term performance awards that may be settled in cash or other property to executive officers and other officers and employees of the Company or any subsidiary of the Company. No awards were granted from the 2007 Incentive Plan during 2007.

Following is a summary of the restricted share award activity under the ICP as of December 29, 2007:

	2007		2006	
Shares in thousands	**Shares**	**Weighted Average Grant Date Fair Value**	Shares	Weighted Average Grant Date Fair Value
Nonvested at beginning of year	**306**	**$ 22.08**	501	$ 20.80
Granted	**–**	**–**	5	28.71
Vested	**(129)**	**32.75**	(197)	18.94
Forfeited	**(16)**	**22.00**	(3)	24.71
Nonvested at end of year	**161**	**$ 22.40**	306	$ 22.08

Following is a summary of the restricted unit award activity under the ICP as of December 29, 2007:

	2007		2006	
Units in thousands	**Units**	**Weighted Average Grant Date Fair Value**	Units	Weighted Average Grant Date Fair Value
Nonvested at beginning of year	**2,009**	**$ 25.22**	1,377	$ 23.10
Granted	**1,129**	**33.75**	673	29.40
Vested	**(198)**	**34.99**	(16)	33.80
Forfeited	**(25)**	**23.24**	(25)	25.22
Nonvested at end of year	**2,915**	**$ 28.23**	2,009	$ 25.22

All grants under the ICP are awarded at fair market value on the date of grant. The fair value of stock options is estimated using the Black-Scholes Option Pricing Model and compensation expense is recognized on a straight-line basis over the requisite service period. Options granted prior to 2004 generally become exercisable over a four-year period from the grant date and expire ten years after the date of grant. Options granted during and subsequent to fiscal 2004 generally become exercisable over a three-year period from the grant date and expire seven years after the date of grant. As of December 29, 2007, there were 73.4 million shares available for future grants under the ICP.

SFAS No. 123(R) requires that the benefit of tax deductions in excess of recognized compensation cost be reported as a financing cash flow, rather than as an operating cash flow as required under prior guidance. Excess tax benefits of $97.8 million and $42.6 million were included in financing activities in the accompanying consolidated statement of cash flow during 2007 and 2006, respectively. Cash received from stock options exercised, which includes the ESPP, totaled $552.4 million and $187.6 million during 2007 and 2006, respectively. The total intrinsic value of options exercised during 2007 was $642.3 million, compared to $117.8 million and $117.5 million in 2006 and 2005, respectively. The fair value of options exercised during 2007 was $1.2 billion, compared to $257.1 million and $263.3 million during 2006 and 2005, respectively.

The fair value of each stock option is estimated using the Black-Scholes Option Pricing Model based on the following assumptions at the time of grant:

	2007	2006	2005
Dividend yield[(1)]	**0.69%**	0.50%	0.56%
Expected volatility[(2)]	**23.84%**	24.58%	34.00%
Risk-free interest rate[(3)]	**4.49%**	4.7%	4.3%
Expected life *(in years)*[(4)]	**5.12**	4.2	5.7
Weighted average grant date fair value	**$ 8.29**	$ 8.46	$ 8.46

(1) The dividend yield is based on annual dividends paid and the fair market value of the Company's stock at the period end date.

(2) The expected volatility is estimated using the Company's historical volatility over a period equal to the expected life of each option grant after adjustments for infrequent events such as stock splits.

(3) The risk-free interest rate is selected based on yields from U.S. Treasury zero-coupon issues with a remaining term equal to the expected term of the options being valued.

(4) The expected life represents the number of years the options are expected to be outstanding from grant date based on historical option holder exercise experience.

As of December 29, 2007, unrecognized compensation expense related to unvested options totaled $126.0 million, which the Company expects to be recognized over a weighted-average period of 1.8 years. After considering anticipated forfeitures, the Company expects approximately 18.7 million of the unvested options to vest over the requisite service period.

Following is a summary of the Company's stock option activity as of December 29, 2007:

Shares in thousands	**Shares**	**Weighted Average Exercise Price**	**Weighted Average Remaining Contractual Term**	**Aggregate Intrinsic Value**
Outstanding at December 30, 2006	**41,617**	**$ 21.35**	–	–
Granted	**12,958**	**34.66**	–	–
Issued in Caremark Merger	**36,838**	**16.44**	–	–
Exercised	**(29,868)**	**16.47**	–	–
Forfeited	**(1,165)**	**30.49**	–	–
Expired	**(358)**	**18.39**	–	–
Outstanding at December 29, 2007	**60,022**	**$ 23.47**	**5.00**	**$ 992,215,995**
Exercisable at December 29, 2007	**40,492**	**$ 19.23**	**4.61**	**$ 840,981,532**

#11 Commitments & Contingencies

Between 1991 and 1997, the Company sold or spun off a number of subsidiaries, including Bob's Stores, Linens 'n Things, Marshalls, Kay-Bee Toys, Wilsons, This End Up and Footstar. In many cases, when a former subsidiary leased a store, the Company provided a guarantee of the store's lease obligations. When the subsidiaries were disposed of, the Company's guarantees remained in place, although each initial purchaser has indemnified the Company for any lease obligations the Company was required to satisfy. If any of the purchasers or any of the former subsidiaries were to become insolvent and failed to make the required payments under a store lease, the Company could be required to satisfy these obligations. As of December 29, 2007, the Company guaranteed approximately 220 such store leases, with the maximum remaining lease term extending through 2022. Assuming that each respective purchaser became insolvent and the Company was required to assume all of these lease obligations, management estimates that the Company could settle the obligations for approximately $325 to $375 million as of December 29, 2007.

Management believes the ultimate disposition of any of the guarantees will not have a material adverse effect on the Company's consolidated financial condition, results of operations or future cash flows.

In 2006, a number of shareholder derivative lawsuits have been filed in the Tennessee state court and the Tennessee federal court against Caremark and various officers and directors of Caremark seeking, among other things, a declaration that the directors breached their fiduciary duties, imposition of a constructive trust upon any illegal profits received by the defendants and punitive and other damages. The cases brought in the Tennessee federal court were consolidated into one action in August 2006, and the consolidated action was voluntarily dismissed without prejudice by the plaintiffs in March 2007. The cases brought in the Tennessee state court were also consolidated into one action, and the plaintiffs amended their complaint to add CVS and its directors as defendants and to allege class action claims. A stipulation of settlement was entered into by the parties on July 5, 2007, which provided, among other things, that (i) the plaintiffs will dismiss the case and release the defendants from claims asserted in the action, (ii) a temporary restraining order issued by the court in March 2007 will be vacated, (iii) defendants will agree to maintain for at least four years a number of corporate governance provisions relating to the granting, exercise and disclosure of stock option awards and (iv) the defendants will not oppose plaintiffs' petition for an award of attorneys' fees and expenses not to exceed $7.5 million. As part of the settlement, the defendants specifically denied any liability or wrongdoing with respect to all claims alleged in the litigation, including claims relating to stock option backdating, and acknowledged that they entered into the settlement solely to avoid the distraction, burden and expense of the pending litigation. The settlement was orally approved by the court, but it remains subject to final court approval. The settlement is also subject to a pending application for extraordinary appeal filed by plaintiffs' counsel relating to the court's prior rulings concerning the settlement and the award of attorney's fees and expenses.

Caremark's subsidiary Caremark, Inc. (now known as Caremark, L.L.C.) is a defendant in a *qui tam* lawsuit initially filed by a relator on behalf of various state and federal government agencies in Texas federal court in 1999. The case was unsealed in May 2005. The case seeks money damages and alleges that Caremark's processing of Medicaid and certain other government claims on behalf of its clients violates applicable federal or state false claims acts and fraud statutes. The U.S. Department of Justice and the States of Texas, Tennessee, Florida, Arkansas, Louisiana and California intervened in the lawsuit, but Tennessee and Florida withdrew from the lawsuit in August 2006 and May 2007, respectively. A phased approach to discovery is ongoing. The parties have filed cross motions for partial summary judgment, argued those motions before the court, and final rulings are pending.

In December 2007, the Company received a document subpoena from the Office of Inspector General within the United States Department of Health and Human Services requesting certain information relating to the processing of Medicaid claims and claims of certain other government programs on an adjudication platform of AdvancePCS (now known as CaremarkPCS, L.L.C.). The Company will cooperate with these requests for information and cannot predict the timing, outcome, or consequence of the review of such information.

Caremark's subsidiary Caremark Inc. (now known as Caremark, L.L.C.) has been named in a putative class action lawsuit filed in July 2004, in Tennessee federal court by an individual named Robert Moeckel, purportedly on behalf of the John Morrell Employee Benefits Plan, which is an employee benefit plan sponsored by a former Caremark client. The lawsuit, which seeks unspecified damages and injunctive relief, alleges that Caremark acts as a fiduciary under ERISA and has breached certain alleged fiduciary duties under ERISA. In November 2007, the court granted Caremark Inc.'s motion for partial summary judgment finding that it is not an ERISA fiduciary under the applicable PBM agreements and that the plaintiff may not sustain claims for breach of fiduciary duty.

In 2004, Caremark received Civil Investigative Demands or similar requests for information relating to certain PBM business practices of its Caremark Inc. (now known as Caremark, L.L.C.) and AdvancePCS, (now known as CaremarkPCS, L.L.C.) subsidiaries under state consumer protection statutes from 28 states plus the District of Columbia. On February 14, 2008, Caremark entered into a settlement concluding this investigation. Caremark agreed to pay $12 million in settlement on behalf of AdvancePCS, $10 million in settlement on behalf of Caremark Inc., $16.5 million in state investigative costs and up to $2.5 million to reimburse certain medical tests. In addition, Caremark entered into a consent order requiring it to maintain certain PBM business practices. Caremark has expressly denied all wrongdoing and entered into the settlement to avoid the uncertainty and expense of the investigation.

Caremark was named in a putative class action lawsuit filed on October 22, 2003 in Alabama state court by John Lauriello, purportedly on behalf of participants in the 1999 settlement of various securities class action and derivative lawsuits against Caremark and others. Other defendants include insurance companies that provided coverage to Caremark with respect to the settled lawsuits. The Lauriello lawsuit seeks approximately $3.2 billion in compensatory damages plus other non-specified damages based on allegations that the amount of insurance coverage available for the settled lawsuits was misrepresented and suppressed. A similar lawsuit was filed on November 5, 2003, by Frank McArthur, also in Alabama state court, naming as defendants Caremark, several insurance companies, attorneys and law firms involved in the 1999 settlement. This lawsuit was subsequently stayed by the court as a later-filed class action.

In 2005, the trial court in the Lauriello case issued an order allowing the Lauriello case to proceed on behalf of the settlement class in the 1999 securities class action. McArthur then sought to intervene in the Lauriello case and to challenge the adequacy of Lauriello as class representative and his lawyers as class counsel. The trial court denied McArthur's motion to intervene, but the Alabama Supreme Court subsequently ordered the lower court to vacate its prior order on class certification and allow McArthur to intervene. Caremark and other defendants filed motions to dismiss the complaint in intervention filed by McArthur. In November 2007, the trial court dismissed the attorneys and law firms named as defendants in the McArthur complaint in intervention and denied the motions to dismiss that complaint filed by Caremark and the insurance company defendants. In January 2008, Lauriello filed a motion to dismiss McArthur's complaint in intervention, appealed the court's dismissal of the attorney and law firm defendants and filed a motion to stay proceedings pending his appeal.

Various lawsuits have been filed alleging that Caremark and its subsidiaries Caremark Inc. (now known as Caremark, L.L.C.) and AdvancePCS (now known as CaremarkPCS, L.L.C.) have violated applicable antitrust laws in establishing and maintaining retail pharmacy networks for client health plans. In August 2003, Bellevue Drug Co., Robert Schreiber, Inc. d/b/a Burns Pharmacy and Rehn-Huerbinger Drug Co. d/b/a Parkway Drugs #4, together with Pharmacy Freedom Fund and the National Community Pharmacists Association filed a putative class action against AdvancePCS in Pennsylvania federal court, seeking treble damages and injunctive relief. The claims were initially sent to arbitration based on contract terms between the pharmacies and AdvancePCS.

In October 2003, two independent pharmacies, North Jackson Pharmacy, Inc. and C&C, Inc. d/b/a Big C Discount Drugs, Inc. filed a putative class action complaint in Alabama federal court against Caremark, Caremark Inc. AdvancePCS and two PBM competitors, seeking treble damages and injunctive relief. The case against Caremark and Caremark Inc. was transferred to Illinois federal court, and the AdvancePCS case was sent to arbitration based on contract terms between the pharmacies and AdvancePCS. The arbitration was then stayed by the parties pending developments in Caremark's court case.

NOTES TO CONSOLIDATED FINANCIAL STATEMENTS

In August 2006, the Bellevue case and the North Jackson Pharmacy case were transferred to Pennsylvania federal court by the Judicial Panel on Multidistrict Litigation for coordinated and consolidated proceedings with other cases before the panel, including cases against other PBMs. Caremark has appealed a decision which vacated the order compelling arbitration and staying the proceedings in the Bellevue case to the Third Circuit Court of Appeals. Motions for class certification in the coordinated cases within the multidistrict litigation, including the North Jackson Pharmacy case, remain pending. The consolidated action is now known as the In Re Pharmacy Benefit Managers Antitrust Litigation.

Caremark and its subsidiaries Caremark Inc. (now known as Caremark, L.L.C.) and AdvancePCS (now known as CaremarkPCS, L.L.C.) have been named in a putative class action lawsuit filed in California state court by an individual named Robert Irwin, purportedly on behalf of California members of non-ERISA health plans and/or all California taxpayers. The lawsuit, which also names other PBMs as defendants, alleges violations of California's unfair competition laws and challenges alleged business practices of PBMs, including practices relating to pricing, rebates, formulary management, data utilization and accounting and administrative processes. Discovery in the case is ongoing.

The Rhode Island Attorney General's Office, the Rhode Island Ethics Commission, and the United States Attorney's Office for the District of Rhode Island have been investigating the business relationships between certain former members of the Rhode Island General Assembly and various Rhode Island companies, including Roger Williams Medical Center, Blue Cross & Blue Shield of Rhode Island and CVS. In connection with the investigation of these business relationships, a former state senator was criminally charged in 2005 by federal and state authorities and has pled guilty to those charges, and a former state representative was criminally charged in October 2007 by federal authorities and pled guilty to those charges. In January 2007, two CVS employees on administrative leave from the Company were indicted on federal charges relating to their involvement in entering into a $12,000 per year consulting agreement with the former state senator eight years ago. The indictment alleges that the two CVS employees concealed the true nature of the Company's relationship with the former state senator from other Company officials and others. CVS will continue to cooperate fully in this investigation, the timing and outcome of which cannot be predicted with certainty at this time.

The Company has been named in a putative class action lawsuit filed in California state court by Gabe Tong, purportedly on behalf of current and former pharmacists working in the Company's California stores. The lawsuit alleges that CVS failed to provide pharmacists in the purported class with meal and rest periods or to pay overtime as required under California law. In October 2007, the Company reached a conditional agreement, subject to the approval by the court, to resolve this matter. In addition, the Company is party to other employment litigation arising in the normal course of its business. The Company cannot predict the outcome of any of these employment litigation matters at this time, however, none of these matters are expected to be material to the Company.

The United States Department of Justice and several state attorneys general are investigating whether any civil or criminal violations resulted from certain practices engaged in by CVS and others in the pharmacy industry with regard to dispensing one of two different dosage forms of a generic drug under circumstances in which some state Medicaid programs at various times reimbursed one dosage form at a different rate from the other. The Company is in discussions with various governmental agencies involved to resolve this matter on a civil basis and without any admission or finding of any violation.

The Company is also a party to other litigation arising in the normal course of its business, none of which is expected to be material to the Company. The Company can give no assurance, however, that our operating results and financial condition will not be materially adversely affected, or that we will not be required to materially change our business practices, based on: (i) future enactment of new healthcare or other laws or regulations; (ii) the interpretation or application of existing laws or regulations, as they may relate to our business or the pharmacy services industry; (iii) pending or future federal or state governmental investigations of our business or the pharmacy services industry; (iv) institution of government enforcement actions against us; (v) adverse developments in any pending qui tam lawsuit against us, whether sealed or unsealed, or in any future qui tam lawsuit that may be filed against us; or (vi) adverse developments in other pending or future legal proceedings against us or affecting the pharmacy services industry.

#12 Income Taxes

The income tax provision consisted of the following for the respective years:

In millions		2007	2006	2005
Current:	Federal	**$ 1,250.8**	$ 676.6	$ 632.8
	State	**241.3**	127.3	31.7
		1,492.1	803.9	664.5
Deferred:	Federal	**206.0**	47.6	17.9
	State	**23.6**	5.4	1.9
		229.6	53.0	19.8
Total		**$ 1,721.7**	$ 856.9	$ 684.3

Following is a reconciliation of the statutory income tax rate to the Company's effective tax rate for the respective years:

	2007	2006	2005
Statutory income tax rate	**35.0%**	35.0%	35.0%
State income taxes, net of federal tax benefit	**4.2**	3.9	3.9
Other	**0.3**	0.1	(0.3)
Federal and net State reserve release	**–**	(0.5)	(2.8)
Effective tax rate	**39.5%**	38.5%	35.8%

Following is a summary of the significant components of the Company's deferred tax assets and liabilities as of the respective balance sheet dates:

In millions	Dec. 29, 2007	Dec. 30, 2006
Deferred tax assets:		
Lease and rents	**$ 276.2**	$ 265.8
Inventory	**56.7**	74.3
Employee benefits	**186.0**	82.4
Accumulated other comprehensive items	**34.7**	41.8
Allowance for bad debt	**74.6**	36.6
Retirement benefits	**6.2**	4.0
Other	**170.9**	68.5
NOL	**26.9**	26.3
Total deferred tax assets	**832.2**	599.7
Deferred tax liabilities:		
Depreciation and amortization	**(3,928.9)**	(234.6)
Total deferred tax liabilities	**(3,928.9)**	(234.6)
Net deferred tax (liability)/assets	**$ (3,096.7)**	$ 365.1

The Company believes it is more likely than not the deferred tax assets included in the above table will be realized during future periods.

During the fourth quarters of 2006 and 2005, an assessment of tax reserves resulted in the Company recording reductions of previously recorded tax reserves through the income tax provision of $11.0 million and $52.6 million, respectively.

The Company adopted FASB Interpretation No. 48, "Accounting for Uncertainty in Income Taxes – an interpretation of FASB Statement No. 109" ("FIN 48"), at the beginning of fiscal year 2007. As a result of the implementation, the Company reduced its reserves for uncertain income tax positions by approximately $4.0 million, which was accounted for as an increase to the December 31, 2006 balance of retained earnings. The income tax reserve increased during 2007 primarily due to the Caremark Merger.

The following is a summary of our income tax reserve:

In millions	2007
Beginning Balance	**$ 43.2**
Additions based on tax positions related to the current year	**207.5**
Additions based on tax positions of prior years	**4.5**
Reductions for tax positions of prior years	**(6.7)**
Expiration of statute of limitations	**(2.0)**
Settlements	**(13.1)**
Ending Balance	**$ 233.4**

The Company and its subsidiaries are subject to U.S. federal income tax as well as income tax of multiple state and local jurisdictions. Substantially all material income tax matters have been concluded for fiscal years through 1992.

On March 30, 2007, the Internal Revenue Service (the "IRS") completed an examination of the consolidated U.S. income tax returns for AdvancePCS and its subsidiaries for the tax years ended March 31, 2002, March 31, 2003 and March 24, 2004, the date on which Caremark acquired AdvancePCS. In July 2007, the IRS completed an examination of the Company's consolidated U.S. income tax returns for fiscal years 2004 and 2005.

During 2007, the IRS commenced an examination of the consolidated U.S. income tax return of the Company for fiscal year 2007 pursuant to the Compliance Assurance Process ("CAP") program. The CAP program is a voluntary program under which taxpayers seek to resolve all or most issues with the IRS prior to the filing of their U.S. income tax returns in lieu of being audited in the traditional manner.

In addition to the CAP examination, the IRS is examining the Company's consolidated U.S. income tax return for fiscal year 2006 and the consolidated U.S. income tax returns of Caremark for fiscal years 2004 and 2005, which benefit from net operating loss carry-forwards going back to 1993. The Company and its subsidiaries are also currently under examination by various state and local jurisdictions. As of December 29, 2007, no examination has resulted in any proposed adjustments that would result in a material change to the Company's results of operations, financial condition or liquidity.

The Company recognizes interest accrued related to unrecognized tax benefits and penalties in income tax expense. During the fiscal year ended December 29, 2007, the Company recognized interest of approximately $17.8 million. The Company had approximately $44.3 million accrued for interest and penalties as of December 29, 2007.

There are no material reserves established at December 29, 2007 for income tax positions for which the ultimate deductibility is highly certain but for which there is uncertainty about the timing of such deductibility. If present, such items would impact deferred tax accounting, not the annual effective income tax rate, and would accelerate the payment of cash to the taxing authority to an earlier period.

The total amount of unrecognized tax benefits that, if recognized, would affect the effective income tax rate is approximately $26.9 million, after considering the federal benefit of state income taxes.

We are currently unable to estimate if there will be any significant changes in the amount of unrecognized tax benefits over the next twelve months. Pursuant to SFAS No. 141, "Business Combinations," and EITF No. 93-7, "Uncertainties Related to Income Taxes in a Purchase Business Combination" ("EITF 93-7"), any income tax adjustments made in the Company's 2008 financial statements that are related to pre-acquisition tax periods will result in modifications to the assets acquired and liabilities assumed in the applicable business combination.

#13 Business Segments

The Company currently operates two business segments: Retail Pharmacy and Pharmacy Services. The operating segments are businesses of the Company for which separate financial information is available and for which operating results are evaluated on a regular basis by executive management in deciding how to allocate resources and in assessing performance. The Company's business segments offer different products and services and require distinct technology and marketing strategies.

As of December 29, 2007, the Retail Pharmacy Segment included 6,245 retail drugstores, the Company's online retail website, CVS.com® and its retail healthcare clinics. The retail drugstores are located in 40 states and the District of Columbia and operate under the CVS® or CVS/pharmacy® name. The retail healthcare clinics utilize nationally recognized medical protocols to diagnose and treat minor health conditions and are staffed by board-certified nurse practitioners and physician assistants. The retail healthcare clinics operate under the MinuteClinic® name and include 462 clinics located in 25 states, 437 of which are located within the Company's retail drugstores.

The Pharmacy Services Segment provides a full range of pharmacy benefit management services to employers, managed care providers and other organizations. These services include mail order pharmacy services, specialty pharmacy services, plan design and administration, formulary management and claims processing, as well as providing insurance and reinsurance services in conjunction with prescription drug benefit plans. The specialty pharmacy business focuses on supporting individuals that require complex and expensive drug therapies. Currently, the Pharmacy Services Segment operates under the Caremark Pharmacy Services®, PharmaCare Management Services® and PharmaCare Pharmacy® names.

As of December 29, 2007, the Pharmacy Services Segment included 56 retail specialty drugstores, 20 specialty mail order pharmacies and 9 mail service pharmacies located in 26 states and the District of Columbia.

The Company evaluates segment performance based on net revenues, gross profit and operating profit before the effect of certain intersegment activities and charges. The accounting policies of the segments are substantially the same as those described in Note 1.

Following is a reconciliation of the Company's business segments to the consolidated financial statements:

In millions	Retail Pharmacy Segment	Pharmacy Services Segment[1]	Intersegment Eliminations[2]	Consolidated Totals
2007:				
Net revenues	**$ 45,086.5**	**$ 34,938.4**	**$ (3,695.4)**	**$ 76,329.5**
Gross profit	**13,110.6**	**2,997.1**		**16,107.7**
Operating profit	**2,691.3**	**2,102.0**		**4,793.3**
Depreciation and amortization	**805.3**	**289.3**		**1,094.6**
Total assets	**19,962.6**	**35,015.1**	**(255.8)**	**54,721.9**
Goodwill	**2,585.7**	**21,336.6**		**23,922.3**
Additions to property and equipment	**1,711.2**	**94.1**		**1,805.3**
2006:				
Net revenues	$ 40,285.6	$ 3,691.3	$ (155.5)	$ 43,821.4
Gross profit	11,283.4	458.8		11,742.2
Operating profit	2,123.5	318.1		2,441.6
Depreciation and amortization	691.9	41.4		733.3
Total assets	19,038.8	1,603.4	(68.1)	20,574.1
Goodwill	2,572.4	622.8		3,195.2
Additions to property and equipment	1,750.5	18.4		1,768.9
2005:				
Net revenues	$ 34,094.6	$ 2,956.7	$ (44.6)	$ 37,006.7
Gross profit	9,349.1	345.5		9,694.6
Operating profit	1,797.1	222.4		2,019.5
Depreciation and amortization	548.5	40.6		589.1
Total assets	13,878.5	1,368.1		15,246.6
Goodwill	1,152.4	637.5		1,789.9
Additions to property and equipment	1,471.3	24.1		1,495.4

(1) Net Revenues of the Pharmacy Services Segment include approximately $4,618.2 million of Retail Co-Payments in 2007.

(2) Intersegment eliminations relate to intersegment revenues and accounts receivable that occur when a Pharmacy Services Segment customer uses a Retail Pharmacy Segment store to purchase covered products. When this occurs, both segments record the revenue on a standalone basis.

NOTES TO CONSOLIDATED FINANCIAL STATEMENTS

#14 Reconciliation of Earnings per Common Share

Following is a reconciliation of basic and diluted earnings per common share for the respective years:

In millions, except per share amounts	**2007**	2006	2005
NUMERATOR FOR EARNINGS PER COMMON SHARE CALCULATION:			
Net earnings	**$ 2,637.0**	$ 1,368.9	$ 1,224.7
Preference dividends, net of income tax benefit	**(14.2)**	(13.9)	(14.1)
Net earnings available to common shareholders, basic	**$ 2,622.8**	$ 1,355.0	$ 1,210.6
Net earnings	**$ 2,637.0**	$ 1,368.9	$ 1,224.7
Dilutive earnings adjustment	**(3.6)**	(4.2)	(4.4)
Net earnings available to common shareholders, diluted	**$ 2,633.4**	$ 1,364.7	$ 1,220.3
DENOMINATOR FOR EARNINGS PER COMMON SHARE CALCULATION:			
Weighted average common shares, basic	**1,328.2**	820.6	811.4
Preference stock	**18.0**	18.8	19.5
Stock options	**22.3**	11.5	9.9
Restricted stock units	**3.3**	2.3	0.8
Weighted average common shares, diluted	**1,371.8**	853.2	841.6
BASIC EARNINGS PER COMMON SHARE:			
Net earnings	**$ 1.97**	$ 1.65	$ 1.49
DILUTED EARNINGS PER COMMON SHARE:			
Net earnings	**$ 1.92**	$ 1.60	$ 1.45

#15 Quarterly Financial Information (Unaudited)

In millions, except per share amounts	First Quarter	Second Quarter	Third Quarter	Fourth Quarter	Fiscal Year
2007:					
Net revenues	**$ 13,188.6**	**$ 20,703.3**	**$ 20,495.2**	**$ 21,942.4**	**$ 76,329.5**
Gross profit	**3,303.2**	**4,158.5**	**4,195.2**	**4,450.8**	**16,107.7**
Operating profit	**736.5**	**1,309.8**	**1,271.1**	**1,475.9**	**4,793.3**
Net earnings	**408.9**	**723.6**	**689.5**	**815.0**	**2,637.0**
Net earnings per common share, basic	**0.45**	**0.48**	**0.47**	**0.56**	**1.97**
Net earnings per common share, diluted	**0.43**	**0.47**	**0.45**	**0.55**	**1.92**
Dividends per common share	**0.04875**	**0.06000**	**0.06000**	**0.06000**	**0.22875**
Stock price: (New York Stock Exchange)					
High	**34.93**	**39.44**	**39.85**	**42.60**	**42.60**
Low	**30.45**	**34.14**	**34.80**	**36.43**	**30.45**
Registered shareholders at year-end					**16,706**
2006:					
Net revenues	$ 9,979.9	$ 10,564.4	$ 11,208.8	$ 12,068.3	$ 43,821.4
Gross profit	2,594.8	2,794.7	3,035.6	3,317.1	11,742.2
Operating profit	560.5	595.0	536.8	749.3	2,441.6
Net earnings[(1)]	329.6	337.9	284.2	417.2	1,368.9
Net earnings per common share, basic[(1)]	0.40	0.41	0.34	0.50	1.65
Net earnings per common share, diluted[(1)]	0.39	0.40	0.33	0.49	1.60
Dividends per common share	0.03875	0.03875	0.03875	0.03875	0.15500
Stock price: (New York Stock Exchange)					
High	30.98	31.89	36.14	32.26	36.14
Low	26.06	27.51	29.85	27.09	26.06

(1) Net earnings and net earnings per common share for the fourth quarter and fiscal year 2006 include the $24.7 million after-tax effect of adopting SAB No. 108.

FIVE-YEAR FINANCIAL SUMMARY

In millions, except per share amounts	**2007 (52 weeks)[1]**	2006 (52 weeks)	2005 (52 weeks)	2004 (52 weeks)	2003 (53 weeks)
STATEMENT OF OPERATIONS DATA:					
Net revenues	**$ 76,329.5**	$ 43,821.4	$ 37,006.7	$ 30,594.6	$ 26,588.2
Gross profit	**16,107.7**	11,742.2	9,694.6	7,915.9	6,803.0
Operating expenses[2][3]	**11,314.4**	9,300.6	7,675.1	6,461.2	5,379.4
Operating profit[4]	**4,793.3**	2,441.6	2,019.5	1,454.7	1,423.6
Interest expense, net	**434.6**	215.8	110.5	58.3	48.1
Income tax provision[5]	**1,721.7**	856.9	684.3	477.6	528.2
Net earnings[6]	**$ 2,637.0**	$ 1,368.9	$ 1,224.7	$ 918.8	$ 847.3
PER COMMON SHARE DATA:					
Net earnings:[6]					
Basic	**$ 1.97**	$ 1.65	$ 1.49	$ 1.13	$ 1.06
Diluted	**1.92**	1.60	1.45	1.10	1.03
Cash dividends per common share	**0.22875**	0.15500	0.14500	0.13250	0.11500
BALANCE SHEET AND OTHER DATA:					
Total assets	**$ 54,721.9**	$ 20,574.1	$ 15,246.6	$ 14,513.3	$ 10,543.1
Long-term debt (less current portion)	**$ 8,349.7**	$ 2,870.4	$ 1,594.1	$ 1,925.9	$ 753.1
Total shareholders' equity	**$ 31,321.9**	$ 9,917.6	$ 8,331.2	$ 6,987.2	$ 6,021.8
Number of stores (at end of period)	**6,301**	6,205	5,474	5,378	4,182

(1) Effective March 22, 2007, pursuant to the Agreement and Plan of Merger dated as of November 1, 2006, as amended (the "Merger Agreement"), Caremark Rx, Inc. ("Caremark") was merged with and into a newly formed subsidiary of CVS Corporation, with the CVS subsidiary, Caremark Rx, L.L.C., continuing as the surviving entity (the "Caremark Merger"). Following the Caremark Merger, the name of the Company was changed to "CVS Caremark Corporation." By virtue of the Caremark Merger, each issued and outstanding share of Caremark common stock, par value $0.001 per share, was converted into the right to receive 1.67 shares of CVS Caremark's common stock, par value $0.01 per share. Cash was paid in lieu of fractional shares.

(2) In 2006, the Company adopted the Securities and Exchange Commission (SEC) Staff Accounting Bulletin ("SAB") No. 108, "Considering the Effects of Prior Year Misstatements when Qualifying Misstatements in Current Year Financial Statements." The adoption of this statement resulted in a $40.2 million pre-tax ($24.7 million after-tax) decrease in operating expenses for 2006.

(3) In 2004, the Company conformed its accounting for operating leases and leasehold improvements to the views expressed by the Office of the Chief Accountant of the Securities and Exchange Commission to the American Institute of Certified Public Accountants on February 7, 2005. As a result, the Company recorded a non-cash pre-tax adjustment of $65.9 million ($40.5 million after-tax) to operating expenses, which represents the cumulative effect of the adjustment for a period of approximately 20 years. Since the effect of this non-cash adjustment was not material to 2004, or any previously reported fiscal year, the cumulative effect was recorded in the fourth quarter of 2004.

(4) Operating profit includes the pre-tax effect of the charge discussed in Note (2) and Note (3) above.

(5) Income tax provision includes the effect of the following: (i) in 2006, an $11.0 million reversal of previously recorded tax reserves through the tax provision principally based on resolving certain state tax matters, (ii) in 2005, a $52.6 million reversal of previously recorded tax reserves through the tax provision principally based on resolving certain state tax matters, and (iii) in 2004, a $60.0 million reversal of previously recorded tax reserves through the tax provision principally based on finalizing certain tax return years and on a 2004 court decision relevant to the industry.

(6) Net earnings and net earnings per common share include the after-tax effect of the charges and gains discussed in Notes (2), (3), (4) and (5) above.

REPORT OF INDEPENDENT REGISTERED PUBLIC ACCOUNTING FIRM

The Board of Directors and Shareholders
CVS Caremark Corporation

We have audited the accompanying consolidated balance sheet of CVS Caremark Corporation as of December 29, 2007, and the related consolidated statements of operations, shareholders' equity and cash flows for the fifty-two week period ended December 29, 2007. These consolidated financial statements are the responsibility of the Company's management. Our responsibility is to express an opinion on these consolidated financial statements based on our audit.

We conducted our audit in accordance with the standards of the Public Company Accounting Oversight Board (United States). Those standards require that we plan and perform the audit to obtain reasonable assurance about whether the financial statements are free of material misstatement. An audit includes examining, on a test basis, evidence supporting the amounts and disclosures in the financial statements. An audit also includes assessing the accounting principles used and significant estimates made by management, as well as evaluating the overall financial statement presentation. We believe that our audit provides a reasonable basis for our opinion.

In our opinion, the 2007 consolidated financial statements referred to above present fairly, in all material respects, the consolidated financial position of CVS Caremark Corporation at December 29, 2007, and the consolidated results of its operations and its cash flows for the fifty-two week period ended December 29, 2007, in conformity with U.S. generally accepted accounting principles.

As discussed in Note 1 to the consolidated financial statements, effective December 31, 2006, CVS Caremark Corporation adopted Financial Accounting Standards Board (FASB) Interpretation No. 48, *Accounting for Uncertainty in Income Taxes – an interpretation of FASB Statement No. 109*.

We also have audited, in accordance with the standards of the Public Company Accounting Oversight Board (United States), CVS Caremark Corporation's internal control over financial reporting as of December 29, 2007, based on criteria established in *Internal Control – Integrated Framework* issued by the Committee of Sponsoring Organizations of the Treadway Commission and our report dated February 25, 2008 expressed an unqualified opinion thereon.

Ernst + Young LLP

Boston, Massachusetts
February 25, 2008

REPORT OF INDEPENDENT REGISTERED PUBLIC ACCOUNTING FIRM

The Board of Directors and Shareholders
CVS Caremark Corporation:

We have audited the accompanying consolidated balance sheet of CVS Caremark Corporation and subsidiaries (formerly CVS Corporation) as of December 30, 2006 and the related consolidated statements of operations, shareholders' equity and cash flows for the fifty-two week periods ended December 30, 2006, and December 31, 2005. These consolidated financial statements are the responsibility of the Company's management. Our responsibility is to express an opinion on these consolidated financial statements based on our audits.

We conducted our audits in accordance with the standards of the Public Company Accounting Oversight Board (United States). Those standards require that we plan and perform the audit to obtain reasonable assurance about whether the financial statements are free of material misstatement. An audit includes examining, on a test basis, evidence supporting the amounts and disclosures in the financial statements. An audit also includes assessing the accounting principles used and significant estimates made by management, as well as evaluating the overall financial statement presentation. We believe that our audits provide a reasonable basis for our opinion.

In our opinion, the consolidated financial statements referred to above present fairly, in all material respects, the financial position of CVS Caremark Corporation and subsidiaries as of December 30, 2006 and the results of their operations and their cash flows for the fifty-two week periods ended December 30, 2006 and December 31, 2005, in conformity with U.S. generally accepted accounting principles.

As discussed in Note 1 to the consolidated financial statements, CVS Caremark Corporation adopted the provisions of Statement of Financial Accounting Standards No. 123 (revised 2004), "Share-Based Payment," effective January 1, 2006.

KPMG LLP

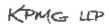

KPMG LLP
Providence, Rhode Island
February 27, 2007

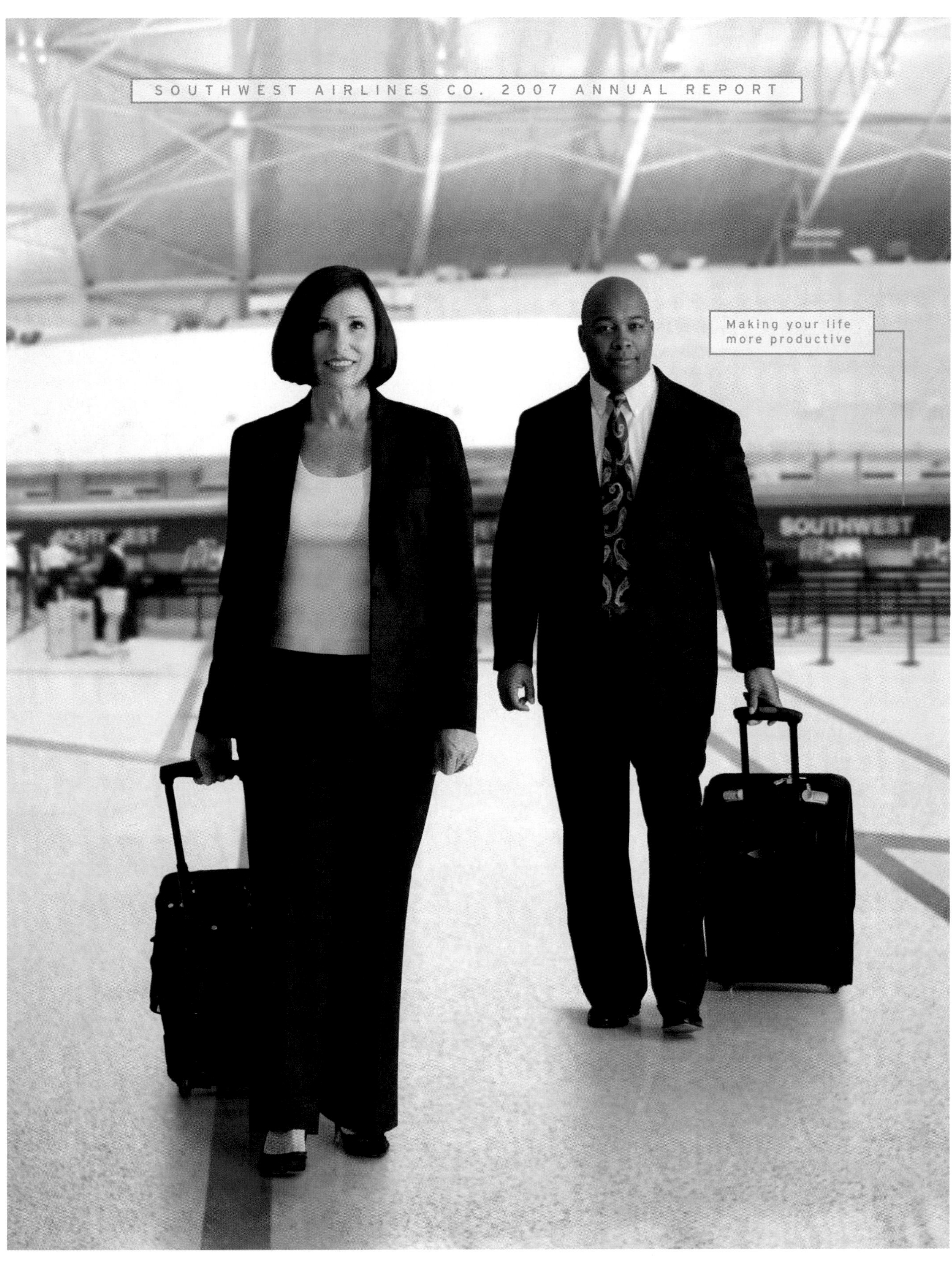
SOUTHWEST AIRLINES CO. 2007 ANNUAL REPORT
Making your life
more productive
SOUTHWEST

Item 8. *Financial Statements and Supplementary Data*

SOUTHWEST AIRLINES CO.

CONSOLIDATED BALANCE SHEET

	December 31, 2007	December 31, 2006
	(In millions, except share data)	
ASSETS		
Current assets:		
Cash and cash equivalents	$ 2,213	$ 1,390
Short-term investments	566	369
Accounts and other receivables	279	241
Inventories of parts and supplies, at cost	259	181
Fuel derivative contracts	1,069	369
Prepaid expenses and other current assets	57	51
Total current assets	4,443	2,601
Property and equipment, at cost:		
Flight equipment	13,019	11,769
Ground property and equipment	1,515	1,356
Deposits on flight equipment purchase contracts	626	734
	15,160	13,859
Less allowance for depreciation and amortization	4,286	3,765
	10,874	10,094
Other assets	1,455	765
	$16,772	$13,460
LIABILITIES AND STOCKHOLDERS' EQUITY		
Current liabilities:		
Accounts payable	$ 759	$ 643
Accrued liabilities	3,107	1,323
Air traffic liability	931	799
Current maturities of long-term debt	41	122
Total current liabilities	4,838	2,887
Long-term debt less current maturities	2,050	1,567
Deferred income taxes	2,535	2,104
Deferred gains from sale and leaseback of aircraft	106	120
Other deferred liabilities	302	333
Commitments and contingencies		
Stockholders' equity:		
Common stock, $1.00 par value: 2,000,000,000 shares authorized; 807,611,634 shares issued in 2007 and 2006	808	808
Capital in excess of par value	1,207	1,142
Retained earnings	4,788	4,307
Accumulated other comprehensive income	1,241	582
Treasury stock, at cost: 72,814,104 and 24,302,215 shares in 2007 and 2006, respectively	(1,103)	(390)
Total stockholders' equity	6,941	6,449
	$16,772	$13,460

SOUTHWEST AIRLINES CO.

CONSOLIDATED STATEMENT OF INCOME

	Years Ended December 31,		
	2007	2006	2005
	(In millions, except per share amounts)		
OPERATING REVENUES:			
Passenger	$9,457	$8,750	$7,279
Freight	130	134	133
Other	274	202	172
Total operating revenues	9,861	9,086	7,584
OPERATING EXPENSES:			
Salaries, wages, and benefits	3,213	3,052	2,782
Fuel and oil	2,536	2,138	1,341
Maintenance materials and repairs	616	468	446
Aircraft rentals	156	158	163
Landing fees and other rentals	560	495	454
Depreciation and amortization	555	515	469
Other operating expenses	1,434	1,326	1,204
Total operating expenses	9,070	8,152	6,859
OPERATING INCOME	791	934	725
OTHER EXPENSES (INCOME):			
Interest expense	119	128	122
Capitalized interest	(50)	(51)	(39)
Interest income	(44)	(84)	(47)
Other (gains) losses, net	(292)	151	(90)
Total other expenses (income)	(267)	144	(54)
INCOME BEFORE INCOME TAXES	1,058	790	779
PROVISION FOR INCOME TAXES	413	291	295
NET INCOME	$ 645	$ 499	$ 484
NET INCOME PER SHARE, BASIC	$ .85	$ .63	$ .61
NET INCOME PER SHARE, DILUTED	$ .84	$ .61	$ .60

SOUTHWEST AIRLINES CO.

CONSOLIDATED STATEMENT OF STOCKHOLDERS' EQUITY

	Years Ended December 31, 2007, 2006, and 2005					
	Common Stock	Capital in Excess of Par Value	Retained Earnings	Accumulated Other Comprehensive Income (Loss)	Treasury Stock	Total
	(In millions, except per share amounts)					
Balance at December 31, 2004	$790	$ 777	$3,614	$ 417	$ (71)	$ 5,527
Purchase of shares of treasury stock	—	—	—	—	(55)	(55)
Issuance of common and treasury stock pursuant to Employee stock plans	12	59	(66)	—	126	131
Tax benefit of options exercised	—	47	—	—	—	47
Share-based compensation	—	80	—	—	—	80
Cash dividends, $.018 per share	—	—	(14)	—	—	(14)
Comprehensive income (loss)						
Net income	—	—	484	—	—	484
Unrealized gain on derivative instruments	—	—	—	474	—	474
Other	—	—	—	1	—	1
Total comprehensive income						959
Balance at December 31, 2005	$802	$ 963	$4,018	$ 892	$ —	$ 6,675
Purchase of shares of treasury stock	—	—	—	—	(800)	(800)
Issuance of common and treasury stock pursuant to Employee stock plans	6	39	(196)	—	410	259
Tax benefit of options exercised	—	60	—	—	—	60
Share-based compensation	—	80	—	—	—	80
Cash dividends, $.018 per share	—	—	(14)	—	—	(14)
Comprehensive income (loss)						
Net income	—	—	499	—	—	499
Unrealized loss on derivative instruments	—	—	—	(306)	—	(306)
Other	—	—	—	(4)	—	(4)
Total comprehensive income						189
Balance at December 31, 2006	$808	$1,142	$4,307	$ 582	$ (390)	$ 6,449
Purchase of shares of treasury stock	—	—	—	—	(1,001)	(1,001)
Issuance of common and treasury stock pursuant to Employee stock plans	—	—	(150)	—	288	138
Tax benefit of options exercised	—	28	—	—	—	28
Share-based compensation	—	37	—	—	—	37
Cash dividends, $.018 per share	—	—	(14)	—	—	(14)
Comprehensive income (loss)						
Net income	—	—	645	—	—	645
Unrealized gain on derivative instruments	—	—	—	636	—	636
Other	—	—	—	23	—	23
Total comprehensive income						1,304
Balance at December 31, 2007	$808	$1,207	$4,788	$1,241	$(1,103)	$ 6,941

SOUTHWEST AIRLINES CO.

CONSOLIDATED STATEMENT OF CASH FLOWS

	Years Ended December 31,		
	2007	2006	2005
		(In millions)	
CASH FLOWS FROM OPERATING ACTIVITIES:			
Net income	$ 645	$ 499	$ 484
Adjustments to reconcile net income to net cash provided by operating activities:			
Depreciation and amortization	555	515	469
Deferred income taxes	328	277	291
Amortization of deferred gains on sale and leaseback of aircraft	(14)	(16)	(16)
Share-based compensation expense	37	80	80
Excess tax benefits from share-based compensation arrangements	(28)	(60)	(47)
Changes in certain assets and liabilities:			
Accounts and other receivables	(38)	(5)	(9)
Other current assets	(229)	87	(59)
Accounts payable and accrued liabilities	1,609	(223)	855
Air traffic liability	131	150	120
Other, net	(151)	102	(50)
Net cash provided by operating activities	2,845	1,406	2,118
CASH FLOWS FROM INVESTING ACTIVITIES:			
Purchases of property and equipment, net	(1,331)	(1,399)	(1,146)
Purchases of short-term investments	(5,086)	(4,509)	(1,804)
Proceeds from sales of short-term investments	4,888	4,392	1,810
Payment for assets of ATA Airlines, Inc.	—	—	(6)
Debtor in possession loan to ATA Airlines, Inc.	—	20	—
Other, net	—	1	—
Net cash used in investing activities	(1,529)	(1,495)	(1,146)
CASH FLOWS FROM FINANCING ACTIVITIES:			
Issuance of long-term debt	500	300	300
Proceeds from Employee stock plans	139	260	132
Payments of long-term debt and capital lease obligations	(122)	(607)	(149)
Payments of cash dividends	(14)	(14)	(14)
Repurchase of common stock	(1,001)	(800)	(55)
Excess tax benefits from share-based compensation arrangements	28	60	47
Other, net	(23)	—	(1)
Net cash provided by (used in) financing activities	(493)	(801)	260
NET INCREASE (DECREASE) IN CASH AND CASH EQUIVALENTS	823	(890)	1,232
CASH AND CASH EQUIVALENTS AT BEGINNING OF PERIOD	1,390	2,280	1,048
CASH AND CASH EQUIVALENTS AT END OF PERIOD	$ 2,213	$ 1,390	$ 2,280
SUPPLEMENTAL DISCLOSURES			
Cash payments for:			
Interest, net of amount capitalized	$ 63	$ 78	$ 71
Income taxes	$ 94	$ 15	$ 8
Noncash rights to airport gates acquired through reduction in debtor in possession loan to ATA Airlines, Inc.	$ —	$ —	$ 20

NOTES TO CONSOLIDATED FINANCIAL STATEMENTS
December 31, 2007

1. Summary of Significant Accounting Policies

Basis of Presentation

Southwest Airlines Co. (the Company or Southwest) is a major domestic airline that provides point-to-point, low-fare service. The Consolidated Financial Statements include the accounts of Southwest and its wholly owned subsidiaries. All significant intercompany balances and transactions have been eliminated. The preparation of financial statements in conformity with accounting principles generally accepted in the United States (GAAP) requires management to make estimates and assumptions that affect the amounts reported in the financial statements and accompanying notes. Actual results could differ from these estimates.

Cash and Cash Equivalents

Cash in excess of that necessary for operating requirements is invested in short-term, highly liquid, income-producing investments. Investments with maturities of three months or less are classified as cash and cash equivalents, which primarily consist of certificates of deposit, money market funds, and investment grade commercial paper issued by major corporations and financial institutions. Cash and cash equivalents are stated at cost, which approximates market value.

Short-Term Investments

Short-term investments consist of auction rate securities with auction reset periods of less than 12 months. These investments are classified as available-for-sale securities and are stated at fair value. At each reset period, the Company accounts for the transaction as "Proceeds from sales of short-term investments" for the security relinquished, and a "Purchase of short-investments" for the security purchased, in the accompanying Consolidated Statement of Cash Flows. Unrealized gains and losses, net of tax, are recognized in "Accumulated other comprehensive income (loss)" in the accompanying Consolidated Balance Sheet. Realized gains and losses on specific investments, which totaled $17 million in 2007, $17 million in 2006, and $4 million in 2005, are reflected in "Interest income" in the accompanying Consolidated Income Statement.

The Company's cash and cash equivalents and short-term investments as of December 31, 2006 and 2007, included $540 million and $2.0 billion, respectively, in collateral deposits received from the counterparties of the Company's fuel derivative instruments. Although these amounts are not restricted in any way, the Company generally must remit the investment earnings from these amounts back to the counterparties. Depending on the fair value of the Company's fuel derivative instruments, the amounts of collateral deposits held at any point in time can fluctuate significantly. Therefore, the Company generally excludes the cash collateral deposits in its decisions related to long-term cash planning and forecasting. See Note 10 for further information on these collateral deposits and fuel derivative instruments.

Accounts and Other Receivables

Accounts and other receivables are carried at cost. They primarily consist of amounts due from credit card companies associated with sales of tickets for future travel and amounts due from counterparties associated with fuel derivative instruments that have settled. The amount of allowance for doubtful accounts as of December 31, 2005, 2006 and 2007 was immaterial. In addition, the provision for doubtful accounts and write-offs for 2005, 2006, and 2007 were immaterial.

Inventories

Inventories primarily consist of flight equipment expendable parts, materials, aircraft fuel, and supplies. All of these items are carried at average cost, less an allowance for obsolescence. These items are generally charged to expense when issued for use. The reserve for obsolescence was immaterial at December 31, 2005, 2006 and 2007. In addition, the Company's provision for obsolescence and write-offs for 2005, 2006, and 2007 were immaterial.

Property and Equipment

Property and equipment is stated at cost. Depreciation is provided by the straight-line method to estimated residual values over periods generally ranging from 23 to 25 years for flight equipment and 5 to 30 years for ground property and equipment once the asset is placed in service. Residual values estimated for aircraft are generally 15 percent and for ground property and equipment range from zero to 10 percent. Property under capital leases and related obligations is recorded at an amount equal to the present value of future minimum lease payments computed on the basis of the Company's incremental borrowing rate or, when known, the interest rate implicit in

NOTES TO CONSOLIDATED FINANCIAL STATEMENTS — (Continued)

the lease. Amortization of property under capital leases is on a straight-line basis over the lease term and is included in depreciation expense.

In estimating the lives and expected residual values of its aircraft, the Company primarily has relied upon actual experience with the same or similar aircraft types, recommendations from Boeing, the manufacturer of the Company's aircraft, and current fair values in markets for similar used aircraft. Subsequent revisions to these estimates, which can be significant, could be caused by changes to the Company's maintenance program, modifications or improvements to the aircraft, changes in utilization of the aircraft (actual flight hours or cycles during a given period of time), governmental regulations on aging aircraft, changing market prices of new and used aircraft of the same or similar types, etc. The Company evaluates its estimates and assumptions each reporting period and, when warranted, adjusts these estimates and assumptions. Generally, these adjustments are accounted for on a prospective basis through depreciation and amortization expense, as required by GAAP.

When appropriate, the Company evaluates its long-lived assets used in operations for impairment. Impairment losses would be recorded when events and circumstances indicate that an asset might be impaired and the undiscounted cash flows to be generated by that asset are less than the carrying amounts of the asset. Factors that would indicate potential impairment include, but are not limited to, significant decreases in the market value of the long-lived asset(s), a significant change in the long-lived asset's physical condition, operating or cash flow losses associated with the use of the long-lived asset, etc. The Company continues to experience positive cash flow and operate all of its aircraft, and there have been no significant impairments of long-lived assets recorded during 2005, 2006, or 2007.

Aircraft and Engine Maintenance

The cost of scheduled inspections and repairs and routine maintenance costs for all aircraft and engines are charged to maintenance expense as incurred. Modifications that significantly enhance the operating performance or extend the useful lives of aircraft or engines are capitalized and amortized over the remaining life of the asset.

Intangible Assets

Intangible assets primarily consist of leasehold rights to airport owned gates. These assets are amortized on a straight-line basis over the expected useful life of the lease, approximately 20 years. The accumulated amortization related to the Company's intangible assets at December 31, 2007, and 2006, was $9 million and $5 million, respectively. The Company periodically assesses its intangible assets for impairment in accordance with SFAS 142, *Goodwill and Other Intangible Assets*; however, no impairments have been noted.

Revenue Recognition

Tickets sold are initially deferred as "Air traffic liability". Passenger revenue is recognized when transportation is provided. "Air traffic liability" primarily represents tickets sold for future travel dates and estimated refunds and exchanges of tickets sold for past travel dates. The majority of the Company's tickets sold are nonrefundable. Tickets that are sold but not flown on the travel date (whether refundable or nonrefundable) can be reused for another flight, up to a year from the date of sale, or refunded (if the ticket is refundable). A small percentage of tickets (or partial tickets) expire unused. The Company estimates the amount of future refunds and exchanges, net of forfeitures, for all unused tickets once the flight date has passed. These estimates are based on historical experience over many years. The Company and many members of the airline industry have consistently applied this accounting method to estimate revenue from forfeited tickets at the date travel is provided. Estimated future refunds and exchanges included in the air traffic liability account are constantly evaluated based on subsequent refund and exchange activity to validate the accuracy of the Company's revenue recognition method with respect to forfeited tickets.

Events and circumstances outside of historical fare sale activity or historical Customer travel patterns can result in actual refunds, exchanges or forfeited tickets differing significantly from estimates; however, these differences have historically not been material. Additional factors that may affect estimated refunds, exchanges, and forfeitures include, but may not be limited to, the Company's refund and exchange policy, the mix of refundable and nonrefundable fares, and fare sale activity. The Company's estimation techniques have been consistently applied from year to year; however, as with any estimates, actual refund and exchange activity may vary from estimated amounts.

The Company is also required to collect certain taxes and fees from Customers on behalf of government agencies and remit these back to the applicable

NOTES TO CONSOLIDATED FINANCIAL STATEMENTS — (Continued)

governmental entity on a periodic basis. These taxes and fees include U.S. federal transportation taxes, federal security charges, and airport passenger facility charges. These items are collected from Customers at the time they purchase their tickets, but are not included in Passenger revenue. The Company records a liability upon collection from the Customer and relieves the liability when payments are remitted to the applicable governmental agency.

Frequent Flyer Program

The Company records a liability for the estimated incremental cost of providing free travel under its Rapid Rewards frequent flyer program at the time an award is earned. The estimated incremental cost includes direct passenger costs such as fuel, food, and other operational costs, but does not include any contribution to overhead or profit.

The Company also sells frequent flyer credits and related services to companies participating in its Rapid Rewards frequent flyer program. Funds received from the sale of flight segment credits are accounted for under the residual value method. Under this method, the Company has determined the portion of funds received for sale of flight segment credits that relate to free travel, currently estimated at 75 percent of the amount received per flight segment credit sold. These amounts are deferred and recognized as "Passenger revenue" when the ultimate free travel awards are flown or the credits expire unused. The remaining 25 percent of the amount received per flight segment credit sold, which is assumed not to be associated with future travel, includes items such as access to the Company's frequent flyer program population for marketing/solicitation purposes, use of the Company's logo on co-branded credit cards, and other trademarks, designs, images, etc. of Southwest for use in marketing materials. This remaining portion is recognized in "Other revenue" in the period earned.

Advertising

The Company expenses the costs of advertising as incurred. Advertising expense for the years ended December 31, 2007, 2006, and 2005 was $191 million, $182 million, and $173 million, respectively.

Share-Based Employee Compensation

The Company has stock-based compensation plans covering the majority of its Employee groups, including a plan covering the Company's Board of Directors and plans related to employment contracts with the Executive Chairman of the Company. The Company accounts for stock-based compensation utilizing the fair value recognition provisions of SFAS No. 123R, "Share-Based Payment." See Note 13.

Financial Derivative Instruments

The Company accounts for financial derivative instruments utilizing Statement of Financial Accounting Standards No. 133 (SFAS 133), "Accounting for Derivative Instruments and Hedging Activities," as amended. The Company utilizes various derivative instruments, including crude oil, unleaded gasoline, and heating oil-based derivatives, to attempt to reduce the risk of its exposure to jet fuel price increases. These instruments primarily consist of purchased call options, collar structures, and fixed-price swap agreements, and upon proper qualification are accounted for as cash-flow hedges, as defined by SFAS 133. The Company has also entered into interest rate swap agreements to convert a portion of its fixed-rate debt to floating rates. These interest rate hedges are accounted for as fair value hedges, as defined by SFAS 133.

Since the majority of the Company's financial derivative instruments are not traded on a market exchange, the Company estimates their fair values. Depending on the type of instrument, the values are determined by the use of present value methods or standard option value models with assumptions about commodity prices based on those observed in underlying markets. Also, since there is not a reliable forward market for jet fuel, the Company must estimate the future prices of jet fuel in order to measure the effectiveness of the hedging instruments in offsetting changes to those prices, as required by SFAS 133. Forward jet fuel prices are estimated through utilization of a statistical-based regression equation with data from market forward prices of like commodities. This equation is then adjusted for certain items, such as transportation costs, that are stated in the Company's fuel purchasing contracts with its vendors.

For the effective portion of settled hedges, as defined in SFAS 133, the Company records the associated gains or losses as a component of Fuel and oil expense in the Consolidated Statement of Income. For amounts representing ineffectiveness, as defined, or changes in fair value of derivative instruments for which hedge accounting is not applied, the Company records any gains or losses as a component of Other (gains) losses, net, in the Consolidated Statement of Income. Amounts that are paid or

NOTES TO CONSOLIDATED FINANCIAL STATEMENTS — (Continued)

received associated with the purchase or sale of financial derivative instruments (i.e., premium costs of option contracts) are classified as a component of Other (gains) losses, net, in the Consolidated Statement of Income in the period in which the instrument settles or expires. All cash flows associated with purchasing and selling derivatives are classified as operating cash flows in the Consolidated Statement of Cash Flows, either as a component of changes in Other current assets or Other, net, depending on whether the derivative will settle within twelve months or beyond twelve months, respectively. See Note 10 for further information on SFAS 133 and financial derivative instruments.

Income Taxes

The Company accounts for deferred income taxes utilizing Statement of Financial Accounting Standards No. 109 (SFAS 109), "Accounting for Income Taxes", as amended. SFAS 109 requires an asset and liability method, whereby deferred tax assets and liabilities are recognized based on the tax effects of temporary differences between the financial statements and the tax bases of assets and liabilities, as measured by current enacted tax rates. When appropriate, in accordance with SFAS 109, the Company evaluates the need for a valuation allowance to reduce deferred tax assets.

Concentration Risk

A significant number of the Company's Employees are unionized and are covered by collective bargaining agreements. The following Employee groups are under agreements that are currently amendable or will become amendable during 2008: the Company's Pilots (became amendable in 2006, and currently in discussions on a new agreement); the Company's Flight Attendants (becomes amendable in June 2008); the Company's Ramp, Operations, Provisioning, and Freight Agents (becomes amendable in July 2008, and began negotiations in January 2008); the Company's Stock Clerks and Mechanics (both become amendable in August 2008); and the Company's Customer Service and Reservations Agents (becomes amendable in November 2008.)

The Company attempts to minimize its concentration risk with regards to its cash, cash equivalents, and its investment portfolio. This is accomplished by diversifying and limiting amounts among different counterparties, the type of investment, and the amount invested in any individual security or money market fund.

To manage risk associated with financial derivative instruments held, the Company selects and will periodically review counterparties based on credit ratings, limits its exposure to a single counterparty, and monitors the market position of the program and its relative market position with each counterparty. At December 31, 2007, the Company had agreements with nine counterparties containing early termination rights and/or bilateral collateral provisions whereby security is required if market risk exposure exceeds a specified threshold amount or credit ratings fall below certain levels. At December 31, 2007, the Company held $2.0 billion in cash collateral deposits under these bilateral collateral provisions. These collateral deposits serve to decrease, but not totally eliminate, the credit risk associated with the Company's hedging program.

The Company operates an all-Boeing 737 fleet of aircraft. If the Company was unable to acquire additional aircraft from Boeing, or Boeing was unable or unwilling to provide adequate support for its products, the Company's operations could be adversely impacted. However, the Company considers its relationship with Boeing to be good and believes the advantages of operating a single fleet type outweigh the risks of such a strategy.

CHAPTER

2 Analyzing Business Transactions

Focus on Financial Statements

INCOME STATEMENT
Revenues
− Expenses
= Net Income

STATEMENT OF RETAINED EARNINGS
Opening Balance
+ Net Income
− Dividends
= Retained Earnings

BALANCE SHEET
Assets | Liabilities
Equity
A = L + E

STATEMENT OF CASH FLOWS
Operating activities
+ Investing activities
+ Financing activities
= Change in Cash
+ Starting Balance
= Ending Cash Balance

Business transactions affect all the financial statements.

All business transactions require the application of three basic accounting concepts: recording a transaction at the right time, placing the right value on it, and calling it by the right name. Most accounting frauds and mistakes violate one or more of these basic accounting concepts. What you learn in this chapter will help you avoid making such mistakes. It will also help you recognize correct accounting practices.

LEARNING OBJECTIVES

LO1 Explain how the concepts of recognition, valuation, and classification apply to business transactions and why they are important factors in ethical financial reporting. *(pp. 114–118)*

LO2 Explain the double-entry system and the usefulness of T accounts in analyzing business transactions. *(pp. 118–122)*

LO3 Demonstrate how the double-entry system is applied to common business transactions. *(pp. 123–130)*

LO4 Prepare a trial balance, and describe its value and limitations. *(pp. 130–132)*

LO5 Show how the timing of transactions affects cash flows and liquidity. *(pp. 132–134)*

SUPPLEMENTAL OBJECTIVE

SO6 Define the *chart of accounts*, record transactions in the general journal, and post transactions to the ledger. *(pp. 134–140)*

DECISION POINT ▶ A USER'S FOCUS

The Boeing Company

In April 2006, the Chinese government announced that it had ordered 80 **Boeing** commercial jet liners, thus fulfilling a commitment it had made to purchase 150 planes from Boeing. Valued at about $4.6 billion, the order for the 80 planes was one of many events that brought about Boeing's resurgence in the stock market. After Boeing received this order, as well as orders from other customers, its stock began trading at an all-time high.

Typically, it takes Boeing almost two years to manufacture a plane. In this case, the aircraft delivery cycle was expected to peak in 2009.[1]

- ▶ An order for airplanes is obviously an important economic event to both the purchaser and the seller. Is there a difference between an economic event and a business transaction that should be recorded in the accounting records?
- ▶ Should Boeing record the order in its accounting records?
- ▶ How important are liquidity and cash flows to Boeing?

Measurement Issues

LO1 Explain how the concepts of recognition, valuation, and classification apply to business transactions and why they are important factors in ethical financial reporting.

Business transactions are economic events that affect a company's financial position. As shown in Figure 1, to measure a business transaction, you must decide when the transaction occurred (the recognition issue), what value to place on the transaction (the valuation issue), and how the components of the transaction should be categorized (the classification issue).

These three issues—recognition, valuation, and classification—underlie almost every major decision in financial accounting today. They are at the heart of accounting for pension plans, mergers of giant companies, and international transactions. In discussing these issues, we follow generally accepted accounting principles (GAAP) and use an approach that promotes an understanding of basic accounting concepts. Keep in mind, however, that measurement issues can be controversial, and resolutions to them are not always as cut-and-dried as the ones presented here.

Recognition

Study Note

In accounting, recognize means to record a transaction or event.

The **recognition** issue refers to the difficulty of deciding *when* a business transaction should be recorded. The resolution of this issue is important because the date on which a transaction is recorded affects amounts in the financial statements.

To illustrate some of the factors involved in the recognition issue, suppose a company wants to purchase an office desk. The following events take place:

1. An employee sends a purchase requisition for the desk to the purchasing department.
2. The purchasing department sends a purchase order to the supplier.
3. The supplier ships the desk.
4. The company receives the desk.
5. The company receives the bill from the supplier.
6. The company pays the bill.

Study Note

A purchase should usually not be recognized (recorded) before title is transferred because until that point, the vendor has not fulfilled its contractual obligation and the buyer has no liability.

According to accounting tradition, a transaction should be recorded when title to merchandise passes from the supplier to the purchaser and creates an obligation to pay. Thus, depending on the details of the shipping agreement for the desk, the transaction should be recognized (recorded) at the time of either event **3** or **4**. This is the guideline we generally use in this book. However, many small businesses that have simple accounting systems do not record a transaction until they receive a bill (event **5**) or pay it (event **6**) because these are the implied

FOCUS ON BUSINESS PRACTICE

Accounting Policies: Where Do You Find Them?

As the text explains, the order of 80 **Boeing** jet liners by the Chinese government, which is the focus of this chapter's Decision Point, was not an event that either the buyer or the seller should have recorded as a transaction. But when do companies record sales or purchase transactions? The answer to this question and others about companies' accounting policies can be found in the Summary of Significant Accounting Policies in their annual reports. For example, in that section of its annual report, Boeing states: "We recognize sales for commercial airplane deliveries as each unit is completed and accepted by the customer."[2]

FIGURE 1
The Role of Measurement Issues

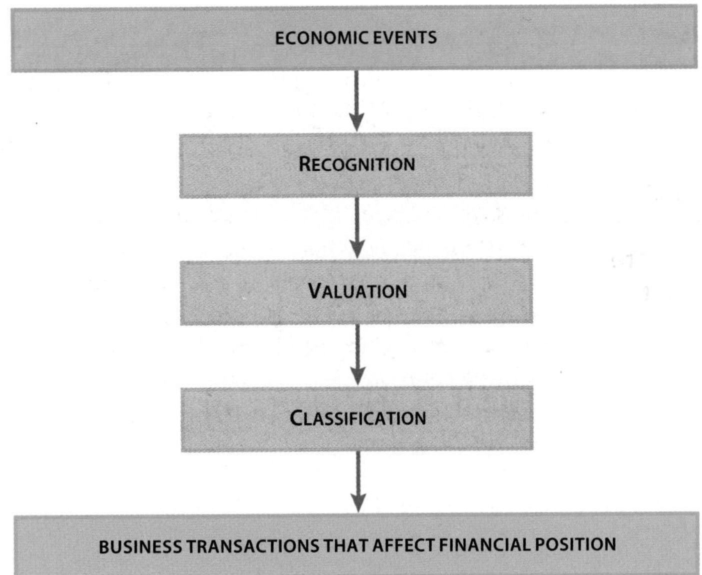

points of title transfer. The predetermined time at which a transaction should be recorded is the **recognition point**.

Although purchase requisitions and purchase orders (events **1** and **2**) are economic events, they do not affect a company's financial position, and they are not recognized in the accounting records. Even the most important economic events may not be recognized in the accounting records. For example, the order of 80 planes described in the Decision Point was a very important economic event for the Chinese government and **Boeing**, but the recognition point for the transaction for both the buyer and the seller is several years in the future—that is, when the planes are delivered and title to them transfers from Boeing to the Chinese government.

Here are some more examples of economic events that should and should not be recorded as business transactions:

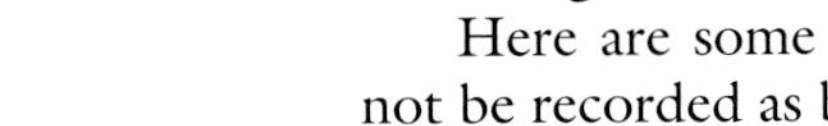

Events That Are Not *Recorded as Transactions*	*Events That* Are *Recorded as Transactions*
A customer inquires about the availability of a service.	A customer buys a service.
A company hires a new employee.	A company pays an employee for work performed.
A company signs a contract to provide a service in the future.	The company performs the service.

The recognition issue can be a difficult one to resolve. For example, consider an advertising agency that is planning a major advertising campaign for one of its clients. Employees may work on the plan several hours a day for a number of weeks. They add value to the plan as they develop it. Should this added value be recognized as the plan is being developed or at the time it is completed? In most cases, the increase in value is recorded at the time the plan is finished and the client is billed for it. However, if a plan is going to take a several months to develop, the agency and the client may agree that the client will be billed at key points during its development. In that case, a transaction is recorded at each billing.

FOCUS ON BUSINESS PRACTICE

IFRS

The Challenge of Fair Value Accounting

The measurement of fair value is a major challenge in merging international financial reporting standards (IFRS) with U.S. GAAP. Both the International Accounting Standards Board (IASB) and the Financial Accounting Standards Board (FASB) are committed to this effort. Fair value is the price to sell an asset or transfer a liability in an orderly market by an arm's-length transaction. Fair value represents a hypothetical transaction that in many cases is difficult to measure: it represents the selling price of an asset or the payment price of a liability. It does not represent the price of acquiring the asset or assuming the liability. In practice, the potential selling price of equipment used in a factory or an investment in a private company for which no ready market exists may not be easy to determine.

Valuation

Study Note

The value of a transaction usually is based on a business document—a canceled check or an invoice.

The **valuation** issue focuses on assigning a monetary value to a business transaction and accounting for the assets and liabilities that result from the business transactions. Generally accepted accounting principles state that all business transactions should be valued at *fair value* when they occur. **Fair value** is defined as the *exchange price* of an actual or potential business transaction between market participants.[3] This practice of recording transactions at exchange price at the point of recognition is commonly referred to as the **cost principle**. It is used because the cost, or exchange price, is verifiable. For example, when the order referred to in the Decision Point is finally complete and **Boeing** delivers the planes to the Chinese government, the two entities will record the transaction in their respective records at the price they have agreed on.

Normally, the value of an asset is held at its initial fair value or cost until the asset is sold, expires, or is consumed. However, if there is evidence that the fair value of the asset or liability has changed, an adjustment to the initial value may be required. There are different rules for the application of fair value to different classes of assets. For example, a building or equipment remains at cost unless there is convincing evidence that the fair value is less than cost. In this case, a loss should be recorded to reduce the value from its cost to fair value. Investments, on the other hand, are often accounted for at fair value, regardless of whether fair value is greater or less than cost. Because these investments are available for sale, the fair value is the best measure of the potential benefit to the company. In its

FOCUS ON BUSINESS PRACTICE

No Dollar Amount: How Can That Be?

Determining the value of a sale or purchase transaction isn't difficult when the value equals the amount of cash that changes hands. However, barter transactions, in which exchanges are made but no cash changes hands, can make valuation more complicated. Barter transactions are quite common in business today. Here are some examples:

- A consulting company provides its services to an auto dealer in exchange for the loan of a car for a year.
- An office supply company provides a year's supply of computer paper to a local weekly newspaper in exchange for an advertisement in 52 issues of the paper.
- Two Internet companies each provide an advertisement and link to the other's website on their own websites.

Determining the value of these transactions is a matter of determining the fair value of the items being traded.

annual report, **Intel Corporation** states: "Investments designated as available-for-sale on the balance sheet date are reported at fair value."[4]

Classification

Study Note

If CVS buys paper towels to resell to customers, the cost would be recorded as an asset in the Inventory account. If the paper towels are used for cleaning in the store, the cost is an expense.

The **classification** issue has to do with assigning all the transactions in which a business engages to appropriate categories, or accounts. Classification of debts can affect a company's ability to borrow money, and classification of purchases can affect its income. For example, purchases of tools may be considered repair expenses (a component of stockholders' equity) or equipment (asset).

As noted in the Decision Point, it will take **Boeing** several years to manufacture the 80 planes that the Chinese government ordered. Over those years, many classification issues will arise. One of the most important is how to classify the numerous costs that Boeing will incur in building the planes. As you will see, generally accepted accounting principles require that these costs be classified as assets until the sale is recorded at the time the planes are delivered. At that time, they will be reclassified as expenses. In this way, the costs will offset the revenues from the sale. It will then be possible to tell whether Boeing made a profit or loss on the transaction.

As we explain later in the chapter, proper classification depends not only on correctly analyzing the effect of each transaction on a business, but also on maintaining a system of accounts that reflects that effect.

Ethics and Measurement Issues

Recognition, valuation, and classification are important factors in ethical financial reporting, and generally accepted accounting principles provide direction about their treatment. These guidelines are intended to help managers meet their obligation to their company's owners and to the public. Many of the most egregious financial reporting frauds over the past several years have resulted from violations of these guidelines.

- **Computer Associates** violated the guidelines for recognition when it kept its books open a few days after the end of a reporting period so revenues could be counted a quarter earlier than they should have been. In all, the company prematurely reported $3.3 billion in revenues from 363 software contracts. When the SEC ordered the company to stop the practice, Computer Associates' stock price dropped by 43 percent in a single day.

Senior WorldCom executives violated standards of good financial reporting and GAAP when they deliberately understated expenses to disguise poor performance. Consequences were devasting for employees, investors, and the public trust. *Left to right*: Melvin Dick of Arthur Andersen, Bernard Ebbers and Scott Sullivan of WorldCom, and Jack Grabman of Salomon Smith Barney are sworn in on July 8, 2002, at a congressional hearing of charges against WorldCom.

- Among its many other transgressions, **Enron Corporation** violated the guidelines for valuation when it valued assets that it transferred to related companies at far more than their actual value.
- By a simple violation of the guidelines for classification, **WorldCom** (now **MCI**) perpetrated the largest financial fraud in history, which resulted in the largest bankruptcy in history. Over a period of several years, the company recorded expenditures that should have been classified as expenses as assets; this had the effect of understating the company's expenses and overstating its income by more than $10 billion.

STOP ► REVIEW ► APPLY

LO1-1 What three issues underlie most major accounting decisions?

LO1-2 A customer asks the owner of a store to save an item for him and says he will pick it up and pay for it next week. The owner agrees to hold it. Should this transaction be recorded as a sale? Explain your answer.

LO1-3 Why is it practical for accountants to rely on original cost for valuation purposes?

LO1-4 Why is classification of a transaction as an expense or an asset a critical issue in accounting?

LO1-5 How are recognition, valuation, and classification related to the ethics of financial reporting?

Suggested answers to all Stop, Review, and Apply questions follow the appendixes.

Double-Entry System

LO2 Explain the double-entry system and the usefulness of T accounts in analyzing business transactions.

> **Study Note**
> Each transaction must include at least one debit and one credit, and the debit totals must equal the credit totals.

The double-entry system, the backbone of accounting, evolved during the Renaissance. The first systematic description of double-entry bookkeeping appeared in 1494, two years after Columbus discovered America, in a mathematics book by Fra Luca Pacioli. Goethe, the famous German poet and dramatist, referred to double-entry bookkeeping as "one of the finest discoveries of the human intellect." Werner Sombart, an eminent economist-sociologist, believed that "double-entry bookkeeping is born of the same spirit as the system of Galileo and Newton."

What is the significance of the double-entry system? The system is based on the *principle of duality*, which means that every economic event has two aspects—effort and reward, sacrifice and benefit, source and use—that offset, or balance, each other. In the **double-entry system**, each transaction must be recorded with at least one debit and one credit, and the total amount of the debits must equal the total amount of the credits. Because of the way it is designed, the whole system is always in balance. All accounting systems, no matter how sophisticated, are based on the principle of duality.

Accounts

Accounts are the basic storage units for accounting data and are used to accumulate amounts from similar transactions. An accounting system has a separate account for each asset, each liability, and each component of stockholders' equity, including revenues and expenses. Whether a company keeps records by hand or by computer, managers must be able to refer to accounts so that they can study their company's financial history and plan for the future. A very small company may need only a few dozen accounts; a multinational corporation may need thousands.

An account title should describe what is recorded in the account. However, account titles can be rather confusing. For example, *Fixed Assets, Plant and Equipment, Capital Assets,* and *Long-Lived Assets* are all titles for long-term assets. Moreover, many account titles change over time as preferences and practices change.

When you come across an account title that you don't recognize, examine the context of the name—whether it is classified in the financial statements as an asset, liability, or component of stockholders' equity—and look for the kind of transaction that gave rise to the account.

The T Account

Study Note

Many students have preconceived ideas about what *debit* and *credit* mean. They think *debit* means "decrease" (or implies something bad) and *credit* means "increase" (or implies something good). It is important to realize that *debit* simply means "left side" and *credit* simply means "right side."

The **T account** is a good place to begin the study of the double-entry system. Such an account has three parts: a title, which identifies the asset, liability, or stockholders' equity account; a left side, which is called the **debit** side; and a right side, which is called the **credit** side. The T account, so called because it resembles the letter *T*, is used to analyze transactions. It looks like this:

Title of Account	
Debit (left) side	Credit (right) side

Any entry made on the left side of the account is a debit, and any entry made on the right side is a credit. The terms *debit* (abbreviated Dr., from the Latin *debere*) and *credit* (abbreviated Cr., from the Latin *credere*) are simply the accountant's words for "left" and "right" (*not* for "increase" or "decrease"). We present a more formal version of the T account, the ledger account form, later in this chapter.

The T Account Illustrated

Suppose a company had several transactions that involved the receipt or payment of cash. These transactions can be summarized in the Cash account by recording receipts on the left (debit) side of a T account and payments on the right (credit) side.

	Cash	
	100,000	70,000
	3,000	400
		1,200
	103,000	**71,600**
Bal.	**31,400**	

The cash receipts on the left total $103,000. (The total is written in smaller, bold figures so that it cannot be confused with an actual debit entry.) The cash payments on the right side total $71,600. These totals are simply working totals, or **footings**. Footings, which are calculated at the end of each month, are an easy way to determine cash on hand. The difference in dollars between the total debit footing and the total credit footing is called the **balance**, or *account balance*. If the balance is a debit, it is written on the left side. If it is a credit, it is written on the right side. Notice that the Cash account has a debit balance of $31,400 ($103,000 − $71,600). This is the amount of cash the business has on hand at the end of the month.

Rules of Double-Entry Accounting

The two rules of the double-entry system are that every transaction affects at least two accounts and that total debits must equal total credits. In other words, for every transaction, one or more accounts must be debited, or entered on the left side of the T account, and one or more accounts must be credited, or entered on the right side of the T account, and the total dollar amount of the debits must equal the total dollar amount of the credits.

Look again at the accounting equation:

Assets = Liabilities + Stockholders' Equity

You can see that if a debit increases assets, then a credit must be used to increase liabilities or stockholders' equity because they are on opposite sides of the equal sign. Likewise, if a credit decreases assets, then a debit must be used to decrease liabilities or stockholders' equity. These rules can be shown as follows:

Assets		=	**Liabilities**		+	**Stockholders' Equity**	
Debit for increases (+)	Credit for decreases (−)		Debit for decreases (−)	Credit for increases (+)		Debit for decreases (−)	Credit for increases (+)

1. Debit increases in assets to asset accounts. Credit decreases in assets to asset accounts.
2. Credit increases in liabilities and stockholders' equity to liability and stockholders' equity accounts. Debit decreases in liabilities and stockholders' equity to liability and stockholders' equity accounts.

One of the more difficult points to understand is the application of double-entry rules to the components of stockholders' equity. The key is to remember that dividends and expenses are deductions from stockholders' equity. Thus, transactions that *increase* dividends or exenses *decrease* stockholders' equity. Consider this expanded version of the accounting equation:

Stockholders' Equity

Assets = Liabilities + Common Stock + Retained Earnings − Dividends + Revenues − Expenses

Assets		**Liabilities**		**Common Stock**		**Retained Earnings**		**Dividends**		**Revenues**		**Expenses**	
+	−	−	+	−	+	−	+	+	−	−	+	+	−
(Dr.)	(Cr.)	(Dr.)	(Cr.)	(Dr.)	(Cr.)	(Dr.)	(Cr.)	(Dr.)	(Cr.)	(Dr.)	(Cr.)	(Dr.)	(Cr.)

TABLE 1
Normal Account Balances of Major Account Categories

Account Category	Increases Recorded by Debit	Increases Recorded by Credit	Normal Balance Debit	Normal Balance Credit
Assets	x		x	
Liabilities		x		x
Stockholders' equity:				
Common stock		x		x
Retained earnings		x		x
Dividends	x		x	
Revenues		x		x
Expenses	x		x	

Normal Balance

The **normal balance** of an account is its usual balance and is the side (debit or credit) that increases the account. Table 1 summarizes the normal account balances of the major account categories. If you have difficulty remembering the normal balances and the rules of debit and credit, try using the acronym ADE: Asset accounts, Dividends, and Expenses are always increased by debits. All other accounts are increased by credits.

Stockholders' Equity Accounts

Study Note
Although dividends are a component of stockholders' equity, they normally appear only in the statement of retained earnings. They do not appear in the stockholders' equity section of the balance sheet.

Figure 2 illustrates how stockholders' equity accounts relate to each other and to the financial statements. The distinctions among these accounts are important for both legal purposes and financial reporting.

- Stockholders' equity accounts represent the legal claims of stockholders to the assets of a corporation. The Common Stock account represents stockholders' claims arising from their investments in the business, and the Retained Earnings account represents stockholders' claims arising from profitable operations. Both are claims against the general assets of the company, not against specific

FIGURE 2
Relationships of Stockholders' Equity Accounts

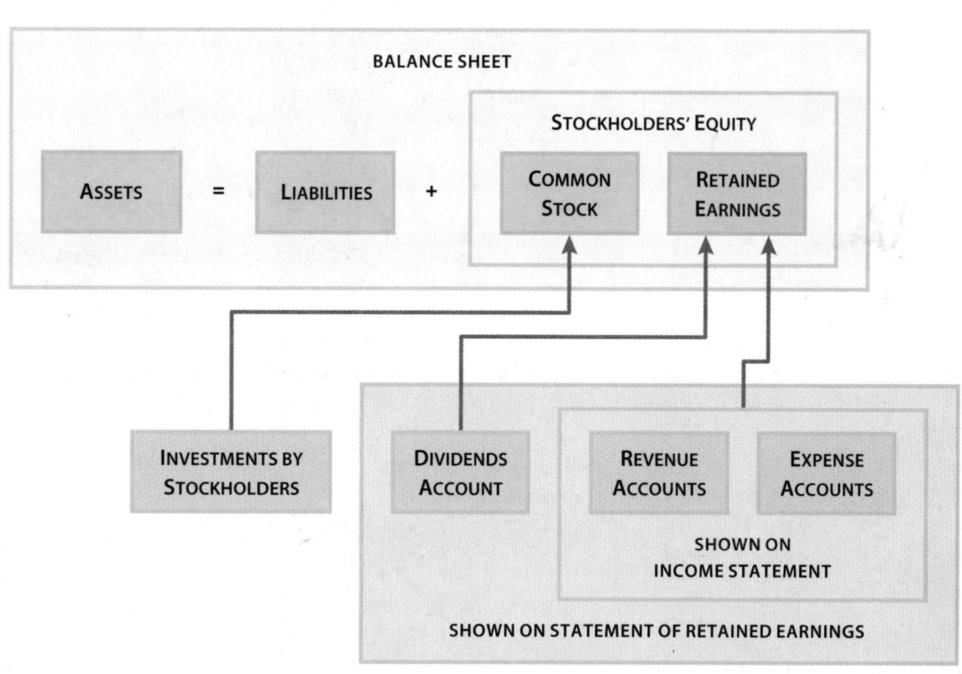

Study Note
Although revenues and expenses are components of stockholders' equity, they appear on the income statement, not in the stockholders' equity section of the balance sheet. Figure 2 illustrates this point.

assets. Dividends are deducted from the stockholders' claims on retained earnings and are shown on the statement of retained earnings.

- By law, investments by stockholders and dividends must be separated from revenues and expenses for both income tax purposes and financial reporting purposes.
- Managers need a detailed breakdown of revenues and expenses for budgeting and operating purposes. From the Revenue and Expense accounts on the income statement, they can identify the sources of all revenues and the nature of all expenses. In this way, accounting gives managers information about whether they have achieved a primary business goal—that is, whether they have enabled their company to earn a net income.

STOP ▸ REVIEW ▸ APPLY

LO2-1 **Why is the system of recording entries called the double-entry system? What is significant about this system?**

LO2-2 **Is the statement "Debits are bad; credits are good" true? Explain your answer.**

LO2-3 **What is an account, and what is its normal balance?**

LO2-4 **What are T accounts, and why are they useful?**

LO2-5 **What are the rules of double entry for (a) assets, (b) liabilities, and (c) stockholders' equity?**

LO2-6 **In the stockholders' equity accounts, why do accountants maintain separate accounts for revenues and expenses rather than using the Retained Earnings account?**

T Accounts, Normal Balance, and the Accounting Equation You are given the following list of accounts with dollar amounts:

Dividends	$ 75	Common Stock	$300
Accounts Payable	200	Fees Revenue	250
Wages Expense	150	Retained Earnings	100
Cash	625		

Insert the account title at the top of its corresponding T account and enter the dollar amount as a normal balance in the account. Then show that the accounting equation is in balance.

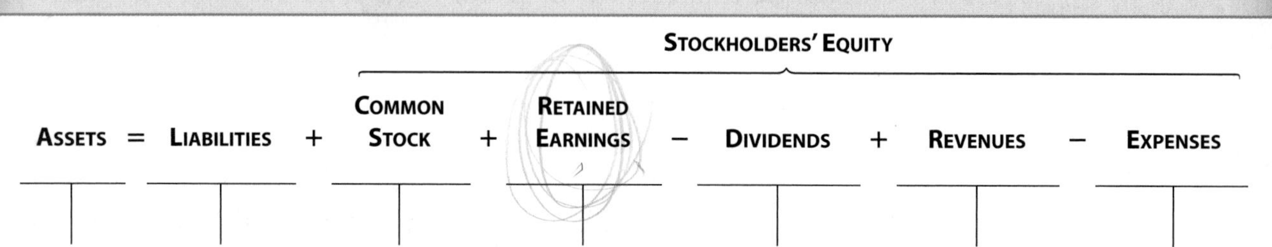

SOLUTION

	Cash	Accounts Payable	Common Stock	Retained Earnings	Dividends	Fees Revenue	Wages Expense
Debit	625				75		150
Credit		200	300	100		250	

Assets = Liabilities + Stockholders' Equity
$625 = $200 + ($300 + $100 − $75 + $250 − $150)
$625 = $200 + $425
$625 = $625

Business Transaction Analysis

LO3 Demonstrate how the double-entry system is applied to common business transactions.

In the next few pages, we show how to apply the double-entry system to some common business transactions. **Source documents**—invoices, receipts, checks, or contracts—usually support the details of a transaction. We focus on the transactions of a small firm, Miller Design Studio, Inc. For each transaction, we follow these steps:

1. State the transaction.
2. Analyze the transaction to determine which accounts are affected.
3. Apply the rules of double-entry accounting by using T accounts to show how the transaction affects the accounting equation.
4. Show the transaction in **journal form**. The journal form is a way of recording a transaction with the date, debit account, and debit amount shown on one line, and the credit account (indented) and credit amount on the next line. The amounts are shown in their respective debit and credit columns. (We discuss journals later in this chapter.)
5. Provide a comment that will help you apply the rules of double entry.

Owner's Investment in the Business

July 1: To begin the business, Joan Miller files articles of incorporation with the state to receive her charter and invests $40,000 in Miller Design Studio, Inc., in exchange for 40,000 shares of $1 par value common stock.

Analysis: An owner's investment in the business *increases* the asset account *Cash* with a debit and *increases* the stockholders' equity account *Common Stock* with a credit.

Application of Double Entry:

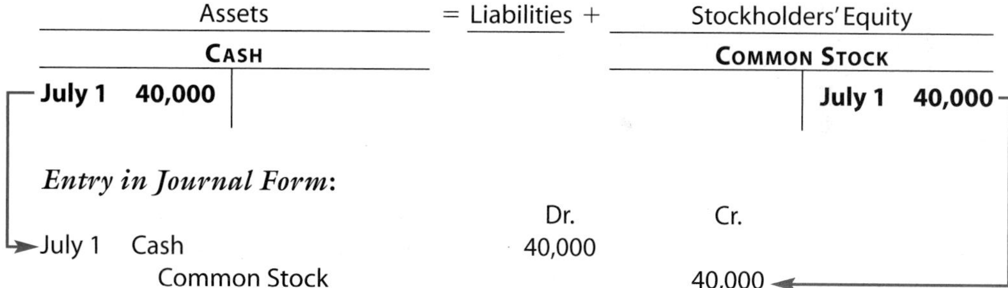

Assets
= Liabilities +
Stockholders' Equity
CASH
July 1 40,000
COMMON STOCK
July 1 40,000
Entry in Journal Form:
Dr.
Cr.
July 1 Cash
40,000
Common Stock
40,000

Comment: If Joan Miller had invested assets other than cash in the business, the appropriate asset accounts would be increased with a debit.

Economic Event That Is Not a Business Transaction

July 2: Orders office supplies, $5,200.

Comment: When an economic event does not constitute a business transaction, no entry is made. In this case, there is no confirmation that the supplies have been shipped or that title has passed.

Prepayment of Expenses in Cash

July 3: Rents an office; pays two months rent in advance, $3,200.

Analysis: The prepayment of office rent in cash *increases* the asset account *Prepaid Rent* with a debit and *decreases* the asset account *Cash* with a credit.

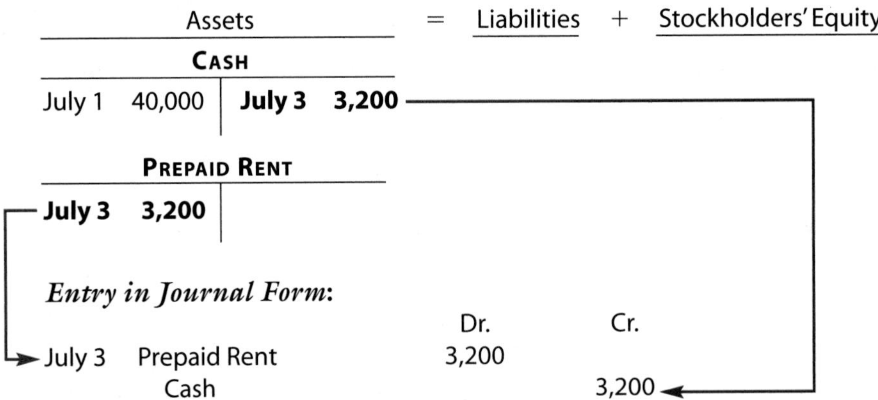

***Comment*:** A prepaid expense is an asset because the expenditure will benefit future operations. This transaction does not affect the totals of assets or liabilities and stockholders' equity because it simply trades one asset for another asset. If the company had paid only July's rent, the stockholders' equity account *Rent Expense* would be debited because the total benefit of the expenditure would be used up in the current month.

Purchase of an Asset on Credit

***July 5*:** Receives office supplies ordered on July 2 and an invoice for $5,200.

***Analysis*:** The purchase of office supplies on credit *increases* the asset account *Office Supplies* with a debit and *increases* the liability account *Accounts Payable* with a credit.

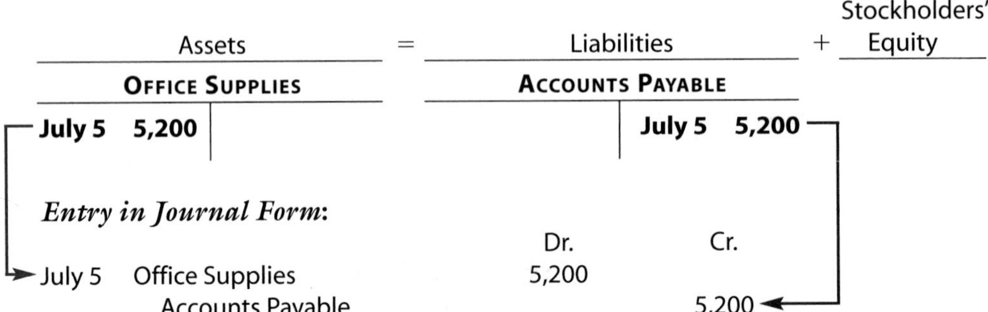

***Comment*:** Office supplies are considered an asset (prepaid expense) because they will not be used up in the current month and thus will benefit future periods. Accounts Payable is used when there is a delay between the time of the purchase and the time of payment.

Purchase of an Asset Partly in Cash and Partly on Credit

***July 6*:** Purchases office equipment, $16,320; pays $13,320 in cash and agrees to pay the rest next month.

***Analysis*:** The purchase of office equipment in cash and on credit *increases* the asset account *Office Equipment* with a debit, *decreases* the asset account *Cash* with a credit, and *increases* the liability account *Accounts Payable* with a credit.

Application of Double Entry:

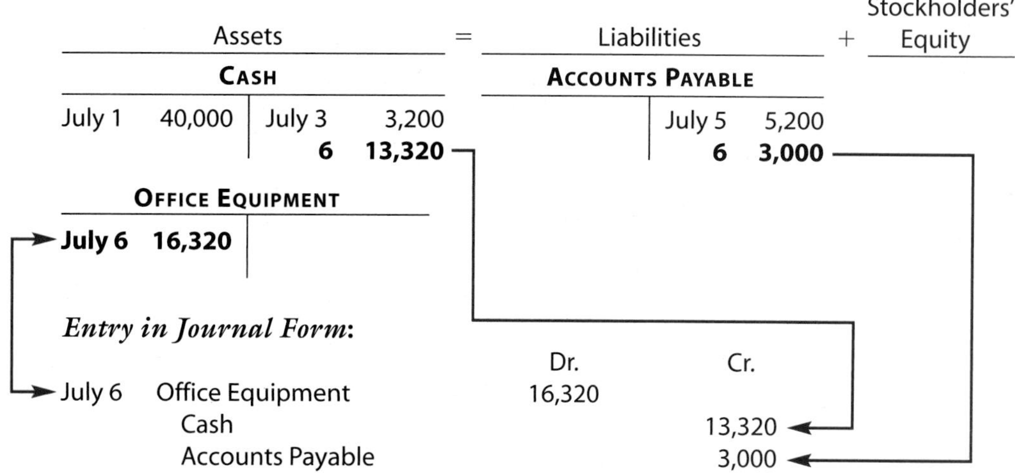

***Comment*:** As this transaction illustrates, assets may be paid for partly in cash and partly on credit. When more than two accounts are involved in a journal entry, as they are in this one, it is called a **compound entry**.

Payment of a Liability

***July 9*:** Makes a partial payment of the amount owed for the office supplies received on July 5, $2,600.

***Analysis*:** A payment of a liability *decreases* the liability account *Accounts Payable* with a debit and *decreases* the asset account *Cash* with a credit.

Application of Double Entry:

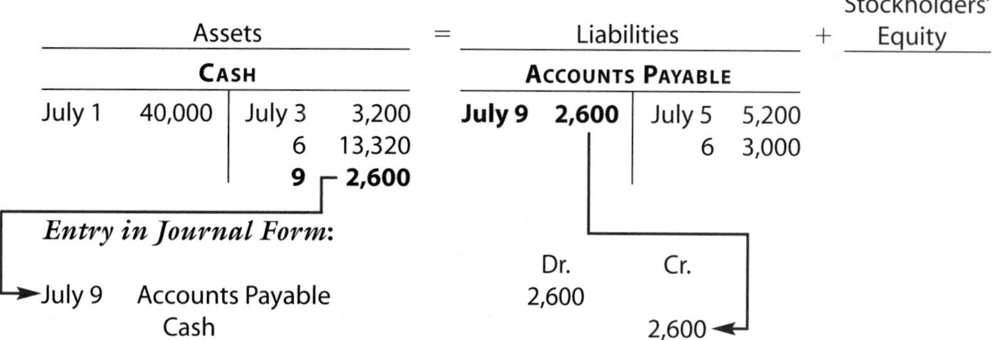

***Comment*:** Note that the office supplies were recorded when they were purchased on July 5.

Revenue in Cash

***July 10*:** Performs a service for an investment advisor by designing a series of brochures and collects a fee in cash, $2,800.

***Analysis*:** A revenue received in cash *increases* the asset account *Cash* with a debit and *increases* the stockholders' equity account *Design Revenue* with a credit.

Application of Double Entry:

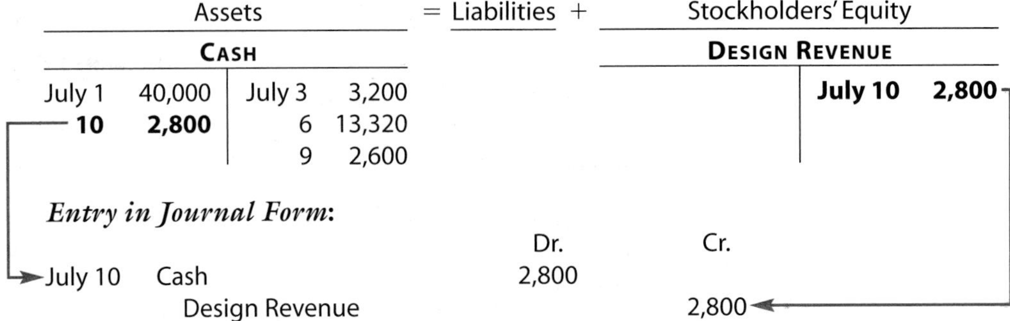

Entry in Journal Form:

		Dr.	Cr.
July 10	Cash	2,800	
	Design Revenue		2,800

Comment: For this transaction, revenue is recognized when the service is provided and the cash is received.

Revenue on Credit

July 15: Performs a service for a department store by designing a TV commercial; bills for the fee now but will be paid later, $9,600.

Analysis: A revenue billed to a customer *increases* the asset account *Accounts Receivable* with a debit and *increases* the stockholders' equity account *Design Revenue* with a credit. Accounts Receivable is used to indicate the customer's obligation until it is paid.

Application of Double Entry:

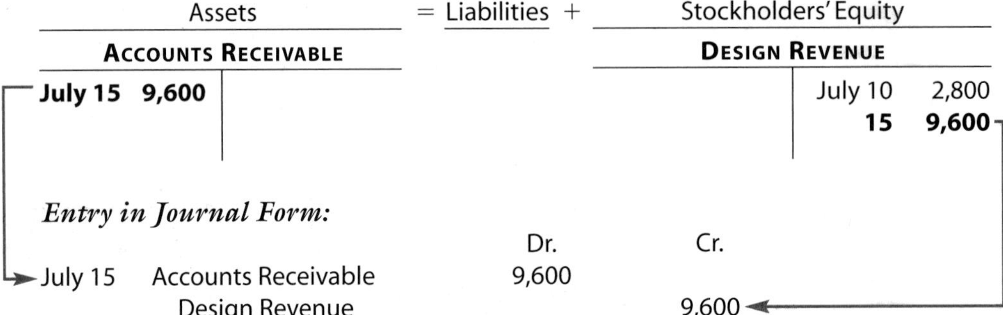

Entry in Journal Form:

		Dr.	Cr.
July 15	Accounts Receivable	9,600	
	Design Revenue		9,600

Comment: In this case, there is a delay between the time revenue is earned and the time the cash is received. Revenues are recorded at the time they are earned and billed regardless of when cash is received.

Revenue Received in Advance

July 19: Accepts an advance fee as a deposit on a series of brochures to be designed, $1,400.

Analysis: A revenue received in advance *increases* the asset account *Cash* with a debit and *increases* the liability account *Unearned Design Revenue* with a credit.

Application of Double Entry:

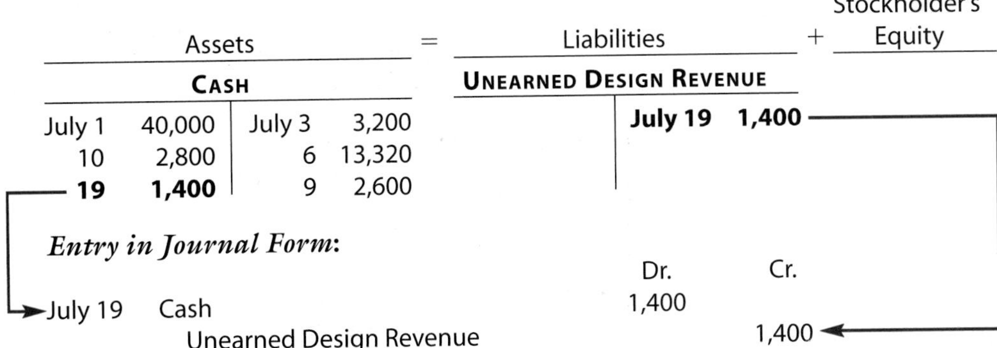

Comment: In this case, payment is received before the fees are earned. Unearned Design Revenue is a liability because the firm must provide the service or return the deposit.

Collection on Account

July 22: Receives partial payment from customer billed on July 15, $5,000.

Analysis: Collection of an account receivable from a customer previously billed *increases* the asset account *Cash* with a debit and *decreases* the asset account *Accounts Receivable* with a credit.

Application of Double Entry:

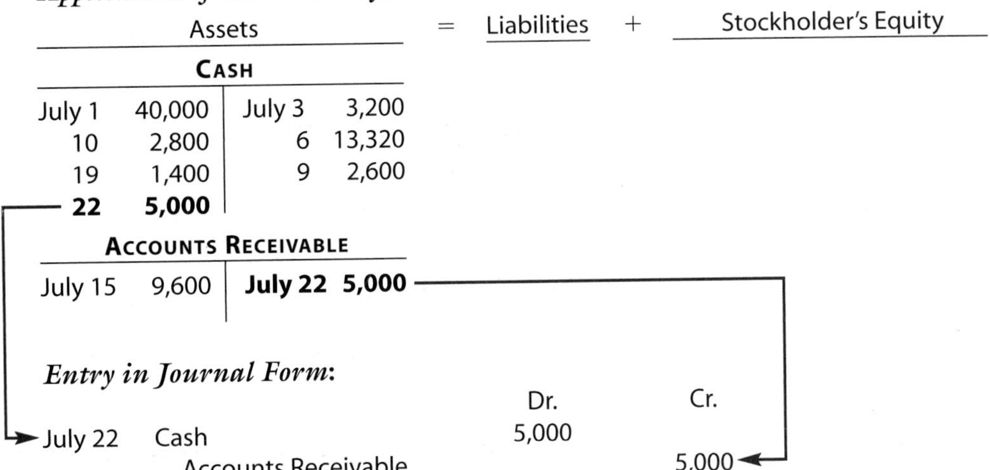

Comment: Note that the revenue related to this transaction was recorded on July 15. Thus, no revenue is recorded at this time.

Expense Paid in Cash

July 26: Pays employees four weeks' wages, $4,800.

Analysis: This cash expense *increases* the stockholders' equity account *Wages Expense* with a debit and *decreases* the asset account *Cash* with a credit.

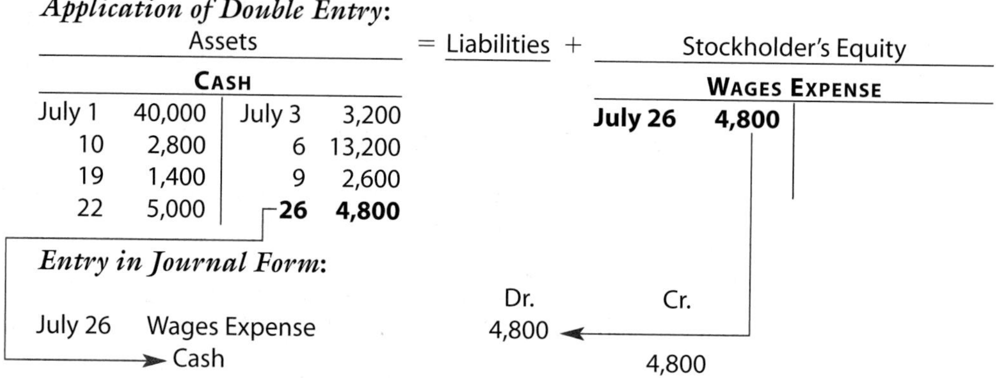

Comment: The increase in Wages Expense will *decrease* stockholders' equity.

Expense to Be Paid Later

July 30: Receives, but does not pay, the utility bill which is due next month, $680.

Analysis: This cash expense *increases* the stockholders' equity account *Utilities Expense* with a debit and *increases* the liability account *Accounts Payable* with a credit.

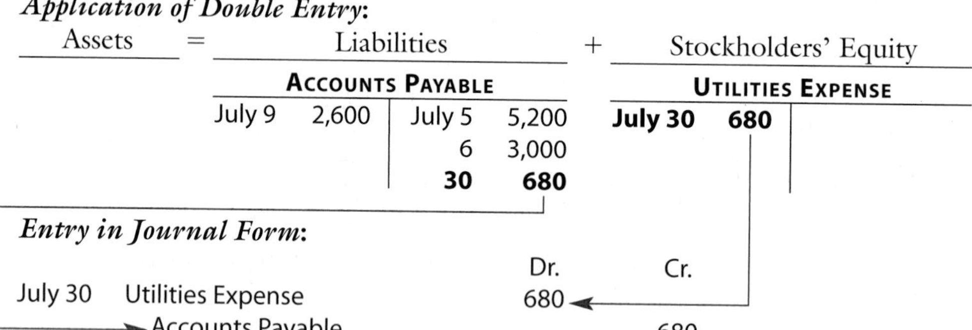

Comment: The expense is recorded if the benefit has been received and the amount is owed, even if the cash is not to be paid until later. Note that the increase in Utility Expense will *decrease* stockholders' equity.

Dividends

July 31: Declares and pays a dividend, $2,800.

Analysis: Payment of a cash dividend *increases* the stockholders' equity account *Dividends* with a debit and *decreases* the asset account *Cash* with a credit.

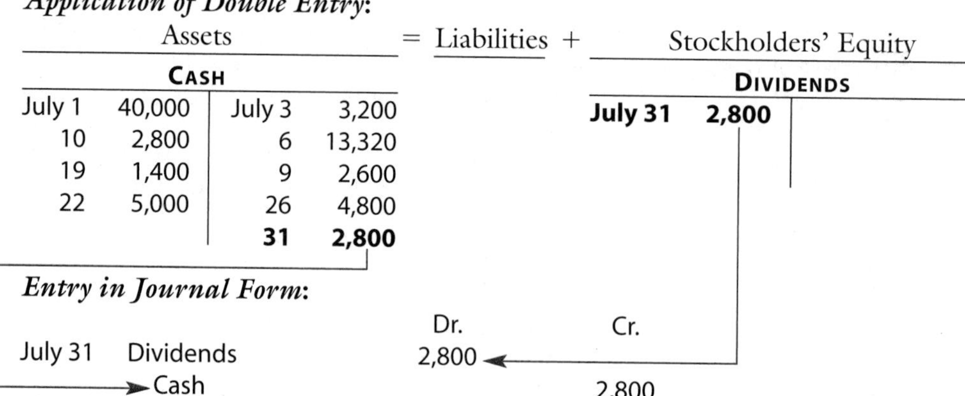

***Comment*:** Note that the increase in Dividends will result in a *decrease* in stockholders' equity.

Summary of Transactions

Exhibit 1 uses the accounting equation to summarize the transactions of Miller Design Studio, Inc. Note that the income statement accounts appear under stockholders' equity and that the transactions in the Cash account will be reflected on the statement of cash flows. No Retained Earnings account appears under stockholders' equity because this is the company's first month of operation.

EXHIBIT 1 Summary of Transactions of Miller Design Studio, Inc.

Assets = **Liabilities** + **Stockholders' Equity**

Cash

July 1	40,000	July 3	3,200
10	2,800	6	13,320
19	1,400	9	2,600
22	5,000	26	4,800
		31	2,800
	49,200		26,720
Bal.	22,480		

This account links to the statement of cash flows.

Accounts Payable

July 9	2,600	July 5	5,200
		6	3,000
		30	680
	2,600		8,880
		Bal.	6,280

Common Stock

		July 1	40,000

Dividends

July 31	2,800		

Accounts Receivable

July 15	9,600	July 22	5,000
Bal.	4,600		

Unearned Design Revenue

		July 19	1,400

Design Revenue

		July 10	2,800
		15	9,600
		Bal.	12,400

Office Supplies

July 5	5,200		

Wages Expense

July 26	4,800		

Prepaid Rent

July 3	3,200		

Utilities Expense

July 30	680		

These accounts link to the income statement.

Office Equipment

July 6	16,320		

Assets	=	Liabilities	+	Stockholders' Equity
$51,800	=	$7,680	+	$44,120

STOP ▸ REVIEW ▸ APPLY

LO3-1 **Explain the meaning of this statement: "The Cash account has a debit balance of $500."**

LO3-2 **Explain why debits, which decrease stockholders' equity, increase expenses, which are a component of stockholders' equity.**

LO3-3 **What steps are followed in analyzing a business transaction?**

LO3-4 **What is the normal balance of Accounts Payable? Under what conditions could Accounts Payable have a debit balance?**

The Trial Balance

LO4 **Prepare a trial balance, and describe its value and limitations.**

For every amount debited, an equal amount must be credited. This means that the total of debits and credits in the T accounts must be equal. To test this, the accountant periodically prepares a **trial balance**. Exhibit 2 shows a trial balance for Miller Design Studio, Inc. It was prepared from the accounts in Exhibit 1.

Preparation and Use of a Trial Balance

Study Note

A trial balance is usually prepared at the end of an accounting period. It is an initial check that the accounts are in balance.

Although a trial balance may be prepared at any time, it is usually prepared on the last day of the accounting period. These are the steps involved in preparing a trial balance:

1. List each account that has a balance, with debit balances in the left column and credit balances in the right column. Accounts are listed in the order in which they appear on the financial statements.
2. Add each column.
3. Compare the totals of the columns.

EXHIBIT 2

Trial Balance

Miller Design Studio, Inc.
Trial Balance
July 31, 2010

Cash	$22,480	
Accounts Receivable	4,600	
Office Supplies	5,200	
Prepaid Rent	3,200	
Office Equipment	16,320	
Accounts Payable		$ 6,280
Unearned Design Revenue		1,400
Common Stock		40,000
Dividends	2,800	
Design Revenue		12,400
Wages Expense	4,800	
Utilities Expense	680	
	$60,080	$60,080

FOCUS ON BUSINESS PRACTICE

Are All Trial Balances Created Equal?

In computerized accounting systems, posting is done automatically, and the trial balance can be easily prepared as often as needed. Any accounts with abnormal balances are highlighted for investigation. Some general ledger software packages for small businesses list the trial balance amounts in a single column and show credit balances as minuses. In such cases, the trial balance is in balance if the total is zero.

Once in a while, a transaction leaves an account with a balance that isn't "normal." For example, when a company overdraws its bank account, its Cash account (an asset) will show a credit balance instead of a debit balance. The "abnormal" balance should be copied into the trial balance columns as it stands, as a debit or a credit.

The trial balance proves whether the accounts are in balance. *In balance* means that the total of all debits recorded equals the total of all credits recorded. But the trial balance does not prove that the transactions were analyzed correctly or recorded in the proper accounts. For example, there is no way of determining from the trial balance that a debit should have been made in the Office Supplies account rather than in the Office Equipment account. And the trial balance does not detect whether transactions have been omitted, because equal debits and credits will have been omitted. Also, if an error of the same amount is made in both a debit and a credit, it will not be evident in the trial balance. The trial balance proves only that the debits and credits in the accounts are in balance.

Finding Trial Balance Errors

If the debit and credit balances in a trial balance are not equal, look for one or more of the following errors:

1. A debit was entered in an account as a credit, or vice versa.
2. The balance of an account was computed incorrectly.
3. An error was made in carrying the account balance to the trial balance.
4. The trial balance was summed incorrectly.

Other than simply adding the columns incorrectly, the two most common mistakes in preparing a trial balance are

1. Recording an account as a credit when it usually carries a debit balance, or vice versa. This mistake causes the trial balance to be out of balance by an amount divisible by 2.
2. Transposing two digits when transferring an amount to the trial balance (for example, entering $23,459 as $23,549). This error causes the trial balance to be out of balance by a number divisible by 9.

So, if a trial balance is out of balance and the addition of the columns is correct, determine the amount by which the trial balance is out of balance and divide it first by 2 and then by 9. If the amount is divisible by 2, look in the trial balance for an amount that is equal to the quotient. If you find such an amount, chances are it's in the wrong column. If the amount is divisible by 9, trace each amount back to the T account balance, checking carefully for a transposition error. If neither of these techniques is successful in identifying the error, first recompute the balance of each T account. Then, if you still have not found the error, retrace each posting to the journal or the T account.

STOP ▶ REVIEW ▶ APPLY

LO4-1 **What is a trial balance, and why is it useful?**

LO4-2 **Is it possible for errors to be present in a trial balance whose debit and credit balances are equal? Explain your answer.**

Cash Flows and the Timing of Transactions

LO5 Show how the timing of transactions affects cash flows and liquidity.

To avoid financial distress, a company must be able to pay its bills on time. Because the timing of cash flows is critical to maintaining adequate liquidity to pay bills, managers and other users of financial information must understand the difference between transactions that generate immediate cash and those that do not. Consider the transactions of Miller Design Studio, Inc., shown in Figure 3. Most of them involve either an inflow or outflow of cash.

As you can see in Figure 3, Miller's Cash account has more transactions than any of its other accounts. Look at the transactions of July 10, 15, and 22:

- July 10: Miller received a cash payment of $2,800.
- July 15: The firm billed a customer $9,600 for a service it had already performed.
- July 22: The firm received a partial payment of $5,000 from the customer, but it had not received the remaining $4,600 by the end of the month.

Because Miller incurred expenses in providing this service, it must pay careful attention to its cash flows and liquidity.

One way Miller can manage its expenditures is to rely on its creditors to give it time to pay. Compare the transactions of July 3, 5, and 9 in Figure 3.

- July 3: Miller prepaid rent of $3,200. That immediate cash outlay may have caused a strain on the business.
- July 5: The firm received an invoice for office supplies in the amount of $5,200. In this case, it took advantage of the opportunity to defer payment.

Study Note

Recording revenues and expenses when they occur will provide a clearer picture of a company's profitability on the income statement. The change in cash flows will provide a clearer picture of the company's liquidity on the statement of cash flows.

FOCUS ON BUSINESS PRACTICE

Should Earnings Be Aligned with Cash Flows?

Electronic Data Systems Corporation (EDS), the large computer services company, recently announced that it was reducing past earnings by $2.24 billion to implement a new accounting rule that would more closely align its earnings with cash flows. Analysts had been critical of EDS for recording revenue from its long-term contracts when the contracts were signed rather than when the cash was received. In fact, about 40 percent of EDC's revenue had been recognized well before the cash was to be received. Analysts' response to the change in EDC's accounting was very positive. "Finally, maybe, we'll see cash flows moving in line with earnings," said one.[5] Although there are natural and unavoidable differences between earnings and cash flows, it is best if accounting rules do not exaggerate these differences.

FIGURE 3
Transactions of Miller Design Studio, Inc.

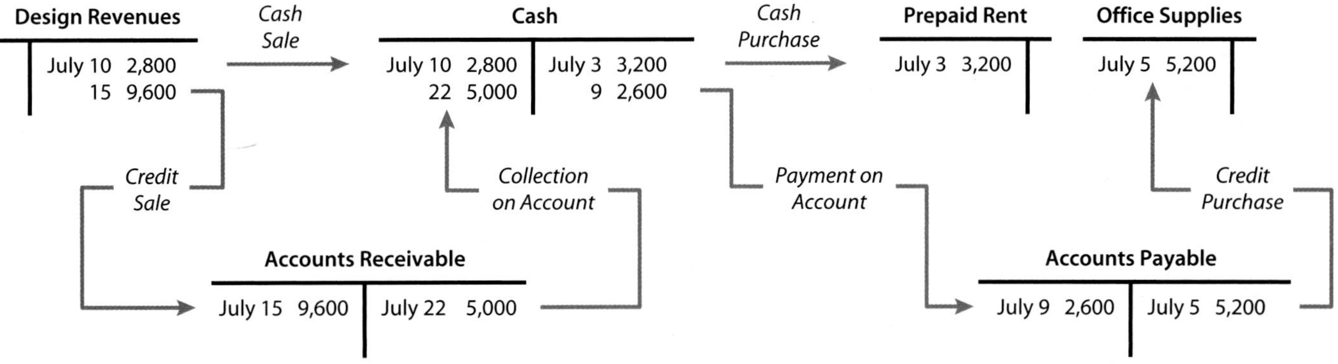

- July 9: The firm paid $2,600, but it deferred paying the remaining $2,600 until after the end of the month.

Of course, Miller expects to receive the rest of the cash from the customer that it billed on July 15, and it must eventually pay the rest of what it owes on the office supplies. In the meantime, the firm must perform a delicate balancing act with its cash flows to ensure that it achieves the goal of liquidity so that it can grow and be profitable.

Large companies face the same challenge, but often on a much greater scale. Recall from the Decision Point that **Boeing** takes years to plan and make the aircraft that the Chinese government and other customers order. At the end of 2006, Boeing had orders for 8,274 airplanes totaling $174.3 billion, or about $21 million per plane.[6] Think of the cash outlays Boeing must make before it delivers the planes and collects payment for them. To maintain liquidity so that Boeing can eventually reap the rewards of delivering the planes, Boeing's management must carefully plan the company's needs for cash.

Because Boeing takes years to plan and make the airplanes that customers have ordered, Boeing's management must carefully plan the company's needs for cash. The timing of cash flows is critical to maintaining adequate liquidity.

STOP ► REVIEW ► APPLY

LO5-1 **Why is the timing of cash flows important?**

LO5-2 **Under what circumstance is there a delay between the time a sale is made and the time cash is collected?**

Cash Flow Analysis A company engaged in the following transactions:

Oct. 1	Performed services for cash, $1,050.	Oct. 4	Performed services on credit, $900.
2	Paid expenses in cash, $550.	5	Paid on account, $350.
3	Incurred expenses on credit, $650.	6	Collected on account, $600.

Enter the correct titles in the following T accounts, and enter the above transactions in the accounts. Determine the cash balance after these transactions, the amount still to be received, and the amount still to be paid.

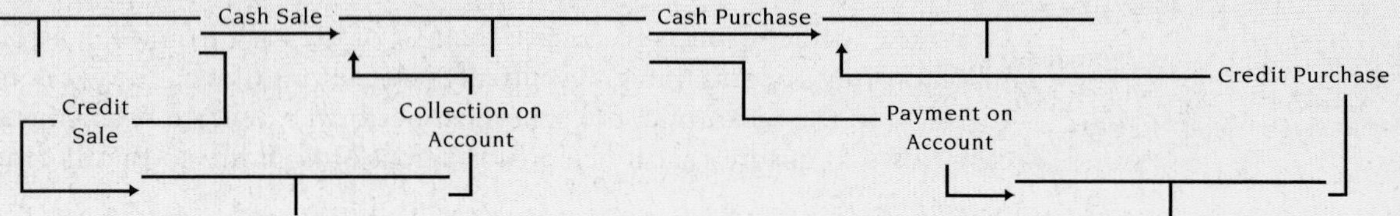

SOLUTION

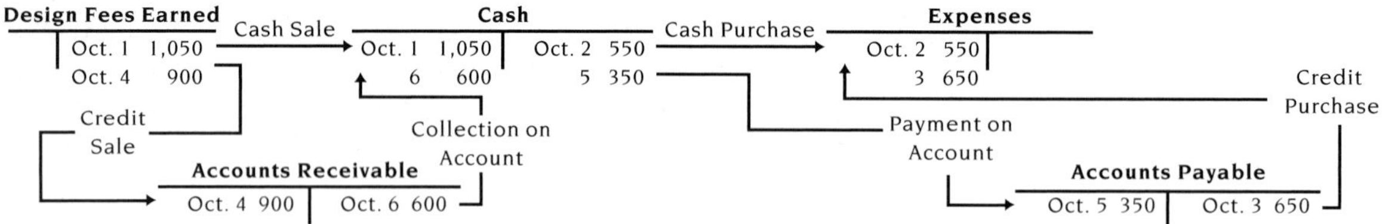

Cash balance after transactions: $1,050 + $600 − $550 − $350 = $750
Amount still to be received: $900 − $600 = $300
Amount still to be paid: $650 − $350 = $300

Recording and Posting Transactions

SO6 **Define the *chart of accounts*, record transactions in the general journal, and post transactions to the ledger.**

Earlier in the chapter, we described how transactions are analyzed according to the rules of double entry and how a trial balance is prepared. As Figure 4 shows, transaction analysis and preparation of a trial balance are the first and last steps in a four-step process. The two intermediate steps are recording the entry in the general journal and posting the entry to the ledger. In this section, we demonstrate how these steps are accomplished in a manual accounting system.

Chart of Accounts

In a manual accounting system, each account is kept on a separate page or card. These pages or cards are placed together in a book or file called the

FIGURE 4
Analyzing and Processing Transactions

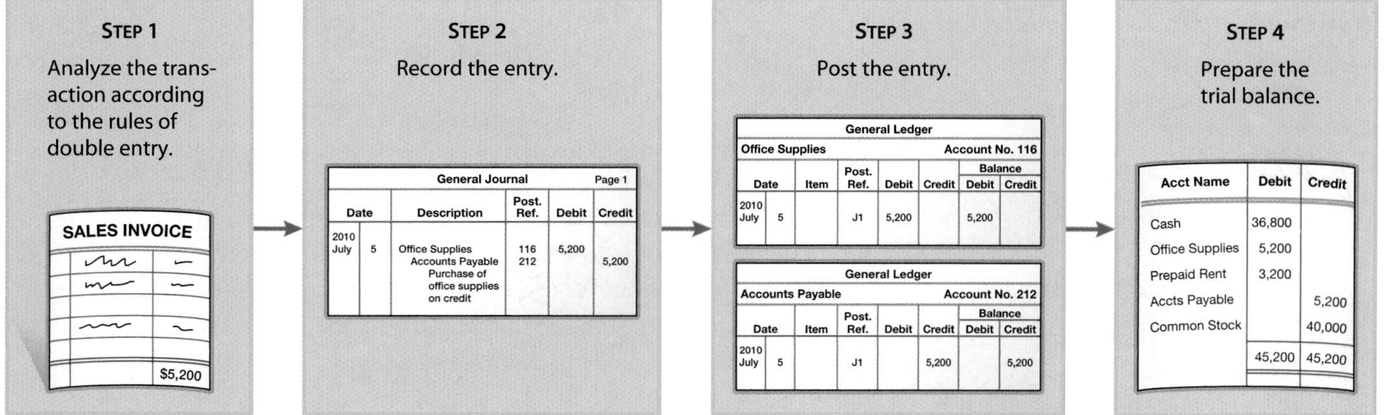

Study Note

A chart of accounts is a table of contents for the ledger. Typically, it lists accounts in the order in which they appear in the ledger, which is usually the order in which they appear on the financial statements. The numbering scheme allows for some flexibility.

general ledger. In the computerized systems that most companies have today, accounts are maintained electronically. However, as a matter of convenience, accountants still refer to the group of company accounts as the *general ledger*, or simply the *ledger*.

To help identify accounts in the ledger and make them easy to find, the accountant often numbers them. A list of these numbers with the corresponding account titles is called a **chart of accounts**. A very simple chart of accounts appears in Exhibit 3. The first digit in the account number identifies the major financial statement classification—that is, an account number that begins with the digit 1 means that the account is an asset account, an account number that begins with a 2 means that the account is a liability account, and so forth. The second and third digits identify individual accounts. The gaps in the sequence of numbers allow the accountant to expand the number of accounts.

General Journal

Study Note

The journal is a chronological record of events.

Although transactions can be entered directly into the ledger accounts, this method makes identifying individual transactions or finding errors very difficult because the debit is recorded in one account and the credit in another. The solution is to record all transactions chronologically in a **journal**. The journal is sometimes called the *book of original entry* because it is where transactions first enter the accounting records. Later, the debit and credit portions of each transaction are transferred to the appropriate accounts in the ledger. A separate **journal entry** is used to record each transaction; the process of recording transactions is called **journalizing**.

Most businesses have more than one kind of journal. The simplest and most flexible kind is the **general journal**, the one we focus on here. Businesses will also have several special-purpose journals, each for recording a common transaction, such as credit sales, credit purchases, cash receipts, and cash disbursements. At this point, we cover only the general journal. Exhibit 4, which displays two of the transactions of Miller Design Studio that we discussed earlier, shows the format for recording entries in a general journal. As you can see in Exhibit 4, the entries in a general journal include the following information about each transaction:

1. The date. The year appears on the first line of the first column, the month on the next line of the first column, and the day in the second column opposite the month. For subsequent entries on the same page for the same month and year, the month and year can be omitted.

EXHIBIT 3 Chart of Accounts for a Small Business

Account Number	Account Name	Description
		Assets
111	Cash	Money and any medium of exchange (coins, currency, checks, money orders, and money on deposit in a bank)
112	Notes Receivable	Promissory notes (written promises to pay definite sums of money at fixed future dates) due from others
113	Accounts Receivable	Amounts due from others for revenues or sales on credit (sales on account)
116	Office Supplies	Prepaid expense; office supplies purchased and not used
117	Prepaid Rent	Prepaid expense; rent paid in advance and not used
118	Prepaid Insurance	Prepaid expense; insurance purchased and not expired
141	Land	Property owned for use in the business
142	Buildings	Structures owned for use in the business
143	Accumulated Depreciation–Buildings	Periodic allocation of the cost of buildings to expense; deducted from Buildings
146	Office Equipment	Office equipment owned for use in the business
147	Accumulated Depreciation–Office Equipment	Periodic allocation of the cost of office equipment to expense; deducted from Office Equipment
		Liabilities
211	Notes Payable	Promissory notes due to others
212	Accounts Payable	Amounts due to others for purchases on credit
213	Unearned Design Revenue	Unearned revenue; advance deposits for website design to be provided in the future
214	Wages Payable	Amounts due to employees for wages earned and not paid
215	Income Taxes Payable	Amounts due to government for income taxes owed and not paid
		Stockholders' Equity
311	Common Stock	Stockholders' investments in a corporation for which they receive shares of stock
312	Retained Earnings	Stockholders' claims against company assets derived from profitable operations
313	Dividends	Distributions of assets (usually cash) that reduce retained earnings
314	Income Summary	Temporary account used at the end of the accounting period to summarize the revenues and expenses for the period
		Revenues
411	Design Revenue	Revenues derived from website design services
		Expenses
511	Wages Expense	Amounts earned by employees
512	Utilities Expense	Amounts for utilities, such as water, electricity, and gas, used
513	Telephone Expense	Amounts of telephone services used
514	Rent Expense	Amounts of rent on property and buildings used
515	Insurance Expense	Amounts for insurance expired
517	Office Supplies Expense	Amounts for office supplies used
518	Depreciation Expense–Buildings	Amount of buildings' cost allocated to expense
520	Depreciation Expense–Office Equipment	Amount of office equipment cost allocated to expense
521	Income Taxes Expense	Amount of tax on income

EXHIBIT 4
The General Journal

A	=	L	+ SE
+ 3,200			
− 3,200			

A	=	L	+ SE
+ 5,200		+ 5,200	

General Journal **Page 1**

Date		Description	Post. Ref.	Debit	Credit
2010					
July	3	Prepaid Rent		3,200	
		Cash			3,200
		Paid two months' rent in advance			
	5	Office Supplies		5,200	
		Accounts Payable			5,200
		Purchase of office supplies on credit			

2. The names of the accounts debited and credited, which appear in the Description column. The names of the accounts that are debited are placed next to the left margin opposite the dates; on the line below, the names of the accounts credited are indented.
3. The debit amounts, which appear in the Debit column opposite the accounts that are debited, and the credit amounts, which appear in the Credit column opposite the accounts credited.
4. An explanation of each transaction, which appears in the Description column below the account names. An explanation should be brief but sufficient to explain and identify the transaction.
5. The account numbers in the Post. Ref. column, if they apply.

At the time the transactions are recorded, nothing is placed in the Post. Ref. (posting reference) column. (This column is sometimes called LP or *Folio*.) Later, if the company uses account numbers to identify accounts in the ledger, the account numbers are filled in. They provide a convenient cross-reference from the general journal to the ledger and indicate that the entry has been posted to the ledger. If the accounts are not numbered, the accountant uses a checkmark (✓) to signify that the entry has been posted.

General Ledger

The general journal is used to record the details of each transaction. The general ledger is used to update each account.

Study Note

A T account is a means of quickly analyzing a set of transactions. It is simply an abbreviated version of a ledger account. Ledger accounts, which provide more information, are used in the accounting records.

The Ledger Account Form The T account is a simple, direct means of recording transactions. In practice, a somewhat more complicated form of the account is needed to record more information. The **ledger account form**, which contains four columns for dollar amounts, is illustrated in Exhibit 5.

The account title and number appear at the top of the account form. As in the journal, the transaction date appears in the first two columns. The Item column is rarely used to identify transactions because explanations already appear in the journal. The Post. Ref. column is used to note the journal page on which the original entry for the transaction can be found. The dollar amount is entered in the appropriate Debit or Credit column, and a new account balance is computed in the last two columns opposite each entry. The advantage of this account form over the T account is that the current balance of the account is readily available.

EXHIBIT 5

Accounts Payable in the General Ledger

General Ledger

Accounts Payable — **Account No. 212**

Date		Item	Post. Ref.	Debit	Credit	Balance Debit	Balance Credit
2010							
July	5		J1		5,200		5,200
	6		J1		3,000		8,200
	9		J1	2,600			5,600
	30		J2		680		6,280

Posting After transactions have been entered in the journal, they must be transferred to the ledger. The process of transferring journal entry information from the journal to the ledger is called **posting**. Posting is usually done after several entries have been made—for example, at the end of each day or less frequently, depending on the number of transactions. As Exhibit 6 shows, in posting, each amount in the Debit column of the journal is transferred to the Debit column of the appropriate

EXHIBIT 6

Posting from the General Journal to the Ledger

A = L + SE
+680 −680

General Journal — **Page 2**

Date		Description	Post. Ref.	Debit	Credit
2010					
July	30	Utilities Expense	512	680	
		Accounts Payable	212		680
		Received bill from utility company			

General Ledger

Accounts Payable — **Account No. 212**

Date		Item	Post. Ref.	Debit	Credit	Balance Debit	Balance Credit
2010							
July	5		J1		5,200		5,200
	6		J1		3,000		8,200
	9		J1	2,600			5,600
	30		J2		680		6,280

General Ledger

Utilities Expense — **Account No. 512**

Date		Item	Post. Ref.	Debit	Credit	Balance Debit	Balance Credit
2010							
July	30		J2	680		680	

account in the ledger, and each amount in the Credit column of the journal is transferred to the Credit column of the appropriate account in the ledger. The steps in the posting process are as follows:

1. In the ledger, locate the debit account named in the journal entry.
2. Enter the date of the transaction in the ledger and, in the Post. Ref. column, the journal page number from which the entry comes.
3. In the Debit column of the ledger account, enter the amount of the debit as it appears in the journal.
4. Calculate the account balance and enter it in the appropriate Balance column.
5. Enter in the Post. Ref. column of the journal the account number to which the amount has been posted.
6. Repeat the same five steps for the credit side of the journal entry.

Notice that step **5** is the last step in the posting process for each debit and credit. As noted earlier, in addition to serving as an easy reference between the journal entry and the ledger account, this entry in the Post. Ref. column of the journal indicates that the entry has been posted to the ledger.

Some Notes on Presentation

A ruled line appears in financial reports before each subtotal or total to indicate that the amounts above are added or subtracted. It is common practice to use a double line under a final total to show that it has been verified.

Dollar signs ($) are required in all financial statements and in the trial balance and other schedules. On these reports, a dollar sign should be placed before the first amount in each column and before the first amount in a column following a ruled line. Dollar signs in the same column are aligned. Dollar signs are not used in journals and ledgers.

On normal, unruled paper, commas and decimal points are used when recording dollar amounts. On the paper used in journals and ledgers, commas and decimal points are unnecessary because ruled columns are provided to properly align dollars and cents. Commas, dollar signs, and decimal points are also unnecessary in electronic spreadsheets. In this book, because most problems and illustrations are in whole dollar amounts, the cents column usually is omitted. When accountants deal with whole dollars, they often use a dash in the cents column to indicate whole dollars rather than taking the time to write zeros.

Account names are capitalized when referenced in text or listed in work documents like the journal or ledger. In financial statements, however, only the first word of an account name is capitalized.

STOP ▶ REVIEW ▶ APPLY

SO6-1 **List the following events in the order in which they occur in an accounting system:**

a. Analysis of the transaction

b. Posting of debits and credits from the journal to the ledger

(continued)

c. Occurrence of the transaction
d. Recording of an entry in the journal
e. Preparation of the trial balance

SO6-2 In recording entries in a journal, which is written first, the debit or the credit? How is indentation used in the journal?

SO6-3 What is the relationship between the journal and the ledger?

SO6-4 Indicate whether each of the following is more closely related to the journal, the ledger, or both:

a. Chart of accounts
b. Book of original entry
c. Post. Ref. column
d. Journalizing
e. Posting
f. Footings

A LOOK BACK AT ▶ THE BOEING COMPANY

The Decision Point at the beginning of the chapter described the order for 80 planes that the Chinese government placed with **Boeing**. It posed the following questions:

- **The order was obviously an important economic event for both the buyer and the seller. Is there a difference between an economic event and a business transaction that should be recorded in the accounting records?**
- **Should Boeing record the order in its accounting records?**
- **How important are liquidity and cash flows to Boeing?**

Despite its importance, the order did not constitute a business transaction, and neither the buyer nor the seller should have recognized it in its accounting records. At the time the Chinese government placed the order, Boeing had not yet built the planes. Until it delivers them and title to them shifts to the Chinese government, Boeing cannot record any revenue.

Even for "firm" orders like this one, Boeing cautions that "an economic downturn could result in airline equipment requirements less than currently anticipated resulting in requests to negotiate the rescheduling or possible cancellation of firm orders."[7] In fact, in the period following the 9/11 attacks on the World Trade Center and the war in Iraq, many airlines cancelled or renegotiated orders they had placed with Boeing. The ongoing energy crisis is also causing airlines to rethink their orders.

Because it takes almost two years to manufacture an airplane, Boeing must pay close attention to its liquidity and cash flows. One measure of liquidity is the **cash return on assets** ratio, which shows how productive assets are in generating cash flows from operations. In other words, it shows how much cash is generated by each dollar of assets invested in operations. This ratio is different from the return on assets ratio, a profitability measure that we introduced in Chapter 1. Using amounts (in millions) from Boeing's balance sheet and statement of cash flows in its annual report, we can calculate the company's cash return on assets as follows:[8]

		2007	2006
K/R Cash Return on Assets =	$\frac{\text{Net Cash Flows from Operating Activities}}{\text{Average Total Assets}}$	$\frac{\$9,584}{(\$58,986 + \$51,794) \div 2}$	$\frac{\$7,499}{(\$51,794 + \$59,996) \div 2}$
		$\frac{\$9,584}{\$55,390}$	$\frac{\$7,499}{\$55,895}$
		.173 (17.3%)	.134 (13.4%)

What do these results tell us? First, in 2007, each dollar of assets that Boeing invested in operations generated about 17.3¢, but that was better than the 13.4¢ generated a year earlier. Second, cash flows from operations increased from $7,499 million to $9,584 million, while average total assets decreased slightly from $55,895 to $55,390. This trend indicates a stronger cash-generating ability and reflects Boeing's dominant position in a growing global market for aircraft.

CHAPTER REVIEW

REVIEW of Learning Objectives

LO1 Explain how the concepts of recognition, valuation, and classification apply to business transactions and why they are important factors in ethical financial reporting.

To measure a business transaction, you must determine when the transaction occurred (the recognition issue), what value to place on the transaction (the valuation issue), and how the components of the transaction should be categorized (the classification issue). In general, recognition should occur when title passes, and a transaction should be valued at the exchange price—the fair value or cost at the time the transaction is recognized. Classification refers to assigning transactions to the appropriate accounts. Generally accepted accounting principles provide guidance about the treatment of these three basic measurement issues. Failure to follow these guidelines is a major reason some companies issue unethical financial statements.

LO2 Explain the double-entry system and the usefulness of T accounts in analyzing business transactions.

In the double-entry system, each transaction must be recorded with at least one debit and one credit, and the total amount of the debits must equal the total amount of the credits. Each asset, liability, and component of stockholders' equity, including revenues and expenses, has a separate account, which is a device for storing transaction data. The T account is a useful tool for quickly analyzing the effects of transactions. It shows how increases and decreases in assets, liabilities, and stockholders' equity are debited and credited to the appropriate accounts.

LO3 Demonstrate how the double-entry system is applied to common business transactions.

The double-entry system is applied by analyzing transactions to determine which accounts are affected and by using T accounts to show how the transactions affect the accounting equation. The transactions may be recorded in journal form with the date, debit account, and debit amount shown on one line, and the credit account (indented) and credit amount on the next line. The amounts are shown in their respective debit and credit columns.

LO4 Prepare a trial balance, and describe its value and limitations.

A trial balance is used to check that the debit and credit balances are equal. It is prepared by listing each account balance in the appropriate Debit or Credit column. The two columns are then added, and the totals are compared. The major limitation of a trial balance is that even when it shows that debit and credit balances are equal, it does not guarantee that the transactions were analyzed correctly or recorded in the proper accounts.

LO5 Show how the timing of transactions affects cash flows and liquidity.

Some transactions generate immediate cash. For those that do not, there is a holding period in either Accounts Receivable or Accounts Payable before the cash is received or paid. The timing of cash flows is critical to a company's ability to maintain adequate liquidity so that it can pay its bills on time.

Supplemental Objective

SO6 Define the *chart of accounts*, record transactions in the general journal, and post transactions to the ledger.

The chart of accounts is a list of account numbers and titles; it serves as a table of contents for the ledger. The general journal is a chronological record of all transactions; it contains the date of each transaction, the titles of the accounts involved, the amounts debited and credited, and an explanation of each entry. After transactions have been entered in the general journal, they are posted to the ledger. Posting is done by transferring the amounts in the Debit and Credit columns of the general journal to the Debit and Credit columns of the corresponding account in the ledger. After each entry is posted, a new balance is entered in the appropriate Balance column.

REVIEW of Concepts and Terminology

The following concepts and terms were introduced in this chapter:

Accounts: Basic units for accumulating and storing accounting data from similar transactions. **(LO2)**

Balance: The difference in dollars between the total debit footing and the total credit footing of an account. Also called *account balance.* **(LO2)**

Chart of accounts: A list of account numbers and titles that facilitates finding accounts in the ledger. **(SO6)**

Classification: The process of assigning transactions to the appropriate accounts. **(LO1)**

Compound entry: An entry that has more than one debit or credit entry. **(LO3)**

Cost principle: The practice of recording transactions at exchange price at the point of recognition. **(LO1)**

Credit: The right side of an account. **(LO2)**

Debit: The left side of an account. **(LO2)**

Double-entry system: The accounting system in which each transaction is recorded with at least one debit and one credit, so that the total amount of debits equals the total amount of credits. **(LO2)**

Fair Value: The *exchange price* of an actual or potential business transaction between market participants. **(LO1)**

Footings: Working totals of columns of numbers. To *foot* means to total a column of numbers. **(LO2)**

General journal: The simplest and most flexible type of journal. **(SO6)**

General ledger: A book or file that contains all of a company's accounts arranged in the order of the chart of accounts. Also called the *ledger*. **(SO6)**

Journal: A chronological record of all transactions; the place where transactions first enter the accounting records. Also called *book of original entry.* **(SO6)**

Journal entry: A journal notation that records a single transaction. **(SO6)**

Journal form: A way of recording a transaction in which the date, debit account, and debit amount appear on one line and the credit account and credit amount appear on the next line. **(LO3)**

Journalizing: The process of recording transactions in a journal. **(SO6)**

Ledger account form: An account form that has four dollar amount columns: one column for debit entries, one column for credit entries, and two columns (debit and credit) for showing the balance of the account. **(SO6)**

Normal balance: The usual balance of an account; the side (debit or credit) that increases the account. **(LO2)**

Posting: The process of transferring journal entry information from the journal to the ledger. **(SO6)**

Recognition: The determination of when a business transaction should be recorded. **(LO1)**

Recognition point: The predetermined time at which a transaction should be recorded; usually, the point at which title passes to the buyer. **(LO1)**

Source documents: Invoices, checks, receipts, or other documents that support a transaction. **(LO3)**

T account: The simplest form of account, which is used to analyze transactions. **(LO2)**

Trial balance: A comparison of the total of debit and credit balances in the accounts to check that they are equal. **(LO4)**

Valuation: The process of assigning a monetary value to a business transaction. **(LO1)**

Key Ratio

Cash return on assets: A ratio that shows how much cash is generated by each dollar of assets; Net Cash Flows from Operating Activities ÷ Average Total Assets.

REVIEW Problem

Transaction Analysis, T Accounts, Journalizing, and the Trial Balance

LO1 LO3 LO4 SO6

After completing yoga school, Tobias Raza started a private practice. The transactions of his company in July are as follows:

2010

July 1 Tobias Raza invested $4,000 in 4,000 shares of $1 par value common stock of his newly chartered company, Yoga Center, Inc.
3 Paid $600 in advance for two months' rent of an office.
9 Purchased supplies for $400 in cash.
12 Purchased $800 of equipment on credit; made a 25 percent down payment.
15 Gave a yoga lesson for a fee of $70 on credit.
18 Made a payment of $100 on the equipment purchased on July 12.
27 Paid a utility bill of $80.

Required

1. Record the company's transactions in journal form.
2. Post the transactions to the following T accounts: Cash, Accounts Receivable, Supplies, Prepaid Rent, Equipment, Accounts Payable, Common Stock, Yoga Fees Earned, and Utilities Expense.
3. Prepare a trial balance for the month of July.
4. How does the transaction of July 15 relate to recognition and cash flows? How do the transactions of July 9 and July 27 relate to classification?

Answer to Review Problem

1. Transactions recorded in journal form:

	A	B	C	D	E	F	G	H
1	July	1		Cash			4,000	
2					Common Stock			4,000
3						Issued 4,000 shares of $1 par		
4						value common stock		
5		3		Prepaid Rent			600	
6					Cash			600
7						Paid two months' rent in advance		
8						for a studio		
9		9		Supplies			400	
10					Cash			400
11						Purchased supplies for cash		
12		12		Equipment			800	
13					Accounts Payable			600
14					Cash			200
15						Purchased equipment on credit,		
16						paying 25 percent down		
17		15		Accounts Receivable			70	
18					Yoga Fees Earned			70
19						Fee on credit for private session		
20		18		Accounts Payable			100	
21					Cash			100
22						Partial payment for equipment		
23						purchsed July 12		
24		27		Utilities Expense			80	
25					Cash			80
26						Paid utility bill		
27								

2. Transactions posted to T accounts:

	A	B	C	D	E	F	G	H	I	J	K	L	M
1			Cash							Accounts Payable			
2	July	1	4,000	July	3	600		July	18	100	July	12	600
3					9	400					*Bal.*		*500*
4					12	200							
5					18	100				Common Stock			
6					27	80					July	1	4,000
7			*4,000*			*1,380*							
8	*Bal.*		*2,620*							Yoga Fees Earned			
9											July	15	70
10			Accounts Receivable										
11	July	15	70							Utilities Expense			
12								July	27	80			
13			Supplies										
14	July	9	400										
15													
16			Prepaid Rent										
17	July	3	600										
18													
19			Equipment										
20	July	12	800										
21													

3. Trial balance:

	A	B	C	D	E
1			**Yoga Center, Inc.**		
2			**Trial Balance**		
3			**July 31, 2010**		
4					
5	Cash			$2,620	
6	Accounts Receivable			70	
7	Supplies			400	
8	Prepaid Rent			600	
9	Equipment			800	
10	Accounts Payable				$ 500
11	Common Stock				4,000
12	Yoga Fees Earned				70
13	Utilities Expense			80	
14				$4,570	$4,570
15					

4. The transaction of July 15 is recorded, or recognized, on that date even though the company received no cash. The company earned the revenue by providing the service, and the customer accepted the service and now has an obligation to pay for it. The transaction is recorded as an account receivable because the company allowed the customer to pay for the service later. The transaction of July 9 is classified as an asset, Supplies, because these supplies will benefit the company in the future. The transaction of July 27 is classified as an expense, Utilities Expense, because the utilities have already been used and will not benefit the company in the future.

CHAPTER ASSIGNMENTS

BUILDING Your Basic Knowledge and Skills

Short Exercises

LO1

Recognition

SE 1. Which of the following events would be recognized and entered in the accounting records of Kazuo Corporation? Why?

Jan. 10 Kazuo Corporation places an order for office supplies.
Feb. 15 Kazuo Corporation receives the office supplies and a bill for them.
Mar. 1 Kazuo Corporation pays for the office supplies.

LO1 LO3

Recognition, Valuation, and Classification

SE 2. Tell how the concepts of recognition, valuation, and classification apply to this transaction:

Cash	
	June 1 1,000

Supplies	
June 1 1,000	

LO1

Classification of Accounts

SE 3. Tell whether each of the following accounts is an asset, a liability, a revenue, an expense, or none of these:

a. Accounts Payable
b. Supplies
c. Dividends
d. Fees Earned
e. Rent Expense
f. Accounts Receivable
g. Unearned Revenue
h. Equipment

LO2

Normal Balances

SE 4. Tell whether the normal balance of each account in **SE 3** is a debit or a credit.

LO3

Transaction Analysis

SE 5. For each transaction that follows, indicate which account is debited and which account is credited.

May 2 Leon Bear started a computer programming business, Bear's Programming Service, Inc., by investing $5,000 in exchange for common stock.
5 Purchased a computer for $2,500 in cash.
7 Purchased supplies on credit for $300.
19 Received cash for programming services performed, $500.
22 Received cash for programming services to be performed, $600.
25 Paid the rent for May, $650.
31 Billed a customer for programming services performed, $250.

LO3

Recording Transactions in T Accounts

SE 6. Set up T accounts and record each transaction in **SE 5**. Determine the balance of each account.

LO4

Preparing a Trial Balance

SE 7. From the T accounts created in **SE 6**, prepare a trial balance dated May 31, 2010.

LO5

Timing and Cash Flows

SE 8. Use the T account for Cash below to record the portion of each of the following transactions, if any, that affect cash. How do these transactions affect the company's liquidity?

CASH	

Jan. 2 Provided services for cash, $1,200
4 Paid expenses in cash, $700
8 Provided services on credit, $1,100
9 Incurred expenses on credit, $800

SO6

Recording Transactions in the General Journal

SE 9. Prepare a general journal form like the one in Exhibit 4 and label it Page 4. Record the following transactions in the journal:

Sept. 6 Billed a customer for services performed, $3,800.
16 Received partial payment from the customer billed on Sept. 6, $1,800.

SO6

Posting to the Ledger Accounts

SE 10. Prepare ledger account forms like the ones in Exhibit 5 for the following accounts: Cash (111), Accounts Receivable (113), and Service Revenue (411). Post the transactions that are recorded in **SE 9** to the ledger accounts, at the same time making the proper posting references. Also prepare a trial balance.

SO6

Recording Transactions in the General Journal

SE 11. Record the transactions in **SE 5** in the general journal.

K/R

Cash Return on Assets

SE 12. Calculate cash return on assets for 2010 using the following data: A company has net cash flows from operating activities of $1,500 in 2010, beginning total assets of $13,000, and ending total assets of $14,000.

Exercises

LO1 LO2 LO3

Discussion Questions

E 1. Develop a brief answer to each of the following questions.

1. Which is the most important issue in recording a transaction: recognition, valuation, or classification?
2. What is an example of how a company could make false financial statements through a violation of the recognition concept?
3. How are assets and expenses related, and why are the debit and credit effects for assets and expenses the same?
4. In what way are unearned revenues the opposite of prepaid expenses?

SO6

Discussion Questions

E 2. Develop a brief answer to each of the following questions.

1. Which account would be most likely to have an account balance that is not normal?
2. A company incurs a cost for a part that is needed to repair a piece of equipment. Is the cost an asset or an expense? Explain.
3. If a company's cash flows for expenses temporarily exceed its cash flows from revenues, how might it make up the difference so that it can maintain liquidity?
4. How would the asset accounts in the chart of accounts for Miller Design Studio, Inc., differ if it were a retail company that sold advertising products instead of a service company that designs ads?

LO1

Recognition

E 3. Which of the following events would be recognized and recorded in the accounting records of Villa Corporation on the date indicated?

Jan. 15	Villa Corporation offers to purchase a tract of land for $140,000. There is a high likelihood that the offer will be accepted.
Feb. 2	Villa Corporation receives notice that its rent will increase from $500 to $600 per month effective March 1.
Mar. 29	Villa Corporation receives its utility bill for the month of March. The bill is not due until April 9.
June 10	Villa Corporation places an order for new office equipment costing $21,000.
July 6	The office equipment Villa Corporation ordered on June 10 arrives. Payment is not due until August 1.

LO1

Application of Recognition Point

E 4. Torez Flower Shop, Inc., uses a large amount of supplies in its business. The following table summarizes selected transaction data for supplies that Torez Flower Shop purchased:

Order	Date Shipped	Date Received	Amount
a	June 26	July 5	$300
b	July 10	15	750
c	16	22	450
d	23	30	600
e	27	Aug. 1	700
f	Aug. 3	7	500

Determine the total purchases of supplies for July alone under each of the following assumptions:

1. Torez Flower Shop, Inc., recognizes purchases when orders are shipped.
2. Torez Flower Shop, Inc., recognizes purchases when orders are received.

LO2

T Accounts, Normal Balance, and the Accounting Equation

E 5. You are given the following list of accounts with dollar amounts:

Rent Expense	$ 450
Cash	1,725
Service Revenue	750
Retained Earnings	300
Dividends	375
Accounts Payable	600
Common Stock	900

Insert each account name at the top of its corresponding T account and enter the dollar amount as a normal balance in the account. Then show that the accounting equation is in balance.

Stockholders' Equity

Assets = Liabilities + Common Stock + Retained Earnings − Dividends + Revenues − Expenses

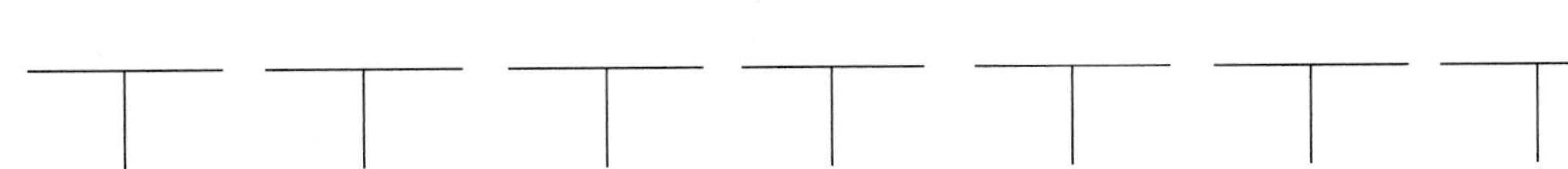

LO2 **Classification of Accounts**

E 6. The following ledger accounts are for the Tuner Service Corporation:

a. Cash
b. Wages Expense
c. Accounts Receivable
d. Common Stock
e. Service Revenue
f. Prepaid Rent
g. Accounts Payable
h. Investments in Securities
i. Income Taxes Payable
j. Income Taxes Expense
k. Land
l. Advertising Expense
m. Prepaid Insurance
n. Utilities Expense
o. Fees Earned
p. Dividends
q. Wages Payable
r. Unearned Revenue
s. Office Equipment
t. Rent Payable
u. Notes Receivable
v. Interest Expense
w. Notes Payable
x. Supplies
y. Interest Receivable
z. Rent Expense

Complete the following table, using X's to indicate each account's classification and normal balance (whether a debit or a credit increases the account).

	Type of Account						Normal Balance (increases balance)	
			Stockholders' Equity					
			Common	Retained Earnings				
Item	**Asset**	**Liability**	**Stock**	**Dividends**	**Revenue**	**Expense**	**Debit**	**Credit**
a.	X						X	

LO3 **Transaction Analysis**

E 7. Analyze transactions **a–g**, using the example that follows.

a. Sarah Lopez established Sarah's Beauty Parlor, Inc., by incorporating and investing $2,500 in exchange for 250 shares of $10 par value common stock.
b. Paid two months' rent in advance, $1,680.
c. Purchased supplies on credit, $120.
d. Received cash for barbering services, $700.
e. Paid for supplies purchased in **c**.
f. Paid utility bill, $72.
g. Declared and paid a dividend of $100.

Example:

a. The asset account Cash was increased. Increases in assets are recorded by debits. Debit Cash $2,500. A component of stockholders' equity, Common Stock, was increased. Increases in stockholders' equity are recorded by credits. Credit Common Stock $2,500.

LO3 **Transaction Analysis**

E 8. The following accounts are applicable to Dale's Lawn Service, Inc., a company that maintains condominium grounds:

1. Cash
2. Accounts Receivable
3. Supplies
4. Equipment
5. Accounts Payable
6. Lawn Services Revenue
7. Wages Expense
8. Rent Expense

Dale's Lawn Service, Inc., completed the following transactions:

	Debit	Credit
a. Paid for supplies purchased on credit last month.	5	1
b. Received cash from customers billed last month.		
c. Made a payment on accounts payable.		
d. Purchased supplies on credit.		
e. Billed a client for lawn services.		
f. Made a rent payment for the current month.		
g. Received cash from customers for current lawn services.		
h. Paid employee wages.		
i. Ordered equipment.		
j. Received and paid for the equipment ordered in **i**.		

Analyze each transaction and show the accounts affected by entering the corresponding numbers in the appropriate debit or credit columns as shown in transaction **a**. Indicate no entry, if appropriate.

LO3 **Recording Transactions in T Accounts**

E 9. Open the following T accounts: Cash; Repair Supplies; Repair Equipment; Accounts Payable; Common Stock; Dividends; Repair Fees Earned; Salaries Expense; and Rent Expense. Record the following transactions for the month of June directly in the T accounts; use the letters to identify the transactions in your T accounts. Determine the balance in each account.

a. Tony Ornega opened Ornega Repair Service, Inc., by investing $4,300 in cash and $1,600 in repair equipment in return for 5,900 shares of the company's $1 par value common stock.
b. Paid $800 for the current month's rent.
c. Purchased repair supplies on credit, $1,100.
d. Purchased additional repair equipment for cash, $600.
e. Paid salary to a helper, $900.
f. Paid $400 of amount purchased on credit in **c**.
g. Accepted cash for repairs completed, $3,720.
h. Declared and paid a dividend of $1,000.

LO4 **Trial Balance**

E 10. After recording the transactions in **E 9**, prepare a trial balance in proper sequence for Ornega Repair Service, Inc., as of June 30, 2010.

LO3 **Analysis of Transactions**

E 11. Explain each transaction (**a–h**) entered in the following T accounts:

Cash			
a.	20,000	b.	7,500
g.	750	e.	1,800
h.	450	f.	2,250

Accounts Receivable			
c.	4,000	g.	750

Equipment			
b.	7,500	h.	450
d.	4,500		

Accounts Payable			
f.	2,250	d.	4,500

Common Stock			
		a.	20,000

Service Revenue			
		c.	4,000

Wages Expense			
e.	1,800		

LO4 **Preparing a Trial Balance**

E 12. The list that follows presents the accounts (in alphabetical order) of the Dymarski Corporation as of March 31, 2010. The list does not include the amount of Accounts Payable.

Accounts Payable	?
Accounts Receivable	$ 2,800
Building	20,400
Cash	5,400
Common Stock	12,000
Equipment	7,200
Land	3,120
Notes Payable	10,000
Prepaid Insurance	660
Retained Earnings	6,870

Prepare a trial balance with the proper heading (see Exhibit 2) and with the accounts listed in the chart of accounts sequence (see Exhibit 3). Compute the balance of Accounts Payable.

LO4 **Effects of Errors on a Trial Balance**

E 13. Which of the following errors would cause a trial balance to have unequal totals? Explain your answers.

a. A payment to a creditor was recorded as a debit to Accounts Payable for $129 and as a credit to Cash for $102.
b. A payment of $150 to a creditor for an account payable was debited to Accounts Receivable and credited to Cash.
c. A purchase of office supplies of $420 was recorded as a debit to Office Supplies for $42 and as a credit to Cash for $42.
d. A purchase of equipment for $450 was recorded as a debit to Supplies for $450 and as a credit to Cash for $450.

LO4 **Correcting Errors in a Trial Balance**

E 14. The trial balance for Marek Services, Inc., at the end of July appears at the top of the next page. It does not balance because of a number of errors. Marek's accountant compared the amounts in the trial balance with the ledger, recomputed the account balances, and compared the postings. He found the following errors:

a. The balance of Cash was understated by $800.
b. A cash payment of $420 was credited to Cash for $240.
c. A debit of $120 to Accounts Receivable was not posted.
d. Supplies purchased for $60 were posted as a credit to Supplies.
e. A debit of $180 to Prepaid Insurance was not posted.

Marek Services, Inc.
Trial Balance
July 31, 2010

Cash	$ 3,440	
Accounts Receivable	5,660	
Supplies	120	
Prepaid Insurance	180	
Equipment	7,400	
Accounts Payable		$ 4,540
Common Stock		3,000
Retained Earnings		7,560
Dividends		700
Revenues		5,920
Salaries Expense	2,600	
Rent Expense	600	
Advertising Expense	340	
Utilities Expense	26	
	$20,366	$21,720

f. The Accounts Payable account had debits of $5,320 and credits of $9,180.
g. The Notes Payable account, with a credit balance of $2,400, was not included on the trial balance.
h. The debit balance of Dividends was listed in the trial balance as a credit.
i. A $200 debit to Dividends was posted as a credit.
j. The actual balance of Utilities Expense, $260, was listed as $26 in the trial balance.

Prepare a corrected trial balance.

LO5

Cash Flow Analysis

E 15. A company engaged in the following transactions:

Dec. 1 Performed services for cash, $750
1 Paid expenses in cash, $550
2 Performed services on credit, $900
3 Collected on account, $600
4 Incurred expenses on credit, $650
5 Paid on account, $350

Enter the correct titles on the following T accounts and enter the above transactions in the accounts. Determine the cash balance after these transactions, the amount still to be received, and the amount still to be paid.

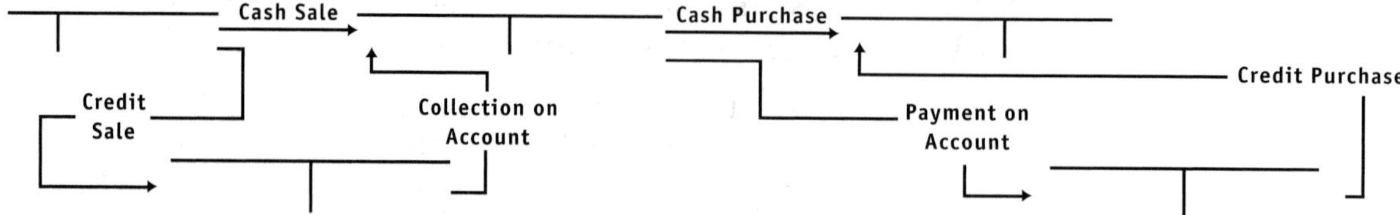

SO6

Recording Transactions in the General Journal

E 16. Record the transactions in **E 9** in the general journal.

LO3 SO6

Analysis of Unfamiliar Transactions

E 17. Managers and accountants often encounter transactions with which they are unfamiliar. Use your analytical skills to analyze and record in journal form the following transactions, which have not yet been discussed in the text.

May 1	Purchased merchandise inventory on account, $1,200.
2	Purchased marketable securities for cash, $3,000.
3	Returned part of merchandise inventory for full credit, $250.
4	Sold merchandise inventory on account, $800 (record sale only).
5	Purchased land and a building for $300,000. Payment is $60,000 cash, and there is a 30-year mortgage for the remainder. The purchase price is allocated as follows: $100,000 to the land and $200,000 to the building.
6	Received an order for $12,000 in services to be provided. With the order was a deposit of $3,500.

SO6

Recording Transactions in the General Journal and Posting to the Ledger Accounts

E 18. Open a general journal form like the one in Exhibit 4, and label it Page 10. After opening the form, record the following transactions in the journal:

Dec. 14	Purchased equipment for $6,000, paying $2,000 as a cash down payment.
28	Paid $3,000 of the amount owed on the equipment.

Prepare three ledger account forms like the one shown in Exhibit 5. Use the following account numbers: Cash, 111; Equipment, 144; and Accounts Payable, 212. Post the two transactions from the general journal to the ledger accounts, being sure to make proper posting references. The Cash account has a debit balance of $8,000 on the day prior to the first transaction.

Cash Return on Assets

E 19. Waksal Company wants to know if its liquidity performance has improved. Calculate cash return on assets for 2009 and 2010 using the following data:

Net cash flows from operating activities, 2009	$ 4,300
Net cash flows from operating activities, 2010	5,000
Total assets, 2008	36,000
Total assets, 2009	40,000
Total assets, 2010	46,000

By this measure has liquidity improved? Why is it important to use average total assets in the calculation?

Problems

T Accounts, Normal Balance, and the Accounting Equation

P 1. Delux Design Corporation creates radio and television advertising for local businesses in the twin cities. The following alphabetical list shows Delux Design's account balances as of January 31, 2010:

Accounts Payable	$ 3,210	Loans Payable	$ 5,000
Accounts Receivable	39,000	Rent Expense	5,940
Cash	9,200	Retained Earnings	22,000
Common Stock	15,000	Telephone Expense	480
Design Revenue	105,000	Unearned Revenue	9,000
Dividends	18,000	Wages Expense	62,000
Equipment	?		

Required

Insert the account title at the top of its corresponding T account and enter the dollar amount as a normal balance in the account. Determine the balance of Equipment and then show that the accounting equation is in balance.

Stockholders' Equity

Assets = Liabilities + Common Stock + Retained Earnings − Dividends + Revenues − Expenses

LO3

Transaction Analysis

P 2. The following accounts are applicable to Tom's Chimney Sweeps, Inc.:

1. Cash
2. Accounts Receivable
3. Supplies
4. Prepaid Insurance
5. Equipment
6. Notes Payable
7. Accounts Payable
8. Common Stock
9. Retained Earnings
10. Dividends
11. Service Revenue
12. Rent Expense
13. Repair Expense

Tom's Chimney Sweeps, Inc., completed the following transactions:

	Debit	Credit
a. Paid for supplies purchased on credit last month.	7	1
b. Billed customers for services performed.		
c. Paid the current month's rent.		
d. Purchased supplies on credit.		
e. Received cash from customers for services performed but not yet billed.		
f. Purchased equipment on account.		
g. Received a bill for repairs.		
h. Returned part of equipment purchased in **f** for a credit.		
i. Received payments from customers previously billed.		
j. Paid the bill received in **g**.		
k. Received an order for services to be performed.		
l. Paid for repairs with cash.		
m. Made a payment to reduce the principal of the note payable.		
n. Declared and paid a dividend.		

Required

Analyze each transaction and show the accounts affected by entering the corresponding numbers in the appropriate debit or credit column as shown in transaction **a**. Indicate no entry, if appropriate.

LO3 LO4 LO5

Transaction Analysis, T Accounts, and Trial Balance

P 3. Carmen Dahlen opened a secretarial school called Star Secretarial Training, Inc.

a. Dahlen contributed the following assets to the business in exchange for 14,300 shares of $1 par value common stock:

Cash	$5,700
Computers	5,000
Office Equipment	3,600

b. Found a location for the business and paid the first month's rent, $260.
c. Paid for an advertisement announcing the opening of the school, $190.
d. Received applications from three students for a four-week secretarial program and two students for a ten-day keyboarding course. The students will be billed a total of $1,300.
e. Purchased supplies on credit, $330.
f. Billed the enrolled students, $2,040.
g. Purchased a second-hand computer, $480, and office equipment, $380, on credit.
h. Paid for the supplies purchased on credit in **e**, $330.
i. Paid cash to repair a broken computer, $40.
j. Received partial payment from students previously billed, $1,380.
k. Paid the utility bill for the current month, $90.
l. Paid an assistant one week's salary, $440.
m. Declared and paid a dividend of $300.

Required

1. Set up the following T accounts: Cash; Accounts Receivable; Supplies; Computers; Office Equipment; Accounts Payable; Common Stock; Dividends; Tuition Revenue; Salaries Expense; Utilities Expense; Rent Expense; Repair Expense; and Advertising Expense.
2. Record the transactions directly in the T accounts, using the transaction letter to identify each debit and credit.
3. Prepare a trial balance using today's date.
4. **User insight ▶** Examine transactions **f** and **j**. What were the revenues and how much cash was received from the revenues? What business issues might you see arising from the differences in these numbers?

LO1 LO3 LO4

Transaction Analysis, Journal Form, T Accounts, and Trial Balance

P 4. Melvin Patel bid for and won a concession to rent bicycles in the local park during the summer. During the month of June, Patel completed the following transactions for his bicycle rental business:

June	2	Began business by placing $7,200 in a business checking account in the name of the corporation in exchange for 7,200 shares of $1 par value common stock.
	3	Purchased supplies on account for $150.
	4	Purchased 10 bicycles for $2,500, paying $1,200 down and agreeing to pay the rest in 30 days.
	5	Paid $2,900 in cash for a small shed to store the bicycles and to use for other operations.
	8	Paid $400 in cash for shipping and installation costs (considered an addition to the cost of the shed) to place the shed at the park entrance.
	9	Hired a part-time assistant to help out on weekends at $7 per hour.

June 10 Paid a maintenance person $75 to clean the grounds.
13 Received $970 in cash for rentals.
17 Paid $150 for the supplies purchased on June 3.
18 Paid a $55 repair bill on bicycles.
23 Billed a company $110 for bicycle rentals for an employee outing.
25 Paid the $100 fee for June to the Park District for the right to operate the bicycle concession.
27 Received $960 in cash for rentals.
29 Paid the assistant wages of $240.
30 Declared and paid a dividend of $500.

Required

1. Prepare entries to record these transactions in journal form.
2. Set up the following T accounts and post all the journal entries: Cash; Accounts Receivable; Supplies; Shed; Bicycles; Accounts Payable; Common Stock; Dividends; Rental Revenue; Wages Expense; Maintenance Expense; Repair Expense; and Concession Fee Expense.
3. Prepare a trial balance for Patel Rentals, Inc., as of June 30, 2010.

User insight ▶

4. Compare and contrast how the issues of recognition, valuation, and classification are settled in the transactions of June 3 and 10.

LO3 LO4 LO5 SO6

Transaction Analysis, General Journal, Ledger Accounts, and Trial Balance

P 5. Alpha Pro Corporation is a marketing firm. The company's trial balance on July 31, 2010, appears below. During the month of August, the company completed the following transactions:

Aug. 2 Paid rent for August, $650.
3 Received cash from customers on account, $2,300.
7 Ordered supplies, $380.
10 Billed customers for services provided, $2,800.
12 Made a payment on accounts payable, $1,300.
14 Received the supplies ordered on August 7 and agreed to pay for them in 30 days, $380.
17 Discovered some of the supplies were not as ordered and returned them for full credit, $80.
19 Received cash from a customer for services provided, $4,800.
24 Paid the utility bill for August, $250.
26 Received a bill, to be paid in September, for advertisements placed in the local newspaper during the month of August to promote Alpha Pro Corporation, $700.

Alpha Pro Corporation
Trial Balance
July 31, 2010

Cash (111)	$10,590	
Accounts Receivable (113)	5,500	
Supplies (115)	610	
Office Equipment (141)	4,200	
Accounts Payable (212)		$ 2,600
Common Stock (311)		12,000
Retained Earnings (312)		6,300
	$20,900	$20,900

Aug. 29 Billed a customer for services provided, $2,700.
30 Paid salaries for August, $3,800.
31 Declared and paid a dividend of $1,200.

Required

1. Open accounts in the ledger for the accounts in the trial balance plus the following accounts: Dividends (313); Marketing Fees (411); Salaries Expense (511); Rent Expense (512); Utilities Expense (513); and Advertising Expense (515).
2. Enter the July 31, 2010, account balances from the trial balance.
3. Enter the above transactions in the general journal (Pages 22 and 23).
4. Post the journal entries to the ledger accounts. Be sure to make the appropriate posting references in the journal and ledger as you post.
5. Prepare a trial balance as of August 31, 2010.

User insight ▶

6. Examine the transactions for August 3, 10, 19, and 29. How much were revenues and how much cash was received from the revenues? What business issues might you see arising from the differences in these numbers?

Alternate Problems

LO2

T Accounts, Normal Balance, and the Accounting Equation

P 6. The Stewart Construction Corporation builds foundations for buildings and parking lots. The following alphabetical list shows Stewart Construction's account balances as of April 30, 2010:

Accounts Payable	$ 1,950	Retained Earnings	$5,000
Accounts Receivable	5,060	Revenue Earned	8,700
Cash	?	Supplies	3,250
Common Stock	15,000	Rent Expense	3,600
Dividends	3,500	Utilities Expense	210
Equipment	13,750	Wages Expense	4,400
Notes Payable	10,000		

Required

Insert the account at the top of its corresponding T account and enter the dollar amount as a normal balance in the account. Determine the balance of cash and then show that the accounting equation is in balance.

Stockholders' Equity

Assets = Liabilities + Common Stock + Retained Earnings − Dividends + Revenues − Expenses

Transaction Analysis, T Accounts, and Trial Balance

P 7. Brad Cupello began an upholstery cleaning business on October 1 and engaged in the following transactions during the month:

Oct.	1	Began business by depositing $15,000 in a bank account in the name of the corporation in exchange for 15,000 shares of $1 par value common stock.
	2	Ordered cleaning supplies, $3,000.
	3	Purchased cleaning equipment for cash, $2,800.
	4	Made two months' van lease payment in advance, $1,200.
	7	Received the cleaning supplies ordered on October 2 and agreed to pay half the amount in 10 days and the rest in 30 days.
	9	Paid for repairs on the van with cash, $1,080.
	12	Received cash for cleaning upholstery, $960.
	17	Paid half the amount owed on supplies purchased on October 7, $1,500.
	21	Billed customers for cleaning upholstery, $1,340.
	24	Paid cash for additional repairs on the van, $80.
	27	Received $600 from the customers billed on October 21.
	31	Declared and paid a dividend of $700.

Required

1. Set up the following T accounts: Cash; Accounts Receivable; Cleaning Supplies; Prepaid Lease; Cleaning Equipment; Accounts Payable; Common Stock; Dividends; Cleaning Revenue; and Repair Expense.
2. Record transactions directly in the T accounts. Identify each entry by date.
3. Prepare a trial balance for Cupello Upholstery Cleaning, Inc., as of October 31, 2010.

User insight ▶

4. Compare and contrast how the issues of recognition, valuation, and classification are settled in the transactions of October 7 and 9.

Transaction Analysis, General Journal, Ledger Accounts, and Trial Balance

P 8. The Golden Nursery School Corporation provides baby-sitting and child-care programs. On January 31, 2010, the company had the following trial balance:

Golden Nursery School Corporation
Trial Balance
January 31, 2010

Cash (111)	$ 2,070	
Accounts Receivable (113)	1,700	
Equipment (141)	1,040	
Buses (143)	17,400	
Notes Payable (211)		$15,000
Accounts Payable (212)		1,640
Common Stock (311)		4,000
Retained Earnings (312)		1,570
	$22,210	$22,210

During the month of February, the company completed the following transactions:

Feb.	2	Paid this month's rent, $400.
	3	Received fees for this month's services, $650.
	4	Purchased supplies on account, $85.
	5	Reimbursed the bus driver for gas expenses, $40.
	6	Ordered playground equipment, $1,000.
	8	Made a payment on account, $170.
	9	Received payments from customers on account, $1,200.
	10	Billed customers who had not yet paid for this month's services, $700.
	11	Paid for the supplies purchased on February 4.
	13	Received and paid cash for playground equipment ordered on February 6, $1,000.
	17	Purchased equipment on account, $290.
	19	Paid this month's utility bill, $145.
	22	Received payment for one month's services from customers previously billed, $500.
	26	Paid part-time assistants for services, $460.
	27	Purchased gas and oil for the bus on account, $325.
	28	Declared and paid a dividend of $200.

Required

1. Open accounts in the ledger for the accounts in the trial balance plus the following ones: Supplies (115); Dividends (313); Service Revenue (411); Rent Expense (511); Gas and Oil Expense (512); Wages Expense (513); and Utilities Expense (514).
2. Enter the January 31, 2010, account balances from the trial balance.
3. Enter the above transactions in the general journal (Pages 17 and 18).
4. Post the entries to the ledger accounts. Be sure to make the appropriate posting references in the journal and ledger as you post.
5. Prepare a trial balance as of February 28, 2010.

User insight ▶

6. Examine the transactions for February 3, 9, 10, and 22. What were the revenues and how much cash was received from the revenues? What business issue might you see arising from the differences in these numbers?

ENHANCING Your Knowledge, Skills, and Critical Thinking

Conceptual Understanding Cases

LO1 LO3

Valuation and Classification of Business Transactions

C1. Tower Garden Center has purchased two pre-owned trucks for delivery of plants and flowers to its customers. The trucks were purchased at a cash-only auction for 15 percent below current market value. The owners have asked you to record these trucks in the financial records at current market value. You don't think that is correct. In response to the owners, write a brief business memorandum in good form based on your knowledge of Chapter 2. Explain how the purchase of the pre-owned trucks will affect the balance sheet, include the entry to record the transaction, and explain why the amount must be at the price paid for the trucks.

LO3

Recording of Rebates

C 2. Is it revenue or a reduction of an expense? That is the question companies that receive manufacturer's rebates for purchasing a large quantity of product must answer. Food companies like **Sara Lee, Kraft Foods,** and **Nestlé** give supermarkets special manufacturer's rebates of up to 45 percent, depending on the quantities purchased. Some firms were recording these rebates as revenue, whereas others were recording them as a reduction of the cost until the SEC said that only one way is correct. What, then, is the correct way for supermarkets to record these rebates? Would your answer change net income?

Interpreting Financial Reports

LO2 LO3

Interpreting a Bank's Financial Statements

C 3. Mellon Bank is a large bank holding company. Selected accounts from the company's 2006 annual report are as follows (in millions):[9]

Cash and Due from Banks	$ 2,840	Securities Available for Sale	$19,377
Loans to Customers	37,506	Deposits by Customers	62,146

1. Indicate whether each of the accounts just listed is an asset, a liability, or a component of stockholders' equity on Mellon Bank's balance sheet.
2. Assume that you are in a position to do business with this large company. Show how Mellon Bank's accountants would prepare the entry in T account form to record each of the following transactions:
   a. You sell securities in the amount of $2,000 to the bank.
   b. You deposit in the bank the $2,000 received from selling the securities.
   c. You borrow $5,000 from the bank.

Cash Flows

C 4. You have been promoted recently and now have access to the firm's monthly financial statements. Business is good. Revenues are increasing rapidly, and income is at an all-time high. The balance sheet shows growth in receivables, and accounts payable have declined. However, the chief financial officer is concerned about the firm's cash flows from operating activities because they are decreasing. What are some reasons why a company with a positive net income may fall short of cash from its operating activities? What could be done to improve this situation?

Decision Analysis Using Excel

LO2 LO3 LO4

Transaction Analysis and Evaluation of a Trial Balance

C 5. Irena Takla hired an attorney to help her start Takla Delivery Service Corporation. On March 1, Takla deposited $14,375 cash in a bank account in the name of the corporation in exchange for 575 shares of $25 par value common stock. When she paid the attorney's bill of $875, the attorney advised her to hire an accountant to keep her records. Takla was so busy that it was March 31 before she hired you to straighten out her records. Your first task is to develop a trial balance based on the March transactions, which are described above and in the next two paragraphs.

After investing in her business and paying her attorney, Takla borrowed $6,250 from the bank. She later paid $325, including interest of $75, on this loan. She also purchased a used pickup truck in the company's name, paying $3,125 down and financing $9,250. The first payment on the truck is due April 15. Takla then rented an office and paid three months' rent, $1,125, in advance. Credit purchases of office equipment of $1,000 and material handling equipment of $625 must be paid by April 10.

In March, Takla Delivery Service completed deliveries of $1,625, of which $500 were cash transactions. Of the credit transactions, $375 were collected during March, and $750 remained to be collected at the end of March. The company paid wages of $562 to its employees. On March 31, the company received a $93 bill for the March utilities expense and a $62 check from a customer for deliveries to be made in April. A customer requested a delivery on March 31 for the following week and agreed to pay $250. Takla is considering recording this agreement as revenue in March to make the business look better.

1. Record all of the transactions for March in journal form. Label each of the entries alphabetically.
2. Set up T accounts. Then post the entries to the T accounts. Identify each posting with the letter corresponding to the transaction.
3. Determine the balance of each account.
4. Prepare a trial balance for Takla Delivery Service Corporation as of March 31, 2010.
5. Irena Takla is unsure how to evaluate the trial balance. The Cash account balance is $15,550, which exceeds the original investment of $14,375 by $1,175. Did the company make a profit of $1,175? Explain why the Cash account is not an indicator of business earnings. Cite specific examples to show why it is difficult to determine net income by looking solely at figures in the trial balance.
6. What are the ethical implications of recording the delivery order received on March 31 as revenue in March?

Annual Report Case: CVS Caremark Corporation

LO1 Recognition, Valuation, and Classification

C 6. Refer to the Summary of Significant Accounting Policies in the notes to the financial statements in the **CVS** annual report in the Supplement to Chapter 1 to answer these questions:

1. How does the concept of recognition apply to advertising costs?
2. How does the concept of valuation apply to inventories?
3. How does the concept of classification apply to cash and cash equivalents?

Comparison Analysis: CVS Versus Southwest

Cash Return on Assets

C 7. Refer to the financial statements of **CVS** and **Southwest Airlines Co.** in the Supplement to Chapter 1. Compute cash return on assets for the past two years for both companies and comment on the results. Total assets in fiscal 2005 were $15,283.4 million for CVS and $14,003 million for Southwest.

Ethical Dilemma Case

LO1 Recognition Point and Ethical Considerations

C 8. Robert Shah, a sales representative for Quality Office Supplies Corporation, is compensated on a commission basis and received a substantial bonus for meeting his annual sales goal. The company's recognition point for sales is the day of shipment. On December 31, Shah realizes he needs sales of $2,000 to reach his sales goal and receive the bonus. He calls a purchaser for a local insurance company, whom he knows well, and asks him to buy $2,000 worth of copier paper today. The purchaser says, "But Jerry, that's more than a year's supply for us." Shah says, "Buy it today. If you decide it's too much, you can return however much you want for full credit next month." The purchaser says, "Okay, ship it." The paper is shipped on December 31 and recorded as a sale. On January 15, the purchaser returns $1,750 worth of paper for full credit (approved by Shah) against the bill. Should the shipment on December 31 be recorded as a sale? Discuss the ethics of Shah's action.

Internet Case

LO1

Financial Measurement Concepts

C 9. Go to the website of any major company. Find the "Investor Relations" or "About Our Company" section and access either the company's annual report or its Form 10-K Annual Report to the Securities and Exchange Commission (SEC). Find the financial statements and look at the notes that follow the financial statements. The first note should relate to significant accounting policies. Find an example of an accounting policy that is an application of each of the following financial measurement concepts: recognition, valuation, and classification. Write a brief report of your findings and be prepared to discuss them in class.

Group Activity Case

LO1 LO3

Valuation and Classification Issues for Dot-Coms

C 10. The dot-com business has raised many issues about accounting practices, some of which are of great concern to both the SEC and the FASB. Important ones relate to the valuation and classification of revenue transactions. Many dot-com companies seek to report as much revenue as possible because revenue growth is seen as a key performance measure for these companies. **Amazon.com** is a good example. Consider the following situations:

a. An Amazon.com customer orders and pays $28 for an electronic Gameboy on the Internet. Amazon sends an email to the company that makes the product, which sends the Gameboy to the customer. Amazon collects $28 from the customer and pays $24 to the other company. Amazon never owns the Gameboy.
b. Amazon agrees to place a banner advertisement on its website for another dot-com company. Instead of paying cash for the advertisement, the other company agrees to let Amazon advertise on its website.
c. Assume the same facts as in situation **b** except that Amazon agrees to accept the other company's common stock in this barter transaction. Over the next six months, the price of that stock declines.

Divide the class into three groups. Assign each group one of the above situations. Each group should discuss the valuation and classification issues that arise in the assigned situation, including how Amazon should account for each transaction.

Business Communication Case

LO1

Valuation Issue

C 11. Nike, Inc. manufactures athletic shoes and related products. In one of its annual reports, Nike made this statement: "Property, plant, and equipment are recorded at cost."[10] Given that the property, plant, and equipment undoubtedly were purchased over several years and that the current value of those assets is likely to be very different from their original cost, what authoritative basis is there for carrying the assets at cost? Does accounting generally recognize changes in value after the purchase of property, plant, and equipment? Assume you are an accountant for Nike. Write a memo to management explaining the rationale underlying Nike's approach.

CHAPTER

3 Measuring Business Income

Focus on Financial Statements

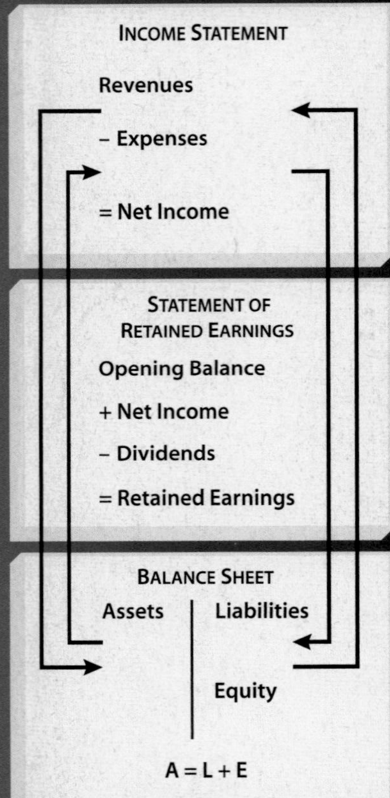

Adjusting entries bring balance sheet and income statement accounts up to date at end of period.

Income, or earnings, is the most important measure of a company's success or failure. Thus, the incentive to manage, or misstate, earnings by manipulating the numbers can be powerful, and because earnings are based on estimates, manipulation can be easy. For these reasons, ethical behavior is extremely important when measuring business income.

LEARNING OBJECTIVES

LO1 **Define *net income*, and explain the assumptions underlying income measurement and their ethical application.** *(pp. 166–169)*

LO2 **Define *accrual accounting*, and explain how it is accomplished.** *(pp. 170–172)*

LO3 **Identify four situations that require adjusting entries, and illustrate typical adjusting entries.** *(pp. 172–182)*

LO4 **Prepare financial statements from an adjusted trial balance.** *(pp. 182–184)*

LO5 **Describe the accounting cycle, and explain the purposes of closing entries.** *(pp. 185–189)*

LO6 **Use accrual-based information to analyze cash flows.** *(pp. 189–191)*

DECISION POINT ▶ A USER'S FOCUS

Netflix, Inc.

Netflix is the world's largest online entertainment subscription service. For a monthly fee, its subscribers have access to more than 90,000 DVD titles, which are shipped free of charge; with certain plans, they also have access to more than 5,000 movies online. At the end of any accounting period, Netflix has many transactions that will affect future periods.[1] Two examples appear in the Financial Highlights below: *prepaid expenses*, which, though paid in the period just ended, will benefit future periods and are therefore recorded as assets; and *accrued expenses*, which the company has incurred but will not pay until a future period. If prepaid and accrued expenses are not accounted for properly at the end of a period, Netflix's income will be misstated. Similar misstatements can occur when a company has received revenue that it has not yet earned or has earned revenue but not yet received it. If misstatements are made, investors will be misled about the company's financial performance.

- ▶ What assumptions must Netflix make to account for transactions that span accounting periods?
- ▶ How does Netflix assign its revenues and expenses to the proper accounting period so that net income is properly measured?
- ▶ Why are the adjustments that these transactions require important to Netflix's financial performance?

NETFLIX'S FINANCIAL HIGHLIGHTS: SELECTED BALANCE SHEET ITEMS (in thousands)

Assets	**2007**	**2006**
Prepaid expenses	$ 6,116	$ 9,456
Liabilities		
Accrued expenses	$36,466	$29,905

Profitability Measurement: Issues and Ethics

LO1 Define *net income*, and explain the assumptions underlying income measurement and their ethical application.

As you know, profitability and liquidity are the two major goals of a business. For a business to succeed, or even to survive, it must earn a profit. **Profit**, however, means different things to different people. Accountants prefer to use the term **net income** because it can be precisely defined from an accounting point of view as the *net increase in stockholders' equity that results from a company's operations.*

Net income is reported on the income statement, and management, stockholders, and others use it to measure a company's progress in meeting the goal of profitability. Readers of income statements need to understand what net income means and be aware of its strengths and weaknesses as a measure of a company's performance.

Net Income

Study Note

The essence of revenue is that something has been earned through the sale of goods or services. That is why cash received through a loan does not constitute revenue.

Net income is accumulated in the Retained Earnings account. In its simplest form, it is measured as the difference between revenues and expenses when revenues exceed expenses:

$$\text{Net Income} = \text{Revenues} - \text{Expenses}$$

When expenses exceed revenues, a **net loss** occurs.

Revenues are *increases in stockholders' equity* resulting from selling goods, rendering services, or performing other business activities. When a business delivers a product or provides a service to a customer, it usually receives cash or a promise from the customer to pay cash in the near future. The promise to pay is recorded in either Accounts Receivable or Notes Receivable. The total of these accounts and the total cash received from customers in an accounting period are the company's revenues for that period.

Study Note

The primary purpose of an expense is to generate revenue.

Expenses are *decreases in stockholders' equity* resulting from the cost of selling goods or rendering services and the cost of the activities necessary to carry on a business, such as attracting and serving customers. In other words, expenses are the cost of the goods and services used in the course of earning revenues. Examples include salaries expense, rent expense, advertising expense, utilities expense, and depreciation (allocation of cost) of a building or office equipment. These expenses are often called the *cost of doing business* or *expired costs.*

Not all increases in stockholders' equity arise from revenues, nor do all decreases in stockholders' equity arise from expenses. Stockholders' investments increase stockholders' equity but are not revenues, and dividends decrease stockholders' equity but are not expenses.

Income Measurement Assumptions

Users of financial reports should be aware that estimates and assumptions play a major role in the measurement of net income and other key indicators of performance. **Netflix's** management acknowledges this in its annual report, as follows:

> The preparation of . . . financial statements in conformity with generally accepted accounting principles in the United States requires estimates and assumptions that affect the reported amounts of assets and liabilities, revenues and expenses and related disclosures. . . .[2]

The major assumptions made in measuring business income have to do with continuity, periodicity, and matching.

Continuity Measuring business income requires that certain expense and revenue transactions be allocated over several accounting periods. Choosing the number of accounting periods raises the issue of **continuity**. What is the expected life of the business? Many businesses last less than five years, and in any given year, thousands of businesses go bankrupt. The majority of companies present annual financial statements on the assumption that the business will continue to operate indefinitely—that is, that the company is a **going concern**. The continuity assumption is as follows:

> Unless there is evidence to the contrary, the accountant assumes that the business will continue to operate indefinitely.

Justification for all the techniques of income measurement rests on the assumption of continuity. Consider, for example, the value of assets on the balance sheet. The continuity assumption allows the cost of certain assets to be held on the balance sheet until a future accounting period, when the cost will become an expense on the income statement. When a firm is facing bankruptcy, the accountant may set aside the assumption of continuity and prepare financial statements based on the assumption that the firm will go out of business and sell all of its assets at liquidation value—that is, for what they will bring in cash.

Periodicity Measuring business income requires assigning revenues and expenses to a specific accounting period. However, not all transactions can be easily assigned to specific periods. For example, when a company purchases a building, it must estimate the number of years the building will be in use. The portion of the cost of the building assigned to each period depends on this estimate and requires an assumption about **periodicity**. The assumption is as follows:

> Although the lifetime of a business is uncertain, it is nonetheless useful to estimate the business's net income in terms of accounting periods.

Study Note
Accounting periods are of equal length so that one period can be compared with the next.

Financial statements may be prepared for any time period, but generally, to make comparisons easier, the periods are of equal length. A 12-month accounting period is called a **fiscal year**; accounting periods of less than a year are called **interim periods**. The fiscal year of many organizations is the calendar year, January 1 to December 31. However, retailers often end their fiscal years during a slack season, and in this case, the fiscal year corresponds to the yearly cycle of business activity.

FOCUS ON BUSINESS PRACTICE

Fiscal Years Vary.

The fiscal years of many schools and governmental agencies end on June 30 or September 30. The table at the right shows the last month of the fiscal year of some well-known companies.

Company	*Last Month of Fiscal Year*
Apple Computer	September
Caesars World	July
Fleetwood Enterprises	April
H.J. Heinz	March
Kelly Services	December
MGM-UA Communications	August
Toys "R" Us	January

Matching Rule To measure net income adequately, revenues and expenses must be assigned to the accounting period in which they occur, regardless of when cash is received or paid. This is an application of the **matching rule**:

> Revenues must be assigned to the accounting period in which the goods are sold or the services performed, and expenses must be assigned to the accounting period in which they are used to produce revenue.

In other words, expenses should be recognized in the same accounting period as the revenues to which they are related. However, a direct cause-and-effect relationship between expenses and revenues is often difficult to identify. When there is no direct means of connecting expenses and revenues, costs are allocated in a systematic way among the accounting periods that benefit from the costs. For example, a building's cost is expensed over the building's expected useful life, and interest on investments is recorded as income even though it may not have been received.

The **cash basis of accounting** differs from the matching rule in that it is the practice of accounting for revenues in the period in which cash is received and for expenses in the period in which cash is paid. Some individuals and businesses use this method to account for income taxes. With this method, taxable income is calculated as the difference between cash receipts from revenues and cash payments for expenses.

Although the cash basis of accounting works well for some small businesses and many individuals, it does not meet the needs of most businesses.

Ethics and the Matching Rule

As shown in Figure 1, applying the matching rule involves making assumptions. It also involves exercising judgment. Consider the assumptions and judgment involved in estimating the useful life of a building. The estimate should be based on realistic assumptions, but management has latitude in making that estimate, and its judgment will affect the final net income that is reported.

The manipulation of revenues and expenses to achieve a specific outcome is called **earnings management**. Research has shown that companies that manage their earnings are much more likely to exceed projected earnings targets by a little than to fall short by a little. Why would management want to manage earnings to keep them from falling short? It may want to

- Meet a previously announced goal and thus meet the expectations of the market.

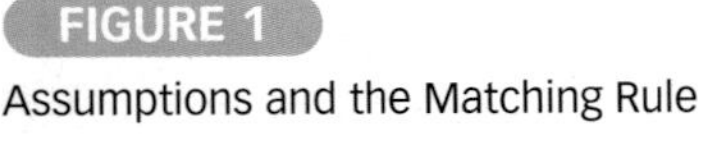
FIGURE 1

Assumptions and the Matching Rule

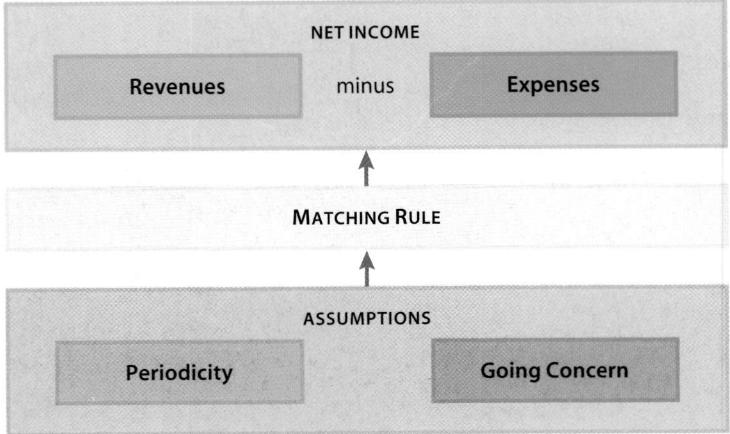

FOCUS ON BUSINESS PRACTICE

Are Misstatements of Earnings Always Overstatements?

Not all misstatements of earnings are overstatements. For instance, privately held companies, which do not have to be concerned about the effect of their earnings announcements on stockholders or investors, may understate income to reduce or avoid income taxes. In an unusual case involving a public company, the SEC cited and fined **Microsoft** for understating its income. Microsoft, a very successful company, accomplished this by overstating its unearned revenue on the balance sheet. The company's motive in trying to appear less successful than it actually was may have been that it was facing government charges of being a monopoly.[3]

- Keep the company's stock price from dropping.
- Meet a goal that will enable it to earn bonuses.
- Avoid embarrassment.

Earnings management, though not the best practice, is not illegal. However, when the estimates involved in earnings management begin moving outside a reasonable range, the financial statements become misleading. For instance, net income is misleading when revenue is overstated by a significant amount or when expenses are understated by a significant amount. As noted earlier in the text, the preparation of financial statements that are intentionally misleading constitutes fraudulent financial reporting.

Most of the enforcement actions that the Securities and Exchange Commission has brought against companies in recent years involve misapplications of the matching rule resulting from improper accrual accounting. For example, **Dell Computer** had to restate four years of its financial results because senior executives improperly applied accrual accounting to give the impression that the company was meeting quarterly earnings targets. After the SEC action, the company conducted an internal investigation that resulted in many changes in its accounting controls.[4] In the rest of this chapter, we focus on accrual accounting and its proper application.

STOP ▸ REVIEW ▸ APPLY

LO1-1 **Why don't accountants refer to *net income* as *profit*?**

LO1-2 **How does the need to assign revenues and expenses to a specific accounting period create problems?**

LO1-3 **What is the significance of the continuity assumption?**

LO1-4 **"The matching rule is the most significant concept in accounting." Do you agree with this statement? Explain your answer.**

Suggested answers to all Stop, Review, and Apply questions follow the appendixes.

Accrual Accounting

LO2 Define *accrual accounting*, and explain how it is accomplished.

Accrual accounting encompasses all the techniques accountants use to apply the matching rule. In accrual accounting, revenues and expenses are recorded in the periods in which they occur rather than in the periods in which they are received or paid.

Accrual accounting is accomplished in the following ways:

1. Recording revenues when they are earned.
2. Recording expenses when they are incurred.
3. Adjusting the accounts.

Recognizing Revenues

As you may recall, the process of determining when revenue should be recorded is called **revenue recognition**. The Securities and Exchange Commission requires that all the following conditions be met before revenue is recognized:[5]

- Persuasive evidence of an arrangement exists.
- A product or service has been delivered.
- The seller's price to the buyer is fixed or determinable.
- Collectibility is reasonably assured.

For example, suppose Miller Design Studio, Inc., has created a website for a customer and that the transaction meets the SEC's four criteria: Miller and the customer agree that the customer owes for the service, the service has been rendered, both parties understand the price, and there is a reasonable expectation that the customer will pay the bill. When Miller bills the customer, it records the transaction as revenue by debiting Accounts Receivable and crediting Design Revenue. Note that revenue can be recorded even though cash has not been collected; all that is required is a reasonable expectation that cash will be paid.

Used to produce revenue

Study Note

Even though certain revenues and expenses theoretically change during the period, there usually is no need to adjust them until the end of the period, when the financial statements are prepared.

Recognizing Expenses

Expenses are recorded when there is an agreement to purchase goods or services, the goods have been delivered or the services rendered, a price has been established or can be determined, and the goods or services have been used to produce revenue. For example, when Miller receives its utility bill, it recognizes the expense as having been incurred and as having helped produce revenue. Miller records this transaction by debiting Utilities Expense and crediting Accounts Payable. Until the bill is paid, Accounts Payable serves as a holding account. Note that recognition of the expense does not depend on the payment of cash.

FOCUS ON BUSINESS PRACTICE

Revenue Recognition: Principles Versus Rules

Revenue recognition highlights the differences between international and U.S. accounting standards. Although U.S. standards are referred to as generally accepted accounting *principles*, the FASB has issued extensive *rules* for revenue recognition in various situations and industries. The IASB, on the other hand, has one broad IFRS for revenue recognition and leaves it to companies and their auditors to determine how to apply the broad *principle*. As a result, revenue recognition is an issue that will provide a challenge to achieving international convergence of accounting practice.

EXHIBIT 1
Trial Balance

Miller Design Studio, Inc.
Trial Balance
July 31, 2010

Cash	$22,480	
Accounts Receivable	4,600	
Office Supplies	5,200	
Prepaid Rent	3,200	
Office Equipment	16,320	
Accounts Payable		$ 6,280
Unearned Design Revenue		1,400
Common Stock		40,000
Dividends	2,800	
Design Revenue		12,400
Wages Expense	4,800	
Utilities Expense	680	
	$60,080	$60,080

Adjusting the Accounts

Accrual accounting also involves adjusting the accounts. Adjustments are necessary because the accounting period, by definition, ends on a particular day. The balance sheet must list all assets and liabilities as of the end of that day, and the income statement must contain all revenues and expenses applicable to the period ending on that day. Although operating a business is a continuous process, there must be a cutoff point for the periodic reports. Some transactions invariably span the cutoff point, and some accounts therefore need adjustment.

As you can see in Exhibit 1, some of the accounts in Miller Design Studio's trial balance as of July 31 do not show the correct balances for preparing the financial statements. The trial balance lists prepaid rent of $3,200. At $1,600 per month, this represents rent for the months of July and August. So, on July 31, one-half of the $3,200 represents rent expense for July, and the remaining $1,600 represents an asset that will be used in August. An adjustment is needed to reflect the $1,600 balance in the Prepaid Rent account on the balance sheet and the $1,600 rent expense on the income statement.

As you will see, several other accounts in Miller Design Studio's trial balance do not reflect their correct balances. Like the Prepaid Rent account, they need to be adjusted.

Adjustments and Ethics

Accrual accounting can be difficult to understand. The account adjustments take time to calculate and enter in the records. Also, adjusting entries do not affect cash flows in the current period because they never involve the Cash account. You might ask, "Why go to all the trouble of making them? Why worry about them?" For one thing, the SEC has identified issues related to accrual accounting and adjustments as an area of utmost importance because of the potential for abuse and misrepresentation.[6]

All adjustments are important because of their effect on performance measures of profitability and liquidity. Adjusting entries affect net income on the income statement, and they affect profitability comparisons from one accounting period to the next. They also affect assets and liabilities on the balance sheet and thus provide information about a company's *future* cash inflows and outflows. This information is needed to assess management's performance in achieving sufficient liquidity to meet the need for cash to pay ongoing obligations. The potential for abuse arises because considerable judgment underlies the application of adjusting entries. When this judgment is misused, performance measures can be misleading.

STOP ▸ REVIEW ▸ APPLY

LO2-1 **What are the conditions for recognizing revenue?**

LO2-2 **What is the difference between the cash basis and the accrual basis of accounting?**

LO2-3 **In what three ways is accrual accounting accomplished?**

LO2-4 **Why are adjusting entries necessary?**

LO2-5 **"Why worry about adjustments? Doesn't it all come out in the wash?" Describe how you would answer these questions.**

The Adjustment Process

LO3 Identify four situations that require adjusting entries, and illustrate typical adjusting entries.

When transactions span more than one accounting period, accrual accounting requires the use of **adjusting entries**. Figure 2 shows the four situations in which adjusting entries must be made. Each adjusting entry affects one balance sheet account and one income statement account. As we have already noted, adjusting entries never affect the Cash account.

The four types of adjusting entries are as follows:

Type 1. Allocating recorded costs between two or more accounting periods. Examples of these costs are prepayments of rent, insurance, and supplies, and the depreciation of plant and equipment. The adjusting entry in this case involves an asset account and an expense account.

FIGURE 2

The Four Types of Adjustments

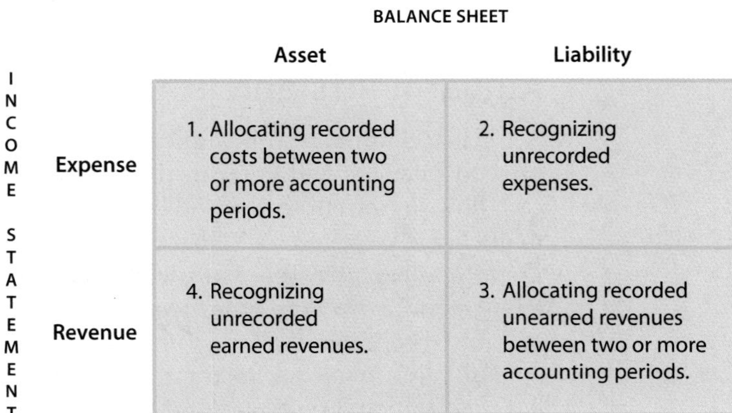
BALANCE SHEET
Asset
Liability
INCOME STATEMENT
Expense
Revenue
1. Allocating recorded costs between two or more accounting periods.
2. Recognizing unrecorded expenses.
4. Recognizing unrecorded earned revenues.
3. Allocating recorded unearned revenues between two or more accounting periods.

When transactions span more than one accounting period, an adjusting entry is necessary. Depreciation of plant and equipment, such as that found in this book warehouse area of Amazon.com's shipping and receiving facility in Fernley, Nevada, is a type of transaction that requires an adjusting entry. In this case, the adjusting entry involves an asset account and an expense account.

Type 2. Recognizing unrecorded expenses. Examples of these expenses are wages, interest, and income taxes that have been incurred but are not recorded during an accounting period. The adjusting entry involves an expense account and a liability account.

Type 3. Allocating recorded, unearned revenues between two or more accounting periods. Examples include payments received in advance and deposits made on goods or services. The adjusting entry involves a liability account and a revenue account.

Type 4. Recognizing unrecorded, earned revenues. An example is revenue that a company has earned for providing a service but for which it has not billed or been paid by the end of the accounting period. The adjusting entry involves an asset account and a revenue account.

Study Note

Adjusting entries provide information about past or future cash flows but never involve an entry to the Cash account.

Adjusting entries are either deferrals or accruals.

- A **deferral** is the postponement of the recognition of an expense already paid (Type 1 adjustment) or of revenue received in advance (Type 3 adjustment). The cash receipt or payment is recorded before the adjusting entry is made.
- An **accrual** is the recognition of a revenue (Type 4 adjustment) or expense (Type 2 adjustment) that has arisen but not been recorded during the accounting period. The cash receipt or payment occurs in a future accounting period, after the adjusting entry has been made.

Type 1 Adjustment: Allocating Recorded Costs (Deferred Expenses)

Companies often make expenditures that benefit more than one period. These costs are debited to an asset account. At the end of an accounting period, the amount of the asset that has been used is transferred from the asset account to an expense account. Two important adjustments of this type are for prepaid expenses and the depreciation of plant and equipment.

FIGURE 3

Adjustment for Prepaid (Deferred) Expenses

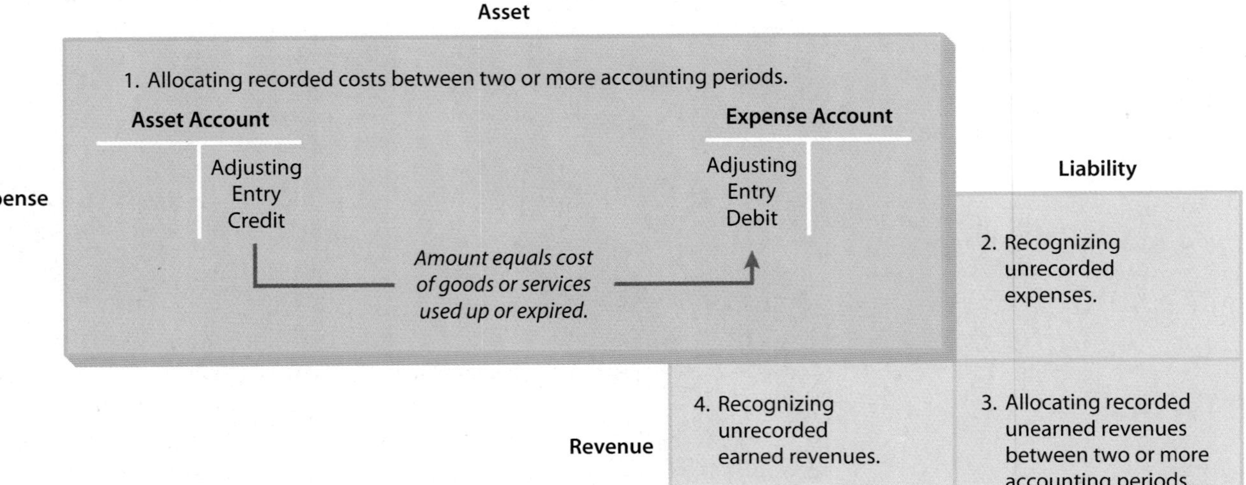

BALANCE SHEET
Asset
1. Allocating recorded costs between two or more accounting periods.
Asset Account
Expense Account
Adjusting Entry Credit
Adjusting Entry Debit
Amount equals cost of goods or services used up or expired.
Liability
2. Recognizing unrecorded expenses.
INCOME STATEMENT
Expense
Revenue
4. Recognizing unrecorded earned revenues.
3. Allocating recorded unearned revenues between two or more accounting periods.

Study Note

The expired portion of a prepayment is converted to an expense; the unexpired portion remains an asset.

Prepaid Expenses Companies customarily pay some expenses, including those for rent, supplies, and insurance, in advance. These costs are called **prepaid expenses**. By the end of an accounting period, a portion or all of prepaid services or goods will have been used or have expired. The required adjusting entry reduces the asset and increases the expense, as shown in Figure 3. The amount of the adjustment equals the cost of the goods or services used or expired.

If adjusting entries for prepaid expenses are not made at the end of an accounting period, both the balance sheet and the income statement will present incorrect information. The company's assets will be overstated, and its expenses will be understated. Thus, stockholders' equity on the balance sheet and net income on the income statement will be overstated.

To illustrate this type of adjusting entry and the others discussed below, we refer again to the transactions of Miller Design Studio, Inc.

At the beginning of July, Miller Design Studio paid two months' rent in advance. The advance payment resulted in an asset consisting of the right to occupy the office for two months. As each day in the month passed, part of the asset's cost expired and became an expense. By July 31, one-half of the asset's cost had expired and had to be treated as an expense. The adjustment is as follows:

Adjustment for Prepaid Rent
July 31: Expiration of one month's rent, $1,600

Analysis: Expiration of prepaid rent *decreases* the asset account *Prepaid Rent* with a credit and *increases* the expense account *Rent Expense* with a debit.

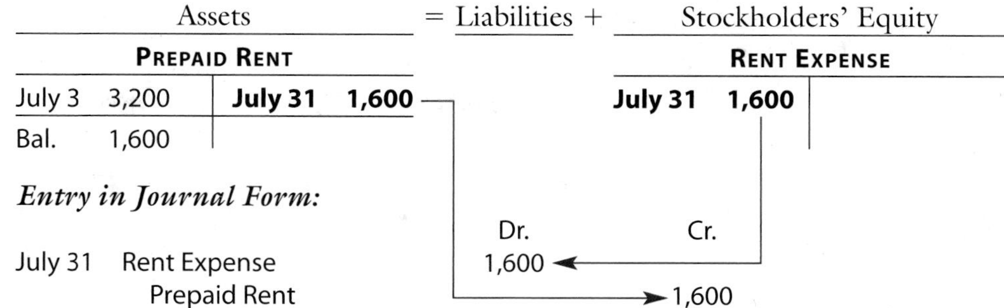

Comment: The Prepaid Rent account now has a balance of $1,600, which represents one month's rent that will be expensed during August. The logic in this analysis applies to all prepaid expenses.

Miller Design Studio purchased $5,200 of office supplies in early July. A careful inventory of the supplies is made at the end of the month. It records the number and cost of supplies that have not yet been consumed and are thus still assets of the company. Suppose the inventory shows that office supplies costing $3,660 are still on hand. This means that of the $5,200 of supplies originally purchased, $1,540 worth were used (became an expense) in July. The adjustment is as follows:

Adjustment for Supplies
July 31: Consumption of supplies, $1,540

Analysis: Consumption of office supplies *decreases* the asset account *Office Supplies* with a credit and *increases* the expense account *Office Supplies Expense* with a debit.

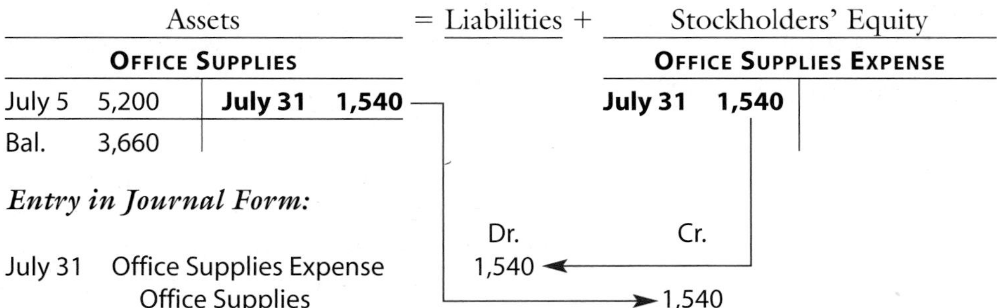

Application of Double Entry:
Assets = Liabilities + Stockholders' Equity
OFFICE SUPPLIES
July 5 5,200
July 31 1,540
Bal. 3,660
OFFICE SUPPLIES EXPENSE
July 31 1,540
Entry in Journal Form:
Dr.
Cr.
July 31 Office Supplies Expense 1,540
Office Supplies 1,540

Comment: The asset account Office Supplies now reflects the correct balance of $3,660 of supplies yet to be consumed. The logic in this example applies to all kinds of supplies.

> **Study Note**
> In accounting, *depreciation* refers only to the *allocation* of an asset's cost, not to any decline in the asset's value.

Depreciation of Plant and Equipment When a company buys a long-term asset—such as a building, truck, computer, or store fixture—it is, in effect, prepaying for the usefulness of that asset for as long as it benefits the company. Because a long-term asset is a deferral of an expense, the accountant must allocate the cost of the asset over its estimated useful life. The amount allocated to any one accounting period is called **depreciation**, or *depreciation expense*. Depreciation, like other expenses, is incurred during an accounting period to produce revenue.

It is often impossible to tell exactly how long an asset will last or how much of the asset has been used in any one period. For this reason, depreciation must be

> **Study Note**
> The difficulty in estimating an asset's useful life is further evidence that the net income figure is, at best, an estimate.

estimated. Accountants have developed a number of methods for estimating depreciation and for dealing with the related complex problems. (In the discussion that follows, we assume that the amount of depreciation has been established.)

To maintain historical cost in specific long-term asset accounts, separate accounts—**Accumulated Depreciation accounts**—are used to accumulate the depreciation on each long-term asset. These accounts, which are deducted from their related asset accounts on the balance sheet, are called *contra accounts.* A **contra account** is a separate account that is paired with a related account—in this case, an asset account. The balance of the contra account is shown on the financial statement as a deduction from its related account. The net amount is called the **carrying value**, or *book value*, of the asset. As the months pass, the amount of the accumulated depreciation grows, and the carrying value shown as an asset declines.

Adjustment for Plant and Equipment
July 31: Depreciation of office equipment, $300

Analysis: Depreciation *decreases* the asset account *Office Equipment* by *increasing* the contra account *Accumulated Depreciation–Office Equipment* with a credit and *increasing* the expense account *Depreciation Expense–Office Equipment* with a debit, as shown below.

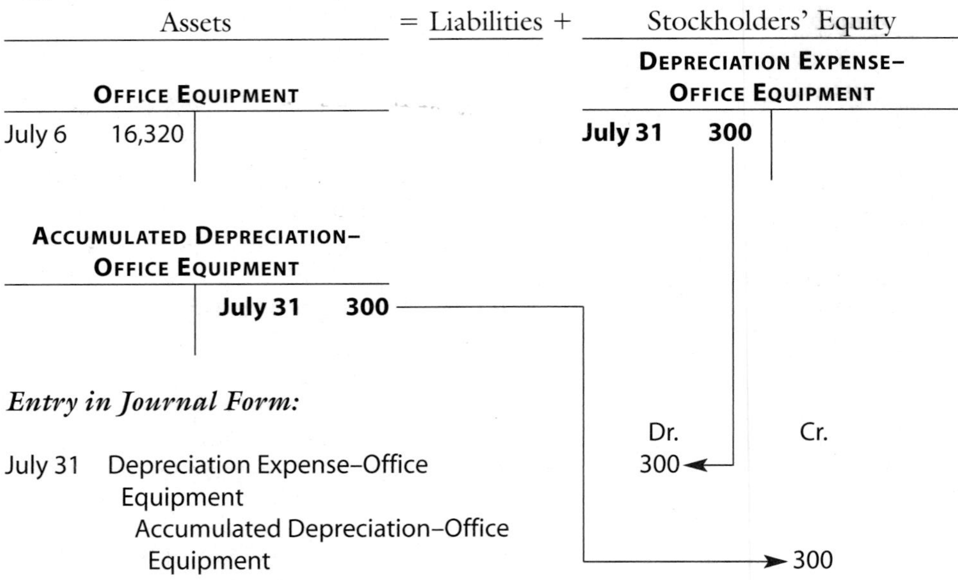

Comment: The carrying value of Office Equipment is $16,020 ($16,320 − $300) and is presented on the balance sheet as follows:

PROPERTY, PLANT, AND EQUIPMENT		
Office equipment	$16,320	
Less accumulated depreciation	300	$16,020

Application to Netflix, Inc. **Netflix** has prepaid expenses and property and equipment similar to those in the examples we have presented. Among Netflix's prepaid expenses are payments made in advance to movie companies for rights to DVDs. By paying in advance, Netflix is able to negotiate lower prices. These fixed payments are debited to Prepaid Expense. When the movies produce revenue, the prepaid amounts are transferred to expense through adjusting entries.[7]

FIGURE 4
Adjustment for Unrecorded (Accrued) Expenses

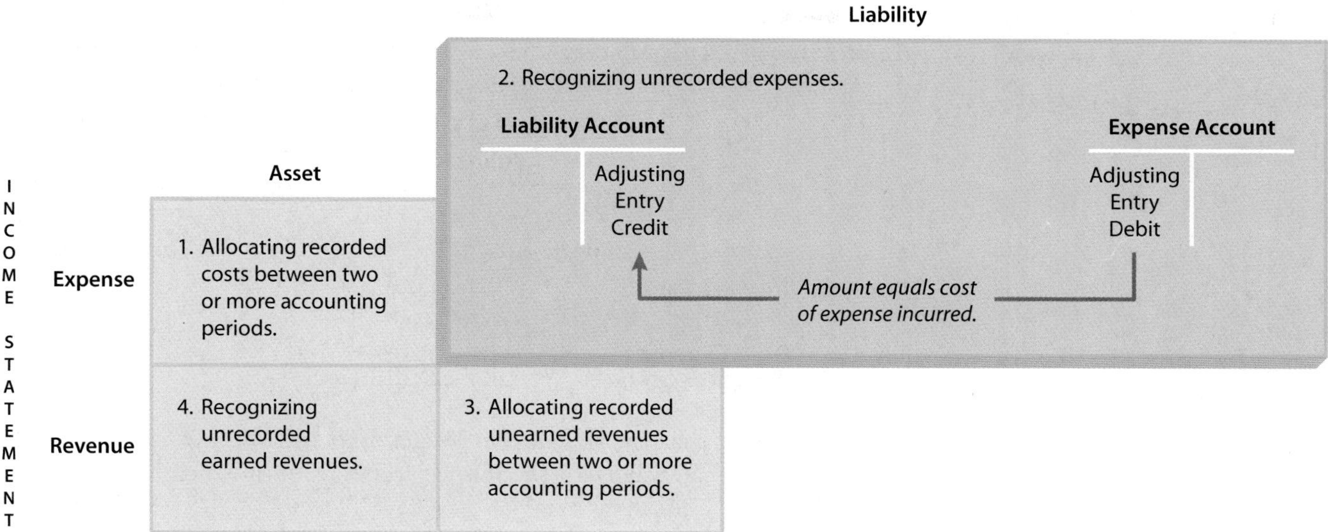

Type 2 Adjustment: Recognizing Unrecorded Expenses (Accrued Expenses)

Study Note

Remember that in accrual accounting an expense must be recorded in the period in which it is incurred, regardless of when payment is made.

Usually, at the end of an accounting period, some expenses incurred during the period have not been recorded in the accounts. These expenses require adjusting entries. One such expense is interest on borrowed money. Each day, interest accumulates on the debt. As shown in Figure 4, at the end of the accounting period, an adjusting entry is made to record the accumulated interest, which is an expense of the period, and the corresponding liability to pay the interest. Other common unrecorded expenses are wages, taxes, and utilities. As the expense and the corresponding liability accumulate, they are said to *accrue*—hence, the term **accrued expenses**.

To illustrate how an adjustment is made for unrecorded wages, suppose Miller Design Studio has two pay periods a month rather than one. In July, its pay periods end on the 12th and the 26th, as indicated in this calendar:

July

Su	M	T	W	Th	F	Sa
	1	2	3	4	5	6
7	8	9	10	11	12	13
14	15	16	17	18	19	20
21	22	23	24	25	26	27
28	29	30	31			

By the end of business on July 31, Miller's assistant will have worked three days (Monday, Tuesday, and Wednesday) beyond the last pay period. The employee has earned the wages for those days but will not be paid until the first payday in August. The wages for these three days are rightfully an expense for July, and the liabilities should reflect that the company owes the assistant for those days. Because the assistant's wage rate is \$2,400 every two weeks, or \$240 per day (\$2,400 ÷ 10 working days), the expense is \$720 (\$240 × 3 days).

Adjustment for Unrecorded Wages
July 31: Accrual of unrecorded wages, $720

Analysis: Accrual of wages *increases* the stockholders' equity account *Wages Expense* with a debit and *increases* the liability account *Wages Payable* with a credit.

Application of Double Entry:

Assets	=	Liabilities		+	Stockholders' Equity			
		WAGES PAYABLE			**WAGES EXPENSE**			
			July 31	**720**	July 26	4,800		
					31	**720**		
					Bal.	5,520		

Entry in Journal Form:

		Dr.	Cr.
July 31	Wages Expense	720	
	Wages Payable		720

Comment: Note that the increase in Wages Expense will *decrease* stockholders' equity and that total wages for the month are $5,520, of which $720 will be paid next month.

As a corporation, Miller Design Studio is subject to federal income taxes. Although the actual amount owed for taxes cannot be determined until after net income is computed at the end of the fiscal year, each month should bear its part of the total year's expense, in accordance with the matching rule. Therefore, the amount of income taxes expense for the current month must be estimated. Assume that after analyzing the firm's operations in its first month of business and conferring with her CPA, Joan Miller estimates July's share of income taxes for the year to be $800.

Adjustment for Estimated Income Taxes
July 31: Accrual of estimated income taxes, $800

Analysis: Accrual of income taxes *increases* the stockholders' equity account *Income Taxes Expense* with a debit and *increases* the liability account *Income Taxes Payable* with a credit.

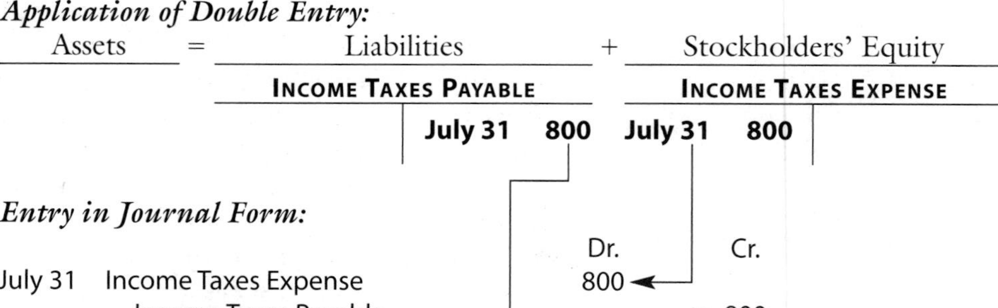

Comment: Note that the increase in Income Taxes Expense will *decrease* stockholders' equity. There are many types of accrued expenses, and the adjustments made for all of them follow the same procedure as the one used for accrued wages and accrued income taxes.

Application to Netflix, Inc. In 2007, **Netflix** had accrued expenses of $36,466,000.[8] If the expenses had not been accrued, Netflix's liabilities would be

FIGURE 5
Adjustment for Unearned (Deferred) Revenues

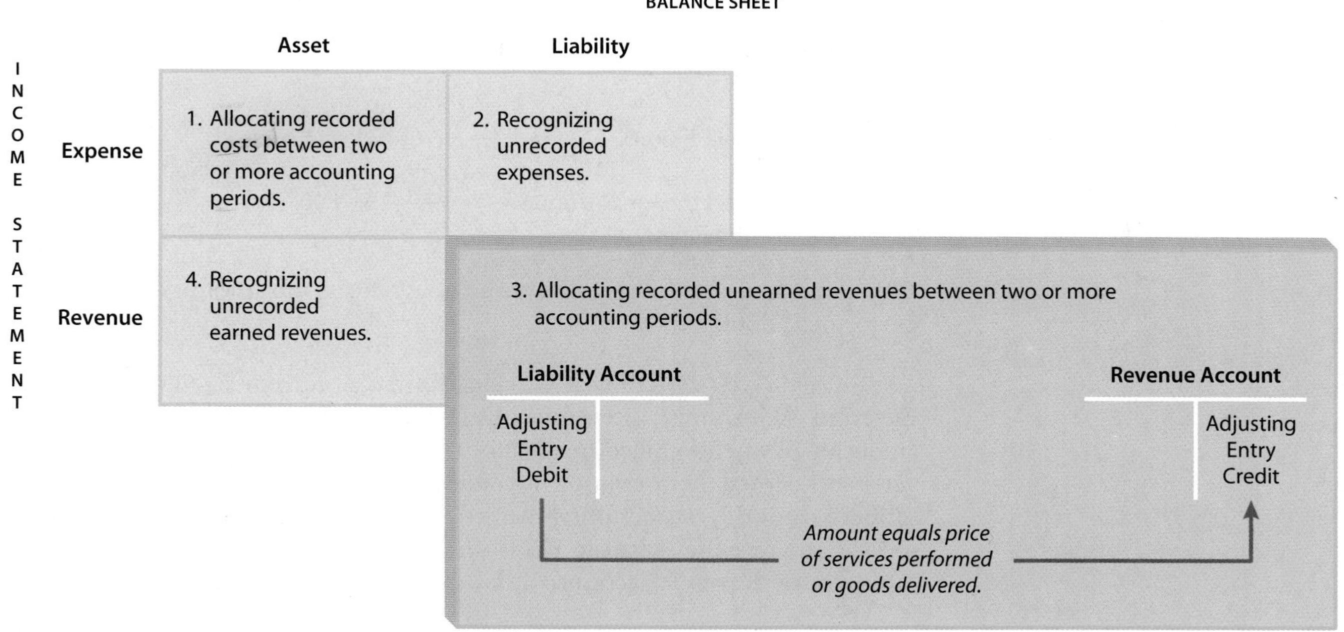

significantly understated, as would the corresponding expenses on Netflix's income statement. The end result would be an overstatement of the company's earnings.

Type 3 Adjustment: Allocating Recorded, Unearned Revenues (Deferred Revenues)

> **Study Note**
> Unearned revenue is a liability because there is an obligation to deliver goods or perform a service, or to return the payment. Once the goods have been delivered or the service performed, the liability is transferred to revenue.

Just as expenses can be paid before they are used, revenues can be received before they are earned. When a company receives revenues in advance, it has an obligation to deliver goods or perform services. **Unearned revenues** are therefore shown in a liability account.

For example, publishing companies usually receive payment in advance for magazine subscriptions. These receipts are recorded in a liability account, Unearned Subscriptions. If the company fails to deliver the magazines, subscribers are entitled to their money back. As the company delivers each issue of the magazine, it earns a part of the advance payments. This earned portion must be transferred from the Unearned Subscriptions account to the Subscription Revenue account, as shown in Figure 5.

During July, Miller Design Studio received $1,400 from another firm as advance payment for a series of brochures. By the end of the month, Miller Design Studio had completed $800 of work on the brochures, and the other firm had accepted the work.

Adjustment for Unearned Revenue
July 31: Performance of services paid for in advance, $800

Analysis: Performance of the services for which payment had been received in advance *increases* the stockholders' equity account *Design Revenue* with a credit and *decreases* the liability account *Unearned Design Revenue* with a debit.

Application of Double Entry:

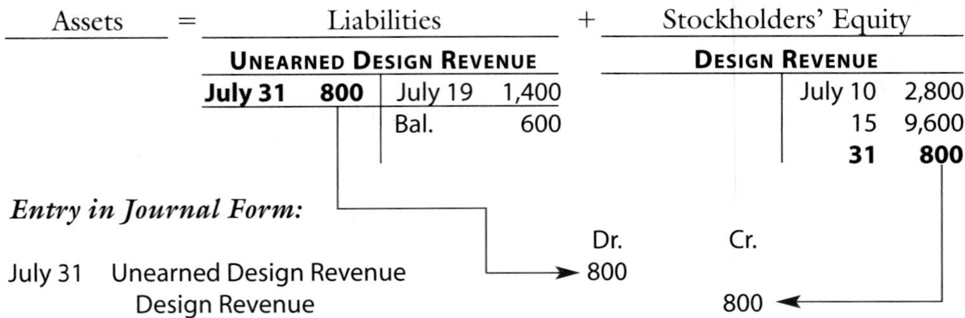

Entry in Journal Form:

		Dr.	Cr.
July 31	Unearned Design Revenue	800	
	Design Revenue		800

Comment: Unearned Design Revenue now reflects the amount of work still to be performed, $600.

Application to Netflix, Inc. **Netflix** has a current liability account called Deferred (Unearned) Revenue. Deferred revenue consists of subscriptions (monthly payments) billed in advance to customers, for which revenues have not yet been earned. Subscription revenues are recognized ratably over each subscriber's monthly subscription period. As time passes and customers use the service, the revenue is transferred from Netflix's Deferred Revenue account to its Subscription Revenue account.

Type 4 Adjustment: Recognizing Unrecorded, Earned Revenues (Accrued Revenues)

Accrued revenues are revenues that a company has earned by performing a service or delivering goods but for which no entry has been made in the accounting records. Any revenues earned but not recorded during an accounting period require an adjusting entry that debits an asset account and credits a revenue account, as shown in Figure 6. For example, the interest on a note receivable is

FIGURE 6

Adjustment for Unrecorded (Accrued) Revenues

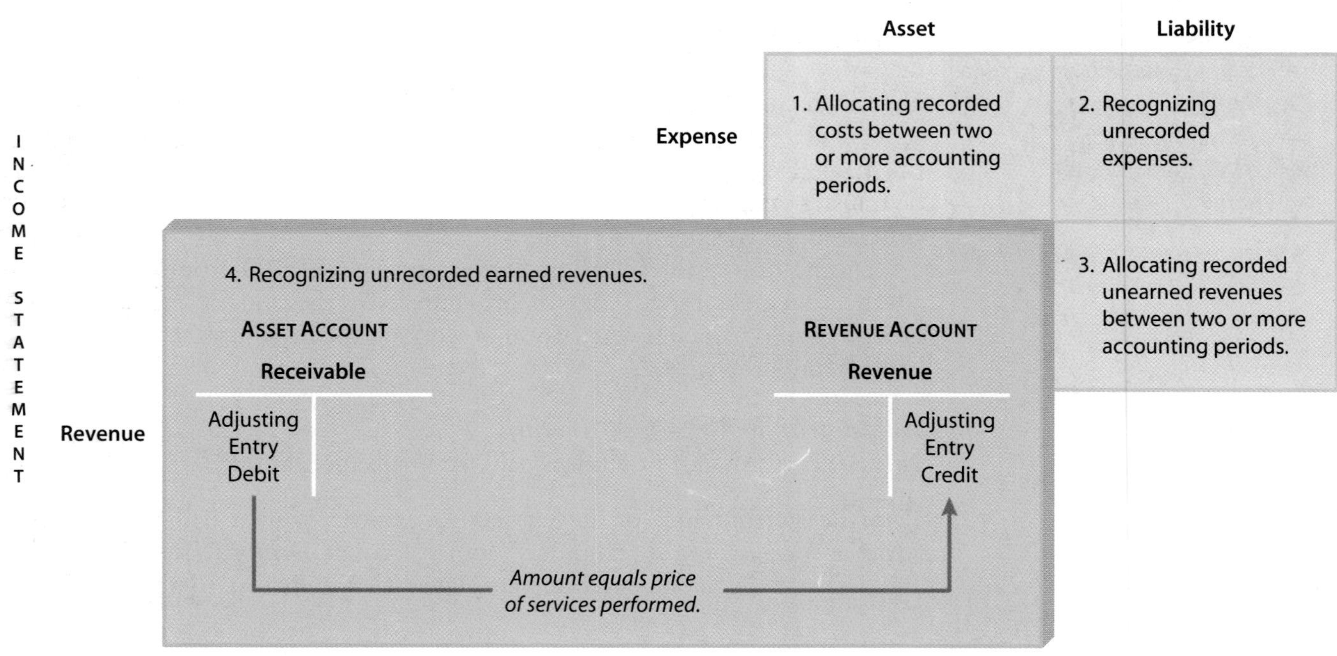

When a company earns revenue by performing a service—such as designing a website or developing marketing plans—but will not receive the revenue for the service until a future accounting period, it must make an adjusting entry. This type of adjusting entry involves an asset account and a revenue account.

earned day by day but may not be received until another accounting period. Interest Receivable should be debited and Interest Income should be credited for the interest accrued at the end of the current period.

During July, Miller Design Studio agreed to create two advertisements for Maggio's Pizza Company. It also agreed that the first advertisement would be finished by July 31. By the end of the month, Miller had earned $400 for completing the first advertisement. The client will not be billed until the entire project has been completed.

Adjustment for Design Revenue
July 31: Accrual of unrecorded revenue, $400

Analysis: Accrual of unrecorded revenue *increases* the stockholders' equity account *Design Revenue* with a credit and *increases* the asset account *Accounts Receivable* with a debit.

Application of Double Entry:

Assets = Liabilities + Stockholders' Equity

ACCOUNTS RECEIVABLE

July 15	9,600	July 22	5,000
31	**400**		
Bal.	5,000		

DESIGN REVENUE

		July 10	2,800
		15	9,600
		31	800
		31	**400**
		Bal.	13,600

Entry in Journal Form:

		Dr.	Cr.
July 31	Accounts Receivable	400	
	Design Revenue		400

Comment: Design Revenue now reflects the total revenue earned during July, $13,600. Some companies prefer to debit an account called Unbilled Accounts Receivable. Other companies simply flag the transactions in Accounts Receivable as "unbilled." On the balance sheet, they are usually combined with accounts receivable.

Application to Netflix, Inc. Since **Netflix's** subscribers pay their subscriptions in advance by credit card, Netflix does not need to bill customers for services provided but not paid. The company is in the enviable position of having no accounts receivable and thus a high degree of liquidity.

A Note About Journal Entries

Thus far, we have presented a full analysis of each journal entry and showed the thought process behind each entry. Because you should now be fully aware of the effects of transactions on the accounting equation and the rules of debit and credit, we present journal entries without full analysis in the rest of the book.

STOP ► REVIEW ► APPLY

LO3-1 What are the four situations that require adjusting entries? Give an example of each.

LO3-2 "Some assets are expenses that have not expired." Explain this statement.

LO3-3 What do plant and equipment, office supplies, and prepaid insurance have in common?

LO3-4 How do accumulated depreciation and depreciation expense differ?

LO3-5 What is a contra account? Give an example.

LO3-6 Why are contra accounts used to record depreciation?

LO3-7 How does unearned revenue arise? Give an example.

LO3-8 Where does unearned revenue appear in the financial statements?

LO3-9 Under what circumstances does a company have accrued revenues? Give an example. What asset arises when an adjustment for accrued revenues is made?

LO3-10 What is an accrued expense? Give two examples.

Identification of Adjusting Entries The four types of adjusting entries are as follows:

Type 1. Allocating recorded costs between two or more accounting periods

Type 2. Recognizing unrecorded expenses

Type 3. Allocating recorded, unearned revenue between two or more accounting periods

Type 4. Recognizing revenues earned but not yet recorded

For each of the following items, identify the type of adjusting entry required:

_____ a. Revenues earned but not yet collected or billed to customers

_____ b. Interest incurred but not yet recorded

_____ c. Unused supplies

_____ d. Costs of plant and equipment

_____ e. Income taxes incurred but not yet recorded

SOLUTION

a. Type 4 b. Type 2 c. Type 1 d. Type 1 e. Type 2

Using the Adjusted Trial Balance to Prepare Financial Statements

LO4 Prepare financial statements from an adjusted trial balance.

After adjusting entries have been recorded and posted, an **adjusted trial balance** is prepared by listing all accounts and their balances. If the adjusting entries have been posted to the accounts correctly, the adjusted trial balance will have equal debit and credit totals. The adjusted trial balance for Miller Design Studio is shown in Exhibit 2.

Notice that some accounts in Exhibit 2, such as Cash and Accounts Payable, have the same balances as in the trial balance in Exhibit 1 because no adjusting entries affected them. The balances of other accounts, such as Office Supplies and Prepaid Rent, differ from those in the trial balance because adjusting entries did affect them. The adjusted trial balance also has some new accounts, such as

EXHIBIT 2 Relationship of the Adjusted Trial Balance to the Income Statement

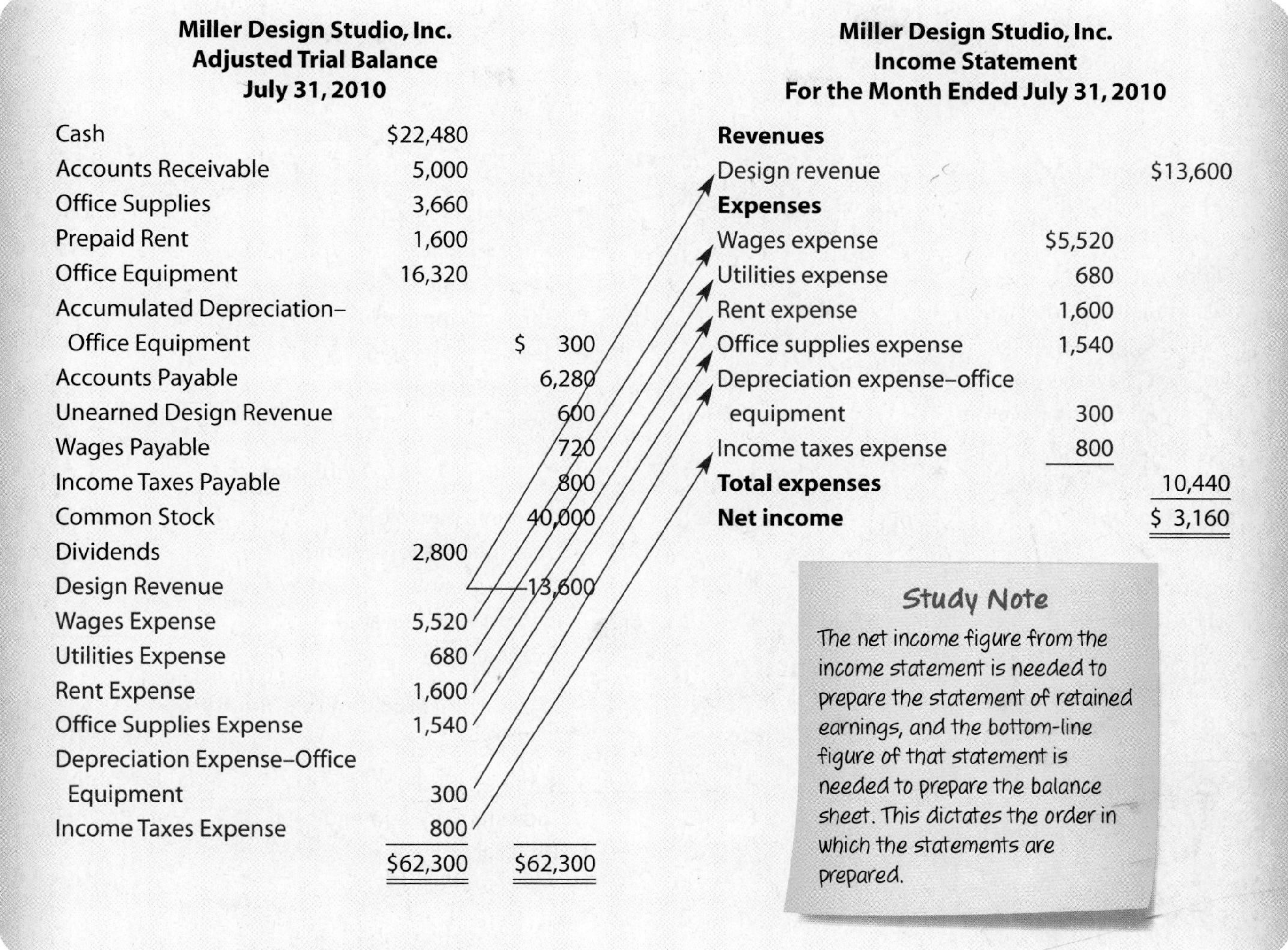

Miller Design Studio, Inc.
Adjusted Trial Balance
July 31, 2010

Cash	$22,480	
Accounts Receivable	5,000	
Office Supplies	3,660	
Prepaid Rent	1,600	
Office Equipment	16,320	
Accumulated Depreciation–Office Equipment		$ 300
Accounts Payable		6,280
Unearned Design Revenue		600
Wages Payable		720
Income Taxes Payable		800
Common Stock		40,000
Dividends	2,800	
Design Revenue		13,600
Wages Expense	5,520	
Utilities Expense	680	
Rent Expense	1,600	
Office Supplies Expense	1,540	
Depreciation Expense–Office Equipment	300	
Income Taxes Expense	800	
	$62,300	$62,300

Miller Design Studio, Inc.
Income Statement
For the Month Ended July 31, 2010

Revenues		
Design revenue		$13,600
Expenses		
Wages expense	$5,520	
Utilities expense	680	
Rent expense	1,600	
Office supplies expense	1,540	
Depreciation expense–office equipment	300	
Income taxes expense	800	
Total expenses		10,440
Net income		$ 3,160

Study Note

The net income figure from the income statement is needed to prepare the statement of retained earnings, and the bottom-line figure of that statement is needed to prepare the balance sheet. This dictates the order in which the statements are prepared.

Study Note

The adjusted trial balance is a second check that the ledger is still in balance. Because it reflects updated information from the adjusting entries, it is used in preparing the formal financial statements. It does not mean there are no accounting errors.

depreciation accounts and Wages Payable, which do not appear in the trial balance.

The adjusted trial balance facilitates the preparation of the financial statements. As shown in Exhibit 2, the revenue and expense accounts are used to prepare the income statement.

Then, as shown in Exhibit 3, the statement of retained earnings and the balance sheet are prepared. Notice that the net income from the income statement is combined with dividends on the statement of retained earnings to give the net change in Miller Design Studio's Retained Earnings account.

The resulting balance of Retained Earnings at July 31 is used in preparing the balance sheet, as are the asset and liability account balances in the adjusted trial balance.

EXHIBIT 3 Relationship of the Adjusted Trial Balance to the Balance Sheet and Statement of Retained Earnings

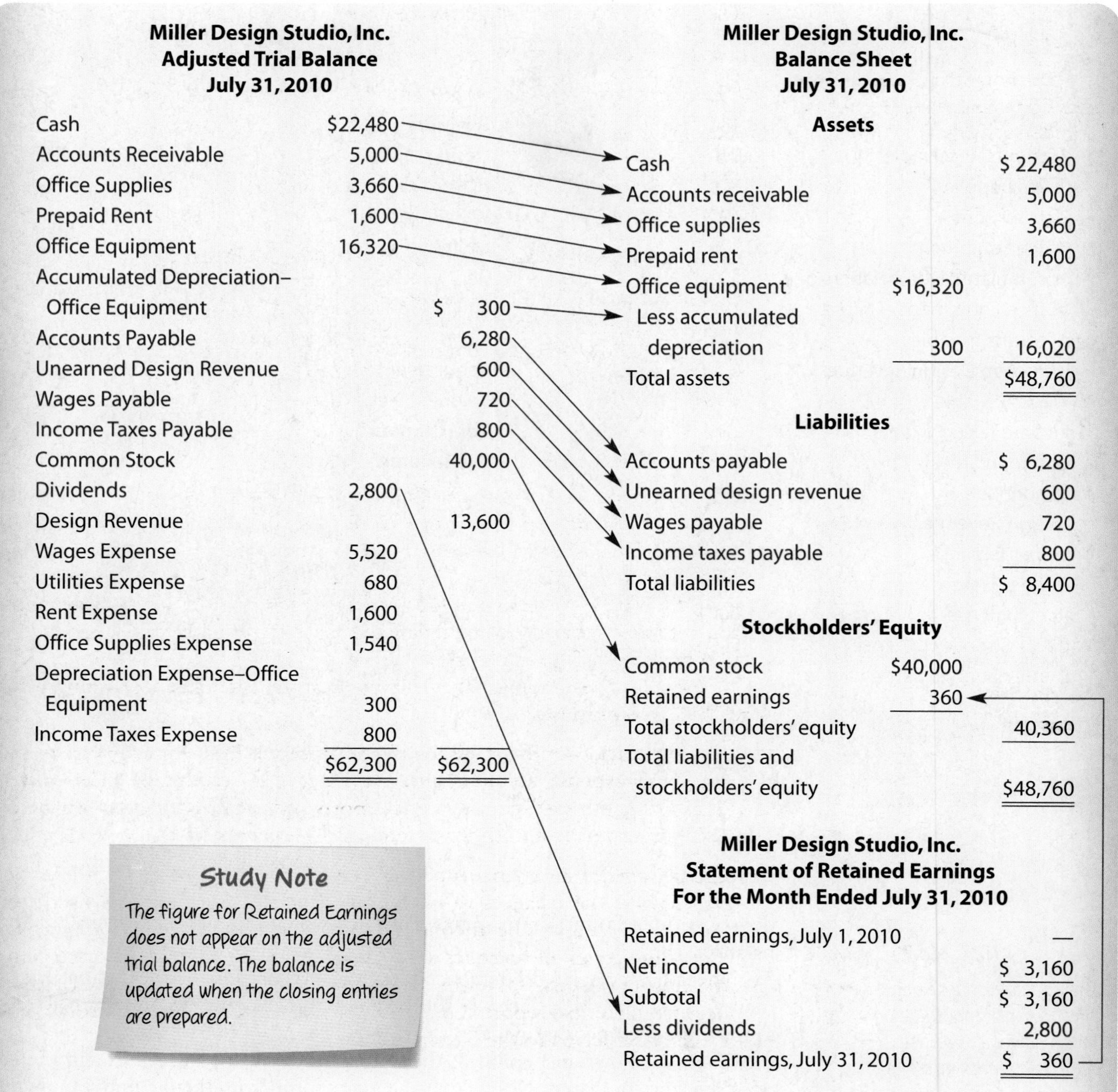

Miller Design Studio, Inc.
Adjusted Trial Balance
July 31, 2010

Cash	$22,480	
Accounts Receivable	5,000	
Office Supplies	3,660	
Prepaid Rent	1,600	
Office Equipment	16,320	
Accumulated Depreciation–Office Equipment		$ 300
Accounts Payable		6,280
Unearned Design Revenue		600
Wages Payable		720
Income Taxes Payable		800
Common Stock		40,000
Dividends	2,800	
Design Revenue		13,600
Wages Expense	5,520	
Utilities Expense	680	
Rent Expense	1,600	
Office Supplies Expense	1,540	
Depreciation Expense–Office Equipment	300	
Income Taxes Expense	800	
	$62,300	$62,300

Miller Design Studio, Inc.
Balance Sheet
July 31, 2010

Assets

Cash		$ 22,480
Accounts receivable		5,000
Office supplies		3,660
Prepaid rent		1,600
Office equipment	$16,320	
Less accumulated depreciation	300	16,020
Total assets		$48,760

Liabilities

Accounts payable		$ 6,280
Unearned design revenue		600
Wages payable		720
Income taxes payable		800
Total liabilities		$ 8,400

Stockholders' Equity

Common stock	$40,000	
Retained earnings	360	
Total stockholders' equity		40,360
Total liabilities and stockholders' equity		$48,760

Miller Design Studio, Inc.
Statement of Retained Earnings
For the Month Ended July 31, 2010

Retained earnings, July 1, 2010	—
Net income	$ 3,160
Subtotal	$ 3,160
Less dividends	2,800
Retained earnings, July 31, 2010	$ 360

Study Note

The figure for Retained Earnings does not appear on the adjusted trial balance. The balance is updated when the closing entries are prepared.

STOP ▸ REVIEW ▸ APPLY

LO4-1 **Why is the income statement usually the first statement prepared from the adjusted trial balance?**

LO4-2 **Why does the ending balance for Retained Earnings not appear on the adjusted trial balance?**

The Accounting Cycle

LO5 Describe the accounting cycle, and explain the purposes of closing entries.

As Figure 7 shows, the **accounting cycle** is a series of steps whose ultimate purpose is to provide useful information to decision makers. These steps are as follows:

1. *Analyze* business transactions from source documents.
2. *Record* the transactions by entering them in the general journal.
3. *Post* the journal entries to the ledger, and prepare a trial balance.
4. *Adjust* the accounts, and prepare an adjusted trial balance.
5. *Prepare* financial statements.
6. *Close* the accounts, and prepare a post-closing trial balance.

Note that steps 3, 4, and 6 entail the preparation of trial balances to ensure that the accounts are in balance.

You are already familiar with steps 1 through 5. In this section, we describe step 6, which may be performed before or after step 5.

Closing Entries

Balance sheet accounts, such as Cash and Accounts Payable, are considered **permanent accounts**, or *real accounts*, because they carry their end-of-period balances into the next accounting period. In contrast, revenue and expense accounts, such as Revenues Earned and Wages Expense, are considered **temporary accounts**, or *nominal accounts*, because they begin each accounting period with a zero balance, accumulate a balance during the period, and are then cleared by means of closing entries.

Closing entries are journal entries made at the end of an accounting period. They have two purposes:

1. Closing entries set the stage for the next accounting period by clearing revenue and expense accounts and the Dividends account of their balances. Recall that the income statement reports net income (or loss) for a single accounting period and shows revenues and expenses for that period only.
2. Closing entries summarize a period's revenues and expenses. This is done by transferring the balances of revenue and expense accounts to the Income Summary account. The **Income Summary account** is a temporary account that summarizes all revenues and expenses for the period. It is used only in the closing process—never in the financial statements. Its balance equals the net income or loss reported on the income statement. The net income or loss is then transferred to the Retained Earnings account.

FOCUS ON BUSINESS PRACTICE

Entering Adjustments with the Touch of a Button

In a computerized accounting system, adjusting entries can be entered just like any other transactions. However, when the adjusting entries are similar for each accounting period, such as those for insurance expense and depreciation expense, or when they always involve the same accounts, such as those for accrued wages, the computer can be programmed to display them automatically. All the accountant has to do is verify the amounts or enter the correct amounts. The adjusting entries are then entered and posted, and the adjusted trial balance is prepared with the touch of a button.

FIGURE 7
Overview of the Accounting Cycle

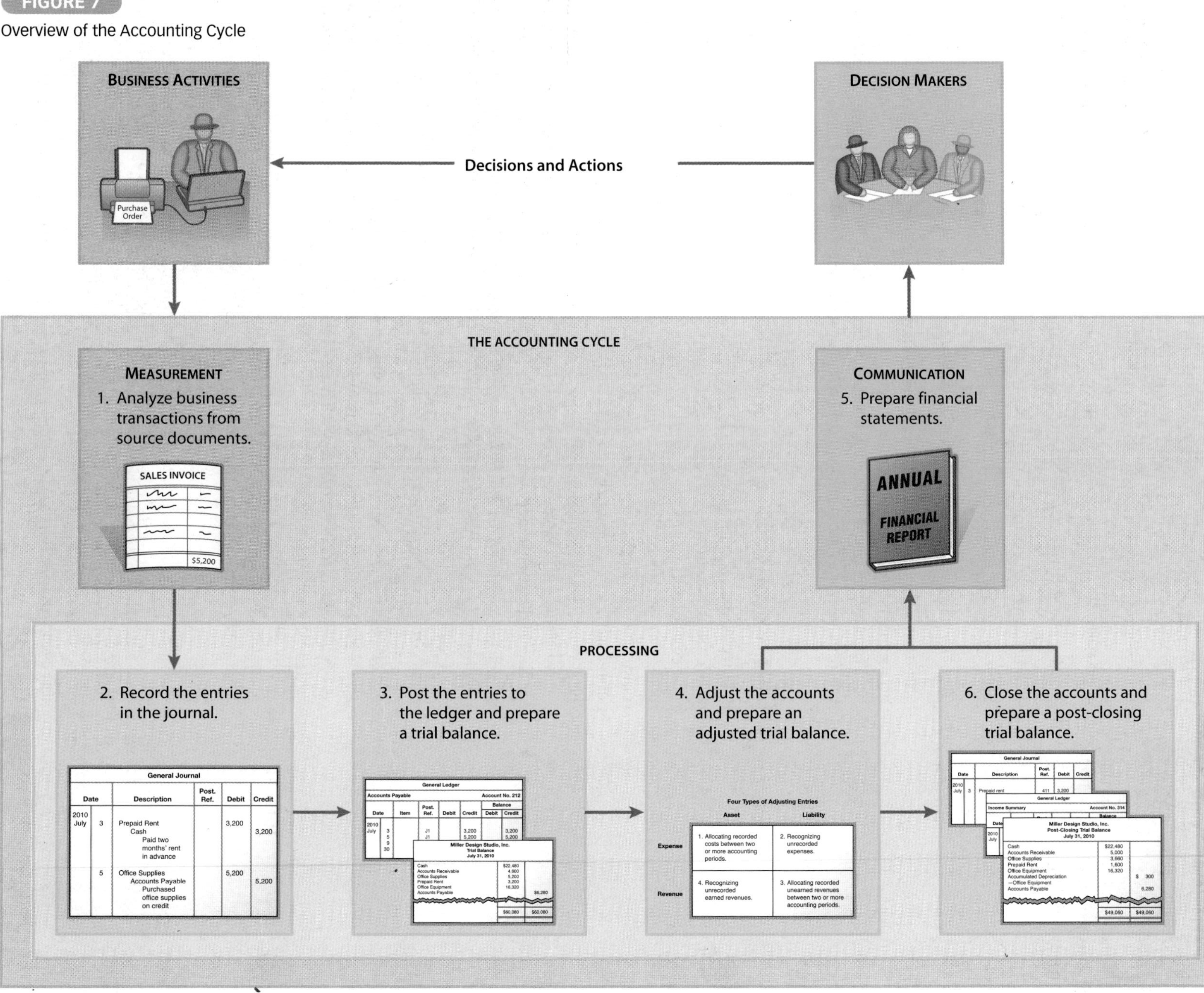

FIGURE 8
Overview of the Closing Process*

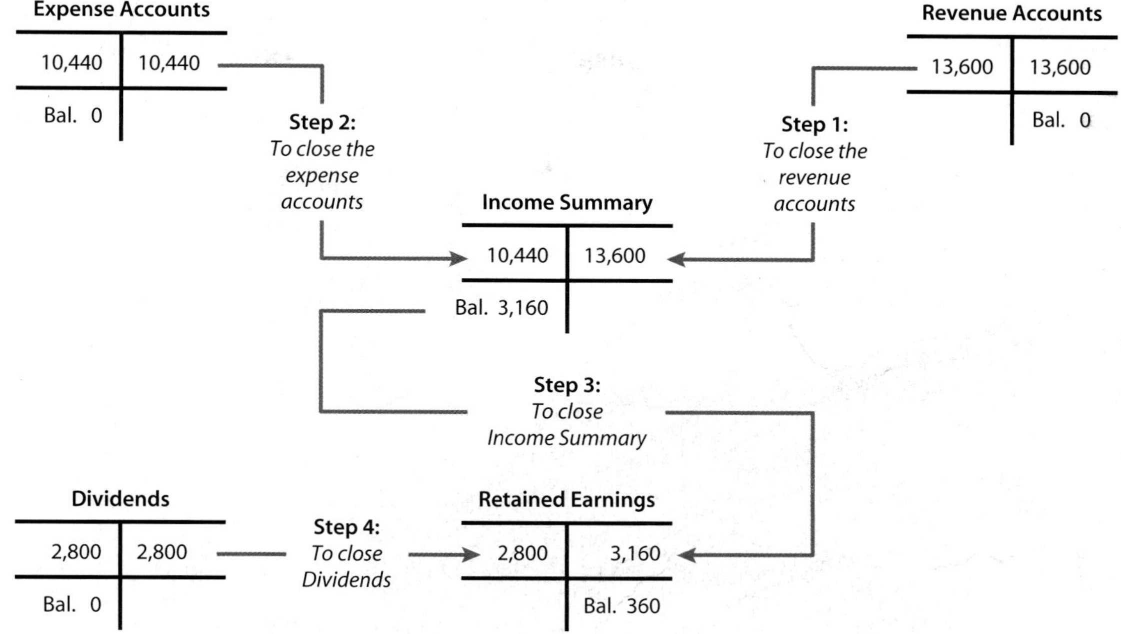

*Amounts for Miller Design Studio. See Exhibit S1 in the Supplement to Chapter 3.

The net income or loss is transferred from the Income Summary account to Retained Earnings because even though revenues and expenses are recorded in revenue and expense accounts, they actually represent increases and decreases in stockholders' equity. Closing entries transfer the net effect of increases (revenues) and decreases (expenses) to stockholders' equity. Figure 8 shows an overview of the closing process.

Closing entries are required at the end of any period for which financial statements are prepared. **Netflix** prepares financial statements each quarter, and when it does, it must close its books. Such interim information is helpful to investors and creditors in assessing a company's ongoing financial performance. Many companies close their books monthly to give management a more timely view of ongoing operations.

The Post-Closing Trial Balance

Because errors can be made in posting closing entries to the ledger accounts, it is necessary to prepare a **post-closing trial balance** to determine that all temporary accounts have zero balances and to double-check that total debits equal total credits. This final trial balance contains only balance sheet accounts because the income statement accounts and the Dividends account have all been closed and now have zero balances.

We discuss closing entries and the post-closing trial balance further in the Supplement to Chapter 3.

STOP ► REVIEW ► APPLY

LO5-1 What are the two purposes of closing entries?

LO5-2 What is the difference between adjusting entries and closing entries?

LO5-3 Which of the following accounts do not show a balance after the closing entries are prepared and posted?

a. Insurance Expense	e. Dividends
b. Accounts Receivable	f. Supplies
c. Commission Revenue	g. Supplies Expense
d. Prepaid Insurance	h. Retained Earnings

LO5-4 What is the significance of the post-closing trial balance?

Preparation of Closing Entries Prepare the necessary closing entries from the following partial adjusted trial balance for MGC Delivery Service, Inc. (except for Retained Earnings, balance sheet accounts have been omitted), and compute the ending balance of retained earnings.

MGC Delivery Service, Inc.
Partial Adjusted Trial Balance
June 30, 2010

Retained Earnings		$12,370
Dividends	$ 9,000	
Delivery Services Revenue		92,700
Driver Wages Expense	44,450	
Fuel Expense	9,500	
Wages Expense	7,200	
Packing Supplies Expense	3,100	
Office Equipment Rental Expense	1,500	
Utilities Expense	2,225	
Insurance Expense	2,100	
Interest Expense	2,550	
Depreciation Expense	5,020	
Income Taxes Expense	4,500	

SOLUTION

Closing entries prepared:

June 30	Delivery Services Revenue	92,700	
	Income Summary		92,700
	To close the revenue account		

(continued)

June 30	Income Summary	82,145	
	Driver Wages Expense		44,450
	Fuel Expense		9,500
	Wages Expense		7,200
	Packing Supplies Expense		3,100
	Office Equipment Rental Expense		1,500
	Utilities Expense		2,225
	Insurance Expense		2,100
	Interest Expense		2,550
	Depreciation Expense		5,020
	Income Taxes Expense		4,500
	To close the expense accounts		
30	Income Summary	10,555	
	Retained Earnings		10,555
	To close the Income Summary account $92,700 − $82,145 = $10,555		
30	Retained Earnings	9,000	
	Dividends		9,000
	To close the Dividends account		

Ending balance of retained earnings computed:

Retained Earnings			
June 30	9,000	Beg. Bal.	12,370
		June 30	10,555
		End. Bal.	13,925

Cash Flows from Accrual-Based Information

LO6 Use accrual-based information to analyze cash flows.

Management has the short-range goal of ensuring that its company has sufficient cash to pay ongoing obligations—in other words, management must ensure the company's liquidity. To plan payments to creditors and assess the need for short-term borrowing, managers must know how to use accrual-based information to analyze cash flows.

Almost every revenue or expense account on the income statement has one or more related accounts on the balance sheet. For instance, Supplies Expense is related to Supplies, Wages Expense is related to Wages Payable, and Design Revenue is related to Unearned Design Revenue. As we have shown, these accounts are related by making adjusting entries, the purpose of which is to apply the matching rule to the measurement of net income.

The cash inflows that a company's operations generate and the cash outflows that they require can also be determined by analyzing these relationships. For example, suppose that after receiving the financial statements in Exhibits 2 and 3,

Study Note

Income as determined by accrual accounting is important to a company's profitability. Cash flows are related to a company's liquidity. Both are important to a company's success.

management wants to know how much cash was expended for office supplies. On the income statement, Office Supplies Expense is $1,540, and on the balance sheet, Office Supplies is $3,660. Because July was the company's first month of operation, there was no prior balance of office supplies, so the amount of cash expended for office supplies during the month was $5,200 ($1,540 + $3,660 = $5,200).

Thus, the cash flow used in purchasing office supplies—$5,200—was much greater than the amount expensed in determining income—$1,540. In planning for August, management can anticipate that the cash needed may be less than the amount expensed because, given the large inventory of office supplies, the company will probably not have to buy office supplies in the coming month. Understanding these cash flow effects enables management to better predict the business's need for cash in August.

The general rule for determining the cash flow received from any revenue or paid for any expense (except depreciation, which is a special case not covered here) is to determine the potential cash payments or cash receipts and deduct the amount not paid or received. As shown below, the application of the general rule varies with the type of asset or liability account:

Type of Account	*Potential Payment or Receipt*		*Not Paid or Received*	*Result*
Prepaid Expense	Ending Balance	+ Expense for the Period	− Beginning Balance	= Cash Payments for Expenses
Unearned Revenue	Ending Balance	+ Revenue for the Period	− Beginning Balance	= Cash Receipts from Revenues
Accrued Payable	Beginning Balance	+ Expense for the Period	− Ending Balance	= Cash Payments for Expenses
Accrued Receivable	Beginning Balance	+ Revenue for the Period	− Ending Balance	= Cash Receipts from Revenues

For instance, suppose that on May 31, a company had a balance of $480 in Prepaid Insurance and that on June 30, the balance was $670. If the insurance expense during June was $120, the amount of cash expended on insurance during June can be computed as follows:

Prepaid Insurance at June 30	$670
Insurance Expense during June	120
Potential cash payments for insurance	$790
Less Prepaid Insurance at May 31	480
Cash payments for insurance during June	$310

The beginning balance is deducted because it was paid in a prior accounting period. Note that the cash payments equal the expense plus the increase in the balance of the Prepaid Insurance account [$120 + ($670 − $480) = $310]. In this case, the cash paid was almost three times the amount of insurance expense. In future months, cash payments are likely to be less than the expense.

STOP ▶ REVIEW ▶ APPLY

LO6-1 **Explain the effect that adjusting entries have on a company's cash flows.**

LO6-2 **Why does the cash paid for expenses in an accounting period often differ from the amount of expenses on the income statement?**

LO6-3 **Why does the cash received for services in an accounting period often differ from the amount of revenue on the income statement?**

A LOOK BACK AT ▶ Netflix, Inc.

In the Decision Point at the beginning of the chapter, we noted that **Netflix** has many transactions that span accounting periods. We asked these questions:

- **What assumptions must Netflix make to account for transactions that span accounting periods?**
- **How does Netflix assign its revenues and expenses to the proper accounting period so that net income is properly measured?**
- **Why are the adjustments that these transactions require important to Netflix's financial performance?**

Two of the assumptions Netflix must make are that it will continue as a going concern for an indefinite time (the continuity assumption) and that it can make useful estimates of its income in terms of accounting periods (the periodicity assumption). These assumptions enable the company to apply the matching rule—that is, revenues are assigned to the accounting period in which goods are sold or services are performed, and expenses are assigned to the accounting period in which they are used to produce revenue.

As you have learned in this chapter, adjusting entries for deferred and accrued expenses and for deferred and accrued revenues have an impact on a company's earnings. By paying close attention to the profit margin ratio, one can assess how well a company is controlling its expenses in relation to its revenues. The **profit margin** shows the percentage of each revenue, or sales dollar, that results in net income. Using data from Netflix's annual report, we can calculate Netflix's profit margin for two successive years as follows (dollars are in thousands):

	2007	2006
Net Income / Revenues*	$66,952 / $1,205,340	$49,082 / $996,600
K/R Profit Margin:	5.6%	4.9%

*Also called *net sales.*

These results show that Netflix's revenues and earnings are increasing very rapidly and that its profitability is improving. Because net income equals revenues minus expenses and adjusting entries affect both revenues and expenses, you can see that without adjusting entries, it would be impossible to make a fair assessment of Netflix's financial performance.

CHAPTER REVIEW

REVIEW of Learning Objectives

LO1 Define *net income*, and explain the assumptions underlying income measurement and their ethical application.

Net income is the net increase in stockholders' equity that results from a company's operations. Net income equals revenues minus expenses; when expenses exceed revenues, a net loss results. Revenues equal the price of goods sold or services rendered during a specific period. Expenses are the costs of goods and services used in the process of producing revenues.

The continuity assumption recognizes that even though businesses face an uncertain future, without evidence to the contrary, accountants must assume that a business will continue to operate indefinitely. The periodicity assumption recognizes that although the lifetime of a business is uncertain, it is nonetheless useful to estimate the business's net income in terms of accounting periods. The matching rule holds that revenues must be assigned to the accounting period in which the goods are sold or the services performed, and expenses must be assigned to the accounting period in which they are used to produce revenue.

Because applying the matching rule involves making assumptions and exercising judgment, it can lead to earnings management, which is the manipulation of revenues and expenses to achieve a specific outcome. When the estimates involved in earnings management move outside a reasonable range, financial statements become misleading. Financial statements that are intentionally misleading constitute fraudulent financial reporting.

LO2 Define *accrual accounting*, and explain how it is accomplished.

Accrual accounting consists of all the techniques accountants use to apply the matching rule. It is accomplished by recognizing revenues when they are earned, by recognizing expenses when they are incurred, and by adjusting the accounts.

LO3 Identify four situations that require adjusting entries, and illustrate typical adjusting entries.

Adjusting entries are required when (1) recorded costs must be allocated between two or more accounting periods, (2) unrecorded expenses exist, (3) recorded, unearned revenues must be allocated between two or more accounting periods, and (4) unrecorded, earned revenues exist. The preparation of adjusting entries is summarized as follows:

	Type of Account		
Type of Adjusting Entry	**Debited**	**Credited**	**Examples of Balance Sheet Accounts**
1. Allocating recorded costs (previously paid, expired)	Expense	Asset (or contra-asset)	Prepaid rent Prepaid insurance Office supplies Accumulated depreciation–office equipment
2. Accrued expenses (incurred, not paid)	Expense	Liability	Wages payable Income taxes payable
3. Allocating recorded, unearned revenues (previously received, earned)	Liability	Revenue	Unearned design revenue
4. Accrued revenues (earned, not received)	Asset	Revenue	Accounts receivable Interest receivable

LO4 Prepare financial statements from an adjusted trial balance.

An adjusted trial balance is prepared after adjusting entries have been posted to the accounts. Its purpose is to test whether the adjusting entries have been posted correctly before the financial statements are prepared. The balances in the revenue and expense accounts in the adjusted trial balance are used to prepare the income statement. The balances in the asset and liability accounts in the adjusted trial balance and in the statement of retained earnings are used to prepare the balance sheet.

LO5 Describe the accounting cycle, and explain the purposes of closing entries.

The accounting cycle has six steps: (1) analyzing business transactions from source documents; (2) recording the transactions by entering them in the journal; (3) posting the entries to the ledger, and preparing a trial balance; (4) adjusting the accounts, and preparing an adjusted trial balance; (5) preparing the financial statements; and (6) closing the accounts, and preparing a post-closing trial balance.

Closing entries have two purposes: (1) they clear the balances of all temporary accounts (revenue, expense, and Dividends accounts) so that they have zero balances at the beginning of the next accounting period, and (2) they summarize a period's revenues and expenses in the Income Summary account so that the net income or loss for the period can be transferred as a total to Retained Earnings. As a final check on the balance of the ledger and to ensure that all temporary accounts have been closed, a post-closing trial balance is prepared after the closing entries have been posted to the ledger accounts.

LO6 Use accrual-based information to analyze cash flows.

To ensure a company's liquidity, managers must know how to use accrual-based information to analyze cash flows. The general rule for determining the cash flow received from any revenue or paid for any expense (except depreciation) is to determine the potential cash payments or cash receipts and deduct the amount not paid or received.

REVIEW of Concepts and Terminology

The following concepts and terms were introduced in this chapter:

Accounting cycle: A series of six steps whose ultimate purpose is to provide useful information to decision makers. **(LO5)**

Accrual: The recognition of an expense or revenue that has arisen but has not yet been recorded. **(LO3)**

Accrual accounting: Recording transactions in the periods in which they occur, rather than in the periods in which cash is received or paid; all the techniques that accountants use to apply the matching rule. **(LO2)**

Accrued expenses: Expenses incurred but not recognized in the accounts; unrecorded expenses. **(LO3)**

Accrued revenues: Revenues for which a service has been performed or goods delivered but for which no entry has been made; unrecorded revenues. **(LO3)**

Accumulated Depreciation accounts: Contra-asset accounts used to accumulate depreciation on specific long-term assets. **(LO3)**

Adjusted trial balance: A trial balance prepared after all adjusting entries have been recorded and posted to the accounts. **(LO4)**

Adjusting entries: Entries made to apply accrual accounting to transactions that span accounting periods. **(LO3)**

Carrying value: The unexpired portion of the cost of an asset. Also called *book value.* **(LO3)**

Cash basis of accounting: Accounting for revenues and expenses on a cash-received and cash-paid basis. **(LO1)**

Closing entries: Journal entries made at the end of a period that set the stage for the next period by clearing the temporary accounts of their balances and transferring them to Retained Earnings; they summarize a period's revenues and expenses. **(LO5)**

Continuity: The difficulty associated with not knowing how long a business will survive. **(LO1)**

Contra account: An account whose balance is subtracted from an associated account in the financial statements. **(LO3)**

Deferral: The postponement of the recognition of an expense already paid or of a revenue received in advance. **(LO3)**

Depreciation: The portion of the cost of a long-term asset allocated to any one accounting period. Also called *depreciation expense.* **(LO3)**

Earnings management: The manipulation of revenues and expenses to achieve a specific outcome. **(LO1)**

Expenses: Decreases in stockholders' equity resulting from the costs of goods and services used in the course of earning revenues. Also called *cost of doing business* or *expired costs.* **(LO1)**

Fiscal year: Any 12-month accounting period. **(LO1)**

Going concern: The assumption that unless there is evidence to the contrary, a business will continue to operate indefinitely. **(LO1)**

Income Summary account: A temporary account used during the closing process that holds a summary of all revenues and expenses before the net income or loss is transferred to the Retained Earnings account. **(LO5)**

Interim periods: Accounting periods of less than one year. **(LO1)**

Matching rule: The principle that revenues must be assigned to the accounting period in which the goods are sold or the services performed, and expenses must be assigned to the accounting period in which they are used to produce revenue. **(LO1)**

Net income: The net increase in stockholders' equity that results from business operations and is accumulated in the Retained Earnings account; revenues less expenses when revenues exceed expenses. **(LO1)**

Net loss: The net decrease in stockholders' equity when expenses exceed revenues. **(LO1)**

Periodicity: The assumption that although the lifetime of a business is uncertain, it is still useful to estimate its net income in terms of accounting periods. **(LO1)**

Permanent accounts: Balance sheet accounts whose balances extend into the next accounting period. Also called *real accounts.* **(LO5)**

Post-closing trial balance: A trial balance prepared at the end of an accounting period after all adjusting and closing entries have been posted; a final check on the balance of the ledger to ensure that all temporary accounts have zero balances and that total debits equal total credits. **(LO5)**

Prepaid expenses: Expenses paid in advance that have not yet expired; an asset account. **(LO3)**

Profit: The increase in stockholders' equity that results from business operations. **(LO1)**

Revenue recognition: The process of determining when revenue is earned. **(LO2)**

Revenues: Increases in stockholders' equity resulting from selling goods, rendering services, or performing other business activities. **(LO1)**

Temporary accounts: Accounts that show the accumulation of revenues and expenses over an accounting period and that at the end of the period are transferred to stockholders' equity. Also called *nominal accounts.* **(LO5)**

Unearned revenues: Revenues received in advance for which the goods have not yet been delivered or the services performed; a liability account. **(LO3)**

Key Ratio

Profit margin: A ratio that shows the percentage of each sales dollar that results in net income; Net Income ÷ Net Revenues.

REVIEW Problem

LO3 LO4

Posting to T Accounts, Determining Adjusting Entries, and Using an Adjusted Trial Balance to Prepare Financial Statements

The following is the unadjusted trial balance for Reliable Lawn Care, Inc., on December 31, 2010:

Reliable Lawn Care, Inc.		
Trial Balance		
December 31, 2010		
Cash	$ 4,320	
Accounts Receivable	2,500	
Office Supplies	360	
Prepaid Insurance	480	
Office Equipment	6,800	
Accumulated Depreciation--Office Equipment		$ 1,200
Accounts Payable		1,400
Unearned Revenue		920
Common Stock		4,000
Retained Earnings		5,740
Dividends	800	
Service Revenue		5,800
Wages Expense	3,000	
Rent Expense	800	
	$19,060	$19,060

The following information is also available:

a. Insurance that expired during December amounted to $80.
b. Office supplies on hand on December 31 totaled $150.
c. Depreciation for December totaled $200.
d. Accrued wages on December 31 totaled $240.
e. Revenues earned for services performed in December but not billed by the end of the month totaled $600.
f. Performance of services paid for in advance, $320.
g. Income taxes for December are estimated to be $500.

Required

1. Prepare T accounts for the accounts in the trial balance, and enter the balances.
2. Determine the required adjusting entries, and record them directly in the T accounts. Open new T accounts as needed.
3. Prepare an adjusted trial balance.
4. Prepare an income statement and a statement of retained earnings for the month ended December 31, 2010, as well as a balance sheet at December 31, 2010.

Answer to Review Problem

1. T accounts set up and amounts from trial balance entered
2. Adjusting entries recorded

	A	B	C	D	E	F	G	H	I	J	K	L	M	N
1	**Cash**					**Accounts Receivable**					**Office Supplies**			
2	Bal.	4,320				Bal.	2,500				Bal.	360	(b)	210
3						(e)	600				*Bal.*	*150*		
4						*Bal.*	*3,100*							
5														
6											**Accumulated Depreciation--**			
7	**Prepaid Insurance**					**Office Equipment**					**Office Equipment**			
8	Bal.	480	(a)	80		Bal.	6,800						Bal.	1,200
9	*Bal.*	400											(c)	200
10													*Bal.*	*1,400*
11														
12	**Accounts Payable**					**Unearned Revenue**					**Wages Payable**			
13			Bal.	1,400		(f)	320	Bal.	920				(d)	240
14								*Bal.*	*600*					
15														
16	**Income Taxes Payable**					**Common Stock**					**Retained Earnings**			
17			(g)	500				Bal.	4,000				Bal.	5,740
18														
19	**Dividends**					**Service Revenue**					**Wages Expense**			
20	Bal.	800						Bal.	5,800		Bal.	3,000		
21								(e)	600		(d)	240		
22								(f)	320		*Bal.*	*3,240*		
23								*Bal.*	*6,720*					
24														
25	**Rent Expense**					**Insurance Expense**					**Office Supplies Expense**			
26	Bal.	800				(a)	80				(b)	210		
27														
28	**Depreciation Expense--**													
29	**Office Equipment**					**Income Taxes Expense**								
30	(c)	200				(g)	500							
31														

3. Adjusted trial balance prepared

Reliable Lawn Care, Inc. Adjusted Trial Balance December 31, 2010		
Cash	$ 4,320	
Accounts Receivable	3,100	
Office Supplies	150	
Prepaid Insurance	400	
Office Equipment	6,800	
Accumulated Depreciation--Office Equipment		$ 1,400
Accounts Payable		1,400
Unearned Revenue		600
Wages Payable		240
Income Taxes Payable		500
Common Stock		4,000
Retained Earnings		5,740
Dividends	800	
Service Revenue		6,720
Wages Expense	3,240	
Rent Expense	800	
Insurance Expense	80	
Office Supplies Expense	210	
Depreciation Expense--Office Equipment	200	
Income Taxes Expense	500	
	$20,600	$20,600

4. Financial statements prepared

Reliable Lawn Care, Inc. Income Statement For the Month Ended December 31, 2010		
Revenue		
Service revenue		$6,720
Expenses		
Wages expense	$3,240	
Rent expense	800	
Insurance expense	80	
Office supplies expense	210	
Depreciation expense--office equipment	200	
Income taxes expense	500	
Total expenses		5,030
Net income		$1,690

(continued)

4. Financial statements prepared *(continued)*

	A	B	C	D
1			**Reliable Lawn Care, Inc.**	
2			**Statement of Retained Earnings**	
3			**For the Month Ended December 31, 2010**	
4				
5	Retained earnings, November 30, 2010			$5,740
6	Net income			1,690
7	Subtotal			$7,430
8	Less dividends			800
9	Retained earnings, December 31, 2010			$6,630
10				

	A	B	C	D	E
1			**Reliable Lawn Care, Inc.**		
2			**Balance Sheet**		
3			**December 31, 2010**		
4					
5			**Assets**		
6	Cash				$ 4,320
7	Accounts receivable				3,100
8	Office supplies				150
9	Prepaid insurance				400
10	Office equipment			$6,800	
11		Less accumulated depreciation		1,400	5,400
12	Total assets				$13,370
13					
14			**Liabilities**		
15	Accounts payable				$ 1,400
16	Unearned revenue				600
17	Wages payable				240
18	Income taxes payable				500
19	Total liabilities				$ 2,740
20					
21			**Stockholders' Equity**		
22	Common stock			$4,000	
23	Retained earnings			6,630	
24	Total stockholders' equity				10,630
25	Total liabilities and stockholders' equity				$13,370
26					

CHAPTER ASSIGNMENTS

BUILDING Your Basic Knowledge and Skills

Short Exercises

LO1 LO2 Accrual Accounting Concepts

SE 1. Match the concepts of accrual accounting on the right with the assumptions or actions on the left:

___ 1. Assumes expenses should be assigned to the accounting period in which they are used to produce revenues		a. Periodicity
___ 2. Assumes a business will last indefinitely		b. Going concern
___ 3. Assumes revenues are earned at a point in time		c. Matching rule
___ 4. Assumes net income that is measured for a short period of time, such as one quarter, is a useful measure		d. Revenue recognition

LO3 Adjustment for Prepaid Insurance

SE 2. The Prepaid Insurance account began the year with a balance of $920. During the year, insurance in the amount of $2,080 was purchased. At the end of the year (December 31), the amount of insurance still unexpired was $1,400. Prepare the year-end entry in journal form to record the adjustment for insurance expense for the year.

LO3 Adjustment for Supplies

SE 3. The Supplies account began the year with a balance of $760. During the year, supplies in the amount of $1,960 were purchased. At the end of the year (December 31), the inventory of supplies on hand was $880. Prepare the year-end entry in journal form to record the adjustment for supplies expense for the year.

LO3 Adjustment for Depreciation

SE 4. The depreciation expense on office equipment for the month of March is $100. This is the third month that the office equipment, which cost $1,900, has been owned. Prepare the adjusting entry in journal form to record depreciation for March and show the balance sheet presentation for office equipment and related accounts after the March 31 adjustment.

LO3 Adjustment for Accrued Wages

SE 5. Wages are paid each Saturday for a six-day workweek. Wages are currently running $1,380 per week. Prepare the adjusting entry required on June 30, assuming July 1 falls on a Tuesday.

LO3 Adjustment for Unearned Revenue

SE 6. During the month of August, deposits in the amount of $2,200 were received for services to be performed. By the end of the month, services in the amount of $1,520 had been performed. Prepare the necessary adjustment for Service Revenue at the end of the month.

LO4

Preparation of an Income Statement and Statement of Retained Earnings from an Adjusted Trial Balance

SE 7. The adjusted trial balance for Shimura Company on December 31, 2010, contains the following accounts and balances: Retained Earnings, $4,300; Dividends, $175; Service Revenue, $1,300; Rent Expense, $200; Wages Expense, $450; Utilities Expense, $100; Telephone Expense, $25; and Income Taxes Expense, $175. Prepare an income statement and statement of retained earnings in proper form for the month of December.

LO5

Preparation of Closing Entries

SE 8. Using the data in **SE 7**, prepare required closing entries for Shimura Company.

LO6

Determination of Cash Flows

SE 9. Unearned Revenue had a balance of $650 at the end of November and $450 at the end of December. Service Revenue was $2,550 for the month of December. How much cash was received for services provided during December?

Profit Margin

SE 10. Calculate profit margin for 2010 using the following data: A company has net income of $14,000 and net sales of $164,000 in 2010.

Exercises

LO1 LO2 LO3

Discussion Questions

E 1. Develop a brief answer to each of the following questions.

1. When a company has net income, what happens to its assets and/or to its liabilities?
2. Why must a company that gives a guaranty or warranty with its product or service show an expense in the year of sale rather than in a later year when a repair or replacement is made?
3. Is accrual accounting more closely related to a company's goal of profitability or liquidity?
4. Under normal circumstances, will the carrying value of a long-term asset be equal to its market value?

LO4

Discussion Questions

E 2. Develop a brief answer to each of the following questions.

1. Why is Retained Earnings not listed on the trial balance for Miller Design Studio, Inc., in Exhibits 1 and 2?
2. If, at the end of the accounting period, you were looking at the T account for a prepaid expense like supplies, would you look for the amounts expended in cash on the debit or credit side? On which side would you find the amount expensed during the period?
3. Would you expect profit margin to be a good measure of a company's liquidity? Why or why not?

LO1 LO2 LO3

Applications of Accounting Concepts Related to Accrual Accounting

E 3. The accountant for Ronaldo Company makes the assumptions or performs the activities in the list that follows. Tell which of these concepts of accrual accounting most directly relates to each assumption or action: (a) periodicity, (b) going concern, (c) matching rule, (d) revenue recognition, (e) deferral, and (f) accrual.

1. In estimating the life of a building, assumes that the business will last indefinitely
2. Records a sale when the customer is billed
3. Postpones the recognition of a one-year insurance policy as an expense by initially recording the expenditure as an asset
4. Recognizes the usefulness of financial statements prepared on a monthly basis even though they are based on estimates
5. Recognizes, by making an adjusting entry, wages expense that has been incurred but not yet recorded
6. Prepares an income statement that shows the revenues earned and the expenses incurred during the accounting period

LO2 **Application of Conditions for Revenue Recognition**

E 4. Four conditions must be met before revenue should be recognized. In each of the following cases, tell which condition has *not* been met.

a. Company A accepts a contract from another company to perform services in the future for $2,000.
b. Company B ships products worth $3,000 to another company without an order from the other company but tells the company it can return the products if it does not sell them.
c. Company C performs services for $10,000 for a company that is in financial difficulty.
d. Company D agrees to work out a price later for services that it performs for another company.

LO3 **Adjusting Entry for Unearned Revenue**

E 5. Fargo Voice, Inc. of Fargo, North Dakota, publishes a monthly magazine featuring local restaurant reviews and upcoming social, cultural, and sporting events. Subscribers pay for subscriptions either one year or two years in advance. Cash received from subscribers is credited to an account called Magazine Subscriptions Received in Advance. On December 31, 2009, the end of the company's fiscal year, the balance of Magazine Subscriptions Received in Advance is $840,000. Expiration of subscriptions revenue is as follows:

During 2009	$175,000
During 2010	415,000
During 2011	250,000

Prepare the adjusting entry in journal form for December 31, 2009.

LO3 **Adjusting Entries for Prepaid Insurance**

E 6. An examination of the Prepaid Insurance account shows a balance of $16,845 at the end of an accounting period, before adjustment. Prepare entries in journal form to record the insurance expense for the period under the following independent assumptions:

1. An examination of the insurance policies shows unexpired insurance that cost $8,270 at the end of the period.
2. An examination of the insurance policies shows insurance that cost $2,150 has expired during the period.

LO3 **Adjusting Entries for Supplies: Missing Data**

E 7. Each of the following columns represents a Supplies account:

	a	b	c	d
Supplies on hand at July 1	$264	$346	$196	$?
Supplies purchased during the month	113	?	174	1,928
Supplies consumed during the month	194	972	?	1,741
Supplies on hand at July 31	?	436	85	1,118

1. Determine the amounts indicated by the question marks.
2. Make the adjusting entry for column **a**, assuming supplies purchased are debited to an asset account.

LO3 **Adjusting Entry for Accrued Salaries**

E 8. Hugo Incorporated has a five-day workweek and pays salaries of $35,000 each Friday.

1. Prepare the adjusting entry required on May 31, assuming that June 1 falls on a Wednesday.
2. Prepare the entry to pay the salaries on June 3, including the amount of salaries payable from requirement **1**.

LO3 **Revenue and Expense Recognition**

E 9. Optima Company produces computer software that Tech Comp, Inc. sells. Optima receives a royalty of 15 percent of sales. Tech Comp pays royalties to Optima Company semiannually—on May 1 for sales made in July through December of the previous year and on November 1 for sales made in January through June of the current year. Royalty expense for Tech Comp and royalty income for Optima Company in the amount of $6,000 were accrued on December 31, 2008. Cash in the amounts of $6,000 and $10,000 was paid and received on May 1 and November 1, 2009, respectively. Software sales during the July to December 2009 period totaled $215,000.

1. Calculate the amount of royalty expense for Tech Comp and royalty income for Optima during 2009.
2. Record the adjusting entry that each company made on December 31, 2009.

LO4 **Preparation of Financial Statements**

E 10. Prepare the monthly income statement, statement of retained earnings, and balance sheet for Alvin Cleaning Company, Inc., from the data provided in the adjusted trial balance at the top of the next page.

LO5 **Preparation of Closing Entries**

E 11. From the adjusted trial balance in **E 10**, prepare the required closing entries for Alvin Cleaning Company, Inc.

LO3 **Adjusting Entries**

E 12. Prepare year-end adjusting entries for each of the following:

1. Office Supplies has a balance of $336 on January 1. Purchases debited to Office Supplies during the year amount to $1,660. A year-end inventory reveals supplies of $1,140 on hand.
2. Depreciation of office equipment is estimated to be $2,130 for the year.
3. Property taxes for six months, estimated at $1,800, have accrued but have not been recorded.
4. Unrecorded interest receivable on U.S. government bonds is $850.

Alvin Cleaning Company, Inc.
Adjusted Trial Balance
August 31, 2010

Cash	$ 4,750	
Accounts Receivable	2,592	
Prepaid Insurance	380	
Prepaid Rent	200	
Cleaning Supplies	152	
Cleaning Equipment	3,875	
Accumulated Depreciation–Cleaning Equipment		$ 320
Truck	7,200	
Accumulated Depreciation–Truck		720
Accounts Payable		420
Wages Payable		295
Unearned Janitorial Revenue		1,590
Income Taxes Payable		900
Common Stock		4,000
Retained Earnings		11,034
Dividends	2,000	
Janitorial Revenue		14,620
Wages Expense	5,680	
Rent Expense	1,350	
Gas, Oil, and Other Truck Expenses	580	
Insurance Expense	380	
Supplies Expense	2,920	
Depreciation Expense–Cleaning Equipment	320	
Depreciation Expense–Truck	720	
Income Taxes Expense	800	
	$33,899	$33,899

5. Unearned Revenue has a balance of $1,800. Services for $750 received in advance have now been performed.
6. Services totaling $800 have been performed; the customer has not yet been billed.

LO3 Accounting for Revenue Received in Advanced

E 13. Robert Shapiro, a lawyer, was paid $84,000 on October 1 to represent a client in real estate negotiations over the next 12 months.

1. Record the entries required in Shapiro's records on October 1 and at the end of the fiscal year, December 31.
2. How would this transaction be reflected on the income statement and balance sheet on December 31?

LO5 Preparation of Closing Entries

E 14. The adjusted trial balance for Burke Consultant Corporation at the end of its fiscal year is at the top of the next page. Prepare the required closing entries.

Burke Consultant Corporation
Trial Balance
December 31, 2010

Cash	$ 7,575	
Accounts Receivable	2,625	
Prepaid Insurance	585	
Office Supplies	440	
Office Equipment	6,300	
Accumulated Depreciation–Office Equipment		$ 765
Automobile	6,750	
Accumulated Depreciation–Automobile		750
Accounts Payable		1,700
Unearned Consulting Fees		1,500
Income Taxes Payable		3,000
Common Stock		10,000
Retained Earnings		4,535
Dividends	7,000	
Consulting Fees Earned		32,550
Office Salaries Expense	13,500	
Advertising Expense	2,525	
Rent Expense	2,650	
Telephone Expense	1,850	
Income Taxes Expense	3,000	
	$54,800	$54,800

LO4 LO5 **Preparation of a Statement of Retained Earnings**

E 15. The Retained Earnings, Dividends, and Income Summary accounts for New Look Hair Salon, Inc., are shown in T account form below. The closing entries have been recorded for the year ended December 31, 2009. Prepare a statement of retained earnings for New Look Hair Salon, Inc.

Retained Earnings

12/31/09	9,500	12/31/08	26,000
		12/31/09	22,000
		Bal.	**38,500**

Income Summary

12/31/09	43,000	12/31/09	65,000
12/31/09	22,000		
Bal.	—		

Dividends

4/1/09	3,000	12/31/09	9,500
7/1/09	3,500		
10/1/09	3,000		
Bal.	—		

LO6 **Determination of Cash Flows**

E 16. After adjusting entries, the balance sheets of Ramiros Company showed the following asset and liability amounts at the end of 2009 and 2010:

	2010	2009
Prepaid insurance	$2,400	$2,900
Wages payable	1,200	2,200
Unearned revenue	4,200	1,900

The following amounts were taken from the 2010 income statement:

Insurance expense	$ 3,800
Wages expense	19,500
Fees earned	8,900

Calculate the amount of cash paid for insurance and wages and the amount of cash received for fees during 2010.

Relationship of Expenses to Cash Paid

E 17. The income statement for Sahan Company included the following expenses for 2010:

Rent expense	$ 75,000
Interest expense	11,700
Salaries expense	121,000

Listed below are the related balance sheet account balances at year end for last year and this year.

	Last Year	This Year
Prepaid rent	$1,500	$ 1,350
Interest payable	—	—
Salaries payable	7,500	14,000

1. Compute the cash paid for rent during the year.
2. Compute the cash paid for interest during the year.
3. Compute the cash paid for salaries during the year.

Profit Margin

E 18. Jarvis Company wants to know if its profitability has improved. Calculate its profit margin for 2010 and 2009 using the following data:

Net Income, 2010	$ 10,000
Net Income, 2009	8,600
Net Sales, 2010	192,000
Net Sales, 2009	160,000

By this measure, has profitability improved?

Problems

LO3

Determining Adjustments

P 1. At the end of the first three months of operation, the trial balance of City Answering Service, Inc., appears as shown at the top of the next page. Oscar Rienzo, the owner of City Answering Service, has hired an accountant to prepare financial statements to determine how well the company is doing after three months. Upon examining the accounting records, the accountant finds the following items of interest:

a. An inventory of office supplies reveals supplies on hand of $150.
b. The Prepaid Rent account includes the rent for the first three months plus a deposit for April's rent.
c. Depreciation on the equipment for the first three months is $416.
d. The balance of the Unearned Answering Service Revenue account represents a 12-month service contract paid in advance on February 1.
e. On March 31, accrued wages total $105.
f. Federal income taxes for the three months are estimated to be $1,110.

City Answering Service, Inc.
Trial Balance
March 31, 2010

Cash	$ 3,582	
Accounts Receivable	4,236	
Office Supplies	933	
Prepaid Rent	800	
Equipment	4,700	
Accounts Payable		$ 2,673
Unearned Answering Service Revenue		888
Common Stock		5,933
Dividends	2,100	
Answering Service Revenue		9,102
Wages Expense	1,900	
Office Cleaning Expense	345	
	$18,596	$18,596

Required

All adjustments affect one balance sheet account and one income statement account. For each of the above situations, show the accounts affected, the amount of the adjustment (using a + or − to indicate an increase or decrease), and the balance of the account after the adjustment in the following format:

Balance Sheet Account	Amount of Adjustment (+ or −)	Balance after Adjustment	Income Statement Account	Amount of Adjustment (+ or −)	Balance after Adjustment

LO2 LO3

Preparing Adjusting Entries

P 2. On November 30, the end of the current fiscal year, the following information is available to assist Caruso Corporation's accountants in making adjusting entries:

a. Caruso Corporation's Supplies account shows a beginning balance of $2,350. Purchases during the year were $4,218. The end-of-year inventory reveals supplies on hand of $1,397.

b. The Prepaid Insurance account shows the following on November 30:

Beginning balance	$4,720
July 1	4,200
October 1	7,272

The beginning balance represents the unexpired portion of a one-year policy purchased the previous year. The July 1 entry represents a new one-year policy, and the October 1 entry represents additional coverage in the form of a three-year policy.

c. The following table contains the cost and annual depreciation for buildings and equipment, all of which Caruso Corporation purchased before the current year:

Account	Cost	Annual Depreciation
Buildings	$298,000	$16,000
Equipment	374,000	40,000

d. On September 1, the company completed negotiations with a client and accepted an advance payment of $18,600 for services to be performed in the next year. The $18,600 was credited to the Unearned Service Revenue account.
e. The company calculated that as of November 30, it had earned $7,000 on an $11,000 contract that would be completed and billed in January.
f. Among the liabilities of the company is a note payable in the amount of $300,000. On November 30, the accrued interest on this note amounted to $18,000.
g. On Saturday, December 2, the company, which is on a six-day workweek, will pay its regular salaried employees $15,000.
h. On November 29, the company completed negotiations and signed a contract to provide services to a new client at an annual rate of $17,500.
i. Management estimates income taxes for the year to be $23,000.

Required

User insight ▶ 1. Prepare adjusting entries for each item listed above.
2. Explain how the conditions for revenue recognition are applied to transactions **e** and **h**.

LO3 LO4 **Determining Adjusting Entries, Posting to T Accounts, and Preparing an Adjusted Trial Balance**

P 3. The schedule below presents the trial balance for Prima Consultants Corporation on December 31, 2010. The following information is also available:

a. Ending inventory of office supplies, $97.
b. Prepaid rent expired, $500.
c. Depreciation of office equipment for the period, $720.
d. Interest accrued on the note payable, $600.

Prima Consultants Corporation
Trial Balance
December 31, 2010

Cash	$ 13,786	
Accounts Receivable	24,840	
Office Supplies	991	
Prepaid Rent	1,400	
Office Equipment	7,300	
Accumulated Depreciation–Office Equipment		$ 2,600
Accounts Payable		1,820
Notes Payable		10,000
Unearned Service Revenue		2,860
Common Stock		11,000
Retained Earnings		19,387
Dividends	15,000	
Service Revenue		58,500
Salaries Expense	33,400	
Utilities Expense	1,750	
Rent Expense	7,700	
	$106,167	$106,167

e. Salaries accrued at the end of the period, $230.
f. Service revenue still unearned at the end of the period, $1,410.
g. Service revenue earned but not billed, $915.
h. Estimated federal income taxes for the period, $2,780.

Required

1. Open T accounts for the accounts in the trial balance plus the following: Interest Payable; Salaries Payable; Income Taxes Payable; Office Supplies Expense; Depreciation Expense–Office Equipment; Interest Expense; and Income Taxes Expense. Enter the account balances.
2. Determine the adjusting entries and post them directly to the T accounts.
3. Prepare an adjusted trial balance.
4. What financial statements do each of the above adjustments affect? What financial statement is *not* affected by the adjustments?

User insight ▶ (item 4)

LO3 LO4

Determining Adjusting Entries and Tracing Their Effects to Financial Statements

P 4. Helen Ortega opened a small tax-preparation service. At the end of its second year of operation, Ortega Tax Service, Inc., had the trial balance shown below. The following information is also available:

a. Office supplies on hand, December 31, 2010, $225.
b. Insurance still unexpired, $100.
c. Estimated depreciation of office equipment, $795.
d. Telephone expense for December, $21; the bill was received but not recorded.
e. The services for all unearned tax fees revenue had been performed by the end of the year.
f. Estimated federal income taxes for the year, $2,430.

Ortega Tax Service, Inc.
Trial Balance
December 31, 2010

Account	Debit	Credit
Cash	$ 3,700	
Accounts Receivable	1,099	
Prepaid Insurance	240	
Office Supplies	780	
Office Equipment	7,100	
Accumulated Depreciation–Office Equipment		$ 770
Accounts Payable		635
Unearned Tax Fees Revenues		219
Common Stock		3,500
Retained Earnings		3,439
Dividends	6,000	
Tax Fees Revenue		21,926
Office Salaries Expense	8,300	
Advertising Expense	650	
Rent Expense	2,400	
Telephone Expense	220	
	$30,489	$30,489

Required

1. Open T accounts for the accounts in the trial balance plus the following: Income Taxes Payable; Insurance Expense; Office Supplies Expense; Depreciation Expense–Office Equipment; and Income Taxes Expense. Record the balances shown in the trial balance.
2. Determine the adjusting entries and post them directly to the T accounts.
3. Prepare an adjusted trial balance, an income statement, a statement of retained earnings, and a balance sheet.

User insight ▶ 4. Why is it not necessary to show the effects of the above transactions on the statement of cash flows?

Determining Adjusting Entries and Tracing Their Effects to Financial Statements

P 5. VIP Limo, Inc., was organized to provide limousine service between the airport and various suburban locations. It has just completed its second year of business. Its trial balance appears below.

VIP Limo, Inc.
Trial Balance
June 30, 2010

Cash (111)	$ 9,812	
Accounts Receivable (112)	14,227	
Prepaid Rent (117)	12,000	
Prepaid Insurance (118)	4,900	
Prepaid Maintenance (119)	12,000	
Spare Parts (141)	11,310	
Limousines (142)	220,000	
Accumulated Depreciation–Limousines (143)		$ 35,000
Notes Payable (211)		45,000
Unearned Passenger Service Revenue (212)		30,000
Common Stock (311)		40,000
Retained Earnings (312)		48,211
Dividends (313)	20,000	
Passenger Service Revenue (411)		428,498
Gas and Oil Expense (511)	89,300	
Salaries Expense (512)	206,360	
Advertising Expense (513)	26,800	
	$626,709	$626,709

The following information is also available:

a. To obtain space at the airport, VIP Limo paid two years' rent in advance when it began the business.
b. An examination of insurance policies reveals that $1,800 expired during the year.
c. To provide regular maintenance for the vehicles, VIP Limo deposited $12,000 with a local garage. An examination of maintenance invoices reveals charges of $10,944 against the deposit.
d. An inventory of spare parts shows $2,016 on hand.

e. VIP Limo depreciates all of its limousines at the rate of 12.5 percent per year. No limousines were purchased during the year.
f. A payment of $11,300 for one full year's interest on notes payable is now due.
g. Unearned Passenger Service Revenue on June 30 includes $17,815 for tickets that employers purchased for use by their executives but which have not yet been redeemed.
h. Federal income taxes for the year are estimated to be $13,250.

Required

1. Determine adjusting entries and enter them in the general journal (Page 14).
2. Open ledger accounts for the accounts in the trial balance plus the following: Interest Payable (213); Income Taxes Payable (214); Rent Expense (514); Insurance Expense (515); Spare Parts Expense (516); Depreciation Expense–Limousines (517); Maintenance Expense (518); Interest Expense (519); and Income Taxes Expense (520). Record the balances shown in the trial balance.
3. Post the adjusting entries from the general journal to the ledger accounts, showing proper references.
4. Prepare an adjusted trial balance, an income statement, a statement of retained earnings, and a balance sheet.

User insight ▶

5. Do adjustments affect the profit margin? After the adjustments, is the profit margin for the year more or less than it would have been if the adjustments had not been made?

Alternate Problems

LO3 Determining Adjustments

P 6. At the end of its fiscal year, the trial balance for Andy's Cleaners, Inc., appears as shown at the top of the next page:

The following information is also available:

a. A study of the company's insurance policies shows that $680 is unexpired at the end of the year.
b. An inventory of cleaning supplies shows $1,150 on hand.
c. Estimated depreciation on the building for the year is $12,800.
d. Accrued interest on the mortgage payable is $1,000.
e. On September 1, the company signed a contract, effective immediately, with Hope County Hospital to dry clean, for a fixed monthly charge of $425, the uniforms used by doctors in surgery. The hospital paid for four months' service in advance.
f. The company pays sales and delivery wages on Saturday. The weekly payroll is $3,060. September 30 falls on a Thursday, and the company has a six-day pay week.
g. Estimated federal income taxes for the period are $2,300.

Required

All adjustments affect one balance sheet account and one income statement account. For each of the above situations, show the accounts affected, the amount of the adjustment (using a + or − to indicate an increase or decrease), and the balance of the account after the adjustment in the following format:

Balance Sheet Account	Amount of Adjustment (+ or −)	Balance after Adjustment	Income Statement Account	Amount of Adjustment (+ or −)	Balance after Adjustment

Andy's Cleaners, Inc.
Trial Balance
September 30, 2010

Cash	$ 11,788	
Accounts Receivable	26,494	
Prepaid Insurance	3,400	
Cleaning Supplies	7,374	
Land	18,000	
Building	186,000	
Accumulated Depreciation–Building		$ 45,600
Accounts Payable		18,400
Unearned Cleaning Revenue		1,700
Mortgage Payable		110,000
Common Stock		40,000
Retained Earnings		16,560
Dividends	9,000	
Cleaning Revenue		159,634
Wages Expense	101,330	
Cleaning Equipment Rental Expense	6,100	
Delivery Truck Expense	4,374	
Interest Expense	11,000	
Other Expenses	7,034	
	$391,894	$391,894

LO2 LO3

Preparing Adjusting Entries

P 7. On June 30, the end of the current fiscal year, the following information is available to Conti Company's accountants for making adjusting entries:

a. One of the company's liabilities is a mortgage payable in the amount of $260,000. On June 30, the accrued interest on this mortgage was $13,000.

b. On Friday, July 2, the company, which is on a five-day workweek and pays employees weekly, will pay its regular salaried employees $18,700.

c. On June 29, the company completed negotiations and signed a contract to provide services to a new client at an annual rate of $7,200.

d. The Supplies account shows a beginning balance of $1,615 and purchases during the year of $4,115. The end-of-year inventory reveals supplies on hand of $1,318.

e. The Prepaid Insurance account shows the following entries on June 30:

Beginning Balance	$1,620
January 1	2,900
May 1	3,366

The beginning balance represents the unexpired portion of a one-year policy purchased a year ago. The January 1 entry represents a new one-year policy; the May 1 entry represents the additional coverage of a three-year policy.

f. The following table contains the cost and annual depreciation for buildings and equipment, all of which were purchased before the current year:

Account	Cost	Annual Depreciation
Buildings	$170,000	$ 7,300
Equipment	218,000	20,650

g. On June 1, the company completed negotiations with another client and accepted a payment of $21,600, representing one year's services paid in advance. The $21,600 was credited to Services Collected in Advance.
h. The company calculates that as of June 30 it had earned $4,500 on a $7,500 contract that will be completed and billed in August.
i. Federal income taxes for the year are estimated to be $6,300.

Required

1. Prepare adjusting entries for each item listed above.
2. Explain how the conditions for revenue recognition are applied to transactions **c** and **h**. (User insight ▶)

LO3

Determining Adjusting Entries, Posting to T Accounts, and Preparing an Adjusted Trial Balance

P 8. The trial balance for Best Advisors Service, Inc., on December 31 follows.

Best Advisors Service, Inc.
Trial Balance
December 31, 2010

Cash	$ 18,500	
Accounts Receivable	8,250	
Office Supplies	2,662	
Prepaid Rent	1,320	
Office Equipment	9,240	
Accumulated Depreciation–Office Equipment		$ 1,540
Accounts Payable		5,940
Notes Payable		11,000
Unearned Service Revenue		2,970
Common Stock		12,000
Retained Earnings		14,002
Dividends	22,000	
Service Revenue		72,600
Salaries Expense	49,400	
Rent Expense	4,400	
Utilities Expense	4,280	
	$120,052	$120,052

The following information is also available:

a. Ending inventory of office supplies, $300.
b. Prepaid rent expired, $610.
c. Depreciation of office equipment for the period, $526.
d. Accrued interest expense at the end of the period, $570.
e. Accrued salaries at the end of the period, $330.
f. Service revenue still unearned at the end of the period, $1,166.
g. Service revenue earned but unrecorded, $3,100.
h. Estimated income taxes for the period, $4,200.

Required

1. Open T accounts for the accounts in the trial balance plus the following: Interest Payable; Salaries Payable; Income Taxes Payable; Office Supplies

Expense; Depreciation Expense–Office Equipment; Interest Expense; and Income Taxes Expense. Enter the balances shown on the trial balance.

2. Determine the adjusting entries and post them directly to the T accounts.
3. Prepare an adjusted trial balance.

User insight ▶ 4. What financial statements do each of the above adjustments affect? What financial statement is *not* affected by the adjustments?

ENHANCING Your Knowledge, Skills, and Critical Thinking

Conceptual Understanding Cases

LO1 LO2 LO3

Importance of Adjustments

C 1. Never Flake Company, which operated in the northeastern part of the United States, provided a rust-prevention coating for the underside of new automobiles. The company advertised widely and offered its services through new car dealers. When a dealer sold a new car, the salesperson attempted to sell the rust-prevention coating as an option. The protective coating was supposed to make cars last longer in the severe northeastern winters. A key selling point was Never Flake's warranty, which stated that it would repair any damage due to rust at no charge for as long as the buyer owned the car.

For several years, Never Flake had been very successful in generating enough cash to continue operations. But in 2008, the company suddenly declared bankruptcy. Company officials said that the firm had only $5.5 million in assets against liabilities of $32.9 million. Most of the liabilities represented potential claims under the company's lifetime warranty. It seemed that owners were keeping their cars longer now than previously. Therefore, more damage was being attributed to rust.

Discuss what accounting decisions could have helped Never Flake to survive under these circumstances.

LO1

Earnings Management and Fraudulent Financial Reporting

C 2. In recent years, the Securities and Exchange Commission (SEC) has been waging a public campaign against corporate accounting practices that manage or manipulate earnings to meet the expectations of Wall Street analysts. Corporations engage in such practices in the hope of avoiding shortfalls that might cause serious declines in their stock price.

For each of the following cases that the Securities and Exchange Commission challenged, tell why each is a violation of the matching rule and how it should be accounted for:

a. **Lucent Technologies** sold telecommunications equipment to companies from which there was no reasonable expectation of payment because of the companies' poor financial condition.
b. **America Online (AOL)** recorded advertising as an asset rather than as an expense.
c. **Eclipsys** recorded software contracts as revenue even though it had not yet rendered the services.
d. **Xerox Corporation** recorded revenue from lease agreements at the time the leases were signed rather than over the lease term.
e. **KnowledgeWare** recorded revenue from sales of software even though it told customers they did not have to pay until they had the software.

Interpreting Financial Reports

LO2 LO3

Application of Accrual Accounting

C 3. The **Lyric Opera of Chicago** is one of the largest and best-managed opera companies in the United States. Managing opera productions requires advance planning, including the development of scenery, costumes, and stage properties and the sale of tickets. To measure how well the company is operating in any given year, management must apply accrual accounting to these and other transactions. At year end, April 30, 2007, Lyric Opera's balance sheet showed deferred production costs of $2,061,756 and deferred ticket revenue of $16,882,165.[9] Be prepared to discuss what accounting policies and adjusting entries are applicable to these accounts. Why are they important to Lyric Opera's management?

LO2 LO3

Analysis of an Asset Account

C 4. **The Walt Disney Company** is engaged in the financing, production, and distribution of motion pictures and television programming. In Disney's 2006 annual report, the balance sheet contains an asset called "film and television costs." Film and television costs, which consist of the costs associated with producing films and television programs less the amount expensed, were $5,235 million. The notes reveal that the amount of film and television costs expensed (amortized) during the year was $3,526 million. The amount spent for new film productions was $2,901 million.[10]

1. What are film and television costs, and why would they be classified as an asset?
2. Prepare an entry in T account form to record the amount the company spent on new film and television production during the year (assume all expenditures are paid for in cash).
3. Prepare an adjusting entry in T account form to record the expense for film and television productions.
4. Suggest a method by which The Walt Disney Company might have determined the amount of the expense in **3** in accordance with the matching rule.

Decision Analysis Using Excel

LO1 LO3

Adjusting Entries, Performance Evaluation, and Dividend Policy

C 5. Tony Mendoza, the owner of a newsletter for managers of hotels and restaurants, has prepared the following condensed amounts from his company's financial statements for 2009:

Revenues	$432,500
Expenses	352,500
Net income	$ 80,000
Total assets	$215,000
Liabilities	$ 60,000
Stockholders' equity	155,000
Total liabilities and stockholders' equity	$215,000

Given these figures, Mendoza is planning a cash dividend of $62,500. However, Mendoza's accountant has found that the following items were overlooked:

a. Although the balance of the Printing Supplies account is $40,000, only $17,500 in supplies is on hand at the end of the year.
b. Depreciation of $25,000 on equipment has not been recorded.
c. Wages of $11,750 have been earned by Mendoza's employees but not recognized in the accounts.

d. No provision has been made for estimated income taxes payable of $13,500.
e. A liability account called Unearned Subscriptions Revenue has a balance of $20,250, although it has been determined that one-third of these subscriptions have been mailed to subscribers.

1. Prepare the necessary adjusting entries.
2. Recast the condensed financial statement figures after you have made the necessary adjustments.
3. Discuss the performance of Mendoza's business after the adjustments have been made. (**Hint**: Compare net income to revenues and total assets before and after the adjustments.) Do you think that paying the dividend is advisable? Why or why not?

Annual Report Case: CVS Caremark Corporation

LO3

Analysis of Balance Sheet and Adjusting Entries

C 6. In the **CVS** annual report in the Supplement to Chapter 1, refer to the balance sheet and the Summary of Significant Accounting Policies in the notes to the financial statements.

1. Examine the accounts in the current assets, property and equipment, and current liabilities sections of CVS's balance sheet. Which are most likely to have had year-end adjusting entries? Describe the nature of the adjusting entries. For more information about the property and equipment section, refer to the notes to the financial statements.
2. Where is depreciation (and amortization) expense disclosed in CVS's financial statements?
3. CVS has a statement on the "Use of Estimates" in its Summary of Significant Accounting Policies. Read this statement and tell how important estimates are to the determination of depreciation expense. What assumptions do accountants make that allow these estimates to be made?

Comparison Analysis: CVS Versus Southwest

Profit Margin

C 7. The profit margin is an important measure of profitability. Use data from **CVS's** income statement and the financial statements of **Southwest Airlines Co.** in the Supplement to Chapter 1 to calculate each company's profit margin for the past two years. By this measure, which company is more profitable?

Ethical Dilemma Case

LO1 LO2 LO3

Importance of Adjustments

C 8. Main Street Service Co., Inc., has achieved fast growth in the St. Louis area by selling service contracts on large appliances, such as washers, dryers, and refrigerators. For a fee, Main Street agrees to provide all parts and labor on an appliance after the regular warranty runs out. For example, by paying a fee of $200, a person who buys a dishwasher can add two years (years 2 and 3) to the regular one-year (year 1) warranty on the appliance. In 2009, the company sold service contracts in the amount of $1.8 million, all of which applied to future years. Management wanted all the sales recorded as revenues in 2009, contending that the amount of the contracts could be determined and the cash had been received. Discuss whether you agree with this logic. How would you record the cash receipts? What assumptions do you think Main Street should make? Would you consider it unethical to follow management's recommendation? Who might be hurt or helped by this action?

Internet Case

LO3 Comparison of Accrued Expenses

C 9. How important are accrued expenses? Randomly choose four different companies. Go to each company's website and find their annual reports. For each company, find the section of the balance sheet labeled "Current Liabilities" and identify the current liabilities that are accrued expenses (sometimes called accrued liabilities). More than one account may be involved. On a pad, write the information you find in four columns: name of company, total current liabilities, total accrued liabilities, and total accrued liabilities as a percentage of total current liabilities. Write a brief statement listing the companies you chose, telling how you obtained their reports, reporting the data you have gathered in the form of a table, and stating a conclusion, with reasons, as to the importance of accrued expenses to the companies you studied.

Group Activity Case

LO3 Types of Adjusting Entries

C 10. In this chapter, we discussed adjusting entries for deferred revenue, deferred expense, accrued revenue, and accrued expense. In informal groups in class, discuss how each type of adjusting entry applies to **Netflix**. Be prepared to present your group's findings to the class.

Business Communication Case

LO3 Real-World Observation of Business Activities

C 11. Visit a company with which you are familiar and observe its operations. (The company can be where you work, where you eat, or where you buy things.) Identify at least two sources of revenue for the company and six types of expenses. For each type of revenue and each type of expense, determine whether it is probable that an adjusting entry is required at the end of the accounting period. Then specify the adjusting entry as a deferred revenue, deferred expense, accrued revenue, or accrued expense. Design a table with columns and rows that summarize your results in an easy-to-understand format.

SUPPLEMENT TO CHAPTER 3

Closing Entries and the Work Sheet

Preparing Closing Entries

As you know, closing entries have two purposes: (1) they clear the balances of all temporary accounts (revenue, expense, and Dividends accounts) so that they have zero balances at the beginning of the next accounting period, and (2) they summarize a period's revenues and expenses in the Income Summary account so that the net income or loss for the period can be transferred as a total to Retained Earnings.

The steps involved in making closing entries are as follows:

Step 1. Close the credit balances on the income statement accounts to the Income Summary account.

Step 2. Close the debit balances on the income statement accounts to the Income Summary account.

Step 3. Close the Income Summary account balance to the Retained Earnings account.

Step 4. Close the Dividends account balance to the Retained Earnings account.

As you will learn in later chapters, not all revenue accounts have credit balances, and not all expense accounts have debit balances. For that reason, when referring to closing entries, we often use the term *credit balances* instead of *revenue accounts* and the term *debit balances* instead of *expense accounts*.

An adjusted trial balance provides all the data needed to record the closing entries. Exhibit S-1 shows the relationships of the four kinds of closing entries to Miller Design Studio's adjusted trial balance.

Study Note

Although it is not absolutely necessary to use the Income Summary account when preparing closing entries, it does simplify the procedure.

Step 1: Closing the Credit Balances

On the credit side of the adjusted trial balance in Exhibit S-1, Design Revenue shows a balance of $13,600. To close this account, a journal entry must be made debiting the account in the amount of its balance and crediting it to the Income Summary account. Exhibit S-2 shows how the entry is posted. Notice that the entry sets the balance of the revenue account to zero and transfers the total revenues to the credit side of the Income Summary account.

Study Note

The Income Summary account now reflects the account balance of the revenue account before it was closed.

Step 2: Closing the Debit Balances

Several expense accounts show balances on the debit side of the adjusted trial balance in Exhibit S-1. A compound entry is needed to credit each of these expense accounts for its balance and to debit the Income Summary account for the total. Exhibit S-3 shows the effect of posting the closing entry. Notice how the entry

EXHIBIT S-1 Preparing Closing Entries from the Adjusted Trial Balance

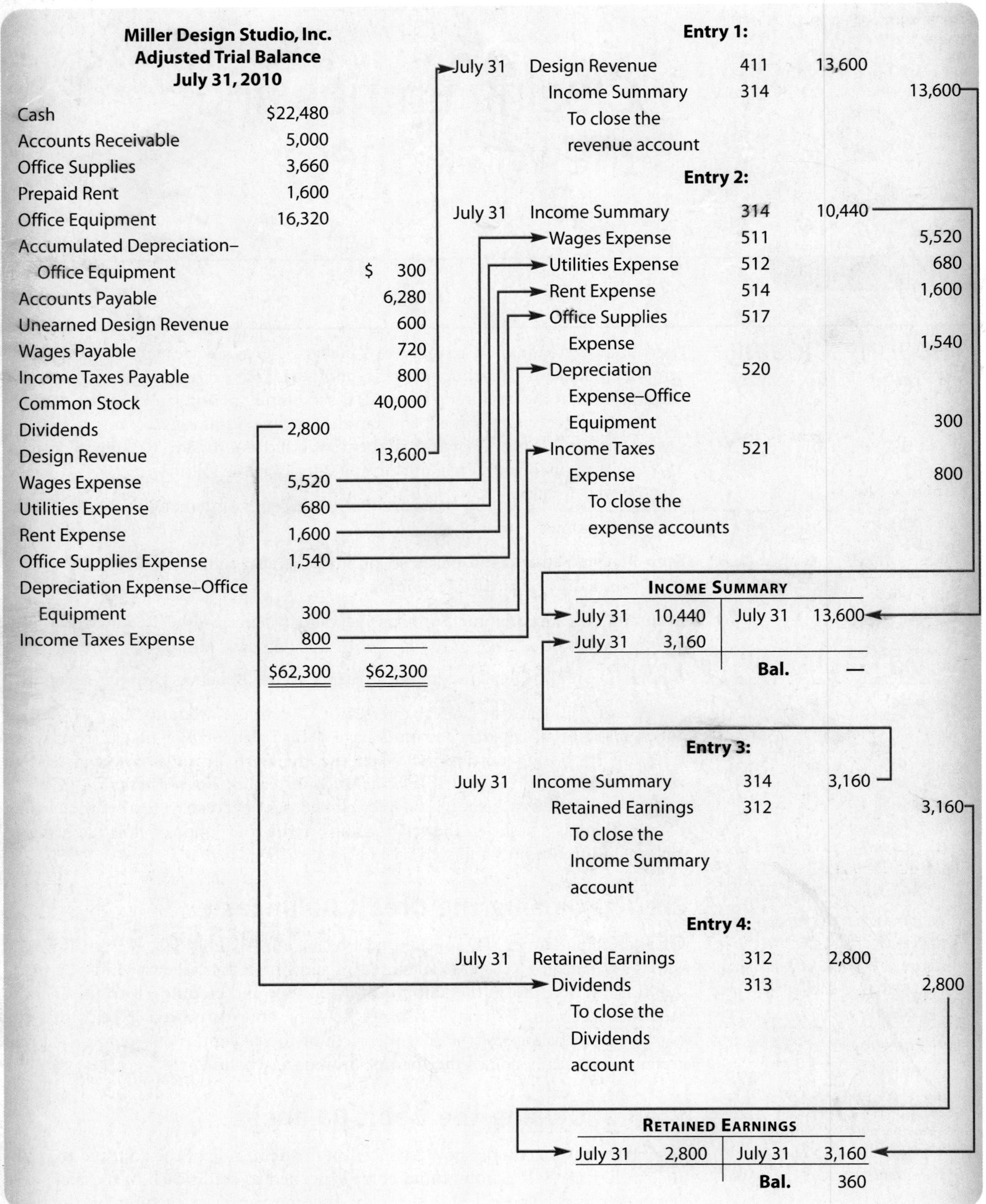

Miller Design Studio, Inc.
Adjusted Trial Balance
July 31, 2010

Account	Debit	Credit
Cash	$22,480	
Accounts Receivable	5,000	
Office Supplies	3,660	
Prepaid Rent	1,600	
Office Equipment	16,320	
Accumulated Depreciation–Office Equipment		$ 300
Accounts Payable		6,280
Unearned Design Revenue		600
Wages Payable		720
Income Taxes Payable		800
Common Stock		40,000
Dividends	2,800	
Design Revenue		13,600
Wages Expense	5,520	
Utilities Expense	680	
Rent Expense	1,600	
Office Supplies Expense	1,540	
Depreciation Expense–Office Equipment	300	
Income Taxes Expense	800	
	$62,300	$62,300

Entry 1:

Date	Account	Ref.	Debit	Credit
July 31	Design Revenue	411	13,600	
	Income Summary	314		13,600
	To close the revenue account			

Entry 2:

Date	Account	Ref.	Debit	Credit
July 31	Income Summary	314	10,440	
	Wages Expense	511		5,520
	Utilities Expense	512		680
	Rent Expense	514		1,600
	Office Supplies Expense	517		1,540
	Depreciation Expense–Office Equipment	520		300
	Income Taxes Expense	521		800
	To close the expense accounts			

INCOME SUMMARY

July 31	10,440	July 31	13,600
July 31	3,160		
		Bal.	—

Entry 3:

Date	Account	Ref.	Debit	Credit
July 31	Income Summary	314	3,160	
	Retained Earnings	312		3,160
	To close the Income Summary account			

Entry 4:

Date	Account	Ref.	Debit	Credit
July 31	Retained Earnings	312	2,800	
	Dividends	313		2,800
	To close the Dividends account			

RETAINED EARNINGS

July 31	2,800	July 31	3,160
		Bal.	360

EXHIBIT S-2

Posting the Closing Entry of a Credit Balance to the Income Summary Account

DESIGN REVENUE — **ACCOUNT NO. 411**

DATE	ITEM	POST. REF.	DEBIT	CREDIT	BALANCE DEBIT	BALANCE CREDIT
July 10		J2		2,800		2,800
15		J2		9,600		12,400
31		J3		800		13,200
31		J3		400		13,600
31	Closing	J4	13,600			—

INCOME SUMMARY — **ACCOUNT NO. 314**

DATE	ITEM	POST. REF.	DEBIT	CREDIT	BALANCE DEBIT	BALANCE CREDIT
July 31	Closing	J4		13,600		13,600

EXHIBIT S-3 Posting the Closing Entry of Debit Balances to the Income Summary Account

INCOME SUMMARY — **ACCOUNT NO. 314**

DATE	ITEM	POST. REF.	DEBIT	CREDIT	BALANCE DEBIT	BALANCE CREDIT
July 31	Closing	J4		13,600		13,600
31	Closing	J4	10,440*			3,160

WAGES EXPENSE — **ACCOUNT NO. 511**

DATE	ITEM	POST. REF.	DEBIT	CREDIT	BALANCE DEBIT	BALANCE CREDIT
July 26		J2	4,800		4,800	
31		J3	720		5,520	
31	Closing	J4		5,520	—	

UTILITIES EXPENSE — **ACCOUNT NO. 512**

DATE	ITEM	POST. REF.	DEBIT	CREDIT	BALANCE DEBIT	BALANCE CREDIT
July 30		J2	680		680	
31	Closing	J4		680	—	

RENT EXPENSE — **ACCOUNT NO. 514**

DATE	ITEM	POST. REF.	DEBIT	CREDIT	BALANCE DEBIT	BALANCE CREDIT
July 31		J3	1,600		1,600	
31	Closing	J4		1,600	—	

OFFICE SUPPLIES EXPENSE — **ACCOUNT NO. 517**

DATE	ITEM	POST. REF.	DEBIT	CREDIT	BALANCE DEBIT	BALANCE CREDIT
July 31		J3	1,540		1,540	
31	Closing	J4		1,540	—	

DEPRECIATION EXPENSE–OFFICE EQUIPMENT — **ACCOUNT NO. 520**

DATE	ITEM	POST. REF.	DEBIT	CREDIT	BALANCE DEBIT	BALANCE CREDIT
July 31		J3	300		300	
31	Closing	J4		300	—	

INCOME TAXES EXPENSE — **ACCOUNT NO. 521**

DATE	ITEM	POST. REF.	DEBIT	CREDIT	BALANCE DEBIT	BALANCE CREDIT
July 31		J3	800		800	
31	Closing	J4		800	—	

*Total of all credit closing entries to expense accounts is debited to the Income Summary account.

EXHIBIT S-4 Posting the Closing Entry of the Income Summary Account Balance to the Retained Earnings Account

INCOME SUMMARY — ACCOUNT NO. 314

Date	Item	Post. Ref.	Debit	Credit	Balance Debit	Balance Credit
July 31	Closing	J4		13,600		13,600
31	Closing	J4	10,440			3,160
31	Closing	J4	3,160			—

RETAINED EARNINGS — ACCOUNT NO. 312

Date	Item	Post. Ref.	Debit	Credit	Balance Debit	Balance Credit
July 31	Closing	J4		3,160		3,160

reduces the expense account balances to zero and transfers the total of the account balances to the debit side of the Income Summary account.

Step 3: Closing the Income Summary Account Balance

Study Note

The credit balance of the Income Summary account at this point ($3,160) represents net income—the key measure of performance. When a net loss occurs, debit the Retained Earnings account (to reduce it) and credit the Income Summary account (to close it).

After the entries closing the revenue and expense accounts have been posted, the balance of the Income Summary account equals the net income or loss for the period. A credit balance in the Income Summary account represents a net income (revenues exceed expenses), and a debit balance represents a net loss (expenses exceed revenues).

At this point, the balance of the Income Summary account, whatever its nature, is closed to the Retained Earnings account, as shown in Exhibit S-1. Exhibit S-4 shows how the closing entry is posted when a company has a net income. Notice the dual effect of closing the Income Summary account and transferring the balance to Retained Earnings.

Step 4: Closing the Dividends Account Balance

Study Note

Notice that the Dividends account is closed to the Retained Earnings account, not to the Income Summary account.

The Dividends account shows the amount by which cash dividends reduce retained earnings during an accounting period. The debit balance of the Dividends account is closed to the Retained Earnings account, as illustrated in Exhibit S-1. Exhibit S-5 shows the posting of the closing entry and the transfer of the balance of the Dividends account to the Retained Earnings account.

The Accounts After Closing

After all the steps in the closing process have been completed and all closing entries have been posted, everything is ready for the next accounting period. The

EXHIBIT S-5 Posting the Closing Entry of the Dividends Account Balance to the Retained Earnings Account

DIVIDENDS — ACCOUNT NO. 313

Date	Item	Post. Ref.	Debit	Credit	Balance Debit	Balance Credit
July 31		J2	2,800		2,800	
31	Closing	J4		2,800		—

RETAINED EARNINGS — ACCOUNT NO. 312

Date	Item	Post. Ref.	Debit	Credit	Balance Debit	Balance Credit
July 31	Closing	J4		3,160		3,160
31	Closing	J4	2,800			360

EXHIBIT S-6

Post-Closing Trial Balance

Miller Design Studio, Inc. Post-Closing Trial Balance July 31, 2010		
Cash	$22,480	
Accounts Receivable	5,000	
Office Supplies	3,660	
Prepaid Rent	1,600	
Office Equipment	16,320	
Accumulated Depreciation–Office Equipment		$ 300
Accounts Payable		6,280
Unearned Design Revenue		600
Wages Payable		720
Income Taxes Payable		800
Common Stock		40,000
Retained Earnings		360
	$49,060	$49,060

revenue, expense, and Dividends accounts (temporary accounts) have zero balances. The Retained Earnings account has been increased or decreased to reflect net income or net loss (net income in our example) and has been decreased for dividends. The balance sheet accounts (permanent accounts) show the correct balances, which are carried forward to the next period, as shown in the post-closing trial balance in Exhibit S-6.

The Work Sheet: An Accountant's Tool

Accountants must collect relevant data to determine what should be included in financial reports. For example, they must examine insurance policies to calculate how much prepaid insurance has expired, examine plant and equipment records to determine depreciation, and compute the amount of accrued wages. To organize such data and avoid omitting important information that might affect the financial statements, accountants use *working papers.* Because working papers provide evidence of past work, they also enable accountants to retrace their steps when they need to verify information in the financial statements.

The *work sheet* is a special kind of working paper. It is often used as a preliminary step in preparing financial statements. Using a work sheet lessens the possibility of leaving out an adjustment and helps the accountant check the arithmetical accuracy of the accounts. The work sheet is never published and is rarely seen by management. It is a tool for the accountant.

Study Note

The work sheet is extremely useful when an accountant must make numerous adjustments. It is not a financial statement, it is not required, and it is not made public.

Because preparing a work sheet is a mechanical process, many accountants use a computer for this purpose. Some accountants use a spreadsheet program to prepare the work sheet. Others use a general ledger system to prepare financial statements from the adjusted trial balance.

Preparing the Work Sheet

A common form of work sheet has one column for account names and/or account numbers and multiple columns with headings like the ones shown in Exhibit S-7. A heading that includes the name of the company and the period of time covered (as on the income statement) identifies the work sheet. As Exhibit S-7 shows, preparation of a work sheet involves five steps.

EXHIBIT S-7 The Work Sheet

Miller Design Studio, Inc.
Work Sheet
For the Month Ended July 31, 2010

	Trial Balance		Adjustments		Adjusted Trial Balance		Income Statement		Balance Sheet	
Account Name	**Debit**	**Credit**	**Debit**	**Credit**	**Debit**	**Credit**	**Debit**	**Credit**	**Debit**	**Credit**
Cash	22,480				22,480				22,480	
Accounts Receivable	4,600		(g) 400		5,000				5,000	
Office Supplies	5,200			(b) 1,540	3,660				3,660	
Prepaid Rent	3,200			(a) 1,600	1,600				1,600	
Office Equipment	16,320				16,320				16,320	
Accumulated Depreciation–Office Equipment		—		(c) 300		300				300
Accounts Payable		6,280				6,280				6,280
Unearned Design Revenue		1,400	(f) 800			600				600
Common Stock		40,000				40,000				40,000
Dividends	2,800				2,800				2,800	
Design Revenue		12,400		(f) 800 (g) 400		13,600		13,600		
Wages Expense	4,800		(d) 720		5,520		5,520			
Utilities Expense	680				680		680			
	60,080	60,080								
Rent Expense			(a) 1,600		1,600		1,600			
Office Supplies Expense			(b) 1,540		1,540		1,540			
Depreciation Expense–Office Equipment			(c) 300		300		300			
Wages Payable				(d) 720		720				720
Income Taxes Expense			(e) 800		800		800			
Income Taxes Payable				(e) 800		800				800
			6,160	6,160	62,300	62,300	10,440	13,600	51,860	48,700
Net Income							3,160			3,160
							13,600	13,600	51,860	51,860

Note: The columns of the work sheet are prepared in the following order: (1) Trial Balance, (2) Adjustments, (3) Adjusted Trial Balance, and (4) Income Statement and Balance Sheet columns. In the fifth step, the Income Statement and Balance Sheet columns are totaled.

Study Note

The Trial Balance columns of a work sheet take the place of the trial balance.

Step 1. Enter and total the account balances in the Trial Balance columns. The debit and credit balances of the accounts as of the last day of an accounting period are copied directly from the ledger into the Trial Balance columns, as shown in Exhibit S-7. When accountants use a work sheet, they do not have to prepare a separate trial balance.

Step 2. Enter and total the adjustments in the Adjustments columns. The required adjustments are entered in the Adjustments columns of the work sheet. As each adjustment is entered, a letter is used to identify its debit and credit parts. For example, in Exhibit S-7, the letter **a** identifies the adjustment made for the rent that Miller Design Studio prepaid on July 3, which results in a debit to Rent Expense and a credit to Prepaid Rent. These identifying letters may be used to reference supporting computations or documentation for the related adjusting entries and can simplify the recording of adjusting entries in the general journal.

A trial balance includes only accounts that have balances; if an adjustment involves an account that does not appear in the trial balance, the new account is added below the accounts listed on the work sheet. For example, Rent Expense has been added to Exhibit S-7. Accumulated depreciation accounts, which have a zero balance only in the initial period of operation, are the only exception to this rule. They are listed immediately after their associated asset accounts.

When all the adjustments have been made, the two Adjustments columns must be totaled. This procedure proves that the debits and credits of the adjustments are equal, and it generally reduces errors in the work sheet.

Step 3. Enter and total the adjusted account balances in the Adjusted Trial Balance columns. The adjusted trial balance in the work sheet is prepared by combining the amount of each account in the Trial Balance columns with the corresponding amount in the Adjustments columns and entering each result in the Adjusted Trial Balance columns.

Exhibit S-7 contains examples of *crossfooting*, or adding and subtracting a group of numbers horizontally. The first line shows Cash with a debit balance of $22,480. Because there are no adjustments to the Cash account, $22,480 is entered in the debit column of the Adjusted Trial Balance columns. On the second line, Accounts Receivable shows a debit of $4,600 in the Trial Balance columns. Because there is a debit of $400 from adjustment **g** in the Adjustments columns, it is added to the $4,600 and carried over to the debit column of the Adjusted Trial Balance columns at $5,000. On the next line, Office Supplies shows a debit of $5,200 in the Trial Balance columns and a credit of $1,540 from adjustment **b** in the Adjustments columns. Subtracting $1,540 from $5,200 results in a $3,660 debit balance in the Adjusted Trial Balance columns. This process is followed for all the accounts, including those added below the trial balance totals. The Adjusted Trial Balance columns are then *footed* (totaled) to check the accuracy of the crossfooting.

Step 4. Extend the account balances from the Adjusted Trial Balance columns to the Income Statement or Balance Sheet columns. Every account in the adjusted trial balance is an income statement account or a balance sheet account. Each account is extended to its proper place as a debit or credit in either the Income Statement columns or the Balance Sheet columns. As shown in Exhibit S-7, revenue and expense accounts are extended to the Income Statement columns, and asset, liability, and the Common Stock and Dividends accounts are extended to the Balance Sheet columns.

To avoid overlooking an account, the accounts are extended line by line, beginning with the first line (Cash) and not omitting any subsequent lines. For instance, the Cash debit balance of $22,480 is extended to the debit column of the Balance Sheet columns; then, the Accounts Receivable debit balance of $5,000 is extended to the debit column of the Balance Sheet columns; and so forth.

Step 5. Total the Income Statement columns and the Balance Sheet columns. Enter the net income or net loss in both pairs of columns as a balancing figure, and recompute the column totals. This last step, shown in Exhibit S-7, is necessary to compute net income or net loss and to prove the arithmetical accuracy of the work sheet.

Net income (or net loss) is equal to the difference between the total debits and credits of the Income Statement columns. It is also equal to the difference between the total debits and credits of the Balance Sheet columns.

Revenues (Income Statement credit column total)	$13,600
Expenses (Income Statement debit column total)	(10,440)
Net Income	$ 3,160

In this case, revenues (credit column) exceed expenses (debit column). Thus, Miller Design Studio has a net income of $3,160. The same difference occurs between the total debits and credits of the Balance Sheet columns.

The $3,160 is entered in the debit side of the Income Statement columns and in the credit side of the Balance Sheet columns to balance the columns. Remember that the excess of revenues over expenses (net income) increases stockholders' equity and that increases in stockholders' equity are recorded by credits.

When a net loss occurs, the opposite rule applies. The excess of expenses over revenues—net loss—is placed in the credit side of the Income Statement columns as a balancing figure. It is then placed in the debit side of the Balance Sheet columns because a net loss decreases stockholders' equity, and decreases in stockholders' equity are recorded by debits.

As a final check, the four columns are totaled again. If the Income Statement columns and the Balance Sheet columns do not balance, an account may have been extended or sorted to the wrong column, or an error may have been made in adding the columns. Of course, equal totals in the two pairs of columns are not absolute proof of accuracy. If an asset has been carried to the Income Statement debit column (or an expense has been carried to the Balance Sheet debit column) or a similar error with revenues or liabilities has been made, the work sheet will balance, but the net income figure will be wrong.

Study Note

Theoretically, adjusting entries can be recorded in the accounting records before the financial statements are prepared, or even before the work sheet is completed. However, they always precede the preparation of closing entries.

Using the Work Sheet

Accountants use the completed work sheet in performing three principal tasks:

1. **Recording the adjusting entries in the general journal.** Because the information needed to record the adjusting entries can be copied from the work sheet, entering the adjustments in the journal is an easy step, as shown in Exhibit S-8. The adjusting entries are then posted to the general ledger.
2. **Recording the closing entries in the general journal.** The Income Statement columns of the work sheet show all the accounts that need to be closed,

EXHIBIT 8 Adjustments from the Work Sheet Entered in the General Journal

General Journal — **Page 3**

Date	Description	Post. Ref.	Debit	Credit
2010				
July 31	Rent Expense	514	1,600	
	Prepaid Rent	117		1,600
	To recognize expiration of one month's rent			
	Office Supplies Expense	517	1,540	
	Office Supplies	116		1,540
	To recognize office supplies used during the month			
	Depreciation Expense–Office Equipment	520	300	
	Accumulated Depreciation–Office Equipment	147		300
	To record depreciation of office equipment for a month			
	Wages Expense	511	720	
	Wages Payable	214		720
	To accrue unrecorded wages			
	Income Taxes Expense	521	800	
	Income Taxes Payable	215		800
	To accrue estimated income taxes			
	Unearned Design Revenue	213	800	
	Design Revenue	411		800
	To recognize payment for services not yet performed			
	Accounts Receivable	113	400	
	Design Revenue	411		400
	To accrue website design fees earned but unrecorded			

except for the Dividends account. Exhibits S-1 through S-5 show how the closing entries are entered in the journal and posted to the ledger.

3. **Preparing the financial statements**. Once the work sheet has been completed, preparing the financial statements is simple because the account balances have been sorted into the Income Statement and Balance Sheet columns.

Supplement Assignments

Questions

1. Which of the following accounts would you expect to find in the post-closing trial balance?
   a. Insurance Expense
   b. Accounts Receivable
   c. Commission Revenue
   d. Prepaid Insurance
   e. Dividends
   f. Supplies
   g. Supplies Expense
   h. Retained Earnings
2. Why are working papers important to accountants?
3. Why are work sheets never published and rarely seen by management?
4. Can the work sheet be used as a substitute for the financial statements? Explain your answer.

5. Why should the Adjusted Trial Balance columns of the work sheet be totaled before the adjusted amounts are carried to the Income Statement and Balance Sheet columns?
6. What sequence should be followed in extending the amounts in the Adjusted Trial Balance columns to the Income Statement and Balance Sheet columns? Discuss your answer.
7. Do the Income Statement columns and the Balance Sheet columns of the work sheet balance after the amounts from the Adjusted Trial Balance columns are extended? Why or why not?
8. Do the totals of the Balance Sheet columns of the work sheet agree with the totals on the balance sheet? Explain your answer.
9. Should adjusting entries be posted to the ledger accounts before or after the closing entries? Explain your answer.
10. At the end of the accounting period, does the posting of adjusting entries to the ledger precede or follow preparation of the work sheet?

Exercises

Preparation of Closing Entries

E 1. The items below are from the Income Statement columns of the work sheet for Best Repair Shop, Inc., for the year ended December 31, 2010.

	Income Statement	
Account Name	**Debit**	**Credit**
Repair Revenue		25,620
Wages Expense	8,110	
Rent Expense	1,200	
Supplies Expense	4,260	
Insurance Expense	915	
Depreciation Expense–Repair Equipment	1,345	
Income Taxes Expense	1,000	
	16,830	25,620
Net Income	8,790	
	25,620	25,620

Prepare entries to close the revenue, expense, Income Summary, and Dividends accounts. Dividends of $5,000 were paid during the year.

Completion of a Work Sheet

E 2. The following is a highly simplified list of trial balance accounts and their normal balances for the month ended October 31, 2010, which was the company's first month of operation:

Trial Balance Accounts and Balances

Cash	$4	Unearned Service Revenue	$ 3
Accounts Receivable	7	Common Stock	5
Prepaid Insurance	2	Retained Earnings	7
Supplies	4	Dividends	6
Office Equipment	8	Service Revenue	23
Accumulated Depreciation–Office Equipment	1	Utilities Expense	2
		Wage Expense	10
Accounts Payable	4		

1. Prepare a work sheet, entering the trial balance accounts in the order they would normally appear and putting the balances in the correct columns.
2. Complete the work sheet using the following information:
   a. Expired insurance, $1.
   b. Of the unearned service revenue balance, $2 has been earned by the end of the month.
   c. Estimated depreciation on office equipment, $1.
   d. Accrued wages, $1.
   e. Unused supplies on hand, $1.
   f. Estimated federal income taxes, $1.

Problems

Closing Entries Using T Accounts and Preparation of Financial Statements

P 1. The adjusted trial balance for Settles Tennis Club, Inc., at the end of the company's fiscal year appears below.

Settles Tennis Club, Inc.
Adjusted Trial Balance
June 30, 2011

Cash	$ 26,200	
Prepaid Advertising	9,600	
Supplies	1,200	
Land	100,000	
Building	645,200	
Accumulated Depreciation–Building		$ 260,000
Equipment	156,000	
Accumulated Depreciation–Equipment		50,400
Accounts Payable		73,000
Wages Payable		9,000
Property Taxes Payable		22,500
Unearned Revenue–Locker Fees		3,000
Income Taxes Payable		20,000
Common Stock		200,000
Retained Earnings		271,150
Dividends	54,000	
Revenue from Court Fees		678,100
Revenue from Locker Fees		9,600
Wages Expense	351,000	
Maintenance Expense	51,600	
Advertising Expense	39,750	
Utilities Expense	64,800	
Supplies Expense	6,000	
Depreciation Expense–Building	30,000	
Depreciation Expense–Equipment	12,000	
Property Taxes Expense	22,500	
Miscellaneous Expense	6,900	
Income Taxes Expense	20,000	
	$1,596,750	$1,596,750

Required

1. Prepare T accounts and enter the balances for Retained Earnings, Dividends, Income Summary, and all revenue and expense accounts.
2. Enter the four required closing entries in the T accounts, labeling the components *a*, *b*, *c*, and *d*, as appropriate.
3. Prepare an income statement, a statement of retained earnings, and a balance sheet for Settles Tennis Club, Inc.
4. Explain why it is necessary to make closing entries at the end of an accounting period.

The Complete Accounting Cycle Without a Work Sheet: Two Months *(second month optional)*

P 2. On May 1, 2010, Javier Munoz opened Javier's Repair Service, Inc. During the month, he completed the following transactions for the company:

May	1	Began business by depositing $5,000 in a bank account in the name of the company in exchange for 500 shares of $10 par value common stock.
	1	Paid the rent for a store for current month, $425.
	1	Paid the premium on a one-year insurance policy, $480.
	2	Purchased repair equipment from Motley Company, $4,200. Terms were $600 down and $300 per month for one year. First payment is due June 1.
	5	Purchased repair supplies from AWD Company on credit, $468.
	8	Paid cash for an advertisement in a local newspaper, $60.
	15	Received cash repair revenue for the first half of the month, $400.
	21	Paid AWD Company on account, $225.
	31	Received cash repair revenue for the second half of May, $975.
	31	Declared and paid a cash dividend, $300.

Required for May

1. Prepare journal entries to record the May transactions.
2. Open the following accounts: Cash (111); Prepaid Insurance (117); Repair Supplies (119); Repair Equipment (144); Accumulated Depreciation–Repair Equipment (145); Accounts Payable (212); Income Taxes Payable (213); Common Stock (311); Retained Earnings (312); Dividends (313); Income Summary (314); Repair Revenue (411); Store Rent Expense (511); Advertising Expense (512); Insurance Expense (513); Repair Supplies Expense (514); Depreciation Expense–Repair Equipment (515); and Income Taxes Expense (516). Post the May journal entries to the ledger accounts.
3. Using the following information, record adjusting entries in the general journal and post to the ledger accounts:
   a. One month's insurance has expired.
   b. The remaining inventory of unused repair supplies is $169.
   c. The estimated depreciation on repair equipment is $70.
   d. Estimated income taxes are $50.
4. From the accounts in the ledger, prepare an adjusted trial balance. (**Note**: Normally a trial balance is prepared before adjustments but is omitted here to save time.)
5. From the adjusted trial balance, prepare an income statement, a statement of retained earnings, and a balance sheet for May.
6. Prepare and post closing entries.
7. Prepare a post-closing trial balance.

(Optional)

During June, Javier Munoz completed these transactions for Javier's Repair Service, Inc.:

June	1	Paid the monthly rent, $425.
	1	Made the monthly payment to Motley Company, $300.
	6	Purchased additional repair supplies on credit from AWD Company, $863.
	15	Received cash repair revenue for the first half of the month, $914.
	20	Paid cash for an advertisement in the local newspaper, $60.
	23	Paid AWD Company on account, $600.
	30	Received cash repair revenue for the last half of the month, $817.
	30	Declared and paid a cash dividend, $300.

8. Prepare and post journal entries to record the June transactions.
9. Using the following information, record adjusting entries in the general journal and post to the ledger accounts:
   a. One month's insurance has expired.
   b. The inventory of unused repair supplies is $413.
   c. The estimated depreciation on repair equipment is $70.
   d. Estimated income taxes are $50.
10. From the accounts in the ledger, prepare an adjusted trial balance.
11. From the adjusted trial balance, prepare the June income statement, statement of retained earnings, and balance sheet.
12. Prepare and post closing entries.
13. Prepare a post-closing trial balance.

Preparation of a Work Sheet, Financial Statements, and Adjusting and Closing Entries

P 3. Beauchamp Theater Corporation's trial balance at the end of its current fiscal year appears at the top of the next page.

Required

1. Enter Beauchamp Theater Corporation's trial balance amounts in the Trial Balance columns of a work sheet and complete the work sheet using the following information:
   a. Expired insurance, $17,400.
   b. Inventory of unused office supplies, $244.
   c. Inventory of unused cleaning supplies, $468.
   d. Estimated depreciation on the building, $14,000.
   e. Estimated depreciation on the theater furnishings, $36,000.
   f. Estimated depreciation on the office equipment, $3,160.
   g. The company credits all gift books sold during the year to the Gift Books Liability account. A gift book is a booklet of ticket coupons that is purchased in advance as a gift. The recipient redeems the coupons at some point in the future. On June 30 it was estimated that $37,800 worth of the gift books had been redeemed.
   h. Accrued but unpaid usher wages at the end of the accounting period, $860.
   i. Estimated federal income taxes, $20,000.
2. Prepare an income statement, a statement of retained earnings, and a balance sheet.
3. Prepare adjusting and closing entries.

Beauchamp Theater Corporation
Trial Balance
June 30, 2010

Cash	$ 31,800	
Accounts Receivable	18,544	
Prepaid Insurance	19,600	
Office Supplies	780	
Cleaning Supplies	3,590	
Land	20,000	
Building	400,000	
Accumulated Depreciation–Building		$ 39,400
Theater Furnishings	370,000	
Accumulated Depreciation–Theater Furnishings		65,000
Office Equipment	31,600	
Accumulated Depreciation–Office Equipment		15,560
Accounts Payable		45,506
Gift Books Liability		41,900
Mortgage Payable		300,000
Common Stock		200,000
Retained Earnings		112,648
Dividends	60,000	
Ticket Sales Revenue		411,400
Theater Rental Revenue		45,200
Usher Wages Expense	157,000	
Office Wages Expense	24,000	
Utilities Expense	112,700	
Interest Expense	27,000	
	$1,276,614	$1,276,614

Preparation of a Work Sheet, Financial Statements, and Adjusting and Closing Entries

P 4. The trial balance on the opposite page was taken from the ledger of Wylie Package Delivery Corporation on August 31, 2010, the end of the company's fiscal year.

Required

1. Enter the trial balance amounts in the Trial Balance columns of a work sheet and complete the work sheet using the following information:
   a. Expired insurance, $1,530.
   b. Inventory of unused delivery supplies, $715.
   c. Inventory of unused office supplies, $93.
   d. Estimated depreciation, building, $7,200.
   e. Estimated depreciation, trucks, $7,725.
   f. Estimated depreciation, office equipment, $1,350.
   g. The company credits the lockbox fees of customers who pay in advance to the Unearned Lockbox Fees account. Of the amount credited to this account during the year, $2,815 had been earned by August 31.

Wylie Package Delivery Corporation
Trial Balance
August 31, 2010

Account	Debit	Credit
Cash	$ 5,036	
Accounts Receivable	14,657	
Prepaid Insurance	2,670	
Delivery Supplies	7,350	
Office Supplies	1,230	
Land	7,500	
Building	98,000	
Accumulated Depreciation–Building		$ 26,700
Trucks	51,900	
Accumulated Depreciation–Trucks		15,450
Office Equipment	7,950	
Accumulated Depreciation–Office Equipment		5,400
Accounts Payable		4,698
Unearned Lockbox Fees		4,170
Mortgage Payable		36,000
Common Stock		20,000
Retained Earnings		44,365
Dividends	15,000	
Delivery Services Revenue		141,735
Lockbox Fees Earned		14,400
Truck Drivers' Wages Expense	63,900	
Office Salaries Expense	22,200	
Gas, Oil, and Truck Repairs Expense	15,525	
	$312,918	$312,918

h. Lockbox fees earned but unrecorded and uncollected at the end of the accounting period, $408.

i. Accrued but unpaid truck drivers' wages at the end of the year, $960.

j. Management estimates federal income taxes to be $6,000.

2. Prepare an income statement, a statement of retained earnings, and a balance sheet.
3. Prepare adjusting and closing entries.

CHAPTER

4

Financial Reporting and Analysis

Focus on Financial Statements

INCOME STATEMENT

Revenues
– Expenses
= Net Income

STATEMENT OF RETAINED EARNINGS

Opening Balance
+ Net Income
– Dividends
= Retained Earnings

BALANCE SHEET

Assets | Liabilities
Equity
A = L + E

STATEMENT OF CASH FLOWS

Operating activities
+ Investing activities
+ Financing activities
= Change in Cash
+ Starting Balance
= Ending Cash Balance

Classifying accounts in groups on the financial statements aids financial analysis.

Stockholders, investors, creditors, and other interested parties rely on the integrity of a company's financial reports. A company's managers and accountants therefore have a responsibility to act ethically in the reporting process. However, what is often overlooked is that the users of financial reports also have a responsibility to recognize and understand the types of judgments and estimates that underlie these reports.

LEARNING OBJECTIVES

LO1 **Describe the objective of financial reporting and identify the qualitative characteristics, conventions, and ethical considerations of accounting information.** *(pp. 234–237)*

LO2 **Define and describe the conventions of *consistency, full disclosure, materiality, conservatism,* and *cost-benefit*.** *(pp. 237–241)*

LO3 **Identify and describe the basic components of a classified balance sheet.** *(pp. 242–248)*

LO4 **Describe the features of multistep and single-step classified income statements.** *(pp. 248–254)*

LO5 **Use classified financial statements to evaluate liquidity and profitability.** *(pp. 254–261)*

DECISION POINT ▶ A USER'S FOCUS

▶ How should financial statements be organized to provide the best information?

▶ What key measures best capture a company's financial performance?

Dell Computer Corporation

In a presentation to financial analysts, **Dell's** management focused on the goals of growth, liquidity, and profitability.[1] In judging whether Dell has achieved those objectives, investors, creditors, managers, and others analyze relationships between key numbers in the financial statements that appear in the company's annual report.

Dell's annual report summarizes the company's financial performance by condensing a tremendous amount of information into a few numbers that managers and external users of financial statements consider most important. As shown in the Financial Highlights below, Dell uses five measures to summarize its operating results and the change in those results from one fiscal year to the next.

DELL'S FINANCIAL HIGHLIGHTS
OPERATING RESULTS
(in millions, except per share)

	2008	2007	Change
Net revenue	$61,133	$57,420	6%
Gross margin	11,671	9,516	23%
Operating income	3,440	3,070	12%
Net income	2,947	2,583	14%
Diluted EPS	1.31	1.14	15%

Foundations of Financial Reporting

LO1 Describe the objective of financial reporting and identify the qualitative characteristics, conventions, and ethical considerations of accounting information.

By issuing stocks and bonds that are traded in financial markets, corporations can raise the cash they need to carry out current and future business activities. Investors in stocks and bonds expect increases in the firm's stock price and returns from dividends. Creditors want to know if the firm can repay a loan plus interest in accordance with specified terms. Very importantly, both investors and creditors need to know if the firm can generate adequate cash flows to maintain its liquidity. Information pertaining to all these matters appears in the financial statements published in a company's annual report.

In the following sections, we describe the objectives of financial reporting and the qualitative characteristics, accounting conventions, and ethical considerations that are involved. Figure 1 illustrates these factors.

Objective of Financial Reporting

Study Note

Although reading financial reports requires some understanding of business, it does not require the skills of a CPA.

The Financial Accounting Standards Board (FASB) emphasizes the needs of capital providers while recognizing the needs of other users when it defines the objective of financial reporting as follows:[2]

> To provide financial information about the reporting entity that is useful to present and potential equity investors, lenders, and other creditors in making decisions in their capacity as capital providers. Information that is decision-useful to capital providers may also be useful to other users of financial reporting who are not capital providers.

To be useful for decision making, financial reporting must enable the user to do the following:

- *Assess cash flow prospects.* Since the ultimate value of an entity and its ability to pay dividends, interest, and otherwise provide returns to capital providers depends on its ability to generate future cash flows, capital providers and other users need information to help make judgments about the entity's ability to generate cash flows.
- *Assess stewardship.* Since management is accountable for the custody and safekeeping of the entity's economic resources and for their efficient and profitable use, capital providers and others need information about the entity's resources (assets), claims against them (liabilities and stockholders' equity), and changes in these resources and claims as impacted by transactions (earnings and cash flows) and other economic events.

Financial reporting includes the financial statements periodically presented to parties outside the business. The statements—the balance sheet, the income statement, the statement of retained earnings, and the statement of cash flows—are important outputs of the accounting system but not the only output. Management's explanations and other information, including underlying assumptions and significant uncertainties about methods and estimates used in the financial reports, constitute important components of financial reporting by an entity. Because of a potential conflict of interest between managers, who must prepare the statements, and investors or creditors, who invest in or lend money to the business, financial statements usually are audited by outside accountants to ensure their reliability.

Qualitative Characteristics of Accounting Information

Students in their first accounting course often get the idea that accounting is 100 percent accurate. Contributing to this perception is that introductory text-

FIGURE 1
Factors Affecting Financial Reporting

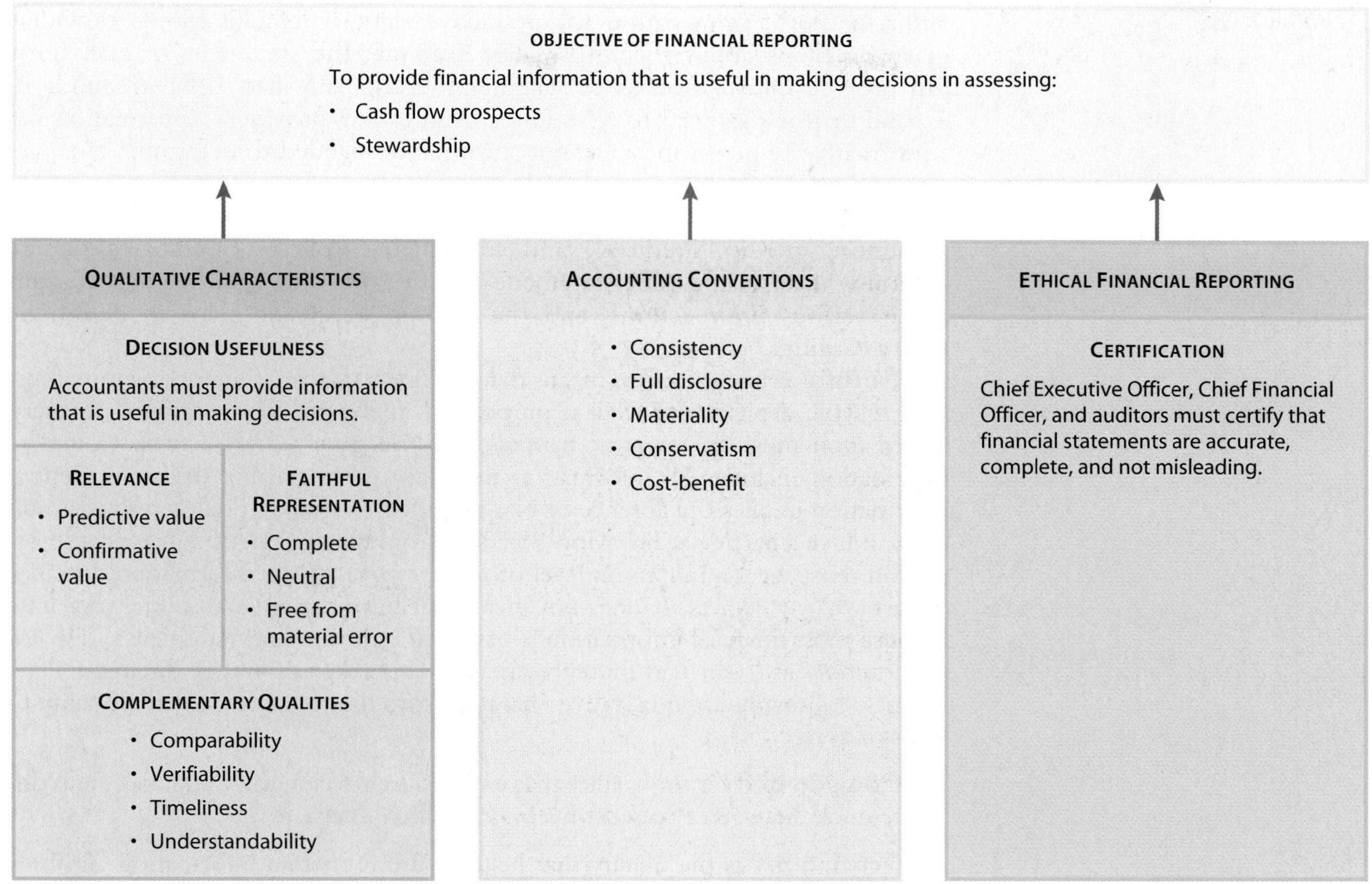

books like this one present the basics of accounting in a simple form to help students understand them. All the problems can be solved, and all the numbers add up; what is supposed to equal something else does. Accounting seems very much like mathematics in its precision. In practice, however, accounting information is neither simple nor precise, and it rarely satisfies all criteria. The FASB emphasizes this fact in the following statement:

> The information provided by financial reporting often results from approximate, rather than exact, measures. The measures commonly involve numerous estimates, classifications, summarizations, judgments and allocations. The outcome of economic activity in a dynamic economy is uncertain and results from combinations of many factors. Thus, despite the aura of precision that may seem to surround financial reporting in general and financial statements in particular, with few exceptions the measures are approximations, which may be based on rules and conventions, rather than exact amounts.[3]

The goal of generating accounting information is to provide data that different users need to make informed decisions for their unique situations. How this goal is achieved provides much of the interest and controversy in accounting. To facilitate interpretation of accounting information, the FASB has established standards, or **qualitative characteristics**, by which to judge the information.[4] The most important or fundamental qualitative characteristics are relevance and faithful representation.

Relevance means that the information has a direct bearing on a decision. In other words, if the information were not available, a different decision would be made. To be relevant, information must have *predictive value, confirmative value,* or both. Information has predictive value if it helps capital providers make decisions about the future. For example, the statement of cash flows can provide information as to whether the company has sufficient funds to expand or if it will need to raise funds from capital providers. Information has confirmative value if it provides the information needed to determine if expectations have been met. For example, the income statement provides information as to whether a company has met earnings expectations for the past accounting period. Predictive and confirmative sources of information are obviously interrelated. The statement of cash flows also confirms expectations about various prior actions, and the income statement helps to determine future earnings.

Faithful representation means that the financial reporting for an entity must be a reliable depiction of what it purports to represent. To be faithful, financial information must be *complete, neutral,* and *free from material error.* Complete information includes all information necessary for a reliable decision. Neutral information implies the absence of bias intended to attain a predetermined result or to induce a particular behavior. Freedom from material error means that information must meet a minimum level of accuracy so that the information does not distort what it depicts. It does not mean that information is absolutely accurate because most financial information is based on estimates and judgments. If major uncertainties as to the faithful representation exist, they should be disclosed.

The following are qualitative characteristics that complement the quality of information:

- **Comparability** is the quality that enables users to identify similarities and differences between two sets of economic phenomena.
- **Verifiability** is the quality that helps assure users that information faithfully represents what it purports to depict.
- **Timeliness** is the quality that enables users to receive information in time to influence a decision.
- **Understandability** is the quality that enables users to comprehend the meaning of the information they receive.

Accounting Conventions

For accounting information to be understandable, accountants must prepare financial statements in accordance with accepted practices. But the decision maker also must know how to interpret the information; in making decisions, he or she must judge what information to use, how to use it, and what it means. Familiarity with the **accounting conventions**, or constraints on accounting, used in preparing financial statements enable the user to better understand accounting information. These conventions, which we discuss later in the chapter, affect how and what information is presented in financial statements.

Ethical Financial Reporting

As we noted earlier in the text, in 2002, in the wake of accounting scandals at **Enron** and **WorldCom**, Congress passed the Sarbanes-Oxley Act. One of the important outcomes of this legislation was that the Securities and Exchange Commission instituted rules requiring the chief executive officers and chief financial officers of all publicly traded companies to certify that, to their knowledge, the

quarterly and annual statements that their companies file with the SEC are accurate and complete. Subsequently, an investigation by the audit committee of **Dell's** Board of Directors and management disclosed weaknesses in the company's controls and led to restatements of the financial statements for the prior four years. After extensive improvements in control and the restatements, the company's chief executive officer, Michael S. Dell, made the following certifying statement in the company's annual report to the SEC:

> Based on my knowledge, the financial statements, and other financial information included in this report, fairly present in all material respects the financial condition, results of operations and cash flows . . . for the periods represented in this report.[5]

The chief financial officer may sign a similar certification.

As the Enron and WorldCom scandals demonstrated, fraudulent financial reporting can have high costs for investors, lenders, employees, and customers. It can also have high costs for the people who condone, authorize, or prepare misleading reports—even those at the highest corporate levels. In March 2005, Bernard J. Ebbers, former CEO of WorldCom, was convicted of seven counts of filing false reports with the SEC and one count each of securities fraud and conspiracy.[6] Each count could carry a prison sentence of five to ten years. In 2006, both Kenneth Lay, former chairman of Enron Corporation, and Jeffrey Skilling, Enron's former CEO, were convicted on charges similar to the ones of which Ebbers was convicted.

STOP ▸ REVIEW ▸ APPLY

LO1-1 **What are the three objectives of financial reporting?**

LO1-2 **What are the qualitative characteristics of accounting information? Explain their significance.**

LO1-3 **Who are the people responsible for preparing financial statements? What does the preparation of reliable financial statements entail?**

Suggested answers to all Stop, Review, and Apply questions follow the appendixes.

Accounting Conventions for Preparing Financial Statements

LO2 **Define and describe the conventions of *consistency, full disclosure, materiality, conservatism,* and *cost-benefit.***

Financial statements are based largely on estimates and the application of accounting rules for recognition and allocation. To deal with the natural constraints on providing financial information, accountants depend on five conventions in recording transactions and preparing financial statements: consistency, full disclosure, materiality, conservatism, and cost-benefit.

Consistency

The **consistency** convention requires that once a company has adopted an accounting procedure, it must use it from one period to the next unless a note to the financial statements informs users of a change in procedure. Generally accepted accounting principles specify what the note must contain:

Like any other company, Goodyear must ensure that the quality of its products is consistent and that its accounting methods are as well. When a company changes an accounting method, it has a duty to inform users of its financial statements of the change. Such information is essential in making effective comparisons of a company's performance over several periods or in comparing its performance with that of other companies.

> The nature of and justification for a change in accounting principle and its effect on income should be disclosed in the financial statements of the period in which the change is made. The justification for the change should explain clearly why the newly adopted accounting principle is preferable.[7]

For example, in the notes to its financial statements, **Goodyear Tire & Rubber Company** disclosed that it had changed its method of accounting for inventories with the approval of its auditors because management felt the new method improved the matching of revenues and costs. Without such an acknowledgment, users of financial statements can assume that the treatment of a particular transaction, account, or item has not changed since the last period. For consistency, all years presented use this new method.

Full Disclosure (Transparency)

The convention of **full disclosure** (or transparency) requires that financial statements present all the information relevant to users' understanding of the statements. That is, the statements must be transparent so that they include any explanation needed to keep them from being misleading. Explanatory notes are therefore an integral part of the financial statements. For instance, as we have already mentioned, the notes should disclose any change that a company has made in its accounting procedures.

A company must also disclose significant events arising after the balance sheet date in the financial statements. Suppose a firm has purchased a piece of land for a future subdivision. Shortly after the end of its fiscal year, the firm is served papers to halt construction because the Environmental Protection Agency asserts that the land was once a toxic waste dump. This information, which obviously affects the users of the financial statements, must be disclosed in the statements for the fiscal year just ended.

Additional note disclosures required by the FASB and other official bodies include the accounting procedures used in preparing the financial statements; and

FOCUS ON BUSINESS PRACTICE

IFRS

How Will Convergence of U.S. GAAP with IFRS Affect Accounting Conventions?

The FASB and the IASB are working toward converging U.S. generally accepted accounting principles (GAAP) with international financial reporting standards (IFRS). Their goal is "to increase the international comparability and the quality of standards used in the United States [which] is consistent with the FASB's obligation to its domestic constituents, who benefit from comparability across national borders."[8] In addition to the comparability convention being affected, other accounting conventions will also be affected by the adoption of IFRS. For instance, conservatism, which has been the bedrock of accounting practice for many decades, would no longer be part of the conceptual framework. The practice of writing up the value of a nonfinancial asset, such as inventory or equipment, that has increased in fair value and recording it as income under IFRS would be considered a violation of the conservatism convention under U.S. GAAP. Such changes will influence the way accountants in the United States analyze financial statements.

important terms of a company's debt, commitments, and contingencies. However, the statements can become so cluttered with notes that they impede rather than help understanding. Beyond the required disclosures, the application of the full-disclosure convention is based on the judgment of management and of the accountants who prepare the financial statements.

In recent years, investors and creditors also have had an influence on full disclosure. To protect them, independent auditors, the stock exchanges, and the SEC have made more demands for disclosure by publicly owned companies. The SEC has pushed especially hard for the enforcement of full disclosure. As a result, more and better information about corporations is available to the public today than ever before.

Materiality

Materiality refers to the relative importance of an item or event. In general, an item or event is material if there is a reasonable expectation that knowing about it would influence the decisions of users of financial statements. Some items or events are so small or insignificant that they would make little difference to decision makers no matter how they are handled. Thus, a large company, like **Dell Computer Corporation**, may decide that expenditures for durable items

FOCUS ON BUSINESS PRACTICE

How Much Is Material? It's Not Only a Matter of Numbers.

The materiality issue was long a pet peeve of the SEC, which contended that companies were increasingly abusing the convention to protect their stocks from taking a pounding when earnings did not reach their targets. In consequence, the SEC issued a rule that put stricter requirements on the use of materiality. In addition to providing quantitative guides, the rule includes qualitative considerations. The percentage assessment of materiality—the rule of thumb of 5 percent or more of net income that accountants and companies have traditionally used—is acceptable as an initial screening. However, the rule states that companies cannot decline to book items in the interest of meeting earnings estimates, preserving a growing earnings trend, converting a loss to a profit, increasing management compensation, or hiding an illegal transaction, such as a bribe.[9]

Study Note

Theoretically, a $10 stapler is a long-term asset and should therefore be capitalized and depreciated over its useful life. However, the convention of materiality allows the stapler to be expensed entirely in the year of purchase because its cost is small and writing it off in one year will have no effect on anyone's decision making.

of less than $500 should be charged as expenses rather than recorded as long-term assets and depreciated.

The materiality of an item normally is determined by relating its dollar value to an element of the financial statements, such as net income or total assets. As a rule, when an item is worth 5 percent or more of net income, accountants treat it as material. However, materiality depends not only on the value of an item, but also on its nature. For example, in a multimillion-dollar company, a mistake of $5,000 in recording an item may not be important, but the discovery of even a small bribe or theft can be very important. Moreover, many small errors can add up to a material amount.

Conservatism

Study Note

The purpose of conservatism is not to produce the lowest net income and lowest asset value. It is a guideline for choosing among GAAP alternatives, and it should be used with care.

When accountants are uncertain about the judgments or estimates they must make, which is often the case, they look to the convention of **conservatism**. This convention holds that when faced with choosing between two equally acceptable procedures or estimates, accountants should choose the one that is least likely to overstate assets and income.

One of the most common applications of the conservatism convention is the use of the lower-of-cost-or-market method in accounting for inventories. Under this method, if an item's market value is greater than its original cost, the more conservative cost figure is used. If the market value is below the original cost, the more conservative market value is used. The latter situation often occurs in the computer industry.

Conservatism can be a useful tool in doubtful cases, but when it is abused, it can lead to incorrect and misleading financial statements. For example, there is no uncertainty about how a long-term asset of material cost should be treated. When conservatism is used to justify expensing such an asset in the period of purchase, income and assets for the current period will be understated, and income in future periods will be overstated. Its cost should be recorded as an asset and spread over the useful life of the asset, as explained in Chapter 3. Accountants therefore depend on the conservatism convention only when uncertain about which accounting procedure or estimate to use.

Cost-Benefit

The **cost-benefit** convention holds that the benefits to be gained from providing accounting information should be greater than the costs of providing it. Of course, minimum levels of relevance and reliability must be reached if accounting information is to be useful. Beyond the minimum levels, however, it is up to the FASB and the SEC, which stipulate the information that must be reported, and the accountant, who provides the information, to judge the costs and benefits in each case.

Firms use the cost-benefit convention for both accounting and non-accounting decisions. Department stores could almost completely eliminate shoplifting if they hired five times as many clerks as they now have and assigned them to watching customers. The benefit would be reduced shoplifting. The cost would be reduced sales (customers do not like being closely watched) and increased wages expense. Although shoplifting is a serious problem for department stores, the benefit of reducing shoplifting in this way does not outweigh the cost.

The costs and benefits of a requirement for accounting disclosure are both immediate and deferred. Judging the final costs and benefits of a far-reaching and

FOCUS ON BUSINESS PRACTICE

When Is "Full Disclosure" Too Much? It's a Matter of Cost and Benefits.

The large accounting firm of **Ernst & Young** reported that over a 20-year period, the total number of pages in the annual reports of 25 large, well-known companies increased an average of 84 percent, and the number of pages of notes increased 325 percent—from 4 to 17 pages. Management's discussion and analysis increased 300 percent, from 3 pages to 12.[10] Because some people feel that "these documents are so daunting that people don't read them at all," the SEC allows companies to issue to the public "summary reports" in which the bulk of the notes can be reduced.

Although more accessible and less costly, summary reports are controversial because many analysts feel that it is in the notes that one gets the detailed information necessary to understand complex business operations. One analyst remarked, "To banish the notes for fear they will turn off readers would be like eliminating fractions from math books on the theory that the average student prefers to work with whole numbers."[11] Where this controversy will end, nobody knows. Detailed reports still must be filed with the SEC, but more and more companies are providing summary reports to the public.

costly requirement for accounting disclosure is difficult. For instance, the FASB allows certain large companies to make a supplemental disclosure in their financial statements of the effects of changes in consumer price levels. Most companies choose not to present this information because they believe the costs of producing and providing it exceed its benefits to the readers of their financial statements. Cost-benefit is a question that the FASB, SEC, and all other regulators face. Even though there are no definitive ways of measuring costs and benefits, much of an accountant's work deals with these concepts.

STOP ▸ REVIEW ▸ APPLY

LO2-1 What are accounting conventions, and why are they important to users of financial statements?

LO2-2 Explain how each of the five accounting conventions helps users interpret financial information.

Examples of Accounting Conventions Each of the items in the numbered list in the left column pertains to one of the five accounting conventions listed below. Match each item to the letter of the appropriate convention.

1. A note to the financial statements explains the company's method of revenue recognition.
2. Inventory is accounted for at its market value, which is less than its original cost.
3. A company uses the same method of revenue recognition year after year.
4. Several accounts are grouped into one category because the total amount of each account is small.
5. A company does not keep detailed records of certain operations because the information gained from the detail is not deemed useful.

a. Consistency
b. Full disclosure
c. Materiality
d. Conservatism
e. Cost-benefit

SOLUTION

1. b 2. d 3. a 4. c 5. e

FOCUS ON BUSINESS PRACTICE

IFRS

IASB Proposes Change in Format of Financial Statements

In the United States, classified financial statements have been used for more than a century and are second nature to all U.S. businesspeople. However, this may not be true in the near future. The International Accounting Standards Board (IABS) is considering a change that will organize the balance sheet and income statement in a format similar to the statement of cash forms. Under the proposal, each statement will have the categories now found on the statement of cash flows: operating, investing and financing activities. The balance sheet form that equates total assets with liabilities and stockholders' equity (A = L + SE) would be replaced with a form in which each category of liabilities would be netted against its corresponding asset category. For example, current operating liabilities would be subtracted from current operating assets, and long-term debt would be subtracted from long-term assets on the asset side of the balance sheet.

Classified Balance Sheet

LO3 Identify and describe the basic components of a classified balance sheet.

As you know, a balance sheet presents a company's financial position at a particular time. The balance sheets we have presented thus far categorize accounts as assets, liabilities, and stockholders' equity. Because even a fairly small company can have hundreds of accounts, simply listing accounts in these broad categories is not particularly helpful to a statement user. Setting up subcategories within the major categories can make financial statements much more useful. This format enables investors and creditors to study and evaluate relationships among the subcategories.

General-purpose external financial statements that are divided into subcategories are called **classified financial statements**. Figure 2 depicts the subcategories into which assets, liabilities, and stockholders' equity are usually broken down.

The subcategories of Cruz Corporation's classified balance sheet, shown in Exhibit 1, typify those used by most corporations in the United States. The subcategories under stockholders' equity would, of course, be different if Cruz Corporation was a sole proprietorship or partnership rather than a corporation.

Assets

As you can see in Exhibit 1, the classified balance sheet of a U.S. company typically divides assets into four categories:

1. Current assets
2. Investments
3. Property, plant, and equipment
4. Intangible assets

FIGURE 2
Classified Balance Sheet

ASSETS		LIABILITIES
• Current Assets • Investments • Property, Plant, and Equipment • Intangible Assets	=	• Current Liabilities • Long-Term Liabilities
		STOCKHOLDERS' EQUITY
		• Contributed Capital • Retained Earnings

EXHIBIT 1 Classified Balance Sheet for Cruz Corporation

Cruz Corporation
Balance Sheet
December 31, 2010

		Assets	
Current assets			
Cash		$ 41,440	
Short-term investments		28,000	
Notes receivable		32,000	
Accounts receivable		141,200	
Merchandise inventory		191,600	
Prepaid insurance		26,400	
Supplies		6,784	
Total current assets			$467,424
Investments			
Land held for future use			50,000
Property, plant, and equipment			
Land		$ 18,000	
Building	$ 82,600		
Less accumulated depreciation	34,560	48,040	
Equipment	$108,000		
Less accumulated depreciation	57,800	50,200	
Total property, plant, and equipment			116,240
Intangible assets			
Trademark			2,000
Total assets			$635,664
		Liabilities	
Current liabilities			
Notes payable		$ 60,000	
Accounts payable		102,732	
Salaries payable		8,000	
Total current liabilities			$ 170,732
Long-term liabilities			
Mortgage payable			71,200
Total liabilities			$241,932
		Stockholders' Equity	
Contributed capital			
Common stock, $10 par value, 20,000 shares authorized, issued, and outstanding		$200,000	
Additional paid-in capital		40,000	
Total contributed capital		$240,000	
Retained earnings		153,732	
Total stockholders' equity			393,732
Total liabilities and stockholders' equity			$635,664

These categories are listed in the order of their presumed ease of conversion into cash. For example, current assets are usually more easily converted to cash than are property, plant, and equipment. For simplicity, some companies group investments, intangible assets, and other miscellaneous assets into a category called **other assets**.

Current Assets **Current assets** are cash and other assets that a company can reasonably expect to convert to cash, sell, or consume within one year or its *normal operating cycle*, whichever is longer. A company's **normal operating cycle** is the average time it needs to go from spending cash to receiving cash. For example, suppose a company uses cash to buy inventory and sells the inventory to a customer on credit. The resulting receivable must be collected in cash before the normal operating cycle ends.

The normal operating cycle for most companies is less than one year, but there are exceptions. For example, because of the length of time it takes **The Boeing Company** to build aircraft, its normal operating cycle exceeds one year. The inventory used in building the planes is nonetheless considered a current asset because the planes will be sold within the normal operating cycle. Another example is a company that sells on an installment basis. The payments for a television set or a refrigerator can extend over 24 or 36 months, but these receivables are still considered current assets.

Cash is obviously a current asset. Short-term investments, notes and accounts receivable, and inventory that a company expects to convert to cash within the next year or the normal operating cycle are also current assets. On the balance sheet, they are listed in the order of their ease of conversion to cash.

Prepaid expenses, such as rent and insurance paid in advance, and inventories of supplies bought for use rather than for sale should be classified as current assets. These assets are current in the sense that if they had not been bought earlier, a current outlay of cash would be needed to obtain them.

In deciding whether an asset is current or noncurrent, the idea of "reasonable expectation" is important. For example, Short-Term Investments, also called *Marketable Securities*, is an account used for temporary investments, such as U.S. Treasury bills, of "idle" cash—that is, cash that is not immediately required for operating purposes. Management can reasonably expect to sell these securities as cash needs arise over the next year or within the company's current operating cycle. Investments in securities that management does not expect to sell within the next year and that do not involve the temporary use of idle cash should be shown in the investments category of a classified balance sheet.

Investments The **investments** category includes assets, usually long term, that are not used in normal business operations and that management does not plan to convert to cash within the next year. Items in this category are securities held for long-term investment, long-term notes receivable, land held for future use, plant or equipment not used in the business, and special funds established to pay off a debt or buy a building. Also included are large permanent investments in another company for the purpose of controlling that company.

> **Study Note**
> For an investment to be classified as current, management must expect to sell it within the next year or the current operating cycle, so it must be readily marketable.

Property, Plant, and Equipment **Property, plant, and equipment** are tangible long-term assets used in a business's day-to-day operations. They represent a place to operate (land and buildings) and the equipment used to produce, sell, and deliver goods or services. They are therefore also called *operating assets* or, sometimes, *fixed assets*, *tangible assets*, *long-lived assets*, or *plant assets*. Through depreciation, the costs of these assets (except land) are spread over the periods they benefit. Past depreciation is recorded in the Accumulated Depreciation account.

To reduce clutter on the balance sheet, property, plant, and equipment are often combined—for example:

Property, plant, and equipment (net) $116,240

The company provides the details in a note to the financial statements.

The property, plant, and equipment category also includes natural resources owned by the company, such as forest lands, oil and gas properties, and coal mines, if they are used in the regular course of business. If they are not, they are listed in the investments category.

Intangible Assets **Intangible assets** are long-term assets with no physical substance whose value stems from the rights or privileges they extend to their owners. Examples are patents, copyrights, goodwill, franchises, and trademarks. These assets are recorded at cost, which is spread over the expected life of the right or privilege. Goodwill, which arises in an acquisition of another company, is an intangible asset that is recorded at cost but is not amortized. It is reviewed each year for possible loss of value, or impairment.

Liabilities

Liabilities are divided into two categories that are based on when the liabilities fall due: current liabilities and long-term liabilities.

Current Liabilities **Current liabilities** are obligations that must be satisfied within one year or within the company's normal operating cycle, whichever is longer. These liabilities are typically paid out of current assets or by incurring new short-term liabilities. They include notes payable, accounts payable, the current portion of long-term debt, salaries and wages payable, taxes payable, and customer advances (unearned revenues).

Study Note

The portion of a mortgage that is due during the next year or the current operating cycle would be classified as a current liability; the portion due after the next year or the current operating cycle would be classified as a long-term liability.

Long-Term Liabilities Debts that fall due more than one year in the future or beyond the normal operating cycle, which will be paid out of noncurrent assets, are **long-term liabilities**. Mortgages payable, long-term notes, bonds payable, employee pension obligations, and long-term lease liabilities generally fall into this category. Deferred income taxes are often disclosed as a separate category in the long-term liability section of the balance sheet of publicly held corporations. This liability arises because the rules for measuring income for tax purposes differ from those for financial reporting. The cumulative annual difference between the income taxes payable to governments and the income taxes expense reported on the income statement is included in the account Deferred Income Taxes.

Stockholders' Equity

As you know, corporations are owned by their stockholders and are separate legal entities. Exhibit 1 shows the stockholders' equity section of a corporation's balance sheet. This section has two parts: contributed capital and retained earnings. Generally, contributed capital is shown on a corporate balance sheet as two amounts: the par value of the issued stock, and additional paid-in capital, which is the amount paid in above par value.

Owner's Equity and Partners' Equity

Although the form of business organization does not usually affect the accounting treatment of assets and liabilities, the equity section of the balance sheet of a sole proprietorship or partnership is very different from the equity section of a corporation's balance sheet.

EXHIBIT 2 Classified Balance Sheet for Dell Computer Corporation

Dell Computer Corporation
Consolidated Statement of Financial Position
(In millions)

	February 1, 2008	February 2, 2007
Assets		
Current assets:		
Cash and cash equivalents	$ 7,764	$ 9,546
Short-term investments	208	752
Accounts receivable, net	5,961	4,622
Financing receivables, net	1,732	1,530
Inventories	1,180	660
Other	3,035	2,829
Total current assets	19,880	19,939
Property, plant, and equipment, net	2,668	2,409
Investments	1,560	2,147
Other non-current assets	3,453	1,140
Total assets	$27,561	$25,635
Liabilities and Stockholders' Equity		
Current liabilities:		
Short-term borrowings	$ 225	$ 188
Accounts payable	11,492	10,430
Accrued and other	6,809	7,173
Total current liabilities	18,526	17,791
Long-term debt	362	569
Other non-current liabilities	4,844	2,836
Total liabilities	23,732	21,196
Stockholders' equity:		
Preferred stock and capital in excess of $.01 par value; shares issued and outstanding: none	—	—
Common stock and capital in excess of $.01 par value; shares authorized: 7,000; shares issued: 3,324* and 3,312,* respectively; shares outstanding: 2,060 and 2,226, respectively	10,683	10,218
Treasury stock, at cost; 785 and 606 shares, respectively	(25,037)	(21,033)
Retained earnings	18,199	15,282
Other comprehensive loss	(16)	(28)
Total stockholders' equity	3,829	4,439
Total liabilities and stockholders' equity	$27,561	$25,635

*Includes an immaterial amount of redeemable common stock.
Source: Dell Computer Corporation, Form 10-K, 2008.

Sole Proprietorship The equity section of a sole proprietorship's balance sheet simply shows the capital in the owner's name at an amount equal to the net assets of the company. It might appear as follows:

Owner's Equity	
Juan Cruz, Capital	$395,732

Because in a sole proprietorship, there is no legal separation between the owner and the business, there is no need to separate contributed capital from earnings retained for use in the business. The Capital account is increased by both the owner's investments and net income. It is decreased by net losses and withdrawals of assets from the business for personal use by the owner. In this kind of business, the formality of declaring and paying dividends is not required.

In fact, the terms *owner's equity*, *proprietorship*, *capital*, and *net worth* are used interchangeably. They all stand for the owner's interest in the company. The first three terms are preferred to *net worth* because most assets are recorded at original cost rather than at current value. For this reason, the ownership section does not represent "worth." It is really a claim against the assets of the company.

Study Note

The only difference in equity between a sole proprietorship and a partnership is the number of Capital accounts.

Partnership The equity section of a partnership's balance sheet is called *partners' equity*. It is much like that of a sole proprietorship's balance sheet. It might appear as follows:

Partners' Equity		
A. J. Martin, Capital	$168,750	
Juan Cruz, Capital	224,982	
Total partners' equity		$393,732

Dell's Balance Sheets

Although balance sheets generally resemble the one shown in Exhibit 1 for Cruz Corporation, no two companies have financial statements that are exactly alike. The balance sheet of **Dell Computer Corporation** is a good example of some of the variations. As shown in Exhibit 2, it provides data for two years so that users can evaluate the change from one year to the next. Note that its major classifications are similar but not identical to those of Cruz Corporation. For instance, Cruz Corporation has asset categories for investments and intangibles, and Dell has an asset category called "other non-current assets," which is a small amount of its total assets. Also note that Dell has a category called "other non-current liabilities." Because this category is listed after long-term debt, it represents longer-term liabilities, due more than one year after the balance sheet date.

STOP ▶ REVIEW ▶ APPLY

LO3-1 **What purpose do classified financial statements serve?**

LO3-2 **What are four common categories of assets on a classified balance sheet?**

LO3-3 **What criteria must an asset meet to be classified as current? Under what condition is an asset considered current even if it will not be realized as cash within a year? What are two examples of assets that fall into this category?**

(continued)

LO3-4 **In what order should current assets be listed?**

LO3-5 **What is the difference between a short-term investment in the current assets section of a balance sheet and a security in the investments section?**

LO3-6 **What is an intangible asset? Give at least three examples.**

LO3-7 **Name the two major categories of liabilities.**

LO3-8 **What are the primary differences between the equity section of the balance sheet of a sole proprietorship or partnership and the equity section of a corporation's balance sheet?**

Balance Sheet Classifications The lettered items below represent a classification scheme for a balance sheet. The numbered items are account titles. Match each account with the letter of the category in which it belongs, or indicate that it does not appear on the balance sheet.

a. Current assets
b. Investments
c. Property, plant, and equipment
d. Intangible assets
e. Current liabilities
f. Long-term liabilities
g. Stockholders' equity
h. Not on balance sheet

1. Trademark
2. Marketable Securities
3. Land Held for Future Use
4. Taxes Payable
5. Bond Payable in Five Years
6. Common Stock
7. Land Used in Operations
8. Accumulated Depreciation
9. Accounts Receivable
10. Interest Expense
11. Unearned Revenue
12. Prepaid Rent

SOLUTION

1. d	5. f	9. a
2. a	6. g	10. h
3. b	7. c	11. e
4. e	8. c	12. a

Forms of the Income Statement

LO4 **Describe the features of multistep and single-step classified income statements.**

In the income statements we have presented thus far, expenses have been deducted from revenue in a single step to arrive at net income. Here, we look at a multistep income statement and a single-step format more complex than the one we presented in earlier chapters.

Multistep Income Statement

A **multistep income statement** goes through a series of steps, or subtotals, to arrive at net income. Figure 3 compares the multistep income statement of a service company with that of a **merchandising company**, which buys and sells products, and a **manufacturing company**, which makes and sells products.

As you can see in Figure 3, in a service company's multistep income statement, the operating expenses are deducted from revenues in a single step to arrive at income from operations. In contrast, because manufacturing and merchandising companies make or buy goods for sale, they must include an additional step for the cost of goods sold. Exhibit 3 shows a multistep income statement for Cruz Corporation, a merchandising company.

Net Sales The first major part of a merchandising or manufacturing company's multistep income statement is **net sales**, often simply called *sales*. Net sales

FIGURE 3
The Components of Multistep Income Statements for Service and Merchandising or Manufacturing Companies

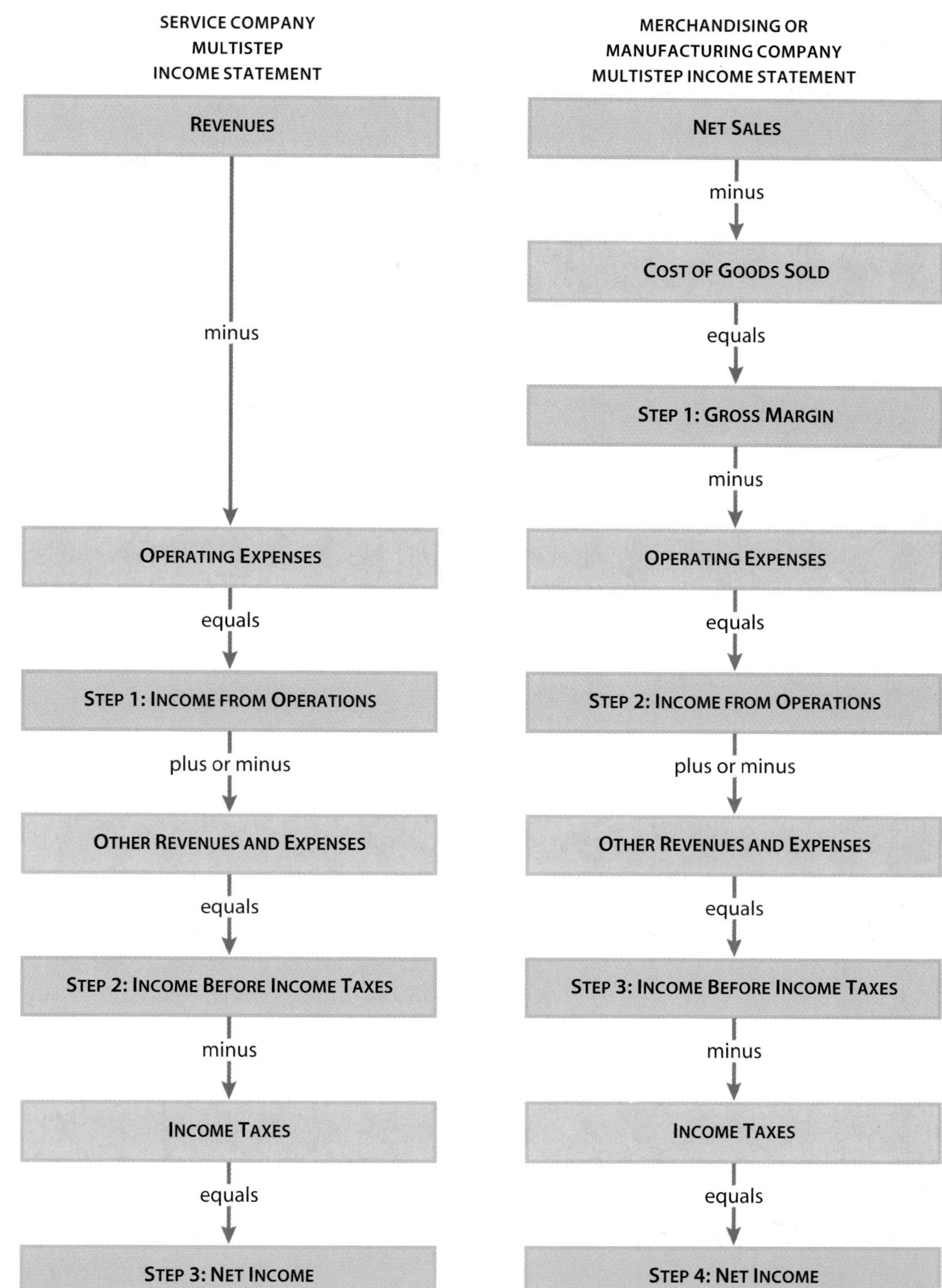

Study Note

The multistep income statement is a valuable analytical tool that is often overlooked. Analysts frequently convert a single-step statement into a multistep one because the latter separates operating sources of income from nonoperating ones. Investors want income to result primarily from operations, not from one-time gains or losses.

consist of the gross proceeds from sales (gross sales) less sales returns and allowances and any discounts allowed.

- **Gross sales** consist of total cash sales and total credit sales during an accounting period. Even though the cash may not be collected until the following accounting period, under the revenue recognition rule, revenue is recorded as earned when title for merchandise passes from seller to buyer at the time of sale.
- **Sales returns and allowances** are cash refunds, credits on account, and discounts from selling prices made to customers who have received defective products or products that are otherwise unsatisfactory. If other discounts are given to customers, they also should be deducted from gross sales.

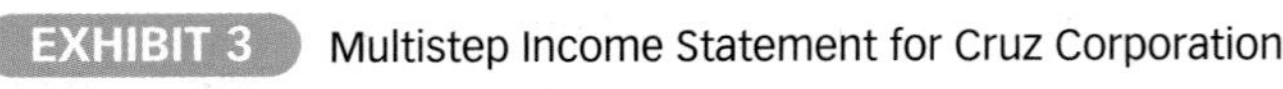
EXHIBIT 3 Multistep Income Statement for Cruz Corporation

Cruz Corporation
Income Statement
For the Year Ended December 31, 2010

Step 1	**Net sales**		$1,248,624
	Cost of goods sold		815,040
	Gross margin		$ 433,584
Step 2	**Operating expenses**		
	Selling expenses	$219,120	
	General and administrative expenses	138,016	
	Total operating expenses		357,136
	Income from operations		$ 76,448
Step 3	**Other revenues and expenses**		
	Interest income	$ 5,600	
	Less interest expense	10,524	
	Excess of other expenses over other revenues		4,924
	Income before income taxes		$ 71,524
	Income taxes		13,524
Step 4	**Net income**		$ 58,000
	Earnings per share		$ 2.90

Managers, investors, and others often use the amount of sales and trends in sales as indicators of a firm's progress. To detect trends, they compare the net sales of different accounting periods. Increasing sales suggest growth; decreasing sales indicate the possibility of decreased future earnings and other financial problems.

Cost of Goods Sold The second part of a multistep income statement for a merchandiser or manufacturer is **cost of goods sold**, also called *cost of sales*. Cost of goods sold (an expense) is the amount a merchandiser paid for the merchandise it sold during an accounting period. For a manufacturer, it is the cost of making the products it sold during an accounting period.

Study Note

Gross margin is an important measure of profitability. When it is less than operating expenses, the company has suffered a net loss from operations.

Gross Margin The third major part of a multistep income statement for a merchandiser or manufacturer is **gross margin**, or *gross profit*, which is the difference between net sales and the cost of goods sold (Step 1 in Exhibit 3). To be successful, companies must achieve a gross margin sufficient to cover operating expenses and provide an adequate after-tax income.

Managers are interested in both the amount and percentage of gross margin. The percentage is computed by dividing the amount of gross margin by net sales. In the case of Cruz Corporation, the amount of gross margin is $433,584, and the percentage of gross margin is 34.7 percent ($433,584 ÷ $1,248,624). This information is useful in planning business operations. For instance, management may try to increase total sales by reducing the selling price. Although this strategy reduces the percentage of gross margin, it will work if the total of items sold increases enough to raise the absolute amount of gross margin. This is the strategy followed by discount warehouse stores like **Sam's Club** and **Costco Wholesale Corporation**.

On the other hand, management may decide to keep a high gross margin from sales and try to increase sales and the amount of gross margin by increasing operating expenses, such as advertising. This is the strategy used by upscale specialty stores like **Neiman Marcus** and **Tiffany & Co.**

Other strategies to increase gross margin from sales include using better purchasing methods to reduce cost of goods sold.

Operating Expenses **Operating expenses**—expenses incurred in running a business other than the cost of goods sold—are the next major part of a multistep income statement. Operating expenses are often grouped into the categories of selling expenses and general and administrative expenses.

- Selling expenses include the costs of storing goods and preparing them for sale; preparing displays, advertising, and otherwise promoting sales; and delivering goods to a buyer if the seller has agreed to pay the cost of delivery.
- General and administrative expenses include expenses for accounting, personnel, credit checking, collections, and any other expenses that apply to overall operations. Although occupancy expenses, such as rent expense, insurance expense, and utilities expense, are often classified as general and administrative expenses, they can also be allocated between selling expenses and general and administrative expenses.

Careful planning and control of operating expenses can improve a company's profitability.

Study Note

Many financial analysts use income from operations as a key measure of profitability.

Income from Operations **Income from operations**, or *operating income*, is the difference between gross margin and operating expenses (Step 2 in Exhibit 3). It represents the income from a company's main business. Income from operations is often used to compare the profitability of two or more companies or divisions within a company.

Other Revenues and Expenses **Other revenues and expenses**, also called *nonoperating revenues and expenses*, are not related to a company's operating activities. This section of a multistep income statement includes revenues from investments (such as dividends and interest on stocks, bonds, and savings accounts) and interest earned on credit or notes extended to customers. It also includes interest expense and other expenses that result from borrowing money or from credit extended to the company. If a company has other kinds of revenues and expenses not related to its normal business operations, they, too, are included in this part of the income statement.

An analyst who wants to compare two companies independent of their financing methods—that is, *before* considering other revenues and expenses—would focus on income from operations.

Income Before Income Taxes **Income before income taxes** is the amount a company has earned from all activities—operating and nonoperating—before taking into account the amount of income taxes it incurred (Step 3 in Exhibit 3). Because companies may be subject to different income tax rates, income before income taxes is often used to compare the profitability of two or more companies or divisions within a company.

Income Taxes **Income taxes**, also called *provision for income taxes*, represent the expense for federal, state, and local taxes on corporate income. Income taxes are shown as a separate item on the income statement. Usually, the word *expense* is not used on the statement. Income taxes do not appear on the income statements of sole proprietorships and partnerships because the individuals who own these businesses are the tax-paying units; they pay income taxes on their share of the business income. Corporations, however, must report and pay income taxes on their earnings.

Because federal, state, and local income taxes for corporations are substantial, they have a significant effect on business decisions. Current federal income tax rates for corporations vary from 15 percent to 35 percent depending on the amount of income before income taxes and other factors. Most other taxes, such as property and employment taxes, are included in operating expenses.

Net Income **Net income** (also called *net earnings*) is the final figure, or "bottom line," of an income statement. It is what remains of gross margin after operating expenses have been deducted, other revenues and expenses have been added or deducted, and income taxes have been deducted (Step 4 in Exhibit 3).

Net income is an important performance measure because it represents the amount of earnings that accrue to stockholders. It is the amount transferred to retained earnings from all the income that business operations have generated during an accounting period. Both managers and investors often use net income to measure a business's financial performance over the past accounting period.

Study Note

Because it is a shorthand measure of profitability, earnings per share is the performance measure most commonly cited in the financial press.

Earnings per Share **Earnings per share**, often called *net income per share*, is the net income earned on each share of common stock. Shares of stock represent ownership in corporations, and the net income per share is reported immediately below net income on the income statement. In the simplest case, it is

EXHIBIT 4 Multistep Income Statement for Dell Computer Corporation

Dell Computer Corporation
Consolidated Statement of Income
(In millions, except per share amounts)

	Fiscal Year Ended		
	February 1, 2008	**February 2, 2007**	**February 3, 2006**
Net revenue	$61,133	$57,420	$55,788
Cost of revenue	49,462	47,904	45,897
Gross margin	11,671	9,516	9,891
Operating expenses:			
Selling, general and administrative	7,538	5,948	5,051
In-process research and development	83	—	—
Research, development and engineering	610	498	458
Total operating expenses	8,231	6,446	5,509
Operating income	3,440	3,070	4,382
Investment and other income, net	387	275	226
Income before income taxes	3,827	3,345	4,608
Income tax provision	880	762	1,006
Net income	$ 2,947	$ 2,583	$ 3,602
Earnings per share*	$ 1.33	$ 1.15	$ 1.50

*Basic

Source: Dell Computer Corporation, Form 10-K, 2008.

computed by dividing the net income by the average number of shares of common stock outstanding during the year. For example, Cruz Corporation's earnings per share of $2.90 was computed by dividing the net income of $58,000 by the 20,000 shares of common stock outstanding (see the stockholders' equity section in Exhibit 1). Investors find the figure useful as a quick way of assessing both a company's profitability and its earnings in relation to the market price of its stock.

Dell's Income Statements

Like balance sheets, income statements vary among companies. You will rarely, if ever, find an income statement exactly like the one we have presented for Cruz Corporation. Companies use both different terms and different structures. For example, as you can see in Exhibit 4, in its multistep income statement, **Dell Computer Corporation** provided three years of data for purposes of comparison.

Single-Step Income Statement

Study Note

If you encounter income statement components not covered in this chapter, refer to the index at the end of the book to find the topic and read about it.

Exhibit 5 shows a **single-step income statement** for Cruz Corporation. In this type of statement, income before income taxes is derived in a single step by putting the major categories of revenues in the first part of the statement and the major categories of costs and expenses in the second part. Income taxes are shown as a separate item, as on the multistep income statement. Both the multistep form and the single-step form have advantages: the multistep form shows the components used in deriving net income, and the single-step form has the advantage of simplicity.

EXHIBIT 5

Single-Step Income Statement for Cruz Corporation

Cruz Corporation
Income Statement
For the Year Ended December 31, 2010

Revenues		
Net sales		$1,248,624
Interest income		5,600
Total revenues		$1,254,224
Costs and expenses		
Cost of goods sold	$815,040	
Selling expenses	219,120	
General and administrative expenses	138,016	
Interest expense	10,524	
Total costs and expenses		1,182,700
Income before income taxes		$ 71,524
Income taxes		13,524
Net income		$ 58,000
Earnings per share		$ 2.90

STOP ▶ REVIEW ▶ APPLY

LO4-1 **What is the primary difference between the operations of a merchandising business and those of a service business? How is this difference reflected on the income statement?**

LO4-2 **Define *gross margin*. Why is it important?**

LO4-3 **Why are other revenues and expenses separated from operating revenues and expenses in a multistep income statement?**

LO4-4 **Define *earnings per share*, and describe how this figure appears on the income statement.**

LO4-5 **Explain how a multistep income statement differs from a single-step income statement. What are the merits of each form?**

Income Statement Classification A classification scheme for a multistep income statement appears below, and to the right is a list of accounts. Match each account with the category in which it belongs, or indicate that it is not on the income statement.

a. Net sales
b. Cost of goods sold
c. Selling expenses
d. General and administrative expenses
e. Other revenues and expenses
f. Not on income statement

1. Sales Returns and allowances
2. Cost of Sales
3. Dividend Income
4. Delivery Expense
5. Office Salaries Expense
6. Wages Payable
7. Sales Salaries Expense
8. Advertising Expense
9. Interest Expense
10. Commissions Expense

SOLUTION

1. a	3. e	5. d	7. c	9. e
2. b	4. c	6. f	8. c	10. c

Using Classified Financial Statements

LO5 **Use classified financial statements to evaluate liquidity and profitability.**

Investors and creditors base their decisions largely on their assessments of a firm's potential liquidity and profitability, and in making those assessments, they often rely on ratios. As you will see in the following pages, ratios use the components of classified financial statements to reflect how well a firm has performed in terms of maintaining liquidity and achieving profitability.

Study Note

Accounts must be classified correctly before the ratios are computed. If they are not classified correctly, the ratios will be incorrect.

Evaluation of Liquidity

As you know, *liquidity* means having enough money on hand to pay bills when they are due and to take care of unexpected needs for cash. In an earlier chapter, we introduced the cash return on assets ratio, a liquidity measure that is computed by dividing net cash flows from operating activities by average total assets. Here, we introduce two additional measures of liquidity: working capital and the current ratio.

Working Capital **Working capital** is the amount by which current assets exceed current liabilities. It is an important measure of liquidity because current liabilities must be satisfied within one year or one operating cycle, whichever is longer, and current assets are used to pay the current liabilities. Thus, the excess

FIGURE 4

Average Current Ratio for Selected Industries

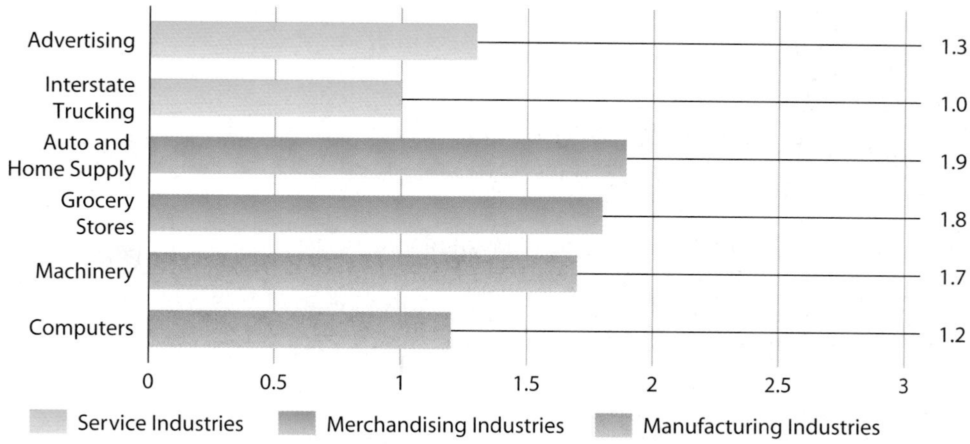

Source: Data from Dun & Bradstreet, *Industry Norms and Key Business Ratios*, 2005–2006

of current assets over current liabilities—the working capital—is what is on hand to continue business operations.

For Cruz Corporation, working capital is computed as follows:

Current assets	$467,424
Less current liabilities	170,732
Working capital	$296,692

Working capital can be used to buy inventory, obtain credit, and finance expanded sales. Lack of working capital can lead to a company's failure.

Current Ratio The current ratio is closely related to working capital. Many bankers and other creditors believe it is a good indicator of a company's ability to pay its debts on time. The **current ratio** is the ratio of current assets to current liabilities. For Cruz Corporation, it is computed like this:

K/R

$$\text{Current Ratio} = \frac{\text{Current Assets}}{\text{Current Liabilities}} = \frac{\$467{,}424}{\$170{,}732} = 2.7$$

Thus, Cruz Corporation has $2.70 of current assets for each $1.00 of current liabilities. Is that good or bad? The answer requires a comparison of this year's current ratio with ratios for earlier years and with similar measures for companies in the same industry, which for Cruz Corporation is auto and home supply.

As Figure 4 illustrates, the average current ratio varies from industry to industry. For the advertising industry, which has no merchandise inventory, the current ratio is 1.3. The auto and home supply industry, in which companies carry large merchandise inventories, has an average current ratio of 1.9. The current ratio for Cruz Corporation, 2.7, exceeds the average for its industry.

A very low current ratio, of course, can be unfavorable, indicating that a company will not be able to pay its debts on time. But that is not always the case. For example, **McDonald's** and various other successful companies have very low current ratios because they carefully plan their cash flows.

A very high current ratio may indicate that a company is not using its assets to the best advantage. In other words, it could probably use its excess funds more effectively to increase its overall profit.

Evaluation of Profitability

Just as important as paying bills on time is *profitability*—the ability to earn a satisfactory income. As a goal, profitability competes with liquidity for managerial

FOCUS ON BUSINESS PRACTICE

IFRS

How Has the Goal of Convergence of U.S. GAAP and IFRS Made Financial Analysis More Difficult?

Although the SEC believes that the ideal outcome of a cooperative international accounting standard-setting process would be worldwide use of a single set of high-quality accounting standards for both domestic and cross-border financial reporting, the reality is that such consistency does not now exist and will be a challenge to implement.[12] For a period of time, users of financial statements will have difficulty comparing companies' performance. Profitability measures of foreign firms that file in the United States using IFRS will not be comparable to profitability measures of companies that file using U.S. GAAP. For instance, consider the reporting earnings of the following European companies under both standards in a recent year:

(Earnings in millions of euros)

	IFRS Earnings	GAAP Earnings	% Diff.
Bayer AG	1,695	269	530.1%
Reed Elsevier	625	399	56.6
Benetton Group	125	100	25.0

Given that assets and equity for these companies are also likely to differ as well as the use of fair value in valuing assets and liabilities, all profitability ratios—profit margin, asset turnover, return of assets, and return on equity—will be affected.

attention because liquid assets, although important, are not the best profit-producing resources. Cash, of course, means purchasing power, but a satisfactory profit can be made only if purchasing power is used to buy profit-producing (and less liquid) assets, such as inventory and long-term assets.

To evaluate a company's profitability, you must relate its current performance to its past performance and prospects for the future, as well as to the averages of other companies in the same industry. The following are the ratios commonly used to evaluate a company's ability to earn income:

1. Profit margin
2. Asset turnover
3. Return on assets
4. Debt to equity ratio
5. Return on equity

In previous chapters, we introduced the profit margin and return on assets ratios. Here, we review these ratios, introduce the other profitability ratios, and show their interrelationships.

Profit Margin The **profit margin** shows the percentage of each sales dollar that results in net income. It should not be confused with gross margin, which is not a ratio but rather the amount by which revenues exceed the cost of goods sold. Cruz Corporation has a profit margin of 4.6 percent. It is computed as follows:

$$\text{Profit Margin} = \frac{\text{Net Income}}{\text{Net Sales}} = \frac{\$58{,}000}{\$1{,}248{,}624} = .046, \text{ or } 4.6\%$$

Thus, on each dollar of net sales, Cruz Corporation makes almost 5 cents. A difference of 1 or 2 percent in a company's profit margin can be the difference between a fair year and a very profitable one.

Asset Turnover The **asset turnover** ratio measures how efficiently assets are used to produce sales. In other words, it shows how many dollars of sales are generated by each dollar of assets. A company with a higher asset turnover uses its assets more productively than one with a lower asset turnover.

The asset turnover ratio is computed by dividing net sales by average total assets. Average total assets are the sum of assets at the beginning of an accounting period and at the end of the period divided by 2. For example, if Cruz Corporation had assets of $594,480 at the beginning of the year, its asset turnover would be computed as follows:

$$\text{Asset Turnover} = \frac{\text{Net Sales}}{\text{Average Total Assets}}$$

$$= \frac{\$1,248,624}{(\$635,664 + \$594,480) \div 2} = \frac{\$1,248,624}{\$615,072} = 2.0 \text{ times}$$

Thus, Cruz Corporation would produce $2.00 in sales for each dollar invested in assets. This ratio shows a relationship between an income statement figure (net sales) and a balance sheet figure (total assets).

Return on Assets Both the profit margin and asset turnover ratios have limitations. The profit margin ratio does not consider the assets necessary to produce income, and the asset turnover ratio does not take into account the amount of income produced. The **return on assets** ratio overcomes these deficiencies by relating net income to average total assets. For Cruz Corporation, it is computed like this:

$$\text{Return on Assets} = \frac{\text{Net Income}}{\text{Average Total Assets}}$$

$$= \frac{\$58,000}{(\$635,664 + \$594,480) \div 2} = \frac{\$58,000}{\$615,072} = .094, \text{ or } 9.4\%$$

Study Note

Return on assets is one of the most widely used measures of profitability because it reflects both the profit margin and asset turnover.

For each dollar invested, Cruz Corporation's assets generate 9.4 cents of net income. This ratio indicates the income-generating strength (profit margin) of the company's resources and how efficiently the company is using all its assets (asset turnover).

Return on assets, then, combines profit margin and asset turnover:

$$\frac{\text{Net Income}}{\text{Net Sales}} \times \frac{\text{Net Sales}}{\text{Average Total Assets}} = \frac{\text{Net Income}}{\text{Average Total Assets}}$$

$$\text{Profit Margin} \times \text{Asset Turnover} = \text{Return on Assets}$$

$$4.6\% \times 2.0 \text{ times} = 9.2\%^*$$

Thus, a company's management can improve overall profitability by increasing the profit margin, the asset turnover, or both. Similarly, in evaluating a company's overall profitability, a financial statement user must consider how these two ratios interact to produce return on assets.

By studying Figures 5, 6, and 7, you can see the different ways in which various industries combine profit margin and asset turnover to produce return on assets. For instance, by comparing the return on assets for grocery stores and auto and home supply companies, you can see how they achieve that return in very different ways. The grocery store industry has a profit margin of 2.3 percent, which when multiplied by an asset turnover of 5.0 times gives a return on assets of 11.5 percent. The auto and home supply industry has a higher profit margin, 2.5 percent, and a lower asset turnover, 3.0 times, and produces a return on assets of 7.5 percent.

Cruz Corporation's profit margin of 4.6 percent is well above the auto and home supply industry's average, but its asset turnover of 2.0 times lags behind the industry average. Cruz is sacrificing asset turnover to achieve a higher profit margin. Clearly, this strategy is working, because Cruz Corporation's return on assets of 9.2 percent exceeds the industry average of 7.5 percent.

*The difference between 9.4 and 9.2 percent is due to rounding.

FIGURE 5
Average Profit Margin for Selected Industries

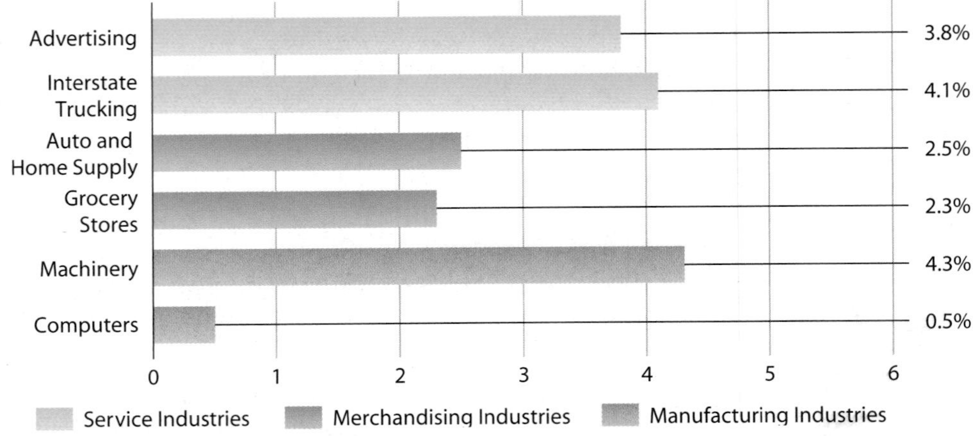

Source: Data from Dun & Bradstreet, *Industry Norms and Key Business Ratios*, 2005–2006

FIGURE 6
Average Asset Turnover for Selected Industries

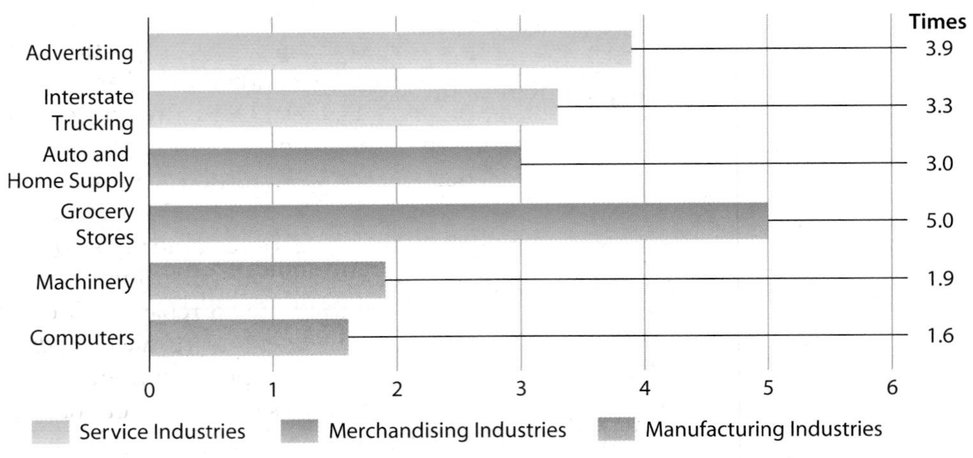

Source: Data from Dun & Bradstreet, *Industry Norms and Key Business Ratios*, 2005–2006

FIGURE 7
Average Return on Assets for Selected Industries

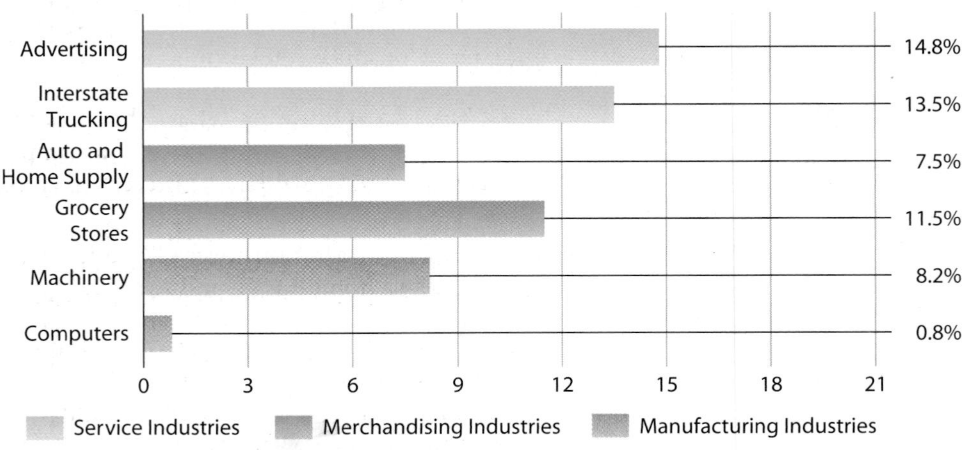

Source: Data from Dun & Bradstreet, *Industry Norms and Key Business Ratios*, 2005–2006

FOCUS ON BUSINESS PRACTICE

What Performance Measures Do Top Companies Use to Compensate Executives?

The boards of directors of public companies often use financial ratios to judge the performance of their top executives and to determine annual bonuses. Public companies must disclose the ratios or performance measures they use in creating these compensation plans. Studies show that the most successful companies over a sustained period of time, like Dell Computer, tend to focus the most on profitability measures. For instance, successful companies use earnings goals combined with sales growth 61 percent of the time compared to 43 percent for not so successful companies. Among the most common earnings goals are return on assets (19 percent for the best companies versus 5 percent for other companies) and return on equity (19 percent versus 7 percent). Clearly, successful companies set objectives that will provide incentives to management to increase profitability.[13]

Debt to Equity Ratio Another useful measure of profitability is the **debt to equity ratio**, which shows the proportion of a company's assets that is financed by creditors and the proportion that is financed by stockholders. This ratio is computed by dividing total liabilities by stockholders' equity. The balance sheets of most public companies do not show total liabilities; a short way of determining them is to deduct the total stockholders' equity from total assets.

A debt to equity ratio of 1.0 means that total liabilities equal stockholders' equity—that half of a company's assets are financed by creditors. A ratio of .5 means that one-third of a company's total assets are financed by creditors. A company with a high debt to equity ratio is at risk in poor economic times because it must continue to repay creditors. Stockholders' investments, on the other hand, do not have to be repaid, and dividends can be deferred when a company suffers because of a poor economy.

Cruz Corporation's debt to equity ratio is computed as follows:

K/R

$$\text{Debt to Equity} = \frac{\text{Total Liabilities}}{\text{Stockholders' Equity}} = \frac{\$241{,}932}{\$393{,}732} = .614, \text{ or } 61.4\%$$

The debt to equity ratio of 61.4 percent means that Cruz Corporation receives less than half its financing from creditors and more than half from investors.

The debt to equity ratio does not fit neatly into either the liquidity or profitability category. It is clearly very important to liquidity analysis because it relates to debt and its repayment. It is also relevant to profitability for two reasons:

1. Creditors are interested in the proportion of the business that is debt-financed because the more debt a company has, the more profit it must earn to ensure the payment of interest to creditors.

2. Stockholders are interested in the proportion of the business that is debt-financed because the amount of interest paid on debt affects the amount of profit left to provide a return on stockholders' investments.

The debt to equity ratio also shows how much expansion is possible through borrowing additional long-term funds.

Figure 8 shows that the debt to equity ratio in selected industries varies from a low of 77.7 percent in the grocery industry to a high of 192.7 percent in the advertising industry.

FIGURE 8

Average Debt to Equity Ratio for Selected Industries

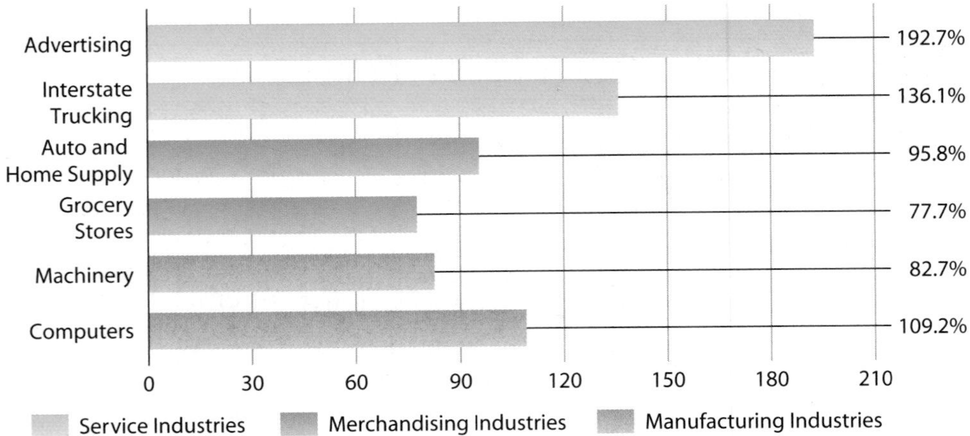

Source: **Data from Dun & Bradstreet, *Industry Norms and Key Business Ratios*, 2005–2006**

Return on Equity Of course, stockholders are interested in how much they have earned on their investment in the business. Their **return on equity** is measured by the ratio of net income to average stockholders' equity. Taking the ending stockholders' equity from the balance sheet and assuming that beginning stockholders' equity is $402,212, Cruz Corporation's return on equity is computed as follows:

K/R

$$\text{Return on Equity} = \frac{\text{Net Income}}{\text{Average Stockholder's Equity}}$$

$$= \frac{\$58{,}000}{(\$393{,}732 + \$402{,}212) \div 2} = \frac{\$58{,}000}{\$397{,}972} = .146, \text{ or } 14.6\%$$

Thus, Cruz Corporation earned 14.6 cents for every dollar invested by stockholders. Whether this is an acceptable return depends on several factors, such as how much the company earned in previous years and how much other companies in the same industry earned. As measured by return on equity, the advertising

Return on equity—the ratio of net income to average stockholder's equity—is an important measure of a company's profitablility. It indicates how much stockholders have earned on their investments. At one time, Coca-Cola Company was among a few companies that earned a 20 percent return on equity.

FIGURE 9

Average Return on Equity for Selected Industries

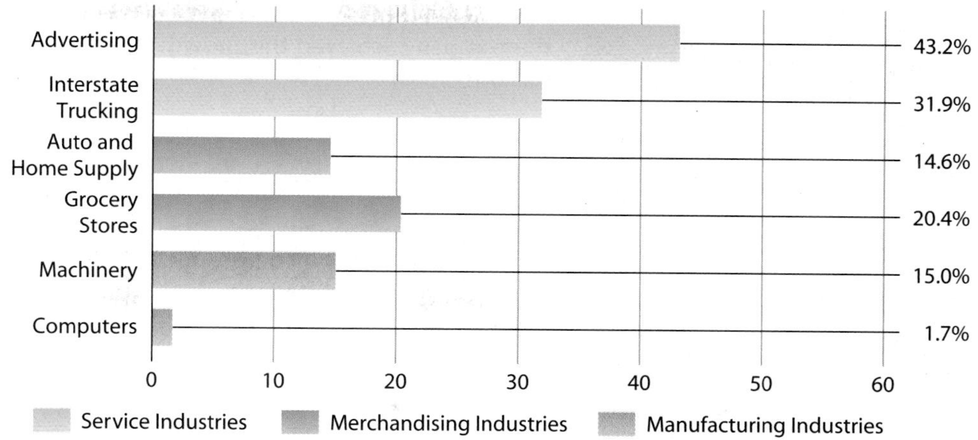

***Source*: Data from Dun & Bradstreet, *Industry Norms and Key Business Ratios*, 2005–2006**

industry is the most profitable of our sample industries, with a return on equity of 43.2 percent (see Figure 9). Cruz Corporation's average return on equity of 14.6 percent is the same as the average of 14.6 percent for the auto and home supply industry.

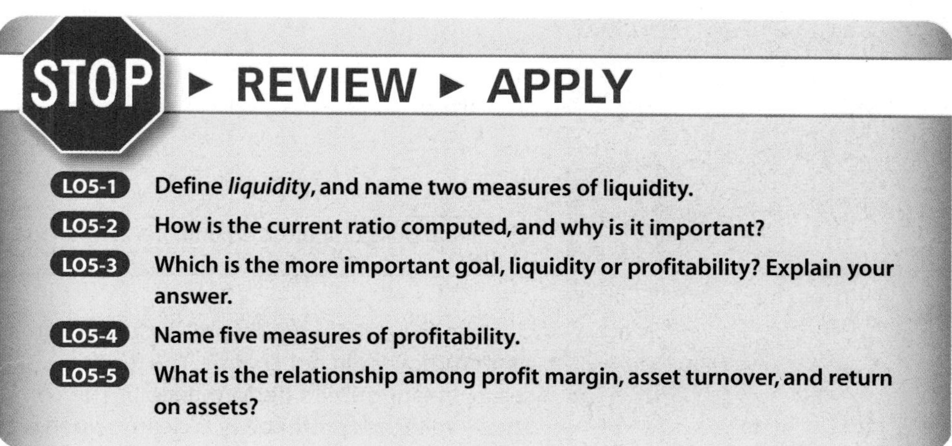

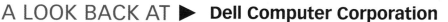

STOP ► REVIEW ► APPLY

LO5-1 **Define *liquidity*, and name two measures of liquidity.**

LO5-2 **How is the current ratio computed, and why is it important?**

LO5-3 **Which is the more important goal, liquidity or profitability? Explain your answer.**

LO5-4 **Name five measures of profitability.**

LO5-5 **What is the relationship among profit margin, asset turnover, and return on assets?**

A LOOK BACK AT ► Dell Computer Corporation

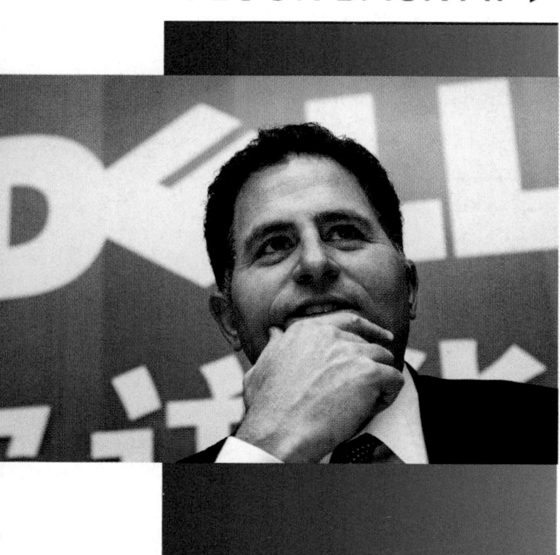

In the Decision Point at the beginning of the chapter, we noted that **Dell's** management focused on the goals of growth, liquidity, and profitability. We also noted that in judging whether a company has achieved its objectives, investors, creditors, and others analyze relationships between key numbers in the company's financial statements. We asked these questions:

- **How should financial statements be organized to provide the best information?**
- **What key measures best capture a company's financial performance?**

As you saw in Exhibits 2 and 4, Dell uses a classified balance sheet and a multistep income statement to communicate its financial results to users. The Financial Highlights that we presented in the Decision Point show that the company increased its revenues by 6 percent between 2007 and 2008. More significant, its operating income and net income increased by 12 percent and 14 percent, respectively.

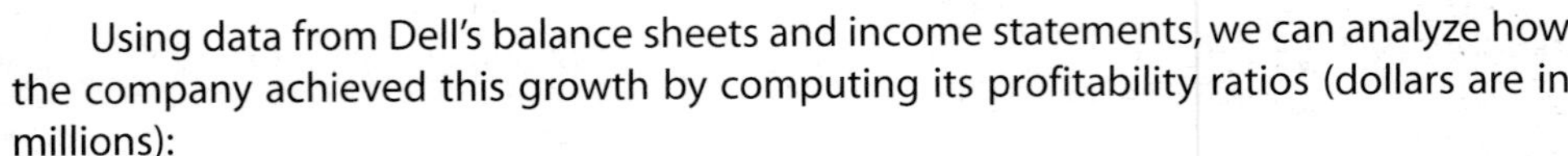

Using data from Dell's balance sheets and income statements, we can analyze how the company achieved this growth by computing its profitability ratios (dollars are in millions):

	2008	2007
$\frac{\text{Net Income}}{\text{Net Revenue}}$	$\frac{\$2,947}{\$61,133}$	$\frac{\$2,583}{\$57,420}$
K/R Profit Margin:	4.8%	4.5%
$\frac{\text{Net Revenue}}{\text{Average Total Assets}}$	$\frac{\$61,133}{(\$27,561 + \$25,635) \div 2}$	$\frac{\$57,420}{(\$25,635 + \$23,252^{*}) \div 2}$
	$\frac{\$61,133}{\$26,598}$	$\frac{\$57,420}{\$24,443.5}$
K/R Asset Turnover:	2.3 times	2.3 times
$\frac{\text{Net Income}}{\text{Average Total Assets}}$	$\frac{\$2,947}{(\$27,561 + \$25,635) \div 2}$	$\frac{\$2,583}{(\$25,635 + \$23,252^{*}) \div 2}$
	$\frac{\$2,947}{\$26,598}$	$\frac{\$2,583}{\$24,443.5}$
K/R Return on Assets:	.111, or 11.1%	.106, or 10.6%

* From Dell Computer Corporation's 2007 annual report.

The increase in net income resulted primarily from the increase in profit margin. Asset turnover did not change. The result is a slightly lower return on assets, but we can see by relating Dell's performance to the computer industry averages in Figures 5, 6, and 7, that Dell's profitability is clearly superior to the industry as follows:

	Profit Margin	×	Asset Turnover	=	Return on Assets
2008:	4.8%	×	2.3 times	=	11.0%*
2007:	4.5%	×	2.3 times	=	10.4%*
Industry Average:	0.5%	×	1.6 times	=	0.8%

* The differences are due to rounding.

Dell also took advantage of debt financing to leverage its profitability into a very high return on equity, as shown by its debt to equity and return on equity ratios:

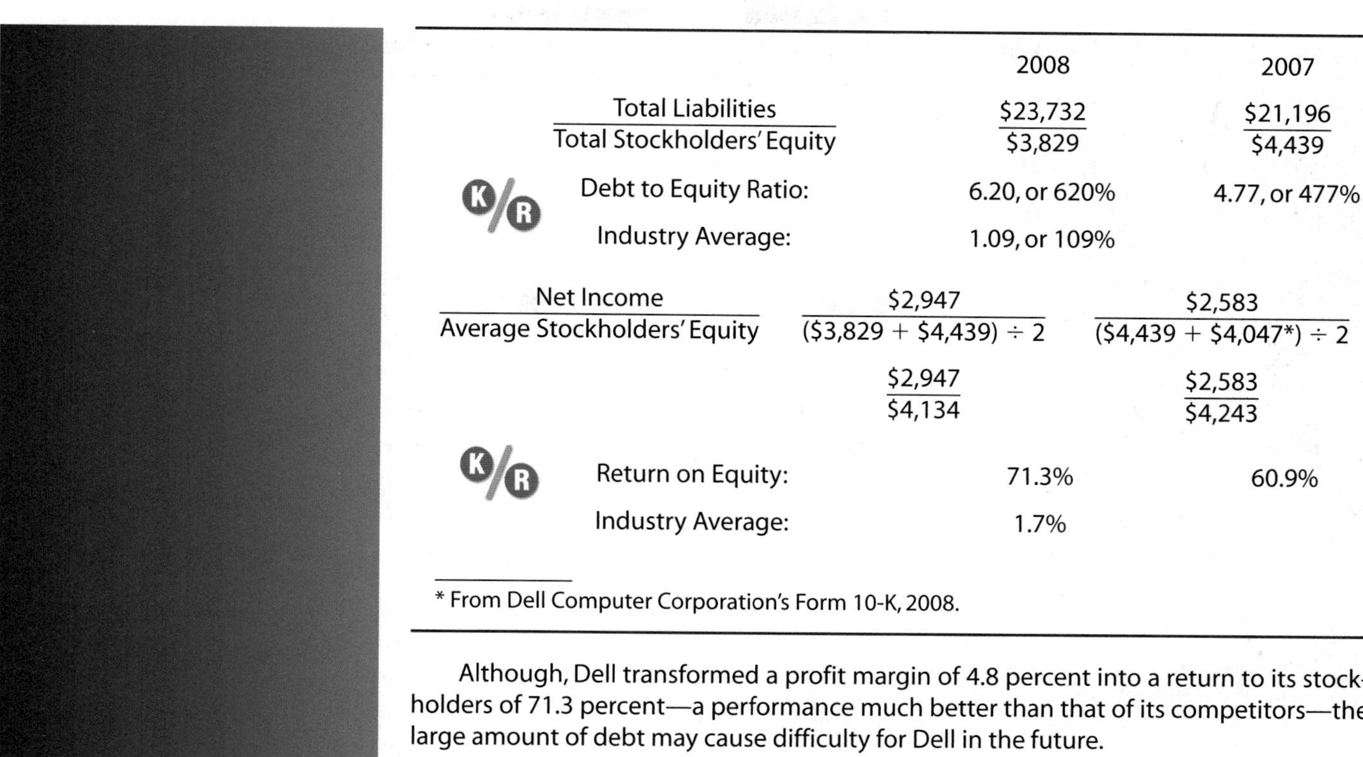

	2008	2007
Total Liabilities / Total Stockholders' Equity	\$23,732 / \$3,829	\$21,196 / \$4,439
Debt to Equity Ratio:	6.20, or 620%	4.77, or 477%
Industry Average:	1.09, or 109%	
Net Income / Average Stockholders' Equity	\$2,947 / (\$3,829 + \$4,439) ÷ 2	\$2,583 / (\$4,439 + \$4,047*) ÷ 2
	\$2,947 / \$4,134	\$2,583 / \$4,243
Return on Equity:	71.3%	60.9%
Industry Average:	1.7%	

* From Dell Computer Corporation's Form 10-K, 2008.

Although, Dell transformed a profit margin of 4.8 percent into a return to its stockholders of 71.3 percent—a performance much better than that of its competitors—the large amount of debt may cause difficulty for Dell in the future.

CHAPTER REVIEW

REVIEW of Learning Objectives

LO1 Describe the objective of financial reporting and identify the qualitative characteristics, conventions, and ethical considerations of accounting information.

The objective of financial reporting is to provide financial information about the reporting entity that is useful to present and potential equity investors, lenders, and other creditors in making decisions in their capacity as capital providers. To be decision-useful, financial information must be useful in assessing cash flow prospects and stewardship. Because of the estimates and judgment that go into preparing financial information, such information must exhibit the qualitative characteristics of relevance and faithful representation. To be relevant, information must have predictive value, confirmative value, or both. To be faithful, financial information must be complete, neutral, and free from material error. Complementing the quality of information are the qualities of comparability, verifiability, timeliness, and understandability. It is also important for users to understand the constraints on financial information or accounting conventions used to prepare financial statements. Since the passage of the Sarbanes-Oxley Act in 2002, CEOs and CFOs have been required to certify to the accuracy and completeness of their companies' financial statements.

LO2 Define and describe the conventions of *consistency, full disclosure, materiality, conservatism,* and *cost-benefit*.

Because accountants' measurements are not exact, certain conventions are applied to help users interpret financial statements. The first of these conventions is consistency. Consistency requires the use of the same accounting procedures from period to period and enhances the comparability of financial statements. Full disclosure means including all relevant information in the financial statements. The materiality convention has to do with determining the relative importance of an item. Conservatism entails using the procedure that is least likely to overstate assets and income. The cost-benefit convention holds that the benefits to be gained from providing accounting information should be greater than the costs of providing it.

LO3 Identify and describe the basic components of a classified balance sheet.

The basic components of a classified balance sheet are as follows:

Assets	**Liabilities**
Current assets	Current liabilities
Investments	Long-term liabilities
Property, plant, and equipment	**Stockholders' Equity**
Intangible assets	Contributed capital
(Other assets)	Retained earnings

Current assets are cash and other assets that a firm can reasonably expect to convert to cash or use up during the next year or the normal operating cycle, whichever is longer. Investments are assets, usually long term, that are not used in the normal operation of a business. Property, plant, and equipment are tangible long-term assets used in day-to-day operations. Intangible assets are long-term assets with no physical substance whose value stems from the rights or privileges they extend to stockholders.

A current liability is an obligation due to be paid or performed during the next year or the normal operating cycle, whichever is longer. Long-term liabilities are debts that fall due more than one year in the future or beyond the normal operating cycle.

The equity section of a corporation's balance sheet differs from the balance sheet of a proprietorship or partnership in that it has subcategories for contributed capital (the assets invested by stockholders) and retained earnings (stockholders' claim to assets earned from operations and reinvested in operations).

LO4 Describe the features of multistep and single-step classified income statements.

Classified income statements for external reporting can be in multistep or single-step form. The multistep form arrives at income before income taxes through a series of steps; the single-step form arrives at income before income taxes in a single step. A multistep income statement usually has a separate section for other revenues and expenses.

LO5 Use classified financial statements to evaluate liquidity and profitability.

In evaluating a company's liquidity and profitability, investors and creditors rely on the data provided in classified financial statements. Two measures of liquidity are working capital and the current ratio. Five measures of profitability are profit margin, asset turnover, return on assets, debt to equity ratio, and return on equity. Industry averages are useful in interpreting these ratios.

REVIEW of Concepts and Terminology

The following concepts and terms were introduced in this chapter:

Accounting conventions: The constraints on accounting used in preparing financial statements that enable the user to better understand accounting information. **(LO1)**

Classified financial statements: General-purpose external financial statements that are divided into subcategories. **(LO3)**

Comparability: The qualitative characteristic of information that enables decision makers to recognize similarities and differences between two sets of economic phenomena. **(LO1)**

Conservatism: The convention that when faced with two equally acceptable alternatives, the accountant chooses the one least likely to overstate assets and income. **(LO2)**

Consistency: The convention requiring that once a company has adopted an accounting procedure, it must use it from one period to the next unless a note to the financial statements informs users of a change in procedure. **(LO2)**

Cost-benefit: The convention that the benefits gained from providing accounting information should be greater than the costs of providing that information. **(LO2)**

Cost of goods sold: The amount a merchandiser paid for the merchandise it sold during an accounting period or the cost to a manufacturer of making the products it sold during an accounting period. Also called *cost of sales.* **(LO4)**

Current assets: Cash and other assets that a company can reasonably expect to convert to cash, sell, or consume within one year or its normal operating cycle, whichever is longer. **(LO3)**

Current liabilities: Obligations due to be paid or performed within one year or within the normal operating cycle, whichever is longer. **(LO3)**

Earnings per share: Net income earned on each share of common stock; net income divided by the average number of common shares outstanding during the year. Also called *net income per share.* **(LO4)**

Faithful representation: The qualitative characteristic of information that financial information must be complete, neutral, and free from material error. **(LO1)**

Full disclosure: The convention requiring that a company's financial statements and their notes present all information relevant to the users' understanding of the statements. **(LO2)**

Gross margin: The difference between net sales and cost of goods sold. Also called *gross profit.* (LO4)

Gross sales: Total sales for cash and on credit during an accounting period. (LO4)

Income before income taxes: The amount a company has earned from all activities—operating and nonoperating—before taking into account the amount of income taxes incurred. (LO4)

Income from operations: Gross margin minus operating expenses. Also called *operating income.* (LO4)

Income taxes: A category for the expense of federal, state, and local taxes that appears only on the income statements of corporations. Also called *provision for income taxes.* (LO4)

Intangible assets: Long-term assets with no physical substance whose value stems from the rights or privileges they extend to their owners. (LO3)

Investments: Assets, usually long term, that are not used in the normal operation of a business and that management does not intend to convert to cash within the next year. (LO3)

Long-term liabilities: Debts that fall due more than one year in the future or beyond the normal operating cycle. (LO3)

Manufacturing company: A company that makes and sells products. (LO4)

Materiality: The convention that refers to the relative importance of an item or event in a financial statement and its influence on the decisions of the users of financial statements. (LO2)

Merchandising company: A company, either a wholesaler or retailer, that buys and sells products. (LO4)

Multistep income statement: An income statement that goes through a series of steps to arrive at net income. (LO4)

Net income: What remains of gross margin after operating expenses have been deducted, other revenues and expenses have been added or deducted, and income taxes have been deducted. Also called *net earnings.* (LO4)

Net sales: The gross proceeds from sales of merchandise (gross sales) less sales returns and allowances and any discounts allowed. Often called *sales.* (LO4)

Normal operating cycle: The average time a company needs to go from spending cash to receiving cash. (LO3)

Operating expenses: Expenses other than cost of goods sold incurred in running a business. (LO4)

Other assets: A balance sheet category that some companies use to group all assets other than current assets and property, plant, and equipment. (LO3)

Other revenues and expenses: The section of a multistep income statement that includes revenues and expenses not related to business operations. Also called *nonoperating revenues and expenses.* (LO4)

Property, plant, and equipment: Tangible long-term assets used in the continuing operation of a business. Also called *operating assets, fixed assets, tangible assets, long-lived assets,* or *plant assets.* (LO3)

Qualitative characteristics: Standards for judging accounting information. (LO1)

Relevance: The qualitative characteristic of information that information must have predictive value, confirmative value, or both. (LO1)

Sales returns and allowances: Refunds, credits, and discounts given to customers who have received defective goods. (LO4)

Single-step income statement: An income statement that arrives at income before income taxes in a single step. (LO4)

Timeliness: The qualitative characteristic of information that enables users to receive information in time to influence a decision. (LO1)

Understandability: The qualitative characteristic of information that enables users to comprehend the meaning of the information they receive. (LO1)

Verifiability: The qualitative characteristic of information that helps assure users that information faithfully represents what it purports to depict. (LO1)

Working capital: A measure of liquidity that shows the net current assets on hand to continue business operations; Total Current Assets − Total Current Liabilities. (LO5)

Key Ratios

Asset turnover: A measure of profitability that shows how efficiently assets are used to produce sales; Net Sales ÷ Average Total Assets. (LO5)

Current ratio: A measure of liquidity; Current Assets ÷ Current Liabilities. (LO5)

Debt to equity ratio: A measure of profitability that shows the proportion of a company's assets that is financed by creditors and the proportion financed by stockholders; Total Liabilities ÷ Stockholders' Equity. **(LO5)**

Profit margin: A measure of profitability that shows the percentage of each sales dollar that results in net income; Net Income ÷ Net Sales. **(LO5)**

Return on assets: A measure of profitability that shows how efficiently a company uses its assets to produce income; Net Income ÷ Average Total Assets. **(LO5)**

Return on equity: A measure of profitability that relates the amount earned by a business to the stockholders' investment in the business; Net Income ÷ Average Stockholders' Equity. **(LO5)**

REVIEW Problem

Using Ratios to Analyze Liquidity and Profitability

Bonalli Shoe Company has been facing increased competition from overseas shoemakers. Its total assets and stockholders' equity at the beginning of 2010 were $690,000 and $590,000, respectively. A summary of the firm's data for 2010 and 2011 follows.

	2011	2010
Current assets	$ 200,000	$ 170,000
Total assets	880,000	710,000
Current liabilities	90,000	50,000
Long-term liabilities	150,000	50,000
Stockholders' equity	640,000	610,000
Sales	1,200,000	1,050,000
Net income	60,000	80,000

Required

Use (1) liquidity analysis and (2) profitability analysis to document Bonalli Shoe Company's declining financial position.

Answer to Review Problem

1. Liquidity analysis:

	A	B	C	D	E
1		**Current Assets**	**Current Liabilities**	**Working Capital**	**Current Ratio**
2	2010	$170,000	$50,000	$120,000	3.40
3	2011	200,000	90,000	110,000	2.22
4	Decrease in working capital			$ 10,000	
5	Decrease in current ratio				1.18
6					

Both working capital and the current ratio declined between 2010 and 2011 because the $40,000 increase in current liabilities ($90,000 − $50,000) was greater than the $30,000 increase in current assets.

2. Profitability analysis:

		Net Income	Sales	Profit Margin	Average Total Assets	Asset Turnover	Return on Assets	Average Stockholders' Equity	Return on Equity
1									
2	2010	$80,000	$1,050,000	7.6%	$700,000 [1]	1.50	11.4%	$600,000 [3]	13.3%
3	2011	60,000	1,200,000	5.0%	795,000 [2]	1.51	7.5%	625,000 [4]	9.6%
4	Increase (decrease)	($20,000)	$ 150,000	-2.6%	$ 95,000	0.01	-3.9%	$ 25,000	-3.7%
5									
6	[1] ($710,000 + $690,000) ÷ 2								
7	[2] ($880,000 + $710,000) ÷ 2								
8	[3] ($610,000 + $590,000) ÷ 2								
9	[4] ($640,000 + $610,000) ÷ 2								
10									

Net income decreased by $20,000 despite an increase in sales of $150,000 and an increase in average total assets of $95,000. Thus, the profit margin fell from 7.6 percent to 5.0 percent, and return on assets fell from 11.4 percent to 7.5 percent. Asset turnover showed almost no change and so did not contribute to the decline in profitability. The decrease in return on equity, from 13.3 percent to 9.6 percent, was not as great as the decrease in return on assets because the growth in total assets was financed mainly by debt rather than by stockholders' equity, as shown in the capital structure analysis below.

	A	B	C	D
1		Total Liabilities	Stockholders' Equity	Debt to Equity Ratio
2	2010	$100,000	$610,000	16.4%
3	2011	240,000	640,000	37.5%
4	Increase	$140,000	$ 30,000	21.1%
5				

Total liabilities increased by $140,000, while stockholders' equity increased by $30,000. Thus, the amount of the business financed by debt in relation to the amount financed by stockholders' equity increased between 2010 and 2011.

CHAPTER ASSIGNMENTS

BUILDING Your Basic Knowledge and Skills

Short Exercises

LO1 **Objectives and Qualitative Characteristics**

SE 1. Identify each of the following statements as related to either the objective (O) of financial information or a qualitative (Q) characteristic of accounting information:

1. Information about business resources, claims to those resources, and changes in them should be provided.

2. Decision makers must be able to interpret accounting information.
3. Information that is useful in making investment and credit decisions should be furnished.
4. Accounting information must exhibit relevance and faithful representation.
5. Information useful in assessing cash flow prospects should be provided.

LO2 **Accounting Conventions**

SE 2. State which of the accounting conventions—consistency, materiality, conservatism, full disclosure, or cost-benefit—is being followed in each of the cases listed below.

1. Management provides detailed information about the company's long-term debt in the notes to the financial statements.
2. A company does not account separately for discounts received for prompt payment of accounts payable because few of these transactions occur and the total amount of the discounts is small.
3. Management eliminates a weekly report on property, plant, and equipment acquisitions and disposals because no one finds it useful.
4. A company follows the policy of recognizing a loss on inventory when the market value of an item falls below its cost but does nothing if the market value rises.
5. When several accounting methods are acceptable, management chooses a single method and follows that method from year to year.

LO3 **Classification of Accounts: Balance Sheet**

SE 3. Tell whether each of the following accounts is a current asset; an investment; property, plant, and equipment; an intangible asset; a current liability; a long-term liability; stockholders' equity; or not on the balance sheet:

1. Delivery Trucks
2. Accounts Payable
3. Note Payable (due in 90 days)
4. Delivery Expense
5. Common Stock
6. Prepaid Insurance
7. Trademark
8. Investment to Be Held Six Months
9. Income Taxes Payable
10. Factory Not Used in Business

LO3 **Classified Balance Sheet**

SE 4. Using the following accounts, prepare a classified balance sheet at year end, May 31, 2010: Accounts Payable, $800; Accounts Receivable, $1,100; Accumulated Depreciation–Equipment, $700; Cash, $200; Common Stock, $1,000; Equipment, $3,000; Franchise, $200; Investments (long-term), $500; Merchandise Inventory, $600; Notes Payable (long-term), $400; Retained Earnings, ?; Wages Payable, $100.

LO4 **Classification of Accounts: Income Statement**

SE 5. Tell whether each of the following accounts is part of net sales, cost of goods sold, operating expenses, or other revenues and expenses, or is not on the income statement:

1. Delivery Expense
2. Interest Expense
3. Unearned Revenue
4. Sales Returns and Allowances
5. Cost of Goods Sold
6. Depreciation Expense
7. Investment Income
8. Retained Earnings

LO4 **Single-Step Income Statement**

SE 6. Using the following accounts, prepare a single-step income statement at year end, May 31, 2010: Cost of Goods Sold, $840; General Expenses, $450; Income Taxes, $105; Interest Expense, $210; Interest Income, $90; Net Sales, $2,400; Selling Expenses, $555. Ignore earnings per share.

Multistep Income Statement

SE 7. Using the accounts presented in **SE 6**, prepare a multistep income statement.

Liquidity Ratios

SE 8. Using the following accounts and balances taken from a year-end balance sheet, compute working capital and the current ratio:

Accounts Payable	$ 7,000
Accounts Receivable	10,000
Cash	4,000
Common Stock	20,000
Marketable Securities	2,000
Merchandise Inventory	12,000
Notes Payable in Three Years	13,000
Property, Plant, and Equipment	40,000
Retained Earnings	28,000

Profitability Ratios

SE 9. Using the following information from a balance sheet and an income statement, compute the (1) profit margin, (2) asset turnover, (3) return on assets, (4) debt to equity ratio, and (5) return on equity. (The previous year's total assets were $200,000, and stockholders' equity was $140,000.)

Total assets	$240,000
Total liabilities	60,000
Total stockholders' equity	180,000
Net sales	260,000
Cost of goods sold	140,000
Operating expenses	80,000
Income taxes	10,000

LO5

Profitability Ratios

SE 10. Assume that a company has a profit margin of 6.0 percent, an asset turnover of 3.2 times, and a debt to equity ratio of 50 percent. What are the company's return on assets and return on equity?

Exercises

LO1 LO2

Discussion Questions

E 1. Develop a brief answer to each of the following questions:

1. How do the four basic financial statements meet the stewardship objective of financial reporting?
2. What are some areas that require estimates to record transactions under the matching rule?
3. How can financial information be consistent but not comparable?
4. When might an amount be material to management but not to the CPA auditing the financial statements?

LO4 LO5

Discussion Questions

E 2. Develop a brief answer to each of the following questions:

1. Why is it that land held for future use and equipment not currently used are classified as investments rather than as property, plant, and equipment?
2. Which is the better measure of a company's performance—income from operations or net income?
3. Why is it important to compare a company's financial performance with industry standards?

4. Is the statement "Return on assets is a better measure of profitability than profit margin" true or false and why?

LO1 LO2

Financial Accounting Concepts

E 3. The lettered items below represent a classification scheme for the concepts of financial accounting. Match each numbered term in the list that follows with the letter of the category in which it belongs.

a. Decision makers (users of accounting information)
b. Business activities or entities relevant to accounting measurement
c. Objective of accounting information
d. Accounting measurement considerations
e. Accounting processing considerations
f. Qualitative characteristics
g. Accounting conventions
h. Financial statements

1. Conservatism
2. Verifiability
3. Statement of cash flows
4. Materiality
5. Faithful representation
6. Recognition
7. Cost-benefit
8. Predictive value
9. Business transactions
10. Consistency
11. Full disclosure
12. Furnishing information that is useful to investors and creditors
13. Specific business entities
14. Classification
15. Management
16. Neutrality
17. Internal accounting control
18. Valuation
19. Investors
20. Completeness
21. Relevance
22. Furnishing information that is useful in assessing cash flow prospects

LO2

Accounting Concepts and Conventions

E 4. Each of the statements below violates a convention in accounting. State which of the following accounting conventions is violated: comparability and consistency, materiality, conservatism, full disclosure, or cost-benefit.

1. Reports that are time-consuming and expensive to prepare are presented to the board of directors each month, even though the reports are never used.
2. A company changes its method of accounting for depreciation.
3. The company in **2** does not indicate in the financial statements that the method of depreciation was changed; nor does it specify the effect of the change on net income.
4. A company's new office building, which is built next to the company's existing factory, is debited to the Factory account because it represents a fairly small dollar amount in relation to the factory.
5. The asset account for a pickup truck still used in the business is written down to what the truck could be sold for, even though the carrying value under conventional depreciation methods is higher.

Classification of Accounts: Balance Sheet

LO3

E 5. The lettered items below represent a classification scheme for a balance sheet, and the numbered items in the list at the top of the next page are account titles. Match each account with the letter of the category in which it belongs.

a. Current assets
b. Investments
c. Property, plant, and equipment
d. Intangible assets
e. Current liabilities
f. Long-term liabilities
g. Stockholders' equity
h. Not on the balance sheet

1. Patent
2. Building Held for Sale
3. Prepaid Rent
4. Wages Payable
5. Note Payable in Five Years
6. Building Used in Operations
7. Fund Held to Pay Off Long-Term Debt
8. Inventory
9. Prepaid Insurance
10. Depreciation Expense
11. Accounts Receivable
12. Interest Expense
13. Unearned Revenue
14. Short-Term Investments
15. Accumulated Depreciation
16. Retained Earnings

LO3 **Classified Balance Sheet Preparation**

E 6. The following data pertain to Branner, Inc.: Accounts Payable, $10,200; Accounts Receivable, $7,600; Accumulated Depreciation–Building, $2,800; Accumulated Depreciation–Equipment, $3,400; Bonds Payable, $12,000; Building, $14,000; Cash, $6,240; Common Stock, $5 par, 4,000 shares authorized, issued, and outstanding, $20,000; Copyright, $1,240; Equipment, $30,400; Inventory, $8,000; Investment in Corporate Securities (long-term), $4,000; Investment in Six-Month Government Securities, $3,280; Land, $1,600; Paid-in Capital in Excess of Par Value, $10,000; Prepaid Rent, $240; Retained Earnings, $17,640; and Revenue Received in Advance, $560.

Prepare a classified balance sheet at December 31, 2010.

LO4 **Classification of Accounts: Income Statement**

E 7. Using the classification scheme below for a multistep income statement, match each account with the letter of the category in which it belongs.

a. Net sales
b. Cost of goods sold
c. Selling expenses
d. General and administrative expenses
e. Other revenues and expenses
f. Not on the income statement

1. Sales Returns and Allowances
2. Cost of Goods Sold
3. Dividend Income
4. Advertising Expense
5. Office Salaries Expense
6. Freight Out Expense
7. Prepaid Insurance
8. Utilities Expense
9. Sales Salaries Expense
10. Rent Expense
11. Depreciation Expense–Delivery Equipment
12. Taxes Payable
13. Interest Expense

LO4 **Preparation of Income Statements**

E 8. The following data pertain to a corporation: net sales, $202,500; cost of goods sold, $110,000; selling expenses, $45,000; general and administrative expenses, $30,000; income taxes, $3,750; interest expense, $2,000; interest income, $1,500; and common stock outstanding, 25,000 shares.

1. Prepare a single-step income statement.
2. Prepare a multistep income statement.

LO4 **Multistep Income Statement**

E 9. A single-step income statement appears at the top of the following page. Present the information in a multistep income statement, and indicate what insights can be obtained from the multistep form as opposed to the single-step form.

SUPPLEMENT TO CHAPTER

4

The Annual Report Project

Many instructors assign a term project that requires reading and analyzing an annual report. The Annual Report Project described here has been successful in our classes. It may be used with the annual report of any company, including CVS Caremark Corporation's annual report and the financial statements from Southwest Airlines Co.'s annual report that appear in the Supplement to Chapter 1.

The extent to which financial analysis is required depends on the point in the course at which the Annual Report Project is assigned. Instruction 3E, below, provides several options.

Instructions:

1. Choose a company, and obtain its most recent annual report online or through your library or another source.
2. Use the Internet or your library to locate at least two articles about the company and the industry in which it operates. Read the articles, as well as the annual report, and summarize your findings. In addition, access the company's Internet home page directly or through the Needles Accounting Resource Center Website (*www.cengage.com/accounting/needles*). Review the company's products and services and its financial information. Summarize what you have learned.
3. Your analysis should consist of five or six double-spaced pages organized according to the following outline:

   A. **Introduction**
   Identify the company by writing a summary that includes the following elements:

   - Name of the chief executive officer
   - Location of the home office
   - Ending date of latest fiscal year
   - Description of the company's principal products or services
   - Main geographic area of activity
   - Name of the company's independent accountants (auditors). In your own words, explain what the accountants said about the company's financial statements.
   - The most recent price of the company's stock and its dividend per share. Be sure to provide the date for this information.

B. Industry Situation and Company Plans
Describe the industry and its outlook. Then summarize the company's future plans based on what you learned from the annual report and your other research. Be sure to include any relevant information from management's letter to the stockholders.

C. Financial Statements
Income Statement: Is the format most like a single-step or multistep format? Determine gross profit, income from operations, and net income for the last two years. Comment on the increases or decreases in these amounts.
Balance Sheet: Show that Assets = Liabilities + Stockholders' Equity for the past two years.
Statement of Cash Flows: Indicate whether the company's cash flows from operations for the past two years were more or less than net income. Also indicate whether the company is expanding through investing activities. Identify the company's most important source of financing. Overall, has cash increased or decreased over the past two years?

D. Accounting Policies
Describe the company's significant accounting policies, if any, relating to revenue recognition, cash, short-term investments, merchandise inventories, and property and equipment. Identify the topics of the notes to the financial statements.

E. Financial Analysis
For the past two years, calculate and discuss the significance of the following ratios:

Option (a): Basic (After Completing Chapter 4)
Liquidity Ratios
- Working capital
- Current ratio

Profitability Ratios
- Profit margin
- Asset turnover
- Return on assets
- Debt to equity ratio
- Return on equity

Option (b): Basic with Enhanced Liquidity Analysis (After Completing Chapter 8)
Liquidity Ratios
- Working capital
- Current ratio
- Receivable turnover
- Days' sales uncollected
- Inventory turnover
- Days' inventory on hand
- Payables turnover
- Days' payable
- Operating cycle
- Financing period

Profitability Ratios
- Profit margin
- Asset turnover
- Return on assets

Debt to equity ratio
Return on equity

Option (c): Comprehensive (After Completing Chapter 13 or 14)

Liquidity Ratios

Working capital
Current ratio
Receivable turnover
Days' sales uncollected
Inventory turnover
Days' inventory on hand
Payables turnover
Days' payable
Operating cycle
Financing period

Profitability Ratios

Profit margin
Asset turnover
Return on assets
Return on equity

Long-Term Solvency Ratios

Debt to equity ratio
Interest coverage

Cash Flow Adequacy

Cash flow yield
Cash flows to sales
Cash flows to assets
Free cash flow

Market Strength Ratios

Price/earnings per share
Dividends yield

CHAPTER

5

The Operating Cycle and Merchandising Operations

Focus on Financial Statements

INCOME STATEMENT

Revenues

− Expenses

= Net Income

STATEMENT OF RETAINED EARNINGS

Opening Balance

+ Net Income

− Dividends

= Retained Earnings

(2)

BALANCE SHEET

Assets | Liabilities

(1)

Equity

A = L + E

STATEMENT OF CASH FLOWS

Operating activities

+ Investing activities

+ Financing activities

= Change in Cash

+ Starting Balance

= Ending Cash Balance

Under the perpetual inventory system, merchandise inventory is updated after every purchase (1) and sale (2).

In the last chapter, we pointed out management's responsibility for ensuring the accuracy and fairness of financial statements. To fulfill that responsibility, management must see that transactions are properly recorded and that the company's assets are protected. That, in turn, requires a system of internal controls. In this chapter, we examine internal controls over the transactions of merchandising companies and the operating cycle in which such transactions take place. The internal controls and other issues that we describe here also apply to manufacturing companies.

LEARNING OBJECTIVES

LO1 Identify the management issues related to merchandising businesses. *(pp. 290–295)*

LO2 Describe the terms of sale related to merchandising transactions. *(pp. 296–298)*

LO3 Prepare an income statement and record merchandising transactions under the perpetual inventory system. *(pp. 299–303)*

LO4 Prepare an income statement and record merchandising transactions under the periodic inventory system. *(pp. 303–308)*

LO5 Describe the components of internal control, control activities, and limitations on internal control. *(pp. 308–311)*

LO6 Apply internal control activities to common merchandising transactions. *(pp. 311–318)*

DECISION POINT ▶ A USER'S FOCUS

- ▶ How can the company efficiently manage its cycle of merchandising operations?
- ▶ How can merchandising transactions be recorded to reflect the company's performance?
- ▶ How can the company maintain control over its merchandising operations?

Costco Wholesale Corporation

Costco is a highly successful and fast-growing merchandising company. Like all other merchandisers, Costco has two key decisions to make: the price at which it will sell goods and the level of service it will provide. A department store may set the price of its merchandise at a relatively high level and provide a great deal of service. A discount store, on the other hand, may price its merchandise at a relatively low level and provide limited service. In the type of discount stores that Costco operates, customers buy memberships that allow them to buy in bulk at wholesale prices. Costco purchases merchandise in large quantities from many suppliers, places the goods on racks in its warehouse-like stores, and sells the goods to customers at very low prices, with less personal service.

Costco's large scale, reflected in its Financial Highlights,[1] presents management with many challenges.

COSTCO'S FINANCIAL HIGHLIGHTS
Operating Results (In millions)

Fiscal-Year Ended	September 2, 2007	September 3, 2006	Change
Net revenue	$64,400	$60,151	7.1%
Cost of sales	56,450	52,745	7.0
Gross margin	$ 7,950	$ 7,406	7.3
Operating expenses	6,342	5,780	9.7
Operating income	$ 1,608	$ 1,626	(1.1)

Managing Merchandising Businesses

LO1 Identify the management issues related to merchandising businesses.

A **merchandising business** earns income by buying and selling goods, which are called **merchandise inventory**. Whether a merchandiser is a wholesaler or a retailer, it uses the same basic accounting methods as a service company. However, the buying and selling of goods adds to the complexity of the business and of the accounting process. To understand the issues involved in accounting for a merchandising business, one must be familiar with the issues involved in managing such a business.

Operating Cycle

Study Note

A company must provide financing for the average days' inventory on hand plus the average number of days to collect credit sales less the average number of days it is allowed to pay its suppliers.

Merchandising businesses engage in a series of transactions called the **operating cycle**. Figure 1 shows the transactions that make up this cycle. Some companies buy merchandise for cash and sell it for cash, but these companies are usually small companies like a produce market or a hot dog stand. Most companies buy merchandise on credit and sell it on credit, thereby engaging in the following four transactions:

1. Purchase of merchandise inventory for cash or on credit
2. Collection of cash from credit sales
3. Payment for purchases made on credit
4. Sales of merchandise inventory for cash or on credit

The first three transactions represent the time it takes to purchase inventory, sell it, and collect for it. Merchandisers must be able to do without the cash for this period of time either by relying on cash flows from other sources within the company or by borrowing. If they lack the cash to pay bills when they come due, they can be forced out of business. Thus managing cash flow is a critical concern.

The suppliers that sold the company the merchandise usually also sell on credit and thus help alleviate the cash flow problem by providing financing for a period of time before they require payment (transaction 4). However, this period is rarely as long as the operating cycle. The period between the time the supplier must be paid and the end of the operating cycle is sometimes referred to as the *cash gap*, and more formally as the financing period.

FIGURE 1
Cash Flows in the Operating Cycle

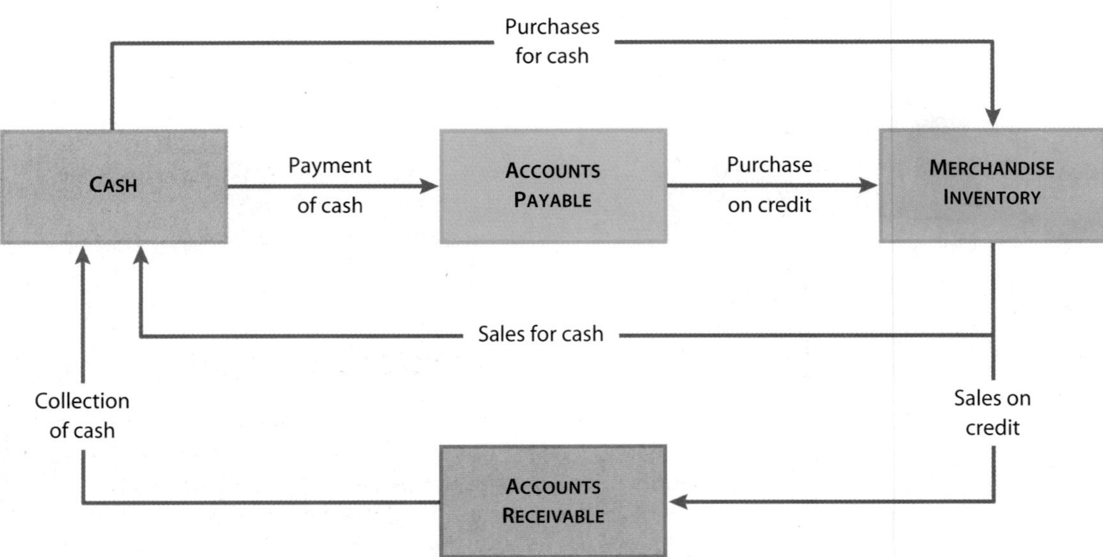

FIGURE 2
The Financing Period

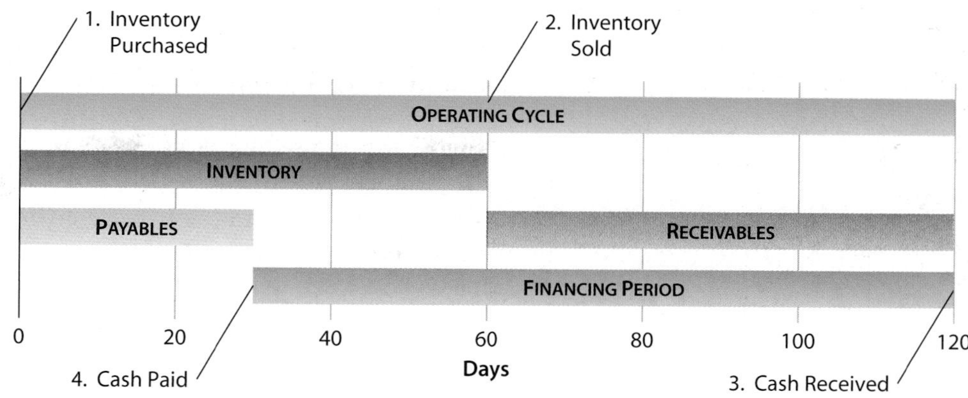

The **financing period**, illustrated in Figure 2, is the amount of time from the purchase of inventory until it is sold and payment is collected, less the amount of time creditors give the company to pay for the inventory. Thus, if it takes 60 days to sell the inventory, 60 days to collect for the sale, and creditors' payment terms are 30 days, the financing period is 90 days. During the financing period, the company will be without cash from this series of transactions and will need either to have funds available internally or to borrow from a bank.

The type of merchandising operation in which a company engages can affect the financing period. For example, compare **Costco's** financing period with that of a traditional discount store chain, **Target Corporation**:

	Target	Costco	Difference
Days' inventory on hand	56 days	31 days	− 25 days
Days' receivable	34	4	− 30
Less days' payable	−59	−31	−(28)
Financing period	**31 days**	**4 days**	**− 27 days**

Costco has an advantage over Target because it holds its inventory for a shorter period before it sells it and collects receivables much faster. Its very short financing period is one of the reasons Costco can charge such low prices. Helpful ratios for calculating the three components of the financing period will be covered in subsequent chapters on inventories, receivables, and current liabilities.

By reducing its financing period, a company can improve its cash flow. Many merchandisers, including Costco, do this by selling as much as possible for cash. Cash sales include sales on bank *credit cards*, such as Visa or MasterCard, and on *debit cards*, which draw directly on the purchaser's bank account. They are considered cash sales because funds from them are available to the merchandiser immediately. Small retail stores may have mostly cash sales and very few credit sales, whereas large wholesale concerns may have almost all credit sales.

Choice of Inventory System

Another issue in managing a merchandising business is the choice of inventory system. Management must choose the system or combination of systems that best achieves the company's goals. The two basic systems of accounting for the many items in merchandise inventory are the perpetual inventory system and the periodic inventory system.

Study Note
Under the perpetual inventory system, the Merchandise Inventory account and the Cost of Goods Sold account are updated with every sale.

Under the **perpetual inventory system**, continuous records are kept of the quantity and, usually, the cost of individual items as they are bought and sold. Under this system, the cost of each item is recorded in the Merchandise Inventory account when it is purchased. As merchandise is sold, its cost is transferred from the Merchandise Inventory account to the Cost of Goods Sold account. Thus, at all times the balance of the Merchandise Inventory account equals the cost of goods on hand, and the balance in Cost of Goods Sold equals the cost of merchandise sold to customers.

Managers use the detailed data that the perpetual inventory system provides to respond to customers' inquiries about product availability, to order inventory more effectively and thus avoid running out of stock, and to control the costs associated with investments in inventory.

Study Note
The value of ending inventory on the balance sheet is determined by multiplying the quantity of each inventory item by its unit cost.

Under the **periodic inventory system**, the inventory not yet sold, or on hand, is counted periodically. This physical count is usually taken at the end of the accounting period. No detailed records of the inventory on hand are maintained during the accounting period. The figure for inventory on hand is accurate only on the balance sheet date. As soon as any purchases or sales are made, the inventory figure becomes a historical amount, and it remains so until the new ending inventory amount is entered at the end of the next accounting period.

Some retail and wholesale companies use the periodic inventory system because it reduces the amount of clerical work. If a company is fairly small, management can maintain control over its inventory simply through observation or by using an offline system of cards or computer records. However, for larger companies, the lack of detailed records may lead to lost sales or high operating costs.

Because of the difficulty and expense of accounting for the purchase and sale of each item, companies that sell items of low value in high volume have traditionally used the periodic inventory system. Examples of such companies include drugstores, automobile parts stores, department stores, and discount stores. In contrast, companies that sell items that have a high unit value, such as appliances or automobiles, have tended to use the perpetual inventory system.

The distinction between high and low unit value for inventory systems has blurred considerably in recent years. Although the periodic inventory system is still widely used, computerization has led to a large increase in the use of the perpetual inventory system. It is important to note that the perpetual inventory system does not eliminate the need for a physical count of the inventory; one should be taken periodically to ensure that the actual number of goods on hand matches the quantity indicated by the computer records.

Foreign Business Transactions

Most large merchandising and manufacturing firms and even many small ones transact some of their business overseas. For example, a U.S. manufacturer may expand by selling its product to foreign customers, or it may lower its product cost by buying a less expensive part from a source in another country. Such sales and purchase transactions may take place in Japanese yen, British pounds, or some other foreign currency.

When an international transaction involves two different currencies, as most such transactions do, one currency has to be translated into another by using an exchange rate. As we noted earlier in the text, an *exchange rate* is the value of one currency stated in terms of another. We also noted that the values of other currencies in relation to the dollar rise and fall daily according to supply and demand. Thus, if there is a delay between the date of sale or purchase and the date of receipt of payment, the amount of cash involved in an international transaction may differ from the amount originally agreed on.

If the billing of an international sale and the payment for it are both in the domestic currency, no accounting problem arises. For example, if a U.S. maker of precision tools sells $160,000 worth of its products to a British company and bills the British company in dollars, the U.S. company will receive $160,000 when it collects payment. However, if the U.S. company bills the British company in British pounds and accepts payment in pounds, it will incur an **exchange gain or loss** if the exchange rate between dollars and pounds changes between the date of sale and the date of payment.

For example, assume that the U.S. company billed the sale of $200,000 at £100,000, reflecting an exchange rate of 2.00 (that is, $2.00 per pound) on the sale date. Now assume that by the date of payment, the exchange rate has fallen to 1.90. When the U.S. company receives its £100,000, it will be worth only $190,000 (£100,000 × $1.90 = $190,000). It will have incurred an exchange loss of $10,000 because it agreed to accept a fixed number of British pounds in payment for its products, and the value of each pound dropped before the payment was made. Had the value of the pound in relation to the dollar increased, the company would have made an exchange gain.

The same logic applies to purchases as to sales, except that the relationship of exchange gains and losses to changes in exchange rates is reversed. For example, assume that the U.S company purchases products from the British company for $200,000. If the payment is to be made in U.S. dollars, no accounting problem arises. However, if the British company expects to be paid in pounds, the U.S. company will have an exchange gain of $10,000 because it agreed to pay a fixed £100,000, and between the dates of purchase and payment, the exchange value of the pound decreased from $2.00 to $1.90. To make the £100,000 payment, the U.S. company has to expend only $190,000.

Exchange gains and losses are reported on the income statement. Because of their bearing on a company's financial performance, they are of considerable interest to managers and investors. Lack of uniformity in international accounting standards is another matter of which investors must be wary.

The Need for Internal Controls

Buying and selling, the principal transactions of merchandising businesses, involve assets—cash, accounts receivable, and merchandise inventory—that are vulnerable to theft and embezzlement. Cash and inventory can, of course, be fairly easy to steal. The reason the potential for embezzlement exists is that the large number of transactions that are usually involved in a merchandising business (for example, cash receipts, receipts on account, payments for purchases, and receipts and shipments of inventory) makes monitoring the accounting records difficult.

If a merchandising company does not take steps to protect its assets, it can suffer high losses of both cash and inventory. Management's responsibility is to establish an environment, accounting systems, and control procedures that will protect the company's assets. These systems and procedures are called **internal controls**.

Study Note

Inventory shortages can result from honest mistakes, such as accidentally tagging inventory with the wrong number.

Taking a **physical inventory** facilitates control over merchandise inventory. This process involves an actual count of all merchandise on hand. It can be a difficult task because it is easy to accidentally omit items or count them twice. As we noted earlier, a physical inventory must be taken under both the periodic and the perpetual inventory systems.

Merchandise inventory includes all goods intended for sale wherever they are located—on store shelves, in warehouses, on car lots, or in transit from suppliers if title to the goods has passed to the merchandiser. To prevent loss of inventory, a merchandiser must have an effective system of internal control.

A company's merchandise inventory includes all goods intended for sale regardless of where they are located—on shelves, in storerooms, in warehouses, or in trucks between warehouses and stores. It also includes goods in transit from suppliers if title to the goods has passed to the merchandiser. Ending inventory does not include merchandise that a company has sold but not yet delivered to customers. Nor does it include goods that it cannot sell because they are damaged or obsolete. If damaged or obsolete goods can be sold at a reduced price, however, they should be included in ending inventory at their reduced value.

Merchandisers usually take a physical inventory after the close of business on the last day of their fiscal year. To facilitate the process, they often end the fiscal year in a slow season, when inventories are at relatively low levels. For example, many department stores end their fiscal year in January or February. After hours—at night, on a weekend, or when the store closes for all or part of a day for taking inventory—employees count all items and record the results on numbered inventory tickets or sheets, following procedures to ensure that no items will be missed. Using bar coding to take inventory electronically has greatly facilitated the process in many companies.

Most companies experience losses of merchandise inventory from spoilage, shoplifting, and theft by employees. When such losses occur, the periodic inventory system provides no means of identifying them because the costs are automatically included in the cost of goods sold. For example, suppose a company has lost $1,250 in stolen merchandise during an accounting period. When the physical inventory is taken, the missing items are not in stock, so they cannot be counted. Because the ending inventory does not contain these items, the amount subtracted from goods available for sale is less than it would be if the goods were in stock. The cost of goods sold, then, is overstated by $1,250. In a sense, the cost of goods sold is inflated by the amount of merchandise that has been lost.

Study Note

An adjustment to the Merchandise Inventory account will be needed if the physical inventory reveals a difference between the actual inventory and the amount in the records.

The perpetual inventory system makes it easier to identify such losses. Because the Merchandise Inventory account is continuously updated for sales, purchases, and returns, the loss will show up as the difference between the inventory records and the physical inventory taken at the end of the accounting period. Once the amount of the loss has been identified, the ending inventory is updated

FOCUS ON BUSINESS PRACTICE

Will Sarbanes-Oxley Stop Fraud?

The Sarbanes-Oxley Act has heightened awareness of internal control and requires increased diligence, but it will never stop fraud from occurring. For instance, NBC Universal, the large media company, recently reported that its treasurer had been arrested for theft of $800,000. The theft occurred due to deficiencies in the internal control system, such as giving the treasurer authorization to set up a legal entity, set up a bank account, make purchases, and pay for them. This situation violated a basic rule of internal control in that the treasurer was able to accomplish both the purchase and the payment with no checks by another person.[2]

by crediting the Merchandise Inventory account. The offsetting debit is usually an increase in Cost of Goods Sold because the loss is considered a cost that reduces the company's gross margin.

Management's Responsibility for Internal Control

Management is responsible for establishing a satisfactory system of internal controls. Such a system includes all the policies and procedures needed to ensure the reliability of financial reporting, compliance with laws and regulations, and the effectiveness and efficiency of operations. In other words, management must safeguard the firm's assets, ensure the reliability of its accounting records, and see that its employees comply with all legal requirements and operate the firm to the best advantage of its owners.

Section 404 of the Sarbanes-Oxley act of 2002 requires that the chief executive officer, the chief financial officer, and the auditors of a public company fully document and certify the company's system of internal controls. For example, in its annual report, **Costco's** management acknowledges its responsibility for internal control as follows:

> [We] are responsible for establishing and maintaining disclosure controls and procedures and internal controls for financial reporting [on behalf of the company].[3]

STOP ► REVIEW ► APPLY

LO1-1 **What is the operating cycle of a merchandising business, and why is it important?**

LO1-2 **What is the financing period, and what are its components?**

LO1-3 **What is the difference between the perpetual inventory system and the periodic inventory system?**

LO1-4 **What conditions cause an exchange gain or loss?**

LO1-5 **Why are internal controls needed, and what is management's responsibility for implementing them?**

Suggested answers to all Stop, Review, and Apply questions follow the appendixes.

Terms of Sale

LO2 Describe the terms of sale related to merchandising transactions.

Study Note

A trade discount applies to the list or catalogue price. A sales discount applies to the sales price.

When goods are sold on credit, both parties should understand the amount and timing of payment as well as other terms of the purchase, such as who pays delivery charges and what warranties or rights of return apply. Sellers quote prices in different ways. Many merchants quote the price at which they expect to sell their goods. Others, particularly manufacturers and wholesalers, quote prices as a percentage (usually 30 percent or more) off their list or catalogue prices. Such a reduction is called a **trade discount**.

For example, if an article is listed at $1,000 with a trade discount of 40 percent, or $400, the seller records the sale at $600, and the buyer records the purchase at $600. The seller may raise or lower the trade discount depending on the quantity purchased. The list or catalogue price and related trade discount are used only to arrive at an agreed-on price; they do not appear in the accounting records.

Sales and Purchases Discounts

The terms of sale are usually printed on the sales invoice and thus constitute part of the sales agreement. Terms differ from industry to industry. In some industries, payment is expected in a short period of time, such as 10 or 30 days. In these cases, the invoice is marked "n/10" ("net 10") or "n/30" ("net 30"), meaning that the amount of the invoice is due either 10 days or 30 days after the invoice date. If the invoice is due 10 days after the end of the month, it is marked "n/10 eom."

Study Note

Early collection also has the advantage of reducing the probability of a customer's defaulting.

In some industries, it is customary to give a discount for early payment. This discount, which is called a **sales discount**, is intended to increase the seller's liquidity by reducing the amount of money tied up in accounts receivable. An invoice that offers a sales discount might be labeled "2/10, n/30," which means that the buyer either can pay the invoice within 10 days of the invoice date and take a 2 percent discount or can wait 30 days and pay the full amount of the invoice. It is often advantageous for a buyer to take the discount because the saving of 2 percent over a period of 20 days (from the 11th day to the 30th day) represents an effective annual rate of 36.5 percent (365 days ÷ 20 days × 2% = 36.5%). Most companies would be better off borrowing money to take the discount. The practice of giving sales discounts has been declining because it is costly to the seller and because, from the buyer's viewpoint, the amount of the discount is usually very small in relation to the price of the purchase.

Because it is not possible to know at the time of a sale whether the customer will pay in time to take advantage of a sales discount, the discounts are recorded only at the time the customer pays. For example, suppose Laboda Sportswear Corporation sells merchandise to a customer on September 20 for $600 on terms of 2/10, n/30. Laboda records the sale on September 20 for the full amount of $600. If the customer takes advantage of the discount by paying on or before September 30, Laboda will receive $588 in cash and will reduce its accounts receivable by $600. The difference of $12 ($600 × .02) will be debited to an account called *Sales Discounts.* Sales Discounts is a contra-revenue account with a normal debit balance that is deducted from sales on the income statement.

The same logic applies to **purchases discounts**, which are discounts that a buyer takes for the early payment of merchandise. For example, the buyer in the transaction described above will record the purchase on September 20 at $600. If the buyer pays on or before September 30, it will record cash paid of $588 and reduce its accounts payable by $600. The difference of $12 is recorded as a credit to an account called Purchases Discounts. The *Purchases Discounts* *account* reduces cost of goods sold or purchases depending on the inventory method used.

Transportation Costs

In some industries, the seller usually pays transportation costs and charges a price that includes those costs. In other industries, it is customary for the purchaser to pay transportation charges. Special terms designate whether the seller or the purchaser pays the freight charges.

FOB shipping point means that the seller places the merchandise "free on board" at the point of origin and the buyer bears the shipping costs. The title to the merchandise passes to the buyer at that point. For example, when the sales agreement for the purchase of a car says "FOB factory," the buyer must pay the freight from the factory where the car was made to wherever he or she is located, and the buyer owns the car from the time it leaves the factory.

FOB destination means that the seller bears the transportation costs to the place where the merchandise is delivered. The seller retains title until the merchandise reaches its destination and usually prepays the shipping costs, in which case the buyer makes no accounting entry for freight.

The effects of these special shipping terms are summarized as follows:

Shipping Term	Where Title Passes	Who Pays the Cost of Transportation
FOB shipping point	At origin	Buyer
FOB destination	At destination	Seller

When the buyer pays the transportation charge, it is called **freight-in**, and it is added to the cost of merchandise purchased. Thus, freight-in increases the buyer's cost of merchandise inventory, as well as the cost of goods sold after they are sold. When freight-in is a relatively small amount, most companies include the cost in the cost of goods sold on the income statement rather than going to the trouble of allocating part of it to merchandise inventory.

Shipping terms affect the financial statements. *FOB shipping point* means the buyer pays the freight charges; when relatively small, these charges are usually included in cost of goods sold on the buyer's income statement. *FOB destination* means the seller pays the frieght charges; they are included in selling expenses on the seller's income statement.

FOCUS ON BUSINESS PRACTICE

Are We Becoming a Cashless Society?

Are checks and cash obsolete? Do you "swipe it"? Most Americans do. About 75 percent of Americans use credit or debit cards rather than checks. Debit cards generate more than 16 billion transactions per year. It is estimated that electronic payments totaling more than $1 trillion outnumber the roughly 40 billion checks written each year. Consumers like the convenience. Retailers, like **McDonald's** and **Starbucks**, like the cards, even though there are fees, because use of cards usually increases the amount of sales.[4]

When the seller pays the transportation charge, it is called **delivery expense**, or *freight-out*. Because the seller incurs this cost to facilitate the sale of its product, the cost is included in selling expenses on the income statement.

Terms of Debit and Credit Card Sales

Many retailers allow customers to use debit or credit cards to charge their purchases. Debit cards deduct directly from a person's bank account, whereas a credit card allows for payment later. Five of the most widely used credit cards are American Express, Discover Card, Diners Club, MasterCard, and Visa. The customer establishes credit with the lender (the credit card issuer) and receives a plastic card to use in making charges. If a seller accepts the card, the customer signs an invoice at the time of the sale. The sale is communicated to the seller's bank, resulting in a cash deposit in the seller's bank account. Thus, the seller does not have to establish the customer's credit, collect from the customer, or tie up money in accounts receivable. As payment, the lender, rather than paying the total amount of the credit card sales, takes a discount of 2 to 6 percent. The discount is a selling expense for the merchandiser. For example, if a restaurant makes sales of $1,000 on Visa credit cards and Visa takes a 4 percent discount on the sales, the restaurant would record Cash in the amount of $960 and Credit Card Expense in the amount of $40.

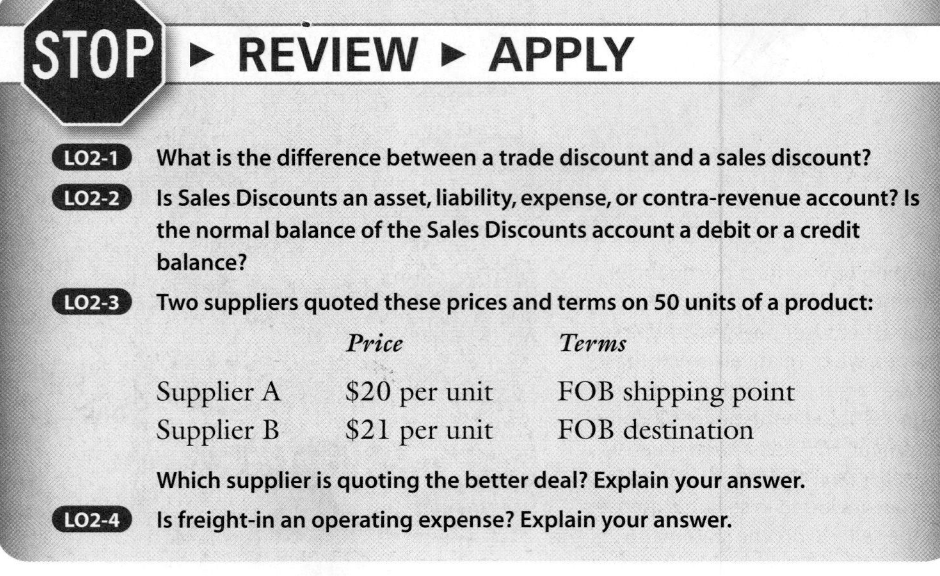

STOP ▸ REVIEW ▸ APPLY

LO2-1 **What is the difference between a trade discount and a sales discount?**

LO2-2 **Is Sales Discounts an asset, liability, expense, or contra-revenue account? Is the normal balance of the Sales Discounts account a debit or a credit balance?**

LO2-3 **Two suppliers quoted these prices and terms on 50 units of a product:**

	Price	*Terms*
Supplier A	$20 per unit	FOB shipping point
Supplier B	$21 per unit	FOB destination

Which supplier is quoting the better deal? Explain your answer.

LO2-4 **Is freight-in an operating expense? Explain your answer.**

Perpetual Inventory System

LO3 Prepare an income statement and record merchandising transactions under the perpetual inventory system.

Exhibit 1 shows how an income statement appears when a company uses the perpetual inventory system. The focal point of the statement is cost of goods sold, which is deducted from net sales to arrive at gross margin. Under the perpetual inventory system, the Merchandise Inventory and Cost of Goods Sold accounts are continually updated during the accounting period as purchases, sales, and other inventory transactions that affect these accounts occur.

Purchases of Merchandise

Figure 3 shows how transactions involving purchases of merchandise are recorded under the perpetual inventory system. As you can see, the focus of these entries is Accounts Payable. In this section, we present a summary of the entries made for merchandise purchases.

Study Note

The Merchandise Inventory account increases when a purchase is made.

Purchases on Credit

Aug. 3: Received merchandise purchased on credit, invoice dated Aug. 1, terms n/10, $4,890.

Aug. 3	Merchandise Inventory	4,890	
	Accounts Payable		4,890
	Purchases on credit		

Comment: Under the perpetual inventory system, the cost of merchandise is recorded in the Merchandise Inventory account at the time of purchase. In the transaction described here, payment is due ten days from the invoice date. If an invoice includes a charge for shipping or if shipping is billed separately, it should be debited to Freight-In.

Purchases Returns and Allowances

Aug. 6: Returned part of merchandise received on Aug. 3 for credit, $480.

Aug. 6	Accounts Payable	480	
	Merchandise Inventory		480
	Returned merchandise from purchase		

EXHIBIT 1

Income Statement Under the Perpetual Inventory System

Kloss Motor Corporation
Income Statement
For the Year Ended December 31, 2010

Net sales	$957,300
Cost of goods sold*	525,440
Gross margin	$431,860
Operating expenses	313,936
Income before income taxes	$117,924
Income taxes	20,000
Net income	$ 97,924

*Freight-in has been included in cost of goods sold.

Study Note

On the income statement, freight-in is included as part of cost of goods sold, and delivery expense (freight-out) is included as an operating (selling) expense.

FIGURE 3

Recording Purchase Transactions Under the Perpetual Inventory System

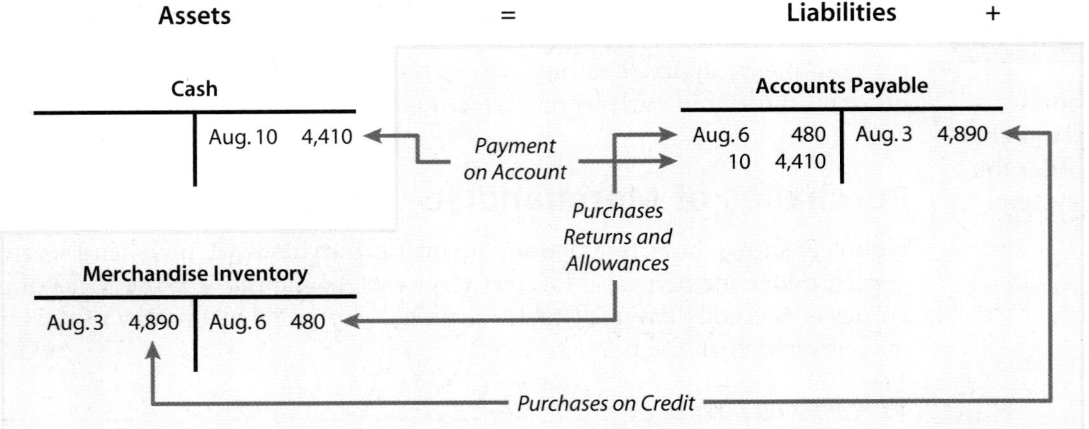

Comment: Under the perpetual inventory system, when a buyer is allowed to return all or part of a purchase or is given an allowance—a reduction in the amount to be paid, Merchandise Inventory is reduced, as is Accounts Payable.

Payments on Account

Aug. 10: Paid amount in full due for the purchase of Aug. 3, part of which was returned on Aug. 6, $4,410.

Aug. 10	Accounts Payable	4,410	
	Cash		4,410
	Made payment on account		

Comment: Payment is made for the net amount due of $4,410 ($4,890 − $480).

Sales of Merchandise

Figure 4 shows how transactions involving sales of merchandise are recorded under the perpetual inventory system. These transactions involve several accounts, including Cash, Accounts Receivable, Merchandise Inventory, Sales Returns and Allowances, and Cost of Goods Sold.

Study Note

The Cost of Goods Sold account is increased and the Merchandise Inventory account is decreased when a sale is made.

Sales on Credit

Aug. 7: Sold merchandise on credit, terms n/30, FOB destination, $1,200; the cost of the merchandise was $720.

Aug. 7	Accounts Receivable	1,200	
	Sales		1,200
	Sold merchandise to Gonzales Distributors		
7	Cost of Goods Sold	720	
	Merchandise Inventory		720
	Transferred cost of merchandise inventory sold to Cost of Goods Sold		

Comment: Under the perpetual inventory system, sales always require two entries, as shown in Figure 4. First, the sale is recorded by increasing Accounts Receivable

FIGURE 4
Recording Sales Transactions Under the Perpetual Inventory System

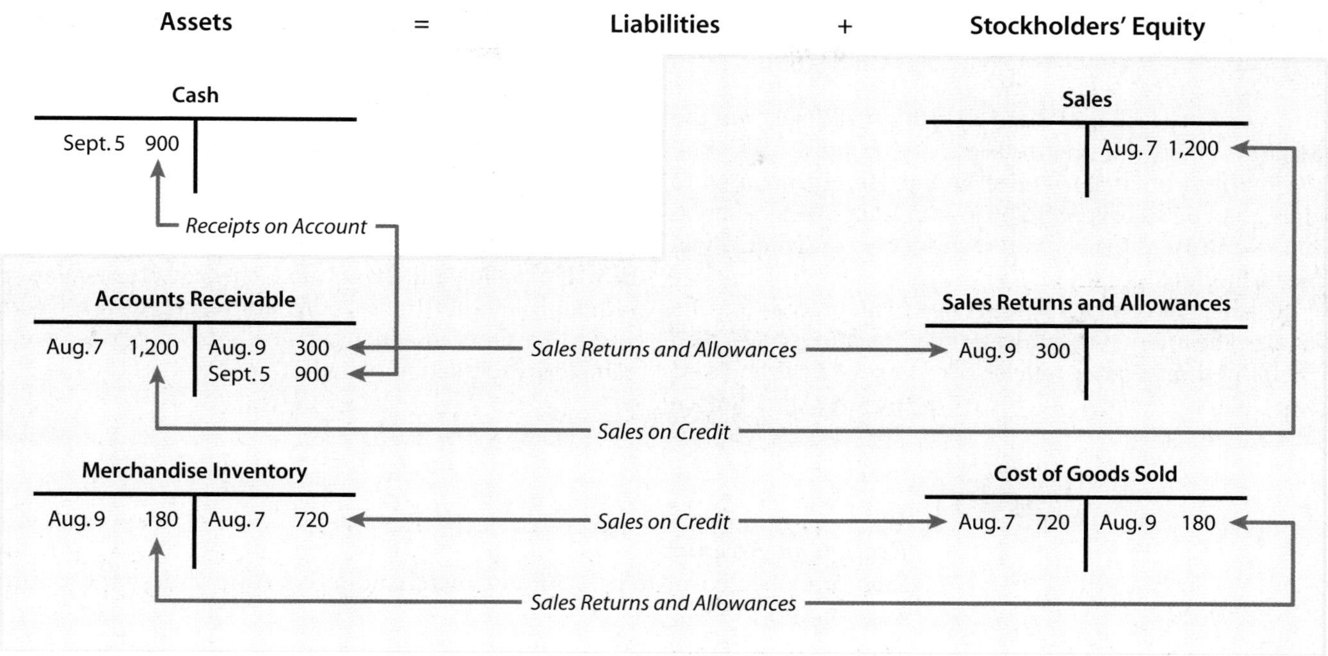

and Sales. Second, Cost of Goods Sold is updated by a transfer from Merchandise Inventory. In the case of cash sales, Cash rather than Accounts Receivable is debited for the amount of the sale. If the seller pays for the shipping, it should be debited to Delivery Expense.

Sales Returns and Allowances
Aug. 9: Accepted return of part of merchandise sold on Aug. 7 for full credit and returned it to merchandise inventory, $300; the cost of the merchandise was $180.

Aug. 9	Sales Returns and Allowances	300	
	Accounts Receivable		300
	Accepted returns of merchandise		
9	Merchandise Inventory	180	
	Cost of Goods Sold		180
	Transferred cost of merchandise returned to Merchandise Inventory		

Study Note
Because the Sales account is established with a credit, its contra account, Sales Returns and Allowances, is established with a debit.

Comment: Under the perpetual inventory system, when a seller allows the buyer to return all or part of a sale or gives an allowance—a reduction in amount—two entries are again necessary. First, the original sale is reversed by reducing Accounts Receivable and debiting the Sales Returns and Allowances account. The **Sales Returns and Allowances account** gives management a readily available measure of unsatisfactory products and dissatisfied customers. This account is a contra-revenue account with a normal debit balance, and it is deducted from sales on the income statement. Second, the cost of the merchandise must also be transferred from the Cost of Goods Sold account back into the Merchandise Inventory account. If the company makes an allowance instead of accepting a return, or if the merchandise cannot be returned to inventory and resold, this transfer is not made.

FOCUS ON BUSINESS PRACTICE

How Are Web Sales Doing?

In spite of the well-publicized dot.com meltdown and the demise of many Internet retailers, merchandise sales over the Internet continue to thrive. Internet sales amounted to more than $233 billion in 2007[5]—up from $44.5 billion in 2001—and were expected to continue to grow rapidly in the near future.

To date, the companies that have been most successful in using the Internet to enhance their operations have been established mail-order retailers like **Lands' End** and **L.L. Bean**. Other retailers, such as **Circuit City** and **Office Depot**, have also benefited from their use of the Internet. Circuit City allows customers to purchase online and pick up the products at stores near their homes. Office Depot, which focuses primarily on business-to-business Internet sales, has set up customized web pages for tens of thousands of corporate clients. These websites allow customers to make online purchases and check store inventories. Although Internet transactions are recorded in the same way as on-site transactions, the technology adds a level of complexity to the transactions.

Receipts on Account

Sept. 5: Collected in full for sale of merchandise on Aug. 7, less the return on Aug. 9, $900.

Sept. 5	Cash	900	
	Accounts Receivable		900
	Received on account		

Comment: Collection is made for the net amount due of $900 ($1,200 − $300).

STOP ▶ REVIEW ▶ APPLY

LO3-1 **Under which inventory system is a Cost of Goods Sold account maintained? Explain why.**

LO3-2 **Discuss this statement: "The perpetual inventory system is the best system because management always needs to know how much inventory is on hand."**

LO3-3 **Why is it advisable to maintain a Sales Returns and Allowances account when the same result could be obtained by debiting each return or allowance to the Sales account?**

Merchandising Transactions: Perpetual Inventory System The numbered items below are account titles, and the lettered items at the top of the next page are types of merchandising transactions. For each transaction, indicate which accounts are debited or credited by placing the account numbers in the appropriate columns.

1. Cash
2. Accounts Receivable
3. Merchandise Inventory
4. Accounts Payable
5. Sales
6. Sales Returns and Allowances
7. Cost of Goods Sold

(continued)

	Account Debited	Account Credited
a. Purchase on credit	______	______
b. Purchase return for credit	______	______
c. Purchase for cash	______	______
d. Sale on credit	______	______
e. Sale for cash	______	______
f. Sales return for credit	______	______
g. Payment on account	______	______
h. Receipt on account	______	______

SOLUTION

	Account Debited	Account Credited
a. Purchase on credit	3	4
b. Purchase return for credit	4	3
c. Purchase for cash	3	1
d. Sale on credit	2, 7	3, 5
e. Sale for cash	1, 7	3, 5
f. Sales return for credit	3, 6	2, 7
g. Payment on account	4	1
h. Receipt on account	1	2

Periodic Inventory System

LO4 Prepare an income statement and record merchandising transactions under the periodic inventory system.

Exhibit 2 shows how an income statement appears when a company uses the periodic inventory system. A major feature of this statement is the computation of cost of goods sold. *Cost of goods sold* must be computed on the income statement because it is not updated for purchases, sales, and other transactions during the accounting period, as it is under the perpetual inventory system. Figure 5 illustrates the components of cost of goods sold.

It is important to distinguish between goods available for sale and cost of goods sold. **Cost of goods available for sale** is the total cost of merchandise that *could* be sold in the accounting period. Cost of goods sold is the cost of merchandise *actually* sold. The difference between the two numbers is the amount *not* sold, or the ending merchandise inventory. Cost of goods available for sale is the sum of the following two factors:

- The amount of merchandise on hand at the beginning of accounting period or beginning inventory.
- The net purchases during the period. (Net purchases consist of total purchases less any deductions such as purchases return and allowances and freight-in.)

As you can see in Exhibit 2, Kloss Motor Corporation has cost of goods available for sale during the period of $718,640 ($211,200 + $507,440). The ending inventory of $193,200 is deducted from this figure to determine the cost of goods sold. Thus, the company's cost of goods sold is $525,440 ($718,640 − $193,200). Figure 5 illustrates these relationships in visual form.

EXHIBIT 2
Income Statement Under the Periodic Inventory System

Study Note
Most published financial statements are condensed, eliminating the detail shown here under cost of goods sold.

Kloss Motor Corporation
Income Statement
For the Year Ended December 31, 2010

Net sales			$957,300
Cost of goods sold			
Merchandise inventory, December 31, 2009		$211,200	
Purchases	$505,600		
Less purchases returns and allowances	31,104		
Net purchases	$474,496		
Freight-in	32,944		
Net cost of purchases		507,440	
Cost of goods available for sale		$718,640	
Less merchandise inventory, December 31, 2010		193,200	
Cost of goods sold			525,440
Gross margin			$431,860
Operating expenses			313,936
Income before income taxes			$117,924
Income taxes			20,000
Net income			$ 97,924

An important component of the cost of goods sold section is **net cost of purchases**. As you can see in Exhibit 2, net cost of purchases is the sum of net purchases and freight-in. **Net purchases** equal total purchases less any deductions, such as purchases returns and allowances and any discounts allowed by suppliers for early payment. Freight-in is added to net purchases because transportation charges are a necessary cost of receiving merchandise for sale.

Purchases of Merchandise

Figure 6 shows how transactions involving purchases of merchandise are recorded under the periodic inventory system. A primary difference between the perpetual and periodic inventory systems is that in the perpetual inventory system, the Merchandise Inventory account is adjusted each time a purchase, sale, or

FIGURE 5
The Components of Cost of Goods Sold

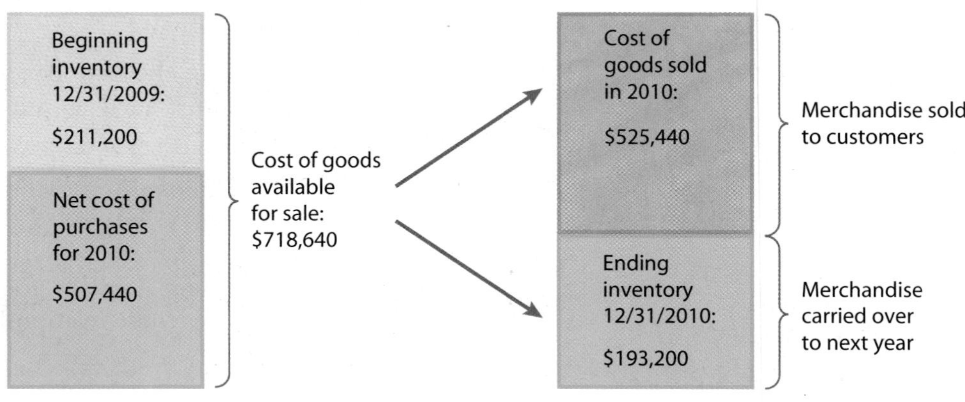

FIGURE 6

Recording Purchase Transactions Under the Periodic Inventory System

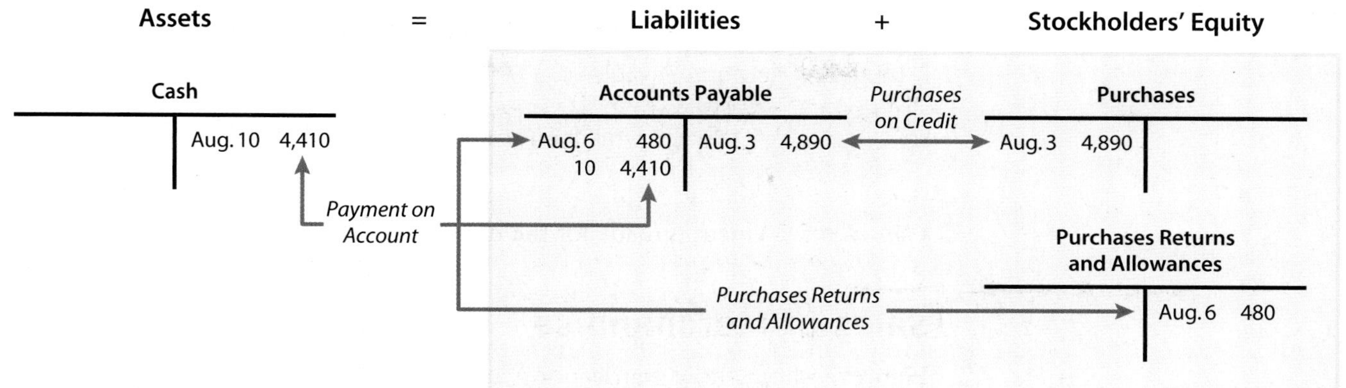

Study Note

Purchases accounts and Purchases Returns and Allowances accounts are used only in conjunction with a periodic inventory system.

other inventory transaction occurs, whereas in the periodic inventory system, the Merchandise Inventory account stays at its beginning balance until the physical inventory is recorded at the end of the period. The periodic system uses a Purchases account to accumulate purchases during an accounting period and a Purchases Returns and Allowances account to accumulate returns of and allowances on purchases.

The following sections illustrate how Kloss Motor Corporation would record purchase transactions under the periodic inventory system.

Study Note

Under the periodic inventory system, the Purchases account increases when a company makes a purchase.

Purchases on Credit

Aug. 3: Received merchandise purchased on credit, invoice dated Aug. 1, terms n/10, $4,890.

		Debit	Credit
Aug. 3	Purchases	4,890	
	Accounts Payable		4,890
	Purchases on credit		

Comment: Under the periodic inventory system, the cost of merchandise is recorded in the **Purchases account** at the time of purchase. This account is a temporary one used only with the periodic inventory system. Its sole purpose is to accumulate the total cost of merchandise purchased for resale during an accounting period. (Purchases of other assets, such as equipment, are recorded in the appropriate asset account, not in the Purchases account.) The Purchases account does not indicate whether merchandise has been sold or is still on hand.

Purchases Returns and Allowances

Aug. 6: Returned part of merchandise received on Aug. 3 for credit, $480.

		Debit	Credit
Aug. 6	Accounts Payable	480	
	Purchases Returns and Allowances		480
	Returned merchandise from purchase		

Study Note

Because the Purchases account is established with a debit, its contra account, Purchases Returns and Allowances, is established with a credit.

Comment: Under the periodic inventory system, the amount of a return or allowance is recorded in the **Purchases Returns and Allowances account**. This is a contra-purchases account with a normal credit balance, and it is deducted from purchases on the income statement. Accounts Payable is also reduced.

Payments on Account
Aug. 10: Paid amount in full due for the purchase of Aug. 3, part of which was returned on Aug. 6, $4,410.

Aug. 10	Accounts Payable	4,410	
	Cash		4,410
	Made payment on account		

Comment: Payment is made for the net amount due of $4,410 ($4,890 − $480).

Sales of Merchandise

Figure 7 shows how transactions involving sales of merchandise are recorded under the periodic inventory system.

Sales on Credit
Aug. 7: Sold merchandise on credit, terms n/30, FOB destination, $1,200; the cost of the merchandise was $720.

Aug. 7	Accounts Receivable	1,200	
	Sales		1,200
	Sold merchandise on credit		

Comment: As shown in Figure 7, under the periodic inventory system, sales require only one entry to increase Sales and Accounts Receivable. In the case of cash sales, Cash rather than Accounts Receivable is debited for the amount of the sale. If the seller pays for the shipping, the amount should be debited to Delivery Expense.

Sales Returns and Allowances
Aug. 9: Accepted return of part of merchandise sold on Aug. 7 for full credit and returned it to merchandise inventory, $300; the cost of the merchandise was $180.

Aug. 9	Sales Returns and Allowances	300	
	Accounts Receivable		300
	Accepted return of merchandise		

FOCUS ON BUSINESS PRACTICE

Are Sales Returns Worth Accounting For?

Some industries routinely have a high percentage of sales returns. More than 6 percent of all nonfood items sold in stores are eventually returned to vendors. This amounts to over $100 billion a year, or more than the gross national product of two-thirds of the world's nations.[6] Book publishers like **Simon & Schuster** often have returns as high as 30 to 50 percent because to gain the attention of potential buyers, they must distribute large numbers of copies to many outlets. Magazine publishers like **AOL Time Warner** expect to sell no more than 35 to 38 percent of the magazines they send to newsstands and other outlets.[7] In all these businesses, it pays management to scrutinize the Sales Returns and Allowances account for ways to reduce returns and increase profitability.

FIGURE 7

Recording Sales Transactions Under the Periodic Inventory System

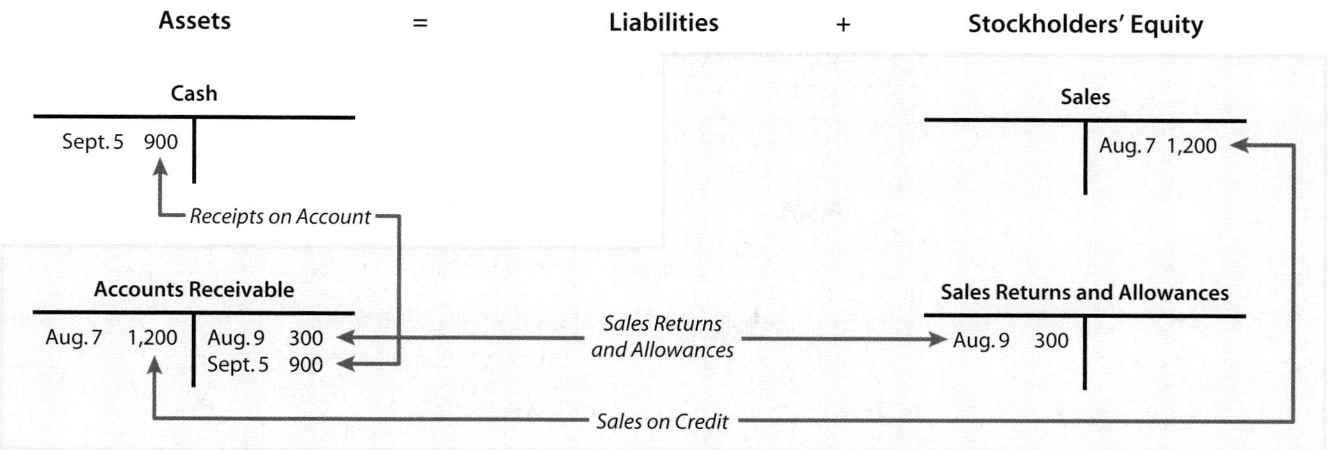

Comment: Under the periodic inventory system, when a seller allows the buyer to return all or part of a sale or gives an allowance, only one entry is needed to reduce Accounts Receivable and debit Sales Returns and Allowances. The Sales Returns and Allowances account is a contra-revenue account with a normal debit balance and is deducted from sales on the income statement.

Receipts on Account

Sept. 5: Collected in full for sale of merchandise on Aug. 7, less the return on Aug. 9, $900.

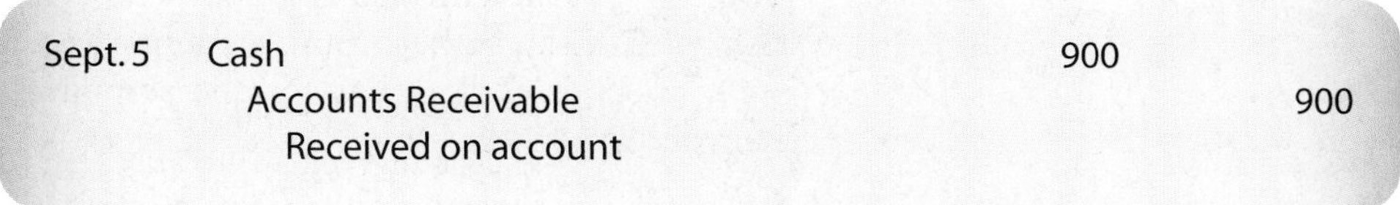

Sept. 5	Cash	900	
	Accounts Receivable		900
	Received on account		

Comment: Collection is made for the net amount due of $900 ($1,200 − $300).

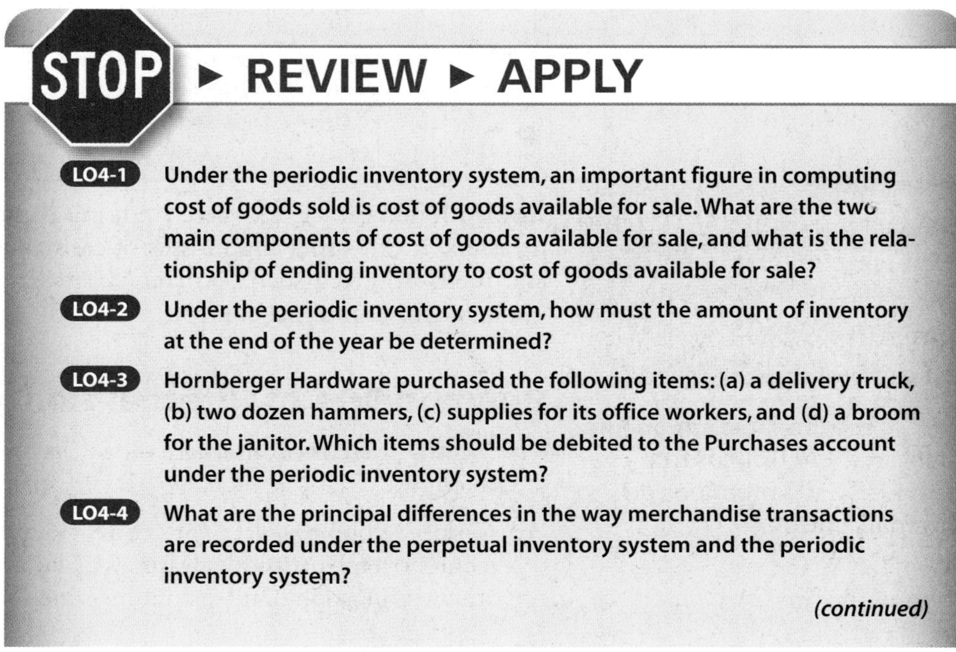

STOP ► REVIEW ► APPLY

LO4-1 **Under the periodic inventory system, an important figure in computing cost of goods sold is cost of goods available for sale. What are the two main components of cost of goods available for sale, and what is the relationship of ending inventory to cost of goods available for sale?**

LO4-2 **Under the periodic inventory system, how must the amount of inventory at the end of the year be determined?**

LO4-3 **Hornberger Hardware purchased the following items: (a) a delivery truck, (b) two dozen hammers, (c) supplies for its office workers, and (d) a broom for the janitor. Which items should be debited to the Purchases account under the periodic inventory system?**

LO4-4 **What are the principal differences in the way merchandise transactions are recorded under the perpetual inventory system and the periodic inventory system?**

(continued)

Merchandising Transactions: Periodic Inventory System The numbered items below are account titles, and the lettered items are types of merchandising transactions. For each transaction, indicate which accounts are debited or credited by placing the account numbers in the appropriate columns.

Accounts	Transactions	Account Debited	Account Credited
1. Cash	a. Purchase on credit	______	______
2. Accounts Receivable	b. Purchase return for credit	______	______
3. Merchandise Inventory	c. Purchase for cash	______	______
4. Accounts Payable	d. Sale on credit	______	______
5. Sales	e. Sale for cash	______	______
6. Sales Returns and Allowances	f. Sales return for credit	______	______
7. Purchases	g. Payment on account	______	______
8. Purchase Returns and Allowances	h. Receipt on account	______	______

SOLUTION

	Account Debited	Account Credited
a. Purchase on credit	7	4
b. Purchase return for credit	4	8
c. Purchase for cash	7	1
d. Sale on credit	2	5
e. Sale for cash	1	5
f. Sales return for credit	6	2
g. Payment on account	4	1
h. Receipt on account	1	2

Internal Control: Components, Activities, and Limitations

LO5 Describe the components of internal control, control activities, and limitations on internal control.

As mentioned earlier, if a merchandising company does not take steps to protect its assets, it can suffer high losses of cash and inventory through embezzlement and theft. To avoid such occurrences, management must set up and maintain a good system of internal control.

Components of Internal Control

An effective system of internal control has five interrelated components.[8] They are as follows:

1. *Control environment* The **control environment** is created by management's overall attitude, awareness, and actions. It encompasses a company's ethics, philosophy and operating style, organizational structure, method of

FOCUS ON BUSINESS PRACTICE

Which Frauds Are Most Common?

A survey of 5,000 large U.S. businesses disclosed that 36 percent suffered losses in excess of $1 million (up from 21 percent in 1998) due to fraud or inventory theft. The frauds most commonly cited were credit card fraud, check fraud, false invoices and phantom vendors, and expense account abuse. The most common reasons for the occurrences of these frauds were poor internal controls, management override of internal controls, and collusion. The most common methods of detecting them were notification by an employee, internal controls, internal auditor review, notification by a customer, and accidental discovery.

Companies that are successful in preventing fraud have a good system of internal control, a formal code of ethics, and a program to monitor compliance that includes a system for reporting incidents of fraud. These companies routinely communicate the existence of the program to their employees.[9]

Study Note

The components of internal control are equally important to manual and computerized accounting systems.

assigning authority and responsibility, and personnel policies and practices. Personnel should be qualified to handle responsibilities, which means that they must be trained and informed about what is expected of them. For example, the manager of a retail store should train employees to follow prescribed procedures for handling cash sales, credit card sales, and returns and refunds.

2. *Risk assessment* **Risk assessment** involves identifying areas in which risks of loss of assets or inaccuracies in accounting records are high so that adequate controls can be implemented. Among the greater risks in a retail store are that employees may steal cash and customers may steal goods.
3. *Information and communication* **Information and communication** pertains to the accounting system established by management—to the way the system gathers and treats information about the company's transactions and to how it communicates individual responsibilities within the system. Employees must understand exactly what their functions are.
4. *Control activities* **Control activities** are the policies and procedures management puts in place to see that its directives are carried out. (Control activities are discussed in more detail below.)
5. *Monitoring* **Monitoring** involves management's regular assessment of the quality of internal control, including periodic review of compliance with all policies and procedures. Large companies often have a staff of internal auditors who review the company's system of internal control to determine if it is working properly and if procedures are being followed. In smaller businesses, owners and managers conduct these reviews.

Control Activities

Control activities are a very important way of implementing internal control. The goal of these activities is to safeguard a company's assets and ensure the reliability of its accounting records.

Control activities include the following:

1. *Authorization* **Authorization** means the approval of certain transactions and activities. In a retail store, for example, cashiers customarily authorize cash sales, but other transactions, such as issuing a refund, may require a manager's approval.

2. *Recording transactions* To establish accountability for assets, all transactions should be recorded. For example, if a retail store uses a cash register that records sales, refunds, and other transactions on a paper tape or computer disk, the cashier can be held accountable for the cash received and the merchandise removed during his or her shift.

3. *Documents and records* Well-designed documents help ensure that transactions are properly recorded. For example, using prenumbered invoices and other documents is a way of ensuring that all transactions are recorded.

4. *Physical controls* **Physical controls** are controls that limit access to assets. For example, in a retail store, only the person responsible for the cash register should have access to it. Other employees should not be able to open the cash drawer when the cashier is not present. Similarly, only authorized personnel should have access to warehouses and storerooms. Access to accounting records, including those stored in company computers, should also be controlled.

5. *Periodic independent verification* **Periodic independent verification** means that someone other than the persons responsible for the accounting records and assets should periodically check the records against the assets. For example, at the end of each shift or day in a retail store, the owner or manager should count the cash in the cash drawer and compare the amount with the amount recorded on the tape or computer disk in the cash register. Other examples of independent verification are periodic counts of physical inventory and reconciliations of monthly bank statements.

6. *Separation of duties* **Separation of duties** means that no one person should authorize transactions, handle assets, or keep records of assets. For example, in a well-managed electronics store, each employee oversees only a single part of a transaction. A sales employee takes the order and creates an invoice. Another employee receives the customer's cash or credit card payment and issues a receipt. Once the customer has a receipt, and only then, a third employee obtains the item from the warehouse and gives it to the customer. A person in the accounting department subsequently compares all sales recorded on the tape or disk in the cash register with the sales invoices and updates the inventory in the accounting records. The separation of duties means that a mistake, careless or not, cannot be made without being seen by at least one other person.

7. *Sound personnel practices* Personnel practices that promote internal control include adequate supervision, rotation of key people among different jobs, insistence that employees take vacations, and bonding of personnel who handle cash or inventory. **Bonding** is the process of carefully checking an employee's background and insuring the company against theft by that person. Bonding does not guarantee against theft, but it does prevent or reduce loss if theft occurs. Prudent personnel practices help ensure that employees know their jobs, are honest, and will find it difficult to carry out and conceal embezzlement over time.

Study Note

No control procedure can guarantee the prevention of theft. However, the more procedures that are in place, the less likely it is that a theft will occur.

Limitations on Internal Control

No system of internal control is without weaknesses. As long as people perform control procedures, an internal control system will be vulnerable to human error. Errors can arise from misunderstandings, mistakes in judgment, carelessness, distraction, or fatigue. And separation of duties can be defeated through collusion by employees who secretly agree to deceive a company. In addition, established procedures may be ineffective against employees' errors or dishonesty, and

FOCUS ON BUSINESS PRACTICE

Shoplifters: Beware!

With theft from shoplifting approaching $30 billion per year, retailers are increasing their use of physical controls beyond the usual electronic warning if a customer tries to walk out without paying. Companies such as **Macy's** and **Babies 'R' Us** have installed more than 6 million video cameras in stores across the country. Advanced surveillance software can compare a shopper's movements between video images and recognize unusual activity. For instance removing 10 items from a shelf or opening a drawer that normally is closed would trigger the system to alert a security guard.[10]

controls that were initially effective may become ineffective when conditions change.

In some cases, the costs of establishing and maintaining elaborate control systems may exceed the benefits. In a small business, for example, active involvement on the part of the owner can be a practical substitute for the separation of some duties.

STOP ▶ REVIEW ▶ APPLY

LO5-1 **Most people think of internal control as a means of making fraud harder to commit and easier to detect. What are some other important purposes of internal control?**

LO5-2 **What are the five components of internal control?**

LO5-3 **What are some examples of control activities?**

LO5-4 **Why is the separation of duties necessary to ensure sound internal control? What does this principle assume about the relationships of employees in a company and the possibility of two or more of them stealing from the company?**

LO5-5 **In a small business, it is sometimes impossible to separate duties completely. What are three other procedures that a small business can use to achieve internal control over cash?**

Internal Control over Merchandising Transactions

LO6 Apply internal control activities to common merchandising transactions.

Sound internal control activities are needed in all aspects of a business, but particularly when assets are involved. Assets are especially vulnerable when they enter and leave a business. When sales are made, for example, cash or other assets enter the business, and goods or services leave. Controls must be set up to prevent theft during those transactions. Purchases of assets and payments of liabilities must also be controlled; adequate purchasing and payment systems can safeguard most such transactions. In addition, assets on hand, such as cash, investments, inventory, plant, and equipment, must be protected.

In this section of the text, you will see how merchandising companies apply internal control activities to such transactions as cash sales, receipts, purchases, and cash payments. Service and manufacturing businesses use similar procedures.

Internal Control and Management Goals

Study Note

Maintaining internal control is especially difficult for a merchandiser. Management must not only establish controls for cash sales receipts, purchases, and cash payments, but also go to great lengths to manage and protect its inventory.

When a system of internal control is applied effectively to merchandising transactions, it can achieve important management goals. As we have noted, it can prevent losses of cash and inventory due to theft or fraud, and it can ensure that records of transactions and account balances are accurate. It can also help managers achieve three broader goals:

1. Keeping enough inventory on hand to sell to customers without overstocking merchandise
2. Keeping sufficient cash on hand to pay for purchases in time to receive discounts
3. Keeping credit losses as low as possible by making credit sales only to customers who are likely to pay on time

One control that managers use to meet these broad goals is the cash budget, which projects future cash receipts and disbursements. By maintaining adequate cash balances, a company is able to take advantage of discounts on purchases, prepare to borrow money when necessary, and avoid the damaging effects of being unable to pay bills when they are due. By investing excess cash, the company can earn interest until the cash is needed.

A more specific control is the separation of duties that involve the handling of cash. Such separation makes theft without detection extremely unlikely unless two or more employees conspire. The separation of duties is easier in large businesses than in small ones, where one person may have to carry out several duties. The effectiveness of internal control over cash varies, based on the size and nature of the company. Most firms, however, should use the following procedures:

1. Separate the functions of authorization, recordkeeping, and custodianship of cash.
2. Limit the number of people who have access to cash, and designate who those people are.
3. Bond all employees who have access to cash.
4. Keep the amount of cash on hand to a minimum by using banking facilities as much as possible.
5. Physically protect cash on hand by using cash registers, cashiers' cages, and safes.
6. Record and deposit all cash receipts promptly, and make payments by check rather than by currency.
7. Have a person who does not handle or record cash make unannounced audits of the cash on hand.
8. Have a person who does not authorize, handle, or record cash transactions reconcile the Cash account each month.

Notice that each of these procedures helps safeguard cash by making it more difficult for any one individual who has access to cash to steal or misuse it without being detected.

Control of Cash Receipts

Cash payments for sales of goods and services can be received by mail or over the counter in the form of checks, credit or debit cards, or currency. Whatever the

FOCUS ON BUSINESS PRACTICE

How Do Computers Promote Internal Control?

One of the more difficult challenges facing computer programmers is to build good internal controls into accounting programs. Such programs must include controls that prevent unintentional errors, as well as unauthorized access and tampering. They prevent errors through reasonableness checks (such as not allowing any transactions over a specified amount), mathematical checks that verify the arithmetic of transactions, and sequence checks that require documents and transactions to be in proper order. They typically use passwords and questions about randomly selected personal data to prevent unauthorized access to computer records. They may also use firewalls, which are strong electronic barriers to unauthorized access, as well as data encryption. Data encryption is a way of coding data so that if they are stolen, they are useless to the thief.

source of the payments, cash should be recorded immediately upon receipt. Such a journal establishes a written record of cash receipts that should prevent errors and make theft more difficult.

Control of Cash Received by Mail Cash received by mail is vulnerable to theft by the employees who handle it. For that reason, companies that deal in mail-order sales generally ask customers to pay by credit card, check, or money order instead of with currency.

When cash is received in the mail, two or more employees should handle it. The employee who opens the mail should make a list in triplicate of the money received. The list should contain each payer's name, the purpose for which the money was sent, and the amount. One copy goes with the cash to the cashier, who deposits the money. The second copy goes to the accounting department for recording. The person who opens the mail keeps the third copy. Errors can be easily caught because the amount deposited by the cashier must agree with the amount received and the amount recorded in the cash receipts journal.

Study Note

The cashier should not be allowed to remove the cash register tape or to record the day's cash receipts.

Control of Cash Received over the Counter Cash registers and prenumbered sales tickets are common tools for controlling cash received over the counter. The amount of a cash sale is rung up on the cash register at the time of the sale. The register should be placed so that the customer can see the amount recorded. Each cash register should have a locked-in tape on which it prints the day's transactions. At the end of the day, the cashier counts the cash in the register and turns it in to the cashier's office. Another employee takes the tape out of the cash register and records the cash receipts for the day in the cash receipts journal. The amount of cash turned in and the amount recorded on the tape should agree; if not, any differences must be explained.

Large retail chains like **Costco** commonly monitor cash receipts by having each cash register tied directly into a computer that records each transaction as it occurs. Whether the elements are performed manually or by computer, separating responsibility for cash receipts, cash deposits, and recordkeeping is necessary to ensure good internal control.

In some stores, internal control is further strengthened by the use of prenumbered sales tickets and a central cash register or cashier's office, where all sales are rung up and collected by a person who does not participate in the sale. The salesperson completes a prenumbered sales ticket at the time of the sale, giving one copy to the customer and keeping a copy. At the end of the day, all sales tickets must be accounted for, and the sales total computed from the sales tickets must equal the total sales recorded on the cash register.

Control of Purchases and Cash Disbursements

Cash disbursements are particularly vulnerable to fraud and embezzlement. In one case, the treasurer of one of the nation's largest jewelry retailers was charged with having stolen over $500,000 by systematically overpaying the company's federal income taxes and keeping the refund checks as they came back to the company.

To avoid this type of theft, cash payments should be made only after they have been specifically authorized and supported by documents that establish the validity and amount of the claims. A company should also separate the duties involved in purchasing goods and services and the duties involved in paying for them. The degree of separation that is possible varies, depending on the size of the business.

Figure 8 shows how a large company can maximize the separation of duties. Five internal units (the requesting department, the purchasing department, the accounting department, the receiving department, and the treasurer) and two firms outside the company (the vendor and the bank) play a role in this control plan. Notice that business documents are crucial components of the plan.

Study Note

A purchase requisition is not the same as a purchase order. A purchase requisition is sent to the purchasing department; a purchase order is sent to the vendor.

Figure 9 illustrates the typical sequence in which documents are used in a company's internal control plan for purchases and cash disbursements (see pages 316–317).

Item 1—Purchase Requisition To begin, the credit office (requesting department) of Laboda Sportswear Corporation fills out a formal request for a purchase, or **purchase requisition**, for office supplies. The head of the requesting department approves it and forwards it to the purchasing department.

FIGURE 8

Internal Controls in a Large Company: Separation of Duties and Documentation

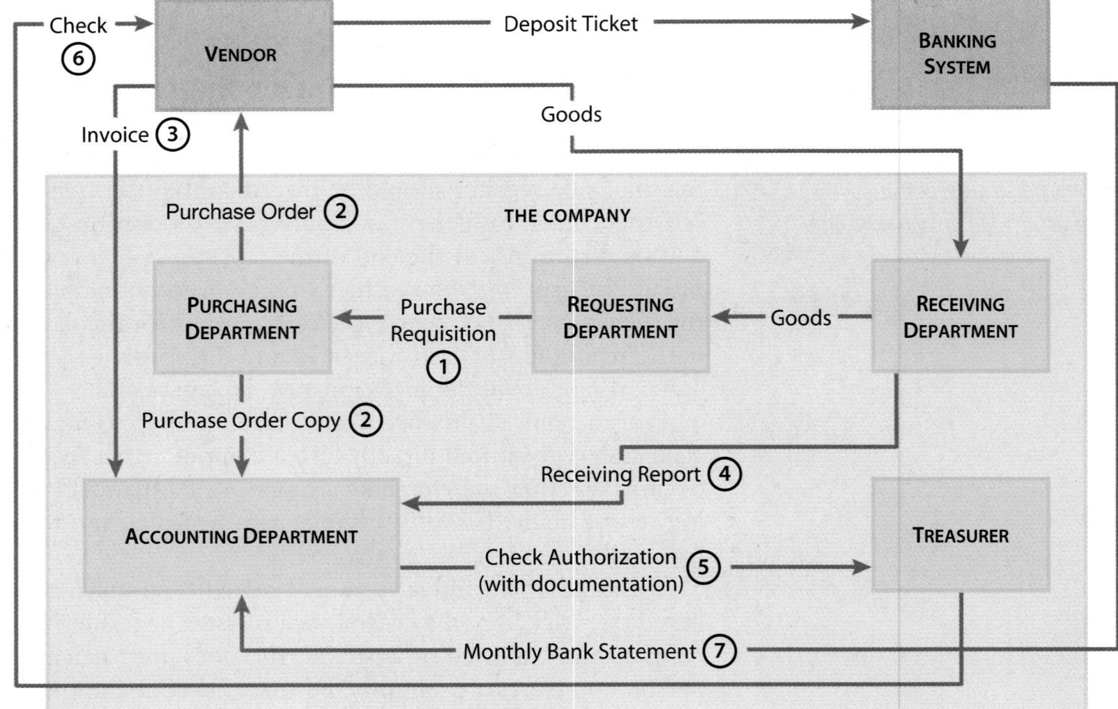

Note: Circled numbers refer to documents in Figure 9

Item 2—Purchase Order The people in the purchasing department prepare a **purchase order**. The purchase order indicates that Laboda will not pay any bill that does include a purchase order number. The purchase order is addressed to the vendor (seller) and contains a description of the quantity and type of items ordered, the expected price, the shipping date and terms, and other instructions.

Study Note

Invoice is the business term for *bill*. Every business document must have a number for purposes of reference.

Item 3—Invoice After receiving the purchase order, the vendor, Henderson Supply Company, ships the goods and sends an **invoice** to Laboda Sportswear. The invoice shows the quantity of goods delivered, describes what they are, and lists the price and terms of payment. If all the goods cannot be shipped immediately, the invoice indicates the estimated date of shipment for the remainder.

Item 4—Receiving Report When the goods reach Laboda's receiving department, an employee notes the quantity, type of goods, and their condition on a **receiving report**. The receiving department does not receive a copy of the purchase order or the invoice, so its employees don't know what should be received or its value. Thus, they are not tempted to steal any excess that may be delivered.

Study Note

Internal control documents sometimes do not exist in paper form in today's computerized accounting systems, but they do exist internally and are subject to the same separation of duties as in manual systems.

Item 5—Check Authorization The receiving report goes to the accounting department, where it is compared with the purchase order and the invoice. If everything is correct, the accounting department completes a **check authorization** and attaches it to the three supporting documents. The check authorization form shown in Figure 9 has a space for each item to be checked off as it is examined. Notice that the accounting department has all the documentary evidence for the transaction but does not have access to the assets purchased. Nor does it write the check for payment. This means that the people doing the accounting cannot conceal fraud by falsifying documents.

Item 6—Check Finally, the treasurer examines all the documents. If the treasurer approves them, he or she signs a check made out to the vendor in the amount of the invoice less any applicable discount. In some systems, the accounting department fills out the check so that all the treasurer has to do is inspect and sign it. The check is then sent to the vendor, with a remittance advice showing what the check is for. A vendor that is not paid the proper amount will complain, of course, thus providing a form of outside control over the payment.

Item 7—Bank Statement The vendor deposits the check in its bank, and the canceled check appears in Laboda Sportswear's next bank statement. If the treasurer has made the check out for the wrong amount (or altered an amount that was already filled in), the problem will show up in the company's bank reconciliation.

As shown in Figure 9, every action is documented and verified by at least one other person. Thus, the requesting department cannot work out a kickback scheme to make illegal payments to the vendor because the receiving department independently records receipts and the accounting department verifies prices. The receiving department cannot steal goods because the receiving report must equal the invoice. For the same reason, the vendor cannot bill for more goods than it ships. The treasurer verifies the accounting department's work, and the accounting department ultimately checks the treasurer's work.

The system we have described is a simple one that provides adequate internal control. There are many variations on it.

FIGURE 9

Internal Control Plan for Purchases and Cash Disbursements

① PURCHASE REQUISITION No. 7077

Laboda Sportswear Corporation

From: Credit Office Date: July 1, 2010

To: Purchasing Department Suggested Vendor: Henderson Supply Company

Please purchase the following items:

Quantity	Number	Description
20 boxes	X 144	Office supplies

Reason for Request: Six months' supply for office

Approved J.P.

To be filled in by Purchasing Department

Date ordered 7/2/2010 P.O. No. J 102

② PURCHASE ORDER No. J 102

Laboda Sportswear Corporation
8428 Rocky Island Avenue
Chicago, Illinois 60643

To: Henderson Supply Company
2525 25th Street
Mesa, Illinois 61611

Date: July 2, 2010
FOB: Destination
Ship by: July 5, 2010
Terms: 2/10, n/30

Ship to: Laboda Sportswear Corporation
Above Address

Please ship the following:

Quantity	✓	Number	Description	Price	Per	Amount
20 boxes		X 144	Office Supplies	260.00	box	$5,200.00

Purchase order number must appear on all shipments and invoices.

Ordered by Marsha Owen

③ INVOICE No. 0468

Henderson Supply Company
2525 25th Street
Mesa, Illinois 61611

Date: July 5, 2010
Your Order No.: J 102

Sold to:
Laboda Sportswear Corporation
8428 Rocky Island Avenue
Chicago, Illinois 60643

Ship to: Same

Sales Representative: Joe Jacobs

Quantity		Description	Price	Per	Amount
Ordered	Shipped				
20	20	Office Supplies	260.00	box	$5,200.00

FOB Destination | Terms: 2/10, n/30 | Date Shipped: 7/5/2010 | Via: Self

④ RECEIVING REPORT No. JR065

Laboda Sportswear Corporation
8428 Rocky Island Avenue
Chicago, Illinois 60643

Date: July 5, 2010

Quantity	Number	Description	Condition
20 boxes	X 144	Office Supplies	O.K.

Received by B.M.

⑤ CHECK AUTHORIZATION

	NO.	CHECK
Purchase Order	J 102	✓
Receiving Report	JR065	✓
INVOICE	0468	✓
Price		✓
Calculations		✓
Terms		✓

Approved for Payment J. Joseph

⑥ Laboda Sportswear Corporation
8428 Rocky Island Avenue
Chicago, Illinois 60643

NO. 2570
61-153/313

7/14 20 10

PAY TO THE ORDER OF Henderson Supply Company $ 5,096.00

Five thousand ninety-six and 00/100 Dollars

THE LAKE PARK NATIONAL BANK
Chicago, Illinois

Laboda Sportswear Corporation

by Arthur Martin

⑆03130153⑆ ⑈8030 647 4⑈

Remittance Advice

Date	P.O. No.	DESCRIPTION	AMOUNT
7/14/2010	J 102	20 X 144 office supplies	
		Supplier Inv. No. 0468	$5,200.00
		Less 2% discount	104.00
		Net	$5,096.00
		Laboda Sportswear Corporation	

Business Document	Prepared by	Sent to	Verification and Related Procedures
① Purchase requisition	Requesting department	Purchasing department	Purchasing verifies authorization.
② Purchase order	Purchasing department	Vendor	Vendor sends goods or services in accordance with purchase order.
③ Invoice	Vendor	Accounting department	Accounting receives invoice from vendor.
④ Receiving report	Receiving department	Accounting department	Accounting compares invoice, purchase order, and receiving report. Accounting verifies prices.
⑤ Check authorization	Accounting department	Treasurer	Accounting attaches check authorization to invoice, purchase order, and receiving report.
⑥ Check	Treasurer	Vendor	Treasurer verifies all documents before preparing check.
⑦ Bank statement	Buyer's bank	Accounting department	Accounting compares amount and payee's name on returned check with check authorization.

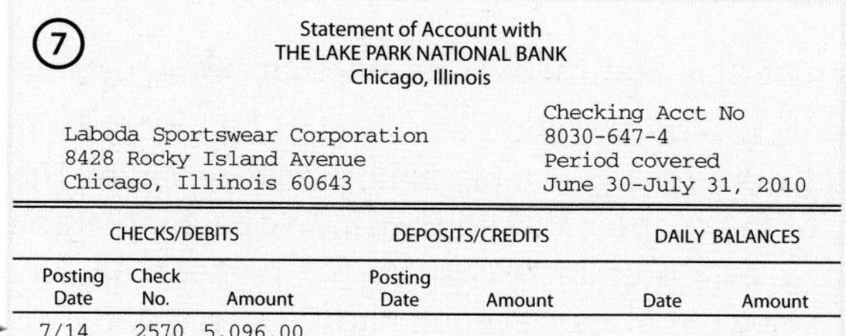
⑦

Statement of Account with
THE LAKE PARK NATIONAL BANK
Chicago, Illinois

Laboda Sportswear Corporation
8428 Rocky Island Avenue
Chicago, Illinois 60643

Checking Acct No
8030-647-4
Period covered
June 30-July 31, 2010

CHECKS/DEBITS			DEPOSITS/CREDITS		DAILY BALANCES	
Posting Date	Check No.	Amount	Posting Date	Amount	Date	Amount
7/14	2570	5,096.00				

STOP ▶ REVIEW ▶ APPLY

LO6-1 **At Thrifty Variety Store, sales clerks count the currency in their cash registers at the end of each day. They then remove the tape from their registers and fill in a daily cash form, in which they note any discrepancies. An employee in the cashier's office counts the cash, compares the total with the daily cash form, and then gives the cash to the company's cashier. What is the weakness in this system of internal control?**

LO6-2 **How does a movie theater control cash receipts?**

Business Documents for Purchases and Cash Disbursements Items **a–e** below are a company's departments. Items **f** and **g** are firms with which the company has transactions:

a. Requesting department
b. Purchasing department
c. Receiving department
d. Accounting department
e. Treasurer
f. Vendor
g. Bank

Use the letter of the department or firm to indicate which one prepares and sends the following business documents:

	Prepared by	Received by
1. Receiving report	____	____
2. Purchase order	____	____
3. Purchase requisition	____	____
4. Check	____	____
5. Invoice	____	____
6. Check authorization	____	____
7. Bank statement	____	____

SOLUTION

	Prepared by	Received by
1. Receiving report	c	d
2. Purchase order	b	f
3. Purchase requisition	a	b
4. Check	d, e	f
5. Invoice	f	d
6. Check authorization	d	e
7. Bank statement	g	d

A LOOK BACK AT ▶ Costco Wholesale Corporation

In this chapter's Decision Point, we noted that **Costco's** managers face many challenges. To ensure the company's success, they must address the following questions:

- **How can the company efficiently manage its cycle of merchandising operations?**
- **How can merchandising transactions be recorded to reflect the company's performance?**
- **How can the company maintain control over its merchandising operations?**

Costco is a very efficiently run organization as reflected by its operating cycle. It sells its inventory every 31 days on average and has almost no receivables. The Financial Highlights at the beginning of the chapter also demonstrate operating efficiency. They show that Costco's operating expenses increased by 9.7 percent, an amount that exceeded the increase of 7.1 percent in net revenue and 7.3 percent in gross margin. Because operating expenses grew faster than gross margin, Costco's operating income declined by 1.1 percent.

Costco's management states that the sales increase was "driven by an increase in comparable sales in warehouses open at least one year and the opening of 30 new

warehouses" and that the increase in operating expenses was caused mostly by "an increase in warehouse payroll and benefits costs."[11]

By buying and selling merchandise in bulk, providing very little service, and keeping its financing period to a minimum, Costco is able to offer its customers wholesale prices. A comparison of gross margin with net revenue in 2007 shows that Costco made only 12.3 percent ($7,950 ÷ $64,400) on each dollar of sales.

To sell for less and still make a profit, Costco must have a system of recording sales and purchase transactions that gives a fair view of its financial performance. It must also maintain a system of internal control that will not only ensure that these transactions are properly recorded, but will also protect the company's assets. In his certification of Costco's financial statements, the CEO stated that the company has the "responsibility to provide adequate internal control over financial reporting . . . to provide reasonable assurance regarding the reliability of financial reporting for external purposes."[12]

CHAPTER REVIEW

REVIEW of Learning Objectives

LO1 Identify the management issues related to merchandising businesses.

Merchandising companies differ from service companies in that they earn income by buying and selling goods. The buying and selling of goods adds to the complexity of the business and raises four issues that management must address. First, the series of transactions in which merchandising companies engage (the operating cycle) requires careful cash flow management. Second, management must choose whether to use the perpetual or the periodic inventory system. Third, if a company has international transactions, it must deal with changing exchange rates. Fourth, management must establish an internal control structure that protects the company's assets—its cash, merchandise inventory, and accounts receivable.

LO2 Describe the terms of sale related to merchandising transactions.

A trade discount is a reduction from the list or catalogue price of a product. A sales discount is a discount given for early payment of a sale on credit. Terms of 2/10, n/30 mean that the buyer can take a 2 percent discount if the invoice is paid within ten days of the invoice date. Otherwise, the buyer is obligated to pay the full amount in 30 days. Discounts on sales are recorded in the Sales Discounts account, and discounts on purchases are recorded in the Purchases Discounts account. FOB shipping point means that the buyer bears the cost of transportation and that title to the goods passes to the buyer at the shipping origin. FOB destination means that the seller bears the cost of transportation and that title does not pass to the buyer until the goods reach their destination. To the seller, debit and credit card sales are similar to cash sales.

LO3 Prepare an income statement and record merchandising transactions under the perpetual inventory system.

Under the perpetual inventory system, the Merchandise Inventory account is continuously adjusted by entering purchases, sales, and other inventory transactions as they occur. Purchases increase the Merchandise Inventory account, and purchases returns decrease it. As goods are sold, their cost is transferred from the Merchandise Inventory account to the Cost of Goods Sold account.

LO4 Prepare an income statement and record merchandising transactions under the periodic inventory system.

When the periodic inventory system is used, the cost of goods sold section of the income statement must include the following elements:

$$\text{Purchases} - \begin{array}{c}\text{Purchases returns and}\\\text{allowances}\end{array} + \text{Freight-in} = \begin{array}{c}\text{Net cost of}\\\text{purchases}\end{array}$$

$$\begin{array}{c}\text{Beginning}\\\text{merchandise inventory}\end{array} + \begin{array}{c}\text{Net cost of}\\\text{purchases}\end{array} = \begin{array}{c}\text{Cost of goods}\\\text{available for sale}\end{array}$$

$$\begin{array}{c}\text{Cost of goods}\\\text{available for sale}\end{array} - \begin{array}{c}\text{Ending merchandise}\\\text{inventory}\end{array} = \begin{array}{c}\text{Cost of}\\\text{goods sold}\end{array}$$

Under the periodic inventory system, the Merchandise Inventory account stays at the beginning level until the physical inventory is recorded at the end of the accounting period. A Purchases account is used to accumulate purchases of merchandise during the accounting period, and a Purchases Returns and Allowances account is used to accumulate returns of purchases and allowances on purchases.

LO5 Describe the components of internal control, control activities, and limitations on internal control.

Internal control consists of all the policies and procedures a company uses to ensure the reliability of financial reporting, compliance with laws and regulations, and the effectiveness and efficiency of operations. Internal control has five components: the control environment, risk assessment, information and communication, control activities, and monitoring. Control activities include having managers authorize certain transactions; recording all transactions to establish accountability for assets; using well-designed documents to ensure proper recording of transactions; instituting physical controls; periodically checking records and assets; separating duties; and using sound personnel practices. A system of internal control relies on the people who implement it. Thus, the effectiveness of internal control is limited by the people involved. Human error, collusion, and failure to recognize changed conditions can contribute to a system's failure.

LO6 Apply internal control activities to common merchandising transactions.

To implement internal control over cash sales, receipts, purchases, and disbursements, the functions of authorization, recordkeeping, and custodianship of cash should be kept separate. The people who have access to cash should be specifically designated and their number limited. Employees who have access to cash should be bonded. The control system should also provide for the use of banking services, physical protection of assets, prompt recording and deposit of cash receipts, and payment by check. A person who does not authorize, handle, or record cash transactions should make unannounced audits of the cash on hand, and the Cash account should be reconciled each month.

REVIEW of Concepts and Terminology

The following concepts and terms were introduced in this chapter:

Authorization: The approval of transactions or activities. **(LO5)**

Bonding: The process of carefully checking an employee's background and insuring the company against theft by that person. **(LO5)**

Check authorization: A form an accounting department prepares that authorizes the issuance of a check to pay an invoice. **(LO6)**

Control activities: Policies and procedures that management establishes to ensure that the objectives of internal control are met. **(LO5)**

Control environment: A company's ethics, philosophy and operating style, organizational structure, method of assigning authority and responsibility, and personnel policies and practices. **(LO5)**

Cost of goods available for sale: The sum of beginning inventory and the net cost of purchases during an accounting period. **(LO4)**

Delivery expense: The transportation cost of delivering merchandise. Also called *freight-out.* **(LO2)**

Exchange gain or loss: A gain or loss due to exchange rate fluctuation, which is reported on the income statement. **(LO1)**

Financing period: The amount of time from the purchase of inventory until it is sold and payment is collected, less the amount of time creditors give the company to pay for the inventory. **(LO1)**

FOB destination: A term indicating that the seller retains title to the merchandise until it reaches its destination and that the seller bears the shipping costs. **(LO2)**

FOB shipping point: A term indicating that the buyer assumes title to the merchandise at the shipping point and bears the shipping costs. **(LO2)**

Freight-in: The transportation cost of receiving merchandise. **(LO2)**

Information and communication: A component of internal control that refers to the way in which the accounting system gathers and treats information and how it communicates responsibilities within the system. **(LO5)**

Internal controls: The systems and procedures that management uses to protect a company's assets. **(LO1)**

Invoice: A form that a vendor sends to a purchaser describing the goods delivered and the quantity, price, and terms of payment. **(LO6)**

Merchandise inventory: The goods on hand at any one time that are available for sale to customers. **(LO1)**

Merchandising business: A business that earns income by buying and selling goods. **(LO1)**

Monitoring: Management's regular assessment of the quality of internal control. (LO5)

Net cost of purchases: Net purchases plus any freight charges on the purchases. (LO4)

Net purchases: Total purchases less any deductions, such as purchases returns and allowances and discounts on purchases. (LO4)

Operating cycle: A series of transactions that includes purchases of merchandise inventory for cash or on credit, payment for purchases made on credit, sales of merchandise inventory for cash or on credit, and collection of cash from credit sales. (LO1)

Periodic independent verification: A periodic check of records against assets by someone other than the person responsible for accounting records and assets. (LO5)

Periodic inventory system: A system for determining inventory on hand by periodically taking a physical count. (LO1)

Perpetual inventory system: A system for determining inventory on hand by keeping continuous records of the quantity and, usually, the cost of individual items as they are bought and sold. (LO1)

Physical controls: Controls that limit access to assets. (LO5)

Physical inventory: An actual count of all merchandise on hand. (LO1)

Purchase order: A form that a company's purchasing department sends to a vendor describing the items ordered and the quantity, price, terms, and shipping date. (LO6)

Purchase requisition: A formal written request for a purchase that a company's credit office (requesting department) sends to the purchasing department. (LO6)

Purchases account: A temporary account used under the periodic inventory system to accumulate the cost of merchandise purchased for resale during an accounting period. (LO4)

Purchases discounts: Discounts that buyers take for early payment of merchandise; the Purchases Discounts account is a contra-purchases account used under the periodic inventory system. (LO2)

Purchases Returns and Allowances account: A contra-purchases account used under the periodic inventory system to accumulate cash refunds, credits on account, and other allowances made by suppliers. (LO4)

Receiving report: A form on which an employee in a company's receiving department notes the quantity, type of goods, and their condition upon delivery from the vendor. (LO6)

Risk assessment: The identification of areas in which risk of loss of assets or inaccuracies in accounting records is high. (LO5)

Sales discount: A discount given to a buyer for early payment of a sale made on credit; the Sales Discounts account is a contra-revenue account. (LO2)

Sales Returns and Allowances account: A contra-revenue account used to accumulate cash refunds, credits on account, and other allowances made to customers who have received defective or otherwise unsatisfactory products. (LO3)

Separation of duties: No one person can authorize transactions, handle assets, or keep records of assets. (LO5)

Trade discount: A deduction (usually 30 percent or more) off a list or catalogue price, which is not recorded in the accounting records. (LO2)

REVIEW Problem

Merchandising Transactions: Perpetual and Periodic Inventory Systems

Fong Company engaged in the following transactions during July:

July 1 Sold merchandise to Pablo Lopez on credit, terms n/30, FOB shipping point, $2,100 (cost, $1,260).

2 Purchased merchandise on credit from Dorothy Company, terms n/30, FOB shipping point, $3,800.

2 Paid Custom Freight $290 for freight charges on merchandise received.

July 9 Purchased merchandise on credit from MNR Company, terms n/30, FOB shipping point, $3,600, including $200 freight costs paid by MNR Company.

11 Accepted from Pablo Lopez a return of merchandise, which was returned to inventory, $300 (cost, $180).

14 Returned for credit $600 of merchandise purchased on July 2.

16 Sold merchandise for cash, $1,000 (cost, $600).

22 Paid Dorothy Company for purchase of July 2 less return on July 14.

23 Received full payment from Pablo Lopez for his July 1 purchase, less return on July 11.

Required

1. Record these transactions in journal form, assuming Fong Company uses the perpetual inventory system.
2. Record the transactions in journal form, assuming Fong Company uses the periodic inventory system.

Answer to Review Problem

Accounts that differ under the two systems are highlighted.

	A	B	C	D	E	F	G	H	I	J	K	L	M	N
1						1. Perpetual Inventory System						2. Periodic Inventory System		
2	July	1		Accounts Receivable			2,100			Accounts Receivable			2,100	
3					Sales			2,100			Sales			2,100
4						Sold merchandise on						Sold merchandise on		
5						account to Pablo Lopez,						account to Pablo Lopez,		
6						terms n/30, FOB shipping						terms n/30. FOB shipping		
7						point						point		
8		1		Cost of Goods Sold			1,260							
9					Merchandise Inventory			1,260						
10						Transferred cost of								
11						merchandise sold to Cost								
12						of Goods Sold account								
13		2		Merchandise Inventory			3,800			Purchases			3,800	
14					Accounts Payable			3,800			Accounts Payable			3,800
15						Purchased merchandise						Purchased merchandise		
16						on account from Dorothy						on account from Dorothy		
17						Company, terms n/30, FOB						Company, terms n/30, FOB		
18						shipping point						shipping point		
19		2		Freight-In			290			Freight-In			290	
20					Cash			290			Cash			290
21						Paid freight on previous						Paid freight on previous		
22						purchase						purchase		
23		9		Merchandise Inventory			3,400			Purchases			3,400	
24				Freight-In			200			Freight-In			200	
25					Accounts Payable			3,600			Accounts Payable			3,600
26						Purchased merchandise on						Purchased merchandise on		
27						account from MNR Company,						account from MNR Company,		
28						terms n/30, FOB shipping						terms n/30, FOB shipping		
29						point, freight paid by supplier						point, freight paid by supplier		

(continued)

	A	B	C	D	E	F	G	H	I	J	K	L	M	N
1						1. Perpetual Inventory System						2. Periodic Inventory System		
2	July	11		Sales Returns and Allowances			300			Sales Returns and Allowances			300	
3					Accounts Receivable			300			Accounts Receivable			300
4						Accepted return of						Accepted return of		
5						merchandise from Pablo						merchandise from Pablo		
6						Lopez						Lopez		
7		11		Merchandise Inventory			180							
8					Cost of Goods Sold			180						
9						Transferred cost of								
10						merchandise returned to								
11						Merchandise Inventory								
12						account								
13		14		Accounts Payable			600			Accounts Payable			600	
14					Merchandise Inventory			600			Purchases Returns and Allowances			600
15						Returned portion of						Returned portion of		
16						merchandise purchased						merchandise purchased		
17						from Dorothy Company						from Dorothy Company		
18		16		Cash			1,000			Cash			1,000	
19					Sales			1,000			Sales			1,000
20						Sold merchandise for cash						Sold merchandise for cash		
21		16		Cost of Goods Sold			600							
22					Merchandise Inventory			600						
23						Transferred cost of								
24						merchandise sold to Cost of								
25						Goods Sold account								
26		22		Accounts Payable			3,200			Accounts Payable			3,200	
27					Cash			3,200			Cash			3,200
28						Made payment on account to						Made payment on account to		
29						Dorothy Company						Dorothy Company		
30						$3,800 – $600 = $3,200						$3,800 – $600 = $3,200		
31		23		Cash			1,800			Cash			1,800	
32					Accounts Receivable			1,800			Accounts Receivable			1,800
33						Received payment on						Received payment on		
34						account from Pablo Lopez						account from Pablo Lopez		
35						$2,100 – $300 = $1,800						$2,100 – $300 = $1,800		

CHAPTER ASSIGNMENTS

BUILDING Your Knowledge and Skills

Short Exercises

Identification of Management Issues

SE 1. Identify each of the following decisions as most directly related to (a) cash flow management, (b) choice of inventory system, (c) foreign merchandising transactions, or (d) internal controls:

1. Determination of how to protect cash from theft or embezzlement
2. Determination of the effects of changes in exchange rates
3. Determination of policies governing sales of merchandise on credit
4. Determination of whether to use the periodic or the perpetual inventory system

LO1 **Operating Cycle**

SE 2. On average, Mason Company holds its inventory 40 days before it is sold, waits 25 days for customers' payments, and takes 33 days to pay suppliers. For how many days must it provide financing in its operating cycle?

LO2 **Terms of Sale**

SE 3. A dealer buys tooling machines from a manufacturer and resells them.

a. The manufacturer sets a list or catalogue price of $12,000 for a machine. The manufacturer offers its dealers a 40 percent trade discount.
b. The manufacturer sells the machine under terms of FOB shipping point. The cost of shipping is $700.
c. The manufacturer offers a sales discount of 2/10, n/30. The sales discount does not apply to shipping costs.

What is the net cost of the tooling machine to the dealer, assuming it is paid for within ten days of purchase?

LO2 **Sales and Purchases Discounts**

SE 4. On April 15, Meier Company sold merchandise to Curran Company for $5,000 on terms of 2/10, n/30. Assume a return of merchandise on April 20 of $850, and payment in full on April 25. What is the payment by Meier to Curran on April 25?

LO3 **Purchases of Merchandise: Perpetual Inventory System**

SE 5. Record in T account form each of the following transactions, assuming the perpetual inventory system is used:

Aug. 2 Purchased merchandise on credit from Indio Company, invoice dated August 1, terms n/10, FOB shipping point, $1,150.

3 Received bill from Lee Shipping Company for transportation costs on August 2 shipment, invoice dated August 1, terms n/30, $105.

7 Returned damaged merchandise received from Indio Company on August 2 for credit, $180.

10 Paid in full the amount due to Indio Company for the purchase of August 2, part of which was returned on August 7.

LO4 **Purchases of Merchandise: Periodic Inventory System**

SE 6. Record in T account form the transactions in **SE 5**, assuming the periodic inventory system is used.

LO4 **Cost of Goods Sold: Periodic Inventory System**

SE 7. Using the following data and assuming cost of goods sold is $273,700, prepare the cost of goods sold section of a merchandising income statement (periodic inventory system). Include the amount of purchases for the month of October.

Freight-in	$13,800
Merchandise inventory, Sept. 30, 2010	37,950
Merchandise inventory, Oct. 31, 2010	50,600
Purchases	?
Purchases returns and allowances	10,350

LO4 **Sales of Merchandise: Periodic Inventory System**

SE 8. Record in T account form the following transactions, assuming the periodic inventory system is used:

Aug. 4 Sold merchandise on credit to Rivera Corporation, terms n/30, FOB destination, $5,040.

Aug. 5 Paid transportation costs for sale of August 4, $462.

9 Part of the merchandise sold on August 4 was accepted back from Rivera Corporation for full credit and returned to the merchandise inventory, $1,470.

Sept. 3 Received payment in full from Rivera Corporation for merchandise sold on August 4, less the return on August 9.

LO5 LO6 **Internal Control Activities**

SE 9. Match the check-writing policies for a small business described below to the following control activities:

a. Authorization
b. Recording transactions
c. Documents and records
d. Physical controls
e. Periodic independent verification
f. Separation of duties
g. Sound personnel practices

1. The person who writes the checks to pay bills is different from the people who authorize the payments and keep records of the payments.
2. The checks are kept in a locked drawer. The only person who has the key is the person who writes the checks.
3. The person who writes the checks is bonded.
4. Once each month the owner compares and reconciles the amount of money shown in the accounting records with the amount in the bank account.
5. The owner of the business approves each check before it is mailed.
6. Information pertaining to each check is recorded on the check stub.
7. Every day, all checks are recorded in the accounting records, using the information on the check stubs.

LO5 **Limitations of Internal Control**

SE 10. Internal control has several inherent limitations. Indicate whether each of the following situations is an example of (a) human error, (b) collusion among employees, (c) changed conditions, or (d) cost-benefit considerations:

1. Effective separation of duties in a restaurant is impractical because the business is too small.
2. The cashier and the manager of a retail shoe store work together to avoid the internal controls for the purpose of embezzling funds.
3. The cashier in a pizza shop does not understand the procedures for operating the cash register and thus fails to ring up all the sales and count the cash at the end of the day.
4. At a law firm, computer supplies are mistakenly delivered to the reception area instead of the receiving area because the supplier began using a different system of shipment. As a result, the receipt of supplies is not recorded.

Exercises

LO1 LO2 **Discussion Questions**

E 1. Develop a brief answer to each of the following questions:

1. Can a company have a "negative" financing period?
2. If you sold goods to a company in Europe and the exchange rate for the dollar is declining as it relates to the euro, would you want the eventual payment to be made in dollars or euros?
3. Who has ultimate responsibility for safeguarding a company's assets with a system of internal control?
4. Assume a large shipment of uninsured merchandise to your company is destroyed when the delivery truck has an accident and burns. Would you want the terms to be FOB shipping point or FOB destination?

LO3 LO4 LO5 LO6

Discussion Questions

E 2. Develop a brief answer to each of the following questions:

1. Under the perpetual inventory system, the Merchandise Inventory account is constantly updated. What would cause it to have the wrong balance?
2. Why is a physical inventory needed under both the periodic and perpetual inventory systems?
3. Which of the following accounts would be assigned a higher level of risk: Building or Merchandising Inventory?
4. Why is it important to write down the amount of cash received through the mail or over the counter?

LO1

Management Issues and Decisions

E 3. The decisions that follow were made by the management of Posad Cotton Company. Indicate whether each decision pertains primarily to (a) cash flow management, (b) choice of inventory system, (c) foreign transactions, or (d) control of merchandising operations.

1. Decided to mark each item of inventory with a magnetic tag that sets off an alarm if the tag is removed from the store before being deactivated.
2. Decided to reduce the credit terms offered to customers from 30 days to 20 days to speed up collection of accounts.
3. Decided that the benefits of keeping track of each item of inventory as it is bought and sold would exceed the costs of such a system.
4. Decided to purchase goods made by a Chinese supplier.
5. Decided to purchase a new type of cash register that can be operated only by a person who knows a predetermined code.
6. Decided to switch to a new cleaning service that will provide the same service at a lower cost with payment due in 30 days instead of 20 days.

LO1

Foreign Merchandising Transactions

E 4. Elm Corporation purchased a machine from Ritholz Corporation on credit for €75,000. At the date of purchase, the exchange rate was $1.00 per euro. On the date of the payment, which was made in euros, the value of the euro was $1.25. Did Elm incur an exchange gain or loss? How much was it?

LO2

Terms of Sale

E 5. An appliance dealer buys refrigerators from a manufacturer and resells them.

a. The manufacturer sets a list or catalogue price of $2,500 for a refrigerator. The manufacturer offers its dealers a 30 percent trade discount.

b. The manufacturer sells the machine under terms of FOB destination. The cost of shipping is $240.

c. The manufacturer offers a sales discount of 2/10, n/30. Sales discounts do not apply to shipping costs.

What is the net cost of the refrigerator to the dealer, assuming it is paid for within ten days of purchase?

LO2 LO4

Sales Involving Discounts: Periodic Inventory System

E 6. Prepare journal entries under the periodic inventory system for the transactions of Sanford Company, and determine the total amount received from Penkas Company:

Mar.	1	Sold merchandise on credit to Penkas Company, terms 2/10, n/30, FOB shipping point, $1,000.
	3	Accepted a return from Penkas Company for full credit, $400.
	10	Received payment from Penkas Company for the sale, less the return and discount.

Mar. 11 Sold merchandise on credit to Penkas Company, terms 2/10, n/30, FOB shipping point, $1,600.
31 Received payment from Penkas Company for the sale of March 11.

LO2 LO3 **Purchases Involving Discounts: Perpetual Inventory System**

E 7. Lien Company engaged in the following transactions:

July 2 Purchased merchandise on credit from Jonak Company, terms 2/10, n/30, FOB destination, invoice dated July 1, $4,000.
6 Returned some merchandise to Jonak Company for full credit, $500.
11 Paid Jonak Company for purchase of July 2 less return and discount.
14 Purchased merchandise on credit from Jonak Company, terms 2/10, n/30, FOB destination, invoice dated July 12, $4,500.
31 Paid amount owed Jonak Company for purchase of July 14.

Prepare journal entries assuming the perpetual inventory system is used and determine the total amount paid to Jonak Company.

LO3 **Preparation of the Income Statement: Perpetual Inventory System**

E 8. Using the selected account balances at December 31, 2010, for Receptions, Etc. that follow, prepare an income statement for the year ended December 31, 2010. Show detail of net sales. The company uses the perpetual inventory system, and Freight-In has not been included in Cost of Goods Sold.

Account Name	Debit	Credit
Sales		$498,000
Sales Returns and Allowances	$ 23,500	
Cost of Goods Sold	284,000	
Freight-In	14,700	
Selling Expenses	43,000	
General and Administrative Expenses	87,000	
Income Taxes	12,000	

LO3 **Recording Purchases: Perpetual Inventory System**

E 9. Give the entries in T account form to record each of the following transactions under the perpetual inventory system:

a. Purchased merchandise on credit, terms n/30, FOB shipping point, $2,500.
b. Paid freight on the shipment in transaction **a**, $135.
c. Purchased merchandise on credit, terms n/30, FOB destination, $1,400.
d. Purchased merchandise on credit, terms n/30, FOB shipping point, $2,600, which includes freight paid by the supplier of $200.
e. Returned part of the merchandise purchased in transaction **c**, $500.
f. Paid the amount owed on the purchase in transaction **a**.
g. Paid the amount owed on the purchase in transaction **d**.
h. Paid the amount owed on the purchase in transaction **c** less the return in **e**.

LO3 **Recording Sales: Perpetual Inventory System**

E 10. On June 15, Palmyra Company sold merchandise for $5,200 on terms of n/30 to Lim Company. On June 20, Lim Company returned some of the merchandise for a credit of $1,200, and on June 25, Lim paid the balance owed. Give Palmyra's entries in T account form to record the sale, return, and receipt of payment under the perpetual inventory system. The cost of the merchandise sold on June 15 was $3,000, and the cost of the merchandise returned to inventory on June 20 was $700.

LO4 **Preparation of the Income Statement: Periodic Inventory System**

E 11. Using the selected year-end account balances at December 31, 2010, for the Morris General Store shown below, prepare a 2010 income statement.

Show detail of net sales. The company uses the periodic inventory system. Beginning merchandise inventory was $28,000; ending merchandise inventory is $21,000.

Account Name	Debit	Credit
Sales		$309,000
Sales Returns and Allowances	$ 15,200	
Purchases	114,800	
Purchases Returns and Allowances		7,000
Freight-In	5,600	
Selling Expenses	56,400	
General and Administrative Expenses	37,200	
Income Taxes	18,000	

LO4 **Merchandising Income Statement: Missing Data, Multiple Years**

E 12. Determine the missing data for each letter in the following three income statements for Sampson Paper Company (in thousands):

	2010	2009	2008
Sales	$ p	$ h	$572
Sales returns and allowances	48	38	a
Net sales	q	634	b
Merchandise inventory, beginning	r	i	76
Purchases	384	338	c
Purchases returns and allowances	62	j	34
Freight-in	s	58	44
Net cost of purchases	378	k	d
Cost of goods available for sale	444	424	364
Merchandise inventory, ending	78	l	84
Cost of goods sold	t	358	e
Gross margin	284	m	252
Selling expenses	u	156	f
General and administrative expenses	78	n	66
Total operating expenses	260	256	g
Income before income taxes	v	o	54
Income taxes	6	4	10
Net income	w	16	44

LO4 **Recording Purchases: Periodic Inventory System**

E 13. Using the data in **E 9**, give the entries in T-account form to record each of the transactions under the periodic inventory system.

LO4 **Recording Sales: Periodic Inventory System**

E 14. Using the relevant data in **E 10**, give the entries in T-account form to record each of the transactions under the periodic inventory system.

LO5 **Use of Accounting Records in Internal Control**

E 15. Careful scrutiny of accounting records and financial statements can lead to the discovery of fraud or embezzlement. Each of the situations that follows may indicate a breakdown in internal control. Indicate the nature of the possible fraud or embezzlement in each of these situations.

1. Wages expense for a branch office was 30 percent higher in 2010 than in 2009, even though the office was authorized to employ only the same four employees and raises were only 5 percent in 2010.
2. Sales returns and allowances increased from 5 percent to 20 percent of sales in the first two months of 2010, after record sales in 2009 resulted in large bonuses for the sales staff.

3. Gross margin decreased from 40 percent of net sales in 2009 to 20 percent in 2010, even though there was no change in pricing. Ending inventory was 50 percent less at the end of 2010 than it was at the beginning of the year. There is no immediate explanation for the decrease in inventory.
4. A review of daily records of cash register receipts shows that one cashier consistently accepts more discount coupons for purchases than do the other cashiers.

LO5 LO6

Control Procedures

E 16. Anna Clapa, who operates a small grocery store, has established the following policies with regard to the checkout cashiers:

1. Each Cashier has his or her own cash drawer, to which no one else has access.
2. Cashiers may accept checks for purchases under $50 with proper identification. For checks over $50, they must receive approval from Clapa.
3. Every sale must be rung up on the cash register and a receipt given to the customer. Each sale is recorded on a tape inside the cash register.
4. At the end of each day, Clapa counts the cash in the drawer and compares it with the amount on the tape inside the cash register.

Match the following conditions for internal control to each of the policies listed above:

a. Transactions are executed in accordance with management's general or specific authorization.
b. Transactions are recorded as necessary to permit preparation of financial statements and maintain accountability for assets.
c. Access to assets is permitted only as allowed by management.
d. At reasonable intervals, the records of assets are compared with the existing assets.

LO5 LO6

Internal Control Procedures

E 17. Mega Hits Video Store maintains the following policies with regard to purchases of new videotapes at each of its branch stores:

1. Employees are required to take vacations, and the duties of employees are rotated periodically.
2. Once each month a person from the home office visits each branch store to examine the receiving records and to compare the inventory of videos with the accounting records.
3. Purchases of new videos must be authorized by purchase order in the home office and paid for by the treasurer in the home office. Receiving reports are prepared in each branch and sent to the home office.
4. All new personnel receive one hour of training in how to receive and catalogue new videos.
5. The company maintains a perpetual inventory system that keeps track of all videos purchased, sold, and on hand.

Match the following control procedures to each of the above policies. (Some may have several answers.)

a. Authorization
b. Recording transactions
c. Documents and records
d. Limited access
e. Periodic independent verification
f. Separation of duties
g. Sound personnel policies

Problems

LO1 LO3

Merchandising Income Statement: Perpetual Inventory System

P 1. At the end of the fiscal year, June 30, 2010, selected accounts from the adjusted trial balance for Barbara's Video Store, Inc., appeared as shown below.

Barbara's Video Store, Inc.
Partial Adjusted Trial Balance
June 30, 2010

Sales		$870,824
Sales Returns and Allowances	$ 25,500	
Cost of Goods Sold	442,370	
Freight-In	20,156	
Store Salaries Expense	216,700	
Office Salaries Expense	53,000	
Advertising Expense	36,400	
Rent Expense	28,000	
Insurance Expense	5,600	
Utilities Expense	18,320	
Store Supplies Expense	3,328	
Office Supplies Expense	3,628	
Depreciation Expense–Store Equipment	3,600	
Depreciation Expense–Office Equipment	3,700	
Income Taxes	5,000	

Required

1. Prepare a multistep income statement for Barbara's Video Store, Inc. Freight-In should be combined with Cost of Goods Sold. Store Salaries Expense; Advertising Expense; Store Supplies Expense; and Depreciation Expense–Store Equipment are selling expenses. The other expenses are general and administrative expenses. The company uses the perpetual inventory system. Show details of net sales and operating expenses.

User insight ▶

2. Based on your knowledge at this point in the course, how would you use the income statement for Barbara's Video Store to evaluate the company's profitability? What other financial statement should you consider and why?

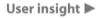

LO3

Merchandising Transactions: Perpetual Inventory System

P 2. Vargo Company engaged in the following transactions in October 2010:

Oct. 7 Sold merchandise on credit to Ken Smith, terms n/30, FOB shipping point, $3,000 (cost, $1,800).

8 Purchased merchandise on credit from Novak Company, terms n/30, FOB shipping point, $6,000.

9 Paid Smart Company for shipping charges on merchandise purchased on October 8, $254.

10 Purchased merchandise on credit from Mara's Company, terms n/30, FOB shipping point, $9,600, including $600 freight costs paid by Mara's.

Oct. 14 Sold merchandise on credit to Rose Milito, terms n/30, FOB shipping point, $2,400 (cost, $1,440).

14 Returned damaged merchandise received from Novak Company on October 8 for credit, $600.

17 Received check from Ken Smith for his purchase of October 7.

19 Sold merchandise for cash, $1,800 (cost, $1,080).

20 Paid Mara's Company for purchase of October 10.

21 Paid Novak Company the balance from the transactions of October 8 and October 14.

24 Accepted from Rose Milito a return of merchandise, which was put back in inventory, $200 (cost, $120).

Required

1. Prepare entries in journal form (refer to the review problem) to record the transactions, assuming use of the perpetual inventory system.

User insight ▶

2. Receiving cash rebates from suppliers based on the past year's purchases is a common practice in some industries. If at the end of the year Vargo Company receives rebates in cash from a supplier, should these cash rebates be reported as revenue? Why or why not?

LO1 LO4

Merchandising Income Statement: Periodic Inventory System

P 3. Selected accounts from the adjusted trial balance for Louise's Gourmet Shop, Inc., as of March 31, 2010, the end of the fiscal year, are shown below.

Louise's Gourmet Shop, Inc.
Partial Adjusted Trial Balance
March 31, 2010

Sales		$168,700
Sales Returns and Allowances	$ 5,700	
Purchases	70,200	
Purchases Returns and Allowances		2,600
Freight-In	2,300	
Store Salaries Expense	33,125	
Office Salaries Expense	12,875	
Advertising Expense	23,800	
Rent Expense	2,400	
Insurance Expense	1,300	
Utilities Expense	1,560	
Store Supplies Expense	2,880	
Office Supplies Expense	1,075	
Depreciation Expense–Store Equipment	1,050	
Depreciation Expense–Office Equipment	800	
Income Taxes	1,000	

The merchandise inventory for Louise's Gourmet Shop was $38,200 at the beginning of the year and $29,400 at the end of the year.

1. Using the information given, prepare an income statement for Louise's Gourmet Shop, Inc. Store Salaries Expense; Advertising Expense; Store Supplies Expense; and Depreciation Expense–Store Equipment are selling expenses. The other expenses are general and administrative expenses. The

company uses the periodic inventory system. Show details of net sales and operating expenses.

User insight ▶ 2. Based on your knowledge at this point in the course, how would you use the income statement for Louise's Gourmet Shop to evaluate the company's profitability? What other financial statements should you consider and why?

LO4

Merchandising Transactions: Periodic Inventory System

P 4. Use the data in **P 2** for this problem.

Required

1. Prepare entries in journal form (refer to the review problem) to record the transactions, assuming use of the periodic inventory system.

User insight ▶ 2. In their published financial statements most companies call the first line on their income statement "net sales." Other companies simply say "sales." Do you think these terms are equivalent and comparable? What would be the content of "net sales"? What might be the reason a company would use "sales" instead of "net sales"?

LO5 LO6

Internal Control

P 5. Handy Andy Company provides maintenance services to factories in the West Bend, Wisconsin, area. The company, which buys a large amount of cleaning supplies, consistently has been over budget in its expenditures for these items. In the past, supplies were left open in the warehouse to be taken each evening as needed by the onsite supervisors. A clerk in the accounting department periodically ordered additional supplies from a long-time supplier. No records were maintained other than to record purchases. Once a year, an inventory of supplies was made for the preparation of the financial statements.

To solve the budgetary problem, management decides to implement a new system for purchasing and controlling supplies. The following actions take place:

1. Management places a supplies clerk in charge of a secured storeroom for cleaning supplies.
2. Supervisors use a purchase requisition to request supplies for the jobs they oversee.
3. Each job receives a predetermined amount of supplies based on a study of each job's needs.
4. In the storeroom, the supplies clerk notes the levels of supplies and completes the purchase requisition when new supplies are needed.
5. The purchase requisition goes to the purchasing clerk, a new position. The purchasing clerk is solely responsible for authorizing purchases and preparing the purchase orders.
6. Supplier prices are monitored constantly by the purchasing clerk to ensure that the lowest price is obtained.
7. When supplies are received, the supplies clerk checks them in and prepares a receiving report. The supplies clerk sends the receiving report to accounting, where each payment to a supplier is documented by the purchase requisition, the purchase order, and the receiving report.
8. The accounting department also maintains a record of supplies inventory, supplies requisitioned by supervisors, and supplies received.
9. Once each month, the warehouse manager takes a physical inventory of cleaning supplies in the storeroom and compares it against the supplies inventory records that the accounting department maintains.

Required

1. Indicate which of the following control activities applies to each of the improvements in the internal control system (more than one may apply):

   a. Authorization
   b. Recording transactions
   c. Documents and records
   d. Physical controls
   e. Periodic independent verification
   f. Separation of duties
   g. Sound personnel practices

User insight ▶ 2. Explain why each new control activity is an improvement over the activities of the old system.

Alternate Problems

Merchandising Income Statement: Perpetual Inventory System

P 6. At the end of the fiscal year, August 31, 2010, selected accounts from the adjusted trial balance for Pasha's Delivery, Inc., appeared as follows:

Pasha's Delivery, Inc.
Partial Adjusted Trial Balance
August 31, 2010

Sales		$169,000
Sales Returns and Allowances	$ 9,000	
Cost of Goods Sold	61,400	
Freight-In	2,300	
Store Salaries Expense	32,825	
Office Salaries Expense	12,875	
Advertising Expense	24,100	
Rent Expense	2,400	
Insurance Expense	1,200	
Utilities Expense	1,560	
Store Supplies Expense	2,680	
Office Supplies Expense	1,175	
Depreciation Expense–Store Equipment	1,250	
Depreciation Expense–Office Equipment	800	
Income Taxes	2,000	

Required

1. Using the information given, prepare an income statement for Pasha's Delivery, Inc. Store Salaries Expense; Advertising Expense; Stores Supplies Expense; and Depreciation Expense–Store Equipment are selling expenses. The other expenses are general and administrative expenses. The company uses the perpetual inventory system. Show details of net sales and operating expenses.

User insight ▶ 2. Based on your knowledge at this point in the course, how would you use the income statement for Pasha's Delivery, Inc. to evaluate the company's profitability? What other financial statement should be considered and why?

Merchandising Transactions: Perpetual Inventory System

P 7. Sarah Company engaged in the following transactions in July 2010:

July 1 Sold merchandise to Chi Dong on credit, terms n/30, FOB shipping point, $2,100 (cost, $1,260).

July 3 Purchased merchandise on credit from Angel Company, terms n/30, FOB shipping point, $3,800.

5 Paid Speed Freight for freight charges on merchandise received, $290.

8 Purchased merchandise on credit from Expo Supply Company, terms n/30, FOB shipping point, $3,600, which includes $200 freight costs paid by Expo Supply Company.

12 Returned some of the merchandise purchased on July 3 for credit, $600.

15 Sold merchandise on credit to Tom Kowalski, terms n/30, FOB shipping point, $1,200 (cost, $720).

17 Sold merchandise for cash, $1,000 (cost, $600).

18 Accepted for full credit a return from Chi Dong and returned merchandise to inventory, $200 (cost, $120).

24 Paid Angel Company for purchase of July 3 less return of July 12.

25 Received check from Chi Dong for July 1 purchase less the return on July 18.

Required

1. Prepare entries in journal form (refer to the review problem) to record the transactions, assuming use of the perpetual inventory system.

User insight ▶ 2. In their published financial statements, most companies call the first line on their income statement "net sales." Other companies simply say "sales." Do you think these terms are equivalent and comparable? What would be the content of "net sales"? What might be the reason a company would use "sales" instead of "net sales"?

LO1 LO4 **Merchandising Income Statement: Periodic Inventory System**

KA KLOOSTER & ALLEN

P 8. The data below are selected accounts from the adjusted trial balance of Daniel's Sports Equipment, Inc., on September 30, 2010, the fiscal year end. The company's beginning merchandise inventory was $81,222 and ending merchandise inventory is $76,664 for the period.

Daniel's Sports Equipment, Inc.
Partial Adjusted Trial Balance
September 30, 2010

Sales		$440,912
Sales Returns and Allowances	$ 18,250	
Purchases	221,185	
Purchases Returns and Allowances		30,238
Freight-In	10,078	
Store Salaries Expense	105,550	
Office Salaries Expense	26,500	
Advertising Expense	20,200	
Rent Expense	15,000	
Insurance Expense	2,200	
Utilities Expense	18,760	
Store Supplies Expense	464	
Office Supplies Expense	814	
Depreciation Expense–Store Equipment	1,800	
Depreciation Expense–Office Equipment	1,850	
Income Taxes	5,000	

Required

1. Prepare a multistep income statement for Daniel's Sports Equipment, Inc. Store Salaries Expense; Advertising Expense; Store Supplies Expense; and Depreciation Expense–Store Equipment are selling expenses. The other expenses are general and administrative expenses. Daniel's Sports Equipment uses the periodic inventory system. Show details of net sales and operating expenses.

User insight ▶

2. Based on your knowledge at this point in the course, how would you use the income statement for Daniel's Sports Equipment to evaluate the company's profitability? What other financial statements should you consider and why?

LO4

Merchandising Transactions: Periodic Inventory System

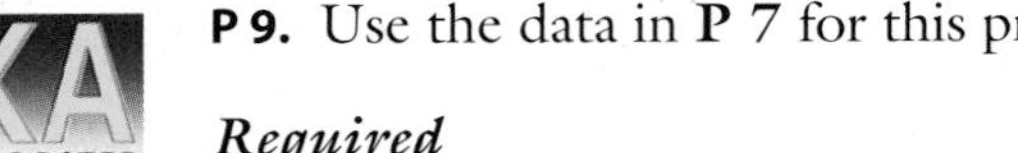

P 9. Use the data in **P 7** for this problem.

Required

1. Prepare entries in journal form (refer to the review problem) to record the transactions, assuming use of the periodic inventory system.

User insight ▶

2. Receiving cash rebates from suppliers based on the past year's purchases is common in some industries. If at the end of the year, Sarah Company receives rebates in cash from a supplier, should these cash rebates be reported as revenue? Why or why not?

ENHANCING Your Knowledge, Skills, and Critical Thinking

Conceptual Understanding Cases

LO1

Cash Flow Management

C 1. Jewell Home Source, Inc., has operated in Kansas for 30 years. The company has always prided itself on providing individual attention to its customers. It carries a large inventory so it can offer a good selection and deliver purchases quickly. It accepts credit cards and checks but also provides 90 days credit to reliable customers who have purchased from the company in the past. It maintains good relations with suppliers by paying invoices quickly.

During the past year, the company has been strapped for cash and has had to borrow from the bank to pay its bills. An analysis of its financial statements reveals that, on average, inventory is on hand for 70 days before being sold, and receivables are held for 90 days before being paid. Accounts payable are paid, on average, in 20 days. What are the operating cycle and the financing period? How long are Jewell's operating cycle and financing period? Describe three ways in which Jewell can improve its cash flow management.

LO1

Periodic Versus Perpetual Inventory Systems

C 2. Books-For-All is a well-established chain of 20 bookstores in western Ohio. In recent years the company has grown rapidly, adding five new stores in regional malls. The manager of each store selects stock based on the market in his or her region. Managers select items from a master list of available titles that the central office provides. Every six months, a physical inventory is taken, and financial statements are prepared using the periodic inventory system. At that time, books that have not sold well are placed on sale or, whenever possible, returned to the publisher.

Management has found that when selecting books, the new managers are not judging the market as well as the managers of the older, established stores. Thus, management is thinking about implementing a perpetual inventory system and carefully monitoring sales from the central office. Do you think Books-For-All should switch to the perpetual inventory system or stay with the periodic inventory system? Discuss the advantages and disadvantages of each system.

LO3

Effects of Weak Dollar

C 3. In 2004, **McDonald's** reported that its sales in Europe exceeded its sales in the United States for the first time. This result has continued in subsequent years. This performance, while reflective of the company's phenomenal success in Europe, was also attributed to the weak dollar in relation to the euro. McDonald's reports its sales wherever they take place in U.S. dollars. Explain why a weak dollar relative to the euro would lead to an increase in McDonald's reported European sales. Why is a weak dollar not relevant to a discussion of McDonald's sales in the United States?

Interpreting Financial Reports

LO5

Internal Control Lapse

C 4. **Starbucks Corporation** has accused an employee and her husband of embezzling $3.7 million by billing the company for services from a fictitious consulting firm. The couple created a phony company called RAD Services Inc. and charged Starbucks for work they never provided. The employee worked in Starbucks' Information Technology Department. RAD Services Inc. charged Starbucks as much as $492,800 for consulting services in a single week.[13] For such a fraud to have taken place, certain control activities were likely not implemented. Identify and describe these activities.

Decision Analysis Using Excel

LO1 LO3 LO4 LO5

Analysis of Merchandising Income Statement

C 5. In 2009, Tanika Jones opened a small retail store in a suburban mall. Called Tanika's Jeans Company, the shop sold designer jeans. Tanika Jones worked 14 hours a day and controlled all aspects of the operation. All sales were for cash or bank credit card. Tanika's Jeans Company was such a success that in 2010, Jones decided to open a second store in another mall. Because the new shop needed her attention, she hired a manager to work in the original store with its two existing sales clerks. During 2010, the new store was successful, but the operations of the original store did not match the first year's performance.

Concerned about this turn of events, Jones compared the two years' results for the original store. The figures are as follows:

	2010	2009
Net sales	$325,000	$350,000
Cost of goods sold	225,000	225,000
Gross margin	$100,000	$125,000
Operating expenses	75,000	50,000
Income before income taxes	$ 25,000	$ 75,000

In addition, Jones' analysis revealed that the cost and selling price of jeans were about the same in both years and that the level of operating expenses was roughly the same in both years, except for the new manager's $25,000 salary. Sales returns and allowances were insignificant amounts in both years.

Studying the situation further, Jones discovered the following facts about the cost of goods sold:

	2010	2009
Purchases	$200,000	$271,000
Total purchases allowances	15,000	20,000
Freight-in	19,000	27,000
Physical inventory, end of year	32,000	53,000

Still not satisfied, Jones went through all the individual sales and purchase records for the year. Both sales and purchases were verified. However, the 2010 ending inventory should have been $57,000, given the unit purchases and sales during the year. After puzzling over all this information, Jones comes to you for accounting help.

1. Using Jones' new information, recompute the cost of goods sold for 2009 and 2010, and account for the difference in income before income taxes between 2009 and 2010.
2. Suggest at least two reasons for the discrepancy in the 2010 ending inventory. How might Jones improve the management of the original store?

Annual Report Case: CVS Caremark Corporation

LO1

Operating Cycle and Financing Period

C 6. Refer to the **CVS** annual report in the Supplement to Chapter 1 and to Figures 1 and 2 in this chapter. Write a memorandum to your instructor briefly describing CVS's operating cycle and financing period. This memorandum should identify the most common transactions in the operating cycle as it applies to CVS. It should refer to the importance of accounts receivable, accounts payable, and merchandise inventory in the CVS financial statements. Complete the memorandum by explaining why the operating cycle and financing period are favorable to the company.

Comparison Case: CVS Versus Walgreens

LO1

Income Statement Analysis

C 7. Refer to the **CVS** annual report in the Supplement to Chapter 1 and to the following data (in millions) for **Walgreens** in 2007: net sales, $53,762.0; cost of sales, $38,518.1; total operating expenses, $12,093.2; and inventories, $6,790.5. Determine which company—CVS or Walgreens—had more profitable merchandising operations in 2007 by preparing a schedule that compares the companies based on net sales, cost of sales, gross margin, total operating expenses, and income from operations as a percentage of sales. (**Hint:** You should put the income statements in comparable formats.) In addition, for each company, compute inventories as a percentage of the cost of sales. Which company has the highest prices in relation to costs of sales? Which company is more efficient in its operating expenses? Which company manages its inventories better? Overall, on the basis of the income statement, which company is more profitable? Explain your answers.

Ethical Dilemma Case

LO1 LO3

Barter Transactions

C 8. Barter transactions in which one company trades goods or services to another company for other goods and services are becoming more common.

Broadcasters, for example, often barter advertising air time for goods or services. In such good-faith transactions, the broadcaster will credit revenue for the fair value of on-air advertising while debiting accounts in equal amounts for the nonmonetary goods and services it receives. **Dynergy**, an energy company, and another company agreed to buy and sell power to each other for the same price, terms, and volume. This resulted in no profit for Dynergy but increased its sales for the year, which perhaps helped it meet its sales goals and management's annual incentive bonus plans.[14] Do you think barter transactions that result in little or no profit for either company are ethical? Are they ethicial in certain situations but not in others? How could you tell the difference?

Internet Case

LO1 LO3

Comparison of Traditional Merchandising with Ecommerce

C 9. *Ecommerce* is a word coined to describe business conducted over the Internet. Ecommerce is similar in some ways to traditional retailing, but it presents new challenges. Go to the website of **Amazon.com**. Investigate and list the steps a customer makes to purchase an item on the site. How do these steps differ from those in a traditional retail store such as **Borders** or **Barnes & Noble**? What are some of the accounting challenges in recording Internet transactions? Be prepared to discuss your results in class.

Group Activity Case

LO5 LO6

Merchandise Inventory and Internal Controls

C 10. Go to a retail business, such as a bookstore, clothing shop, gift shop, grocery, hardware store, or car dealership in your local shopping area or a shopping mall. Ask to speak to someone who is knowledgeable about the store's inventory methods. Your instructor will assign groups to find the answers to the following questions. Be prepared to discuss your findings in class.

1. *Inventory systems* How is each item of inventory identified? Does the business have a computerized or a manual inventory system? Which inventory system, periodic or perpetual, is used? How often do employees take a physical inventory? What procedures are followed in taking a physical inventory? What kinds of inventory reports are prepared or received?
2. *Internal control structure* How does the company protect itself against inventory theft and loss? What control activities, including authorization, recording transactions, documents and records, physical controls, periodic checks, separation of duties, and sound personnel policies, does the company use? Can you see these control procedures in use?

Business Communication Case

LO5 LO6

Internal Control in a Small Company

C 11. Dan Markus runs a small company called Markus Construction. In the past, Markus's site managers have each purchased construction materials for their jobs. Markus thinks that a centralized purchasing department would help reduce waste and possibly theft. He has asked you, the company's accountant, to write a short memorandum describing such a purchasing system, the accompanying internal controls, and the forms needed to implement it. The company has a central warehouse where material could be received.

CHAPTER

6 Inventories

Focus on Financial Statements

INCOME STATEMENT
Revenues
– Expenses
= Net Income

STATEMENT OF RETAINED EARNINGS
Opening Balance
+ Net Income
– Dividends
= Retained Earnings

BALANCE SHEET
Assets | Liabilities
Equity
A = L + E

STATEMENT OF CASH FLOWS
Operating activities
+ Investing activities
+ Financing activities
= Change in Cash
+ Starting Balance
= Ending Cash Balance

Valuation of merchandise inventory on the balance sheet is linked to measurement of cost of goods sold on the income statement.

For any company that makes or sells merchandise, inventory is an extremely important asset. Managing this asset is a challenging task. It requires not only protecting goods from theft or loss, but also ensuring that operations are highly efficient. Further, as you will see in this chapter, proper accounting of inventory is essential because misstatements will affect net income in at least two years.

LEARNING OBJECTIVES

LO1 **Explain the management decisions related to inventory accounting, evaluation of inventory level, and the effects of inventory misstatements on income measurement.** *(pp. 342–348)*

LO2 **Define *inventory cost*, contrast goods flow and cost flow, and explain the lower-of-cost-or-market (LCM) rule.** *(pp. 348–351)*

LO3 **Calculate inventory cost under the periodic inventory system using various costing methods.** *(pp. 351–355)*

LO4 **Explain the effects of inventory costing methods on income determination and income taxes.** *(pp. 355–358)*

SUPPLEMENTAL OBJECTIVES

SO5 **Calculate inventory cost under the perpetual inventory system using various costing methods.** *(pp. 358–360)*

SO6 **Use the retail method and gross profit method to estimate the cost of ending inventory.** *(pp. 360–362)*

DECISION POINT ► A USER'S FOCUS

► What is the impact of inventory decisions on operating results?

► How should inventory be valued?

► How should the level of inventory be evaluated?

Toyota Motor Corporation

Toyota Motor Corporation manufactures and sells automobiles and other vehicles globally. This world-leading Japanese company, which is known for the quality of its products and the efficiency of its operations, is one of the largest employers in the United States. As you can see in Toyota's Financial Highlights,[1] inventory is an important component of the company's total assets.

TOYOTA'S FINANCIAL HIGHLIGHTS
(In millions)

	2007	2006	Change
Product sales	$192,038	$170,763	12.5%
Cost of goods sold	155,495	139,059	11.8
Operating income	18,964	15,990	18.6
Inventories	15,281	13,799	10.7
Total current assets	99,823	91,387	9.2

Managing Inventories

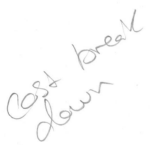

LO1 Explain the management decisions related to inventory accounting, evaluation of inventory level, and the effects of inventory misstatements on income measurement.

Inventory is considered a current asset because a company normally sells it within a year or within its operating cycle. For a merchandising company like **CVS** or **Walgreens**, inventory consists of all goods owned and held for sale in the regular course of business. Because manufacturing companies like **Toyota** are engaged in making products, they have three kinds of inventory:

- Raw materials (goods used in making products)
- Work in process (partially completed products)
- Finished goods ready for sale

In a note to its financial statements, Toyota showed the following breakdown of its inventories (figures are in millions):[2]

Inventories	*2007*	*2006*
Raw materials (includes supplies)	$ 3,072	$ 2,421
Work in process	2,006	2,038
Finished goods	10,203	9,340
Total inventories	$15,281	$13,799

The work in process and the finished goods inventories have three cost components:

- Cost of the raw materials that go into the product
- Cost of the labor used to convert the raw materials to finished goods
- Overhead costs that support the production process

Overhead costs include the costs of indirect materials (such as packing materials), indirect labor (such as the salaries of supervisors), factory rent, depreciation of plant assets, utilities, and insurance.

Inventory Decisions

Study Note

Management considers the behavior of inventory prices over time when selecting inventory costing methods.

The primary objective of inventory accounting is to determine income properly by matching costs of the period against revenues for the period. As you can see in Figure 1, in accounting for inventory, management must choose among different processing systems, costing methods, and valuation methods. These different systems and methods usually result in different amounts of reported net income. Thus, management's choices affect investors' and creditors' evaluations of a company, as well as internal evaluations, such as the performance reviews on which bonuses and executive compensation are based.

The consistency convention requires that once a company has decided on the systems and methods it will use in accounting for inventory, it must use them from one accounting period to the next unless management can justify a change. When a change is justifiable, the full disclosure convention requires that the company clearly describe the change and its effects in the notes to its financial statements.

Because the valuation of inventory affects income, it can have a considerable impact on the amount of income taxes a company pays—and the amount of taxes it pays can have a considerable impact on its cash flows. Federal income tax regulations are specific about the valuation methods a company may use. As a result, management is sometimes faced with the dilemma of how to apply GAAP to income determination and still minimize income taxes.

FIGURE 1
Management Choices in Accounting for Inventories

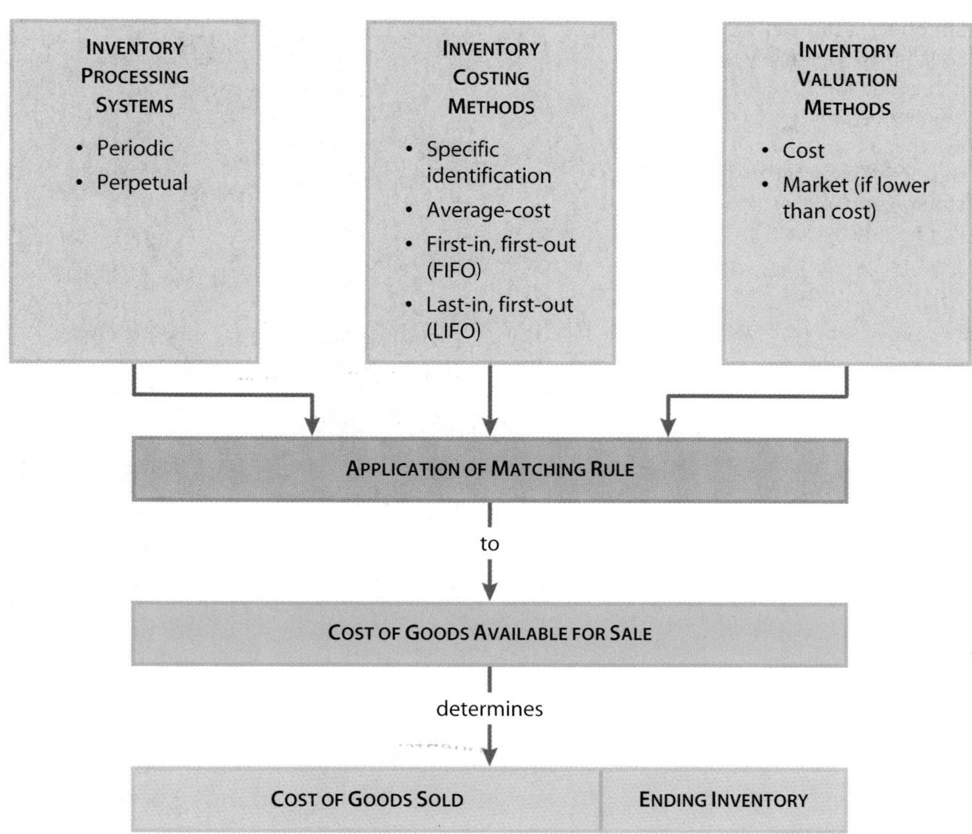

Evaluating the Level of Inventory

Study Note

Some of the costs of carrying inventory are insurance, property tax, and storage costs. Other costs may result from spoilage and employee theft.

The level of inventory a company maintains has important economic consequences. Ideally, management wants to have a great variety and quantity of goods on hand so that customers have a large choice and do not have to wait for an item to be restocked. But implementing such a policy can be expensive. Handling and storage costs and the interest cost of the funds needed to maintain high inventory levels are usually substantial. On the other hand, low inventory levels can result in disgruntled customers and lost sales.

FOCUS ON BUSINESS PRACTICE

A Whirlwind Inventory Turnover—How Does Dell Do It?

Dell Computer Corporation turns its inventory over every five days. How can it do this when other computer companies have inventory on hand for 60 days or even longer? Technology and good inventory management are a big part of the answer.

Dell's speed from order to delivery sets the standard for the computer industry. Consider that a computer ordered by 9 A.M. can be delivered the next day by 9 P.M. How can Dell do this when it does not start ordering components and assembling computers until a customer places an order? First, Dell's suppliers keep components warehoused just minutes from Dell's factories, making efficient, just-in-time operations possible. Another time and money saver is the handling of computer monitors. Monitors are no longer shipped first to Dell and then on to buyers. Dell sends an email message to a shipper, such as **United Parcel Service**, and the shipper picks up a monitor from a supplier and schedules it to arrive with the PC. In addition to contributing to a high inventory turnover, this practice saves Dell about $30 per monitor in freight costs. Dell is showing the world how to run a business in the cyber age by selling more than $1 million worth of computers a day on its website.[3]

Shoppers at this well-stocked Toys "R" Us store are very likely to find the items they want. Maintaining such a high level of inventory reduces the risk that a company will lose sales, but this policy has a price. The handling, storage, and interest costs involved can be substantial.

One measure that managers commonly use to evaluate inventory levels is **inventory turnover**, which is the average number of times a company sells its inventory during an accounting period. It is computed by dividing cost of goods sold by average inventory. For example, using the data presented in this chapter's Decision Point, we can compute **Toyota's** inventory turnover for 2007 as follows (figures are in millions):

K/R

$$\text{Inventory Turnover} = \frac{\text{Cost of Goods Sold}}{\text{Average Inventory}}$$

$$= \frac{\$155{,}495}{(\$15{,}281 + \$13{,}799) \div 2}$$

$$= \frac{\$155{,}495}{\$14{,}540} = 10.7 \text{ times}$$

Another common measure of inventory levels is **days' inventory on hand**, which is the average number of days it takes a company to sell the inventory it has in stock. For Toyota, it is computed as follows:

K/R

$$\text{Days' Inventory on Hand} = \frac{\text{Number of Days in a Year}}{\text{Inventory Turnover}}$$

$$= \frac{365 \text{ days}}{10.7 \text{ times}} = 34.1 \text{ days}$$

Toyota turned its inventory over 10.7 times in 2007 or, on average, every 34.1 days. Thus, it had to provide financing for the inventory for a little more than one month before it sold it.

Toyota's great efficiency is demonstrated by the fact that its inventory ratios are much better than the ratios for the machinery and computer industries in Figures 2 and 3. It is also better than those of other automobile manufacturers whose day's inventory on hand can often exceed 90 days. Although inventory turnover and days' inventory on hand vary by industry, companies like Toyota that maintain their inventories at low levels and still satisfy customers' needs are the most successful.

Study Note

Inventory turnover will be systematically higher if year-end inventory levels are low. For example, many merchandisers' year-end is in January when inventories are lower than at any other time of the year.

FIGURE 2
Inventory Turnover for Selected Industries

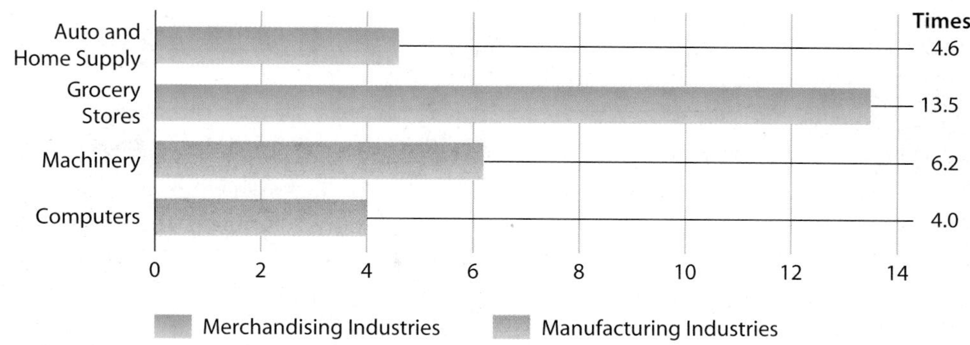

Source: **Data from Dun & Bradstreet, *Industry Norms and Key Business Ratios*, 2005–2006**

To reduce their levels of inventory, many merchandisers and manufacturers use supply-chain management in conjunction with a just-in-time operating environment. With **supply-chain management**, a company uses the Internet to order and track goods that it needs immediately. A **just-in-time operating environment** is one in which goods arrive just at the time they are needed.

Toyota uses supply-chain management to increase inventory turnover. It manages its inventory purchases through business-to-business transactions that it conducts over the Internet. Toyota also uses a just-in-time operating environment in which it works closely with suppliers to coordinate and schedule shipments so that the shipments arrive exactly when they are needed. The major benefits of using supply-chain management in a just-in-time operating environment are that Toyota has less money tied up in inventory and its cost of carrying inventory is reduced.

Effects of Inventory Misstatements on Income Measurement

The reason inventory accounting is so important to income measurement is the way income is measured on the income statement. Recall that gross margin is the difference between net sales and cost of goods sold and that cost of goods sold depends on the portion of cost of goods available for sale assigned to ending inventory. These relationships lead to the following conclusions:

- The higher the value of ending inventory, the lower the cost of goods sold and the higher the gross margin.

FIGURE 3
Days' Inventory on Hand for Selected Industries

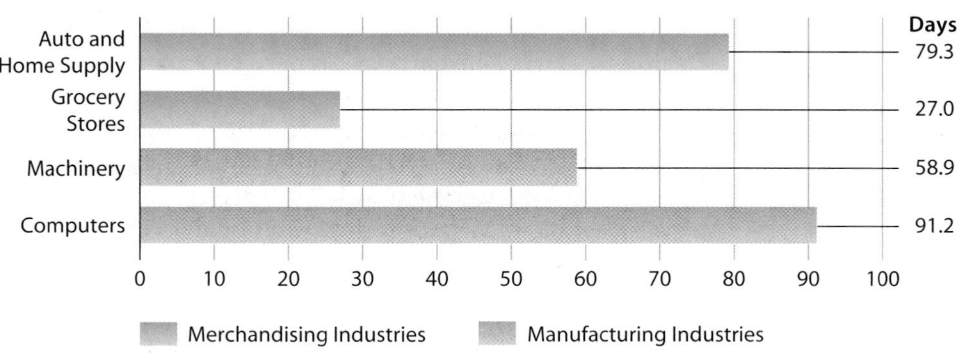

Source: **Data from Dun & Bradstreet, *Industry Norms and Key Business Ratios*, 2005–2006**

FOCUS ON BUSINESS PRACTICE

What Do You Do to Cure a Bottleneck Headache?

A single seat belt can have as many as 50 parts, and getting the parts from suppliers was once a big problem for **Autoliv, Inc.**, a Swedish maker of auto safety devices. Autoliv's plant in Indianapolis was encountering constant bottlenecks in dealing with 125 different suppliers. To keep the production lines going required high-priced, rush shipments on a daily basis. To solve the problem, the company began using supply-chain management, keeping in touch with suppliers through the Internet rather than through faxes and phone calls. This system allowed suppliers to monitor the inventory at Autoliv and thus to anticipate problems. It also provided information on quantity and time of recent shipments, as well as continuously updated forecasts of parts that would be needed in the next 12 weeks. With supply-chain management, Autoliv reduced inventory by 75 percent and rush freight costs by 95 percent.[4]

- Conversely, the lower the value of ending inventory, the higher the cost of goods sold and the lower the gross margin.

Because the amount of gross margin has a direct effect on net income, the value assigned to ending inventory also affects net income. In effect, the value of ending inventory determines what portion of the cost of goods available for sale is assigned to cost of goods sold and what portion is assigned to the balance sheet as inventory to be carried over into the next accounting period.

The basic issue in separating goods available for sale into two components—goods sold and goods not sold—is to assign a value to the goods not sold, the ending inventory. The portion of goods available for sale not assigned to the ending inventory is used to determine the cost of goods sold. Because the figures for ending inventory and cost of goods sold are related, a misstatement in the inventory figure at the end of an accounting period will cause an equal misstatement in gross margin and income before income taxes in the income statement. The amount of assets and stockholders' equity on the balance sheet will be misstated by the same amount.

Inventory is particularly susceptible to fraudulent financial reporting. For example, it is easy to overstate or understate inventory by including end-of-the-year purchase and sales transactions in the wrong fiscal year or by simply misstating inventory. A misstatement can occur because of mistakes in the accounting process. It can also occur because of deliberate manipulation of operating results motivated by a desire to enhance the market's perception of the company, obtain bank financing, or achieve compensation incentives.

In one spectacular case of fraudulent financial reporting, **Rite Aid Corporation**, the large drugstore chain, falsified income by manipulating its computerized inventory system to cover losses it had sustained from shoplifting, employee theft, and spoilage. In another case, bookkeepers at **RentWay, Inc.**, a company that rents furniture to apartment dwellers, boosted income artificially over several years by overstating inventory in small increments that were not noticed by top management.

Whatever the causes of an overstatement or understatement of inventory, the three examples that follow illustrate the effects. In each case, beginning inventory, net cost of purchases, and cost of goods available for sale are stated correctly. In Example 1, ending inventory is correctly stated; in Example 2, it is overstated by $3,000; and in Example 3, it is understated by $3,000.

Autoliv's use of supply-chain management is an example of how this system has benefited businesses. By using the Internet to order and track the numerous parts involved in the manufacture of the seat belts pictured here, Autoliv prevented delays in the shipments of parts by allowing its suppliers to monitor inventory and thus to anticipate problems. The firm also drastically reduced its inventory and freight costs.

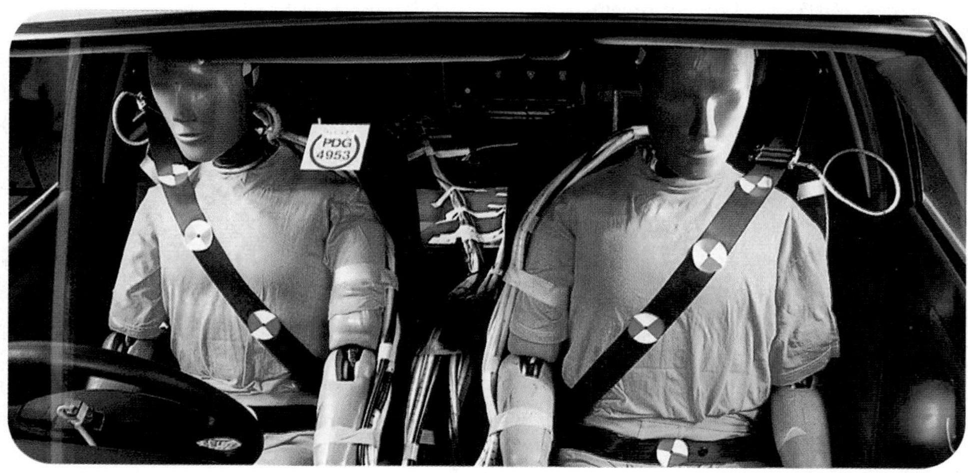

Example 1. Ending Inventory Correctly Stated at $5,000

Cost of Goods Sold for the Year		*Income Statement for the Year*	
Beginning inventory	$ 6,000	Net sales	$50,000
Net cost of purchases	29,000	→ Cost of goods sold	30,000
Cost of goods available for sale	$35,000	Gross margin	$20,000
Ending inventory	5,000	Operating expenses	16,000
Cost of goods sold	$30,000	Income before income taxes	$ 4,000

Example 2. Ending Inventory Overstated by $3,000

Cost of Goods Sold for the Year		*Income Statement for the Year*	
Beginning inventory	$ 6,000	Net sales	$50,000
Net cost of purchases	29,000	→ Cost of goods sold	27,000
Cost of goods available for sale	$35,000	Gross margin	$23,000
Ending inventory	8,000	Operating expenses	16,000
Cost of goods sold	$27,000	Income before income taxes	$ 7,000

Example 3. Ending Inventory Understated by $3,000

Cost of Goods Sold for the Year		*Income Statement for the Year*	
Beginning inventory	$ 6,000	Net sales	$50,000
Net cost of purchases	29,000	→ Cost of goods sold	33,000
Cost of goods available for sale	$35,000	Gross margin	$17,000
Ending inventory	2,000	Operating expenses	16,000
Cost of goods sold	$33,000	Income before income taxes	$ 1,000

In all three examples, the cost of goods available for sale was $35,000. The difference in income before income taxes resulted from how this $35,000 was divided between ending inventory and cost of goods sold.

Study Note

A misstatement of inventory has the opposite effect in two successive accounting periods.

Because the ending inventory in one period becomes the beginning inventory in the following period, a misstatement in inventory valuation affects not only the current period but the following period as well. Over two periods, the errors in income before income taxes will offset, or counterbalance, each other. For instance, in Example 2, the overstatement of ending inventory will cause a $3,000 overstatement of beginning inventory in the following year, which will result in a $3,000 understatement of income. Because the total income before income taxes for the two periods is the same, it may appear that one need not worry about inventory misstatements. However, the misstatements violate the matching rule. In addition, management, creditors, and investors base many decisions on the accountant's determination of net income. The accountant has an obligation to make the net income figure for each period as useful as possible.

The effects of inventory misstatements on income before income taxes are as follows:

Year 1	*Year 2*
Ending inventory overstated	**Beginning inventory overstated**
Cost of goods sold understated	Cost of goods sold overstated
Income before income taxes overstated	Income before income taxes understated
Ending inventory understated	**Beginning inventory understated**
Cost of goods sold overstated	Cost of goods sold understated
Income before income taxes understated	Income before income taxes overstated

STOP ► REVIEW ► APPLY

LO1-1 **How does a manufacturing company's inventory differ from that of a merchandising company?**

LO1-2 **What is the primary objective of inventory accounting?**

LO1-3 **Why is the level of inventory important, and what are two common measures of inventory level?**

LO1-4 **Why is inventory particularly vulnerable to fraudulent financial reporting?**

LO1-5 **If inventory is overstated at the end of 2008, what is the effect on the (a) 2008 net income, (b) 2008 year-end balance sheet value, (c) 2009 net income, and (d) 2009 year-end balance sheet value?**

Suggested answers to all Stop, Review, and Apply questions follow the appendixes.

Inventory Cost and Valuation

LO2 Define *inventory cost*, contrast goods flow and cost flow, and explain the lower-of-cost-or-market (LCM) rule.

The primary basis of accounting for inventories is cost, the price paid to acquire an asset. **Inventory cost** includes the following:

- Invoice price less purchases discounts
- Freight-in, including insurance in transit
- Applicable taxes and tariffs

Other costs—for ordering, receiving, and storing—should in principle be included in inventory cost. In practice, however, it is so difficult to allocate such costs to specific inventory items that they are usually considered expenses of the accounting period rather than inventory costs.

Inventory costing and valuation depend on the prices of the goods in inventory. The prices of most goods vary during the year. A company may have purchased identical lots of merchandise at different prices. Also, when a company deals in identical items, it is often impossible to tell which have been sold and which are still in inventory. When that is the case, it is necessary to make an assumption about the order in which items have been sold. Because the assumed order of sale may or may not be the same as the actual order of sale, the assumption is really about the *flow of costs* rather than the *flow of physical inventory*.

Goods Flows and Cost Flows

Study Note

The assumed flow of inventory costs does not have to correspond to the physical flow of goods.

Goods flow refers to the actual physical movement of goods in the operations of a company. **Cost flow** refers to the association of costs with their *assumed* flow in the operations of a company. The assumed cost flow may or may not be the same as the actual goods flow. The possibility of a difference between cost flow and goods flow may seem strange at first, but it arises because several choices of assumed cost flow are available under generally accepted accounting principles. In fact, it is sometimes preferable to use an assumed cost flow that bears no relationship to goods flow because it gives a better estimate of income, which is the main goal of inventory valuation.

Merchandise in Transit Because merchandise inventory includes all items that a company owns and holds for sale, the status of any merchandise in transit, whether the company is selling it or buying it, must be evaluated to see if the merchandise should be included in the inventory count. Neither the seller nor the buyer has *physical* possession of merchandise in transit. As Figure 4 shows, ownership is determined by the terms of the shipping agreement, which indicate when title passes. Outgoing goods shipped FOB (free on board) destination are included in the seller's merchandise inventory, whereas those shipped FOB shipping point are not. Conversely, incoming goods shipped FOB shipping point are included in the buyer's merchandise inventory, but those shipped FOB destination are not.

Merchandise on Hand Not Included in Inventory At the time a company takes a physical inventory, it may have merchandise on hand to which it does

FIGURE 4
Merchandise in Transit

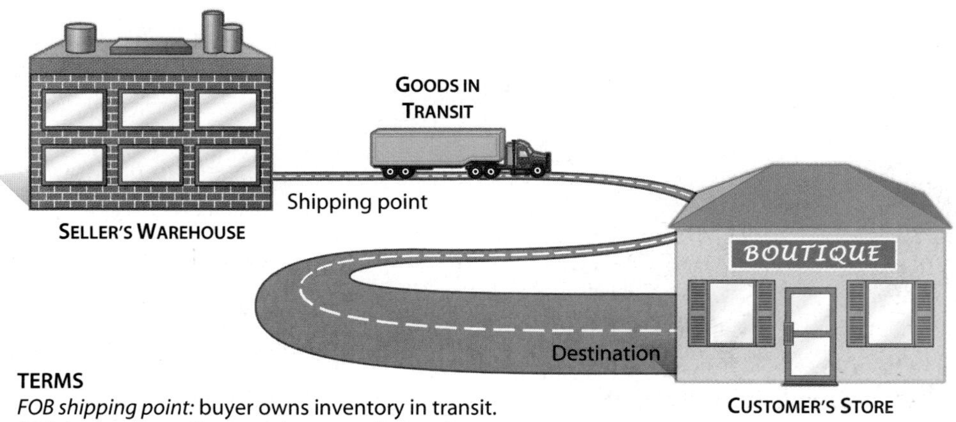

not hold title. For example, it may have sold goods but not yet delivered them to the buyer, but because the sale has been completed, title has passed to the buyer. Thus, the merchandise should be included in the buyer's inventory, not the seller's. Goods held on consignment also fall into this category.

A **consignment** is merchandise that its owner (the consignor) places on the premises of another company (the consignee) with the understanding that payment is expected only when the merchandise is sold and that unsold items may be returned to the consignor. Title to consigned goods remains with the consignor until the consignee sells the goods. Consigned goods should not be included in the consignee's physical inventory because they still belong to the consignor.

Lower-of-Cost-or-Market (LCM) Rule

Study Note

Cost must be determined by one of the inventory costing methods before it can be compared with the market value.

Although cost is usually the most appropriate basis for valuation of inventory, inventory may at times be properly shown in the financial statements at less than its historical, or original, cost. If the market value of inventory falls below its historical cost because of physical deterioration, obsolescence, or decline in price level, a loss has occurred. This loss is recognized by writing the inventory down to **market**—that is, to its current replacement cost. For a merchandising company, market is the amount that it would pay at the present time for the same goods, purchased from the usual suppliers and in the usual quantities.

When the replacement cost of inventory falls below its historical cost (as determined by an inventory costing method), the **lower-of-cost-or-market (LCM) rule** requires that the inventory be written down to the lower value and that a loss be recorded. This rule is an example of the application of the conservatism convention because the loss is recognized before an actual transaction takes place. Under historical cost accounting, the inventory would remain at cost until it is sold. According to an AICPA survey, approximately 82 percent of 600 large companies apply the LCM rule to their inventories for financial reporting.[5]

Disclosure of Inventory Methods

The full disclosure convention requires that companies disclose their inventory methods, including the use of LCM, in the notes to their financial statements, and users should pay close attention to them. For example, Toyota discloses that it uses the lower-of-cost-or-market method in this note to its financial statements:

> Inventories are valued at cost, not in excess of market, cost being determined on the "average cost" basis, . . .[6]

FOCUS ON BUSINESS PRACTICE

Lower of Cost or Market Can Be Costly

When the lower-of-cost-or-market rule comes into play, it can be an indication of how bad things are for a company. When the market for Internet and telecommunications equipment had soured, **Cisco Systems**, a large Internet supplier, found itself faced with probably the largest inventory loss in history. It had to write down to zero almost two-thirds of its $2.5 billion inventory, 80 percent of which consisted of raw materials that would never be made into final products.[7] In another case, through poor management, a downturn in the economy, and underperforming stores, **Kmart**, the discount department store, found itself with a huge amount of excess merchandise, including more than 5,000 truckloads of goods stored in parking lots, which it could not sell except at drastically reduced prices. The company had to mark down its inventory by $1 billion in order to sell it, which resulted in a debilitating loss.[8]

STOP ► REVIEW ► APPLY

LO2-1 **What items should be included in the cost of inventory?**

LO2-2 **What is the difference between goods flow and cost flow?**

LO2-3 **At the end of its fiscal year on June 30, Fargo Sales Company has an order for 130 units of product in its warehouse. Although the shipping department tries, it cannot ship the product by June 30, and title to the goods has not yet passed. Should the 130 units be included in the year-end count of inventory? Why or why not?**

LO2-4 **In the phrase *lower of cost or market*, what does *market* mean?**

LO2-5 **Why is it important for a company to disclose its method of accounting for inventory costs?**

Inventory Costs and Valuation Concepts

Match the letter of each item below with the numbers of the related items:

a. An inventory cost
b. An assumption used in the valuation of inventory
c. Full disclosure convention
d. Conservatism convention
e. Consistency convention
f. Not an inventory cost or assumed flow

1. Cost of consigned goods
2. A note to the financial statements explaining inventory policies
3. Application of the LCM rule
4. Goods flow
5. Transportation charge for merchandise shipped FOB shipping point
6. Cost flow
7. Choosing a method and sticking with it
8. Transportation charge for merchandise shipped FOB destination

SOLUTION

1. f	3. d	5. a	7. e
2. c	4. b	6. f	8. f

Inventory Cost Under the Periodic Inventory System

LO3 Calculate inventory cost under the periodic inventory system using various costing methods.

The value assigned to ending inventory is the result of two measurements: quantity and cost. Under the periodic inventory system, quantity is determined by taking a physical inventory; under the perpetual inventory system, quantities are updated as purchases and sales take place. Cost is determined by using one of the following methods, each based on a different assumption of cost flow:

1. Specific identification method
2. Average-cost method
3. First-in, first-out (FIFO) method
4. Last-in, first-out (LIFO) method

The choice of method depends on the nature of the business, the financial effects of the method, and the cost of implementing the method.

To illustrate how each method is used under the periodic inventory system, we use the following data for April, a month in which prices were rising:

April 1	Inventory	160 units @ $10.00	$ 1,600
6	Purchase	440 units @ $12.50	5,500
25	Purchase	400 units @ $14.00	5,600
Goods available for sale		1,000 units	$12,700
Sales		560 units	
On hand April 30		440 units	

Study Note

If the prices of merchandise purchased never changed, there would be no need for inventory methods. It is price changes that make some assumption about the order in which goods are sold necessary.

The problem of inventory costing is to divide the cost of the goods available for sale ($12,700) between the 560 units sold and the 440 units on hand.

Specific Identification Method

The **specific identification method** identifies the cost of each item in ending inventory. It can be used only when it is possible to identify the units in ending inventory as coming from specific purchases. For instance, if the April 30 inventory consisted of 100 units from the April 1 inventory, 200 units from the April 6 purchase, and 140 units from the April 25 purchase, the specific identification method would assign the costs as follows:

Periodic Inventory System—Specific Identification Method

100 units @ $10.00	$1,000	Cost of goods available	
200 units @ $12.50	2,500	for sale	$12,700
140 units @ $14.00	1,960	Less April 30 inventory	5,460
440 units at a cost of	$5,460	Cost of goods sold	$ 7,240

Although the specific identification method may appear logical, most companies do not use it for the following reasons:

1. It is usually impractical, if not impossible, to keep track of the purchase and sale of individual items.
2. When a company deals in items that are identical but that it bought at different prices, deciding which items were sold becomes arbitrary. If the company were to use the specific identification method, it could raise or lower income by choosing the lower- or higher-priced items.

Average-Cost Method

Under the **average-cost method**, inventory is priced at the average cost of the goods available for sale during the accounting period. Average cost is computed by dividing the total cost of goods available for sale by the total units available for sale. This gives an average unit cost that is applied to the units in ending inventory.

In our illustration, the ending inventory would be $5,588, or $12.70 per unit, determined as follows:

Periodic Inventory System—Average-Cost Method

Cost of Goods Available for Sale ÷ Units Available for Sale = Average Unit Cost

$12,700 ÷ 1,000 units = $12.70

Ending inventory: 440 units @ $12.70	=	$ 5,588
Cost of goods available for sale		$12,700
Less April 30 inventory		5,588
Cost of goods sold		$ 7,112

The average-cost method tends to level out the effects of cost increases and decreases because the cost of the ending inventory is influenced by all the prices paid during the year and by the cost of beginning inventory. Some analysts, however, criticize this method because they believe recent costs are more relevant for income measurement and decision making.

First-In, First-Out (FIFO) Method

The **first-in, first-out (FIFO) method** assumes that the costs of the first items acquired should be assigned to the first items sold. The costs of the goods on

Study Note

Because of their perishable nature, some products, such as milk, require a physical flow of first-in, first-out. However, the inventory method used to account for them can be based on an assumed cost flow that differs from FIFO, such as average-cost or LIFO.

hand at the end of a period are assumed to be from the most recent purchases, and the costs assigned to goods that have been sold are assumed to be from the earliest purchases. Any business, regardless of its goods flow, can use the FIFO method because the assumption underlying it is based on the flow of costs, not the flow of goods. In our illustration, the FIFO method would result in an ending inventory of $6,100, computed as follows:

Periodic Inventory System—FIFO Method

400 units @ $14.00 from purchase of April 25	$ 5,600
40 units @ $12.50 from purchase of April 6	500
440 units at a cost of	$ 6,100
Cost of goods available for sale	$12,700
Less April 30 inventory	6,100
Cost of goods sold	$ 6,600

Thus, the FIFO method values ending inventory at the most recent costs and includes earlier costs in cost of goods sold. During periods of rising prices, FIFO yields the highest possible amount of net income because cost of goods sold shows the earliest costs incurred, which are lower during periods of inflation. Another reason for this is that businesses tend to raise selling prices as costs increase, even when they purchased the goods before the cost increase. In periods of declining prices, FIFO tends to charge the older and higher prices against revenues, thus reducing income. Consequently, a major criticism of FIFO is that it magnifies the effects of the business cycle on income.

Study Note

Physical flow under LIFO can be likened to the changes in a gravel pile as the gravel is sold. As the gravel on top leaves the pile, more is purchased and added to the top. The gravel on the bottom may never be sold. Although the physical flow is last-in, first-out, any acceptable cost flow assumption can be made.

Last-In, First-Out (LIFO) Method

The **last-in, first-out (LIFO) method** of costing inventories assumes that the costs of the last items purchased should be assigned to the first items sold and that the cost of ending inventory should reflect the cost of the goods purchased earliest. Under LIFO, the April 30 inventory would be $5,100:

Periodic Inventory System—LIFO Method

160 units @ $10.00 from April 1 inventory	$ 1,600
280 units @ $12.50 from purchase of April 6	3,500
440 units at a cost of	$ 5,100
Cost of goods available for sale	$12,700
Less April 30 inventory	5,100
Cost of goods sold	$ 7,600

FOCUS ON BUSINESS PRACTICE **IFRS**

How Widespread Is LIFO?

Achieving convergence in inventory methods between U.S. and international accounting standards will be very difficult. As may be seen in Figure 6 (on page 356), LIFO is the second most popular inventory method in the United States. However, outside the United States, hardly any companies use LIFO because it is not allowed under international financial reporting standards (IFRS). Further, U.S. companies may use different inventory methods for different portions of their inventory as long as there is proper disclosure. International standards only allow this practice in very limited cases. Also, as noted earlier in the chapter, U.S. and international standards have different ways of measuring "market" value of inventories. Because these differences are so significant, there is no current effort to resolve them.[9]

FOCUS ON BUSINESS PRACTICE

IFRS

Is "Market" the Same as Fair Value?

When the lower-of-cost-or-market rule is used, what does "market" mean? Under International Financial Reporting Standards (IFRS), market is determined to be fair value, which is understood to be the amount at which an asset can be sold. However, under U.S. standards, market in valuing inventory is normally considered to be replacement cost or the amount at which the asset can be purchased. The two "market" values, selling price and purchasing price, can often be quite different for the same asset. This is an issue that will have to be addressed if the U.S. and international standards are to achieve convergence.

The effect of LIFO is to value inventory at the earliest prices and to include the cost of the most recently purchased goods in the cost of goods sold. This assumption, of course, does not agree with the actual physical movement of goods.

There is, however, a strong logical argument to support LIFO. A certain size of inventory is necessary in a going concern—when inventory is sold, it must be replaced with more goods. The supporters of LIFO reason that the fairest determination of income occurs if the current costs of merchandise are matched against current sales prices, regardless of which physical units of merchandise are sold. When prices are moving either up or down, the cost of goods sold will, under LIFO, show costs closer to the price level at the time the goods are sold. Thus, the LIFO method tends to show a smaller net income during inflationary times and a larger net income during deflationary times than other methods of inventory valuation. The peaks and valleys of the business cycle tend to be smoothed out.

Study Note

In inventory valuation, the flow of costs—and hence income determination—is more important than the physical movement of goods and balance sheet valuation.

An argument can also be made against LIFO. Because the inventory valuation on the balance sheet reflects earlier prices, it often gives an unrealistic picture of the inventory's current value. Balance sheet measures like working capital and current ratio may be distorted and must be interpreted carefully.

Summary of Inventory Costing Methods

Figure 5 summarizes how the four inventory costing methods affect the cost of goods sold on the income statement and inventory on the balance sheet when a company uses the periodic inventory system. In periods of rising prices, FIFO yields the highest inventory valuation, the lowest cost of goods sold, and hence a higher net income; LIFO yields the lowest inventory valuation, the highest cost of goods sold, and thus a lower net income.

FIGURE 5

The Impact of Costing Methods on the Income Statement and Balance Sheet Under the Periodic Inventory System

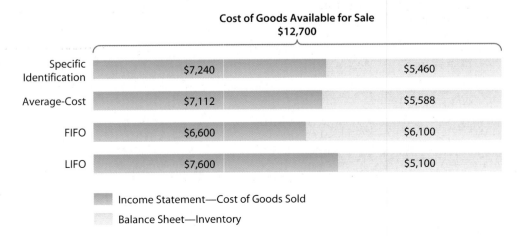

Cost of Goods Available for Sale $12,700

Method	Income Statement—Cost of Goods Sold	Balance Sheet—Inventory
Specific Identification	$7,240	$5,460
Average-Cost	$7,112	$5,588
FIFO	$6,600	$6,100
LIFO	$7,600	$5,100

STOP ▶ REVIEW ▶ APPLY

LO3-1 **Do the FIFO and LIFO inventory costing methods result in different quantities of ending inventory? Explain your answer.**

LO3-2 **Under which inventory costing methods are (a) the earliest costs assigned to inventory, (b) the latest costs assigned to inventory, and (c) the average costs assigned to inventory?**

LO3-3 **What are the relative advantages and disadvantages of FIFO and LIFO from management's point of view?**

Impact of Inventory Decisions

LO4 Explain the effects of inventory costing methods on income determination and income taxes.

Table 1 shows how the specific identification, average-cost, FIFO, and LIFO methods of pricing inventory affect gross margin. The table uses the same data as in the previous section and assumes April sales of $10,000.

Keeping in mind that April was a period of rising prices, you can see in Table 1 that LIFO, which charges the most recent—and, in this case, the highest—prices to cost of goods sold, resulted in the lowest gross margin. Conversely, FIFO, which charges the earliest—and, in this case, the lowest—prices to cost of goods sold, produced the highest gross margin. The gross margin under the average-cost method falls between the gross margins produced by LIFO and FIFO, so this method clearly has a less pronounced effect.

During a period of declining prices, the LIFO method would produce a higher gross margin than the FIFO method. It is apparent that both these methods have the greatest impact on gross margin during prolonged periods of price changes, whether up or down. Because the specific identification method depends on the particular items sold, no generalization can be made about the effect of changing prices on gross margin.

Effects on the Financial Statements

As Figure 6 shows, the FIFO, LIFO, and average-cost methods of inventory costing are widely used. Each method has its advantages and disadvantages—none is perfect. Among the factors managers should consider in choosing an

TABLE 1

Effects of Inventory Costing Methods on Gross Margin

	Specific Identification Method	Average-Cost Method	FIFO Method	LIFO Method
Sales	$10,000	$10,000	$10,000	$10,000
Cost of goods sold				
Beginning inventory	$ 1,600	$ 1,600	$ 1,600	$ 1,600
Purchases	11,100	11,100	11,100	11,100
Cost of goods available for sale	$12,700	$12,700	$12,700	$12,700
Less ending inventory	5,460	5,588	6,100	5,100
Cost of goods sold	$ 7,240	$ 7,112	$ 6,600	$ 7,600
Gross margin	$ 2,760	$ 2,888	$ 3,400	$ 2,400

FIGURE 6

Inventory Costing Methods Used by 600 Large Companies

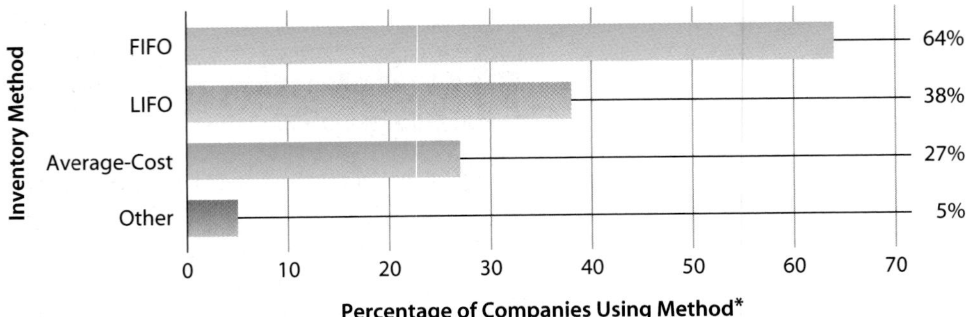

* *Totals more than 100% due to use of more than one method.*

Source: **"Industry Costing Methods Used by 600 Large Companies." Copyright © 2007 by AICPA. Reproduced with permission.**

inventory costing method are the trend of prices and the effects of each method on financial statements, income taxes, and cash flows.

As we have pointed out, inventory costing methods have different effects on the income statement and balance sheet. The LIFO method is best suited for the income statement because it matches revenues and cost of goods sold. But it is not the best method for valuation of inventory on the balance sheet, particularly during a prolonged period of price increases or decreases. FIFO, on the other hand, is well suited to the balance sheet because the ending inventory is closest to current values and thus gives a more realistic view of a company's current assets. Readers of financial statements must be alert to the inventory methods a company uses and be able to assess their effects.

Effects on Income Taxes

The Internal Revenue Service governs how inventories must be valued for federal income tax purposes. IRS regulations give companies a wide choice of inventory costing methods, including specific identification, average-cost, FIFO, and LIFO, and, except when the LIFO method is used, it allows them to apply the lower-of-cost-or-market rule. However, if a company wants to change the valuation method it uses for income tax purposes, it must have advance approval from the IRS.* This requirement conforms to the consistency convention. A company should change its inventory method only if there is a good reason to do so. The company must show the nature and effect of the change in its financial statements.

Many accountants believe that using the FIFO and average-cost methods in periods of rising prices causes businesses to report more than their actual profit, resulting in excess payment of income tax. Profit is overstated because cost of goods sold is understated relative to current prices. Thus, the company must buy replacement inventory at higher prices, while additional funds are needed to pay income taxes. During periods of rapid inflation, billions of dollars reported as profits and paid in income taxes were believed to be the result of poor matching of current costs and revenues under the FIFO and average-cost methods. Consequently, many companies, believing that prices would continue to rise, switched to the LIFO inventory method.

Study Note

In periods of rising prices, LIFO results in lower net income and thus lower taxes.

When a company uses the LIFO method to report income for tax purposes, the IRS requires that it use the same method in its accounting records, and, as we

* A single exception to this rule is that when companies change to LIFO from another method, they do not need advance approval from the IRS.

have noted, it disallows use of the LCM rule. The company may, however, use the LCM rule for financial reporting purposes.

Over a period of rising prices, a business that uses the LIFO method may find that for balance sheet purposes, its inventory is valued at a figure far below what it currently pays for the same items. Management must monitor such a situation carefully, because if it lets the inventory quantity at year end fall below the level at the beginning of the year, the company will find itself paying higher income taxes. Higher income before taxes results because the company expenses the historical costs of inventory, which are below current costs. When sales have reduced inventories below the levels set in prior years, it is called a **LIFO liquidation**—that is, units sold exceed units purchased for the period.

Managers can prevent a LIFO liquidation by making enough purchases before the end of the year to restore the desired inventory level. Sometimes, however, a LIFO liquidation cannot be avoided because products are discontinued or supplies are interrupted, as in the case of a strike. In 2006, 26 out of 600 large companies reported a LIFO liquidation in which their net income increased due to the matching of historical costs with present sales dollars.[10]

Effects on Cash Flows

Generally speaking, the choice of accounting methods does not affect cash flows. For example, a company's choice of average cost, FIFO, or LIFO does not affect what it pays for goods or the price at which it sells them. However, the fact that income tax law requires a company to use the same method for income tax purposes and financial reporting means that the choice of inventory method will affect the amount of income tax paid. Therefore, choosing a method that results in lower income will result in lower income taxes due. In most other cases where there is a choice of accounting method, a company may choose different methods for income tax computations and financial reporting.

STOP ▸ REVIEW ▸ APPLY

LO4-1 **In periods of steadily rising prices, which inventory method—average-cost, FIFO, or LIFO—will give the (a) highest ending inventory cost, (b) lowest ending inventory cost, (c) highest net income, and (d) lowest net income?**

LO4-2 **What is the relationship between income tax rules and the inventory valuation methods?**

Characteristics of Inventory Costing Methods
Match each of the descriptions listed below to these inventory costing methods:

a. Specific identification
b. Average-cost
c. First-in, first-out (FIFO)
d. Last-in, first-out (LIFO)

1. Matches recent costs with recent revenues
2. Assumes that each item of inventory is identifiable
3. Results in the most realistic balance sheet valuation
4. Results in the lowest net income in periods of deflation
5. Results in the lowest net income in periods of inflation
6. Matches the oldest costs with recent revenues
7. Results in the highest net income in periods of inflation
8. Results in the highest net income in periods of deflation
9. Tends to level out the effects of inflation
10. Is unpredictable as to the effects of inflation

(continued)

SOLUTION

1. d	6. c
2. a	7. c
3. c	8. d
4. c	9. b
5. d	10. a

Inventory Cost Under the Perpetual Inventory System

SO5 Calculate inventory cost under the perpetual inventory system using various costing methods.

Study Note

The costs of an automated perpetual system are considerable. They include the costs of automating the system, maintaining the system, and taking a physical inventory.

Under the perpetual inventory system, cost of goods sold is accumulated as sales are made and costs are transferred from the Inventory account to the Cost of Goods Sold account. The cost of the ending inventory is the balance of the Inventory account. To illustrate costing methods under the perpetual inventory system, we use the following data:

Inventory Data—April 30

April	1	Inventory	160 units @ $10.00
	6	Purchase	440 units @ $12.50
	10	Sale	560 units
	25	Purchase	400 units @ $14.00
	30	Inventory	440 units

The specific identification method produces the same inventory cost and cost of goods sold under the perpetual system as under the periodic system because cost of goods sold and ending inventory are based on the cost of the identified items sold and on hand. The detailed records of purchases and sales maintained under the perpetual system facilitate the use of the specific identification method.

The average-cost method uses a different approach under the perpetual and periodic systems, and it produces different results. Under the periodic system, the average cost is computed for all goods available for sale during the period. Under the perpetual system, an average is computed after each purchase or series of purchases, as follows:

Perpetual Inventory System—Average-Cost Method

April	1	Inventory	160 units @ $10.00	$1,600
	6	Purchase	440 units @ $12.50	5,500
	6	Balance	600 units @ $11.83*	$7,100
				(new average computed)
	10	Sale	560 units @ $11.83*	(6,625)
	10	Balance	40 units @ $11.83*	$ 475
	25	Purchase	400 units @ $14.00	5,600
	30	Inventory	440 units @ $13.80*	$6,075
				(new average computed)
Cost of goods sold				$6,625

The costs applied to sales become the cost of goods sold, $6,625. The ending inventory is the balance, $6,075.

*Rounded.

When costing inventory with the FIFO and LIFO methods, it is necessary to keep track of the components of inventory at each step of the way because as sales are made, the costs must be assigned in the proper order. The FIFO method is applied as follows:

Perpetual Inventory System—FIFO Method

April	1	Inventory	160 units @ $10.00		$1,600
	6	Purchase	440 units @ $12.50		5,500
	10	Sale	160 units @ $10.00	($1,600)	
			400 units @ $12.50	(5,000)	(6,600)
	10	Balance	40 units @ $12.50		$ 500
	25	Purchase	400 units @ $14.00		5,600
	30	Inventory	40 units @ $12.50	$ 500	
			400 units @ $14.00	5,600	$6,100
Cost of goods sold					$6,600

Note that the ending inventory of $6,100 and the cost of goods sold of $6,600 are the same as the figures computed earlier under the periodic inventory system. This will always occur because the ending inventory under both systems consists of the last items purchased—in this case, the entire purchase of April 25 and 40 units from the purchase of April 6.

The LIFO method is applied as follows:

Perpetual Inventory System—LIFO Method

April	1	Inventory	160 units @ $10.00		$1,600
	6	Purchase	440 units @ $12.50		5,500
	10	Sale	440 units @ $12.50	($5,500)	
			120 units @ $10.00	(1,200)	(6,700)
	10	Balance	40 units @ $10.00		$ 400
	25	Purchase	400 units @ $14.00		5,600
	30	Inventory	40 units @ $10.00	$ 400	
			400 units @ $14.00	5,600	$6,000
Cost of goods sold					$6,700

Notice that the ending inventory of $6,000 includes 40 units from the beginning inventory and 400 units from the April 25 purchase.

Figure 7 compares the average-cost, FIFO, and LIFO methods under the perpetual inventory system. The rank of the results is the same as under the periodic inventory system, but some amounts have changed. For example, LIFO has

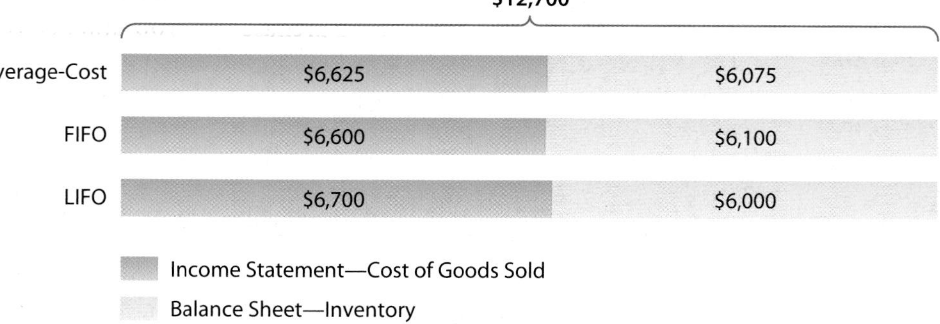

FIGURE 7
The Impact of Costing Methods on the Income Statement and Balance Sheet Under the Perpetual Inventory System

FOCUS ON BUSINESS PRACTICE

More Companies Enjoy LIFO!

The availability of better technology may partially account for the increasing use of LIFO in the United States. Using the LIFO method under the perpetual inventory system has always been a tedious process, especially if done manually. The development of faster and less expensive computer systems has made it easier for companies that use the perpetual inventory system to switch to LIFO and enjoy that method's economic benefits.

the lowest balance sheet inventory valuation regardless of the inventory system used, but the amount is $6,000 using the perpetual system versus $5,100 using the periodic system.

STOP ▶ REVIEW ▶ APPLY

SO5-1 **Why would it be more expensive to maintain a perpetual inventory system than a periodic inventory system?**

SO5-2 **Under the perpetual inventory system, why should a physical inventory be taken periodically?**

Valuing Inventory by Estimation

SO6 Use the retail method and gross profit method to estimate the cost of ending inventory.

It is sometimes necessary or desirable to estimate the value of ending inventory. The retail method and gross profit method are most commonly used for this purpose.

Retail Method

The **retail method** estimates the cost of ending inventory by using the ratio of cost to retail price. Retail merchandising businesses use this method for two main reasons:

1. To prepare financial statements for each accounting period, one must know the cost of inventory; the retail method can be used to estimate the cost without taking the time or going to the expense of determining the cost of each item in the inventory.
2. Because items in a retail store normally have a price tag or a universal product code, it is common practice to take the physical inventory at retail from these price tags or codes and to reduce the total value to cost by using the retail method. The term *at retail* means the amount of the inventory at the marked selling prices of the inventory items.

When the retail method is used to estimate ending inventory, the records must show the beginning inventory at cost and at retail. They must also show the amount of goods purchased during the period at cost and at retail. The net sales at retail is the balance of the Sales account less returns and allowances. A simple example of the retail method is shown in Table 2.

TABLE 2

Retail Method of Inventory Estimation

	Cost	Retail
Beginning inventory	$ 80,000	$110,000
Net purchases for the period (excluding freight-in)	214,000	290,000
Freight-in	6,000	
Goods available for sale	$300,000	$400,000
Ratio of cost to retail price: $\frac{\$300,000}{\$400,000} = 75\%$		
Net sales during the period		320,000
Estimated ending inventory at retail		$ 80,000
Ratio of cost to retail	75%	
Estimated cost of ending inventory	$ 60,000	

Study Note

Freight-in does not appear in the Retail column because retailers automatically price their goods high enough to cover freight charges.

Study Note

When estimating inventory by the retail method, the inventory need not be counted.

Goods available for sale is determined at cost and at retail by listing beginning inventory and net purchases for the period at cost and at their expected selling price, adding freight-in to the cost column, and totaling. The ratio of these two amounts (cost to retail price) provides an estimate of the cost of each dollar of retail sales value. The estimated ending inventory at retail is then determined by deducting sales for the period from the retail price of the goods that were available for sale during the period. The inventory at retail is then converted to cost on the basis of the ratio of cost to retail.

The cost of ending inventory can also be estimated by applying the ratio of cost to retail price to the total retail value of the physical count of the ending inventory. Applying the retail method in practice is often more difficult than this simple example because of such complications as changes in retail price during the period, different markups on different types of merchandise, and varying volumes of sales for different types of merchandise.

Gross Profit Method

The **gross profit method** (also known as the *gross margin method*) assumes that the ratio of gross margin for a business remains relatively stable from year to year. The gross profit method is used in place of the retail method when records of the retail prices of beginning inventory and purchases are not available. It is a useful way of estimating the amount of inventory lost or destroyed by theft, fire, or other hazards; insurance companies often use it to verify loss claims. The gross profit method is acceptable for estimating the cost of inventory for interim reports, but it is not acceptable for valuing inventory in the annual financial statements.

As Table 3 shows, the gross profit method is simple to use. First, figure the cost of goods available for sale in the usual way (add purchases to beginning inventory).

TABLE 3

Gross Profit Method of Inventory Estimation

1. Beginning inventory at cost		$100,000
Purchases at cost (including freight-in)		580,000
Cost of goods available for sale		$680,000
2. Less estimated cost of goods sold		
Sales at selling price	$800,000	
Less estimated gross margin		
($800,000 × 30%)	240,000	
Estimated cost of goods sold		560,000
3. Estimated cost of ending inventory		$120,000

Second, estimate the cost of goods sold by deducting the estimated gross margin of 30 percent from sales. Finally, deduct the estimated cost of goods sold from the goods available for sale to arrive at the estimated cost of ending inventory.

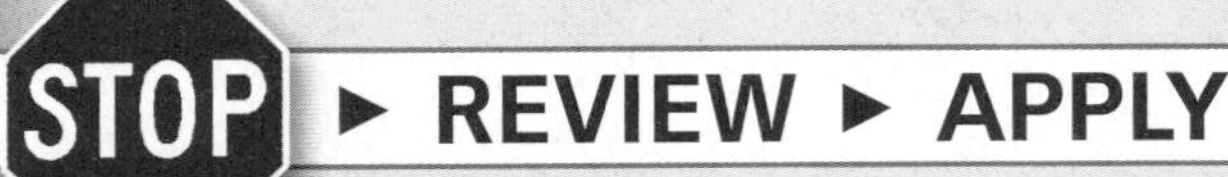

SO6-1 **Does using the retail method mean that inventories are measured at retail value on the balance sheet? Explain your answer.**

SO6-2 **For what reasons might managers use the gross profit method of estimating inventory?**

A LOOK BACK AT ► Toyota Motor Corporation

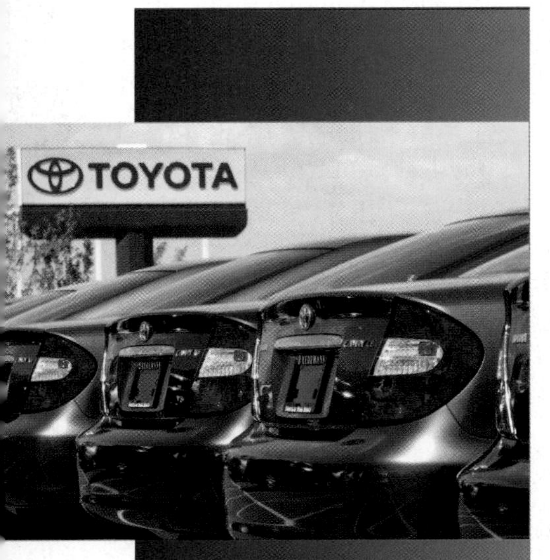

In this chapter's Decision Point, we posed the following questions:

- **What is the impact of inventory decisions on operating results?**
- **How should inventory be valued?**
- **How should the level of inventory be evaluated?**

As we pointed out in the chapter, Toyota uses supply-chain management and a just-in-time operating environment to manage its inventory. By doing so, it reduces its operating costs. We also pointed out that a note in Toyota's annual report disclosed that the company used the average costing method and applied the lower-of-cost-or-market rule to its inventories. Toyota's approach to valuation adheres to the conservatism convention because it may recognize losses in value before the products are sold if their value decreases.

Using data from Toyota's Financial Highlights, we can evaluate the company's success in managing its inventories by comparing its inventory turnover ratio and days' inventory on hand in 2007 and 2006 (dollar amounts are in millions; inventory in 2005 is $12,568):

	2007	2006
Cost of Goods Sold / Average Inventory	$155,495 / ($15,281 + $13,799) ÷ 2	$139,059 / ($13,799 + $12,568) ÷ 2
K/R	$155,495 / $14,540	$139,059 / $13,183.5
Inventory Turnover:	10.7 times	10.5 times
Number of Days in a Year / Inventory Turnover	365 days / 10.7 times	365 days / 10.5 times
K/R		
Days' Inventory on Hand:	34.1 days	34.8 days

Thus, in 2007, Toyota experienced a small improvement in its inventory turnover, as well as a small reduction in the number of days it had inventory on hand. This is a very good performance, especially in light of the decline in the housing market and economy in the latter part of 2007.

CHAPTER REVIEW

REVIEW of Learning Objectives

LO1 Explain the management decisions related to inventory accounting, evaluation of inventory level, and the effects of inventory misstatements on income measurement.

The objective of inventory accounting is the proper determination of income through the matching of costs and revenues. In accounting for inventories, management must choose the type of processing system, costing method, and valuation method the company will use. Because the value of inventory affects a company's net income, management's choices will affect not only external and internal evaluations of the company, but also the amount of income taxes the company pays and its cash flows.

The level of inventory a company maintains has important economic consequences. To evaluate inventory levels, managers commonly use inventory turnover and its related measure, days' inventory on hand. Supply-chain management and a just-in-time operating environment are a means of increasing inventory turnover and reducing inventory carrying costs. If the value of ending inventory is understated or overstated, a corresponding error—dollar for dollar—will be made in income before income taxes. Furthermore, because the ending inventory of one period is the beginning inventory of the next, the misstatement affects two accounting periods, although the effects are opposite.

LO2 Define *inventory cost*, contrast goods flow and cost flow, and explain the lower-of-cost-or-market (LCM) rule.

Inventory cost includes the invoice price less purchases discounts; freight-in, including insurance in transit; and applicable taxes and tariffs. Goods flow refers to the actual physical flow of merchandise in a business, whereas cost flow refers to the assumed flow of costs. The lower-of-cost-or-market rule states that if the replacement cost (market cost) of the inventory is lower than the original cost, the lower figure should be used.

LO3 Calculate inventory cost under the periodic inventory system using various costing methods.

The value assigned to ending inventory is the result of two measurements: quantity and cost. Quantity is determined by taking a physical inventory. Cost is determined by using one of four inventory methods, each based on a different assumption of cost flow. Under the periodic inventory system, the specific identification method identifies the actual cost of each item in inventory. The average-cost method assumes that the cost of inventory is the average cost of goods available for sale during the period. The first-in, first-out (FIFO) method assumes that the costs of the first items acquired should be assigned to the first items sold. The last-in, first-out (LIFO) method assumes that the costs of the last items acquired should be assigned to the first items sold.

LO4 Explain the effects of inventory costing methods on income determination and income taxes.

During periods of rising prices, the LIFO method will show the lowest net income; FIFO, the highest; and average-cost, in between. LIFO and FIFO have the opposite effects in periods of falling prices. No generalization can be made regarding the specific identification method. The Internal Revenue Service requires that if LIFO is used for tax purposes, it must be used for financial statements; it also does not allow the lower-of-cost-or-market rule to be applied to the LIFO method.

Supplemental Objectives

SO5 Calculate inventory cost under the perpetual inventory system using various costing methods.

Under the perpetual inventory system, cost of goods sold is accumulated as sales are made and costs are transferred from the Inventory account to the Cost of Goods Sold account. The cost of the ending inventory is the balance of the Inventory account. The specific identification method and the FIFO method produce the same results under both the perpetual and periodic inventory systems. The results differ for the average-cost method because an average is calculated after each sale rather than at the end of the accounting period. Results also differ for the LIFO method because the cost components of inventory change constantly as goods are bought and sold.

SO6 Use the retail method and gross profit method to estimate the cost of ending inventory.

Two methods of estimating the value of inventory are the retail method and the gross profit method. Under the retail method, inventory is determined at retail prices and is then reduced to estimated cost by applying a ratio of cost to retail price. Under the gross profit method, cost of goods sold is estimated by reducing sales by estimated gross margin. The estimated cost of goods sold is then deducted from the cost of goods available for sale to estimate the cost of ending inventory.

REVIEW of Concepts and Terminology

The following concepts and terms were introduced in this chapter:

Average-cost method: An inventory costing method in which inventory is priced at the average cost of the goods available for sale during the period. **(LO3)**

Consignment: Merchandise that its owner (the consignor) places on the premises of another company (the consignee) with the understanding that payment is expected only when the merchandise is sold and that unsold items may be returned to the consignor. **(LO2)**

Cost flow: The association of costs with their assumed flow in the operations of a company. **(LO2)**

First-in, first-out (FIFO) method: An inventory costing method based on the assumption that the costs of the first items acquired should be assigned to the first items sold. **(LO3)**

Goods flow: The actual physical movement of goods in the operations of a company. **(LO2)**

Gross profit method: A method of inventory estimation based on the assumption that the ratio of gross margin for a business remains relatively stable from year to year. Also called *gross margin method.* **(SO6)**

Inventory cost: The invoice price of an asset less purchases discounts, plus freight-in, plus applicable taxes and tariffs. **(LO2)**

Just-in-time operating environment: A method of reducing levels of inventory by working in close collaboration with suppliers to coordinate and schedule deliveries so that goods arrive just at the time they are needed. **(LO1)**

Last-in, first-out (LIFO) method: An inventory costing method based on the assumption that the costs of the last items purchased should be assigned to the first items sold. **(LO3)**

LIFO liquidation: The reduction of inventory below previous levels because sales of older, lower-priced units have exceeded the purchases of units for the current period. **(LO4)**

Lower-of-cost-or-market (LCM) rule: A method of valuing inventory at an amount less than cost when the replacement cost falls below historical cost. **(LO2)**

Market: Current replacement cost of inventory. **(LO2)**

Retail method: A method of inventory estimation, used in retail merchandising businesses, in which inventory at retail value is reduced by the ratio of cost to retail price. **(SO6)**

Specific identification method: An inventory costing method in which the cost of each item in ending inventory is identified as coming from a specific purchase. **(LO3)**

Supply-chain management: A system of managing inventory and purchasing through business-to-business transactions over the Internet. **(LO1)**

Key Ratios

Days' inventory on hand: The average number of days required to sell the inventory on hand; Number of Days in a Year ÷ Inventory Turnover. **(LO1)**

Inventory turnover: A ratio indicating the number of times a company's average inventory is sold during an accounting period; Cost of Goods Sold ÷ Average Inventory. **(LO1)**

REVIEW Problem

LO1 LO3 SO5

Periodic and Perpetual Inventory Systems

The following table summarizes the beginning inventory, purchases, and sales of Zeta Company's single product during May:

	A	B	C	D	E	F	G	H
1					Beginning Inventory and Purchases			
2	Date				Units	Cost	Total	Sales Units
3	May	1		Inventory	2,800	$20	$ 56,000	
4		8		Purchase	1,200	22	26,400	
5		10		Sale				3,200
6		24		Purchase	1,600	24	38,400	
7								
8	Totals				5,600		$120,800	3,200
9								

Required

1. Assuming that the company uses the periodic inventory system, compute the cost that should be assigned to ending inventory and to cost of goods sold using (a) the average-cost method, (b) the FIFO method, and (c) the LIFO method.
2. Assuming that the company uses the perpetual inventory system, compute the cost that should be assigned to ending inventory and to cost of goods sold using (a) the average-cost method, (b) the FIFO method, and (c) the LIFO method.
3. Compute inventory turnover and days' inventory on hand under each of the inventory cost flow assumptions in **1**. What conclusion can you draw from this comparison?

Answer to Review Problem

	Units	Amount
Beginning inventory	2,800	$ 56,000
Purchases	2,800	64,800
Available for sale	5,600	$120,800
Sales	3,200	
Ending inventory	2,400	

1. Periodic inventory system:
   a. Average-cost method

Cost of goods available for sale	$120,800
Less ending inventory consisting of 2,400 units at $21.57*	51,768
Cost of goods sold	$ 69,032

*$120,800 ÷ 5,600 units = $21.57 (rounded).

b. FIFO method

Cost of goods available for sale		$120,800
Less ending inventory consisting of		
May 24 purchase (1,600 × $24)	$38,400	
May 8 purchase (800 × $22)	17,600	56,000
Cost of goods sold		$ 64,800

c. LIFO method

Cost of goods available for sale	$120,800
Less ending inventory consisting of	
beginning inventory (2,400 × $20)	48,000
Cost of goods sold	$72,800

2. Perpetual inventory system:

a. Average-cost method

Date	Units	Cost	Amount
May 1 Inventory	2,800	$20.00	$56,000
8 Purchase	1,200	22.00	26,400
8 Balance	4,000	20.60	$82,400
10 Sale	(3,200)	20.60	(65,920)
10 Balance	800	20.60	$16,480
24 Purchase	1,600	24.00	38,400
31 Inventory	2,400	22.87*	$54,880
Cost of goods sold			$65,920

*Rounded.

b. FIFO method

Date	Units	Cost	Amount
May 1 Inventory	2,800	$20	$56,000
8Purchase	1,200	22	26,400
8Balance	2,800	20	
	1,200	22	$82,400
10 Sale	(2,800)	20	
	(400)	22	(64,800)
10 Balance	800	22	$17,600
24 Purchase	1,600	24	38,400
31 Inventory	800	22	
	1,600	24	$56,000
Cost of goods sold			$64,800

c. LIFO method

Date	Units	Cost	Amount
May 1 Inventory	2,800	$20	$56,000
8 Purchase	1,200	22	26,400
8 Balance	2,800	20	
	1,200	22	$82,400
10 Sale	(1,200)	22	
	(2,000)	20	(66,400)
10 Balance	800	20	$16,000
24 Purchase	1,600	24	38,400
31 Inventory	800	20	
	1,600	24	$54,400
Cost of goods sold			$66,400

3. Ratios computed:

	Average-Cost	FIFO	LIFO
Cost of Goods Sold / Average Inventory	$\frac{\$69,032}{\$53,884} = 1.3$	$\frac{\$64,800}{\$56,000} = 1.2$	$\frac{\$72,800}{\$52,000} = 1.4$
	(\$51,768 + \$56,000) ÷ 2	(\$56,000 + \$56,000) ÷ 2	(\$48,000 + \$56,000) ÷ 2
Inventory Turnover:	1.3 times	1.2 times	1.4 times
Days' Inventory on Hand:	(365 days ÷ 1.3 times) 280.8 days	(365 days ÷ 1.2 times) 304.2 days	(365 days ÷ 1.4 times) 260.7 days

In periods of rising prices, the LIFO method will always result in a higher inventory turnover and lower days' inventory on hand than the other costing methods. When comparing inventory ratios for two or more companies, their inventory methods should be considered.

CHAPTER ASSIGNMENTS

BUILDING Your Basic Knowledge and Skills

Short Exercises

LO1 **Management Issues**

SE 1. Indicate whether each of the following items is associated with (a) allocating the cost of inventories in accordance with the matching rule, (b) assessing the impact of inventory decisions, (c) evaluating the level of inventory, or (d) engaging in an unethical practice.

1. Calculating days' inventory on hand
2. Ordering a supply of inventory to satisfy customer needs
3. Valuing inventory at an amount to achieve a specific profit objective
4. Calculating the income tax effect of an inventory method
5. Deciding the cost to place on ending inventory

LO1 **Inventory Turnover and Days' Inventory on Hand**

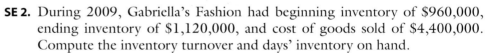

SE 2. During 2009, Gabriella's Fashion had beginning inventory of \$960,000, ending inventory of \$1,120,000, and cost of goods sold of \$4,400,000. Compute the inventory turnover and days' inventory on hand.

LO3 **Specific Identification Method**

SE 3. Assume the following data with regard to inventory for Caciato Company:

Aug. 1	Inventory	40 units @ \$10 per unit	\$ 400
8	Purchase	50 units @ \$11 per unit	550
22	Purchase	35 units @ \$12 per unit	420
Goods available for sale		125 units	\$1,370
Aug. 15	Sale	45 units	
28	Sale	25 units	
Inventory, Aug. 31		55 units	

Assuming that the inventory consists of 30 units from the August 8 purchase and 25 units from the purchase of August 22, calculate the cost of ending inventory and cost of goods sold.

LO3 **Average-Cost Method: Periodic Inventory System**

SE 4. Using the data in **SE 3**, calculate the cost of ending inventory and cost of goods sold according to the average-cost method under the periodic inventory system.

LO3 **FIFO Method: Periodic Inventory System**

SE 5. Using the data in **SE 3**, calculate the cost of ending inventory and cost of goods sold according to the FIFO method under the periodic inventory system.

LO3 **LIFO Method: Periodic Inventory System**

SE 6. Using the data in **SE 3**, calculate the cost of ending inventory and cost of goods sold according to the LIFO method under the periodic inventory system.

LO4 **Effects of Inventory Costing Methods and Changing Prices**

SE 7. Using Table 1 as an example, prepare a table with four columns that shows the ending inventory and cost of goods sold for each of the results from your calculations in **SE 3** through **SE 6**, including the effects of the different prices at which the merchandise was purchased. Which method(s) would result in the lowest income taxes?

SO5 **Average-Cost Method: Perpetual Inventory System**

SE 8. Using the data in **SE 3**, calculate the cost of ending inventory and cost of goods sold according to the average-cost method under the perpetual inventory system.

SO5 **FIFO Method: Perpetual Inventory System**

SE 9. Using the data in **SE 3**, calculate the cost of ending inventory and cost of goods sold according to the FIFO method under the perpetual inventory system.

SO5 **LIFO Method: Perpetual Inventory System**

SE 10. Using the data in **SE 3**, calculate the cost of ending inventory and cost of goods sold according to the LIFO method under the perpetual inventory system.

Exercises

LO1 LO2 **Discussion Questions**

E 1. Develop a brief answer to each of the following questions:

1. Is it good or bad for a retail store to have a large inventory?
2. Which is more important from the standpoint of inventory costing: the flow of goods or the flow of costs?
3. Why is misstatement of inventory one of the most common means of financial statement fraud?
4. Given that the LCM rule is an application of the conservatism convention in the current accounting period, is the effect of this application also conservative in the next period?

LO4 SO5 SO6

Discussion Questions

E 2. Develop a brief answer to each of the following questions:

1. Under what condition would all four methods of inventory pricing produce exactly the same results?
2. Under the perpetual inventory system, why is the cost of goods sold not determined by deducting the ending inventory from the cost of goods available for sale, as it is under the periodic inventory method?
3. Which of the following methods do not require a physical inventory: periodic inventory system, perpetual inventory method, retail method, or gross profit method?

LO1

Management Issues

E 3. Indicate whether each of the following items is associated with (a) allocating the cost of inventories in accordance with the matching rule, (b) assessing the impact of inventory decisions, (c) evaluating the level of inventory, or (d) engaging in an unethical action.

1. Computing inventory turnover
2. Valuing inventory at an amount to meet management's targeted net income
3. Application of the just-in-time operating environment
4. Determining the effects of inventory decisions on cash flows
5. Apportioning the cost of goods available for sale to ending inventory and cost of goods sold
6. Determining the effects of inventory methods on income taxes
7. Determining the assumption about the flow of costs into and out of the company

LO1

Inventory Ratios

E 4. Just a Buck Discount Stores is assessing its levels of inventory for 2009 and 2010 and has gathered the following data:

	2010	2009	2008
Ending inventory	$ 96,000	$ 81,000	$69,000
Cost of goods sold	480,000	450,000	

Compute the inventory turnover and days' inventory on hand for 2009 and 2010 and comment on the results.

LO1

Effects of Inventory Errors

E 5. Condensed income statements for Ken-Du Company for two years are shown below.

	2010	2009
Sales	$504,000	$420,000
Cost of goods sold	300,000	216,000
Gross margin	$204,000	$204,000
Operating expenses	120,000	120,000
Income before income taxes	$ 84,000	$ 84,000

After the end of 2010, the company discovered that an error had resulted in a $36,000 understatement of the 2009 ending inventory.

Compute the corrected income before income taxes for 2009 and 2010. What effect will the error have on income before income taxes and stockholders' equity for 2011?

LO1 LO2 LO3

Accounting Conventions and Inventory Valuation

E 6. Turnbow Company, a telecommunications equipment company, has used the LIFO method adjusted for lower of cost or market for a number of years. Due to falling prices of its equipment, it has had to adjust (reduce) the cost of inventory to market each year for two years. The company is considering changing its method to FIFO adjusted for lower of cost or market in the future.

Explain how the accounting conventions of consistency, full disclosure, and conservatism apply to this decision. If the change were made, why would management expect fewer adjustments to market in the future?

LO3

Periodic Inventory System and Inventory Costing Methods

E 7. Gary's Parts Shop recorded the following purchases and sales during the past year:

Jan.	1	Beginning inventory	125 cases @ $46	$ 5,750
Feb.	25	Purchase	100 cases @ $52	5,200
June	15	Purchase	200 cases @ $56	11,200
Oct.	15	Purchase	150 cases @ $56	8,400
Dec.	15	Purchase	100 cases @ $60	6,000
Goods available for sale			675	$36,550
Total sales			500 cases	
Dec.	31	Ending inventory	175 cases	

Assume that Gary's Parts Shop sold all of the June 15 purchase and 100 cases each from the January 1 beginning inventory, the October 15 purchase, and the December 15 purchase.

Determine the costs that should be assigned to ending inventory and cost of goods sold under each of the following assumptions: (1) costs are assigned by the specific identification method; (2) costs are assigned by the average-cost method; (3) costs are assigned by the FIFO method; (4) costs are assigned by the LIFO method. What conclusions can be drawn about the effect of each method on the income statement and the balance sheet of Gary's Parts Shop? Round your answers to the nearest whole number and assume the periodic inventory system.

LO3

Periodic Inventory System and Inventory Costing Methods

E 8. During its first year of operation, Deja Vu Company purchased 5,600 units of a product at $21 per unit. During the second year, it purchased 6,000 units of the same product at $24 per unit. During the third year, it purchased 5,000 units at $30 per unit. Deja Vu Company managed to have an ending inventory each year of 1,000 units. The company uses the periodic inventory system.

Prepare cost of goods sold statements that compare the value of ending inventory and the cost of goods sold for each of the three years using (1) the FIFO inventory costing method and (2) the LIFO method. From the resulting data, what conclusions can you draw about the relationships between the changes in unit price and the changes in the value of ending inventory?

LO3

Periodic Inventory System and Inventory Costing Methods

E 9. In chronological order, the inventory, purchases, and sales of a single product for a recent month are as follows:

			Units	Amount per Unit
June	1	Beginning inventory	150	$ 60
	4	Purchase	400	66
	12	Purchase	800	72
	16	Sale	1,300	120
	24	Purchase	300	78

Using the periodic inventory system, compute the cost of ending inventory, cost of goods sold, and gross margin. Use the following inventory costing methods: average-cost, FIFO, and LIFO. Explain the differences in gross margin produced by the three methods, and round the unit costs to cents and the totals to dollars.

LO4

Effects of Inventory Costing Methods on Cash Flows

E 10. Infinite Products, Inc., sold 120,000 cases of glue at $40 per case during 2010. Its beginning inventory consisted of 20,000 cases at a cost of $24 per case. During 2010, it purchased 60,000 cases at $28 per case and later 50,000 cases at $30 per case. Operating expenses were $1,100,000, and the applicable income tax rate was 30 percent.

Using the periodic inventory system, compute net income using the FIFO method and the LIFO method for costing inventory. Which alternative produces the larger cash flow?

The company is considering a purchase of 10,000 cases at $30 per case just before the year end. What effect on net income and on cash flow will this proposed purchase have under each method? (**Hint:** What are the income tax consequences?)

SO5

Perpetual Inventory System and Inventory Costing Methods

E 11. Referring to the data provided in **E 9** and using the perpetual inventory system, compute the cost of ending inventory, cost of goods sold, and gross margin. Use the average-cost, FIFO, and LIFO inventory costing methods. Explain the reasons for the differences in gross margin produced by the three methods. Round unit costs to cents and totals to dollars.

LO3 SO5

Periodic and Perpetual Systems and Inventory Costing Methods

E 12. During July 2010, Tricoci, Inc., sold 250 units of its product Empire for $4,000. The following units were available:

	Units	Cost
Beginning inventory	100	$ 2
Purchase 1	40	4
Purchase 2	60	6
Purchase 3	150	9
Purchase 4	90	12

A sale of 250 units was made after purchase 3. Of the units sold, 100 came from beginning inventory and 150 came from purchase 3.

Determine the goods available for sale in units and in dollars and ending inventory in units. Then determine the costs that should be assigned to cost of goods sold and ending inventory under each of the following assumptions: (1) Costs are assigned under the periodic inventory system using (a) the specific identification method, (b) the average-cost method, (c) the FIFO method, and (d) the LIFO method. (2) Costs are assigned under the perpetual inventory system using (a) the average-cost method, (b) the FIFO method, and (c) the LIFO method. For each alternative, show the gross margin. Round unit costs to cents and totals to dollars.

SO6

Retail Method

E 13. Olivia's Dress Shop had net retail sales of $125,000 during the current year. The following additional information was obtained from the company's accounting records:

	At Cost	At Retail
Beginning inventory	$ 20,000	$ 30,000
Net purchases (excluding freight-in)	70,000	110,000
Freight-in	5,200	

1. Using the retail method, estimate the company's ending inventory at cost.
2. Assume that a physical inventory taken at year end revealed an inventory on hand of $9,000 at retail value. What is the estimated amount of inventory shrinkage (loss due to theft, damage, etc.) at cost using the retail method?

SO6

Gross Profit Method

E 14. Chen Mo-Wan was at home when he received a call from the fire department telling him his store had burned. His business was a total loss. The insurance company asked him to prove his inventory loss. For the year, until the date of the fire, Chen's company had sales of $900,000 and purchases of $560,000. Freight-in amounted to $27,400, and beginning inventory was $90,000. Chen always priced his goods to achieve a gross margin of 40 percent.

Compute Chen's estimated inventory loss.

Problems

LO1 LO3

Periodic Inventory System and Inventory Costing Methods

P 1. El Faro Company merchandises a single product called Smart. The following data represent beginning inventory and purchases of Smart during the past year: January 1 inventory, 34,000 units at $11.00; February purchases, 40,000 units at $12.00; March purchases, 80,000 units at $12.40; May purchases, 60,000 units at $12.60; July purchases, 100,000 units at $12.80; September purchases, 80,000 units at $12.60; and November purchases, 30,000 units at $13.00. Sales of Smart totaled 393,000 units at $20.00 per unit. Selling and administrative expenses totaled $2,551,000 for the year. El Faro Company uses the periodic inventory system.

Required

1. Prepare a schedule to compute the cost of goods available for sale.
2. Compute income before income taxes under each of the following inventory cost flow assumptions: (a) the average-cost method; (b) the FIFO method; and (c) the LIFO method.
3. Compute inventory turnover and days' inventory on hand under each of the inventory cost flow assumptions listed in requirement **2**. What conclusion can you draw? (User insight ▶)

LO1 LO3

Periodic Inventory System and Inventory Costing Methods

P 2. The inventory of Product PIT and data on purchases and sales for a two-month period follow. The company closes its books at the end of each month. It uses the periodic inventory system.

Apr.	1	Beginning inventory	50 units @ $204
	10	Purchase	100 units @ $220
	17	Sale	90 units
	30	Ending inventory	60 units
May	2	Purchase	100 units @ $216
	14	Purchase	50 units @ $224
	22	Purchase	60 units @ $234
	30	Sale	200 units
	31	Ending inventory	70 units

Required

1. Compute the cost of ending inventory of Product PIT on April 30 and May 31 using the average-cost method. In addition, determine cost of goods sold for April and May. Round unit costs to cents and totals to dollars.
2. Compute the cost of the ending inventory on April 30 and May 31 using the FIFO method. In addition, determine cost of goods sold for April and May.
3. Compute the cost of the ending inventory on April 30 and May 31 using the LIFO method. In addition, determine cost of goods sold for April and May.

User insight ▶ 4. Do the cash flows from operations for April and May differ depending on which inventory costing method is used? Explain.

LO4 SO5

Perpetual Inventory System and Inventory Costing Methods

P 3. Use the data provided in **P 2**, but assume that the company uses the perpetual inventory system. (**Hint:** In preparing the solutions required below, it is helpful to determine the balance of inventory after each transaction, as shown in the Review Problem in this chapter.)

Required

1. Determine the cost of ending inventory and cost of goods sold for April and May using the average-cost method. Round unit costs to cents and totals to dollars.
2. Determine the cost of ending inventory and cost of goods sold for April and May using the FIFO method.
3. Determine the cost of ending inventory and cost of goods sold for April and May using the LIFO method.

User insight ▶ 4. Assume that this company grows for many years in a long period of rising prices. How realistic do you think the balance sheet value for inventory would be and what effect would it have on the inventory turnover ratio?

SO6

Retail Method

P 4. Ptak Company operates a large discount store and uses the retail method to estimate the cost of ending inventory. Management suspects that in recent weeks there have been unusually heavy losses from shoplifting or employee pilferage. To estimate the amount of the loss, the company has taken a physical inventory and will compare the results with the estimated cost of inventory. Data from the accounting records of Ptak Company are as follows:

	At Cost	At Retail
October 1 beginning inventory	$102,976	$148,600
Purchases	143,466	217,000
Purchases returns and allowances	(4,086)	(6,400)
Freight-in	1,900	
Sales		218,366
Sales returns and allowances		(1,866)
October 31 physical inventory at retail		124,900

Required

1. Using the retail method, prepare a schedule to estimate the dollar amount of the store's month-end inventory at cost.
2. Use the store's cost to retail ratio to reduce the retail value of the physical inventory to cost.
3. Calculate the estimated amount of inventory shortage at cost and at retail.

User insight ▶ 4. Many retail chains use the retail method because it is efficient. Why do you think using this method is an efficient way for these companies to operate?

SO6

Gross Profit Method

P 5. Rudy Brothers is a large retail furniture company that operates in two adjacent warehouses. One warehouse is a showroom, and the other is used to store merchandise. On the night of April 22, 2010, a fire broke out in the storage warehouse and destroyed the merchandise stored there. Fortunately, the fire did not reach the showroom, so all the merchandise on display was saved.

Although the company maintained a perpetual inventory system, its records were rather haphazard, and the last reliable physical inventory had been taken on December 31. In addition, there was no control of the flow of goods between the showroom and the warehouse. Thus, it was impossible to tell what goods should have been in either place. As a result, the insurance company required an independent estimate of the amount of loss. The insurance company examiners were satisfied when they received the following information:

Merchandise inventory on December 31, 2009	$ 363,700.00
Purchases, January 1 to April 22, 2010	603,050.00
Purchases returns, January 1 to April 22, 2010	(2,676.50)
Freight-in, January 1 to April 22, 2010	13,275.00
Sales, January 1 to April 22, 2010	989,762.50
Sales returns, January 1 to April 22, 2010	(7,450.00)
Merchandise inventory in showroom on April 22, 2010	100,740.00
Average gross margin	44%

Required

1. Prepare a schedule that estimates the amount of the inventory loss that Rudy Brothers suffered in the fire.

User insight ▶ 2. What are some other reasons management might need to estimate the amount of inventory?

Alternate Problems

LO1 LO3

Periodic Inventory System and Inventory Costing Methods

P 6. The Jarmen Cabinet Company sold 2,200 cabinets during 2010 at $80 per cabinet. Its beginning inventory on January 1 was 130 cabinets at $28. Purchases made during the year were as follows:

February	225 cabinets @ $31.00
April	350 cabinets @ $32.50
June	700 cabinets @ $35.00
August	300 cabinets @ $33.00
October	400 cabinets @ $34.00
November	250 cabinets @ $36.00

The company's selling and administrative expenses for the year were $50,500. The company uses the periodic inventory system.

Required

1. Prepare a schedule to compute the cost of goods available for sale.
2. Compute income before income taxes under each of the following inventory cost flow assumptions: (a) the average-cost method, (b) the FIFO method, and (c) the LIFO method.

User insight ▶

3. Compute inventory turnover and days' inventory on hand under each of the inventory cost flow assumptions in requirement **2**. What conclusion can you draw from this comparison?

LO1 LO3

Periodic Inventory System and Inventory Costing Methods

P 7. The inventory, purchases, and sales of Product CAT for March and April are listed below. The company closes its books at the end of each month. It uses the periodic inventory system.

Mar.	1	Beginning inventory	60 units @ $98
	10	Purchase	100 units @ $104
	19	Sale	90 units
	31	Ending inventory	70 units
Apr.	4	Purchase	120 units @ $106
	15	Purchase	50 units @ $108
	23	Sale	200 units
	25	Purchase	100 units @ $110
	30	Ending inventory	140 units

Required

1. Compute the cost of the ending inventory on March 31 and April 30 using the average-cost method. In addition, determine cost of goods sold for March and April. Round unit costs to cents and totals to dollars.
2. Compute the cost of the ending inventory on March 31 and April 30 using the FIFO method. Also determine cost of goods sold for March and April.
3. Compute the cost of the ending inventory on March 31 and April 30 using the LIFO method. Also determine cost of goods sold for March and April.

User insight ▶

4. Do the cash flows from operations for March and April differ depending on which inventory costing method is used—average-cost, FIFO, or LIFO? Explain.

Perpetual Inventory System and Inventory Costing Methods

P 8. Use the data provided in **P 7**, but assume that the company uses the perpetual inventory system. (**Hint:** In preparing the solutions required below, it is helpful to determine the balance of inventory after each transaction, as shown in the Review Problem in this chapter.)

Required

1. Determine the cost of ending inventory and cost of goods sold for March and April using the average-cost method. Round unit costs to cents and totals to dollars.
2. Determine the cost of ending inventory and cost of goods sold for March and April using the FIFO method.
3. Determine the cost of ending inventory and cost of goods sold for March and April using the LIFO method.

User insight ▶ 4. Assume that this company grows for many years in a long period of rising prices. How realistic do you think the balance sheet value for inventory would be and what effect would it have on the inventory turnover ratio?

ENHANCING Your Knowledge, Skills, and Critical Thinking

Conceptual Understanding Cases

LO1 **Evaluation of Inventory Levels**

C 1. J. C. Penney, a large retail company with many stores, has an inventory turnover of 3.7 times. **Dell Computer Corporation**, an Internet mail-order company, has an inventory turnover of 77.8. Dell achieves its high turnover through supply-chain management in a just-in-time operating environment. Why is inventory turnover important to companies like J. C. Penney and Dell? Why are comparisons among companies important? Are J. C. Penney and Dell a good match for comparison? Describe supply-chain management and a just-in-time operating environment. Why are they important to achieving a favorable inventory turnover?

LO1 **Misstatement of Inventory**

C 2. Crazy Eddie, Inc., a discount consumer electronics chain, seemed to be missing \$52 million in merchandise inventory. "It was a shock," the new management was quoted as saying. It was also one of the nation's largest swindles. Investors lost \$145.6 million when the company declared bankruptcy. A count turned up only \$75 million in inventory, compared with \$126.7 million reported by former management. Net sales could account for only \$6.7 million of the difference. At the time, it was not clear whether bookkeeping errors in prior years or an actual physical loss created the shortfall, although at least one store manager felt it was a bookkeeping error because security was strong. "It would be hard for someone to steal anything," he said. Former management was eventually fined \$72.7 million.[11]

1. What is the effect of the misstatement of inventory on Crazy Eddie's reported earnings in prior accounting periods?
2. Is this a situation you would expect in a company that is experiencing financial difficulty? Explain.

LO4 **LIFO Inventory Method**

C 3. Seventy-six percent of chemical companies use the LIFO inventory method for the costing of inventories, whereas only 11 percent of computer equipment companies use LIFO.[12]

Describe the LIFO inventory method. What effects does it have on reported income, cash flows, and income taxes during periods of price changes? Why do you think so many chemical companies use LIFO while most companies in the computer industry do not?

Interpreting Financial Reports

LO2 **LCM and Conservatism**

C 4. Exxon Mobil Corporation, the world's largest company, uses the LIFO inventory method for most of its inventories. Its inventory costs are heavily dependent on the cost of oil. In a recent year when the price of oil was down, Exxon Mobil, following the lower-of-cost-or-market (LCM) rule, wrote down its inventory by $325 million. In the next year, when the price of oil recovered, the company reported that market price exceeded the LIFO carrying values by $6.8 billion.[13] Explain why the LCM rule resulted in a write-down in the first year. What is the inconsistency between the first- and second-year treatments of the change in the price of oil? How does the accounting convention of conservatism explain the inconsistency? If the price of oil declined substantially in a third year, what would be the likely consequence?

LO1 LO4

FIFO and LIFO

C 5. Exxon Mobil Corporation had net income of $39.5 billion in 2006. Inventories under the LIFO method used by the company were $9.0 billion in 2006. Inventory would have been $15.9 billion higher if the company had used FIFO.[14] Why do you suppose Exxon Mobil's management chooses to use the LIFO inventory method? On what economic conditions, if any, do those reasons depend?

Decision Analysis Using Excel

LO3 LO4

FIFO versus LIFO Analysis

C 6. Semi Truck Sales Company (STS Company) buys large trucks from the manufacturer and sells them to companies and independent truckers who haul goods over long distances. STS has been successful in this niche of the industry. Because of the high cost of the trucks and of financing inventory, STS tries to maintain as small an inventory as possible. In fact, at the beginning of July the company had no inventory or liabilities, as shown on the balance sheet below.

On July 9, STS took delivery of a truck at a price of $150,000. On July 19, an identical truck was delivered to the company at a price of $160,000. On July 28, the company sold one of the trucks for $195,000. During July, expenses totaled $15,000. All transactions were paid in cash.

STS Company
Balance Sheet
July 1, 2010

Assets		Stockholders' Equity	
Cash	$400,000	Common stock	$400,000
Total assets	$400,000	Total stockholders' equity	$400,000

1. Prepare income statements and balance sheets for STS on July 31 using (a) the FIFO method of inventory valuation and (b) the LIFO method of inventory valuation. Assume an income tax rate of 40 percent. Explain the effects of each method on the financial statements.
2. Assume that the management of STS Company has a policy of declaring a cash dividend each period that is exactly equal to net income. What effects does this action have on each balance sheet prepared in requirement 1? How do the resulting balance sheets compare with the balance sheet at the beginning of the month? Which inventory method, if either, do you feel is more realistic in representing STS's income?
3. Assume that STS receives notice of another price increase of $10,000 on trucks, to take effect on August 1. How does this information relate to management's dividend policy, and how will it affect next month's operations?

Annual Report Case: CVS Caremark Corporation

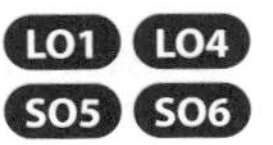

Inventory Costing Methods and Ratios

C 7. Refer to the note related to inventories in the **CVS** annual report in the Supplement to Chapter 1 to answer the following questions: What inventory method(s) does CVS use? If LIFO inventories had been valued at FIFO, why would there be no difference? Do you think many of the company's inventories are valued at market? Why or why not? Few companies use the retail method, so why do you think CVS uses it? Compute and compare the inventory turnover and days' inventory on hand for CVS for 2007 and 2006. Ending 2005 inventories were $6,484.8 million.

Comparison Case: CVS Versus Walgreens

Inventory Efficiency

C 8. Refer to **CVS's** annual report in the Supplement to Chapter 1 and to the following data (in millions) for **Walgreens**: cost of goods sold, $38,518.1 and $34,240.4 for 2007 and 2006, respectively; inventories, $6,790.5, $6,050.4 and $5,674.7 for 2007, 2006, and 2005, respectively. Ending inventories for 2005 for CVS were $6,484.8 million.

Calculate inventory turnover and days' inventory on hand for 2007 and 2006. If you did C 7, refer to your answer there for CVS. Has either company improved its performance over the past two years? What advantage does the superior company's performance provide to it? Which company appears to make the most efficient use of inventories? Explain your answers.

Ethical Dilemma Case

Inventories, Income Determination, and Ethics

C 9. Jazz, Inc., which has a December 31 year end, designs and sells fashions for young professional women. Lyla Hilton, president of the company, fears that the forecasted 2010 profitability goals will not be reached. She is pleased when Jazz receives a large order on December 30 from The Executive Woman, a retail chain of upscale stores for businesswomen. Hilton immediately directs the controller to record the sale, which represents 13 percent of Jazz's annual sales. At the same time, she directs the inventory control department not to separate the goods for shipment until after January 1. Separated goods are not included in inventory because they have been sold.

On December 31, the company's auditors arrive to observe the year-end taking of the physical inventory under the periodic inventory system. How will Hilton's actions affect Jazz's 2010 profitability? How will they affect Jazz's 2011 profitability? Were Hilton's actions ethical? Why or why not?

Internet Case

Effect of LIFO on Income and Cash Flows

C 10. **Maytag Corporation**, an appliance manufacturer, uses the LIFO inventory method. Go to its website and select "About Maytag." Then select "Financial Center." After finding the income statement and inventory note, calculate what net income would have been had the company used FIFO. Calculate how much cash the company saved for the year and cumulatively by using LIFO. What is the difference between the LIFO and FIFO gross margin and profit margin results? Which reporting alternative is better for the company?

Group Activity Case

LO2 LO4

Retail Business Inventories

C 11. Assign teams to various types of stores in your community—a grocery, clothing, book, music, or appliance store. Make an appointment to interview the manager for 30 minutes to discuss the company's inventory accounting system. The store may be a branch of a larger company. Ask the following questions, summarize your findings in a paper, and be prepared to discuss your results in class:

1. What is the physical flow of merchandise into the store, and what documents are used in connection with this flow?
2. What documents are prepared when merchandise is sold?
3. Does the store keep perpetual inventory records? If so, does it keep the records in units only, or does it keep track of cost as well? If not, what system does the store use?
4. How often does the company take a physical inventory?
5. How are financial statements generated for the store?
6. What inventory method does the company use to cost its inventory for financial statements?

Business Communication Case

LO1 LO2 LO3

Inventory Ratio Analysis

C 12. Yamaha Corporation and **Pioneer Corporation** are two large, diversified Japanese electronics companies. Both use the average-cost method and the lower-of-cost-or-market rule to account for inventories. The following data are for their 2007 fiscal years (in millions of yen):[15]

	Yamaha	Pioneer
Beginning inventory	¥ 25,815	¥104,226
Ending inventory	26,788	105,331
Cost of goods sold	244,594	614,444

Assume you have been asked to analyze the inventory efficiency of the two companies. Prepare a memorandum to your boss that compares the inventory efficiency of Yamaha and Pioneer by computing the inventory turnover and days' inventory on hand for both companies in 2007. Show and comment on the relative efficiency of the two companies. Also comment on how the inventory method would affect your evaluation if you were to compare Yamaha and Pioneer to each other and to a U.S. company given the fact that most companies in the United States use the LIFO inventory method. Mention what could be done to make the results comparable.

CHAPTER

7 Cash and Receivables

Focus on Financial Statements

INCOME STATEMENT
Revenues
– Expenses
= Net Income

STATEMENT OF RETAINED EARNINGS
Opening Balance
+ Net Income
– Dividends
= Retained Earnings

BALANCE SHEET
Assets | Liabilities
Equity
A = L + E

STATEMENT OF CASH FLOWS
Operating activities
+ Investing activities
+ Financing activities
= Change in Cash
+ Starting Balance
= Ending Cash Balance

Valuation of accounts receivable on the balance sheet is linked to measurement of uncollectible accounts expense on the income statement.

Cash and receivables require careful oversight to ensure that they are ethically handled. If cash is mismanaged or stolen, it can bring about the downfall of a business. Because accounts receivable and notes receivable require estimates of future losses, they can be easily manipulated to show improvement in reported earnings. Improved earnings can, of course, enhance a company's stock price, as well as the bonuses of its executives. In this chapter, we address the management of cash and demonstrate the importance of estimates in accounting for receivables.

LEARNING OBJECTIVES

LO1 **Identify and explain the management and ethical issues related to cash and receivables.** *(pp. 382–389)*

LO2 **Define *cash equivalents*, and explain methods of controlling cash, including bank reconciliations.** *(pp. 390–394)*

LO3 **Apply the allowance method of accounting for uncollectible accounts.** *(pp. 394–401)*

LO4 **Define *promissory note*, and make common calculations for promissory notes receivable.** *(pp. 401–404)*

DECISION POINT ▶ A USER'S FOCUS

- How can the company control its cash needs?
- How can the company evaluate credit policies and the level of its receivables?
- How should the company estimate the value of its receivables?

Nike, Inc.

Nike, one of the world's largest and best-known athletic sportswear companies, must give the retail stores that buy its products time to pay for their purchases. At the same time, however, Nike must have enough cash on hand to pay its suppliers. As you can see in Nike's Financial Highlights, cash and accounts receivable have made up roughly 50 percent of its current assets in recent years.[1] The company must therefore plan and control its cash flows very carefully.

NIKE'S FINANCIAL HIGHLIGHTS
(In millions)

	2007	2006	2005
Cash	$ 1,856.7	$ 954.2	$ 1,388.1
Accounts receivable, net	2,494.7	2,382.9	2,468.0
Total current assets	8,076.5	7,346.0	7,234.7
Net sales	16,325.9	14,954.9	17,739.7

Management Issues Related to Cash and Receivables

LO1 Identify and explain the management and ethical issues related to cash and receivables.

The management of cash and accounts and notes receivable is critical to maintaining adequate liquidity. These assets are important components of the operating cycle, which also includes inventories and accounts payable. In dealing with cash and receivables, management must address five key issues: managing cash needs, setting credit policies, evaluating the level of accounts receivable, financing receivables, and making ethical estimates of credit losses.

Cash Management

On the balance sheet, **cash** usually consists of currency and coins on hand, checks and money orders from customers, and deposits in checking and savings accounts. Cash is the most liquid of all assets and the most readily available to pay debts. It is central to the operating cycle because all operating transactions eventually use or generate cash.

Cash may include a *compensating balance*, an amount that is not entirely free to be spent. A **compensating balance** is a minimum amount that a bank requires a company to keep in its bank account as part of a credit-granting arrangement. Such an arrangement restricts cash; in effect, it increases the interest on the loan and reduces a company's liquidity. The Securities and Exchange Commission therefore requires companies that have compensating balances to disclose the amounts involved.

Most companies experience seasonal cycles of business activity during the year. During some periods, sales are weak; during others, they are strong. There are also periods when expenditures are high, and periods when they are low. For toy companies, college textbook publishers, amusement parks, construction companies, and manufacturers of sports equipment, the cycles are dramatic, but all companies experience them to some degree.

Seasonal cycles require careful planning of cash inflows, cash outflows, borrowing, and investing. Figure 1 shows the seasonal cycles typical of an athletic sportswear company like **Nike**. As you can see, cash receipts from sales are highest in the late spring, summer, and fall because that is when most people engage in outdoor sports. Sales are relatively low in the winter months. On the other hand, cash expenditures are highest in late winter and spring as the company builds up inventory for spring and summer selling. During the late summer, fall, and winter, the company has excess cash on hand that it needs to invest in a way

FOCUS ON BUSINESS PRACTICE

How Do Good Companies Deal with Bad Times?

Good companies manage their cash well even in bad times. When a slump in the technology market caused **Texas Instrument's** sales to decline by more than 40 percent, resulting in a loss of nearly $120 million, this large electronics firm actually increased its cash by acting quickly to cut its purchases of plant assets by two-thirds. It also reduced its payroll and lowered the average number of days it had inventory on hand from 71 to 58.[2]

In similar circumstances, some companies have not reacted as quickly as Texas Instruments. For example, before 9/11, the Big Three automakers—**General Motors**, **Ford**, and **DaimlerChrysler**—were awash in cash. However, in little over a year, the three companies went through $28 billion in cash through various purchases, losses, dividends, and share buybacks. Then, with increasing losses from rising costs, big rebates, and zero percent financing, they were suddenly faced with a shortage of cash. As a result, Standard & Poor's lowered their credit ratings, which raises the interest cost of borrowing money. Perhaps the Big Three should have held on to some of that cash.[3]

FIGURE 1

Seasonal Cycles and Cash Requirements for an Athletic Sportswear Company

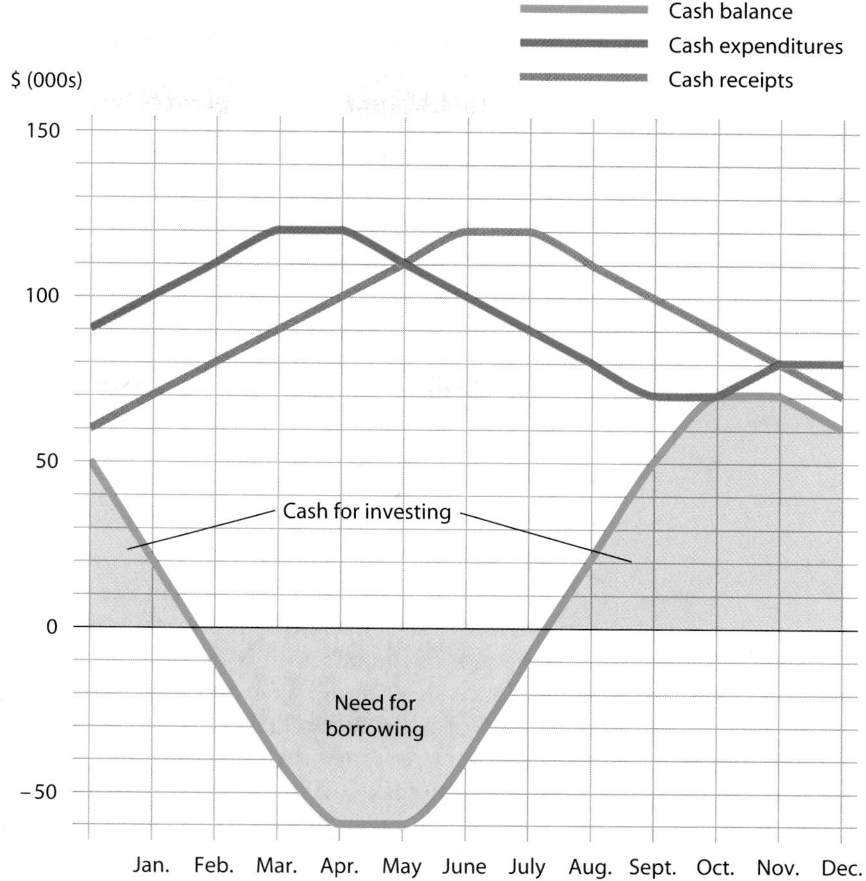

that will earn a return but still permit access to cash as needed. During late spring and early summer, the company needs to plan for short-term borrowing to tide it over until cash receipts pick up later in the year.

Accounts Receivable and Credit Policies

Like cash, accounts receivable and notes receivable are major types of **short-term financial assets**. Both kinds of receivables result from extending credit to individual customers or to other companies. Retailers like **Sears** (now merged with **Kmart**) have made credit available to nearly every responsible person in the United States. Every field of retail trade has expanded by allowing customers to make payments a month or more after the date of sale. What is not so apparent is that credit has expanded even more among wholesalers and manufacturers like **Nike** than at the retail level. Figure 2 shows the levels of accounts receivable in selected industries.

As we have indicated, **accounts receivable** are the short-term financial assets of a wholesaler or retailer that arise from sales on credit. This type of credit is often called **trade credit**. Terms of trade credit usually range from 5 to 60 days, depending on industry practice. For some companies that sell to consumers, **installment accounts receivable**, which allow the buyer to make a series of time payments, constitute a significant portion of accounts receivable. Department stores, appliance stores, furniture stores, used car dealers, and other retail businesses often offer installment credit. The installment accounts receivable of retailers like **Sears** and **J. C. Penney** can amount to millions of dollars. Although the payment period may be 24 months or more, installment accounts receivable are classified as current assets if such credit policies are customary in the industry.

FIGURE 2

Accounts Receivable as a Percentage of Total Assets for Selected Industries

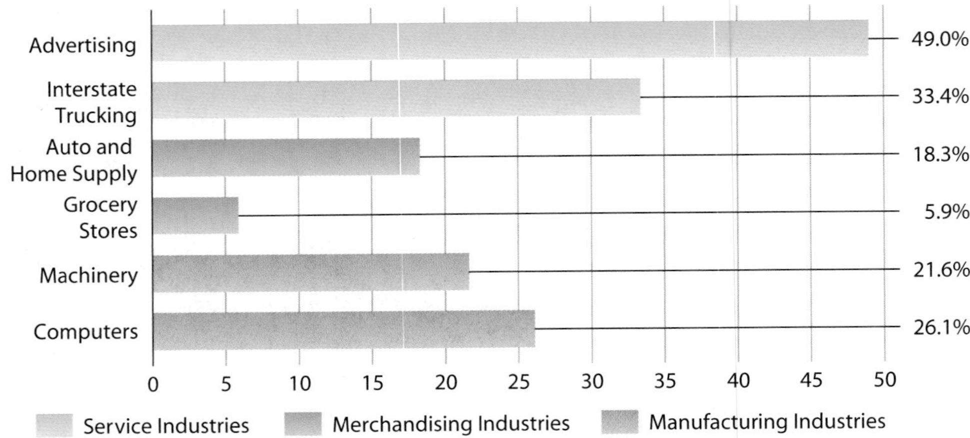

Source: **Data from Dun & Bradstreet, *Industry Norms and Key Business Ratios,* 2005–2006.**

On the balance sheet, *accounts receivable* designates amounts arising from credit sales made to customers in the ordinary course of business. Because loans or credit sales made to employees, officers, or owners of the corporation increase the risk of uncollectibility and conflict of interest, they appear separately on the balance sheet under asset titles like *receivables from employees.*

Normally, individual accounts receivable have debit balances, but sometimes customers overpay their accounts either by mistake or in anticipation of making future purchases. When these accounts show credit balances, the company should show the total credits on its balance sheet as a current liability. The reason for this is that if the customers make no future purchases, the company will have to grant them refunds.

Companies that sell on credit do so to be competitive and to increase sales. In setting credit terms, a company must keep in mind the credit terms of its competitors and the needs of its customers. Obviously, any company that sells on credit wants customers who will pay their bills on time. To increase the likelihood of selling only to customers who will pay on time, most companies develop control procedures and maintain a credit department. The credit department's responsibilities include examining each person or company that applies for credit and approving or rejecting a credit sale to that customer. Typically, the credit department asks for information about the customer's financial resources and debts. It may also check personal references and credit bureaus for further information. Then, based on the information it has gathered, it decides whether to extend credit to the customer.

Companies that are too lenient in granting credit can run into difficulties when customers don't pay. For example, **Sprint**, one of the weaker companies in the highly competitive cell phone industry, targeted customers with poor credit histories. It attracted so many who failed to pay their bills that its stock dropped by 50 percent to $2.50 because of the losses that resulted.[4]

Evaluating the Level of Accounts Receivable

Two common measures of the effect of a company's credit policies are receivable turnover and days' sales uncollected. The **receivable turnover** shows how many times, on average, a company turned its receivables into cash during an accounting period. This measure reflects the relative size of a company's accounts receivable and the success of its credit and collection policies. It may also be affected by external factors, such as seasonal conditions and interest rates. **Days' sales uncollected** is a related measure that shows, on average, how long it takes to collect accounts receivable.

The receivable turnover is computed by dividing net sales by average accounts receivable (net of allowances). Theoretically, the numerator should be net credit sales, but the amount of net credit sales is rarely available in public reports, so investors use total net sales. Using data from **Nike's** Financial Highlights at the beginning of the chapter, we can compute the company's receivable turnover as follows (dollar amounts are in millions):

K/R

$$\text{Receivable Turnover} = \frac{\text{Net Sales}}{\text{Average Accounts Receivable}}$$

$$= \frac{\$16{,}325.9}{(\$2{,}494.7 + \$2{,}382.9) \div 2}$$

$$= \frac{\$16{,}325.9}{\$2{,}438.8} = 6.7 \text{ times}$$

To find days' sales uncollected, the number of days in a year is divided by the receivable turnover, as follows:

K/R

$$\text{Days' Sales Uncollected} = \frac{365 \text{ days}}{\text{Receivable Turnover}} = \frac{365 \text{ days}}{6.7 \text{ times}} = 54.5 \text{ days}$$

Thus, Nike turned its receivables 6.7 times a year, or an average of every 54.5 days. A turnover period of this length is not unusual among apparel companies because their credit terms allow retail outlets time to sell products before paying for them. However, it is longer than the turnover period of many companies in other industries. To interpret a company's ratios, you must take into consideration the norms of the industry in which it operates.

As Figure 3 shows, the receivable turnover ratio varies substantially from industry to industry. Because grocery stores have few receivables, they have a very quick turnover. The turnover in interstate trucking is 9.9 times because the typical credit terms in that industry are 30 days. The turnover in the machinery and computer industries is lower because those industries tend to have longer credit terms.

Figure 4 shows the days' sales uncollected for the industries listed in Figure 3. Grocery stores, which have the lowest ratio (4.3 days) require the least amount of receivables financing; the computer industry, with days' sales uncollected of 58.9 days, requires the most.

Study Note

For many businesses with seasonal sales activity, such as **Nordstrom, Dillard's, Marshall Field's,** and **Macy's,** the fourth quarter produces more than 25 percent of annual sales. For these businesses, receivables are highest at the balance sheet date, resulting in an artificially low receivable turnover and high days' sales uncollected.

FIGURE 3

Receivable Turnover for Selected Industries

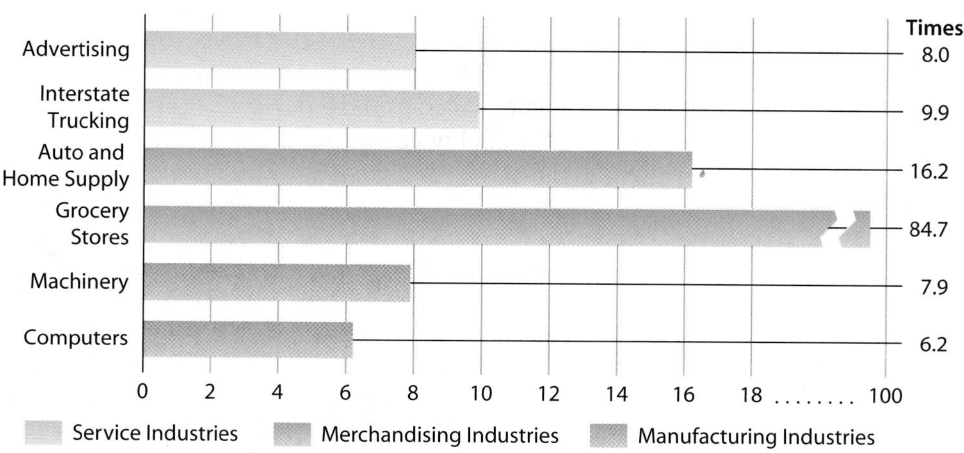

Source: Data from Dun & Bradstreet, *Industry Norms and Key Business Ratios,* 2005–2006.

FIGURE 4
Days' Sales Uncollected for Selected Industries

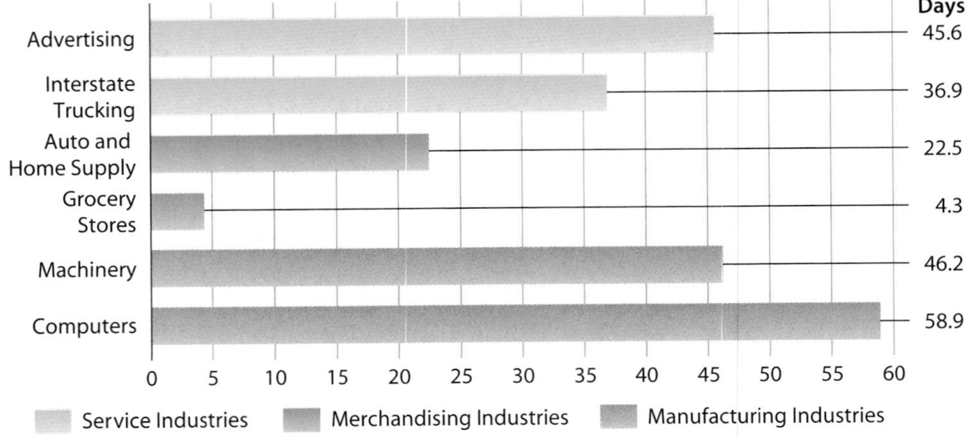

Source: Data from Dun & Bradstreet, *Industry Norms and Key Business Ratios,* 2005–2006.

Financing Receivables

Financial flexibility is important to most companies. Companies that have significant amounts of assets tied up in accounts receivable may be unwilling or unable to wait until they collect cash from their receivables. Many corporations have set up finance companies to help their customers pay for the purchase of their products. For example, **Ford** has set up Ford Motor Credit Company (FMCC), **General Motors** has set up General Motors Acceptance Corporation (GMAC), and **Sears** has set up Sears Roebuck Acceptance Corporation (SRAC). Other companies borrow funds by pledging their accounts receivable as collateral. If a company does not pay back its loan, the creditor can take the collateral (in this case, the accounts receivable) and convert it to cash to satisfy the loan.

Study Note
A company that factors its receivables will have a better receivable turnover and days' sales uncollected than a company that does not factor them.

Companies can also raise funds by selling or transferring accounts receivable to another entity, called a **factor**, as illustrated in Figure 5. The sale or transfer of accounts receivable, called **factoring**, can be done with or without recourse. *With recourse* means that the seller of the receivables is liable to the factor (i.e., the purchaser) if a receivable cannot be collected. *Without recourse* means that the factor bears any losses from unpaid accounts. A company's acceptance of credit cards like Visa, MasterCard, or American Express is an example of factoring without recourse because the issuers of the cards accept the risk of nonpayment.

FOCUS ON BUSINESS PRACTICE

How Do Powerful Buyers Cause Problems for Small Suppliers?

Big buyers often have significant power over small suppliers, and their cash management decisions can cause severe cash flow problems for the little companies that depend on them. For instance, in an effort to control costs and optimize cash flow, **Ameritech Corp**. told 70,000 suppliers that it would begin paying its bills in 45 days instead of 30. Other large companies routinely take 90 days or more to pay. Some small suppliers are so anxious to get the big companies' business that they fail to realize the implications of the deals they make until it is too late. When **Earthly Elements, Inc.**, accepted a $10,000 order for dried floral gifts from a national home shopping network, its management was ecstatic because the deal increased sales by 25 percent. But in four months, the resulting cash crunch forced the company to close down. When the shopping network finally paid for the order six months later, it was too late to revive Earthly Elements.[5]

FIGURE 5
How Factoring Works

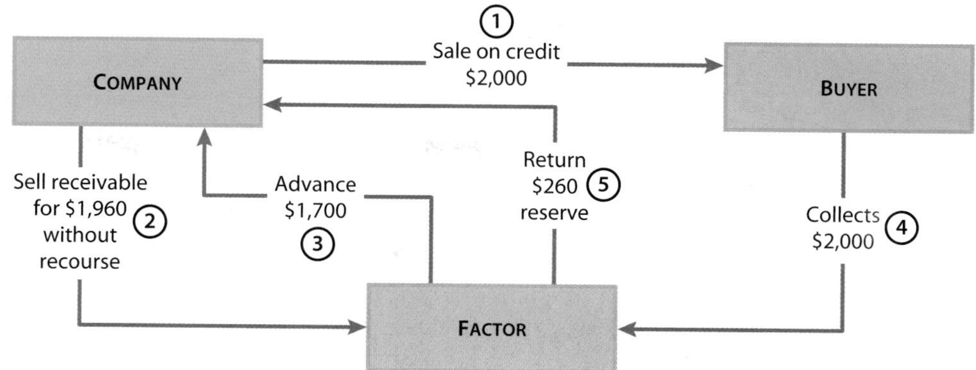

Note: Factor will keep $260 reserve if buyer does not pay.

The factor, of course, charges a fee for its service. The fee for sales with recourse is usually about 2 percent of the accounts receivable. The fee is higher for sales without recourse because the factor's risk is greater. In accounting terminology, a seller of receivables with recourse is said to be contingently liable. A **contingent liability** is a potential liability that can develop into a real liability if a particular event occurs. In this case, the event would be a customer's nonpayment of a receivable. A contingent liability generally requires disclosure in the notes to the financial statements.

Nike does not factor or otherwise directly finance its receivables, but **Circuit City Stores**, one of the nation's largest electronics and appliance retailers, does. To promote sales, Circuit City offers generous terms through its installment programs, under which customers pay over a number of months. However, because of its rapid growth, the company needs the cash from these installment receivables sooner than the customers have agreed to pay. To generate cash immediately from these receivables, Circuit City sells them through a process called *securitization*.

Under **securitization**, a company groups its receivables in batches and sells them at a discount to companies and investors. When the receivables are paid, the buyers get the full amount; their profit depends on the amount of the discount. Circuit City sells all its receivables without recourse, which means that after it sells

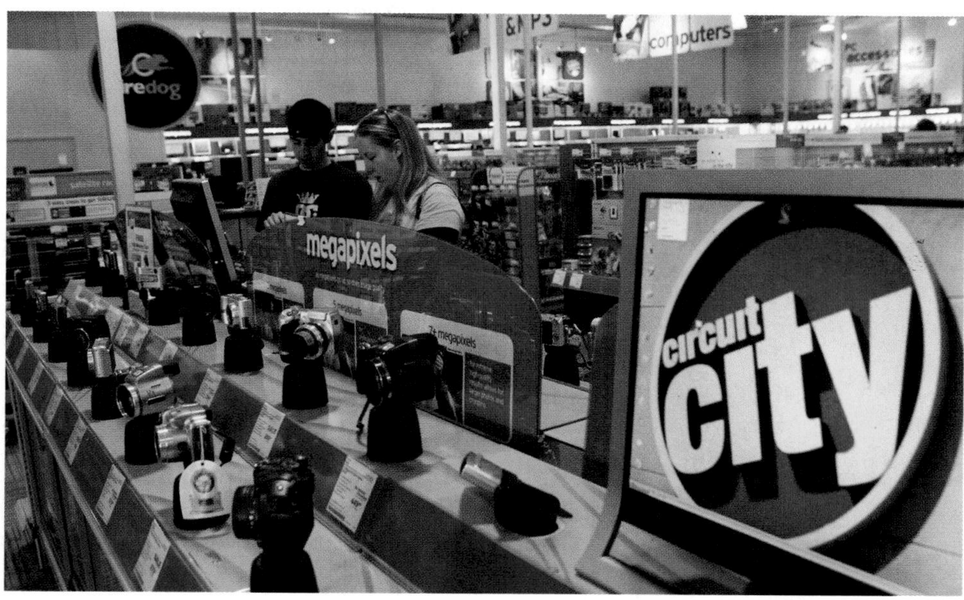

To encourage sales, Circuit City offers installment programs, under which customers pay over time. When the company needs cash from these installment receivables sooner than customers have agreed to pay, Circuit City sells the receivables in batches at a discount to companies and investors—a process called *securitization*.

FOCUS ON BUSINESS PRACTICE

Why Are Subprime Loans Bad?

Although subprime loans (home loans to individuals with poor credit ratings and low incomes) represent only a small portion of the mortgage loan market, they have caused huge problems in the real estate market in recent years. These loans are a form of securitization in that they are batched together and sold in units as safe investments, when in fact they are quite risky. As just one of many examples, when people by the thousands were unable to keep up with their mortgage payments, the investments were marked down to their fair value. This loss of value led to the demise of such venerable firms as Lehman Brothers, the sale of Merrill Lynch, and ultimately to a massive government bailout.[6]

them, it has no further liability, even if no customers were to pay. If Circuit City sold its receivables with recourse and a customer did not pay, it would have to make good on the debt.[7]

Another method of financing receivables is to sell promissory notes held as notes receivable to a financial lender, usually a bank. This practice is called **discounting** because the bank derives its profit by deducting the interest from the maturity value of the note. The holder of the note (usually the payee) endorses the note and turns it over it to the bank. The bank expects to collect the maturity value of the note (principal plus interest) on the maturity date, but it also has recourse against the note's endorser.

For example, if Company X holds a $20,000 note from Company Z and the note will pay $1,200 in interest, a bank may be willing to buy the note for $19,200. If Company Z pays, the bank will receive $21,200 at maturity and realize a $2,000 profit. If it fails to pay, Company X is liable to the bank for payment. In the meantime, Company X has a contingent liability in the amount of the discounted note plus interest that it must disclose in the notes to its financial statements.

Ethics and Estimates in Accounting for Receivables

As we have noted, companies extend credit to customers because they expect it will increase their sales and earnings, but they know they will always have some credit customers who cannot or will not pay. The accounts of such customers are called **uncollectible accounts**, or *bad debts*, and they are expenses of selling on credit. To match these expenses, or losses, to the revenues they help generate, they should be recognized at the time credit sales are made.

Of course, at the time a company makes credit sales, it cannot identify which customers will not pay their bills, nor can it predict the exact amount of money it will lose. Therefore, to adhere to the matching rule, it must estimate losses from uncollectible accounts. The estimate becomes an expense in the fiscal year in which the sales are made.

Because the amount of uncollectible accounts can only be estimated and the exact amount will not be known until later, a company's earnings can be easily manipulated. Earnings can be overstated by underestimating the amount of losses from uncollectible accounts and understated by overestimating the amount of the losses. Misstatements of earnings can occur simply because of a bad estimate. But, as we have noted, they can be deliberately made to meet analysts' estimates of earnings, reduce income taxes, or meet benchmarks for bonuses.

Among the many examples of unethical or questionable practices in dealing with uncollectible accounts are the following:

- **WorldCom** (now **MCI**) increased revenues and hid losses by continuing to bill customers for service for years after the customers had quit paying.
- The policy of **Household International**, a large personal finance company, seems to be flexible about when to declare loans delinquent. As a result, the company can vary its estimates of uncollectible accounts from year to year.[8]
- By making large allowances for estimated uncollectible accounts and then gradually reducing them, **Bank One** improved its earnings over several years.[9]
- **HealthSouth** manipulated its income by varying its estimates of the difference between what it charged patients and what it could collect from insurance companies.[10]

Companies with high ethical standards try to be accurate in their estimates of uncollectible accounts, and they disclose the basis of their estimates. For example, **Nike's** management describes its estimates as follows:

> We make ongoing estimates relating to the collectibility of our accounts receivables and maintain an allowance for estimated losses resulting from the inability of our customers to make required payments. In determining the amount of the allowance, we consider our historical level of credit losses and make judgments about the creditworthiness of significant customers based on ongoing credit evaluations. Since we cannot predict future changes in the financial stability of our customers, actual future losses from uncollectible accounts may differ from our estimates.[11]

STOP ► REVIEW ► APPLY

LO1-1 **What items are included in the Cash account? What is a compensating balance?**

LO1-2 **Why does a company sell on credit if it expects that some of its accounts receivable will not be paid? What role does a credit department play in selling on credit?**

LO1-3 **Indicate which of the following items should be included in accounts receivable on the balance sheet (if an item does not belong there, indicate where on the balance sheet it should appear): (a) installment accounts receivable from regular customers, due monthly for three years; (b) debit balances in customers' accounts; (c) receivables from employees; (d) credit balances in customers' accounts; and (e) receivables from officers of the company.**

LO1-4 **How does the receivable turnover ratio help in evaluating the level of receivables?**

LO1-5 **What is a factor, and what do the terms *factoring with recourse* and *factoring without recourse* mean?**

LO1-6 **How is accounting for receivables susceptible to unethical financial reporting?**

Suggested answers to all Stop, Review, and Apply questions follow the appendixes.

Cash Equivalents and Cash Control

LO2 Define *cash equivalents*, and explain methods of controlling cash, including bank reconciliations.

Study Note

The statement of cash flows explains the change in the balance of cash and cash equivalents from one accounting period to the next.

Cash Equivalents

As we noted earlier, cash is the asset most readily available to pay debts, but at times a company may have more cash on hand than it needs to pay its debts. Excess cash should not remain idle, especially during periods of high interest rates. Management may decide to invest the excess cash in short-term interest-bearing accounts or certificates of deposit (CDs) at banks and other financial institutions, in government securities (such as U.S. Treasury notes), or in other securities. If these investments have a term of 90 days or less when they are purchased, they are called **cash equivalents** because the funds revert to cash so quickly they are treated as cash on the balance sheet.

Nike describes its treatment of cash and cash equivalents as follows:

> Cash and equivalents represent cash and short-term, highly liquid investments with maturities of three months or less at date of purchase. The carrying amounts reflected in the consolidated balance sheet for cash and equivalents approximate fair value.[12]

According to a recent survey of 600 large U.S. corporations, 6 percent use the term *cash* as the balance sheet caption, and 89 percent use either *cash and cash equivalents* or *cash and equivalents.* The rest either combine cash with marketable securities or have no cash.[13]

Fair Value of Cash and Cash Equivalents

Cash and cash equivalents are financial instruments that are valued at fair value. In most cases the amount recorded in the records approximates fair value, and most businesses and other entities consider cash equivalents to be very safe investments. Companies often invest these funds in money market funds to earn interest with cash when they don't need cash for current operations. Money market funds usually invest in very safe securities, such as commercial paper, which is short-term debt of other entities. Although money market funds are not guaranteed, investors do not expect losses on these investments. However, in recent years a few of these funds invested in batches of subprime mortgages in an attempt to earn a little higher interest rate. The result has been traumatic for all parties. **Bank of America**, for instance, shut down its $34 billion Columbia Strategic Cash Portfolio money market fund when investors pulled out $21 billion because the fund was losing so much money from investing in subprime loans.[14]

Cash Control Methods

In an earlier chapter, we discussed the concept of internal control and how it applies to cash transactions. Here, we address three additional ways of controlling cash: imprest systems; banking services, including electronic funds transfer; and bank reconciliations.

Imprest Systems Most companies need to keep some currency and coins on hand. Currency and coins are needed for cash registers, for paying expenses that are impractical to pay by check, and for situations that require cash advances—for example, when sales representatives need cash for travel expenses. One way to control a cash fund and cash advances is by using an **imprest system**.

A common form of imprest system is a petty cash fund, which is established at a fixed amount. A receipt documents each cash payment made from the fund. The fund is periodically reimbursed, based on the documented expenditures, by the exact amount necessary to restore its original cash balance. The person responsible for the petty cash fund must always be able to account for its contents by showing that total cash and receipts equal the original fixed amount.

Banking Services All businesses rely on banks to control cash receipts and cash disbursements. Banks serve as safe depositories for cash, negotiable instruments, and other valuable business documents, such as stocks and bonds. The checking accounts that banks provide improve control by minimizing the amount of currency a company needs to keep on hand and by supplying permanent records of all cash payments. Banks also serve as agents in a variety of transactions, such as the collection and payment of certain kinds of debts and the exchange of foreign currencies.

> **Study Note**
> Periodically, banks detect individuals who are *kiting*. Kiting is the illegal issuing of checks when there is insufficient money to cover them. Before one kited check clears the bank, a kited check from another account is deposited to cover it, making an endless circle.

Electronic funds transfer (EFT) is a method of conducting business transactions that does not involve the actual transfer of cash. With EFT, a company electronically transfers cash from its bank to another company's bank. For the banks, the electronic transfer is simply a bookkeeping entry. Companies today rely heavily on this method of payment. **Wal-Mart**, for example, makes 75 percent of its payments to suppliers through EFT.

Because of EFT and other electronic banking services, we are rapidly becoming a cashless society. Automated teller machines (ATMs) allow bank customers to make deposits, withdraw cash, transfer funds among accounts, and pay bills. Large consumer banks like **Citibank**, **Chase**, and **Bank of America** process hundreds of thousands of ATM transactions each week. Many banks also give customers the option of paying bills over the telephone and with *debit cards*. In 2007, debit cards accounted for more than $1 trillion in transactions.[15] When a customer makes a retail purchase using a debit card, the amount of the purchase is deducted directly from the buyer's bank account. The bank usually documents debit card transactions for the retailer, but the retailer must develop new internal controls to ensure that the transactions are recorded properly and that unauthorized transfers do not occur. It is expected that within a few years, a majority of all retail activity will be handled electronically.

> **Study Note**
> The ending balance on a company's bank statement does not represent the amount of cash that should appear on its balance sheet. At the balance sheet date, deposits may be in transit to the bank, and some checks may be outstanding. That is why companies must prepare a bank reconciliation.

Bank Reconciliations Rarely does the balance of a company's Cash account exactly equal the cash balance on its bank statement. The bank may not yet have recorded certain transactions that appear in the company's records, and the company may not yet have recorded certain bank transactions. A bank reconciliation is therefore a necessary step in internal control. A **bank reconciliation** is the process of accounting for the difference between the balance on a company's bank statement and the balance in its Cash account. This process involves making additions to and subtractions from both balances to arrive at the adjusted cash balance.

The following are the transactions that most commonly appear in a company's records but not on its bank statement:

1. *Outstanding checks*: These are checks that a company has issued and recorded but that do not yet appear on its bank statement.
2. *Deposits in transit*: These are deposits a company has sent to its bank but that the bank did not receive in time to enter on the bank statement.

Transactions that may appear on the bank statement but not in the company's records include the following:

1. *Service charges* (SC): Banks often charge a fee, or service charge, for the use of a checking account. Many banks base the service charge on a number of

Study Note

Bank reconciliations perform an important function in internal control. If carried out by someone who does not have access to the bank account, they provide an independent check on the person or persons who do have that access.

Study Note

A credit memorandum means that an amount was added to the bank balance; a debit memorandum means that an amount was deducted.

factors, such as the average balance of the account during the month or the number of checks drawn.

2. NSF *(nonsufficient funds) checks*: An NSF check is a check that a company has deposited but that is not paid when the bank presents it to the issuer's bank. The bank charges the company's account and returns the check so that the company can try to collect the amount due. If the bank has deducted the NSF check on the bank statement but the company has not deducted it from its book balance, an adjustment must be made in the bank reconciliation. The company usually reclassifies the NSF check from Cash to Accounts Receivable because it must now collect from the person or company that wrote the check.
3. *Miscellaneous debits and credits*: Banks also charge for other services, such as stopping payment on checks and printing checks. The bank notifies the depositor of each deduction by including a debit memorandum with the monthly statement. A bank also sometimes serves as an agent in collecting on promissory notes for the depositor. When it does, it includes a credit memorandum in the bank statement, along with a debit memorandum for the service charge.
4. *Interest income*: Banks commonly pay interest on a company's average balance. Accounts that pay interest are sometimes called NOW or money market accounts.

An error by either the bank or the depositor will, of course, require immediate correction.

To illustrate the preparation of a bank reconciliation, suppose that Terry Services Company's bank statement for August shows a balance of $1,735.53 on August 31 and that on the same date, the company's records show a cash balance of $1,207.95. The purpose of a bank reconciliation is to identify the items that make up the difference between these amounts and to determine the correct cash balance. Exhibit 1 shows Terry Services Company's bank reconciliation for August. The circled numbers in the exhibit refer to the following:

1. The bank has not recorded a deposit in the amount of $138.00 that the company mailed to the bank on August 31.
2. The bank has not paid the five checks that the company issued in July and August: Even though the July 14 check was deducted in the July 30 reconciliation, it must be deducted again in each subsequent month in which it remains outstanding.
3. The company incorrectly recorded a $150 deposit from cash sales as $165.00. On August 6, the bank received the deposit and corrected the amount.
4. Among the returned checks was a credit memorandum showing that the bank had collected a promissory note from K. Diaz in the amount of $140.00, plus $10.00 in interest on the note. A debit memorandum was also enclosed for the $2.50 collection fee. The company had not entered these amounts in its records.
5. Also returned with the bank statement was an NSF check for $64.07 that the company had received from a customer named Austin Chase. The NSF check was not reflected in the company's records.
6. A debit memorandum was enclosed for the regular monthly service charge of $6.25. The company had not yet recorded this charge.
7. Interest earned on the company's average balance was $7.81.

Bank Reconciliation

Terry Services Company
Bank Reconciliation
August 31, 2010

Balance per bank, August 31		$1,735.53
① Add deposit of August 31 in transit		138.00
		$1,873.53
② Less outstanding checks:		
No. 551, issued on July 14	$ 75.00	
No. 576, issued on Aug. 30	20.34	
No. 578, issued on Aug. 31	250.00	
No. 579, issued on Aug. 31	185.00	
No. 580, issued on Aug. 31	65.25	595.59
Adjusted bank balance, August 31		**$1,277.94**
Balance per books, August 31		$1,207.95
Add:		
④ Note receivable collected by bank	$140.00	
④ Interest income on note	10.00	
⑦ Interest income	7.81	157.81
		$1,365.76
Less:		
③ Overstatement of deposit of August 6	$ 15.00	
④ Collection fee	2.50	
⑤ NSF check of Austin Chase	64.07	
⑥ Service charge	6.25	87.82
Adjusted book balance, August 31		**$1,277.94**

Study Note

It is possible to place an item in the wrong section of a bank reconciliation and still have it balance. The *correct* adjusted balance must be obtained.

As you can see in Exhibit 1, starting from their separate balances, both the bank and book amounts are adjusted to the amount of $1,277.94. This adjusted balance is the amount of cash the company owns on August 31 and thus is the amount that should appear on its August 31 balance sheet.

When outstanding checks are presented to the bank for payment and the bank receives and records the deposit in transit, the bank balance will automatically become correct. However, the company must update its book balance by recording all the items reported by the bank. Thus, Terry Services Company would record an increase (debit) in Cash with the following items:

- Decrease (credit) in Notes Receivable, $140.00
- Increase (credit) in Interest Income, $10.00 (interest on note)
- Increase (credit) in Interest Income, $7.81 (interest on average bank balance)

The company would record a reduction (credit) in Cash with the following items:

- Decrease (debit) in Sales, $15.00 (error in recording deposit)
- Increase (debit) in Accounts Receivable, $64.07 (return of NSF check)
- Increase (debit) in Bank Service Charges, $8.75 ($6.25 + $2.50)

As the use of electronic funds transfer, automatic payments, and debit cards increases, the items that most businesses will have to deal with in their bank reconciliations will undoubtedly grow.

STOP ▸ REVIEW ▸ APPLY

LO2-1 How do cash equivalents differ from cash?
LO2-2 Why is an imprest system an effective control over cash?
LO2-3 What is a bank reconciliation? What two amounts need to be reconciled?

Uncollectible Accounts

LO3 Apply the allowance method of accounting for uncollectible accounts.

Study Note
The direct charge-off method does not conform to the matching rule.

Some companies recognize a loss at the time they determine that an account is uncollectible by reducing Accounts Receivable and increasing Uncollectible Accounts Expense. Federal regulations require companies to use this method of recognizing a loss—called the **direct charge-off method**—in computing taxable income. Although small companies may use this method for all purposes, companies that follow generally accepted accounting principles do not use it in their financial statements. The reason they do not is that a direct charge-off is usually recorded in a different accounting period from the one in which the sale takes place, and the method therefore does not conform to the matching rule. Companies that follow GAAP prefer the allowance method.

The Allowance Method

Study Note
The allowance method relies on an estimate of uncollectible accounts but is in accord with the matching rule.

Under the **allowance method**, losses from bad debts are matched against the sales they help to produce. As mentioned earlier, when management extends credit to increase sales, it knows it will incur some losses from uncollectible accounts. Losses from credit sales should be recognized at the time the sales are made so that they are matched to the revenues they help generate. Of course, at the time a company makes credit sales, management cannot identify which customers will not pay their debts, nor can it predict the exact amount of money the company will lose. Therefore, to observe the matching rule, losses from uncollectible accounts must be estimated, and the estimate becomes an expense in the period in which the sales are made.

For example, suppose that Sharon Sales Company made most of its sales on credit during its first year of operation, 2010. At the end of the year, accounts receivable amounted to $200,000. On December 31, 2010, management reviewed the collectible status of the accounts receivable. Approximately $12,000 of the $200,000 of accounts receivable were estimated to be uncollectible. This adjusting entry would be made on December 31 of that year:

A	= L +	SE
−12,000		−12,000

2010			
Dec. 31	Uncollectible Accounts Expense	12,000	
	Allowance for Uncollectible Accounts		12,000
	To record the estimated uncollectible accounts expense for the year		

Disclosure of Uncollectible Accounts

Study Note

Allowance for Uncollectible Accounts reduces the gross accounts receivable to the amount estimated to be collectible (net realizable value). The purpose of another contra account, Accumulated Depreciation, is *not* to reduce the gross plant and equipment accounts to realizable value. Rather, its purpose is to show how much of the cost of the plant and equipment has been allocated as an expense to previous accounting periods.

Uncollectible Accounts Expense appears on the income statement as an operating expense. **Allowance for Uncollectible Accounts** appears on the balance sheet as a contra account that is deducted from accounts receivable. It reduces the accounts receivable to the amount expected to be collected in cash, as follows:

Current assets:		
Cash		$ 20,000
Short-term investments		30,000
Accounts receivable	$200,000	
Less allowance for uncollectible accounts	12,000	188,000
Inventory		112,000
Total current assets		$350,000

Accounts receivable may also be shown on the balance sheet as follows:

Accounts receivable (net of allowance for uncollectible accounts of $12,000)	$188,000

Study Note

The allowance account is necessary because the specific uncollectible accounts will not be identified until later.

Or accounts receivable may be shown at "net," with the amount of the allowance for uncollectible accounts identified in a note to the financial statements. For most companies, the "net" amount of accounts receivable approximates fair value. Fair value disclosures are not required for accounts receivable but 341 of 600 large companies made this disclosure voluntarily. Of those, 325, or 95 percent, indicated that the net accounts receivable approximated fair value.[16]

The allowance account often has other titles, such as *Allowance for Doubtful Accounts* and *Allowance for Bad Debts.* Once in a while, the older phrase *Reserve for Bad Debts* will be seen, but in modern practice it should not be used. *Bad Debts Expense* is a title often used for Uncollectible Accounts Expense.

Estimating Uncollectible Accounts Expense

Study Note

The accountant looks at both local and national economic conditions in determining the estimated uncollectible accounts expense.

As noted, expected losses from uncollectible accounts must be estimated. Of course, estimates can vary widely. If management takes an optimistic view and projects a small loss from uncollectible accounts, the resulting net accounts receivable will be larger than if management takes a pessimistic view. The net income will also be larger under the optimistic view because the estimated expense will be smaller. The company's accountant makes an estimate based on past experience and current economic conditions. For example, losses from uncollectible accounts are normally expected to be greater in a recession than

FOCUS ON BUSINESS PRACTICE

Cash Collections Can Be Hard to Estimate

Companies must not only sell goods and services; they must also generate cash flows by collecting on those sales. When there are changes in the economy, some companies make big mistakes in estimating the amount of accounts they will collect. For example, when the dot-com bubble burst in the early 2000s, companies like **Nortel Networks**, **Cisco Systems**, and **Lucent Technologies** increased their estimates of allowances for uncollectible accounts — actions that eliminated previously reported earnings and caused the companies' stock prices to fall.[17] However, it turned out that these companies had overestimated how bad the losses would be. In later years, they reduced their allowances for credit losses, thereby increasing their reported earnings.[18]

during a period of economic growth. The final decision, made by management, on the amount of the expense will depend on objective information, such as the accountant's analyses, and on certain qualitative factors, such as how investors, bankers, creditors, and others view the performance of the debtor company. Regardless of the qualitative considerations, the estimated losses from uncollectible accounts should be realistic.

Two common methods of estimating uncollectible accounts expense are the percentage of net sales method and the accounts receivable aging method.

Study Note

Unlike the direct charge-off method, the percentage of net sales method matches revenues with expenses.

Percentage of Net Sales Method The **percentage of net sales method** asks the question, How much of this year's *net sales* will not be collected? The answer determines the amount of uncollectible accounts expense for the year. For example, the following balances represent Shivar Company's ending figures for 2012:

SALES

		Dec. 31	322,500

SALES RETURNS AND ALLOWANCES

Dec. 31	20,000		

SALES DISCOUNTS

Dec. 31	2,500		

ALLOWANCE FOR UNCOLLECTIBLE ACCOUNTS

		Dec. 31	1,800

The following are Shivar's actual losses from uncollectible accounts for the past three years:

Year	*Net Sales*	*Losses from Uncollectible Accounts*	*Percentage*
2009	$260,000	$ 5,100	1.96
2010	297,500	6,950	2.34
2011	292,500	4,950	1.69
Total	$850,000	$17,000	2.00

Credit sales often constitute most of a company's sales. If a company has substantial cash sales, it should use only its net credit sales in estimating uncollectible accounts.

Shivar's management believes that its uncollectible accounts will continue to average about 2 percent of net sales. The uncollectible accounts expense for the year 2012 is therefore estimated as follows:

$$.02 \times (\$322,500 - \$20,000 - \$2,500) = .02 \times \$300,000 = \$6,000$$

The following entry would be made to record the estimate:

A	= L +	SE
−6,000		−6,000

2012			
Dec. 31	Uncollectible Accounts Expense	6,000	
	Allowance for Uncollectible Accounts		6,000
	To record uncollectible accounts expense at 2 percent of $300,000 net sales		

Allowance for Uncollectible Accounts will now have a balance of $7,800:

ALLOWANCE FOR UNCOLLECTIBLE ACCOUNTS

		Dec. 31	1,800
		Dec. 31 Adj.	6,000
		Dec. 31 Bal.	**7,800**

The balance consists of the $6,000 estimated uncollectible accounts receivable from 2012 sales and the $1,800 estimated uncollectible accounts receivable from previous years.

Accounts Receivable Aging Method The **accounts receivable aging method** asks the question, How much of the *ending balance of accounts receivable* will not be collected? With this method, the ending balance of Allowance for Uncollectible Accounts is determined directly through an analysis of accounts receivable. The difference between the amount determined to be uncollectible and the actual balance of Allowance for Uncollectible Accounts is the expense for the period. In theory, this method should produce the same result as the percentage of net sales method, but in practice it rarely does.

The **aging of accounts receivable** is the process of listing each customer's receivable account according to the due date of the account. If the customer's account is past due, there is a possibility that the account will not be paid. And that possibility increases as the account extends further beyond the due date. The aging of accounts receivable helps management evaluate its credit and collection policies and alerts it to possible problems.

> **Study Note**
> An aging of accounts receivable is an important tool in cash management because it helps to determine what amounts are likely to be collected in the months ahead.

Exhibit 2 illustrates the aging of accounts receivable for Gomez Company. Each account receivable is classified as being not yet due or as being 1–30 days, 31–60 days, 61–90 days, or over 90 days past due. Based on past experience, the estimated percentage for each category is determined and multiplied by the amount in each category to determine the estimated, or target, balance of Allowance for Uncollectible Accounts. In total, it is estimated that $4,918 of the $88,800 in accounts receivable will not be collected.

> **Study Note**
> When the write-offs in an accounting period exceed the amount of the allowance, a debit balance in the Allowance for Uncollectible Accounts account results.

Once the target balance for Allowance for Uncollectible Accounts has been found, it is necessary to determine the amount of the adjustment. The amount depends on the current balance of the allowance account. Let us assume two cases for the December 31 balance of Gomez Company's Allowance for Uncollectible Accounts: (1) a credit balance of $1,600 and (2) a debit balance of $1,600.

EXHIBIT 2 Analysis of Accounts Receivable by Age

Gomez Company
Analysis of Accounts Receivable by Age
December 31, 2010

Customer	Total	Not Yet Due	1–30 Days Past Due	31–60 Days Past Due	61–90 Days Past Due	Over 90 Days Past Due
K. Wu	$ 300		$ 300			
R. List	800			$ 800		
B. Smith	2,000	$ 1,800	200			
T. Vigo	500				$ 500	
Others	85,200	42,000	28,000	7,600	4,400	$3,200
Totals	$88,800	$43,800	$28,500	$8,400	$4,900	$3,200
Estimated percentage uncollectible		1.0	2.0	10.0	30.0	50.0
Allowance for Uncollectible Accounts	$ 4,918	$ 438	$ 570	$ 840	$1,470	$1,600

In the first case, an adjustment of $3,318 is needed to bring the balance of the allowance account to a $4,918 credit balance:

Targeted balance for allowance for uncollectible accounts	$4,918
Less current credit balance of allowance for uncollectible accounts	1,600
Uncollectible accounts expense	$3,318

The uncollectible accounts expense is recorded as follows:

A	= L +	SE
−3,318		−3,318

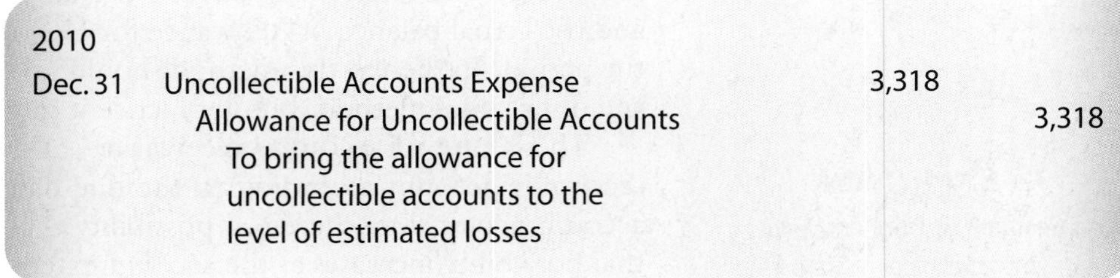

2010			
Dec. 31	Uncollectible Accounts Expense	3,318	
	Allowance for Uncollectible Accounts		3,318
	To bring the allowance for uncollectible accounts to the level of estimated losses		

The resulting balance of Allowance for Uncollectible Accounts is $4,918:

Allowance for Uncollectible Accounts

		Dec. 31	1,600
		Dec. 31 Adj.	3,318
		Dec. 31 Bal.	**4,918**

In the second case, because Allowance for Uncollectible Accounts has a debit balance of $1,600, the estimated uncollectible accounts expense for the year will have to be $6,518 to reach the targeted balance of $4,918. This calculation is as follows:

Targeted balance for allowance for uncollectible accounts	$4,918
Plus current debit balance of allowance for uncollectible accounts	1,600
Uncollectible accounts expense	**$6,518**

The uncollectible accounts expense is recorded as follows:

A	= L +	SE
−6,518		−6,518

2010			
Dec. 31	Uncollectible Accounts Expense	6,518	
	Allowance for Uncollectible Accounts		6,518
	To bring the allowance for uncollectible accounts to the level of estimated losses		

After this entry, Allowance for Uncollectible Accounts has a credit balance of $4,918:

Allowance for Uncollectible Accounts

Dec. 31	1,600	Dec. 31 Adj.	6,518
		Dec. 31 Bal.	**4,918**

FIGURE 6
Two Methods of Estimating Uncollectible Accounts

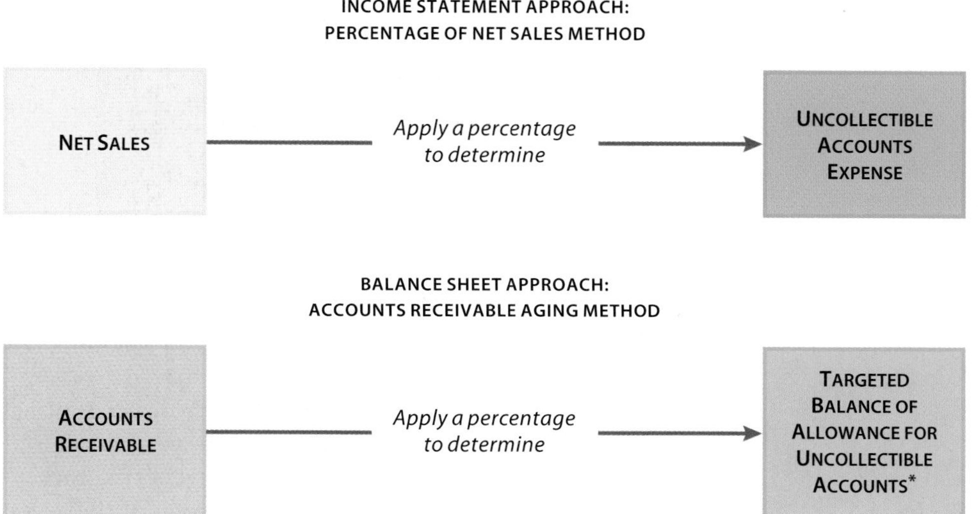

Study Note

Describing the aging method as the balance sheet method emphasizes that the computation is based on ending accounts receivable rather than on net sales for the period.

Comparison of the Two Methods Both the percentage of net sales method and the accounts receivable aging method estimate the uncollectible accounts expense in accordance with the matching rule, but as shown in Figure 6, they do so in different ways. The percentage of net sales method is an income statement approach. It assumes that a certain proportion of sales will not be collected, and this proportion is the *amount of Uncollectible Accounts Expense* for the period. The accounts receivable aging method is a balance sheet approach. It assumes that a certain proportion of accounts receivable outstanding will not be collected. This proportion is the *targeted balance of the Allowance for Uncollectible Accounts account*. The expense for the accounting period is the difference between the targeted balance and the current balance of the allowance account.

Writing Off Uncollectible Accounts

Regardless of the method used to estimate uncollectible accounts, the total of accounts receivable written off in an accounting period will rarely equal the estimated uncollectible amount. The allowance account will show a credit balance when the total of accounts written off is less than the estimated uncollectible amount. It will show a debit balance when the total of accounts written off is greater than the estimated uncollectible amount.

Study Note

When writing off an individual account, debit Allowance for Uncollectible Accounts, not Uncollectible Accounts Expense.

When it becomes clear that a specific account receivable will not be collected, the amount should be written off to Allowance for Uncollectible Accounts. Remember that the uncollectible amount was already accounted for as an expense when the allowance was established. For example, assume that on January 15, 2011, T. Vigo, who owes Gomez Company $500, is declared bankrupt by a federal court. The entry to *write off* this account is as follows:

A	= L +	SE
+500		
−500		

2011			
Jan. 15	Allowance for Uncollectible Accounts	500	
	Accounts Receivable		500
	To write off receivable from T. Vigo as uncollectible because of his bankruptcy		

Although the write-off removes the uncollectible amount from Accounts Receivable, it does not affect the estimated net realizable value of accounts receivable. It simply reduces T. Vigo's account to zero and reduces Allowance for Uncollectible Accounts by $500, as shown below:

	Balances Before Write-off	*Balances After Write-off*
Accounts receivable	$88,800	$88,300
Less allowance for uncollectible accounts	4,918	4,418
Estimated net realizable value of accounts receivable	$83,882	$83,882

Occasionally, a customer whose account has been written off as uncollectible will later be able to pay some or all of the amount owed. When that happens, two entries must be made: one to reverse the earlier write-off (which is now incorrect) and another to show the collection of the account.

STOP ▸ REVIEW ▸ APPLY

LO3-1 **What accounting principle does the direct charge-off method of recognizing uncollectible accounts violate? Why?**

LO3-2 **According to generally accepted accounting principles, at what point in the cycle of sales and collections does a loss on an uncollectible account occur?**

LO3-3 **What is the effect on net income when management takes an optimistic rather than a pessimistic view of estimated uncollectible accounts?**

LO3-4 **Why is the percentage of net sales method of estimating uncollectible accounts called an income statement approach, and why is the accounts receivable aging method called a balance sheet approach?**

LO3-5 **What is the reasoning behind the percentage of net sales method and the accounts receivable aging method?**

LO3-6 **Suppose that after adjusting and closing accounts at the end of a fiscal year, Accounts Receivable is $176,000 and Allowance for Uncollectible Accounts is $14,500. (a) What is the collectible value of Accounts Receivable? (b) If the $450 account of a bankrupt customer is written off in the first month of the new year, what will the collectible value of Accounts Receivable be?**

Aging and Net Sales Methods Contrasted
Jazz Instruments, Inc., sells its merchandise on credit. In the company's last fiscal year, which ended July 31, it had net sales of $7,000,000. At the end of the fiscal year, it had Accounts Receivable of $1,800,000 and a credit balance in Allowance for Uncollectible Accounts of $11,200. In the past, the company has been unable to collect on approximately 1 percent of its net sales. An aging analysis of accounts receivable has indicated that $80,000 of current receivables are uncollectible.

1. Calculate the amount of uncollectible accounts expense, and use T accounts to determine the resulting balance of Allowance for Uncollectible Accounts under the percentage of net sales method and the accounts receivable aging method.

2. How would your answers change if Allowance for Uncollectible Accounts had a debit balance of $11,200 instead of a credit balance?

(continued)

SOLUTION

1. **Percentage of net sales method:**

ALLOWANCE FOR UNCOLLECTIBLE ACCOUNTS

	July 31		11,200
	31	UA Exp.	70,000*
	July 31	Bal.	81,200

*Uncollectible Accounts Expense = $7,000,000 × .01

Aging Method:

ALLOWANCE FOR UNCOLLECTIBLE ACCOUNTS

	July 31		11,200
	31	UA Exp.	68,800*
	July 31	Bal.	80,000

*Uncollectible Accounts Expense = $80,000 − $11,200

2. Under the percentage of net sales method, the amount of the expense is the same in **1** and **2** but the ending balance will be $58,800 ($70,000 − $11,200). Under the aging method, the ending balance is the same, but the amount of the expense will be $91,200 ($80,000 + $11,200).

Notes Receivable

LO4 Define *promissory note*, and make common calculations for promissory notes receivable.

A **promissory note** is an unconditional promise to pay a definite sum of money on demand or at a future date. The person or company that signs the note and thereby promises to pay is the *maker* of the note. The entity to whom payment is to be made is the *payee*. The promissory note shown in Figure 7 is an unconditional promise by the maker, Samuel Mason, to pay a definite sum—or principal

FIGURE 7 A Promissory Note

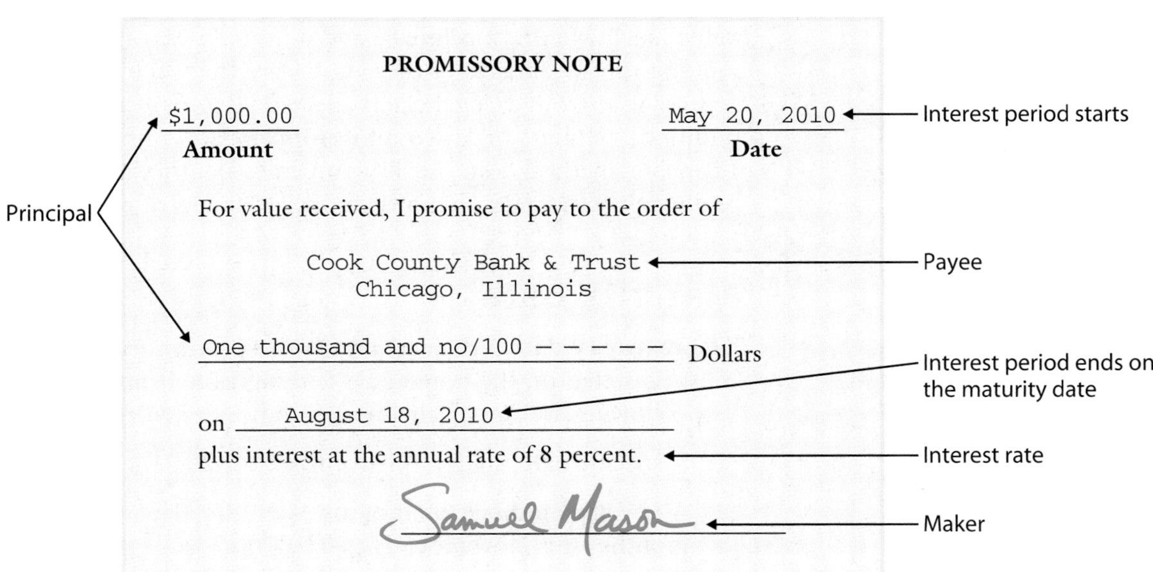
PROMISSORY NOTE

$1,000.00 — Amount

May 20, 2010 — Date

For value received, I promise to pay to the order of

Cook County Bank & Trust
Chicago, Illinois

One thousand and no/100 - - - - - Dollars

on August 18, 2010

plus interest at the annual rate of 8 percent.

Samuel Mason

Automobile manufacturers like Toyota, whose assembly line is pictured here, often accept promissory notes, which are unconditional promises to pay a definite sum of money on demand or at a future date. These notes produce interest income and represent a stronger legal claim against a debtor than do accounts receivable. In addition, firms commonly raise money by selling—or discounting—promissory notes to banks.

($1,000)—to the payee, Cook County Bank & Trust, on August 18, 2010. As you can see, this promissory note is dated May 20, 2010, and bears an interest rate of 8 percent.

Study Note

Notes receivable and notes payable are distinguished from accounts receivable and accounts payable because the latter were not created by a formal promissory note.

A payee includes all the promissory notes it holds that are due in less than one year in **notes receivable** in the current assets section of its balance sheet. A maker includes them in **notes payable** in the current liabilities section of its balance sheet. Since notes receivable and notes payable are financial instruments, companies may voluntarily disclose their fair value. In most cases, fair value approximates the amount in the account records, but sometimes the adjustments to fair value are significant, such as in the recent cases of subprime loans gone bad.

The nature of a company's business generally determines how frequently it receives promissory notes from customers. Firms that sell durable goods of high value, such as farm machinery and automobiles, often accept promissory notes. Among the advantages of these notes are that they produce interest income and represent a stronger legal claim against a debtor than do accounts receivable. In addition, selling—or discounting—promissory notes to banks is a common financing method. Almost all companies occasionally accept promissory notes, and many companies obtain them in settlement of past-due accounts.

Maturity Date

The **maturity date** is the date on which a promissory note must be paid. This date must be stated on the note or be determinable from the facts stated on the note. The following are among the most common statements of maturity date:

1. A specific date, such as "November 14, 2010"
2. A specific number of months after the date of the note, such as "three months after November 14, 2010"

3. A specific number of days after the date of the note, such as "60 days after November 14, 2010"

The maturity date is obvious when a specific date is stated. And when the maturity date is a number of months from the date of the note, one simply uses the same day in the appropriate future month. For example, a note dated January 20 that is due in two months would be due on March 20.

When the maturity date is a specific number of days from the date of the note, however, the exact maturity date must be determined. In computing the maturity date, it is important to exclude the date of the note. For example, a note dated May 20 and due in 90 days would be due on August 18, determined as follows:

Days remaining in May (31 − 20)	11
Days in June	30
Days in July	31
Days in August	18
Total days	90

Duration of a Note

Study Note

Another way to compute the duration of notes is to begin with the interest period, as in this example:

90	Interest period
− 11	days remaining in May (31 − 20)
79	
− 30	days in June
49	
− 31	days in July
18	due date in August

The **duration of a note** is the time between a promissory note's issue date and its maturity date. Knowing the exact number of days in the duration of a note is important because interest is calculated on that basis. Identifying the duration is easy when the maturity date is stated as a specific number of days from the date of the note because the two numbers are the same. However, when the maturity date is stated as a specific date, the exact number of days must be determined. Assume that a note issued on May 10 matures on August 10. The duration of the note is 92 days:

Days remaining in May (31 − 10)	21
Days in June	30
Days in July	31
Days in August	10
Total days	92

Interest and Interest Rate

Interest is the cost of borrowing money or the return on lending money, depending on whether one is the borrower or the lender. The amount of interest is based on three factors: the principal (the amount of money borrowed or lent), the rate of interest, and the loan's length of time. The formula used in computing interest is as follows:

$$\text{Principal} \times \text{Rate of Interest} \times \text{Time} = \text{Interest}$$

Interest rates are usually stated on an annual basis. For example, the interest on a one-year, 8 percent, \$1,000 note would be \$80 (\$1,000 × 8/100 × 1 = \$80). If the term, or time period, of the note is three months instead of a year, the interest charge would be \$20 (\$1,000 × 8/100 × 3/12 = \$20).

When the term of a note is expressed in days, the exact number of days must be used in computing the interest. Thus, if the term of the note described above was 45 days, the interest would be \$10, computed as follows: \$1,000 × 8/100 × 45/365 = \$9.86.

Maturity Value

The **maturity value** is the total proceeds of a promissory note—face value plus interest—at the maturity date. The maturity value of a 90-day, 8 percent, $1,000 note is computed as follows:

$$\begin{aligned}\text{Maturity Value} &= \text{Principal} + \text{Interest}\\ &= \$1{,}000 + (\$1{,}000 \times 8/100 \times 90/365)\\ &= \$1{,}000 + \$19.73\\ &= \$1{,}019.73\end{aligned}$$

There are also so-called non-interest-bearing notes. The maturity value is the face value, or principal amount. In this case, the principal includes an implied interest cost.

Accrued Interest

A promissory note received in one accounting period may not be due until a later period. The interest on a note accrues by a small amount each day of the note's duration. As we described in an earlier chapter, the matching rule requires that the accrued interest be apportioned to the periods in which it belongs. For example, assume that the $1,000, 90-day, 8 percent note discussed above was received on August 31 and that the fiscal year ended on September 30. In this case, 30 days interest, or $6.58 ($1,000 × 8/100 × 30/365 = $6.58), would be earned in the fiscal year that ends on September 30. An adjusting entry would be made to record the interest receivable as an asset and the interest income as revenue. The remainder of the interest income, $13.15 ($1,000 × 8/100 × 60/365), would be recorded as income, and the interest receivable ($6.58) would be shown as received when the note is paid. Note that all the cash for the interest is received when the note is paid, but the interest income is apportioned to two fiscal years.

Dishonored Note

When the maker of a note does not pay the note at maturity, it is said to be a **dishonored note**. The holder, or payee, of a dishonored note should make an entry to transfer the total amount due (including interest income) from Notes Receivable to an account receivable from the debtor. Two objectives are accomplished by transferring a dishonored note into an Accounts Receivable account. First, it leaves only notes that have not matured and are presumably negotiable and collectible in the Notes Receivable account. Second, it establishes a record in the borrower's accounts receivable account that the customer has dishonored a note receivable. Such information may be helpful in deciding whether to extend credit to the customer in the future.

STOP ▸ REVIEW ▸ APPLY

LO4-1 **What is a promissory note?**

LO4-2 **Who is the maker of a promissory note? Who is the payee?**

LO4-3 **What is the difference between interest and interest rate?**

LO4-4 **What are the maturity dates of the following notes: (a) a three-month note that is dated August 16, (b) a 90-day note that is dated August 16, and (c) a 60-day note that is dated March 25?**

A LOOK BACK AT ▶ Nike, Inc.

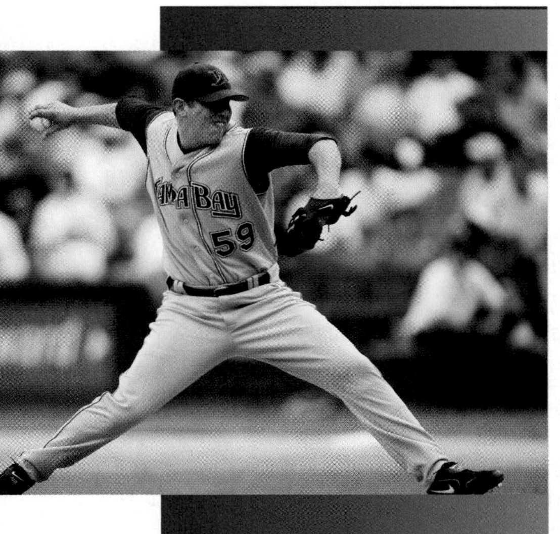

In this chapter's Decision Point, we noted that **Nike** must give the retailers that buy its products time to pay for their purchases, but at the same time, Nike must have enough cash on hand to pay its suppliers. To plan the company's cash flows, Nike's management must address the following questions:

- **How can the company control its cash needs?**
- **How can the company evaluate credit policies and the level of its receivables?**
- **How should the company estimate the value of its receivables?**

As you saw in Figure 1, companies like Nike go through seasonal cycles that affect their cash flows. At times, Nike may have excess cash available that it can invest in a way that earns a return but still permits ready access to cash. At other times, it may have to borrow funds. To ensure that it can borrow funds when it needs to, Nike maintains good relations with its banks.

To evaluate the company's credit policies and the level of its accounts receivable, management can compare the current year's receivable turnover and days' sales uncollected with those ratios in previous years. Using data from Nike's Financial Highlights, we can compute these ratios for 2006 and 2007 as follows (dollars are in millions):

		2007	2006
Receivable Turnover:	$\frac{\text{Net Sales}}{\text{Average Accounts Receivable}}$	$\frac{\$16,325.9}{(\$2,494.7 + \$2,382.9) \div 2}$	$\frac{\$14,954.9}{(\$2,382.9 + \$2,468.0) \div 2}$
		$\frac{\$16,325.9}{\$2,438.8}$	$\frac{\$14,954.9}{\$2,425.5}$
		6.7 times	6.2 times
Days' Sales Uncollected:	$\frac{\text{Number of Days in a Year}}{\text{Receivable Turnover}}$	$\frac{\text{365 days}}{\text{6.7 times}}$	$\frac{\text{365 days}}{\text{6.2 times}}$
		54.5 days	58.9 days

Thus, in 2007, Nike achieved an improvement in its receivable turnover. It also reduced the number of days it takes to collect accounts receivable.

A decline of 4.4 days may not seem like much, but it represents almost $200 million in cash. Nike's management comments as follows: "Accounts Receivable provided cash to the Company due to the improved account management through better utilization of supply chain systems."[19]

CHAPTER REVIEW

REVIEW of Learning Objectives

LO1 Identify and explain the management and ethical issues related to cash and receivables.

The management of cash and receivables is critical to maintaining adequate liquidity. In dealing with these assets, management must (1) consider the need for short-term investing and borrowing as the business's balance of cash fluctuates during seasonal cycles, (2) establish credit policies that balance the need for sales with the ability to collect, (3) evaluate the level of receivables using receivable turnover and days' sales uncollected, (4) assess the need to increase cash flows through the financing of receivables, and (5) understand the importance of ethics in estimating credit losses.

LO2 Define *cash equivalents*, and explain methods of controlling cash, including bank reconciliations.

Cash equivalents are investments that have a term of 90 days or less. Cash and cash equivalents are financial instruments that are valued at fair value. Methods of controlling cash include imprest systems; banking services, including electronic funds transfer; and bank reconciliations. A bank reconciliation accounts for the difference between the balance on a company's bank statement and the balance in its Cash account. It involves adjusting for outstanding checks, deposits in transit, service charges, NSF checks, miscellaneous debits and credits, and interest income.

LO3 Apply the allowance method of accounting for uncollectible accounts.

Because of the time lag between credit sales and the time accounts are judged uncollectible, the allowance method is used to match the amount of uncollectible accounts against revenues in any given period. Uncollectible accounts expense is estimated by using either the percentage of net sales method or the accounts receivable aging method. When the first method is used, bad debts are judged to be a certain percentage of sales during the period. When the second method is used, certain percentages are applied to groups of accounts receivable that have been arranged by due dates.

Allowance for Uncollectible Accounts is a contra-asset account to Accounts Receivable. The estimate of uncollectible accounts is debited to Uncollectible Accounts Expense and credited to the allowance account. When an individual account is determined to be uncollectible, it is removed from Accounts Receivable by debiting the allowance account and crediting Accounts Receivable. If the written-off account is later collected, the earlier entry is reversed and the collection is recorded in the normal way.

LO4 Define *promissory note* and make common calculations for promissory notes receivable.

A promissory note is an unconditional promise to pay a definite sum of money on demand or at a future date. Companies that sell durable goods of high value, such as farm machinery and automobiles, often accept promissory notes. Selling these notes to banks is a common financing method. In accounting for promissory notes, it is important to know how to calculate the maturity date, duration of a note, interest and interest rate, and maturity value.

REVIEW of Concepts and Terminology

The following concepts and terms were introduced in this chapter:

Accounts receivable: Short-term financial assets that arise from sales on credit at the wholesale or retail level. **(LO1)**

Accounts receivable aging method: A method of estimating uncollectible accounts based on the assumption that a predictable proportion of each dollar of accounts receivable outstanding will not be collected. **(LO3)**

Aging of accounts receivable: The process of listing each customer's receivable account according to the due date of the account. **(LO3)**

Allowance for Uncollectible Accounts: A contra-asset account that reduces accounts receivable to the amount expected to be collected in cash. Also called *Allowance for Doubtful Accounts* and *Allowance for Bad Debts.* **(LO3)**

Allowance method: A method of accounting for uncollectible accounts by expensing estimated uncollectible accounts in the period in which the related sales take place. **(LO3)**

Bank reconciliation: The process of accounting for the difference between the balance appearing on a company's bank statement and the balance in its Cash account. **(LO2)**

Cash: Coins and currency on hand, checks and money orders from customers, and deposits in checking and savings accounts. **(LO1)**

Cash equivalents: Short-term investments that will revert to cash in 90 days or less from the time they are purchased. **(LO2)**

Compensating balance: A minimum amount that a bank requires a company to keep in its bank account as part of a credit-granting arrangement. **(LO1)**

Contingent liability: A potential liability that can develop into a real liability if a particular event occurs. **(LO1)**

Direct charge-off method: A method of accounting for uncollectible accounts by directly debiting an expense account when bad debts are discovered; it violates the matching rule but is required for computing federal income tax. **(LO3)**

Discounting: A method of selling notes receivable to a bank in which the bank derives its profit by deducting the interest from the maturity value of the note. **(LO1)**

Dishonored note: A promissory note that the maker cannot or will not pay at the maturity date. **(LO4)**

Duration of a note: The time between a promissory note's issue date and its maturity date. **(LO4)**

Electronic funds transfer (EFT): The transfer of funds from one bank to another through electronic communication. **(LO2)**

Factor: An entity that buys accounts receivable. **(LO1)**

Factoring: The sale or transfer of accounts receivable. **(LO1)**

Imprest system: A system for controlling small cash disbursements by establishing a fund at a fixed amount and periodically reimbursing the fund by the amount necessary to restore its original cash balance. **(LO2)**

Installment accounts receivable: Accounts receivable that are payable in a series of time payments. **(LO1)**

Interest: The cost of borrowing money or the return on lending money, depending on whether one is the borrower or the lender. **(LO4)**

Maturity date: The date on which a promissory note must be paid. **(LO4)**

Maturity value: The total proceeds of a promissory note—face value plus interest—at the maturity date. **(LO4)**

Notes payable: Collective term for promissory notes owed by the entity (maker) who promises payment to other entities. **(LO4)**

Notes receivable: Collective term for promissory notes held by the entity to whom payment is promised (payee). **(LO4)**

Percentage of net sales method: A method of estimating uncollectible accounts based on the assumption that a predictable proportion of each dollar of sales will not be collected. **(LO3)**

Promissory note: An unconditional promise to pay a definite sum of money on demand or at a future date. **(LO4)**

Securitization: The grouping of receivables into batches for sale at a discount to companies and investors. **(LO1)**

Short-term financial assets: Assets that arise from cash transactions, the investment of cash, and the extension of credit. **(LO1)**

Trade credit: Credit granted to customers by wholesalers or retailers. **(LO1)**

Uncollectible accounts: Accounts receivable owed by customers who cannot or will not pay. Also called *bad debts.* **(LO1)**

Key Ratios

Days' sales uncollected: A ratio that shows on average how long it takes to collect accounts receivable; 365 Days ÷ Receivable Turnover. **(LO1)**

Receivable turnover: A ratio for measuring the average number of times receivables are turned into cash during an accounting period; Net Sales ÷ Average Accounts Receivable. **(LO1)**

REVIEW Problem

Estimating Uncollectible Accounts and Receivables Analysis

Pente Metal Corporation sells merchandise on credit and also accepts notes as payment. During the year ended June 30, the company had net sales of $2,400,000. At the end of the year, it had Accounts Receivable of $800,000 and a debit balance in Allowance for Uncollectible Accounts of $4,200. In the past, approximately 1.5 percent of net sales has been uncollectible. Also, an aging analysis of accounts receivable reveals that $34,000 in accounts receivable appears to be uncollectible.

Required

1. Compute Uncollectible Accounts Expense, and determine the ending balance of Allowance for Uncollectible Accounts and Accounts Receivable, Net, under (a) the percentage of net sales method and (b) the accounts receivable aging method.
2. Compute the receivable turnover and days' sales uncollected using the data from the accounts receivable aging method in requirement **1** and assuming that the prior year's net accounts receivable were $706,000.

Answer to Review Problem

1. Uncollectible Accounts Expense and ending account balances
   a. Percentage of net sales method:
      Uncollectible Accounts Expense = 1.5 percent × $2,400,000 = $36,000
      Allowance for Uncollectible Accounts = $36,000 − $4,200 = $31,800
      Accounts Receivable, Net = $800,000 − $31,800 = $768,200
   b. Accounts receivable aging method:
      Uncollectible Accounts Expense = $4,200 + $34,000 = $38,200
      Allowance for Uncollectible Accounts = $34,000
      Accounts Receivable, Net = $800,000 − $34,000 = $766,000
2. Receivable turnover and days' sales uncollected

$$\text{Receivable Turnover} = \frac{\$2{,}400{,}000}{(\$766{,}000 + \$706{,}000) \div 2} = 3.3 \text{ times}$$

$$\text{Days' Sales Uncollected} = \frac{365 \text{ days}}{3.3 \text{ times}} = 110.6 \text{ days}$$

CHAPTER ASSIGNMENTS

BUILDING Your Basic Knowledge and Skills

Short Exercises

LO1 **Management Issues**

SE 1. Indicate whether each of the following actions is related to (a) managing cash needs, (b) setting credit policies, (c) financing receivables, or (d) ethically reporting receivables:

1. Selling accounts receivable to a factor
2. Borrowing funds for short-term needs during slow periods
3. Conducting thorough checks of new customers' ability to pay
4. Making every effort to reflect possible future losses accurately

LO1 **Short-Term Liquidity Ratios**

SE 2. Graff Company has cash of $40,000, net accounts receivable of $90,000, and net sales of $720,000. Last year's net accounts receivable were $70,000. Compute the following ratios: (a) receivable turnover and (b) days' sales uncollected.

LO2 **Cash and Cash Equivalents**

SE 3. Compute the amount of cash and cash equivalents on Car Wash Company's balance sheet if, on the balance sheet date, it has currency and coins on hand of $125, deposits in checking accounts of $750, U.S. Treasury bills due in 80 days of $7,500, and U.S. Treasury bonds due in 200 days of $12,500.

LO2 **Bank Reconciliation**

SE 4. Prepare a bank reconciliation from the following information:

a. Balance per bank statement as of June 30, $4,862.77
b. Balance per books as of June 30, $2,479.48
c. Deposits in transit, $654.24
d. Outstanding checks, $3,028.89
e. Interest on average balance, $8.64

LO3 **Percentage of Net Sales Method**

SE 5. At the end of October, Zion Company's management estimates the uncollectible accounts expense to be 1 percent of net sales of $1,500,000. Prepare the entry to record the uncollectible accounts expense, assuming the Allowance for Uncollectible Accounts has a debit balance of $7,000.

LO3 **Accounts Receivable Aging Method**

SE 6. An aging analysis on June 30 of the accounts receivable of Sung Corporation indicates that uncollectible accounts amount to $86,000. Prepare the entry to record uncollectible accounts expense under each of the following independent assumptions:

a. Allowance for Uncollectible Accounts has a credit balance of $18,000 before adjustment.
b. Allowance for Uncollectible Accounts has a debit balance of $14,000 before adjustment.

LO3

Write-off of Accounts Receivable

SE 7. Windy Corporation, which uses the allowance method, has accounts receivable of $50,800 and an allowance for uncollectible accounts of $9,800. An account receivable from Tom Novak of $4,400 is deemed to be uncollectible and is written off. What is the amount of net accounts receivable before and after the write-off?

LO4

Notes Receivable Calculations

SE 8. On August 25, Champion Company received a 90-day, 9 percent note in settlement of an account receivable in the amount of $20,000. Determine the maturity date, amount of interest on the note, and maturity value.

Exercises

LO1 LO2

Discussion Questions

E 1. Develop a brief answer to each of the following questions:

1. Name some businesses whose needs for cash fluctuate during the year. Name some whose needs for cash are relatively stable over the year.
2. Why is it advantageous for a company to finance its receivables?
3. To increase its sales, a company decides to increase its credit terms from 15 to 30 days. What effect will this change in policy have on receivable turnover and days' sales uncollected?
4. How might the receivable turnover and days' sales uncollected reveal that management is consistently underestimating the amount of losses from uncollectible accounts? Is this action ethical?

LO3 LO4

Discussion Questions

E 2. Develop a brief answer to each of the following questions:

1. What accounting rule is violated by the direct charge-off method of recognizing uncollectible accounts? Why?
2. In what ways is Allowance for Uncollectible Accounts similar to Accumulated Depreciation? In what ways is it different?
3. Under what circumstances would an accrual of interest income on an interest-bearing note receivable not be required at the end of an accounting period?

LO1

Management Issues

E 3. Indicate whether each of the following actions is primarily related to (a) managing cash needs, (b) setting credit policies, (c) financing receivables, or (d) ethically reporting accounts receivable:

1. Buying a U.S. Treasury bill with cash that is not needed for a few months
2. Comparing receivable turnovers for two years
3. Setting a policy that allows customers to buy on credit
4. Selling notes receivable to a financing company
5. Making careful estimates of losses from uncollectible accounts
6. Borrowing funds for short-term needs in a period when sales are low
7. Changing the terms for credit sales in an effort to reduce the days' sales uncollected
8. Revising estimated credit losses in a timely manner when economic conditions change
9. Establishing a department whose responsibility is to approve customers' credit

LO1 **Short-Term Liquidity Ratios**

E 4. Using the following data from Lopez Corporation's financial statements, compute the receivable turnover and the days' sales uncollected:

Current assets	
Cash	$ 35,000
Short-term investments	85,000
Notes receivable	120,000
Accounts receivable, net	200,000
Inventory	250,000
Prepaid assets	25,000
Total current assets	$ 715,000
Current liabilities	
Notes payable	$ 300,000
Accounts payable	75,000
Accrued liabilities	10,000
Total current liabilities	$ 385,000
Net sales	$1,600,000
Last period's accounts receivable, net	$ 180,000

LO2 **Cash and Cash Equivalents**

E 5. At year end, Lam Company had currency and coins in cash registers of \$2,800, money orders from customers of \$5,000, deposits in checking accounts of \$32,000, U.S. Treasury bills due in 80 days of \$90,000, certificates of deposit at the bank that mature in six months of \$100,000, and U.S. Treasury bonds due in one year of \$50,000. Calculate the amount of cash and cash equivalents that will be shown on the company's year-end balance sheet.

LO2 **Bank Reconciliation**

E 6. Prepare a bank reconciliation from the following information:

a. Balance per bank statement as of May 31, \$17,755.44
b. Balance per books as of May 31, \$12,211.94
c. Deposits in transit, \$2,254.81
d. Outstanding checks, \$7,818.16
e. Bank service charge, \$19.85

LO3 **Percentage of Net Sales Method**

E 7. At the end of the year, Emil Enterprises estimates the uncollectible accounts expense to be 0.8 percent of net sales of \$7,575,000. The current credit balance of Allowance for Uncollectible Accounts is \$12,900. Prepare the entry to record the uncollectible accounts expense. What is the balance of Allowance for Uncollectible Accounts after this adjustment?

LO3 **Accounts Receivable Aging Method**

E 8. The Accounts Receivable account of Samson Company shows a debit balance of \$52,000 at the end of the year. An aging analysis of the individual accounts indicates estimated uncollectible accounts to be \$3,350.

Prepare the entry to record the uncollectible accounts expense under each of the following independent assumptions: (a) Allowance for Uncollectible Accounts has a credit balance of \$400 before adjustment, and (b) Allowance for Uncollectible Accounts has a debit balance of \$400 before adjustment. What is the balance of Allowance for Uncollectible Accounts after each of these adjustments?

LO3 **Aging Method and Net Sales Method Contrasted**

E 9. At the beginning of 2010, the balances for Accounts Receivable and Allowance for Uncollectible Accounts were $430,000 and $31,400 (credit), respectively. During the year, credit sales were $3,200,000, and collections on account were $2,950,000. In addition, $35,000 in uncollectible accounts was written off.

Using T accounts, determine the year-end balances of Accounts Receivable and Allowance for Uncollectible Accounts. Then prepare the year-end adjusting entry to record the uncollectible accounts expense under each of the following conditions. Also show the year-end balance sheet presentation of accounts receivable and allowance for uncollectible accounts.

a. Management estimates the percentage of uncollectible credit sales to be 1.4 percent of total credit sales.
b. Based on an aging of accounts receivable, management estimates the end-of-year uncollectible accounts receivable to be $38,700.

Post the results of each of the entries to the T account for Allowance for Uncollectible Accounts.

LO3 **Aging Method and Net Sales Method Contrasted**

E 10. During 2010, Omega Company had net sales of $11,400,000. Most of the sales were on credit. At the end of 2010, the balance of Accounts Receivable was $1,400,000, and Allowance for Uncollectible Accounts had a debit balance of $48,000.

Omega Company's management uses two methods of estimating uncollectible accounts expense: the percentage of net sales method and the accounts receivable aging method. The percentage of uncollectible sales is 1.5 percent of net sales, and based on an aging of accounts receivable, the end-of-year uncollectible accounts total $140,000.

Prepare the end-of-year adjusting entry to record the uncollectible accounts expense under each method. What will the balance of Allowance for Uncollectible Accounts be after each adjustment? Why are the results different? Which method is likely to be more reliable? Why?

LO3 **Aging Method and Net Sales Method Contrasted**

E 11. The First Fence Company sells merchandise on credit. During the fiscal year ended July 31, the company had net sales of $1,150,000. At the end of the year, it had Accounts Receivable of $300,000 and a debit balance in Allowance for Uncollectible Accounts of $1,700. In the past, approximately 1.4 percent of net sales have proved to be uncollectible. Also, an aging analysis of accounts receivable reveals that $15,000 of the receivables appears to be uncollectible.

Prepare entries in journal form to record uncollectible accounts expense using (a) the percentage of net sales method and (b) the accounts receivable aging method. What is the resulting balance of Allowance for Uncollectible Accounts under each method? How would your answers under each method change if Allowance for Uncollectible Accounts had a credit balance of $1,700 instead of a debit balance? Why do the methods result in different balances?

LO3 **Write-off of Accounts Receivable**

E 12. Colby Company, which uses the allowance method, has Accounts Receivable of $65,000 and an allowance for uncollectible accounts of $6,400 (credit). The company sold merchandise to Irma Hegerman for $7,200 and later received $2,400 from Hegerman. The rest of the amount due from Hegerman had to be written off as uncollectible. Using T accounts, show the beginning balances and the effects of the Hegerman transactions on Accounts Receivable and Allowance for Uncollectible Accounts. What is the amount of net accounts receivable before and after the write-off?

LO4 **Interest Computations**

E 13. Determine the interest on the following notes:

a. $77,520 at 10 percent for 90 days
b. $54,400 at 12 percent for 60 days
c. $61,200 at 9 percent for 30 days
d. $102,000 at 15 percent for 120 days
e. $36,720 at 6 percent for 60 days

LO4 **Notes Receivable Calculations**

E 14. Determine the maturity date, interest at maturity, and maturity value for a 90-day, 10 percent, $36,000 note from Archer Corporation dated February 15.

LO4 **Notes Receivable Calculations**

E 15. Determine the maturity date, interest in 2010 and 2011, and maturity value for a 90-day, 12 percent, $30,000 note from a customer dated December 1, 2010, assuming a December 31 year-end.

LO4 **Notes Receivable Calculations**

E 16. Determine the maturity date, interest at maturity, and maturity value for each of the following notes:

a. A 60-day, 10 percent, $4,800 note dated January 5 received from A. Gal for granting a time extension on a past-due account.
b. A 60-day, 12 percent, $3,000 note dated March 9 received from T. Kawa for granting a time extension on a past-due account.

Problems

LO2 **Bank Reconciliation**

P 1. The following information is available for Unique Globe, Inc., as of May 31, 2010:

a. Cash on the books as of May 31 amounted to $43,784.16. Cash on the bank statement for the same date was $53,451.46.
b. A deposit of $5,220.94, representing cash receipts of May 31, did not appear on the bank statement.
c. Outstanding checks totaled $3,936.80.
d. A check for $1,920.00 returned with the statement was recorded incorrectly in the check register as $1,380.00. The check was for a cash purchase of merchandise.
e. The bank service charge for May amounted to $30.
f. The bank collected $12,200.00 for Unique Globe, Inc., on a note. The face value of the note was $12,000.00.
g. An NSF check for $178.56 from a customer, Eve Lay, was returned with the statement.
h. The bank mistakenly charged to the company account a check for $750.00 drawn by another company.

i. The bank reported that it had credited the account for $250.00 in interest on the average balance for May.

Required

1. Prepare a bank reconciliation for Unique Globe, Inc., as of May 31, 2010.
2. Prepare the entries in journal form necessary to adjust the accounts.
3. What amount of cash should appear on Unique Globe, Inc.'s balance sheet as of May 31?

User insight ▶
4. Why is a bank reconciliation considered an important control over cash?

Methods of Estimating Uncollectible Accounts and Receivables Analysis

P 2. Moore Company had an Accounts Receivable balance of $640,000 and a credit balance in Allowance for Uncollectible Accounts of $33,400 at January 1, 2010. During the year, the company recorded the following transactions:

a. Sales on account, $2,104,000
b. Sales returns and allowances by credit customers, $106,800
c. Collections from customers, $1,986,000
d. Worthless accounts written off, $39,600

The company's past history indicates that 2.5 percent of its net credit sales will not be collected.

Required

1. Prepare T accounts for Accounts Receivable and Allowance for Uncollectible Accounts. Enter the beginning balances, and show the effects on these accounts of the items listed above, summarizing the year's activity. Determine the ending balance of each account.
2. Compute Uncollectible Accounts Expense and determine the ending balance of Allowance for Uncollectible Accounts under (a) the percentage of net sales method and (b) the accounts receivable aging method, assuming an aging of the accounts receivable shows that $48,000 may be uncollectible.
3. Compute the receivable turnover and days' sales uncollected, using the data from the accounts receivable aging method in requirement **2**.

User insight ▶
4. How do you explain that the two methods used in requirement **2** result in different amounts for Uncollectible Accounts Expense? What rationale underlies each method?

Accounts Receivable Aging Method

P 3. The Ciao Style Store uses the accounts receivable aging method to estimate uncollectible accounts. On February 1, 2010, the balance of the Accounts Receivable account was a debit of $442,341, and the balance of Allowance for Uncollectible Accounts was a credit of $43,700. During the year, the store had sales on account of $3,722,000, sales returns and allowances of $60,000, worthless accounts written off of $44,300, and collections from customers of $3,211,000. As part of the end-of-year (January 31, 2011) procedures, an aging analysis of accounts receivable is prepared. The analysis, which is partially complete, is as follows:

Customer Account	Total	Not Yet Due	1–30 Days Past Due	31–60 Days Past Due	61–90 Days Past Due	Over 90 Days Past Due
Balance Forward	$793,791	$438,933	$149,614	$106,400	$57,442	$41,402

To finish the analysis, the following accounts need to be classified:

Account	Amount	Due Date
J. Kras	$11,077	Jan. 15
T. Lopez	9,314	Feb. 15 (next fiscal year)
L. Zapal	8,664	Dec. 20
R. Caputo	780	Oct. 1
E. Rago	14,710	Jan. 4
S. Smith	6,316	Nov. 15
A. Quinn	4,389	Mar. 1 (next fiscal year)
	$55,250	

From past experience, the company has found that the following rates are realistic for estimating uncollectible accounts:

Time	Percentage Considered Uncollectible
Not yet due	2
1–30 days past due	5
31–60 days past due	15
61–90 days past due	25
Over 90 days past due	50

Required

1. Complete the aging analysis of accounts receivable.
2. Compute the end-of-year balances (before adjustments) of Accounts Receivable and Allowance for Uncollectible Accounts.
3. Prepare an analysis computing the estimated uncollectible accounts.
4. How much is Ciao Style Store's estimated uncollectible accounts expense for the year? (Round the adjustment to the nearest whole dollar.)

User insight ▶ 5. What role do estimates play in applying the aging analysis? What factors might affect these estimates?

Notes Receivable Calculations

P 4. Rich Importing Company engaged in the following transactions involving promissory notes:

May	3	Sold engines to Kabel Company for $30,000 in exchange for a 90-day, 12 percent promissory note.
	16	Sold engines to Vu Company for $16,000 in exchange for a 60-day, 13 percent note.
	31	Sold engines to Vu Company for $15,000 in exchange for a 90-day, 11 percent note.

Required

1. For each of the notes, determine the (a) maturity date, (b) interest on the note, and (c) maturity value.
2. Assume that the fiscal year for Rich Importing Company ends on June 30. How much interest income should be recorded on that date?

User insight ▶ 3. What are the effects of the transactions in May on cash flows for the year ended June 30?

Alternate Problems

Bank Reconciliation

P 5. The following information is available for Prime Corporation as of April 30, 2010:

a. Cash on the books as of April 30 amounted to $113,175.28. Cash on the bank statement for the same date was $140,717.08.
b. A deposit of $14,349.84, representing cash receipts of April 30, did not appear on the bank statement.
c. Outstanding checks totaled $7,302.64.
d. A check for $2,420.00 returned with the statement was recorded as $2,024.00. The check was for advertising.
e. The bank service charge for April amounted to $35.00.
f. The bank collected $36,300.00 for Prime Corporation on a note. The face value of the note was $36,000.00.
g. An NSF check for $1,140.00 from a customer, Tom Jones, was returned with the statement.
h. The bank mistakenly deducted a check for $700.00 that was drawn by Tiger Corporation.
i. The bank reported a credit of $560.00 for interest on the average balance.

Required

1. Prepare a bank reconciliation for Prime Corporation as of April 30, 2010.
2. Prepare the necessary entries in journal form from the reconciliation.
3. State the amount of cash that should appear on Prime Corporation's balance sheet as of April 30.
4. **User insight ▶** Why is a bank reconciliation a necessary internal control?

Methods of Estimating Uncollectible Accounts and Receivables Analysis

P 6. On December 31 of last year, the balance sheet of Korab Company had Accounts Receivable of $149,000 and a credit balance in Allowance for Uncollectible Accounts of $10,150. During the current year, Korab Company's financial records included the following selected activities: (a) sales on account, $597,500; (b) sales returns and allowances, $36,500; (c) collections from customers, $575,000; and (d) accounts written off as worthless, $8,000. In the past, 1.6 percent of Korab Company's net sales have been uncollectible.

Required

1. Prepare T accounts for Accounts Receivable and Allowance for Uncollectible Accounts. Enter the beginning balances, and show the effects on these accounts of the items listed above, summarizing the year's activity. Determine the ending balance of each account.
2. Compute Uncollectible Accounts Expense and determine the ending balance of Allowance for Uncollectible Accounts under (a) the percentage of net sales method and (b) the accounts receivable aging method. Assume that an aging of the accounts receivable shows that $10,000 may be uncollectible.
3. Compute the receivable turnover and days' sales uncollected, using the data from the accounts receivable aging method in requirement **2**.
4. **User insight ▶** How do you explain that the two methods used in requirement **2** result in different amounts for Uncollectible Accounts Expense? What rationale underlies each method?

Accounts Receivable Aging Method

P 7. Garcia Company uses the accounts receivable aging method to estimate uncollectible accounts. At the beginning of the year, the balance of the Accounts Receivable account was a debit of $90,430, and the balance of Allowance for Uncollectible Accounts was a credit of $8,100. During the year, the store had sales on account of $475,000, sales returns and allowances of $6,200, worthless accounts written off of $8,800, and collections from customers of $452,730. At the end of year (December 31, 2010), a junior accountant for Garcia Company was preparing an aging analysis of accounts receivable. At the top of page 6 of the report, the following totals appeared:

Customer Account	Total	Not Yet Due	1–30 Days Past Due	31–60 Days Past Due	61–90 Days Past Due	Over 90 Days Past Due
Balance Forward	$89,640	$49,030	$24,110	$9,210	$3,990	$3,300

To finish the analysis, the following accounts need to be classified:

Account	Amount	Due Date
B. Smith	$ 930	Jan. 14 (next year)
L. Wing	645	Dec. 24
A. Rak	1,850	Sept. 28
T. Cat	2,205	Aug. 16
M. Nut	350	Dec. 14
S. Prince	1,785	Jan. 23 (next year)
J. Wind	295	Nov. 5
	$8,060	

From past experience, the company has found that the following rates are realistic for estimating uncollectible accounts:

Time	Percentage Considered Uncollectible
Not yet due	2
1–30 days past due	5
31–60 days past due	15
61–90 days past due	25
Over 90 days past due	50

Required

1. Complete the aging analysis of accounts receivable.
2. Compute the end-of-year balances (before adjustments) of Accounts Receivable and Allowance for Uncollectible Accounts.
3. Prepare an analysis computing the estimated uncollectible accounts.
4. Calculate Garcia Company's estimated uncollectible accounts expense for the year (round the amount to the nearest whole dollar).

User insight ▶

5. What role do estimates play in applying the aging analysis? What factors might affect these estimates?

ENHANCING Your Knowledge, Skills, and Critical Thinking

Conceptual Understanding Cases

LO1

Role of Credit Sales

C 1. **Mitsubishi Corp.**, a broadly diversified Japanese corporation, instituted a credit plan called Three Diamonds for customers who buy its major electronic products, such as large-screen televisions and videotape recorders, from specified retail dealers.[20] Under the plan, approved customers who make purchases in July of one year do not have to make any payments until September of the next year. Nor do they have to pay interest during the intervening months. Mitsubishi pays the dealer the full amount less a small fee, sends the customer a Mitsubishi credit card, and collects from the customer at the specified time.

What was Mitsubishi's motivation for establishing such generous credit terms? What costs are involved? What are the accounting implications?

LO1 LO3

Role of Estimates in Accounting for Receivables

C 2. **CompuCredit** is a credit card issuer in Atlanta. It prides itself on making credit cards available to almost anybody in a matter of seconds over the Internet. The cost to the consumer is an interest rate of 28 percent, about double that of companies that provide cards only to customers with good credit. Despite its high interest rate, CompuCredit has been successful, reporting 1.9 million accounts and an income of approximately $100 million in a recent year. To calculate its income, the company estimates that 10 percent of its $1.3 billion in accounts receivable will not be paid; the industry average is 7 percent. Some analysts have been critical of CompuCredit for being too optimistic in its projections of losses.[21]

Why are estimates necessary in accounting for receivables? If CompuCredit were to use the same estimate of losses as other companies in its industry, what would its income have been for the year? How would one determine if CompuCredit's estimate of losses is reasonable?

LO1

Receivables Financing

C 3. Bernhardt Appliances, Inc., located in central Ohio, is a small manufacturer of washing machines and dryers. Bernhardt sells most of its appliances to large, established discount retail companies that market the appliances under their own names. Bernhardt sells the appliances on trade credit terms of n/60. If a customer wants a longer term, however, Bernhardt will accept a note with a term of up to nine months. At present, the company is having cash flow troubles and needs $10 million immediately. Its cash balance is $400,000, its accounts receivable balance is $4.6 million, and its notes receivable balance is $7.4 million.

How might Bernhardt Appliance's management use its accounts receivable and notes receivable to raise the cash it needs? What are the company's prospects for raising the needed cash?

Interpreting Financial Reports

LO1

Comparison and Interpretation of Ratios

C 4. **Fosters Group Limited** and **Heineken N.V.** are two well-known beer companies. Fosters is an Australian company, and Heineken is Dutch. Fosters is about half the size of Heineken.

Ratios can help in comparing and understanding companies that are different in size and that use different currencies. For example, the receivable turnovers for Fosters and Heineken in 2007 and 2006 were as follows:[22]

	2007	2006
Fosters	5.3 times	5.0 times
Heineken	6.2 times	6.0 times

What do the ratios tell you about the credit policies of the two companies? How long does it take each, on average, to collect a receivable? What do the ratios tell you about the companies' relative needs for capital to finance receivables? Which company is improving? Can you tell which company has a better credit policy? Explain your answers.

Decision Analysis Using Excel

LO1 LO3

Accounting for Accounts Receivable

C 5. Makay Products Co. is a major consumer goods company that sells over 3,000 products in 135 countries. The company's annual report to the Securities and Exchange Commission presented the following data (in thousands) pertaining to net sales and accounts related to accounts receivable for 2008, 2009, and 2010.

	2010	2009	2008
Net sales	$9,820,000	$9,730,000	$9,888,000
Accounts receivable	1,046,000	1,048,000	1,008,000
Allowance for uncollectible accounts	37,200	42,400	49,000
Uncollectible accounts expense	30,000	33,400	31,600
Uncollectible accounts written off	38,600	40,200	35,400
Recoveries of accounts previously written off	3,400	200	2,000

1. Compute the ratio of uncollectible accounts expense to net sales and to accounts receivable, and the ratio of allowance for uncollectible accounts to accounts receivable for 2008, 2009, and 2010.
2. Compute the receivable turnover and days' sales uncollected for each year, assuming 2007 net accounts receivable were $930,000,000.
3. What is your interpretation of the ratios? Describe management's attitude toward the collectibility of accounts receivable over the three-year period.

Annual Report Case: CVS Caremark Corporation

LO1 LO2 LO3

CASH FLOW

Cash and Receivables

C 6. Refer to the **CVS** annual report in the Supplement to Chapter 1 to answer the following questions:

1. What amount of cash and cash equivalents did CVS have in 2007? Do you suppose most of that amount is cash in the bank or cash equivalents?
2. What customers represent the main source of CVS's accounts receivable, and how much is CVS's allowance for uncollectible accounts?
3. What do you think CVS's seasonal needs for cash are? Where in CVS's financial statements is the seasonality of sales discussed?

Comparison Case: CVS Versus Walgreens

Accounts Receivable Analysis

C 7. Refer to the **CVS** annual report in the Supplement to Chapter 1 and to the following data (in millions) for Walgreens: net sales, $53,762.0 and $47,409.0 for 2007 and 2006, respectively; accounts receivable, net, $2,236.5 and $2,062.7 for 2007 and 2006, respectively.

1. Compute receivable turnover and days' sales uncollected for 2007 and 2006 for CVS and Walgreens. Accounts Receivable in 2005 were $1,841.6 million for CVS and $1,442.2 million for Walgreens.
2. Do you discern any differences in the two companies' credit policies? Explain your answer.

Ethical Dilemma Case

LO1 LO3

Ethics and Uncollectible Accounts

C 8. Caldwell Interiors, a successful retail furniture company, is located in an affluent suburb where a major insurance company has just announced a restructuring that will lay off 4,000 employees. Caldwell Interiors sells quality furniture, usually on credit. Accounts Receivable is one of its major assets. Although the company's annual uncollectible accounts losses are not out of line, they represent a sizable amount. The company depends on bank loans for its financing. Sales and net income have declined in the past year, and some customers are falling behind in paying their accounts.

Abby Caldwell, the owner of the business, knows that the bank's loan officer likes to see a steady performance. She has therefore instructed the company's controller to underestimate the uncollectible accounts this year to show a small growth in earnings. Caldwell believes this action is justified because earnings in future years will average out the losses, and since the company has a history of success, she believes the adjustments are meaningless accounting measures anyway.

Are Caldwell's actions ethical? Would any parties be harmed by her actions? How important is it to try to be accurate in estimating losses from uncollectible accounts?

Internet Case

LO1 LO3

Comparison of J.C. Penney, Inc., and Dillard's, Inc.

C 9. Access the annual reports of **J.C. Penney** and **Dillard's**. Find the accounts receivable on each company's balance sheet and the notes to the financial statements that are related to those accounts. Which company has the most accounts receivable as a percentage of total assets? What is the percentage of the allowance account to gross accounts receivable for each company? Which company experienced the highest loss rate on its receivables? Why do you think there is a difference? Do the companies finance their receivables? Be prepared to discuss your findings in class.

Group Activity Case

Effects of Credit Policies

C 10. **Tenet Healthcare Corp.**, the second largest publicly traded hospital chain in the United States, had a large amount of uncollectible accounts expense because so many patients were unable to pay their medical bills. Its uncollectible accounts expense amounted to about 11 percent of its revenues. After management analyzed the problem, they found that 70 percent of the losses came from uninsured patients and 30 percent from those who had insurance. The company realized that many of the uninsured could not be expected to pay and that the large amount of the bills simply discouraged patients from seeking health care. The company decided to start charging these patients less, hoping it could eliminate 40 to 60 percent of its bad debts loss. The company's chief financial officer said, "A significant amount of the revenue will never be recorded in the first place due to this pricing, so that it will not have to be written off as bad debt."[23]

In informal groups in class, discuss and report on the following questions: What effect will the new pricing policy have on the company's reported earnings? Why would the company want to show lower uncollectible accounts expense? Do you think the new policy has ethical ramifications?

Business Communication Case

LO1 LO2

Cash Management and Cash Equivalents

C 11. Collegiate Publishing Company publishes college textbooks in the sciences and humanities. More than 50 percent of Collegiate Publishing's sales occur in July, August, and December. The company's cash balance builds up until sometime after the sales take place and the books are paid for. During the rest of the year, its sales are low. The company's treasurer keeps the cash in a bank checking account earning little or no interest and pays bills from this account as they come due. To survive periods when cash receipts are low, Collegiate Publishing Company sometimes borrows money, and it repays the loans in the months when cash receipts are largest.

The company is currently considering two plans of action. First, it would work with the bookstores to implement electronic funds transfer (EFT) for payment. Second, it would invest in short-term (less than 90 days) securities that pay a higher rate of interest than the checking account.

Write a memorandum to the president that lays out the advantages of EFT and states the accounting implications (if any) of the plan to invest in short-term securities.

CHAPTER

8 Current Liabilities and Fair Value Accounting

Focus on Financial Statements

INCOME STATEMENT
Revenues
– Expenses
= Net Income

STATEMENT OF RETAINED EARNINGS
Opening Balance
+ Net Income
– Dividends
= Retained Earnings

BALANCE SHEET
Assets | Liabilities
Equity
A = L + E

STATEMENT OF CASH FLOWS
Operating activities
+ Investing activities
+ Financing activities
= Change in Cash
+ Starting Balance
= Ending Cash Balance

Valuation of unearned revenues and accrued liabilities on the balance sheet is linked to measurement of revenues and expenses on the income statement.

Although some current liabilities, such as accounts payable, are recorded when a company makes a purchase, others accrue during an accounting period and are not recorded until adjusting entries are made at the end of the period. In addition, the value of some accruals must be estimated. If accrued liabilities are not recognized and valued properly, both liabilities and expenses will be understated on the financial statements, making the company's performance look better than it actually is.

LEARNING OBJECTIVES

LO1 Identify the management issues related to current liabilities. *(pp. 424–428)*

LO2 Identify, compute, and record definitely determinable and estimated current liabilities. *(pp. 428–438)*

LO3 Distinguish *contingent liabilities* from *commitments*. *(pp. 438–439)*

LO4 Identify the valuation approaches to fair value accounting, and define *time value of money* and *interest* and apply them to present values. *(pp. 439–444)*

LO5 Apply present value to simple valuation situations. *(pp. 444–446)*

DECISION POINT ►A USER'S FOCUS

Microsoft

Microsoft is the world's leading computer software company. It earns revenue by developing, manufacturing, licensing, and supporting a wide range of software products, including its new Windows Vista® and Xbox360™. As you can see in Microsoft's Financial Highlights, its total liabilities in 2007 were almost $23.8 billion, or about 76.5 percent of its stockholders' equity of $31.1 billion.[1]

Managing liabilities is obviously important to achieving profitability and liquidity. If a company has too few liabilities, it may not be earning up to its potential. If it has too many liabilities, it may be incurring excessive risks. A company that does not manage its debt carefully is vulnerable to failure.

MICROSOFT'S FINANCIAL HIGHLIGHTS (In millions)

Current Liabilities	**2007**	**2006**
Accounts payable	$ 3,247	$ 2,909
Accrued compensation	2,325	1,938
Income taxes payable	1,040	1,557
Short-term unearned revenue	10,779	9,138
Securities lending payable and other	6,363	6,900
Total current liabilities	$23,754	$22,442
Long-term unearned revenue and other long-term liabilities	8,320	7,051
Total liabilities	$32,074	$29,493

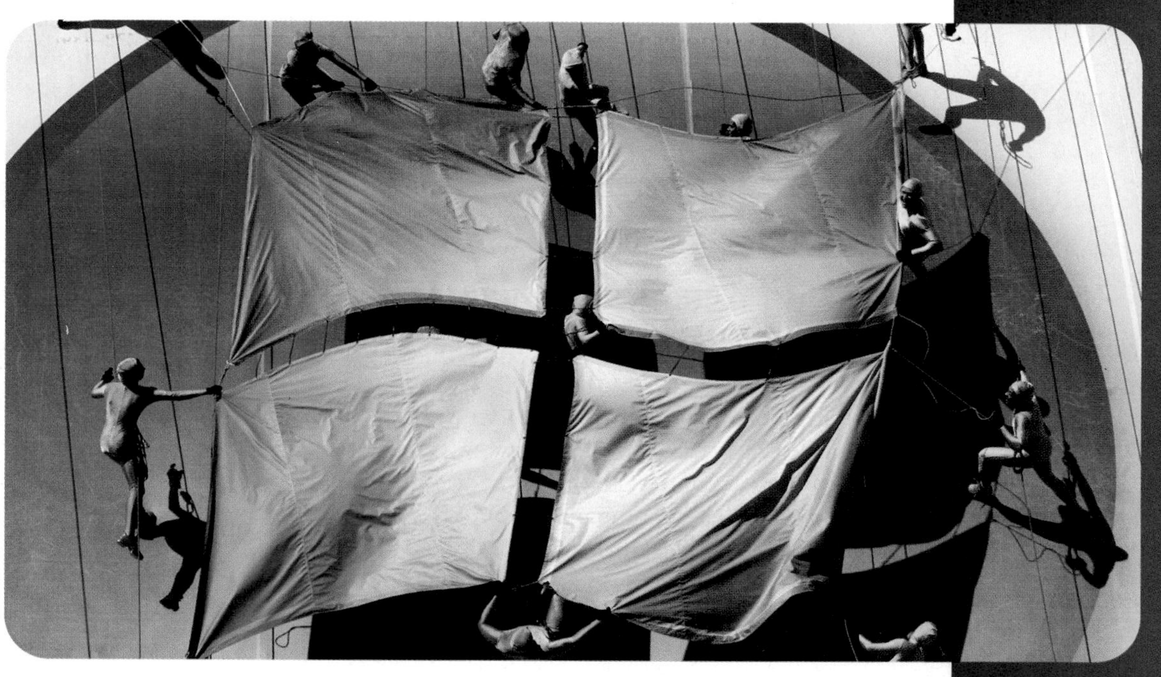

- ► How does Microsoft's decision to incur debt relate to the goals of the business?
- ► Is the level of accounts payable in the operating cycle satisfactory?
- ► Has the company properly identified and accounted for all its current liabilities?

Management Issues Related to Current Liabilities

LO1 Identify the management issues related to current liabilities.

Current liabilities require not only careful management of liquidity and cash flows, but close monitoring of accounts payable as well. In reporting on current liabilities, managers must understand how they should be recognized, valued, classified, and disclosed.

Managing Liquidity and Cash Flows

The primary reason a company incurs current liabilities is to meet its needs for cash during the operating cycle. As explained in Chapter 5, the operating cycle is the length of time it takes to purchase inventory, sell the inventory, and collect the resulting receivable. Most current liabilities arise in support of this cycle, as when accounts payable arise from purchases of inventory, accrued expenses arise from operating costs, and unearned revenues arise from customers' advance payments. Companies incur short-term debt to raise cash during periods of inventory build-up or while waiting for collection of receivables. They use the cash to pay the portion of long-term debt that is currently due and to pay liabilities arising from operations.

Failure to manage the cash flows related to current liabilities can have serious consequences for a business. For instance, if suppliers are not paid on time, they may withhold shipments that are vital to a company's operations. Continued failure to pay current liabilities can lead to bankruptcy. To evaluate a company's ability to pay its current liabilities, analysts often use two measures of liquidity—working capital and the current ratio, both of which we defined in an earlier chapter. Current liabilities are a key component of both these measures. They typically equal from 25 to 50 percent of total assets.

As shown below (in millions), **Microsoft's** short-term liquidity as measured by working capital and the current ratio was positive in 2006 and declined somewhat in 2007.

	Current Assets	−	Current Liabilities	=	Working Capital	Current Ratio*
2006	$49,010	−	$22,442	=	$26,568	2.18
2007	$40,168	−	$23,754	=	$16,414	1.69

The decline in Microsoft's working capital and current ratio from 2006 to 2007 was caused primarily by a large increase in cash purchases of its own stock. Overall, Microsoft is in a strong current situation and exercises very good management of its cash flow. Note the large amounts of both short-term and long-term unearned revenue. These are fees for licenses and services that customers pay in advance, thus helping cash flow. Microsoft will, of course, have to perform the services to earn the revenues.

Evaluating Accounts Payable

Another consideration in managing liquidity and cash flows is the time suppliers give a company to pay for purchases. Measures commonly used to assess a company's ability to pay within a certain time frame are **payables turnover** and **days' payables**. Payables turnover is the number of times, on average, that a company pays its accounts payable in an accounting period. Days' payable shows how long, on average, a company takes to pay its accounts payables.

To measure payables turnover for **Microsoft**, we must first calculate purchases by adjusting cost of goods sold for the change in inventory. An increase in

*Current assets divided by current liabilities

FOCUS ON BUSINESS PRACTICE

Debt Problems Can Plague Even Well-Known Companies.

In a Wall Street horror story that illustrates the importance of managing current liabilities, **Xerox Corporation**, one of the most storied names in American business, found itself combating rumors that it was facing bankruptcy. Following a statement by Xerox's CEO that the company's financial model was "unsustainable," management was forced to defend the company's liquidity by saying it had adequate funds to continue operations. But in a report filed with the SEC, management acknowledged that it had tapped into its $7 billion line of bank credit for more than $3 billion to pay off short-term debt that was coming due. Unable to secure more money from any other source to pay these debts, Xerox had no choice but to turn to the line of credit from its bank. Had it run out, the company might well have gone bankrupt.[2] Fortunately, Xerox was able to restructure its line of credit to stay in business.

inventory means purchases were more than cost of goods sold; a decrease means purchases were less than cost of goods sold. Microsoft's cost of goods sold in 2007 was $10,693 million, and its inventory decreased by $351 million. Much of its inventory consists of its new consumer product, Xbox360. Its payables turnover is computed as follows (in millions):

K/R

$$\text{Payables Turnover} = \frac{\text{Cost of Goods Sold} + \text{Change in Merchandise Inventory}}{\text{Average Accounts Payable}}$$

$$= \frac{\$10{,}693 - \$351}{(\$3{,}247 + \$2{,}909) \div 2}$$

$$= \frac{\$10{,}342}{\$3{,}078} = 3.4 \text{ times}$$

To find the days' payable, the number of days in a year is divided by the payables turnover:

K/R

$$\text{Days' Payable} = \frac{365 \text{ days}}{\text{Payables Turnover}} = \frac{365 \text{ days}}{3.4 \text{ times}} = 107.4 \text{ days}$$

The payables turnover of 3.4 times and days' payable of 107.4 days indicate that the credit terms Microsoft receives from its suppliers are excellent. These results also stem partly from the fact that some product costs are small relative to sales price. After development, some software is not costly to produce, because products such as Windows Vista can be licensed to businesses and sold and delivered online. In other industries, credit terms and product costs are not nearly as favorable. As you can see in Figures 1 and 2, companies in other industries have higher payables turnover and lower days' payable than Microsoft. These key ratios have been a major factor in Microsoft's ability to maintain adequate liquidity. To get a full picture of a company's operating cycle and liquidity, analysts also consider payables turnover and days' payable in relation to the other components of the operating cycle: inventory and receivable turnovers and their related number of days' ratios.

Reporting Liabilities

In deciding whether to buy stock in a company or lend money to it, investors and creditors must evaluate not only the company's current liabilities, but its future obligations as well. In doing so, they have to rely on the integrity of the company's financial statements.

FIGURE 1
Payables Turnover for Selected Industries

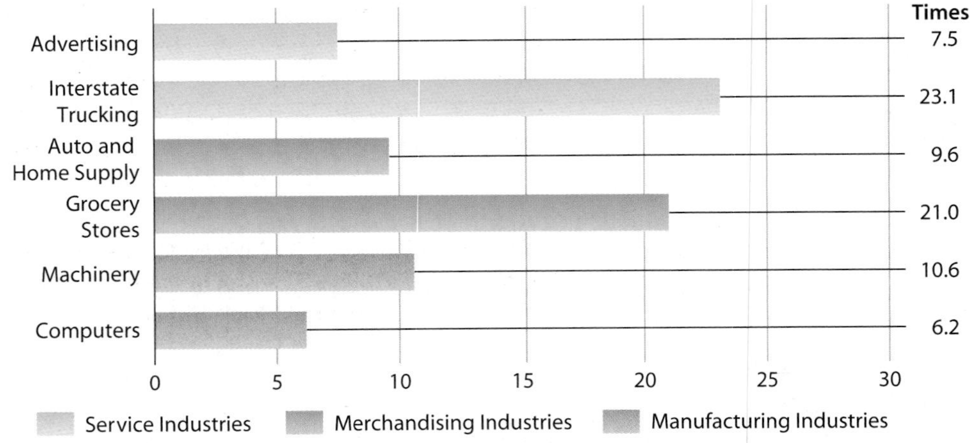

Source: Data from Dun & Bradstreet, *Industry Norms and Key Business Ratios*, 2005–2006.

Ethical reporting of liabilities requires that they be properly recognized, valued, classified, and disclosed. In one notable case involving unethical reporting of liabilities, the CEO and other employees of **Nortel Networks Corporation**, a Canadian manufacturer of telecommunications equipment, understated accrued liabilities (and corresponding expenses) in order to report a profit and obtain salary bonuses. After all accrued liabilities had been identified, it was evident that the company was in fact losing money. The board of directors of the corporation fired all who had been involved.[3]

Recognition Timing is important in the recognition of liabilities. Failure to record a liability in an accounting period very often goes along with failure to record an expense. The two errors lead to an understatement of expense and an overstatement of income.

Generally accepted accounting principles require that a liability be recorded when an obligation occurs. This rule is harder to apply than it might appear. When a transaction obligates a company to make future payments, a liability arises and is recognized, as when goods are bought on credit. However, some current liabilities are not the result of direct transactions. One of the key reasons for making adjusting entries at the end of an accounting period is to recognize unrecorded liabilities that accrue during the period. Accrued liabilities include

FIGURE 2
Days' Payable for Selected Industries

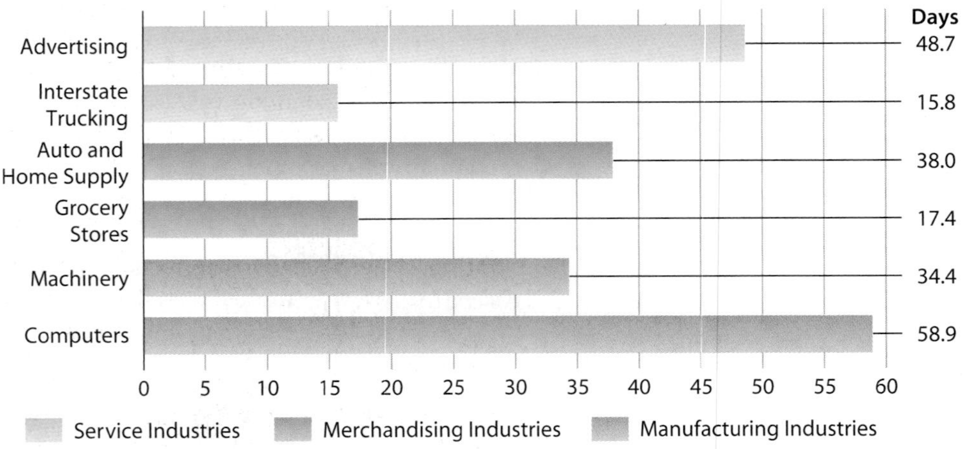

Source: Data from Dun & Bradstreet, *Industry Norms and Key Business Ratios*, 2005–2006.

salaries payable and interest payable. Other liabilities that can only be estimated, such as taxes payable, must also be recognized through adjusting entries.

Agreements for future transactions do not have to be recognized. For instance, **Microsoft** might agree to pay an executive $250,000 a year for a period of three years, or it might agree to buy an unspecified amount of advertising at a certain price over the next five years. Such contracts, though they are definite commitments, are not considered liabilities because they are for future—not past—transactions. Because there is no current obligation, no liability is recognized, but they would be mentioned in the notes to the financial statements and SEC filings if material.

Study Note

Disclosure of the fair value and the bases for estimating the fair value of short-term notes payable, loans payable, and other short-term debt are required unless it is not practical to estimate the value. Guidance for determining fair value is covered later in this chapter.

Valuation On the balance sheet, a liability is generally valued at the amount of money needed to pay the debt or at the fair market value of the goods or services to be delivered.

The amount of most liabilities is definitely known. For example, **Amazon.com** sells a large number of gift certificates that are redeemable in the future. The amount of the liability (unearned revenue) is known, but the exact timing is not known.

Some companies, however, must estimate future liabilities. For example, an automobile dealer that sells a car with a one-year warranty must provide parts and service during the year. The obligation is definite because the sale has occurred, but the amount of the obligation can only be estimated. Such estimates are usually based on past experience and anticipated changes in the business environment.

Classification As you may recall from our discussion of classified balance sheets in an earlier chapter, **current liabilities** are debts and obligations that a company expects to satisfy within one year or within its normal operating cycle, whichever is longer. These liabilities are normally paid out of current assets or with cash generated by operations. **Long-term liabilities** are liabilities due beyond one year or beyond the normal operating cycle. For example, Microsoft incurs long-term liabilities to finance its software development among other objectives. The distinction between current and long-term liabilities is important because it affects the evaluation of a company's liquidity. Microsoft carefully distinguishes between short-term unearned revenues, which represent services to be performed in the next year, and long-term unearned revenues, which represent services that will be performed in future years.

Disclosure A company may have to include additional explanation of some liability accounts in the notes to its financial statements. For example, if a company's Notes Payable account is large, it should disclose the balances, maturity dates, interest rates, and other features of the debts in an explanatory note. Any special credit arrangements should also be disclosed. For example, in a note to its financial statements, **Hershey Foods Corporation**, the famous candy company, discloses the rationale for its credit arrangements:

> **Short-Term Debt and Financing Arrangements**
>
> We maintain debt levels we consider prudent based on our cash flow, interest coverage ratio and percentage of debt to capital. We use financing to lower our overall cost of capital, which increases our return on stockholders' equity.[4]

Unused lines of credit allow a company to borrow on short notice up to the credit limit, with little or no negotiation. Thus, the type of disclosure in Hershey's note is helpful in assessing whether a company has additional borrowing power.

STOP ► REVIEW ► APPLY

LO1-1 What are three examples of current liabilities?

LO1-2 What are two measures of liquidity used in evaluating a firm's ability to pay its current liabilities?

LO1-3 What does payables turnover tell you about a company's liquidity?

LO1-4 Why is the timing of liability recognition important?

LO1-5 What is the rule for classifying a liability as current?

LO1-6 Manly Company has an unused line of bank credit of $100,000. Should Manly record this line of credit as a liability and disclose it in its financial statements?

Suggested answers to all Stop, Review, and Apply questions follow the appendixes.

Common Types of Current Liabilities

LO2 Identify, compute, and record definitely determinable and estimated current liabilities.

As noted earlier, a company incurs current liabilities to meet its needs for cash during the operating cycle. These liabilities fall into two major groups: definitely determinable liabilities and estimated liabilities.

Definitely Determinable Liabilities

Current liabilities that are set by contract or statute and that can be measured exactly are called **definitely determinable liabilities**. The problems in accounting for these liabilities are to determine their existence and amount and to see that they are recorded properly. The most common definitely determinable liabilities are described below.

Study Note

On the balance sheet, the order of presentation for current liabilities is not as strict as for current assets. Generally, accounts payable or notes payable appear first, and the rest of current liabilities follow.

Accounts Payable Accounts payable (sometimes called *trade accounts payable*) are short-term obligations to suppliers for goods and services. The amount in the Accounts Payable account is generally supported by an accounts payable subsidiary ledger, which contains an individual account for each person or company to which money is owed. As shown in the Financial Highlights at the beginning of the chapter, accounts payable make up more than half of **Microsoft's** current liabilities.

Bank Loans and Commercial Paper Management often establishes a **line of credit** with a bank. This arrangement allows the company to borrow funds when they are needed to finance current operations. In a note to its financial statements, **Goodyear Tire & Rubber Company** describes its lines of credit as follows: "In aggregate, we had credit arrangements of $8,208 million available at December 31, 2006, of which $533 million were unused."[5]

Although a company signs a promissory note for the full amount of a line of credit, it has great flexibility in using the available funds. It can increase its borrowing up to the limit when it needs cash and reduce the amount borrowed when it generates enough cash of its own. Both the amount borrowed and the interest rate charged by the bank may change daily. The bank may require the company to meet certain financial goals (such as maintaining specific profit margins, current ratios, or debt to equity ratios) to retain its line of credit.

Companies with excellent credit ratings can borrow short-term funds by issuing **commercial paper**. *Commercial paper* refers to unsecured loans (i.e., loans not backed up by any specific assets) that are sold to the public, usually through professionally managed investment firms. Highly rated companies rely heavily on commercial paper to raise short-term funds, but they can quickly lose access to this means of borrowing if their credit rating drops. Because of disappointing operating results in recent years, well-known companies like **DaimlerChrysler**, **Lucent Technologies**, and **Motorola** have lost some or all of their ability to issue commercial paper.

Study Note

Only the used portion of a line of credit is recognized as a liability in the financial statements.

The portion of a line of credit currently borrowed and the amount of commercial paper issued are usually combined with notes payable in the current liabilities section of the balance sheet. Details are disclosed in a note to the financial statements.

Notes Payable Short-term notes payable are obligations represented by promissory notes. A company may sign promissory notes to obtain bank loans, pay suppliers for goods and services, or secure credit from other sources.

Interest is usually stated separately on the face of the note, as shown in Figure 3. The entries to record the note in Figure 3 are as follows:

ISSUANCE

A	=	L	+	SE
+10,000.00		+10,000.00		

Aug. 31	Cash	10,000.00	
	Notes Payable		10,000.00
	Issued 60-day, 12% promissory note		

PAYMENT

A	=	L	+	SE
−10,197.26		−10,000.00		−197.26

Oct. 30	Notes Payable	10,000.00	
	Interest Expense	197.26	
	Cash		10,197.26
	Payment of promissory note with interest		

$$\$10{,}000 \times \frac{12}{100} \times \frac{60}{365} = \$197.26$$

Accrued Liabilities As we noted earlier, a key reason for making adjusting entries at the end of an accounting period is to recognize liabilities that are not already in the accounting records. This practice applies to any type of liability. As

FIGURE 3
Promissory Note

Chicago, Illinois August 31, 2010

Sixty days after date I promise to pay First Federal Bank the sum of $10,000 with interest at the rate of 12% per annum.

Sandra Caron
Caron Corporation

you will see, accrued liabilities (also called *accrued expenses*) can include estimated liabilities. For example, as can be seen in **Microsoft's** Financial Highlights, the company had accrued compensation of over $2,325 million in 2007.

Here, we focus on interest payable, a definitely determinable liability. Interest accrues daily on interest-bearing notes. In accordance with the matching rule, an adjusting entry is made at the end of each accounting period to record the interest obligation up to that point. For example, if the accounting period of the maker of the note in Figure 3 ends on September 30, or 30 days after the issuance of the 60-day note, the adjusting entry would be as follows:

A	=	L	+	SE
		+98.63		−98.63

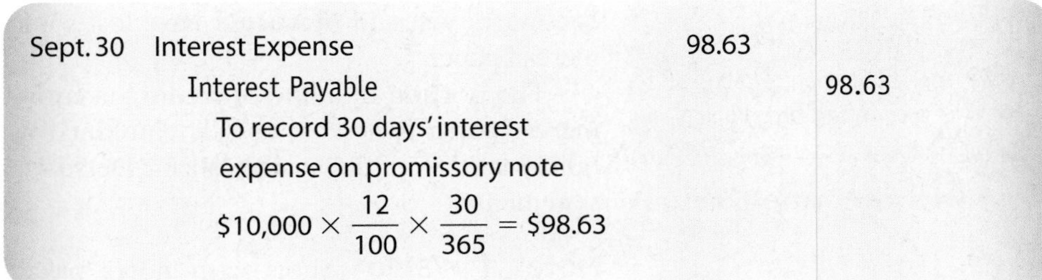

Sept. 30	Interest Expense	98.63	
	Interest Payable		98.63
	To record 30 days' interest expense on promissory note		
	$\$10{,}000 \times \frac{12}{100} \times \frac{30}{365} = \$98.63$		

Dividends Payable As you know, cash dividends are a distribution of earnings to a corporation's stockholders, and a corporation's board of directors has the sole authority to declare them. The corporation has no liability for dividends until the date of declaration. The time between that date and the date of payment of dividends is usually short. During this brief interval, the dividends declared are considered current liabilities of the corporation.

Sales and Excise Taxes Payable Most states and many cities levy a sales tax on retail transactions, and the federal government imposes an excise tax on some products, such as gasoline. A merchant that sells goods subject to these taxes must collect the taxes and forward them periodically to the appropriate government agency. Until the merchant remits the amount it has collected to the government, that amount represents a current liability.

For example, suppose a merchant makes a $200 sale that is subject to a 5 percent sales tax and a 10 percent excise tax. If the sale takes place on June 1, the entry to record it is as follows:

A	=	L	+	SE
+230		+10		+200
		+20		

June 1	Cash	230	
	Sales		200
	Sales Tax Payable		10
	Excise Tax Payable		20
	Sales of merchandise and collection of sales and excise tax		

The sale is properly recorded at $200, and the taxes collected are recorded as liabilities to be remitted to the appropriate government agencies.

Companies that have a physical presence in many cities and states require a complex accounting system for sales taxes because the rates vary from state to state and city to city. For Internet companies, the sales tax situation is simpler. For example, **Amazon.com** is an Internet company without a physical presence in most states and thus does not always have to collect sales tax from its customers. This situation may change in the future, but so far Congress has exempted most Internet sales from sales tax.

FOCUS ON BUSINESS PRACTICE

Small Businesses Offer Benefits, Too.

A survey of small business in the Midwest focused on the employee benefits that these companies offer. The graph at the right presents the results. As you can see, 77 percent of respondents provided both paid vacation and health/medical benefits, and 23 percent even offered their employees tuition reimbursement.[6]

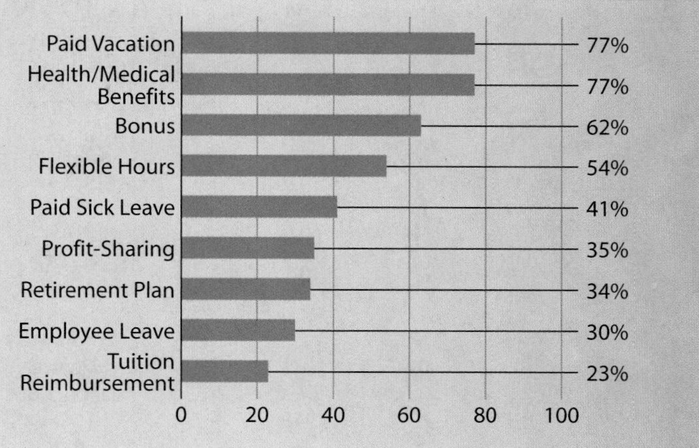

Current Portion of Long-Term Debt If a portion of long-term debt is due within the next year and is to be paid from current assets, that portion is classified as a current liability. It is common for companies to have portions of long-term debt, such as notes or mortgages, due in the next year. No journal entry is necessary when this is case. The total debt is simply reclassified or divided into two categories—short-term and long-term—when the company prepares its balance sheet and other financial statements.

Payroll Liabilities For most organizations, the cost of labor and payroll taxes is a major expense. In the banking and airlines industries, payroll costs represent more than half of all operating costs. Payroll accounting is important because complex laws and significant liabilities are involved. The employer is liable to employees for wages and salaries and to various agencies for amounts withheld from wages and salaries and for related taxes. **Wages** are compensation of employees at an hourly rate; **salaries** are compensation of employees at a monthly or yearly rate.

Because payroll accounting applies only to an organization's employees, it is important to distinguish between employees and independent contractors. Employees are paid a wage or salary by the organization and are under its direct supervision and control. Independent contractors are not employees of the organization and so are not accounted for under the payroll system. They offer services to the organization for a fee, but they are not under its direct control or supervision. Certified public accountants, advertising agencies, and lawyers, for example, often act as independent contractors.

Study Note

In many organizations, a large portion of the cost of labor is not reflected in employees' regular paychecks. Vacation pay, sick pay, personal days, health insurance, life insurance, and pensions are some of the additional cost that may be negotiated between employers and employees.

Figure 4 shows how payroll liabilities relate to employee earnings and employer taxes and other costs. When accounting for payroll liabilities, it is important to keep the following in mind:

- The amount payable to employees is less than the amount of their earnings. This occurs because employers are required by law or are requested by employees to withhold certain amounts from wages and send them directly to government agencies or other organizations.
- An employer's total liabilities exceed employees' earnings because the employer must pay additional taxes and make other contributions (e.g., for pensions and medical care) that increase the cost and liabilities.

FIGURE 4
Illustration of Payroll Costs

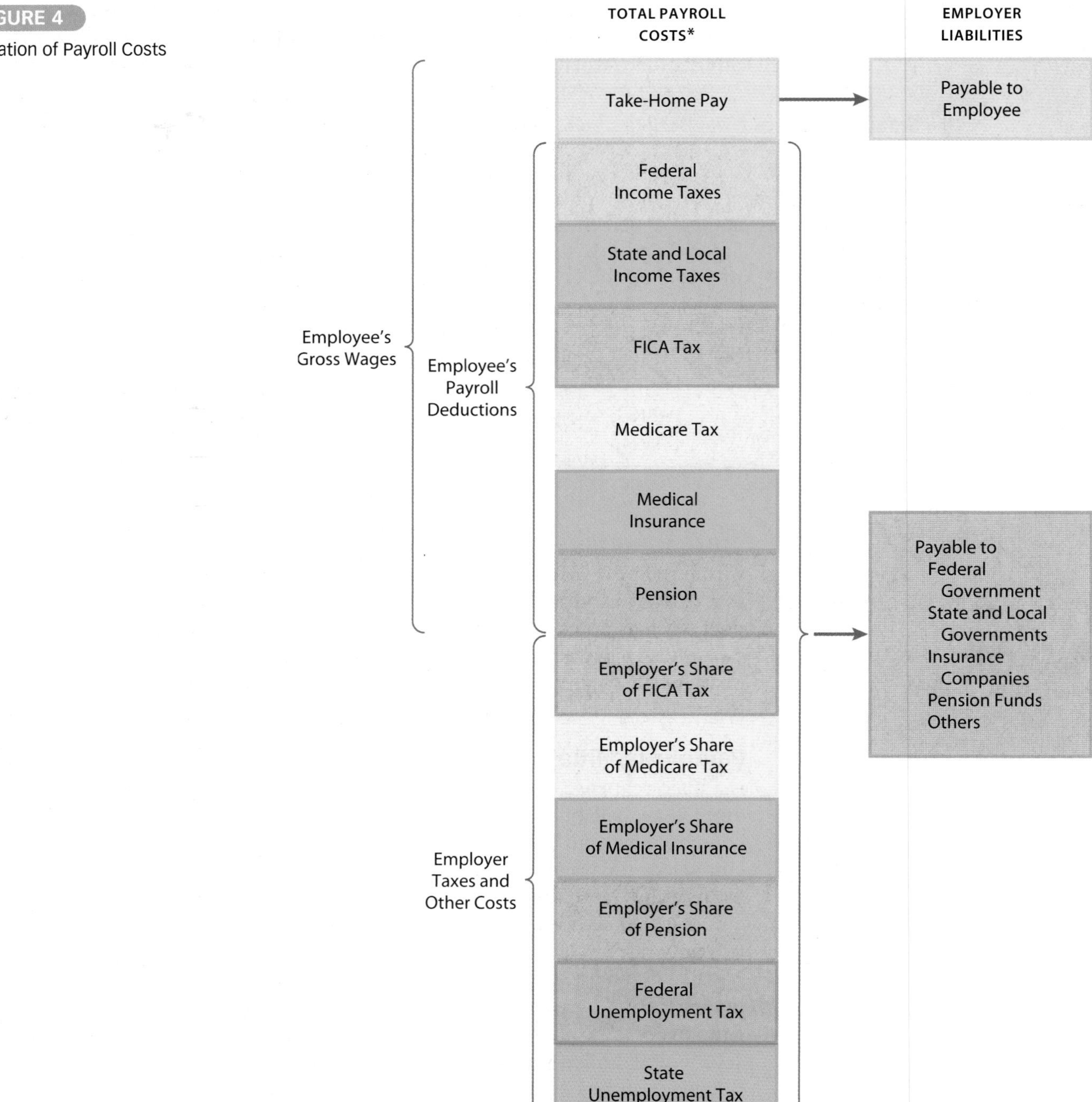

Boxes are not proportional to amounts.

Study Note

The employee pays all federal, state, and local taxes on income. The employer and employee share FICA and Medicare taxes. The employer bears FUTA and state unemployment taxes.

The most common withholdings, taxes, and other payroll costs are described below.

Federal Income Taxes Employers are required to withhold federal income taxes from employees' paychecks and pay them to the United States Treasury. These taxes are collected each time an employee is paid.

State and Local Income Taxes Most states and some local governments levy income taxes. In most cases, the procedures for withholding are similar to those for federal income taxes.

Social Security (FICA) Tax The social security program (the Federal Insurance Contribution Act) provides retirement and disability benefits and survivor's benefits. About 90 percent of the people working in the United States fall under the provisions of this program. The 2008 social security tax rate of 6.2 percent was paid by *both* employee and employer on the first $102,000 earned by an employee during the calendar year. Both the rate and the base to which it applies are subject to change in future years.

Medicare Tax A major extension of the social security program is Medicare, which provides hospitalization and medical insurance for persons over age 65. In 2008, the Medicare tax rate was 1.45 percent of gross income, with no limit, paid by *both* employee and employer.

Medical Insurance Many organizations provide medical benefits to employees. Often, the employee contributes a portion of the cost through withholdings from income and the employer pays the rest—usually a greater amount—to the insurance company.

Pension Contributions Many organizations also provide pension benefits to employees. A portion of the pension contribution is withheld from the employee's income, and the organization pays the rest of the amount into the pension fund.

Federal Unemployment Insurance (FUTA) Tax This tax pays for programs for unemployed workers. It is paid *only* by employers and recently was 6.2 percent of the first $7,000 earned by each employee (this amount may vary from state to state). The employer is allowed a credit for unemployment taxes it pays to the state. The maximum credit is 5.4 percent of the first $7,000 earned by each employee. Most states set their rate at this maximum. Thus, the FUTA tax most often paid is .8 percent (6.2 percent − 5.4 percent) of the taxable wages.

State Unemployment Insurance Tax State unemployment programs provide compensation to eligible unemployed workers. The compensation is paid out of the fund provided by the 5.4 percent of the first $7,000 (or the amount the state sets) earned by each employee. In some states, employers with favorable employment records may be entitled to pay less than 5.4 percent.

To illustrate the recording of a payroll, suppose that on February 15, a company's wages for employees are $65,000 and withholdings for employees are as follows: $10,800 for federal income taxes, $2,400 for state income taxes, $4,030 for social security tax, $942 for Medicare tax, $1,800 for medical insurance, and $2,600 for pension contributions. The entry to record this payroll is:

A	=	L	+	SE
		+10,800		−65,000
		+2,400		
		+4,030		
		+942		
		+1,800		
		+2,600		
		+42,428		

Date	Account	Debit	Credit
Feb. 15	Wages Expense	65,000	
	Employees' Federal Income Taxes Payable		10,800
	Employees' State Income Taxes Payable		2,400
	Social Security Tax Payable		4,030
	Medicare Tax Payable		942
	Medical Insurance Premiums Payable		1,800
	Pension Contributions Payable		2,600
	Wages Payable		42,428
	To record payroll		

Note that although the employees earned $65,000, their take-home pay was only $42,428.

Using the same data but assuming that the employer pays 80 percent of the medical insurance premiums and half of the pension contributions, the employer's taxes and benefit costs would be recorded as follows:

A =	L	+ SE
	+4,030	−18,802
	+942	
	+7,200	
	+2,600	
	+520	
	+3,510	

Feb. 15	Payroll Taxes and Benefits Expense	18,802	
	Social Security Tax Payable		4,030
	Medicare Tax Payable		942
	Medical Insurance Premiums Payable		7,200
	Pension Contributions Payable		2,600
	Federal Unemployment Tax Payable		520
	State Unemployment Tax Payable		3,510
	To record payroll taxes and other costs		

Note that the payroll taxes and benefits expense increase the total cost of the payroll to $83,802 ($18,802 + $65,000), which exceeds the amount earned by employees by almost 29 percent. This is a typical situation. **Microsoft** has all these payroll liabilities in its internal records, but for simplicity combines them all into a single account called Accrued Compensation, as shown in the Financial Highlights at the beginning of this chapter.

Unearned Revenues **Unearned revenues** are advance payments for goods or services that a company must provide in a future accounting period. It then recognizes the revenue over the period in which it provides the products or services. Microsoft, for example, states in its annual report that unearned revenue represents advance customer billings, which it is accounting for as subscriptions with revenue recognized over the period covered by the billing. Assume that Microsoft bills a customer in advance for a one-year subscription. The following entry would be made:

A =	L	+ SE
+3,600	+3,600	

Accounts Receivable	3,600	
Unearned Revenue		3,600
Subscriptions billed in advance		

Microsoft will soon receive cash in the amount of $3,600, but it also has a liability of $3,600 that will slowly be reduced over the year as it provides the service. After the first month, the company records the recognition of revenue as follows:

A =	L	+ SE
	−300	+300

Unearned Revenue	300	
Revenue		300
Recognition of revenue for services provided		

Many businesses, including repair companies, construction companies, and special-order firms, ask for a deposit before they will begin work. Until they deliver the goods or services, these deposits are current liabilities.

FOCUS ON BUSINESS PRACTICE

Those Little Coupons Can Add Up.

Many companies promote their products by issuing coupons that offer "cents off" or other enticements. Because four out of five shoppers use coupons, companies are forced by competition to distribute them. The total value of unredeemed coupons, each of which represents a potential liability for the issuing company, is staggering. *PROMO Magazine* estimates that almost 300 billion coupons are issued annually. Of course, the liability depends on how many coupons will actually be redeemed. *PROMO* estimates that number at approximately 3.6 billion, or about 1.2 percent. Thus, a big advertiser that puts a cents-off coupon in Sunday papers to reach 60 million people can be faced with liability for 720,000 coupons. The total value of coupons redeemed each year is estimated at more than $3.6 billion.[7]

Estimated Liabilities

Study Note

Estimated liabilities are recorded and presented on the financial statements in the same way as definitely determinable liabilities. The only difference is that the computation of estimated liabilities involves some uncertainty.

Estimated liabilities are definite debts or obligations whose exact dollar amount cannot be known until a later date. Because there is no doubt that a legal obligation exists, the primary accounting problem is to estimate and record the amount of the liability. The following are examples of estimated liabilities.

Income Taxes Payable The federal government, most state governments, and some cities and towns levy a tax on a corporation's income. The amount of the liability depends on the results of a corporation's operations, which are often not known until after the end of the corporation's fiscal year. However, because income taxes are an expense in the year in which income is earned, an adjusting entry is necessary to record the estimated tax liability. **Microsoft**, for example, has income taxes payable in 2007 of $1,040 million, as shown in the Financial Highlights at the beginning of this chapter.

Sole proprietorships and partnerships do *not* pay income taxes. However, their owners must report their share of the firm's income on their individual tax returns.

Property Taxes Payable Property taxes are a main source of revenue for local governments. They are levied annually on real property, such as land and buildings, and on personal property, such as inventory and equipment. Because the fiscal years of local governments rarely correspond to a company's fiscal year,

FOCUS ON BUSINESS PRACTICE

What Is the Cost of Frequent Flyer Miles?

In the early 1980s, **American Airlines** developed a frequent flyer program that awards free trips and other bonuses to customers based on the number of miles they fly on the airline. Since then, many other airlines have instituted similar programs, and it is estimated that 40 million people now participate in them. Today, U.S. airlines have more than 4 trillion "free miles" outstanding, and 8 percent of passengers travel on "free" tickets. Estimated liabilities for these tickets have become an important consideration in evaluating an airline's financial position. Complicating the estimate is that almost half the miles have been earned through purchases from hotels, car rental and telephone companies, Internet service providers like **AOL**, and bank credit cards.[8]

Today, because of frequent flyer programs, U.S. airline companies have more than 4 trillion "free miles" outstanding. What are the accounting implications of these programs? Airlines usually record the costs as a reduction in sales (a contra-sales account) rather than as an expense with a corresponding current liability.

it is necessary to estimate the amount of property taxes that applies to each month of the year.

Promotional Costs You are no doubt familiar with the coupons and rebates that are part of many companies' marketing programs and with the frequent flyer programs that airlines have been offering for more than 20 years. Companies usually record the costs of these programs as a reduction in sales (a contra-sales account) rather than as an expense with a corresponding current liability. As **Hershey Foods Corporation** acknowledges in its annual report, promotional costs are hard to estimate:

> Accrued liabilities requiring the most difficult or subjective judgments include liabilities associated with marketing promotion programs. . . . We recognize the costs of marketing programs as a reduction to net sales with a corresponding accrued liability based on estimates at the time of revenue recognition. . . . We determine the amount of the accrued liability by analysis of programs offered, historical trends, expectations regarding customer and consumer participation, sales and payment trends and experience . . . with previously offered programs.[9]

Hershey accrues over $600 million in promotional costs each year and reports that its estimates are usually accurate within about 4 percent, or $24 million.

Study Note

Recording a product warranty expense in the period of the sale is an application of the matching rule.

Product Warranty Liability When a firm sells a product or service with a warranty, it has a liability for the length of the warranty. The warranty is a feature of the product and is included in the selling price; its cost should therefore be debited to an expense account in the period of the sale. Based on past experience, it should be possible to estimate the amount the warranty will cost in the future. Some products will require little warranty service; others may require much. Thus, there will be an average cost per product.

For example, suppose a muffler company like **Midas** guarantees that it will replace free of charge any muffler it sells that fails during the time the buyer owns the car. The company charges a small service fee for replacing the muffler. In the past, 6 percent of the mufflers sold have been returned for replacement under the warranty. The average cost of a muffler is $50. If the company sold 700 mufflers during July, the accrued liability would be recorded as an adjustment at the end of July, as shown in the following entry:

A	=	L	+	SE
		+2,100		−2,100

July 31	Product Warranty Expense	2,100	
	Estimated Product Warranty Liability		2,100
	To record estimated product warranty expense:		
	Number of units sold	700	
	Rate of replacement under warranty	× .06	
	Estimated units to be replaced	42	
	Estimated cost per unit	$ 50	
	Estimated liability for product warranty	$2,100	

When a muffler is returned for replacement under the warranty, the cost of the muffler is charged against the Estimated Product Warranty Liability account. For example, suppose that on December 5, a customer returns a defective muffler, which cost $60, and pays a $30 service fee to have it replaced. The entry is:

A	=	L	+	SE
+30		−60		+30
−60				

Dec. 5	Cash	30	
	Estimated Product Warranty Liability	60	
	Service Revenue		30
	Merchandise Inventory		60
	Replacement of muffler under warranty		

Vacation Pay Liability In most companies, employees accrue paid vacation as they work during the year. For example, an employee may earn two weeks of paid vacation for each 50 weeks of work. Thus, the person is paid 52 weeks' salary for 50 weeks' work. The cost of the two weeks' vacation should be allocated as an expense over the whole year so that month-to-month costs will not be distorted. The vacation pay represents 4 percent (two weeks' vacation divided by 50 weeks) of a worker's pay. Every week worked earns the employee a small fraction (2 percent) of vacation pay, which is 4 percent of total annual salary.

Vacation pay liability can represent a substantial amount of money. As an example, in the 10-K form that **US Airways** submitted to the SEC for 2007, the airline reported accrued salaries, wages, and vacation liabilities of $225 million.

Suppose that a company with a vacation policy of two weeks of paid vacation for each 50 weeks of work has a payroll of $42,000 and that it paid $2,000 of that amount to employees on vacation for the week ended April 20. Because of turnover and rules regarding term of employment, the company assumes that only 75 percent of employees will ultimately collect vacation pay. The computation of vacation pay expense based on the payroll of employees not on vacation ($42,000 − $2,000) is as follows: $40,000 × 4 percent × 75 percent = $1,200. The company would make the following entry to record vacation pay expense for the week ended April 20:

A	=	L	+	SE
		+1,200		−1,200

Apr. 20	Vacation Pay Expense	1,200	
	Estimated Liability for Vacation Pay		1,200
	Estimated vacation pay expense		

At the time employees receive their vacation pay, an entry is made debiting Estimated Liability for Vacation Pay and crediting Cash or Wages Payable. The following entry records the $2,000 paid to employees on vacation during the month of August:

A*	=	L	+ SE
−2,000		−2,000	

* Assumes cash paid.

Aug. 31	Estimated Liability for Vacation Pay	2,000	
	Cash (or Wages Payable)		2,000
	Wages of employees on vacation		

The treatment of vacation pay presented here can also be applied to other payroll costs, such as bonus plans and contributions to pension plans.

STOP ► REVIEW ► APPLY

LO2-1 What is the difference between a line of credit and commercial paper?

LO2-2 When can a portion of long-term debt be classified as a current liability?

LO2-3 What are three types of employer-related payroll liabilities?

LO2-4 Who pays social security and Medicare taxes?

LO2-5 Why are unearned revenues classified as liabilities?

LO2-6 What is definite about an estimated liability?

LO2-7 Why are income taxes payable considered to be estimated liabilities?

LO2-8 In accounting for discount coupons, how is recording the estimate of how much will be redeemed as a contra-sales account similar to and different from recording it as a promotional expense?

LO2-9 When does a company incur a liability for a product warranty?

Identification of Current Liabilities Identify each of the following as either (1) a definitely determinable liability or (2) an estimated liability:

_____ a. Bank loan
_____ b. Dividends payable
_____ c. Product warranty liabilities
_____ d. Interest payable
_____ e. Income taxes payable
_____ f. Vacation pay liability
_____ g. Notes payable
_____ h. Property taxes payable
_____ i. Commercial paper
_____ j. Gift certificate liability

SOLUTION

a. 1
b. 1
c. 2
d. 1
e. 2
f. 2
g. 1
h. 2
i. 1
j. 2

Contingent Liabilities and Commitments

LO3 **Distinguish *contingent liabilities* from *commitments*.**

The FASB requires companies to disclose in a note to their financial statements any contingent liabilities and commitments they may have. A **contingent liability** is not an *existing* obligation. Rather, it is a *potential* liability because it depends on a future event arising out of a past transaction. Contingent liabilities often involve lawsuits, income tax disputes, discounted notes receivable, guarantees of debt, and failure to follow government regulations. For instance, a construction company that built a bridge may have been sued by the state for using poor materials. The past transaction is the building of the bridge under contract. The future event is the outcome of the lawsuit, which is not yet known.

The FASB has established two conditions for determining when a contingency should be entered in the accounting records:

1. The liability must be probable.
2. The liability can be reasonably estimated.[10]

Study Note

Contingencies are recorded when they are probable and can be reasonably estimated.

Estimated liabilities like the income tax, warranty, and vacation pay liabilities that we have described meet those conditions. They are therefore accrued in the accounting records.

In a survey of 600 large companies, the most common types of contingencies reported were litigation, which can involve many different issues, and environmental concerns, such as toxic waste cleanup.[11] In a note to its financial statements, **Microsoft** describes contingent liabilities in the area of lawsuits involving potential infringement of European competition law, antitrust and overcharge actions, patent and intellectual property claims, and others. Microsoft's management states:

> While we intend to vigorously defend these matters, there exists the possibility of adverse outcomes that we estimate could be up to $4.15 billion in aggregate beyond recorded amounts.[12]

A **commitment** is a legal obligation that does not meet the technical requirements for recognition as a liability and so is not recorded. The most common examples are purchase agreements and leases.[13]

For example, Microsoft also reports in its notes to the financial statements construction commitments in the amount of $821 million and purchase commitments in the amount of $1,824 million. Knowledge of these amounts is very important for planning cash flows in the coming year.

STOP ▶ REVIEW ▶ APPLY

LO3-1 **What is a contingent liability? How does a contingent liability differ from a commitment?**

LO3-2 **What are two examples of contingent liabilities? Why is each a contingent liability?**

LO3-3 **What is an example of a commitment?**

Valuation Approaches to Fair Value Accounting

LO4 Identify the valuation approaches to fair value accounting, and define *time value of money* and *interest* and apply them to present values.

Recall that fair value is the price for which an asset or liability could be sold. As pointed out previously, the concept of fair value applies to financial assets, such as cash equivalents, accounts receivable, and investments, and to liabilities, such as accounts payable and short-term loans. Fair value is also applicable to determining whether tangible assets such as inventories and long-term assets have sustained a permanent decline in value below their cost. The FASB identifies three approaches to measurement of fair value:[14]

- *Market approach.* When available, external market transactions involving identical or comparable assets or liabilities are ideal. For example, the market approach is good for valuing investments and liabilities for which there is a ready market. However, a ready market is not always available. For example, there may not be a market for special-purpose equipment. In these cases, other approaches must be used.

- *Income (or cash flow) approach.* The income approach, as defined by the FASB, converts future cash flows to a single present value. This approach is based on management's best determination of the future cash amounts generated by an asset or payments that will be made for a liability. It is based on internally generated information, which should be reasonable for the circumstances.
- *Cost approach.* The cost approach is based on the amount that currently would be required to replace an asset. For example, inventory is usually valued at lower of cost or market, where market is the replacement cost. For a plant asset, the replacement cost of a new asset must be adjusted to take into account the asset's age, condition, depreciation, and obsolescence.

Complicating factors may arise in applying the market and cost approaches, but conceptually they are relatively straightforward. The income or cash flow approach requires knowledge of interest and the time value of money, and present value techniques, as presented in the following sections.

Interest and the Time Value of Money

"Time is money" is a common expression. It derives from the concept of the **time value of money**, which refers to the costs or benefits derived from holding or not holding money over time. **Interest** is the cost of using money for a specific period.

The interest associated with the time value of money is an important consideration in any kind of business decision. For example, if you sell a bicycle for $100 and hold that amount for one year without putting it in a savings account, you have forgone the interest that the money would have earned. However, if you accept a note payable instead of cash and add the interest to the price of the bicycle, you will not forgo the interest that the cash could have earned.

Study Note

In business, compound interest is the most useful concept of interest because it helps decision makers choose among alternative courses of action.

Simple interest is the interest cost for one or more periods when the principal sum—the amount on which interest is computed—stays the same from period to period. **Compound interest** is the interest cost for two or more periods when after each period, the interest earned in that period is added to the amount on which interest is computed in future periods. In other words, the principal sum is increased at the end of each period by the interest earned in that period. The following two examples illustrate these concepts:

Example of Simple Interest Willy Wang accepts an 8 percent, $15,000 note due in 90 days. How much will he receive at that time? The interest is calculated as follows:

$$\begin{aligned}\text{Interest} &= \text{Principal} \times \text{Rate} \times \text{Time}\\ &= \$15{,}000 \times 8/100 \times 90/365\\ &= \$295.89\end{aligned}$$

Therefore, the total that Wang will receive is $15,295.89, calculated as follows:

$$\begin{aligned}\text{Total} &= \text{Principal} + \text{Interest}\\ &= \$15{,}000.00 + \$295.89\\ &= \$15{,}295.89\end{aligned}$$

Example of Compound Interest Terry Soma deposits $10,000 in an account that pays 6 percent interest. She expects to leave the principal and accumulated interest in the account for three years. How much will the account total at the end of three years? Assume that the interest is paid at the end of the year and is added to the principal at that time, and that this total in turn earns interest. The amount at the end of three years is computed as follows:

(1)	(2)	(3)	(4)
Year	Principal Amount at Beginning of Year	Annual Amount of Interest (Col. 2 × 6%)	Accumulated Amount at End of Year (Col. 2 + Col. 3)
1	$10,000.00	$600.00	$10,600.00
2	10,600.00	636.00	11,236.00
3	11,236.00	674.16	11,910.16

At the end of three years, Soma will have $11,910.16 in her account. Note that the amount of interest increases each year by the interest rate times the interest of the previous year. For example, between year 1 and year 2, the interest increased by $36, which equals 6 percent times $600. The final amount of $11,910.16 is referred to as the **future value**, which is the amount an investment ($10,000 in this case), will be worth at a future date if invested at compound interest.

Calculating Present Value

Study Note

Present value is a method of valuing future cash flows. Financial analysts commonly compute present value to determine the value of potential investments.

Suppose you had the choice of receiving $100 today or one year from today. No doubt, you would choose to receive it today. Why? If you have the money today, you can put it in a savings account to earn interest so you will have more than $100 a year from today. In other words, an amount to be received in the future (future value) is not worth as much today as an amount received today (present value). **Present value** is the amount that must be invested today at a given rate of interest to produce a given future value. Thus, present value and future value are closely related.

For example, suppose Kelly Fontaine needs $10,000 one year from now. How much does she have to invest today to achieve that goal if the interest rate is 5 percent? From earlier examples, we can establish the following equation:

Present Value	× (1.0 + Interest Rate)	=	Future Value
Present Value	× 1.05	=	$10,000.00
Present Value		=	$10,000.00 ÷ 1.05
Present Value		=	$9,523.81

To achieve a future value of $10,000, Fontaine must invest a present value of $9,523.81. Interest of 5 percent on $9,523.81 for one year equals $476.19, and these two amounts added together equal $10,000.

Present Value of a Single Sum Due in the Future

When more than one period is involved, the calculation of present value is more complicated. For example, suppose Ron More wants to be sure of having $8,000 at the end of three years. How much must he invest today in a 5 percent savings account to achieve this goal? We can compute the present value of $8,000 at compound interest of 5 percent for three years by adapting the above equation:

Year	Amount at End of Year		Divide by		Present Value at Beginning of Year
3	$8,000.00	÷	1.05	=	$7,619.05
2	7,619.05	÷	1.05	=	7,256.24
1	7,256.24	÷	1.05	=	6,910.70

TABLE 1

Present Value of $1 to Be Received at the End of a Given Number of Periods

Period	1%	2%	3%	4%	5%	6%	7%	8%	9%	10%
1	0.990	0.980	0.971	0.962	0.952	0.943	0.935	0.926	0.917	0.909
2	0.980	0.961	0.943	0.925	0.907	0.890	0.873	0.857	0.842	0.826
3	0.971	0.942	0.915	0.889	0.864	0.840	0.816	0.794	0.772	0.751
4	0.961	0.924	0.888	0.855	0.823	0.792	0.763	0.735	0.708	0.683
5	0.951	0.906	0.863	0.822	0.784	0.747	0.713	0.681	0.650	0.621
6	0.942	0.888	0.837	0.790	0.746	0.705	0.666	0.630	0.596	0.564
7	0.933	0.871	0.813	0.760	0.711	0.665	0.623	0.583	0.547	0.513
8	0.923	0.853	0.789	0.731	0.677	0.627	0.582	0.540	0.502	0.467
9	0.914	0.837	0.766	0.703	0.645	0.592	0.544	0.500	0.460	0.424
10	0.905	0.820	0.744	0.676	0.614	0.558	0.508	0.463	0.422	0.386

Ron More must invest $6,910.70 today to achieve a value of $8,000 in three years.

Again, we can simplify the calculation by using the appropriate table. In Table 1, the point at which the 5 percent column and the row for period 3 intersect shows a factor of .864. This factor, when multiplied by $1, gives the present value of $1 to be received three years from now at 5 percent interest. Thus, we solve the problem as follows:

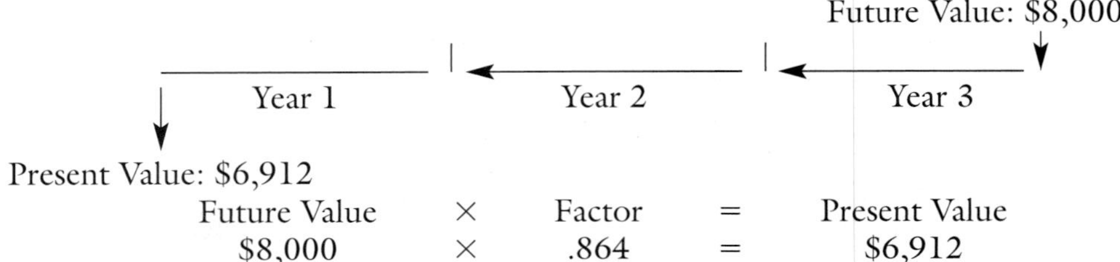

Future Value	×	Factor	=	Present Value
$8,000	×	.864	=	$6,912

Except for a rounding difference of $1.30, this result is the same as our earlier one.

Present Value of an Ordinary Annuity It is often necessary to compute the present value of a series of receipts or payments equally spaced over time—in other words, the present value of an **ordinary annuity**. For example, suppose Vickie Long has sold a piece of property and is to receive $18,000 in three equal annual payments of $6,000 beginning one year from today. What is the present value of this sale if the current interest rate is 5 percent?

Using Table 1, we can compute the present value by calculating a separate value for each of the three payments and summing the results, as follows:

Future Receipts (Annuity)				Present Value Factor at 5 Percent		
Year 1	**Year 2**	**Year 3**		**(from Table 1)**		**Present Value**
$6,000			×	.952	=	$ 5,712
	$6,000		×	.907	=	5,442
		$6,000	×	.864	=	5,184
Total Present Value						$16,338

The present value of the sale is $16,338. Thus, there is an implied interest cost (given the 5 percent rate) of $1,662 associated with the payment plan that allows the purchaser to pay in three installments.

TABLE 2

Present Value of an Ordinary $1 Annuity Received in Each Period for a Given Number of Periods

Period	1%	2%	3%	4%	5%	6%	7%	8%	9%	10%
1	0.990	0.980	0.971	0.962	0.952	0.943	0.935	0.926	0.917	0.909
2	1.970	1.942	1.913	1.886	1.859	1.833	1.808	1.783	1.759	1.736
3	2.941	2.884	2.829	2.775	2.723	2.673	2.624	2.577	2.531	2.487
4	3.902	3.808	3.717	3.630	3.546	3.465	3.387	3.312	3.240	3.170
5	4.853	4.713	4.580	4.452	4.329	4.212	4.100	3.993	3.890	3.791
6	5.795	5.601	5.417	5.242	5.076	4.917	4.767	4.623	4.486	4.355
7	6.728	6.472	6.230	6.002	5.786	5.582	5.389	5.206	5.033	4.868
8	7.652	7.325	7.020	6.733	6.463	6.210	5.971	5.747	5.535	5.335
9	8.566	8.162	7.786	7.435	7.108	6.802	6.515	6.247	5.995	5.759
10	9.471	8.983	8.530	8.111	7.722	7.360	7.024	6.710	6.418	6.145

We can make this calculation more easily by using Table 2. The point at which the 5 percent column intersects the row for period 3 shows a factor of 2.723. When multiplied by $1, this factor gives the present value of a series of three $1 payments (spaced one year apart) at compound interest of 5 percent. Thus, we solve the problem as follows:

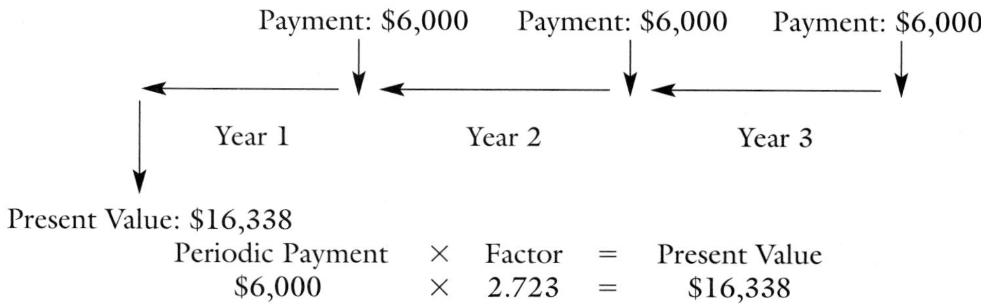

Periodic Payment	×	Factor	=	Present Value
$6,000	×	2.723	=	$16,338

This result is the same as the one we computed earlier.

Study Note

The interest rate used when compounding interest for less than one year is the annual rate divided by the number of periods in a year.

Time Periods As in all our examples, the compounding period is in most cases one year, and the interest rate is stated on an annual basis. However, the left-hand column in Tables 1 and 2 refers not to years but rather to periods. This wording accommodates compounding periods of less than one year. Savings accounts that record interest quarterly and bonds that pay interest semiannually are cases in which the compounding period is less than one year. To use the tables in these cases, it is necessary to (1) divide the annual interest rate by the number of periods in the year, and (2) multiply the number of periods in one year by the number of years.

For example, suppose we want to compute the present value of a $6,000 payment that is to be received in two years, assuming an annual interest rate of 8 percent. The compounding period is semiannual. Before using Table 1 in this computation, we must compute the interest rate that applies to each compounding period and the total number of compounding periods. First, the interest rate to use is 4 percent (8% annual rate ÷ 2 periods per year). Second, the total number of compounding periods is 4 (2 periods per year × 2 years). From Table 1, therefore, the maturity value of the payment is computed as follows:

Principal	×	Factor	=	Present Value
$6,000	×	.855	=	$5,130

The present value of the payment is $5,130. This procedure is used anytime the corresponding period is less than one year. For example, a monthly compounding requires dividing the annual interest rate by 12 and multiplying the number of years by 12 to use the tables.

This method of determining the interest rate and the number of periods when the compounding period is less than one year can be used with Tables 1 and 2.

STOP ▶ REVIEW ▶ APPLY

LO4-1 What are the three approaches to measuring fair value?

LO4-2 What is the time value of money?

LO4-3 What is the difference between simple and compound interest?

LO4-4 What is an ordinary annuity?

LO4-5 What is the key variable that relates present value to future value?

LO4-6 How does a compounding period of less than one year affect the computation of present value?

Applications Using Present Value

LO5 Apply present value to simple valuation situations.

The concept of present value is widely used in business decision making and financial reporting. As mentioned above, the FASB has made it the foundation of its approach in determining the fair value of assets and liabilities when a ready market price is not available. For example, the value of a long-term note receivable or payable can be determined by calculating the present value of the future interest payments.

The Office of the Chief Accountant of the SEC has issued guidance on how to apply fair value accounting.[15] For instance, it says that management's internal assumptions about expected cash flows may be used to measure fair value and that market quotes may be used when they are from an orderly, active market as opposed to a distressed, inactive market. Thus, **Microsoft** may determine the expected present value of the future cash flows of an investment by using its internal cash flow projections and a market rate of interest. By comparing the result to the current value of the investment, Microsoft can determine if an adjustment needs to be made to record a gain or loss.

In the sections that follow, we illustrate two simple, useful applications of present value, which will be helpful in understanding the uses of present value in subsequent chapters.

Valuing an Asset

An asset is something that will provide future benefits to the company that owns it. Usually, the purchase price of an asset represents the present value of those future benefits. It is possible to evaluate a proposed purchase price by comparing it with the present value of the asset to the company.

For example, Mike Yeboah is thinking of buying a new machine that will reduce his annual labor cost by $1,400 per year. The machine will last eight years. The interest rate that Yeboah assumes for making managerial decisions is 10 percent. What is the maximum amount (present value) that Yeboah should pay for the machine?

The present value of the machine to Yeboah is equal to the present value of an ordinary annuity of $1,400 per year for eight years at compound interest of 10 percent. Using the factor from Table 2, we compute the value as follows:

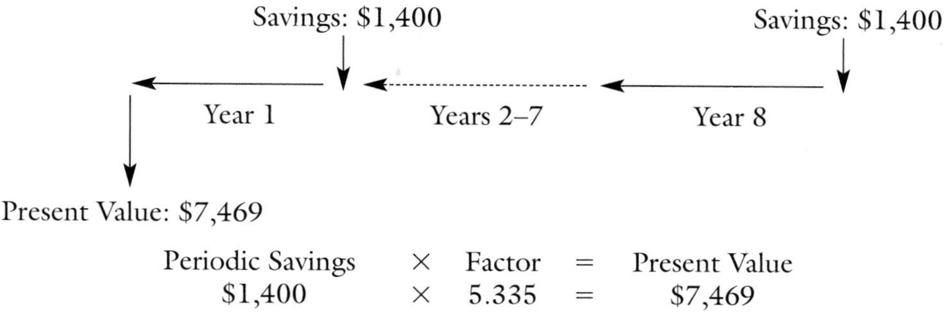

Periodic Savings	×	Factor	=	Present Value
$1,400	×	5.335	=	$7,469

Yeboah should not pay more than $7,469 for the machine because this amount equals the present value of the benefits he would receive from owning it.

Deferred Payment

To encourage buyers to make a purchase, sellers sometimes agree to defer payment for a sale. This practice is common among companies that sell agricultural equipment; to accommodate farmers who often need new equipment in the spring but cannot pay for it until they sell their crops in the fall, these companies are willing to defer payment.

Suppose Field Helpers Corporation sells a tractor to Sasha Ptak for $100,000 on February 1 and agrees to take payment ten months later, on December 1. When such an agreement is made, the future payment includes not only the selling price, but also an implied (imputed) interest cost. If the prevailing annual interest rate for such transactions is 12 percent compounded monthly, the actual price of the tractor would be the present value of the future payment, computed

Companies that sell agricultural equipment like these combine harvesters often agree to defer payment for a sale. This practice is common because farmers often need new equipment in the spring but cannot pay for it until they sell their crops in the fall. Deferred payment is a useful application of the time value of money.

using the factor from Table 1 (10 periods, 1 percent [12 percent divided by 12 months]), as follows:

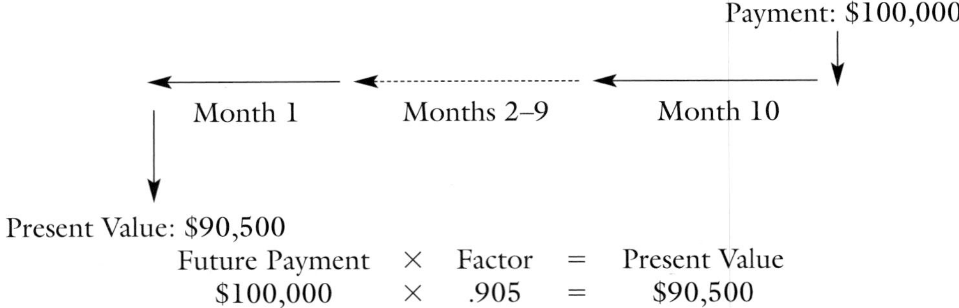

Present Value: $90,500

Future Payment	×	Factor	=	Present Value
$100,000	×	.905	=	$90,500

Ptak records the present value, $90,500, in his purchase records, and Field Helpers Corporation records it in its sales records. The balance consists of interest expense or interest income.

Other Applications

There are many other applications of present value in accounting, including computing imputed interest on non-interest-bearing notes, accounting for installment notes, valuing a bond, and recording lease obligations. Present value is also applied in accounting for pension obligations; valuing debt; depreciating property, plant, and equipment; making capital expenditure decisions; and generally in accounting for any item in which time is a factor.

STOP ▸ REVIEW ▸ APPLY

LO5-1 **Why is present value important in making business decisions?**

LO5-2 **What are the applications of present value to financial reporting?**

LO5-3 **What are some of the ways in which businesses use present value?**

Valuing an Asset When Making a Purchasing Decision Jerry owns a restaurant and has the opportunity to buy a high-quality espresso coffee machine for $5,000. After carefully studying projected costs and revenues, Jerry estimates that the machine will produce a net cash flow of $1,600 annually and will last for five years. He determines that an interest rate of 10 percent is an adequate return on investment for his business.

Calculate the present value of the machine to Jerry. Based on your calculation, do you think a decision to purchase the machine would be wise?

SOLUTION

Calculation of the present value:

Annual cash flow	$1,600.00
Factor from Table 2 (5 years at 10%)	× 3.791
Present value of net cash flows	$6,065.60
Less purchase price	− 5,000.00
Net present value	$1,065.60

The present value of the net cash flows from the machine exceeds the purchase price. Thus, the investment will return more than 10 percent to Jerry's business. A decision to purchase the machine would therefore be wise.

A LOOK BACK AT ▶ Microsoft

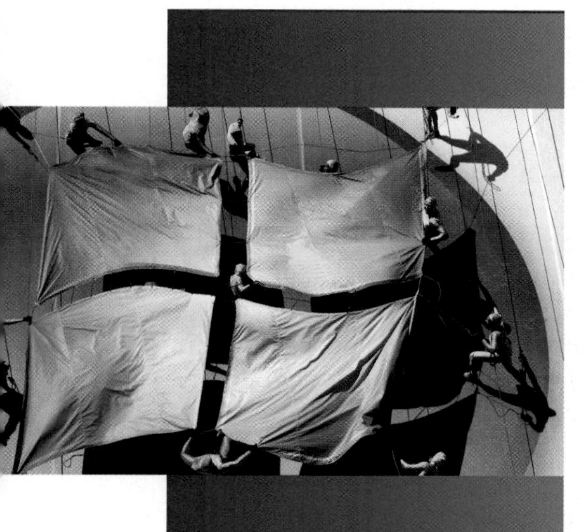

At the beginning of the chapter, we noted that Microsoft is the market leader in software. To stay a leader Microsoft must continue to develop new products and services. To accomplish this, the company has to provide investors and creditors with satisfactory answers to these questions:

- **How does Microsoft's decision to incur heavy debt relate to the goals of the business?**
- **Is the level of accounts payable in the operating cycle satisfactory?**
- **Has the company properly identified and accounted for all its current liabilities?**

The development of new products and services requires a lot of capital, much of which the company has raised by borrowing money. Management has committed $7.12 billion to research and development. It has analyzed its future cash flows in terms of present value and carefully planned its cash needs by making very good use of the operating cycle. By using advance billings, keeping inventories low, and making maximum use of credit from its suppliers, it has been able to keep its cash needs to a minimum. This is particularly evident when we compare its payables turnover and days' payable for 2006 and 2007 (dollar amounts are in millions):

		2007	2006
(Cost of Goods Sold ± Change in Merchandise Inventory) / Average Accounts Payable	=	($10,693 − $351) / (($3,247 + $2,909) ÷ 2)	($7,650 + $987) / (($2,909 + $1,662) ÷ 2)
	=	$10,342 / $3,078	$8,637 / $2,285.5
K/R Payables Turnover	=	3.4 times	3.8 times
365 days / Payables Turnover	=	365 days / 3.4 times	365 days / 3.8 times
K/R Days' Payable	=	107.4 days	96.1 days

Clearly, Microsoft maintained a favorable payables turnover and days' payable ratio over the two-year period. The list of current liabilities that it presents in its 2007 annual report gives readers a clear picture of the company's short-term obligations.

CHAPTER REVIEW

REVIEW of Learning Objectives

LO1 Identify the management issues related to current liabilities.

Current liabilities are an important consideration in managing a company's liquidity and cash flows. Key measures of liquidity are working capital, payables turnover, and days' payable. Liabilities result from past transactions and should be recognized at the time a transaction obligates a company to make future payments. They are valued at the amount of money necessary to satisfy the obligation or at the fair value of the goods or services to be delivered. Liabilities are classified as current or long term. Companies are required to provide supplemental disclosure when the nature or details of the obligations would help in understanding the liability.

LO2 Identify, compute, and record definitely determinable and estimated current liabilities.

The two major categories of current liabilities are definitely determinable liabilities and estimated liabilities. Definitely determinable liabilities can be measured exactly. These liabilities include accounts payable, bank loans and commercial paper, notes payable, accrued liabilities, dividends payable, sales and excise taxes payable, the current portion of long-term debt, payroll liabilities, and unearned revenues.

Estimated liabilities definitely exist, but their amounts are uncertain and must be estimated. They include liabilities for income taxes, property taxes, promotional costs, product warranties, and vacation pay.

LO3 Distinguish *contingent liabilities* from *commitments*.

A contingent liability is a potential liability that arises from a past transaction and is dependent on a future event. Contingent liabilities often involve lawsuits, income tax disputes, discounted notes receivable, guarantees of debt, and failure to follow government regulations. A commitment is a legal obligation, such as a purchase agreement, that is not recorded as a liability.

LO4 Identify the valuation approaches to fair value accounting, and define *time value of money* and *interest* and apply them to present values.

Three approaches to measurement of fair value are market, income (or cash flow), and cost. The time value of money refers to the costs or benefits derived from holding or not holding money over time.

Interest is the cost of using money for a specific period. In the computation of simple interest, the amount on which the interest is computed stays the same from period to period. In the computation of compound interest, the interest for a period is added to the principal amount before the interest for the next period is computed.

Future value is the amount an investment will be worth at a future date if invested at compound interest. Present value is the amount that must be invested today at a given rate of interest to produce a given future value.

An ordinary annuity is a series of equal payments made at the end of equal intervals of time, with compound interest on the payments. The present value of an ordinary annuity is the present value of a series of payments. Calculations of present values are simplified by using the appropriate tables, which appear in an appendix to the book.

LO5 Apply the time value of money to simple valuation situations.

Present value is commonly used in determining fair value and may be used in determining the value of an asset, in computing the present value of deferred payments, in establishing a fund for loan repayment, and in numerous other accounting situations in which time is a factor.

REVIEW of Concepts and Terminology

The following concepts and terms were introduced in this chapter:

Commercial paper: Unsecured loans sold to the public, usually through professionally managed investment firms, as a means of borrowing short-term funds. (LO2)

Commitment: A legal obligation that does not meet the technical requirements for recognition as a liability. (LO3)

Compound interest: The interest cost for two or more periods when after each period, the interest of that period is added to the amount on which interest is computed in future periods. (LO4)

Contingent liability: A potential liability that arises from a past transaction and is dependent on a future event. (LO3)

Current liabilities: Debts and obligations that a company expects to satisfy within one year or within the normal operating cycle, whichever is longer. (LO1)

Definitely determinable liabilities: Current liabilities that are set by contract or statute and that can be measured exactly. (LO2)

Estimated liabilities: Definite debts or obligations whose exact amounts cannot be known until a later date. (LO2)

Future value: The amount an investment will be worth at a future date if invested at compound interest. (LO4)

Interest: The cost of using money for a specific period. (LO4)

Line of credit: An arrangement with a bank that allows a company to borrow funds as needed. (LO2)

Long-term liabilities: Debts and obligations due beyond one year or beyond the normal operating cycle. (LO1)

Ordinary annuity: A series of equal payments made at the end of equal intervals of time, with compound interest on the payments. (LO4)

Present value: The amount that must be invested today at a given rate of interest to produce a given future value. (LO4)

Salaries: Compensation of employees at a monthly or yearly rate. (LO2)

Simple interest: The interest cost for one or more periods when the amount on which the interest is computed stays the same from period to period. (LO4)

Time value of money: The costs or benefits derived from holding or not holding money over time. (LO4)

Unearned revenues: Revenues received in advance for goods or services that will not be delivered during the current accounting period. (LO2)

Wages: Compensation of employees at an hourly rate. (LO2)

Key Ratios

Days' payable: How long, on average, a company takes to pay its accounts payable; 365 days ÷ Payables Turnover. (LO1)

Payables turnover: The number of times, on average, that a company pays its accounts payable in an accounting period; (Cost of Goods Sold +/− Change in Merchandise Inventory) ÷ Average Accounts Payable. (LO1)

REVIEW Problem

Identification and Evaluation of Current Liabilities

Maggie Lee started a fitness business, Maggie's Fitness Center, last year. In addition to offering exercise classes, she sells nutritional supplements. She has not yet filed any tax reports for her business and therefore owes taxes. Because she has limited experience in running a business, she has brought you all her business records—a checkbook, canceled checks, deposit slips, suppliers' invoices, a notice of annual property taxes of $3,600 due to the city, and a promissory note to her bank for $16,000. She wants you to determine what her business owes the government and other parties.

You analyze all her records and determine the following as of December 31, 2010:

Unpaid invoices for supplements	$ 12,000
Sales of supplements (excluding sales tax)	57,000
Cost of supplements sold	33,600
Exercise instructor salaries	22,800
Exercise revenues	81,400
Current assets	40,000
Supplements inventory (12/31/10)	27,000
Supplements inventory (12/31/09)	21,000

You learn that the company has sold gift certificates in the amount of $700 that have not been redeemed and that it has deducted $1,374 from its two employees' salaries for federal income taxes owed to the government. The current social security tax is 6.2 percent on maximum earnings of $102,000 for each employee, and the current Medicare tax is 1.45 percent (no maximum earnings). The FUTA tax is 5.4 percent to the state and .8 percent to the federal government on the first $7,000 earned by each employee; no employee earned more than $7,000. Lee has not filed a sales tax report to the state (6 percent of supplements sales).

Required

1. Given these facts, determine the company's current liabilities as of December 31, 2010.

User insight ▶ 2. Your analysis of the company's current liabilities has been based on documents that the owner showed you. What liabilities may be missing from your analysis?

User insight ▶ 3. Evaluate the company's liquidity by calculating working capital, payables turnover, and days' payable. Comment on the results. (Assume average accounts payable were the same as year-end accounts payable.)

Answer to Review Problem

1. The current liabilities of Maggie's Fitness Center as of December 31, 2010, are as follows:

	A	B	C	D	E	F	G
1	Accounts payable						$12,000.00
2	Notes payable						16,000.00
3	Property taxes payable						3,600.00
4	Sales tax payable	(	$57,000	x	0.06	)	3,420.00
5	Social security tax payable	(	$22,800	x	0.062	)	1,413.60
6	Medicare tax payable	(	$22,800	x	0.0145	)	330.60
7	State unemployment tax payable	(	$22,800	x	0.054	)	1,231.20
8	Federal unemployment tax payable	(	$22,800	x	0.008	)	182.40
9	Employees' federal income taxes payable						1,374.00
10	Unearned revenues						700.00
11	Total current liabilities						$40,251.80

2. The company may have current liabilities for which you have not seen any documentary evidence. For instance, invoices for accounts payable could be missing. In addition, the company may have accrued liabilities, such as vacation pay

for its two employees, which would require establishing an estimated liability. If the promissory note to Lee's bank is interest-bearing, it also would require an adjustment to accrue interest payable, and the company could have other loans outstanding for which you have not seen documentary evidence. Moreover, it may have to pay penalties and interest to the federal and state governments because of its failure to remit tax payments on a timely basis. City and state income tax withholding for the employees could be another overlooked liability.

3. Liquidity ratios computed and evaluated:

	A	B	C	D	E	F	G
1	Working Capital	=	Current Assets		–	Current Liabilities	
2		=	$40,000.00		–	$40,251.80	
3		=	($251.80)				
4							
5	Payables Turnover	=	Cost of Goods Sold +/– Change in Merchandise Inventory				
6						Accounts Payable	
7							
8		=	$33,600		+	$6,000	
9					$12,000		
10							
11		=	$39,600				
12			$12,000				
13							
14		=	3.3	times			
15							
16	Days' Payable	=	365	days			
17			Payables Turnover				
18							
19		=	365	days			
20			3.3	times			
21							
22		=	110.6	days			
23							

Maggie's Fitness Center has a negative working capital of $251.80, its payables turnover is only 3.3 times, and it takes an average of 110.6 days to pay its accounts payable. Its liquidity is therefore highly questionable. Many of its current assets are inventory, which it must sell to generate cash, and it must pay most of its current liabilities sooner than the 110.6 days would indicate.

CHAPTER ASSIGNMENTS

BUILDING Your Basic Knowledge and Skills

Short Exercises

Issues in Accounting for Liabilities

SE 1. Indicate whether each of the following actions relates to (a) managing liquidity and cash flow, (b) recognition of liabilities, (c) valuation of liabilities, (d) classification of liabilities, or (e) disclosure of liabilities:

1. Determining that a liability will be paid in less than one year
2. Estimating the amount of a liability

3. Providing information about when liabilities are due and their interest rates
4. Determining when a liability arises
5. Assessing working capital and payables turnover

LO1 **Measuring Short-Term Liquidity**

SE 2. Robinson Company has current assets of $65,000 and current liabilities of $40,000, of which accounts payable are $35,000. Robinson's cost of goods sold is $230,000, its merchandise inventory increased by $10,000, and accounts payable were $25,000 the prior year. Calculate Robinson's working capital, payables turnover, and days' payable.

LO2 LO3 **Types of Liabilities**

SE 3. Indicate whether each of the following is (a) a definitely determinable liability, (b) an estimated liability, (c) a commitment, or (d) a contingent liability:

1. Dividends payable
2. Pending litigation
3. Income taxes payable
4. Current portion of long-term debt
5. Vacation pay liability
6. Guaranteed loans of another company
7. Purchase agreement

LO2 **Interest Expense on Note Payable**

SE 4. On the last day of August, Avenue Company borrowed $240,000 on a bank note for 60 days at 12 percent interest. Assume that interest is stated separately. Prepare the following entries in journal form: (1) August 31, recording of note; and (2) October 30, payment of note plus interest.

LO2 **Payroll Expenses**

SE 5. The following payroll totals for the month of April are from the payroll register of Young Corporation: salaries, $223,000; federal income taxes withheld, $31,440; social security tax withheld, $13,826; Medicare tax withheld, $3,234; medical insurance deductions, $6,580; and salaries subject to unemployment taxes, $156,600.

Determine the total and components of (1) the monthly payroll and (2) employer's payroll expense, assuming social security and Medicare taxes equal to the amounts for employees, a federal unemployment insurance tax of .8 percent, a state unemployment tax of 5.4 percent, and medical insurance premiums for which the employer pays 80 percent of the cost.

LO2 **Product Warranty Liability**

SE 6. Harper Corp. manufactures and sells travel clocks. Each clock costs $12.50 to produce and sells for $25. In addition, each clock carries a warranty that provides for free replacement if it fails during the two years following the sale. In the past, 5 percent of the clocks sold have had to be replaced under the warranty. During October, Harper sold 52,000 clocks, and 2,800 clocks were replaced under the warranty. Prepare entries in journal form to record the estimated liability for product warranties during the month and the clocks replaced under warranty during the month.

Note: Tables 1 and 2 in the appendix on present value tables may be used where appropriate to solve **SE 7** and **SE 8**.

LO4 **Simple and Compound Interest**

SE 7. Ursus Motors, Inc., receives a one-year note that carries a 12 percent annual interest rate on $6,000 for the sale of a used car. Compute the maturity value under each of the following assumptions: (1) Simple interest is charged. (2) The interest is compounded semiannually. (3) The interest is compounded quarterly. (4) The interest is compounded monthly.

LO4 **Present Value Calculations**

SE 8. Find the present value of (1) a single payment of $24,000 at 6 percent for 12 years, (2) 12 annual payments of $2,000 at 6 percent, (3) a single payment of $5,000 at 9 percent for five years, and (4) five annual payments of $5,000 at 9 percent.

LO5 **Valuing an Asset for the Purpose of Making a Purchasing Decision**

SE 9. Hogan Whitner owns a machine shop and has the opportunity to purchase a new machine for $30,000. After carefully studying projected costs and revenues, Whitner estimates that the new machine will produce a net cash flow of $7,200 annually and will last for eight years. Whitner believes that an interest rate of 10 percent is adequate for his business.

Calculate the present value of the machine to Whitner. Does the purchase appear to be a smart business decision?

Exercises

LO1 LO2 LO3 **Discussion Questions**

E 1. Develop a brief answer to each of the following questions:

1. Nimish Banks, a star college basketball player, received a contract from the Midwest Blazers to play professional basketball. The contract calls for a salary of $420,000 a year for four years, dependent on his making the team in each of those years. Should this contract be considered a liability and recorded on the books of the basketball team? Why or why not?
2. Is an increasing payables turnover good or bad for a company? Why or why not?
3. Do adjusting entries involving estimated liabilities and accruals ever affect cash flows?
4. When would a commitment be recognized in the accounting records?

LO4 **Discussion Questions**

E 2. Develop a brief answer to each of the following questions:

1. Is a friend who borrows money from you for three years and agrees to pay you interest after each year paying you simple or compound interest?
2. Ordinary annuities assume that the first payment is made at the end of each year. In a transaction, who is better off in this arrangement, the payer or the receiver? Why?
3. Why is present value one of the most useful concepts in making business decisions?

LO1 **Issues in Accounting for Liabilities**

E 3. Indicate whether each of the following actions relates to (a) managing liquidity and cash flows, (b) recognition of liabilities, (c) valuation of liabilities, (d) classification of liabilities, or (e) disclosure of liabilities:

1. Setting a liability at the fair market value of goods to be delivered
2. Relating the payment date of a liability to the length of the operating cycle
3. Recording a liability in accordance with the matching rule
4. Providing information about financial instruments on the balance sheet
5. Estimating the amount of "cents-off" coupons that will be redeemed

6. Categorizing a liability as long-term debt
7. Measuring working capital
8. Comparing days' payable with last year

LO1 **Measuring Short-Term Liquidity**

E 4. In 2010, Hagler Company had current assets of $310,000 and current liabilities of $200,000, of which accounts payable were $130,000. Cost of goods sold was $850,000, merchandise inventory increased by $80,000, and accounts payable were $110,000 in the prior year. In 2011, Hagler had current assets of $420,000 and current liabilities of $320,000, of which accounts payable were $150,000. Cost of goods sold was $950,000, and merchandise inventory decreased by $30,000. Calculate Hagler's working capital, payables turnover, and days' payable for 2010 and 2011. Assess Hagler's liquidity and cash flows in relation to the change in the payables turnover from 2010 to 2011.

LO2 **Interest Expense on Note Payable**

E 5. On the last day of October, Wicker Company borrows $120,000 on a bank note for 60 days at 11 percent interest. Interest is not included in the face amount. Prepare the following entries in journal form: (1) October 31, recording of note; (2) November 30, accrual of interest expense; and (3) December 30, payment of note plus interest.

LO2 **Sales and Excise Taxes**

E 6. Web Design Services billed its customers a total of $490,200 for the month of August, including 9 percent federal excise tax and 5 percent sales tax.

1. Determine the proper amount of service revenue to report for the month.
2. Prepare an entry in journal form to record the revenue and related liabilities for the month.

LO2 **Payroll Expenses**

E 7. At the end of October, the payroll register for Global Tool Corporation contained the following totals: wages, $742,000; federal income taxes withheld, $189,768; state income taxes withheld, $31,272; social security tax withheld, $46,004; Medicare tax withheld, $10,759; medical insurance deductions, $25,740; and wages subject to unemployment taxes, $114,480.

Determine the total and components of the (1) monthly payroll and (2) employer payroll expenses, assuming social security and Medicare taxes equal to the amount for employees, a federal unemployment insurance tax of .8 percent, a state unemployment tax of 5.4 percent, and medical insurance premiums for which the employer pays 80 percent of the cost.

LO2 **Product Warranty Liability**

E 8. Sanchez Company manufactures and sells electronic games. Each game costs $50 to produce, sells for $90, and carries a warranty that provides for free replacement if it fails during the two years following the sale. In the past, 7 percent of the games sold had to be replaced under the warranty. During July, Sanchez sold 6,500 games, and 700 games were replaced under the warranty.

1. Prepare an entry in journal form to record the estimated liability for product warranties during the month.
2. Prepare an entry in journal form to record the games replaced under warranty during the month.

LO2 **Vacation Pay Liability**

E 9. Angel Corporation gives three weeks' paid vacation to each employee who has worked at the company for one year. Based on studies of employee turnover and previous experience, management estimates that 65 percent of the employees will qualify for vacation pay this year.

1. Assume that Angel's July payroll is $150,000, of which $10,000 is paid to employees on vacation. Figure the estimated employee vacation benefit for the month.
2. Prepare an entry in journal form to record the employee benefit for July.
3. Prepare an entry in journal form to record the pay to employees on vacation.

Note: Tables 1 and 2 in the appendix on present value tables may be used where appropriate to solve **E10** through **E15**.

LO4 LO5 **Determining an Advance Payment**

E 10. Tracy Collins is contemplating paying five years' rent in advance. Her annual rent is $25,200. Calculate the single sum that would have to be paid now for the advance rent if we assume compound interest of 8 percent.

LO4 **Present Value Calculations**

E 11. Find the present value of (1) a single payment of $12,000 at 6 percent for 12 years, (2) 12 annual payments of $1,000 at 6 percent, (3) a single payment of $2,500 at 9 percent for five years, and (4) five annual payments of $2,500 at 9 percent.

LO4 LO5 **Present Value of a Lump-Sum Contract**

E 12. A contract calls for a lump-sum payment of $15,000. Find the present value of the contract, assuming that (1) the payment is due in five years, and the current interest rate is 9 percent; (2) the payment is due in ten years, and the current interest rate is 9 percent; (3) the payment is due in five years, and the current interest rate is 5 percent; and (4) the payment is due in ten years, and the current interest rate is 5 percent.

LO4 LO5 **Present Value of an Annuity Contract**

E 13. A contract calls for annual payments of $1,200. Find the present value of the contract, assuming that (1) the number of payments is seven, and the current interest rate is 6 percent; (2) the number of payments is 14, and the current interest rate is 6 percent; (3) the number of payments is seven, and the current interest rate is 8 percent; and (4) the number of payments is 14, and the current interest rate is 8 percent.

LO4 LO5 **Valuing an Asset for the Purpose of Making a Purchasing Decision**

E 14. Robert Baka owns a service station and has the opportunity to purchase a car wash machine for $30,000. After carefully studying projected costs and revenues, Baka estimates that the car wash machine will produce a net cash flow of $5,200 annually and will last for eight years. He determines that an interest rate of 14 percent is adequate for his business. Calculate the present value of the machine to Baka. Does the purchase appear to be a smart business decision?

LO4 LO5 **Deferred Payment**

E 15. Larson Equipment Corporation sold a precision tool machine with computer controls to Bondie Corporation for $200,000 on January 2 and agreed to take payment nine months later on October 2. Assuming that the prevailing annual interest rate for such a transaction is 16 percent compounded quarterly, what is the actual sale (purchase) price of the machine tool?

LO4 LO5

Negotiating the Sale of a Business

E 16. Eva Prokop is attempting to sell her business to Joseph Kahn. The company has assets of $3,600,000, liabilities of $3,200,000, and stockholders' equity of $400,000. Both parties agree that the proper rate of return to expect is 12 percent; however, they differ on other assumptions. Prokop believes that the business will generate at least $400,000 per year of cash flows for 20 years. Kahn thinks that $320,000 in cash flows per year is more reasonable and that only ten years in the future should be considered. Using Table 2 in the appendix on present value tables, determine the range for negotiation by computing the present value of Prokop's offer to sell and of Kahn's offer to buy.

Problems

LO1 LO2 LO3

Identification of Current Liabilities, Contingencies, and Commitments

P 1. Listed below are common types of current liabilities, contingencies, and commitments:

a. Accounts payable
b. Bank loans and commercial paper
c. Notes payable
d. Dividends payable
e. Sales and excise taxes payable
f. Current portion of long-term debt
g. Payroll liabilities
h. Unearned revenues
i. Income taxes payable
j. Property taxes payable
k. Promotional costs
l. Product warranty liability
m. Vacation pay liability
n. Contingent liability
o. Commitment

Required

1. For each of the following statements, identify the category above to which it gives rise or with which it is most closely associated:
   1. A company agrees to replace parts of a product if they fail.
   2. An employee earns one day off for each month worked.
   3. A company signs a contract to lease a building for five years.
   4. A company puts discount coupons in the newspaper.
   5. A company agrees to pay insurance costs for employees.
   6. A portion of a mortgage on a building is due this year.
   7. The board of directors declares a dividend.
   8. A company has trade payables.
   9. A company has a pending lawsuit against it.
   10. A company arranges for a line of credit.
   11. A company signs a note due in 60 days.
   12. A company operates in a state that has a sales tax.
   13. A company earns a profit that is taxable.
   14. A company owns buildings that are subject to property taxes.

User insight ▶

2. Of the items listed from **a** to **o** above, which ones would you not expect to see listed on the balance sheet with a dollar amount? Of those items that would be listed on the balance sheet with a dollar amount, which ones would you consider to involve the most judgment or discretion on the part of management?

LO2 **Notes Payable and Wages Payable**

P 2. **Part A**: State Mill Company, whose fiscal year ends December 31, completed the following transactions involving notes payable:

2010

Nov. 25	Purchased a new loading cart by issuing a 60-day, 10 percent note for $86,400.
Dec. 31	Made the end-of-year adjusting entry to accrue interest expense.

2011

Jan. 24	Paid off the loading cart note.

Required

1. Prepare entries in journal form for State Mill's notes payable transactions.
2. (User insight ▶) When notes payable appears on the balance sheet, what other current liability would you look for to be associated with the notes? What would it mean if this other current liability did not appear?

Part B: At the end of October 2011, the payroll register for State Mill Company contained the following totals: wages, $185,500; federal income taxes withheld, $47,442; state income taxes withheld, $7,818; social security tax withheld, $11,501; Medicare tax withheld, $2,690; medical insurance deductions, $6,400; and wages subject to unemployment taxes, $114,480.

Required

Prepare entries to record the (1) monthly payroll and (2) employer payroll expenses, assuming social security and Medicare taxes equal to the amount for employees, a federal unemployment insurance tax of .8 percent, a state unemployment tax of 5.4 percent, and medical insurance premiums for which the employer pays 80 percent of the cost.

LO2 **Product Warranty Liability**

P 3. The Smart Way Products Company manufactures and sells wireless video cell phones, which it guarantees for five years. If a cell phone fails, it is replaced free, but the customer is charged a service fee for handling. In the past, management has found that only 3 percent of the cell phones sold required replacement under the warranty. The average cell phone costs the company $120. At the beginning of September, the account for estimated liability for product warranties had a credit balance of $104,000. During September, 250 cell phones were returned under the warranty. The company collected $4,930 of service fees for handling. During the month, the company sold 2,800 cell phones.

Required

1. Prepare entries in journal form to record (a) the cost of cell phones replaced under warranty and (b) the estimated liability for product warranties for cell phones sold during the month.
2. Compute the balance of the Estimated Product Warranty Liability account at the end of the month.
3. (User insight ▶) If the company's product warranty liability is underestimated, what are the effects on current and future years' income?

LO1 **Identification and Evaluation of Current Liabilities**

P 4. Tony Garcia opened a small motorcycle repair shop, Garcia Cycle Repair, on January 2, 2010. The shop also sells a limited number of motorcycle parts. In January 2010, Garcia realized he had never filed any tax reports for his business and therefore probably owes a considerable amount of taxes. Since he has limited experience in running a business, he has brought you all his business records, including a checkbook, canceled checks, deposit slips, suppliers' invoices, a notice of annual property taxes of $2,310 due to the city, and a promissory note to his father-in-law for $2,500. He wants you to determine what his business owes the government and other parties.

You analyze all his records and determine the following as of December 31, 2009:

Unpaid invoices for motorcycle parts	$ 9,000
Parts sales (excluding sales tax)	44,270
Cost of Parts Sold	31,125
Workers' salaries	18,200
Repair revenues	60,300
Current assets	16,300
Motorcycle parts inventory	11,750

You learn that the company has deducted $476 from the two employees' salaries for federal income taxes owed to the government. The current social security tax is 6.2 percent on maximum earnings of $102,000 for each employee, and the current Medicare tax is 1.45 percent (no maximum earnings). The FUTA tax is 5.4 percent to the state and .8 percent to the federal government on the first $7,000 earned by each employee, and both employees earned more than $7,000. Garcia has not filed a sales tax report to the state (5 percent of sales).

Required

1. Given these limited facts, determine Garcia Cycle Repair's current liabilities as of December 31, 2009.

User insight ▶ 2. What additional information would you want from Garcia to satisfy yourself that all current liabilities have been identified?

User insight ▶ 3. Evaluate Garcia's liquidity by calculating working capital, payables turnover, and days' payable. Comment on the results. (Assume average accounts payable were the same as year-end accounts payable.)

LO4 LO5

Applications of Present Value

P 5. Andy Corporation's management took the following actions, which went into effect on January 2, 2010. Each action involved an application of present value.

a. Andy Corporation enters into a purchase agreement that calls for a payment of $500,000 three years from now.
b. Bought out the contract of a member of top management for a payment of $50,000 per year for four years beginning January 2, 2011.

Required

1. Assuming an annual interest rate of 10 percent and using Tables 1 and 2 in this chapter, answer the following questions:
   a. In action **a**, what is the present value of the liability for the purchase agreement?
   b. In action **b**, what is the cost (present value) of the buyout?

User insight ▶ 2. Many businesses analyze present value extensively when making decisions about investing in long-term assets. Why is this type of analysis particularly appropriate for such decisions?

Alternate Problems

Notes Payable and Wages Payable

P 6. **Part A**: Nazir Corporation, whose fiscal year ended June 30, 2010, completed the following transactions involving notes payable:

May	21	Obtained a 60-day extension on an $18,000 trade account payable owed to a supplier by signing a 60-day, $18,000 note. Interest is in addition to the face value, at the rate of 14 percent.
June	30	Made the end-of-year adjusting entry to accrue interest expense.
July	20	Paid off the note plus interest due the supplier.

Required

1. Prepare journal entries for the notes payable transactions.

2. When notes payable appears on the balance sheet, what other current liability would you look for to be associated with the notes? What would it mean if this other current liability did not appear?

Part B: The payroll register for Nazir Corporation contained the following totals at the end of July 2010: wages, $139,125; federal income taxes withheld, $35,582; state income taxes withheld, $5,863; social security tax withheld, $8,626; Medicare tax withheld, $2,017; medical insurance deductions, $4,800; and wages subject to unemployment taxes, $85,860.

Required

Prepare entries to record the (1) monthly payroll and (2) employer payroll expenses, assuming social security and Medicare taxes equal to the amount for employees, a federal unemployment insurance tax of .8 percent, a state unemployment tax of 5.4 percent, and medical insurance premiums for which the employer pays 80 percent of the cost.

Product Warranty Liability

P 7. Telemix Company is engaged in the retail sale of high-definition televisions (HDTVs). Each HDTV has a 24-month warranty on parts. If a repair under warranty is required, a charge for the labor is made. Management has found that 20 percent of the HDTVs sold require some work before the warranty expires. Furthermore, the average cost of replacement parts has been $60 per repair. At the beginning of January, the account for the estimated liability for product warranties had a credit balance of $14,300. During January, 112 HDTVs were returned under the warranty. The cost of the parts used in repairing the HDTVs was $8,765, and $9,442 was collected as service revenue for the labor involved. During January, the month before the Super Bowl, Telemix Company sold 450 new HDTVs.

Required

1. Prepare entries in journal form to record each of the following: (a) the warranty work completed during the month, including related revenue; (b) the estimated liability for product warranties for HDTVs sold during the month.
2. Compute the balance of the Estimated Product Warranty Liability account at the end of the month.

User insight ▶

3. If the company's product warranty liability is overestimated, what are the effects on current and future years' income?

Applications of Present Value

P 8. The management of K&S, Inc., took the following actions that went into effect on January 2, 2010. Each action involved an application of present value.

a. Asked for another fund to be established by a single payment to accumulate to $75,000 in four years.
b. Approved the purchase of a parcel of land for future plant expansion. Payments are to start January 2, 2011, at $50,000 per year for five years.

Required

1. Assuming an annual interest rate of 8 percent and using Tables 1 and 2 in this chapter, answer the following questions:
   a. In action **a**, how much will need to be deposited initially to accumulate the desired amount?
   b. In action **b**, what is the purchase price (present value) of the land?

User insight ▶ 2. What is the fundamental reason present value analysis is a useful tool in making business decisions?

ENHANCING Your Knowledge, Skills, and Critical Thinking

Conceptual Understanding Cases

LO2

Frequent Flyer Plan

C 1. JetGreen Airways instituted a frequent flyer program in which passengers accumulate points toward a free flight based on the number of miles they fly on the airline. One point was awarded for each mile flown, with a minimum of 750 miles being given for any flight. Because of competition in 2010, the company began a bonus plan in which passengers receive triple the normal mileage points. In the past, about 1.5 percent of passenger miles were flown by passengers who had converted points to free flights. With the triple mileage program, JetGreen expects that a 2.5 percent rate will be more appropriate for future years.

During 2010, the company had passenger revenues of $966.3 million and passenger transportation operating expenses of $802.8 million before depreciation and amortization. Operating income was $86.1 million. What is the appropriate rate to use to estimate free miles? What would be the effect of the estimated liability for free travel by frequent flyers on 2010 net income? Describe several ways to estimate the amount of this liability. Be prepared to discuss the arguments for and against recognizing this liability.

LO3

Lawsuits and Contingent Liabilities

C 2. When faced with lawsuits, many companies recognize a loss and therefore credit a liability or reserve account for any future losses that may result. For instance, in the famous **WorldCom** case, **Citibank**, the world's largest financial services firm, announced it was setting up reserves or liabilities of $5.6 billion in connection with pending lawsuits related to its relationship with WorldCom.[16] Are these lawsuits contingent liabilities? Using the two criteria established by the FASB for recording a contingency, what conditions must exist for Citibank to record these lawsuits when they have not yet been heard in court?

LO4 LO5

Present Value

C 3. In its "Year-End Countdown Sale," a local **Cadillac** auto dealer advertised "0% interest for 60 months!"[17] What role does the time value of money play in this promotion? Assuming that Cadillac is able to borrow funds at 8 percent interest, what is the cost to Cadillac of every customer who takes advantage of this offer? If you were able to borrow to pay cash for this car, which rate would be more relevant in determining how much you might offer for the car—the rate at which you borrow money or the rate Cadillac borrows money?

Interpreting Financial Reports

LO1

Comparison of Two Companies' Ratios with Industry Ratios

K/R

C 4. Both **Sun Microsystems Inc**. and **Cisco Systems** are in the computer industry. These data (in millions) are for their fiscal year ends:[18]

	Sun	Cisco
Accounts payable	$1,428	$ 786
Cost of goods sold	7,608	12,586
Increase (decrease) in inventory	(16)	(49)

Compare the payables turnover ratio and days' payable for both companies. How are cash flows affected by days' payable? How do Sun Microsystems' and Cisco Systems' ratios compare with the computer industry ratios shown in Figures 1 and 2 in this chapter? (Use year-end amounts for ratios.)

LO2

Nature and Recognition of an Estimated Liability

C 5. The decision to recognize and record a liability is sometimes a matter of judgment. People who use **General Motors** credit cards earn rebates toward the purchase or lease of GM vehicles in relation to the amount of purchases they make with their cards. General Motors chooses to treat these outstanding rebates as a commitment in the notes to its financial statements:

> GM sponsors a credit card program . . . which offers rebates that can be applied primarily against the purchase or lease of GM vehicles. The amount of rebates available to qualified cardholders (net of deferred program income) was $4.9 billion and $4.7 billion at December 31, 2006, and 2005, respectively.[19]

Using the two criteria established by the FASB for recording a contingency, explain GM's reasoning in treating this liability as a commitment in the notes, where it will likely receive less attention by analysts, rather than including it on the income statement as an expense and on the balance sheet as an estimated liability. Do you agree with this position? (**Hint**: Apply the matching rule.)

Decision Analysis Using Excel

LO4 LO5

Baseball Contract

C 6. The Houston Texans' fifth-year pitcher Juan Alvarez made the All-Star team in 2010. Alvarez has three years left on a contract that is to pay him $2.4 million a year. He wants to renegotiate his contract because other players who have equally outstanding records (although they also have more experience) are receiving as much as $10.5 million per year for five years. Management has a policy of never renegotiating a current contract but is willing to consider extending the contract to additional years. In fact, the Texans have offered Alvarez an additional three years at $6.0 million, $9.0 million, and $12.0 million, respectively. In addition, they have added an option year at $15.0 million. Management points out that this package is worth $42.0 million, or $10.5 million per year on average. Alvarez is considering this offer and is also considering asking for a bonus to be paid upon signing the contract. Write a memorandum to Alvarez that comments on management's position and evaluates the offer, assuming a current interest rate of 10 percent. (**Hint**: Use present values.) Propose a range for the signing bonus. Finally, include other considerations that may affect the value of the offer.

Annual Report Case: CVS Caremark Corporation

LO1 LO3

Short-Term Liabilities and Seasonality; Commitments and Contingencies

C 7. Refer to the quarterly financial report near the end of the notes to the financial statements in **CVS's** annual report. Is CVS a seasonal business? Would you expect short-term borrowings and accounts payable to be unusually high or unusually low at the balance sheet date of December 29, 2007?

Read CVS's note on commitments and contingencies. What commitments and contingencies does the company have? Why is it important to consider this information in connection with payables analysis?

Comparison Case: CVS Versus Walgreens

LO1

Payables Analysis

C 8. Refer to **CVS's** financial statements in the Supplement to Chapter 1 and to the following data for **Walgreens**:

	2007	2006	2005
Cost of goods sold	$38,518.1	$34,240.4	$30,413.8
Accounts payable	3,733.3	4,039.2	3,163.6
Increase in merchandise inventory	676.2	375.7	854.0

Compute the payables turnover and days' payable for CVS and Walgreens for the past two years. In 2005, CVS had accounts payable of $2,124.8 million, and its merchandise inventory increased by $624.1 in 2006. Which company do you think makes the most use of creditors for financing the needs of the operating cycle? Has the trend changed?

Ethical Dilemma Case

LO2

Known Legal Violations

C 9. Harbor Restaurant is a large steak restaurant in the suburbs of Detroit. Jake Takas, an accounting student at a nearby college, recently secured a full-time accounting job at the restaurant. He felt fortunate to have a good job that accommodated his class schedule because the local economy was very bad. After a few weeks on the job, Takas realized that his boss, the owner of the business, was paying the kitchen workers in cash and was not withholding federal and state income taxes or social security and Medicare taxes. Takas understands that federal and state laws require these taxes to be withheld and paid to the appropriate agency in a timely manner. He also realizes that if he raises this issue, he could lose his job. What alternatives are available to Takas? What action would you take if you were in his position? Why did you make this choice?

Internet Case

Pain in the Drug Industry

C 10. Pain medications have been in the news. The big drug company **Merck** had to withdraw its pain killer Vioxx from the market when it became known that the drug increased the risk of heart attacks. Other drugs are under scrutiny, like Celebrex from **Pfizer**. Do an Internet search on these terms and companies. Find out if any lawsuits have been initiated and how these companies are reacting. Access their annual reports and find out what they report under contingent liabilities in the notes to the financial statements and elsewhere. Have they set aside any reserves for liabilities? What are the criteria for recognizing potential liabilities in the accounting records?

Group Activity Case

LO2 LO5

Nature and Recognition of an Estimated Liability

C 11. Assume that you work for Theater-At-Home, Inc., a retail company that sells basement movie projection systems for $10,000. Your boss is considering two types of promotions:

1. Offering customers a $1,000 coupon that they can apply to future purchases, including the purchase of annual maintenance.
2. Offering credit terms that allow payments of $2,000 down and $2,000 per year for four years starting one year after the purchase. Theater-At-Home would have to borrow money at 7 percent interest to finance these credit arrangements.

Divide the class into groups. After discussing the relative merits of these two plans, including their implications for accounting and the time value of money, each group should decide on the best alternative. The groups may recommend changes in the plans. A representative of each group should report the group's findings to the class.

Business Communication Case

LO5

Evaluation of an Auto Lease

C 12. Ford Credit ran an advertisement offering three alternatives for a 24-month lease on a new Lincoln automobile. The three alternatives were zero dollars down and $587 per month for 24 months, $1,975 down and $499 per month for 24 months, or $12,283 down and no monthly payments.[20] Your boss asks you to prepare an analysis of the three alternatives assuming a 12 percent annual return compounded monthly is the relevant interest rate for the company. Present your analysis and make a recommendation to your boss in a one-page business memorandum. Use Table 2 in the appendix on present value tables to determine which is the best deal. How would your recommendation change if the interest rate were higher? If it were lower?

CHAPTER

9 Long-Term Assets

Focus on Financial Statements

INCOME STATEMENT

Revenues

– Expenses

= Net Income

STATEMENT OF RETAINED EARNINGS

Opening Balance

+ Net Income

– Dividends

= Retained Earnings

BALANCE SHEET

Assets	Liabilities
	Equity

A = L + E

STATEMENT OF CASH FLOWS

Operating activities

+ Investing activities

+ Financing activities

= Change in Cash

+ Starting Balance

= Ending Cash Balance

Allocating cost of long-term assets on balance sheet affects income statement. Buying/disposing of long-term assets affects statement of cash flows.

Long-term assets include tangible assets, such as land, buildings, and equipment; natural resources, such as timberland and oil fields; and intangible assets, such as patents and copyrights. These assets represent a company's strategic commitments well into the future. The judgments related to their acquisition, operation, and disposal and to the allocation of their costs will affect a company's performance for years to come. Investors and creditors rely on accurate and full reporting of the assumptions and judgments that underlie the measurement of long-term assets.

LEARNING OBJECTIVES

LO1 **Define *long-term assets*, and explain the management issues related to them.** *(pp. 466–471)*

LO2 **Distinguish between *capital expenditures* and *revenue expenditures*, and account for the cost of property, plant, and equipment.** *(pp. 471–475)*

LO3 **Compute depreciation under the straight-line, production, and declining-balance methods.** *(pp. 475–482)*

LO4 **Account for the disposal of depreciable assets.** *(pp. 482–484)*

LO5 **Identify the issues related to accounting for natural resources, and compute depletion.** *(pp. 484–487)*

LO6 **Identify the issues related to accounting for intangible assets, including research and development costs and goodwill.** *(pp. 487–492)*

DECISION POINT ▶ A USER'S FOCUS

Apple Computer, Inc.

Long known for its innovative technology and design of computers, **Apple** revolutionized the music industry with its digital iPod music player. The company's success stems from its willingness to invest in research and development and long-term assets to create new products. Each year, it spends almost $782 million on research and development and about $735 million on new long-term assets. About 15 percent of its assets are long term. You can get an idea of the extent and importance of Apple's long-term assets by looking at the Financial Highlights from its balance sheet.[1]

APPLE COMPUTER'S FINANCIAL HIGHLIGHTS (In millions)

	2007	2006
Property, Plant, and Equipment:		
Land and buildings	$ 762	$ 626
Machinery, equipment, and internal-use software	954	595
Office furniture and equipment	106	94
Leasehold improvements	1,019	760
	2,841	2,075
Less accumulated depreciation and amortization	1,009	794
Total property, plant, and equipment, net	$1,832	$1,281
Other Noncurrent Assets:		
Goodwill	$ 38	$ 38
Acquired intangible assets	299	139
Capitalized software development costs	83	21
Other noncurrent assets	1,139	1,217
Total other noncurrent assets	$1,559	$1,415

- ▶ What are Apple's long-term assets?
- ▶ What are its policies in accounting for long-term assets?
- ▶ Does the company generate enough cash flow to finance its continued growth?

Management Issues Related to Long-Term Assets

LO1 Define *long-term assets*, and explain the management issues related to them.

> **Study Note**
> For an asset to be classified as property, plant, and equipment, it must be "put in use," which means it is available for its intended purpose. An emergency generator is "put in use" when it is available for emergencies, even if it is never used.

> **Study Note**
> A computer that a company uses in an office is a long-term plant asset. An identical computer that a company sells to customers is considered inventory.

Long-term assets were once called fixed assets, but this term has fallen out of favor because it implies that the assets last forever, which they do not. Long-term assets have the following characteristics:

- *They have a useful life of more than one year.* This distinguishes them from current assets, which a company expects to use up or convert to cash within one year or during its operating cycle, whichever is longer. They also differ from current assets in that they support the operating cycle, rather than being part of it. Although there is no strict rule for defining the useful life of a long-term asset, the most common criterion is that the asset be capable of repeated use for at least a year. Included in this category is equipment used only in peak or emergency periods, such as electric generators.
- *They are used in the operation of a business.* Assets not used in the normal course of business, such as land held for speculative reasons or buildings no longer used in ordinary business operations, should be classified as long-term investments, not as long-term assets.
- *They are not intended for resale to customers.* An asset that a company intends to resell to customers should be classified as inventory—not as a long-term asset—no matter how durable it is. For example, a printing press that a manufacturer offers for sale is part of the manufacturer's inventory, but it is a long-term asset for a printing company that buys it to use in its operations.

Figure 1 shows the relative importance of long-term assets in various industries. Figure 2 shows how long-term assets are classified and defines the methods of accounting for them. Plant assets, which are **tangible assets**, are accounted for through **depreciation**, the periodic allocation of the cost of a tangible long-lived asset over its estimated useful life. (Although land is a tangible asset, it is not depreciated because it has an unlimited life.) **Natural resources**, which are also tangible assets, are accounted for through **depletion**, the proportional allocation of the cost of a natural resource to the units extracted. Most **intangible assets** are accounted for through **amortization**, the periodic allocation of the cost of the asset to the periods it benefits. However, some intangible assets, including goodwill, are not subject to amortization if their fair value is below the carrying value.

Carrying value (also called *book value*) is the unexpired part of an asset's cost (see Figure 3). Long-term assets are generally reported at carrying value. If a long-term asset loses any of its potential to generate revenue before the end of its useful life, it is deemed *impaired*, and its carrying value is reduced.

FIGURE 1
Long-Term Assets as a Percentage of Total Assets for Selected Industries

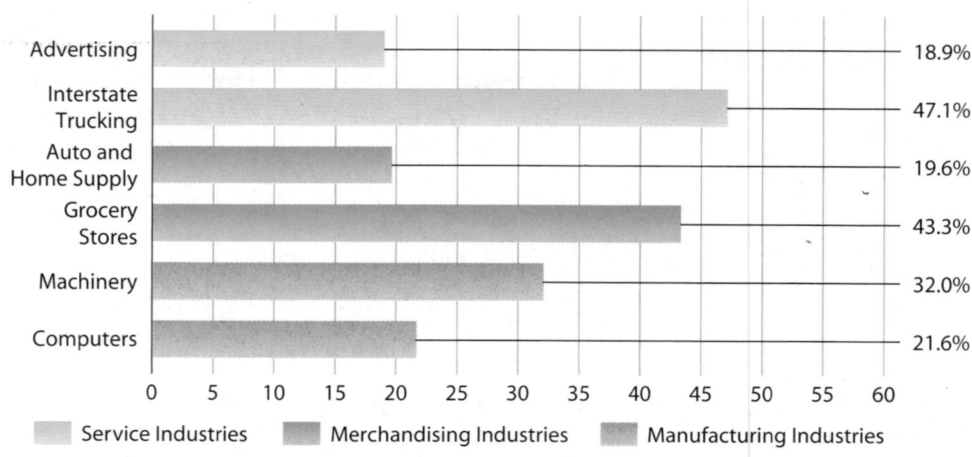

Source: Data from Dun & Bradstreet, *Industry Norms and Key Business Ratios*, 2005–2006

FIGURE 2

Classification of Long-Term Assets and Methods of Accounting for Them

BALANCE SHEET Long-Term Assets		INCOME STATEMENT Expenses
	**Tangible Assets:** long-term assets that have physical substance Land Plant, Buildings, Equipment (plant assets)	Land is not expensed because it has an unlimited life. **Depreciation:** periodic allocation of the cost of a tangible long-lived asset (other than land and natural resources) over its estimated useful life
	**Natural Resources:** long-term assets purchased for the economic value that can be taken from the land and used up, as with ore, lumber, oil, and gas or other resources contained in the land Mines Timberland Oil and Gas Fields	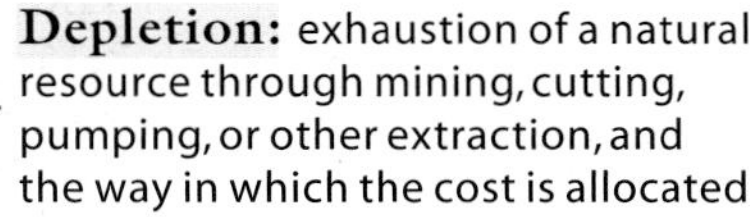 **Depletion:** exhaustion of a natural resource through mining, cutting, pumping, or other extraction, and the way in which the cost is allocated
	**Intangible Assets:** long-term assets that have no physical substance but have a value based on rights or advantages accruing to the owner Patents, Copyrights, Software, Trademarks, Licenses, Brands, Franchises, Leaseholds, Noncompete Covenants, Customer Lists, Goodwill	**Amortization:** periodic allocation of the cost of an intangible asset to the periods it benefits

Study Note

To be classified as intangible, an asset must lack physical substance, be long term, and represent a legal right or advantage.

All long-term assets, including intangible assets that are not subject to amortization, are subject to an annual impairment evaluation. **Asset impairment** occurs when the carrying value of a long-term asset exceeds its fair value.[2] *Fair value* is the amount for which the asset could be bought or sold in a current transaction. For example, if the sum of the expected cash flows from an asset is less than its carrying value, the asset would be impaired. Reducing carrying value to fair value, as measured by the present value of future cash flows, is an application of conservatism. A reduction in carrying value as the result of impairment is recorded as a loss. When the market prices used to establish fair value are not available, the amount of an impairment must be estimated from the best available information.

In 2004, **Apple** recognized losses of $5.5 million in asset impairments, but it recognized none in subsequent years. A few years earlier, in the midst of an

FIGURE 3

Carrying Value of Long-Term Assets on the Balance Sheet

Plant Assets	Natural Resources	Intangible Assets
Less Accumulated Depreciation	Less Accumulated Depletion	Less Accumulated Amortization
Carrying Value	Carrying Value	Carrying Value

economic slowdown in the telecommunications industry, **WorldCom** recorded asset impairments that totaled $79.8 billion, the largest impairment write-down in history. Since then, other telecommunications companies, including **AT&T** and **Qwest Communications**, have taken large impairment write-downs. Due to these companies' declining revenues, the carrying value of some of their long-term assets no longer exceeded the cash flows that they were meant to help generate.[3] Because of the write-downs, these companies reported large operating losses.

Taking a large write-down in a bad year is often called "taking a big bath" because it "cleans" future years of the bad year's costs and thus can help a company return to a profitable status. In other words, by taking the largest possible loss on a long-term asset in a bad year, companies hope to reduce the costs of depreciation or amortization on the asset in subsequent years.[4]

In the next few pages, we discuss the management issues related to long-term assets—how management decides whether it will acquire them, how it will finance them, and how it will account for them.

Acquiring Long-Term Assets

The decision to acquire a long-term asset is a complex process. For example, **Apple's** decision to invest capital in establishing its own retail stores throughout the country required very careful analysis. Methods of evaluating data to make rational decisions about acquiring long-term assets are grouped under a topic called capital budgeting, which is usually covered as a managerial accounting topic. However, an awareness of the general nature of the problem is helpful in understanding the management issues related to long-term assets.

To illustrate an acquisition decision, suppose that Apple's management is considering the purchase of a $100,000 customer-relations software package. Management estimates that the new software will save net cash flows of $40,000 per year for four years, the usual life of new software, and that the software will be worth $20,000 at the end of that period. These data are shown in Table 1.

To put the cash flows on a comparable basis, it is helpful to use present value tables, such as Tables 1 and 2 in the appendix on present value tables. If the interest rate set by management as a desirable return is 10 percent compounded annually, the purchase decision would be evaluated as follows:

		Present Value
Acquisition cost	Present value factor = 1.000	
	1.000 × $100,000	($100,000)
Net annual savings in cash flows	Present value factor = 3.170	
	(Table 2: 4 periods, 10%)	
	3.170 × $40,000	126,800
Disposal price	Present value factor = .683	
	(Table 1: 4 periods, 10%)	
	.683 × $20,000	13,660
Net present value		$ 40,460

As long as the net present value is positive, Apple will earn at least 10 percent on the investment. In this case, the return is greater than 10 percent because the net present value is a positive $40,460. Moreover, the net present value is large relative to the investment. Based on this analysis, it appears that Apple's management should make the decision to purchase. However, in making its decision, it

TABLE 1
Illustration of an Acquisition Decision

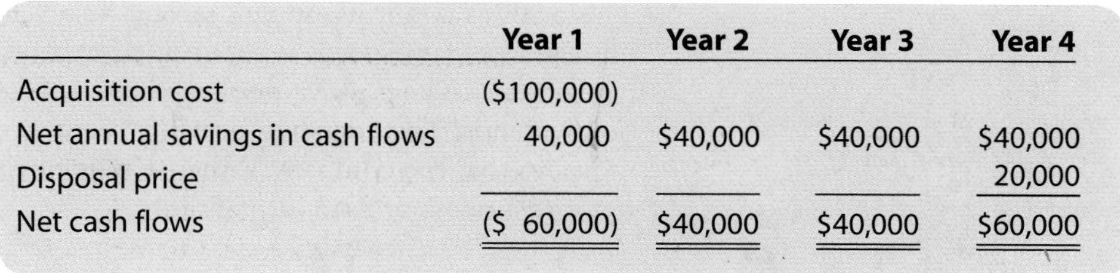

	Year 1	Year 2	Year 3	Year 4
Acquisition cost	($100,000)			
Net annual savings in cash flows	40,000	$40,000	$40,000	$40,000
Disposal price				20,000
Net cash flows	($ 60,000)	$40,000	$40,000	$60,000

should take other important considerations into account, including the costs of training personnel to use the software. It should also allow for the possibility that because of unforeseen circumstances, the savings may not be as great as expected.

Information about acquisitions of long-term assets appears in the investing activities section of the statement of cash flows. In referring to this section of its 2007 annual report, Apple's management makes the following statement:

> The company's total capital expenditures were $822 million during fiscal 2007. . . . The company currently anticipates it will utilize approximately $1.1 billion for capital expenditures during 2008, approximately $400 million for further expansion of the Company's Retail segment and [the remainder] utilized to support normal replacement of existing capital assets.

Financing Long-Term Assets

When management decides to acquire a long-term asset, it must also decide how to finance the purchase. Many financing arrangements are based on the life of the asset. For example, an automobile loan generally spans 4 or 5 years, whereas a mortgage on a house may span 30 years. For a major long-term acquisition, a company may issue stock, long-term notes, or bonds. Some companies are profitable enough to pay for long-term assets out of cash flows from operations. A good place to study a company's investing and financing activities is its statement of cash flows, and a good measure of its ability to finance long-term assets is free cash flow.

Free cash flow is the amount of cash that remains after deducting the funds a company must commit to continue operating at its planned level. The commitments to be covered include current or continuing operations, interest, income taxes, dividends, and net capital expenditures (purchases of plant assets minus sales of plant assets). If a company fails to pay for current or continuing operations, interest, and income taxes, its creditors and the government can take legal action. Although the payment of dividends is not strictly required, dividends normally represent a commitment to stockholders. If they are reduced or eliminated, stockholders will be unhappy, and the price of the company's stock will fall. Net capital expenditures represent management's plans for the future.

A positive free cash flow means that a company has met all its cash commitments and has cash available to reduce debt or to expand its operations. A negative free cash flow means that it will have to sell investments, borrow money, or issue stock in the short term to continue at its planned level. If free cash flow remains negative for several years, a company may not be able to raise cash by issuing stock or bonds.

Using data from **Apple's** statement of cash flows in its 2007 annual report, we can compute the company's free cash flow as follows (in millions):

Free Cash Flow = Net Cash Flows from Operating Activities − Dividends − Purchases of Plant Assets + Sales of Plant Assets
= $5,470 − $0 − $735
= $4,735

This analysis confirms Apple's strong financial position. Its cash flow from operating activities far exceeds its net capital expenditures of $735 million. A factor that contributes to its positive free cash flow of $5,470 million is that the company pays no dividends. The financing activities section of Apple's statement of cash flows also indicates that the company, rather than incurring debt for expansion, actually made net investments of $2,312 million.

Applying the Matching Rule

When a company records an expenditure as a long-term asset, it is deferring an expense until a later period. Thus, the current period's profitability looks better than it would if the expenditure had been expensed immediately. Management has considerable latitude in making the judgments and estimates necessary to account for all types and aspects of long-term assets. Sometimes, this latitude is used unwisely and unethically. For example, in the infamous **WorldCom** accounting fraud, management ordered that certain expenditures that should have been recorded as operating expenses be capitalized as long-term assets and written off over several years. The result was an overstatement of income by about $10 billion, which ultimately led to the largest bankruptcy in the history of U.S. business.

To avoid fraudulent reporting of long-term assets, a company's management must apply the matching rule in resolving two important issues. The first is how much of the total cost of a long-term asset to allocate to expense in the current accounting period. The second is how much to retain on the balance sheet as an asset that will benefit future periods. To resolve these issues, management must answer four important questions about the acquisition, use, and disposal of each long-term asset (see Figure 4):

1. How is the cost of the long-term asset determined?
2. How should the expired portion of the cost of the long-term asset be allocated against revenues over time?

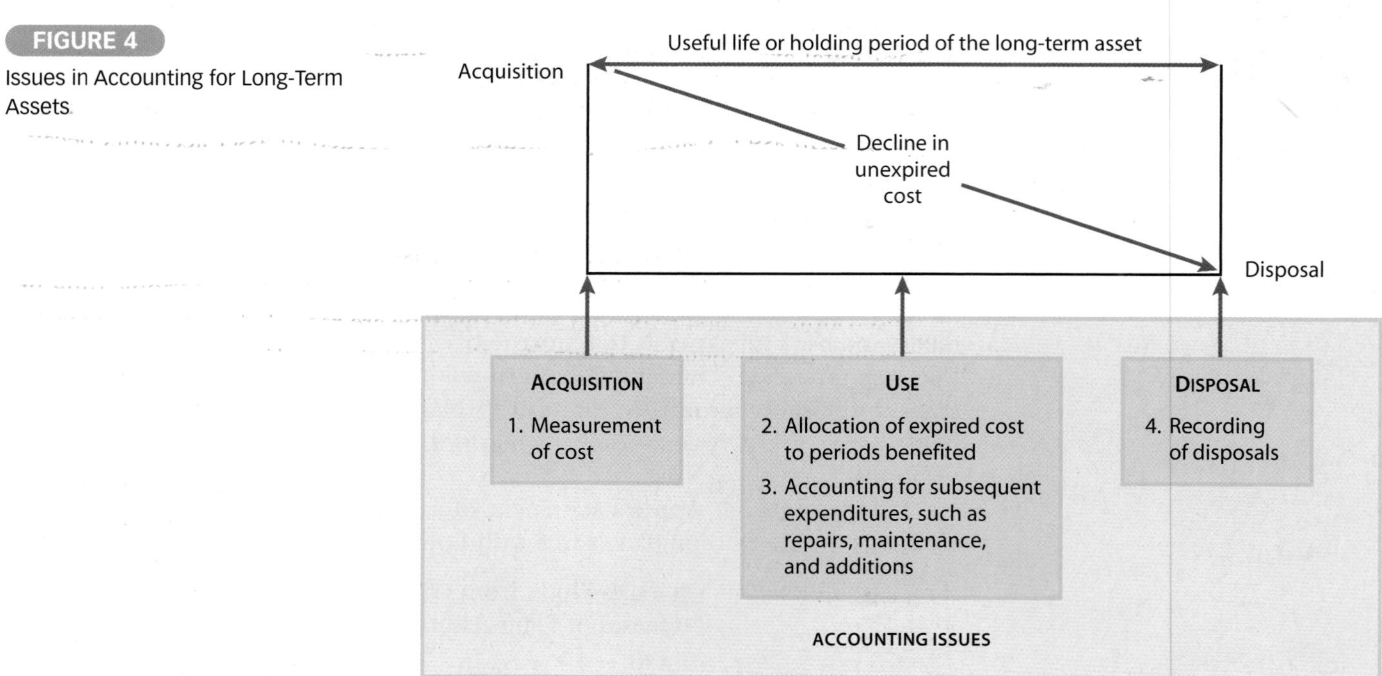

FIGURE 4
Issues in Accounting for Long-Term Assets

3. How should subsequent expenditures, such as repairs and additions, be treated?
4. How should disposal of the long-term asset be recorded?

Management's answers to these questions can be found in the company's annual report under management's discussion and analysis and in the notes to the financial statements.

STOP ► REVIEW ► APPLY

LO1-1 **What are the characteristics of long-term assets?**

LO1-2 **Why is land different from other long-term assets?**

LO1-3 **What do accountants mean by *depreciation*, and how does depreciation differ from depletion and amortization?**

LO1-4 **What is asset impairment, and how does it affect the valuation of long-term assets?**

LO1-5 **How do cash flows relate to the decision to acquire a long-term asset, and how does an asset's useful life relate to the means of financing it?**

LO1-6 **Define *free cash flow*, and identify its components. What do *positive free cash flow* and *negative free cash flow* mean?**

LO1-7 **What four questions are important in accounting for long-term assets?**

Suggested answers to all Stop, Review, and Apply questions follow the appendixes.

Acquisition Cost of Property, Plant, and Equipment

LO2 Distinguish between *capital expenditures* and *revenue expenditures*, and account for the cost of property, plant, and equipment.

Expenditure refers to a payment or an obligation to make a future payment for an asset, such as a truck, or for a service, such as a repair. Expenditures are classified as capital expenditures or revenue expenditures.

- A **capital expenditure** is an expenditure for the purchase or expansion of a long-term asset. Capital expenditures are recorded in asset accounts because they benefit several future accounting periods.
- A **revenue expenditure** is an expenditure made for the ordinary repairs and maintenance needed to keep a long-term asset in good operating condition. For example, trucks, machines, and other equipment require periodic tune-ups and routine repairs. Expenditures of this type are recorded in expense accounts because their benefits are realized in the current period.

Capital expenditures include outlays for plant assets, natural resources, and intangible assets. They also include expenditures for the following:

- **Additions**, which are enlargements to the physical layout of a plant asset. For example, if a new wing is added to a building, the benefits from the expenditure will be received over several years, and the amount paid should be debited to an asset account.
- **Betterments**, which are improvements to a plant asset but that do not add to the plant's physical layout. Installation of an air-conditioning system is an

example. Because betterments provide benefits over a period of years, their costs should be debited to an asset account.

- **Extraordinary repairs**, which are repairs that significantly enhance a plant asset's estimated useful life or residual value. For example, a complete overhaul of a building's heating and cooling system may extend the system's useful life by five years. Extraordinary repairs are typically recorded by reducing the Accumulated Depreciation account; the assumption in doing so is that some of the depreciation previously recorded on the asset has now been eliminated. The effect of the reduction is to increase the asset's carrying value by the cost of the extraordinary repair. The new carrying value should be depreciated over the asset's new estimated useful life.

The distinction between capital and revenue expenditures is important in applying the matching rule. For example, if the purchase of a machine that will benefit a company for several years is mistakenly recorded as a revenue expenditure, the total cost of the machine becomes an expense on the income statement in the current period. As a result, current net income will be reported at a lower amount (understated), and in future periods, net income will be reported at a higher amount (overstated). If, on the other hand, a revenue expenditure, such as the routine overhaul of a piece of machinery, is charged to an asset account, the expense of the current period will be understated. Current net income will be overstated by the same amount, and the net income of future periods will be understated.

General Approach to Acquisition Costs

Study Note

Expenditures necessary to prepare an asset for its intended use are a cost of the asset.

The acquisition cost of property, plant, and equipment includes all expenditures reasonable and necessary to get an asset in place and ready for use. For example, the cost of installing and testing a machine is a legitimate cost of acquiring the machine. However, if the machine is damaged during installation, the cost of repairs is an operating expense, not an acquisition cost.

Acquisition cost is easiest to determine when a purchase is made for cash. In that case, the cost of the asset is equal to the cash paid for it plus expenditures for freight, insurance while in transit, installation, and other necessary related costs. Expenditures for freight, insurance while in transit, and installation are included in the cost of the asset because they are necessary if the asset is to function. In accordance with the matching rule, these expenditures are allocated over the asset's useful life rather than charged as expenses in the current period.

Any interest charges incurred in purchasing an asset are not a cost of the asset; they are a cost of borrowing the money to buy the asset and are therefore an operating expense. An exception to this rule is that interest costs incurred during the construction of an asset are properly included as a cost of the asset.[5]

As a matter of practicality, many companies establish policies that define when an expenditure should be recorded as an expense or as an asset. For example, small expenditures for items that qualify as long-term assets may be treated as expenses because the amounts involved are not material in relation to net income. Thus, although a wastebasket may last for years, it would be recorded as supplies expense rather than as a depreciable asset.

Specific Applications

In the sections that follow, we discuss some of the problems of determining the cost of long-term plant assets.

Study Note

Many costs may be incurred to prepare land for its intended use and condition. All such costs are a cost of the land.

Land The purchase price of land should be debited to the Land account. Other expenditures that should be debited to the Land account include commissions to real estate agents; lawyers' fees; accrued taxes paid by the purchaser; costs of preparing the land to build on, such as the costs of tearing down old buildings and grading the land; and assessments for local improvements, such as putting in streets and sewage systems. The cost of landscaping is usually debited to the Land account because such improvements are relatively permanent. Land is not subject to depreciation because it has an unlimited useful life.

Study Note

The costs of tearing down existing buildings can be major. Companies may spend millions of dollars imploding buildings so they can remove them and build new ones.

Let us assume that a company buys land for a new retail operation. The net purchase price is $340,000. The company also pays brokerage fees of $12,000, legal fees of $4,000, $20,000 to have an old building on the site torn down, and $2,000 to have the site graded. It receives $8,000 in salvage from the old building. The cost of the land is $370,000, calculated as follows:

Net purchase price		$340,000
Brokerage fees		12,000
Legal fees		4,000
Tearing down old building	$20,000	
Less salvage	8,000	12,000
Grading		2,000
Total cost		$370,000

Land Improvements Some improvements to real estate, such as driveways, parking lots, and fences, have a limited life and thus are subject to depreciation. They should be recorded in an account called Land Improvements rather than in the Land account.

Buildings When a company buys a building, the cost includes the purchase price of the building and all repairs and other expenditures required to put the

To make way for its new headquarters in Birmingham, Alabama, Energen Corporation had this ten-story building imploded. Like other costs involved in preparing land for use, the cost of implosion is debited to the Land account. Other expenditures debited to the Land account include the purchase price of the land, brokerage and legal fees involved in the purchase, taxes paid by the purchaser, and landscaping.

building in usable condition. When a company uses a contractor to construct a building, the cost includes the net contract price plus other expenditures necessary to put the building in usable condition. When a company constructs its own building, the cost includes all reasonable and necessary expenditures. Reasonable and necessary expenditures include the costs of materials, labor, part of the overhead and other indirect costs, architects' fees, insurance during construction, interest on construction loans during the period of construction, lawyers' fees, and building permits. Because buildings have a limited useful life, they are subject to depreciation.

Leasehold Improvements Improvements to leased property that become the property of the lessor (the owner of the property) at the end of the lease are called **leasehold improvements**.

For example, a tenant's installation of light fixtures, carpets, or walls would be considered a leasehold improvement. These improvements are usually classified as tangible assets in the property, plant, and equipment section of the balance sheet. Sometimes, they are included in the intangible assets section; the theory in reporting them as intangibles is that because they revert to the lessor at the end of the lease, they are more of a right than a tangible asset. The cost of a leasehold improvement is depreciated or amortized over the remaining term of the lease or the useful life of the improvement, whichever is shorter.

Leasehold improvements are fairly common in large businesses. A study of large companies showed that 22 percent report leasehold improvements. The percentage is likely to be much higher for small businesses because they generally operate in leased premises.[6]

Study Note

The wiring and plumbing of a dental chair are included in the cost of the asset because they are a necessary cost of preparing the asset for use.

Equipment The cost of equipment includes all expenditures connected with purchasing the equipment and preparing it for use. Among these expenditures are the invoice price less cash discounts; freight, including insurance; excise taxes and tariffs; buying expenses; installation costs; and test runs to ready the equipment for operation. Equipment is subject to depreciation.

Group Purchases Companies sometimes purchase land and other assets for a lump sum. Because land has an unlimited life and is a nondepreciable asset, it must have a separate ledger account, and the lump-sum purchase price must be apportioned between the land and the other assets.

For example, suppose a company buys a building and the land on which it is situated for a lump sum of $170,000. The company can apportion the costs by determining what it would have paid for the building and for the land if it had purchased them separately and applying the appropriate percentages to the lump-sum price. Assume that appraisals yield estimates of $20,000 for the land and $180,000 for the building if purchased separately. In that case, 10 percent of the lump-sum price, or $17,000, would be allocated to the land, and 90 percent, or $153,000, would be allocated to the building.

The allocation would be as follows:

	Appraisal	Percentage		Apportionment	
Land	$ 20,000	10%	($20,000 ÷ $200,000)	$ 17,000	($170,000 × 10%)
Building	180,000	90%	($180,000 ÷ $200,000)	153,000	($170,000 × 90%)
Totals	$200,000	100%		$170,000	

STOP ▶ REVIEW ▶ APPLY

LO2-1 **What is the difference between revenue expenditures and capital expenditures, and why is it important?**

LO2-2 **In what ways do an addition, a betterment, and an extraordinary repair differ?**

LO2-3 **When an addition to a building is charged as a repair expense, how will it affect income in future years?**

LO2-4 **What, in general, is included in the acquisition cost of a long-term asset?**

LO2-5 **The following expenditures relate to the purchase of a computer system: (a) purchase price, (b) interest charges incurred in purchasing the equipment, (c) freight charges, (d) installation charges, (e) cost of special communications outlets at the computer site, (f) cost of repairing a part damaged during installation, and (g) cost of adjustments to the system during the first month of operation. Which of these expenditures should be charged to an asset account?**

LO2-6 **Tom's Grocery obtained bids on the construction of a receiving dock at the back of its store. The lowest bid was $44,000. The company decided to build the dock itself and was able to do so for $40,000, which it borrowed. It recorded the expenditures by debiting its Buildings account for $44,000 and crediting its Notes Payable account for $40,000 and its Gain on Construction account for $4,000. Do you agree with this entry? Why or why not?**

Identification of Capital Expenditures Match each term below with the corresponding action in the list that follows by writing the appropriate numbers in the blanks:

1. Addition
2. Betterment
3. Extraordinary repair
4. Land
5. Land improvement
6. Leasehold improvement
7. Buildings
8. Equipment
9. Not a capital expenditure

___ a. Purchase of a computer

___ b. Purchase of a lighting system for a parking lot

___ c. Repainting of an existing building

___ d. Installation of a new roof that extends an existing building's useful life

___ e. Construction of a foundation for a new building

___ f. Erection of a new storage facility at the back of an existing building

___ g. Installation of partitions and shelves in a leased space

___ h. Clearing of land in preparation for construction of a new building

___ i. Installation of a new heating system in an existing building

SOLUTION

a. 8	f. 1
b. 5	g. 6
c. 9	h. 4
d. 3	i. 2
e. 7	

Depreciation

LO3 Compute depreciation under the straight-line, production, and declining-balance methods.

As we noted earlier, *depreciation* is the periodic allocation of the cost of a tangible asset (other than land and natural resources) over the asset's estimated useful life. In accounting for depreciation, it is important to keep the following points in mind:

▶ *All tangible assets except for land have a limited useful life, and the costs of these assets must be distributed as expenses over the years they benefit.* Physical deterioration and obsolescence are the major factors in limiting a depreciable asset's useful life.

— **Physical deterioration** results from use and from exposure to the elements, such as wind and sun. Periodic repairs and a sound maintenance policy may keep buildings and equipment in good operating order and prolong their useful lives, but every machine or building must at some point be discarded. Repairs do not eliminate the need for depreciation.

— **Obsolescence** refers to the process of going out of date. Because of fast-changing technology and fast-changing demands, machinery and even buildings often become obsolete before they wear out.

Study Note

A computer may be functioning as well as it did on the day it was purchased four years ago, but because much faster, more efficient computers have become available, the old computer is now obsolete.

Accountants do not distinguish between physical deterioration and obsolescence because they are interested in the length of an asset's useful life, not in what limits its useful life.

- *Depreciation refers to the allocation of the cost of a plant asset to the periods that benefit from the asset, not to the asset's physical deterioration or decrease in market value.* The term *depreciation* describes the gradual conversion of the cost of the asset into an expense.

Study Note

Depreciation is the allocation of the acquisition cost of a plant asset, and any similarity between undepreciated cost and current market value is pure coincidence.

- *Depreciation is not a process of valuation.* Accounting records are not indicators of changing price levels; they are kept in accordance with the cost principle. Because of an advantageous purchase price and market conditions, the value of a building may increase. Nevertheless, because depreciation is a process of allocation, not valuation, depreciation on the building must continue to be recorded. Eventually, the building will wear out or become obsolete regardless of interim fluctuations in market value.

Factors in Computing Depreciation

Four factors affect the computation of depreciation:

1. *Cost.* As explained earlier, cost is the net purchase price of an asset plus all reasonable and necessary expenditures to get it in place and ready for use.
2. *Residual value.* **Residual value** is the portion of an asset's acquisition cost that a company expects to recover when it disposes of the asset. Other terms used to describe residual value are *salvage value*, *disposal value*, and *trade-in value*.
3. *Depreciable cost.* **Depreciable cost** is an asset's cost less its residual value. For example, a truck that cost $24,000 and that has a residual value of $6,000

FOCUS ON BUSINESS PRACTICE

How Long Is the Useful Life of an Airplane?

Most airlines depreciate their planes over an estimated useful life of 10 to 20 years. But how long will a properly maintained plane really last? Western Airlines paid $3.3 million for a new Boeing 737 in July 1968. More than 78,000 flights and 30 years later, this aircraft was still flying for Vanguard Airlines, a no-frills airline. Among the other airlines that have owned this plane are Piedmont, **Delta**, and **US Airways**. Virtually every part of the plane has been replaced over the years. **Boeing** believes the plane could theoretically make double the number of flights before it is retired.

The useful lives of many types of assets can be extended indefinitely if the assets are correctly maintained, but proper accounting in accordance with the matching rule requires depreciation over a "reasonable" useful life. Each airline that owned the plane would have accounted for the plane in this way.

Study Note

It is depreciable cost, not acquisition cost, that is allocated over a plant asset's useful life.

would have a depreciable cost of $18,000. Depreciable cost must be allocated over the useful life of the asset.

4. *Estimated useful life.* **Estimated useful life** is the total number of service units expected from a long-term asset. Service units may be measured in terms of the years an asset is expected to be used, the units it is expected to produce, the miles it is expected to be driven, or similar measures. In computing an asset's estimated useful life, an accountant should consider all relevant information, including past experience with similar assets, the asset's present condition, the company's repair and maintenance policy, and current technological and industry trends.

Depreciation is recorded at the end of an accounting period with an adjusting entry that takes the following form:

A	= L +	SE
−XXX		−XXX

Depreciation Expense–Asset Name	XXX	
Accumulated Depreciation–Asset Name		XXX
To record depreciation for the period		

Methods of Computing Depreciation

Many methods are used to allocate the cost of plant assets to accounting periods through depreciation. Each is appropriate in certain circumstances. The most common methods are the straight-line method, the production method, and an accelerated method known as the declining-balance method.

Straight-Line Method When the **straight-line method** is used to calculate depreciation, the asset's depreciable cost is spread evenly over the estimated useful life of the asset. The straight-line method is based on the assumption that depreciation depends only on the passage of time. The depreciation expense for each period is computed by dividing the depreciable cost (the cost of the depreciating asset less its estimated residual value) by the number of accounting periods in the asset's estimated useful life. The rate of depreciation is the same in each year.

Study Note

Residual value and useful life are, at best, educated guesses.

Suppose, for example, that a delivery truck cost $20,000 and has an estimated residual value of $2,000 at the end of its estimated useful life of five years. Under the straight-line method, the annual depreciation would be $3,600, calculated as follows:

$$\frac{\text{Cost} - \text{Residual Value}}{\text{Estimated Useful Life}} = \frac{\$20{,}000 - \$2{,}000}{5 \text{ years}} = \$3{,}600 \text{ per year}$$

Table 2 shows the depreciation schedule for the five years. Note that in addition to annual depreciation's being the same each year, the accumulated depreciation

SL

TABLE 2

Depreciation Schedule, Straight-Line Method

	Cost	Annual Depreciation	Accumulated Depreciation	Carrying Value
Date of purchase	$20,000	—	—	$20,000
End of first year	20,000	$3,600	$ 3,600	16,400
End of second year	20,000	3,600	7,200	12,800
End of third year	20,000	3,600	10,800	9,200
End of fourth year	20,000	3,600	14,400	5,600
End of fifth year	20,000	3,600	18,000	2,000

TABLE 3

Depreciation Schedule, Production Method

	Cost	Miles	Annual Depreciation	Accumulated Depreciation	Carrying Value
Date of purchase	$20,000	—	—	—	$20,000
End of first year	20,000	20,000	$4,000	$ 4,000	16,000
End of second year	20,000	30,000	6,000	10,000	10,000
End of third year	20,000	10,000	2,000	12,000	8,000
End of fourth year	20,000	20,000	4,000	16,000	4,000
End of fifth year	20,000	10,000	2,000	18,000	2,000

increases uniformly, and the carrying value decreases uniformly until it reaches the estimated residual value.

Study Note

The production method is appropriate when a company has widely fluctuating rates of production. For example, carpet mills often close during the first two weeks in July but may run double shifts in September. With the production method, depreciation would be in direct relation to a mill's units of output.

Production Method The **production method** is based on the assumption that depreciation is solely the result of use and that the passage of time plays no role in the process. If we assume that the delivery truck in the previous example has an estimated useful life of 90,000 miles, the depreciation cost per mile would be determined as follows:

$$\frac{\text{Cost} - \text{Residual Value}}{\text{Estimated Units of Useful Life}} = \frac{\$20{,}000 - \$2{,}000}{90{,}000 \text{ miles}} = \$0.20 \text{ per mile}$$

If the truck was driven 20,000 miles in the first year, 30,000 miles in the second, 10,000 miles in the third, 20,000 miles in the fourth, and 10,000 miles in the fifth, the depreciation schedule for the truck would be as shown in Table 3.

As you can see, the amount of depreciation each year is directly related to the units of use. The accumulated depreciation increases annually in direct relation to these units, and the carrying value decreases each year until it reaches the estimated residual value.

The production method should be used only when the output of an asset over its useful life can be estimated with reasonable accuracy. In addition, the unit used to measure the estimated useful life of an asset should be appropriate for the asset. For example, the number of items produced may be an appropriate measure for one machine, but the number of hours of use may be a better measure for another.

Study Note

Accelerated depreciation is appropriate for assets that provide the greatest benefits in their early years. Under an accelerated method, depreciation charges will be highest in years when revenue generation from the asset is highest.

Declining-Balance Method An **accelerated method** of depreciation results in relatively large amounts of depreciation in the early years of an asset's life and smaller amounts in later years. This type of method, which is based on the passage of time, assumes that many plant assets are most efficient when new and so provide the greatest benefits in their first years. It is consistent with the matching rule to allocate more depreciation to an asset in its earlier years than to later ones if the benefits it provides in its early years are greater than those it provides later on.

Fast-changing technologies often cause equipment to become obsolescent and lose service value rapidly. In such cases, using an accelerated method is appropriate because it allocates more depreciation to earlier years than to later ones. Another argument in favor of using an accelerated method is that repair expense is likely to increase as an asset ages. Thus, the total of repair and depreciation expense will remain fairly constant over the years. This result naturally assumes that the services received from the asset are roughly equal from year to year.

The **declining-balance method** is the most common accelerated method of depreciation. With this method, depreciation is computed by applying a fixed rate to the carrying value (the declining balance) of a tangible long-term asset. It

TABLE 4

Depreciation Schedule, Double-Declining-Balance Method

	Cost	Annual Depreciation	Accumulated Depreciation	Carrying Value
Date of purchase	$20,000	—	—	$20,000
End of first year	20,000	(40% × $20,000) = $8,000	$ 8,000	12,000
End of second year	20,000	(40% × $12,000) = 4,800	12,800	7,200
End of third year	20,000	(40% × $ 7,200) = 2,880	15,680	4,320
End of fourth year	20,000	(40% × $ 4,320) = 1,728	17,408	2,592
End of fifth year	20,000	592*		2,000

***Depreciation is limited to the amount necessary to reduce carrying value to residual value: $2,592 (previous carrying value) − $2,000 (residual value) = $592.**

Study Note

The double-declining-balance method is the only method presented here in which the residual value is not deducted before beginning the depreciation calculation.

therefore results in higher depreciation charges in the early years of the asset's life. Though any fixed rate can be used, the most common rate is a percentage equal to twice the straight-line depreciation percentage. When twice the straight-line rate is used, the method is usually called the **double-declining-balance method**.

In our example of the straight-line method, the delivery truck had an estimated useful life of five years, and the annual depreciation rate for the truck was therefore 20 percent (100 percent ÷ 5 years). Under the double-declining-balance method, the fixed rate would be 40 percent (2 × 20 percent). This fixed rate is applied to the carrying value that remains at the end of each year. With this method, the depreciation schedule would be as shown in Table 4.

Note that the fixed rate is always applied to the carrying value at the end of the previous year. Depreciation is greatest in the first year and declines each year after that. The depreciation in the last year is limited to the amount necessary to reduce carrying value to residual value.

Comparison of the Three Methods Figure 5 compares yearly depreciation and carrying value under the three methods. The graph on the left shows yearly depreciation. As you can see, straight-line depreciation is uniform at $3,600 per year over the five-year period. The double-declining-balance method begins at $8,000 and decreases each year to amounts that are less than straight-line (ultimately, $592). The production method does not generate a regular pattern because of the random fluctuation of the depreciation from year to year.

FIGURE 5

Graphic Comparison of Three Methods of Determining Depreciation

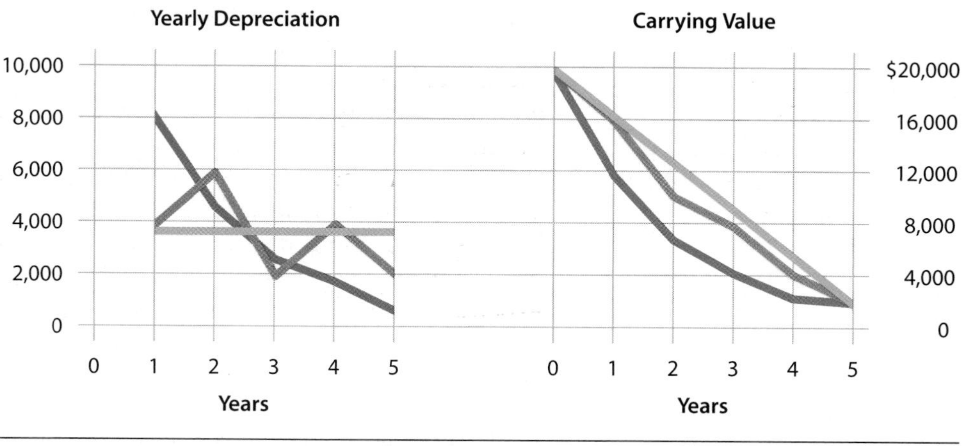

FOCUS ON BUSINESS PRACTICE

Accelerated Methods Save Money!

As shown in the figure below, an AICPA study of 600 large companies found that the overwhelming majority used the straight-line method of depreciation for financial reporting. Only about 8 percent used some type of accelerated method, and 4 percent used the production method. These figures tend to be misleading about the importance of accelerated depreciation methods, however, especially when it comes to income taxes. Federal income tax laws allow either the straight-line method or an accelerated method, and for tax purposes, about 75 percent of the 600 companies studied preferred an accelerated method.

Companies use different methods of depreciation for good reason. The straight-line method can be advantageous for financial reporting because it can produce the highest net income, and an accelerated method can be beneficial for tax purposes because it can result in lower income taxes.

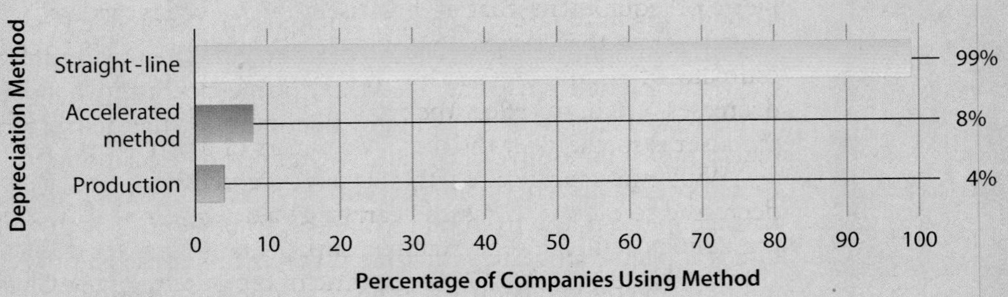

Note: **Total percentage exceeds 100 because some companies used different methods for different types of depreciable assets.**

Source: **"Depreciation Methods Used by 600 Large Companies." Copyright © 2007 by AICPA. Reproduced with permission.**

The graph on the right side of Figure 5 shows the carrying value under the three methods. Each method starts in the same place (cost of $20,000) and ends at the same place (residual value of $2,000). However, the patterns of carrying value during the asset's useful life differ. For instance, the carrying value under the straight-line method is always greater than under the double-declining-balance method, except at the beginning and end of the asset's useful life.

Special Issues in Depreciation

Other issues in depreciating assets include group depreciation, depreciation for partial years, revision of depreciation rates, and accelerated cost recovery for tax purposes.

Group Depreciation The estimated useful life of an asset is the average length of time assets of the same type are expected to last. For example, the average useful life of a particular type of machine may be six years, but some machines in this category may last only two or three years, while others may last eight or nine years or longer. For this reason, and for convenience, large companies group similar assets, such as machines, trucks, and pieces of office equipment, to calculate depreciation. This method, called **group depreciation** is widely used in all fields of industry and business. A survey of large businesses indicated that 65 percent used group depreciation for all or part of their plant assets.[7]

Depreciation for Partial Years To simplify our examples of depreciation, we have assumed that plant assets were purchased at the beginning or end of an accounting period. Usually, however, businesses buy assets when they are needed and sell or discard them when they are no longer needed or useful. The time of year is normally not a factor in the decision. Thus, it is often necessary to calculate depreciation for partial years. Some companies compute depreciation to the nearest month. Others use the half-year convention, in which one-half year of depreciation is taken in the year the asset is purchased and one-half year is taken in the year the asset is sold.

Revision of Depreciation Rates Because a depreciation rate is based on an estimate of an asset's useful life, the periodic depreciation charge is seldom precise. It is sometimes very inadequate or excessive. Such a situation may result from an underestimate or overestimate of the asset's useful life or from a wrong estimate of its residual value. What should a company do when it discovers that a piece of equipment that it has used for several years will last a shorter—or longer—time than originally estimated? Sometimes, it is necessary to revise the estimate of useful life so that the periodic depreciation expense increases or decreases. Then, to reflect the revised situation, the remaining depreciable cost of the asset is spread over the remaining years of useful life.

With this technique, the annual depreciation expense is increased or decreased to reduce the asset's carrying value to its residual value at the end of its remaining useful life. For example, suppose a delivery truck cost $14,000 and has a residual value of $2,000. At the time of the purchase, the truck was expected to last six years, and it was depreciated on the straight-line basis. However, after two years of intensive use, it is determined that the truck will last only two more years, but its residual value at the end of the two years will still be $2,000. In other words, at the end of the second year, the truck's estimated useful life is reduced from six years to four years. At that time, the asset account and its related accumulated depreciation account would be as follows:

Delivery Truck				Accumulated Depreciation–Delivery Truck	
Cost	14,000			Depreciation, Year 1	2,000
				Depreciation, Year 2	2,000

The remaining depreciable cost is computed as follows:

Cost	−	Depreciation Already Taken	−	Residual Value	
$14,000	−	$4,000	−	$2,000	= $8,000

The new annual periodic depreciation charge is computed by dividing the remaining depreciable cost of $8,000 by the remaining useful life of two years. Therefore, the new periodic depreciation charge is $4,000. This method of revising depreciation is used widely in industry. It is also supported by *Opinion No. 9* and *Opinion No. 20* of the Accounting Principles Board of the AICPA.

Special Rules for Tax Purposes Over the years, to encourage businesses to invest in new plant and equipment, Congress has revised the federal income tax law to provide an economic stimulus to the economy. For instance, for tax purposes the law allows rapid write-offs of plant assets through accelerated depreciation, which differs considerably from the depreciation methods most companies

Study Note

For financial reporting purposes, the objective is to measure performance accurately. For tax purposes, the objective is to minimize tax liability.

use for financial reporting. Tax methods of depreciation are usually not acceptable for financial reporting because the periods over which deductions may be taken are often shorter than the assets' estimated useful lives. The most recent changes in the federal income tax law—the **Economic Stimulus Act of 2008**—allows a small company to expense the first $250,000 of equipment expenditures rather than recording them as assets and depreciating them over their useful lives. Also, for assets that are subject to depreciation, there is a bonus first-year deduction. These laws are quite complex and are the subject of more advanced courses.

STOP ▶ REVIEW ▶ APPLY

- **LO3-1** Why is it useful to think of a plant asset as a bundle of service units?
- **LO3-2** A firm buys technical equipment that is expected to last 12 years. Why might the firm have to depreciate the equipment over a shorter time?
- **LO3-3** A company purchased a building five years ago. The building's market value is now greater than when the building was purchased. Should the company stop depreciating the building?
- **LO3-4** Evaluate the following statement: "A parking lot should not be depreciated because adequate repairs will make it last for an indefinite period."
- **LO3-5** Is the purpose of depreciation to determine the value of equipment? Explain your answer.
- **LO3-6** How do the assumptions underlying the straight-line and production methods of depreciation differ?
- **LO3-7** What is the principal argument in favor of an accelerated depreciation method?
- **LO3-8** On what basis is depreciation taken on a group of assets rather than on individual items?
- **LO3-9** What procedure should be followed in revising a depreciation rate?

Disposal of Depreciable Assets

LO4 Account for the disposal of depreciable assets.

When plant assets are no longer useful because they have physically deteriorated or become obsolete, a company can dispose of them by discarding them, selling them for cash, or trading them in on the purchase of a new asset. Regardless of how a company disposes of a plant asset, it must record depreciation expense for the partial year up to the date of disposal. This step is required because the company used the asset until that date and, under the matching rule, the accounting period should receive the proper allocation of depreciation expense.

In the next sections, we show how to record each type of disposal. As our example, we assume that KOT Company buys a machine on January 2, 2009, for $13,000 and plans to depreciate it on a straight-line basis over an estimated useful life of eight years. The machine's residual value at the end of eight years is estimated to be $600. On December 31, 2014, the balances of the relevant accounts are as shown below, and on January 2, 2015, management disposes of the asset.

Study Note

When it disposes of an asset, a company must bring the depreciation up to date and remove all evidence of ownership of the asset, including the contra account Accumulated Depreciation.

Machinery		Accumulated Depreciation–Machinery	
13,000			9,300

Discarded Plant Assets

A plant asset rarely lasts exactly as long as its estimated life. If it lasts longer, it is not depreciated past the point at which its carrying value equals its residual value. The purpose of depreciation is to spread the depreciable cost of an asset over its estimated life. Thus, the total accumulated depreciation should never exceed the total depreciable cost. If an asset remains in use beyond the end of its estimated life, its cost and accumulated depreciation remain in the ledger accounts. Proper records will thus be available for maintaining control over plant assets. If the residual value is zero, the carrying value of a fully depreciated asset is zero until the asset is disposed of. If such an asset is discarded, no gain or loss results. In our example, however, the discarded equipment has a carrying value of $3,700 at the time of its disposal. The carrying value is computed from the T accounts as machinery of $13,000 less accumulated depreciation of $9,300. A loss equal to the carrying value should be recorded when the machine is discarded, as follows:

A	= L +	SE
+ 9,300		−3,700
−13,000		

2015			
Jan. 2	Accumulated Depreciation–Machinery	9,300	
	Loss on Disposal of Machinery	3,700	
	Machinery		13,000
	Disposal of machine no longer in use		

Gains and losses on disposals of plant assets are classified as other revenues and expenses on the income statement.

Plant Assets Sold for Cash

Study Note

When an asset is discarded or sold for cash, the gain or loss equals cash received minus the carrying value.

The entry to record a plant asset sold for cash is similar to the one just illustrated, except that the receipt of cash should also be recorded. The following entries show how to record the sale of a machine under three assumptions about the selling price. In the first case, the $3,700 cash received is exactly equal to the $3,700 carrying value of the machine; therefore, no gain or loss occurs:

A	= L +	SE
+ 3,700		
+ 9,300		
−13,000		

2015			
Jan. 2	Cash	3,700	
	Accumulated Depreciation–Machinery	9,300	
	Machinery		13,000
	Sale of machine for carrying value; no gain or loss		

In the second case, the $2,000 cash received is less than the carrying value of 3,700, so a loss of $1,700 is recorded:

A	= L +	SE
+ 2,000		−1,700
+ 9,300		
−13,000		

2015			
Jan. 2	Cash	2,000	
	Accumulated Depreciation–Machinery	9,300	
	Loss on Sale of Machinery	1,700	
	Machinery		13,000
	Sale of machine at less than carrying value; loss of $1,700 ($3,700 − $2,000) recorded		

In the third case, the $4,000 cash received exceeds the carrying value of $3,700, so a gain of $300 is recorded:

A	= L +	SE
+ 4,000		+ 300
+ 9,300		
−13,000		

2015			
Jan. 2	Cash	4,000	
	Accumulated Depreciation–Machinery	9,300	
	Machinery		13,000
	Gain on Sale of Machinery		300
	Sale of machine at more than the carrying value; gain of $300 ($4,000 − $3,700) recorded		

Exchanges of Plant Assets

As we have noted, businesses can dispose of plant assets by trading them in on the purchase of other plant assets. Exchanges may involve similar assets, such as an old machine traded in on a newer model, or dissimilar assets, such as a cement mixer traded in on a truck. In either case, the purchase price is reduced by the amount of the trade-in allowance.

Basically, accounting for exchanges of plant assets is similar to accounting for sales of plant assets for cash. If the trade-in allowance is greater than the asset's carrying value, the company realizes a gain. If the allowance is less, it suffers a loss. (Some special rules apply and are addressed in more advanced courses.)

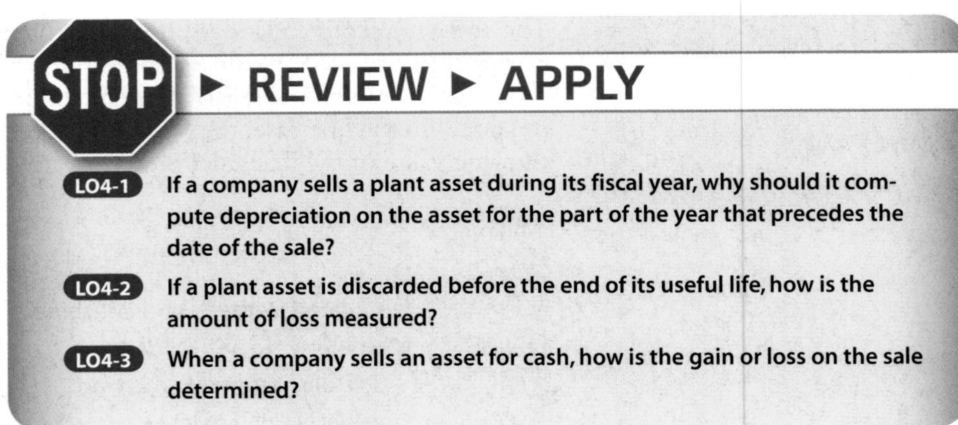

STOP ▶ REVIEW ▶ APPLY
LO4-1 If a company sells a plant asset during its fiscal year, why should it compute depreciation on the asset for the part of the year that precedes the date of the sale?
LO4-2 If a plant asset is discarded before the end of its useful life, how is the amount of loss measured?
LO4-3 When a company sells an asset for cash, how is the gain or loss on the sale determined?

Natural Resources

LO5 Identify the issues related to accounting for natural resources, and compute depletion.

Natural resources are long-term assets that appear on a balance sheet with descriptive titles like Timberlands, Oil and Gas Reserves, and Mineral Deposits. The distinguishing characteristic of these assets is that they are converted to inventory by cutting, pumping, mining, or other extraction methods.

Natural resources are recorded at acquisition cost, which may include some costs of development. As a natural resource is extracted and converted to inventory, its asset account must be proportionally reduced. For example, the carrying value of oil reserves on the balance sheet is reduced by the proportional cost of the barrels pumped during the period. As a result, the original cost of the oil reserves is gradually reduced, and depletion is recognized in the amount of the decrease.

When you season your food with salt, you probably don't think of it as using a natural resource, but that is what salt is. Table salt is produced by evaporation methods; rock salt, which is used for highway maintenance, is mined. Natural resources are considered components of property, plant, and equipment. These long-term assets are recorded at acquistion cost, which may include some costs of development.

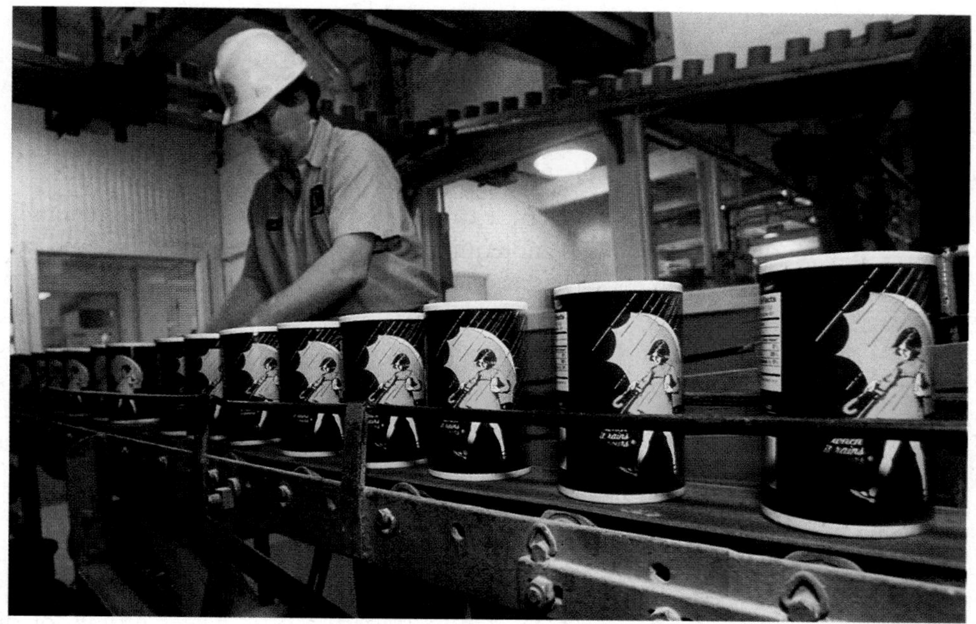

Depletion

Depletion refers not only to the exhaustion of a natural resource, but also to the proportional allocation of the cost of a natural resource to the units extracted. The way in which the cost of a natural resource is allocated closely resembles the production method of calculating depreciation. When a natural resource is purchased or developed, the total units that will be available, such as barrels of oil, tons of coal, or board-feet of lumber, must be estimated. The depletion cost per unit is determined by dividing the cost of the natural resource (less residual value, if any) by the estimated number of units available. The amount of the depletion cost for each accounting period is then computed by multiplying the depletion cost per unit by the number of units extracted and sold.

For example, suppose a mine was purchased for $3,600,000 and that it has an estimated residual value of $600,000 and contains an estimated 3,000,000 tons of coal. The depletion charge per ton of coal is $1, calculated as follows:

$$\frac{\$3{,}600{,}000 - \$600{,}000}{3{,}000{,}000 \text{ tons}} = \$1 \text{ per ton}$$

Thus, if 230,000 tons of coal are mined and sold during the first year, the depletion charge for the year is $230,000. This charge would be recorded as follows:

A	= L +	SE
−230,000		−230,000

Dec. 31	Depletion Expense–Coal Deposits	230,000	
	Accumulated Depletion–Coal Deposits		230,000
	To record depletion of coal mine: $1 per ton for 230,000 tons mined and sold		

On the balance sheet, data for the mine would be presented as follows:

Coal deposits	$3,600,000	
Less accumulated depletion	230,000	$3,370,000

Sometimes, a natural resource is not sold in the year it is extracted. It is important to note that it would then be recorded as a depletion *expense* in the year it is *sold*. The part not sold is considered inventory.

Depreciation of Related Plant Assets

Study Note

A company may abandon equipment that is still in good working condition because of the expense involved in dismantling the equipment and moving it to another site.

The extraction of natural resources generally requires special on-site buildings and equipment (e.g., conveyors, drills, and pumps). The useful life of these plant assets may be longer than the estimated time it will take to deplete the resources. However, a company may plan to abandon these assets after all the resources have been extracted because they no longer serve a useful purpose. In this case, they should be depreciated on the same basis as the depletion.

For example, if machinery with a useful life of ten years is installed on an oil field that is expected to be depleted in eight years, the machinery should be depreciated over the eight-year period, using the production method. That way, each year's depreciation will be proportional to the year's depletion. If one-sixth of the oil field's total reserves is pumped in one year, then the depreciation should be one-sixth of the machinery's cost minus the residual value.

If the useful life of a long-term plant asset is less than the expected life of the resource, the shorter life should be used to compute depreciation. In such cases, or when an asset will not be abandoned after all reserves have been depleted, other depreciation methods, such as straight-line or declining-balance, are appropriate.

Development and Exploration Costs in the Oil and Gas Industry

The costs of exploring and developing oil and gas resources can be accounted for under one of two methods. Under **successful efforts accounting**, the cost of successful exploration—for example, producing an oil well—is a cost of the resource. It should be recorded as an asset and depleted over the estimated life of the resource. The cost of an unsuccessful exploration—such as the cost of a dry well—is written off immediately as a loss. Because of these immediate write-offs, successful efforts accounting is considered the more conservative method and is used by most large oil companies.

On the other hand, smaller, independent oil companies argue that the cost of dry wells is part of the overall cost of the systematic development of an oil field and is thus a part of the cost of producing wells. Under the **full-costing method**, all costs, including the cost of dry wells, are recorded as assets and depleted over the

FOCUS ON BUSINESS PRACTICE

How Do You Measure What's Underground? With a Good Guess.

Accounting standards require publicly traded energy companies to disclose in their annual reports their production activities, estimates of their proven oil and gas reserves, and estimates of the present value of the future cash flows those reserves are expected to generate. The figures are not easy to estimate. After all, the reserves are often miles underground or beneath deep water. As a result, these figures are considered "supplementary" and not reliable enough to be audited independently. Nevertheless, it appears that some companies, including **Royal Dutch/Shell Group**, have overestimated their reserves and thus overestimated their future prospects. Apparently, some managers at Royal Dutch/Shell Group receive bonuses based on the amount of new reserves added to the annual report. When the company recently announced that it was reducing its reported reserves by 20 percent, the price of its stock dropped.[8]

estimated life of the producing resources. This method tends to improve a company's earnings performance in its early years.

The Financial Accounting Standards Board permits the use of either method.[9]

STOP ► REVIEW ► APPLY

LO5-1 **What circumstance would cause the amount of annual depletion to differ from the amount of depletion expense?**

LO5-2 **Under what circumstances can a mining company depreciate its plant assets over a period that is less than the assets' useful lives?**

LO5-3 **What is the difference between successful efforts accounting and full-costing accounting?**

Natural Resource Depletion and Depreciation of Related Plant Assets Ouyang Mining Company paid \$8,800,000 for land containing an estimated 40 million tons of ore. The land without the ore is estimated to be worth \$2,000,000. The company spent \$1,380,000 to erect buildings on the site and \$2,400,000 on installing equipment. The buildings have an estimated useful life of 30 years, and the equipment has an estimated useful life of 10 years. Because of the remote location, neither the buildings nor the equipment has a residual value. The company expects that it can mine all the usable ore in 10 years. During its first year of operation, it mined and sold 2,800,000 tons of ore.

1. Compute the depletion charge per ton.
2. Compute the depletion expense that Ouyang Mining should record for its first year of operation.
3. Determine the depreciation expense for the year for the buildings, making it proportional to the depletion.
4. Determine the depreciation expense for the year for the equipment under two alternatives: (a) making the expense proportional to the depletion, and (b) using the straight-line method.

SOLUTION

1. $\dfrac{\$8{,}800{,}000 - \$2{,}000{,}000}{40{,}000{,}000 \text{ tons}} = \$0.17 \text{ per ton}$

2. 2,800,000 tons × \$0.17 per ton = \$476,000

3. $\dfrac{2{,}800{,}000 \text{ tons}}{40{,}000{,}000 \text{ tons}} \times \$1{,}380{,}000 = \$96{,}600$

4. a. $\dfrac{2{,}800{,}000 \text{ tons}}{40{,}000{,}000 \text{ tons}} \times \$2{,}400{,}000 = \$168{,}000$

   b. $\dfrac{\$2{,}400{,}000}{10 \text{ years}} \times 1 \text{ year} = \$240{,}000$

Intangible Assets

LO6 **Identify the issues related to accounting for intangible assets, including research and development costs and goodwill.**

An intangible asset is both long term and nonphysical. Its value comes from the long-term rights or advantages it affords its owner. Table 5 describes the most common types of intangible assets—goodwill, trademarks and brand names, copyrights, patents, franchises and licenses, leaseholds, software, noncompete covenants, and customer lists—and their accounting treatment. Like intangible assets, some current assets—for example, accounts receivable and certain prepaid expenses—have no physical substance, but because current assets are short term, they are not classified as intangible assets.

Figure 6 shows the percentage of companies that report the various types of intangible assets. For some companies, intangible assets make up a substantial portion of total assets. As was noted in the Decision Point, **Apple Computer's**

TABLE 5

Accounting for Intangible Assets

Type	Description	Usual Accounting Treatment
	Subject to Amortization and Annual Impairment Test	
Copyright	An exclusive right granted by the federal government to reproduce and sell literary, musical, and other artistic materials and computer programs for a period of the author's life plus 70 years	Record at acquisition cost, and amortize over the asset's useful life, which is often much shorter than its legal life. For example, the cost of paperback rights to a popular novel would typically be amortized over a useful life of two to four years.
Patent	An exclusive right granted by the federal government for a period of 20 years to make a particular product or use a specific process. A design may be granted a patent for 14 years.	The cost of successfully defending a patent in a patent infringement suit is added to the acquisition cost of the patent. Amortize over the asset's useful life, which may be less than its legal life.
Leasehold	A right to occupy land or buildings under a long-term rental contract. For example, if Company A sells or subleases its right to use a retail location to Company B for ten years in return for one or more rental payments, Company B has purchased a leasehold.	The lessor (Company A) debits Leasehold for the amount of the rental payment and amortizes it over the remaining life of the lease. The lessee (Company B) debits payments to Lease Expense.
Software	Capitalized costs of computer programs developed for sale, lease, or internal use	Record the amount of capitalizable production costs, and amortize over the estimated economic life of the product.
Noncompete covenant	A contract limiting the rights of others to compete in a specific industry or line of business for a specified period	Record at acquisition cost, and amortize over the contract period.
Customer list	A list of customers or subscribers	Debit Customer Lists for amount paid, and amortize over the asset's expected life.
	Subject to Annual Impairment Test Only	
Goodwill	The excess of the amount paid for a business over the fair market value of the business's net assets	Debit Goodwill for the acquisition cost, and review impairment annually.
Trademark, brand name	A registered symbol or name that can be used only by its owner to identify a product or service	Debit Trademark or Brand Name for the acquisition cost, and amortize it over a reasonable life.
Franchise, license	A right to an exclusive territory or market, or the right to use a formula, technique, process, or design	Debit Franchise or License for the acquisition cost, and amortize it over a reasonable life, not to exceed 40 years.

goodwill, other acquired intangible assets, and capitalized software costs amounted to $420 million in 2007. How these assets are accounted for has a major effect on Apple's performance.

The purchase of an intangible asset is a special kind of capital expenditure. Such assets are accounted for at acquisition cost—that is, the amount that a company paid for them. Some intangible assets, such as goodwill and trademarks, may be acquired at little or no cost. Even though these assets may have great value and be needed for profitable operations, a company should include them on its balance sheet only if it purchased them from another party at a price established in the marketplace. When a company develops its own intangible assets, it should record the costs of development as expenses. An exception to this is the cost of internally

that 75 percent of new-product expenses go to unsuccessful products. Thus, their costs do not represent future benefits.

Computer Software Costs

The costs that companies incur in developing computer software for sale or lease or for their own internal use are considered research and development costs until the product has proved technologically feasible. Thus, costs incurred before that point should be charged to expense as they are incurred. A product is deemed technologically feasible when a detailed working program has been designed. Once that occurs, all software production costs are recorded as assets and are amortized over the software's estimated economic life using the straight-line method. Capitalized software costs are becoming more prevalent and as shown in Figure 7 appear on 23 percent of 600 large companies' balance sheets, including $83 million for Apple (see Decision Point at the beginning of the chapter). If at any time a company cannot expect to realize from the software the amount of the unamortized costs on the balance sheet, the asset should be written down to the amount expected to be realized.[16]

Goodwill

Goodwill means different things to different people. Generally, it refers to a company's good reputation. From an accounting standpoint, goodwill exists when a purchaser pays more for a business than the fair market value of the business's net assets. In other words, the purchaser would pay less if it bought the assets separately. Most businesses are worth more as going concerns than as collections of assets.

When the purchase price of a business is more than the fair market value of its physical assets, the business must have intangible assets. If it does not have patents, copyrights, trademarks, or other identifiable intangible assets of value, the excess payment is assumed to be for goodwill. Goodwill reflects all the factors that allow a company to earn a higher-than-market rate of return on its assets, including customer satisfaction, good management, manufacturing efficiency, the advantages of having a monopoly, good locations, and good employee relations. The payment above and beyond the fair market value of the tangible assets and other specific intangible assets is properly recorded in the Goodwill account.

The FASB requires that purchased goodwill be reported as a separate line item on the balance sheet and that it be reviewed annually for impairment. If the fair value of goodwill is less than its carrying value on the balance sheet, goodwill is considered impaired. In that case, goodwill is reduced to its fair value, and the

FOCUS ON BUSINESS PRACTICE

Wake up, Goodwill Is Growing!

As Figure 7 shows, 87 percent of 600 large companies separately report goodwill as an asset. Because much of the growth of these companies has come through purchasing other companies, goodwill as a percentage of total assets has also grown. As the table at the right shows, the amount of goodwill can be material.[17]

	Goodwill (in billions)	Percentage of Total Assets
General Mills	$6,835	38%
Heinz	$2,835	28%
Cisco Systems	$9,298	21%

impairment charge is reported on the income statement. A company can perform the fair value measurement for each reporting unit at any time as long as the measurement date is consistent from year to year.[18]

A company should record goodwill only when it acquires a controlling interest in another business. The amount to be recorded as goodwill can be determined by writing the identifiable net assets up to their fair market values at the time of purchase and subtracting the total from the purchase price. For example, suppose a company pays $11,400,000 to purchase another business. If the net assets of the business (total assets − total liabilities) are fairly valued at $10,000,000, then the amount of the goodwill is $1,400,000 ($11,400,000 − $10,000,000). If the fair market value of the net assets is more or less than $10,000,000, an entry is made in the accounting records to adjust the assets to the fair market value. The goodwill would then represent the difference between the adjusted net assets and the purchase price of $11,400,000.

STOP ► REVIEW ► APPLY

LO6-1 **Accounts receivable have no physical substance. Why are they then not classified as intangible assets?**

LO6-2 **Under what circumstances can a company have intangible assets that do not appear on the balance sheet?**

LO6-3 **What is the FASB's rule for treating research and development costs?**

LO6-4 **How is accounting for software development costs similar to and different from accounting for research and development costs?**

LO6-5 **Under what conditions should goodwill be recorded? Should it remain in the records permanently once it is recorded?**

A LOOK BACK AT ► Apple Computer, Inc.

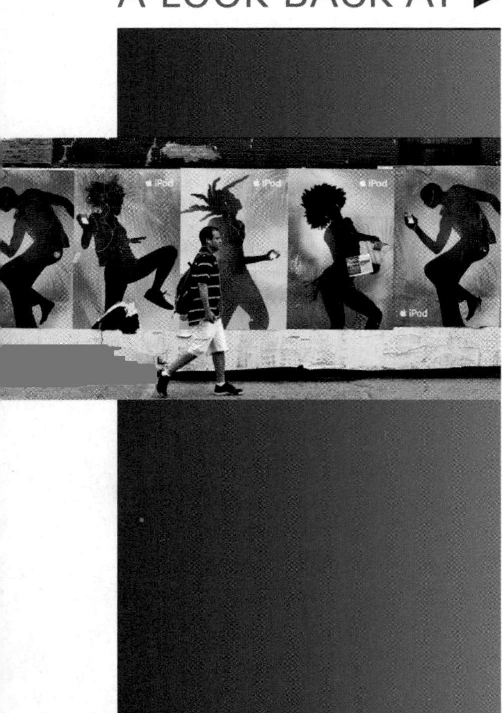

We began the chapter by emphasizing that **Apple's** success as an innovator and marketer comes from wise and steady investments in long-term assets and related expenditures like research and development. In evaluating Apple's performance, investors and creditors look for answers to the following questions:

- **What are Apple's long-term assets?**
- **What are its policies in accounting for long-term assets?**
- **Does the company generate enough cash flow to finance its continued growth?**

Apple's tangible long-term assets include land, manufacturing facilities, office buildings, machinery, equipment, and leasehold improvements to its retail stores. Its balance sheet also includes goodwill and intangible assets that it acquired through acquisitions. Because internally developed intangible assets are not recorded as assets, the value of Apple's own brand name is not reflected on the balance sheet. Clearly, however, it far exceeds the value of the intangible assets that are listed.

In accordance with GAAP, Apple's accounting policies include using the straight-line depreciation method for tangible assets, amortizing intangible assets over a reasonable useful life, and expensing research and development costs. In addition, it evaluates its long-term assets for impairment each year to ensure that it is not carrying assets on its balance sheet at amounts that exceed their value.

A good measure of the funds that Apple has available for growth is its free cash flow:

Free Cash Flow = Net Cash Flows from Operating Activities − Dividends − Purchases of Plant Assets + Sales of Plant Assets

		2007		2006
Free Cash Flow	=	\$5,470 − \$0 − \$735		\$2,220 − \$0 − \$657
	=	\$4,735	=	\$1,563

This two-year view of Apple's free cash flow shows great improvement in 2007 due to the phenomenal success of the iPod and iPhone. The company obviously generated enough cash to finance its continued growth. Its policy of not paying dividends contributes to the amount of cash it has available for this purpose. Although Apple may have sold some plant assets, the amounts were sufficiently immaterial that it did not report them separately.

CHAPTER REVIEW

REVIEW of Learning Objectives

LO1 Define *long-term assets*, and explain the management issues related to them.

Long-term assets have a useful life of more than one year, are used in the operation of a business, and are not intended for resale. They can be tangible or intangible. In the former category are land, plant assets, and natural resources. In the latter are patents, trademarks, franchises, and other rights, as well as goodwill. The management issues related to long-term assets include decisions about whether to acquire the assets, how to finance them, and how to account for them.

LO2 Distinguish between *capital expenditures* and *revenue expenditures*, and account for the cost of property, plant, and equipment.

Capital expenditures are recorded as assets, whereas revenue expenditures are recorded as expenses of the current period. Capital expenditures include not only outlays for plant assets, natural resources, and intangible assets, but also expenditures for additions, betterments, and extraordinary repairs that increase an asset's residual value or extend its useful life. Revenue expenditures are made for ordinary repairs and maintenance. The error of classifying a capital expenditure as a revenue expenditure, or vice versa, has an important effect on net income.

The acquisition cost of property, plant, and equipment includes all expenditures reasonable and necessary to get the asset in place and ready for use. Among these expenditures are purchase price, installation cost, freight charges, and insurance during transit. The acquisition cost of a plant asset is allocated over the asset's useful life.

LO3 Compute depreciation under the straight-line, production, and declining-balance methods.

Depreciation—the periodic allocation of the cost of a plant asset over its estimated useful life—is commonly computed by using the straight-line method, the production method, or an accelerated method. The straight-line method is related directly to the passage of time, whereas the production method is related directly to use or output. An accelerated method, which results in relatively large amounts of depreciation in earlier years and reduced amounts in later years, is based on the assumption that plant assets provide greater economic benefits in their earlier years than in later ones. The most common accelerated method is the declining-balance method.

LO4 Account for the disposal of depreciable assets.

A company can dispose of a long-term plant asset by discarding or selling it or exchanging it for another asset. Regardless of the way in which a company disposes of such an asset, it must record depreciation up to the date of disposal. To do so, it must remove the carrying value from the asset account and the depreciation to date from the accumulated depreciation account. When a company sells a depreciable long-term asset at a price that differs from its carrying value, it should report the gain or loss on its income statement. In recording exchanges of similar plant assets, a gain or loss may arise.

LO5 Identify the issues related to accounting for natural resources, and compute depletion.

Natural resources are depletable assets that are converted to inventory by cutting, pumping, mining, or other forms of extraction. They are recorded at cost as long-term assets. As natural resources are sold, their costs are allocated as expenses through depletion charges. The depletion charge is based on the ratio of the resource extracted to the total estimated resource. A major issue related to this subject is accounting for oil and gas reserves.

LO6 Identify the issues related to accounting for intangible assets, including research and development costs and goodwill.

The purchase of an intangible asset should be treated as a capital expenditure and recorded at acquisition cost. All intangible assets are subject to annual tests for impairment of value. Intangible assets with a definite life are also amortized annually. The FASB requires that research and development costs be treated as revenue expenditures and charged as expenses in the periods of expenditure. Software costs are treated as research and development costs and expensed until a feasible working program is developed, after which time the costs may be capitalized and amortized over a reasonable estimated life. Goodwill is the excess of the amount paid for a business over the fair market value of the net assets and is usually related to the business's superior earning potential. It should be recorded only when a company purchases an entire business, and it should be reviewed annually for possible impairment.

REVIEW of Concepts and Terminology

The following concepts and terms were introduced in this chapter:

Accelerated method: A method of depreciation that allocates relatively large amounts of the depreciable cost of an asset to earlier years and smaller amounts to later years. **(LO3)**

Additions: Enlargements to the physical layout of a plant asset. **(LO2)**

Amortization: The periodic allocation of the cost of an intangible asset to the periods it benefits. **(LO1)**

Asset impairment: Loss of revenue-generating potential of a long-lived asset before the end of its useful life; the difference between an asset's carrying value and its fair value, as measured by the present value of the expected cash flows. **(LO1)**

Betterments: Improvements that do not add to the physical layout of a plant asset. **(LO2)**

Brand name: A registered name that can be used only by its owner to identify a product or service. **(LO6)**

Capital expenditure: An expenditure for the purchase or expansion of a long-term asset, which is recorded in an asset account. **(LO2)**

Carrying value: The unexpired part of an asset's cost. Also called *book value*. **(LO1)**

Copyright: An exclusive right granted by the federal government to reproduce and sell literary, musical, and other artistic materials and computer programs for a period of the author's life plus 70 years. **(LO6)**

Customer list: A list of customers or subscribers. **(LO6)**

Declining-balance method: An accelerated method of depreciation in which depreciation is computed by applying a fixed rate to the carrying value (the declining balance) of a tangible long-lived asset. **(LO3)**

Depletion: The exhaustion of a natural resource through mining, cutting, pumping, or other extraction, and the way in which the cost is allocated. **(LO1)**

Depreciable cost: The cost of an asset less its residual value. **(LO3)**

Depreciation: The periodic allocation of the cost of a tangible long-lived asset (other than land and natural resources) over its estimated useful life. **(LO1)**

Double-declining-balance method: An accelerated method of depreciation in which a fixed rate equal to twice the straight-line percentage is applied to the carrying value (the declining balance) of a tangible long-lived asset. **(LO3)**

Economic Stimulus Act of 2008: A federal income tax law that allows a small company to expense the first $250,000 of equipment expenditures **(LO3)**

Estimated useful life: The total number of service units expected from a long-term asset. **(LO3)**

Expenditure: A payment or an obligation to make future payment for an asset or a service. **(LO2)**

Extraordinary repairs: Repairs that significantly enhance a plant asset's estimated useful life or residual value and thereby increase its carrying value. **(LO2)**

Franchise: The right to an exclusive territory or market. **(LO6)**

Free cash flow: Amount of cash that remains after deducting the funds a company must commit to continue operating at its planned level; Net Cash Flows from Operating Activities − Dividends − Purchases of Plant Assets + Sales of Plant Assets. **(LO1)**

Full-costing method: A method of accounting for the costs of exploring and developing oil and gas resources in which all costs are recorded as assets and depleted over the estimated life of the producing resources. **(LO5)**

Goodwill: The excess of the amount paid for a business over the fair market value of the business's net assets. **(LO6)**

Group depreciation: The grouping of similar items to calculate depreciation. **(LO3)**

Intangible assets: Long-term assets with no physical substance whose value is based on rights or advantages accruing to the owner. **(LO1)**

Leasehold: A right to occupy land or buildings under a long-term rental contract. **(LO6)**

Leasehold improvements: Improvements to leased property that become the property of the lessor at the end of the lease. **(LO2)**

License: The right to use a formula, technique, process, or design. **(LO6)**

Long-term assets: Assets that have a useful life of more than one year, are used in the operation of a business, and are not intended for resale. Less commonly called *fixed assets.* **(LO1)**

Natural resources: Long-term assets purchased for the economic value that can be taken from the land and used up. **(LO1)**

Noncompete covenant: A contract limiting the rights of others to compete in a specific industry or line of business for a specified period. **(LO6)**

Obsolescence: The process of becoming out of date, which is a factor in the limited useful life of tangible assets. **(LO3)**

Patent: An exclusive right granted by the federal government for a period of 20 years to make a particular product or use a specific process. **(LO6)**

Physical deterioration: A decline in the useful life of a depreciable asset resulting from use and from exposure to the elements. **(LO3)**

Production method: A method of depreciation that assumes depreciation is solely the result of use and that allocates depreciation based on the units of use or output during each period of an asset's useful life. **(LO3)**

Residual value: The portion of acquisition cost expected to be recovered at date of its disposal. Also called *salvage value*, *disposal value*, or *trade-in value*. **(LO3)**

Revenue expenditure: An expenditure for ordinary repairs and maintenance of a long-term asset, which is recorded by a debit to an expense account. **(LO2)**

Software: Capitalized costs associated with computer programs developed for sale, lease, or internal use and amortized over the estimated economic life of the programs. **(LO6)**

Straight-line method: A method of depreciation that assumes depreciation depends only on the passage of time and that allocates an equal amount of depreciation to each accounting period in an asset's useful life. **(LO3)**

Successful efforts accounting: A method of accounting for the costs of exploring and developing oil and gas resources in which successful exploration is recorded as an asset and depleted over the estimated life of the resource and all unsuccessful efforts are immediately written off as losses. **(LO5)**

Tangible assets: Long-term assets that have physical substance. **(LO1)**

Trademark: A registered symbol that can be used only by its owner to identify a product or service. **(LO6)**

REVIEW Problem

LO3 Comparison of Depreciation Methods

Peter Construction Company purchased a cement mixer on January 2, 2010, for $29,000. The mixer was expected to have a useful life of five years and a residual value of $2,000. The company's engineers estimated that the mixer would have a useful life of 15,000 hours. It was used for 3,000 hours in 2010, 5,250 hours in

2011, 4,500 hours in 2012, 1,500 hours in 2013, and 750 hours in 2014. The company's fiscal year ends on December 31.

Required

1. Compute the depreciation expense and carrying value for 2010 to 2014, using the following methods: (a) straight-line, (b) production, and (c) double-declining-balance.
2. Show the balance sheet presentation for the cement mixer on December 31, 2010. Assume the straight-line method.
3. What conclusions can you draw from the patterns of yearly depreciation?

Answer to Review Problem

1. Depreciation computed:

	Depreciation Method	Year	Computation			Depreciation	Carrying Value
a.	Straight-line	2010	$27,000	÷	5	$ 5,400	$23,600
		2011	27,000	÷	5	5,400	18,200
		2012	27,000	÷	5	5,400	12,800
		2013	27,000	÷	5	5,400	7,400
		2014	27,000	÷	5	5,400	2,000
b.	Production	2010	$27,000	x	$\frac{3,000}{15,000}$	$ 5,400	$23,600
		2011	27,000	x	$\frac{5,250}{15,000}$	9,450	14,150
		2012	27,000	x	$\frac{4,500}{15,000}$	8,100	6,050
		2013	27,000	x	$\frac{1,500}{15,000}$	2,700	3,350
		2014	27,000	x	$\frac{750}{15,000}$	1,350	2,000
c.	Double-declining-balance	2010	$29,000	x	0.40	$11,600	$17,400
		2011	17,400	x	0.40	6,960	10,440
		2012	10,440	x	0.40	4,176	6,264
		2013	6,264	x	0.40	2,506	3,758
		2014	3,758	–	2,000	1,758*	2,000

* Remaining depreciation to reduce carrying value to residual value ($3,758 – $2,000).

2. Balance sheet presentation on December 31, 2010:

Property, plant, and equipment	
Cement mixer	$29,000
Less accumulated depreciation	5,400
	$23,600

3. The pattern of depreciation for the straight-line method differs significantly from the pattern for the double-declining-balance method. In the earlier years, the amount of depreciation under the double-declining-balance method is significantly greater than the amount under the straight-line method. In the later years, the opposite is true. The carrying value under the straight-line method is greater than under the double-declining-balance method at the end of all years except the fifth year. Depreciation under the production method differs from depreciation under the other methods in that it follows no regular pattern. It varies with the amount of use. Consequently, depreciation is greatest in 2011 and 2012, which are the years of greatest use. Use declined significantly in the last two years.

CHAPTER ASSIGNMENTS

BUILDING Your Basic Knowledge and Skills

Short Exercises

LO1 **Management Issues**

SE 1. Indicate whether each of the following actions is primarily related to (a) acquisition of long-term assets, (b) evaluating the adequacy of financing of long-term assets, or (c) applying the matching rule to long-term assets.

1. Deciding between common stock and long-term notes for the raising of funds
2. Relating the acquisition cost of a long-term asset to the cash flows generated by the asset
3. Determining how long an asset will benefit the company
4. Deciding to use cash flows from operations to purchase long-term assets
5. Determining how much an asset will sell for when it is no longer useful to the company
6. Calculating free cash flow

LO1 **Free Cash Flow**

SE 2. Rak Corporation had cash flows from operating activities during the past year of $97,000. During the year, the company expended $12,500 for dividends; expended $79,000 for property, plant, and equipment; and sold property, plant, and equipment for $6,000. Calculate the company's free cash flow. What does the result tell you about the company?

LO2 **Determining Cost of Long-Term Assets**

SE 3. Smith Auto purchased a neighboring lot for a new building and parking lot. Indicate whether each of the following expenditures is properly charged to (a) Land, (b) Land Improvements, or (c) Buildings.

1. Paving costs
2. Architects' fee for building design
3. Cost of clearing the property
4. Cost of the property
5. Building construction costs
6. Lights around the property
7. Building permit
8. Interest on the construction loan

LO2 **Group Purchase**

SE 4. Lian Company purchased property with a warehouse and parking lot for $1,500,000. An appraiser valued the components of the property if purchased separately as follows:

Land	$ 400,000
Land improvements	200,000
Building	1,000,000
Total	$1,600,000

Determine the cost to be assigned to each component.

LO3 **Straight-Line Method**

SE 5. Kelly's Fitness Center purchased a new step machine for $16,500. The apparatus is expected to last four years and have a residual value of $1,500. What will the depreciation expense be for each year under the straight-line method?

LO3 **Production Method**

SE 6. Assume that the step machine in **SE 5** has an estimated useful life of 8,000 hours and was used for 2,400 hours in year 1, 2,000 hours in year 2, 2,200 hours in year 3, and 1,400 hours in year 4. How much would depreciation expense be in each year?

LO3 **Double-Declining-Balance Method**

SE 7. Assume that the step machine in **SE 5** is depreciated using the double-declining-balance method. How much would depreciation expense be in each year?

LO4 **Disposal of Plant Assets: No Trade-In**

SE 8. Alarico Printing owned a piece of equipment that cost $16,200 and on which it had recorded $9,000 of accumulated depreciation. The company disposed of the equipment on January 2, the first day of business of the current year.

1. Calculate the carrying value of the equipment.
2. Calculate the gain or loss on the disposal under each of the following assumptions:
   a. The equipment was discarded as having no value.
   b. The equipment was sold for $3,000 cash.
   c. The equipment was sold for $8,000 cash.

LO5 **Natural Resources**

SE 9. Narda Company purchased land containing an estimated 4,000,000 tons of ore for $16,000,000. The land will be worth $2,400,000 without the ore after eight years of active mining. Although the equipment needed for the mining will have a useful life of 20 years, it is not expected to be usable and will have no value after the mining on this site is complete. Compute the depletion charge per ton and the amount of depletion expense for the first year of operation, assuming that 600,000 tons of ore are mined and sold. Also, compute the first-year depreciation on the mining equipment using the production method, assuming a cost of $19,200,000 with no residual value.

LO6 **Intangible Assets: Computer Software**

SE 10. Danya Company has created a new software application for PCs. Its costs during research and development were $250,000. Its costs after the working program was developed were $175,000. Although the company's copyright may be amortized over 40 years, management believes that the product will be viable for only five years. How should the costs be accounted for? At what value will the software appear on the balance sheet after one year?

Exercises

LO1 LO2 LO3

Discussion Questions

E 1. Develop a brief answer for each of the following questions:

1. Is carrying value ever the same as market value?
2. What major advantage does a company that has positive free cash flow have over a company that has negative free cash flow?
3. What incentive does a company have to allocate more of a group purchase price to land than to building?
4. Which depreciation method would best reflect the risk of obsolescence from rapid technological changes?

LO4 LO5 LO6

Discussion Questions

E 2. Develop a brief answer for each of the following questions:

1. When would the disposal of a long-term asset result in no gain or loss?
2. When would annual depletion not equal depletion expense?
3. Why would a firm amortize a patent over fewer years than the patent's life?
4. Why would a company spend millions of dollars on goodwill?

Management Issues

E 3. Indicate whether each of the following actions is primarily related to (a) acquisition of long-term assets, (b) evaluating the financing of long-term assets, or (c) applying the matching rule to long-term assets.

1. Deciding to use the production method of depreciation
2. Allocating costs on a group purchase
3. Determining the total units a machine will produce
4. Deciding to borrow funds to purchase equipment
5. Estimating the savings a new machine will produce and comparing that amount to cost
6. Examining the trend of free cash flow over several years
7. Deciding whether to rent or buy a piece of equipment

LO1

Purchase Decision—Present Value Analysis

E 4. Management is considering the purchase of a new machine for a cost of $12,000. It is estimated that the machine will generate positive net cash flows of $3,000 per year for five years and will have a disposal price at the end of that time of $1,000. Assuming an interest rate of 9 percent, determine if management should purchase the machine. Use Tables 1 and 2 in the appendix on present value tables to determine the net present value of the new machine.

Free Cash Flow

E 5. Zedek Corporation had cash flows from operating activities during the past year of $216,000. During the year, the company expended $462,000 for property, plant, and equipment; sold property, plant, and equipment for $54,000; and paid dividends of $50,000. Calculate the company's free cash flow. What does the result tell you about the company?

LO2 **Special Types of Capital Expenditures**

E 6. Tell whether each of the following transactions related to an office building is a revenue expenditure (RE) or a capital expenditure (CE). In addition, indicate whether each transaction is an ordinary repair (OR), an extraordinary repair (ER), an addition (A), a betterment (B), or none of these (N).

1. The hallways and ceilings in the building are repainted at a cost of $6,250.
2. The hallways, which have tile floors, are carpeted at a cost of $28,000.
3. A new wing is added to the building at a cost of $105,470.
4. Furniture is purchased for the entrance to the building at a cost of $13,250.
5. The air-conditioning system is overhauled at a cost of $21,153. The overhaul extends the useful life of the air-conditioning system by ten years.
6. A cleaning firm is paid $150 per week to clean the newly installed carpets.

LO2 **Determining Cost of Long-Term Assets**

E 7. Colletta Manufacturing purchased land next to its factory to be used as a parking lot. The expenditures incurred by the company were as follows: purchase price, $600,000; broker's fees, $48,000; title search and other fees, $4,400; demolition of a cottage on the property, $16,000; general grading of property, $8,400; paving parking lots, $80,000; lighting for parking lots, $64,000; and signs for parking lots, $12,800. Determine the amounts that should be debited to the Land account and the Land Improvements account.

LO2 **Group Purchase**

E 8. Joanna Mak purchased a car wash for $480,000. If purchased separately, the land would have cost $120,000, the building $270,000, and the equipment $210,000. Determine the amount that should be recorded in the new business's records for land, building, and equipment.

LO2 LO3 **Cost of Long-Term Asset and Depreciation**

E 9. Nick Santiago purchased a used tractor for $35,000. Before the tractor could be used, it required new tires, which cost $2,200, and an overhaul, which cost $2,800. Its first tank of fuel cost $150. The tractor is expected to last six years and have a residual value of $4,000. Determine the cost and depreciable cost of the tractor and calculate the first year's depreciation under the straight-line method.

LO3 **Depreciation Methods**

E 10. On January 13, 2010, Silverio Oil Company purchased a drilling truck for $45,000. Silverio expects the truck to last five years or 200,000 miles, with an estimated residual value of $7,500 at the end of that time. During 2011, the truck is driven 48,000 miles. Silverio's year end is December 31. Compute the depreciation for 2011 under each of the following methods: (1) straight-line, (2) production, and (3) double-declining-balance. Using the amount computed in **(3)**, prepare the entry in journal form to record depreciation expense for the second year, and show how the Drilling Truck account would appear on the balance sheet.

LO3 **Double-Declining-Balance Method**

E 11. Stop Burglar Alarm Systems Company purchased a computer for $2,240. It has an estimated useful life of four years and an estimated residual value of $240. Compute the depreciation charge for each of the four years using the double-declining-balance method.

LO3 **Revision of Depreciation Rates**

E 12. Hope Hospital purchased a special x-ray machine. The machine, which cost $311,560, was expected to last ten years, with an estimated residual value of $31,560. After two years of operation (and depreciation charges using the straight-line method), it became evident that the x-ray machine would last a total of only seven years. The estimated residual value, however, would remain the same. Given this information, determine the new depreciation charge for the third year on the basis of the revised estimated useful life.

LO4 **Disposal of Plant Assets**

E 13. A piece of equipment that cost $32,400 and on which $18,000 of accumulated depreciation had been recorded was disposed of on January 2, the first day of business of the current year. For each of the following assumptions, compute the gain or loss on the disposal.

1. The equipment was discarded as having no value.
2. The equipment was sold for $6,000 cash.
3. The equipment was sold for $18,000 cash.

LO4 **Disposal of Plant Assets**

E 14. Samson Company purchased a computer on January 2, 2009, at a cost of $1,250. The computer is expected to have a useful life of five years and a residual value of $125. Assume that the computer is disposed of on July 1, 2012. Record the depreciation expense for half a year and the disposal under each of the following assumptions:

1. The computer is discarded.
2. The computer is sold for $200.
3. The computer is sold for $550.

LO5 **Natural Resource Depletion and Depreciation of Related Plant Assets**

E 15. Nelson Company purchased land containing an estimated 2.5 million tons of ore for a cost of $4,400,000. The land without the ore is estimated to be worth $250,000. During its first year of operation, the company mined and sold 375,000 tons of ore. Compute the depletion charge per ton. Compute the depletion expense that Nelson should record for the year.

LO6 **Copyrights and Trademarks**

E 16. The following exercise is about amortizing copyrights and trademarks.

1. Fulton Publishing Company purchased the copyright to a basic computer textbook for $80,000. The usual life of a textbook is about four years. However, the copyright will remain in effect for another 50 years. Calculate the annual amortization of the copyright.
2. Sloan Company purchased a trademark from a well-known supermarket for $640,000. The management of the company argued that the trademark's useful life was indefinite. Explain how the cost should be accounted for.

LO6 **Accounting for a Patent**

E 17. At the beginning of the fiscal year, Andy Company purchased for $2,060,000 a patent that applies to the manufacture of a unique tamper-proof lid for medicine bottles. Andy incurred legal costs of $900,000 in successfully defending use of the lid by a competitor. Andy estimated that the patent would be valuable for at least ten years. During the first two years of operations, Andy successfully marketed the lid. At the beginning of the third year, a study appeared in a consumer magazine showing that children could in fact remove the lid. As a result, all orders for the lids were canceled, and the patent was rendered worthless.

Prepare entries in journal form to record the following: (a) purchase of the patent; (b) successful defense of the patent; (c) amortization expense for the first year; and (d) write-off of the patent as worthless.

Problems

LO1 LO2

Identification of Long-Term Assets Terminology

P 1. Listed below are common terms associated with long-term assets:

a. Tangible assets
b. Natural resources
c. Intangible assets
d. Additions
e. Betterments
f. Extraordinary repair
g. Depreciation
h. Depletion
i. Amortization
j. Revenue expenditure
k. Free cash flow

Required

1. For each of the following statements, identify the term listed above with which it is associated. (If two terms apply, choose the one that is most closely associated.)
   1. Periodic cost associated with intangible assets
   2. Cost of constructing a new wing on a building
   3. A measure of funds available for expansion
   4. A group of assets encompassing property, plant, and equipment
   5. Cost associated with enhancing a building but not expanding it
   6. Periodic cost associated with tangible assets
   7. A group of assets that gain their value from contracts or rights
   8. Cost of normal repairs to a building
   9. Assets whose value derives from what can be extracted from them
   10. Periodic cost associated with natural resources
   11. Cost of a repair that extends the useful life of a building

User insight ▶

2. Assuming the company uses cash for all its expenditures, which of the items listed above would you expect to see on the income statement? Which ones would not result in an outlay of cash?

Determining Cost of Assets

P 2. Siber Computers constructed a new training center in 2010. You have been hired to manage the training center. A review of the accounting records shows the following expenditures debited to an asset account called Training Center:

Attorney's fee, land acquisition	$ 35,200
Cost of land	597,000
Architect's fee, building design	102,000
Building	1,025,000
Parking lot and sidewalk	135,600
Electrical wiring, building	168,000
Landscaping	55,000
Cost of surveying land	8,900
Training equipment, tables, and chairs	136,400
Installation of training equipment	65,600
Cost of grading the land	14,000
Cost of changes in building to soundproof rooms	58,700
Total account balance	$2,401,400

An employee of Siber Computers worked full time overseeing the construction project. He spent two months on the purchase and preparation of the site, six months on the construction, one month on land improvements, and one month on equipment installation and training room furniture purchase and setup. His salary of $72,000 during these ten months was charged to Administrative Expense. The training center was placed in operation on November 1.

Required

1. Prepare a schedule with the following four column (account) headings: Land, Land Improvements, Building, and Equipment. Place each of the above expenditures in the appropriate column. Total the columns.

User insight ▶

2. What impact does the classification of the items among several accounts have on evaluating the profitability performance of the company?

LO3 LO4

Comparison of Depreciation Methods

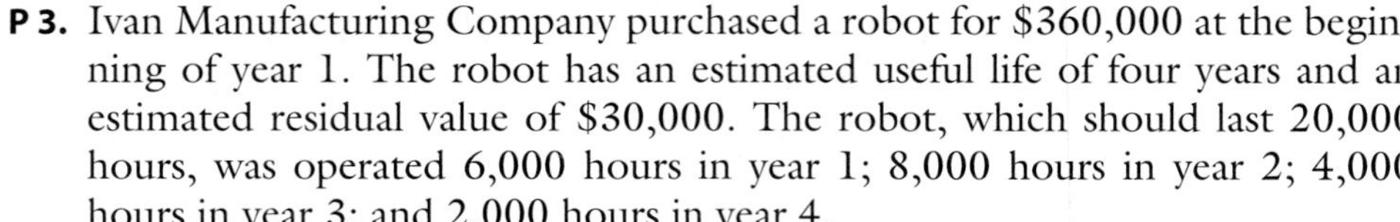

P 3. Ivan Manufacturing Company purchased a robot for $360,000 at the beginning of year 1. The robot has an estimated useful life of four years and an estimated residual value of $30,000. The robot, which should last 20,000 hours, was operated 6,000 hours in year 1; 8,000 hours in year 2; 4,000 hours in year 3; and 2,000 hours in year 4.

Required

1. Compute the annual depreciation and carrying value for the robot for each year assuming the following depreciation methods: (a) straight-line, (b) production, and (c) double-declining-balance.
2. If the robot is sold for $375,000 after year 2, what would be the amount of gain or loss under each method?

User insight ▶

3. What conclusions can you draw from the patterns of yearly depreciation and carrying value in requirement **1**? Do the three methods differ in their effect on the company's profitability? Do they differ in their effect on the company's operating cash flows? Explain.

LO3 LO4

Comparison of Depreciation Methods

P 4. Roman's Construction Company purchased a new crane for $721,000 at the beginning of year 1. The crane has an estimated residual value of $70,000 and an estimated useful life of six years. The crane is expected to last 10,000 hours. It was used 1,800 hours in year 1; 2,000 in year 2; 2,500 in year 3; 1,500 in year 4; 1,200 in year 5; and 1,000 in year 6.

Required

1. Compute the annual depreciation and carrying value for the new crane for each of the six years (round to the nearest dollar where necessary) under each of the following methods: (a) straight-line, (b) production, and (c) double-declining-balance.
2. If the crane is sold for $500,000 after year 3, what would be the amount of gain or loss under each method?

User insight ▶

3. Do the three methods differ in their effect on the company's profitability? Do they differ in their effect on the company's operating cash flows? Explain.

LO5

Natural Resource Depletion and Depreciation of Related Plant Assets

KA KLOOSTER & ALLEN

P 5. Kulig Company purchased land containing an estimated 10 million tons of ore for a cost of $3,300,000. The land without the ore is estimated to be worth $600,000. The company expects that all the usable ore can be mined in 10 years. Buildings costing $300,000 with an estimated useful life of 20 years were erected on the site. Equipment costing $360,000 with an estimated useful life of 10 years was installed. Because of the remote location, neither the buildings nor the equipment has an estimated residual value. During its first year of operation, the company mined and sold 450,000 tons of ore.

Required

1. Compute the depletion charge per ton.
2. Compute the depletion expense that Kulig should record for the year.
3. Determine the depreciation expense for the year for the buildings, making it proportional to the depletion.
4. Determine the depreciation expense for the year for the equipment under two alternatives: (a) making the expense proportional to the depletion and (b) using the straight-line method.

User insight ▶

5. Suppose the company mined and sold 250,000 tons of ore (instead of 450,000) during the first year. Would the change in the results in requirement **2** or **3** affect earnings or cash flows? Explain.

Alternate Problems

LO2

Determining Cost of Assets

P 6. Global Company was formed on January 1, 2010, and began constructing a new plant. At the end of 2010, its auditor discovered that all expenditures involving long-term assets had been debited to an account called Fixed Assets. An analysis of the Fixed Assets account, which had a year-end balance of $2,659,732, disclosed that it contained the following items:

Cost of land	$ 320,600
Surveying costs	4,100
Transfer of title and other fees required by the county	920
Broker's fees for land	21,144
Attorney's fees associated with land acquisition	7,048
Cost of removing timber from land	49,600
Cost of grading land	4,200
Cost of digging building foundation	35,100
Architect's fee for building and land improvements (80 percent building)	67,200
Cost of building construction	715,000
Cost of sidewalks	11,400
Cost of parking lots	54,400
Cost of lighting for grounds	80,300
Cost of landscaping	11,800
Cost of machinery	993,000
Shipping cost on machinery	55,300
Cost of installing machinery	176,200
Cost of testing machinery	21,600
Cost of changes in building to comply with safety regulations pertaining to machinery	12,540
Cost of repairing building that was damaged in the installation of machinery	8,900
Cost of medical bill for injury received by employee while installing machinery	2,560
Cost of water damage to building during heavy rains prior to opening the plant for operation	6,820
Account balance	$2,659,732

Global Company sold the timber it cleared from the land to a firewood dealer for \$7,000. This amount was credited to Miscellaneous Income.

During the construction period, two of Global's supervisors devoted full time to the construction project. Their annual salaries were \$51,000 and \$39,000, respectively. They spent two months on the purchase and preparation of the land, six months on the construction of the building (approximately one-sixth of which was devoted to improvements on the grounds), and one month on machinery installation. When the plant began operation on October 1, the supervisors returned to their regular duties. Their salaries were debited to Factory Salaries Expense.

Required

1. Prepare a schedule with the following column headings: Land, Land Improvements, Buildings, Machinery, and Expense. Place each of the above expenditures in the appropriate column. Negative amounts should be shown in parentheses. Total the columns.

User insight ▶

2. What impact does the classification of the items among several accounts have on evaluating the profitability performance of the company?

LO3 LO4

Comparison of Depreciation Methods

P 7. Relax Designs, Inc., purchased a computerized blueprint printer that will assist in the design and display of plans for factory layouts. The cost of the printer was \$45,000, and its expected useful life is four years. The company can probably sell the printer for \$5,000 at the end of four years. The printer is expected to last 6,000 hours. It was used 1,200 hours in year 1; 1,800 hours in year 2; 2,400 hours in year 3; and 600 hours in year 4.

Required

1. Compute the annual depreciation and carrying value for the new blueprint printer for each of the four years (round to the nearest dollar where necessary) under each of the following methods: (a) straight-line, (b) production, and (c) double-declining-balance.
2. If the printer is sold for \$24,000 after year 2, what would be the gain or loss under each method?

User insight ▶

3. What conclusions can you draw from the patterns of yearly depreciation and carrying value in requirement **1**? Do the three methods differ in their impact on profitability? Do they differ in their effect on the company's operating cash flows? Explain.

LO5

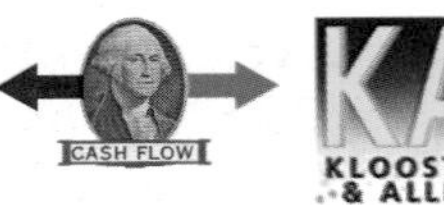

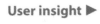

Natural Resource Depletion and Depreciation of Related Plant Assets

P 8. Fuentez Mining Company purchased land containing an estimated 20 million tons of ore for a cost of \$8,800,000. The land without the ore is estimated to be worth \$1,600,000. The company expects that all the usable ore can be mined in 10 years. Buildings costing \$800,000 with an estimated useful life of 30 years were erected on the site. Equipment costing \$960,000 with an estimated useful life of 10 years was installed. Because of the remote location, neither the buildings nor the equipment has an estimated residual value. During its first year of operation, the company mined and sold 1,600,000 tons of ore.

Required

1. Compute the depletion charge per ton.
2. Compute the depletion expense that should be recorded for the year.
3. Determine the depreciation expense for the year for the buildings, making it proportional to the depletion.

4. Determine the depreciation expense for the year for the equipment under two alternatives: (a) making the expense proportional to the depletion and (b) using the straight-line method.

User insight ▶ 5. Suppose the company mined and sold 2,000,000 tons of ore (instead of 1,600,000) during the first year. Would the change in the results in requirements **2** or **3** affect earnings or cash flows? Explain.

ENHANCING Your Knowledge, Skills, and Critical Thinking

Conceptual Understanding Cases

LO1

Effect of Change in Estimates

C 1. The airline industry was hit particularly hard after the 9/11 attacks on the World Trade Center in 2001. In 2002, **Southwest Airlines**, one of the healthier airlines companies, made a decision to lengthen the useful lives of its aircraft from 22 to 27 years. Shortly thereafter, following Southwest's leadership, other airlines made the same move.[19] What advantage, if any, can the airlines gain by making this change in estimate? Will it change earnings or cash flows and, if it does, will the change be favorable or negative?

Some people argue that the useful lives and depreciation of airplanes are irrelevant. They claim that because of the extensive maintenance and testing that airline companies are required by law to perform, the planes theoretically can be in service for an indefinite future period. What is wrong with this argument?

LO1

Impairment Test

C 2. The annual report for **Costco Wholesale Corporation**, the large discount company, contains the following statement:

> The company periodically evaluates the realizability of long-lived assets for impairment when [circumstances] may indicate the carrying amount of the asset may not be recoverable.[20]

What does the concept of impairment mean in accounting? What effect does impairment have on profitability and cash flows? Why would the concept of impairment be referred to as a conservative accounting approach?

LO3

Accounting Policies

C 3. IBM, the large computer equipment and services company, states in its annual report that "plant, rental machines and other property are carried at cost and depreciated over their useful lives using the straight-line method."[21] What estimates are necessary to carry out this policy? What factors should be considered in making each of the estimates?

Interpreting Financial Reports

LO6

Brands

C 4. Hilton Hotels Corporation and **Marriott International** provide hospitality services. Hilton Hotels' well-known brands include Hilton, Doubletree, Hampton Inn, Embassy Suites, Red Lion Hotels and Inns, and Homewood Suites. Marriott also owns or manages properties with recognizable brand names, such as Marriott Hotels, Resorts and Suites; Ritz-Carlton; Renaissance Hotels; Residence Inn; Courtyard; and Fairfield Inn.

On its balance sheet, Hilton Hotels Corporation includes brands (net of amortization) of $1.7 billion, or 19.5 percent of total assets. Marriott International, however, does not list brands among its intangible assets.[22] What principles of accounting for intangibles would cause Hilton to record brands as an asset while Marriott does not? How will these differences in accounting for brands generally affect the net income and return on assets of these two competitors?

LO3

Effects of Change in Accounting Method

C 5. Depreciation expense is a significant cost for companies in which plant assets are a high proportion of assets. The amount of depreciation expense in a given year is affected by estimates of useful life and choice of depreciation method. In 2010, Century Steelworks Company, a major integrated steel producer, changed the estimated useful lives for its major production assets. It also changed the method of depreciation for other steel-making assets from straight-line to the production method.

In its 2010 annual report, Century Steelworks makes the following statement:

> A recent study conducted by management shows that actual years-in-service figures for our major production equipment and machinery are, in most cases, higher than the estimated useful lives assigned to these assets. We have recast the depreciable lives of such assets so that equipment previously assigned a useful life of 8 to 26 years now has an extended depreciable life of 10 to 32 years.

The report goes on to explain the new production method of depreciation, as follows:

> [The method] recognizes that depreciation of production equipment and machinery correlates directly to both physical wear and tear and the passage of time. The production method of depreciation, which we have now initiated, more closely allocates the cost of these assets to the periods in which products are manufactured.

The report summarizes the effects of the changes in estimated useful lives and depreciation method on the year 2010 as shown in the following table:

Incremental Increase in Net Income	In Millions	Per Share
Lengthened lives	$11.0	$ .80
Production method		
Current year	7.3	.53
Prior years	2.8	.20
Total increase	$21.1	$1.53

During 2010, Century Steelworks reported a net loss of $83,156,500 ($6.03 per share). Depreciation expense for 2010 was $87,707,200.

In explaining the changes the company has made, the controller of Century Steelworks was quoted in an article in *Business Journal* as follows: "There is no reason for Century Steelworks to continue to depreciate our assets more conservatively than our competitors do." But the article also quotes an industry analyst who argues that by slowing its method of depreciation, Century Steelworks could be viewed as reporting lower-quality earnings.

1. Explain the accounting treatment when there is a change in the estimated lives of depreciable assets. What circumstances must exist for the production method to produce the effect it did in relation to the straight-line method? What would Century Steelworks' net income or loss have been if the changes

had not been made? What might have motivated management to make the changes?

2. What does the controller of Century Steelworks mean when he says that Century had been depreciating "more conservatively than our competitors do"? Why might the changes at Century Steelworks indicate, as the analyst asserts, "lower-quality earnings"? What risks might Century face as a result of its decision to use the production method of depreciation?

Decision Analysis Using Excel

LO1

Purchase Decision and Time Value of Money

C 6. Page Machine Works has obtained a subcontract from the government to manufacture special parts for a new military aircraft. The parts are to be delivered over the next five years, and the company will be paid as the parts are delivered.

To make the parts, Page Machine Works will have to purchase new equipment. Two types are available. Type A is conventional equipment that can be put into service immediately; Type B requires one year to be put into service but is more efficient than Type A. Type A requires an immediate cash investment of $1,000,000 and will produce enough parts to provide net cash receipts of $340,000 each year for the five years. Type B may be purchased by signing a two-year non-interest-bearing note for $1,346,000. It is projected that Type B will produce net cash receipts of zero in year 1, $500,000 in year 2, $600,000 in year 3, $600,000 in year 4, and $200,000 in year 5. Neither type of equipment can be used on other contracts, and neither type will have any useful life remaining at the end of the contract. Page currently pays an interest rate of 16 percent to borrow money.

1. What is the present value of the investment required for each type of equipment? (Use Table 1 in the appendix on present value tables.)
2. Compute the net present value of each type of equipment based on your answer in **1** and the present value of the net cash receipts projected to be received. (Use Tables 1 and 2 in the appendix on present value tables.)
3. Write a memorandum to the board of directors recommending the best option for Page. Explain your reasoning and include **1** and **2** as attachments.

Annual Report Case: CVS Caremark Corporation

Long-Term Assets

LO3 LO6

C 7. To answer the following questions, refer to the **CVS** annual report in the Supplement to Chapter 1. Examine the balance sheets and the summary of significant accounting policies on property and equipment in the notes to the financial statements.

1. What percentage of total assets in the most recent year was property and equipment, net? Identify the major categories of CVS's property and equipment. Which is the most significant type of property and equipment? What are leasehold improvements? How significant are these items, and what are their effects on the earnings of the company?
2. Continue with the summary of significant accounting policies item on property and equipment in the CVS annual report. What method of depreciation does CVS use? How long does management estimate its buildings will last as compared with furniture and equipment? What does this say about the company's need to remodel its stores?

3. Refer to the note on impairment of long-lived assets in the summary of significant accounting policies in CVS Corporation's annual report. How does the company determine if it has impaired assets?

Comparison Case: CVS Versus Southwest

LO1

Long-Term Assets and Free Cash Flows

C 8. Refer to the **CVS** annual report and to the financial statements of **Southwest Airlines Co.** in the Supplement to Chapter 1 to answer the questions below.

1. Prepare a table that shows the net amount each company spent on property and equipment (from the statement of cash flows), the total property and equipment (from the balance sheet), and the percentage of the first figure to the second for each of the past two years. Which company grew its property and equipment at a faster rate?
2. Calculate free cash flow for each company for the past two years. What conclusions can you draw about the need for each company to raise funds from debt and equity and the ability of each company to grow?

Ethical Dilemma Case

LO2

Ethics and Allocation of Acquisition Costs

C 9. Raintree Company has purchased land and a warehouse for $18,000,000. The warehouse is expected to last 20 years and to have a residual value equal to 10 percent of its cost. The chief financial officer (CFO) and the controller are discussing the allocation of the purchase price. The CFO believes that the largest amount possible should be assigned to the land because this action will improve reported net income in the future. Depreciation expense will be lower because land is not depreciated. He suggests allocating one-third, or $6,000,000, of the cost to the land. This results in depreciation expense each year of $540,000 [($12,000,000 − $1,200,000) ÷ 20 years].

The controller disagrees. She argues that the smallest amount possible, say one-fifth of the purchase price, should be allocated to the land, thereby saving income taxes, since the depreciation, which is tax-deductible, will be greater. Under this plan, annual depreciation would be $648,000 [($14,400,000 − $1,440,000) ÷ 20 years]. The annual tax savings at a 30 percent tax rate is $32,400 [($648,000 − $540,000) × .30]. How would each decision affect the company's cash flows? Ethically, how should the purchase cost be allocated? Who will be affected by the decision?

Internet Case

LO3 LO4 LO6

SEC and Forms 10-K

C 10. Public corporations are required not only to communicate with their stockholders by means of an annual report but also to submit an annual report to the Securities and Exchange Commission (SEC). The annual report to the SEC is called a Form 10-K and is a source of the latest information about a company.

Access the SEC's EDGAR files to locate either **H.J. Heinz Company's** or **Ford Motor Company's** Form 10-K. Find the financial statements and the notes to the financial statements. Scan through the notes to the financial statements and prepare a list of information related to long-term assets, including intangibles. For instance, what depreciation methods does the company use? What are the useful lives of its property, plant, and equipment? What intangible assets does the company have? Does the company have goodwill? How much does the company spend on research and development? How much did the company spend on new property, plant, and equipment (capital expenditures)? Summarize your results and be prepared to discuss them in class as well as your experience in using the SEC's EDGAR database.

Group Activity Case

LO2 LO6

Ethics of Aggressive Accounting Policies

C 11. Is it ethical to choose aggressive accounting practices to advance a company's business? During the 1990s, **America Online (AOL)**, the largest Internet service provider in the United States, was one of the hottest stocks on Wall Street. After its initial stock offering in 1992, AOL's stock price shot up by several thousand percent.

Accounting is very important to a company like AOL because earnings enable it to sell shares of stock and raise more cash to fund its growth. In its early years, AOL was one of the most aggressive companies in its choice of accounting principles. AOL's strategy called for building the largest customer base in the industry. Consequently, it spent many millions of dollars each year marketing its services to new customers. Such costs are usually recognized as operating expenses in the year in which they are incurred. However, AOL treated these costs as long-term assets, called "deferred subscriber acquisition costs," and expensed them over several years, because it said the average customer was going to stay with the company for three years or more. The company also recorded research and development costs as "product development costs" and amortized them over five years.

Both of these practices are justifiable theoretically, but they are not common practice. If the standard, more conservative practice had been followed, the company would have had a net loss in every year it has been in business.[23] This result would have greatly limited AOL's ability to raise money and grow.

Form groups to discuss this case. Determine whether your group thinks AOL was justified in adopting the "aggressive" accounting techniques. What was "aggressive" about these techniques? What was management's rationale for adopting the accounting policies that it did? What could go wrong with such a plan? How would you evaluate the ethics of AOL's actions? Who benefits from the actions? Who is harmed by these actions? Be prepared to support your conclusions in class.

Business Communication Case

Motivation for Change of Depreciation Method

C 12. Polaroid Corporation, a manufacturer of instant cameras and film, changed from an accelerated depreciation method for financial reporting purposes to the straight-line method for assets acquired after January 1, 1997. As noted in Polaroid's 1997 annual report:

> The company changed its method of depreciation for financial reporting for the cost of buildings, machinery, and equipment acquired on or after January 1, 1997, from a primarily accelerated method to the straight-line method.[24]

Polaroid's deteriorating financial position led it to declare bankruptcy in 2001. Write a one-page memorandum that argues that the change in accounting method may have been a signal that the company was in financial trouble. In your memorandum, discuss the effects of the change on future earnings and cash flows. In addition, discuss which of the two depreciation methods is more conservative.

CHAPTER

10 Long-Term Liabilities

Focus on Financial Statements

INCOME STATEMENT

Revenues

− Expenses

= Net Income

STATEMENT OF RETAINED EARNINGS

Opening Balance

+ Net Income

− Dividends

= Retained Earnings

BALANCE SHEET

Assets	Liabilities
	Equity

A = L + E

STATEMENT OF CASH FLOWS

Operating activities

+ Investing activities

+ Financing activities

= Change in Cash

+ Starting Balance

= Ending Cash Balance

Interest on long-term liabilities on balance sheet is an expense on income statement. Borrowing/repaying long-term liabilities affects statement of cash flows.

Long-term liabilities can be an attractive means of financing the expansion of a business. By incurring long-term debt to fund growth, a company may be able to earn a return that exceeds the interest it pays on the debt. When it does, it increases earnings for stockholders—that is, return on equity. Many companies reward top managers with bonuses for improving return on equity. This incentive provides a temptation to incur too much debt, which increases a company's financial risk. Thus, in deciding on an appropriate level of debt, as in so many other management issues, ethics is a major concern.

LEARNING OBJECTIVES

LO1 Identify the management issues related to long-term debt. *(pp. 514–522)*

LO2 Describe the features of a bond issue and the major characteristics of bonds. *(pp. 523–525)*

LO3 Record bonds issued at face value and at a discount or premium. *(pp. 526–529)*

LO4 Use present values to determine the value of bonds. *(pp. 529–530)*

LO5 Amortize bond discounts and bond premiums using the straight-line and effective interest methods. *(pp. 531–539)*

SUPPLEMENTAL OBJECTIVES

SO6 Account for the retirement of bonds and the conversion of bonds into stock. *(pp. 539–541)*

SO7 Record bonds issued between interest dates and year-end adjustments. *(pp. 541–543)*

DECISION POINT ▶ A USER'S FOCUS

- ▶ What are McDonald's most important long-term debts?
- ▶ What are its considerations in deciding to issue long-term debt?
- ▶ How does one evaluate whether a company has too much debt?

McDonald's Corporation

McDonald's, the world's largest restaurant chain, passed a milestone when it earned more revenues in Europe than in the United States. To finance its continued global expansion, the company raises funds by issuing both debt and capital stock. As you can see in its Financial Highlights, McDonald's relies heavily on debt financing. In 2006, its long-term liabilities were 68 percent of total stockholders' equity, and, together with current liabilities, they were over 87 percent of stockholders' equity. In 2007, its total current and long-term liabilities amounted to over 92 percent of stockholders' equity. McDonald's long-term obligations also include numerous leases on real estate, as well as employee pension and health plans.[1]

MCDONALD'S FINANCIAL HIGHLIGHTS (In millions)

	2007	2006
Total current liabilities	$ 4,498.5	$ 2,951.6
Long-term debt	$ 7,310.0	$ 8,389.9
Other long-term liabilities	1,342.5	1,098.4
Deferred income taxes	960.9	1,076.3
Total long-term liabilities	$ 9,613.4	$10,564.6
Total stockholders' equity	$15,279.8	$15,458.3
Total liabilities and stockholders' equity	$29,391.7	$28,974.5

Management Issues Related to Issuing Long-Term Debt

LO1 Identify the management issues related to long-term debt.

Profitable operations and short-term credit seldom provide sufficient cash for a growing business. Growth usually requires investment in long-term assets and in research and development and other activities that will produce income in future years. To finance these assets and activities, a company needs funds that will be available for long periods. Two key sources of long-term funds are the issuance of capital stock and the issuance of long-term debt. The management issues related to long-term debt financing are whether to take on long-term debt, how much long-term debt to carry, and what types of long-term debt to incur.

Deciding to Issue Long-Term Debt

A key decision for management is whether to rely solely on stockholders' equity—capital stock issued and retained earnings—for long-term funds or to rely partially on long-term debt. Some companies, such as **Microsoft** and **Apple Computer**, do not issue long-term debt, but like **McDonald's**, most companies find it useful to do so.

Because long-term debt must be paid at maturity and because it usually requires periodic payments of interest, issuing common stock has two advantages over issuing long-term debt: (1) it does not have to be paid back, and (2) a company normally pays dividends on common stock only if it earns sufficient income. Issuing long-term debt, however, has the following advantages over issuing common stock:

- **No loss of stockholder control**. When a corporation issues long-term debt, common stockholders do not relinquish any of their control over the company because bondholders and other creditors do not have voting rights. But when a corporation issues additional shares of common stock, the votes of the new stockholders may force current stockholders and management to give up some control.
- **Tax effects**. The interest on debt is tax-deductible, whereas dividends on common stock are not. For example, if a corporation pays $100,000 in interest and its income tax rate is 30 percent, its net cost will be $70,000 because it will save $30,000 on income taxes. To pay $100,000 in dividends on common stock, the corporation would have to earn $142,857 before income taxes [($100,000 ÷ (1 − .30)].
- **Financial leverage**. If a corporation earns more from the funds it raises by incurring long-term debt than it pays in interest on the debt, the excess will increase its earnings for the stockholders. This concept is called **financial leverage**, or *trading on equity*. For example, if a company earns 12 percent on a $1,000,000 investment financed by long-term 10 percent notes, it will earn $20,000 before income taxes ($120,000 − $100,000). The debt to equity ratio is considered an overall measure of a company's financial leverage.

Despite these advantages, debt financing is not always in a company's best interest. It may entail the following:

- **Financial risk**. A high level of debt exposes a company to financial risk. A company whose plans for earnings do not pan out, whose operations are subject to the ups and downs of the economy, or whose cash flow is weak may be unable to pay the principal amount of its debt at the maturity date or even to make periodic interest payments. Creditors can then force the company into bankruptcy—something that has occurred often in the heavily debt-financed airline industry. **TWA**, **Continental Airlines**, and **United Airlines** filed for bankruptcy protection because they could not make payments on their long-term debt and other liabilities. (While in bankruptcy, they restructured their debt and interest payments: TWA sold off its assets, Continental survived, and United is still trying to come out of bankruptcy.)

- **Negative financial leverage**. Financial leverage can work against a company if the earnings from its investments do not exceed its interest payments. For example, many small Internet companies failed in recent years because they relied too heavily on debt financing before developing sufficient resources to ensure their survival.

Evaluating Long-Term Debt

The amount of long-term debt that companies carry varies widely. For many companies, it is less than 100 percent of stockholders' equity. However, as Figure 1 shows, the average debt to equity for selected industries often exceeds 100 percent of stockholders' equity. The range is from 77.7 percent to 192.7 percent of equity. To assess how much debt to carry, managers compute the debt to equity ratio. Using data from **McDonald's** Financial Highlights, we can compute its debt to equity ratio in 2007 as follows (in millions):

K/R

$$\text{Debt to Equity} = \frac{\text{Total Liabilities}}{\text{Total Stockholders' Equity}}$$

$$= \frac{\$4{,}498.5 + \$9{,}613.4}{\$15{,}279.8} = \frac{\$14{,}111.9}{\$15{,}279.8} = 0.9 \text{ times}$$

A debt to equity ratio of 0.9 is relatively large, but it does not tell the whole story. McDonald's also has long-term leases on property at about 13,000 locations. McDonald's structures these leases in such a way that they do not appear as liabilities on its balance sheet. This practice is called **off-balance-sheet financing** and, as used by McDonald's, is entirely legal. The leases are, however, long-term commitments of cash payments and so have the effect of long-term liabilities. McDonald's total commitment for its leases, which average 20 to 25 years, is $10,513 million.[2] If we add the discounted present value of these lease obligations to McDonald's balance sheet debt, it brings the total debt to about $20,000 million.

FIGURE 1

Average Debt to Equity for Selected Industries

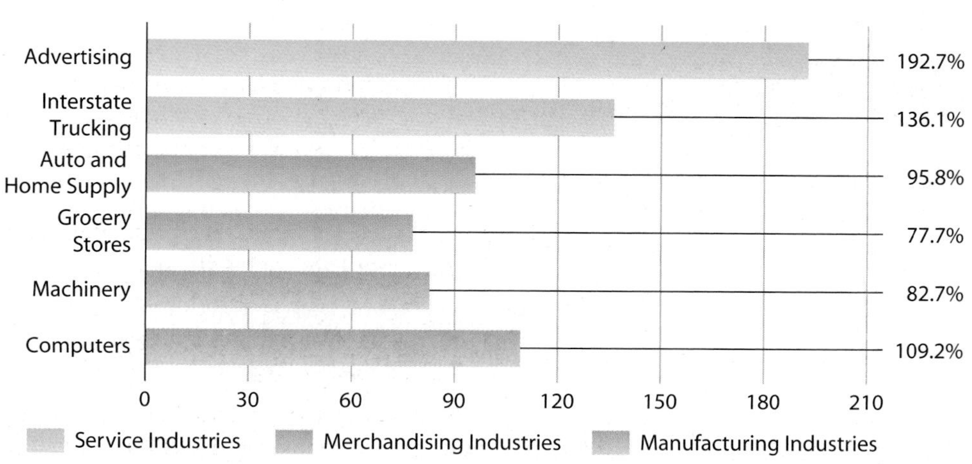

Source: Data from Dun & Bradstreet, *Industry Norms and Key Business Ratios*, 2005–2006.

Financial leverage—using long-term debt to fund investments or operations that increase return on equity—is advantageous as long as a company is able to make timely interest payments and repay the debt at maturity. Because failure to do so can force a company into bankruptcy, companies must assess the financial risk involved. A common measure of how much risk a company undertakes by assuming long-term debt is the **interest coverage ratio**. It measures the degree of protection a company has from default on interest payments. Most analysts want to see an interest coverage ratio of at least 3 or 4 times. Lower interest coverage would mean the company is at risk from a downturn in the economy.

McDonald's 2007 annual report shows that the company had income before taxes of $3,572.1 million and interest expense of $410.1 million. Using these figures, we can compute McDonald's interest coverage ratio as follows:

$$\text{Interest Coverage Ratio} = \frac{\text{Income Before Income Taxes} + \text{Interest Expense}}{\text{Interest Expense}}$$

$$= \frac{\$3{,}572.1 + \$410.1}{\$410.1}$$

$$= \frac{\$3{,}982.2}{\$410.1}$$

$$= 9.7 \text{ times}$$

McDonald's strong interest coverage ratio of 9.7 times shows that it was in no danger of being unable to make interest payments. However, in computing this ratio, management will add the company's off-balance-sheet rent expense of $1,053.8 to its interest expense. This procedure decreases the coverage ratio to 3.4 times. Although still adequate to cover interest payments, the adjusted coverage ratio is far less robust, which shows the significant effect that off-balance-sheet financing for leases can have on a company's financial situation.

Types of Long-Term Debt

To structure long-term financing to the best advantage of their companies, managers must know the characteristics of the various types of long-term debt.

FOCUS ON BUSINESS PRACTICE

How Does Debt Affect a Company's Ability to Borrow?

Credit ratings by agencies like Standard & Poor's reflect the fact that the greater a company's debt, the greater its financial risk. Standard & Poor's rates companies from AAA (best) to CCC (worst) based on various factors, including a company's debt to equity ratio, as shown in the table below.

Rating	AAA	AA	A	BBB	BB	B	CCC
Debt/Equity Ratio*	4.5	34.1	42.9	47.9	59.8	76.0	75.7

*Averages of companies with similar ratings.

These ratings affect not only how much a company can borrow, but also what the interest will cost. The lower its rating, the more a company must pay in interest, and vice versa.

In the heavily debt-laden auto industry, a change in debt rating can mean millions of dollars. For instance, when S & P lowered **General Motors'** and **Ford Motor Company's** credit ratings to "junk status"—BB—it meant that these companies might have to pay 1 or more percentage points in additional interest, which on a debt of $291 billion for GM and $161 billion for Ford would amount to about $2 billion.[3] Thus, companies must pay close attention to their financial risk as expressed by the debt to equity ratio. **McDonald's** solid credit is reflected in an A rating.

The most common are bonds payable, notes payable, mortgages payable, long-term leases, pension liabilities, other postretirement benefits, and deferred income taxes.

Bonds Payable Long-term bonds are the most common type of long-term debt. They can have many different characteristics, including the amount of interest, whether the company can elect to repay them before their maturity date, and whether they can be converted to common stock. We cover bonds in detail in later sections of this chapter.

Notes Payable Long-term notes payable, those that come due in more than one year, are also very common. They differ from bonds mainly in the way the contract with the creditor is structured. A long-term note is a promissory note that represents a loan from a bank or other creditor, whereas a bond is a more complex financial instrument that usually involves debt to many creditors. Analysts often do not distinguish between long-term notes and bonds because they have similar effects on the financial statements. Recently, in one of the largest debt offerings in history, **Deutsche Telekom International Finance** raised $14.6 billion by issuing a series of long-term notes denominated in dollars, Euros, pounds, and yen. Some notes were due in 2005, 2010, and 2030.[4]

Mortgages Payable A **mortgage** is a long-term debt secured by real property. It is usually paid in equal monthly installments. Each monthly payment includes interest on the debt and a reduction in the debt. Table 1 shows the first three monthly payments on a $100,000, 12 percent mortgage. The mortgage was obtained on June 1, and the monthly payments are $1,600. The entry to record the July 1 payment would be as follows:

A	=	L	+ SE
−1,600		−600	−1,000

July 1	Mortgage Payable	600	
	Mortgage Interest Expense	1,000	
	Cash		1,600
	Made monthly mortgage payment		

Notice from the entry and from Table 1 that the July 1 payment represents interest expense of $1,000 ($100,000 × .12 × 1/12) and a reduction in the debt of $600 ($1,600 − $1,000). Therefore, the July payment reduces the unpaid balance to $99,400. August's interest expense is slightly less than July's because of the decrease in the debt.

TABLE 1
Monthly Payment Schedule on a $100,000, 12 Percent Mortgage

Payment Date	A Unpaid Balance at Beginning of Period	B Monthly Payment	C Interest for 1 Month at 1% on Unpaid Balance* (1% × A)	D Reduction in Debt (B − C)	E Unpaid Balance at End of Period (A − D)
June 1					$100,000
July 1	$100,000	$1,600	$1,000	$600	99,400
Aug. 1	99,400	1,600	994	606	98,794
Sept. 1	98,794	1,600	988	612	98,182

***Rounded to the nearest dollar.**

Long-Term Leases A company can obtain an operating asset in three ways:

1. By borrowing money and buying the asset
2. By renting the asset on a short-term lease
3. By obtaining the asset on a long-term lease

The first two methods do not create accounting problems. When a company uses the first method, it records the asset and liability at the amount paid, and the asset is subject to periodic depreciation.

When a company uses the second method, the lease is short in relation to the useful life of the asset, and the risks of ownership remain with the lessor. This type of agreement is called an **operating lease**. Payments on operating leases are properly treated as rent expense.

The third method is one of the fastest-growing ways of financing plant assets in the United States today. A long-term lease on a plant asset has several advantages. It requires no immediate cash payment, the rental payment is deducted in full for tax purposes, and it costs less than a short-term lease. Acquiring the use of plant assets under long-term leases does create several accounting challenges, however.

Long-term leases may be carefully structured, as they are by **McDonald's**, so that they can be accounted for as operating leases. Accounting standards require, however, that a long-term lease be treated as a **capital lease** when it meets the following conditions:

Study Note

Under a capital lease, the lessee should record depreciation, using any allowable method.

- It cannot be canceled.
- Its duration is about the same as the useful life of the asset.
- It stipulates that the lessee has the option to buy the asset at a nominal price at the end of the lease.

Study Note

A capital lease is in substance an installment purchase, and the leased asset and related liability must be recognized at their present value.

A capital lease is thus more like a purchase or sale on installment than a rental. The lessee in a capital lease should record an asset, depreciation on the asset, and a long-term liability equal to the present value of the total lease payments during the lease term.[5] Much like a mortgage payment, each lease payment consists partly of interest expense and partly of repayment of debt.

Suppose, for example, that Polany Manufacturing Company enters into a long-term lease for a machine. The lease terms call for an annual payment of $8,000 for six years, which approximates the useful life of the machine. At the end of the lease period, the title to the machine passes to Polany. This lease is clearly a capital lease and should be recorded as an asset and a liability.

Present value techniques can be used to place a value on the asset and on the corresponding liability in a capital lease. Suppose Polany's interest cost on the unpaid part of its obligation is 16 percent. Using the factor for 16 percent and six periods in Table 2 in the appendix on present values tables, we can compute the present value of the lease payments as follows:

$$\text{Periodic Payment} \times \text{Factor} = \text{Present Value}$$
$$\$8,000 \times 3.685 = \$29,480$$

The entry to record the lease is as follows:

A	=	L	+ SE
+29,480		+29,480	

Capital Lease Equipment	29,480	
Capital Lease Obligations		29,480
To record capital lease on machinery		

Capital Lease Equipment is classified as a long-term asset. Capital Lease Obligations is classified as a long-term liability.

Each year, Polany must record depreciation on the leased asset. Using straight-line depreciation, a six-year life, and no residual value, the following entry would record the depreciation:

A	=	L	+ SE
−4,913			−4,913

Depreciation Expense, Capital Lease Equipment	4,913	
Accumulated Depreciation, Capital Lease Equipment		4,913
To record depreciation expense on capital lease		

The interest expense for each year is computed by multiplying the interest rate (16 percent) by the amount of the remaining lease obligation. Table 2 shows these calculations. Using the data in the table, the first lease payment would be recorded as follows:

A	=	L	+ SE
−8,000		−3,283	−4,717

Interest Expense (Column B)	4,717	
Capital Lease Obligations (Column C)	3,283	
Cash (Column A)		8,000
Made payment on capital lease		

This example suggests why companies are motivated to engage in off-balance-sheet financing for leases. By structuring long-term leases so that they can be accounted for as operating leases, companies avoid recording them on the balance sheet as long-term assets and liabilities. This practice, which, as we have noted, is legal and which **McDonald's** uses with skill, not only improves the debt to equity ratio by showing less debt on the balance sheet; it also improves the return on assets by reducing the total assets.

Pension Liabilities Most employees of medium-sized and large companies are covered by a **pension plan**, a contract that requires a company to pay benefits to its employees after they retire. Some companies pay the full cost of the pension plan, but in many companies, employees share the cost by contributing part of their salaries or wages. The contributions from employer and employees are usually paid into a **pension fund**, which is invested on behalf of the employees and from which

TABLE 2

Payment Schedule on a 16 Percent Capital Lease

Year	A Lease Payment	B Interest (16%) on Unpaid Obligation* (D × 16%)	C Reduction of Lease Obligation (A − B)	D Balance of Lease Obligation (D − C)
Beginning				$29,480
1	$ 8,000	$ 4,717	$ 3,283	26,197
2	8,000	4,192	3,808	22,389
3	8,000	3,582	4,418	17,971
4	8,000	2,875	5,125	12,846
5	8,000	2,055	5,945	6,901
6	8,000	1,099†	6,901	—
	$48,000	$18,520	$29,480	

*Rounded to the nearest dollar.

†The last year's interest equals $1,099 ($8,000 − $6,901); it does not exactly equal $1,104 ($6,901 × $\frac{16}{100}$ × 1) because of the cumulative effect of rounding.

benefits are paid to retirees. Pension benefits typically consist of monthly payments to retired employees and other payments upon disability or death.

Employers whose pension plans do not have sufficient assets to cover the present value of their pension obligations must record the amount of the shortfall as a liability on their balance sheets. If a pension plan has sufficient assets to cover its obligations, no balance sheet reporting is required or permitted.

There are two kinds of pension plans:

Study Note

Companies prefer defined contribution plans because the employees assume the risk that their pension assets will earn a sufficient return to meet their retirement needs.

- *Defined contribution plan.* Under a defined contribution plan, the employer makes a fixed annual contribution, usually a percentage of the employee's gross pay; the amount of the contribution is specified in an agreement between the company and the employees. Retirement payments vary depending on how much the employee's retirement account earns. Employees usually control their own investment accounts, can make additional contributions of their own, and can transfer the funds if they leave the company. Examples of defined contribution plans include 401(k) plans, profit-sharing plans, and employee stock ownership plans (ESOPs).

Study Note

Accounting for a defined benefit plan is far more complex than accounting for a defined contribution plan. Fortunately, accountants can rely on the calculations of professional actuaries, whose expertise includes the mathematics of pension plans.

- *Defined benefit plan.* Under a defined benefit plan, the employer contributes an amount annually required to fund estimated future pension liability arising from employment in the current year. The exact amount of the liability will not be known until the retirement and death of the current employees. Although the amount of future benefits is fixed, the annual contributions vary depending on assumptions about how much the pension fund will earn.

Annual pension expense under a defined contribution plan is simple and predictable. Pension expense equals the fixed amount of the annual contribution. In contrast, annual expense under a defined benefit plan is one of the most complex topics in accounting. The intricacies are reserved for advanced courses, but in concept, the procedure is simple. Computation of the annual expense takes into account the estimation of many factors, such as the average remaining service life of active employees, the long-run return on pension plan assets, and future salary increases. A new accounting standard requires companies and other entities with defined benefit plans not backed by a fund sufficient to pay them to record the unfunded portion as a liability.[6] For many companies this can amount to millions or even billions of dollars. **General Motors Corporation,** for example, has a pension liability of $11.4 billion.[7]

Because pension expense under a defined benefit plan is not predictable and can vary from year to year, many companies are adopting the more predictable

FOCUS ON BUSINESS PRACTICE

Postretirement Liabilities Affect Everyone

The rule requiring recognition of unfunded pension plans as liabilities impacts even government entities. Most government entities have defined benefit pension plans and provide postretirement medical benefits. As a result, states, school districts, and municipalities are all encountering previously ignored pension and health care liabilities. For example, a series of evasive tactics in San Diego led to a $1.1 billion shortfall, which almost caused the city to declare bankruptcy.[8] The state of New Jersey actually stopped setting aside funds to pay for health care in order to give a tax cut. No one added up the cost until the new accounting rule required it. The estimated cost to provide the health care promised to New Jersey's current and future retirees is $58 billion, or twice the state's annual budget.[9] These cases, while extreme, are not unusual. Citizens across the country will face tax increases to pay for these liabilities.

Postretirement benefits, such as health care, are a type of long-term debt for the company that provides them. Recent accounting standards hold that employees earn these benefits during their employment and that the benefits should therefore be estimated and accrued while the employee is working.

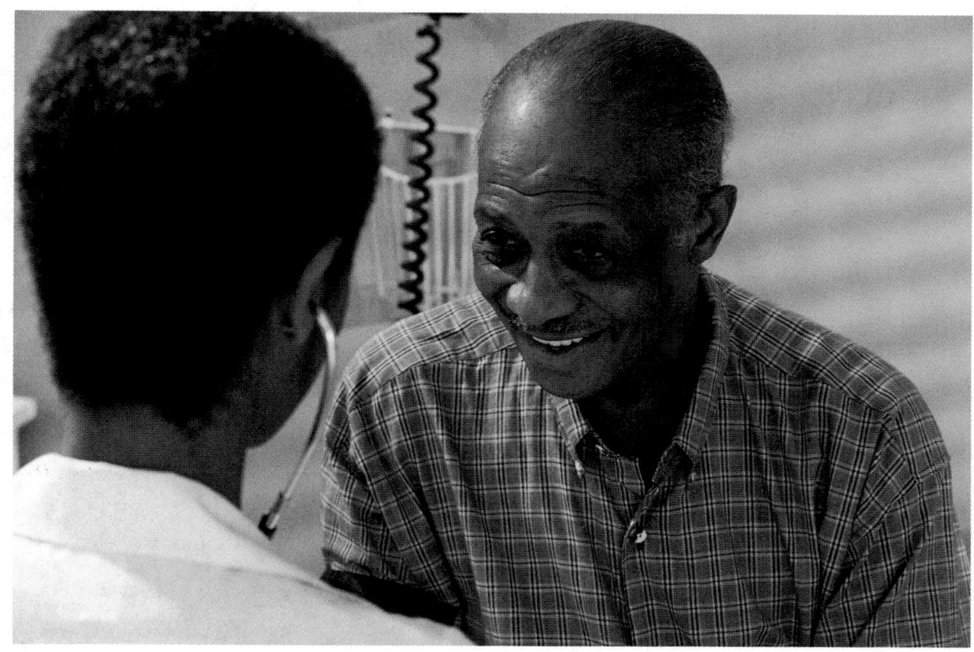

defined contribution plans. For example, in its 2007 annual report, **McDonald's** states that its plan "includes profit sharing, 401(k) and . . . ESOP features."

Study Note

Other postretirement benefits should be expensed as the employee earns them, not when they are paid after the employee retires. This practice conforms to the matching rule.

Other Postretirement Benefits Many companies provide retired employees not only with pensions, but also with health care and other benefits. In the past, these **other postretirement benefits** were accounted for on a cash basis—that is, they were expensed when the benefits were paid, after an employee had retired. More recent accounting standards hold that employees earn these benefits during their employment and that, in accordance with the matching rule, they should be estimated and accrued during the time the employee is working.[10]

The estimates must take into account assumptions about retirement age, mortality, and, most significantly, future trends in health care benefits. Like pension benefits, such future benefits should be discounted to the current period. A field test conducted by the Financial Executives Research Foundation determined that the change to accrual accounting increased postretirement benefits by two to seven times the amount recognized on a cash basis. **General Motors**, the nation's largest private purchaser of health care, recently reported that its future health care liabilities for retirees exceeded $47 billion.[11]

Deferred Income Taxes Among the long-term liabilities on the balance sheets of many companies, including **McDonald's**, is an account called **Deferred Income Taxes**. Deferred income taxes are the result of using different accounting methods to calculate income taxes on the income statement and income tax liability on the income tax return. For instance, companies often use straight-line depreciation for financial reporting and an accelerated method to calculate income tax liability. Because straight-line depreciation is less than accelerated depreciation in the early years of an asset's life, the presumption is that the income taxes will eventually have to be paid. Thus, the difference is listed as a long-term liability, deferred income taxes. Because companies try to manage their affairs to minimize income taxes paid, deferred income taxes can become quite large. In McDonald's case, as shown in the company's Financial Highlights, they amounted to almost $1 billion in 2007. We cover deferred income taxes in greater detail in a later chapter.

Cash Flow Information

The best source of information concerning cash flows about short-term and long-term debt is the financing activities section of the statement of cash flows. For instance, McDonald's cash flows from these activities are clearly revealed in this partial section of the company's statement of cash flows (in millions):

	2007	2006	2005
Financing Activities			
Net short-term borrowings	$ 101.3	$ 34.5	$ 22.7
Long-term financing issuances	2,116.8	1.9	3,107.9
Long-term financing repayments	(1,645.5)	(2,301.1)	(1,518.3)

Note that McDonald's has little short-term borrowing and that the company's cash outflows for long-term borrowing exceeded cash inflows by $238.3 million.

STOP ▸ REVIEW ▸ APPLY

LO1-1 What are the advantages and disadvantages of issuing long-term debt?

LO1-2 Why is interest coverage important in evaluating long-term debt?

LO1-3 What are the two components of a uniform monthly mortgage payment?

LO1-4 What is a capital lease? Why should an accountant record both an asset and a liability in connection with this type of lease?

LO1-5 What is a pension plan? What is a pension fund?

LO1-6 What is the difference between a defined contribution plan and a defined benefit plan?

LO1-7 What are other postretirement benefits, and how is the matching rule applied to them?

Suggested answers to all Stop, Review, and Apply questions follow the appendixes.

Identification of Long-Term Debt Each type of long-term liability below is closely related to one of the statements in the list that follows. Write the number of the liability next to the statement to which it applies.

1. Bonds payable
2. Long-term notes payable
3. Mortgage payable
4. Long-term lease
5. Pension liabilities
6. Other postretirement benefits
7. Deferred income taxes

_____ a. Cost of health care after employees' retirement
_____ b. The most common type of long-term debt
_____ c. The result of differences between accounting income and taxable income
_____ d. Debt that is secured by real estate
_____ e. Promissory note that is due in more than one year
_____ f. May be based on a percentage of employees' wages or on future benefits
_____ g. Can be similar in form to an installment purchase

SOLUTION

a. 6
b. 1
c. 7
d. 3
e. 2
f. 5
g. 4

The Nature of Bonds

LO2 Describe the features of a bond issue and the major characteristics of bonds.

Study Note

An investor who purchases debt securities, such as bonds or notes, is a creditor of the organization, not an owner.

A **bond** is a security, usually long term, representing money that a corporation borrows from the investing public. (The federal, state, and local governments also issue bonds to raise money, as do foreign countries.) A bond entails a promise to repay the amount borrowed, called the *principal*, on a specified date and to pay interest at a specified rate at specified times—usually semiannually. In contrast to stockholders, who are the owners of a corporation, bondholders are a corporation's creditors.

When a public corporation decides to issue bonds, it must submit the appropriate legal documents to the Securities and Exchange Commission for permission to borrow the funds. The SEC reviews the corporation's financial health and the specific terms of the **bond indenture**, which is a contract that defines the rights, privileges, and limitations of the bondholders. The bond indenture generally describes such things as the maturity date of the bonds, interest payment dates, and the interest rate. It may also cover repayment plans and restrictions. Once the bond issue is approved, the corporation has a limited time in which to issue the authorized bonds. As evidence of its debt to the bondholders, the corporation provides each of them with a **bond certificate**.

Bond Issue: Prices and Interest Rates

Study Note

When bonds with an interest rate different from the market rate are issued, they sell at a discount or premium. The discount or premium acts as an equalizing factor.

A **bond issue** is the total value of bonds issued at one time. For example, a $1,000,000 bond issue could consist of a thousand $1,000 bonds. The prices of bonds are stated in terms of a percentage of the face value, or principal, of the bonds. A bond issue quoted at 103 1/2 means that a $1,000 bond costs $1,035 ($1,000 × 1.035). When a bond sells at exactly 100, it is said to sell at face (or par) value. When it sells below 100, it is said to sell at a discount; above 100, at a premium. For instance, a $1,000 bond quoted at 87.62 would be selling at a discount and would cost the buyer $876.20.

Face Interest Rate and Market Interest Rate Two interest rates relevant to bond prices are the face interest rate and market interest rate:

- The **face interest rate** is the fixed rate of interest paid to bondholders based on the face value of the bonds. The rate and amount are fixed over the life of

FOCUS ON BUSINESS PRACTICE

Check Out Those Bond Prices!

The price of many bonds can be found daily in business publications like *The Wall Street Journal*. For instance, shown below are quotations for the bonds of Ford Motor Company and Abbott Laboratories, two very active corporate bond traders:[12]

	Face Rate	Maturity	Last Price	Last Yield
Ford Motor	9.980	2/47	82.500	12.112
Abbott	5.150	11/02	102.106	4.666

Abbott is one of the strongest companies financially, while Ford Motor is one of the weaker ones. Note that the face rate on Abbott's bond is lower than the face rate on Ford Motor's (5.150 percent versus 9.980 percent). In addition, the last price on Ford Motor's bond is less than 100 (82.500); thus, the market rate of interest on the bond (last yield of 12.112 percent) is greater than the face rate. This means that investors are not willing to settle for the 9.980 percent face rate and are demanding a higher rate by paying less than 100. Conversely, Abbott's bond sells for more than 100 (102.106), which means that investors are willing to accept a market rate (4.666 percent) that is even less than the bond's face rate. The prices of bonds vary daily as companies' fortunes and interest rates change.

Study Note

A bond sells at face value when the face interest rate of the bond is identical to the market interest rate for similar bonds on the date of issue.

the bond. To allow time to file with the SEC, publicize the bond issue, and print the bond certificates, a company must decide in advance what the face interest rate will be. Most companies try to set the face interest rate as close as possible to the market interest rate.

- The **market interest rate** is the rate of interest paid in the market on bonds of similar risk.* It is also called the *effective interest rate.* The market interest rate fluctuates daily. Because a company has no control over it, the market interest rate often differs from the face interest rate on the issue date.

Discounts and Premiums If the market interest rate fluctuates from the face interest rate before the issue date, the issue price of bonds will not equal their face value. This fluctuation in market interest rate causes the bonds to sell at either a discount or premium:

- A **discount** equals the excess of the face value over the issue price. The issue price will be less than the face value when the market interest rate is higher than the face interest rate.
- A **premium** equals the excess of the issue price over the face value. The issue price will be more than the face value when the market interest rate is lower than the face interest rate.

Discounts or premiums are contra-accounts that are subtracted from or added to bonds payable on the balance sheet.

Characteristics of Bonds

Study Note

Do not confuse the terms *indenture* and *debenture*. They sound alike, but an indenture is a bond contract, whereas a debenture is an unsecured bond. A debenture bond of a stable company actually might be a less risky investment than a secured bond of an unstable company.

A bond indenture can be written to fit an organization's financing needs. As a result, the bonds issued in today's financial markets have many different features. We describe several of the more important features of bonds in the following paragraphs.

Unsecured and Secured Bonds Bonds can be either unsecured or secured. **Unsecured bonds** (also called *debenture bonds*) are issued on the basis of a corporation's general credit. **Secured bonds** carry a pledge of certain corporate assets as a guarantee of repayment. A pledged asset may be a specific asset, such as a truck, or a general category of asset, such as property, plant, or equipment.

Term and Serial Bonds When all the bonds of an issue mature at the same time, they are called **term bonds**. For instance, a company may decide to issue $1,000,000 worth of bonds, all due 20 years from the date of issue.

Study Note

An advantage of issuing serial bonds is that the organization retires the bonds over a period of years, rather than all at once.

When the bonds of an issue mature on different dates, they are called **serial bonds**. For example, suppose a $1,000,000 bond issue calls for paying $200,000 of the principal every five years. This arrangement means that after the first $200,000 payment is made, $800,000 of the bonds would remain outstanding for the next five years, $600,000 for the next five years, and so on. A company may issue serial bonds to ease the task of retiring its debt—that is, paying off what it owes on the bonds.

Callable and Convertible Bonds When bonds are callable and convertible, a company may be able to retire them before their maturity dates. When a company

*At the time this chapter was written, the market interest rates on corporate bonds were volatile. Therefore, we use a variety of interest rates in our examples.

does retire a bond issue before its maturity date, it is called **early extinguishment of debt**. Doing so can be to a company's advantage.

Callable bonds give the issuer the right to buy back and retire the bonds before maturity at a specified **call price**, which is usually above face value. Callable bonds give a company flexibility in financing its operations. For example, if bond interest rates drop, the company can call the bonds and reissue debt at a lower interest rate. A company might also call its bonds if it has earned enough to pay off the debt, if the reason for having the debt no longer exists, or if it wants to restructure its debt to equity ratio. The bond indenture states the time period and the prices at which the bonds can be redeemed.

Convertible bonds allow the bondholder to exchange a bond for a specified number of shares of common stock. The face value of a convertible bond when issued is greater than the market value of the shares to which it can be converted. However, if the market price of the common stock rises above a certain level, the value of the bond rises in relation to the value of the common stock. Even if the stock price does not rise, the investor still holds the bond and receives both the periodic interest payments and the face value at the maturity date.

One advantage of issuing convertible bonds is that the interest rate is usually lower because investors are willing to give up some current interest in the hope that the value of the stock will increase and the value of the bonds will therefore also increase. In addition, if the bonds are both callable and convertible and the market value of the stock rises to a level at which the bond is worth more than face value, management can avoid repaying the bonds by calling them for redemption, thereby forcing the bondholders to convert their bonds into common stock. The bondholders will agree to convert because no gain or loss results from the transaction.

Registered and Coupon Bonds **Registered bonds** are issued in the names of the bondholders. The issuing organization keeps a record of the bondholders' names and addresses and pays them interest by check on the interest payment date. Most bonds today are registered.

Coupon bonds are not registered with the organization. Instead, they bear coupons stating the amount of interest due and the payment date. The bondholder removes the coupons from the bonds on the interest payment dates and presents them at a bank for collection.

STOP ▶ REVIEW ▶ APPLY

LO2-1 **What are a bond issue, a bond certificate, and a bond indenture? What information is in a bond indenture?**

LO2-2 **Napier Corporation sold a $500,000 bond issue of 5 percent, $1,000 bonds. What would the proceeds from the sale be if the bonds were issued at 95, at 100, and at 102?**

LO2-3 **If you were about to buy bonds on which the face interest rate was less than the market interest rate, would you expect to pay more or less than par value for the bonds?**

LO2-4 **What are the essential differences between (a) a discount and premium, (b) secured and unsecured (debenture) bonds, (c) term and serial bonds, (d) callable and convertible bonds, and (e) registered and coupon bonds?**

Accounting for the Issuance of Bonds

LO3 Record bonds issued at face value and at a discount or premium.

When the board of directors of a public corporation decides to issue bonds, the company must submit the appropriate legal documents to the Securities and Exchange Commission for authorization to borrow the funds. It is not necessary to make a journal entry to record the authorization of a bond issue. However, most companies disclose the authorization in the notes to their financial statements. The note lists the number and value of bonds authorized, the interest rate, the interest payment dates, and the life of the bonds.

In sections that follow, we show how to record bonds issued at face value, at a discount, and at a premium.

Bonds Issued at Face Value

Suppose Bharath Corporation issues $200,000 of 9 percent, five-year bonds on January 1, 2010, and sells them on the same date for their face value. The bond indenture states that interest is to be paid on January 1 and July 1 of each year. The entry to record the bond issue is as follows:

A	=	L	+ SE
+200,000		+200,000	

2010			
Jan. 1	Cash	200,000	
	Bonds Payable		200,000
	Sold $200,000 of 9%, 5-year bonds at face value		

Study Note

When calculating semiannual interest, do not use the annual rate (9 percent in this case). Rather, use half the annual rate.

Once a corporation issues bonds, it must pay interest to the bondholders over the life of the bonds, usually semiannually, and the principal of the bonds at maturity. In this example, interest is paid on January 1 and July 1 of each year. Thus, Bharath Corporation would owe the bondholders $9,000 interest on July 1, 2010:

$$\begin{aligned} \text{Interest} &= \text{Principal} \times \text{Rate} \times \text{Time} \\ &= \$200{,}000 \times \frac{9}{100} \times 6/12 \text{ year} \\ &= \$9{,}000 \end{aligned}$$

Bharath would record the interest paid to the bondholders on each semiannual interest payment date (January 1 or July 1) as follows:

A*	=	L	+ SE
−9,000			−9,000

*Assumes cash paid.

Bond Interest Expense	9,000	
Cash (or Interest Payable)		9,000
Paid (or accrued) semiannual interest to bondholders of 9%, 5-year bonds		

Bonds Issued at a Discount

Suppose Bharath Corporation issues $200,000 of 9 percent, five-year bonds at 96.149 on January 1, 2010, when the market interest rate is 10 percent. In this case, the bonds are being issued at a discount because the market interest rate exceeds the face interest rate. The following entry records the issuance of the bonds at a discount:

FOCUS ON BUSINESS PRACTICE

100-Year Bonds Are Not for Everyone.

In 1993, interest rates on long-term debt were at historically low levels, which induced some companies to attempt to lock in those low costs for long periods. One of the most aggressive companies in that regard was **The Walt Disney Company**, which issued $150 million of 100-year bonds at a yield of only 7.5 percent. It was the first time since 1954 that 100-year bonds had been issued. Among the others that followed Walt Disney's lead by issuing 100-year bonds were the **Coca-Cola Company**, **Columbia HCA Healthcare**, **Bell South**, **IBM**, and even the People's Republic of China. Some analysts wondered if even Mickey Mouse could survive 100 years. Investors who purchase such bonds take a financial risk because if interest rates rise, which is always likely, the market value of the bonds will decrease.[13]

A	=	L	+ SE
+192,298		−7,702	
		+200,000	

2010				
Jan. 1	Cash		192,298	
	Unamortized Bond Discount		7,702	
	Bonds Payable			200,000
	Sold $200,000 of 9%, 5-year bonds at 96.149			
	Face amount of bonds	$200,000		
	Less purchase price of bonds ($200,000 × .96149)	192,298		
	Unamortized bond discount	$ 7,702		

In 1993, the Walt Disney Company issued $150 million of 100-year bonds at a yield of 7.5 percent. At the time, some analysts wondered if even Mickey Mouse could survive 100 years. However, Mickey, who first appeared in 1928 in the animated short film *Steamboat Willie*, goes on. In 2003, he celebrated his 75th birthday. The bonds must be paid by 2093, but Disney has the option of repaying the bonds beginning in 2023.

In this entry, Cash is debited for the amount received ($192,298), Bonds Payable is credited for the face amount ($200,000) of the bond liability, and the difference ($7,702) is debited to Unamortized Bond Discount. If a balance sheet is prepared right after the bonds are issued at a discount, the liability for bonds payable is reported as follows:

Long-term liabilities		
9% bonds payable, due 1/1/2015	$200,000	
Less unamortized bond discount	7,702	$192,298

Unamortized Bond Discount is a contra-liability account. Its balance is deducted from the face amount of the bonds to arrive at the carrying value, or present value, of the bonds. The bond discount is described as unamortized because it will be amortized (written off) over the life of the bonds.

Bonds Issued at a Premium

When bonds have a face interest rate above the market rate for similar investments, they are issued at a price above the face value, or at a premium. For example, suppose Bharath Corporation issues $200,000 of 9 percent, five-year bonds for $208,200 on January 1, 2010, when the market interest rate is 8 percent. This means that investors will purchase the bonds at 104.1 percent of their face value. The issuance would be recorded as follows:

A	=	L	+ SE
+208,200		+8,200	
		+200,000	

2010			
Jan. 1	Cash	208,200	
	Unamortized Bond Premium		8,200
	Bonds Payable		200,000
	Sold $200,000 of 9%, 5-year bonds at 104.1 ($200,000 × 1.041)		

Right after this entry is made, bonds payable would be presented on the balance sheet as follows:

Long-term liabilities		
9% bonds payable, due 1/1/2015	$200,000	
Unamortized bond premium	8,200	$208,200

Study Note

The carrying amount is always the face value of the bonds plus the unamortized discount or less the unamortized premium. The carrying amount always approaches the face value over the life of the bond.

The carrying value of the bonds payable is $208,200, which equals the face value of the bonds plus the unamortized bond premium. The cash received from the bond issue is also $208,200. This means that the purchasers were willing to pay a premium of $8,200 to buy these bonds because their face interest rate was higher than the market interest rate.

Bond Issue Costs

The costs of issuing bonds can amount to as much as 5 percent of a bond issue. These costs often include the fees of underwriters, whom corporations hire to take care of the details of marketing a bond issue. Because the issue costs benefit the whole life of a bond issue, it makes sense to spread them over that period. It is generally accepted practice to establish a separate account for these costs and to amortize them over the life of the bonds.

Because issue costs decrease the amount of money a company receives from a bond issue, they have the effect of raising the discount or lowering the premium on the issue. Thus, bond issue costs can be spread over the life of the bonds through the amortization of a discount or premium. This method simplifies recordkeeping. In the rest of our discussion, we assume that all bond issue costs increase the discounts or decrease the premiums on bond issues.

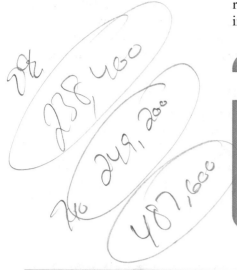

STOP ▶ REVIEW ▶ APPLY

LO3-1 **When bonds are issued at a discount, will the market interest rate be more or less than the face interest rate?**

LO3-2 **When bonds are issued at a premium, how is the bond liability shown on the balance sheet?**

LO3-3 **Why do bond issue costs increase the discount on a bond issue?**

Using Present Value to Value a Bond

LO4 Use present values to determine the value of bonds.

A bond's value is based on the present value of two components of cash flow: a series of fixed interest payments, and a single payment at maturity. The amount of interest a bond pays is fixed over its life, but the market interest rate varies from day to day. Thus, the amount investors are willing to pay for a bond varies as well.

Case 1: Market Rate Above Face Rate

Suppose a bond has a face value of $20,000 and pays fixed interest of $900 every six months (a 9 percent annual rate). The bond is due in five years. If the market interest rate today is 12 percent, what is the present value of the bond?

To answer this question, we use Table 2 in the appendix on present value tables to calculate the present value of the periodic interest payments of $900, and we use Table 1 in the same appendix to calculate the present value of the single payment of $20,000 at maturity. Because interest payments are made every six months, the compounding period is half a year. Thus, we have to convert the annual rate to a semiannual rate of 6 percent (12 percent divided by two six-month periods per year) and use ten periods (five years multiplied by two six-month periods per year). With this information, we can compute the present value of the bond as follows:

Present value of 10 periodic payments at 6%:	
$900 × 7.360 (from Table 2 in the appendix)	$ 6,624
Present value of a single payment at the end of 10 periods at 6%: $20,000 × .558 (from Table 1 in the appendix):	11,160
Present value of $20,000 bond	$17,784

The market interest rate has increased so much since the bond was issued—from 9 percent to 12 percent—that the value of the bond today is only $17,784. That amount is all investors would be willing to pay at this time for a bond that provides income of $900 every six months and a return of the $20,000 principal in five years.

Case 2: Market Rate Below Face Rate

As Figure 2 shows, if the market interest rate on the bond described above falls below the face interest rate, say to 8 percent (4 percent semiannually), the present value of the bond will be greater than the face value of $20,000:

FIGURE 2

Using Present Value to Value a $20,000, 9 Percent, Five-Year Bond

Case 1: Face Rate = 9%
Market Rate = 12%

Interest Payments: $900 each six-month period

Period 1 Period 2 Period 3 Period 4 Period 5 Period 6 Period 7 Period 8 Period 9 Period 10

10 6-month periods = 5 years

Present Value
$900 x 7.360 = $6,624.00

Repayment
$20,000

Present Value
$20,000 x .558 = $11,160.00

Present Value of Bond
$17,784.00

Case 2: Face Rate = 9%
Market Rate = 8%

Interest Payments: $900 each six-month period

Period 1 Period 2 Period 3 Period 4 Period 5 Period 6 Period 7 Period 8 Period 9 Period 10

10 6-month periods = 5 years

Present Value
$900 x 8.111 = $7,299.90

Repayment
$20,000

Present Value
$20,000 x .676 = $13,520.00

Present Value of Bond
$20,819.90

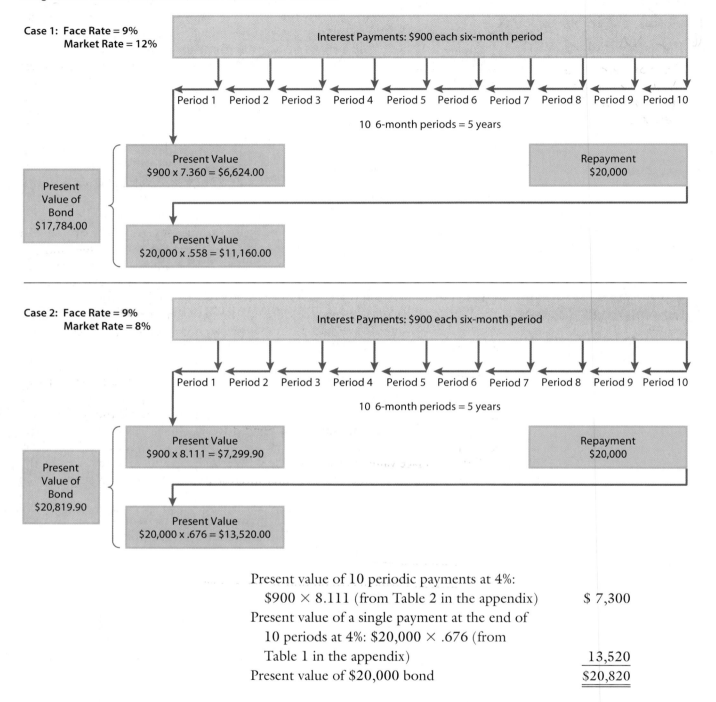

Present value of 10 periodic payments at 4%:	
$900 × 8.111 (from Table 2 in the appendix)	$ 7,300
Present value of a single payment at the end of 10 periods at 4%: $20,000 × .676 (from Table 1 in the appendix)	13,520
Present value of $20,000 bond	$20,820

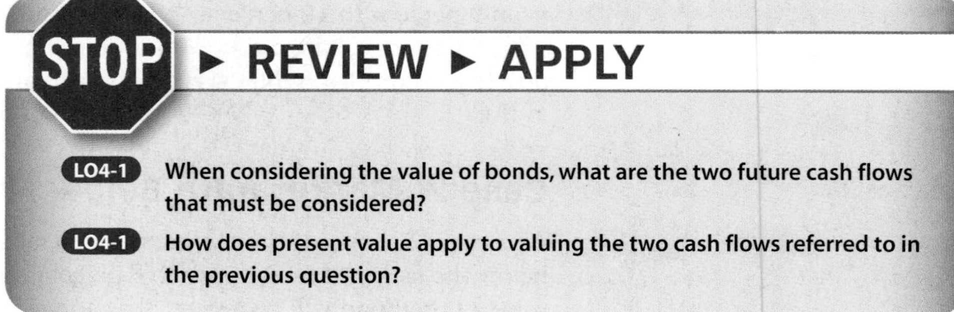

LO4-1 When considering the value of bonds, what are the two future cash flows that must be considered?
LO4-1 How does present value apply to valuing the two cash flows referred to in the previous question?

Amortization of Bond Discounts and Premiums

LO5 Amortize bond discounts and bond premiums using the straight-line and effective interest methods.

A bond discount or premium represents the amount by which the total interest cost is higher or lower than the total interest payments. To record interest expense properly and ensure that the carrying value of bonds payable at maturity equals face value, it is necessary to systematically reduce the bond discount or premium—that is, to amortize them—over the life of the bonds. This can be accomplished by using either the straight-line method or the effective interest method.

Amortizing a Bond Discount

In one of our earlier examples, Bharath Corporation issued $200,000 of five-year bonds at a time when the market interest rate of 10 percent exceeded the face interest rate of 9 percent. The bonds sold for $192,298, resulting in an unamortized bond discount of $7,702.

Study Note

A bond discount is a component of interest cost because it represents the amount in excess of the issue price that a corporation must pay on the maturity date.

Because a bond discount affects interest expense in each year of a bond issue, the bond discount should be amortized over the life of the bond issue. In this way, the unamortized bond discount will decrease gradually over time, and the carrying value of the bond issue (face value less unamortized discount) will gradually increase. By the maturity date, the carrying value of the bond issue will equal its face value, and the unamortized bond discount will be zero.

In the following sections, we calculate Bharath Corporation's total interest cost and amortize its bond discount using the straight-line and the effective interest methods.

Calculating Total Interest Cost When a corporation issues bonds at a discount, the market (or effective) interest rate that it pays is greater than the face interest rate on the bonds. The reason is that the interest cost is the stated interest payments *plus* the amount of the bond discount. That is, although the company does not receive the full face value of the bonds on issue, it still must pay back the full face value at maturity. The difference between the issue price and the face value must be added to the total interest payments to arrive at the actual interest expense.

The full cost to Bharath of issuing its bonds at a discount is as follows:

Cash to be paid to bondholders	
Face value at maturity	$200,000
Interest payments ($200,000 × .09 × 5 years)	90,000
Total cash paid to bondholders	$290,000
Less cash received from bondholders	192,298
Total interest cost	$ 97,702

Or, alternatively:

Interest payments ($200,000 × .09 × 5 years)	$ 90,000
Bond discount	7,702
Total interest cost	$ 97,702

The total interest cost of $97,702 is made up of $90,000 in interest payments and the $7,702 bond discount. Thus, the bond discount increases the interest paid on the bonds from the face interest rate to the market interest rate. The market (or effective) interest rate is the real interest cost of the bond over its life.

To have each year's interest expense reflect the market interest rate, the discount must be allocated over the remaining life of the bonds as an increase in the interest expense each period. Thus, the interest expense for each period will exceed the actual payment of interest by the amount of the bond discount that is amortized over the period. This process of allocation is called *amortization of the bond discount.*

Study Note

The discount on a zero coupon bond represents the interest that will be paid (in its entirety) on the maturity date.

Some bonds do not require periodic interest payments. These bonds, called **zero coupon bonds**, are simply a promise to pay a fixed amount at the maturity date. They are issued at a large discount because the only interest that the buyer earns or the issuer pays is the discount. For example, a five-year, $200,000 zero coupon bond issued when the market rate is 14 percent, compounded semiannually, would sell for only $101,600. That amount is the present value of a single payment of $200,000 at the end of five years. The discount of $98,400 ($200,000 − $101,600) is the total interest cost, which is amortized over the life of the bond.

Straight-Line Method The **straight-line method** equalizes amortization of a bond discount for each interest period. Using our example of Bharath Corporation, the interest payment dates of the bond issue are January 1 and July 1 of each year, and the bonds mature in five years. With the straight-line method, the amount of the bond discount amortized and the interest expense for each semiannual period are calculated in four steps:

1. Total Interest Payments = Interest Payments per Year × Life of Bonds

$$= 2 \times 5 = 10$$

2. Amortization of Bond Discount per Interest Period $= \dfrac{\text{Bond Discount}}{\text{Total Interest Payments}}$

$$= \frac{\$7{,}702}{10}$$

$$= \$770^{*}$$

3. Cash Interest Payment = Face Value × Face Interest Rate × Time

$$= \$200{,}000 \times .09 \times 6/12 = \$9{,}000$$

4. Interest Expense per Interest Period = Interest Payment + Amortization of Bond Discount

$$= \$9{,}000 + \$770 = \$9{,}770$$

On July 1, 2010, the first semiannual interest date, the entry would be:

A*	=	L	+	SE
−9,000		+770		−9,770

*Assumes cash paid.

2010			
July 1	Bond Interest Expense	9,770	
	Unamortized Bond Discount		770
	Cash (or Interest Payable)		9,000
	Paid (or accrued) semiannual interest to bondholders and amortized the discount on 9%, 5-year bonds		

Notice that the bond interest expense is $9,770, but the amount paid to the bondholders is the $9,000 face interest payment. The difference of $770 is the credit to Unamortized Bond Discount. This lowers the debit balance of Unamortized Bond Discount and raises the carrying value of the bonds payable by $770 each interest period. If no changes occur in the bond issue, this entry will be made every six months for the life of the bonds. When the bond issue

*Rounded.

matures, the Unamortized Bond Discount account will have a zero balance, and the carrying value of the bonds will be $200,000—exactly equal to the amount due the bondholders.

Although the straight-line method has long been used, it has a certain weakness. When it is used to amortize a discount, the carrying value goes up each period, but the bond interest expense stays the same; thus, the rate of interest falls over time. Conversely, when this method is used to amortize a premium, the rate of interest rises over time. The Accounting Principles Board therefore holds that the straight-line method should be used only when it does not lead to a material difference from the effective interest method.[14] A material difference is one that affects the evaluation of a company.

Effective Interest Method When the **effective interest method** is used to compute the interest and amortization of a bond discount, a constant interest rate is applied to the carrying value of the bonds at the beginning of each interest period. This constant rate is the market rate (i.e., the effective rate) at the time the bonds were issued. The amount amortized each period is the difference between the interest computed by using the market rate and the actual interest paid to bondholders.

As an example, we use the same facts we used earlier—a $200,000 bond issue at 9 percent, with a five-year maturity and interest to be paid twice a year. The market rate at the time the bonds were issued was 10 percent, so the bonds sold for $192,298, a discount of $7,702. Table 3 shows the interest and amortization of the bond discount.

Study Note

Whether a bond is sold at a discount or a premium, its carrying value will equal its face value on the maturity date.

The amounts in the table for period 1 were computed as follows:

Column A: The carrying value of the bonds is their face value less the unamortized bond discount ($200,000 − $7,702 = $192,298).

TABLE 3

Interest and Amortization of a Bond Discount: Effective Interest Method

Semiannual Interest Period	A Carrying Value at Beginning of Period	B Semiannual Interest Expense at 10% to Be Recorded* (5% × A)	C Semiannual Interest Payment to Bondholders (4½% × $200,000)	D Amortization of Bond Discount (B − C)	E Unamortized Bond Discount at End of Period (E − D)	F Carrying Value at End of Period (A + D)
0					$7,702	$192,298
1	$192,298	$9,615	$9,000	$615	7,087	192,913
2	192,913	9,646	9,000	646	6,441	193,559
3	193,559	9,678	9,000	678	5,763	194,237
4	194,237	9,712	9,000	712	5,051	194,949
5	194,949	9,747	9,000	747	4,304	195,696
6	195,696	9,785	9,000	785	3,519	196,481
7	196,481	9,824	9,000	824	2,695	197,305
8	197,305	9,865	9,000	865	1,830	198,170
9	198,170	9,908	9,000	908	922	199,078
10	199,078	9,922†	9,000	922	—	200,000

*Rounded to the nearest dollar.

†Last period's interest expense equals $9,922 ($9,000 + $922); it does not equal $9,954 ($199,078 × .05) because of the cumulative effect of roundin-

Column B: The interest expense to be recorded is the effective interest. It is found by multiplying the carrying value of the bonds by the market interest rate for one-half year ($192,298 × .10 × 6/12 = $9,615).

Column C: The interest paid in the period is a constant amount computed by multiplying the face value of the bonds by their face interest rate by the interest time period ($200,000 × .09 × 6/12 = $9,000).

Column D: The discount amortized is the difference between the effective interest expense to be recorded and the interest to be paid on the interest payment date ($9,615 − $9,000 = $615).

Column E: The unamortized bond discount is the balance of the bond discount at the beginning of the period less the current period amortization of the discount ($7,702 − $615 = $7,087). The unamortized discount decreases in each interest payment period because it is amortized as a portion of interest expense.

Column F: The carrying value of the bonds at the end of the period is the carrying value at the beginning of the period plus the amortization during the period ($192,298 + $615 = $192,913). Notice that the sum of the carrying value and the unamortized discount (Column F + Column E) always equals the face value of the bonds ($192,913 + $7,087 = $200,000).

The entry to record the interest expense is exactly like the one when the straight-line method is used. However, the amounts debited and credited to the various accounts are different. Using the effective interest method, the entry for July 1, 2010, would be as follows:

A*	=	L	+	SE
−9,000		+615		−9,615

*Assumes cash paid.

2010			
July 1	Bond Interest Expense	9,615	
	Unamortized Bond Discount		615
	Cash (or Interest Payable)		9,000
	Paid (or accrued) semiannual interest to bondholders and amortized the discount on 9%, 5-year bonds		

Study Note

The bond interest expense recorded exceeds the amount of interest paid because of the amortization of the bond discount. The matching rule dictates that the discount be amortized over the life of the bond.

Although an interest and amortization table is useful because it can be prepared in advance for all periods, it is not necessary to have one to determine the amortization of a discount for any one interest payment period. It is necessary only to multiply the carrying value by the effective interest rate and subtract the interest payment from the result. For example, the amount of discount to be amortized in the seventh interest payment period is $824, calculated as follows: ($196,481 × .05) − $9,000.

Figure 3, which is based on the data in Table 3, shows how the effective interest method affects the amortization of a bond discount. Notice that the carrying value (the issue price) is initially less than the face value, but that it gradually increases toward face value over the life of the bond issue. Notice also that interest expense exceeds interest payments by the amount of the bond discount amortized. Interest expense increases gradually over the life of the bond because it is based on the gradually increasing carrying value (multiplied by the market interest rate).

Study Note

The bond interest *increases* each period because the carrying value of the bonds (the principal on which the interest is calculated) increases each period.

FIGURE 3

Carrying Value and Interest Expense—Bonds Issued at a Discount

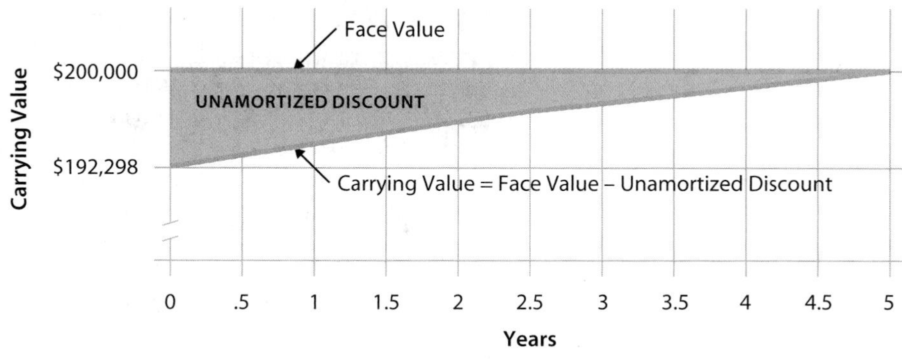

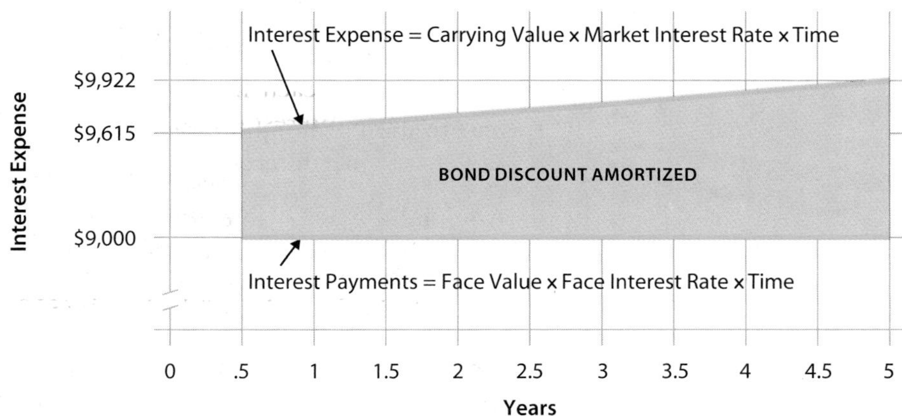

Amortizing a Bond Premium

In our earlier example of bonds issued at a premium, Bharath Corporation issued $200,000 of five-year bonds at a time when the market interest rate was 8 percent and the face interest rate was 9 percent. The bonds sold for $208,200, which resulted in an unamortized bond premium of $8,200. Like a discount, a premium must be amortized over the life of the bonds so that it can be matched to its effects on interest expense during that period.

In the following sections, we calculate Bharath Corporation's total interest cost and amortize its bond premium using the straight-line and effective interest methods.

Study Note

A bond premium is deducted from interest payments in calculating total interest because a bond premium represents an amount over the face value of a bond that the corporation never has to return to the bondholders. In effect, it reduces the higher-than-market interest the corporation is paying on the bond.

Calculation of Total Interest Cost Because the bondholders paid more than face value for the bonds, the premium of $8,200 ($208,200 − $200,000) represents an amount that the bondholders will not receive at maturity. The premium is in effect a reduction, in advance, of the total interest paid on the bonds over the life of the bond issue. The total interest cost over the issue's life can be computed as follows:

Cash to be paid to bondholders	
Face value at maturity	$200,000
Interest payments ($200,000 × .09 × 5 years)	90,000
Total cash paid to bondholders	$290,000
Less cash received from bondholders	208,200
Total interest cost	$ 81,800

Alternatively, the total interest cost can be computed as follows:

Interest payments ($200,000 × .09 × 5 years)	$ 90,000
Less bond premium	8,200
Total interest cost	$ 81,800

Notice that the total interest payments of $90,000 exceed the total interest cost of $81,800 by $8,200, the amount of the bond premium.

Straight-Line Method Under the straight-line method, the bond premium is spread evenly over the life of the bond issue. As with bond discounts, the amount of the bond premium amortized and the interest expense for each semiannual period are computed in four steps:

1. Total Interest Payments = Interest Payments per Year × Life of Bonds

$$= 2 \times 5 = 10$$

2. $$\text{Amortization of Bond Premium per Interest Period} = \frac{\text{Bond Premium}}{\text{Total Interest Payments}} = \frac{\$8{,}200}{10} = \$820$$

3. Cash Interest Payment = Face Value × Face Interest Rate × Time

$$= \$200{,}000 \times .09 \times 6/12 = \$9{,}000$$

4. $$\text{Interest Expense per Interest Period} = \text{Interest Payment} - \text{Amortization of Bond Premium}$$

$$= \$9{,}000 - \$820 = \$8{,}180$$

On July 1, 2010, the first semiannual interest date, the entry would be like this:

A*	=	L	+	SE
−9,000		−820		−8,180

*Assumes cash paid.

2010			
July 1	Bond Interest Expense	8,180	
	Unamortized Bond Premium	820	
	Cash (or Interest Payable)		9,000
	Paid (or accrued) semiannual interest to bondholders and amortized the premium on 9%, 5-year bonds		

Study Note

The bond interest expense recorded is less than the amount of the interest paid because of the amortization of the bond premium. The matching rule dictates that the premium be amortized over the life of the bond.

Note that the bond interest expense is $8,180, but the amount that bondholders receive is the $9,000 face interest payment. The difference of $820 is the debit to Unamortized Bond Premium. This lowers the credit balance of the Unamortized Bond Premium account and the carrying value of the bonds payable by $820 each interest period. If the bond issue remains unchanged, the same entry will be made on every semiannual interest date over the life of the bond issue. When the bond issue matures, the balance in the Unamortized Bond Premium account will be zero, and the carrying value of the bonds payable will be $200,000—exactly equal to the amount due the bondholders.

As noted earlier, the straight-line method should be used only when it does not lead to a material difference from the effective interest method.

Effective Interest Method Under the straight-line method, the effective interest rate changes constantly, even though the interest expense is fixed,

TABLE 4

Interest and Amortization of a Bond Premium: Effective Interest Method

Semiannual Interest Period	A Carrying Value at Beginning of Period	B Semiannual Interest Expense at 8% to Be Recorded* (4% × A)	C Semiannual Interest Payment to Bondholders (4½% × $200,000)	D Amortization of Bond Premium (C − B)	E Unamortized Bond Premium at End of Period (E − D)	F Carrying Value at End of Period (A − D)
0					$8,200	$208,200
1	$208,200	$8,328	$9,000	$672	7,528	207,528
2	207,528	8,301	9,000	699	6,829	206,829
3	206,829	8,273	9,000	727	6,102	206,102
4	206,102	8,244	9,000	756	5,346	205,346
5	205,346	8,214	9,000	786	4,560	204,560
6	204,560	8,182	9,000	818	3,742	203,742
7	203,742	8,150	9,000	850	2,892	202,892
8	202,892	8,116	9,000	884	2,008	202,008
9	202,008	8,080	9,000	920	1,088	201,088
10	201,088	7,912†	9,000	1,088	—	200,000

***Rounded to the nearest dollar**

†Last period's interest expense equals $7,912 ($9,000 − $1,088); it does not equal $8,044 ($201,088 × .04) because of the cumulative effect of rounding.

because the effective interest rate is determined by comparing the fixed interest expense with a carrying value that changes as a result of amortizing the discount or premium. To apply a fixed interest rate over the life of the bonds based on the actual market rate at the time of the bond issue, one must use the effective interest method. With this method, the interest expense decreases slightly each period (see Table 4, Column B) because the amount of the bond premium amortized increases slightly (Column D). This occurs because a fixed rate is applied each period to the gradually decreasing carrying value (Column A). The first interest payment is recorded as follows:

A*	=	L	+	SE
−9,000		−672		−8,328

*Assumes cash paid.

2010			
July 1	Bond Interest Expense	8,328	
	Unamortized Bond Premium	672	
	Cash (or Interest Payable)		9,000
	Paid (or accrued) semiannual interest to bondholders and amortized the premium on 9%, 5-year bonds		

Note that the unamortized bond premium (Column E) decreases gradually to zero as the carrying value decreases to the face value (Column F). To find the amount of premium amortized in any one interest payment period, subtract the effective interest expense (the carrying value times the effective interest rate, Column B) from the interest payment (Column C). In semiannual interest period 5, for example, the amortization of premium is $786, which is calculated in the following manner: $9,000 − ($205,346 × .04).

FIGURE 4
Carrying Value and Interest Expense—Bonds Issued at a Premium

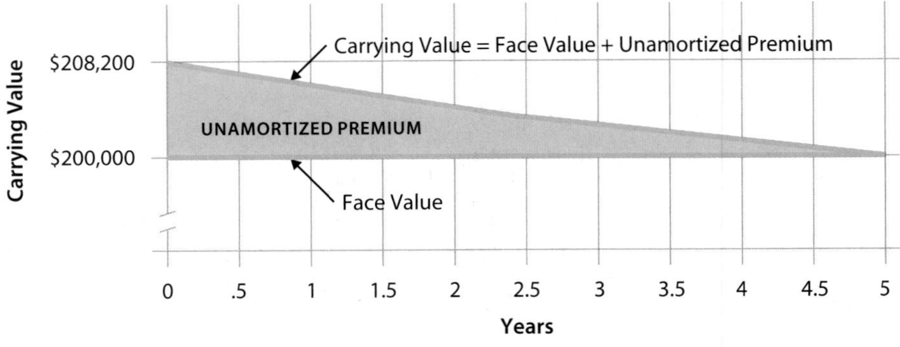

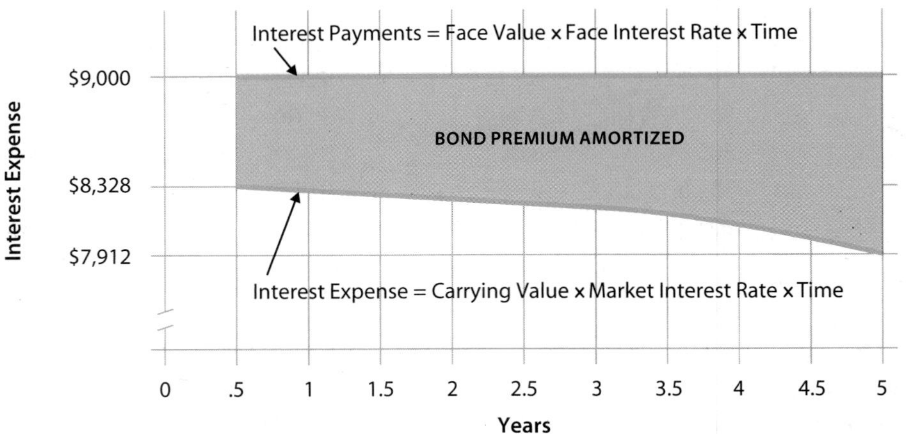

Figure 4, which is based on the data in Table 4, shows how the effective interest method affects the amortization of a bond premium. Note that the carrying value (issue price) is initially greater than the face value, but it gradually decreases toward the face value over the bond issue's life. Note also that interest payments exceed interest expense by the amount of the premium amortized. Interest expense decreases gradually over the life of the bond because it is based on the gradually decreasing carrying value (multiplied by the market interest rate).

STOP ▶ REVIEW ▶ APPLY

LO5-1 **What is included in the calculation of the total interest cost of a bond issue other than interest payments?**

LO5-2 **Why is the straight-line method of amortization usually acceptable even though it is not the most theoretically correct method?**

LO5-3 **Why does amortizing a bond discount result in an interest expense greater than the interest paid? Why does amortization of a premium have the opposite effect?**

LO5-4 **When the effective interest method of amortizing a bond discount or premium is used, why does the amount of interest expense change from period to period?**

Bond Transactions On June 1, Lazo Corporation issues $4,000,000 of 8 percent, 20-year bonds at 97. Interest is payable semiannually, on May 31 and November 30. Lazo's fiscal year ends on November 30.

1. Using the straight-line method of amortization, prepare entries in journal form for June 1 and November 30.
2. Using the effective interest method and assuming the same facts as above except that the market rate of interest is 8.5 percent, prepare the entry for November 30.

(continued)

SOLUTION

1. Straight-line method

June 1	Cash	3,880,000	
	Unamortized Bond Discount	120,000	
	Bonds Payable		4,000,000
	Issue of $4,000,000 of 8%, 20-year bonds at 97		
	$4,000,000 × .97 = $3,880,000		
Nov. 30	Bond Interest Expense	163,000	
	Unamortized Bond Discount		3,000
	Cash		160,000
	Paid bondholders semiannual interest and amortized the discount on 8%, 20-year bonds		
	$120,000 ÷ 40 periods = $3,000		
	$4,000,000 × .04 = $160,000		

2. Effective interest method

Nov. 30	Bond Interest Expense	164,900	
	Unamortized Bond Discount		4,900
	Cash		160,000
	Paid bondholders semiannual interest and amortized the discount on 8%, 20-year bonds		
	$3,880,000 × .0425 = $164,900		
	$4,000,000 × .04 = $160,000		

Retirement of Bonds

SO6 Account for the retirement of bonds and the conversion of bonds into stock.

Usually, companies pay bonds when they are due—on the maturity date. However, as noted in our discussion of callable and convertible bonds, retiring a bond issue before its maturity date can be to a company's advantage. For example, when interest rates drop, many companies refinance their bonds at the lower rate, much like homeowners who refinance their mortgage loans when interest rates go down. Although companies usually pay a premium for early extinguishment of bond debt, what they save on interest can make the refinancing cost-effective.

Calling Bonds

Suppose Bharath Corporation can call, or retire, at 105 the $200,000 of bonds it issued at a premium (104.1) on January 1, 2010, and it decides to do so on July 1, 2013. The retirement thus takes place on the seventh interest payment date. Assume the entry for the required interest payment and the amortization of the premium has been made. The entry to record the retirement of the bonds is:

A	=	L	+	SE
−210,000		−200,000		−7,108
		−2,892		

2013			
July 1	Bonds Payable	200,000	
	Unamortized Bond Premium	2,892	
	Loss on Retirement of Bonds	7,108	
	Cash		210,000
	Retired 9% bonds at 105		

In this entry, the cash paid is the face value times the call price ($200,000 × 1.05 = $210,000). The unamortized bond premium can be found in Column E of Table 4. The loss on retirement of bonds occurs because the call price of the bonds is greater than the carrying value ($210,000 − $202,892 = $7,108).

Sometimes, a rise in the market interest rate can cause the market value of bonds to fall considerably below their face value. If it has the cash to do so, the company may find it advantageous to purchase the bonds on the open market and retire them, rather than wait and pay them off at face value. A gain is recognized for the difference between the purchase price of the bonds and the carrying value of the retired bonds.

For example, suppose that because of a rise in interest rates, Bharath Corporation is able to purchase the $200,000 bond issue on the open market at 85. The entry would be as follows:

A	=	L	+	SE
−170,000		−200,000		+32,892
		−2,892		

2013			
July 1	Bonds Payable	200,000	
	Unamortized Bond Premium	2,892	
	Cash		170,000
	Gain on Retirement of Bonds		32,892
	Purchased and retired 9% bonds at 85		

Converting Bonds

When a bondholder converts bonds to common stock, the company records the common stock at the carrying value of the bonds. The bond liability and the unamortized discount or premium are written off the books. For this reason, no gain or loss on the transaction is recorded. For example, suppose Bharath Corporation does not call its bonds on July 1, 2013. Instead, the corporation's bondholders decide to convert all their bonds to $8 par value common stock under a convertible provision of 40 shares of common stock for each $1,000 bond. The entry would be as follows:

A	=	L	+	SE
		−200,000		+64,000
		−2,892		+138,892

2013			
July 1	Bonds Payable	200,000	
	Unamortized Bond Premium	2,892	
	Common Stock		64,000
	Additional Paid-in Capital		138,892
	Converted 9% bonds payable into $8 par value common stock at a rate of 40 shares for each $1,000 bond		

The unamortized bond premium is found in Column E of Table 4. At a rate of 40 shares for each $1,000 bond, 8,000 shares will be issued, with a total par value of $64,000 (8,000 × $8). The Common Stock account is credited for the amount of the par value of the stock issued. In addition, Additional Paid-in Capital is credited for the difference between the carrying value of the bonds and the par value of the stock issued ($202,892 − $64,000 = $138,892). No gain or loss is recorded.

STOP ▶ REVIEW ▶ APPLY

LO6-1 When may a company want to exercise the call provision of a bond?

LO6-2 Why are convertible bonds advantageous to both the company and the bondholder?

Other Bonds Payable Issues

SO7 Record bonds issued between interest dates and year-end adjustments.

Among the other issues involved in accounting for bonds payable are the sale of bonds between interest payment dates and the year-end accrual of bond interest expense.

Sale of Bonds Between Interest Dates

Although corporations may issue bonds on an interest payment date, as in our previous examples, they often issue them between interest payment dates. When that is the case, they generally collect from the investors the interest that would have accrued for the partial period preceding the issue date, and at the end of the first interest period, they pay the interest for the entire period. In other words, the interest collected when bonds are sold is returned to investors on the next interest payment date.

There are two reasons for following this procedure:

1. From a practical standpoint, if a company issued bonds on several different days and did not collect the accrued interest, records would have to be maintained for each bondholder and date of purchase. The interest due each bondholder would therefore have to be computed for a different time period. Clearly, this procedure would involve large bookkeeping costs. On the other hand, if accrued interest is collected when the bonds are sold, the corporation can pay the interest due for the entire period on the interest payment date, thereby eliminating the extra computations and costs.
2. When accrued interest is collected in advance, the amount is subtracted from the full interest paid on the interest payment date. Thus, the resulting interest expense represents the amount for the time the money was borrowed.

For example, suppose Bharath Corporation sold $200,000 of 9 percent, five-year bonds for face value on May 1, 2010, rather than on January 1, 2010. The entry to record the sale of the bonds is as follows:

A	=	L	+	SE
+206,000		+200,000		+6,000

2010			
May 1	Cash	206,000	
	Bond Interest Expense		6,000
	Bonds Payable		200,000
	Sold 9%, 5-year bonds at face value plus 4 months' accrued interest $200,000 × .09 × 4/12 = $6,000		

Cash is debited for the amount received, $206,000 (the face value of $200,000 plus four months' accrued interest of $6,000). Bond Interest Expense is credited for the $6,000 of accrued interest, and Bonds Payable is credited for the face value of $200,000.

When the first semiannual interest payment date arrives, the following entry is made:

A*	=	L	+	SE
−9,000				−9,000

*Assumes cash paid.

2010			
July 1	Bond Interest Expense	9,000	
	Cash (or Interest Payable)		9,000
	Paid (or accrued) semiannual interest		
	$200,000 × .09 × 6/12 = $9,000		

Notice that the entire half-year interest is debited to Bond Interest Expense and credited to Cash because the corporation pays bond interest every six months, in full six-month amounts. Figure 5 illustrates this process. The actual interest expense for the two months that the bonds were outstanding is $3,000. This amount is the net balance of the $9,000 debit to Bond Interest Expense on July 1 less the $6,000 credit to Bond Interest Expense on May 1. You can see these steps clearly in the following T account:

BOND INTEREST EXPENSE

Bal.	0	May 1	6,000
July 1	9,000		
Bal.	**3,000**		

Year-End Accrual of Bond Interest Expense

Study Note

Remember that adjusting entries never affect cash.

Bond interest payment dates rarely correspond with a company's fiscal year. Therefore, an adjustment must be made to accrue the interest expense on the bonds from the last interest payment date to the end of the fiscal year. In addition, any discount or premium on the bonds must be amortized for the partial period.

In our example of bonds issued at a premium, Bharath Corporation issued $200,000 of bonds on January 1, 2010, at 104.1 percent of face value. Suppose Bharath's fiscal year ends on September 30, 2010. In the period since the interest payment and amortization of the premium on July 1, three months' worth of interest has accrued. Under the effective interest method, the following adjusting entry would be made:

A	=	L	+	SE
		−349.50		−4,150.50
		+4,500.00		

2010			
Sept. 30	Bond Interest Expense	4,150.50	
	Unamortized Bond Premium	349.50	
	Bond Interest Payable		4,500.00
	To record accrual of interest on 9% bonds payable for 3 months and amortization of one-half of the premium for the second interest payment period		

FIGURE 5

Interest Expense When Bonds Are Issued Between Interest Dates

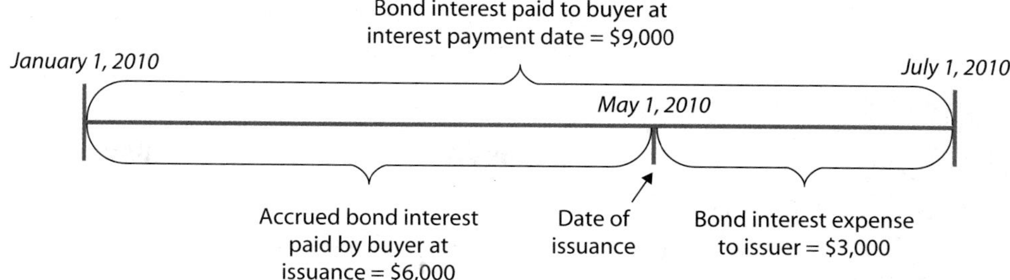

This entry covers one-half of the second interest period. Unamortized Bond Premium is debited for $349.50, which is one-half of $699, the amortization of the premium for the second period from Table 4. Bond Interest Payable is credited for $4,500, three months' interest on the face value of the bonds ($200,000 × .09 × 3/12). The net debit figure of $4,150.50 ($4,500.00 − $349.50) is the bond interest expense for the three-month period.

On the interest payment date of January 1, 2011, the entry to pay the bondholders and amortize the premium is as follows:

A	=	L	+	SE
−9,000.00		−4,500.00		−4,150.50
		−349.50		

2011			
Jan. 1	Bond Interest Expense	4,150.50	
	Bond Interest Payable	4,500.00	
	Unamortized Bond Premium	349.50	
	Cash		9,000.00
	Paid semiannual interest, including interest previously accrued, and amortized the premium for the period since the end of the fiscal year		

Study Note

The matching rule dictates that both the accrued interest and the amortization of a premium or discount be recorded at year end.

One-half ($4,500) of the amount paid ($9,000) was accrued on September 30. Unamortized Bond Premium is debited for $349.50, the remaining amount to be amortized for the period ($699.00 − $349.50). The resulting bond interest expense is the amount that applies to the three-month period from October 1 to December 31.

Bond discounts are recorded at year end in the same way as bond premiums. The difference is that the amortization of a bond discount increases interest expense instead of decreasing it.

STOP ▶ REVIEW ▶ APPLY

LO7-1 **When a company issues bonds between interest dates, why does it collect an amount equal to accrued interest from the buyer?**

LO7-2 **In making the year-end accrual for interest on bonds payable, what two computations affect the amount of interest expense?**

A LOOK BACK AT ▶ McDonald's Corporation

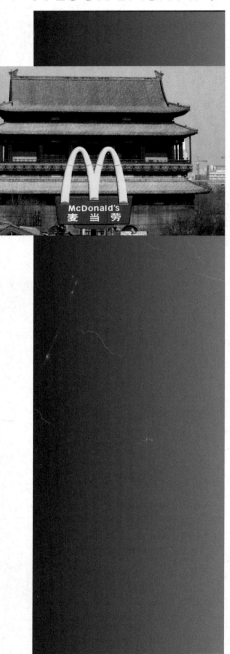

As we noted in this chapter's Decision Point, McDonald's relies on both debt and equity financing to support its continued global expansion. Because of the extent of the company's long-term debt, potential investors and creditors need to address the following questions:

- **What are McDonald's most important long-term debts?**
- **What are its considerations in deciding to issue long-term debt?**
- **How does one evaluate whether a company has too much debt?**

In addition to bonds, notes, and mortgages, McDonald's long-term debt includes leases on numerous properties. The company also has deferred income taxes and pension and health plans. Its purpose in taking on long-term debt is to foster growth and increase earnings. By using financial leverage in this way, McDonald's, like any other company, assumes financial risk. In McDonald's case, the risk is partially offset because much of its long-term debt relates to leases on real estate, an area in which the company has long experience and great expertise. McDonald's management commits the company to long-term leases not only because it believes the company will stay in the leased locations for a long time, but also because it is a way of financing expansion.

McDonald's 2007 annual report includes a detailed description of management's approach to debt financing. It points out that Standard & Poor's gives the company an "A" credit rating and that management carefully monitors key credit ratios that "incorporate capitalized operating leases to estimate total adjusted debt."

We can evaluate whether McDonald's maintains an appropriate level of debt by computing its interest coverage ratio over a two-year period, as follows:

$$\text{Interest Coverage Ratio} = \frac{\text{Income Before Income Taxes} + \text{Interest Expense}}{\text{Interest Expense}}$$

	2007	2006
Interest Coverage Ratio =	$\frac{\$3{,}572.1 + \$410.1}{\$410.1}$	$\frac{\$4{,}154.4 + \$401.9}{\$401.9}$
=	$\frac{\$3{,}982.2}{\$410.1}$	$\frac{\$4{,}556.3}{\$401.9}$
=	9.7 times	11.3 times

This analysis shows that McDonald's can easily cover its interest payments. Even though its ability to do so decreased over the two-year period, there is plenty of cushion in this ratio to cover all of McDonald's balance sheet commitments, including long-term leases.

CHAPTER REVIEW

REVIEW of Learning Objectives

LO1 Identify the management issues related to long-term debt.

Long-term debt is used to finance assets and business activities, such as research and development, that will produce income in future years. The management issues related to long-term debt are whether to take on long-term debt, how much debt to carry, and what types of debt to incur. The advantages of issuing long-term debt are that common stockholders do not relinquish any control, interest on debt is tax-deductible, and financial leverage can increase earnings. The disadvantages are that interest and principal must be paid on time and financial leverage can work against a company if an investment is not successful. The level of debt can be evaluated using the debt to equity ratio and the interest coverage ratio. Common types of long-term debt are bonds, notes, mortgages, long-term leases, pension liabilities, other postretirement benefits, and deferred income taxes.

LO2 Describe the features of a bond issue and the major characteristics of bonds.

A bond is a security that represents money borrowed from the investing public. When a corporation issues bonds, it enters into a contract, called a bond indenture, with the bondholders. The bond indenture defines the terms of the bond issue. A bond issue is the total value of bonds issued at one time. The prices of bonds are stated in terms of a percentage of the face value, or principal, of the bonds. The face interest rate is the fixed rate of interest paid to bondholders based on the face value. The market interest rate is the rate of interest paid in the market on bonds of similar risk. If the market rate fluctuates from the face interest rate before the bond issue date, the bonds will sell at either a discount or a premium.

A corporation can issue several types of bonds, each having different characteristics. For example, a bond issue may or may not require security (secured versus unsecured bonds). It may be payable at a single time (term bonds) or at several times (serial bonds). And the holder may receive interest automatically (registered bonds) or may have to return coupons to receive interest payable (coupon bonds). Bonds may also be callable and convertible.

LO3 Record bonds issued at face value and at a discount or premium.

Bondholders pay face value for bonds when the interest rate on the bonds approximates the market rate for similar investments. The issuing corporation records the bond issue at face value as a long-term liability in the Bonds Payable account. Bonds are issued at a discount when their face interest rate is lower than the market rate for similar investments. The difference between the face value and the issue price is debited to Unamortized Bond Discount. Bonds are issued at a premium when their face interest rate is greater than the market interest rate on similar investments. The difference between the issue price and the face value is credited to Unamortized Bond Premium.

LO4 Use present values to determine the value of bonds.

The value of a bond is determined by summing the present values of (1) the series of fixed interest payments of the bond issue and (2) the single payment of the face value at maturity. Tables 1 and 2 in the appendix on present value tables should be used in making these computations.

LO5 Amortize bond discounts and bond premiums using the straight-line and effective interest methods.

The straight-line method allocates a fixed portion of a bond discount or premium each interest period to adjust the interest payment to interest expense. The effective interest method, which is used when the effects of amortization are material, applies a constant rate of interest to the carrying value of the bonds. To find interest and the amortization of discounts or premiums, the effective interest rate is applied to the carrying value of the bonds (face value minus the discount or plus the premium) at the beginning of the interest period. The amount of the discount or premium to be amortized is the difference between the interest figured by using the effective rate and that obtained by using the face rate. The results of using the effective interest method on bonds issued at a discount or a premium are summarized below and compared with issuance at face value:

	Bonds Issued at		
	Face Value	**Discount**	**Premium**
Trend in carrying value over bond term	Constant	Increasing	Decreasing
Trend in interest expense over bond term	Constant	Increasing	Decreasing
Interest expense versus interest payments	Interest expense = interest payments	Interest expense > interest payments	Interest expense < interest payments
Classification of bond discount or premium	Not applicable	Contra-liability (deducted from Bonds Payable)	Liability (added to Bonds Payable)

Supplemental Objectives

SO6 Account for the retirement of bonds and the conversion of bonds into stock.

Callable bonds can be retired before maturity at the option of the issuing corporation. The call price is usually an amount greater than the face value of the bonds, in which case the corporation recognizes a loss on the retirement of the bonds. Sometimes, a rise in the market interest rate causes the market value of the bonds to fall below face value. If a company purchases its bonds on the open market at a price below carrying value, it recognizes a gain on the transaction.

Convertible bonds allow the bondholder to convert bonds to the issuing corporation's common stock. When bondholders exercise this option, the common stock issued is recorded at the carrying value of the bonds being converted. No gain or loss is recognized.

SO7 Record bonds issued between interest dates and year-end adjustments.

When bonds are sold between the interest payment dates, the issuing corporation collects from investors the interest that has accrued since the last interest payment date. When the next interest payment date arrives, the corporation pays the bondholders interest for the entire interest period.

When the end of a corporation's fiscal year does not fall on an interest payment date, the corporation must accrue bond interest expense from the last interest payment date to the end of its fiscal year. This accrual results in the inclusion of the interest expense in the year it is incurred.

REVIEW of Concepts and Terminology

The following concepts and terms were introduced in this chapter:

Bond: A security, usually long term, representing money that a corporation or other entity borrows from the investing public. **(LO2)**

Bond certificate: Evidence of an organization's debt to a bondholder. **(LO2)**

Bond indenture: A contract that defines the terms of a bond issue. **(LO2)**

Bond issue: The total value of bonds issued at one time. **(LO2)**

Callable bonds: Bonds that the issuing corporation can buy back and retire at a call price before their maturity dates. **(LO2)**

Call price: A specified price, usually above face value, at which a corporation can buy back its bonds before maturity. **(LO2)**

Capital lease: A long-term lease that resembles a purchase or sale on installment and in which the lessee assumes the risk of ownership. **(LO1)**

Convertible bonds: Bonds that can be exchanged for the issuing corporation's common stock. **(LO2)**

Coupon bonds: Bonds not registered with the issuing organization that bear coupons stating the amount of interest due and the payment date. **(LO2)**

Deferred income taxes: The result of using different methods to calculate income taxes for financial reporting and tax purposes. **(LO1)**

Discount: The amount by which a bond's face value exceeds its issue price, which occurs when the market interest rate is higher than the face interest rate. **(LO2)**

Early extinguishment of debt: The retirement of a bond issue before its maturity date. **(LO2)**

Effective interest method: A method of amortizing bond discounts or premiums that applies a constant interest rate (the market rate when the bonds were issued) to the bonds' carrying value at the beginning of each interest period. **(LO5)**

Face interest rate: The fixed rate of interest paid to bondholders based on the face value of the bonds. **(LO2)**

Financial leverage: A corporation's ability to increase earnings for stockholders by earning more on assets than it pays in interest on the debt it incurred to finance the assets. Also called *trading on equity*. **(LO1)**

Market interest rate: The rate of interest paid in the market on bonds of similar risk. Also called *effective interest rate*. **(LO2)**

Mortgage: A debt secured by real property. **(LO1)**

Off-balance-sheet financing: Structuring long-term debts in such a way that they do not appear as liabilities on the balance sheet. **(LO1)**

Operating lease: A short-term lease in which the risks of ownership remain with the lessor and for which payments are recorded as rent expense. **(LO1)**

Other postretirement benefits: Health care and other nonpension benefits paid after retirement but earned while the employee is still working. **(LO1)**

Pension fund: A fund established by the contributions of an employer and often of employees from which payments are made to employees after retirement or upon disability or death. **(LO1)**

Pension plan: A contract requiring a company to pay benefits to its employees after they retire. **(LO1)**

Premium: The amount by which a bond's issue price exceeds its face value, which occurs when the market interest rate is lower than the face interest rate. **(LO2)**

Registered bonds: Bonds that the issuing company registers in the names of the bondholders. **(LO2)**

Secured bonds: Bonds that carry a pledge of certain assets as a guarantee of repayment. **(LO2)**

Serial bonds: Bonds in one issue that mature on different dates. **(LO2)**

Straight-line method: A method of amortizing bond discounts or premiums that allocates the discount or premium equally over each interest period of the life of a bond. **(LO5)**

Term bonds: Bonds in one issue that mature at the same time. **(LO2)**

Unsecured bonds: Bonds issued on an organization's general credit. Also called *debenture bonds*. **(LO2)**

Zero coupon bonds: Bonds that do not pay periodic interest but that pay a fixed amount on the maturity date. **(LO5)**

Key Ratio

Interest coverage ratio: A measure of the degree of protection a company has from default on interest payments; (Income Before Income Taxes + Interest Expense) ÷ Interest Expense. **(LO1)**

REVIEW Problem

Accounting for a Bond Discount, Bond Retirement, and Bond Conversion

When Wilson Manufacturing Company wanted to expand its metal window division, it did not have enough capital to finance the project. To fund it, management sought and received approval from the board of directors to issue bonds. The bond indenture stated that the company would issue $2,500,000 of 8 percent, five-year bonds on January 1, 2009, and would pay interest semiannually, on June 30 and December 31 of each of the five years. It also stated that the bonds would be callable at 104 and that each $1,000 bond would be convertible to 30 shares of $10 par value common stock. Wilson sold the bonds on January 1, 2009, at 96 because the market rate of interest for similar investments was 9 percent. It decided to amortize the bond discount by using the effective interest method. On July 1, 2011, management called and retired half the bonds, and investors converted the other half to common stock.

Required

1. Prepare an interest and amortization schedule for the first five interest periods.
2. Prepare entries in journal form to record the sale of the bonds, the first two interest payments, the bond retirement, and the bond conversion.

Answer to Review Problem

1. Schedule for the first five interest periods:

	A	B	C–F	G–L	M	N	O
1	**Interest and Amortization of Bond Discount**						
2–3	**Semiannual Interest Payment Date**	**Carrying Value at Beginning of Period**	**Seminannual Interest Expense* (9% x 1/2)**	**Seminannual Interest Expense (8% x 1/2)**	**Amortization of Discount**	**Unamortized Bond Discount at End of Period**	**Carrying Value at End of Period**
4	Jan. 1, 2009					$100,000	$2,400,000
5	June 30, 2009	$2,400,000	$108,000	$100,000	$8,000	92,000	2,408,000
6	Dec. 31, 2009	2,408,000	108,360	100,000	8,360	83,640	2,416,360
7	June 30, 2010	2,416,360	108,736	100,000	8,736	74,904	2,425,096
8	Dec. 31, 2010	2,425,096	109,129	100,000	9,129	65,774 **	2,434,226
9	June 30, 2011	2,434,226	109,540	100,000	9,540	56,234	2,443,766
10							
11	*Rounded to the nearest dollar.						
12	**Rounded.						

2. Entries in journal form:

	A	B	C–E	F	G
1	2009				
2	Jan.	1	Cash	2,400,000	
3			Unamortized Bond Discount	100,000	
4			Bonds Payable		2,500,000
5			Sold $2,500,000 of 8%, 5-year bonds at 96		
6	June	30	Bond Interest Expense	108,000	
7			Unamortized Bond Discount		8,000
8			Cash		100,000
9			Paid semiannual interest and amortized		
10			the discount on 8%, 5-year bonds		

(continued)

A	B	C	D	E	F	G
2009						
Dec.	31	Bond Interest Expense			108,360	
			Unamortized Bond Discount			8,360
			Cash			100,000
				To record accrued semiannual interest and		
				amortize the discount on 8%, 5-year bonds		
2011						
July	1	Bonds Payable			1,250,000	
		Loss on Retirement of Bonds			78,118	
			Unamortized Bond Discount			28,118
			Cash			1,300,000
				Called $1,250,000 of 8% bonds and retired		
				them at 104 ($56,235 x 1/2 = $28,118*)		
		Bonds Payable			1,250,000	
			Unamortized Bond Discount			28,117
			Common Stock			375,000
			Additional Paid-in Capital			846,883
				Converted $1,250,000 of 8% bonds into		
				common stock		
				1,250 x 30 shares = 37,500 shares		
				37,500 shares x $10 = $375,000		
				$56,235 – $28,118 = $28,117		
				$1,250,000 – ($28,117 + $375,000) = $846,883		

CHAPTER ASSIGNMENTS

BUILDING Your Basic Knowledge and Skills

Short Exercises

LO1 **Bond Versus Common Stock Financing**

SE 1. Indicate whether each of the following is an advantage or a disadvantage of using long-term bond financing rather than issuing common stock.

1. Interest paid on bonds is tax-deductible.
2. Investments are sometimes not as successful as planned.
3. Financial leverage can have a negative effect when investments do not earn as much as the interest payments on the related debt.
4. Bondholders do not have voting rights in a corporation.
5. Positive financial leverage may be achieved.

LO1 **Types of Long-Term Liabilities**

SE 2. Place the number of the liability next to the statement to which it applies.

1. Bonds payable
2. Long-term notes
3. Mortgage payable
4. Long-term lease

____ a. May result in a capital lease
____ b. Differences in income taxes on accounting income and taxable income
____ c. The most popular form of long-term financing
____ d. Often used to purchase land and buildings

5. Pension liabilities ___ e. Often used interchangeably with bonds payable
6. Other postretirement benefits ___ f. Future health care costs are a major component
7. Deferred income taxes ___ g. May include 401(k), ESOPs, or profit-sharing

LO1 **Mortgage Payable**

SE 3. Karib Corporation purchased a building by signing a $150,000 long-term mortgage with monthly payments of $1,200. The mortgage carries an interest rate of 8 percent. Prepare a monthly payment schedule showing the monthly payment, the interest for the month, the reduction in debt, and the unpaid balance for the first three months. (Round to the nearest dollar.)

LO4 **Valuing Bonds Using Present Value**

SE 4. Rogers Paints, Inc., is considering the sale of two bond issues. Choice A is a $600,000 bond issue that pays semiannual interest of $32,000 and is due in 20 years. Choice B is a $600,000 bond issue that pays semiannual interest of $30,000 and is due in 15 years. Assume that the market interest rate for each bond is 12 percent. Calculate the amount that Rogers Paints will receive if both bond issues occur. (Calculate the present value of each bond issue and sum.)

LO3 LO5 **Straight-Line Method**

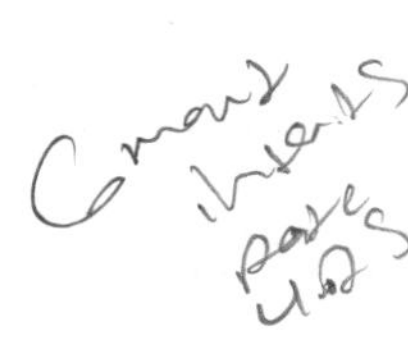

SE 5. On April 1, 2009, Morimoto Corporation issued $8,000,000 in 8.5 percent, five-year bonds at 98. The semiannual interest payment dates are April 1 and October 1. Prepare entries in journal form for the issue of the bonds by Morimoto on April 1, 2009, and the first two interest payments on October 1, 2009, and April 1, 2010. Use the straight-line method and ignore year-end accruals.

LO3 LO5 SO7 **Effective Interest Method**

SE 6. On March 1, 2010, Fast Freight Company sold $400,000 of its 9.5 percent, 20-year bonds at 106. The semiannual interest payment dates are March 1 and September 1. The market interest rate is 8.9 percent. The firm's fiscal year ends August 31. Prepare entries in journal form to record the sale of the bonds on March 1, the accrual of interest and amortization of premium on August 31, and the first interest payment on September 1. Use the effective interest method to amortize the premium.

SO6 **Bond Retirement**

SE 7. The Silk Corporation has outstanding $200,000 of 8 percent bonds callable at 104. On December 1, immediately after the payment of the semiannual interest and the amortization of the bond discount were recorded, the unamortized bond discount equaled $5,250. On that date, $120,000 of the bonds were called and retired. Prepare the entry to record the retirement of the bonds on December 1.

SO6 **Bond Conversion**

SE 8. The Tramot Corporation has $2,000,000 of 6 percent bonds outstanding. There is $40,000 of unamortized discount remaining on the bonds after the March 1, 2009, semiannual interest payment. The bonds are convertible at the rate of 20 shares of $10 par value common stock for each $1,000 bond. On March 1, 2009, bondholders presented $1,200,000 of the bonds for conversion. Prepare the entry to record the conversion of the bonds.

SO7

Bond Issue Between Interest Dates

SE 9. Downey Corporation sold $400,000 of 9 percent, ten-year bonds for face value on September 1, 2010. The issue date of the bonds was May 1, 2010. The company's fiscal year ends on December 31, and this is its only bond issue. Record the sale of the bonds on September 1 and the first semiannual interest payment on November 1, 2010. What is the bond interest expense for the year ended December 31, 2010?

LO3 LO5 SO7

Year-End Accrual of Bond Interest

SE 10. On October 1, 2010, Tender Corporation issued $500,000 of 9 percent bonds at 96. The bonds are dated October 1 and pay interest semiannually. The market rate of interest is 10 percent, and the company's year end is December 31. Prepare the entries to record the issuance of the bonds, the accrual of the interest on December 31, 2010, and the payment of the first semiannual interest on April 1, 2011. Assume the company uses the effective interest method to amortize the bond discount.

Exercises

LO1 LO2 SO6

Discussion Questions

E 1. Develop brief answers to each of the following questions:

1. How does a lender assess the risk that a borrower may default—that is, not pay interest and principal when due?
2. If a company with a high debt to equity ratio wants to increase its debt when the economy is weak, what kind of bond might it issue?
3. Why might a company lease a long-term asset rather than buy it and issue long-term bonds?
4. Why are callable and convertible bonds considered to add to management's future flexibility in financing a business?

LO3 LO4 LO5 SO7

Discussion Questions

E 2. Develop brief answers to each of the following questions:

1. What determines whether bonds are issued at a discount, premium, or face value?
2. Why does the market price of a bond vary over time?
3. When is it acceptable to use the straight-line method to amortize a bond discount or premium?
4. Why must the accrual of bond interest be recorded at the end of an accounting period?

LO1

Interest Coverage Ratio

E 3. Compute the interest coverage ratios for 2010 and 2011 from the partial income statements of Chimney Company that appear below. State whether the ratio improved or worsened over time.

	2011	2010
Income from operations	$23,890	$18,460
Interest expense	5,800	3,300
Income before income taxes	$18,090	$15,160
Income taxes	5,400	4,500
Net income	$12,690	$10,660

LO1 **Mortgage Payable**

E 4. Victory Corporation purchased a building by signing a $150,000 long-term mortgage with monthly payments of $2,000. The mortgage carries an interest rate of 12 percent.

1. Prepare a monthly payment schedule showing the monthly payment, the interest for the month, the reduction in debt, and the unpaid balance for the first three months. (Round to the nearest dollar.)
2. Prepare entries in journal form to record the purchase and the first two monthly payments.

LO1 **Recording Lease Obligations**

E 5. Tapas Corporation has leased a piece of equipment that has a useful life of 12 years. The terms of the lease are payments of $43,000 per year for 12 years. Tapas currently is able to borrow money at a long-term interest rate of 15 percent. (Round answers to the nearest dollar.)

1. Calculate the present value of the lease.
2. Prepare the entry to record the lease agreement.
3. Prepare the entry to record depreciation of the equipment for the first year using the straight-line method.
4. Prepare the entries to record the lease payments for the first two years.

LO4 **Valuing Bonds Using Present Value**

E 6. Avanti, Inc., is considering the sale of two bond issues. Choice A is an $800,000 bond issue that pays semiannual interest of $64,000 and is due in 20 years. Choice B is an $800,000 bond issue that pays semiannual interest of $60,000 and is due in 15 years. Assume that the market interest rate for each bond is 12 percent. Calculate the amount that Avanti, Inc., will receive if both bond issues are made. (**Hint:** Calculate the present value of each bond issue and sum.)

LO4 **Valuing Bonds Using Present Value**

E 7. Use the present value tables in the appendix on present value tables to calculate the issue price of a $300,000 bond issue in each of the following independent cases. Assume interest is paid semiannually.

a. A 10-year, 8 percent bond issue; the market interest rate is 10 percent.
b. A 10-year, 8 percent bond issue; the market interest rate is 6 percent.
c. A 10-year, 10 percent bond issue; the market interest rate is 8 percent.
d. A 20-year, 10 percent bond issue; the market interest rate is 12 percent.
e. A 20-year, 10 percent bond issue; the market interest rate is 6 percent.

LO4 **Zero Coupon Bonds**

E 8. The state of Ohio needs to raise $25,000,000 for highway repairs. Officials are considering issuing zero coupon bonds, which do not require periodic interest payments. The current market interest rate for the bonds is 10 percent. What face value of bonds must be issued to raise the needed funds, assuming the bonds will be due in 30 years and compounded annually? How would your answer change if the bonds were due in 50 years? How would both answers change if the market interest rate were 8 percent instead of 10 percent?

LO3 LO5 **Straight-Line Method**

E 9. DNA Corporation issued $4,000,000 in 10.5 percent, ten-year bonds on February 1, 2010, at 104. Semiannual interest payment dates are January 31 and July 31. Use the straight-line method and ignore year-end accruals.

1. With regard to the bond issue on February 1, 2010:
   a. How much cash is received?
   b. How much is Bonds Payable?
   c. What is the difference between **a** and **b** called and how much is it?
2. With regard to the bond interest payment on July 31, 2010:
   a. How much cash is paid in interest?
   b. How much is the amortization?
   c. How much is interest expense?
3. With regard to the bond interest payment on January 31, 2011:
   a. How much cash is paid in interest?
   b. How much is the amortization?
   c. How much is interest expense?

LO3 LO5

Straight-Line Method

E 10. Nina Corporation issued $8,000,000 in 8.5 percent, five-year bonds on March 1, 2010, at 96. The semiannual interest payment dates are September 1 and March 1. Prepare entries in journal form for the issue of the bonds by Nina on March 1, 2010, and the first two interest payments on September 1, 2010, and March 1, 2011. Use the straight-line method and ignore year-end accruals.

LO3 LO5

Effective Interest Method

E 11. Smart Toy Company sold $500,000 of 9.5 percent, 20-year bonds on April 1, 2009, at 106. The semiannual interest payment dates are March 31 and September 30. The market interest rate is 8.9 percent. The company's fiscal year ends September 30. Use the effective interest method to calculate the amortization.

1. With regard to the bond issue on April 1, 2009:
   a. How much cash is received?
   b. How much is Bonds Payable?
   c. What is the difference between **a** and **b** called and how much is it?
2. With regard to the bond interest payment on September 30, 2009:
   a. How much cash is paid in interest?
   b. How much is the amortization?
   c. How much is interest expense?
3. With regard to the bond interest payment on March 31, 2010:
   a. How much cash is paid in interest?
   b. How much is the amortization?
   c. How much is interest expense?

LO3 LO5

Effective Interest Method

E 12. On March 1, 2010, Knap Corporation issued $1,200,000 of 10 percent, five-year bonds. The semiannual interest payment dates are February 28 and August 31. Because the market rate for similar investments was 11 percent, the bonds had to be issued at a discount. The discount on the issuance of the bonds was $48,670. The company's fiscal year ends February 28. Prepare entries in journal form to record the bond issue on March 1, 2010, the payment of interest, and the amortization of the discount on August 31, 2010 and on February 28, 2011. Use the effective interest method. (Round answers to the nearest dollar.)

SO6

Bond Retirement

E 13. The Rondo Corporation has outstanding $400,000 of 8 percent bonds callable at 104. On September 1, immediately after recording the payment of the semiannual interest and the amortization of the discount, the unamortized bond discount equaled $10,500. On that date, $240,000 of the bonds was called and retired.

1. How much cash must be paid to retire the bonds?
2. Is there a gain or loss on retirement, and if so, how much is it?

SO6 **Bond Conversion**

E 14. The Jolly Corporation has $400,000 of 6 percent bonds outstanding. There is $20,000 of unamortized discount remaining on these bonds after the July 1, 2011, semiannual interest payment. The bonds are convertible at the rate of 20 shares of $5 par value common stock for each $1,000 bond. On July 1, 2011, bondholders presented $300,000 of the bonds for conversion.

1. Is there a gain or loss on conversion, and if so, how much is it?
2. How many shares of common stock are issued in exchange for the bonds?
3. In dollar amounts, how does this transaction affect the total liabilities and the total stockholders' equity of the company? In your answer, show the effects on four accounts.

LO5 SO7 **Effective Interest Method and Interest Accrual**

E 15. The long-term debt section of the Midwest Corporation's balance sheet at the end of its fiscal year, December 31, 2009, is as follows:

Long-term liabilities		
Bonds payable—8%, interest payable 1/1 and 7/1, due 12/31/16	$250,000	
Less unamortized bond discount	20,000	$230,000

Prepare entries in journal form relevant to the interest payments on July 1, 2010, December 31, 2010, and January 1, 2011. Assume a market interest rate of 10 percent.

LO4 SO6 **Time Value of Money and Early Extinguishment of Debt**

E 16. Anna's, Inc., has a $350,000, 8 percent bond issue that was issued a number of years ago at face value. There are now ten years left on the bond issue, and the market interest rate is 16 percent. Interest is paid semiannually. The company purchases the bonds on the open market at the calculated current market value and retires the bonds.

1. Using present value tables, calculate the current market value of the bond issue.
2. Is there a gain or loss on retirement of bonds, and if so, how much is it?

LO3 SO7 **Bond Issue on and Between Interest Dates**

E 17. Jigar Tech, Inc., is authorized to issue $1,800,000 in bonds on June 1. The bonds carry a face interest rate of 9 percent, which is to be paid on June 1 and December 1. Prepare entries in journal form for the issue of the bonds by Jigar Tech, Inc., under the assumptions that (a) the bonds are issued on September 1 at 100 and (b) the bonds are issued on June 1 at 105.

SO7 **Bond Issue Between Interest Dates**

E 18. Arif Corporation sold $400,000 of 12 percent, ten-year bonds at face value on September 1, 2010. The issue date of the bonds was May 1, 2010.

1. Record the sale of the bonds on September 1 and the first semiannual interest payment on November 1, 2010.
2. Arif's fiscal year ends on December 31, and this is its only bond issue. What is the bond interest expense for the year ended December 31, 2010?

LO3 LO5 SO7

Year-End Accrual of Bond Interest

E 19. Hinali Corporation issued $1,000,000 of 9 percent bonds on October 1, 2010, at 96. The bonds are dated October 1 and pay interest semiannually. The market interest rate is 10 percent, and Hinali's fiscal year ends on December 31. Prepare the entries to record the issuance of the bonds, the accrual of the interest on December 31, 2010, and the first semiannual interest payment on April 1, 2011. Assume the company uses the effective interest method to amortize the bond discount.

Problems

LO1

Lease Versus Purchase

P 1. Shen Corporation can either lease or buy a small garage next to its business that will provide parking for its customers. The company can lease the building for a period of 12 years, which approximates the useful life of the facility and thus qualifies as a capital lease. The terms of the lease are payments of $12,000 per year for 12 years. Shen currently is able to borrow money at a long-term interest rate of 9 percent. The company can purchase the building by signing an $80,000 long-term mortgage with monthly payments of $1,000. The mortgage also carries an interest rate of 9 percent.

Required

1. With regard to the lease option,
   a. Calculate the present value of the lease. (Round answers to the nearest dollar.)
   b. Prepare the entry to record the lease agreement.
   c. Prepare the entry to record depreciation of the equipment for the first year using the straight-line method.
   d. Prepare the entries to record the lease payments for the first two years.
2. With regard to the purchase option,
   a. Prepare a monthly payment schedule showing the monthly payment, the interest for the month, the reduction in debt, and the unpaid balance for the first three months. (Round to the nearest dollar.)
   b. Prepare entries in journal form to record the purchase and the first two monthly payments.

User insight ▶

3. Based on your calculations, which option seems to be best? Aside from cost, name an advantage and a disadvantage of each option.

LO1 LO2 LO3

Bond Terminology

P 2. Listed below are common terms associated with bonds:

a. Bond certificate
b. Bond issue
c. Bond indenture
d. Unsecured bonds
e. Debenture bonds
f. Secured bonds
g. Term bonds
h. Serial bonds
i. Registered bonds
j. Coupon bonds
k. Callable bonds
l. Convertible bonds
m. Face interest rate
n. Market interest rate
o. Effective interest rate
p. Bond premium
q. Bond discount

Required

1. For each of the following statements, identify the term with which it is associated. (If more than one statement applies, choose the term with which it is most closely associated.)
    1. Occurs when bonds are sold at more than face value
    2. Rate of interest that will vary depending on economic conditions
    3. Bonds that may be exchanged for common stock
    4. Bonds that are not registered
    5. A bond issue in which all bonds are due on the same date
    6. Occurs when bonds are sold at less than face value
    7. Rate of interest that will be paid regardless of market conditions
    8. Bonds that may be retired at management's option
    9. A document that is evidence of a company's debt
    10. Same as market rate of interest
    11. Bonds for which the company knows who owns them
    12. A bond issue for which bonds are due at different dates
    13. The total value of bonds issued at one time
    14. Bonds whose payment involves a pledge of certain assets
    15. Same as debenture bonds
    16. Contains the terms of the bond issue
    17. Bonds issued on the general credit of the company

User insight ▶ 2. What effect will a decrease in interest rates below the face interest rate and before a bond is issued have on the cash received from the bond issue? What effect will the decrease have on interest expense? What effect will the decrease have on the amount of cash paid for interest?

Bond Basics—Straight-Line Method, Retirement and Conversion

P 3. Murcia Corporation has $4,000,000 of 9.5 percent, 25-year bonds dated May 1, 2009, with interest payable on April 30 and October 31. The company's fiscal year ends on December 31, and it uses the straight-line method to amortize bond premiums or discounts. The bonds are callable after ten years at 103 or convertible into 40 shares of $10 par value common stock.

Required

1. Assume the bonds are issued at 103.5 on May 1, 2009.
    a. How much cash is received?
    b. How much is Bonds Payable?
    c. What is the difference between **a** and **b** called and how much is it?
    d. With regard to the bond interest payment on October 31, 2009:
        (1) How much cash is paid in interest?
        (2) How much is the amortization?
        (3) How much is interest expense?
2. Assume the bonds are issued at 96.5 on May 1, 2009.
    a. How much cash is received?
    b. How much is Bonds Payable?
    c. What is the difference between **a** and **b** called and how much is it?
    d. With regard to the bond interest payment on October 31, 2009:
        (1) How much cash is paid in interest?
        (2) How much is the amortization?
        (3) How much is interest expense?
3. Assume the issue price in requirement **1** and that the bonds are called and retired ten years later.
    a. How much cash will have to be paid to retire the bonds?

   b. Is there a gain or loss on the retirement? If there is a gain or loss, how much is it?
4. Assume the issue price in requirement **2** and that the bonds are converted to common stock ten years later.
   a. Is there a gain or loss on conversion, and if so, how much is it?
   b. How many shares of common stock are issued in exchange for the bonds?
   c. In dollar amounts, how does this transaction affect the total liabilities and the total stockholders' equity of the company? In your answer, show the effects on four accounts.

User insight ▶

5. Assume that after ten years market interest rates have dropped significantly and that the price of the company's common stock has risen significantly. Also assume that management wants to improve its credit rating by reducing its debt to equity ratio and that it needs what cash it currently has for expansion. Would management prefer the approach and result in requirement **3** or **4**? Explain your answer. What would be a disadvantage of the approach you chose?

LO3 LO5

Bond Transactions—Effective Interest Method

P 4. Dygat Corporation has $10,000,000 of 10.5 percent, 20-year bonds dated June 1, 2010 with interest payment dates of May 31 and November 30. The company's fiscal year ends November 30. It uses the effective interest method to amortize bond premiums or discounts.

Required

1. Assume the bonds are issued at 103 on June 1 to yield an effective interest rate of 10.1 percent. Prepare entries in journal form for June 1, 2010, November 30, 2010, and May 31, 2011. (Round amounts to the nearest dollar.)
2. Assume the bonds are issued at 97 on June 1 to yield an effective interest rate of 10.9 percent. Prepare entries in journal form for June 1, 2010, November 30, 2010, and May 31, 2011. (Round amounts to the nearest dollar.)

User insight ▶

3. Explain the role that market interest rates play in causing a premium in requirement **1** and a discount in requirement **2**.

Bonds Issued at a Discount and a Premium—Effective Interest Method

P 5. Johnson Corporation issued bonds twice during 2010. The transactions were as follows:

2010		
Jan.	1	Issued $1,000,000 of 9.2 percent, ten-year bonds dated January 1, 2010, with interest payable on June 30 and December 31. The bonds were sold at 98.1, resulting in an effective interest rate of 9.5 percent.
Apr.	1	Issued $2,000,000 of 9.8 percent, ten-year bonds dated April 1, 2010, with interest payable on March 31 and September 30. The bonds were sold at 101, resulting in an effective interest rate of 9.5 percent.
June	30	Paid semiannual interest on the January 1 issue and amortized the discount, using the effective interest method.
Sept.	30	Paid semiannual interest on the April 1 issue and amortized the premium, using the effective interest method.
Dec.	31	Paid semiannual interest on the January 1 issue and amortized the discount, using the effective interest method.
	31	Made an end-of-year adjusting entry to accrue interest on the April 1 issue and to amortize half the premium applicable to the second interest period.

2011
Mar. 31 Paid semiannual interest on the April 1 issue and amortized the premium applicable to the second half of the second interest period.

Required

1. Prepare entries in journal form to record the bond transactions. (Round amounts to the nearest dollar.)

User insight ▶

2. Describe the effect of the above transactions on profitability and liquidity by answering the following questions.
   a. What is the total interest expense in 2010 for each of the bond issues?
   b. What is the total cash paid in 2010 for each of the bond issues?
   c. What differences, if any, do you observe and how do you explain them?

Alternate Problems

Bond Basics—Straight-line Method, Retirement, and Conversion

P 6. Golden Corporation has $20,000,000 of 10.5 percent, 20-year bonds dated June 1, 2010, with interest payment dates of May 31 and November 30. After ten years the bonds are callable at 104, and each $1,000 bond is convertible into 25 shares of $20 par value common stock. The company's fiscal year ends on December 31. It uses the straight-line method to amortize bond premiums or discounts.

Required

1. Assume the bonds are issued at 103 on June 1, 2010.
   a. How much cash is received?
   b. How much is Bonds Payable?
   c. What is the difference between **a** and **b** called and how much is it?
   d. With regard to the bond interest payment on November 30, 2010:
      (1) How much cash is paid in interest?
      (2) How much is the amortization?
      (3) How much is interest expense?
2. Assume the bonds are issued at 97 on June 1, 2010.
   a. How much cash is received?
   b. How much is Bonds Payable?
   c. What is the difference between **a** and **b** called and how much is it?
   d. With regard to the bond interest payment on November 30, 2010:
      (1) How much cash is paid in interest?
      (2) How much is the amortization?
      (3) How much is interest expense?
3. Assume the issue price in requirement **1** and that the bonds are called and retired ten years later.
   a. How much cash will have to be paid to retire the bonds?
   b. Is there a gain or loss on the retirement, and if so, how much is it?
4. Assume the issue price in requirement **2** and that the bonds are converted to common stock ten years later.
   a. Is there a gain or loss on the conversion, and if so, how much is it?
   b. How many shares of common stock are issued in exchange for the bonds?
   c. In dollar amounts, how does this transaction affect the total liabilities and the total stockholders' equity of the company? In your answer, show the effects on four accounts.

User insight ▶

5. Assume that after ten years, market interest rates have dropped significantly and that the price of the company's common stock has risen significantly.

Also assume that management wants to improve its credit rating by reducing its debt to equity ratio and that it needs what cash it has for expansion. Which approach would management prefer—the approach and result in requirement **3** or **4**? Explain your answer. What would be a disadvantage of the approach you chose?

LO3 LO5

Effective Interest Method

P 7. Jose Corporation has $4,000,000 of 9.5 percent, 25-year bonds dated March 1, 2010, with interest payable on February 28 and August 31. The company's fiscal year end is February 28. It uses the effective interest method to amortize bond premiums or discounts. (Round amounts to the nearest dollar.)

Required

1. Assume the bonds are issued at 102.5 on March 1, 2010, to yield an effective interest rate of 9.2 percent. Prepare entries in journal form for March 1, 2010, August 31, 2010, and February 28, 2011.
2. Assume the bonds are issued at 97.5 on March 1, 2010, to yield an effective interest rate of 9.8 percent. Prepare entries in journal form for March 1, 2010, August 31, 2010, and February 28, 2011.

User insight ▶

3. Explain the role that market interest rates play in causing a premium in requirement **1** and a discount in requirement **2**.

LO3 LO5 SO7

Bonds Issued at a Discount and a Premium—Effective Interest Method

P 8. Rago Corporation issued bonds twice during 2010. A summary of the transactions involving the bonds follows.

2010		
Jan.	1	Issued $3,000,000 of 9.9 percent, ten-year bonds dated January 1, 2010, with interest payable on June 30 and December 31. The bonds were sold at 102.6, resulting in an effective interest rate of 9.4 percent.
Mar.	1	Issued $2,000,000 of 9.2 percent, ten-year bonds dated March 1, 2010, with interest payable March 1 and September 1. The bonds were sold at 98.2, resulting in an effective interest rate of 9.5 percent.
June	30	Paid semiannual interest on the January 1 issue and amortized the premium, using the effective interest method.
Sept.	1	Paid semiannual interest on the March 1 issue and amortized the discount, using the effective interest method.
Dec.	31	Paid semiannual interest on the January 1 issue and amortized the premium, using the effective interest method.
	31	Made an end-of-year adjusting entry to accrue interest on the March 1 issue and to amortize two-thirds of the discount applicable to the second interest period.
2011		
Mar.	1	Paid semiannual interest on the March 1 issue and amortized the remainder of the discount applicable to the second interes period.

Required

1. Prepare entries in journal form to record the bond transacti amounts to the nearest dollar.)

User insight ▶ 2. Describe the effect on profitability and liquidity by answering the following questions.

a. What is the total interest expense in 2010 for each of the bond issues?
b. What is the total cash paid in 2010 for each of the bond issues?
c. What differences, if any, do you observe and how do you explain these differences?

ENHANCING Your Knowledge, Skills, and Critical Thinking

Conceptual Understanding Cases

Effect of Long-Term Leases

C 1. Many companies use long-term leases to finance long-term assets. Although these leases are similar to mortgage payments, they are structured in such a way that they qualify as operating leases. As a result, the lease commitments do not appear on the companies' balance sheets.

In a recent year, **Continental Airlines** had almost $20 billion in total operating lease commitments, of which $1.5 billion was due in the current year. Further, the airline had total assets of $11.3 billion and total liabilities of $11.0 billion. Because of heavy losses in previous years, its stockholders' equity was only $0.3 billion.[15]

What effect do these types of leases have on the balance sheet? Why would the use of these long-term leases make a company's debt to equity ratio, interest coverage ratio, and free cash flow look better than they really are? What is a capital lease? How does the application of capital lease accounting provide insight into a company's financial health?

LO2 LO6

Bond Issue

C 2. Eastman Kodak, the photography company, issued a $1 billion bond issue. Even though the company's credit rating was low, the bond issue was well received by the investment community because the company offered attractive terms. The offering comprised $500 million of 10-year unsecured notes and $500 million of 30-year convertible bonds. The convertibles were callable after seven years and would be convertible into common stock about 40 to 45 percent higher than the current price.[16]

What are unsecured notes? Why would they carry a relatively high interest rate? What are convertible securities? Why are they good for the investor and for the company? Why would they carry a relatively low interest rate? What does *callable* mean? What advantage does this feature give the company?

LO2 LO3

Bond Interest Rates and Market Prices

C 3. Dow Chemical is one of the largest chemical companies in the world. Among its long-term liabilities was a bond due in 2011 that carried a face interest rate of 6.125 percent.[17] Recently, this bond sold on the New York Stock Exchange at 104⅜.

Did this bond sell at a discount or a premium? Assuming the bond was originally issued at face value, did interest rates rise or decline after the date of issue? Would you have expected the market rate of interest on this bond to be more or less than 6.125 percent? Did the current market price affect either the amount that the company paid in semiannual interest or the amount of interest expense for the same period? Explain your answers.

Interpreting Financial Reports

Leverage, Debt to Equity and Financial Risk

C 4. *The Wall Street Journal* reported recently that many public companies are "loading up on debt to improve returns for the shareholders. . . . **Domino's Pizza Inc.**, **Health Management Associates, Inc.**, and **Dean Foods Co.** unveiled plans to take on significant debt and distribute much of their cash to shareholders through dividends or one-time share buybacks. This is resulting in higher leverage [and] making the per-share earnings they report look better."[18] With higher earnings per share, the price of the companies' stock should go up.

What is leverage? Why does this plan result in higher leverage and what ratio reflects the higher leverage? Will the companies have more or less financial risk after these transactions? Why will this plan make earnings per share look better?

LO2

Characteristics of Convertible Debt

C 5. **Amazon.com, Inc.**, gained fame as an online marketplace for books, records, and other products. Although the increase in its stock price was initially meteoric, only recently has the company begun to earn a profit. To support its enormous growth, Amazon.com issued $500,000,000 in 6.845 percent convertible notes due in 2010 at face value. Interest is payable on February 1 and August 1. The notes are convertible into common stock at a price of $112 per share, which at the time of issue was above the market price. The market value of Amazon.com's common stock has been quite volatile, from $39 to $95 in 2007.[19]

What reasons can you suggest for Amazon.com's management choosing notes that are convertible into common stock rather than simply issuing nonconvertible notes or issuing common stock directly? Are there any disadvantages to this approach? If the price of the company's common stock goes to $100 per share, what would be the total theoretical value of the notes? If the holders of the notes were to elect to convert the notes into common stock, what would be the effect on the company's debt to equity ratio, and what would be the effect on the percentage ownership of the company by other stockholders?

Decision Analysis Using Excel

Issuance of Long-Term Bonds Versus Leasing

C 6. The Fertile Corporation plans to build or lease a new plant that will produce liquid fertilizer for the agricultural market. The plant is expected to cost $800,000,000 and will be located in the southwestern United States. The company's chief financial officer, Sharon Weiss, has spent the last several weeks studying different means of financing the plant. Following her talks with bankers and other financiers, she has decided that there are two basic choices: the plant can be financed through the issuance of a long-term bond or through a long-term lease. Details for the two options are as follows:

1. Issue $800,000,000 of 25-year, 16 percent bonds secured by the new plant. Interest on the bonds would be payable semiannually.
2. Sign a 25-year lease for an existing plant calling for lease payments of $65,400,000 on a semiannual basis.

Weiss wants to know what effect each choice would have on the company's financial statements. She estimates that the useful life of the plant is 25 years, at which time the plant is expected to have an estimated residual value of $80,000,000.

Weiss is planning a meeting to discuss the alternatives. Write a short memorandum to her identifying the issues that should be considered at this meeting.

(**Note:** You are not asked to make any calculations, discuss the factors, or recommend an action.)

Annual Report Case: CVS Caremark Corporation

LO1 **Business Practice, Long-Term Debt, Leases, and Pensions**

C 7. To answer the following questions, refer to the financial statements and the notes to the financial statements in the **CVS** annual report in the Supplement to Chapter 1:

1. Is it the practice of CVS to own or lease most of its buildings?
2. Does CVS lease property predominantly under capital leases or under operating leases? How much was rental expense for operating leases in 2007?
3. Does CVS have a defined benefit pension plan? Does it offer postretirement benefits?

Comparison Case: CVS Versus Southwest

LO1 **Use of Debt Financing**

C 8. Refer to the **CVS** annual report and the financial statements of **Southwest Airlines Co.** in the Supplement to Chapter 1. Calculate the debt to equity ratio and the interest coverage ratio for both companies' two most recent years. Find the note to the financial statements that contains information on leases and lease commitments by CVS. Southwest's lease expenses were $469 million and $433 million in 2006 and 2007, respectively, and total lease commitments for future years were $2,339 million. What effect do the total lease commitments and lease expense have on your assessment of the ratios you calculated? Evaluate and comment on the relative performance of the two companies with regard to debt financing. Which company has more risk of not being able to meet its interest obligations? How does leasing affect the analysis? Explain.

Ethical Dilemma Case

LO2 **Bond Indenture and Ethical Reporting**

C 9. Bio-Phar Technology, Inc., a biotech company, has a $24,000,000 bond issue outstanding. The bond indenture has several restrictive provisions, including requirements that current assets exceed current liabilities by a ratio of 2 to 1 and that income before income taxes exceed the annual interest on the bonds by a ratio of 3 to 1. If those requirements are not met, the bondholders can force the company into bankruptcy. The company is still awaiting Food and Drug Administration (FDA) approval of its new product, CMZ-12, a cancer treatment drug. Management has been counting on sales of CMZ-12 this year to meet the provisions of the bond indenture. As the end of the fiscal year approaches, the company does not have sufficient current assets or income before income taxes to meet the requirements.

Joan Miller, the chief financial officer, proposes, "Since we can assume that FDA approval will occur early next year, I suggest we book sales and receivables from our major customers now in anticipation of next year's sales. This action will increase our current assets and our income before income taxes. It is essential that we do this to save the company. Look at all the people who will be hurt if we don't do it."

Is Miller's proposal acceptable accounting? Is it ethical? Who could be harmed by it? What steps might management take?

Internet Case

LO2

Bond Rating Changes

C 10. During economic or industry recessions, it is common to see downward revisions of bond ratings. Access Standard & Poor's list of companies with lowered bond ratings and identify three whose names you recognize. Based on your general knowledge of these companies, give reasons that you believe contributed to the downgrade of the ratings.

Group Activity Case

LO4

Nature of Zero Coupon Notes

C 11. *The Wall Street Journal* reported, "Financially ailing **Trans World Airlines** has renegotiated its agreement to sell its 40 landing and takeoff slots and three gates at O'Hare International Airport to **American Airlines**."[20] Instead of receiving a lump-sum cash payment in the amount of $162.5 million, TWA elected to receive a zero coupon note from American that would be paid off in monthly installments over a 20-year period. Since the 240 monthly payments totaled $500 million, TWA placed a value of $500 million on the note and indicated that the bankruptcy court would not have accepted the lower lump-sum cash payment.[21]

Divide into groups to discuss the following questions:

1. How does this zero coupon note differ from the zero coupon bonds that were described earlier in this chapter?
2. How do you explain the difference between the $162.5 million cash payment and the $500 million note?
3. Do you think TWA was right in placing a $500 million price on the sale?

Business Communication Case

LO1

Comparison of Interest Coverage

C 12. Japanese companies have historically relied more on debt financing and are more highly leveraged than U.S. companies, but this has changed for some of the most successful companies. Assume you have been asked to assess the riskiness of **Sony Corporation** and **Panasonic Co.**, two large Japanese electronics companies with debt to equity ratios of about 2.3 and 1.1, respectively, in 2007.[22] From the selected data from the companies' annual reports shown in the table that follows (in millions of yen), compute the interest coverage ratios for the two companies for the two years.

	Sony		Panasonic	
	2007	2006	2007	2006
Interest expense	24,578	28,996	21,686	22,827
Income before income taxes	157,207	286,329	371,312	246,913

Write a one-page memorandum that assesses the risk of default on debt payments of the companies. Compare debt to equity to the computer industry in Figure 1. Also, compute interest coverage ratios for each company for the two years. Use the rule of thumb measures mentioned in the text in your evaluation.

CHAPTER

11 Contributed Capital

Focus on Financial Statements

INCOME STATEMENT

Revenues

– Expenses

= Net Income

STATEMENT OF RETAINED EARNINGS

Opening Balance

+ Net Income

– Dividends

= Retained Earnings

BALANCE SHEET

Assets	Liabilities
	Equity

A = L + E

STATEMENT OF CASH FLOWS

Operating activities
+ Investing activities
+ Financing activities
= Change in Cash
+ Starting Balance
= Ending Cash Balance

Sale/repurchase of capital stock and payment of cash dividends on the balance sheet are financing activities on the statement of cash flows.

In the last chapter, we focused on long-term *debt* financing. Here, we focus on long-term *equity* financing—that is, on the capital that stockholders contribute to a corporation. The issues involved in equity financing—including the type of stock a corporation issues, the dividends that it pays, and the treasury stock that it purchases—can significantly affect return on equity and other measures of profitability on which management's compensation is based. Thus, as with the management issues involved in long-term debt financing, ethics is a major concern. Management's decisions must be based not on personal gain, but on the value created for the corporation's owners.

LEARNING OBJECTIVES

LO1 Identify and explain the management issues related to contributed capital. *(pp. 566–574)*

LO2 Identify the components of stockholders' equity. *(pp. 575–578)*

LO3 Identify the characteristics of preferred stock. *(pp. 578–582)*

LO4 Account for the issuance of stock for cash and other assets. *(pp. 582–585)*

LO5 Account for treasury stock. *(pp. 585–588)*

DECISION POINT ▶ A USER'S FOCUS

Google, Inc.

When a company issues stock to the public for the first time, it is called an **initial public offering (IPO)**. There are many initial public offerings in any given year, but when **Google**, the popular Internet search engine company, went to market with its IPO in August 2004, it created a national sensation for two reasons. First, it was the largest IPO by an Internet company after the tech-bust in 2001 and 2002. Second, Google provides a very well known and widely used search service. Those who were fortunate enough to get shares saw the price per share soar to $135 in a few days and reach $700 per share in 2008 before dropping down to between $400 and $500. Google's Financial Highlights show the components of Google's stockholders' equity.[1]

GOOGLE'S FINANCIAL HIGHLIGHTS (In thousands)

	Dec. 31 2007	Dec. 31 2006
Stockholders' equity		
Preferred stock	$ —	$ —
Common stock	313	309
Additional paid-in capital	13,241,221	11,882,906
Retained earnings	9,334,772	5,133,314
Other items	113,373	23,311
Total stockholders' equity	$ 22,689,679	$ 17,039,840
Total assets	$ 25,335,806	$ 18,473,351

- ▶ Why did Google's management choose to issue common stock to satisfy its needs for new capital?
- ▶ What are some of the advantages and disadvantages of this approach to financing a business?
- ▶ What measures should an investor use in evaluating management's performance?

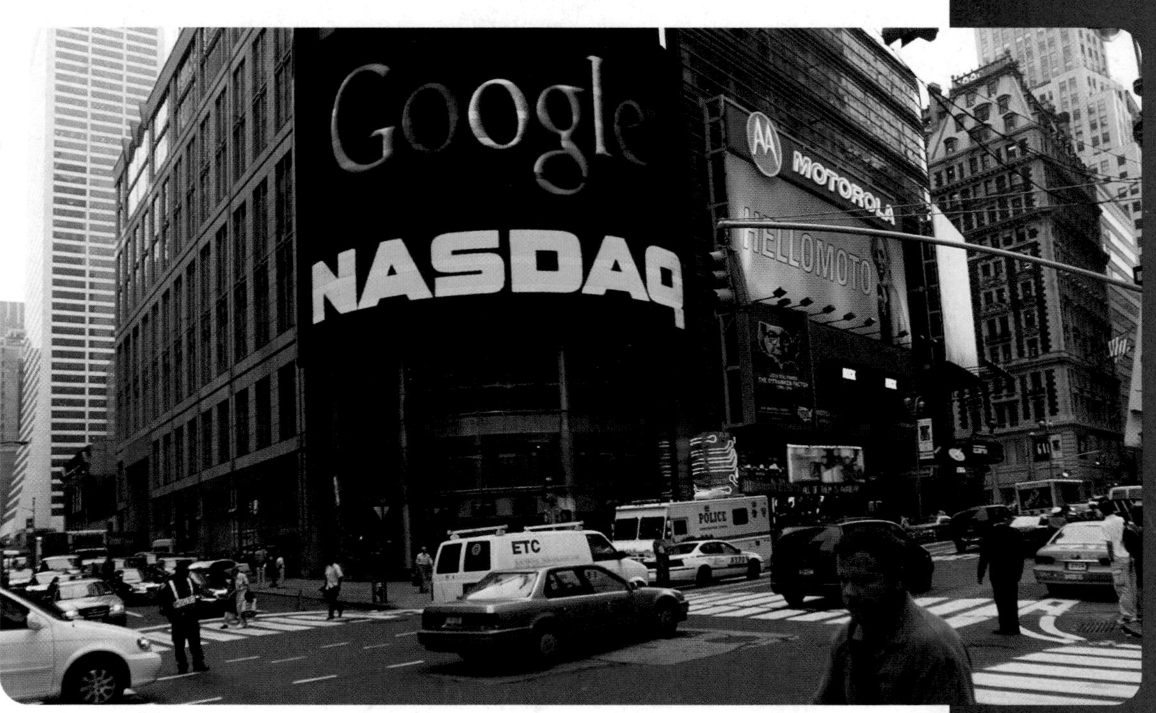

Management Issues Related to Contributed Capital

LO1 Identify and explain the management issues related to contributed capital.

In Chapter 1, we defined a *corporation* as a business unit chartered by the state and legally separate from its owners—that is, its stockholders. *Contributed capital*, which refers to stockholders' investments in a corporation, is a major means of financing a corporation. Managing contributed capital requires an understanding of the advantages and disadvantages of the corporate form of business and of the issues involved in equity financing. It also requires familiarity with dividend policies, with how to use return on equity to evaluate performance, and with stock option plans.

The Corporate Form of Business

The corporate form of business is well suited to today's trends toward large organizations, international trade, and professional management. Although fewer in number than sole proprietorships and partnerships, corporations dominate the U.S. economy in part because of their ability to raise large amounts of capital. Figure 1 shows the amount and sources of capital that corporations have raised in recent years. As you can see, the amount increased dramatically after 1995. In 2004, the amount of new corporate capital was $2,859 billion. Of this amount, $2,656 billion, or 93 percent, came from new bond issues; $170 billion, or 6 percent, came from new common stock issues; and $33 billion, or 1 percent, came from preferred stock issues.

Advantages of Incorporation Managers of a corporation must be familiar with the advantages and disadvantages of this form of business. Some of the advantages are as follows:

- **Separate Legal Entity** As a separate legal entity, a corporation can buy and sell property, sue other parties, enter into contracts, hire and fire employees, and be taxed.
- **Limited Liability** Because a corporation is a legal entity, separate from its owners, its creditors can satisfy their claims only against the assets of the corporation, not against the personal property of the corporation's owners. Because the owners are not responsible for the corporation's debts, their liability is limited to the amount of their investment. In contrast, the personal property of sole proprietors and partners generally is available to creditors.
- **Ease of Capital Generation** It is fairly easy for a corporation to raise capital because shares of ownership in the business are available to a great number of potential investors for a small amount of money. As a result, a single corporation can have many owners.
- **Ease of Transfer of Ownership** A **share of stock**, a unit of ownership in a corporation, is easily transferable. A stockholder can normally buy and sell shares without affecting the corporation's activities or needing the approval of other owners.
- **Lack of Mutual Agency** Mutual agency is not a characteristic of the corporate form of business. If a stockholder tries to enter into a contract for the corporation, the corporation is not bound by the contract. But in a partnership, because of mutual agency, all the partners can be bound by one partner's actions.
- **Continuous Existence** Because a corporation is a separate legal entity, an owner's death, incapacity, or withdrawal does not affect the life of the corporation. A corporation's life is set by its charter and regulated by state laws.

FIGURE 1
Sources of Capital Raised by Corporations in the United States

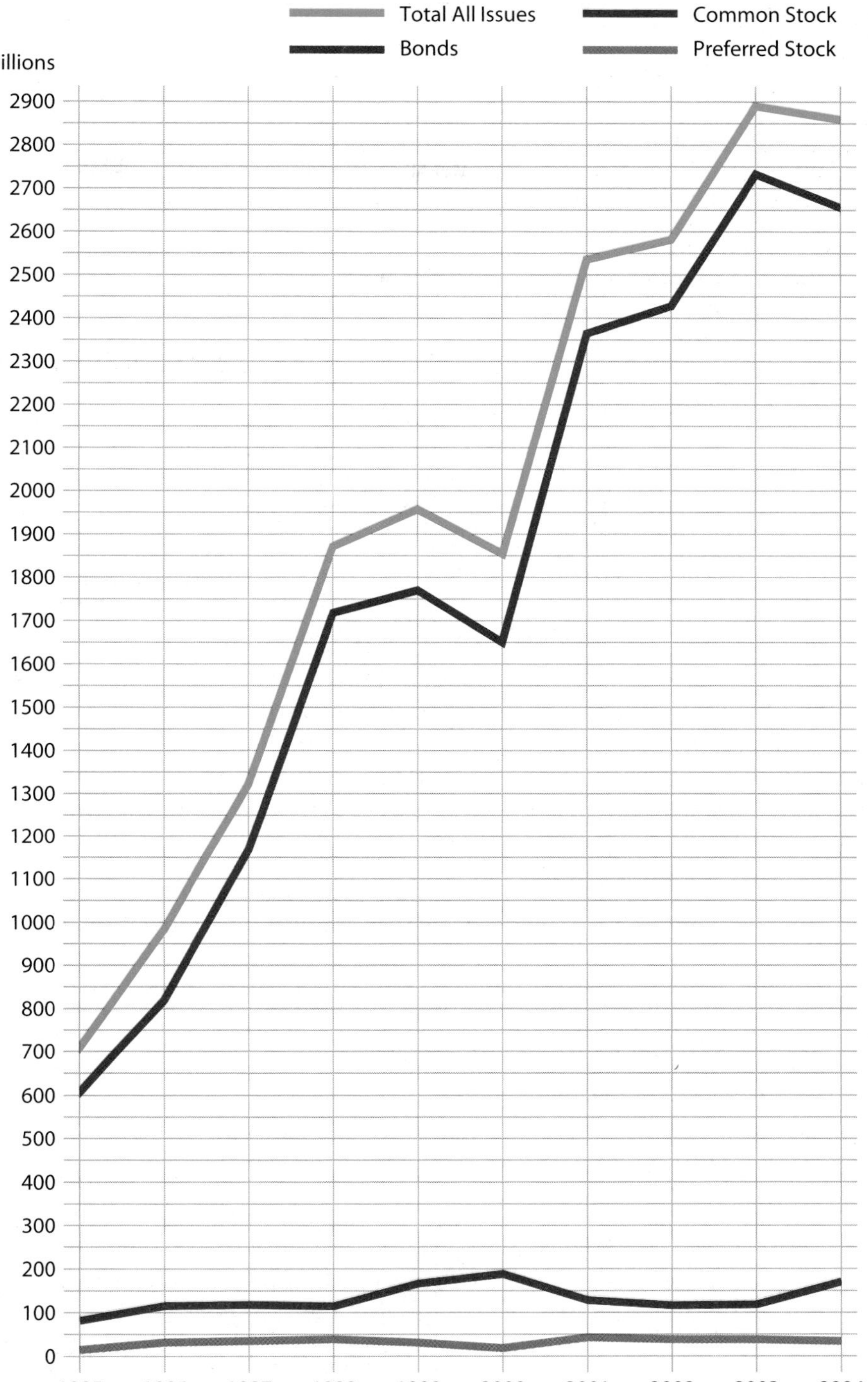

Source: "Sources of Capital Raised by Corporations in the United States" from *Securities Industry Yearbook 2004–2005*. Reprinted by permission of Securities Industry Association.

Centralized Authority and Responsibility The board of directors represents the stockholders and delegates the responsibility and authority for the day-to-day operation of the corporation to a single person, usually the president. Operating power is not divided among the many owners of the business. The president may delegate authority over certain segments of the business to others, but he or she is held accountable to the board of directors. If the board is dissatisfied with the performance of the president, it can replace that person.

- **Professional Management** Large corporations have many owners, the vast majority of whom are unequipped to make timely decisions about business operations. So, in most cases, management and ownership are separate. This allows a corporation to hire the best talent available to manage the business.

Disadvantages of Incorporation The disadvantages of corporations include the following:

- **Government Regulation** Corporations must meet the requirements of state laws. As "creatures of the state," they are subject to greater state control and regulation than are other forms of business. They must file many reports with the state in which they are chartered. Publicly held corporations must also file reports with the Securities and Exchange Commission and with the stock exchanges on which they are listed. Meeting these requirements is very costly.
- **Taxation** A major disadvantage of the corporate form of business is **double taxation**. Because a corporation is a separate legal entity, its earnings are subject to federal and state income taxes, which may be as much as 35 percent of corporate earnings. If any of the corporation's after-tax earnings are paid out as dividends, the earnings are taxed again as income to the stockholders. In contrast, the earnings of sole proprietorships and partnerships are taxed only once, as personal income to the owners.
- **Limited Liability** Although limited liability is an advantage of incorporation, it can also be a disadvantage. Limited liability restricts the ability of a small corporation to borrow money. Because creditors can lay claim only to the assets of a corporation, they may limit their loans to the level secured by those assets or require stockholders to guarantee the loans personally.
- **Separation of Ownership and Control** Just as limited liability can be a drawback, so can the separation of ownership and control. Management sometimes makes decisions that are not good for the corporation as a whole. Poor communication can also make it hard for stockholders to exercise control over the corporation or even to recognize that management's decisions are harmful.

Study Note

Among the agencies that regulate corporations are the Public Company Accounting Oversight Board (PCAOB), Securities and Exchange Commission (SEC), the Occupational Safety and Health Administration (OSHA), the Federal Trade Commission (FTC), the Environmental Protection Agency (EPA), the Nuclear Regulatory Commission (NRC), the Equal Employment Opportunity Commission (EEOC), the Interstate Commerce Commission (ICC), the National Transportation Safety Board (NTSB), the Federal Aviation Administration (FAA), and the Federal Communications Commission (FCC).

Study Note

Lenders to a small corporation may require the corporation's officers to sign a promissory note, which makes them personally liable for the debt.

Equity Financing

Equity financing is accomplished through the issuance of stock to investors in exchange for assets, usually cash. Once the stock has been issued to them, the stockholders can transfer their ownership at will. When they do, they must sign their **stock certificates**, documents showing the number of shares that they own, and send them to the corporation's secretary. In large corporations that are listed on the stock exchanges, stockholders' records are hard to maintain. Such companies can have millions of shares of stock, thousands of which change ownership every day. Therefore, they often appoint independent registrars and transfer agents (usually banks and trust companies) to help perform the secretary's duties. The outside agents are responsible for transferring the corporation's stock, maintaining stockholders' records, preparing a list of stockholders for stockholders' meetings, and paying dividends.

Par value and *legal capital* are important terms in equity financing:

- **Par value** is an arbitrary amount assigned to each share of stock. It must be recorded in the capital stock accounts, and it constitutes a corporation's legal capital.
- **Legal capital** is the number of shares issued times the par value. It is the minimum amount that a corporation can report as contributed capital.

Par value usually bears little if any relationship to the market value or book value of the shares. For example, although **Google's** stock initially sold for $85 per share and the market value is now much higher, its par value per share is only $.001. Google's legal capital is only about $313,000 (313 million shares × $.001) even though the total market value of its shares exceeds $150 billion.

To help with its initial public offering (IPO), a corporation often uses an **underwriter**—an intermediary between the corporation and the investing public. For a fee—usually less than 1 percent of the selling price—the underwriter guarantees the sale of the stock. The corporation records the amount of the net proceeds of the offering—what the public paid less the underwriter's fees, legal and printing expenses, and any other direct costs of the offering—in its capital stock and additional paid-in capital accounts. Because of the size of its IPO, Google used a group of investment banks headed by two well-known investment bankers, **Morgan Stanley** and **Credit Suisse First Boston**.

The costs of forming a corporation are called **start-up and organization costs**. These costs, which are incurred before a corporation begins operations, include state incorporation fees and attorneys' fees for drawing up the articles of incorporation. They also include the cost of printing stock certificates, accountants' fees for registering the firm's initial stock, and other expenditures necessary for the formation of the corporation. Because Google's IPO was so large, the fees of the lawyers, accountants, and underwriters who helped arrange the IPO amounted to millions of dollars.

Study Note

Start-up and organization costs are expensed when incurred.

Theoretically, start-up and organization costs benefit the entire life of a corporation. For that reason, a case can be made for recording them as intangible assets and amortizing them over the life of the corporation. However, a corporation's life normally is not known, so accountants expense start-up and organization costs as they are incurred.

Advantages of Equity Financing Financing a business by issuing common stock has several advantages:

- It is less risky than financing with bonds because a company does not pay dividends on common stock unless the board of directors decides to pay them. In contrast, if a company does not pay interest on bonds, it can be forced into bankruptcy.
- When a company does not pay a cash dividend, it can plow the cash generated by profitable operations back into the company's operations. **Google**, for instance, does not currently pay any dividends, and its issuance of common stock provides it with funds for expansion.
- A company can use the proceeds of a common stock issue to maintain or improve its debt to equity ratio.

Disadvantages of Equity Financing Issuing common stock also has certain disadvantages:

- Unlike interest on bonds, dividends paid on stock are not tax-deductible.
- When a corporation issues more stock, it dilutes its ownership. Thus, the current stockholders must yield some control to the new stockholders.

Dividend Policies

A **dividend** is a distribution among stockholders of the assets that a corporation's earnings have generated. Stockholders receive these assets, usually cash, in proportion to the number of shares they own. A corporation's board of directors has sole authority to declare dividends, but senior managers, who usually serve as members of the board, influence dividend policies. Receiving dividends is one of two ways in which stockholders can earn a return on their investment in a corporation. The other way is to sell their shares for more than they paid for them.

Although a corporation may have sufficient cash and retained earnings to pay a dividend, its board of directors may not declare one for several reasons. The corporation may need the cash for expansion; it may want to improve its overall financial position by liquidating debt; or it may be facing major uncertainties, such as a pending lawsuit or strike or a projected decline in the economy, which makes it prudent to preserve resources.

A corporation pays dividends quarterly, semiannually, annually, or at other times declared by its board of directors. Most states do not allow a corporation to declare a dividend that exceeds its retained earnings. When a corporation does declare a dividend that exceeds retained earnings, it is, in essence, returning to the stockholders part of their contributed capital. This is called a **liquidating dividend**. A corporation usually pays a liquidating dividend only when it is going out of business or reducing its operations.

Having sufficient retained earnings in itself does not justify the declaration of a dividend. If a corporation does not have cash or other assets readily available for distribution, it might have to borrow money to pay the dividend—an action most boards of directors want to avoid.

Study Note

Journal entries for dividends are made only on the declaration date and the payment date.

Dividend Dates Three important dates are associated with dividends:

- The **declaration date** is the date on which the board of directors formally declares that the corporation is going to pay a dividend. Because the legal obligation to pay the dividend arises at this time, a liability for Dividends Payable is recorded and the Dividends account is debited on this date. In the accounting process, Retained Earnings will be reduced by the total dividends declared during the period.

- The **record date** is the date on which ownership of stock, and therefore the right to receive a dividend, is determined. Persons who own the stock on the record date will receive the dividend. No journal entry is made on this date. Between the record date and the date of payment, the stock is said to be **ex-dividend**. If the owner on the date of record sells the shares of stock before the date of payment, the right to the dividend remains with that person; it does not transfer with the shares to the second owner.

- The **payment date** is the date on which the dividend is paid to the stockholders of record. On this date, the Dividends Payable account is eliminated, and the Cash account is reduced.

Because an accounting period may end between the record date and the payment date, dividends declared during the period may exceed the amount paid for dividends. For example, in Figure 2, the accounting period ends on December 31. The declaration date for the dividends is December 21, the record date is December 31, and the payment date is January 11. In this case, the statement of retained earnings for the accounting period will show a decrease in the amount of the dividends declared, but the statement of cash flows will not show the dividends because the cash has not yet been paid out.

Evaluating Dividend Policies To evaluate the amount of dividends they receive, investors use the **dividends yield** ratio. Dividends yield is computed by dividing the dividends per share by the market price per share. **Microsoft's** his-

FIGURE 2
Dividend Dates

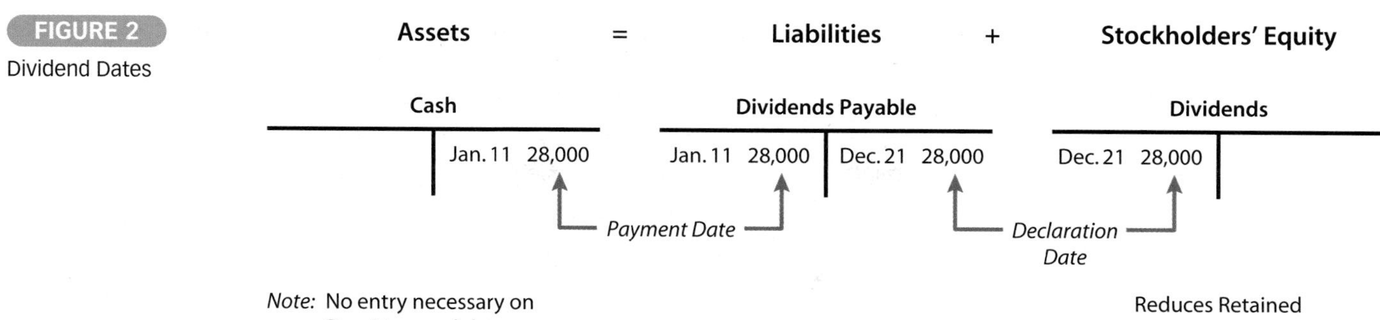

tory of dividend payments provides an interesting example. Having built up a large cash balance through its years of profitable operations, Microsoft increased its annual dividend to $3.8 billion ($.40 per share) in 2007.[2] Using Microsoft's regular annual dividend as a more realistic measure of what investors can expect in the future, its dividends yield is computed as follows:

K/R

$$\text{Dividends Yield} = \frac{\text{Dividends per Share}}{\text{Market Price per Share}} = \frac{\$.40}{\$27.87} = 1.4\%$$

Figure 3 shows how Microsoft's dividends yield and last price are quoted on NASDAQ. Because the yield on corporate bonds exceeds 7 percent, Microsoft shareholders must expect some of their return to come from increases in the price of the shares.

Companies usually pay dividends only when they have had profitable operations. For example, **Apple Computer** began paying dividends in 1987, but it stopped those payments in 1996 to conserve cash after it suffered large operating losses in 1995. Now that Apple is profitable again, it may resume paying dividends. However, factors other than earnings affect the decision to pay dividends. Among them are the following:

- **Industry policies** A company may change its dividend policy to bring it into line with the prevailing policy in its industry. For example, despite positive

FIGURE 3
Stock Quotations on NASDAQ

NASDAQ NATIONAL MARKET EXCHANGE

YTD % CHG	STOCK	SYM	YLD	PE	LAST	NET CHG
− 8.6	♦ MicrosSys	MCRS	...	29	32.08	0.11
− 3.8	Microsemi	MSCC	...	Cc	21.30	−0.35
−21.7	♦ Microsoft	MSFT	1.6	16	27.87	0.30
−30.7	MicroStrat	MSTR	...	14	65.93	0.38
−31.5	Microtune	TUNE	...	Cc	4.47	...
▼ −39.5	McrsEndovasc	MEND	...	Dd	11.91	−0.07
−19.6	Middleby	MIDD	...	20	61.59	−1.02
− 2.4	MidsexWtr	MSEX	3.8	23	18.50	0.01
− 0.4	Midland	MLAN	.6	14	64.46	...
▼ −18.0	MdwstBanc	MBHI	5.1	14	10.18	0.45
−12.7	MillnmPhrm	MLNM	...	Cc	13.08	−0.40
−10.6	MillerHrm	MLHR	1.2	13	28.95	0.20
− 8.4	MillicmInt	MICC	...	28	108.07	−2.06

***Source*: Stock quotes on the NASDAQ from *The Wall Street Journal*, March 9, 2008. Copyright © 2008 Dow Jones & Co., Inc. Reprinted by permission of Dow Jones & Company via Copyright Clearance Center.**

earnings, **AT&T Corporation** slashed its dividends by 83 percent. This action put AT&T's policy more in line with the policies of its peers in the telecommunications industry, most of which do not pay dividends.[3]

- **Volatility of earnings** If a company has years of good earnings followed by years of poor earnings, it may want to keep dividends low to avoid giving a false impression of sustained high earnings. For example, for years, **General Motors** paid a fairly low but stable dividend but declared a bonus dividend in especially good years.

- **Effect on cash flows** A company may not pay dividends because its operations do not generate enough cash to do so or because it wants to invest cash in future operations. **Abbott Laboratories** increases its dividends per share each year to reward its stockholders but also keeps back a portion of its earnings to spend for other purposes, such as researching and developing new drugs that will generate revenue in the future. In a recent year, for example, the company paid $1.18 per share dividend on earnings per share of $2.53.[4]

In recent years, because of a 15 percent reduction in the tax rate on dividends, attitudes toward dividends have changed. Many companies have either increased their dividends or started to pay dividends for the first time. The special dividend by Microsoft mentioned above is a good example of this effect.

Using Return on Equity to Measure Performance

Return on equity is the most important ratio associated with stockholders' equity. It is also a common measure of management's performance. For instance, when *BusinessWeek* and *Forbes* rate companies on their success, return on equity is the major basis of their evaluations. In addition, the compensation of top executives is often tied to return on equity benchmarks.

Google's return on equity in 2007 is computed as follows:[5]

$$\text{Return on Equity} = \frac{\text{Net Income}}{\text{Average Stockholders' Equity}}$$

$$= \frac{\$4,203,720}{(\$22,689,679 + \$17,039,840) \div 2}$$

$$= \frac{\$\ 4,203,720}{\$19,864,759}$$

$$= 21.2\%$$

Google's healthy return on equity of 21.2 percent depends, of course, on the amount of net income the company earns. However, it also depends on the level of stockholders' equity, which in turn depends on management decisions about the amount of stock the company sells to the public. As the company sells more shares, stockholders' equity increases, and as a result, return on equity decreases. Management can keep stockholders' equity at a minimum by financing the business with cash flows from operations and by issuing debt instead of stock. However, as we have pointed out, issuing bonds and other types of debt increases a company's risk because the interest and principal of the debt must be paid in a timely manner.

Management can also reduce the number of shares in the hands of the public by buying back the company's shares on the open market. The cost of these shares, which are called **treasury stock**, has the effect of reducing stockholders' equity and thereby increasing return on equity. Many companies follow this practice instead of paying or increasing dividends. Their reason for doing so is that it puts money into the hands of stockholders in the form of market price appreciation without creating a commitment to higher dividends in the future. For instance, in 2007, **Microsoft** purchased $27.6 billion of its common stock on the open market.[6] Microsoft's stock repurchases will improve the company's return on equity, increase its earnings per share, and lower its price/earnings ratio.

The **price/earnings (P/E) ratio** is a measure of investors' confidence in a company's future. It is calculated by dividing the market price per share by the earnings per share. The price/earnings ratio will vary as market price per share fluctuates daily and the amount of earnings per share changes. If you look back at Figure 3, you will see that it shows a P/E ratio of 16 for Microsoft. It was computed using the annual earnings per share from Microsoft's most recent income statement, as follows:

$$\text{Price/Earnings (P/E) Ratio} = \frac{\text{Market Price per Share}}{\text{Earnings per Share}} = \frac{\$27.87}{\$1.74} = 16 \text{ times}$$

Because the market price is 16 times earnings, investors are paying a good price in relation to earnings. They do so in the expectation that this software company will continue to be successful.

Stock Options as Compensation

More than 97 percent of public companies encourage employees to invest in their common stock through **stock option plans**.[7] Most such plans give employees the right to purchase stock in the future at a fixed price. Some companies offer stock option plans only to management personnel, but others, including **Google**, make them available to all employees. Because the market value of a company's stock is tied to a company's performance, these plans are a means of both motivating and compensating employees. As the market value of the stock goes up, the difference between the option price and the market price grows, which increases the amount of compensation. Another key benefit of stock option plans is that compensation expense is tax-deductible.

On the date stock options are granted, the fair value of the options must be estimated. The amount in excess of the exercise price is recorded as compensation expense over the grant period.[8]

For example, suppose that on July 1, 2010, a company grants its top executives the option to purchase 50,000 shares of $10 par value common stock at its current market value of $15 per share. The fair value of the option must be estimated on that date to determine compensation expense. Any one of several methods of estimating the fair value of options at the grant date may be used; they are dealt with in more advanced courses. Later, when the market price is $25 per share, one of the firm's vice presidents exercises her option and purchases 2,000 shares. Although the vice president has a gain of $20,000 (the $50,000 market value less the $30,000 option price), no compensation expense is recorded. The company receives only the option price, not the current market value.

In one example of how firms value stock options, **Google** recognized $868,646 of stock-based compensation expense in 2007. This amount represented about 7.5 percent of the company's total expenses and almost 21 percent of the net income. Management used a well-known statistical method to estimate the option values.[9]

FOCUS ON BUSINESS PRACTICE

Politics and Accounting Don't Mix

The FASB has long held that stock options should be treated as an expense, but in trying to pass this rule, it has encountered heavy opposition from the technology industry, which is the largest user of stock options. Leaders of the technology industry have maintained that expensing stock options would hurt their companies' profits and growth. The FASB argued that stock options are a form of compensation and therefore have value. The U.S. Congress got involved and pressured the FASB to back down, using the companies' reasoning that stock options essentially have no value and thus are not an expense on the income statement, although they should be mentioned in a note to the financial statements. What was happening was that many stock options were granted, and companies granting them were very loose in how they accounted for them. Many of the stock transactions were back-dated so that the exercise price would be most advantageous to the executives who were benefitting. The SEC has more than 100 ongoing criminal investigations of backdating practices. Estimates are that between 1994 and 2005, when the FASB finally ruled that all publicly traded companies must expense stock options, \$246 billion of options compensation expense had been ignored, overstating reported earnings by 7 percent.[10]

Cash Flow Information

The best source of information concerning cash flows related to stock transactions and dividends is the financing activities section of the statement of cash flows. For instance, **Microsoft's** cash flows from these activities are clearly revealed in this partial section of the company's statement of cash flows (in millions):

	2007	2006	2005
Financing Activities			
Common stock issued	\$ 6,782	\$ 2,101	\$ 3,109
Common stock repurchased	(27,575)	(19,207)	(8,057)
Common stock cash dividend	**(3,805)**	**(3,545)**	**(36,112)**

Note the increasing amounts of common stock repurchased (treasury stock) and the large special dividend the company paid in 2005. Both actions are a reflection of the company's success.

STOP ▶ REVIEW ▶ APPLY

LO1-1 **Identify and explain the advantages of the corporate form of business.**

LO1-2 **Identify and explain the disadvantages of the corporate form of business.**

LO1-3 **What three dates are important in paying dividends?**

LO1-4 **What is the dividends yield ratio, and what do investors learn from it?**

LO1-5 **What are two general ways in which management can improve a company's return on equity?**

LO1-6 **What is the price/earnings (P/E) ratio, and what does it measure?**

LO1-7 **What is a stock option plan, and why would a company want to have one?**

Suggested answers to all Stop, Review, and Apply questions follow the appendixes.

Components of Stockholders' Equity

LO2 Identify the components of stockholders' equity.

In a corporation's balance sheet, the owners' claims to the business are called *stockholders' equity*. As shown in Exhibit 1, this section of a corporate balance sheet usually has at least three components.

- **Contributed capital**—the stockholders' investments in the corporation
- **Retained earnings**—the earnings of the corporation since its inception, less any losses, dividends, or transfers to contributed capital. Retained earnings are reinvested in the business. They are not a pool of funds to be distributed to the stockholders; instead, they represent the stockholders' claim to assets resulting from profitable operations.
- **Treasury stock**—shares of its own stock that the corporation has bought back on the open market. The cost of these shares is treated not as an investment, but as a reduction in stockholders' equity. By buying back the shares, the corporation reduces the ownership of the business..

As you can see in **Google's** Financial Highlights at the beginning of the chapter, "other items" may also appear in the stockholders' equity section. We discuss these items in a later chapter.

A corporation can issue two types of stock:

- **Common stock** is the basic form of stock that a corporation issues; that is, if a corporation issues only one type of stock, it is common stock. Because shares of common stock carry voting rights, they generally provide their owners with the means of controlling the corporation. Common stock is also called **residual equity**, which means that if the corporation is liquidated, the claims of all creditors and usually those of preferred stockholders rank ahead of the claims of common stockholders.
- To attract investors whose goals differ from those of common stockholders, a corporation may also issue **preferred stock**. Preferred stock gives its owners preference over common stockholders, usually in terms of receiving dividends and in terms of claims to assets if the corporation is liquidated. (We describe these preferences in more detail later in the chapter.)

EXHIBIT 1

Stockholders' Equity Section of a Balance Sheet

Stockholders' Equity		
Contributed capital		
Preferred stock, $50 par value, 2,000 shares authorized, issued, and outstanding		$100,000
Common stock, $5 par value, 60,000 shares authorized, 40,000 shares issued, 36,000 shares outstanding	$200,000	
Additional paid-in capital	100,000	300,000
Total contributed capital		$400,000
Retained earnings		120,000
Total contributed capital and retained earnings		$520,000
Less treasury stock, common (4,000 shares at cost)		40,000
Total stockholders' equity		$480,000

FOCUS ON BUSINESS PRACTICE

Are You a First-Class or Second-Class Stockholder?

When companies go public, insiders—usually the founders of the company or top management—often get first-class shares with extra votes, while outsiders get second-class shares with fewer votes. The class A and class B shares of **Adolph Coors Company**, the large brewing firm, are an extreme example. The company's class B shares, owned by the public, have no votes except in the case of a merger. Its class A shares, held by the Coors family trust, have all the votes on other issues.

Google also has two classes of common shares. Both classes are identical except that each class B share is entitled to ten votes and each class A share is entitled to only one vote. Class A shares are the ones that Google offered to the public in its IPO. As a result, Class B holders controls78 percent of the company.[11]

Shareholder advocates denounce the class division of shares as undemocratic. They maintain that this practice gives a privileged few shareholders all or most of the control of a company and that it denies other shareholders voting power consistent with the risk they are taking. Defenders of the practice argue that it shields top executives from the market's obsession with short-term results and allows them to make better long-term decisions. They also point out that many investors don't care about voting rights as long as the stock performs well.

In keeping with the convention of full disclosure, the stockholders' equity section of a corporate balance sheet gives a great deal of information about the corporation's stock. Under contributed capital, it lists the kinds of stock; their par value; and the number of shares authorized, issued, and outstanding.

- **Authorized shares** are the maximum number of shares that a corporation's state charter allows it to issue. Most corporations are authorized to issue more shares than they need to issue at the time they are formed. Thus, they are able to raise more capital in the future by issuing additional shares. When a corporation issues all of its authorized shares, it cannot issue more without a change in its state charter.

Larry Page *(left)* and Sergey Brin, who founded Google, Inc., in 1998, have a lot to look happy about. In its IPO in August 2004, Google issued about 22.5 million shares at $85 per share for a total of $1.9 billion. The price per share soared to $135 in a few days and reached $300 in 2005 and $700 in 2008. The ability to raise large amounts of capital by issuing stocks and bonds is part of the reason corporations dominate the U.S. economy.

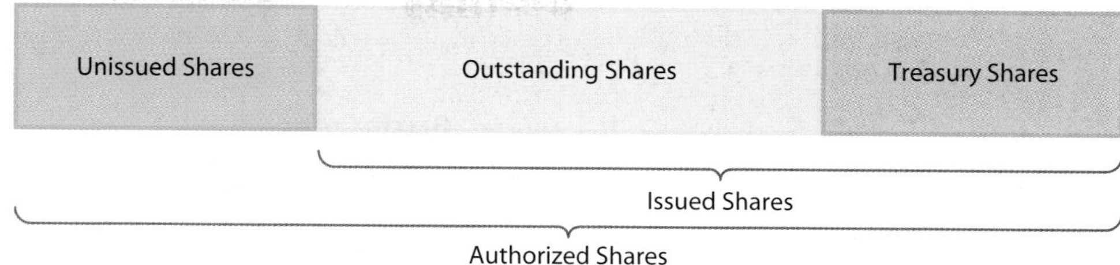

FIGURE 4
Relationship of Authorized Shares to Unissued, Issued, Outstanding, and Treasury Shares

- **Issued shares** are those that a corporation sells or otherwise transfers to stockholders. The owners of a corporation's issued shares own 100 percent of the business. Unissued shares have no rights or privileges until they are issued.
- **Outstanding shares** are shares that a corporation has issued and that are still in circulation. Treasury stock is not outstanding because it consists of shares that a corporation has issued but that it has bought back and thereby put out of circulation. Thus, a corporation can have more shares issued than are currently outstanding.

Figure 4 shows the relationship of authorized shares to issued, unissued, outstanding, and treasury shares. In this regard, Google is an interesting example. The company has 9 billion authorized shares of stock and only about 309 million shares issued. With its excess of authorized issues, Google obviously has plenty of flexibility for future stock transactions.

STOP ▸ REVIEW ▸ APPLY

LO2-1 **Why is common stock called *residual equity*?**

LO2-2 **How does preferred stock differ from common stock?**

LO2-3 **What distinguishes authorized shares from issued shares and outstanding shares?**

LO2-4 **What is the difference between issued shares and outstanding shares?**

Components of Stockholders' Equity The following data are from the records of Garcia Corporation on December 31, 2010:

	Balance
Preferred stock, $100 par value, 6 percent noncumulative, 5,000 shares authorized, issued, and outstanding	$500,000
Common stock, $2 par value, 100,000 shares authorized, 90,000 shares issued, and 85,000 shares outstanding	180,000
Additional paid-in capital	489,000
Retained earnings	172,500
Treasury stock, common (5,000 shares, at cost)	110,000

Prepare a stockholders' equity section for Garcia Corporation's balance sheet.

(continued)

SOLUTION

Garcia Corporation
Balance Sheet
December 31, 2010

Stockholders' Equity

Contributed capital		
Preferred stock, $100 par value, 6 percent noncumulative, 5,000 shares authorized, issued, and outstanding		$ 500,000
Common stock, $2 par value, 100,000 shares authorized, 90,000 shares issued, 85,000 shares outstanding	$180,000	
Additional paid-in capital	489,000	669,000
Total contributed capital		$1,169,000
Retained earnings		172,500
Total contributed capital and retained earnings		$1,341,500
Less treasury stock, common (5,000 shares at cost)		110,000
Total stockholders' equity		$1,231,500

Preferred Stock

LO3 Identify the characteristics of preferred stock.

Most preferred stock has one or more of the following characteristics: preference as to dividends, preference as to assets if a corporation is liquidated, convertibility, and a callable option. A corporation may offer several different classes of preferred stock, each with distinctive characteristics to attract different investors.

Study Note

Preferred stock has many different characteristics. They are rarely exactly the same from company to company.

Preference as to Dividends

Preferred stockholders ordinarily must receive a certain amount of dividends before common stockholders receive anything. The amount that preferred stockholders must be paid before common stockholders can be paid is usually stated in dollars per share or as a percentage of the par value of the preferred shares. For example, a company might pay an annual dividend of $4 per share on preferred stock, or it might issue preferred stock at $50 par value and pay an annual dividend of 8 percent of par value, which would also be $4 per share.

Preferred stockholders have no guarantee of ever receiving dividends. A company must have earnings and its board of directors must declare dividends on preferred stock before any liability arises. The consequences of not granting an annual dividend on preferred stock vary according to whether the stock is noncumulative or cumulative:

- If the stock is **noncumulative preferred stock** and the board of directors fails to declare a dividend on it in any given year, the company is under no obligation to make up the missed dividend in future years.
- If the stock is **cumulative preferred stock**, the dividend amount per share accumulates from year to year, and the company must pay the whole amount before it pays any dividends on common stock.

Dividends not paid in the year they are due are called **dividends in arrears**. For example, suppose that a corporation has 20,000 shares of $100 par value, 5 percent cumulative preferred stock outstanding. If the corporation pays no dividends in 2011, preferred dividends in arrears at the end of the year would amount to $100,000 (20,000 shares × $100 × .05 = $100,000). If the corporation's board declares dividends in 2012, the corporation must pay preferred stockholders the dividends in arrears plus their current year's dividends before paying any dividends on common stock.

Dividends in arrears are not recognized as liabilities because no liability exists until the board of directors declares a dividend. A corporation cannot be sure it is going to make a profit, so, of course, it cannot promise dividends to stockholders. However, if it has dividends in arrears, it should report the amount either in the body of its financial statements or in a note to its financial statements.

The following note is typical of one that might appear in a company's annual report:

> On December 31, 2010, the company was in arrears by $37,851,000 ($1.25 per share) on dividends to its preferred stockholders. The company must pay all dividends in arrears to preferred stockholders before paying any dividends to common stockholders.

Suppose that on January 1, 2011, a corporation issued 20,000 shares of $10 par value, 6 percent cumulative preferred stock and 100,000 shares of common stock. Operations in 2011 produced income of only $8,000. However, in the same year, the corporation's board of directors declared a $6,000 cash dividend to the preferred stockholders. Thus, the dividend picture at the end of 2011 was as follows:

2011 dividends due preferred stockholders ($200,000 × .06)	$12,000
Less 2011 dividends declared to preferred stockholders	6,000
2011 preferred stock dividends in arrears	$ 6,000

Now suppose that in 2012, the corporation earns income of $60,000 and wants to pay dividends to both the preferred and the common stockholders. Because the preferred stock is cumulative, the corporation must pay the $6,000 in arrears on the preferred stock, plus the current year's dividends on the preferred stock, before it can distribute a dividend to the common stockholders. If the corporation's board of directors now declares a $24,000 dividend to be distributed to preferred and common stockholders, the distribution would be as follows:

2012 declaration of dividends	$24,000
Less 2011 preferred stock dividends in arrears	6,000
Amount available for 2012 dividends	$18,000
Less 2012 dividends due preferred stockholders ($200,000 × .06)	12,000
Remainder available to common stockholders	$ 6,000

Preference as to Assets

Preferred stockholders often have preference in terms of their claims to a corporation's assets if the corporation is liquidated. If a corporation does go out of business, these preferred stockholders have a right to receive the par value of their stock or a larger stated liquidation value per share before the common stockholders

FOCUS ON BUSINESS PRACTICE

How Does a Stock Become a Debt?

Some companies have used the flexibility of preferred stocks to create a type of stock that is similar to debt. Usually, stocks do not have maturity dates, and companies do not buy them back except at the option of management. However, **CMS Energy**, **Time Warner**, **Xerox**, and other companies have issued preferred stock that is "mandatorily redeemable." This means that the issuing companies are required to buy back the stock at fixed future dates or under predetermined conditions. Thus, these special preferred stocks are similar to bonds in that they have a fixed maturity date. In addition, in much the same way as bonds require periodic interest payments at a fixed rate, these stocks require an annual dividend payment, also at a fixed rate. Even though companies list these stocks in the stockholders' equity section of their balance sheets, the astute analyst will treat them as debt when calculating a company's debt to equity ratio.[12] The FASB is considering a proposal that would require these special preferred stocks to be classified as a liability on the balance sheet.[13]

receive any share of the corporation's assets. This preference can also extend to any dividends in arrears owed to the preferred stockholders.

Convertible Preferred Stock

Study Note

When preferred stockholders convert their shares to common stock, they gain voting rights but lose the dividend and liquidation preference. Conversion back to preferred stock is not an option.

Like all preferred stockholders, owners of **convertible preferred stock** are more likely than common stockholders to receive regular dividends. In addition, they can exchange their shares of preferred stock for shares of common stock at a ratio stated in the company's preferred stock contract. If the market value of the company's common stock increases, the conversion feature allows these stockholders to share in the increase by converting their stock to common stock. For example, if you look back at **Google's** Financial Highlights at the beginning of the chapter, you will see that Google has preferred stock but none is issued. The reason is that the initial investors in the company received convertible preferred stock. These stockholders took advantage of the steep increase in the price of the common stock by converting their shares to common stock. Thus, by including the conversion feature, Google was able to make its preferred stock more attractive to investors. The stock is still authorized, and the company may decide to issue it again in the future.

Suppose, for instance, that a company issues 1,000 shares of 8 percent, $100 par value convertible preferred stock for $100 per share. Each share of stock can be converted to five shares of the company's common stock at any time. The market value of the common stock at the time the company issues the convertible preferred stock is $15 per share. In the past, an owner of the common stock could expect dividends of about $1 per share per year. The owner of one share of preferred stock, on the other hand, now holds an investment that has a market value of about $75 and is also more likely than a common stockholder to receive dividends.

Now suppose that in the next several years, the corporation's earnings increase, the dividends paid to common stockholders increase to $3 per share, and the market value of a share of common stock increases from $15 to $30. Preferred stockholders can convert each of their preferred shares to five common shares, thereby increasing their dividends from $8 on each preferred share to $15 ($3 on each of five common shares). Moreover, the market value of each share of preferred stock will be close to the $150 value of the five shares of common stock because each share can be converted to five shares of common stock.

Callable Preferred Stock

Most preferred stock is **callable preferred stock**—that is, the issuing corporation can redeem or retire it at a price stated in the preferred stock contract. An owner of nonconvertible preferred stock must surrender it to the issuing corporation when asked to do so. If the preferred stock is convertible, the stockholder can either surrender the stock to the corporation or convert it to common stock when the corporation calls the stock. The *call price*, or redemption price, is usually higher than the stock's par value. For example, preferred stock that has a $100 par value might be callable at $103 per share.

When preferred stock is called and surrendered, the stockholder is entitled to the following:

- The par value of the stock
- The call premium
- Any dividends in arrears
- The current period's dividend prorated by the proportion of the year to the call date

A corporation may decide to call its preferred stock for any of the following reasons:

- It may want to force conversion of the preferred stock to common stock because the dividend that it pays on preferred shares is higher than the dividend that it pays on the equivalent number of common shares.
- It may be able to replace the outstanding preferred stock with a preferred stock at a lower dividend rate or with long-term debt, which can have a lower after-tax cost.
- It may simply be profitable enough to retire the preferred stock.

STOP ▸ REVIEW ▸ APPLY

LO3-1 **What does preferred stock's preference as to dividends and assets mean?**

LO3-2 **What is cumulative preferred stock, and how does it relate to dividends in arrears? How should dividends in arrears be disclosed in the financial statements?**

LO3-3 **Define the terms *convertible* and *callable* as they apply to preferred stock.**

Cash Dividends with Dividends in Arrears
Sung Corporation has 2,000 shares of $100 par value, 7 percent cumulative preferred stock outstanding and 200,000 shares of $1 par value common stock outstanding. In the corporation's first three years of operation, its board of directors declared cash dividends as follows:

2010: none

2011: $20,000

2012: $30,000

Determine the total cash dividends paid to the preferred and common stockholders during each of the three years.

(continued)

SOLUTION

2010:	None	
2011:	Preferred dividends in arrears (2,000 shares × $100 × .07)	$14,000
	Current year remainder to preferred ($20,000 − $14,000)	6,000
	Total to preferred stockholders	$20,000
2012:	Preferred dividends in arrears ($14,000 − $6,000)	$ 8,000
	Current year to preferred (2,000 shares × $100 × .07)	14,000
	Total to preferred stockholders	$22,000
	Total to common stockholders ($30,000 − $22,000)	8,000
	Total dividends in 2012	$30,000

Issuance of Common Stock

LO4 Account for the issuance of stock for cash and other assets.

Study Note

Legal capital is the minimum amount a corporation can report as contributed capital. To protect creditors, a corporation cannot declare a dividend that would reduce capital below the amount of legal capital.

A share of capital stock may be either par or no-par. The value of par stock is stated in the corporate charter and must be printed on each stock certificate. It can be $.01, $1, $5, $100, or any other amount established by the organizers of the corporation. For instance, the par value of **Google's** common stock is $.001. The par values of common stocks tend to be lower than those of preferred stocks.

As noted earlier, par value is the amount per share that is recorded in a corporation's capital stock accounts, and it constitutes a corporation's legal capital. A corporation cannot declare a dividend that would cause stockholders' equity to fall below the firm's legal capital. Par value is thus a minimum cushion of capital that protects a corporation's creditors. Any amount in excess of par value that a corporation receives from a stock issue is recorded in its Additional Paid-in Capital account and represents a portion of its contributed capital.

No-par stock is capital stock that does not have a par value. A corporation may issue stock without a par value for several reasons. For one thing, rather than recognizing par value as an arbitrary figure, investors may confuse it with the stock's market value. For another, most states do not allow a stock issue below par value, and this limits a corporation's flexibility in obtaining capital.

State laws often require corporations to place a **stated value** on each share of stock that they issue, but even when this is not required, a corporation's board of directors may do so as a matter of convenience. The stated value can be any value set by the board unless the state specifies a minimum amount, which is sometimes the case. The stated value can be set before or after the shares are issued if the state law is not specific.

Par Value Stock

When a corporation issues par value stock, the appropriate capital stock account (usually Common Stock or Preferred Stock) is credited for the par value regardless of whether the proceeds are more or less than the par value.

When a corporation issues stock at a price greater than par value, as is usually the case, the proceeds in excess of par are credited to an account called Additional Paid-in Capital. For example, suppose Nocek Corporation is authorized to issue 10,000 shares of $10 par value common stock and that it issues 5,000 shares at

$12 each on January 1, 2010. The entry to record the issuance of the stock at the price in excess of par value would be as follows:

A	= L +	SE
+60,000		+50,000
		+10,000

Jan. 1	Cash	60,000	
	Common Stock		50,000
	Additional Paid-in Capital		10,000
	Issued 5,000 shares of $10 par value common stock for $12 per share		

Cash is debited for the proceeds of $60,000 (5,000 shares × $12), and Common Stock is credited for the total par value of $50,000 (5,000 shares × $10). Additional Paid-in Capital is credited for the difference of $10,000 (5,000 shares × $2).

The amount in excess of par value is part of Nocek Corporation's contributed capital and will be included in the stockholders' equity section of its balance sheet. Immediately after the stock issue, this section of Nocek's balance sheet would appear as follows:

Contributed capital	
Common stock, $10 par value, 10,000 shares authorized, 5,000 shares issued and outstanding	$50,000
Additional paid-in capital	10,000
Total contributed capital	$60,000
Retained earnings	—
Total stockholders' equity	$60,000

If a corporation issues stock for less than par value, an account called Discount on Capital Stock is debited for the difference. The issuance of stock at a discount rarely occurs; it is illegal in many states.

No-Par Stock

Study Note

When no-par stock has a stated value, the stated value serves the same purpose as par value in that it represents the minimum legal capital.

Most states require that all or part of the proceeds from a corporation's issuance of no-par stock be designated as legal capital, which cannot be used unless the corporation is liquidated. The purpose of this requirement is to protect the corporation's assets for creditors.

Suppose that on January 1, 2010, Nocek Corporation issues 5,000 shares of no-par common stock at $15 per share. The $75,000 (5,000 shares × $15) in proceeds would be recorded as follows:

A	= L +	SE
+75,000		+75,000

Jan. 1	Cash	75,000	
	Common Stock		75,000
	Issued 5,000 shares of no-par common stock for $15 per share		

Because the stock does not have a stated or par value, all proceeds of the issue are credited to Common Stock and are part of the company's legal capital.

As noted earlier, state laws may require corporations to put a stated value on each share of stock that they issue. Assuming the same facts as above except that Nocek puts a $10 stated value on each share of its no-par stock, the entry would be as follows:

A	= L +	SE
+75,000		+50,000
		+25,000

Jan. 1	Cash	75,000	
	Common Stock		50,000
	Additional Paid-in Capital		25,000
	Issued 5,000 shares of no-par common stock with $10 stated value for $15 per share		

Notice that the legal capital credited to Common Stock is the stated value decided by Nocek's board of directors. Also note that the Additional Paid-in Capital account is credited for $25,000, which is the difference between the proceeds ($75,000) and the total stated value ($50,000).

Issuance of Stock for Noncash Assets

A corporation may issue stock in return for assets or services other than cash. Transactions of this kind usually involve a corporation's exchange of stock for land or buildings or for the services of attorneys and others who help organize the corporation. In such cases, the problem is to determine the dollar amount at which the exchange should be recorded.

A corporation's board of directors has the right to determine the fair market value of the assets or services that the corporation receives in exchange for its stock. Generally, this kind of transaction is recorded at the fair market value of the stock that the corporation is giving up. If the stock's fair market value cannot be determined, the fair market value of the assets or services received can be used.

Study Note

In establishing the fair market value of property that a corporation exchanges for stock, a board of directors cannot be arbitrary; it must use all the information at its disposal.

For example, suppose that when Nocek Corporation was formed on January 1, 2010, its attorney agreed to accept 200 shares of its $10 par value common stock for services rendered. At that time, the market value of the stock could not be determined. However, for similar services, the attorney would have charged Nocek $3,000. The entry to record this noncash transaction is as follows:

A	= L +	SE
		−3,000
		+2,000
		+1,000

Jan. 1	Start-up and Organization Costs	3,000	
	Common Stock		2,000
	Additional Paid-in Capital		1,000
	Issued 200 shares of $10 par value common stock for attorney's services		

Now suppose that two years later, Nocek Corporation exchanged 500 shares of its $10 par value common stock for a piece of land. At the time of the exchange, Nocek's stock was selling on the market for $16 per share. The following entry records this exchange:

A	= L +	SE
+8,000		+5,000
		+3,000

Jan. 1	Land	8,000	
	Common Stock		5,000
	Additional Paid-in Capital		3,000
	Issued 500 shares of $10 par value common stock with a market value of $16 per share for a piece of land		

STOP ▶ REVIEW ▶ APPLY

LO4-1 **What is the significance of the following terms: *par value, no-par value*, and *stated value*?**

LO4-2 **Which is more relevant to the analyst: par value, additional paid-in capital, or the total of the two?**

LO4-3 **What two methods are used to value stock when it is issued for noncash assets, and when should each be used?**

Accounting for Treasury Stock

LO5 Account for treasury stock.

Study Note

Treasury stock is not the same as unissued stock. Treasury stock represents shares that have been issued but are no longer outstanding. Unissued shares, on the other hand, have never been in circulation.

As we noted earlier, treasury stock is stock that the issuing company has reacquired, usually by purchasing shares on the open market. Although repurchasing its own stock can be a severe drain on a corporation's cash, it is common practice. In a recent year, 386, or 64 percent, of 600 large companies held treasury stock.[14]

Among the reasons a company may want to buy back its own stock are the following:

- It may want stock to distribute to employees through stock option plans.
- It may be trying to maintain a favorable market for its stock.
- It may want to increase its earnings per share or stock price per share.
- It may want to have additional shares of stock available for purchasing other companies.
- It may want to prevent a hostile takeover.

A purchase of treasury stock reduces a company's assets and stockholders' equity. It is not considered a purchase of assets, as the purchase of shares in another company would be. A company can hold treasury shares for an indefinite period or reissue or retire them. Treasury shares have no rights until they are reissued. Like unissued shares, they do not have voting rights, rights to dividends, or rights to assets during liquidation of the company. However, there is one major difference between unissued shares and treasury shares. A share of stock issued at par value or greater and that was reacquired as treasury stock can be reissued at less than par value without negative results.

Purchase of Treasury Stock

When treasury stock is purchased, it is recorded at cost. The par value, stated value, or original issue price of the stock is ignored. As noted above, the purchase reduces both a firm's assets and its stockholders' equity. For example, suppose that on September 15, Amber Corporation purchases 2,000 shares of its common stock on the market at a price of $50 per share. The purchase would be recorded as follows:

A	= L +	SE
−100,000		−100,000

Sept. 15	Treasury Stock, Common	100,000	
	Cash		100,000
	Acquired 2,000 shares of the company's common stock for $50 per share		

FOCUS ON BUSINESS PRACTICE

Are Share Buybacks Really Good?

Corporate America sets new records for share buybacks every year: $10 billion in 1991, $123 billion in 2000; $197 billion in 2004; and an estimated $500 billion in 2007. **Home Depot, Inc, Wal-Mart, Inc, General Electric, Johnson & Johnson** and **Microsoft**, along with many other companies, spent billions to boost their stock prices—but to no avail. The stated aim is to boost stock prices and earnings per share by reducing the supply of stock in public hands.

According to renowned investor Warren Buffett and others, share buybacks are ill-advised. Many of the purchases in 2007, for example, occurred when the market was experiencing record highs. Also, what is often not stated publicly is that many shares do not stay out of public hands because the companies recycle the stock into generous stock options for management and thus do not achieve the stated goal of reducing outstanding shares. Estimates are that perhaps half of the stock purchased is little more than a "backdoor compensation" for employees. Furthermore, many companies have borrowed money to repurchase stock, thereby increasing their debt to equity ratios. These companies later suffered reductions in their credit ratings and severe declines in their stock prices.[15]

Study Note

Because treasury stock reduces stockholder's equity—the denominator of the return on equity ratio—the return on equity will increase when treasury shares are purchased even though there is no increase in earnings.

The stockholders' equity section of Amber's balance sheet shows the cost of the treasury stock as a deduction from the total of contributed capital and retained earnings:

Contributed capital	
Common stock, $5 par value, 200,000 shares authorized, 60,000 shares issued, 58,000 shares outstanding	$ 300,000
Additional paid-in capital	60,000
Total contributed capital	$ 360,000
Retained earnings	1,800,000
Total contributed capital and retained earnings	$2,160,000
Less treasury stock, common (2,000 shares at cost)	100,000
Total stockholders' equity	$2,060,000

Notice that the number of shares issued, and therefore the legal capital, has not changed. However, the number of shares outstanding has decreased as a result of the transaction.

Sale of Treasury Stock

Treasury shares can be sold at cost, above cost, or below cost. For example, suppose that on November 15, Amber Corporation sells its 2,000 treasury shares for $50 per share. The following entry records the transaction:

A	= L +	SE
+100,000		+100,000

Date	Account	Debit	Credit
Nov. 15	Cash	100,000	
	Treasury Stock, Common		100,000
	Reissued 2,000 shares of treasury stock for $50 per share		

When treasury shares are sold for an amount greater than their cost, the excess of the sales price over cost should be credited to Paid-in Capital, Treasury Stock. No gain should be recorded.

In 2004, Microsoft's board approved a plan to buy back $30 billion of the company's common stock over the next four years. By 2007, the company had repurchased more than $60 billion of its own stock. When are share buybacks not a good idea? According to investor Warren Buffett, shown here offering his hand to Microsoft's Bill Gates, buybacks are ill-advised when a company buys high and sells low and when it borrows money to finance a buyback.

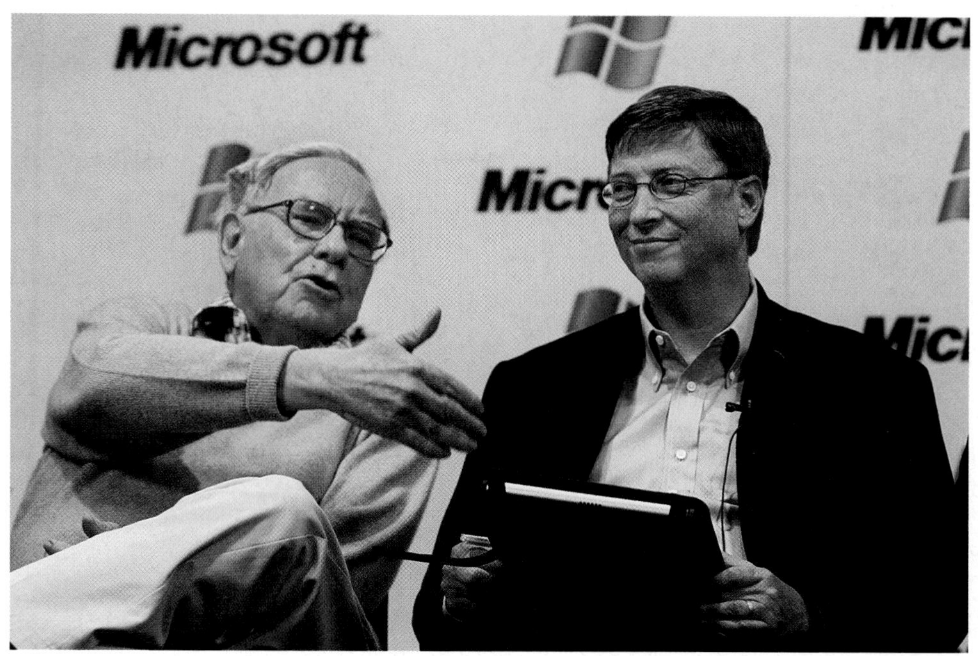

For instance, suppose that on November 15, Amber Corporation sells its 2,000 treasury shares for $60 per share. The entry for the reissue would be as follows:

A	= L +	SE
+120,000		+100,000
		+ 20,000

Nov. 15	Cash	120,000	
	Treasury Stock, Common		100,000
	Paid-in Capital, Treasury Stock		20,000
	Sold 2,000 shares of treasury stock for $60 per share; cost was $50 per share		

Study Note

Gains and losses on the reissue of treasury stock are never recognized as such. Instead, the Retained Earnings and Paid-in Capital, Treasury Stock accounts are used.

When treasury shares are sold below their cost, the difference is deducted from Paid-in Capital, Treasury Stock. If this account does not exist or if its balance is insufficient to cover the excess of cost over the reissue price, Retained Earnings absorbs the excess. No loss is recorded.

For example, suppose that on September 15, Amber bought 2,000 shares of its common stock on the market at a price of $50 per share. On October 15, the company sold 800 shares for $60 per share, and on December 15, it sold the remaining 1,200 shares for $42 per share.

The entries for these three transactions are as follows:

A	= L +	SE
−100,000		−100,000

Sept. 15	Treasury Stock, Common	100,000	
	Cash		100,000
	Purchased 2,000 shares of treasury stock at $50 per share		

A	= L +	SE
+48,000		+40,000
		+ 8,000

Oct. 15	Cash	48,000	
	Treasury Stock, Common		40,000
	Paid-in Capital, Treasury Stock		8,000
	Sold 800 shares of treasury stock for $60 per share; cost was $50 per share		

A	= L +	SE
+50,400		− 8,000
		− 1,600
		+60,000

Dec. 15	Cash	50,400	
	Paid-in Capital, Treasury Stock	8,000	
	Retained Earnings	1,600	
	Treasury Stock, Common		60,000
	Sold 1,200 shares of treasury stock for $42 per share; cost was $50 per share		

Study Note

Retained Earnings is debited only when the Paid-in Capital, Treasury Stock account has been depleted. In this case, the credit balance of $8,000 is completely exhausted before Retained Earnings absorbs the excess.

In the entry for the December 15 transaction, Retained Earnings is debited for $1,600 because the 1,200 shares were sold for $9,600 less than cost. That amount is $1,600 greater than the $8,000 of paid-in capital generated by the sale of the 800 shares of treasury stock on October 15.

Retirement of Treasury Stock

If a company decides that it will not reissue treasury stock, it can, with the approval of its stockholders, retire the stock. All items related to those shares are then removed from the associated capital accounts. If the cost of buying back the treasury stock is less than the company received when it issued the stock, the difference is recorded in Paid-in Capital, Retirement of Stock. If the cost is more than was received when the stock was first issued, the difference is a reduction in stockholders' equity and is debited to Retained Earnings. For instance, suppose that on November 15, Amber Corporation decides to retire the 2,000 shares of stock that it bought back for $100,000. If the $5 par value common stock was originally issued at $6 per share, this entry would record the retirement:

A	= L +	SE
		−10,000
		−2,000
		−88,000
		+100,000

Nov. 15	Common Stock	10,000	
	Additional Paid-in Capital	2,000	
	Retained Earnings	88,000	
	Treasury Stock, Common		100,000
	Retired 2,000 shares that cost $50 per share and were issued originally at $6 per share		

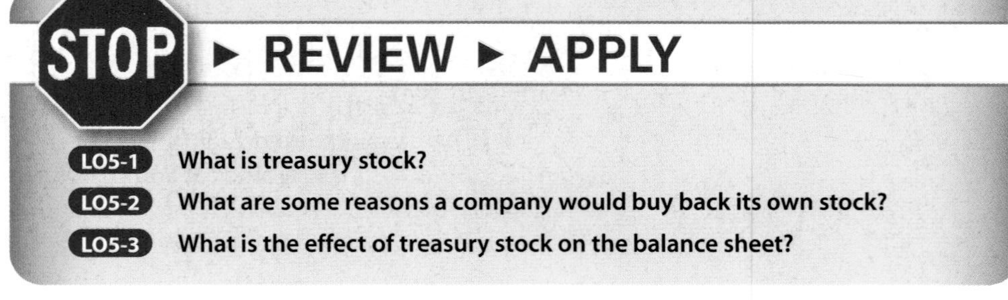

STOP ▸ REVIEW ▸ APPLY
LO5-1 What is treasury stock?
LO5-2 What are some reasons a company would buy back its own stock?
LO5-3 What is the effect of treasury stock on the balance sheet?

A LOOK BACK AT ▶ Google, Inc.

This chapter's Decision Point focused on one of the most exciting financing events of recent history, **Google's** IPO. In evaluating Google's performance since its IPO, those who invested in its stock should consider the following questions:

- **Why did Google's management choose to issue common stock to satisfy its needs for new capital?**
- **What are some of the advantages and disadvantages of this approach to financing a business?**
- **What measures should an investor use in evaluating management's performance?**

As a relatively new company, Google needed to raise capital so that it could expand its operations. The company's management decided to do so by issuing common stock. This approach to financing does not burden a company with debt or interest payments. In addition, the company has the option of paying or not paying dividends. Because Google currently does not pay dividends, it can invest cash from its earnings in expanding the company. Issuing stock does, however, dilute the ownership of a company's current owners, and if the company pays dividends, they are not tax-deductible, as interest on debt is.

Return on equity is, of course, a key measure of management's performance. Using the data from Google's Financial Highlights and Google's 2005 stockholders' equity of $9,418,957 thousand, we can compute the company's return on equity for 2007 and 2006 as follows (in thousands):

$$\text{Return on Equity} = \frac{\text{Net Income}}{\text{Average Stockholders' Equity}}$$

K/R

	2007	2006
Return on Equity =	$\frac{\$4{,}203{,}720}{(\$22{,}689{,}679 + \$17{,}039{,}840) \div 2}$	$\frac{\$3{,}077{,}446}{(\$17{,}039{,}840 + \$9{,}418{,}957) \div 2}$
	= 21.2%	= 23.3%

Google's return on equity declined from 23.3 percent to 21.2 percent but still remains at a very good level.

At the time of the IPO, when Google's stock sold for $85 per share, its P/E ratio was 74.6 times. During the last two years its ratios have been as follows:

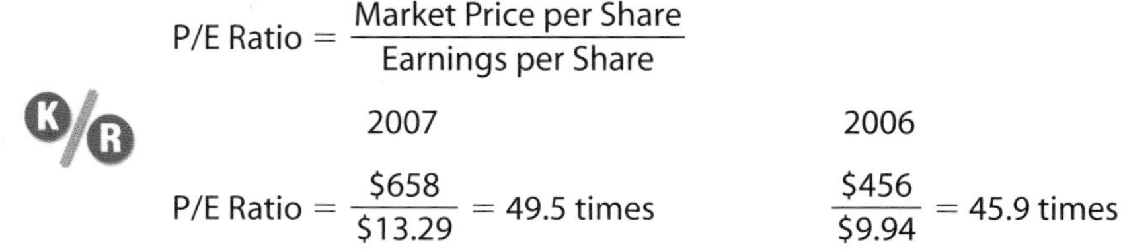

$$\text{P/E Ratio} = \frac{\text{Market Price per Share}}{\text{Earnings per Share}}$$

K/R

	2007	2006
P/E Ratio =	$\frac{\$658}{\$13.29}$ = 49.5 times	$\frac{\$456}{\$9.94}$ = 45.9 times

These are very high P/E ratios; the average for the S&P 500 stocks at the time was about 15. Evidently, despite Google's not paying dividends, investors are rewarding the company's high return on equity and think the company's future is very bright.

CHAPTER REVIEW

REVIEW of Learning Objectives

LO1 Identify and explain the management issues related to contributed capital.

Contributed capital is a critical component in corporate financing. Managing contributed capital requires an understanding of the advantages and disadvantages of the corporate form of business and of the issues involved in using equity financing. Managers must also know how to determine dividend policies and how to evaluate these policies using dividends yield, return on equity, and the price/earnings ratio. The liability for payment of dividends arises on the date the board of directors declares a dividend. The declaration is recorded with a debit to Dividends and a credit to Dividends Payable. The record date—the date on which ownership of the stock, and thus of the right to receive a dividend, is determined—requires no entry. On the payment date, the Dividends Payable account is eliminated, and the Cash account is reduced. Another issue involved in managing contributed capital is using stock options as compensation.

LO2 Identify the components of stockholders' equity.

The stockholders' equity section of a corporate balance sheet usually has at least three components: contributed capital, retained earnings, and treasury stock. Contributed capital consists of money raised through stock issues. A corporation can issue two types of stock: common stock and preferred stock. Common stockholders have voting rights; they also share in the corporation's earnings. Preferred stockholders usually have preference over common stockholders in one or more areas. Retained earnings are reinvested in the corporation; they represent stockholders' claims to assets resulting from profitable operations. Treasury stock is stock that the issuing corporation has reacquired. It is treated as a deduction from stockholders' equity.

LO3 Identify the characteristics of preferred stock.

Preferred stock generally gives its owners first right to dividend payments. Only after these stockholders have been paid can common stockholders receive any portion of a dividend. If the preferred stock is cumulative and dividends are in arrears, a corporation must pay the amount in arrears to preferred stockholders before it pays any dividends to common stockholders. Preferred stockholders also usually have preference over common stockholders in terms of their claims to corporate assets if the corporation is liquidated. In addition, preferred stock may be convertible to common stock, and it is often callable at the option of the corporation.

LO4 Account for the issuance of stock for cash and other assets.

Corporations normally issue their stock in exchange for cash or other assets. Most states require corporations to issue stock at a minimum value called *legal capital.* Legal capital is represented by the stock's par or stated value.

When stock is issued for cash at par or stated value, Cash is debited and Common Stock or Preferred Stock is credited. When stock is sold at an amount greater than par or stated value, the excess is recorded in Additional Paid-in Capital.

When stock is issued for noncash assets, the general rule is to record the stock at its market value. If this value cannot be determined, the fair market value of the asset received is used to record the transaction.

LO5 Account for treasury stock.

Treasury stock is stock that the issuing company has reacquired. A company may buy back its own stock for several reasons, including a desire to create stock option plans, maintain a favorable market for the stock, increase earnings per share, or purchase other companies. Treasury stock is recorded at cost and is deducted from stockholders' equity. It can be reissued or retired. It is similar to unissued stock in that it does not have rights until it is reissued.

REVIEW of Concepts and Terminology

The following concepts and terms were introduced in this chapter:

Authorized shares: The maximum number of shares a corporation can issue without a change in its state charter. **(LO2)**

Callable preferred stock: Preferred stock that the issuing corporation can redeem or retire at a stated price. **(LO3)**

Common stock: Shares of stock that carry voting rights but that rank below preferred stock in terms of dividends and the distribution of assets. **(LO2)**

Convertible preferred stock: Preferred stock that the owner can exchange for common stock. **(LO3)**

Cumulative preferred stock: Preferred stock on which unpaid dividends accumulate over time and that must be satisfied before a dividend can be paid to common stockholders. **(LO3)**

Declaration date: The date on which a board of directors declares a dividend. **(LO1)**

Dividend: A distribution of a corporation's assets (usually cash generated by past earnings) to its stockholders. **(LO1)**

Dividends in arrears: Past dividends on cumulative preferred stock that remain unpaid. **(LO3)**

Double taxation: Taxation of corporate earnings twice—once as income of the corporation and once as income to stockholders in the form of dividends. **(LO1)**

Ex-dividend: A description of stock between the record date and the date of payment, during which the right to the dividend remains with the person who owned the stock on the record date. **(LO1)**

Initial public offering (IPO): A company's first issue of capital stock to the public. **(Decision Point)**

Issued shares: The shares of stock sold or otherwise transferred to stockholders. **(LO2)**

Legal capital: The number of shares of stock issued times the par value; the minimum amount a corporation can report as contributed capital. **(LO1)**

Liquidating dividend: A dividend that exceeds retained earnings and that a corporation usually pays only when it is going out of business or reducing its operations. **(LO1)**

Noncumulative preferred stock: Preferred stock that does not oblige the issuer to make up a missed dividend in a subsequent year. **(LO3)**

No-par stock: Capital stock that does not have a par value. **(LO4)**

Outstanding shares: Shares that have been issued and that are still in circulation. **(LO2)**

Par value: An arbitrary amount assigned to each share of stock; constitutes a corporation's legal capital. **(LO1)**

Payment date: The date on which a dividend is paid. **(LO1)**

Preferred stock: Stock that has preference over common stock, usually in terms of dividends and the distribution of assets. **(LO2)**

Record date: The date on which ownership of stock, and thus the right to receive a dividend, is determined. **(LO1)**

Residual equity: The equity of common stockholders after all other claims have been satisfied. **(LO2)**

Share of stock: A unit of ownership in a corporation. **(LO1)**

Start-up and organization costs: The costs of forming a corporation. **(LO1)**

Stated value: A value that a board of directors assigns to no-par stock. **(LO4)**

Stock certificates: Documents issued to stockholders showing the number of shares that they own. **(LO1)**

Stock option plans: Plans that give employees the right to purchase their companies' stock under specified terms. **(LO1)**

Treasury stock: Capital stock, either common or preferred, that the issuing company has reacquired and has not subsequently resold or retired. **(LO1)**

Underwriter: An intermediary between the corporation and the investing public who facilitates an issue of stock or other securities for a fee. **(LO1)**

Key Ratios

Dividends yield: Current return to stockholders in the form of dividends; Dividends per Share ÷ Market Price per Share. **(LO1)**

Price/earnings (P/E) ratio: A measure of confidence in a company's future; Market Price per Share ÷ Earnings per Share. **(LO1)**

Return on equity: A measure of management's performance; Net Income ÷ Average Stockholders' Equity. **(LO1)**

REVIEW Problem

Recording Stock Issues and Calculating Related Ratios

Fisher Corporation was organized in 2010 in Arizona. Its state charter authorized it to issue 2 million shares of $1 par value common stock and 50,000 shares of 4 percent, $20 par value cumulative and convertible preferred stock. Fisher's stock transactions during 2010 were as follows:

Feb.	1	Issued 200,000 shares of common stock for $250,000.
	15	Issued 6,000 shares of common stock for accounting and legal services. The bills for these services totaled $7,200.
Mar.	15	Issued 240,000 shares of common stock to Tom Lee in exchange for a building and land appraised at $200,000 and $50,000, respectively.
Apr.	2	Purchased 40,000 shares of common stock for the treasury at $1.25 per share from a person who changed her mind about investing in the company.
July	1	Issued 50,000 shares of preferred stock for $1,000,000.
Sept.	30	Sold 20,000 of the shares in the treasury for $1.50 per share.
Dec.	31	Fisher's board of directors declared dividends of $49,820 payable on January 15, 2011, to stockholders of record on January 7. Dividends included preferred stock dividends of $20,000 for one-half year.

For the period ended December 31, 2010, Fisher reported net income of $80,000 and earnings per common share of $.14. At December 31, the market price per common share was $1.60.

Required

1. Record Fisher's stock transactions in T accounts.
2. Prepare the stockholders' equity section of Fisher's balance sheet as of December 31, 2010. (**Hint**: Use net income and dividends to calculate retained earnings.)
3. Calculate Fisher's dividends yield on common stock, price/earnings ratio of common stock, and return on equity.

Answer to Review Problem

1. Entries in T accounts:

Assets = Liabilities + Stockholders' Equity

Assets

Cash

Feb.	1	250,000	April	2	50,000
July	1	1,000,000			
Sept.	30	30,000			

Building

Mar.	15	200,000			

Land

Mar.	15	50,000			

Liabilities

Dividends Payable

			Dec.	31	49,820

Stockholders' Equity

Preferred Stock

			July	1	1,000,000

Common Stock

			Feb.	1	200,000
				15	6,000
			Mar.	15	240,000
			Bal.		446,000

Additional Paid-in Capital

			Feb.	1	50,000
				15	1,200
			Mar.	15	10,000
			Bal.		61,200

Paid-in Capital, Treasury Stock

			Sept.	30	5,000

Dividends

Dec.	31	49,820			

Treasury Stock

April	2	50,000	Sept.	30	25,000
Bal.		25,000			

Start-up and Organization Costs

Feb.	15	7,200			

2. Stockholders' equity section of the balance sheet:

Fisher Corporation
Balance Sheet
December 31, 2010

Stockholders' Equity		
Contributed capital		
Preferred stock, 4 percent cumulative convertible, $20 par value, 50,000 shares authorized, issued, and outstanding		$1,000,000
Common stock, $1 par value, 2,000,000 shares authorized, 446,000 shares issued, and 426,000 shares outstanding	$446,000	
Additional paid-in capital	61,200	
Paid-in capital, treasury stock	5,000	512,200
Total contributed capital		$1,512,200
Retained earnings		30,180 *
Total contributed capital and retained earnings		$1,542,380
Less treasury stock (20,000 shares, at cost)		25,000
Total stockholders' equity		$1,517,380

* Retained Earnings = Net Income − Cash Dividends Declared
Retained Earnings = $80,000 − $49,820 = $30,180

3. Dividends yield on common stock, price/earnings ratio of common stock, and return on equity:

$$\text{Dividends per Share} = \frac{\text{Common Stock Dividend}}{\text{Common Shares Outstanding}} = \frac{\$29{,}820}{426{,}000} = \$.07$$

$$\text{Dividends Yield} = \frac{\text{Dividends per Share}}{\text{Market Price per Share}} = \frac{\$0.07}{\$1.60} = 4.4\%$$

$$\text{Price/Earnings Ratio} = \frac{\text{Market Price per Share}}{\text{Earnings per Share}} = \frac{\$1.60}{\$0.14} = 11.4 \text{ times}$$

The opening balance of stockholders' equity on February 1, 2010, was $250,000.

$$\text{Return on Equity} = \frac{\text{Net Income}}{\text{Average Stockholders' Equity}}$$

$$= \frac{\$80{,}000}{(\$1{,}517{,}380 + \$250{,}000) \div 2}$$

$$= \frac{\$80{,}000}{\$883{,}690}$$

$$= 9.1\%$$

CHAPTER ASSIGNMENTS

BUILDING Your Basic Knowledge and Skills

Short Exercises

LO1

Management Issues

SE 1. Indicate whether each of the following actions is related to (a) managing under the corporate form of business, (b) using equity financing, (c) determining dividend policies, (d) evaluating performance using return on equity, or (e) issuing stock options:

1. Considering whether to make a distribution to stockholders
2. Controlling day-to-day operations
3. Determining whether to issue preferred or common stock
4. Compensating management based on the company's meeting or exceeding the targeted return on equity
5. Compensating employees by giving them the right to purchase shares at a given price
6. Transferring shares without the approval of other owners

LO1

Advantages and Disadvantages of a Corporation

SE 2. Identify whether each of the following characteristics is an advantage or a disadvantage of the corporate form of business:

1. Ease of transfer of ownership
2. Taxation
3. Separate legal entity
4. Lack of mutual agency
5. Government regulation
6. Continuous existence

LO2 **Effect of Start-up and Organization Costs**

SE 3. At the beginning of 2009, Patel Company incurred the following start-up and organization costs: (1) attorneys' fees with a market value of $20,000, paid with 12,000 shares of $1 par value common stock, and (2) incorporation fees of $12,000. Calculate total start-up and organization costs. What will be the effect of these costs on the income statement and balance sheet?

LO1 **Exercise of Stock Options**

SE 4. On June 6, Aretha Dafoe received an option to purchase 20,000 shares of Shalom Company $1 par value common stock at an option price of $8 per share, which is equal to the market price on that date. The market price of the common stock on the date Dafoe exercises the option is $25 per share. (1) What value must be estimated to determine the expense of the option on June 6? (2) What relevance does the market price per share have when Dafoe later exercises the option?

LO2 **Stockholders' Equity**

SE 5. Prepare the stockholders' equity section of Fina Corporation's balance sheet from the following accounts and balances on December 31, 2010:

Common Stock, $10 par value, 30,000 shares authorized, 20,000 shares issued, and 19,500 shares outstanding	$200,000
Additional Paid-in Capital	100,000
Retained Earnings	15,000
Treasury Stock, Common (500 shares, at cost)	7,500

LO1 **Cash Dividends**

SE 6. Tone Corporation has authorized 200,000 shares of $1 par value common stock, of which 160,000 are issued and 140,000 are outstanding. On May 15, the board of directors declared a cash dividend of $.20 per share, payable on June 15 to stockholders of record on June 1. Prepare the entries in T accounts, as necessary, for each of the three dates.

LO3 **Preferred Stock Dividends with Dividends in Arrears**

SE 7. The Ferris Corporation has 2,000 shares of $100, 8 percent cumulative preferred stock outstanding and 40,000 shares of $1 par value common stock outstanding. In the company's first three years of operation, its board of directors paid cash dividends as follows: 2009, none; 2010, $40,000; and 2011, $80,000. Determine the total cash dividends and dividends per share paid to the preferred and common stockholders during each of the three years.

LO4 **Issuance of Stock**

SE 8. Rattich Company is authorized to issue 50,000 shares of common stock. The company sold 2,500 shares at $12 per share. Prepare entries in journal form to record the sale of stock for cash under each of the following independent alternatives: (1) The stock has a par value of $5, and (2) the stock has no par value but a stated value of $1 per share.

LO4 **Issuance of Stock for Noncash Assets**

SE 9. Embossing Corporation issued 32,000 shares of its $1 par value common stock in exchange for land that had a fair market value of $200,000. Prepare in journal form the entries necessary to record the issuance of the stock for the land under each of these conditions: (1) The stock was selling for $7 per share on the day of the transaction; (2) management attempted to place a value on the common stock but could not do so.

LO5 **Treasury Stock Transactions**

SE 10. Prepare in journal form the entries necessary to record the following stock transactions of the Seoul Company during 2010:

Oct. 1 Purchased 2,000 shares of its own $2 par value common stock for $20 per share, the current market price.

17 Sold 500 shares of treasury stock purchased on October 1 for $25 per share.

LO5 **Retirement of Treasury Stock**

SE 11. On October 28, 2010, the Seoul Company (**SE 10**) retired the remaining 1,500 shares of treasury stock. The shares were originally issued at $5 per share. Prepare the necessary entry in journal form.

Exercises

LO1 LO2 **Discussion Questions**

E 1. Develop brief answers to each of the following questions:

1. Why are most large companies established as corporations rather than as partnerships?
2. Why do many companies like to give stock options as compensation?
3. If an investor sells shares after the declaration date but before the date of record, does the seller still receive the dividend?
4. Why does a company usually not want to issue all its authorized shares?

LO3 LO4 LO5 **Discussion Questions**

E 2. Develop brief answers to each of the following questions:

1. Why would a company want to issue callable preferred stock?
2. What arguments can you give for treating preferred stock as debt rather than equity when carrying out financial analysis?
3. What relevance does par value or stated value have to a financial ratio, such as return on equity or debit to equity?
4. Why is treasury stock not considered an investment or an asset?

LO1 **Dividends Yield and Price/Earnings Ratio**

E 3. In 2011, Rainbow Corporation earned $8.80 per share and paid a dividend of $4.00 per share. At year end, the price of its stock was $132.00 per share. Calculate the dividends yield and the price/earnings ratio.

LO2 **Stockholders' Equity**

E 4. The following accounts and balances are from the records of Stuard Corporation on December 31, 2010:

Preferred Stock, $100 par value, 9 percent cumulative, 10,000 shares authorized, 3,000 shares issued and outstanding	$300,000
Common Stock, $12 par value, 22,500 shares authorized, 15,000 shares issued, and 14,250 shares outstanding	180,000
Additional Paid-in Capital	97,000
Retained Earnings	11,500
Treasury Stock, Common (750 shares, at cost)	15,000

Prepare the stockholders' equity section for Stuard Corporation's balance sheet as of December 31, 2010.

LO2 LO3

Characteristics of Common and Preferred Stock

E 5. Indicate whether each of the following characteristics is more closely associated with common stock (C) or preferred stock (P):

1. Often receives dividends at a set rate
2. Is considered the residual equity of a company
3. Can be callable
4. Can be convertible
5. More likely to have dividends that vary in amount from year to year
6. Can be entitled to receive dividends not paid in past years
7. Likely to have full voting rights
8. Receives assets first in liquidation
9. Generally receives dividends before other classes of stock

LO2 LO4

Stock Entries Using T Accounts; Stockholders' Equity

E 6. Shark School Supply Corporation was organized in 2010. It was authorized to issue 200,000 shares of no-par common stock with a stated value of $5 per share, and 40,000 shares of $100 par value, 6 percent noncumulative preferred stock. On March 1, the company issued 60,000 shares of its common stock for $15 per share and 8,000 shares of its preferred stock for $100 per share.

1. Record the issuance of the stock in T accounts.
2. Prepare the stockholders' equity section of Shark School Supply Corporation's balance sheet as it would appear immediately after the company issued the common and preferred stock.

LO1

Cash Dividends

E 7. Pine Corporation secured authorization from the state for 100,000 shares of $10 par value common stock. It has 40,000 shares issued and 35,000 shares outstanding. On June 5, the board of directors declared a $0.25 per share cash dividend to be paid on June 25 to stockholders of record on June 15. Prepare entries in T accounts to record these events.

LO1 LO5

Cash Dividends

E 8. Avena Corporation has 250,000 authorized shares of $1 par value common stock, of which 100,000 are issued, including 10,000 shares of treasury stock. On October 15, the corporation's board of directors declared a cash dividend of $0.50 per share payable on November 15 to stockholders of record on November 1. Prepare entries in T accounts for each of the three dates.

LO3

Cash Dividends with Dividends in Arrears

E 9. Ghana Corporation has 10,000 shares of its $100 par value, 7 percent cumulative preferred stock outstanding, and 50,000 shares of its $1 par value common stock outstanding. In Ghana's first four years of operation, its board of directors paid cash dividends as follows: 2009, none; 2010, $120,000; 2011, $140,000; 2012, $140,000. Determine the dividends per share and total cash dividends paid to the preferred and common stockholders during each of the four years.

LO3

Cash Dividends on Preferred and Common Stock

E 10. Dylan Corporation pays dividends at the end of each year. The dividends that it paid for 2009, 2010, and 2011 were $80,000, $60,000, and

$180,000, respectively. Calculate the total amount of dividends Dylan Corporation paid in each of these years to its common and preferred stockholders under both of the following capital structures: (1) 20,000 shares of $100 par, 6 percent noncumulative preferred stock and 60,000 shares of $10 par common stock; (2) 10,000 shares of $100 par, 7 percent cumulative preferred stock and 60,000 shares of $10 par common stock. Dylan Corporation had no dividends in arrears at the beginning of 2009.

LO4 **Issuance of Stock**

E 11. Power Net Company is authorized to issue 50,000 shares of common stock. On August 1, the company issued 2,500 shares at $25 per share. Prepare entries in journal form to record the issuance of stock for cash under each of the following alternatives:

1. The stock has a par value of $25.
2. The stock has a par value of $10.
3. The stock has no par value.
4. The stock has a stated value of $1 per share.

LO4 **Issuance of Stock for Noncash Assets**

E 12. On July 1, 2010, Kosa, a new corporation, issued 20,000 shares of its common stock to finance a corporate headquarters building. The building has a fair market value of $600,000 and a book value of $400,000. Because Kosa is a new corporation, it is not possible to establish a market value for its common stock. Record the issuance of stock for the building, assuming the following conditions: (1) the par value of the stock is $10 per share; (2) the stock is no-par stock; and (3) the stock has a stated value of $4 per share.

LO5 **Treasury Stock Transactions**

E 13. Record in T accounts the following stock transactions of Pigua Company, which represent all of the company's treasury stock transactions during 2010:

May	5	Purchased 1,600 shares of its own $2 par value common stock for $40 per share, the current market price.
	17	Sold 600 shares of treasury stock purchased on May 5 for $44 per share.
	21	Sold 400 shares of treasury stock purchased on May 5 for $40 per share.
	28	Sold the remaining 600 shares of treasury stock purchased on May 5 for $38 per share.

LO5 **Treasury Stock Transactions Including Retirement**

E 14. Record in T accounts the following stock transactions of Lopez Corporation, which represent all its treasury stock transactions for the year:

June	1	Purchased 2,000 shares of its own $15 par value common stock for $35 per share, the current market price.
	10	Sold 500 shares of treasury stock purchased on June 1 for $40 per share.
	20	Sold 700 shares of treasury stock purchased on June 1 for $29 per share.
	30	Retired the remaining shares purchased on June 1. The original issue price was $21 per share.

Problems

LO1 LO2 LO4

Common Stock Transactions and Stockholders' Equity

KLOOSTER & ALLEN

P 1. On March 1, 2010, Dora Corporation began operations with a charter it received from the state that authorized 50,000 shares of $4 par value common stock. Over the next quarter, the company engaged in the transactions that follow.

Mar.	1	Issued 15,000 shares of common stock, $100,000.
	2	Paid fees associated with obtaining the charter and starting up and organizing the corporation, $12,000.
Apr.	10	Issued 6,500 shares of common stock, $65,000.
	15	Purchased 2,500 shares of common stock, $25,000.
May	31	The board of directors declared a $.20 per share cash dividend to be paid on June 15 to shareholders of record on June 10.

Required

1. Record the above transactions in T accounts.
2. Prepare the stockholders' equity section of Dora Corporation's balance sheet on May 31, 2010. Net income earned during the first quarter was $15,000.
3. What effect, if any, will the cash dividend declaration on May 31 have on Dora Corporation's net income, retained earnings, and cash flows? (User insight ▶)

Preferred and Common Stock Dividends and Dividends Yield

P 2. The Rago Corporation had the following stock outstanding from 2009 through 2012:

Preferred stock: $100 par value, 8 percent cumulative, 5,000 shares authorized, issued, and outstanding

Common stock: $10 par value, 100,000 shares authorized, issued, and outstanding

The company paid $30,000, $30,000, $94,000, and $130,000 in dividends during 2009, 2010, 2011, and 2012, respectively. The market price per common share was $7.25 and $8.00 per share at the end of years 2011 and 2012, respectively.

Required

1. Determine the dividends per share and the total dividends paid to common stockholders and preferred stockholders in the years 2009, 2010, 2011, and 2012.
2. Perform the same computations, with the assumption that the preferred stock was noncumulative.
3. Calculate the 2011 and 2012 dividends yield for common stock, using the dividends per share computed in requirement **2**.
4. How are cumulative preferred stock and noncumulative preferred stock similar to long-term bonds? How do they differ from long-term bonds? (User insight ▶)

LO4 LO5

Comprehensive Stockholders' Equity Transactions

KLOOSTER & ALLEN

P 3. In January 2010, the Janas Corporation was organized and authorized to issue 1,000,000 shares of no-par common stock and 25,000 shares of 5 percent, $50 par value, noncumulative preferred stock.

The stock-related transactions for the first year's operations are listed on the following page.

		Account	
		Debited	Credited
Jan. 19	Sold 7,500 shares of common stock for $15,750. State law requires a minimum of $1 stated value per share.	110 ($15,750)	310 ($7,500) 312 ($8,250)
21	Issued 2,500 shares of common stock to attorneys and accountants for services valued at $5,500 and provided during the organization of the corporation.		
Feb. 7	Issued 15,000 shares of common stock for a building that had an appraised value of $39,000.		
Mar. 22	Purchased 5,000 shares of its common stock at $3 per share.		
July 15	Issued 2,500 shares of common stock to employees under a stock option plan that allows any employee to buy shares at the current market price, which is now $3 per share.		
Aug. 1	Sold 1,250 shares of treasury stock for $4 per share.		
Sept. 1	Declared a cash dividend of $.15 per common share to be paid on September 25 to stockholders of record on September 15.		
15	Date of record for cash dividends		
25	Paid cash dividends to stockholders of record on September 15.		
Oct. 30	Issued 2,000 shares of common stock for a piece of land. The stock was selling for $3 per share, and the land had a fair market value of $6,000.		
Dec. 15	Issued 1,100 shares of preferred stock for $50 per share.		

Required

1. For each of the above transactions, enter in the blanks provided the account numbers and dollar amounts (as shown in the example) for the account(s) debited and credited. The account numbers are listed below.

110 Cash	312 Additional Paid-in Capital
120 Land	313 Paid-in Capital, Treasury Stock
121 Building	340 Retained Earnings
220 Dividends Payable	341 Dividends
305 Preferred Stock	350 Treasury Stock, Common
310 Common Stock	510 Start-up and Organization Costs

User insight ▶ 2. Why is the stockholders' equity section of the balance sheet an important consideration in analyzing the performance of a company?

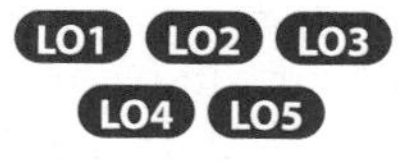

Comprehensive Stockholders' Equity Transactions and Stockholders' Equity

P 4. Kras, Inc., was organized and authorized to issue 5,000 shares of $100 par value, 9 percent preferred stock and 50,000 shares of no-par, $5 stated value common stock on July 1, 2010. Stock-related transactions for Kras are as follows:

July	1	Issued 10,000 shares of common stock at $11 per share.
	1	Issued 500 shares of common stock at $11 per share for services rendered in connection with the organization of the company.
	2	Issued 1,000 shares of preferred stock at par value for cash.
	10	Issued 2,500 shares of common stock for land on which the asking price was $70,000. Market value of the stock was $12. Management wishes to record the land at full market value of the stock.
Aug.	2	Purchased 1,500 shares of its common stock at $13 per share.
	10	Declared a cash dividend for one month on the outstanding preferred stock and $.02 per share on common stock outstanding, payable on August 22 to stockholders of record on August 12.
	12	Date of record for cash dividends.
	22	Paid cash dividends.

Required

1. Record the transactions in journal form.
2. Prepare the stockholders' equity section of the balance sheet as it would appear on August 31, 2010. The Company's net income for July and August was $11,500.

User insight ▶ 3. Calculate dividends yield, price/earnings ratio, and return on equity. Assume earnings per common share are $1.00 and market price per common share is $20. For beginning stockholders' equity, use the balance after the July transactions.

User insight ▶ 4. Discuss the results in requirement **3**, including the effect on investors' returns and the company's profitability as it relates to stockholders' equity.

LO1 LO5

Treasury Stock

P 5. The Rolek Company was involved in the following treasury stock transactions during 2010:

a. Purchased 40,000 shares of its $1 par value common stock on the market for $2.50 per share.
b. Purchased 8,000 shares of its $1 par value common stock on the market for $2.80 per share.
c. Sold 22,000 shares purchased in **a** for $65,500.
d. Sold the other 18,000 shares purchased in **a** for $36,000.
e. Sold 3,000 of the remaining shares of treasury stock for $1.60 per share.
f. Retired all the remaining shares of treasury stock. All shares originally were issued at $1.50 per share.

Required

1. Record the treasury stock transactions in T accounts.

User insight ▶ 2. What do you think is the reasoning behind treating the purchase of treasury stock as a reduction in stockholders' equity as opposed to treating it as an investment asset?

Alternate Problems

LO1 LO2 LO4 LO5

Common Stock Transactions and Stockholders' Equity

P 6. Glass Corporation began operations on September 1, 2010. The corporation's charter authorized 150,000 shares of $8 par value common stock. Glass Corporation engaged in the following transactions during its first quarter:

Sept.	1	Issued 25,000 shares of common stock, $250,000.
	1	Paid an attorney $16,000 to help start up and organize the corporation and obtain a corporate charter from the state.
Oct.	2	Issued 40,000 shares of common stock, $480,000.
	15	Purchased 5,000 shares of common stock for $75,000.
Nov.	30	Declared a cash dividend of $.40 per share to be paid on December 15 to stockholders of record on December 10.

Required

1. Prepare entries in T accounts to record the above transactions.
2. Prepare the stockholders' equity section of Glass Corporation's balance sheet on November 30, 2010. Net income for the quarter was $40,000.

User insight ▶

3. What effect, if any, will the cash dividend declaration on November 30 have on net income, retained earnings, and cash flows?

Preferred and Common Stock Dividends and Dividend Yield

P 7. The Vegas Corporation had both common stock and preferred stock outstanding from 2009 through 2011. Information about each stock for the three years is as follows:

Type	Par Value	Shares Outstanding	Other
Preferred	$100	20,000	7% cumulative
Common	20	300,000	

The company paid $70,000, $400,000, and $550,000 in dividends for 2009 through 2011, respectively. The market price per common share was $15 and $17 per share at the end of years 2010 and 2011, respectively.

Required

1. Determine the dividends per share and total dividends paid to the common and preferred stockholders each year.
2. Assuming that the preferred stock was noncumulative, repeat the computations performed in requirement **1**.
3. Calculate the 2010 and 2011 dividends yield for common stock using dividends per share computed in requirement **2**.

User insight ▶

4. How are cumulative preferred stock and noncumulative preferred stock similar to long-term bonds? How do they differ from long-term bonds?

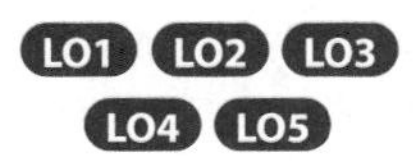

Comprehensive Stockholders' Equity Transactions and Financial Ratios

P 8. Stavski Plastics Corporation was chartered in the state of Massachusetts. The company was authorized to issue 10,000 shares of $100 par value, 6 percent preferred stock and 50,000 shares of no-par common stock. The common stock has a $2 stated value. The stock-related transactions for the quarter ended October 31, 2010, were as follows:

Aug.	3	Issued 10,000 shares of common stock at $22 per share.
	15	Issued 8,000 shares of common stock for land. Asking price for the land was $100,000. Common stock's market value was $12 per share.
	22	Issued 5,000 shares of preferred stock for $500,000.

Oct.	4	Issued 5,000 shares of common stock for $60,000.
	10	Purchased 2,500 shares of common stock for the treasury for $6,500.
	15	Declared a quarterly cash dividend on the outstanding preferred stock and $.10 per share on common stock outstanding, payable on October 31 to stockholders of record on October 25.
	25	Date of record for cash dividends.
	31	Paid cash dividends.

Required

1. Record transactions for the quarter ended October 31, 2010, in T accounts.
2. Prepare the stockholders' equity section of the balance sheet as of October 31, 2010. Net income for the quarter was $23,000.
3. **User insight ▶** Calculate dividends yield, price/earnings ratio, and return on equity. Assume earnings per common share are $1.97 and market price per common share is $25. For beginning stockholders' equity, use the balance after the August transactions.
4. **User insight ▶** Discuss the results in requirement **3**, including the effect on investors' returns and the firm's profitability as it relates to stockholders' equity.

ENHANCING Your Knowledge, Skills, and Critical Thinking

Conceptual Understanding Cases

LO1 Reasons for Issuing Common Stock

C 1. **DreamWorks Animation**, led by billionaire Microsoft founder Paul Allen, went public in a recent year with its class A common stock at $28 per share, raising $650 million. By the end of the first day, it was up 27 percent to $38 per share, giving the company a value of almost $1 billion.[16] This initial enthusiasm did not last. By the end of 2007, the price was only around $25 per share. As a growing company that has produced such animated hits as *Shrek* and *Shrek II*, DreamWorks could have borrowed significant funds by issuing long-term debt. What are some advantages of issuing common stock as opposed to bonds? What are some disadvantages?

LO3 Reasons for Issuing Preferred Stock

C 2. Preferred stock is a hybrid security; it has some of the characteristics of stock and some of the characteristics of bonds. Historically, preferred stock has not been a popular means of financing. In the past few years, however, it has become more attractive to companies and individual investors alike, and investors are buying large amounts because of high yields. Large preferred stock issues have been made by such banks as **Chase**, **Citibank**, **HSBC Bank USA**, and **Wells Fargo**, as well as by other companies. The dividends yields on these stocks are over 9 percent, higher than the interest rates on bonds of comparable risk.[17] Especially popular are preferred equity redemption convertible stocks, or PERCs, which are automatically convertible into common stock after three years if the company does not call them first and retire them. What reasons can you give for the popularity of preferred stock, and of PERCs in particular, when the tax-deductible interest on bonds is lower? Discuss from both the company's and the investor's standpoint.

LO5 **Purposes of Treasury Stock**

C 3. Many companies in recent years have bought back their common stock. For example, **IBM**, with large cash holdings, spent almost $18 billion over three years repurchasing its stock.[18] What are the reasons companies buy back their own shares? What is the effect of common stock buybacks on earnings per share, return on equity, return on assets, debt to equity, and the current ratio?

Interpreting Financial Reports

LO4 **Effect of Stock Issue**

C 4. When **Google, Inc.** went public with an IPO, it used an auction system that allowed everyone to participate rather than allocating shares of stock to a few insiders. As mentioned in the Decision Point at the beginning of this chapter, the company's IPO drew widespread attention. Announcements of the IPO would have been similar to the following:

22,500,000 Shares
GOOGLE, INC.
$0.001 Par Value Common Stock
Price $85 a share

The gross proceeds of the IPO before issue costs were $1.9 billion.

Shown below is a portion of the stockholders' equity section of the balance sheet adapted from Google's annual report, which was issued prior to this stock offering:

Stockholders' Equity
(In thousands)

Common Stock, $0.001 par value, 700,000 shares authorized; 161,000 shares issued and outstanding	$ 161
Additional paid-in capital	725,219
Retained earnings	191,352

1. Assume that the net proceeds to Google after issue costs were $1.8 billion. Record the stock issuance on Google's accounting records in journal form.
2. Prepare the portion of the stockholders' equity section of the balance sheet shown above after the issue of the common stock, based on the information given. Round all answers to the nearest thousand.
3. Based on your answer in **2**, did Google have to increase its authorized shares to undertake this stock issue?
4. What amount per share did Google receive and how much did Google's underwriters receive to help in issuing the stock? What do underwriters do to earn their fee?

Effect of Deferring Preferred Dividends

C 5. **US Airways** had indefinitely deferred the quarterly dividend on its $358 million of cumulative convertible 9 1/4 percent preferred stock.[19] According to a US Airways spokesperson, the company did not want to "continue to pay a dividend while the company is losing money." Others interpreted the action as "an indication of a cash crisis situation."

At the time, **Berkshire Hathaway**, the large company run by Warren Buffett and the owner of the preferred stock, was not happy. However, US Airways was able to turn around, become profitable, and return to paying its cumulative dividends on preferred stock. Berkshire Hathaway was able to convert the preferred stock into 9.24 million common shares of US Airways' common stock at $38.74 per share at a time when the market value had risen to $62.[20]

What is cumulative convertible preferred stock? Why is deferring dividends on those shares a drastic action? What is the impact on profitability and liquidity? Why did using preferred stock instead of long-term bonds as a financing method probably save the company from bankruptcy? What was Berkshire Hathaway's gain on its investment at the time of the conversion?

Decision Analysis Using Excel

LO1 LO2

Analysis of Alternative Financing Methods

K/R

C 6. Westec Corporation, which offers services to the computer industry, has expanded rapidly in recent years. Because of its profitability, the company has been able to grow without obtaining external financing. This fact is reflected in its current balance sheet, which contains no long-term debt. The liabilities and stockholders' equity sections of the company's balance sheet on March 31, 2010, appear below.

Westec Corporation
Balance Sheet
March 31, 2010

Liabilities		
Current liabilities		$ 500,000
Stockholders' Equity		
Common stock, $10 par value, 500,000 shares authorized, 100,000 shares issued and outstanding	$1,000,000	
Additional paid-in capital	1,800,000	
Retained earnings	1,700,000	
Total stockholders' equity		4,500,000
Total liabilities and stockholders' equity		$5,000,000

The company now has the opportunity to double its size by purchasing the operations of a rival company for $4,000,000. If the purchase goes through, Westec will become one of the top companies in its specialized industry. The problem for management is how to finance the purchase. After much study and discussion with bankers and underwriters, management has prepared the following three financing alternatives to present to the board of directors, which must authorize the purchase and the financing:

Alternative A The company could issue $4,000,000 of long-term debt. Given the company's financial rating and the current market rates, management believes the company will have to pay an interest rate of 12 percent on the debt.

Alternative B The company could issue 40,000 shares of 8 percent, $100 par value preferred stock.

Alternative C The company could issue 100,000 additional shares of $10 par value common stock at $40 per share.

Management explains to the board that the interest on the long-term debt is tax-deductible and that the applicable income tax rate is 40 percent. The board members know that a dividend of $.80 per share of common stock was paid last year, up from $.60 and $.40 per share in the two years before that. The board has had a policy of regular increases in dividends of $.20 per share. The board believes each of the three financing alternatives is feasible and now wants to study the financial effects of each alternative.

1. Prepare a schedule to show how the liabilities and stockholders' equity sections of Westec's balance sheet would look under each alternative, and compute the debt to equity ratio (total liabilities ÷ total stockholders' equity) for each.
2. Compute and compare the cash needed to pay the interest or dividends for each kind of new financing, net of income taxes, in the first year.
3. How might the cash needed to pay for the financing change in future years under each alternative?
4. Prepare a memorandum to the board of directors that evaluates the alternatives in order of preference based on cash flow effects, giving arguments for and against each one.

Annual Report Case: CVS Caremark Corporation

LO5

Stockholders' Equity

C 7. Refer to the **CVS** annual report in the Supplement to Chapter 1 to answer the following questions:

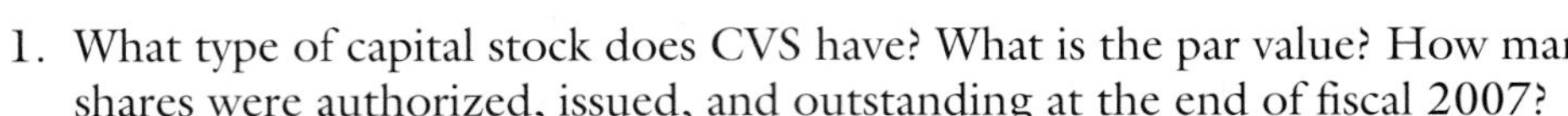

1. What type of capital stock does CVS have? What is the par value? How many shares were authorized, issued, and outstanding at the end of fiscal 2007?
2. What is the dividends yield (use average price of stock in last quarter) for CVS and its relationship to the investors' total return? Does the company rely mostly on stock or on earnings for its stockholders' equity?
3. Does the company have a stock option plan? To whom do the stock options apply? Do employees have significant stock options? Given the market price of the stock shown in the report, do these options represent significant value to the employees?

Comparison Case: CVS Versus Southwest

Return on Equity, Treasury Stock, and Dividends Policy

C 8. Refer to the **CVS** annual report and the financial statements of **Southwest Airlines Co.** in the Supplement to Chapter 1.

1. Compute the return on equity for both companies for fiscal 2007 and 2006. Total stockholders' equity for CVS and Southwest in 2005 was $8,331.2 million and $6,675 million, respectively.
2. Did either company purchase treasury stock during these years? How will the purchase of treasury stock affect return on equity and earnings per share?
3. Did either company issue stock during these years? What are the details?
4. Compare the dividend policy of the two companies.

Ethical Dilemma Case

LO1 LO5

Ethics, Management Compensation, and Treasury Stock

C 9. Compensation of senior management is often tied to earnings per share or return on equity. Treasury stock purchases have a favorable impact on both these measures. In the recent buyback boom, many companies borrowed money to purchase treasury shares. In some cases, the motivation for the borrowing and repurchase of shares was the desire of executives to secure their year-end cash bonuses. Did these executives act ethically? Were their actions in the best interests of stockholders? Why or why not? How might such behavior be avoided in the future?

Internet Case

LO1 LO2 LO3 LO4 LO5

Comprehensive Analysis of Stockholders' Equity

C 10. Many Internet companies have gone public in recent years. These companies are generally unprofitable in their start-up years and require a great deal of cash to finance expansion. They also reward their employees with stock options. Choose any one of the following Internet companies: **Amazon.com**, **Yahoo!**, or **eBay**. Go to the website of the company you have selected. In the company's latest annual report, look at the financing section of the statement of cash flows for the last three years. How has the company financed its business? Has it issued stock or long-term debt? Has it purchased treasury stock, paid dividends, or issued stock under stock option plans? Is the company profitable (see net income or earnings at the top of the statement)? Are your findings in line with your expectations about Internet companies? Find the company's stock price, either on its website or in a newspaper, and compare it with the average issue price of the company's past stock issues. Summarize your findings and conclusions.

Group Activity Case

LO1 LO5

Treasury Stock or Dividends?

C 11. In your class, divide into small groups. Assume the president of a small company that has been profitable for several years but has not paid a dividend has hired your group. The company has built up a cash reserve. It has 20 stockholders, but the president owns 40 percent of the company's shares. Several of the stockholders with smaller numbers of shares would like to sell their shares, but there is no ready market. The president of the company has asked your group to determine whether it would be better to recommend to the board of directors that they pay a dividend to all stockholders or whether they should buy out the smaller stockholders to hold in the treasury shares and possibly retire them. In your group, decide which recommendation you will make to the president. Develop a series of points to support your argument. Participate in a class debate among teams who have chosen opposing positions.

Business Communication Case

Debt or Equity Financing

C 12. As noted in Case 4, **Google, Inc.**, announced a common stock issue:

22,500,000 Shares
$0.001 Par Value Common Stock
Price $85 a share

The net proceeds before issue costs were approximately $1.9 billion.

Given Google's successful track record as a start-up company, it is likely the company could have borrowed over $1.9 billion in debt financing rather than issue common stock. Write a one-page business memorandum that takes either the position that (1) Google should have issued debt at an interest rate of 8 percent or (2) Google is correct in issuing common stock. Be sure to include in your presentation the effect of your alternative on the debt to equity ratio and return on equity.

CHAPTER 12

The Corporate Income Statement and the Statement of Stockholders' Equity

Focus on Financial Statements

INCOME STATEMENT
Revenues
– Expenses
= Net Income

STATEMENT OF RETAINED EARNINGS
Opening Balance
+ Net Income
– Dividends
= Retained Earnings

BALANCE SHEET
Assets | Liabilities
Equity
A = L + E

STATEMENT OF CASH FLOWS
Operating activities
+ Investing activities
+ Financing activities
= Change in Cash
+ Starting Balance
= Ending Cash Balance

Net income from income statement is on statement of retained earnings; retained earnings is often component on statement of stockholders' equity.

As we pointed out in an earlier chapter, earnings management—the practice of manipulating revenues and expenses to achieve a specific outcome—is unethical when companies use it to create misleading financial statements. Users of financial statements consider the possibility of earnings management by assessing the quality, or sustainability, of a company's earnings. To do so, they evaluate how the components of the company's income statement affect earnings. In this chapter, we focus on those components. We also cover earnings per share, the statement of stockholders' equity, stock dividends and stock splits, and book value per share.

LEARNING OBJECTIVES

LO1 **Define *quality of earnings*, and identify the components of a corporate income statement.** *(pp. 610–616)*

LO2 **Show the relationships among income taxes expense, deferred income taxes, and net of taxes.** *(pp. 616–620)*

LO3 **Compute earnings per share.** *(pp. 620–622)*

LO4 **Define *comprehensive income*, and describe the statement of stockholders' equity.** *(pp. 623–625)*

LO5 **Account for stock dividends and stock splits.** *(pp. 625–630)*

LO6 **Calculate book value per share.** *(pp. 630–631)*

DECISION POINT ▶ A USER'S FOCUS

Motorola, Inc.

Motorola, a well-known maker of cell phones and other telecommunications equipment, has had its ups and downs in recent years. As shown in its Financial Highlights, the company had good earnings in 2005 and 2006 but a big decrease in revenue and an operating loss in 2007. These results reflect the initial success of the Razr phone, followed by the company's difficulty in extending the phone's popularity.[1]

How does one use complex income statements like Motorola's to evaluate a company's performance? It is not enough to simply look at the "bottom line" (i.e., net earnings) or even at net sales and operating income. To gain a proper perspective on a company's performance, one must examine the components of its income statement.

MOTOROLA'S FINANCIAL HIGHLIGHTS (In millions)

		2007		2006		2005
Net sales		$36,622		$42,847		$35,310
Operating earnings (loss)		(553)		4,092		4,605
Net earnings (loss)		(49)		3,661		4,578
Basic earnings per share						
Continuing operations	(0.05)		1.33		1.83	
Discontinued operations	0.03	(0.02)	0.17	1.50	0.02	1.85
Cash flows from operating activities		3,066		1,991		1,151

- ▶ What items other than normal operating activities contributed to Motorola's performance?
- ▶ What does the company's income statement indicate about its quality of earnings?
- ▶ How does one put the various measures of performance (some of which are shown in Motorola's financial highlights) in perspective?

Performance Measurement: Quality of Earnings Issues

LO1 Define *quality of earnings*, and identify the components of a corporate income statement.

Net income (net earnings) is the measure most commonly used to evaluate a company's performance. In fact, a survey of 2,000 members of the Association for Investment Management and Research indicated that the two most important economic measures in evaluating common stocks were expected changes in earnings per share and expected return on equity.[2] Net income is a key component of both measures.

Because of the importance of net income, or the "bottom line," in measuring a company's prospects, there is significant interest in evaluating the quality of the net income figure, or the **quality of earnings**. The quality of a company's earnings refers to the substance of earnings and their sustainability into future accounting periods. For example, if earnings increase because of a gain on the sale of an asset, this portion of earnings will not be sustained in the future.

The accounting estimates and methods that a company uses affect the quality of its earnings, as do these components of the income statement:

- Gains and losses on transactions
- Write-downs and restructurings
- Nonoperating items

Because management has choices in the content and positioning of these income statement components, there is a potential for managing earnings to achieve specific income targets. It is therefore critical for users of income statements to understand these factors and take them into consideration when evaluating a company's performance.

Study Note

It is important to know which items included in earnings are recurring and which are one-time items. Income from continuing operations before nonoperating items gives a clear signal about future results. In assessing a company's future earnings potential, nonoperating items are excluded because they are not expected to continue.

Exhibit 1 shows the components of a typical corporate income statement. Net income or loss (the "bottom line" of the income statement) includes all revenues, expenses, gains, and losses over the accounting period. When a company has both continuing and discontinued operations, the operating income section is called **income from continuing operations**. Income from continuing operations before income taxes may include gains or losses on the sale of assets, write-downs, and restructurings. The income taxes expense section of the statement is subject to special accounting rules.

As you can see in Exhibit 1, the section of a corporate income statement that follows income taxes contains such nonoperating items as discontinued operations and extraordinary gains (or losses). Another item that may appear in this section is the write-off of goodwill when its value has been impaired. Earnings per share information appears at the bottom of the statement.

FOCUS ON BUSINESS PRACTICE

Why Do Investors Study Quality of Earnings?

Analysts for **Twentieth Century Mutual Funds**, a major investment company now merged with **American Century Investments Corporation**, make adjustments to a company's reported financial performance to create a more accurate picture of the company's ongoing operations. For example, suppose a paper manufacturer reports earnings of $1.30 per share. Further investigation, however, shows that the per share number includes a one-time gain on the sale of assets, which accounts for an increase of $.25 per share. Twentieth Century would list the company as earning only $1.05 per share. "These kinds of adjustments help assure long-term decisions aren't based on one-time events."[3]

EXHIBIT 1 Corporate Income Statement

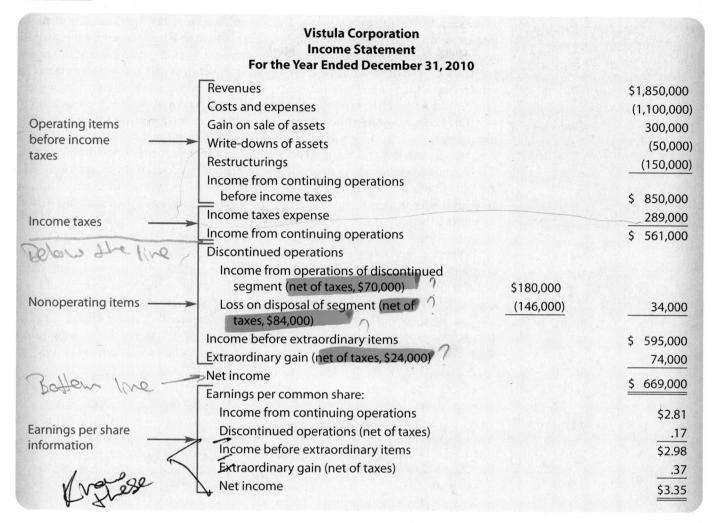

Vistula Corporation
Income Statement
For the Year Ended December 31, 2010

Operating items before income taxes	Revenues		$1,850,000
	Costs and expenses		(1,100,000)
	Gain on sale of assets		300,000
	Write-downs of assets		(50,000)
	Restructurings		(150,000)
	Income from continuing operations before income taxes		$ 850,000
Income taxes	Income taxes expense		289,000
	Income from continuing operations		$ 561,000
Nonoperating items	Discontinued operations		
	Income from operations of discontinued segment (net of taxes, $70,000)	$180,000	
	Loss on disposal of segment (net of taxes, $84,000)	(146,000)	34,000
	Income before extraordinary items		$ 595,000
	Extraordinary gain (net of taxes, $24,000)		74,000
	Net income		$ 669,000
Earnings per share information	Earnings per common share:		
	Income from continuing operations		$2.81
	Discontinued operations (net of taxes)		.17
	Income before extraordinary items		$2.98
	Extraordinary gain (net of taxes)		.37
	Net income		$3.35

The Effect of Accounting Estimates and Methods

Users of financial statements need to be aware of the impact that accounting estimates and methods have on the income that a firm reports. As you know, to comply with the matching rule, accountants must assign revenues and expenses to the periods in which they occur. If they cannot establish a direct relationship between revenues and expenses, they systematically allocate the expenses among the accounting periods that benefit from them, and in doing so, they must make estimates and exercise judgment. An accounting estimate should be based on realistic assumptions, but there is latitude in making the estimate, and the final judgment will affect the net income that appears on a company's income statement.

For example, when a company acquires an asset, the accountant must estimate the asset's useful life. Technological obsolescence could shorten the asset's expected useful life, and regular maintenance and repairs could lengthen it. Although the actual useful life cannot be known with certainty until some future date, the accountant's estimate of it affects both current and future operating income. Other areas that require accounting estimates include the residual value of assets, uncollectible accounts receivable, sales returns, total units of production, total recoverable units of natural resources, amortization periods, warranty claims, and environmental cleanup costs.

Study Note

Although companies in the same industry may have comparable earnings, their quality of earnings may not be comparable. To assess the quality of a company's reported earnings, you must know the estimates and methods it uses to compute income. Generally accepted accounting principles allow several methods, all yielding different results.

The importance of accounting estimates depends on the industry in which a firm operates. For example, estimated uncollectible receivables for a credit card firm, such as **American Express**, or for a financial services firm, such as **Bank of America**, can have a material impact on earnings, but estimated useful life may be less important because depreciable assets represent a small percentage of the firm's total assets. **Walgreens** has very few receivables, but it has major investments in depreciable assets. Thus, estimates of useful life and residual value are more important to Walgreens than an estimate of uncollectible accounts receivable.

The accounting methods a firm uses also affect its operating income. Generally accepted accounting methods include uncollectible receivable methods (percentage of net sales and aging of accounts receivable), inventory methods (LIFO, FIFO, and average-cost), depreciation methods (accelerated, production, and straight-line), and revenue recognition methods. All these methods are designed to match revenues and expenses, but the expenses are estimates, and the period or periods benefited cannot be demonstrated conclusively. In practice, it is hard to justify one method of estimation over another.

Different accounting methods have different effects on net income. Some methods are more conservative than others because they tend to produce a lower net income in the current period. For example, suppose that two companies have similar operations, but one uses FIFO for inventory costing and the straight-line (SL) method for computing depreciation, whereas the other uses LIFO for inventory costing and the double-declining-balance (DDB) method for computing depreciation. The income statements of the two companies might appear as follows:

	FIFO and SL	LIFO and DDB
Net sales	$462,500	$462,500
Cost of goods available for sale	$200,000	$200,000
Less ending inventory	30,000	25,000
Cost of goods sold	$170,000	$175,000
Gross margin	$292,500	$287,500
Less depreciation expense	$ 20,000	$ 40,000
Less other expenses	85,000	85,000
Total operating expenses	$105,000	$125,000
Income from continuing operations before income taxes	$187,500	$162,500

The income from continuing operations before income taxes for the firm that uses LIFO and DDB is lower because in periods of rising prices, the LIFO method produces a higher cost of goods sold, and in the early years of an asset's useful life, accelerated depreciation yields a higher depreciation expense. The result is lower operating income. However, future operating income should be higher.

Although the choice of accounting method does not affect cash flows except for possible differences in income taxes, the $25,000 difference in operating income stems solely from the choice of accounting methods. Estimates of the useful lives and residual values of plant assets could lead to an even greater difference. In practice, of course, differences in net income occur for many reasons, but the user of financial statements must be aware of the discrepancies that can occur as a result of the accounting methods used in preparing the statements. In general, an accounting method or estimate that results in lower current earnings produces a better quality of operating income.

The latitude that companies have in their choice of accounting methods and estimates could cause problems in the interpretation of financial statements were it not for the conventions of full disclosure and consistency. As noted in an

FOCUS ON BUSINESS PRACTICE

Beware of the "Bottom Line!"

In the second quarter of 2007, **McDonald's** posted its second-ever loss: $711.7 million. Is this cause for concern? In fact, it is misleading: the company is actually in a period of rapidly growing revenues and profits. The loss resulted from a one-time, noncash impairment of $1.6 billion, related to investments in Latin America. In another example, **Campbell Soup** showed unrealistically positive results in a recent year. Its income jumped by 31 percent, due to a tax settlement and an accounting restatement. Without these items, its revenue and income would have been up less than 1 percent, and soup sales—its main product—actually dropped by 6 percent. The lesson to be learned is to look beyond the "bottom line" to the components of the income statement when evaluating a company's performance.[4]

earlier chapter, full disclosure requires management to explain the significant accounting policies used in preparing the financial statements in a note to the statements. Consistency requires that the same accounting procedures be followed from year to year. If a change in procedure is made, the nature of the change and its monetary effect must be explained in a note. For instance, in a note to its financial statements, **Motorola** discloses that it uses the FIFO method for inventory accounting and a combination of straight-line and accelerated depreciation methods for various groups of long-term assets.

Gains and Losses

When a company sells or otherwise disposes of operating assets or marketable securities, a gain or loss generally results. Although these gains or losses appear in the operating section of the income statement, they usually represent one-time events. They are not sustainable, ongoing operations, and management often has some choice as to their timing. Thus, from an analyst's point of view, they should be ignored when considering operating income.

Write-downs and Restructurings

When management decides that an asset is no longer of value to the company, a write-down or restructuring occurs.

- A **write-down**, also called a *write-off*, is a reduction in the value of an asset below its carrying value on the balance sheet.
- A **restructuring** is the estimated cost of a change in a company's operations. It usually involves the closing of facilities and the laying off of personnel.

Both write-downs and restructurings reduce current operating income and boost future income by shifting future costs to the current accounting period. They are often an indication of poor management decisions in the past, such as paying too much for the assets of another company or making operational changes that do not work out. Companies sometimes take all possible losses in the current year so that future years will be "clean" of these costs. Such "big baths," as they are called, commonly occur when a company is having a bad year. They also often occur in years when there is a change in management. The new management takes a "big bath" in the current year so it can show improved results in future years.

In a recent year, 35 percent of 600 large companies had write-downs of tangible assets, and 42 percent had restructurings. Another 112 percent had write-downs or charges related to intangible assets, often involving goodwill.[5]

FOCUS ON BUSINESS PRACTICE

Can You Believe "Pro Forma" Earnings?

Companies must report earnings in accordance with GAAP, but many also report "pro forma" earnings. Pro forma reporting of earnings, in the words of one analyst, means that they "have thrown out the bad stuff."[6] In other words, when companies report pro forma earnings, they are telling the investment community to ignore one-time losses and nonoperating items, which may reflect bad decisions in the past. In the late 1990s, technology firms with high growth rates and volatile or low earnings and firms that unexpectedly miss earnings targets widely relied on pro forma results. More recent research has shown that after the bubble burst in 2001–2002 and after the Enron collapse, the number of companies reporting pro forma earnings declined significantly.[7] The investment community learned that GAAP earnings are a better benchmark of a company's performance because they are based on recognized standards used by all companies, whereas there is no generally accepted way to report pro forma earnings. They are whatever the company wants you to see.

Nonoperating Items

The nonoperating items that appear on the income statement include discontinued operations and extraordinary gains and losses, both of which can significantly affect net income. In Exhibit 1, earnings per common share for income from continuing operations are $2.81, but when all the nonoperating items are taken into consideration, net income per share is $3.35. **Discontinued operations** are segments of a business, such as a separate major line of business, or serve a separate class of customer that is no longer part of a company's operations. To make it easier to evaluate a company's ongoing operations, generally accepted accounting principles require that gains and losses from discontinued operations be reported separately on the income statement.

In Exhibit 1, the disclosure of discontinued operations has two parts. One part shows that after the decision to discontinue, the income from operations of the disposed segment was $180,000 (net of $70,000 taxes). The other part shows that the loss from the disposal of the segment was $146,000 (net of $84,000 tax savings). (The computation of the gains or losses involved in discontinued operations is covered in more advanced accounting courses.)

Extraordinary items are "events or transactions that are distinguished by their unusual nature *and* by the infrequency of their occurrence."[8] Items usually treated as extraordinary include the following:

1. An uninsured loss from flood, earthquake, fire, or theft
2. A gain or loss resulting from the passage of a new law
3. The expropriation (taking) of property by a foreign government

In Exhibit 1, the extraordinary gain was $74,000 after taxes of $24,000.

Quality of Earnings and Cash Flows

K/R

The reason for considering quality of earnings issues is to assess how various components of the income statement affect cash flows and performance measures affected by earnings, such as profit margin, return on assets, and return on equity. Generally, except for their effect on income taxes, gains and losses, asset write-downs, restructurings, and nonoperating items have no effect on cash flows because the cash for these items has already been expended. Thus, the focus of analysis is on sustainable earnings, which generally have a relationship to future cash flows.

Motorola provides communications equipment to the National Football League. Shown here wearing a Motorola headset is Bill Belichick, head coach of the New England Patriots. Despite Motorola's sluggish results in recent years, its CEO pointed out in 2005 that the company's quality of earnings had improved from year to year. *Quality of earnings* refers to the substance and sustainability of earnings into future accounting periods.

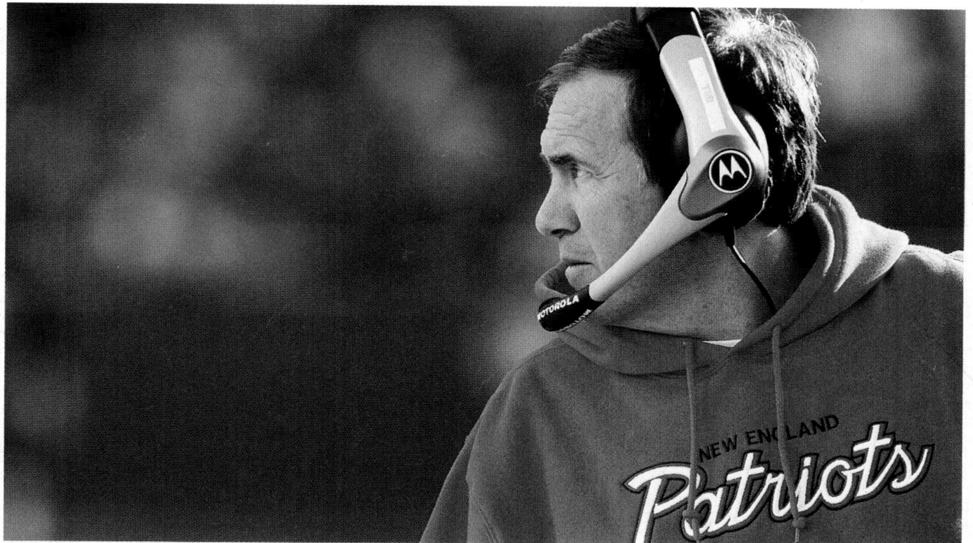

Because **Motorola** has a history of reporting nonrecurring special items, including restructuring expenses and investment and inventory write-offs, analysts have questioned the quality of its earnings.[9] Recently, the company had 7 straight years of such items. The nonrecurring special items in Motorola's income statement, shown in Exhibit 2, include other charges, gains on sales of

EXHIBIT 2 Motorola's Income Statement

	Year Ended December 31		
(In millions)	**2007**	**2006**	**2005**
Net sales	**$36,622**	$42,847	$35,310
Cost of sales	**26,670**	30,120	23,881
Gross margin	**$ 9,952**	$12,727	$11,429
Selling, general, and administrative costs	**$ 5,092**	$ 4,504	$ 3,628
Research and development expenditures	**4,429**	4,106	3,600
Other charges (income)	**984**	25	(404)
Operating earnings (loss)	**$ (553)**	$ 4,092	$ 4,605
Other income (expense):			
Interest income, net	**$ 91**	$ 326	$ 71
Gains on sales of investments and businesses, net	**50**	41	1,845
Other	**22**	151	(109)
Total other income (expense)	**$ 163**	$ 518	$ 1,807
Earnings (loss) from continuing operations before income taxes	**$ (390)**	$ 4,610	$ 6,412
Income tax expense (benefit)	**(285)**	1,349	1,893
Earnings (loss) from continuing operations	**$ (105)**	$ 3,261	$ 4,519
Earnings from discontinued operations, net of tax	**56**	400	59
Net earnings (loss)	**$ (49)**	$ 3,661	$ 4,578

Note: Highlighted items are discussed in the text.
Source: Motorola, Inc., *Annual Report*, 2007.

investments and businesses, and earnings from discontinued operations. However, if you look back at Motorola's Financial Highlights at the start of this chapter, you will see that the company's cash flows from operating activities were positive even in 2007 when it suffered a net loss but then did not exceed net earnings in 2005 and 2006 by a factor of more than 2 to 1. By this measure, Motorola's earnings are of relatively high quality.

STOP ► REVIEW ► APPLY

LO1-1 **What is quality of earnings? What are three components of the income statement that affect quality of earnings?**

LO1-2 **Why would the reader of financial statements be interested in management's choice of accounting methods and estimates? Give an example.**

LO1-3 **What is the difference between a write-down and a restructuring, and where do these items appear on a corporate income statement?**

LO1-4 **How do cash flows relate to quality of earnings?**

Suggested Answers to all Stop, Review, and Apply questions follow the appendixes.

Income Taxes

LO2 Show the relationships among income taxes expense, deferred income taxes, and net of taxes.

Corporations determine their taxable income (the amount on which they pay taxes) by deducting allowable expenses from taxable income. The federal tax laws determine which expenses corporations may deduct. (Rules for calculating and reporting taxable income in specialized industries, such as banking, insurance, mutual funds, and cooperatives, are highly technical and may vary significantly from the ones we discuss in this chapter.)

Table 1 shows the tax rates that apply to a corporation's taxable income. A corporation with taxable income of $70,000 would have a federal income tax liability of $12,500: $7,500 (the tax on the first $50,000 of taxable income) plus $5,000 (25 percent of the $20,000 earned in excess of $50,000).

Income taxes expense is recognized in the accounting records on an accrual basis. It may or may not equal the amount of taxes a corporation actually pays. The amount a corporation pays is determined by the rules of the income tax code. As we noted earlier in the text, small businesses often keep both their accounting records and tax records on a cash basis, so that the income taxes expense on their income statements equals their income taxes. This practice is acceptable as long as the difference between the income calculated on an accounting basis and the income calculated for tax purposes is not material. However, the purpose of accounting is not to determine taxable income and tax liability, but to determine net income in accordance with GAAP.

Management has an incentive to use methods that minimize its firm's tax liability. But accountants, who are bound by accrual accounting and the materiality concept, cannot let tax procedures dictate their method of preparing financial statements if the result would be misleading. The difference between accounting income and taxable income, especially in large businesses, can be material. This

Study Note

Many people think it is illegal to keep accounting records on a different basis from income tax records. However, the Internal Revenue Code and GAAP often do not agree. To work with two conflicting sets of guidelines, the accountant must keep two sets of records.

TABLE 1

Tax Rate Schedule for Corporations, 2007

Taxable Income Over	Taxable Income But Not Over	Tax Liability	Tax Liability Of the Amount Over
	$ 50,000	0 + 15%	—
$ 50,000	75,000	$ 7,500 + 25%	$ 50,000
75,000	100,000	13,750 + 34%	75,000
100,000	335,000	22,250 + 39%	100,000
335,000	10,000,000	113,900 + 34%	335,000
10,000,000	15,000,000	3,400,000 + 35%	10,000,000
15,000,000	18,333,333	5,150,000 + 38%	15,000,000
18,333,333	—	6,416,667 + 35%	18,333,333

Note: Tax rates are subject to change by Congress.

discrepancy can result from differences in the timing of the recognition of revenues and expenses under accrual accounting and the tax method. The following are some possible variations:

	Accrual Accounting	Tax Method
Expense recognition	Accrual or deferral	At time of expenditure
Accounts receivable	Allowance	Direct charge-off
Inventories	Average-cost	FIFO
Depreciation	Straight-line	Accelerated cost recovery

Deferred Income Taxes

Study Note

The discrepancy between GAAP-based tax expense and Internal Revenue Code-based tax liability creates the need for the Deferred Income Taxes account.

Income tax allocation is the method used to accrue income taxes expense on the basis of accounting income when accounting income and taxable income differ. The account used to record the difference between income taxes expense and income taxes payable is called **Deferred Income Taxes**. For example, in the income statement in Exhibit 1, Vistula Corporation has income taxes expense on income from continuing operations of $289,000. Suppose, however, that Vistula's actual income taxes payable are $184,000. The following entry shows how income tax allocation would treat this situation:

A	=	L	+	SE
		+184,000		−289,000
		+105,000		

Dec. 31	Income Taxes Expense	289,000	
	Income Taxes Payable		184,000
	Deferred Income Taxes		105,000
	To record estimated current and deferred income taxes		

Study Note

Deferred Income Taxes is classified as a liability when it has a credit balance and as an asset when it has a debit balance. It is further classified as either current or long-term depending on when it is expected to reverse.

In other years, Vistula's Income Taxes Payable may exceed its Income Taxes Expense. In this case, the entry is the same except that Deferred Income Taxes is debited.

The Financial Accounting Standards Board has issued specific rules for recording, measuring, and classifying deferred income taxes.[10] Deferred income taxes are recognized for the estimated future tax effects resulting from temporary differences in the valuation of assets, liabilities, equity, revenues, expenses, gains, and losses for tax and financial reporting purposes. Temporary differences include revenues and expenses or gains and losses that are included in taxable income before or after they are included in financial income. In other words, the recognition point for revenues, expenses, gains, and losses is not the same for tax and financial reporting.

For example, advance payments for goods and services, such as magazine subscriptions, are not recognized as income until the products are shipped. However, for tax purposes, advance payments are usually recognized as revenue when cash is received. As a result, taxes paid exceed taxes expense, which creates a deferred income taxes asset (or prepaid taxes).

Classification of deferred income taxes as current or noncurrent depends on the classification of the asset or liability that created the temporary difference. For example, the deferred income taxes asset mentioned above would be classified as current if unearned subscription revenue were classified as a current liability. On the other hand, the temporary difference arising from depreciation is related to a long-term depreciable asset. Therefore, the resulting deferred income taxes would be classified as long-term. If a temporary difference is not related to an asset or liability, it is classified as current or noncurrent based on its expected date of reversal. (Temporary differences and the classification of deferred income taxes that results are covered in depth in more advanced courses.)

Each year, the balance of the Deferred Income Taxes account is evaluated to determine whether it still accurately represents the expected asset or liability in light of legislated changes in income tax laws and regulations.

In any given year, the amount a company pays in income taxes is determined by subtracting (or adding) the deferred income taxes for that year from (or to) income taxes expense. In subsequent years, the amount of deferred income taxes can vary based on changes in tax laws and rates.

A survey of the financial statements of 600 large companies indicates the importance of deferred income taxes to financial reporting. About 68 percent reported deferred income taxes with a credit balance in the long-term liability section of their balance sheets.[11]

Net of Taxes

The phrase **net of taxes** indicates that taxes (usually income taxes) have been taken into account in reporting an item in the financial statements. The phrase is used in a corporate income statement when a company has items that must be disclosed in a separate section. Each such item should be reported net of the applicable income taxes to avoid distorting the income taxes expense associated with ongoing operations and the resulting net operating income.

For example, assume that a corporation with operating income before income taxes of $240,000 has a total tax expense of $132,000 and that the total income includes a gain of $200,000 on which a tax of $60,000 is due. Also assume that the gain is not part of the corporation's normal operations and must be disclosed separately on the income statement as an extraordinary item. This is how the income taxes expense would be reported on the income statement:

Operating income before income taxes	$240,000
Income taxes expense	72,000
Income before extraordinary item	$168,000
Extraordinary gain (net of taxes, $60,000)	140,000
Net income	$308,000

If all the income taxes expense were deducted from operating income before income taxes, both the income before extraordinary item and the extraordinary gain would be distorted.

The procedure is the same in the case of an extraordinary loss. For example, given the same facts except that the income taxes expense is only $12,000 because of a $200,000 extraordinary loss, the result is a $60,000 tax savings:

Operating income before income taxes	$240,000
Income taxes expense	72,000
Income before extraordinary item	$168,000
Extraordinary loss (net of taxes, $60,000)	(140,000)
Net income	$ 28,000

In Exhibit 1, the total of the income tax items for Vistula Corporation is $299,000. That amount is allocated among five statement components, as follows:

Income taxes expense on income from continuing operations	$289,000
Income taxes on income from a discontinued segment	70,000
Income tax savings on the loss on the disposal of the segment	(84,000)
Income taxes on extraordinary gain	24,000
Total income taxes expense	$299,000

STOP ▸ REVIEW ▸ APPLY

LO2-1 **"Accounting income should be geared to the concept of taxable income because the public understands that concept." Comment on this statement, and explain why income tax allocation is necessary.**

LO2-2 **What are deferred income taxes?**

LO2-3 **How does the concept of net of taxes affect the income statement?**

Income Tax Allocation Jose Corporation reported the accounting income before income taxes, income taxes expense, and net income for 2010 and 2011 shown in the opposite column.

	2010	2011
Income before income taxes	$42,000	$42,000
Income taxes expense	13,245	13,245
Net income	$28,755	$28,755

On the balance sheet, deferred income taxes liability increased by $5,760 in 2010 and decreased by $2,820 in 2011.

1. How much was actually payable in income taxes for 2010 and 2011?
2. Prepare entries in journal form to record estimated current and deferred income taxes for 2010 and 2011.

SOLUTION

1. Income taxes calculated:

	2010	2011
Income taxes expense	$13,245	$13,245
Decrease (increase) in deferred income taxes	(5,760)	2,820
Income taxes payable	$ 7,485	$16,065

(continued)

2. Entries prepared:

2010	Income Taxes Expense	13,245	
	Deferred Income Taxes		5,760
	Income Taxes Payable		7,485
	To record estimated current and deferred income taxes for 2010		
2011	Income Taxes Expense	13,245	
	Deferred Income Taxes	2,820	
	Income Taxes Payable		16,065
	To record estimated current and deferred income taxes for 2011		

Earnings per Share

LO3 Compute earnings per share.

Study Note

Earnings per share is a measure of a corporation's profitability. It is one of the most closely watched financial ratios in the business world. Its disclosure on the income statement is required.

Readers of financial statements use earnings per share to judge a company's performance and to compare it with the performance of other companies. Because this information is so important, the Accounting Principles Board concluded that earnings per share of common stock should be presented on the face of the income statement.[12] As shown in Exhibit 1, this information is usually disclosed just below net income.

A corporate income statement always shows earnings per share for income from continuing operations and other major components of net income. For example, if a company has a gain or loss on discontinued operations or on extraordinary items, its income statement may present earnings per share amounts for the gain or loss.

Exhibit 3 shows how **Motorola** presents earnings per share on its income statement. As you can see, the statement covers three years, and discontinued operations had a positive effect on earnings per share in all three years. However, the earnings per share for continuing operations is a better indicator of the company's future performance. The company is discontinuing some operations by selling or otherwise disposing of noncore divisions. Note that earnings per share are reported as basic and diluted.

Basic Earnings per Share

Basic earnings per share is the net income applicable to common stock divided by the weighted-average number of common shares outstanding. To compute this figure, one must determine if the number of common shares outstanding changed during the year and if the company paid dividends on preferred stock.

When a company has only common stock and the number of shares outstanding is the same throughout the year, the earnings per share computation is simple. Exhibit 1 shows that Vistula Corporation had net income of $669,000. If Vistula had 200,000 shares of common stock outstanding during the entire year, the earnings per share of common stock would be computed as follows:

$$\text{Earnings per Share} = \frac{\$669{,}000}{200{,}000} = \$3.35^{*} \text{ per share}$$

*This number is rounded, as are some other results of computations that follow.

EXHIBIT 3

Motorola's Earnings Per Share Presentation

	Years Ended December 31		
	2007	**2006**	**2005**
Earnings (loss) per common share:			
Basic:			
Continuing operations	**$ (0.05)**	$1.33	$1.83
Discontinued operations	**0.03**	0.17	0.02
	$ (0.02)	$1.50	$1.85
Diluted:			
Continuing operations	**$ (0.05)**	$1.30	$1.79
Discontinued operations	**0.03**	0.16	0.02
	$ (0.02)	$1.46	$1.81
Weighted averages common shares outstanding:			
Basic	**2,312.7**	2,446.3	2,471.3
Diluted	**2,312.7**	2,504.2	2,527.0

Source: Motorola, Inc., *Annual Report,* 2007.

If the number of shares outstanding changes during the year, it is necessary to figure the weighted-average number of shares outstanding for the year. Suppose that from January 1 to March 31, Vistula Corporation had 200,000 shares outstanding; from April 1 to September 30, it had 240,000 shares outstanding; and from October 31 to December 31, it had 260,000 shares outstanding. The weighted-average number of common shares outstanding and basic earnings per share would be determined this way:

200,000 shares × $\frac{3}{12}$ year	50,000
240,000 shares × $\frac{6}{12}$ year	120,000
260,000 shares × $\frac{3}{12}$ year	65,000
Weighted-average common shares outstanding	235,000

$$\text{Basic Earnings per Share} = \frac{\text{Net Income}}{\text{Weighted-Average Common Shares Outstanding}}$$

$$= \frac{\$669{,}000}{235{,}000 \text{ shares}} = \$2.85 \text{ per share}$$

If a company has nonconvertible preferred stock outstanding, the dividend for that stock must be subtracted from net income before earnings per share for common stock are computed. For example, suppose that Vistula Corporation has preferred stock on which it pays an annual dividend of $47,000. Earnings per share on common stock would be $2.65 [($669,000 − $47,000) ÷ 235,000 shares].

Diluted Earnings per Share

Companies can have a simple capital structure or a complex capital structure.

- A company has a **simple capital structure** if it has no preferred stocks, bonds, or stock options that can be converted to common stock. A company with a simple capital structure computes earnings per share as shown above.

- A company that has issued securities or stock options that can be converted to common stock has a **complex capital structure**. These securities and options have the potential of diluting the earnings per share of common stock.

Potential dilution means that the conversion of stocks or bonds or the exercise of stock options can increase the total number of shares of common stock that a company has outstanding and thereby reduce a current stockholder's proportionate share of ownership in the company. For example, suppose that a person owns 10,000 shares of a company's common stock, which equals 2 percent of the outstanding shares of 500,000. Now suppose that holders of convertible bonds convert the bonds into 100,000 shares of stock. The person's 10,000 shares would then equal only 1.67 percent (10,000 ÷ 600,000) of the outstanding shares. In addition, the added shares outstanding would lower earnings per share and would most likely lower market price per share.

When a company has a complex capital structure, it must report two earnings per share figures: basic earnings per share and diluted earnings per share.[13] **Diluted earnings per share** are calculated by adding all potentially dilutive securities to the denominator of the basic earnings per share calculation. This figure shows stockholders the maximum potential effect of dilution on their ownership position. As you can see in Exhibit 3, the dilution effect for **Motorola** is not large, only 4 cents per share in 2006 ($1.50 − $1.46) and none in 2007, because the company's only dilutive securities are a relatively few stock options.

STOP ▶ REVIEW ▶ APPLY

LO3-1 **Where are earnings per share disclosed in the financial statements?**

LO3-2 **When does a company have a simple capital structure? A complex capital structure?**

LO3-3 **What is the difference between basic and diluted earnings per share?**

Earnings per Share During 2011, Sasha Corporation reported a net income of $1,529,500. On January 1, 2011, Sasha had 350,000 shares of common stock outstanding, and it issued an additional 210,000 shares of common stock on October 1. The company has a simple capital structure.

1. Determine the weighted-average number of common shares outstanding.
2. Compute earnings per share.

SOLUTION

1. Weighted-average number of common shares outstanding:

350,000 shares × 9/12	262,500
560,000 shares × 3/12	140,000
Weighted-average number of common shares outstanding	402,500

2. Earnings per share:
   $1,529,500 ÷ 402,500 shares = $3.80

Comprehensive Income and the Statement of Stockholders' Equity

LO4 Define *comprehensive income*, and describe the statement of stockholders' equity.

The concept of comprehensive income and the statement of stockholders' equity provide further explanation of the income statement and the balance sheet and serve as links between those two statements.

Comprehensive Income

Some items that are not stock transactions affect stockholders' equity. These items, which come from sources other than stockholders and that account for the change in a company's equity during an accounting period, are called **comprehensive income**. Comprehensive income includes net income, changes in unrealized investment gains and losses, and other items affecting equity, such as foreign currency translation adjustments. The FASB holds that these changes in stockholders' equity should be summarized as income for a period.[14] Companies may report comprehensive income and its components in a separate financial statement, as **eBay** does in Exhibit 4, or as a part of another financial statement.

In a recent survey of 600 large companies, 579 reported comprehensive income. Of these, 83 percent reported comprehensive income in the statement of stockholders' equity (as in Exhibit 5), 13 percent reported it in a separate statement, and only 4 percent reported it in the income statement.[15]

The Statement of Stockholders' Equity

Study Note

The statement of stockholders' equity is a labeled calculation of the change in each stockholders' equity account over an accounting period.

The **statement of stockholders' equity**, also called the *statement of changes in stockholders' equity*, summarizes changes in the components of the stockholders' equity section of the balance sheet. Most companies use this statement in place of the statement of retained earnings because it reveals much more about the stockholders' equity transactions that took place during the accounting period.

For example, in Crisanti Corporation's statement of stockholders' equity in Exhibit 5, the first line shows the beginning balance of each account in the stockholders' equity section of the balance sheet. Each subsequent line discloses the effects of transactions on those accounts. Crisanti had a net income of $540,000 and a foreign currency translation loss of $20,000, which it reported as accumulated other comprehensive income. These two items together resulted in comprehensive income of $520,000.

EXHIBIT 4

eBay's Statement of Comprehensive Income

	Year Ended December 31		
(In thousands)	2007	2006	2005
Net income	$1,082,043	$1,125,639	$ 348,251
Other comprehensive income			
Foreign currency translation	(140,459)	588,150	645,202
Unrealized gains (losses) on investments, net	1,922	8,327	589,566
Unrealized gains (losses) on cash flow hedges	1,297	(194)	(175)
Estimated tax provision on above items	(1,272)	(3,216)	(229,514)
Net change in other comprehensive income	(138,512)	593,097	1,005,079
Comprehensive income	$ 943,531	$1,718,706	$1,353,330

Source: eBay Inc., *Annual Report*, 2007.

EXHIBIT 5 Statement of Stockholders' Equity

Crisanti Corporation
Statement of Stockholders' Equity
For the Year Ended December 31, 2010

	Preferred Stock $100 Par Value 8% Convertible	Common Stock $10 Par Value	Additional Paid-in Capital	Retained Earnings	Treasury Stock	Accumulated Other Comprehensive Income	Total
Balance, December 31, 2009	$800,000	$600,000	$600,000	$1,200,000			$3,200,000
Net income				540,000			540,000
Foreign currency translation adjustment						($20,000)	(20,000)
Issuance of 10,000 shares of common stock		100,000	400,000				500,000
Conversion of 2,000 shares of preferred stock to 6,000 shares of common stock	(200,000)	60,000	140,000				—
10 percent stock dividend on common stock, 7,600 shares		76,000	304,000	(380,000)			—
Purchase of 1,000 shares of treasury stock					($48,000)		(48,000)
Cash dividends							
Preferred stock				(48,000)			(48,000)
Common stock				(95,200)			(95,200)
Balance, December 31, 2010	$600,000	$836,000	$1,444,000	$1,216,800	($48,000)	($20,000)	$4,028,800

Study Note

The ending balances on the statement of stockholders' equity are transferred to the stockholders' equity section of the balance sheet.

Crisanti's statement of stockholders' equity also shows that during 2010, the firm issued 10,000 shares of common stock for $500,000, had a conversion of $200,000 of preferred stock to common stock, declared and issued a 10 percent stock dividend on common stock, purchased treasury stock for $48,000, and paid cash dividends on both preferred and common stock. The ending balances of the accounts appear at the bottom of the statement. Those accounts and balances make up the stockholders' equity section of Crisanti's balance sheet on December 31, 2010, as shown in Exhibit 6.

Retained Earnings

The Retained Earnings column in Exhibit 5 has the same components as the statement of retained earnings. As we explained earlier in the text, **retained earnings** represent the claims by stockholders to assets that arise from the earnings of the business. Retained earnings equal a company's profits since its inception, minus any losses, dividends to stockholders, or transfers to contributed capital.

It is important to remember that retained earnings are not the assets themselves. The existence of retained earnings means that assets generated by profitable operations have been kept in the company to help it grow or meet other business needs. A credit balance in Retained Earnings is *not* directly associated

EXHIBIT 6

Stockholders' Equity Section of a Balance Sheet

Crisanti Corporation
Balance Sheet
December 31, 2010

Stockholders' Equity

Contributed capital		
Preferred stock, $100 par value, 8 percent convertible, 20,000 shares authorized, 6,000 shares issued and outstanding		$ 600,000
Common stock, $10 par value, 200,000 shares authorized, 83,600 shares issued, 82,600 shares outstanding	$ 836,000	
Additional paid-in capital	1,444,000	2,280,000
Total contributed capital		$2,880,000
Retained earnings		1,216,800
Total contributed capital and retained earnings		$4,096,800
Less: Treasury stock, common (1,000 shares, at cost)	$ 48,000	
Foreign currency translation adjustment	20,000	68,000
Total stockholders' equity		$4,028,800

Study Note

A deficit is a negative (debit) balance in Retained Earnings. It is not the same as a net loss, which reflects a firm's performance in just one accounting period.

with a specific amount of cash or designated assets. Rather, it means that assets as a whole have increased.

Retained Earnings can have a debit balance. Generally, this happens when a company's dividends and subsequent losses are greater than its accumulated profits from operations. In this case, the company is said to have a **deficit** (debit balance) in Retained Earnings. A deficit is shown in the stockholders' equity section of the balance sheet as a deduction from contributed capital.

STOP ▸ REVIEW ▸ APPLY

LO4-1 **What is comprehensive income? How does comprehensive income differ from net income?**

LO4-2 **How do the statement of stockholders' equity and the stockholders' equity section of the balance sheet differ?**

LO4-3 **When does a company have a deficit in retained earnings?**

Stock Dividends and Stock Splits

LO5 Account for stock dividends and stock splits.

Two transactions that commonly modify the content of stockholders' equity are stock dividends and stock splits. In the discussion that follows, we describe how to account for both kinds of transactions.

Stock Dividends

A **stock dividend** is a proportional distribution of shares among a corporation's stockholders. Unlike a cash dividend, a stock dividend involves no distribution of assets, and so it has no effect on a firm's assets or liabilities. A board of directors may declare a stock dividend for the following reasons:

1. To give stockholders some evidence of the company's success without affecting working capital, which would be the case if it paid a cash dividend.
2. To reduce the stock's market price by increasing the number of shares outstanding. (This goal is, however, more often met by a stock split.)
3. To make a nontaxable distribution to stockholders. Stock dividends that meet certain conditions are not considered income and are thus not taxed.
4. To increase the company's permanent capital by transferring an amount from retained earnings to contributed capital.

Study Note

The declaration of a stock dividend results in a reshuffling of stockholders' equity—that is, a portion of retained earnings is converted to contributed capital (by closing the Stock Dividends account). Total stockholders' equity is not affected.

A stock dividend does not affect total stockholders' equity. Basically, it transfers a dollar amount from retained earnings to contributed capital. The amount transferred is the fair market value (usually, the market price) of the additional shares that the company issues. The laws of most states specify the minimum value of each share transferred, which is normally the minimum legal capital (par or stated value). When stock distributions are small—less than 20 to 25 percent of a company's outstanding common stock—generally accepted accounting principles hold that market value reflects their economic effect better than par or stated value. For this reason, market price should be used to account for small stock dividends.[16]

Study Note

For a small stock dividend, the portion of retained earnings transferred is determined by multiplying the number of shares to be distributed by the stock's market price on the declaration date.

To illustrate how to account for a stock dividend, suppose that stockholders' equity in Rivera Corporation is as follows:

Contributed capital	
Common stock, $5 par value, 50,000 shares authorized, 15,000 shares issued and outstanding	$ 75,000
Additional paid-in capital	15,000
Total contributed capital	$ 90,000
Retained earnings	450,000
Total stockholders' equity	$540,000

Now suppose that on February 24, the market price of Rivera's stock is $20 per share, and on that date, its board of directors declares a 10 percent stock dividend to be distributed on March 31 to stockholders of record on March 15. No entry is needed for the date of record (March 15). The entries for the declaration and distribution of the stock dividend are as follows:

Declaration Date

A	=	L	+	SE
				−30,000
				+7,500
				+22,500

Date	Account	Debit	Credit
Feb. 24	Stock Dividends	30,000	
	Common Stock Distributable		7,500
	Additional Paid-in Capital		22,500
	Declared a 10 percent stock dividend on common stock, distributable on March 31 to stockholders of record on March 15: 15,000 shares × .10 = 1,500 shares 1,500 shares × $20/share = $30,000 1,500 shares × $5/share = $7,500		

Date of Distribution

A	=	L	+	SE
				−7,500
				+7,500

		Dr.	Cr.
Mar. 31	Common Stock Distributable	7,500	
	Common Stock		7,500
	Distributed a stock dividend of 1,500 shares		

This stock dividend permanently transfers the market value of the stock, \$30,000, from retained earnings to contributed capital and increases the number of shares outstanding by 1,500.

The Stock Dividends account is used to record the total amount of the stock dividend. When the Stock Dividends account is closed to Retained Earnings at the end of the accounting period, Retained Earnings is reduced by the amount of the stock dividend. The Common Stock Distributable account is credited for the par value of the stock to be distributed (1,500 × \$5 = \$7,500).

In addition, when the market value is greater than the par value of the stock, the Additional Paid-in Capital account must be credited for the amount by which the market value exceeds the par value. In our example, the total market value of the stock dividend (\$30,000) exceeds the total par value (\$7,500) by \$22,500. On the date of distribution, the Common Stock Distributable account is debited, and the Common Stock account is credited for the par value of the stock (\$7,500).

Study Note

Common Stock Distributable is a contributed capital (stockholders' equity) account, not a liability account. When the shares are issued, Common Stock Distributable is converted to the Common Stock account.

Common Stock Distributable is not a liability account because there is no obligation to distribute cash or other assets. The obligation is to distribute additional shares of capital stock. If financial statements are prepared between the declaration date and the date of distribution, Common Stock Distributable should be reported as part of contributed capital:

Contributed capital	
Common stock, \$5 par value, 50,000 shares authorized, 15,000 shares issued and outstanding	\$ 75,000
Common stock distributable, 1,500 shares	7,500
Additional paid-in capital	37,500
Total contributed capital	\$ 120,000
Retained earnings	420,000
Total stockholders' equity	\$540,000

This example demonstrates the following points:

1. Total stockholders' equity is the same before and after the stock dividend.
2. The assets of the corporation are not reduced, as they would be by a cash dividend.
3. The proportionate ownership in the corporation of any individual stockholder is the same before and after the stock dividend.

To illustrate these points, suppose a stockholder owns 500 shares before the stock dividend. After the corporation distributes the 10 percent stock dividend, this stockholder would own 550 shares, as shown in the partial balance sheet that follows.

	Stockholders' Equity	
	Before Dividend	After Dividend
Common stock	$ 75,000	$ 82,500
Additional paid-in capital	15,000	37,500
Total contributed capital	$ 90,000	$120,000
Retained earnings	450,000	420,000
Total stockholders' equity	$540,000	$540,000
Shares outstanding	15,000	16,500
Stockholders' equity per share	$36.00	$32.73

	Stockholders' Investment	
Shares owned	500	550
Shares outstanding	15,000	16,500
Percentage of ownership	3⅓%	3⅓%
Proportionate investment ($540,000 × 3⅓%)	$18,000	$18,000

Both before and after the stock dividend, stockholders' equity totals $540,000, and the stockholder owns 3⅓ percent of the company. The proportionate investment (stockholders' equity times percentage of ownership) remains at $18,000.

> **Study Note**
> When a stock dividend greater than 20 to 25 percent is declared, the transfer from retained earnings is based on the stock's par or stated value, not on its market value.

All stock dividends have an effect on the market price of a company's stock. But some stock dividends are so large that they have a material effect. For example, a 50 percent stock dividend would cause the market price of the stock to drop about 33 percent because the increase is now one-third of shares outstanding. The AICPA has decided that large stock dividends—those greater than 20 to 25 percent—should be accounted for by transferring the par or stated value of the stock on the declaration date from retained earnings to contributed capital.[17]

Stock Splits

> **Study Note**
> Stock splits and stock dividends reduce earnings per share because they increase the number of shares issued and outstanding. Cash dividends have no effect on earnings per share.

A **stock split** occurs when a corporation increases the number of shares of stock issued and outstanding and reduces the par or stated value proportionally. A company may plan a stock split when it wants to lower its stock's market value per share and increase the demand for the stock at this lower price. It may do so if the market price has become so high that it hinders the trading of the stock or if it wants to signal to the market its success in achieving its operating goals.

Nike achieved these strategic objectives in a recent year by declaring a 2-for-1 stock split and increasing its cash dividend.[18] After the stock split, the number of the company's outstanding shares doubled, thereby cutting the share price from about $80 per share to $40 per share. The stock split left each stockholder's total wealth unchanged but increased the income stockholders received from dividends. The stock split was a sign that Nike has continued to do well.

To illustrate a stock split, suppose that MUI Corporation has 15,000 shares of $5.00 par value stock outstanding and the market value is $70.00 per share. The corporation plans a 2-for-1 split. This split will lower the par value to $2.50 per share and increase the number of shares outstanding to 30,000. A stockholder who previously owned 200 shares of the $5.00 par value stock would own 400 shares of the $2.50 par value stock after the split. When a stock split occurs, the market value tends to fall in proportion to the increase in outstanding shares

FOCUS ON BUSINESS PRACTICE

Do Stock Splits Help Increase a Company's Market Price?

Stock splits tend to follow the market. When the market went up dramatically in 1998, 1999, and 2000, there were record numbers of stock splits—more than 1,000 per year. At the height of the market in early 2000, stock splitters included such diverse companies as **Alcoa**, **Apple Computer**, **Chase Manhattan**, **Intel**, **NVIDIA**, **Juniper Networks**, and **Tiffany & Co.** Some analysts liken stock splits to the air a chef whips into a mousse: it doesn't make it any sweeter, just frothier. There is no fundamental reason a stock should go up because of a stock split. When **Rambus Inc.**, a developer of high-speed memory technology, announced a four-for-one split on March 10, 2000, its stock rose more than 50 percent, to $471 per share.[19] But when the market deflated in 2001, its stock dropped to less than $10 per share. Research shows that stock splits have no long-term effect on stock prices.

of stock. For example, MUI's 2-for-1 stock split would cause the price of its stock to drop by approximately 50 percent, to about $35.00. It would also halve earnings per share and cash dividends per share (unless the board increased the dividend). The lower price and increase in shares tend to promote the buying and selling of shares.

A stock split does not increase the number of shares authorized, nor does it change the balances in the stockholders' equity section of the balance sheet. It simply changes the par value and number of shares issued, both shares outstanding and treasury stock. Thus, an entry is unnecessary. However, it is appropriate to document the change with a memorandum entry in the general journal. For example:

July 15	The 15,000 shares of $5 par value common stock issued and outstanding were split 2 for 1, resulting in 30,000 shares of $2.50 par value common stock issued and outstanding.

The change for MUI Corporation is as follows:

Before Stock Split

Contributed capital	
Common stock, $5 par value, 50,000 shares authorized; 15,000 shares issued and outstanding	$ 75,000
Additional paid-in capital	15,000
Total contributed capital	$ 90,000
Retained earnings	450,000
Total stockholders' equity	$540,000

After Stock Split

Contributed capital	
Common stock, $2.50 par value, 50,000 shares authorized, 30,000 shares issued and outstanding	$ 75,000
Additional paid-in capital	15,000
Total contributed capital	$ 90,000
Retained earnings	450,000
Total stockholders' equity	$540,000

Study Note

A stock split affects only the calculation of common stock. In this case, there are twice as many shares after the split, but par value is half of what it was.

How do stock splits affect stockholders? In a recent year, almost 10 percent of large companies declared stock splits. In most cases, stockholders received one additional share for each share owned (2 for 1). Since there are now twice as many shares, the market value of the stock will drop to about half, and each stockholder's interest in the company will be in the same proportion as before the split. Thus, a stockholder's wealth and ownership interest in the company are not materially affected by a stock split.

Although the per share amount of stockholders' equity is half as much after the split, each stockholder's proportionate interest in the company remains the same.

If the number of split shares will exceed the number of authorized shares, the corporation's board of directors must secure state and stockholders' approval before it can issue the additional shares.

STOP ▶ REVIEW ▶ APPLY

LO5-1 **How does the accounting treatment of stock dividends differ from that of cash dividends?**

LO5-2 **What is the difference between a stock dividend and a stock split?**

LO5-3 **What is the effect of a stock dividend and a stock split on a corporation's capital structure?**

Book Value

LO6 Calculate book value per share.

K/R

The word *value* is associated with shares of stock in several ways. Par value or stated value is set when the stock is authorized, and it establishes a company's legal capital. Neither par value nor stated value has any relationship to a stock's book value or market value. The **book value** of stock represents a company's total assets less its liabilities. It is simply the stockholders' equity in a company or, to put it another way, it represents a company's net assets. The **book value per share** is therefore the equity of the owner of one share of stock in the net assets of a company. That value, of course, generally does not equal the amount a stockholder receives if the company is sold or liquidated because in most cases, assets are recorded at historical cost, not at their current market value.

If a company has only common stock outstanding, book value per share is calculated by dividing stockholders' equity by the number of common shares outstanding. Common stock distributable is included in the number of shares outstanding, but treasury stock is not. For example, if a firm has total stockholders' equity of $2,060,000 and 58,000 shares outstanding, the book value per share of its common stock would be $35.52 ($2,060,000 ÷ 58,000 shares).

If a company has both preferred and common stock, determining the book value per share is not so simple. Generally, the preferred stock's call value (or par value, if a call value is not specified) and any dividends in arrears are subtracted from stockholders' equity to determine the equity pertaining to common stock. As an illustration, refer to the stockholders' equity section of Crisanti Corporation's balance sheet in Exhibit 6. If Crisanti has no dividends in arrears and its preferred stock is callable at $105, the equity pertaining to its common stock would be calculated as follows:

Total stockholders' equity	$ 4,028,800
Less equity allocated to preferred stockholders (6,000 shares × $105)	630,000
Equity pertaining to common stockholders	$3,398,800

As indicated in Exhibit 6, Crisanti has 82,600 shares of common stock outstanding (83,600 shares issued less 1,000 shares of treasury stock). Its book values per share are computed as follows:

Preferred stock: $630,000 ÷ 6,000 Shares = $105 per Share
Common stock: $3,398,800 ÷ 82,600 Shares = $41.15 per Share

If we assume the same facts except that Crisanti's preferred stock is 8 percent cumulative and that one year of dividends is in arrears, the stockholders' equity would be allocated as follows:

Total stockholders' equity		$ 4,028,800
Less call value of outstanding preferred shares	$630,000	
Dividends in arrears ($600,000 × .08)	48,000	
Equity allocated to preferred stockholders		678,000
Equity pertaining to common stockholders		$3,350,800

The book values per share would then be as follows:

Preferred stock: $678,000 ÷ 6,000 Shares = $113 per Share
Common stock: $3,350,800 ÷ 82,600 Shares = $40.57 per Share

STOP ► REVIEW ► APPLY

LO6-1 **What is the formula for computing book value per share when a corporation has no preferred stock?**

LO6-2 **Would you expect a corporation's book value per share to equal its market value per share? Why or why not?**

A LOOK BACK AT ▶ Motorola, Inc.

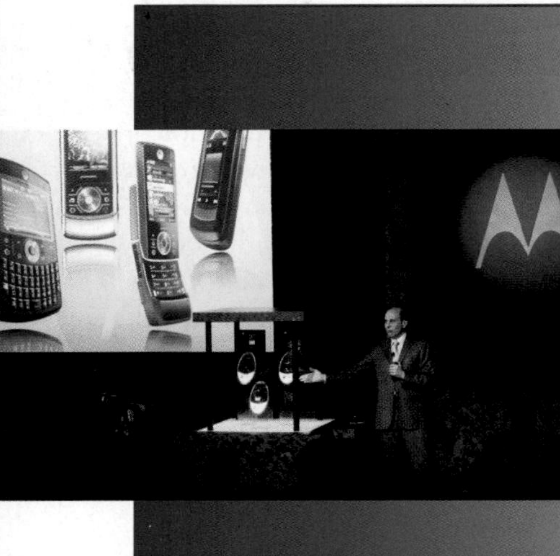

In this chapter's Decision Point, we observed that in evaluating a company's performance, it is important to look beyond "bottom line" earnings and other common indicators of performance. We pointed out that to gain a proper perspective on a company's performance, one must examine the components of its income statement. Users of Motorola's income statement should ask questions like the following:

- **What items other than normal operating activities contributed to Motorola's performance?**
- **What does the company's income statement indicate about its quality of earnings?**
- **How does one put the various measures of performance (some of which are shown in Motorola's financial highlights) in perspective?**

The astute user of **Motorola's** income statement, shown in Exhibit 2, will take the following into account:

- ***Other charges*, which appear in the operating section of Motorola's income statement, were present in all three years. These changes had a material effect on the company's performance in 2007 when they reduced operating income by almost $1 billion, causing an operating loss. They were less important in 2006 and 2005.**
- **Gains on sales of investments and businesses occurred in all three years. Although such gains increase income, they lower the quality of earnings because they are one-time events, and the income they produce will not be sustained in the future. This is reflected by the large gain in 2005, which contributed more than 40 percent of net earnings, but was not repeated in 2006 or 2007. The analyst should therefore ignore them.**
- **Motorola had earnings from discontinued operations in all three years. Earnings from discontinued operations increase earnings, but these earnings are not likely to be repeated in future years. When a company eliminates unprofitable operations, it does so with the expectation of better results in the future.**

To put Motorola's performance in perspective, the company's operating earnings performance has deteriorated significantly over the three-year period. All is not negative though. As may be seen in the Financial Highlights at the beginning of the chapter, Motorola's operations produced strong and growing cash flows.

CHAPTER REVIEW

REVIEW of Learning Objectives

LO1 Define *quality of earnings*, and identify the components of a corporate income statement.

The quality of earnings refers to the substance of earnings and their sustainability into future accounting periods. The quality of a company's earnings may be affected by the accounting methods and estimates it uses and by the gains and losses, write-downs and restructurings, and nonoperating items that it reports on its income statement.

When a company has both continuing and discontinued operations, the operating income section of its income statement is called income from continuing operations. Income from continuing operations before income taxes is affected by choices of accounting methods and estimates and may contain gains and losses on the sale of assets, write-downs, and restructurings. The income taxes expense section of the statement is subject to special accounting rules. The lower part of the statement may contain such nonoperating items as discontinued operations and extraordinary gains and losses. Earnings per share information appears at the bottom of the statement.

The reason for considering quality of earnings issues is to assess their effect on cash flows and performance measures. Except for possible income tax effects, gains and losses, asset write-downs, restructurings, and nonoperating items generally have no effect on cash flows. However, quality of earnings issues can affect key performance ratios like profit margin, return on assets, and return on equity because the cash for these items has already been expended.

LO2 Show the relationships among income taxes expense, deferred income taxes, and net of taxes.

Income taxes expense is the tax applicable to income from operations on an accrual basis. Income tax allocation is necessary when there is a material difference between accrual-based accounting income and taxable income—that is, between the income taxes expense reported on the income statement and actual income tax liability. The difference between income taxes expense and income taxes payable is debited or credited to an account called Deferred Income Taxes. The phrase *net of taxes* indicates that taxes have been taken into account in reporting an item in the financial statements.

LO3 Compute earnings per share.

Readers of financial statements use earnings per share to evaluate a company's performance and to compare it with the performance of other companies. Earnings per share of common stock are presented on the face of the income statement. The amounts are computed by dividing the income applicable to common stock by the number of common shares outstanding for the year. If the number of shares outstanding varied during the year, the weighted-average number of common shares outstanding is used in the computation. A company that has a complex capital structure must disclose both basic and diluted earnings per share on the face of its income statement.

LO4 Define *comprehensive income*, and describe the statement of stockholders' equity.

Comprehensive income includes all items from sources other than stockholders that account for changes in stockholders' equity during an accounting period. The statement of stockholders' equity summarizes changes over the period in each component of the stockholders' equity section of the balance sheet. This statement reveals much more than the statement of retained earnings does about the transactions that affect stockholders' equity.

LO5 Account for stock dividends and stock splits.

A stock dividend is a proportional distribution of shares among a corporation's stockholders. The following is a summary of the key dates and accounting treatments of stock dividends:

Key Date	Stock Dividend
Declaration date	Debit Stock Dividends for the market value of the stock to be distributed (if the stock dividend is small), and credit Common Stock Distributable for the stock's par value and Additional Paid-in Capital for the excess of the market value over the stock's par value.
Record date	No entry is needed.
Date of distribution	Debit Common Stock Distributable and credit Common Stock for the par value of the stock.

A company usually declares a stock split to reduce the market value of its stock and thereby improve the demand for the stock. Because the par value of the stock normally decreases in proportion to the number of additional shares issued, a stock split has no effect on the dollar amount in stockholders' equity. A stock split does not require a journal entry, but a memorandum entry in the general journal is appropriate.

LO6 Calculate book value per share.

Book value per share is stockholders' equity per share. It is calculated by dividing stockholders' equity by the number of common shares outstanding. When a company has both preferred and common stock, the call or par value of the preferred stock and any dividends in arrears are deducted from stockholders' equity before dividing by the common shares outstanding.

REVIEW of Concepts and Terminology

The following concepts and terms were introduced in this chapter:

Book value: A company's total assets less its liabilities; stockholders' equity or net assets. **(LO6)**

Complex capital structure: A capital structure that includes preferred stocks, bonds, and stock options that can be converted to common stock. **(LO3)**

Comprehensive income: Items from sources other than owners that account for the change in stockholders' equity during an accounting period. **(LO4)**

Deferred Income Taxes: The account used to record the difference between income taxes expense and income taxes payable. **(LO2)**

Deficit: A debit balance in the Retained Earnings account. **(LO4)**

Discontinued operations: Segments that are no longer part of a company's operations. **(LO1)**

Extraordinary items: Events or transactions that are unusual in nature and infrequent in occurrence. **(LO1)**

Income from continuing operations: The operating income section of the income statement when a company has both continuing and discontinued operations. **(LO1)**

Income tax allocation: The accounting method used to accrue income taxes expense on the basis of accounting income when accounting income and taxable income differ. **(LO2)**

Net of taxes: A phrase indicating that taxes have been taken into account in reporting an item in the financial statements. **(LO2)**

Quality of earnings: The substance of earnings and their sustainability into the future. **(LO1)**

Restructuring: The estimated cost of a change in a company's operations, usually involving the closing of facilities and the laying off of personnel. **(LO1)**

Retained earnings: Stockholders' claims to assets arising from the earnings of the business; the accumulated earnings of a corporation since its inception, minus any losses, dividends, or transfers to contributed capital. **(LO4)**

Simple capital structure: A capital structure in which there are no stocks, bonds, or stock options that can be converted to common stock. **(LO3)**

Statement of stockholders' equity: A financial statement that summarizes changes in the components of the stockholders' equity section of the balance sheet. Also called the *statement of changes in stockholders' equity*. **(LO4)**

Stock dividend: A proportional distribution of shares among a corporation's stockholders. **(LO5)**

Stock split: An increase in the number of outstanding shares of stock accompanied by a proportionate reduction in the par or stated value. **(LO5)**

Write-down: A reduction in the value of an asset below its carrying value on the balance sheet. Also called a *write-off*. **(LO1)**

Key Ratios

Basic earnings per share: The net income applicable to common stock divided by the weighted-average number of common shares outstanding. **(LO3)**

Book value per share: The equity of the owner of one share of stock in a corporation's net assets. **(LO6)**

Diluted earnings per share: The net income applicable to common stock divided by the sum of the weighted-average number of common shares outstanding and potentially dilutive securities. **(LO3)**

REVIEW Problem

LO4 LO5 LO6

Comprehensive Stockholders' Equity Transactions

The stockholders' equity of Kowalski Company on June 30, 2010, was as follows:

Contributed capital	
Common stock, no par value, $6 stated value, 500,000 shares authorized, 125,000 shares issued and outstanding	$ 750,000
Additional paid-in capital	410,000
Total contributed capital	$ 1,160,000
Retained earnings	485,000
Total stockholders' equity	$1,645,000

Stockholders' equity transactions in the next fiscal year were as follows:

a. The board of directors declared a 2-for-1 stock split.
b. The board of directors obtained authorization to issue 25,000 shares of $100 par value, 6 percent noncumulative preferred stock, callable at $104.
c. Issued 6,000 shares of common stock for a building appraised at $48,000.
d. Purchased 4,000 shares of the company's common stock for $32,000.
e. Issued 10,000 shares of preferred stock for $100 per share.
f. Sold 2,500 shares of treasury stock for $17,500.
g. Declared cash dividends of $6 per share on preferred stock and $.20 per share on common stock.
h. Declared a 10 percent stock dividend on common stock to be distributed after the end of the fiscal year. The market value was $10 per share.
i. Closed net income for the year, $170,000.
j. Closed the Dividends and Stock Dividends accounts to Retained Earnings.

Required:

1. Record the stockholders' equity components of the preceding transactions in T accounts. Indicate when there is no entry.
2. Prepare the stockholders' equity section of the company's balance sheet on June 30, 2011.

3. Compute the book values per share of common stock on June 30, 2010 and 2011, and of preferred stock on June 30, 2011, using the end-of-year shares outstanding.

Answer to Review Problem

1. Entries in T accounts:
   a. No entry (memorandum in journal)
   b. No entry (memorandum in journal)

	A	B	C	D	E	F	G	H	I
1		**Preferred Stock**					**Common Stock**		
2			e.	1,000,000				Beg. Bal.	750,000
3								c.	18,000
4								End. Bal.	768,000
5									
6		**Common Stock Distributable**					**Additional Paid-in Capital**		
7			h.	76,350				Beg. Bal.	410,000
8								c.	30,000
9								h.	178,150
10								End. Bal.	618,150
11									
12		**Retained Earnings**					**Treasury Stock**		
13	f.	2,500	Beg. Bal.	485,000		d.	32,000	f.	20,000
14	j.	365,400	i.	170,000		End. Bal.	12,000		
15			End. Bal.	287,100					
16									
17		**Dividends**					**Stock Dividends**		
18	g.	110,900*	j.	110,900		h.	254,000**	j.	254,500
19									
20	*10,000 x $6 =		$ 60,000			**254,500 shares x 0.10 x $10 = $254,500			
21	254,500 x $0.20 =		50,900						
22			$110,900						
23									

2. Stockholders' equity section of the balance sheet:

	A	B	C	D
1		**Kowalski Company**		
2		**Balance Sheet**		
3		**June 30, 2011**		
4				
5		**Stockholders' Equity**		
6	Contributed capital			
7		Preferred stock, $100 par value, 6 percent		
8		noncumulative, 25,000 shares authorized,		
9		10,000 shares issued and outstanding		$ 1,000,000
10		Common stock, no par value, $3 stated value,		
11		500,000 shares authorized, 256,000 shares		
12		issued, 254,500 shares outstanding	$768,000	
13		Common stock distributable, 25,450 shares	76,350	
14		Additional paid-in capital	618,150	1,462,500
15		Total contributed capital		$2,462,500
16	Retained earnings			287,100
17	Total contributed capital and retained earnings			$2,749,600
18	Less treasury stock (1,500 shares, at cost)			12,000
19	Total stockholders' equity			$2,737,600
20				

3. Book values:
   June 30, 2010
   Common Stock: $1,645,000 ÷ 125,000 shares = $13.16 per share
   June 30, 2011
   Preferred Stock: Call price of $104 per share equals book value per share
   Common Stock:
   ($2,737,600 − $1,040,000) ÷ (254,500 shares + 25,450 shares)
   $1,697,600 ÷ 279,950 shares = $6.06 per share (rounded)

CHAPTER ASSIGNMENTS

BUILDING Your Basic Knowledge and Skills

Short Exercises

LO1 **Quality of Earnings**

SE 1. Each of the items listed below is a quality of earnings issue. Indicate whether the item is (a) an accounting method, (b) an accounting estimate, or (c) a nonoperating item. For any item for which the answer is (a) or (b), indicate which alternative is usually the more conservative choice.

1. LIFO versus FIFO
2. Extraordinary loss
3. 10-year useful life versus 15-year useful life
4. Straight-line versus accelerated method
5. Discontinued operations
6. Immediate write-off versus amortization
7. Increase versus decrease in percentage of uncollectible accounts

LO1 **Corporate Income Statement**

SE 2. Assume that Jefferson Company's chief financial officer gave you the following information: net sales, $360,000; cost of goods sold, $175,000; loss from discontinued operations (net of income tax benefit of $35,000), $100,000; loss on disposal of discontinued operations (net of income tax benefit of $8,000), $25,000; operating expenses, $65,000; income taxes expense on continuing operations, $50,000. From this information, prepare the company's income statement for the year ended June 30, 2010. (Ignore earnings per share information.)

LO2 **Corporate Income Tax Rate Schedule**

SE 3. Using the corporate tax rate schedule in Table 1, compute the income tax liability for taxable income of (1) $800,000 and (2) $40,000,000.

LO3 **Earnings per Share**

SE 4. During 2010, Wells Corporation reported a net income of $1,338,400. On January 1, Wells had 720,000 shares of common stock outstanding. The company issued an additional 480,000 shares of common stock on August 1. In 2010, the company had a simple capital structure. During 2011, there were no transactions involving common stock, and the company reported net income of $1,740,000. Determine the weighted-average number of

common shares outstanding for 2010 and 2011. Also compute earnings per share for 2010 and 2011.

LO4 **Statement of Stockholders' Equity**

SE 5. Refer to the statement of stockholders' equity for Crisanti Corporation in Exhibit 5 to answer the following questions: (1) At what price per share were the 5,000 shares of common stock sold? (2) What was the conversion price per share of the common stock? (3) At what price was the common stock selling on the date of the stock dividend? (4) At what price per share was the treasury stock purchased?

LO4 LO5 **Effects of Stockholders' Equity Actions**

SE 6. Tell whether the following actions will increase, decrease, or have no effect on total assets, total liabilities, and total stockholders' equity: (1) Declaration of a stock dividend; (2) Declaration of a cash dividend; (3) Stock split; (4) Purchase of treasury stock.

LO5 **Stock Dividends**

SE 7. On February 15, Asher Corporation's board of directors declared a 2 percent stock dividend applicable to the outstanding shares of its $10 par value common stock, of which 400,000 shares are authorized, 260,000 are issued, and 40,000 are held in the treasury. The stock dividend was distributed on March 15 to stockholders of record on March 1. On February 15, the market value of the common stock was $15 per share. On March 30, the board of directors declared a $.50 per share cash dividend. No other stock transactions have occurred. Record, as necessary, the transactions of February 15, March 1, March 15, and March 30.

LO5 **Stock Split**

SE 8. On August 10, 2010, the board of directors of Karton Inc. declared a 3-for-1 stock split of its $9 par value common stock, of which 200,000 shares were authorized and 62,500 were issued and outstanding. The market value on that date was $60 per share, the balance of additional paid-in capital was $1,500,000, and the balance of retained earnings was $1,625,000. Prepare the stockholders' equity section of the company's balance sheet after the stock split. What journal entry, if any, is needed to record the stock split?

LO6 **Book Value for Preferred and Common Stock**

SE 9. Using data from Soong Corporation's partial balance sheet below, compute the book value per share for both the preferred and the common stock.

Contributed capital	
Preferred stock, $100 par value, 8 percent cumulative, 20,000 shares authorized, 1,000 shares issued and outstanding*	$ 100,000
Common stock, $10 par value, 200,000 shares authorized, 80,000 shares issued and outstanding	800,000
Additional paid-in capital	1,032,000
Total contributed capital	$1,932,000
Retained earnings	550,000
Total stockholders' equity	$2,482,000

*The preferred stock is callable at $108 per share, and one year's dividends are in arrears.

Exercises

LO1 LO2

Discussion Questions

E 1. Develop brief answers to each of the following questions:

1. In what way is selling an investment for a gain potentially a negative in evaluating quality of earnings?
2. Is it unethical for new management to take an extra large write-off (a "big bath") in order to reduce future costs? Why or why not?
3. What is an argument against the recording of deferred income taxes?
4. Why is it useful to disclose discontinued operations separately on the income statement?

LO3 LO4 LO5 LO6

Discussion Questions

E 2. Develop brief answers to each of the following questions:

1. What is one way a company can improve its earnings per share without improving its earnings or net income?
2. Why is comprehensive income a part of stockholders' equity?
3. Upon receiving shares of stock from a stock dividend, why should the stockholder not consider the value of the stock as income?
4. What is the effect of a stock dividend or a stock split on book value per share?

LO1

Effect of Alternative Accounting Methods

E 3. At the end of its first year of operations, a company calculated its ending merchandise inventory according to three different accounting methods, as follows: FIFO, $95,000; average-cost, $90,000; LIFO, $86,000. If the company used the average-cost method, its net income for the year would be $34,000.

1. Determine net income if the company used the FIFO method.
2. Determine net income if the company used the LIFO method.
3. Which method is more conservative?
4. Will the consistency convention be violated if the company chooses to use the LIFO method? Why or why not?
5. Does the full-disclosure convention require disclosure of the inventory method used in the financial statements?

LO1

Corporate Income Statement

E 4. Assume that Cetnar Company's chief financial officer gave you the following information: net sales, $1,900,000; cost of goods sold, $1,050,000; extraordinary gain (net of income taxes of $3,500), $12,500; loss from discontinued operations (net of income tax benefit of $30,000), $50,000; loss on disposal of discontinued operations (net of income tax benefit of $13,000), $35,000; selling expenses, $50,000; administrative expenses, $40,000; income taxes expense on continuing operations, $300,000. From this information, prepare the company's income statement for the year ended June 30, 2010. (Ignore earnings per share information.)

LO1

Corporate Income Statement

E 5. The items at the top of the next page are components of Patel Company's income statement for the year ended December 31, 2010. Recast the income statement in proper multistep form, including allocating income taxes to appropriate items (assume a 30 percent income tax rate) and showing earnings per share figures (100,000 shares outstanding).

Sales	$555,000
Cost of goods sold	(275,000)
Operating expenses	(112,500)
Restructuring	(55,000)
Total income taxes expense for period	(89,550)
Income from operations of a discontinued segment	80,000
Gain on disposal of segment	70,000
Extraordinary gain	36,000
Net income	$208,950
Earnings per share	$ 2.09

LO2 **Corporate Income Tax Rate Schedule**

E 6. Using the corporate tax rate schedule in Table 1, compute the income tax liability for the following situations:

Situation	Taxable Income
A	$ 70,000
B	85,000
C	320,000

LO2 **Income Tax Allocation**

E 7. Fabio Corporation's income statement showed the following data for 2009 and 2010:

	2009	2010
Income before income taxes	$280,000	$280,000
Income taxes expense	88,300	88,300
Net income	$191,700	$191,700

On the balance sheet, deferred income taxes liability increased by $38,400 in 2009 and decreased by $18,800 in 2010.

1. How much did Fabio actually pay in income taxes for 2009 and 2010?
2. Prepare entries in journal form to record income taxes expense for 2009 and 2010.

LO3 **Earnings per Share**

E 8. During 2009, Arthur Corporation reported a net income of $3,059,000. On January 1, Arthur had 2,800,000 shares of common stock outstanding. The company issued an additional 1,680,000 shares of common stock on October 1. In 2009, the company had a simple capital structure. During 2010, there were no transactions involving common stock, and the company reported net income of $4,032,000.

1. Determine the weighted-average number of common shares outstanding each year.
2. Compute earnings per share for each year.

LO4 **Statement of Stockholders' Equity**

E 9. The stockholders' equity section of Erich Corporation's balance sheet on December 31, 2010, follows.

Contributed capital	
Common stock, $2 par value, 500,000 shares authorized, 400,000 shares issued and outstanding	$ 800,000
Additional paid-in capital	1,200,000
Total contributed capital	$ 2,000,000
Retained earnings	4,200,000
Total stockholders' equity	$6,200,000

Prepare a statement of stockholders' equity for the year ended December 31, 2011, assuming these transactions occurred in sequence in 2011:

a. Issued 10,000 shares of $100 par value, 9 percent cumulative preferred stock at par after obtaining authorization from the state.
b. Issued 40,000 shares of common stock in connection with the conversion of bonds having a carrying value of $600,000.
c. Declared and issued a 2 percent common stock dividend. The market value on the date of declaration was $14 per share.
d. Purchased 10,000 shares of common stock for the treasury at a cost of $16 per share.
e. Earned net income of $460,000.
f. Declared and paid the full year's dividend on preferred stock and a dividend of $.40 per share on common stock outstanding at the end of the year.
g. Had foreign currency translation adjustment of minus $100,000.

LO5 **Journal Entries: Stock Dividends**

E 10. Snols Company has 30,000 shares of its $1 par value common stock outstanding. Record in journal form the following transactions as they relate to the company's common stock:

July	17	Declared a 10 percent stock dividend on common stock to be distributed on August 10 to stockholders of record on July 31. Market value of the stock was $5 per share on this date.
	31	Date of record.
Aug.	10	Distributed the stock dividend declared on July 17.
Sept.	1	Declared a $.50 per share cash dividend on common stock to be paid on September 16 to stockholders of record on September 10.

LO5 **Stock Split**

E 11. Fernandez Company currently has 500,000 shares of $1 par value common stock authorized with 200,000 shares outstanding. The board of directors declared a 2-for-1 split on May 15, 2010, when the market value of the common stock was $2.50 per share. The retained earnings balance on May 15 was $700,000. Additional paid-in capital on this date was $20,000. Prepare the stockholders' equity section of the company's balance sheet before and after the stock split. What entry, if any, would be necessary to record the stock split?

LO5 **Stock Split**

E 12. On January 15, 2010, the board of directors of Tower International declared a 3-for-1 stock split of its $12 par value common stock, of which 3,200,000 shares were authorized and 800,000 were issued and outstanding. The market value on that date was $45 per share. On the same date, the balance of additional paid-in capital was $16,000,000, and the balance of retained earnings was $32,000,000. Prepare the stockholders' equity section of the company's balance sheet before and after the stock split. What entry, if any, is needed to record the stock split?

LO6 **Book Value for Preferred and Common Stock**

E 13. Below is the stockholders' equity section of Hegel Corporation's balance sheet. Determine the book value per share for both the preferred and the common stock.

Contributed capital	
Preferred stock, $100 per share, 6 percent cumulative, 10,000 shares authorized, 200 shares issued and outstanding*	$ 20,000
Common stock, $5 par value, 100,000 shares authorized, 10,000 shares issued, 9,000 shares outstanding	50,000
Additional paid-in capital	28,000
Total contributed capital	$ 98,000
Retained earnings	95,000
Total contributed capital and retained earnings	$193,000
Less treasury stock, common (1,000 shares at cost)	15,000
Total stockholders' equity	$178,000

*The preferred stock is callable at $105 per share, and one year's dividends are in arrears.

Problems

LO1 **Effect of Alternative Accounting Methods**

P 1. Matka Company began operations in 2010. At the beginning of the year, the company purchased plant assets of $450,000, with an estimated useful life of ten years and no residual value. During the year, the company had net sales of $650,000, salaries expense of $100,000, and other expenses of $40,000, excluding depreciation. In addition, Matka Company purchased inventory as follows:

Jan. 15	200 units at $400	$ 80,000
Mar. 20	100 units at $408	40,800
June 15	400 units at $416	166,400
Sept. 18	300 units at $412	123,600
Dec. 9	150 units at $420	63,000
Total	1,150 units	$473,800

At the end of the year, a physical inventory disclosed 250 units still on hand. The managers of Matka Company know they have a choice of accounting methods, but they are unsure how those methods will affect net income.

They have heard of the FIFO and LIFO inventory methods and the straight-line and double-declining-balance depreciation methods.

Required

1. Prepare two income statements for Matka Company, one using the FIFO and straight-line methods and the other using the LIFO and double-declining-balance methods. Ignore income taxes.
2. Prepare a schedule accounting for the difference in the two net income figures obtained in requirement **1**.
3. User insight ▶ What effect does the choice of accounting method have on Matka's inventory turnover? What conclusions can you draw? Use the year-end balance to compute the ratio.
4. User insight ▶ How does the choice of accounting methods affect Matka's return on assets? Assume the company's only assets are cash of $40,000, inventory, and plant assets. Use year-end balances to compute the ratios. Is your evaluation of Matka's profitability affected by the choice of accounting methods?

LO1 LO2 LO3

KLOOSTER & ALLEN

Corporate Income Statement

P 2. Information concerning operations of Camping Gear Corporation during 2010 is as follows:

a. Administrative expenses, $90,000
b. Cost of goods sold, $420,000
c. Extraordinary loss from an earthquake (net of taxes, $36,000), $60,000
d. Sales (net), $900,000
e. Selling expenses, $80,000
f. Income taxes expense applicable to continuing operations, $105,000

Required

1. Prepare the corporation's income statement for the year ended December 31, 2010, including earnings per share information. Assume a weighted average of 50,000 common shares outstanding during the year.

2. User insight ▶ Which item in Camping Gear Corporation's income statement affects the company's quality of earnings? Why does it have an effect on quality of earnings?

LO1 LO2 LO3

KLOOSTER & ALLEN

Corporate Income Statement and Evaluation of Business Operations

P 3. During 2010, Vitos Corporation engaged in two complex transactions to improve the business—selling off a division and retiring bonds. The company has always issued a simple single-step income statement, and the accountant has accordingly prepared the December 31 year-end income statements for 2009 and 2010, as shown at the top of the next page.

Joseph Vitos, the president of Vitos Corporation, is pleased to see that both net income and earnings per share increased by almost 33 percent from 2009 to 2010 and he intends to announce to the company's stockholders that the plan to improve the business has been successful.

Required

1. Recast the 2010 and 2009 income statements in proper multistep form, including allocating income taxes to appropriate items (assume a 30 percent income tax rate) and showing earnings per share figures (400,000 shares outstanding).
2. User insight ▶ What is your assessment of Vitos Corporation's plan and business operations in 2010?

Vitos Corporation
Income Statements
For the Years Ended December 31, 2010 and 2009

	2010	2009
Net sales	$2,000,000	$2,400,000
Cost of goods sold	(1,100,000)	(1,200,000)
Operating expenses	(450,000)	(300,000)
Income taxes expense	(358,200)	(270,000)
Income from operations of a discontinued segment	320,000	
Gain on disposal of discontinued segment	280,000	
Extraordinary gain on retirement of bonds	144,000	
Net income	$ 835,800	$ 630,000
Earnings per share	$2.09	$1.58

LO4 LO5 **Dividends, Stock Splits, and Stockholders' Equity**

P 4. The stockholders' equity section of Lim Mills, Inc., as of December 31, 2009, was as follows:

Contributed capital	
Common stock, $3 par value, 1,000,000 shares authorized, 80,000 shares issued and outstanding	$240,000
Additional paid-in capital	75,000
Total contributed capital	$315,000
Retained earnings	240,000
Total stockholders' equity	$555,000

A review of the stockholders' equity records of Lim Mills, Inc., disclosed the following transactions during 2010:

Mar. 25 The board of directors declared a 5 percent stock dividend to stockholders of record on April 20 to be distributed on May 1. The market value of the common stock was $21 per share.
Apr. 20 Date of record for stock dividend.
May 1 Issued stock dividend.
Sept. 10 Declared a 3-for-1 stock split.
Dec. 15 Declared a 10 percent stock dividend to stockholders of record on January 15 to be distributed on February 15. The market price on this date is $9 per share.

Required

1. Record the stockholders' equity components of the transactions for Lim Mills, Inc., in T accounts.
2. Prepare the stockholders' equity section of the company's balance sheet as of December 31, 2010. Assume net income for 2010 is $494,000.

User insight ▶

3. If you owned 2,000 shares of Lim Mills stock on March 1, 2010, how many shares would you own on February 15, 2011? Would your proportionate share of the ownership of the company be different on the latter date than it was on the former date? Explain your answer.

LO4 LO5

Dividends and Stock Split Transactions and Stockholder's Equity

P 5. The stockholders' equity section of Acerin Moving and Storage Company's balance sheet as of December 31, 2010, appears below.

Contributed capital	
Common stock, $2 par value, 6,000,000 shares authorized, 1,000,000 shares issued and outstanding	$2,000,000
Additional paid-in capital	800,000
Total contributed capital	$2,800,000
Retained earnings	2,160,000
Total stockholders' equity	$4,960,000

The company engaged in the following stockholders' equity transactions during 2010:

Mar. 5	Declared a $.40 per share cash dividend to be paid on April 6 to stockholders of record on March 20.
20	Date of record.
Apr. 6	Paid the cash dividend.
June 17	Declared a 10 percent stock dividend to be distributed August 17 to stockholders of record on August 5. The market value of the stock was $14 per share.
Aug. 5	Date of record for the stock dividend.
17	Distributed the stock dividend.
Oct. 2	Split its stock 2 for 1.
Dec. 27	Declared a cash dividend of $.20 payable January 27, 2011, to stockholders of record on January 14, 2011.

Required

1. Record the 2010 transactions in journal form.
2. Prepare the stockholders' equity section of Acerin Moving and Storage Company's balance sheet as of December 31, 2010. Assume net income for the year is $800,000.

User insight ▶

3. If you owned some shares of Acerin, would you expect the total value of your shares to go up or down as a result of the stock dividends and stock split? What intangibles might affect the stock value?

LO4 LO5 LO6

Comprehensive Stockholders' Equity Transactions

P 6. On December 31, 2010, the stockholders' equity section of Koval Company's balance sheet appeared as follows:

Contributed capital	
Common stock, $8 par value, 400,000 shares authorized, 120,000 shares issued and outstanding	$ 960,000
Additional paid-in capital	2,560,000
Total contributed capital	$ 3,520,000
Retained earnings	1,648,000
Total stockholders' equity	$5,168,000

The following are selected transactions involving stockholders' equity in 2011:

Jan. 4	The board of directors obtained authorization for 40,000 shares of $40 par value noncumulative preferred stock that carried an indicated dividend rate of $4 per share and was callable at $42 per share.
Jan. 14	The company sold 24,000 shares of the preferred stock at $40 per share and issued another 4,000 in exchange for a building valued at $160,000.
Mar. 8	The board of directors declared a 2-for-1 stock split on the common stock.
Apr. 20	After the stock split, the company purchased 6,000 shares of common stock for the treasury at an average price of $12 per share.
May 4	The company sold 2,000 of the shares purchased on April 20, at an average price of $16 per share.
Jul. 15	The board of directors declared a cash dividend of $4 per share on the preferred stock and $.40 per share on the common stock.
Jul. 25	Date of record.
Aug. 15	Paid the cash dividend.
Nov. 28	The board of directors declared a 15 percent stock dividend when the common stock was selling for $20 per share to be distributed on January 5.
Dec. 15	Date of record for the stock dividend.

Required

1. Record the above transactions in journal form.
2. Prepare the stockholders' equity section of the company's balance sheet as of December 31, 2011. Net loss for 2011 was $436,000. (**Hint:** Use T accounts to keep track of transactions.)

User insight ▶

3. Compute the book value per share for preferred and common stock (including common stock distributable) on December 31, 2010 and 2011, using end-of-year shares outstanding. What effect would you expect the change in book value to have on the market price per share of the company's stock?

Alternate Problems

Corporate Income Statement

P 7. Income statement information for Nguyen Corporation in 2009 is as follows:

a. Administrative expenses, $110,000
b. Cost of goods sold, $440,000
c. Extraordinary loss from a storm (net of taxes, $10,000), $20,000
d. Income taxes expense, continuing operations, $42,000
e. Net sales, $890,000
f. Selling expenses, $190,000

Required

1. Prepare Nguyen Corporation's income statement for 2009, including earnings per share, assuming a weighted average of 100,000 shares of common stock outstanding for 2009.

User insight ▶

2. Which item in Nguyen Corporation's income statement affects the company's quality of earnings? Why does it have this effect?

Dividends, Stock Splits, and Stockholders' Equity

P 8. The stockholders' equity section of the balance sheet of Rago Corporation as of December 31, 2010, appears at the top of the next page.

Contributed capital	
Common stock, $4 par value, 250,000 shares authorized, 100,000 shares issued and outstanding	$ 400,000
Additional paid-in capital	500,000
Total contributed capital	$ 900,000
Retained earnings	600,000
Total stockholders' equity	$1,500,000

Rago Corporation had the following transactions in 2011:

Feb. 28	The board of directors declared a 10 percent stock dividend to stockholders of record on March 25 to be distributed on April 5. The market value on this date is $16.
Mar. 25	Date of record for stock dividend.
Apr. 5	Issued stock dividend.
Aug. 3	Declared a 2-for-1 stock split.
Nov. 20	Purchased 9,000 shares of the company's common stock at $8 per share for the treasury.
Dec. 31	Declared a 5 percent stock dividend to stockholders of record on January 25 to be distributed on February 5. The market value per share was $9.

Required

1. Record the stockholders' equity components of the transactions for Rago Corporation in T accounts.
2. Prepare the stockholders' equity section of the company's balance sheet as of December 31, 2011. Assume net income for 2011 is $54,000.

User insight ▶

3. If you owned 500 shares of Rago stock on February 1, 2011, how many shares would you own February 5, 2012? Would your proportionate share of the ownership of the company be different on the latter date than it was on the former date? Explain your answer.

ENHANCING Your Knowledge, Skills, and Critical Thinking

Conceptual Understanding Cases

LO5 **Stock Split**

C 1. When **Croc's**, the shoe company, reported in early 2007 that its first quarter earnings had increased from the previous year, its stock price jumped to over $80 per share. At the same time, the company announced a 2-for-1 stock split.[20] What is a stock split and what effect does it have on the company's stockholders' equity? What effect will it likely have on the market value of the company's stock? In light of your answers, do you think the stock split is positive for the company and for its stockholders?

LO1 **Classic Quality of Earnings Case**

C 2. On Tuesday, January 19, 1988, **IBM** reported greatly increased earnings for the fourth quarter of 1987. Despite this reported gain in earnings, the price of IBM's stock on the New York Stock Exchange declined by $6 per share to $111.75. In sympathy with this move, most other technology stocks also declined.[21]

IBM's fourth-quarter net earnings rose from $1.39 billion, or $2.28 a share, to $2.08 billion, or $3.47 a share, an increase of 49.6 percent and 52.2 percent over the same period a year earlier. Management declared that these results demonstrated the effectiveness of IBM's efforts to become more competitive and that, despite the economic uncertainties of 1988, the company was planning for growth.

The apparent cause of the stock price decline was that the huge increase in income could be traced to nonrecurring gains. Investment analysts pointed out that IBM's high earnings stemmed primarily from such factors as a lower tax rate. Despite most analysts' expectations of a tax rate between 40 and 42 percent, IBM's was a low 36.4 percent, down from the previous year's 45.3 percent. Analysts were also disappointed in IBM's revenue growth. Revenues within the United States were down, and much of the company's growth in revenues came through favorable currency translations, increases that might not be repeated. In fact, some estimates of IBM's fourth-quarter earnings attributed $.50 per share to currency translations and another $.25 to tax-rate changes.

Other factors contributing to IBM's rise in earnings were one-time transactions, such as the sale of Intel Corporation stock and bond redemptions, along with a corporate stock buyback program that reduced the amount of stock outstanding in the fourth quarter by 7.4 million shares.

The analysts were concerned about the quality of IBM's earnings. Identify four quality of earnings issues reported in the case and the analysts' concern about each. In percentage terms, what is the impact of the currency changes on fourth-quarter earnings? Comment on management's assessment of IBM's performance. Do you agree with management? (Optional question: What has IBM's subsequent performance been?) Be prepared to discuss your answers in class.

Interpreting Financial Reports

LO1 LO4 **Interpretation of Statement of Stockholders' Equity**

C 3. The consolidated statement of stockholders' equity for Jackson Electronics, Inc., a manufacturer of a broad line of electrical components, is presented below. It has nine summary transactions.

Jackson Electronics, Inc.
Consolidated Statement of Stockholders' Equity
For the Year Ended September 30, 2011
(In thousands)

	Preferred Stock	Common Stock	Additional Paid-in Capital	Retained Earnings	Treasury Stock, Common	Accumulated Other Comprehensive Income	Total
Balance at September 30, 2010	$2,756	$3,902	$14,149	$119,312	($ 942)		$139,177
(1) Net income				18,753			18,753
(2) Unrealized gain on available for sale securities						$12,000	12,000
(3) Redemption and retirement of preferred stock (27,560 shares)	(2,756)						(2,756)
(4) Stock options exercised (89,000 shares)		89	847				936
(5) Purchases of common stock for treasury (501,412 shares)					(12,552)		(12,552)
(6) Issuance of common stock (148,000 shares) in exchange for convertible subordinated debentures		148	3,635				3,783
(7) Issuance of common stock (715,000 shares) for cash		715	24,535				25,250
(8) Issuance of 500,000 shares of common stock in exchange for investment in Electrix Company shares		500	17,263				17,763
(9) Cash dividends—common stock ($.80 per share)				(3,086)			(3,086)
Balance at September 30, 2011	$	$5,354	$60,429	$134,979	($13,494)	$12,000	$199,268

1. Show that you understand it by preparing an explanation for each transaction. In each case, if applicable, determine the average price per common share. At times, you will have to make assumptions about an offsetting part of the entry. For example, assume debentures (long-term bonds) are recorded at face value and that employees pay cash for stock purchased under company incentive plans.
2. Define comprehensive income and determine the amount for Jackson Electronics.

LO2

Analysis of Income Taxes from Annual Report

C 4. In its 2007 annual report, **Nike, Inc.**, the athletic sportswear company, provided the following data about its current and deferred income tax provisions (in millions):

	2007
Current income taxes due	$674.1
Deferred income taxes	34.3
Total provision for income taxes	$708.4

1. What were the 2007 income taxes on the income statement? Record in journal form the overall income tax liability for 2007, using income tax allocation procedures.
2. Nike's balance sheet contains both deferred income tax assets and deferred tax liabilities. How do such deferred income tax assets arise? How do such deferred income tax liabilities arise? Given the definition of assets and liabilities, do you see a potential problem with the company's classifying deferred income taxes as a liability? Why or why not?

Decision Analysis Using Excel

LO4 LO5 LO6

Analyzing Effects of Stockholders' Equity Transactions

C 5. Kolmeyer Steel Corporation (KSC) is a small specialty steel manufacturer located in northern Alabama. The Kolmeyer family has owned the company for several generations. Robert Kolmeyer is a major shareholder in KSC by virtue of his having inherited 200,000 shares of common stock in the company. Kolmeyer has not shown much interest in the business because of his enthusiasm for archaeology. However, when he received the minutes of the last board of directors meeting, he questioned a number of transactions involving stockholders' equity. He asks you as a person with knowledge of accounting to help him interpret the effect of these transactions on his interest in KSC.

You begin by examining the stockholders' equity section of KSC's December 31, 2010, balance sheet, which appears at the top of the opposite page. Then you read these relevant parts of the minutes of the board of directors meeting on December 15, 2011:

> **Item A** The president reported the following transactions involving the company's stock during the last quarter:
>
> *October 15.* Sold 500,000 shares of authorized common stock through the investment banking firm of T.R. Kendall at a net price of $50 per share.
>
> *November 1.* Purchased 100,000 shares for the corporate treasury from Lucy Kolmeyer at a price of $55 per share.
>
> **Item B** The board declared a 2-for-1 stock split (accomplished by halving the par value and doubling each stockholder's shares), followed by a 10 percent stock dividend. The board then declared a cash dividend of $2 per share on the resulting shares. Cash dividends are declared on outstanding shares and shares distributable. All these transactions are applicable to stockholders of record on December 20 and are payable on January 10. The market value of KSC stock on the board meeting date after the stock split was estimated to be $30.

Kolmeyer Steel Corporation
Balance Sheet
December 31, 2010

Stockholders' Equity

Contributed capital	
Common stock, $10 par value, 5,000,000 shares authorized, 1,000,000 shares issued and outstanding	$10,000,000
Additional paid-in capital	25,000,000
Total contributed capital	$35,000,000
Retained earnings	20,000,000
Total stockholders' equity	$55,000,000

Item C The chief financial officer stated that he expected the company to report net income for the year of $4,000,000.

1. Prepare a stockholders' equity section of KSC's balance sheet as of December 31, 2011 that reflects the above transactions. (**Hint:** Use T accounts to analyze the transactions. Also use a T account to keep track of the shares of common stock outstanding.)
2. Write a memorandum to Robert Kolmeyer that shows the book value per share and Kolmeyer's percentage of ownership at the beginning and end of the year. Explain the difference and state whether Kolmeyer's position has improved during the year. Tell why or why not and state how Kolmeyer may be able to maintain his percentage of ownership.

Annual Report Case: CVS Caremark Corporation

LO1 LO4

Corporate Income Statement and Statement of Stockholders' Equity

C 6. Refer to the **CVS** annual report in the Supplement to Chapter 1 to answer the following questions:

1. Does CVS have discontinued operations or extraordinary items? Are there any items that would lead you to question the quality of CVS's earnings? Would you say the income statement for CVS is relatively simple or relatively complex? Why?
2. What transactions most often affect the stockholders' equity section of the CVS balance sheet? (**Hint:** Examine the corporation's statements of stockholders' equity.)

Comparison Case: CVS Versus Southwest

Book Value and Market Value

C 7. Refer to the **CVS** annual report and the financial statements for **Southwest Airlines Co.** in the Supplement to Chapter 1. Compute the 2007 and 2006 book value per share for both companies and compare the results to the average stock price of each in the fourth quarter of 2007 as shown in the notes to the financial statements. Southwest's average price per share was $13.59 in 2007 and $15.82 in 2006. How do you explain the differences in book value per share, and how do you interpret their relationship to market prices?

Ethical Dilemma Case

Ethics and Stock Dividends

C 8. For 20 years, Armand Service Corporation, a public corporation that has promoted itself to investors as a stable, reliable company, has paid a cash dividend every quarter. Recent competition from Asian companies has negatively affected the company's earnings and cash flows. As a result, Judy Armand, president of the company, is proposing that the board of directors declare a stock dividend of 5 percent this year instead of a cash dividend. She stated: "This will maintain our consecutive dividend record and will not require any cash outflow." What is the difference between a cash dividend and a stock dividend? Why does a corporation usually distribute either kind of dividend, and how does each affect the financial statements? Is the action that Judy Armand proposed ethical? Why or why not?

Internet Case

Comparison of Comprehensive Income Disclosures

C 9. When the FASB ruled that public companies should report comprehensive income, it did not issue specific guidelines for how this amount and its components should be disclosed. Choose two companies in the same industry. Go to the annual reports on the websites of the two companies you have selected. In the latest annual report, look at the financial statements. How have your two companies reported comprehensive income—as part of the income statement, as part of stockholders' equity, or as a separate statement? What items create a difference between net income and comprehensive income? Is comprehensive income greater or less than net income? Is comprehensive income more volatile than net income? Which measure of income is used to compute basic earnings per share?

Group Activity Case

C 10. Divide into groups of three or four students each. Each group should choose a company in the technology industry, such as **Yahoo!**, **ebay**, **Apple**, or **Microsoft**. Obtain the company's annual report or SEC Form 10-K from the Internet. Find the corporate income statement and summary of significant accounting policies (usually the first note to the financial statements).

1. As a team, prepare a one-page executive summary that highlights the quality of earnings, the relationship of book value and market value, and the existence or absence of stock splits or dividends, including reference to management's assessment. Include a table with your report and answers to the following questions:
   a. Did the company report any discontinued operations or extraordinary items?
   b. What percentage of impact did these items have on earnings per share? (Summarize in your table the methods and estimates the company uses.)
   c. How would you evaluate the quality of earnings for the company?
   d. Did the company provide a statement of stockholders' equity or summarize changes in stockholders' equity in the notes only?
   e. Did the company declare any stock dividends or stock splits? Calculate book value per common share.
2. Find in the financial section of your local paper the current market prices of the company's common stock. Discuss the difference between market price per share and book value per share.

3. Find and read references to earnings per share in management's discussion and analysis in the company's annual report. Be prepared to share your report with the reports of other teams in class.

Business Communication Case

LO1

C 11. When analysts expected **IBM** to earn $1.32 per share, the company actually earned $1.33. In the same year, **Microsoft** was expected to earn $.43 per share, but it earned only $.41. The corporate income statements of these companies show that Microsoft had a special charge (with corresponding liability) of $660 million, or $.06 per share, based on settlement of a class-action lawsuit filed on behalf of consumers, whereas IBM had no such charge.[22]

Assume you work for an investment manager who has asked you to write a memorandum in one page or less that assesses these results. Specifically, who did better, Microsoft or IBM? Use quality of earnings to support your answer and comment on the effect of Microsoft's special charge on current and future cash flows.

CHAPTER

13 The Statement of Cash Flows

Focus on Financial Statements

INCOME STATEMENT
Revenues
– Expenses
= Net Income

STATEMENT OF RETAINED EARNINGS
Opening Balance
+ Net Income
– Dividends
= Retained Earnings

BALANCE SHEET
Assets | Liabilities
Equity
A = L + E

STATEMENT OF CASH FLOWS
Operating activities
+ Investing activities
+ Financing activities
= Change in Cash
+ Starting Balance
= Ending Cash Balance

Changes in all noncash balance sheet accounts are used to explain changes in cash.

Cash flows are the lifeblood of a business. They enable a company to pay expenses, debts, employees' wages, and taxes, and to invest in the assets it needs for its operations. Without sufficient cash flows, a company cannot grow and prosper. Because of the importance of cash flows, one must be alert to the possibility that items may be incorrectly classified in a statement of cash flows and that the statement may not fully disclose all pertinent information. This chapter identifies the classifications used in a statement of cash flows and explains how to analyze the statement.

LEARNING OBJECTIVES

LO1 Describe the principal purposes and uses of the statement of cash flows, and identify its components. *(pp. 656–661)*

LO2 Analyze the statement of cash flows. *(pp. 661–665)*

LO3 Use the indirect method to determine cash flows from operating activities. *(pp. 665–672)*

LO4 Determine cash flows from investing activities. *(pp. 672–675)*

LO5 Determine cash flows from financing activities. *(pp. 676–679)*

DECISION POINT ▶ A USER'S FOCUS

Amazon.com, Inc.

Founded in 1995, **Amazon.com, Inc.,** is now the largest on-line merchandising company in the world and one of the 500 largest companies in the United States. The company's financial focus is on "long-term sustainable growth" in cash flows.

Strong cash flows are critical to achieving and maintaining liquidity. If cash flows exceed the amount a company needs for operations and expansion, it will not have to borrow additional funds. It can use its excess cash to reduce debt, thereby lowering its debt to equity ratio and improving its financial position. That, in turn, can increase the market value of its stock, which will increase shareholders' value.

The Financial Highlights below summarize key components of Amazon.com's statement of cash flows.[1]

- ▶ Are operations generating sufficient operating cash flows?
- ▶ Is the company growing by investing in long-term assets?
- ▶ Has the company had to borrow money or issue stock to finance its growth?

AMAZON.COM'S FINANCIAL HIGHLIGHTS:
Consolidated Statement of Cash Flows (In millions)

	2007	2006	2005
Net cash provided by operating activities	$1,405	$ 702	$ 733
Net cash provided by (used in) investing activities	42	(333)	(778)
Net cash provided by (used in) financing activities	50	(400)	(193)
Foreign currency effects	20	40	(52)
Increase (decrease) in cash and equivlalents	$1,517	$ 9	($ 290)

Overview of the Statement of Cash Flows

LO1 Describe the principal purposes and uses of the statement of cash flows, and identify its components.

The **statement of cash flows** shows how a company's operating, investing, and financing activities have affected cash during an accounting period. It explains the net increase (or decrease) in cash during the period. For purposes of preparing this statement, **cash** is defined as including both cash and cash equivalents. **Cash equivalents** are investments that can be quickly converted to cash; they have a maturity of 90 days or less when they are purchased. They include money market accounts, commercial paper, and U.S. Treasury bills. A company invests in cash equivalents to earn interest on cash that would otherwise be temporarily idle.

Suppose, for example, that a company has $1,000,000 that it will not need for 30 days. To earn a return on this amount, the company could place the cash in an account that earns interest (such as a money market account), lend the cash to another corporation by purchasing that corporation's short-term notes (commercial paper), or purchase a short-term obligation of the U.S. government (a Treasury bill).

Because cash includes cash equivalents, transfers between the Cash account and cash equivalents are not treated as cash receipts or cash payments. On the statement of cash flows, cash equivalents are combined with the Cash account. Cash equivalents should not be confused with short-term investments, or marketable securities. These items are not combined with the Cash account on the statement of cash flows; rather, purchases of marketable securities are treated as cash outflows, and sales of marketable securities are treated as cash inflows.

Study Note

Money market accounts, commercial paper (short-term notes), and U.S. Treasury bills are considered cash equivalents because they are highly liquid, temporary (90 days or less) holding places for cash not currently needed to operate the business.

Purposes of the Statement of Cash Flows

The primary purpose of the statement of cash flows is to provide information about a company's cash receipts and cash payments during an accounting period. A secondary purpose is to provide information about a company's operating, investing, and financing activities during the accounting period. Some information about those activities may be inferred from other financial statements, but the statement of cash flows summarizes *all* transactions that affect cash.

Uses of the Statement of Cash Flows

The statement of cash flows is useful to management, as well as to investors and creditors.

- Management uses the statement of cash flows to assess liquidity, to determine dividend policy, and to evaluate the effects of major policy decisions involving investments and financing. Examples include determining if short-term financing is needed to pay current liabilities, deciding whether to raise or lower dividends, and planning for investing and financing needs.
- Investors and creditors use the statement to assess a company's ability to manage cash flows, to generate positive future cash flows, to pay its liabilities, to pay dividends and interest, and to anticipate its need for additional financing.

Classification of Cash Flows

The statement of cash flows has three major classifications: operating, investing, and financing activities. The components of these activities are illustrated in Figure 1 and summarized below.

1. **Operating activities** involve the cash inflows and outflows from activities that enter into the determination of net income. Cash inflows in this category include cash receipts from the sale of goods and services and from the sale of

FIGURE 1

Classification of Cash Inflows and Cash Outflows

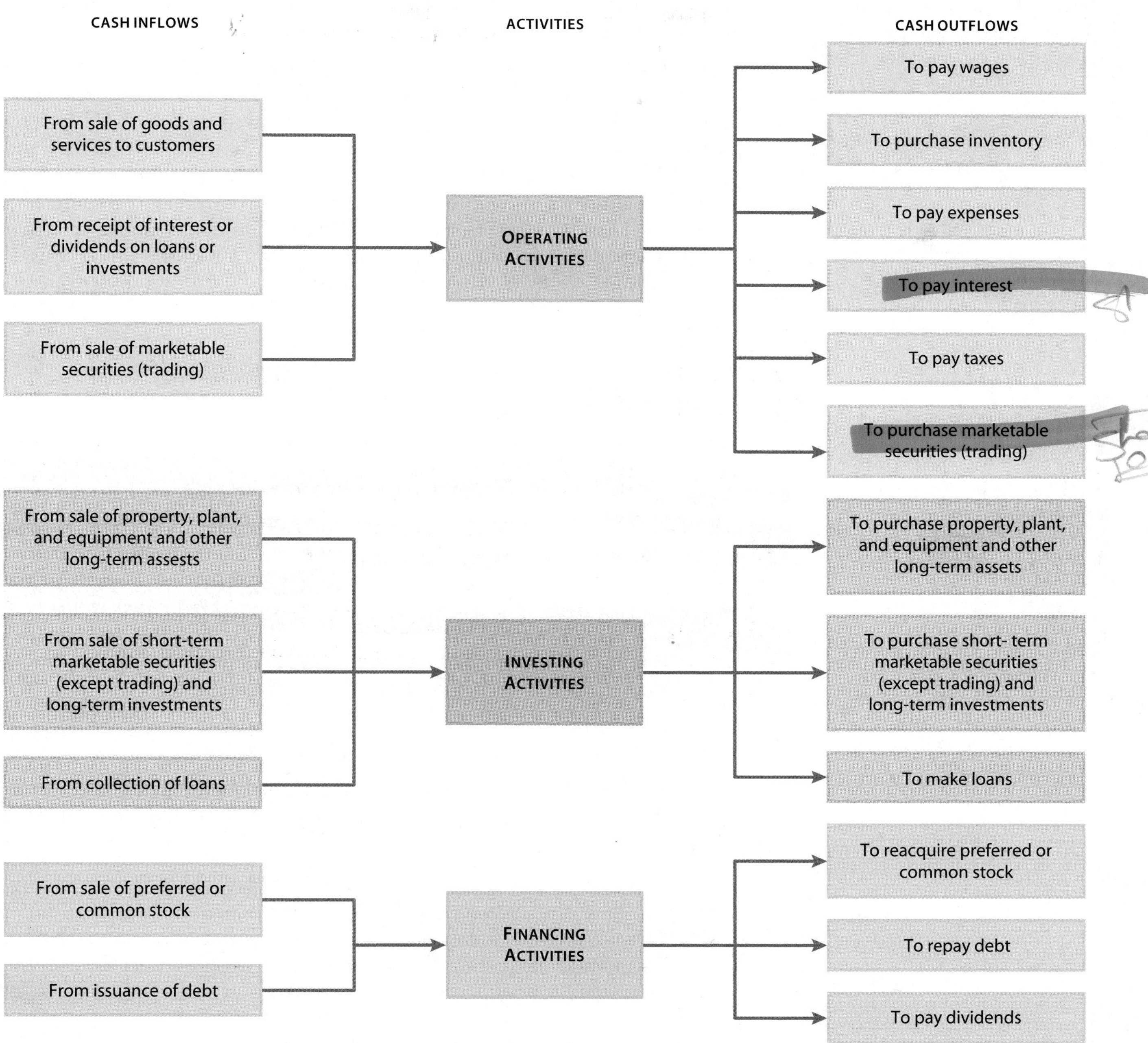

trading securities. Trading securities are a type of marketable security that a company buys and sells for the purpose of making a profit in the near term. Cash inflows also include interest and dividends received on loans and investments. Cash outflows include cash payments for wages, inventory, expenses, interest, taxes, and the purchase of trading securities. In effect, accrual-based income from the income statement is changed to reflect cash flows.

2. **Investing activities** involve the acquisition and sale of property, plant, and equipment and other long-term assets, including long-term investments. They also involve the acquisition and sale of short-term marketable securities, other than trading securities, and the making and collecting of loans.

Study Note

Operating activities involve the day-to-day sale of goods and services, investing activities involve long-term assets and investments, and financing activities deal with stockholders' equity accounts and debt (borrowing).

Cash inflows include the cash received from selling marketable securities and long-term assets and from collecting on loans. Cash outflows include the cash expended on purchasing these securities and assets and the cash lent to borrowers.

3. **Financing activities** involve obtaining resources from stockholders and providing them with a return on their investments, and obtaining resources from creditors and repaying the amounts borrowed or otherwise settling the obligations. Cash inflows include the proceeds from stock issues and from short- and long-term borrowing. Cash outflows include the repayments of loans (excluding interest) and payments to owners, including cash dividends. Treasury stock transactions are also considered financing activities. Repayments of accounts payable or accrued liabilities are not considered repayments of loans; they are classified as cash outflows under operating activities.

Required Disclosure of Noncash Investing and Financing Transactions

Companies occasionally engage in significant **noncash investing and financing transactions**. These transactions involve only long-term assets, long-term liabilities, or stockholders' equity. For instance, a company might exchange a long-term asset for a long-term liability, settle a debt by issuing capital stock, or take out a long-term mortgage to purchase real estate. Noncash transactions represent significant investing and financing activities, but they are not reflected on the statement of cash flows because they do not affect current cash inflows or outflows. They will, however, affect future cash flows. For this reason, it is required that they be disclosed in a separate schedule or as part of the statement of cash flows.

Format of the Statement of Cash Flows

The Financial Highlights at the beginning of the chapter summarize the key components of **Amazon.com's** statement of cash flows. Exhibit 1 presents the full statement.

- The first section of the statement of cash flows is cash flows from operating activities. When the indirect method is used to prepare this section, it begins with net income and ends with cash flows from operating activities. This is the method most commonly used; we discuss it in detail later in the chapter.
- The second section, cash flows from investing activities, shows cash transactions involving capital expenditures (for property and equipment) and loans. Cash outflows for capital expenditures are usually shown separately from cash inflows from their disposal, as they are in Amazon.com's statement. However, when the inflows are not material, some companies combine these two lines to show the net amount of outflow.
- The third section, cash flows from financing activities, shows debt and common stock transactions, as well as payments for dividends and treasury stock.
- A reconciliation of the beginning and ending balances of cash appears at the bottom of the statement. These cash balances will tie into the cash balances of the balance sheets.

EXHIBIT 1 Consolidated Statements of Cash Flows

Amazon.com, Inc.
Consolidated Statements of Cash flows

	For the Years Ended		
(In millions)	**2007**	**2006**	**2005**
OPERATING ACTIVITIES			
Net income	$ 476	$ 190	$ 359
Adjustments to reconcile net income to net cash from operating activities:			
Depreciation and amortization	246	205	121
Stock-based compensation	185	101	87
Deferred income taxes	(99)	22	70
Excess tax benefits from stock-based compensation	(257)	(102)	(7)
Other	22	2	(31)
Cumulative effect of change in accounting principle	—	—	(26)
Changes in operating assets and liabilities:			
Inventories	(303)	(282)	(104)
Accounts receivable, net and other	(255)	(103)	(84)
Accounts payable	928	402	274
Accrued expenses and other	429	241	67
Additions to unearned revenue and other	33	26	7
Net cash provided by operating activities	$ 1,405	$ 702	$ 733
INVESTING ACTIVITIES			
Purchases of fixed assets, including software and website development	$ (224)	$ (216)	$ (204)
Acquisitions, net of cash received and other	(75)	(32)	(24)
Sales and maturities of marketable securities and other investments	1,271	1,845	836
Purchases of marketable securities and other investments	(930)	(1,930)	(1,386)
Net cash provided by (used in) investing activities	$ 42	$ (333)	$ (778)
FINANCING ACTIVITIES			
Proceeds from exercises of stock options	$ 91	$ 35	$ 59
Excess tax benefits from exercises of stock options	257	102	7
Common stock repurchased (Treasury stock)	(248)	(252)	—
Proceeds from long-term debt and other	24	98	11
Repayments of long-term debt and capital lease obligations	(74)	(383)	(270)
Net cash provided by (used in) financing activities	$ 50	$ (400)	$ (193)
Foreign-currency effect on cash and cash equivalents	$ 20	$ 40	$ (52)
NET (DECREASE) INCREASE IN CASH AND CASH EQUIVALENTS	$ 1,517	$ 9	$ (290)
CASH AND CASH EQUIVALENTS, beginning of year	1,022	1,013	1,303
CASH AND CASH EQUIVALENTS, end of year	$ 2,539	$ 1,022	$ 1,013

Source: Amazon.com, Inc., *Annual Report*, 2007 (adapted).

FOCUS ON BUSINESS PRACTICE

IFRS

How Universal Is the Statement of Cash Flows?

Despite the importance of the statement of cash flows in assessing the liquidity of companies in the United States, there has been considerable variation in its use and format in other countries. For example, in many countries, the statement shows the change in working capital rather than the change in cash and cash equivalents. Although the European Union's principal directives for financial reporting do not address the statement of cash flows, international accounting standards require it, and international financial markets expect it to be presented. As a result, most multinational companies include the statement in their financial reports. Most European countries adopted the statement of cash flows when the European Union adopted international accounting standards.

Ethical Considerations and the Statement of Cash Flows

Although cash inflows and outflows are not as subject to manipulation as earnings are, managers are acutely aware of users' emphasis on cash flows from operations as an important measure of performance. Thus, an incentive exists to overstate these cash flows.

In earlier chapters, we cited an egregious example of earnings management. As you may recall, by treating operating expenses of about $10 billion over several years as purchases of equipment, **WorldCom** reduced reported expenses and improved reported earnings. In addition, by classifying payments of operating expenses as investments on the statement of cash flows, it was able to show an improvement in cash flows from operations. The inclusion of the expenditures in the investing activities section did not draw special attention because the company normally had large capital expenditures.

Another way a company can show an apparent improvement in its performance is through lack of transparency, or lack of full disclosure, in its financial statements. For instance, securitization—the sale of batches of accounts receivable—is clearly a means of financing, and the proceeds from it should be shown in the financing section of the statement of cash flows. However, because the accounting standards are somewhat vague about where these proceeds should go, some companies net the proceeds against the accounts receivable in the operating section of the statement and bury the explanation in the notes to the financial statements. By doing so, they make collections of receivables in the operating activities section look better than they actually were. It is not illegal to do this, but from an ethical standpoint, it obscures the company's true performance.

STOP ▶ REVIEW ▶ APPLY

LO1-1 **In the statement of cash flows, what does cash include?**

LO1-2 **What are the purposes of the statement of cash flows?**

LO1-3 **What are the three classifications of cash flows? Give two examples of each.**

(continued)

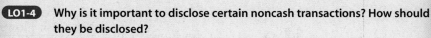

LO1-4 **Why is it important to disclose certain noncash transactions? How should they be disclosed?**

LO1-5 **Why would a company want to classify an item that belongs in the operating activities section of the statement of cash flows in the investing or financing sections?**

Suggested answers to all Stop, Review, and Apply questions follow the appendixes.

Analyzing Cash Flows

LO2 Analyze the statement of cash flows.

Like the analysis of other financial statements, an analysis of the statement of cash flows can reveal significant relationships. Two areas on which analysts focus when examining a company's statement of cash flows are cash-generating efficiency and free cash flow.

Can a Company Have Too Much Cash?

Before the bull market ended in 2007, many companies had accumulated large amounts of cash. **Exxon Mobil**, **Microsoft**, and **Cisco Systems**, for example, had amassed more than $100 billion in cash. At that time, the average large company in the United States had 7 percent of its assets in cash.

Increased cash can be a benefit or a potential risk. Many companies put their cash to good use. Of course they are wise to have cash on hand for emergencies. They may also invest in productive assets, conduct research and development, pay off debt, buy back stock, or pay dividends. Sometimes, however, shareholders suffer when executives are too conservative and keep the money in low-paying money market accounts or make unwise acquisitions. For the user of financial statements, the lesson is that it is important to look closely at the components of the statement of cash flows to see how management is spending its cash.[2]

Cash-Generating Efficiency

Managers accustomed to evaluating income statements usually focus on the bottom-line result. While the level of cash at the bottom of the statement of cash flows is certainly an important consideration, such information can be obtained from the balance sheet. The focal point of cash flow analysis is on cash inflows and outflows from operating activities. These cash flows are used in ratios that measure **cash-generating efficiency**, which is a company's ability to generate cash from its current or continuing operations. The ratios that analysts use to compute cash-generating efficiency are cash flow yield, cash flows to sales, and cash flows to assets.

In this section, we compute these ratios for **Amazon.com** in 2007 using data for net income and net cash flows from Exhibit 1 and the following information from Amazon.com's 2007 annual report. (All dollar amounts are in millions.)

	2007	2006	2005
Net Sales	$14,835	$10,711	$8,490
Total Assets	6,485	4,363	3,696

Cash flow yield is the ratio of net cash flows from operating activities to net income:

$$\text{Cash Flow Yield} = \frac{\text{Net Cash Flows from Operating Activities}}{\text{Net Income}}$$

$$= \frac{\$1{,}405}{\$476}$$

$$= 3.0 \text{ times*}$$

For most companies, the cash flow yield should exceed 1.0. In 2007, Amazon.com performed much better than this minimum. With a cash flow yield of 3.0 times, Amazon.com generated about $3 of cash for every dollar of net income.

The cash flow yield needs to be examined carefully. Keep in mind, for instance, that a firm with significant depreciable assets should have a cash flow yield greater than 1.0 because depreciation expense is added back to net income to arrive at cash flows from operating activities. If special items, such as discontinued operations, appear on the income statement and are material, income from continuing operations should be used as the denominator. Also, an artificially high cash flow yield may result because a firm has very low net income, which is the denominator in the ratio.

Cash flows to sales is the ratio of net cash flows from operating activities to sales:

$$\text{Cash Flows to Sales} = \frac{\text{Net Cash Flows from Operating Activities}}{\text{Sales}}$$

$$= \frac{\$1{,}405}{\$14{,}835}$$

$$= 9.5\%*$$

Thus, Amazon.com generated positive cash flows to sales of 9.5 percent. Another way to state this result is that every dollar of sales generates 9.5 cents in cash.

Cash flows to assets is the ratio of net cash flows from operating activities to average total assets:

$$\text{Cash Flows to Assets} = \frac{\text{Net Cash Flows from Operating Activities}}{\text{Average Total Assets}}$$

$$= \frac{\$1{,}405}{(\$6{,}485 + \$4{,}363) \div 2}$$

$$= 25.9\%*$$

At 25.9 percent, Amazon.com's cash flows to assets ratio indicates that for every dollar of assets, the company generates almost 26 cents. This excellent result is higher than its cash flows to sales ratio because of its good asset turnover ratio (sales ÷ average total assets) of 2.7 times (25.9% ÷ 9.5%). Cash flows to sales and cash flows to assets are closely related to the profitability measures of profit margin and return on assets. They exceed those measures by the amount of the cash flow yield ratio because cash flow yield is the ratio of net cash flows from operating activities to net income.

Asking the Right Questions About the Statement of Cash Flows

Most readers of financial statements are accustomed to looking at the "bottom line" to get an overview of a company's financial status. They look at total assets

---

*Rounded.

on the balance sheet and net income on the income statement. However, the statement of cash flows requires a different approach because the bottom line of cash on hand does not tell the reader very much; changes in the components of the statement during the year are far more revealing.

In interpreting a statement of cash flows, it pays to know the right questions to ask. To illustrate, let's use **Amazon.com** as an example.

- In our discussion of cash flow yield, we saw that Amazon.com generated about $3 of cash from operating activities for every dollar of net income in 2007. What are the primary reasons that cash flows from operating activities differed from net income?

For Amazon.com, the largest positive items in 2007 were accounts payable and depreciation. They are added to net income for different reasons. Accounts payable represents an increase in the amount owed to creditors, whereas depreciation represents a noncash expense that is deducted in arriving at net income. Amazon.com's two largest negative items were increases in inventories and receivables. As a growing company, Amazon.com was managing its operating cycle by generating cash from creditors to pay for increases in inventories and receivables.

- Amazon.com had only a small increase in cash from investing activities in 2007. What were its most important investing activities other than capital expenditures?

The company was managing its investing activities by making active use of investments. Sales of marketable securities and other investments were sufficient to offset the purchase of marketable securities and other investments and the purchase of various assets.

- Amazon.com's financing activities showed a small increase in cash in 2007. How did the company manage its financing activities during that fiscal year?

Exercise of stock options and the tax effects of stock-based compensation provided funds to buy back treasury stock and pay off some long-term debt. Because of its good cash flow from operations, Amazon.com did not need long-term financing.

FOCUS ON BUSINESS PRACTICE

Cash Flows Tell All.

In early 2001, the telecommunications industry began one of the biggest market crashes in history. Could it have been predicted? The capital expenditures that telecommunications firms must make for equipment, such as cable lines and computers, are sizable. When the capital expenditures (a negative component of free cash flow) of 41 telecommunications companies are compared with their cash flows from sales over the six years preceding the crash, an interesting pattern emerges. In the first three years, both capital expenditures and cash flows from sales were about 20 percent of sales. In other words, operations were generating enough cash flows to cover capital expenditures. Although, cash flows from sales in the next three years stayed at about 20 percent of sales, free cash flows turned very negative, and almost half of capital expenditures had to be financed by debt instead of operations, making these companies more vulnerable to the downturn in the economy that occurred in 2001[3] and especially in 2008. The predictive reliability of free cash flow was confirmed in a later study that showed that of 100 different measures, stock price to free cash flow was the best predictor of future increases in stock price.[4]

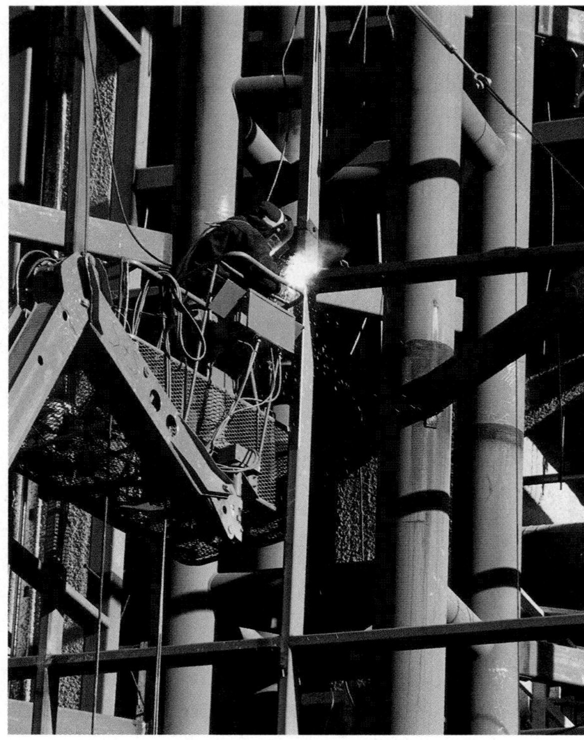

Construction firms must make large capital expenditures for plant assets, such as the equipment shown here. These expenditures are a negative component of free cash flow, which is the amount of cash that remains after deducting the funds a company needs to operate at its planned level. In 2007, negative free cash flows forced a number of construction firms to rely heavily on debt to finance their capital expenditures, thus increasing their vulnerability to the ecconomic downturn of 2008.

Free Cash Flow

As we noted in an earlier chapter, **free cash flow** is the amount of cash that remains after deducting the funds a company must commit to continue operating at its planned level. If free cash flow is positive, it means that the company has met all of its planned cash commitments and has cash available to reduce debt or to expand. A negative free cash flow means that the company will have to sell investments, borrow money, or issue stock in the short term to continue at its planned level; if a company's free cash flow remains negative for several years, it may not be able to raise cash by issuing stocks or bonds. On the statement of cash flows, cash commitments for current and continuing operations, interest, and income taxes are incorporated in cash flows from current operations.

Amazon.com has a stated primary financial objective of "long-term sustainable growth in free cash flow."[5] The company definitely achieved this objective in 2007. Its free cash flow for this year is computed as follows (in millions):

FOCUS ON BUSINESS PRACTICE

What Do You Mean, "Free Cash Flow"?

Because the statement of cash flows has been around for less than 20 years, no generally accepted analyses have yet been developed. For example, the term *free cash flow* is commonly used in the business press, but there is no agreement on its definition. An article in *Forbes* defines *free cash flow* as "cash available after paying out capital expenditures and dividends, but *before taxes and interest*"[6] [emphasis added]. An article in *The Wall Street Journal* defines it as "operating income less maintenance-level capital expenditures."[7] The definition with which we are most in agreement is the one used in *BusinessWeek*: free cash flow is net cash flows from operating activities less net capital expenditures and dividends. This "measures truly discretionary funds—company money that an owner could pocket without harming the business."[8]

K/R

$$\text{Free Cash Flow} = \text{Net Cash Flows from Operating Activities} - \text{Dividends} - \text{Purchases of Plant Assets} + \text{Sales of Plant Assets}$$

$$= \$1{,}405 - \$0 - \$224 + \$0$$

$$= \$1{,}181$$

Study Note

The computation for free cash flow sometimes uses *net capital expenditures* in place of (*purchases of plant assets* + *sales of plant assets*).

Purchases of plant assets (capital expenditures) and sales (dispositions) of plant assets, if any, appear in the investing activities section of the statement of cash flows. Dividends, if any, appear in the financing activities section. Amazon.com is a growing company and does not have material sales of plant assets and does not pay dividends. The company's positive free cash flow of $1,181 million was due primarily to its strong operating cash flow of $1,405 million. Consequently, the company does not have to borrow money to expand.

Because cash flows can vary from year to year, analysts should look at trends in cash flow measures over several years. It is also important to consider the effect of seasonality on a company's sales. Because Amazon.com's sales peak toward the end of the year, the cash situation at that time may not be representative of the rest of the year. For example, Amazon.com's management states that

> Our cash, cash equivalents, and marketable securities balances typically reach their highest level [at the end of each year.] This operating cycle results in a corresponding increase in accounts payable at December 31. Our accounts payable balance generally declines during the first three months of the year, resulting in a corresponding decline in cash . . ."[9]

STOP ► REVIEW ► APPLY

- **LO2-1** **What is cash-generating efficiency?**
- **LO2-2** **What are three ratios that measure cash-generating efficiency?**
- **LO2-3** **What is free cash flow?**
- **LO2-4** **What do *positive* and *negative free cash flows* mean?**

Operating Activities

LO3 Use the indirect method to determine cash flows from operating activities.

To demonstrate the preparation of the statement of cash flows, we will work through an example step by step. The data for this example are presented in Exhibit 2, which shows Laguna Corporation's income statement for 2010, and in Exhibit 3, which shows Laguna's balance sheets for December 31, 2010 and 2009. Exhibit 3 shows the balance sheet accounts that we use for analysis and whether the change in each account is an increase or a decrease.

The first step in preparing the statement of cash flows is to determine cash flows from operating activities. The income statement indicates how successful a company has been in earning an income from its operating activities, but because that statement is prepared on an accrual basis, it does not reflect the inflow and outflow of cash related to operating activities. Revenues are recorded even though the company may not yet have received the cash, and expenses are recorded even though the company may not yet have expended the cash. Thus, to ascertain cash flows from operations, the figures on the income statement must be converted from an accrual basis to a cash basis.

EXHIBIT 2
Income Statement

Laguna Corporation Income Statement For the Year Ended December 31, 2010		
Sales		$ 698,000
Cost of goods sold		520,000
Gross margin		$ 178,000
Operating expenses (including depreciation expense of $37,000)		147,000
Operating income		$ 31,000
Other income (expenses)		
Interest expense	($23,000)	
Interest income	6,000	
Gain on sale of investments	12,000	
Loss on sale of plant assets	(3,000)	(8,000)
Income before income taxes		$ 23,000
Income taxes expense		7,000
Net income		$ 16,000

Study Note

The direct and indirect methods relate only to the operating activities section of the statement of cash flows. They are both acceptable for financial reporting purposes.

There are two methods of accomplishing this:

- The **direct method** adjusts each item on the income statement from the accrual basis to the cash basis. The result is a statement that begins with cash receipts from sales and interest and deducts cash payments for purchases, operating expenses, interest payments, and income taxes to arrive at net cash flows from operating activities.
- The **indirect method** does not require the adjustment of each item on the income statement. It lists only the adjustments necessary to convert net income to cash flows from operations.

The direct and indirect methods always produce the same net figure. The average person finds the direct method easier to understand because its presentation of operating cash flows is more straightforward than that of the indirect method. However, the indirect method is the overwhelming choice of most companies and

FOCUS ON BUSINESS PRACTICE IFRS

The Direct Method May Become More Important

At present, the direct method of preparing the operating section of the statement of cash flows is not important, but this may change if the International Accounting Standards Board (IASB) has its way. As mentioned earlier in the text, 99 percent of public companies in the United States presently use the indirect method to show the operating activities section of the statement of cash flows. However, in the interest of converging U.S. GAAP with international financial reporting standards (IFRS), the IASB is promoting the use of the direct method, even though it is more costly for companies to prepare. IFRS will continue to require a reconciliation of net income and net cash flows from operating activities similar to what is now done in the indirect method. **CVS's** statement of cash flows, as shown in the Supplement to Chapter 1, is one of the few U.S. companies to use the direct method with a reconciliation. Thus, its approach is very similar to what all companies may do if IFRS are adopted in the United States.

EXHIBIT 3 Comparative Balance Sheets Showing Changes in Accounts

Laguna Corporation
Comparative Balance Sheets
December 31, 2010 and 2009

	2010	2009	Change	Increase or Decrease
Assets				
Current assets				
Cash	$ 46,000	$ 15,000	$ 31,000	Increase
Accounts receivable (net)	47,000	55,000	(8,000)	Decrease
Inventory	144,000	110,000	34,000	Increase
Prepaid expenses	1,000	5,000	(4,000)	Decrease
Total current assets	$238,000	$185,000	$ 53,000	
Investments	$115,000	$127,000	($ 12,000)	Decrease
Plant assets	$715,000	$505,000	$210,000	Increase
Less accumulated depreciation	(103,000)	(68,000)	(35,000)	Increase
Total plant assets	$612,000	$437,000	$175,000	
Total assets	$965,000	$749,000	$216,000	
Liabilities				
Current liabilities				
Accounts payable	$ 50,000	$ 43,000	$ 7,000	Increase
Accrued liabilities	12,000	9,000	3,000	Increase
Income taxes payable	3,000	5,000	(2,000)	Decrease
Total current liabilities	$ 65,000	$ 57,000	$ 8,000	
Long-term liabilities				
Bonds payable	295,000	245,000	50,000	Increase
Total liabilities	$360,000	$302,000	$ 58,000	
Stockholders' Equity				
Common stock, $5 par value	$276,000	$200,000	$ 76,000	Increase
Additional paid-in capital	214,000	115,000	99,000	Increase
Retained earnings	140,000	132,000	8,000	Increase
Treasury stock	(25,000)	0	(25,000)	Increase
Total stockholders' equity	$605,000	$447,000	$158,000	
Total liabilities and stockholders' equity	$965,000	$749,000	$216,000	

accountants. A survey of large companies shows that 99 percent use this method.[10] From an analyst's perspective, the indirect method is superior to the direct method because it begins with net income and derives cash flows from operations; the analyst can readily identify the factors that cause cash flows from operations. From a company's standpoint, the indirect method is easier and less expensive to prepare. For these reasons, we use the indirect method in our example.

FIGURE 2

Indirect Method of Determining Net Cash Flows from Operating Activities

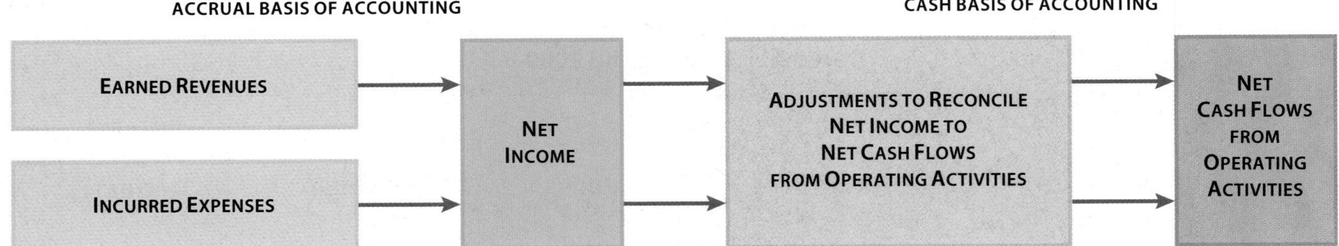

As Figure 2 shows, the indirect method focuses on adjusting items on the income statement to reconcile net income to net cash flows from operating activities. These items include depreciation, amortization, and depletion; gains and losses; and changes in the balances of current asset and current liability accounts. The schedule in Exhibit 4 shows the reconciliation of Laguna Corporation's net income to net cash flows from operating activities. We discuss each adjustment in the sections that follow.

Depreciation

> **Study Note**
> Operating expenses on the income statement include depreciation expense, which does not require a cash outlay.

The investing activities section of the statement of cash flows shows the cash payments that the company made for plant assets, intangible assets, and natural resources during the accounting period. Depreciation expense, amortization expense, and depletion expense for these assets appear on the income statement as allocations of the costs of the original purchases to the current accounting period. The amount of these expenses can usually be found in the income statement or in a note to the financial statements. As you can see in Exhibit 2, Laguna

EXHIBIT 4

Schedule of Cash Flows from Operating Activities: Indirect Method

Laguna Corporation
Schedule of Cash Flows from Operating Activities
For the Year Ended December 31, 2010

Cash flows from operating activities		
Net income		$16,000
Adjustments to reconcile net income to net cash flows from operating activities		
Depreciation	$37,000	
Gain on sale of investments	(12,000)	
Loss on sale of plant assets	3,000	
Changes in current assets and current liabilities		
Decrease in accounts receivable	8,000	
Increase in inventory	(34,000)	
Decrease in prepaid expenses	4,000	
Increase in accounts payable	7,000	
Increase in accrued liabilities	3,000	
Decrease in income taxes payable	(2,000)	14,000
Net cash flows from operating activities		$30,000

Corporation's income statement discloses depreciation expense of $37,000, which would have been recorded as follows:

A	= L +	SE
−37,000		−37,000

Depreciation Expense	37,000	
Accumulated Depreciation		37,000
To record annual depreciation on plant assets		

Even though depreciation expense appears on the income statement, it involves no outlay of cash and so does not affect cash flows in the current period. Thus, to arrive at cash flows from operations on the statement of cash flows, an adjustment is needed to increase net income by the amount of depreciation expense shown on the income statement.

Gains and Losses

Study Note

Gains and losses by themselves do not represent cash flows; they are merely bookkeeping adjustments. For example, when a long-term asset is sold, it is the proceeds (cash received), not the gain or loss, that constitute cash flow.

Like depreciation expense, gains and losses that appear on the income statement do not affect cash flows from operating activities and need to be removed from this section of the statement of cash flows. The cash receipts generated by the disposal of the assets that resulted in the gains or losses are included in the investing activities section of the statement of cash flows. Thus, to reconcile net income to cash flows from operating activities (and prevent double counting), gains and losses must be removed from net income.

For example, on its income statement, Laguna Corporation shows a $12,000 gain on the sale of investments. This amount is subtracted from net income to reconcile net income to net cash flows from operating activities. The reason for doing this is that the $12,000 is included in the investing activities section of the statement of cash flows as part of the cash from the sale of the investment. Because the gain has already been included in the calculation of net income, the $12,000 gain must be subtracted to prevent double counting.

Laguna's income statement also shows a $3,000 loss on the sale of plant assets. This loss is already reflected in the sale of plant assets in the investing activities section of the statement of cash flows. Thus, the $3,000 is added to net income to reconcile net income to net cash flows from operating activities.

Changes in Current Assets

Decreases in current assets other than cash have positive effects on cash flows, and increases in current assets have negative effects on cash flows. A decrease in a current asset frees up invested cash, thereby increasing cash flow. An increase in a current asset consumes cash, thereby decreasing cash flow. For example, look at Laguna Corporation's income statement and balance sheets in Exhibits 2 and 3. Note that net sales in 2010 were $698,000 and that Accounts Receivable decreased by $8,000. Thus, collections were $8,000 more than sales recorded for the year, and the total cash received from sales was $706,000 ($698,000 + $8,000 = $706,000). The effect on accounts receivable can be illustrated as follows:

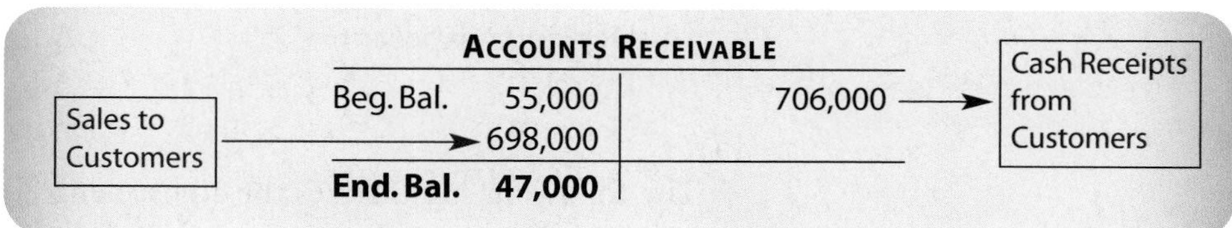

To reconcile net income to net cash flows from operating activities, the $8,000 decrease in Accounts Receivable is added to net income.

Inventory can be analyzed in the same way. For example, Exhibit 3 shows that Laguna's Inventory account increased by $34,000 between 2009 and 2010. This means that Laguna expended $34,000 more in cash for purchases than it included in cost of goods sold on its income statement. Because of this expenditure, net income is higher than net cash flows from operating activities, so $34,000 must be deducted from net income. By the same logic, the decrease of $4,000 in Prepaid Expenses shown on the balance sheets must be added to net income to reconcile net income to net cash flows from operations.

Changes in Current Liabilities

The effect that changes in current liabilities have on cash flows is the opposite of the effect of changes in current assets. An increase in a current liability represents a postponement of a cash payment, which frees up cash and increases cash flow in the current period. A decrease in a current liability consumes cash, which decreases cash flow. To reconcile net income to net cash flows from operating activities, increases in current liabilities are added to net income, and decreases are deducted. For example, Exhibit 3 shows that from 2009 to 2010, Laguna's accounts payable increased by $7,000. This means that Laguna paid $7,000 less to creditors than the amount indicated in the cost of goods sold on its income statement. The following T account illustrates this relationship:

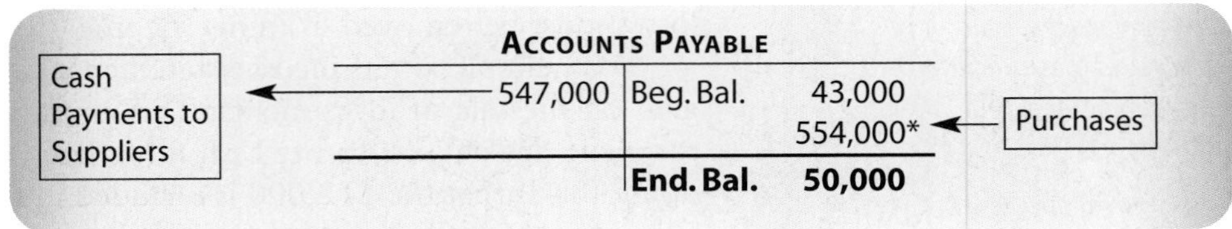

Thus, $7,000 must be added to net income to reconcile net income to net cash flows from operating activities. By the same logic, the increase of $3,000 in accrued liabilities shown on the balance sheets must be added to net income, and the decrease of $2,000 in income taxes payable must be deducted from net income.

Schedule of Cash Flows from Operating Activities

In summary, Exhibit 4 shows that by using the indirect method, net income of $16,000 has been adjusted by reconciling items totaling $14,000 to arrive at net cash flows from operating activities of $30,000. This means that although Laguna's net income was $16,000, the company actually had net cash flows of $30,000 available from operating activities to use for purchasing assets, reducing debts, and paying dividends. The treatment of income statement items that do not affect cash flows can be summarized as follows:

	Add to or Deduct from Net Income
Depreciation expense	Add
Amortization expense	Add
Depletion expense	Add
Losses	Add
Gains	Deduct

The following summarizes the adjustments for increases and decreases in current assets and current liabilities:

*Purchases = Cost of Goods Sold ($520,000) + Increase in Inventory ($34,000)

FOCUS ON BUSINESS PRACTICE

What Is EBITDA, and Is It Any Good?

Some companies and analysts like to use EBITDA (an acronym for Earnings Before Interest, Taxes, Depreciation, and Amortization) as a short-cut measure of cash flows from operations. But recent events have caused many analysts to reconsider this measure of performance. For instance, when **WorldCom** transferred $3.8 billion from expenses to capital expenditures in one year, it touted its EBITDA; at the time, the firm was, in fact, nearly bankrupt. The demise of **Vivendi**, the big French company that imploded when it did not have enough cash to pay its debts and that also touted its EBIDTA, is another reason that analysts have had second thoughts about relying on this measure of performance.

Some analysts are now saying that EBITDA is "to a great extent misleading" and that it "is a confusing metric. . . . Some take it for a proxy for profits and some take it for a proxy for cash flow, and it's neither."[11] Cash flows from operations and free cash flow, both of which take into account interest, taxes, and depreciation, are better and more comprehensive measures of a company's cash-generating efficiency.

	Add to Net Income	*Deduct from Net Income*
Current assets		
Accounts receivable (net)	Decrease	Increase
Inventory	Decrease	Increase
Prepaid expenses	Decrease	Increase
Current liabilities		
Accounts payable	Increase	Decrease
Accrued liabilities	Increase	Decrease
Income taxes payable	Increase	Decrease

STOP ▶ REVIEW ▶ APPLY

LO3-1 **What is the basic difference between the direct method and the indirect method of determining cash flows from operations?**

LO3-2 **What conditions might cause a corporation that had a net loss of $12,000 to have a positive cash flow from operations of $9,000?**

LO3-3 **Why is depreciation added to net income in arriving at cash flows from operating activities?**

LO3-4 **Why is a gain subtracted from net income in arriving at cash flows from operating activities?**

LO3-5 **Why do changes in current assets and current liabilities appear in the operating section of the statement of cash flows?**

LO3-6 **When the indirect method is used to determine net cash flows from operating activities, should (a) an increase in accounts receivable, (b) a decrease in inventory, (c) an increase in accounts payable, (d) a decrease in wages payable, (e) depreciation expense, and (f) amortization of patents be added to or subtracted from net income?**

Cash Flows from Operating Activities: Indirect Method For the year ended June 30, 2010, Hoffer Corporation's net income was $7,400. Its depreciation expense was $2,000. During the year, its Accounts Receivable increased by $4,400, Inventories increased by $7,000, Prepaid Rent decreased by $1,400, Accounts Payable increased by $14,000, Salaries Payable increased by $1,000, and Income Taxes Payable decreased by $600. The company also had a gain on the sale of investments of $1,800. Use the indirect method to prepare a schedule of cash flows from operating activities.

(continued)

SOLUTION

Hoffer Corporation
Schedule of Cash Flows from Operating Activities
For the Year Ended June 30, 2010

Cash flows from operating activities		
Net income		$ 7,400
Adjustments to reconcile net income to net cash flows from operating activities		
Depreciation	$ 2,000	
Gain on sale of investments	(1,800)	
Changes in current assets and current liabilities		
Increase in accounts receivable	(4,400)	
Increase in inventories	(7,000)	
Decrease in prepaid rent	1,400	
Increase in accounts payable	14,000	
Increase in salaries payable	1,000	
Decrease in income taxes payable	(600)	4,600
Net cash flows from operating activities		$12,000

Investing Activities

LO4 Determine cash flows from investing activities.

Study Note

Investing activities involve long-term assets and short- and long-term investments. Inflows and outflows of cash are shown in the investing activities section of the statement of cash flows.

To determine cash flows from investing activities, accounts involving cash receipts and cash payments from investing activities are examined individually. The objective is to explain the change in each account balance from one year to the next.

Although investing activities center on the long-term assets shown on the balance sheet, they also include any short-term investments shown under current assets on the balance sheet and any investment gains and losses on the income statement. The balance sheets in Exhibit 3 show that Laguna had no short-term investments and that its long-term assets consisted of investments and plant assets. The income statement in Exhibit 2 shows that Laguna had a gain on the sale of investments and a loss on the sale of plant assets.

The following transactions pertain to Laguna's investing activities in 2010:

1. Purchased investments in the amount of $78,000.
2. Sold investments that cost $90,000 for $102,000.
3. Purchased plant assets in the amount of $120,000.
4. Sold plant assets that cost $10,000 and that had accumulated depreciation of $2,000 for $5,000.
5. Issued $100,000 of bonds at face value in a noncash exchange for plant assets.

In the following sections, we analyze the accounts related to investing activities to determine their effects on Laguna's cash flows.

Investments

Our objective in this section is to explain Laguna Corporation's $12,000 decrease in investments. We do this by analyzing the increases and decreases in Laguna's Investments account to determine their effects on the Cash account.

Item **1** in the list of Laguna's transactions states that its purchases of investments totaled $78,000 during 2010. This transaction, which caused a $78,000 decrease in cash flows, is recorded as follows:

A	= L +	SE
+78,000		
−78,000		

Investments	78,000	
Cash		78,000
Purchase of investments		

Item **2** states that Laguna sold investments that cost $90,000 for $102,000. This transaction resulted in a gain of $12,000. It is recorded as follows:

A	= L +	SE
+102,000		+12,000
− 90,000		

Cash	102,000	
Investments		90,000
Gain on Sale of Investments		12,000
Sale of investments for a gain		

Study Note

The $102,000 price obtained, not the $12,000 gained, constitutes the cash flow.

The effect of this transaction is a $102,000 increase in cash flows. Note that the gain on the sale is included in the $102,000. This is the reason we excluded it in computing cash flows from operations. If it had been included in that section, it would have been counted twice. We have now explained the $12,000 decrease in the Investments account during 2010, as illustrated in the following T account:

INVESTMENTS

Beg. Bal.	127,000	Sales	90,000
Purchases	78,000		
End. Bal.	**115,000**		

The cash flow effects of these transactions are shown in the investing activities section of the statement of cash flows as follows:

Purchase of investments	($ 78,000)
Sale of investments	102,000

Purchases and sales are listed separately as cash outflows and inflows to give analysts a complete view of investing activity. However, some companies prefer to list them as a single net amount. If Laguna Corporation had short-term investments or marketable securities, the analysis of cash flows would be the same.

Plant Assets

For plant assets, we have to explain changes in both the Plant Assets account and the related Accumulated Depreciation account. Exhibit 3 shows that from 2009 to 2010, Laguna Corporation's plant assets increased by $210,000 and that accumulated depreciation increased by $35,000.

Item **3** in the list of Laguna's transactions in 2010 states that the company purchased plant assets totaling $120,000. This entry records the cash outflow:

A	=	L	+	SE
+120,000				
−120,000				

Plant Assets	120,000	
Cash		120,000
Purchase of plant assets		

Item **4** states that Laguna Corporation sold plant assets that cost $10,000 and that had accumulated depreciation of $2,000 for $5,000. Thus, this transaction resulted in a loss of $3,000. The entry to record it is as follows:

A	=	L	+	SE
+ 5,000				−3,000
+ 2,000				
−10,000				

Cash	5,000	
Accumulated Depreciation	2,000	
Loss on Sale of Plant Assets	3,000	
Plant Assets		10,000
Sale of plant assets at a loss		

Study Note

Even though Laguna had a loss on the sale of plant assets, it realized a positive cash flow of $5,000, which will be reported in the investing activities section of its statement of cash flows. When the indirect method is used, the loss is eliminated with an "add-back" to net income.

Note that in this transaction, the positive cash flow is equal to the amount of cash received, $5,000. The loss on the sale of plant assets is included in the investing activities section of the statement of cash flows and excluded from the operating activities section by adjusting net income for the amount of the loss. The amount of a loss or gain on the sale of an asset is determined by the amount of cash received and does not represent a cash outflow or inflow.

The investing activities section of Laguna's statement of cash flows reports the firm's purchase and sale of plant assets as follows:

Purchase of plant assets	($120,000)
Sale of plant assets	5,000

Cash outflows and cash inflows are listed separately here, but companies sometimes combine them into a single net amount, as they do the purchase and sale of investments.

Item **5** in the list of Laguna's transactions is a noncash exchange that affects two long-term accounts, Plant Assets and Bonds Payable. It is recorded as follows:

A	=	L	+	SE
+100,000		+100,000		

Plant Assets	100,000	
Bonds Payable		100,000
Issued bonds at face value for plant assets		

Although this transaction does not involve an inflow or outflow of cash, it is a significant transaction involving both an investing activity (the purchase of plant assets) and a financing activity (the issue of bonds payable). Because one purpose of the statement of cash flows is to show important investing and financing activities, the transaction is listed at the bottom of the statement of cash flows or in a separate schedule, as follows:

Schedule of Noncash Investing and Financing Transactions

Issue of bonds payable for plant assets	$100,000

We have now accounted for all the changes related to Laguna's plant asset accounts. The following T accounts summarize these changes:

PLANT ASSETS

Beg. Bal.	505,000	Sale	10,000
Cash Purchase	120,000		
Noncash Purchase	100,000		
End. Bal.	**715,000**		

ACCUMULATED DEPRECIATION			
Sale	2,000	Beg. Bal.	68,000
		Dep. Exp.	37,000
		End. Bal.	**103,000**

Had the balance sheet included specific plant asset accounts (e.g., Equipment and the related accumulated depreciation account) or other long-term asset accounts (e.g., Intangibles), the analysis would have been the same.

STOP ▸ REVIEW ▸ APPLY

LO4-1 **What are the two major categories of assets that relate to the investing activities section of the statement of cash flows?**

LO4-2 **What is the proper treatment on the statement of cash flows of a transaction in which a company had a loss of $5,000 when it sold a building that it had bought for $50,000 and that had accumulated depreciation of $32,000?**

LO4-3 **What is the proper treatment on the statement of cash flows of a transaction in which a company purchased buildings and land by taking out a mortgage for $234,000?**

Cash Flows from Investing Activities: Plant Assets The following T accounts show Matiz Company's plant assets and accumulated depreciation at the end of 2010:

PLANT ASSETS			
Beg. Bal.	65,000	Disposals	23,000
Purchases	33,600		
End. Bal.	**75,600**		

ACCUMULATED DEPRECIATION			
Disposals	14,700	Beg. Bal.	34,500
		Depreciation	10,200
		End. Bal.	**30,000**

Matiz's income statement shows a gain on the sale of plant assets of $4,400. Compute the amounts that should be shown as cash flows from investing activities, and show how they should appear on Matiz's 2010 statement of cash flows.

SOLUTION

Cash flows from investing activities:

Purchase of plant assets	($33,600)
Sale of plant assets	12,700

The T accounts show total purchases of plant assets of $33,600, which is an outflow of cash, and disposal of plant assets that cost $23,000 and that had accumulated depreciation of $14,700. The income statement shows a $4,400 gain on the sale of the plant assets. The cash inflow from the disposal was as follows:

Plant assets	$23,000
Less accumulated depreciation	14,700
Book value	$ 8,300
Add gain on sale	4,400
Cash inflow from sale of plant assets	$12,700

Because the gain on the sale is included in the $12,700 in the investing activities section of the statement of cash flows, it should be deducted from net income in the operating activities section.

Financing Activities

LO5 Determine cash flows from financing activities.

Determining cash flows from financing activities is very similar to determining cash flows from investing activities, but the accounts analyzed relate to short-term borrowings, long-term liabilities, and stockholders' equity. Because Laguna Corporation does not have short-term borrowings, we deal only with long-term liabilities and stockholders' equity accounts.

The following transactions pertain to Laguna's financing activities in 2010:

1. Issued $100,000 of bonds at face value in a noncash exchange for plant assets.
2. Repaid $50,000 of bonds at face value at maturity.
3. Issued 15,200 shares of $5 par value common stock for $175,000.
4. Paid cash dividends in the amount of $8,000.
5. Purchased treasury stock for $25,000.

Bonds Payable

Exhibit 3 shows that Laguna's Bonds Payable account increased by $50,000 in 2010. Both items **1** and **2** in the list above affect this account. We analyzed item **1** in connection with plant assets, but it also pertains to the Bonds Payable account. As we noted, this transaction is reported on the schedule of noncash investing and financing transactions. Item **2** results in a cash outflow, which is recorded as follows:

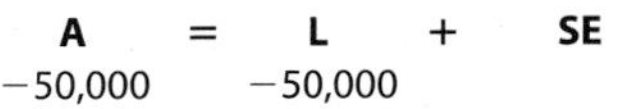

	Debit	Credit
Bonds Payable	50,000	
Cash		50,000
Repayment of bonds at face value at maturity		

This appears in the financing activities section of the statement of cash flows as follows:

Repayment of bonds ($50,000)

The following T account explains the change in Bonds Payable:

Bonds Payable

Repayment	50,000	Beg. Bal.	245,000
		Noncash Issue	100,000
		End. Bal.	**295,000**

If Laguna Corporation had any notes payable, the analysis would be the same.

Common Stock

Like the Plant Asset account and its related accounts, accounts related to stockholders' equity should be analyzed together. For example, the Additional Paid-in Capital account should be examined along with the Common Stock account. In 2010, Laguna's Common Stock account increased by $76,000, and its Additional Paid-in Capital account increased by $99,000. Item **3** in the list of Laguna's transactions, which states that the company issued 15,200 shares of $5 par value common stock for $175,000, explains these increases. The entry to record the cash inflow is as follows:

FOCUS ON BUSINESS PRACTICE

How Much Cash Does a Company Need?

Some kinds of industries are more vulnerable to downturns in the economy than others. Historically, because of the amount of debt they carry and their large interest and loan payments, companies in the airline and automotive industries have been hard hit by economic downturns. But research has shown that high-tech companies with large amounts of intangible assets are also hard hit. Biotechnology, pharmaceutical, and computer hardware and software companies can lose up to 80 percent of their value in times of financial stress. In contrast, companies with large amounts of tangible assets, such as oil companies and railroads, can lose as little as 10 percent. To survive during economic downturns, it is very important for high-tech companies to use their cash-generating efficiency to build cash reserves. It makes sense for these companies to hoard cash and not pay dividends to the extent that companies in other industries do.[12]

A	=	L	+	SE
+175,000				+76,000
				+99,000

Cash	175,000	
Common Stock		76,000
Additional Paid-in Capital		99,000
Issued 15,200 shares of $5 par value common stock		

This appears in the financing activities section of the statement of cash flows as:

Issuance of common stock $175,000

The following analysis of this transaction is all that is needed to explain the changes in the two accounts during 2010:

Common Stock

	Beg. Bal. 200,000
	Issue 76,000
	End. Bal. 276,000

Additional Paid-in Capital

	Beg. Bal. 115,000
	Issue 99,000
	End. Bal. 214,000

Retained Earnings

At this point, we have dealt with several items that affect retained earnings. The only item affecting Laguna's retained earnings that we have not considered is the payment of $8,000 in cash dividends (item **4** in the list of Laguna's transactions). At the time it declared the dividend, Laguna would have debited its Dividends account. After paying the dividend, it would have closed the Dividends account to Retained Earnings and recorded the closing with the following entry:

A	=	L	+	SE
				−8,000
				+8,000

Retained Earnings	8,000	
Dividends		8,000
To close the Dividends account		

Cash dividends would be displayed in the financing activities section of Laguna's statement of cash flows as follows:

Payment of dividends ($8,000)

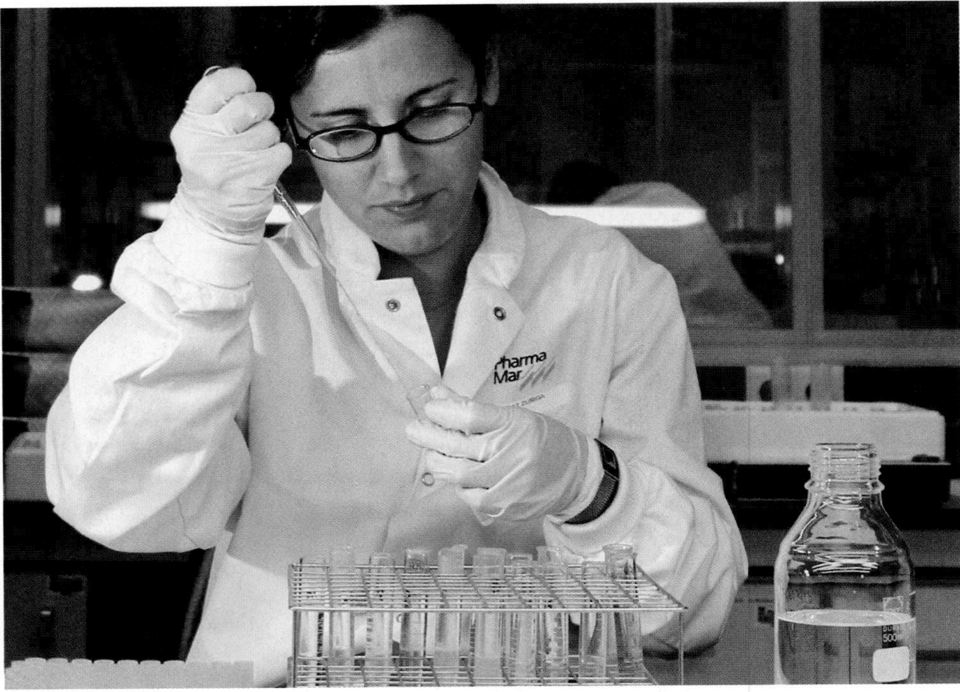

High-tech companies with large amounts of intangible assets, such as PharmaMar, a pharmaceutical firm based in Madrid, can lose up to 80 percent of their value in times of financial stress. As a hedge against economic downturns, these companies need to build cash reserves, and they may therefore choose to hoard cash rather than pay dividends.

Study Note

It is dividends paid, not dividends declared, that appear on the statement of cash flows.

This T account shows the change in the Retained Earnings account:

Retained Earnings			
Dividends	8,000	Beg. Bal.	132,000
		Net Income	16,000
		End. Bal.	**140,000**

Treasury Stock

As we noted in the chapter on contributed capital, many companies buy back their own stock on the open market. These buybacks use cash, as this entry shows:

A	=	L	+	SE
−25,000				−25,000

Treasury Stock	25,000	
Cash		25,000

Study Note

The purchase of treasury stock qualifies as a financing activity, but it is also a cash outflow.

This use of cash is classified in the statement of cash flows as a financing activity:

Purchase of treasury stock ($25,000)

The T account for this transaction is as follows:

Treasury Stock			
Purchase	25,000		

We have now analyzed all of Laguna Corporation's income statement items, explained all balance sheet changes, and taken all additional information into account. Exhibit 5 shows how our data are assembled in Laguna's statement of cash flows.

EXHIBIT 5 Statement of Cash Flows: Indirect Method

Laguna Corporation
Statement of Cash Flows
For the Year Ended December 31, 2010

Cash flows from operating activities		
Net income		$ 16,000
Adjustments to reconcile net income to net cash flows from operating activities		
Depreciation	$ 37,000	
Gain on sale of investments	(12,000)	
Loss on sale of plant assets	3,000	
Changes in current assets and current liabilities		
Decrease in accounts receivable	8,000	
Increase in inventory	(34,000)	
Decrease in prepaid expenses	4,000	
Increase in accounts payable	7,000	
Increase in accrued liabilities	3,000	
Decrease in income taxes payable	(2,000)	14,000
Net cash flows from operating activities		$ 30,000
Cash flows from investing activities		
Purchase of investments	($ 78,000)	
Sale of investments	102,000	
Purchase of plant assets	(120,000)	
Sale of plant assets	5,000	
Net cash flows from investing activities		(91,000)
Cash flows from financing activities		
Repayment of bonds	($ 50,000)	
Issuance of common stock	175,000	
Payment of dividends	(8,000)	
Purchase of treasury stock	(25,000)	
Net cash flows from financing activities		92,000
Net increase in cash		$ 31,000
Cash at beginning of year		15,000
Cash at end of year		$ 46,000
Schedule of Noncash Investing and Financing Transactions		
Issue of bonds payable for plant assets		$100,000

STOP ▶ REVIEW ▶ APPLY

LO5-1 **What major categories of liabilities and stockholders' equity relate to the financing activities section of the statement of cash flows?**

LO5-2 **What is the proper treatment on the statement of cash flows of a transaction in which $50,000 of bonds payable are converted to 2,500 shares of $6 par value common stock?**

A LOOK BACK AT ▶ Amazon.com, Inc.

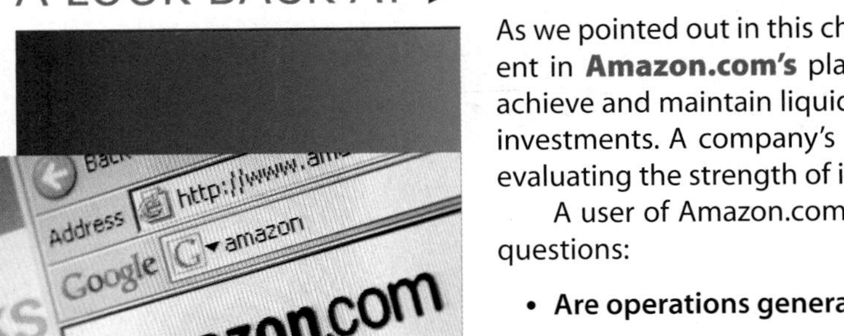

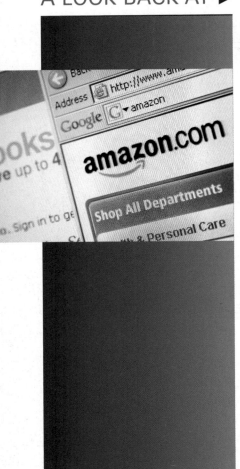

As we pointed out in this chapter's Decision Point, strong cash flows are a basic ingredient in **Amazon.com's** plans for the future. Strong cash flows enable a company to achieve and maintain liquidity, to expand, and to increase the value of its shareholders' investments. A company's statement of cash flows provides information essential to evaluating the strength of its cash flows and its liquidity.

A user of Amazon.com's statement of cash flows would want to ask the following questions:

- **Are operations generating sufficient operating cash flows?**
- **Is the company growing by investing in long-term assets?**
- **Has the company had to borrow money or issue stock to finance its growth?**

Using data from Exhibit 1, which presents Amazon.com's statements of cash flows, we can answer these questions. We can gauge Amazon.com's ability to generate cash flows from operations by calculating its cash flow yields in 2007 and 2006:

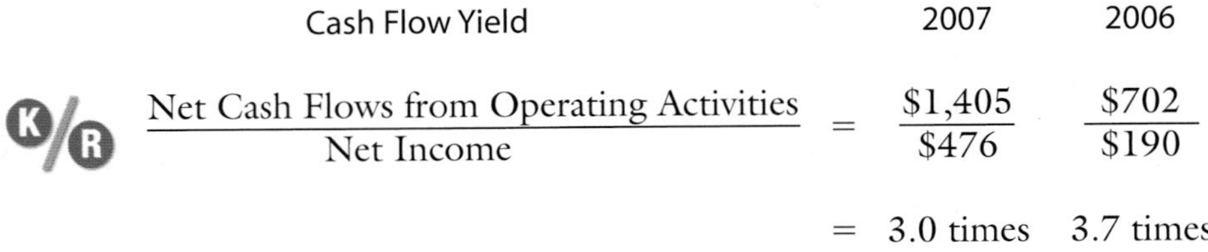

Cash Flow Yield		2007	2006
$\frac{\text{Net Cash Flows from Operating Activities}}{\text{Net Income}}$	=	$\frac{\$1,405}{\$476}$	$\frac{\$702}{\$190}$
	=	3.0 times	3.7 times

As you can see, Amazon.com's cash flow yield decreased somewhat over the two years, from 3.7 to 3.0 times, but both years easily exceeded the 1.0 level normally considered the minimum acceptable cash flow yield. Although both net cash flows from activities and net income increased significantly from 2006 to 2007, net income grew more rapidly.

Free cash flow measures the sufficiency of cash flows in a different way, and as mentioned earlier in the chapter, it is a key financial objective for Amazon.com's management. The computations below show that the company is meeting its objectives. Its free cash flow grew by almost $700 million from 2006 to 2007:

Free Cash Flow		2007	2006
Net Cash Flows from Operating Activities − Dividends − Purchases of Plant Assets + Sales of Plant Assets	=	$1,405 − $0 − $224 + $0	$702 − $0 − $216 + $0
	=	$1,181	$486

An examination of Amazon.com' s statement of cash flows in Exhibit 1 shows how the company is investing its free cash flow. In addition to investing in long-term assets ($224 million in 2007 and $216 million in 2006), the company decreased its investment in marketable securities. Thus, the company did not have to rely on borrowing money (because repayments exceeded proceeds from debt) or issuing stock to finance its growth. In fact, although it did not pay a cash dividend, Amazon.com did repurchase common stock in the amount of $248 million. Finally, it increased its cash balance from $1,022 million in 2006 to $2,539 million in 2007. One must conclude that Amazon.com is a very successful and growing company. It will be interesting to see if it can keep up its success.

CHAPTER REVIEW

REVIEW of Learning Objectives

LO1 Describe the principal purposes and uses of the statement of cash flows, and identify its components.

The statement of cash flows shows how a company's operating, investing, and financing activities have affected cash during an accounting period. For the statement of cash flows, *cash* is defined as including both cash and cash equivalents. The primary purpose of the statement is to provide information about a firm's cash receipts and cash payments during an accounting period. A secondary purpose is to provide information about a firm's operating, investing, and financing activities. Management uses the statement to assess liquidity, determine dividend policy, and plan investing and financing activities. Investors and creditors use it to assess the company's cash-generating ability.

The statement of cash flows has three major classifications: (1) operating activities, which involve the cash effects of transactions and other events that enter into the determination of net income; (2) investing activities, which involve the acquisition and sale of marketable securities and long-term assets and the making and collecting of loans; and (3) financing activities, which involve obtaining resources from stockholders and creditors and providing the former with a return on their investments and the latter with repayment. Noncash investing and financing transactions are also important because they affect future cash flows; these exchanges of long-term assets or liabilities are of interest to potential investors and creditors.

LO2 Analyze the statement of cash flows.

In examining a company's statement of cash flows, analysts tend to focus on cash-generating efficiency and free cash flow. Cash-generating efficiency is a firm's ability to generate cash from its current or continuing operations. The ratios used to measure cash-generating efficiency are cash flow yield, cash flows to sales, and cash flows to assets. Free cash flow is the cash that remains after deducting the funds a firm must commit to continue operating at its planned level. These commitments include current and continuing operations, interest, income taxes, dividends, and capital expenditures.

LO3 Use the indirect method to determine cash flows from operating activities.

The indirect method adjusts net income for all items in the income statement that do not have cash flow effects (such as depreciation, amortization, and gains and losses on sales of assets) and for changes in liabilities that affect operating cash flows. Generally, increases in current assets have a negative effect on cash flows, and decreases have a positive effect. Conversely, increases in current liabilities have a positive effect on cash flows, and decreases have a negative effect.

LO4 Determine cash flows from investing activities.

Investing activities involve the acquisition and sale of property, plant, and equipment and other long-term assets, including long-term investments. They also involve the acquisition and sale of short-term marketable securities, other than trading securities, and the making and collecting of loans. Cash flows from investing activities are determined by analyzing the cash flow effects of changes in each account related to investing activities. The effects of gains and losses reported on the income statement must also be considered.

LO5 Determine cash flows from financing activities.

Determining cash flows from financing activities is almost identical to determining cash flows from investing activities. The difference is that the accounts analyzed relate to short-term borrowings, long-term liabilities, and stockholders' equity. After the changes in the balance sheet accounts from one accounting period to the next have been explained, all the cash flow effects should have been identified.

REVIEW of Concepts and Terminology

The following concepts and terms were introduced in this chapter:

Cash: For purposes of the statement of cash flows, both cash and cash equivalents. **(LO1)**

Cash equivalents: Short-term (90 days or less), highly liquid investments, including money market accounts, commercial paper, and U.S. Treasury bills. **(LO1)**

Cash-generating efficiency: A firm's ability to generate cash from current or continuing operations. **(LO2)**

Direct method: The procedure for converting the income statement from an accrual basis to a cash basis by adjusting each item on the statement. **(LO3)**

Financing activities: Business activities that involve obtaining resources from stockholders and creditors and providing the former with a return on their investments and the latter with repayment. **(LO1)**

Free cash flow: The amount of cash that remains after deducting the funds a company must commit to continue operating at its planned level; Net Cash Flows from Operating Activities − Dividends − Purchases of Plant Assets + Sales of Plant Assets. **(LO2)**

Indirect method: The procedure for converting the income statement from an accrual basis to a cash basis by adjusting net income for items that do not affect cash flows, including depreciation, amortization, depletion, gains, losses, and changes in current assets and current liabilities. **(LO3)**

Investing activities: Business activities that involve the acquisition and sale of marketable securities and long-term assets and the making and collecting of loans. **(LO1)**

Noncash investing and financing transactions: Significant investing and financing transactions involving only long-term assets, long-term liabilities, or stockholders' equity that do not affect current cash inflows or outflows. **(LO1)**

Operating activities: Business activities that involve the cash effects of transactions and other events that enter into the determination of net income. **(LO1)**

Statement of cash flows: A financial statement that shows how a company's operating, investing, and financing activities have affected cash during an accounting period. **(LO1)**

Key Ratios

Cash flows to assets: Net Cash Flows from Operating Activities ÷ Average Total Assets. **(LO2)**

Cash flows to sales: Net Cash Flows from Operating Activities ÷ Sales. **(LO2)**

Cash flow yield: Net Cash Flows from Operating Activities ÷ Net Income. **(LO2)**

REVIEW Problem

LO2 LO3 LO4 LO5

The Statement of Cash Flows

Lopata Corporation's income statement for 2011 and its comparative balance sheets for 2011 and 2010 are presented on the opposite page. The company's records for 2011 provide this additional information:

a. Sold long-term investments that cost $35,000 for a gain of $6,250; made other long-term investments in the amount of $10,000.
b. Purchased five acres of land to build a parking lot for $12,500.
c. Sold equipment that cost $18,750 and that had accumulated depreciation of $12,650 at a loss of $1,150; purchased new equipment for $15,000.
d. Repaid notes payable in the amount of $50,000; borrowed $15,000 by signing new notes payable.
e. Converted $50,000 of bonds payable into 3,000 shares of common stock.
f. Reduced the Mortgage Payable account by $10,000.
g. Declared and paid cash dividends of $25,000.
h. Purchased treasury stock for $5,000.

Lopata Corporation Income Statement For the Year Ended December 31, 2011		
Net sales		$825,000
Cost of goods sold		460,000
Gross margin		$365,000
Operating expenses (including depreciation expense of $6,000 on buildings and $11,550 on equipment and amortization expense of $2,400)		235,000
Operating income		$130,000
Other income		
Interest expense	($27,500)	
Dividend income	1,700	
Gain on sale of investments	6,250	
Loss on disposal of equipment	(1,150)	(20,700)
Income before income taxes		$109,300
Income taxes expense		26,100
Net income		$ 83,200

Lopata Corporation Comparative Balance Sheets December 31, 2011 and 2010	2011	2010	Change	Increase or Decrease
Assets				
Cash	$ 52,925	$ 60,925	($ 8,000)	Decrease
Accounts receivable (net)	148,000	157,250	(9,250)	Decrease
Inventory	161,000	150,500	10,500	Increase
Prepaid expenses	3,900	2,900	1,000	Increase
Long-term investments	18,000	43,000	(25,000)	Decrease
Land	75,000	62,500	12,500	Increase
Buildings	231,000	231,000	—	—
Accumulated depreciation, buildings	(45,500)	(39,500)	(6,000)	Increase
Equipment	79,865	83,615	(3,750)	Decrease
Accumulated depreciation, equipment	(21,700)	(22,800)	1,100	Decrease
Intangible assets	9,600	12,000	(2,400)	Decrease
Total assets	$712,090	$741,390	($29,300)	
Liabilities and Stockholders' Equity				
Accounts payable	$ 66,875	$116,875	($50,000)	Decrease
Notes payable (current)	37,850	72,850	(35,000)	Decrease
Accrued liabilities	2,500	—	2,500	Increase
Income taxes payable	10,000	—	10,000	Increase
Bonds payable	105,000	155,000	(50,000)	Decrease
Mortgage payable	165,000	175,000	(10,000)	Decrease
Common stock, $10 par value	200,000	170,000	30,000	Increase
Additional paid-in capital	45,000	25,000	20,000	Increase
Retained earnings	104,865	46,665	58,200	Increase
Treasury stock	(25,000)	(20,000)	(5,000)	Increase
Total liabilities and stockholders' equity	$712,090	$741,390	($29,300)	

Required

1. Prepare a statement of cash flows using the indirect method.
2. Compute cash flow yield, cash flows to sales, cash flows to assets, and free cash flow for 2011.

Answer to Review Problem

1. Statement of cash flows using the indirect method:

Lopata Corporation Statement of Cash Flows For the Year Ended December 31, 2011		
Cash flows from operating activities		
Net income		$83,200
Adjustments to reconcile net income to net cash flows		
from operating activities		
Depreciation expense, buildings	$ 6,000	
Depreciation expense, equipment	11,550	
Amortization expense, intangible assets	2,400	
Gain on sale of investments	(6,250)	
Loss on disposal of equipment	1,150	
Changes in current assets and current liabilities		
Decrease in accounts receivable	9,250	
Increase in inventory	(10,500)	
Increase in prepaid expenses	(1,000)	
Decrease in accounts payable	(50,000)	
Increase in accrued liabilities	2,500	
Increase in income taxes payable	10,000	(24,900)
Net cash flows from operating activities		$58,300
Cash flows from investing activities		
Sale of long-term investments	$41,250 [a]	
Purchase of long-term investments	(10,000)	
Purchase of land	(12,500)	
Sale of equipment	4,950 [b]	
Purchase of equipment	(15,000)	
Net cash flows from investing activities		8,700
Cash flows from financing activities		
Repayment of notes payable	($50,000)	
Issuance of notes payable	15,000	
Reduction in mortgage	(10,000)	
Dividends paid	(25,000)	
Purchase of treasury stock	(5,000)	
Net cash flows from financing activities		(75,000)
Net (decrease) in cash		($ 8,000)
Cash at beginning of year		60,925
Cash at end of year		$52,925
Schedule of Noncash Investing and Financing Transactions		
Conversion of bonds payable into common stock		$50,000
a $35,000 + $6,250 (gain) = $41,250		
b $18,750 − $12,650 = $6,100 (book value) − $1,150 (loss) = $4,950		

2. Cash flow yield, cash flows to sales, cash flows to assets, and free cash flow for 2011:

$$\text{Cash Flow Yield} = \frac{\$58{,}300}{\$83{,}200} = .7 \text{ times}$$

$$\text{Cash Flows to Sales} = \frac{\$58{,}300}{\$825{,}000} = 7.1\%$$

$$\text{Cash Flows to Assets} = \frac{\$58{,}300}{(\$712{,}090 + \$741{,}390) \div 2} = 8.0\%$$

$$\text{Free Cash Flow} = \$58{,}300 - \$25{,}000 - \$12{,}500 - \$15{,}000 + \$4{,}950 = \$10{,}750$$

CHAPTER ASSIGNMENTS

BUILDING Your Basic Knowledge and Skills

Short Exercises

LO1 **Classification of Cash Flow Transactions**

SE 1. The list that follows itemizes Furlong Corporation's transactions. Identify each as (a) an operating activity, (b) an investing activity, (c) a financing activity, (d) a noncash transaction, or (e) none of the above.

1. Sold land.
2. Declared and paid a cash dividend.
3. Paid interest.
4. Issued common stock for plant assets.
5. Issued preferred stock.
6. Borrowed cash on a bank loan.

LO2 **Cash-Generating Efficiency Ratios and Free Cash Flow**

SE 2. In 2010, Ross Corporation had year-end assets of $550,000, sales of $790,000, net income of $90,000, net cash flows from operating activities of $180,000, purchases of plant assets of $120,000, and sales of plant assets of $20,000, and it paid dividends of $40,000. In 2009, year-end assets were $500,000. Calculate the cash-generating efficiency ratios of cash flow yield, cash flows to sales, and cash flows to assets. Also calculate free cash flow.

LO2 **Cash-Generating Efficiency Ratios and Free Cash Flow**

SE 3. Examine the cash flow measures in requirement **2** of the review problem in this chapter. Discuss the meaning of these ratios.

LO3 **Computing Cash Flows from Operating Activities: Indirect Method**

SE 4. Wachowski Corporation had a net income of $33,000 during 2010. During the year, the company had depreciation expense of $14,000. Accounts Receivable increased by $11,000, and Accounts Payable increased by $5,000. Those were the company's only current assets and current liabilities. Use the indirect method to determine net cash flows from operating activities.

LO3

Computing Cash Flows from Operating Activities: Indirect Method

SE 5. During 2010, Minh Corporation had a net income of $144,000. Included on its income statement were depreciation expense of $16,000 and amortization expense of $1,800. During the year, Accounts Receivable decreased by $8,200, Inventories increased by $5,400, Prepaid Expenses decreased by $1,000, Accounts Payable decreased by $14,000, and Accrued Liabilities decreased by $1,700. Use the indirect method to determine net cash flows from operating activities.

LO4

Cash Flows from Investing Activities and Noncash Transactions

SE 6. During 2010, Howard Company purchased land for $375,000. It paid $125,000 in cash and signed a $250,000 mortgage for the rest. The company also sold a building that originally cost $90,000, on which it had $70,000 of accumulated depreciation, for $95,000 cash, making a gain of $75,000. Prepare the cash flows from investing activities section and the schedule of noncash investing and financing transactions of the statement of cash flows.

LO5

Cash Flows from Financing Activities

SE 7. During 2010, Arizona Company issued $500,000 in long-term bonds at 96, repaid $75,000 of bonds at face value, paid interest of $40,000, and paid dividends of $25,000. Prepare the cash flows from the financing activities section of the statement of cash flows.

LO1 LO3 LO4 LO5

Identifying Components of the Statement of Cash Flows

SE 8. Assuming the indirect method is used to prepare the statement of cash flows, tell whether each of the following items would appear (a) in cash flows from operating activities, (b) in cash flows from investing activities, (c) in cash flows from financing activities, (d) in the schedule of noncash investing and financing transactions, or (e) not on the statement of cash flows at all:

1. Dividends paid
2. Cash receipts from customers
3. Decrease in accounts receivable
4. Sale of plant assets
5. Gain on sale of investments
6. Issue of stock for plant assets
7. Issue of common stock
8. Net income

Exercises

LO1 LO2

Discussion Questions

E 1. Develop brief answers to each of the following questions:

1. Which statement is more useful—the income statement or the statement of cash flows?
2. How would you respond to someone who says that the most important item on the statement of cash flows is the change in the cash balance for the year?
3. If a company's cash flow yield is less than 1.0, would its cash flows to sales and cash flows to assets be greater or less than profit margin and return on assets, respectively?

LO3 LO4 LO5

Discussion Questions

E 2. Develop brief answers to each of the following questions:

1. If a company has positive earnings, can cash flows from operating activities ever be negative?
2. Which adjustments to net income in the operating activities section of the statement of cash flows are directly related to cash flows in other sections?
3. In computing free cash flow, what is an argument for treating the purchases of treasury stock like dividend payments?

LO1

Classification of Cash Flow Transactions

E 3. Koral Corporation engaged in the transactions listed below. Identify each transaction as (a) an operating activity, (b) an investing activity, (c) a financing activity, (d) a noncash transaction, or (e) not on the statement of cash flows. (Assume the indirect method is used.)

1. Declared and paid a cash dividend.
2. Purchased a long-term investment.
3. Increased accounts receivable.
4. Paid interest.
5. Sold equipment at a loss.
6. Issued long-term bonds for plant assets.
7. Increased dividends receivable.
8. Issued common stock.
9. Declared and issued a stock dividend.
10. Repaid notes payable.
11. Decreased wages payable.
12. Purchased a 60-day Treasury bill.
13. Purchased land.

LO2

Cash-Generating Efficiency Ratios and Free Cash Flow

E 4. In 2011, Heart Corporation had year-end assets of \$1,200,000, sales of \$1,650,000, net income of \$140,000, net cash flows from operating activities of \$195,000, dividends of \$60,000, purchases of plant assets of \$250,000, and sales of plant assets of \$45,000. In 2010, year-end assets were \$1,050,000. Calculate free cash flow and the cash-generating efficiency ratios of cash flow yield, cash flows to sales, and cash flows to assets.

LO3

Cash Flows from Operating Activities: Indirect Method

E 5. The condensed single-step income statement for the year ended December 31, 2010, of Sunderland Chemical Company, a distributor of farm fertilizers and herbicides, appears as follows:

Sales		\$13,000,000
Less: Cost of goods sold	\$7,600,000	
Operating expenses (including depreciation of \$820,000)	3,800,000	
Income taxes expense	400,000	11,800,000
Net income		\$ 1,200,000

Selected accounts from Sunderland Chemical Company's balance sheets for 2010 and 2009 are as follows:

	2010	2009
Accounts receivable	$2,400,000	$1,700,000
Inventory	840,000	1,020,000
Prepaid expenses	260,000	180,000
Accounts payable	960,000	720,000
Accrued liabilities	60,000	100,000
Income taxes payable	140,000	120,000

Present in good form a schedule of cash flows from operating activities using the indirect method.

LO3 **Computing Cash Flows from Operating Activities: Indirect Method**

E 6. During 2010, Diaz Corporation had net income of $41,000. Included on its income statement were depreciation expense of $2,300 and amortization expense of $300. During the year, Accounts Receivable increased by $3,400, Inventories decreased by $1,900, Prepaid Expenses decreased by $200, Accounts Payable increased by $5,000, and Accrued Liabilities decreased by $450. Determine net cash flows from operating activities using the indirect method.

LO3 **Preparing a Schedule of Cash Flows from Operating Activities: Indirect Method**

E 7. For the year ended June 30, 2010, net income for Silk Corporation was $7,400. Depreciation expense was $2,000. During the year, Accounts Receivable increased by $4,400, Inventories increased by $7,000, Prepaid Rent decreased by $1,400, Accounts Payable increased by $14,000, Salaries Payable increased by $1,000, and Income Taxes Payable decreased by $600. Use the indirect method to prepare a schedule of cash flows from operating activities.

LO4 **Computing Cash Flows from Investing Activities: Investments**

E 8. CUD Company's T account for long-term available-for-sale investments at the end of 2010 is as follows:

Investments			
Beg. Bal.	152,000	Sales	156,000
Purchases	232,000		
End. Bal.	**228,000**		

In addition, CUD Company's income statement shows a loss on the sale of investments of $26,000. Compute the amounts to be shown as cash flows from investing activities and show how they are to appear in the statement of cash flows.

LO4 **Computing Cash Flows from Investing Activities: Plant Assets**

E 9. The T accounts for plant assets and accumulated depreciation for CUD Company at the end of 2010 are as follows:

Plant Assets			
Beg. Bal.	260,000	Disposals	92,000
Purchases	134,400		
End. Bal.	**302,400**		

Accumulated Depreciation			
Disposals	58,800	Beg. Bal.	138,000
		Depreciation	40,800
		End. Bal.	**120,000**

In addition, CUD Company's income statement shows a gain on sale of plant assets of $17,600. Compute the amounts to be shown as cash flows from investing activities and show how they are to appear on the statement of cash flows.

LO5

Determining Cash Flows from Financing Activities: Notes Payable

E 10. All transactions involving Notes Payable and related accounts of Pearl Company during 2010 are recorded as follows:

Cash	18,000	
Notes Payable		18,000
Bank loan		
Patent	30,000	
Notes Payable		30,000
Purchase of patent by issuing note payable		
Notes Payable	5,000	
Interest Expense	500	
Cash		5,500
Repayment of note payable at maturity		

Determine the amounts of the transactions affecting financing activities and show how they are to appear on the statement of cash flows for 2010.

LO3 LO4 LO5

Preparing the Statement of Cash Flows: Indirect Method

E 11. Olbrot Corporation's income statement for the year ended June 30, 2010 and its comparative balance sheets for June 30, 2010 and 2009 follow.

Olbrot Corporation
Income Statement
For the Year Ended June 30, 2010

Sales	$244,000
Cost of goods sold	148,100
Gross margin	$ 95,900
Operating expenses	45,000
Operating income	$ 50,900
Interest expense	2,800
Income before income taxes	$ 48,100
Income taxes expense	12,300
Net income	$ 35,800

Olbrot Corporation
Comparative Balance Sheets
June 30, 2010 and 2009

	2010	2009
Assets		
Cash	$ 139,800	$ 25,000
Accounts receivable (net)	42,000	52,000
Inventory	86,800	96,800
Prepaid expenses	6,400	5,200
Furniture	110,000	120,000
Accumulated depreciation, furniture	(18,000)	(10,000)
Total assets	$367,000	$289,000

(continued)

Liabilities and Stockholders' Equity

Accounts payable	$ 26,000	$ 28,000
Income taxes payable	2,400	3,600
Notes payable (long-term)	74,000	70,000
Common stock, $10 par value	230,000	180,000
Retained earnings	34,600	7,400
Total liabilities and stockholders' equity	$367,000	$289,000

Olbrot issued a $44,000 note payable for purchase of furniture; sold furniture that cost $54,000 with accumulated depreciation of $30,600 at carrying value; recorded depreciation on the furniture for the year, $38,600; repaid a note in the amount of $40,000; issued $50,000 of common stock at par value; and paid dividends of $8,600. Prepare Olbrot's statement of cash flows for the year 2010 using the indirect method.

Problems

LO1 Classification of Cash Flow Transactions

P 1. Analyze each transaction listed in the table that follows and place X's in the appropriate columns to indicate the transaction's classification and its effect on cash flows using the indirect method.

	Cash Flow Classification				Effect on Cash Flows		
Transaction	**Operating Activity**	**Investing Activity**	**Financing Activity**	**Noncash Trans-action**	**Increase**	**Decrease**	**No Effect**
1. Paid a cash dividend.							
2. Decreased accounts receivable.							
3. Increased inventory.							
4. Incurred a net loss.							
5. Declared and issued a stock dividend.							
6. Retired long-term debt with cash.							
7. Sold available-for-sale securities at a loss.							
8. Issued stock for equipment.							
9. Decreased prepaid insurance.							
10. Purchased treasury stock with cash.							
11. Retired a fully depreciated truck (no gain or loss).							
12. Increased interest payable.							
13. Decreased dividends receivable on investment.							
14. Sold treasury stock.							
15. Increased income taxes payable.							
16. Transferred cash to money market account.							
17. Purchased land and building with a mortgage.							

LO1

Interpreting and Analyzing the Statement of Cash Flows

P 2. The comparative statements of cash flows for Executive Style Corporation, a manufacturer of high-quality suits for men, appear below. To expand its markets and familiarity with its brand, the company attempted a new strategic diversification in 2010 by acquiring a chain of retail men's stores in outlet malls. Its plan was to expand in malls around the country, but department stores viewed the action as infringing on their territory.

Executive Style Corporation
Statement of Cash Flows
For the Years Ended December 31, 2010 and 2009
(In thousands)

	2010	**2009**
Cash flows from operating activities		
Net income (loss)	($ 21,545)	$ 38,015
Adjustments to reconcile net income to net cash flows from operating activities		
Depreciation	$ 35,219	$ 25,018
Loss on closure of retail outlets	35,000	
Changes in current assets and current liabilities		
Decrease (increase) in accounts receivable	50,000	(44,803)
Decrease (increase) in inventory	60,407	(51,145)
Decrease (increase) in prepaid expenses	1,367	2,246
Increase (decrease) in accounts payable	30,579	1,266
Increase (decrease) in accrued liabilities	1,500	(2,788)
Increase (decrease) in income taxes payable	(8,300)	(6,281)
	$205,772	($ 76,487)
Net cash flows from operating activities	$184,227	($ 38,472)
Cash flows from investing activities		
Capital expenditures, net	($ 16,145)	($ 33,112)
Purchase of Retail Division, cash portion	—	(201,000)
Net cash flows from investing activities	($ 16,145)	($234,112)
Cash flows from financing activities		
Increase (decrease) in notes payable to banks	($123,500)	$228,400
Reduction in long-term debt	(9,238)	(10,811)
Payment of dividends	(22,924)	(19,973)
Purchase of treasury stock	—	(12,500)
Net cash flows from financing activities	($155,662)	$185,116
Net increase (decrease) in cash	$ 12,420	($ 87,468)
Cash at beginning of year	16,032	103,500
Cash at end of year	$ 28,452	$ 16,032

Schedule of Noncash Investing and Financing Transactions

Issue of bonds payable for retail acquisition		$ 50,000

Required

Evaluate the success of the company's strategy by answering the questions that follow.

1. What are the primary reasons cash flows from operating activities differ from net income? What is the effect on the acquisition in 2009? What conclusions can you draw from the changes in 2010?
2. Compute free cash flow for both years. What was the total cost of the acquisition? Is the company able to finance expansion in 2009 by generating internal cash flow? What was the situation in 2010?
3. (User insight ▶) What are the most significant financing activities in 2009? How did the company finance the acquisition? Do you think this is a good strategy? What other issues might you question in financing activities?
4. (User insight ▶) Based on results in 2010, what actions was the company forced to take and what is your overall assessment of the company's diversification strategy?

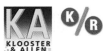

LO2 LO3 LO4 LO5

Statement of Cash Flows: Indirect Method

P 3. The comparative balance sheets for Arif Fabrics, Inc., for December 31, 2010 and 2009 appear below.

Arif Fabrics, Inc.
Comparative Balance Sheets
December 31, 2010 and 2009

	2010	2009
Assets		
Cash	$ 94,560	$ 27,360
Accounts receivable (net)	102,430	75,430
Inventory	112,890	137,890
Prepaid expenses	—	20,000
Land	25,000	—
Building	137,000	—
Accumulated depreciation–building	(15,000)	—
Equipment	33,000	34,000
Accumulated depreciation–equipment	(14,500)	(24,000)
Patents	4,000	6,000
Total assets	$479,380	$276,680
Liabilities and Stockholders' Equity		
Accounts payable	$ 10,750	$ 36,750
Notes payable (current)	10,000	—
Accrued liabilities	—	12,300
Mortgage payable	162,000	—
Common stock, $10 par value	180,000	150,000
Additional paid-in capital	57,200	37,200
Retained earnings	59,430	40,430
Total liabilities and stockholders' equity	$479,380	$276,680

Additional information about Arif Fabrics's operations during 2010 is as follows: (a) net income, $28,000; (b) building and equipment depreciation expense amounts, $15,000 and $3,000, respectively; (c) equipment that cost $13,500 with accumulated depreciation of $12,500 sold at a gain of $5,300; (d) equipment purchases, $12,500; (e) patent amortization, $3,000; purchase of patent, $1,000; (f) funds borrowed by issuing notes payable, $25,000; notes payable repaid, $15,000; (g) land and building purchased for

$162,000 by signing a mortgage for the total cost; (h) 1,500 shares of $20 par value common stock issued for a total of $50,000; and (i) paid cash dividend, $9,000.

Required

1. Using the indirect method, prepare a statement of cash flows for Arif Fabrics.
2. User insight ▶ Why did Arif Fabrics have an increase in cash of $67,200 when it recorded net income of only $28,000? Discuss and interpret.
3. User insight ▶ Compute and assess cash flow yield and free cash flow for 2010. What is your assessment of Arif's cash-generating ability?

LO2 LO3 LO4 LO5

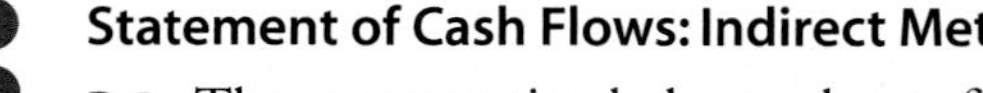

Statement of Cash Flows: Indirect Method

P 4. The comparative balance sheets for Lopez Ceramics, Inc., for December 31, 2010 and 2009 follow. During 2010, the company had net income of $48,000 and building and equipment depreciation expenses of $40,000 and $30,000, respectively. It amortized intangible assets in the amount of $10,000; purchased investments for $58,000; sold investments for $75,000, on which it recorded a gain of $17,000; issued $120,000 of long-term bonds at face value; purchased land and a warehouse through a $160,000 mortgage; paid $20,000 to reduce the mortgage; borrowed $30,000 by issuing notes payable; repaid notes payable in the amount of $90,000; declared and paid cash dividends in the amount of $18,000; and purchased treasury stock in the amount of $10,000.

Required

1. Using the indirect method, prepare a statement of cash flows for Lopez Ceramics, Inc.
2. User insight ▶ Why did Lopez Ceramics experience a decrease in cash in a year in which it had a net income of $48,000? Discuss and interpret.
3. User insight ▶ Compute and assess cash flow yield and free cash flow for 2010. Why is each of these measures important in assessing cash-generating ability?

Lopez Ceramics, Inc.
Comparative Balance Sheets
December 31, 2010 and 2009

	2010	2009
Assets		
Cash	$ 128,800	$ 152,800
Accounts receivable (net)	369,400	379,400
Inventory	480,000	400,000
Prepaid expenses	7,400	13,400
Long-term investments	220,000	220,000
Land	180,600	160,600
Building	600,000	460,000
Accumulated depreciation, building	(120,000)	(80,000)
Equipment	240,000	240,000
Accumulated depreciation, equipment	(58,000)	(28,000)
Intangible assets	10,000	20,000
Total assets	$2,058,200	$1,938,200

(continued)

Liabilities and Stockholders' Equity		
Accounts payable	$ 235,400	$ 330,400
Notes payable (current)	20,000	80,000
Accrued liabilities	5,400	10,400
Mortgage payable	540,000	400,000
Bonds payable	500,000	380,000
Common stock	650,000	650,000
Additional paid-in capital	40,000	40,000
Retained earnings	127,400	97,400
Treasury stock	(60,000)	(50,000)
Total liabilities and stockholders' equity	$2,058,200	$1,938,200

LO2 LO3 LO4 LO5

KA KLOOSTER & ALLEN K/R

Statement of Cash Flows: Indirect Method

P 5. Wu Corporation's comparative balance sheets as of December 31, 2011 and 2010 and its income statement for the year ended December 31, 2011 are presented below and on the opposite page. During 2011, Wu Corporation engaged in these transactions:

a. Sold furniture and fixtures that cost $35,600, on which it had accumulated depreciation of $28,800, at a gain of $7,000.
b. Purchased furniture and fixtures in the amount of $39,600.
c. Paid a $20,000 note payable and borrowed $40,000 on a new note.
d. Converted bonds payable in the amount of $100,000 into 4,000 shares of common stock.
e. Declared and paid $6,000 in cash dividends.

Required

1. Using the indirect method, prepare a statement of cash flows for Wu Corporation. Include a supporting schedule of noncash investing transactions and financing transactions.
2. User insight ▶ What are the primary reasons for Wu Corporation's large increase in cash from 2010 to 2011, despite its low net income?
3. User insight ▶ Compute and assess cash flow yield and free cash flow for 2011. Compare and contrast what these two performance measures tell you about Wu's cash-generating ability.

Wu Corporation
Comparative Balance Sheets
December 31, 2011 and 2010

	2011	2010
Assets		
Cash	$ 164,800	$ 50,000
Accounts receivable (net)	165,200	200,000
Merchandise inventory	350,000	450,000
Prepaid rent	2,000	3,000
Furniture and fixtures	148,000	144,000
Accumulated depreciation, furniture and fixtures	(42,000)	(24,000)
Total assets	$788,000	$823,000

(continued)

Liabilities and Stockholders' Equity		
Accounts payable	$ 143,400	$ 200,400
Income taxes payable	1,400	4,400
Notes payable (long-term)	40,000	20,000
Bonds payable	100,000	200,000
Common stock, $20 par value	240,000	200,000
Additional paid-in capital	181,440	121,440
Retained earnings	81,760	76,760
Total liabilities and stockholders' equity	$788,000	$823,000

Wu Corporation
Income Statement
For the Year Ended December 31, 2011

Sales		$1,609,000
Cost of goods sold		1,127,800
Gross margin		$ 481,200
Operating expenses (including depreciation expense of $46,800)		449,400
Income from operations		$ 31,800
Other income (expenses)		
Gain on sale of furniture and fixtures	$ 7,000	
Interest expense	(23,200)	(16,200)
Income before income taxes		$ 15,600
Income taxes expense		4,600
Net income		$ 11,000

Alternate Problems

LO1 **Classification of Cash Flow Transactions**

P 6. Analyze each transaction listed in the table that follows and place X's in the appropriate columns to indicate the transaction's classification and its effect on cash flows using the indirect method.

	Cash Flow Classification				Effect on Cash Flows		
Transaction	**Operating Activity**	**Investing Activity**	**Financing Activity**	**Noncash Trans-action**	**Increase**	**Decrease**	**No Effect**
1. Increased accounts payable.							
2. Decreased inventory.							
3. Increased prepaid insurance.							
4. Earned a net income.							
5. Declared and paid a cash dividend.							
6. Issued stock for cash.							
7. Retired long-term debt by issuing stock.							
8. Purchased a long-term investment with cash.							

(continued)

Transaction	Cash Flow Classification: Operating Activity	Investing Activity	Financing Activity	Noncash Transaction	Effect on Cash Flows: Increase	Decrease	No Effect
9. Sold trading securities at a gain.							
10. Sold a machine at a loss.							
11. Retired fully depreciated equipment.							
12. Decreased interest payable.							
13. Purchased available-for-sale securities (long-term).							
14. Decreased dividends receivable.							
15. Decreased accounts receivable.							
16. Converted bonds to common stock.							
17. Purchased 90-day Treasury bill.							

LO2 LO3 LO4 LO5

Statement of Cash Flows: Indirect Method

P 7. Ortega Corporation's income statement for the year ended June 30, 2010 and its comparative balance sheets as of June 30, 2010 and 2009 appear below and on the next page. During 2010, the corporation sold equipment that cost \$24,000, on which it had accumulated depreciation of \$17,000, at a loss of \$4,000. It also purchased land and a building for \$100,000 through an increase of \$100,000 in Mortgage Payable; made a \$20,000 payment on the mortgage; repaid notes but borrowed an additional \$30,000 through the issuance of a new note payable of \$80,000; and declared and paid a \$60,000 cash dividend.

Ortega Corporation
Income Statement
For the Year Ended June 30, 2010

Sales		$4,040,900
Cost of goods sold		3,656,300
Gross margin		$ 384,600
Operating expenses (including depreciation expense of $60,000)		189,200
Income from operations		$ 195,400
Other income (expenses)		
Loss on sale of equipment	($ 4,000)	
Interest expense	(37,600)	(41,600)
Income before income taxes		$ 153,800
Income taxes expense		34,200
Net income		$ 119,600

Required

1. Using the indirect method, prepare a statement of cash flows. Include a supporting schedule of noncash investing and financing transactions.

User insight ▶ 2. What are the primary reasons for Ortega Corporation's large increase in cash from 2009 to 2010?

User insight ▶ 3. Compute and assess cash flow yield and free cash flow for 2010. How would you assess the corporation's cash-generating ability?

Ortega Corporation
Comparative Balance Sheets
June 30, 2010 and 2009

	2010	2009
Assets		
Cash	$ 167,000	$ 20,000
Accounts receivable (net)	100,000	120,000
Inventory	180,000	220,000
Prepaid expenses	600	1,000
Property, plant, and equipment	628,000	552,000
Accumulated depreciation, property, plant, and equipment	(183,000)	(140,000)
Total assets	$892,600	$773,000
Liabilities and Stockholders' Equity		
Accounts payable	$ 64,000	$ 42,000
Notes payable (due in 90 days)	30,000	80,000
Income taxes payable	26,000	18,000
Mortgage payable	360,000	280,000
Common stock, $5 par value	200,000	200,000
Retained earnings	212,600	153,000
Total liabilities and stockholders' equity	$892,600	$773,000

ENHANCING Your Knowledge, Skills, and Critical Thinking

Conceptual Understanding Cases

LO1 LO3

EBITDA and the Statement of Cash Flows

C 1. When **Fleetwood Enterprises, Inc.**, a large producer of recreational vehicles and manufactured housing, warned that it might not be able to generate enough cash to satisfy debt requirements and could be in default of a loan agreement, its cash flow, defined in the financial press as "EBITDA" (earnings before interest, taxes, depreciation, and amortization), was a negative $2.7 million. The company would have had to generate $17.7 million in the next accounting period to comply with the loan terms.[13] To what section of the statement of cash flows does EBITDA most closely relate? Is EBITDA a good approximation for this section of the statement of cash flows? Explain your answer, which should include an identification of the major differences between EBITDA and the section of the statement of cash flows you chose.

Interpreting Financial Reports

Anatomy of a Disaster

C 2. On October 16, 2001, Kenneth Lay, then chairman and CEO of **Enron Corporation**, announced the company's earnings for the first nine months of 2001 as follows:

> Our 26 percent increase in recurring earnings per diluted share shows the very strong results of our core wholesale and retail energy businesses and our natural gas pipelines. The continued excellent prospects in these businesses and Enron's leading market position make us very confident in our strong earnings outlook.[14]

Less than six months later, the company filed for the biggest bankruptcy in U.S. history. Its stock dropped to less than $1 per share, and a major financial scandal was underway.

Presented on the opposite page is Enron's statement of cash flows for the first nine months of 2001 and 2000 (restated to correct the previous accounting errors). Assume you report to an investment analyst who has asked you to analyze this statement for clues as to why the company went under.

1. For the two time periods shown, compute the cash-generating efficiency ratios of cash flow yield, cash flows to sales (Enron's revenues were $133,762 million in 2001 and $55,494 million in 2000), and cash flows to assets (use total assets of $61,783 million for 2001 and $64,926 million for 2000). Also compute free cash flows for the two years.
2. Prepare a memorandum to the investment analyst that assesses Enron's cash-generating efficiency in light of the chairman's remarks and that evaluates the company's available free cash flow, taking into account its financing activities. Identify significant changes in Enron's operating items and any special operating items that should be considered. Include your computations as an attachment.

LO2

Cash-Generating Efficiency Ratios and Free Cash Flow

C 3. The data that follow pertain to two of Japan's best-known and most successful companies, **Sony Corporation** and **Panasonic, Inc.**[15] (Numbers are in billions of yen.)

	Sony Corporation		Panasonic, Inc.	
	2007	2006	2007	2006
Sales	¥ 8,296	¥ 7,511	¥9,108	¥8,894
Net income	126	124	212	154
Average total assets	11,163	10,054	8,931	8,011
Net cash flows from operating activities	561	400	533	575
Dividends paid	25	25	55	39
Purchases of plant assets	414	384	418	386

Calculate the ratios of cash flow yield, cash flows to sales, and cash flows to assets, as well as free cash flow, for the two years, for both Sony Corporation and Panasonic, Inc. Which company is most efficient in generating cash flow? Which company has the best year-to-year trend? Which company do you think will most probably need external financing?

Decision Analysis Using Excel

Analysis of Cash Flow Difficulty

C 4. Sol Stein, certified public accountant, has just given his employer Sing Moy, the president of Moy Print Gallery, Inc., the income statement that appears on page 700.

After examining the statement, Moy said to Stein, "Sol, the statement seems to be well done, but what I need to know is why I don't have enough cash to pay

Enron Corporation
Statement of Cash Flows
For the Nine Months Ended September 30, 2001 and 2000

(In millions)	**2001**	**2000**
Cash Flows from Operating Activities		
Reconciliation of net income to net cash provided by operating activities		
Net income	$ 225	$ 797
Cumulative effect of accounting changes, net of tax	(19)	0
Depreciation, depletion and amortization	746	617
Deferred income taxes	(134)	8
Gains on sales of non-trading assets	(49)	(135)
Investment losses	768	0
Changes in components of working capital		
Receivables	987	(3,363)
Inventories	1	339
Payables	(1,764)	2,899
Other	464	(455)
Trading investments		
Net margin deposit activity	(2,349)	541
Other trading activities	173	(555)
Other, net	198	(566)
Net Cash Provided by (Used in) Operating Activities	$ (753)	$ 127
Cash Flows from Investing Activities		
Capital expenditures	$(1,584)	$(1,539)
Equity investments	(1,172)	(858)
Proceeds from sales of non-trading investments	1,711	222
Acquisition of subsidiary stock	0	(485)
Business acquisitions, net of cash acquired	(82)	(773)
Other investing activities	(239)	(147)
Net Cash Used in Investing Activities	$(1,366)	$(3,580)
Cash Flows from Financing Activities		
Issuance of long-term debt	$ 4,060	$ 2,725
Repayment of long-term debt	(3,903)	(579)
Net increase in short-term borrowings	2,365	1,694
Issuance of common stock	199	182
Net redemption of company-obligated preferred securities of subsidiaries	0	(95)
Dividends paid	(394)	(396)
Net (acquisition) disposition of treasury stock	(398)	354
Other financing activities	(49)	(12)
Net Cash Provided by Financing Activities	$ 1,880	$ 3,873
Increase (Decrease) in Cash and Cash Equivalents	$ (239)	$ 420
Cash and Cash Equivalents, Beginning of Period	1,240	333
Cash and Cash Equivalents, End of Period	$ 1,001	$ 753

Source: Adapted from Enron Corporation, SEC filings, 2001.

Moy Print Gallery, Inc.
Income Statement
For the Year Ended December 31, 2010

Sales	$ 884,000
Cost of goods sold	508,000
Gross margin	$ 376,000
Operating expenses (including depreciation expense of $20,000)	204,000
Operating income	$ 172,000
Interest expense	24,000
Income before income taxes	$ 148,000
Income taxes expense	28,000
Net income	$120,000

my bills this month. You show that I earned $120,000 in 2010, but I have only $24,000 in the bank. I know I bought a building on a mortgage and paid a cash dividend of $48,000, but what else is going on?"

Stein replied, "To answer your question, we have to look at comparative balance sheets and prepare another type of statement. Take a look at these balance sheets." The statement handed to Moy follows.

Moy Print Gallery, Inc.
Comparative Balance Sheets
December 31, 2010 and 2009

	2010	2009
Assets		
Cash	$ 24,000	$ 40,000
Accounts receivable (net)	178,000	146,000
Inventory	240,000	180,000
Prepaid expenses	10,000	14,000
Building	400,000	—
Accumulated depreciation	(20,000)	—
Total assets	$832,000	$380,000
Liabilities and Stockholders' Equity		
Accounts payable	$ 74,000	$ 96,000
Income taxes payable	6,000	4,000
Mortgage payable	400,000	—
Common stock	200,000	200,000
Retained earnings	152,000	80,000
Total liabilities and stockholders' equity	$832,000	$380,000

1. To what other statement is Stein referring? From the information given, prepare the additional statement using the indirect method.

2. Moy Print Gallery, Inc., has a cash problem despite profitable operations. Why is this the case?

Annual Report Case: CVS Caremark Corporation

Analysis of the Statement of Cash Flows

C 5. Refer to the statement of cash flows in the **CVS** annual report to answer the following questions:

1. Does CVS use the indirect method of reporting cash flows from operating activities? Other than net earnings, what are the most important factors affecting the company's cash flows from operating activities? Explain the trend of each of these factors.
2. Based on the cash flows from investing activities in 2006 and 2007, would you say that CVS is a contracting or an expanding company? Explain your answer.
3. Has CVS used external financing during 2006 and 2007? If so, where did it come from?

Comparison Case: CVS Versus Southwest

Cash Flows Analysis

C 6. Refer to the **CVS** annual report and the financial statements of **Southwest Airlines Co.** in the Supplement to Chapter 1. Calculate for two years each company's cash flow yield, cash flows to sales, cash flows to assets, and free cash flow. At the end of 2005, Southwest's total assets were $14,003 million and CVS's total assets were $15,246.6 million.

Discuss and compare the trends of the cash-generating ability of CVS and Southwest. Comment on each company's change in cash and cash equivalents over the two-year period.

Ethical Dilemma Case

Ethics and Cash Flow Classifications

C 7. Specialty Metals, Inc., a fast-growing company that makes metals for equipment manufacturers, has an $800,000 line of credit at its bank. One section in the credit agreement says that the ratio of cash flows from operations to interest expense must exceed 3.0. If this ratio falls below 3.0, the company must reduce the balance outstanding on its line of credit to one-half the total line if the funds borrowed against the line of credit exceed one-half of the total line.

After the end of the fiscal year, during a meeting with the president of the company, the controller made the following statement: "We will not meet the ratio requirements on our line of credit in 2010 because interest expense was $1.2 million and cash flows from operations were $3.2 million. Also, we have borrowed 100 percent of our line of credit. We do not have the cash to reduce the credit line by $400,000."

The president replied, "This is a serious situation. To pay our ongoing bills, we need our bank to increase our line of credit, not decrease it. What can we do about this?"

"Do you recall the $500,000 two-year note payable for equipment?" answered the controller. "It is now classified as 'Proceeds from Notes Payable' in cash flows provided from financing activities in the statement of cash flows. If we moved it to cash flows from operations and called it 'Increase in Payables,' it would increase cash flows from operations to $3.7 million and put us over the limit."

"Well, do it," ordered the president. "It surely doesn't make any difference where it appears on the statement. It is an increase in both places. It would be much worse for our company in the long term if we failed to meet this ratio requirement."

What is your opinion of the controller and president's reasoning? Is the president's order ethical? Who benefits and who is harmed if the controller follows the president's order? What alternatives are available to management? What would you do?

Internet Case

LO2

Follow-up Analysis of Cash Flows

C 8. Go to **CVS Caremark Corporation's** website and find the statement of cash flows in its latest annual report. Compare it with the 2007 statement in the Supplement to Chapter 1 by doing the following:

1. Identify major changes in operating, investing, and financing activities.
2. Read management's financial review of cash flows.
3. Calculate the cash flow ratios (cash flow yield, cash flows to sales, cash flows to assets) and free cash flow for the most recent year.

How does CVS's cash flow performance differ between these two years? Be prepared to discuss your conclusions in class.

Group Activity Case

LO1

Cash Flow Versus Net Income

C 9. The excerpt that follows is from a recent article on the financial reporting of **Amazon.com**, the famous Internet seller.

> From the beginning, Bezos [Amazon.com's Chairman and CEO] told shareholders that his goal was to build a company, not an artificial bottom line. "When forced to choose between optimizing the appearance of our GAAP accounting and maximizing the present value of future cash flows, we'll take the cash flows." . . . Amazon has since become famous for emphasizing its so-called pro-forma results, which exclude certain costs and highlight Bezo's beloved cash flow. Cash flow—is indeed a critical indicator of whether Amazon will avoid being crushed by its debt. But ultimately Bezos will have to show that Amazon can make honest-to-God net profits under old-school accounting.[16]

Divide into class groups in order to develop a position in support of or against Bezo's reasoning. Then participate in a debate, defending your group's position. The basic question to address is, Which is more important for a young growing company—cash flows from operating activities or net income under generally accepted accounting principles?

Business Communication Case

LO1 LO2

Alternative Uses of Cash

C 10. Perhaps because of hard times in their start-up years, companies in the high-tech sector of American industry seem more prone than those in other sectors to building up cash reserves. For example, companies like **Cisco Systems**, **Intel**, **Dell**, and **Oracle** have amassed large cash balances.[17]

Assume you work for a company in the high-tech industry that has built up a substantial amount of cash. The company is still growing through development of new products, has some debt, and has never paid a dividend or bought treasury stock. The price of the company's stock is lagging. Write a one-page memo to the CEO that outlines at least four strategies for using the company's cash to improve the company's financial outlook.

CHAPTER

14 Financial Performance Measurement

Focus on Financial Statements

INCOME STATEMENT

Revenues

− Expenses

= Net Income

STATEMENT OF RETAINED EARNINGS

Opening Balance

+ Net Income

− Dividends

= Retained Earnings

BALANCE SHEET

Assets | Liabilities

Equity

A = L + E

STATEMENT OF CASH FLOWS

Operating activities

+ Investing activities

+ Financing activities

= Change in Cash

+ Starting Balance

= Ending Cash Balance

Users assess performance by comparing categories within and across the financial statements.

The ultimate purpose of financial reporting is to enable managers, creditors, investors, and other interested parties to evaluate a company's financial performance. In earlier chapters, we discussed the various measures used in assessing a company's financial performance; here, we provide a comprehensive summary of those measures. Because these measures play a key role in executive compensation, there is always the risk that they will be manipulated. Users of financial statements therefore need to be familiar with the analytical tools and techniques used in performance measurement and the assumptions that underlie them.

LEARNING OBJECTIVES

LO1 Describe the objectives, standards of comparison, sources of information, and compensation issues in measuring financial performance. *(pp. 706–713)*

LO2 Apply horizontal analysis, trend analysis, vertical analysis, and ratio analysis to financial statements. *(pp. 714–720)*

LO3 Apply ratio analysis to financial statements in a comprehensive evaluation of a company's financial performance. *(pp. 721–729)*

DECISION POINT ▶ A USER'S FOCUS

Starbucks Corporation

Formed in 1985, **Starbucks** is today a well-known specialty retailer. The company purchases and roasts whole coffee beans and sells them, along with a variety of freshly brewed coffees and other beverages and food items, in its retail shops. It also produces and sells bottled coffee drinks and a line of premium ice creams.

Like many other companies, Starbucks uses financial performance measures, primarily earnings per share, in determining compensation for top management. Earnings per share and some of the measures that drive earnings per share appear in the company's Financial Highlights below.[1] By linking compensation to financial performance, Starbucks provides its executives with incentive to improve the company's performance. Compensation and financial performance are thus linked to increasing shareholders' value.

STARBUCKS' FINANCIAL HIGHLIGHTS
(In thousands, except profit margin and earnings per share)

	2007	2006	2005
Net revenues	$9,411,497	$7,786,942	$6,369,300
Net earnings	$ 672,638	$ 564,259	$ 494,370
Profit margin	7.1%	7.2%	7.8%
Earnings per share—basic	$0.90	$0.74	$0.63

▶ What standards should be used to evaluate Starbucks' performance?

▶ What analytical tools are available to measure performance?

▶ How successful has the company been in creating value for shareholders?

Foundations of Financial Performance Measurement

LO1 Describe the objectives, standards of comparison, sources of information, and compensation issues in measuring financial performance.

Financial performance measurement, also called *financial statement analysis*, uses all the techniques available to show how important items in a company's financial statements relate to the company's financial objectives. Persons with a strong interest in measuring a company's financial performance fall into two groups:

1. A company's top managers, who set and strive to achieve financial performance objectives; middle-level managers of business processes; and lower-level employees who own stock in the company
2. Creditors and investors, as well as customers who have cooperative agreements with the company

Financial Performance Measurement: Management's Objectives

All the strategic and operating plans that management formulates to achieve a company's goals must eventually be stated in terms of financial objectives. A primary objective is to increase the wealth of the company's stockholders, but this objective must be divided into categories. A complete financial plan should have financial objectives and related performance objectives in all the following categories:

Financial Objective	Performance Objective
Liquidity	The company must be able to pay bills when due and meet unexpected needs for cash.
Profitability	It must earn a satisfactory net income.
Long-term solvency	It must be able to survive for many years.
Cash flow adequacy	It must generate sufficient cash through operating, investing, and financing activities.
Market strength	It must be able to increase stockholders' wealth.

Management's main responsibility is to carry out its plan to achieve the company's financial objectives. This requires constant monitoring of key financial performance measures for each objective listed above, determining the cause of any deviations from the measures, and proposing ways of correcting the deviations. Management compares actual performance with the key performance measures in monthly, quarterly, and annual reports. The information in management's annual reports provides data for long-term trend analyses.

Financial Performance Measurement: Creditors' and Investors' Objectives

Creditors and investors use financial performance evaluation to judge a company's past performance and present position. They also use it to assess a company's future potential and the risk connected with acting on that potential. An investor focuses on a company's potential earnings ability because that ability will affect the market price of the company's stock and the amount of dividends the company will pay. A creditor focuses on the company's potential debt-paying ability.

Past performance is often a good indicator of future performance. To evaluate a company's past performance, creditors and investors look at trends in past sales, expenses, net income, cash flow, and return on investment. To evaluate its current position, they look at its assets, liabilities, cash position, debt in relation to equity, and levels of inventories and receivables. Knowing a company's past performance and current position can be important in judging its future potential and the related risk.

The risk involved in making an investment or loan depends on how easy it is to predict future profitability or liquidity. If an investor can predict with confidence that a company's earnings per share will be between $2.50 and $2.60 in the next year, the investment is less risky than if the earnings per share are expected to fall between $2.00 and $3.00. For example, the potential of an investment in an established electric utility company is relatively easy to predict on the basis of the company's past performance and current position. In contrast, the potential of an investment in a new Internet firm that has not yet established a record of earnings is very hard to predict. Investing in the Internet firm is therefore riskier than investing in the electric utility company.

In return for taking a greater risk, investors often look for a higher expected return (an increase in market price plus dividends). Creditors who take a greater risk by advancing funds to a company like the new Internet firm mentioned above may demand a higher interest rate and more assurance of repayment (a secured loan, for instance). The higher interest rate reimburses them for assuming the higher risk.

Standards of Comparison

When analyzing financial statements, decision makers must judge whether the relationships they find in the statements are favorable or unfavorable. Three standards of comparison that they commonly use are rule-of-thumb measures, a company's past performance, and industry norms.

Study Note

Rules of thumb evolve and change as the business environment changes. Not long ago, an acceptable current ratio was higher than today's 2:1.

Rule-of-Thumb Measures Many financial analysts, investors, and lenders apply general standards, or rule-of-thumb measures, to key financial ratios. For example, most analysts today agree that a current ratio (current assets divided by current liabilities) of 2:1 is acceptable.

In its *Industry Norms and Key Business Ratios*, the credit-rating firm of Dun & Bradstreet offers such rules of thumb as the following:

> *Current debt to tangible net worth*: A business is usually in trouble when this relationship exceeds 80 percent.
>
> *Inventory to net working capital*: Ordinarily, this relationship should not exceed 80 percent.

Although rule-of thumb measures may suggest areas that need further investigation, there is no proof that the levels they specify apply to all companies. A company with a current ratio higher than 2:1 may have a poor credit policy (causing accounts receivable to be too large), too much inventory, or poor cash management. Another company may have a ratio lower than 2:1 but still have excellent management in all three of those areas. Thus, rule-of-thumb measures must be used with caution.

Past Performance Comparing financial measures or ratios of the same company over time is an improvement over using rule-of-thumb measures. Such a comparison gives the analyst some basis for judging whether the measure or ratio is getting better or worse. Thus, it may be helpful in showing future trends. However, trends reverse at times, so such projections must be made with care.

FOCUS ON BUSINESS PRACTICE

Look Carefully at the Numbers

In recent years, companies have increasingly used pro forma statements—statements as they would appear without certain items—as a way of presenting a better picture of their operations than would be the case in reports prepared under GAAP. In one quarter, **Amazon.com** reported a "pro forma net" loss of $76 million; under GAAP, its net loss was $234 million. Pro forma statements, which are unaudited, have come to mean whatever a company's management wants them to mean. As a result, the SEC has issued new rules that prohibit companies from giving more prominence to non-GAAP measures and from using terms that are similar to GAAP measures.[2] Nevertheless, companies still report pro forma results. A common practice used by such companies as **Google**, **eBay**, and **Starbucks** is to provide in the notes to the financial statements income as it would be without the expense related to compensation for stock options.[3] Analysts should rely exclusively on financial statements that are prepared using GAAP and that are audited by an independent CPA.

Another problem with trend analysis is that past performance may not be enough to meet a company's present needs. For example, even though a company improves its return on investment from 3 percent in one year to 4 percent the next year, the 4 percent return may not be adequate for the company's current needs. In addition, using a company's past performance as a standard of comparison is not helpful in judging its performance relative to that of other companies.

Industry Norms Using industry norms as a standard of comparison overcomes some of the limitations of comparing a company's measures or ratios over time. Industry norms show how a company compares with other companies in the same industry. For example, if companies in a particular industry have an average rate of return on investment of 8 percent, a 3 or 4 percent rate of return is probably not adequate.

Industry norms can also be used to judge trends. Suppose that because of a downturn in the economy, a company's profit margin dropped from 12 percent to 10 percent, while the average drop in profit margin of other companies in the same industry was from 12 to 4 percent. By this standard, the company would have done relatively well.

Sometimes, instead of industry averages, data for the industry leader or a specific competitor are used for analysis.

Using industry norms as standards has three limitations:

1. Companies in the same industry may not be strictly comparable. For example, consider two companies in the oil industry. One purchases oil products and markets them through service stations. The other, an international company, discovers, produces, refines, and markets its own oil products. Because of the disparity in their operations, these two companies cannot be directly compared.

Study Note

Each segment of a diversified company represents an investment that the home office or parent company evaluates and reviews frequently.

2. Many large companies have multiple segments and operate in more than one industry. Some of these **diversified companies**, or *conglomerates*, operate in many unrelated industries. The individual segments of a diversified company generally have different rates of profitability and different degrees of risk. In analyzing a diversified company's consolidated financial statements, it is often impossible to use industry norms as a standard because there simply are no comparable companies.

EXHIBIT 1
Selected Segment Information for Goodyear Tire & Rubber Company

(In millions)	2006	2005	2004
Sales			
North American Tire	$ 9,089	$ 9,091	$ 8,569
European Union Tire	4,990	4,676	4,476
Eastern Europe, Africa, and Middle East Tire	1,562	1,437	1,279
Latin American Tire	1,604	1,466	1,245
Asia Pacific Tire	1,503	1,423	1,312
Total Tires	**18,748**	**18,093**	**16,881**
Engineered Products	1,510	1,630	1,472
Net Sales	**20,258**	**19,723**	**18,353**
Segment Operating Income			
North American Tire	($233)	$167	$ 74
European Union Tire	286	317	253
Eastern Europe, Africa, and Middle East Tire	229	198	194
Latin American Tire	326	295	251
Asia Pacific Tire	104	84	60
Total Tires	**712**	**1,061**	**832**
Engineered Products	74	103	114
Total Segment Operating Income	**786**	**1,164**	**946**
Assets*			
North American Tire	$ 4,798	$ 5,478	$ 5,091
European Union Tire	4,367	3,844	4,264
Eastern Europe, Africa, and Middle East Tire	1,391	1,262	1,315
Latin American Tire	986	899	847
Asia Pacific Tire	1,236	1,123	1,154
Total Tires	**12,778**	**12,606**	**12,671**
Engineered Products	794	748	765
Chemical Products	—	—	650
Total Segment Assets	**13,572**	**13,354**	**14,086**

*2004 assets estimated.

Source: Goodyear Tire & Rubber Company, *Annual Report*, 2006.

The FASB provides a partial solution to this problem. It requires diversified companies to report profit or loss, certain revenue and expense items, and assets for each of their segments. Segment information may be reported for operations in different industries or different geographical areas, or for major customers.[4] Exhibit 1 shows how **Goodyear Tire & Rubber Company** reports data on sales, income, and assets for its engineered and chemical products segments. These data allow the analyst to compute important profitability performance measures, such as profit margin, asset turnover, and return on assets, for each segment and to compare them with the appropriate industry norms.

3. Another limitation of industry norms is that even when companies in the same industry have similar operations, they may use different acceptable accounting procedures. For example, they may use different methods of valuing inventories and different methods of depreciating assets.

Shown here is Goodyear Tire & Rubber Company's polymer plant in Beaumont, Texas. The Beaumont plant is Goodyear's major supplier of tire polymers and the largest in its chemical products segment, which includes facilities in Houston, Niagara Falls, and Akron. The FASB requires diversified companies to report financial information for each of their segments. Goodyear has seven segments in all.

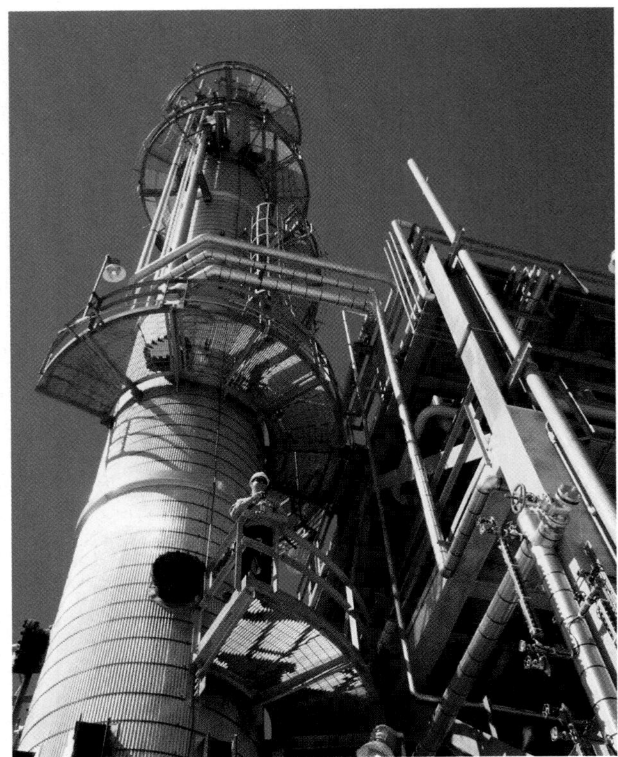

Despite these limitations, if little information about a company's past performance is available, industry norms probably offer the best available standards for judging current performance—as long as they are used with care.

Sources of Information

The major sources of information about public corporations are reports published by the corporations themselves, reports filed with the SEC, business peri3.odicals, and credit and investment advisory services.

Reports Published by the Corporation A public corporation's annual report is an important source of financial information. From a financial analyst's perspective, the main parts of an annual report are management's analysis of the past year's operations; the financial statements; the notes to the financial statements, which include a summary of significant accounting policies; the auditors' report; and financial highlights for a five- or ten-year period.

Most public corporations also publish **interim financial statements** each quarter and sometimes each month. These reports, which present limited information in the form of condensed financial statements, are not subject to a full audit by an independent auditor. The financial community watches interim statements closely for early signs of change in a company's earnings trend.

Reports Filed with the SEC Public corporations in the United States must file annual reports, quarterly reports, and current reports with the Securities and Exchange Commission (SEC). If they have more than $10 million in assets and more than 500 shareholders, they must file these reports electronically at *www.sec.gov/edgar.shtml*, where anyone can access them free of charge.

The SEC requires companies to file their annual reports on a standard form, called Form 10-K. Form 10-K contains more information than a company's annual report and is therefore a valuable source of information.

Companies file their quarterly reports with the SEC on Form 10-Q. This report presents important facts about interim financial performance.

The current report, which is filed on Form 8-K, must be submitted to the SEC within a few days of the date of certain significant events, such as the sale or purchase of a division or a change in auditors. The current report is often the first indicator of significant changes that will affect a company's financial performance in the future.

Business Periodicals and Credit and Investment Advisory Services

Financial analysts must keep up with current events in the financial world. A leading source of financial news is *The Wall Street Journal.* It is the most complete financial newspaper in the United States and is published every business day. Useful periodicals that are published every week or every two weeks include *Forbes*, *Barron's*, *Fortune*, and the *Financial Times.*

Credit and investment advisory services also provide useful information. The publications of Moody's Investors Service and Standard & Poor's provide details about a company's financial history. Data on industry norms, average ratios, and credit ratings are available from agencies like Dun & Bradstreet. Dun & Bradstreet's *Industry Norms and Key Business Ratios* offers an annual analysis of 14 ratios for each of 125 industry groups, classified as retailing, wholesaling, manufacturing, and construction. *Annual Statement Studies*, published by Risk Management Association (formerly Robert Morris Associates), presents many facts and ratios for 223 different industries. The publications of a number of other agencies are also available for a yearly fee.

An example of specialized financial reporting readily available to the public is *Mergent's Dividend Achievers.* It profiles companies that have increased their dividends consistently over the past ten years. A listing from that publication—for **PepsiCo Inc.**—is presented in Exhibit 2. As you can see, a wealth of information about the company, including the market action of its stock, its business operations, recent developments and prospects, and earnings and dividend data, is summarized on one page. We use the kind of data contained in Mergent's summaries in many of the analyses and ratios that we present later in this chapter.

Executive Compensation

As we noted earlier in the text, one intent of the Sarbanes-Oxley Act of 2002 was to strengthen the corporate governance of public corporations. Under this act, a public corporation's board of directors must establish a **compensation committee** made up of independent directors to determine how the company's top executives will be compensated. The company must disclose the components of compensation and the criteria it uses to remunerate top executives in documents that it files with the SEC.

The components of **Starbucks'** compensation of executive officers are typical of those used by many companies:

- Annual base salary
- Incentive bonuses
- Stock option awards[5]

Incentive bonuses are based on financial performance measures that the compensation committee identifies as important to the company's long-term success. Many companies tie incentive bonuses to measures like growth in revenues and return on assets or return on equity. Starbucks bases 80 percent of its incentive bonus on an "earnings per share target approved by the compensation

EXHIBIT 2

Listing from Mergent's Dividend Achievers

PEPSICO INC.

Exchange	Symbol	Price	52Wk Range	Yield	P/E
NYS	PEP	$68.03 (8/31/2007)	69.94-61.24	2.20	19.22

*7 Year Price Score 89.69 *NYSE Composite Index=100 *12 Month Price Score 99.39

Interim Earnings (Per Share)

Qtr.	Mar	Jun	Aug	Dec
2004	0.46	0.61	0.79	0.58
2005	0.53	0.70	0.51	0.65
2006	0.60	0.80	0.88	1.06
2007	0.65	0.94	...	...

Interim Dividends (Per Share)

Amt	Decl	Ex	Rec	Pay
0.30Q	11/17/2006	12/6/2006	12/8/2006	1/2/2007
0.30Q	2/2/2007	3/7/2007	3/9/2007	3/30/2007
0.375Q	5/2/2007	6/6/2007	6/8/2007	6/29/2007
0.375Q	7/19/2007	9/5/2007	9/7/2007	9/28/2007

Indicated Div: $1.50 (Div. Reinv. Plan)

Valuation Analysis

Forecast P/E	15.48 (1/10/2007)		
Market Cap	$110.3 Billion	Book Value	16.0 Billion
Price/Book	6.91	Price/Sales	3.03

Dividend Achiever Status

10 Year Growth Rate	10.00%
Total Years of Dividend Growth	35

Business Summary: Food (MIC: 4.1 SIC: 2086 NAIC: 312111)

PepsiCo is engaged in manufacturing, marketing and selling a range of salty, sweet and grain-based snacks, carbonated and non-carbonated beverages and foods. Co. is organized into four divisions: Frito-Lay North America (FLNA); PepsiCo Beverages North America (PBNA); PepsiCo International (PI); and Quaker Foods North America (QFNA). FLNA branded snacks include Lay's potato chips, Doritos tortilla chips and Rold Gold pretzels. PBNA's brands include Pepsi, Mountain Dew, Gatorade, Tropicana Pure Premium, and Lipton. PI's brands include Lay's, Walkers, Cheetos, Doritos, Ruffles, Gamesa and Sabritas. QFNA's brands include Quaker oatmeal, Rice-A-Roni and Near East side dishes.

Recent Developments: For the quarter ended June 16 2007, net income increased 13.2% to US$1.56 billion from US$1.38 billion in the year-earlier quarter. Revenues were US$9.61 billion, up 10.2% from US$8.71 billion the year before. Operating income was US$1.96 billion versus US$1.80 billion in the prior-year quarter, an increase of 8.8%. Direct operating expenses rose 12.4% to US$4.34 billion from US$3.86 billion in the comparable period the year before. Indirect operating expenses increased 8.3% to US$3.31 billion from US$3.05 billion in the equivalent prior-year period.

Prospects: Co. is seeing an increase in its net revenue, driven by robust snacks and beverage growth at its PepsiCo International division. Specifically, international snacks volume growth is being driven by double-digit growth in Russia and India, partially offset by low-single-digit declines at Sabritas in Mexico and Walkers in the U.K., while beverage volume growth is being fueled by double-digit growth in Pakistan, Russia, the Middle East and the U.K., partially offset by a mid-single-digit decline in Mexico and a double-digit decline in Thailand. Accordingly, Co. is raising its full year 2007 earnings guidance to at least $3.35 per share.

Financial Data (US$ in Thousands)	6 Mos	3 Mos	12/30/2006	12/31/2005	12/25/2004	12/27/2003	12/28/2002	12/29/2001
Earnings Per Share	3.54	3.40	3.34	2.39	2.44	2.05	1.85	1.47
Cash Flow Per Share	3.86	3.95	3.70	3.45	2.99	2.53	2.65	2.39
Tang Book Value Per Share	5.71	5.51	5.50	5.20	4.84	3.82	4.93	2.17
Dividends Per Share	1.275	1.200	1.160	1.010	0.850	0.630	0.595	0.575
Dividend Payout %	36.02	35.32	34.73	42.26	34.84	30.73	32.16	39.12
Income Statement								
Total Revenue	16,957,000	7,350,000	35,137,000	32,562,000	29,261,000	26,971,000	25,112,000	26,935,000
EBITDA	4,233,000	1,769,000	8,399,000	7,732,000	6,848,000	6,269,000	6,077,000	5,189,000
Depn & Amortn	608,000	276,000	1,344,000	1,253,000	1,209,000	1,165,000	1,067,000	1,008,000
Income Before Taxes	3,590,000	1,473,000	6,989,000	6,382,000	5,546,000	4,992,000	4,868,000	4,029,000
Income Taxes	937,000	377,000	1,347,000	2,304,000	1,372,000	1,424,000	1,555,000	1,367,000
Net Income	2,653,000	1,096,000	5,642,000	4,078,000	4,212,000	3,568,000	3,313,000	2,662,000
Average Shares	1,665,000	1,673,000	1,687,000	1,706,000	1,729,000	1,739,000	1,789,000	1,807,000
Balance Sheet								
Total Assets	31,925,000	29,830,000	29,930,000	31,727,000	27,987,000	25,327,000	23,474,000	21,695,000
Current Liabilities	7,589,000	7,522,000	6,860,000	9,406,000	6,752,000	6,415,000	6,052,000	4,998,000
Long-Term Obligations	3,261,000	1,807,000	2,550,000	2,313,000	2,397,000	1,702,000	2,187,000	2,651,000
Total Liabilities	16,052,000	14,482,000	14,562,000	17,476,000	14,464,000	13,453,000	14,183,000	13,021,000
Stockholders' Equity	15,956,000	15,429,000	15,447,000	14,320,000	13,572,000	11,896,000	9,298,000	8,648,000
Shares Outstanding	1,621,000	1,631,000	1,638,000	1,656,000	1,679,000	1,705,000	1,722,000	1,756,000
Statistical Record								
Return on Assets %	18.73	18.84	18.35	13.44	15.84	14.66	14.71	13.34
Return on Equity %	37.96	37.90	38.01	28.77	33.17	33.76	37.02	33.58
EBITDA Margin %	24.96	24.07	23.90	23.75	23.40	23.24	24.20	19.26
Net Margin %	15.65	14.91	16.06	12.52	14.39	13.23	13.19	9.88
Asset Turnover	1.15	1.16	1.14	1.07	1.10	1.11	1.11	1.35
Current Ratio	1.29	1.16	1.33	1.11	1.28	1.08	1.06	1.17
Debt to Equity	0.20	0.12	0.17	0.16	0.18	0.14	0.24	0.31
Price Range	69.48-58.91	65.91-57.20	65.91-56.77	59.90-51.57	55.55-45.39	48.71-37.30	53.12-35.50	50.28-41.26
P/E Ratio	19.63-16.64	19.39-16.82	19.73-17.00	25.06-21.58	22.77-18.60	23.76-18.20	28.71-19.19	34.20-28.07
Average Yield %	1.99	1.93	1.90	1.82	1.66	1.43	1.29	1.25

Address: 700 Anderson Hill Road, Purchase, NY 10577-1444 **Telephone:** 914-253-2000 **Web Site:** www.pepsico.com	**Officers:** Steven S. Reinemund - Chmn., C.E.O. Indra K. Nooyi - Pres., C.F.O. **Transfer Agents:** The Bank of New York	**Investor Contact:** 914-253-3035 **No of Institutions:** 1292 **Shares:** 1,121,669,888 **% Held:** 68.49

Source: PepsiCo listing from *Mergent's Dividend Achievers Fall 2007: Featuring Second-Quarter Results for 2007.* Reprinted by permission of John Wiley & Sons Inc.

committee" and 20 percent on the executive's "specific individual performance." The Financial Highlights at the beginning of the chapter show the growth in the Starbucks' earnings per share.

Stock option awards are usually based on how well the company is achieving its long-term strategic goals. In 2006, a very good year for Starbucks, the company's CEO received a base salary of $100,000,000 and an incentive bonus of twice that amount. In November 2005, he received a stock option award of 966,469 shares of common stock.[6]

From one vantage point, earnings per share is a "bottom-line" number that encompasses all the other performance measures. However, using a single performance measure as the basis for determining compensation has the potential of leading to practices that are not in the best interests of the company or its stockholders. For instance, management could boost earnings per share by reducing the number of shares outstanding (the denominator in the earnings per share equation) while not improving earnings. It could accomplish this by using cash to repurchase shares of the company's stock (treasury stock), rather than investing the cash in more profitable operations.

As you study the comprehensive financial analysis of Starbucks in the coming pages, consider that knowledge of performance measurement not only is important for evaluating a company but also leads to an understanding of the criteria by which a board of directors evaluates and compensates management.

STOP ► REVIEW ► APPLY

LO1-1 **How are the objectives of investors and creditors in using financial performance evaluation similar? How do they differ?**

LO1-2 **What role does risk play in making loans and investments?**

LO1-3 **What standards of comparison are commonly used to evaluate financial statements, and what are their relative merits?**

LO1-4 **Why would a financial analyst compare the ratios of Steelco, a steel company, with the ratios of other companies in the steel industry? What factors might invalidate such a comparison?**

LO1-5 **Where can investors find information about public corporations in which they are thinking of investing?**

LO1-6 **What is the role of a corporation's compensation committee, and what are three common components of executive compensation?**

Suggested answers to all Stop, Review, and Apply questions follow the appendixes.

Performance Measurement Components

Identify each of the following as (a) an objective of financial statement analysis, (b) a standard for financial statement analysis, (c) a source of information for financial statement analysis, or (d) an executive compensation issue:

1. A company's past performance
2. Investment advisory services
3. Assessment of a company's future potential
4. Incentive bonuses
5. Industry norms
6. Annual report
7. Creating shareholder value
8. Form 10-K

SOLUTION

1. b	5. b
2. c	6. c
3. a	7. d
4. d	8. c

Tools and Techniques of Financial Analysis

LO2 Apply horizontal analysis, trend analysis, vertical analysis, and ratio analysis to financial statements.

Study Note

It is important to ascertain the base amount used when a percentage describes an item. For example, inventory may be 50 percent of total current assets but only 10 percent of total assets.

To gain insight into a company's financial performance, one must look beyond the individual numbers to the relationship between the numbers and their change from one period to another. The tools of financial analysis—horizontal analysis, trend analysis, vertical analysis, and ratio analysis—are intended to show these relationships and changes. To illustrate how these tools are used, we devote the rest of this chapter to a comprehensive financial analysis of **Starbucks Corporation**.

Horizontal Analysis

Comparative financial statements provide financial information for the current year and the previous year. To gain insight into year-to-year changes, analysts use **horizontal analysis**, in which changes from the previous year to the current year are computed in both dollar amounts and percentages. The percentage change relates the size of the change to the size of the dollar amounts involved.

Exhibits 3 and 4 present **Starbuck Corporation's** comparative balance sheets and income statements and show both the dollar and percentage changes. The percentage change is computed as follows:

$$\text{Percentage Change} = 100 \times \left(\frac{\text{Amount of Change}}{\text{Base Year Amount}}\right)$$

The **base year** is always the first year to be considered in any set of data. For example, when comparing data for 2006 and 2007, 2006 is the base year. As the balance sheets in Exhibit 3 show, between 2006 and 2007, Starbucks' total current assets increased by \$166,699 thousand, from \$1,529,788 thousand to \$1,696,487 thousand, or by 10.9 percent. This is computed as follows:

$$\text{Percentage Change} = 100 \times \left(\frac{\$166{,}699 \text{ thousand}}{\$1{,}529{,}788 \text{ thousand}}\right) = 10.9\%$$

When examining such changes, it is important to consider the dollar amount of the change as well as the percentage change in each component. For example, the difference between the percentage increase in short-term investments (11.6 percent) and inventories (8.7 percent) is not great. However, the dollar increase in inventories is more than three times the dollar increase in short-term investments (\$55,436 thousand versus \$16,395 thousand). Thus, even though the percentage changes are not very different, inventories require much more investment.

Starbucks' balance sheets for this period, illustrated in Exhibit 3, also show an increase in total assets of \$914,937 thousand, or 20.7 percent. In addition, they show that stockholders' equity increased by \$55,611 thousand, or 2.5 percent. All of this indicates that Starbucks is a growing company.

Starbucks' income statements in Exhibit 4 show that net revenues increased by \$1,624,555 thousand, or 20.9 percent, while gross margin increased by \$804,222 thousand, or 17.5 percent. This indicates that cost of sales grew faster than net revenues. In fact, cost of sales increased by 25.8 percent compared with the 20.9 percent increase in net revenues.

Starbucks' total operating expenses increased by \$658,298 thousand, or 17.3 percent, not as fast as the 20.9 percent increase in net revenues. As a result, operating income increased by \$145,924 thousand, or 18.2 percent, and net income increased by \$108,379 thousand, or 19.2 percent. The primary reason for the increases in operating income and net income is that total operating expenses increased at a slower rate (17.3 percent) than net revenues (20.9 percent).

EXHIBIT 3 Comparative Balance Sheets with Horizontal Analysis

Starbucks Corporation
Consolidated Balance Sheets
September 30, 2007, and October 1, 2006

(Dollar amounts in thousands)	**2007**	**2006**	**Increase (Decrease) Amount**	**Increase (Decrease) Percentage**
	Assets			
Current assets:				
Cash and cash equivalents	$ 281,261	$ 312,606	($ 31,345)	(10.0)
Short-term investments	157,433	141,038	16,395	11.6
Accounts receivable, net	287,925	224,271	63,654	28.4
Inventories	691,658	636,222	55,436	8.7
Prepaid and other current assets	148,757	126,874	21,883	17.2
Deferred income taxes, net	129,453	88,777	40,676	45.8
Total current assets	$1,696,487	$1,529,788	$ 166,699	10.9
Property, plant, and equipment, net	2,890,433	2,287,899	602,534	26.3
Long-term investments	279,868	224,904	54,964	24.4
Other assets	219,422	186,917	32,505	17.4
Goodwill	215,625	161,478	54,147	33.5
Other intangible assets	42,043	37,955	4,088	10.8
Total assets	$5,343,878	$4,428,941	$ 914,937	20.7
	Liabilities and Shareholders' Equity			
Current liabilities:				
Commercial paper and short-term borrowings	$ 710,248	$ 700,000	$ 10,248	1.5
Accounts payable	390,836	340,937	49,899	14.6
Accrued compensation and related costs	332,331	288,963	43,368	15.0
Accrued occupancy costs	74,591	54,868	19,723	35.9
Accrued taxes	92,516	94,010	(1,494)	(1.6)
Other accrued expenses	257,369	224,154	33,215	14.8
Deferred revenue	296,900	231,926	64,974	28.0
Current portion of long-term debt	775	762	13	1.7
Total current liabilities	$2,155,566	$1,935,620	$ 219,946	11.4
Long-term debt and other liabilities	904,195	264,815	639,380	241.4
Shareholders' equity	2,284,117	2,228,506	55,611	2.5
Total liabilities and shareholders' equity	$5,343,878	$4,428,941	$ 914,937	20.7

Source: Data from Starbucks Corporation, Form 10-K, 2007.

Trend Analysis

Trend analysis is a variation of horizontal analysis. With this tool, the analyst calculates percentage changes for several successive years instead of for just two years. Because of its long-term view, trend analysis can highlight basic changes in the nature of a business.

EXHIBIT 4 Comparative Income Statements with Horizontal Analysis

Starbucks Corporation
Consolidated Income Statements
For the Years Ended September 30, 2007, and October 1, 2006

			Increase (Decrease)	
(Dollar amounts in thousands, except per share amounts)	**2007**	**2006**	**Amount**	**Percentage**
Net revenues	$9,411,497	$7,786,942	$1,624,555	20.9
Cost of sales, including occupancy costs	3,999,124	3,178,791	820,333	25.8
Gross margin	$5,412,373	$4,608,151	$ 804,222	17.5
Operating expenses				
Store operating expenses	$3,215,889	$2,687,815	$ 528,074	19.6
Other operating expenses	294,136	253,724	40,412	15.9
Depreciation and amortization expenses	467,160	387,211	79,949	20.6
General and administrative expenses	489,249	479,386	9,863	2.1
Total operating expenses	$4,466,434	$3,808,136	$ 658,298	17.3
Operating income	$ 945,939	$ 800,015	$ 145,924	18.2
Other income, net	110,425	106,228	4,197	4.0
Income before taxes	$1,056,364	$ 906,243	$ 150,121	16.6
Provision for income taxes	383,726	324,770	58,956	18.2
Income before cumulative change for FIN 47, net of taxes	$ 672,638	581,473	91,165	15.7
Cumulative effect of accounting change for FIN 47, net of taxes	—	(17,214)	17,214	100.0
Net income	$ 672,638	$ 564,259	$ 108,379	19.2
Per common share:				
Net income per common share before cumulative effect of change in accounting principle—basic	$ 0.90	$ 0.76	$ 0.14	18.4
Cumulative effect of accounting change for FIN 47, net of taxes	—	(0.02)	0.02	100.0
Net income per common share—basic	$ 0.90	$ 0.74	$ 0.16	21.6
Net income per common share before cumulative effect of change in accounting principle—diluted	$ 0.87	$ 0.73	$ 0.14	19.2
Cumulative effect of accounting change for FIN 47, net of taxes	—	(0.02)	0.02	100.0
Net income per common share—diluted	$ 0.87	$ 0.71	$ 0.16	22.5
Shares used in calculation of net income per common share—basic	749,763	766,144	(16,381)	(2.1)
Shares used in calculation of net income per common share—diluted	770,091	792,556	(22,465)	(2.8)

Source: Data from Starbucks Corporation, Form 10-K, 2007.

EXHIBIT 5
Trend Analysis

Starbucks Corporation Net Revenues and Operating Income Trend Analysis					
	2007	**2006**	**2005**	**2004**	**2003**
Dollar values					
(In thousands)					
Net revenues	$9,411,497	$7,786,942	$6,369,300	$5,294,247	$4,075,522
Operating income	945,939	800,015	703,870	549,460	386,317
Trend analysis					
(In percentages)					
Net revenues	230.9	191.1	156.3	129.9	100.0
Operating income	244.9	207.1	182.2	142.2	100.0

Source: Data from Starbucks Corporation, Form 10-K, 2007.

Study Note

To reflect the general five-year economic cycle of the U.S. economy, trend analysis usually covers a five-year period. Cycles of other lengths exist and are tracked by the National Bureau of Economic Research. Trend analysis needs to be of sufficient length to show a company's performance in both up and down markets.

In addition to presenting comparative financial statements, many companies present a summary of key data for five or more years. Exhibit 5 shows a trend analysis of **Starbucks'** five-year summary of net revenues and operating income.

Trend analysis uses an **index number** to show changes in related items over time. For an index number, the base year is set at 100 percent. Other years are measured in relation to that amount. For example, the 2007 index for Starbucks' net revenues is figured as follows (dollar amounts are in thousands):

$$\text{Index} = 100 \times \left(\frac{\text{Index Year Amount}}{\text{Base Year Amount}}\right)$$

$$= 100 \times \left(\frac{\$9{,}411{,}497}{\$4{,}075{,}522}\right) = 230.9\%$$

The trend analysis in Exhibit 5 shows that Starbucks' net revenues increased over the five-year period, as did operating income. However, operating income grew faster than net revenues in every year. Figure 1 illustrates these trends.

FIGURE 1
Graph of Trend Analysis Shown in Exhibit 5

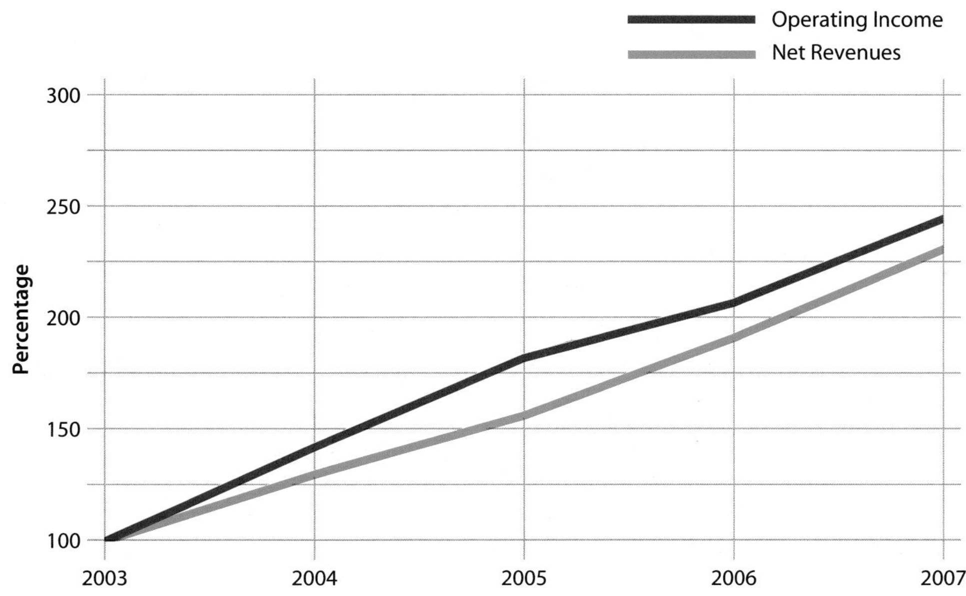

FIGURE 2

Common-Size Balance Sheets Presented Graphically

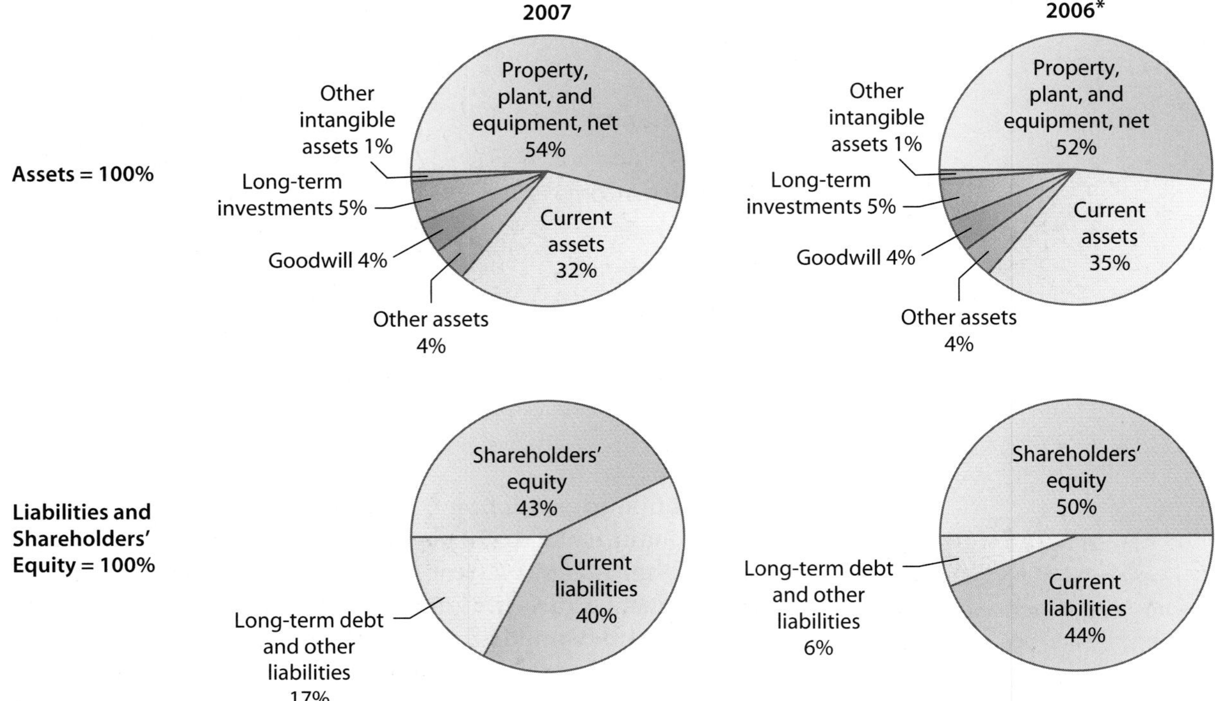

** Rounding causes some additions not to total precisely.*

EXHIBIT 6

Common-Size Balance Sheets

Starbucks Corporation
Common-Size Balance Sheets
September 30, 2007, and October 1, 2006

	2007	**2006**
Assets		
Current assets	31.7%	34.5%
Property, plant, and equipment, net	54.1	51.7
Long-term investments	5.2	5.1
Other assets	4.1	4.2
Goodwill	4.0	3.6
Other intangible assets	0.8	0.9
Total assets	100.0%	100.0%
Liabilities and Shareholders' Equity		
Current liabilities	40.3%	43.7%
Long-term debt and other liabilities	16.9	6.0
Shareholders' equity	42.7	50.3
Total liabilities and shareholders' equity	100.0%	100.0%

Note: Amounts do not precisely total 100 percent in all cases due to rounding.
Source: Data from Starbucks Corporation, Form 10-K, 2007.

FIGURE 3
Common-Size Income Statements Presented Graphically

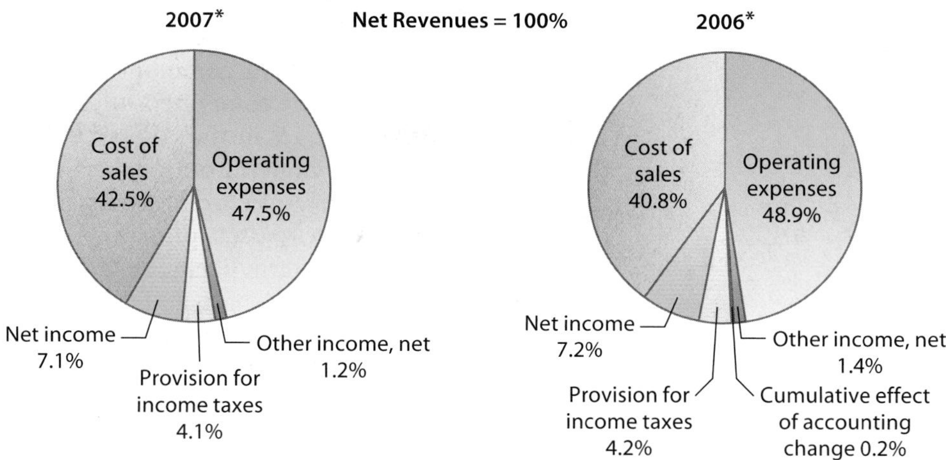

* *Rounding causes some additions not to total precisely.*
Note: Not all items are presented.

Vertical Analysis

Vertical analysis shows how the different components of a financial statement relate to a total figure in the statement. The analyst sets the total figure at 100 percent and computes each component's percentage of that total. The resulting financial statement, which is expressed entirely in percentages, is called a **common-size statement**. Common-size balance sheets and common-size income statements for **Starbucks Corporation** are shown in pie-chart form in Figures 2 and 3 and in financial statement form in Exhibits 6 and 7. (On the

EXHIBIT 7
Common-Size Income Statements

Starbucks Corporation
Common-Size Income Statements
For the Years Ended September 30, 2007, and October 1, 2006

	2007	2006
Net revenues	100.0%	100.0%
Cost of sales, including occupancy costs	42.5	40.8
Gross margin	57.5%	59.2%
Operating expenses:		
Store operating expenses	34.2%	34.5%
Other operating expenses	3.1	3.3
Depreciation and amortization expenses	5.0	5.0
General and administrative expenses	5.2	6.2
Total operating expenses	47.5%	48.9%
Operating income	10.1%	10.3%
Other income, net	1.2	1.4
Income before taxes	11.2%	11.6%
Provision for income taxes	4.1	4.2
Income before cumulative change for FIN 47, net of taxes	7.1	7.5
Cumulative effect of accounting change for FIN 47, net of taxes	—	(0.2)
Net income	7.1%	7.2%

Note: Amounts do not precisely total 100 percent in all cases due to rounding.
Source: Data from Starbucks Corporation, Form 10-K, 2007.

balance sheet, the total figure is total assets or total liabilities and stockholders' equity, and on the income statement, it is net revenues or net sales.)

Vertical analysis and common-size statements are useful in comparing the importance of specific components in the operation of a business and in identifying important changes in the components from one year to the next. The main conclusions to be drawn from our analysis of Starbucks are that the company's assets consist largely of current assets and property, plant, and equipment; that the company finances assets primarily through equity and current liabilities; and that it has few long-term liabilities.

Looking at the pie charts in Figure 2 and the common-size balance sheets in Exhibit 6, you can see that the composition of Starbucks' assets shifted from property, plant, and equipment to current assets. You can also see that the relationship of liabilities and equity shifted slightly from stockholders' equity to current liabilities. The common-size income statements in Exhibit 7, illustrated in Figure 3, show that Starbucks reduced its operating expenses from 2006 to 2007 by 1.4 percent of revenues (48.9% − 47.5%). In other words, operating expenses did not grow as fast as revenues.

Common-size statements are often used to make comparisons between companies. They allow an analyst to compare the operating and financing characteristics of two companies of different size in the same industry. For example, the analyst might want to compare Starbucks with other specialty retailers in terms of percentage of total assets financed by debt or in terms of operating expenses as a percentage of net revenues. Common-size statements would show those and other relationships. These statements can also be used to compare the characteristics of companies that report in different currencies.

Ratio Analysis

Ratio analysis identifies key relationships between the components of the financial statements. Ratios are useful tools for evaluating a company's financial position and operations and may reveal areas that need further investigation. To interpret ratios correctly, one must have a general understanding of the company and its environment, financial data for several years or for several companies, and an understanding of the data underlying the numerator and denominator.

Ratios can be expressed in several ways. For example, a ratio of net income of $100,000 to sales of $1,000,000 can be stated as follows:

1. Net income is 1/10, or 10 percent, of sales.
2. The ratio of sales to net income is 10 to 1 (10:1), or sales are 10 times net income.
3. For every dollar of sales, the company has an average net income of 10 cents.

STOP ▸ REVIEW ▸ APPLY

LO2-1 **Why would an investor want to see both horizontal and trend analyses of a company's financial statements?**

LO2-2 **What does this sentence mean: "Based on a 1990 index equaling 100, net income increased from 240 in 2000 to 260 in 2001"?**

LO2-3 **What is the difference between horizontal and vertical analysis?**

LO2-4 **What is the purpose of ratio analysis?**

Comprehensive Illustration of Ratio Analysis

LO3 Apply ratio analysis to financial statements in a comprehensive evaluation of a company's financial performance.

In this section, to illustrate how analysts use ratio analysis in evaluating a company's financial performance, we perform a comprehensive ratio analysis of **Starbucks'** performance in 2006 and 2007. The following excerpt from the discussion and analysis section of Starbucks' 2007 annual report provides the context for our evaluation of the company's liquidity, profitability, long-term solvency, cash flow adequacy, and market strength:

> Starbucks achieved solid performance in fiscal 2007—meeting its targets for store openings, revenue growth, comparable store sales growth, and earnings per share—despite a challenging economic and operating environment, and significant cost increases from dairy. The Company completed the fiscal year with encouraging trends and momentum in its International business but faced increasing challenges in its U.S. business. While U.S. comparable store sales were within the Company's stated target range, it was accomplished through two price increases which offset flat-to-negative transaction count trends in the U.S. business. The pressure on traffic is consistent with similar trends reported across both the retail and restaurant industry. Management believes that the combination of the economic slowdown and the price increases implemented in fiscal 2007 to help mitigate significant cost pressures have impacted the frequency of customer visits to Starbucks stores.

Evaluating Liquidity

As you know, liquidity is a company's ability to pay bills when they are due and to meet unexpected needs for cash. Because debts are paid out of working capital, all liquidity ratios involve working capital or some part of it. (Cash flow ratios are also closely related to liquidity.)

Study Note

When examining ratios in published sources, be aware that publishers often redefine the content of the ratios provided by the companies. While the general content is similar, variations occur. Be sure to ascertain and evaluate the information that a published source uses to calculate ratios.

Exhibit 8 presents **Starbucks'** liquidity ratios in 2006 and 2007. The **current ratio** and the **quick ratio** are measures of short-term debt-paying ability. The principal difference between the two ratios is that the numerator of the current ratio includes inventories and prepaid expenses. Inventories take longer to convert to cash than the current assets included in the numerator of the quick ratio. Starbucks' quick ratio was 0.4 times in 2006 and decreased to 0.3 times in 2007. Its current ratio was 0.8 times in 2006 and 0.8 in 2007. From 2006 to 2007, its current assets grew at the same rate as current liabilities.

Starbucks' management of receivables declined from 2006 to 2007. The **receivable turnover**, which measures the relative size of accounts receivable and the effectiveness of credit policies, fell from 37.5 times in 2006 to 36.7 times in 2007. The related ratio of **days' sales uncollected** increased, from 9.7 days in 2006 to 9.9 days in 2007. The number of days is quite low because the majority of Starbucks' revenues are from cash sales.

Starbucks' **inventory turnover**, which measures the relative size of inventories, increased from 5.4 times in 2006 to 6.0 times in 2007. This resulted in a favorable decrease in **days' inventory on hand**, from 67.6 days in 2006 to 60.8 days in 2007.

The **operating cycle** is the time it takes to sell products and collect for them. Starbucks' operating cycle decreased from 77.3 days in 2006 (9.7 days + 67.6 days, or the days' sales uncollected plus the days' inventory on hand) to 70.7 days in 2007 (9.9 days + 60.8 days).

Related to the operating cycle is the number of days a company takes to pay its accounts payable. Starbucks' **payables turnover** decreased from 11.6 times in 2006 to 11.1 times in 2007. This resulted in **days' payable** of 31.5 days in 2006 and 32.9 days in 2007. If the days' payable is subtracted from the operating cycle, Starbucks' financing period—the number of days of financing required—was

EXHIBIT 8 Liquidity Ratios of Starbucks Corporation

(Dollar amounts in thousands)	2007	2006
Current ratio: Measure of short-term debt-paying ability		
$\frac{\text{Current Assets}}{\text{Current Liabilities}}$	$\frac{\$1{,}696{,}487}{\$2{,}155{,}566} = 0.8$ times	$\frac{\$1{,}529{,}788}{\$1{,}935{,}620} = 0.8$ times
Quick ratio: Measure of short-term debt-paying ability		
$\frac{\text{Cash + Marketable Securities + Receivables}}{\text{Current Liabilities}}$	$\frac{\$281{,}261 + \$157{,}433 + \$287{,}925}{\$2{,}155{,}566}$	$\frac{\$312{,}606 + \$141{,}038 + \$224{,}271}{\$1{,}935{,}620}$
	$= \frac{\$726{,}619}{\$2{,}155{,}566} = 0.3$ times	$= \frac{\$677{,}915}{\$1{,}935{,}620} = 0.4$ times
Receivable turnover: Measure of relative size of accounts receivable and effectiveness of credit policies		
$\frac{\text{Net Sales}}{\text{Average Accounts Receivable}}$	$\frac{\$9{,}411{,}497}{(\$287{,}925 + \$224{,}271) \div 2}$	$\frac{\$7{,}786{,}942}{(\$224{,}271 + \$190{,}762^{*}) \div 2}$
	$= \frac{\$9{,}411{,}497}{\$256{,}098} = 36.7$ times	$= \frac{\$7{,}786{,}942}{\$207{,}517} = 37.5$ times
Days' sales uncollected: Measure of average days taken to collect receivables		
$\frac{\text{Days in Year}}{\text{Receivable Turnover}}$	$\frac{365 \text{ days}}{36.7 \text{ times}} = 9.9$ days	$\frac{365 \text{ days}}{37.5 \text{ times}} = 9.7$ days
Inventory turnover: Measure of relative size of inventory		
$\frac{\text{Costs of Goods Sold}}{\text{Average Inventory}}$	$\frac{\$3{,}999{,}124}{(\$691{,}658 + \$636{,}222) \div 2}$	$\frac{\$3{,}178{,}791}{(\$636{,}222 + \$546{,}299^{*}) \div 2}$
	$= \frac{\$3{,}999{,}124}{\$663{,}940} = 6.0$ times	$= \frac{\$3{,}178{,}791}{\$591{,}261} = 5.4$ times
Days' inventory on hand: Measure of average days taken to sell inventory		
$\frac{\text{Days in Year}}{\text{Inventory Turnover}}$	$\frac{365 \text{ days}}{6.0 \text{ times}} = 60.8$ days	$\frac{365 \text{ days}}{5.4 \text{ times}} = 67.6$ days
Payables turnover: Measure of relative size of accounts payable		
$\frac{\text{Costs of Goods Sold +/− Change in Inventory}}{\text{Average Accounts Payable}}$	$\frac{\$3{,}999{,}124 + \$55{,}436}{(\$390{,}836 + \$340{,}937) \div 2}$	$\frac{\$3{,}178{,}791 + \$89{,}923^{*}}{(\$340{,}937 + \$220{,}975^{*}) \div 2}$
	$= \frac{\$4{,}054{,}560}{\$365{,}887} = 11.1$ times	$= \frac{\$3{,}268{,}714}{\$280{,}956} = 11.6$ times
Days' payable: Measure of average days taken to pay accounts payable		
$\frac{\text{Days in Year}}{\text{Payables Turnover}}$	$\frac{365 \text{ days}}{11.1 \text{ times}} = 32.9$ days	$\frac{365 \text{ days}}{11.6 \text{ times}} = 31.5$ days

*Figures for 2005 are from the balance sheet in Starbucks' Form 10-K, 2006.
Source: Data from Starbucks Corporation, Form 10-K, 2007, and Form 10-K, 2006.

FIGURE 4
Starbucks' Operating Cycle

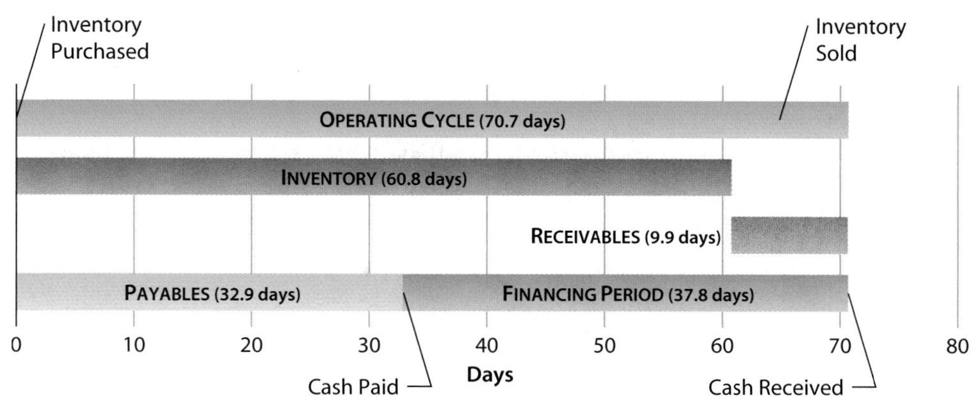

45.8 days in 2006 and 37.8 days in 2007 (see Figure 4). Overall, the company's liquidity improved.

Study Note

In accounting literature, profit is expressed in different ways—for example, as income before income taxes, income after income taxes, or operating income. To draw appropriate conclusions from profitability ratios, analysts must be aware of the content of net income data.

Evaluating Profitability

Investors and creditors are interested in evaluating not only a company's liquidity, but also its profitability—that is, its ability to earn a satisfactory income. Profitability is closely linked to liquidity because earnings ultimately produce the cash flow needed for liquidity. Exhibit 9 shows **Starbucks'** profitability ratios in 2006 and 2007.

Profit margin measures how well a company manages its costs per dollar of sales. Starbucks' profit margin decreased from 7.2 to 7.1 percent between 2006

EXHIBIT 9 Profitability Ratios of Starbucks Corporation

(Dollar amounts in thousands)	2007	2006
Profit margin: Measure of net income produced by each dollar of sales		
$\frac{\text{Net Income}}{\text{Net Sales}}$	$\frac{\$672{,}638}{\$9{,}411{,}497} = 7.1\%$	$\frac{\$564{,}259}{\$7{,}786{,}942} = 7.2\%$
Asset turnover: Measure of how efficiently assets are used to produce sales		
$\frac{\text{Net Sales}}{\text{Average Total Assets}}$	$\frac{\$9{,}411{,}497}{(\$5{,}343{,}878 + \$4{,}428{,}941) \div 2}$	$\frac{\$7{,}786{,}942}{(\$4{,}428{,}941 + \$3{,}513{,}693^{*}) \div 2}$
	$= \frac{\$9{,}411{,}497}{\$4{,}886{,}410} = 1.9 \text{ times}$	$= \frac{\$7{,}786{,}942}{\$3{,}971{,}317} = 2.0 \text{ times}$
Return on assets: Measure of overall earning power or profitability		
$\frac{\text{Net Income}}{\text{Average Total Assets}}$	$\frac{\$672{,}638}{\$4{,}886{,}410} = 13.8\%$	$\frac{\$564{,}259}{\$3{,}971{,}317} = 14.2\%$
Return on equity: Measure of the profitability of stockholders' investments		
$\frac{\text{Net Income}}{\text{Average Stockholders' Equity}}$	$\frac{\$672{,}638}{(\$2{,}284{,}117 + \$2{,}228{,}506) \div 2}$	$\frac{\$564{,}259}{(\$2{,}228{,}506 + \$2{,}090{,}262^{*}) \div 2}$
	$= \frac{\$672{,}638}{\$2{,}256{,}312} = 29.8\%$	$= \frac{\$564{,}259}{\$2{,}159{,}384} = 26.1\%$

*Figures for 2005 are from the five-year selected financial data in Starbucks' Form 10-K, 2006.
Source: Data from Starbucks Corporation, Form 10-K, 2007, and Form 10-K, 2006.

FOCUS ON BUSINESS PRACTICE

What's the Best Way to Measure Performance for Management Compensation?

Efforts to link management compensation to performance measures and the creation of shareholder wealth are increasing. **Starbucks** uses earning per share (EPS) for this purpose. Some other companies, including **Walgreens**, use a better approach. Its use of return on invested capital, which is closely related to return on assets, shows whether or not management is employing the assets profitably. Better still would be to compare the company's return on assets to its cost of debt and equity capital, as does **Target**.[7] Many analysts believe that this measure, which is called *economic value added (EVA)*, is superior to EPS. If the return on assets exceeds the cost of financing the assets with debt and equity, then management is indeed creating value for the shareholders.

Study Note

The analysis of both asset turnover and return on assets is improved if only productive assets are used in the calculations. For example, when investments in unfinished new plant construction or in plants that are now obsolete or nonoperating are removed from the asset base, the result is a better picture of the productivity of assets.

and 2007. Its **asset turnover**, which measures how efficiently assets are used to produce sales, decreased from 2.0 to 1.9 times. The result is a decrease in the company's earning power, or **return on assets**, from 14.2 percent in 2006 to 13.8 percent in 2007. These computations show the relationships (the small difference in the two sets of return on assets figures results from the rounding of the ratios):

	Profit Margin		*Asset Turnover*		*Return on Assets*
	$\frac{\text{Net Income}}{\text{Net Sales}}$	×	$\frac{\text{Net Sales}}{\text{Average Total Assets}}$	=	$\frac{\text{Net Income}}{\text{Average Total Assets}}$
2006	7.2%	×	2.0	=	14.4%
2007	7.1%	×	1.9	=	13.5%

Starbucks' **return on equity** also improved, from 26.1 percent in 2006 to 29.8 percent in 2007.

Although we have used net income in computing profitability ratios for Starbucks, net income is not always a good indicator of a company's sustainable earnings. For instance, if a company has discontinued operations, income from

In addition to using EVA (economic value added) to determine executive compensation, Target uses it to guide capital investment decisions. The company uses a benchmark of 9 percent for the estimated after-tax cost of capital invested in retail operations and a benchmark of 5 percent for capital invested in credit card operations. Target believes that a focus on EVA fosters its objective of increasing average annual earnings per share by 15 percent or more over time.

continuing operations may be a better measure of sustainable earnings. For a company that has one-time items on its income statement—such as restructurings, gains, or losses—income from operations before these items may be a better measure. Some analysts like to use earnings before interest and taxes, or EBIT, for the earnings measure because it excludes the effects of the company's borrowings and the tax rates from the analysis. Whatever figure one uses for earnings, it is important to try to determine the effects of various components on future operations.

Evaluating Long-Term Solvency

Long-term solvency has to do with a company's ability to survive for many years. The aim of evaluating long-term solvency is to detect early signs that a company is headed for financial difficulty. Increasing amounts of debt in a company's capital structure mean that the company is becoming more heavily leveraged. This condition has a negative effect on long-term solvency because it represents increasing legal obligations to pay interest periodically and the principal at maturity. Failure to make those payments can result in bankruptcy.

Study Note

Liquidity is a firm's ability to meet its current obligations; solvency is its ability to meet maturing obligations as they come due without losing the ability to continue operations.

Declining profitability and liquidity ratios are key indicators of possible failure. Two other ratios that analysts consider when assessing long-term solvency are debt to equity and interest coverage, which are shown in Exhibit 10. The **debt to equity ratio** measures capital structure and leverage by showing the amount of a company's assets provided by creditors in relation to the amount provided by stockholders. **Starbucks'** debt to equity ratio increased from 1.0 times in 2006 to 1.3 times in 2007, representing an increased reliance on debt financing. Recall from Exhibit 3 that Starbucks' long-term debt and other liabilities more than doubled. However, the company has little short-term debt and a strong current ratio. Starbucks' long-term solvency is not in danger.

If debt is risky, why have any? The answer is that the level of debt is a matter of balance. Despite its riskiness, debt is a flexible means of financing certain business operations. The interest paid on debt is tax-deductible, whereas dividends on stock are not. Because debt usually carries a fixed interest charge, the cost of financing can be limited, and leverage can be used to advantage. If a company can earn a return on assets greater than the cost of interest, it makes an overall profit. In addition, being a debtor in periods of inflation has advantages because the debt, which is a fixed dollar amount, can be repaid with cheaper dollars.

EXHIBIT 10 Long-term Solvency Ratios of Starbucks Corporation

(Dollar amounts in thousands)	2007	2006
Debt to equity ratio: Measure of capital structure and leverage		
$\frac{\text{Total Liabilities}}{\text{Stockholders' Equity}}$	$\frac{\$3{,}059{,}761}{\$2{,}284{,}117} = 1.3$ times	$\frac{\$2{,}200{,}435}{\$2{,}228{,}506} = 1.0$ times
Interest coverage ratio: Measure of creditors' protection from default on interest payments		
$\frac{\text{Income Before Income Taxes + Interest Expense}}{\text{Interest Expense}}$	$\frac{\$1{,}056{,}364 + \$42{,}100}{\$42{,}100}$	$\frac{\$906{,}243 + \$11{,}100}{\$11{,}100}$
	$= \frac{\$1{,}098{,}464}{\$42{,}100} = 26.1$ times	$= \frac{\$917{,}343}{\$11{,}100} = 82.6$ times

Source: Starbucks Corporation, Form 10-K, 2007.

However, the company runs the risk of not earning a return on assets equal to the cost of financing the assets, thereby incurring a loss.

The **interest coverage ratio** measures the degree of protection creditors have from default on interest payments. Starbucks' interest coverage declined from 82.6 times to 26.1 times due to almost four times as much interest. Nevertheless, interest coverage is still at a very safe level.

Study Note

Because of innovative financing plans and other means of acquiring assets, lease payments and similar types of fixed obligations should be considered when evaluating long-term solvency.

Evaluating the Adequacy of Cash Flows

Because cash flows are needed to pay debts when they are due, cash flow measures are closely related to liquidity and long-term solvency. Exhibit 11 presents **Starbucks'** cash flow adequacy ratios in 2006 and 2007.

Cash flow yield shows the cash-generating ability of a company's operations; it is measured by dividing cash flows from operating activities by net income. Starbucks' net cash flows from operating activities increased from \$1,131,633 thousand in 2006 to \$1,331,221 thousand in 2007. Its cash flow yield was stable at 2.0 times in 2006 and 2007.

Starbucks' ratios for cash flows to sales and cash flows to assets decreased. The company's net sales and average total assets increased faster than the cash flows provided by its operations. **Cash flows to sales**, or the cash-generating ability of sales, decreased from 14.5 to 14.1 percent. **Cash flows to assets**, or the ability of assets to generate operating cash flows, decreased from 28.5 to 27.2 percent.

Starbucks' **free cash flow**, the cash remaining after providing for commitments, also decreased. While the company's net capital expenditures (the difference

EXHIBIT 11 Cash Flow Adequacy Ratios of Starbucks Corporation

(Dollar amounts in thousands)	2007	2006
Cash flow yield: Measure of the ability to generate operating cash flows in relation to net income		
Net Cash Flows from Operating Activities / Net Income	\$1,331,221* / \$672,638 = 2.0 times	\$1,131,633* / \$564,259 = 2.0 times
Cash flows to sales: Measure of the ability of sales to generate operating cash flows		
Net Cash Flows from Operating Activities / Net Sales	\$1,331,221 / \$9,411,497 = 14.1%	\$1,131,633 / \$7,786,942 = 14.5%
Cash flows to assets: Measure of the ability of assets to generate operating cash flows		
Net Cash Flows from Operating Activities / Average Total Assets	\$1,331,221 / (\$5,343,878 + \$4,428,941) ÷ 2	\$1,131,633 / (\$4,428,941 + \$3,513,693*) ÷ 2
	\$1,331,221 / \$4,886,410 = 27.2%	= \$1,131,633 / \$3,971,317 = 28.5%
Free cash flow: Measure of cash remaining after providing for commitments		
Net Cash Flows from Operating Activities − Dividends − Net Capital Expenditures	\$1,331,221 − \$0 − \$1,080,348**	\$1,131,633* − \$0 − \$771,230*
	= \$250,873	= \$360,403

*These figures are from the statement of cash flows in Starbucks' Form 10-K, 2007.
**The 2005 figure is from the five-year selected financial data in Starbucks' Form 10-K, 2006.
Source: Data from Starbucks Corporation, Form 10-K, 2007, and Form 10-K, 2006.

> **Study Note**
>
> When the computation for free cash flow uses "net capital expenditures" in place of "purchases of plant assets minus sales of plant assets," it means that the company's sales of plant assets were too small or immaterial to be broken out.

between purchases and sales of plant assets) increased by over $309 million, the net cash provided by operating activities increased by almost $200 million. Another factor in Starbucks' free cash flows is that the company pays no dividends. Note management's comment regarding future liquidity and cash flows:

> The primary sources of the Company's liquidity are cash flows generated from retail store operations and other business channels, borrowings under available commercial paper programs and credit agreements, proceeds from the issuance of long-term debt securities and the Company's existing cash and liquid investments, which were $460 million and $459 million as of September 30, 2007 and October 1, 2006, respectively. . . . The Company intends to use its cash and liquid investments, including any borrowings under its revolving credit facility, commercial paper program and proceeds from the issuance of long-term debt securities, to invest in its core businesses and other new business opportunities related to its core businesses.[8]

Evaluating Market Strength

Market price is the price at which a company's stock is bought and sold. It indicates how investors view the potential return and risk connected with owning the stock. Market price by itself is not very informative, however, because companies have different numbers of shares outstanding, different earnings, and different dividend policies. Thus, market price must be related to earnings by considering the price/earnings (P/E) ratio and the dividends yield. Those ratios for **Starbucks** appear in Exhibit 12. We computed them by using the average market prices of Starbucks' stock during the fourth quarter of 2006 and 2007.

The **price/earnings (P/E) ratio**, which measures investors' confidence in a company, is the ratio of the market price per share to earnings per share. The P/E ratio is useful in comparing the earnings of different companies and the value of a company's shares in relation to values in the overall market. With a higher P/E ratio, the investor obtains less underlying earnings per dollar invested. Despite an increase in earnings per share from $0.74 in 2006 to $0.90 in 2007, Starbucks' P/E ratio declined from 45.6 times to 30.1 times because the market value of its stock declined from about $34 to about $27. The implication is that investors are not expecting Starbucks to grow as fast in the future as it has in the past.

The **dividends yield** measures a stock's current return to an investor in the form of dividends. Because Starbucks pays no dividends, we can conclude that those who invest in the company expect their return to come from increases in the stock's market value.

EXHIBIT 12 Market Strength Ratios of Starbucks Corporation

	2007	2006
Price/earnings (P/E) ratio: Measure of investors' confidence in a company		
Market Price per Share / Earnings per Share	$27.08* / $0.90 = 30.1 times	$33.78* / $0.74 = 45.6 times
Dividends yield: Measure of a stock's current return to an investor		
Dividends per Share / Market Price per Share	Starbucks does not pay a dividend.	

*Market price is the average for the fourth quarter reported in Starbucks' annual report.
Source: Data from Starbucks Corporation, Form 10-K, 2007.

STOP ▶ REVIEW ▶ APPLY

LO3-1 **Company A and Company B both have net incomes of $1,000,000. Is it possible to conclude from this information that these companies are equally successful? Why or why not?**

LO3-2 **Circo Company has a return on assets of 12 percent and a debt to equity ratio of 0.5. Would you expect return on equity to be more or less than 12 percent?**

LO3-3 **Consider the following statement: "Supermarket executives are beginning to look back with some nostalgia on the days when the standard profit margin was 1 percent of sales. Last year the industry overall margin came to a thin 0.72 percent." How could a supermarket earn a satisfactory return on assets with such a small profit margin?**

LO3-4 **What amount is common to all cash flow adequacy ratios? To what other groups of ratios are the cash flow adequacy ratios most closely related?**

LO3-5 **Which ratios are most relevant to determining the financing period?**

LO3-6 **Company J's stock and Company Q's stock have the same market price. How might you determine whether investors are equally confident about the future of these companies?**

Effects of Transactions on Ratios Sasah's, a retail company, engaged in the transactions listed in the first column of the table below. Opposite each transaction is a ratio and space to mark the effect of each transaction on the ratio.

Transaction	Ratio	Effect: Increase	Effect: Decrease	Effect: None
a. Accrued salaries.	Current ratio			
b. Purchased inventory.	Quick ratio			
c. Increased allowance for uncollectible accounts.	Receivable turnover			
d. Purchased inventory on credit.	Payables turnover			
e. Sold treasury stock.	Profit margin			
f. Borrowed cash by issuing bond payable.	Asset turnover			
g. Paid wages expense.	Return on assets			
h. Repaid bond payable.	Debt to equity			
i. Accrued interest expense.	Interest coverage			
k. Sold merchandise on account.	Return on equity			
l. Recorded depreciation expense.	Cash flow yield			
m. Sold equipment.	Free cash flow			

Show that you understand the effect of business activities on performance measures by placing an *X* in the appropriate column to show whether the transaction increased, decreased, or had no effect on the ratio.

(continued)

SOLUTION

Transaction	Ratio	Effect: Increase	Decrease	None
a. Accrued salaries.	Current ratio		X	
b. Purchased inventory.	Quick ratio		X	
c. Increased allowance for uncollectible accounts.	Receivable turnover	X		
d. Purchased inventory on credit.	Payables turnover		X	
e. Sold treasury stock.	Profit margin			X
f. Borrowed cash by issuing bond payable.	Asset turnover		X	
g. Paid wages expense.	Return on assets		X	
h. Repaid bond payable.	Debt to equity	X		
i. Accrued interest expense.	Interest coverage		X	
k. Sold merchandise on account.	Return on equity	X		
l. Recorded depreciation expense.	Cash flow yield	X		
m. Sold equipment.	Free cash flow	X		

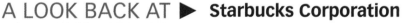

A LOOK BACK AT ▶ Starbucks Corporation

To assess a company's financial performance, managers, stockholders, creditors, and other interested parties use measures that are linked to creating shareholder value. The Financial Highlights at the beginning of the chapter show steady increases in **Starbucks'** revenues, earnings, profit margin, and earnings per share—all good signs, but for a comprehensive view of the company's performance, users of its financial statements must consider the following questions:

- **What standards should be used to evaluate Starbucks' performance?**
- **What analytical tools are available to measure performance?**
- **How successful has the company been in creating value for shareholders?**

Starbucks' performance should be compared with the performance of other companies in the same industry—the specialty retail business. In addition, Starbucks' performance in the current year should be compared with its performance in past years. To make this comparison, users of Starbucks' financial statements employ such techniques as horizontal or trend analysis, vertical analysis, and ratio analysis.

Our comprehensive ratio analysis of Starbucks clearly shows that the company's financial condition improved from 2006 to 2007, as measured by its liquidity, profitability, long-term solvency, and cash flow adequacy ratios. This performance resulted in an increase in earnings per share from $0.74 to $0.90, but was not accompanied by a corresponding increase in shareholder value due to the decline in share price from $34 to $27.

CHAPTER REVIEW

REVIEW of Learning Objectives

LO1 Describe the objectives, standards of comparison, sources of information, and compensation issues in measuring financial performance.

A primary objective in management's use of financial performance measurement is to increase the wealth of the company's stockholders. Creditors and investors use financial performance measurement to judge a company's past performance and current position, as well as its future potential and the risk associated with it. Creditors use the information gained from their analyses to make reliable loans that will be repaid with interest. Investors use the information to make investments that will provide a return that is worth the risk.

Three standards of comparison commonly used in evaluating financial performance are rule-of-thumb measures, a company's past performance, and industry norms. Rule-of-thumb measures are weak because of a lack of evidence that they can be widely applied. A company's past performance can offer a guideline for measuring improvement, but it is not helpful in judging performance relative to the performance of other companies. Although the use of industry norms overcomes this last problem, its disadvantage is that firms are not always comparable, even in the same industry.

The main sources of information about public corporations are reports that the corporations publish themselves, such as annual reports and interim financial statements; reports filed with the SEC; business periodicals; and credit and investment advisory services.

In public corporations, a committee made up of independent directors appointed by the board of directors determines the compensation of top executives. Although earnings per share can be regarded as a "bottom-line" number that encompasses all the other performance measures, using it as the sole basis for determining executive compensation may lead to management practices that are not in the best interests of the company or its stockholders.

LO2 Apply horizontal analysis, trend analysis, vertical analysis, and ratio analysis to financial statements.

Horizontal analysis involves the computation of changes in both dollar amounts and percentages from year to year.

Trend analysis is an extension of horizontal analysis in that it calculates percentage changes for several years. The analyst computes the changes by setting a base year equal to 100 and calculating the results for subsequent years as percentages of the base year.

Vertical analysis uses percentages to show the relationship of the component parts of a financial statement to a total figure in the statement. The resulting financial statements, which are expressed entirely in percentages, are called common-size statements.

Ratio analysis is a technique of financial performance evaluation that identifies key relationships between the components of the financial statements. To interpret ratios correctly, the analyst must have a general understanding of the company and its environment, financial data for several years or for several companies, and an understanding of the data underlying the numerators and denominators.

LO3 Apply ratio analysis to financial statements in a comprehensive evaluation of a company's financial performance.

A comprehensive ratio analysis includes the evaluation of a company's liquidity, as well as its profitability, long-term solvency, cash flow adequacy, and market strength. The ratios for measuring these characteristics are illustrated in Exhibits 8 through 12.

REVIEW of Concepts and Terminology

The following concepts and terms were introduced in this chapter:

Base year: In financial analysis, the first year to be considered in any set of data. **(LO2)**

Common-size statement: A financial statement in which the components are expressed as percentages of a total figure in the statement. **(LO2)**

Compensation committee: A committee of independent directors appointed by a public corporation's board of directors to determine how top executives will be compensated. **(LO1)**

Diversified companies: Companies that operate in more than one industry. Also called *conglomerates.* **(LO1)**

Financial performance measurement: An evaluation method that uses all the techniques available to show how important items in financial statements relate to a company's financial objectives. Also called *financial statement analysis.* **(LO1)**

Free cash flow: A measure of cash remaining after providing for commitments; Net Cash Flows from Operating Activities − Dividends − Purchases of Plant Assets + Sales of Plant Assets. **(LO3)**

Horizontal analysis: A technique for analyzing financial statements in which changes from the previous year to the current year are computed in both dollar amounts and percentages. **(LO2)**

Index number: In trend analysis, a number that shows changes in related items over time and that is calculated by setting the base year equal to 100 percent. **(LO2)**

Interim financial statements: Financial statements issued for a period of less than one year, usually a quarter or a month. **(LO1)**

Operating cycle: The time it takes to sell products and collect for them; days' inventory on hand plus days' sales uncollected. **(LO3)**

Ratio analysis: A technique of financial performance evaluation that identifies key relationships between components of the financial statements. **(LO2)**

Trend analysis: A variation of horizontal analysis in which percentage changes are calculated for several successive years instead of for two years. **(LO2)**

Vertical analysis: A technique for analyzing financial statements that uses percentages to show how the different components of a statement relate to a total figure in the statement. **(LO2)**

Key Ratios

Asset turnover: A measure of how efficiently assets are used to produce sales; Net Sales ÷ Average Total Assets. **(LO3)**

Cash flows to assets: A measure of the ability of assets to generate operating cash flows; Net Cash Flows from Operating Activities ÷ Average Total Assets. **(LO3)**

Cash flows to sales: A measure of the ability of sales to generate operating cash flows; Net Cash Flows from Operating Activities ÷ Net Sales. **(LO3)**

Cash flow yield: A measure of a company's ability to generate operating cash flows in relation to net income; Net Cash Flows from Operating Activities ÷ Net Income. **(LO3)**

Current ratio: A measure of short-term debt-paying ability; Current Assets ÷ Current Liabilities. **(LO3)**

Days' inventory on hand: A measure that shows the average number of days taken to sell inventory; Days in Year ÷ Inventory Turnover. **(LO3)**

Days' payable: A measure that shows the average number of days taken to pay accounts payable; Days in Year ÷ Payables Turnover. **(LO3)**

Days' sales uncollected: A measure that shows the number of days, on average, that a company must wait to receive payment for credit sales; Days in Year ÷ Receivable Turnover. **(LO3)**

Debt to equity ratio: A measure that shows the relationship of debt financing to equity financing, or the extent to which a company is leveraged; Total Liabilities ÷ Stockholders' Equity. **(LO3)**

Dividends yield: A measure of a stock's current return to an investor; Dividends per Share ÷ Market Price per Share. **(LO3)**

Interest coverage ratio: A measure of the degree of protection creditors have from default on interest payments; (Income Before Income Taxes + Interest Expense) ÷ Interest Expense. **(LO3)**

Inventory turnover: A measure of the relative size of inventory; Cost of Goods Sold ÷ Average Inventory. **(LO3)**

Payables turnover: A measure of the relative size of accounts payable; (Cost of Goods Sold +/− Change in Inventory) ÷ Average Accounts Payable. **(LO3)**

Price/earnings (P/E) ratio: A measure of investors' confidence in a company and a means of comparing stock values; Market Price per Share ÷ Earnings per Share. **(LO3)**

Profit margin: A measure that shows the percentage of each revenue dollar that contributes to net income; Net Income ÷ Net Sales. **(LO3)**

Quick ratio: A measure of short-term debt-paying ability; (Cash + Marketable Securities + Receivables) ÷ Current Liabilities. **(LO3)**

Receivable turnover: A measure of the relative size of accounts receivable and the effectiveness of credit policies; Net Sales ÷ Average Accounts Receivable. **(LO3)**

Return on assets: A measure of overall earning power, or profitability, that shows the amount earned on each dollar of assets invested; Net Income ÷ Average Total Assets. **(LO3)**

Return on equity: A measure of how much income was earned on each dollar invested by stockholders; Net Income ÷ Average Stockholders' Equity. **(LO3)**

REVIEW Problem

LO3

Comparative Analysis of Two Companies

Maggie Washington is considering investing in a fast-food restaurant chain because she believes the trend toward eating out more often will continue. She has narrowed her choice to Quik Burger or Big Steak. The balance sheets and income statements of Quik Burger and Big Steak are presented on the opposite page.

The following information pertaining to 2010 is also available to Maggie Washington:

1. Quik Burger's statement of cash flows shows that it had net cash flows from operations of $2,200,000. Big Steak's statement of cash flows shows that its net cash flows from operations were $3,000,000.
2. Net capital expenditures were $2,100,000 for Quik Burger and $1,800,000 for Big Steak.
3. Quik Burger paid dividends of $500,000, and Big Steak paid dividends of $600,000.
4. The market prices of the stocks of Quik Burger and Big Steak were $30 and $20, respectively.

Financial information pertaining to prior years is not readily available to Maggie Washington.

Required

Perform a comprehensive ratio analysis of both Quik Burger and Big Steak following the steps outlined below. Assume that all notes payable of these two companies are current liabilities and that all their bonds payable are long-term liabilities. Show dollar amounts in thousands, use end-of-year balances for averages, assume no change in inventory, and round all ratios and percentages to one decimal place.

1. Prepare an analysis of liquidity.
2. Prepare an analysis of profitability.
3. Prepare an analysis of long-term solvency.
4. Prepare an analysis of cash flow adequacy.
5. Prepare an analysis of market strength.

	Balance Sheets December 31, 2010 (in thousands)	
	Quik Burger	**Big Steak**
Assets		
Cash	$ 2,000	$ 4,500
Accounts receivable (net)	2,000	6,500
Inventory	2,000	5,000
Property, plant, and equipment (net)	20,000	35,000
Other assets	4,000	5,000
Total assets	$30,000	$56,000
Liabilities and Stockholders' Equity		
Accounts payable	$ 2,500	$ 3,000
Notes payable	1,500	4,000
Bonds payable	10,000	30,000
Common stock, $1 par value	1,000	3,000
Additional paid-in capital	9,000	9,000
Retained earnings	6,000	7,000
Total liabilities and stockholders' equity	$30,000	$56,000

	Income Statements For the Year Ended December 31, 2010 (in thousands, except per share amounts)	
	Quik Burger	**Big Steak**
Net sales	$53,000	$86,000
Costs and expenses		
Cost of goods sold	$37,000	$61,000
Selling expenses	7,000	10,000
Administrative expenses	4,000	5,000
Total costs and expenses	$48,000	$76,000
Income from operations	$ 5,000	$10,000
Interest expense	1,400	3,200
Income before income taxes	$ 3,600	$ 6,800
Income Taxes	1,800	3,400
Net income	$ 1,800	$ 3,400
Earnings per share	$ 1.80	$ 1.13

6. In each analysis, indicate the company that apparently had the more favorable ratio. (Consider differences of .1 or less to be neutral.)
7. In what ways would having access to prior years' information aid this analysis?

Answer to Review Problem

Ratio Name	Quik Burger	Big Steak	6. Company with More Favorable Ratio
1. Liquidity analysis			
a. Current ratio	($2,000 + $2,000 + $2,000) / ($2,500 + $1,500) = $6,000 / $4,000 = 1.5 times	($4,500 + $6,500 + $5,000) / ($3,000 + $4,000) = $16,000 / $7,000 = 2.3 times	Big Steak
b. Quick ratio	($2,000 + $2,000) / ($2,500 + $1,500) = $4,000 / $4,000 = 1.0 times	($4,500 + $6,500) / ($3,000 + $4,000) = $11,000 / $7,000 = 1.6 times	Big Steak
c. Receivable turnover	$53,000 / $2,000 = 26.5 times	$86,000 / $6,500 = 13.2 times	Quik Burger
d. Days' sales uncollected	365 days / 26.5 times = 13.8 days	365 days / 13.2 times = 27.6 days	Quik Burger
e. Inventory turnover	$37,000 / $2,000 = 18.5 times	$61,000 / $5,000 = 12.2 times	Quik Burger
f. Days' inventory on hand	365 days / 18.5 times = 19.7 days	365 days / 12.2 times = 29.9 days	Quik Burger
g. Payables turnover	$37,000 / $2,500 = 14.8 times	$61,000 / $3,000 = 20.3 times	Big Steak
h. Days' payable	365 days / 14.8 times = 24.7 days	365 days / 20.3 times = 18.0 days	Big Steak

Note: This analysis indicates the company with the apparently more favorable ratio. Class discussion may focus on conditions under which different conclusions may be drawn.

Ratio Name	Quik Burger	Big Steak	6. Company with More Favorable Ratio
2. Profitability analysis			
a. Profit margin	$1,800 / $53,000 = 3.4%	$3,400 / $86,000 = 4.0%	Big Steak
b. Asset turnover	$53,000 / $30,000 = 1.8 times	$86,000 / $56,000 = 1.5 times	Quik Burger
c. Return on assets	$1,800 / $30,000 = 6.0%	$3,400 / $56,000 = 6.1%	Neutral
d. Return on equity	$1,800 / ($1,000 + $9,000 + $6,000) = $1,800 / $16,000 = 11.3%	$3,400 / ($3,000 + $9,000 + $7,000) = $3,400 / $19,000 = 17.9%	Big Steak

	Ratio Name	Quik Burger	Big Steak	6. Company with More Favorable Ratio
3.	**Long-term solvency analysis**			
a.	Debt to equity ratio	($2,500 + $1,500 + $10,000) / ($1,000 + $9,000 + $6,000)	($3,000 + $4,000 + $30,000) / ($3,000 + $9,000 + $7,000)	Quik Burger
		= $14,000 / $16,000 = 0.9 times	= $37,000 / $19,000 = 1.9 times	
b.	Interest coverage ratio	($3,600 + $1,400) / $1,400	($6,800 + $3,200) / $3,200	Quik Burger
		= $5,000 / $1,400 = 3.6 times	= $10,000 / $3,200 = 3.1 times	

	Ratio Name	Quik Burger	Big Steak	6. Company with More Favorable Ratio
4.	**Cash flow adequacy analysis**			
a.	Cash flow yield	$2,200 / $1,800 = 1.2 times	$3,000 / $3,400 = 0.9 times	Quik Burger
b.	Cash flows to sales	$2,200 / $53,000 = 4.2%	$3,000 / $86,000 = 3.5%	Quik Burger
c.	Cash flows to assets	$2,200 / $30,000 = 7.3%	$3,000 / $56,000 = 5.4%	Quik Burger
d.	Free cash flow	$2,200 – $500 – $2,100	$3,000 – $600 – $1,800	Big Steak
		= ($400)	= $600	

	Ratio Name	Quik Burger	Big Steak	6. Company with More Favorable Ratio
5.	**Market strength analysis**			
a.	Price/earnings ratio	$30 / $1.80 = 16.7 times	$20 / $1.13 = 17.7 times	Big Steak
b.	Dividends yield	($500,000 ÷ 1,000,000) / $30	($600,000 ÷ 3,000,000) / $20	
		= $0.50 / $30 = 1.7%	= $0.20 / $20 = 1.0%	Quik Burger

7. Prior years' information would be helpful in two ways. First, turnover, return, and cash flows to assets ratios could be based on average amounts. Second, a trend analysis could be performed for each company.

CHAPTER ASSIGNMENTS

BUILDING Your Basic Knowledge and Skills

Short Exercises

LO1 **Objectives and Standards of Financial Performance Evaluation**

SE 1. Indicate whether each of the following items is (a) an objective or (b) a standard of comparison of financial statement analysis:

1. Industry norms
2. Assessment of a company's past performance
3. The company's past performance
4. Assessment of future potential and related risk
5. Rule-of-thumb measures

LO1 **Sources of Information**

SE 2. For each piece of information in the list that follows, indicate whether the best source would be (a) reports published by the company, (b) SEC reports, (c) business periodicals, or (d) credit and investment advisory services.

1. Current market value of a company's stock
2. Management's analysis of the past year's operations
3. Objective assessment of a company's financial performance
4. Most complete body of financial disclosures
5. Current events affecting the company

LO2 **Trend Analysis**

SE 3. Using 2009 as the base year, prepare a trend analysis for the following data, and tell whether the results suggest a favorable or unfavorable trend. (Round your answers to one decimal place.)

	2011	2010	2009
Net sales	$158,000	$136,000	$112,000
Accounts receivable (net)	43,000	32,000	21,000

LO2 **Horizontal Analysis**

SE 4. The comparative income statements and balance sheets of Sarot, Inc., appear on the opposite page. Compute the amount and percentage changes for the income statements, and comment on the changes from 2009 to 2010. (Round the percentage changes to one decimal place.)

LO2 **Vertical Analysis**

SE 5. Express the comparative balance sheets of Sarot, Inc., (shown on the opposite page) as common-size statements, and comment on the changes from 2009 to 2010. (Round computations to one decimal place.)

LO3 **Liquidity Analysis**

SE 6. Using the information for Sarot, Inc., in **SE 4** and **SE 5**, compute the current ratio, quick ratio, receivable turnover, days' sales uncollected, inven-

Sarot, Inc.
Comparative Income Statements
For the Years Ended December 31, 2010 and 2009

	2010	2009
Net sales	$720,000	$580,000
Cost of goods sold	448,000	352,000
Gross margin	$272,000	$228,000
Operating expenses	160,000	120,000
Operating income	$112,000	$108,000
Interest expense	28,000	20,000
Income before income taxes	$ 84,000	$ 88,000
Income taxes expense	28,000	32,000
Net income	$ 56,000	$ 56,000
Earnings per share	$ 2.80	$ 2.80

Sarot, Inc.
Comparative Balance Sheets
December 31, 2010 and 2009

	2010	2009
Assets		
Current assets	$ 96,000	$ 80,000
Property, plant, and equipment (net)	520,000	400,000
Total assets	$616,000	$480,000
Liabilities and Stockholders' Equity		
Current liabilities	$ 72,000	$ 88,000
Long-term liabilities	360,000	240,000
Stockholders' equity	184,000	152,000
Total liabilities and stockholders' equity	$616,000	$480,000

tory turnover, days' inventory on hand, payables turnover, and days' payable for 2009 and 2010. Inventories were $16,000 in 2008, $20,000 in 2009, and $28,000 in 2010. Accounts receivable were $24,000 in 2008, $32,000 in 2009, and $40,000 in 2010. Accounts payable were $36,000 in 2008, $40,000 in 2009, and $48,000 in 2010. The company had no marketable securities or prepaid assets. Comment on the results. (Round computations to one decimal place.)

LO3 **Profitability Analysis**

SE 7. Using the information for Sarot, Inc., in **SE 4** and **SE 5**, compute the profit margin, asset turnover, return on assets, and return on equity for 2009 and 2010. In 2008, total assets were $400,000 and total stockholders' equity was $120,000. Comment on the results. (Round computations to one decimal place.)

LO3

Long-term Solvency Analysis

SE 8. Using the information for Sarot, Inc., in **SE 4** and **SE 5**, compute the debt to equity ratio and the interest coverage ratio for 2009 and 2010. Comment on the results. (Round computations to one decimal place.)

LO3

Cash Flow Adequacy Analysis

SE 9. Using the information for Sarot, Inc., in **SE 4**, **SE 5**, and **SE 7**, compute the cash flow yield, cash flows to sales, cash flows to assets, and free cash flow for 2009 and 2010. Net cash flows from operating activities were $84,000 in 2009 and $64,000 in 2010. Net capital expenditures were $120,000 in 2009 and $160,000 in 2010. Cash dividends were $24,000 in both years. Comment on the results. (Round computations to one decimal place.)

LO3

Market Strength Analysis

SE 10. Using the information for Sarot, Inc., in **SE 4**, **SE 5**, and **SE 9**, compute the price/earnings (P/E) ratio and dividends yield for 2009 and 2010. The company had 20,000 shares of common stock outstanding in both years. The price of Sarot's common stock was $60 in 2009 and $40 in 2010. Comment on the results. (Round computations to one decimal place.)

Exercises

LO1 LO2

Discussion Questions

E 1. Develop brief answers to each of the following questions:

1. Why is it essential that management compensation, including bonuses, be linked to financial goals and strategies that achieve shareholder value?
2. How are past performance and industry norms useful in evaluating a company's performance? What are their limitations?
3. In a five-year trend analysis, why do the dollar values remain the same for their respective years while the percentages usually change when a new five-year period is chosen?

LO3

Discussion Questions

E 2. Develop brief answers to each of the following questions:

1. Why does a decrease in receivable turnover create the need for cash from operating activities?
2. Why would ratios that include one balance sheet account and one income statement account, such as receivable turnover or return on assets, be questionable if they came from quarterly or other interim financial reports?
3. What is a limitation of free cash flow in comparing one company to another?

LO1

Issues in Financial Performance Evaluation: Objectives, Standards, Sources of Information, and Executive Compensation

E 3. Identify each of the following as (a) an objective of financial statement analysis, (b) a standard for financial statement analysis, (c) a source of information for financial statement analysis, or (d) an executive compensation issue:

1. Average ratios of other companies in the same industry
2. Assessment of the future potential of an investment
3. Interim financial statements
4. Past ratios of the company
5. SEC Form 10-K
6. Assessment of risk
7. A company's annual report
8. Linking performance to shareholder value

LO2

Trend Analysis

E 4. Using 2006 as the base year, prepare a trend analysis of the following data, and tell whether the situation shown by the trends is favorable or unfavorable. (Round your answers to one decimal place.)

	2010	2009	2008	2007	2006
Net sales	$25,520	$23,980	$24,200	$22,880	$22,000
Cost of goods sold	17,220	15,400	15,540	14,700	14,000
General and administrative expenses	5,280	5,184	5,088	4,896	4,800
Operating income	3,020	3,396	3,572	3,284	3,200

LO2

Horizontal Analysis

E 5. Compute the amount and percentage changes for the following balance sheets for Davis Company, and comment on the changes from 2009 to 2010. (Round the percentage changes to one decimal place.)

Davis Company
Comparative Balance Sheets
December 31, 2010 and 2009

	2010	2009
Assets		
Current assets	$ 18,600	$ 12,800
Property, plant, and equipment (net)	109,464	97,200
Total assets	$128,064	$110,000
Liabilities and Stockholders' Equity		
Current liabilities	$ 11,200	$ 3,200
Long-term liabilities	35,000	40,000
Stockholders' equity	81,864	66,800
Total liabilities and stockholders' equity	$128,064	$110,000

LO2

Vertical Analysis

E 6. Express the partial comparative income statements for Davis Company that follow as common-size statements, and comment on the changes from 2009 to 2010. (Round computations to one decimal place.)

Davis Company
Partial Comparative Income Statements
For the Years Ended December 31, 2010 and 2009

	2010	2009
Net sales	$212,000	$184,000
Cost of goods sold	127,200	119,600
Gross margin	$ 84,800	$ 64,400
Selling expenses	$ 53,000	$ 36,800
General expenses	25,440	18,400
Total operating expenses	$ 78,440	$ 55,200
Operating income	$ 6,360	$ 9,200

Liquidity Analysis

E 7. Partial comparative balance sheet and income statement information for Smith Company is as follows:

	2011	2010
Cash	$ 27,200	$ 20,800
Marketable securities	14,400	34,400
Accounts receivable (net)	89,600	71,200
Inventory	108,800	99,200
Total current assets	$ 240,000	$225,600
Accounts payable	$ 80,000	$ 56,400
Net sales	$ 645,120	$441,440
Cost of goods sold	435,200	406,720
Gross margin	$ 209,920	$ 34,720

In 2009, the year-end balances for Accounts Receivable and Inventory were $64,800 and $102,400, respectively. Accounts Payable was $61,200 in 2009 and is the only current liability. Compute the current ratio, quick ratio, receivable turnover, days' sales uncollected, inventory turnover, days' inventory on hand, payables turnover, and days' payable for each year. (Round computations to one decimal place.) Comment on the change in the company's liquidity position, including its operating cycle and required days of financing from 2010 to 2011.

Turnover Analysis

E 8. Modern Suits Rental has been in business for four years. Because the company has recently had a cash flow problem, management wonders whether there is a problem with receivables or inventories. Here are selected figures from the company's financial statements (in thousands):

	2011	2010	2009	2008
Net sales	$288.0	$224.0	$192.0	$160.0
Cost of goods sold	180.0	144.0	120.0	96.0
Accounts receivable (net)	48.0	40.0	32.0	24.0
Merchandise inventory	56.0	44.0	32.0	20.0
Accounts payable	26.0	20.0	16.0	10.0

Compute the receivable turnover, inventory turnover, and payables turnover for each of the four years, and comment on the results relative to the cash flow problem that the firm has been experiencing. Merchandise inventory was $22,000, accounts receivable were $22,000, and accounts payable were $8,000 in 2007. (Round computations to one decimal place.)

Profitability Analysis

E 9. Barr Company had total assets of $320,000 in 2008, $340,000 in 2009, and $380,000 in 2010. The company's debt to equity ratio was .67 times in all three years. In 2009, Barr had net income of $38,556 on revenues of $612,000. In 2010, it had net income of $49,476 on revenues of $798,000. Compute the profit margin, asset turnover, return on assets, and return on equity for 2009 and 2010. Comment on the apparent cause of the increase or decrease in profitability. (Round the percentages and other ratios to one decimal place.)

LO3 **Long-term Solvency and Market Strength Ratios**

E 10. An investor is trying to decide whether to invest in the long-term bonds and common stock of Companies P and R. Both companies operate in the same industry. Both also pay a dividend per share of $4 and have a yield of 5 percent on their long-term bonds. Other data for the two companies are as follows:

	Company P	Company R
Total assets	$2,400,000	$1,080,000
Total liabilities	1,080,000	594,000
Income before income taxes	288,000	129,600
Interest expense	97,200	53,460
Earnings per share	3.20	5.00
Market price of common stock	40.00	47.50

Compute the debt to equity, interest coverage, and price/earnings (P/E) ratios, as well as the dividends yield, and comment on the results. (Round computations to one decimal place.)

LO3 **Cash Flow Adequacy Analysis**

E 11. Using the data below from the financial statements of Bali, Inc., compute the company's cash flow yield, cash flows to sales, cash flows to assets, and free cash flow. (Round computations to one decimal place.)

Net sales	$1,600,000
Net income	176,000
Net cash flows from operating activities	228,000
Total assets, beginning of year	1,445,000
Total assets, end of year	1,560,000
Cash dividends	60,000
Net capital expenditures	149,000

Problems

LO2 **Horizontal and Vertical Analysis**

P 1. Robert Corporation's condensed comparative balance sheets and condensed comparative income statements for 2011 and 2010 follow.

Robert Corporation
Comparative Balance Sheets
December 31, 2011 and 2010

	2011	2010
Assets		
Cash	$ 40,600	$ 20,400
Accounts receivable (net)	117,800	114,600
Inventory	287,400	297,400
Property, plant, and equipment (net)	375,000	360,000
Total assets	$820,800	$792,400

(continued)

Liabilities and Stockholders' Equity

Accounts payable	$133,800	$238,600
Notes payable (short-term)	100,000	200,000
Bonds payable	200,000	—
Common stock, $10 par value	200,000	200,000
Retained earnings	187,000	153,800
Total liabilities and stockholders' equity	$820,800	$792,400

Robert Corporation
Comparative Income Statements
For the Years Ended December 31, 2011 and 2010

	2011	2010
Net sales	$1,638,400	$1,573,200
Cost of goods sold	1,044,400	1,004,200
Gross margin	$ 594,000	$ 569,000
Operating expenses		
Selling expenses	$ 238,400	$ 259,000
Administrative expenses	223,600	211,600
Total operating expenses	$ 462,000	$ 470,600
Income from operations	$ 132,000	$ 98,400
Interest expense	32,800	19,600
Income before income taxes	$ 99,200	$ 78,800
Income taxes expense	31,200	28,400
Net income	$ 68,000	$ 50,400
Earnings per share	$ 3.40	$ 2.52

Required

1. Prepare schedules showing the amount and percentage changes from 2010 to 2011 for the comparative income statements and the balance sheets.
2. Prepare common-size income statements and balance sheets for 2010 and 2011.

User insight ▶ 3. Comment on the results in requirements **1** and **2** by identifying favorable and unfavorable changes in the components and composition of the statements.

Effects of Transactions on Ratios

P 2. Sung Corporation, a clothing retailer, engaged in the transactions listed in the first column of the table that follows. Opposite each transaction is a ratio and space to mark the effect of each transaction on the ratio.

Transaction	Ratio	Effect: Increase	Effect: Decrease	Effect: None
a. Issued common stock for cash.	Asset turnover			
b. Declared cash dividend.	Current ratio			
c. Sold treasury stock.	Return on equity			
d. Borrowed cash by issuing note payable.	Debt to equity ratio			
e. Paid salaries expense.	Inventory turnover			
f. Purchased merchandise for cash.	Current ratio			
g. Sold equipment for cash.	Receivable turnover			

(continued)

Transaction	Ratio	Effect: Increase	Decrease	None
h. Sold merchandise on account.	Quick ratio			
i. Paid current portion of long-term debt.	Return on assets			
j. Gave sales discount.	Profit margin			
k. Purchased marketable securities for cash.	Quick ratio			
l. Declared 5% stock dividend.	Current ratio			
m. Purchased a building.	Free cash flow			

Required

User insight ▶ Show that you understand the effect of business activities on performance measures by placing an X in the appropriate column to show whether the transaction increased, decreased, or had no effect on the indicated ratio.

Comprehensive Ratio Analysis

P 3. The condensed comparative income statements of Tola Corporation appear below. The corporation's condensed comparative balance sheets are presented on the next page. All figures are given in thousands of dollars, except earnings per share and market price per share.

Additional data for Tola Corporation in 2011 and 2010 are as follows:

	2011	2010
Net cash flows from operating activities	$32,000	$49,500
Net capital expenditures	$59,500	$19,000
Dividends paid	$15,700	$17,500
Number of common shares	15,000	15,000
Market price per share	$40	$60

Balances of selected accounts at the end of 2009 were accounts receivable (net), $26,350; inventory, $49,700; accounts payable, $32,400; total assets, $323,900; and stockholder's equity, $188,300. All of the bonds payable were long-term liabilities.

Tola Corporation
Comparative Income Statements
For the Years Ended December 31, 2011 and 2010

	2011	2010
Net sales	$400,200	$371,300
Cost of goods sold	227,050	198,100
Gross margin	$173,150	$173,200
Operating expenses		
Selling expenses	$ 65,050	$ 52,300
Administrative expenses	70,150	57,750
Total operating expenses	$135,200	$110,050
Income from operations	$ 37,950	$ 63,150
Interest expense	12,500	10,000
Income before income taxes	$ 25,450	$ 53,150
Income taxes expense	7,000	17,500
Net income	$ 18,450	$ 35,650
Earnings per share	$ 1.23	$ 2.38

Tola Corporation
Comparative Balance Sheets
December 31, 2011 and 2010

	2011	2010
Assets		
Cash	$ 15,550	$ 13,600
Accounts receivable (net)	36,250	21,350
Inventory	61,300	53,900
Property, plant, and equipment (net)	288,850	253,750
Total assets	$401,950	$342,600
Liabilities and Stockholders' Equity		
Accounts payable	$ 52,350	$ 36,150
Notes payable	25,000	25,000
Bonds payable	100,000	55,000
Common stock, $10 par value	150,000	150,000
Retained earnings	74,600	76,450
Total liabilities and stockholders' equity	$401,950	$342,600

Required

Perform the following analyses. Round percentages and ratios to one decimal place.

1. Prepare a liquidity analysis by calculating for each year the (a) current ratio, (b) quick ratio, (c) receivable turnover, (d) days' sales uncollected, (e) inventory turnover, (f) days' inventory on hand, (g) payables turnover, and (h) days' payable.
2. Prepare a profitability analysis by calculating for each year the (a) profit margin, (b) asset turnover, (c) return on assets, and (d) return on equity.
3. Prepare a long-term solvency analysis by calculating for each year the (a) debt to equity ratio and (b) interest coverage ratio.
4. Prepare a cash flow adequacy analysis by calculating for each year the (a) cash flow yield, (b) cash flows to sales, (c) cash flows to assets, and (d) free cash flow.
5. Prepare an analysis of market strength by calculating for each year the (a) price/earnings (P/E) ratio and (b) dividends yield.

User insight ▶ 6. After making the calculations, indicate whether each ratio improved or deteriorated from 2010 to 2011 (use *F* for favorable and *U* for unfavorable and consider changes of .1 or less to be neutral).

LO3 **Comprehensive Ratio Analysis of Two Companies**

P 4. Agnes Ball is considering an investment in the common stock of a chain of retail department stores. She has narrowed her choice to two retail companies, Fast Corporation and Style Corporation, whose income statements and balance sheets are presented on the opposite page.

During the year, Fast Corporation paid a total of $50,000 in dividends. The market price per share of its stock is currently $60. In comparison, Style Corporation paid a total of $114,000 in dividends, and the current market price of its stock is $76 per share. Fast Corporation had net cash flows from operations of $271,500 and net capital expenditures of $625,000. Style Corporation had net cash flows from operations of $492,500 and net capital

Income Statements

	Fast	Style
Net sales	$12,560,000	$25,210,000
Costs and expenses		
Cost of goods sold	$ 6,142,000	$14,834,000
Selling expenses	4,822,600	7,108,200
Administrative expenses	986,000	2,434,000
Total costs and expenses	$11,950,600	$24,376,200
Income from operations	$ 609,400	$ 833,800
Interest expense	194,000	228,000
Income before income taxes	$ 415,400	$ 605,800
Income taxes expense	200,000	300,000
Net income	$ 215,400	$ 305,800
Earnings per share	$ 4.31	$ 10.19

Balance Sheets

	Fast	Style
Assets		
Cash	$ 80,000	$ 192,400
Marketable securities (at cost)	203,400	84,600
Accounts receivable (net)	552,800	985,400
Inventory	629,800	1,253,400
Prepaid expenses	54,400	114,000
Property, plant, and equipment (net)	2,913,600	6,552,000
Intangibles and other assets	553,200	144,800
Total assets	$4,987,200	$9,326,600
Liabilities and Stockholders' Equity		
Accounts payable	$ 344,000	$ 572,600
Notes payable	150,000	400,000
Income taxes payable	50,200	73,400
Bonds payable	2,000,000	2,000,000
Common stock, $20 par value	1,000,000	600,000
Additional paid-in capital	609,800	3,568,600
Retained earnings	833,200	2,112,000
Total liabilities and stockholders' equity	$4,987,200	$9,326,600

expenditures of $1,050,000. Information for prior years is not readily available. Assume that all notes payable are current liabilities and all bonds payable are long-term liabilities and that there is no change in inventory.

Required

Conduct a comprehensive ratio analysis for each company, following the steps outlined on the next page. Compare the results. Round percentages and ratios to one decimal place, and consider changes of .1 or less to be indeterminate.

1. Prepare a liquidity analysis by calculating for each company the (a) current ratio, (b) quick ratio, (c) receivable turnover, (d) days' sales uncollected, (e) inventory turnover, (f) days' inventory on hand, (g) payables turnover, and (h) days' payable.
2. Prepare a profitability analysis by calculating for each company the (a) profit margin, (b) asset turnover, (c) return on assets, and (d) return on equity.
3. Prepare a long-term solvency analysis by calculating for each company the (a) debt to equity ratio and (b) interest coverage ratio.
4. Prepare a cash flow adequacy analysis by calculating for each company the (a) cash flow yield, (b) cash flows to sales, (c) cash flows to assets, and (d) free cash flow.
5. Prepare an analysis of market strength by calculating for each company the (a) price/earnings (P/E) ratio and (b) dividends yield.

User insight ▶ 6. Compare the two companies by inserting the ratio calculations from 1 through 5 in a table with the following column headings: Ratio, Name, Fast, Style, and Company with More Favorable Ratio. Indicate in the last column which company had the more favorable ratio in each case.

User insight ▶ 7. How could the analysis be improved if information about these companies' prior years were available?

Alternate Problems

LO3

Effects of Transactions on Ratios

P 5. Lim Corporation engaged in the transactions listed in the first column of the following table. Opposite each transaction is a ratio and space to indicate the effect of each transaction on the ratio.

Transaction	Ratio	Effect: Increase	Effect: Decrease	Effect: None
a. Sold merchandise on account.	Current ratio			
b. Sold merchandise on account.	Inventory turnover			
c. Collected on accounts receivable.	Quick ratio			
d. Wrote off an uncollectible account.	Receivable turnover			
e. Paid on accounts payable.	Current ratio			
f. Declared cash dividend.	Return on equity			
g. Incurred advertising expense.	Profit margin			
h. Issued stock dividend.	Debt to equity ratio			
i. Issued bonds payable.	Asset turnover			
j. Accrued interest expense.	Current ratio			
k. Paid previously declared cash dividend.	Dividends yield			
l. Purchased treasury stock.	Return on assets			
m. Recorded depreciation expense.	Cash flow yield			

Required

User insight ▶ Show that you understand the effect of business activities on performance measures by placing an *X* in the appropriate column to show whether the transaction increased, decreased, or had no effect on the indicated ratio.

LO3

Comprehensive Ratio Analysis

P 6. Data for Robert Corporation in 2011and 2010 follow. These data should be used in conjunction with the data in **P 1**.

	2011	2010
Net cash flows from operating activities	($98,000)	$72,000
Net capital expenditures	$20,000	$32,500
Dividends paid	$22,000	$17,200
Number of common shares	20,000	20,000
Market price per share	$18	$30

Selected balances at the end of 2009 were accounts receivable (net), $103,400; inventory, $273,600; total assets, $732,800; accounts payable, $193,300; and stockholders' equity, $320,600. All Robert's notes payable were current liabilities; all its bonds payable were long-term liabilities.

Required

Perform a comprehensive ratio analysis following the steps outlined below. Round all answers to one decimal place.

1. Prepare a liquidity analysis by calculating for each year the (a) current ratio, (b) quick ratio, (c) receivable turnover, (d) days' sales uncollected, (e) inventory turnover, (f) days' inventory on hand, (g) payables turnover, and (h) days' payable.
2. Prepare a profitability analysis by calculating for each year the (a) profit margin, (b) asset turnover, (c) return on assets, and (d) return on equity.
3. Prepare a long-term solvency analysis by calculating for each year the (a) debt to equity ratio and (b) interest coverage ratio.
4. Prepare a cash flow adequacy analysis by calculating for each year the (a) cash flow yield, (b) cash flows to sales, (c) cash flows to assets, and (d) free cash flow.
5. Prepare a market strength analysis by calculating for each year the (a) price/earnings (P/E) ratio and (b) dividends yield.

User insight ▶

6. After making the calculations, indicate whether each ratio improved or deteriorated from 2010 to 2011 (use *F* for favorable and *U* for unfavorable and consider changes of .1 or less to be neutral).

ENHANCING Your Knowledge, Skills, and Critical Thinking

Conceptual Understanding Cases

LO1 LO3

Standards for Financial Performance Evaluation

C 1. In a dramatic move, **Standard & Poor's Ratings Group**, the large financial company that evaluates the riskiness of companies' debt, downgraded its rating of **General Motors** and **Ford Motor Co**. debt to "junk" bond status because of concerns about the companies' profitability and cash flows. Despite aggressive cost cutting, both companies still face substantial future liabilities for health-care and pension obligations. They are losing money or barely breaking even on auto operations that concentrate on slow-selling SUVs. High gas prices and competition force them to sell the cars at a discount. The companies are counting on SUVs to make a comeback.[9]

What standards do you think Standard & Poor's would use to evaluate Ford's progress? What performance measures would Standard & Poor's most likely use in making its evaluation?

LO1

Using Segment Information

C 2. Refer to Exhibit 1, which shows the segment information of **Goodyear Tire & Rubber Company**. In what business segments does Goodyear operate? What is the relative size of its business segments in terms of sales and income in the most recent year shown? Which segment is most profitable in terms of return on assets? In which region of the world is the tires segment largest, and which tire segment is most profitable in terms of return on assets?

LO1

Using Investors' Services

C 3. Refer to Exhibit 2, which contains the **PepsiCo Inc.** listing from Mergent's *Handbook of Dividend Achievers*. Assume that an investor has asked you to assess PepsiCo's recent history and prospects. Write a memorandum to the investor that addresses the following points:

1. PepsiCo's earnings history. What has been the general relationship between PepsiCo's return on assets and its return on equity over the last seven years? What does this tell you about the way the company is financed? What figures back up your conclusion?
2. The trend of PepsiCo's stock price and price/earnings (P/E) ratio for the seven years shown.
3. PepsiCo's prospects, including developments likely to affect the company's future.

Interpreting Financial Reports

LO2

Trend Analysis

C 4. H. J. Heinz Company is a global company engaged in several lines of business, including food service, infant foods, condiments, pet foods, and weight-control food products. Below is a five-year summary of operations and other related data for Heinz.[10] (Amounts are expressed in thousands.)

H. J. Heinz Company and Subsidiaries
Five-Year Summary of Operations and Other Related Data

	2007	2006	2005	2004	2003
Summary of operations					
Sales	$ 9,001,630	$8,643,438	$ 8,103,456	$7,625,831	$7,566,800
Cost of products sold	5,608,730	5,550,364	5,069,926	4,733,314	4,825,462
Interest expense	333,270	316,296	232,088	211,382	222,729
Provision for income taxes	332,797	250,700	299,511	352,117	283,541
Net income (before special items)	791,602	442,761	688,004	715,451	400,491
Other related data					
Dividends paid: common	461,224	408,137	398,854	379,910	521,592
Total assets	10,033,026	9,737,767	10,577,718	9,877,189	9,224,751
Total debt	4,881,884	4,411,982	4,695,253	4,974,430	4,930,929
Shareholders' equity	1,841,683	2,048,823	2,602,573	1,894,189	1,199,157

Prepare a trend analysis for Heinz with 2003 as the base year and discuss the results. Identify important trends and state whether the trends are favorable or unfavorable. Discuss significant relationships among the trends.

Decision Analysis Using Excel

LO2 LO3

Effect of a One-Time Item on a Loan Decision

C 5. Apple a Day, Inc., and Unforgettable Edibles, Inc. are food catering businesses that operate in the same metropolitan area. Their customers include Fortune 500 companies, regional firms, and individuals. The two firms reported similar profit margins for the current year, and both base bonuses for managers on the achievement of a target profit margin and return on equity. Each firm has submitted a loan request to you, a loan officer for City National Bank. They have provided you with the following information:

	Apple a Day	Unforgettable Edibles
Net sales	$625,348	$717,900
Cost of goods sold	225,125	287,080
Gross margin	$400,223	$430,820
Operating expenses	281,300	371,565
Operating income	$118,923	$ 59,255
Gain on sale of real estate	—	81,923
Interest expense	(9,333)	(15,338)
Income before income taxes	$109,590	$125,840
Income taxes expense	25,990	29,525
Net income	$ 83,600	$ 96,315
Average stockholders' equity	$312,700	$390,560

1. Perform a vertical analysis and prepare a common-size income statement for each firm. Compute profit margin and return on equity.
2. Discuss these results, the bonus plan for management, and loan considerations. Identify the company that is the better loan risk.

Annual Report Case: CVS Caremark Corporation

Comprehensive Ratio Analysis

C 6. Using data from the **CVS** annual report in the Supplement to Chapter 1, conduct a comprehensive ratio analysis that compares the company's performance in 2007 and 2006. If you have computed ratios for CVS in previous chapters, you may prepare a table that summarizes the ratios and show calculations only for the ratios you have not previously calculated. If this is the first ratio analysis you have done for CVS, show all your computations. In either case, after each group of ratios, comment on the performance of CVS. Round your calculations to one decimal place. Prepare and comment on the following categories of ratios:

Liquidity analysis: current ratio, quick ratio, receivable turnover, days' sales uncollected, inventory turnover, days' inventory on hand, payables turnover, and days' payable. (Accounts Receivable, Inventories, and Accounts Payable were [in millions] $1,841.6, $6,484.8, and $2,125.4, respectively, in 2005.)

Profitability analysis: profit margin, asset turnover, return on assets, and return on equity. (Total assets and total shareholders' equity were [in millions] $15,246.6 and $8,331.2, respectively, in 2005.)

Long-term solvency analysis: debt to equity ratio and interest coverage ratio.

Cash flow adequacy analysis: cash flow yield, cash flows to sales, cash flows to assets, and free cash flow.

Market strength analysis: price/earnings (P/E) ratio and dividends yield.

Comparison Case: CVS Versus Southwest

Comparison of Key Financial Performance Measures

LO3

K/R

C 7. Refer to the annual report of **CVS** and the financial statements of **Southwest Airlines Co.** in the Supplement to Chapter 1. Prepare a table for the following key financial performance measures for the two most recent years for both companies. Use your computations in **C6** or perform those analyses if you have not done so. Total assets for Southwest in 2005 were $14,003 million.

Profitability:	profit margin asset turnover return on assets
Long-term solvency:	debt to equity ratio
Cash flow adequacy:	cash flow yield free cash flow

Evaluate and comment on the relative performance of the two companies with respect to each of the above categories.

Ethical Dilemma Case

Executive Compensation

LO1

C 8. Executive compensation is often based on meeting certain targets for revenue growth, earnings, earnings per share, return on assets, or other performance measures. But what if performance is not living up to expectations? Some companies are simply changing the targets. For instance, **Sun Microsystems'** proxy as quoted in *The Wall Street Journal* states that "due to economic challenges experienced during the last fiscal year, our earnings per share and revenues are significantly below plan. As such, the Bonus Plan was amended to reduce the target bonus to 50% of the original plan and base the target bonus solely on the third and fourth quarters."[11] Sun Microsystems was not alone. Other companies, such as **AT&T Wireless**, **Estee Lauder**, and **UST**, also lowered targets for executive bonuses.

Do you think it is acceptable to change the bonus targets for executives during the year if the year turns out to be not as successful as planned? What if an unexpected, world-shaking event occurs and has a negative effect on business, such as 9/11 had on the airline industry? What are three standards of comparison? Which of these might justify changing the bonus targets during the year?

Internet Case

Using Investors' Services

LO1

C 9. Go to the website for **Moody's Investors Service**. Click on "ratings," which will show revisions of debt ratings issued by Moody's in the past few days. Choose a rating that has been upgraded or downgraded and read the short press announcement related to it. What reasons does Moody's give for the change in rating? What is Moody's assessment of the future of the company or institution? What financial performance measures are mentioned in the article? Summarize your findings and be prepared to share them in class.

Group Activity Case

LO3

Analyzing the Airline Industry

C 10. Divide into groups. Assume your group is analyzing the fate of the larger airlines, such as **United** and **American**. You have the following information:

a. Between 1999 and now, the long-term debt, including lease obligations, of the largest airlines more than doubled.
b. The price of fuel has increased by one-third.
c. Passenger loads are only now getting back to pre-9/11 levels.
d. Severe price competition from discount airlines exists.

Identify the ratios that you consider most important to consider in assessing the future of the large airlines and discuss the effect of each of the above factors on the ratios. Be prepared to present all or part of your findings in class.

Business Communication Case

Comparison of International Companies' Operating Cycles

C 11. Ratio analysis enables one to compare the performance of companies whose financial statements are presented in different currencies. Selected data from 2006 for two large pharmaceutical companies—one American, **Pfizer, Inc.**, and one Swiss, **Roche**—are presented below (in millions).[12]

	Pfizer, Inc. (U.S.)	Roche (Swiss)
Net sales	$48,371	SF42,041
Cost of goods sold	7,640	10,616
Accounts receivable	9,392	8,960
Inventories	6,111	5,592
Accounts payable	2,019	2,213

For each company, calculate the receivable turnover, days' sales uncollected, inventory turnover, days' inventory on hand, payables turnover, and days' payable. Then determine the operating cycle and days of financing required for each company. (Accounts receivable in 2005 were $9,103 for Pfizer and SF7,698 for Roche. Inventories in 2005 were $5,478 for Pfizer and SF5,041 for Roche. Accounts payable in 2005 were $2,073 for Pfizer and SF2,373 for Roche.) Prepare a memo containing your analysis of the operating cycles of these companies.

CHAPTER

15 Investments

Focus on Financial Statements

INCOME STATEMENT
Revenues
– Expenses
= Net Income

STATEMENT OF RETAINED EARNINGS
Opening Balance
+ Net Income
– Dividends
= Retained Earnings

BALANCE SHEET
Assets | Liabilities
Equity
A = L + E

STATEMENT OF CASH FLOWS
Operating activities
+ Investing activities
+ Financing activities
= Change in Cash
+ Starting Balance
= Ending Cash Balance

Sales of investments for cash, a financing activity on cash flow statement, may result in gain/loss on income statement and affect operating activities on cash flow statement.

Many companies invest in the stock or debt securities of other firms. They may do so for several reasons. A company may temporarily have excess funds on which it can earn a return, or investments may be an integral part of its business, as in the case of a bank. A company may also invest in other firms for the purpose of partnering with or controlling them. This chapter presents an overview of both short-term and long-term investments, including the importance of avoiding unethical trading in securities.

LEARNING OBJECTIVES

LO1 **Identify and explain the management issues related to investments.** *(pp. 754–758)*

LO2 **Explain the financial reporting implications of short-term investments.** *(pp. 758–761)*

LO3 **Explain the financial reporting implications of long-term investments in stock and the cost-adjusted-to-market and equity methods used to account for them.** *(pp. 761–766)*

LO4 **Explain the financial reporting implications of consolidated financial statements.** *(pp. 766–774)*

LO5 **Explain the financial reporting implications of debt investments.** *(pp. 774–776)*

DECISION POINT ▶ A USER'S FOCUS

eBAY, INC.

eBay, the world's largest online trading company, enables a global community of buyers and sellers to interact and trade with one another. Since the company went public in 1998, it has grown very rapidly. In addition to having expanded its core business, it has grown by investing in and acquiring other companies. It has also invested cash in the debt securities of other companies. As you can see in eBay's Financial Highlights, these investments and the related accounts are important components of its financial statements.[1]

▶ **What are the effects of eBay's investments on its financial performance?**

▶ **How does eBay's acquisition of other companies affect its financial performance?**

EBAY'S FINANCIAL HIGHLIGHTS (In millions)

	2007	2006
Balance sheet		
Short-term investments	$ 667	$ 555
Long-term investments	138	278
Goodwill	6,257	6,544
Total assets	15,366	13,494
Income Statement		
Interest and other income, net	$ 154	$ 130
Impairment of goodwill	1,391	0
Income from operations	613	1,423
Statement of Cash Flows		
Cash flows from investing activities		
Purchases of investments	($ 271)	($ 583)
Sales of investments	889	1,380
Acquisitions, net of cash required	(864)	(46)

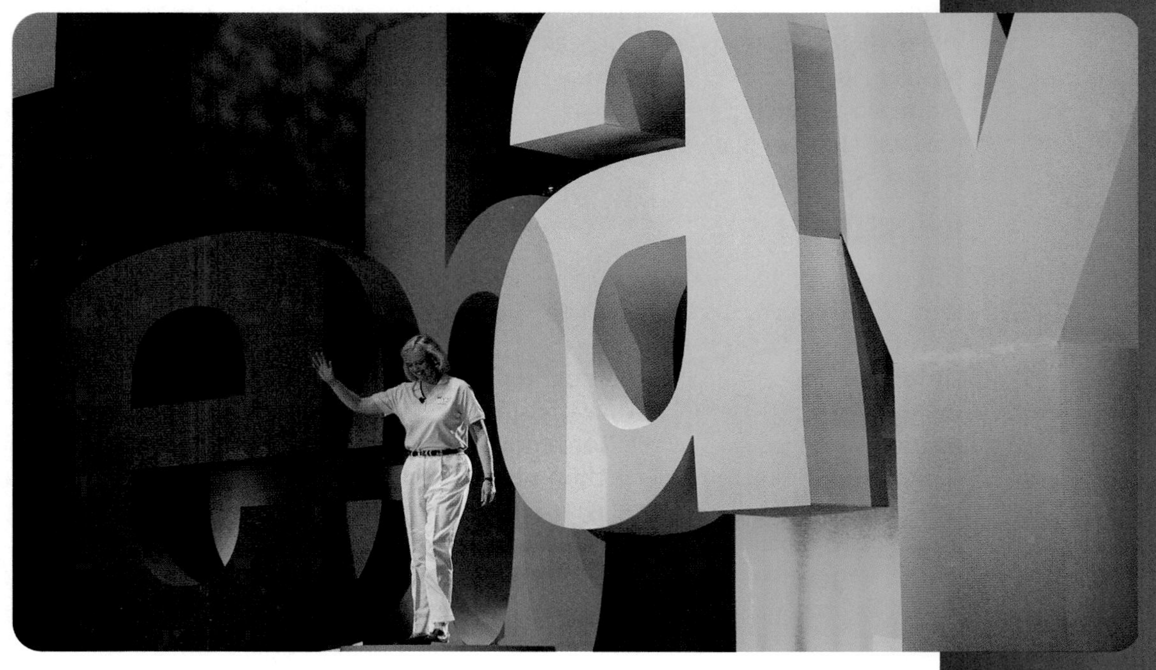

Management Issues Related to Investments

LO1 Identify and explain the management issues related to investments.

In making investments, **eBay's** management, like the management of any company, must understand issues related to the recognition, valuation, classification, disclosure, and ethics of investments.

Recognition

Recognition of investments as assets follows the general rule for recording transactions that we described earlier in the text. Purchases of investments are recorded on the date on which they are made, and sales of investments are reported on the date of sale. At the time of the transaction, there is either a transfer of funds or a definite obligation to pay. Income from investments is reported as other income on the income statement. Any gains or losses on investments are also reported on the income statement. Gains and losses appear as adjustments in the operating activities section of the statement of cash flows. The cash amounts of purchases and sales of investments appear in the investing activities section of the statement of cash flows.

CASH FLOW

Valuation

Like other purchase transactions, investments are valued according to the *cost principle*—that is, they are valued in terms of their cost at the time they are purchased. The cost, or purchase price, includes any commissions or fees. However, after the purchase, the value of investments on the balance sheet is adjusted to reflect subsequent conditions. These conditions may reflect changes in the market value or fair value of the investments, changes caused by the passage of time (as in amortization), or changes in the operations of the investee companies. Long-term investments must be evaluated annually for any impairment or decline in value that is more than temporary. If such an impairment exists, a loss on the investment must be recorded.

Under a new accounting standard, companies may elect to measure investments at fair value. Recall that **fair value** is defined as the *exchange price* associated with an actual or potential business transaction between market participants. This option applies to all investments discussed in this chapter, except in the case of an investment in a subsidiary that is consolidated with the parent's financial statements. Generally, companies can elect the investments to which they want to apply fair value, but having done so, they cannot change the use of fair value in the future. Fair value is not difficult to determine when there is a ready market in which there are buyers and sellers for an asset, but its determination becomes more problematic when there is no ready market. In the latter case, the fair value must be estimated through a method such as net present value.[2] The goal is to bring U.S. practices more in line with international financial reporting standards.

Classification

Investments in debt and equity securities are classified as either short-term or long-term. **Short-term investments**, also called **marketable securities**, have a maturity of more than 90 days but are intended to be held only until cash is needed for current operations. (As we pointed out in an earlier chapter, investments with a maturity of *less* than 90 days are classified as cash equivalents.) *Long-term investments* are intended to be held for more than one year. Long-term investments are reported in the investments section of the balance sheet, not in the current assets section. Although long-term investments may be just as marketable as short-term assets, management intends to hold them for an indefinite time.

Short-term and long-term investments must be further classified as trading securities, available-for-sale securities, or held-to-maturity securities.[3]

FOCUS ON BUSINESS PRACTICE

What Role Did Accounting Play in the Sub-Prime Mortgage Collapse?

Investment banks and brokers have been in the news as they have experienced spectacular losses related to sub-prime mortgage securities. **UBS**, the large Swiss bank, had write-offs of $18.4 billion. **Bear Stearns**, the large U.S. brokerage company, saw its stock drop from more than $90 per share to $2 per share in less than a week when it was bailed out by the Federal Reserve and **J.P. Morgan**. What is going on? When interest rates rose and home prices fell, the fair value of the mortgages that backed up securities held by these companies dropped. Under accounting standards, the companies were required to write drown the securities to their fair value, which was now substantially below the carrying value. The accounting rules that brought these losses to light are challenged in an editorial in *The Wall Street Journal*, which called fair value accounting a "fabulous failure" and predicts substantial write-ups once the crisis is over.[4] The supporters of fair value argue that the write-offs are not caused by accounting but reflect a real decline in value and that investors should have been able to act on this information as soon as possible.

- **Trading securities** are debt or equity securities bought and held principally for the purpose of being sold in the near term.
- **Available-for-sale securities** are debt or equity securities that do not meet the criteria for either trading or held-to-maturity securities. They may be short-term or long-term depending on what management intends to do with them.
- **Held-to-maturity securities** are debt securities that management intends to hold until their maturity date.

Figure 1 illustrates the classification of short-term and long-term investments. Table 1 shows the relationship between the percentage of ownership in a company's stock and the investing company's level of control, as well as the classifications and accounting treatments of these stock investments. These classifications are important because each one requires a different accounting treatment. We discuss the accounting treatments later in this chapter.

In general, the percentage of ownership in another company's stock has the following effects:

- *Noninfluential and noncontrolling investment*: A firm that owns less than 20 percent of the stock of another company has no influence on the other company's operations.

FIGURE 1 Classification of Investments

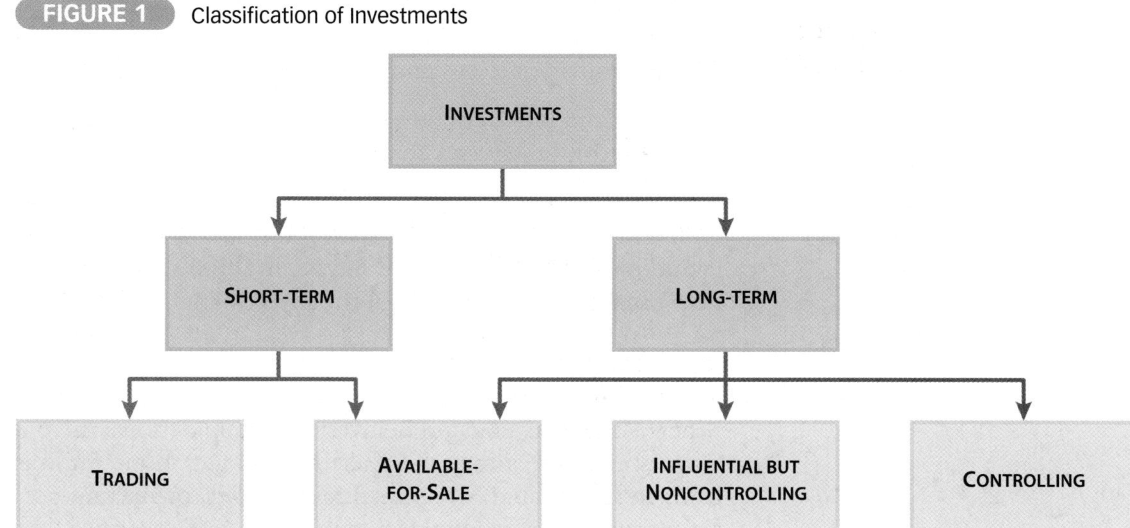

TABLE 1
Accounting for Equity Investments

Level of Control	Percentage of Ownership	Classification	Accounting Treatment
Noninfluential and noncontrolling	Less than 20%	Short-term investments—trading securities	Recorded at cost initially; cost adjusted after purchase for changes in market value; unrealized gains and losses reported on income statement
		Short-term or long-term investments—available-for-sale securities	Recorded at cost initially; cost adjusted for changes in market value with unrealized gains and losses to stockholders' equity
Influential but noncontrolling	Between 20% and 50%	Long-term investments	Equity method: recorded at cost initially; cost subsequently adjusted for investor's share of net income or loss and for dividends received
Controlling	More than 50%	Long-term investments	Financial statements consolidated

- *Influential but noncontrolling investment*: A firm that owns between 20 to 50 percent of another company's stock can exercise **significant influence** over that company's operating and financial policies, even though it holds 50 percent or less of the voting stock. Indications of significant influence include representation on the board of directors, participation in policymaking, exchange of managerial personnel, and technological dependency between the two companies.
- *Controlling investment*: A firm that owns more than 50 percent of another company's stock can exercise **control** over that company's operating and financial policies.

Study Note

Influence and control are related specifically to equity holdings, not debt holdings.

Disclosure

Companies provide detailed information about their investments and how they account for them in the notes to their financial statements. For instance, in 2007, in a note summarizing its significant accounting policies, **eBay** made this disclosure:

> Short and long-term investments, which include marketable equity securities, government and corporate bonds, are classified as available for sale and reported at fair value. . . .[5]

eBay's notes also provide detailed information about the company's acquisitions, including Stubhub, Inc., and Skype, in 2005, 2006, and 2007. Such disclosures help users assess the impact of the investments.

Ethics of Investing

When a company engages in investment transactions, there is always the possibility that its employees may use their knowledge about the transactions for personal gain. In the United States, **insider trading**, or making use of inside information for personal gain, is unethical and illegal. Before a publicly held company releases

FOCUS ON BUSINESS PRACTICE

What Are Special-Purpose Entities?

When **Enron** imploded in 2001 and its use of special purpose entities (SPEs) was widely reported, many accountants were unaware of the intricacies of accounting for these entities. SPEs are firms with limited lives that are created to achieve a specific objective (or objectives) of the parent company. They may take the form of a partnership, corporation, trust, or joint venture. SPEs have been around since the 1970s and have been used primarily by banks and other financial institutions as a way of raising funds by bundling together receivables and other loans into packages that can be sold to investors or used to borrow funds. Enron turned this use of SPEs on its head. It used its SPEs to transfer assets and any related debt off its balance sheet, conceal its losses and borrow money, and generally make its financial statements look far better than they actually were. By setting up the SPEs as partnerships and using the arcane accounting rules for SPEs, Enron was able to avoid consolidating these entities even though it kept a 97 percent ownership in them. The FASB has since clarified the accounting rules for SPEs, which it calls Variable Interest Entities (VIEs).[6]

significant information about an investment to its stockholders and the general public, its officers and employees are not allowed to buy or sell stock in the company or in the firm whose shares the company is buying. Only after the information is released to the public can insiders engage in such trading. The Securities and Exchange Commission vigorously prosecutes any individual, whether employed by the company in question or not, who buys or sells shares of a publicly held company based on information not yet available to the public.

Not all countries prohibit insider trading. Until recently, insider trading was legal in Germany, but with the goal of expanding its securities markets, that country reformed its securities laws. It established the Federal Authority for Securities Trading (FAST), in part to oversee insider trading. However, only seven FAST staff members handle investigations of insider trading, as compared with the more than fifty staff members who handle the SEC's investigations.[7] Other countries continue to permit insider trading.

A bear and a bull guard the Frankfurt Stock Exchange in Germany. In 1995, Germany outlawed insider trading, eliminating what had been considered a management perk. It also required companies to warn investors of potential bad news. "In the U.S., the [SEC] has always been pretty ruthless with companies that didn't come clean, and it will be interesting to see what happens here," says Marco Becht, co-author of *The Control of Corporate Europe*.

STOP ▶ REVIEW ▶ APPLY

LO1-1 **In general, how are investments recognized and valued at date of purchase?**

LO1-2 **What is the difference between trading securities, available-for-sale securities, and held-to-maturity securities?**

LO1-3 **Why are the level and percentage of ownership important in accounting for equity investments?**

LO1-4 **Why is disclosure of investments important?**

LO1-5 **What is insider trading?**

Suggested answers to all Stop, Review, and Apply questions follow the appendixes.

Investment Accounting Terminology Indicate whether each phrase listed below is most closely related to (a) trading securities, (b) available-for-sale securities, (c) held-to-maturity securities, (d) noninfluential and noncontrolling ownership, (e) influential but noncontrolling ownership, or (f) controlling ownership:

1. No significant influence over investee
2. Securities bought and sold for short-term profit
3. Ability to make decisions for investee
4. Significant influence over investee
5. Securities that may be sold at any time
6. Debt securities that will be held until they are repaid

SOLUTION

1. d	4. e
2. a	5. b
3. f	6. c

Short-Term Investments in Equity Securities

LO2 Explain the financial reporting implications of short-term investments.

As we pointed out earlier, all trading securities are short-term investments, while available-for-sale securities may be either short-term or long-term.

Trading Securities

Trading securities are frequently bought and sold to generate profits on short-term changes in their prices. They are classified as current assets on the balance sheet and are valued at fair value, which is usually the same as market value. An increase or decrease in the fair value of a company's total trading portfolio (the group of securities it holds for trading purposes) is included in net income in the accounting period in which the increase or decrease occurs.

For example, suppose Norman Company buys 5,000 shares of **IBM** for $450,000 ($90 per share) and 5,000 shares of **Microsoft** for $150,000 ($30 per share) on October 25, 2010. The purchase is made for trading purposes—that is, Norman's management intends to realize a gain by holding the shares for only a short period. The entry to record the investment at cost is as follows:

Purchase

A	=	L	+	SE
+600,000				
−600,000				

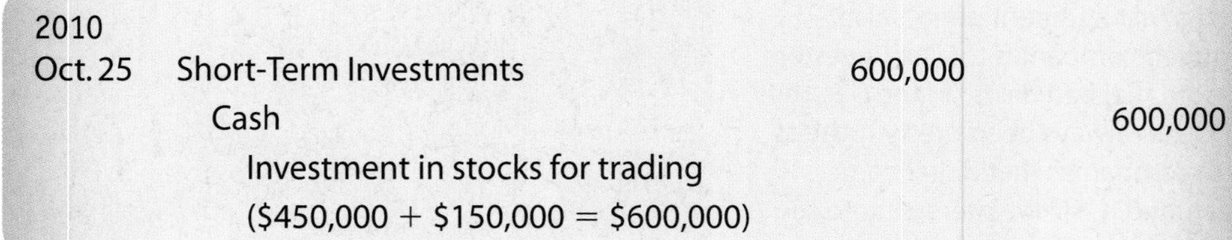

2010			
Oct. 25	Short-Term Investments	600,000	
	Cash		600,000
	Investment in stocks for trading ($450,000 + $150,000 = $600,000)		

Assume that at year end, IBM's stock price has decreased to $80 per share and Microsoft's has risen to $32 per share. The trading portfolio is now valued at $560,000:

Security	*Market Value*	*Cost*	*Gain* (Loss)
IBM (5,000 shares)	$400,000	$450,000	
Microsoft (5,000 shares)	160,000	150,000	
Totals	$560,000	$600,000	($40,000)

Because the current fair value of the portfolio is $40,000 less than the original cost of $600,000, the following adjusting entry is needed:

Year-End Adjustment

A	= L +	SE
−40,000		−40,000

2010			
Dec. 31	Unrealized Loss on Short-Term Investments	40,000	
	Allowance to Adjust Short-Term Investments to Market		40,000
	Recognition of unrealized loss on trading portfolio		

Study Note

The Allowance to Adjust Short-Term Investments to Market account is never changed when securities are sold. It changes only when an adjusting entry is made at year end.

The unrealized loss will appear on the income statement as a reduction in income. The loss is unrealized because the securities have not been sold; if unrealized gains occur, they are treated the same way. The Allowance to Adjust Short-Term Investments to Market account appears on the balance sheet as a contra-asset, as follows:

Short-term investments (at cost)	$600,000
Less allowance to adjust short-term investments to market	40,000
Short-term investments (at market)	$560,000

or, more simply,

Short-term investments (at market value, cost is $600,000)	$560,000

If Norman sells its 5,000 shares of Microsoft for $35 per share on March 2, 2011, a realized gain on trading securities is recorded as follows:

Sale

A	= L +	SE
+175,000		+25,000
−150,000		

2011			
Mar. 2	Cash	175,000	
	Short-Term Investments		150,000
	Gain on Sale of Investments		25,000
	Sale of 5,000 shares of Microsoft for $35 per share; cost was $30 per share		

The realized gain will appear on the income statement. Note that the realized gain is unaffected by the adjustment for the unrealized loss at the end of 2010. The two transactions are treated independently. If the stock had been sold for less than cost, a realized loss on investments would have been recorded. Realized losses also appear on the income statement.

Now let's assume that during 2011, Norman buys 2,000 shares of **Apple Computer** at $32 per share and has no transactions involving its shares of IBM. Also assume that by December 31, 2011, the price of IBM's stock has risen to

FOCUS ON BUSINESS PRACTICE

How Can Even a Big Company Make an Accounting Mistake?

Like many companies, **General Electric**, one of America's largest corporations, protects itself against future increases in interest rates on debt by hedging its debt transactions with *derivatives*, which are agreements to buy or sell stocks, bonds, or other securities in the future. A derivative can be set up in such a way that it has no value and therefore entails no gain or loss. But when a derivative has value, it is considered a trading security and a money-making (or money-losing) tool rather than a true hedge; in this case, any gain or loss that results from valuing the derivative at fair value must be reported on the income statement. General Electric thought it had no gains or losses on its derivatives, but when it recalculated their value over a two-year period, it found that it had gains amounting to about $.02 per share in each year. When the company issued a press release reporting the error, its CFO stated that "there are no exceptions to hedge accounting. . . . At the end of the day, the standard is the standard."[8]

$95 per share, or $5 per share more than the original cost, and that Apple's stock price has fallen to $29, or $3 less than the original cost. We can now analyze Norman's trading portfolio as follows:

Security	*Market Value*	*Cost*	*Gain* (Loss)
IBM (5,000 shares)	$ 475,000	$ 450,000	
Apple (2,000 shares)	58,000	64,000	
Totals	$533,000	$514,000	$19,000

The market value of Norman's trading portfolio now exceeds the cost by $19,000 ($533,000 − $514,000). This amount represents the targeted ending balance for the Allowance to Adjust Short-Term Investments to Market account. Recall that at the end of 2010, that account had a credit balance of $40,000, meaning that the market value of the trading portfolio was less than the cost. Because no entries are made to the account during 2011, it retains its balance until adjusting entries are made at the end of the year. The adjustment for 2011 must be $59,000—enough to result in a debit balance of $19,000 in the allowance account:

Year-End Adjustment

A	= L +	SE
+59,000		+59,000

2011			
Dec. 31	Allowance to Adjust Short-Term Investments to Market	59,000	
	Unrealized Gain on Short-Term Investments		59,000
	Recognition of unrealized gain on trading portfolio ($40,000 + $19,000 = $59,000)		

Study Note

The entry in the Allowance to Adjust Short-Term Investments to Market account is equal to the change in the market value. Compute the new allowance, and then compute the amount needed to change the account. The unrealized loss or gain is the other half of the entry.

The 2011 ending balance of Norman's allowance account can be determined as follows:

ALLOWANCE TO ADJUST SHORT-TERM INVESTMENTS TO MARKET

Dec. 31, 2011 Adj.	59,000	Dec. 31, 2010 Bal.	40,000
Dec. 31, 2011 Bal.	19,000		

The balance sheet presentation of short-term investments is as follows:

Short-term investments (at cost)	$514,000
Plus allowance to adjust short-term investments to market	19,000
Short-term investments (at market)	$533,000

or, more simply,

Short-term investments (at market value, cost is $514,000)	$533,000

If the company also has held-to-maturity securities that will mature within one year, they are included in short-term investments at cost adjusted for the effects of interest.

Available-for-Sale Securities

Short-term available-for-sale securities are accounted for in the same way as trading securities with two exceptions: (1) an unrealized gain or loss is reported as a special item in the stockholders' equity section of the balance sheet, not as a gain or loss on the income statement; (2) if a decline in the value of a security is considered permanent, it is charged as a loss on the income statement.

For example, **eBay's** summary of significant accounting policies contains the following statement: "Unrealized gains and losses [on available-for-sale securities] are excluded from earnings and reported as a component of comprehensive income (loss)." The company's statement of comprehensive income shows unrealized gains on investments of $8.3 million in 2006 and $589.6 million in 2007. In addition, eBay's income statement shows impairment charges of $1.4 billion in 2007. The $1.4 billion represents the amount by which the carrying value of goodwill associated with its Skype Technologies (voice-over Internet) division exceeded its fair value. The company reported no impairment charges in 2006.[9]

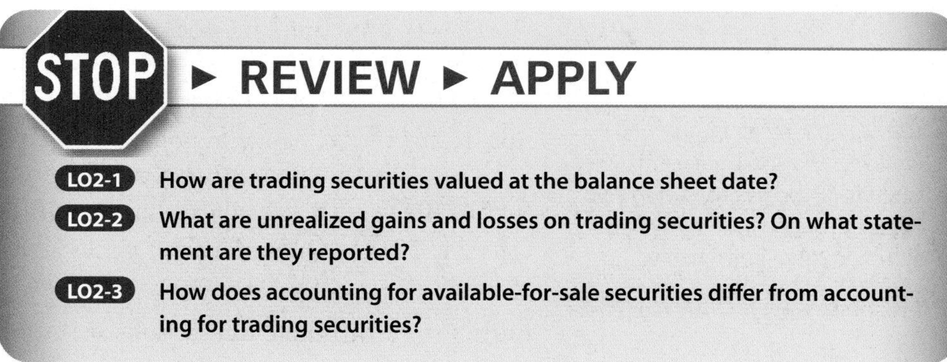

LO2-1 How are trading securities valued at the balance sheet date?

LO2-2 What are unrealized gains and losses on trading securities? On what statement are they reported?

LO2-3 How does accounting for available-for-sale securities differ from accounting for trading securities?

Long-Term Investments in Equity Securities

LO3 Explain the financial reporting implications of long-term investments in stock and the cost-adjusted-to-market and equity methods used to account for them.

The accounting treatment of long-term investments in equity securities, such as common stock, depends on the extent to which the investing company can exercise control over the other company.

Noninfluential and Noncontrolling Investment

As noted earlier, available-for-sale securities are debt or equity securities that cannot be classified as trading or held-to-maturity securities. When long-term equity securities are involved, a further criterion for classifying them as available for sale is that they be noninfluential and noncontrolling investments of less than 20 percent of the voting stock. Accounting for long-term available-for-sale securities requires using the **cost-adjusted-to-market method**. With this method, the securities are initially recorded at cost and are thereafter adjusted periodically for changes in market value by using an allowance account.[10]

Available-for-sale securities are classified as long term if management intends to hold them for more than one year. When accounting for long-term available-for-sale securities, the unrealized gain or loss resulting from the adjustment is not reported on the income statement. Instead, the gain or loss is reported as a special item in the stockholders' equity section of the balance sheet and in the disclosure of comprehensive income.

At the end of each accounting period, the total cost and the total market value of these long-term stock investments must be determined. If the total market value is less than the total cost, the difference must be credited to a contra-asset account called Allowance to Adjust Long-Term Investments to Market. Because of the long-term nature of the investment, the debit part of the entry, which represents a decrease in value below cost, is treated as a temporary decrease and does not appear as a loss on the income statement. It is shown in a contra-stockholders' equity account called Unrealized Loss on Long-Term Investments.* Thus, both of these accounts are balance sheet accounts. If the market value exceeds the cost, the allowance account is added to Long-Term Investments, and the unrealized gain appears as an addition to stockholders' equity.

When a company sells its long-term investments in stock, the difference between the sale price and the cost of the stock is recorded as a realized gain or loss on the income statement. Dividend income from such investments is recorded by a debit to Cash and a credit to Dividend Income. For example, assume these facts about the long-term stock investments of Hoska Corporation:

June 1, 2010	Paid cash for the following long-term investments: 5,000 shares of Murcia Corporation common stock (representing 2 percent of outstanding stock) at $25 per share; 2,500 shares of Rava Corporation common stock (representing 3 percent of outstanding stock) at $15 per share.
Dec. 31, 2010	Quoted market prices at year end: Murcia common stock, $21; Rava common stock, $17.
Apr. 1, 2011	Change in policy required the sale of 1,000 shares of Murcia common stock at $23.
July 1, 2011	Received cash dividend from Rava equal to $.20 per share.
Dec. 31, 2011	Quoted market prices at year end: Murcia common stock, $24; Rava common stock, $13.

Study Note

Hoska's sale of stock on April 1, 2011, was the result of a change in policy. This illustrates that intent is often the only difference between long-term investments and short-term investments.

Entries to record these transactions are as follows:

Investment

A	=	L	+	SE
+162,500				
−162,500				

2010			
June 1	Long-Term Investments	162,500	
	Cash		162,500
	Investments in Murcia common stock (5,000 shares × $25 = $125,000) and Rava common stock (2,500 shares × $15 = $37,500)		

*If the decrease in market value of a long-term investment is deemed permanent or if the investment is deemed impaired, the decline or impairment is recorded by debiting a loss account on the income statement instead of the Unrealized Loss account.

Year-End Adjustment

A	= L +	SE
−15,000		−15,000

2010			
Dec. 31	Unrealized Loss on Long-Term Investments	15,000	
	Allowance to Adjust Long-Term Investments to Market		15,000
	To record reduction of long-term investment to market		

This adjustment involves the following computations:

Company	*Shares*	*Market Price*	*Total Market*	*Total Cost*
Murcia	5,000	$21	$105,000	$125,000
Rava	2,500	17	42,500	37,500
			$147,500	$162,500

Total Cost − Total Market Value = $162,500 − $147,500 = $15,000

Other entries are as follows:

Sale

A	= L +	SE
+23,000		−2,000
−25,000		

2011			
Apr. 1	Cash	23,000	
	Loss on Sale of Investments	2,000	
	Long-Term Investments		25,000
	Sale of 1,000 shares of Murcia common stock		
	1,000 × $23 = $23,000		
	1,000 × $25 = 25,000		
	Loss $ 2,000		

Dividend Received

A	= L +	SE
+500		+500

2011			
July 1	Cash	500	
	Dividend Income		500
	Receipt of cash dividend from Rava stock		
	2,500 × $.20 = $500		

Year-End Adjustment

A	= L +	SE
+6,000		+6,000

2011			
Dec. 31	Allowance to Adjust Long-Term Investments to Market	6,000	
	Unrealized Loss on Long-Term Investments		6,000
	To record the adjustment in long-term investments so it is reported at market		

The adjustment equals the previous balance ($15,000 from the December 31, 2010, entry) minus the new balance ($9,000), or $6,000. The new balance of $9,000 is the difference at the present time between the total market value and the total cost of all investments. It is figured as follows:

Company	*Shares*	*Market Price*	*Total Market*	*Total Cost*
Murcia	4,000	$24	$ 96,000	$100,000
Rava	2,500	13	32,500	37,500
			$128,500	$137,500

Total Cost − Total Market Value = $137,500 − $128,500 = $9,000

The Allowance to Adjust Long-Term Investments to Market and the Unrealized Loss on Long-Term Investments are reciprocal contra accounts, each with the same dollar balance, as shown by the effects of these transactions on the T accounts:

CONTRA-ASSET ACCOUNT

ALLOWANCE TO ADJUST LONG-TERM INVESTMENTS TO MARKET

Dec. 31, 2011 Adj.	6,000	Dec. 31, 2010 Bal.	15,000
		Dec. 31, 2011 Bal.	9,000

CONTRA-STOCKHOLDERS' EQUITY ACCOUNT

UNREALIZED LOSS ON LONG-TERM INVESTMENTS

Dec. 31, 2010 Bal.	15,000	Dec. 31, 2011 Adj.	6,000
Dec. 31, 2011 Bal.	9,000		

The Allowance account reduces long-term investments by the amount by which the cost of the investments exceeds market; the Unrealized Loss account reduces stockholders' equity by a similar amount. The opposite effects will exist if market value exceeds cost, resulting in an unrealized gain.

Influential but Noncontrolling Investment

As we have noted, ownership of 20 percent or more of a company's voting stock is considered sufficient to influence the company's operations. When that is the case, the **equity method** should be used to account for the stock investment. The equity method presumes that an investment of 20 percent or more is not a passive investment and that the investor should therefore share proportionately in the success or failure of the company. The three main features of this method are as follows:

1. The investor records the original purchase of the stock at cost.
2. The investor records its share of the company's periodic net income as an increase in the Investment account, with a corresponding credit to an income account. Similarly, it records its share of a periodic loss as a decrease in the Investment account, with a corresponding debit to a loss account.
3. When the investor receives a cash dividend, the asset account Cash is increased, and the Investment account is decreased.

eBay owns a minority interest of approximately 25 percent in **craigslist.inc.**, an online community featuring classified ad forums. Because the investment is more than 20 percent, eBay is presumed to have significant influence over craigslist's operations. Thus, eBay uses the equity method to account for the investment and classifies this investment and others that use the equity method as long-term investments.[11]

To illustrate the equity method, suppose that on January 1 of the current year, Shafer Corporation acquired 40 percent of Nica Corporation's voting common stock for $90,000. With this share of ownership, Shafer can exert significant influence over Nica's operations. During the year, Nica reported net income of $40,000 and paid cash dividends of $10,000. Shafer recorded these transactions as follows:

Investment

A	= L +	SE
+90,000		
−90,000		

Investment in Nica Corporation	90,000	
Cash		90,000
Investment in Nica Corporation common stock		

Recognition of Income

A	= L +	SE
+16,000		+16,000

Investment in Nica Corporation	16,000	
Income, Nica Corporation Investment		16,000
Recognition of 40% of income reported by Nica Corporation		
40% × $40,000 = $16,000		

Receipt of Cash Dividend

A	= L +	SE
+4,000		
−4,000		

Cash	4,000	
Investment in Nica Corporation		4,000
Cash dividend from Nica Corporation		
40% × $10,000 = $4,000		

The balance of the Investment in Nica Corporation account after these transactions is $102,000, as shown here:

Investment in Nica Corporation

Investment	90,000	Dividend Received	4,000
Share of Income	16,000		
Bal.	102,000		

Study Note

Under the equity method, dividends received represent a return on investment and decrease the Investment account with a credit entry.

The share of income is reported as a separate line item on the income statement as a part of income from operations. The dividends received affect cash flows

FOCUS ON BUSINESS PRACTICE

Accounting for International Joint Ventures

When U.S. companies make investments abroad, they often find it wise or necessary to partner with a local company or with the government of the country. Some countries require that their citizens own a minimum percentage of each business. In other countries—among them, Brazil, China, India, and the former United Soviet Socialist Republics—the government has traditionally had a share of ownership. Such business arrangements are usually called *joint ventures*. Because the resulting enterprise is jointly owned, it is appropriate to treat the U.S. company's status as "influential but noncontrolling." Thus, the most appropriate accounting method for these arrangements is the equity method.

from operating activities on the statement of cash flows. The reported income exceeds the cash received by $12,000 ($16,000 − $4,000).

Controlling Investment Some investing firms that own less than 50 percent of a company's voting stock exercise such powerful influence that for all practical purposes, they control the policies of the other company. Nevertheless, ownership of more than 50 percent of the voting stock is required for accounting recognition of control. When a firm has a controlling interest in another company, a parent-subsidiary relationship is said to exist. The investing company is the **parent company**; the other company is a **subsidiary**.

Because a parent company and its subsidiaries are separate legal entities, each prepares separate financial statements. However, because of their special relationship, they are viewed for external financial reporting purposes as a single economic entity. For this reason, the FASB requires that they combine their financial statements into a single set of statements called **consolidated financial statements**.[12] For example, in its summary of significant accounting policies, **eBay** states that "the accompanying financial statements are consolidated and include the financial statements of eBay and our majority-owned subsidiaries. All significant intercompany balances and transactions have been eliminated in consolidation."[13]

Study Note

Parents and subsidiaries are separate legal entities even though they combine their financial reports at year end.

STOP ▶ REVIEW ▶ APPLY

LO3-1 **What percentage of ownership applies to each of the following: (a) noninfluential and noncontrolling investment, (b) influential but noncontrolling investment, and (c) controlling investment? What is the appropriate accounting treatment for each of these investments?**

LO3-2 **What is a parent-subsidiary relationship?**

LO3-3 **American Home Products Corporation has many subsidiaries. Would its stockholders be more interested in its consolidated financial statements or in the individual statements of its subsidiaries? Explain your answer.**

LO3-4 **Merchant Corporation's summary of significant accounting policies contained this statement: "Investments in companies in which Merchant has significant influence in management are on the equity basis." What is the equity method of accounting for investments, and why did Merchant use it in this case?**

Consolidated Financial Statements

LO4 Explain the financial reporting implications of consolidated financial statements.

Most major corporations find it convenient for economic, legal, tax, or other reasons to operate in parent-subsidiary relationships. When we speak of a large company, such as **PepsiCo** or **IBM**, we generally think of the parent company, not of its many subsidiaries. Potential investors, however, want a clear financial picture of the total economic entity. The main purpose of consolidated financial statements is to give such a view of the parent and subsidiary firms by treating them as if they were one company. On a consolidated balance sheet, the Inventory account includes the inventory held by the parent and all its subsidiaries. Similarly, on the consolidated income statement, the Sales account is the total revenue from sales by the parent and all its subsidiaries. This overview helps management, stockholders, and creditors of the parent company judge the company's progress in meeting its goals.

Consolidated Balance Sheet

The **purchase method** of preparing consolidated financial statements combines similar accounts from the separate statements of the parent and the subsidiaries. Some accounts result from transactions between the parent and the subsidiary—for example, sales and purchases between the two entities, and debt owed by one of the entities to the other. It is not appropriate to include these accounts in the consolidated financial statements; the sales and purchases are only transfers between different parts of the business, and the payables and receivables do not represent amounts due to or receivable from outside parties. For this reason, it is important that certain **eliminations** be made. These eliminations avoid the duplication of accounts and reflect the financial position and operations from the standpoint of a single entity. Eliminations appear only on the work sheets used in preparing consolidated financial statements. They are never shown in the accounting records of either the parent or the subsidiary.

Study Note

As separate entities, the parent and subsidiary maintain individual accounting records. Work sheet eliminations remove only duplications that occur in consolidation and the effects of intercompany transactions.

Another good example of accounts that result from transactions between a parent and its subsidiary is the Investment in Subsidiary account on the parent's balance sheet and the stockholders' equity accounts of the subsidiary. When the balance sheets of the two companies are combined, these accounts must be eliminated to avoid duplicating them in the consolidated financial statements.

To illustrate the preparation of a consolidated balance sheet under the purchase method, we use the following balance sheet data for Parent Company and Subsidiary Company:

Accounts	*Parent Company*	*Subsidiary Company*
Cash	$ 50,000	$12,500
Other assets	380,000	30,000
Total assets	$430,000	$42,500
Liabilities	$ 30,000	$ 5,000
Common stock	300,000	27,500
Retained earnings	100,000	10,000
Total liabilities and stockholders' equity	$430,000	$42,500

100 Percent Purchase at Book Value Suppose that Parent Company purchases 100 percent of the stock of Subsidiary Company for an amount exactly equal to Subsidiary's book value. The book value of Subsidiary Company is $37,500 ($42,500 − $5,000). Parent Company would record the purchase as follows:

A	= L +	SE
+37,500		
−37,500		

Investment in Subsidiary Company	37,500	
Cash		37,500
Purchase of 100 percent of Subsidiary Company at book value		

It is helpful to use a work sheet like the one shown in Exhibit 1 in preparing consolidated financial statements. Note that the balance of Parent Company's

EXHIBIT 1 Work Sheet for Preparing a Consolidated Balance Sheet

Parent and Subsidiary Companies
Work Sheet for Consolidated Balance Sheet
As of Acquisition Date

Accounts	Balance Sheet, Parent Company	Balance Sheet, Subsidiary Company	Eliminations Debit	Eliminations Credit	Consolidated Balance Sheet
Cash	12,500	12,500			25,000
Investment in subsidiary company	37,500			(1) 37,500	—
Other assets	380,000	30,000			410,000
Total assets	430,000	42,500			435,000
Liabilities	30,000	5,000			35,000
Common stock	300,000	27,500	(1) 27,500		300,000
Retained earnings	100,000	10,000	(1) 10,000		100,000
Total liabilities and stockholders' equity	430,000	42,500	37,500	37,500	435,000

(1) Elimination of intercompany investment

Cash account is now $12,500 and that Investment in Subsidiary Company is shown as an asset in Parent Company's balance sheet, reflecting the purchase of the subsidiary. To prepare a consolidated balance sheet, it is necessary to eliminate the investment in the subsidiary, as shown in elimination entry **1** in Exhibit 1. This entry accomplishes two things. First, it eliminates the double counting that would take place when the net assets of the two companies are combined. Second, it eliminates the stockholders' equity section of Subsidiary Company.

As we have pointed out, the theory underlying consolidated financial statements is that parent and subsidiary are a single entity. Thus, the stockholders' equity section of the consolidated balance sheet is the same for Parent Company and Subsidiary Company.

So, after eliminating the Investment in Subsidiary Company account and the stockholders' equity accounts of the subsidiary, we can take the information from the Consolidated Balance Sheet column in Exhibit 1 and present it in the following form:

Parent and Subsidiary Companies
Consolidated Balance Sheet
As of Acquisition Date

Cash	$ 25,000	Liabilities	$ 35,000
Other assets	410,000	Common stock	300,000
		Retained earnings	100,000
		Total liabilities and	
Total assets	$435,000	stockholders' equity	$435,000

EXHIBIT 2 Work Sheet Showing Elimination When Purchase Is for Less than 100 Percent Ownership

Parent and Subsidiary Companies
Work Sheet for Consolidated Balance Sheet
As of Acquisition Date

Accounts	Balance Sheet, Parent Company	Balance Sheet, Subsidiary Company	Eliminations: Debit	Eliminations: Credit	Consolidated Balance Sheet
Cash	16,250	12,500			28,750
Investment in subsidiary company	33,750			(1) 33,750	—
Other assets	380,000	30,000			410,000
Total assets	430,000	42,500			438,750
Liabilities	30,000	5,000			35,000
Common stock	300,000	27,500	(1) 27,500		300,000
Retained earnings	100,000	10,000	(1) 10,000		100,000
Minority interest	—	—		(1) 3,750	3,750
Total liabilities and stockholders' equity	430,000	42,500	37,500	37,500	438,750

(1) Elimination of intercompany investment. Minority interest equals 10 percent of subsidiary's total stockholders' equity.

Study Note

When the elimination entry is made, all of the subsidiary's stockholders' equity accounts are eliminated. The percentage not owned by the parent company is assigned to minority interest.

Less Than 100 Percent Purchase at Book Value When a parent company purchases less than 100 percent but more than 50 percent of a subsidiary's voting stock, it will have control over the subsidiary, and it must prepare consolidated financial statements. It must also account for the interests of the subsidiary's stockholders who own less than 50 percent of the voting stock. These are the minority stockholders, and their **minority interest** must appear on the consolidated balance sheet (as part of stockholders' equity) as an amount equal to their percentage of ownership times the subsidiary's net assets.[14]

Suppose that Parent Company buys 90 percent of Subsidiary Company's voting stock for \$33,750. In this case, the portion of the company purchased has a book value of \$33,750 (90% × \$37,500). The work sheet used to prepare the consolidated balance sheet appears in Exhibit 2. The elimination is made just as in Exhibit 1, except that the minority interest must be accounted for. All of the Investment in Subsidiary Company account (\$33,750) is eliminated against all of Subsidiary Company's stockholders' equity accounts (totaling \$37,500). The difference (\$3,750, or 10% × \$37,500) is set as minority interest.

There are two ways to classify minority interest on a consolidated balance sheet. One way is to place the entry between long-term liabilities and stockholders' equity. The other way is to consider the stockholders' equity section as consisting of minority interest and the parent company's stockholders' equity, as shown here:

Minority interest	\$ 3,750
Common stock	300,000
Retained earnings	100,000
Total stockholders' equity	\$403,750

Purchase at More or Less than Book Value The purchase price of a business depends on many factors, such as the current market price, the relative strength of the buyer's and seller's bargaining positions, and the prospects for future earnings. Thus, it is only by chance that the purchase price of a subsidiary equals the book value of its equity. Usually, it does not.

For example, a parent company may pay more than the subsidiary's book value for a controlling interest if the subsidiary's assets are understated. This happens when the historical cost less depreciation of the subsidiary's assets does not reflect current market values. The parent may also pay more than book value if the subsidiary has something the parent wants, such as an important technical process, a new and different product, or a new market. On the other hand, the parent may pay less than book value if the subsidiary's assets are not worth their depreciated cost. It may also pay less than book value if heavy losses suffered by the subsidiary have caused its stock price to drop.

Study Note

Regardless of the circumstances, the Investment in Subsidiary Company account must be eliminated completely and should not appear on the consolidated balance sheet.

The Accounting Principles Board has provided the following guidelines for consolidating a purchased subsidiary and its parent when the parent pays more than book value for its investment in the subsidiary:

> First, all identifiable assets acquired . . . and liabilities assumed in a business combination . . . should be assigned a portion of the cost of the acquired company, normally equal to their fair values at date of acquisition.
>
> Second, the excess of the cost of the acquired company over the sum of the amounts assigned to identifiable assets acquired less liabilities assumed should be recorded as goodwill.[15]

As explained in the chapter on long-term assets, goodwill is carried on the balance sheet at cost and is subject to an annual impairment test. **eBay** describes its treatment of goodwill as follows:

> Goodwill represents the excess of the purchase price over the fair value of the net tangible and identifiable intangible assets acquired. Intangible assets resulting from the acquisition of entities accounted for using the purchase method of accounting are estimated by management. . . . Goodwill is not subject to amortization, but is subject to at least an annual assessment for impairment, applying a fair-value based test.[16]

To illustrate the application of these principles, suppose that Parent Company purchases 100 percent of Subsidiary Company's voting stock for $46,250, or $8,750 more than book value. Parent Company considers $5,000 of the $8,750 to be due to the increased value of Subsidiary's other assets and $3,750 of the $8,750 to be due to the overall strength that Subsidiary Company would add to Parent Company's organization. The work sheet used to prepare the consolidated balance sheet appears in Exhibit 3. All of the Investment in Subsidiary Company ($46,250) has been eliminated against all of Subsidiary Company's stockholders' equity ($37,500). The excess of cost over book value ($8,750) has been debited in the amounts of $5,000 to Other Assets and $3,750 to a new account called **Goodwill**, or *Goodwill from Consolidation.*

Study Note

Goodwill is recorded when the purchase price of a business exceeds the fair market value of the net assets purchased.

The amount of goodwill is determined as follows:

Cost of investment in subsidiary	$46,250
Book value of subsidiary	37,500
Excess of cost over book value	$ 8,750
Portion of excess attributable to undervalued other assets of subsidiary	5,000
Portion of excess attributable to goodwill	$ 3,750

EXHIBIT 3 Work Sheet Showing Elimination When Purchase Cost Is Greater than Book Value

Parent and Subsidiary Companies
Work Sheet for Consolidated Balance Sheet
As of Acquisition Date

Accounts	Balance Sheet, Parent Company	Balance Sheet, Subsidiary Company	Eliminations Debit	Eliminations Credit	Consolidated Balance Sheet
Cash	3,750	12,500			16,250
Investment in subsidiary company	46,250			(1) 46,250	—
Other assets	380,000	30,000	(1) 5,000		415,000
Goodwill	—	—	(1) 3,750		3,750
Total assets	430,000	42,500			435,000
Liabilities	30,000	5,000			35,000
Common stock	300,000	27,500	(1) 27,500		300,000
Retained earnings	100,000	10,000	(1) 10,000		100,000
Total liabilities and stockholders' equity	430,000	42,500	46,250	46,250	435,000

(1) Elimination of intercompany investment. Excess of cost over book value ($46,250 − $37,500 = $8,750) is allocated to Other Assets ($5,000) and Goodwill ($3,750).

Study Note

In this example, neither company has goodwill on its balance sheet. Goodwill is "created" when consolidated statements are prepared.

On the consolidated balance sheet, goodwill appears as an asset representing the portion of the excess of the cost of the investment over book value that cannot be allocated to any specific asset. Other assets appears on the consolidated balance sheet at the combined total of $415,000 ($380,000 + $30,000 + $5,000).

When the parent company pays less than book value for its investment in the subsidiary, *Opinion No. 16* of the Accounting Principles Board requires that the excess of book value over cost of the investment be used to lower the carrying value of the subsidiary's long-term assets. The reasoning behind this is that market values of long-lived assets (other than marketable securities) are among the least reliable of estimates, since a ready market does not usually exist for such assets. In other words, the Accounting Principles Board advises against using negative goodwill, except in very special cases.

Intercompany Receivables and Payables If a subsidiary owes money to the parent company, there will be a receivable on the parent company's individual balance sheet and a payable on the subsidiary company's individual balance sheet. Conversely, if a parent owes money to a subsidiary, there will be a receivable on the subsidiary's balance sheet and a payable on the parent's balance sheet. When a consolidated balance sheet is prepared, both the receivable and the payable should be eliminated because from the viewpoint of the consolidated entity, neither the asset nor the liability exists. In other words, it does not make sense for a company to owe money to itself. The eliminating entry is made on the work sheet by debiting the payable and crediting the receivable for the amount of the intercompany loan.

Consolidated Income Statement

A consolidated income statement is prepared by combining the revenues and expenses of the parent and subsidiary companies. The procedure is the same as the one used to prepare a consolidated balance sheet—that is, intercompany transactions are eliminated to prevent double counting of revenues and expenses. The following intercompany transactions affect the consolidated income statement:

1. Sales and purchases of goods and services between parent and subsidiary
2. Income and expenses related to loans, receivables, or bond indebtedness between parent and subsidiary
3. Other income and expenses from intercompany transactions.

Study Note

Intercompany sales or purchases are not revenues or expenses to the consolidated entity. True revenues and expenses occur only when transactions are with parties outside the firm.

To illustrate the eliminating entries, suppose that Parent Company sold $60,000 of goods to Subsidiary Company, which in turn sold all the goods to others. Subsidiary Company paid Parent Company $1,000 interest on a loan.

The work sheet in Exhibit 4 shows how to prepare a consolidated income statement. Because the purpose of the eliminating entries is to treat the two companies as a single entity, it is important to include in Sales only sales made to outsiders and to include in Cost of Goods Sold only purchases made from outsiders. This goal is met with the first eliminating entry, which eliminates the $60,000 of intercompany sales and purchases by a debit of that amount to Sales and a credit of that amount to Cost of Goods Sold. As a result, only sales to outsiders ($255,000) and purchases from outsiders ($120,000) are included in the Consolidated Income Statement column. The intercompany interest income and expense are eliminated by a debit to Other Revenues and a credit to Other Expenses.

Public corporations also prepare consolidated statements of stockholders' equity and consolidated statements of cash flows. For examples of these statements, see the **CVS** annual report in the Supplement to Chapter 1.

EXHIBIT 4 Work Sheet for Preparing a Consolidated Income Statement

Parent and Subsidiary Companies
Work Sheet for Consolidated Income Statement
For the Year Ended December 31, 2010

Accounts	Income Statement, Parent Company	Income Statement, Subsidiary Company	Eliminations: Debit	Eliminations: Credit	Consolidated Income Statement
Sales	215,000	100,000	(1) 60,000		255,000
Other revenues	30,000	5,000	(2) 1,000		34,000
Total revenues	245,000	105,000			289,000
Cost of goods sold	105,000	75,000		(1) 60,000	120,000
Other expenses	70,000	25,000		(2) 1,000	94,000
Total costs and expenses	175,000	100,000			214,000
Net income	70,000	5,000	61,000	61,000	75,000

(1) Elimination of intercompany sales and purchases
(2) Elimination of intercompany interest income and interest expense

An art installation of euro currency in Ludwigsburg, Germany, preceded the adoption of the Euro on January 1, 2002, as the only form of legal tender in twelve European countries. When a U.S. company owns more than 50 percent of a foreign company, it must prepare consolidated financial statements. The statements of the foreign subsidiary must be restated in dollars—not euros or other foreign currencies—before consolidation can take place.

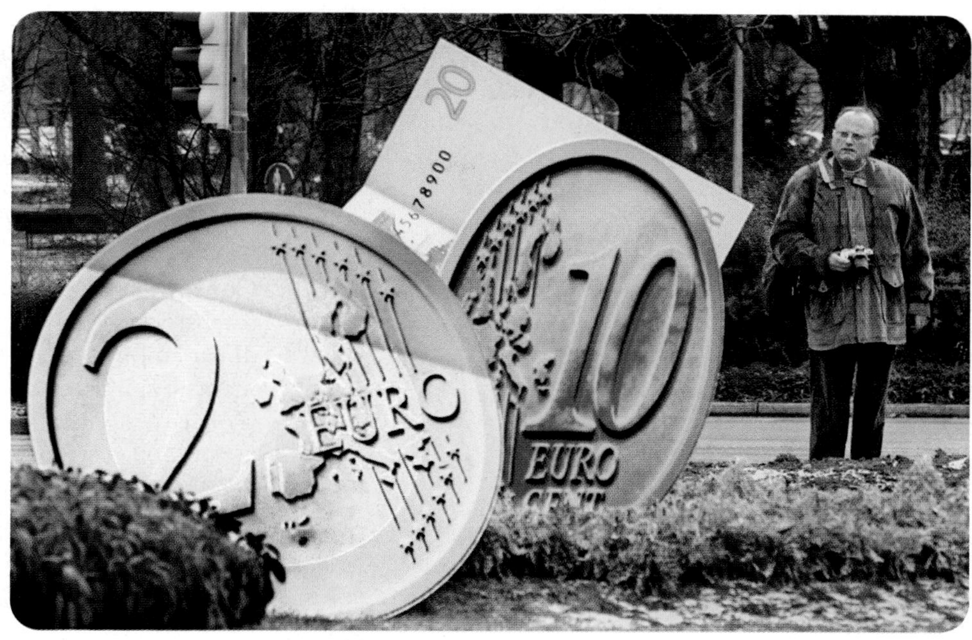

Restatement of Foreign Subsidiary Financial Statements

Companies often expand by establishing or buying foreign subsidiaries. Such companies are called **multinational** or **transnational corporations**. If a company owns more than 50 percent of a foreign subsidiary and thus exercises control, the foreign subsidiary should be included in the consolidated financial statements. The consolidation procedure is the same as the one for domestic subsidiaries, except that the foreign subsidiary's statements must be restated in the reporting currency before consolidation takes place. The **reporting currency** is the currency in which the consolidated financial statements are presented, which for U.S. companies is usually the U.S. dollar. For example, **eBay** purchased a German firm and an Indian firm in 2004. Clearly, it makes no sense to combine the assets of German and Indian subsidiaries stated in euros and rupees with the assets of the U.S. parent company stated in dollars. Thus, **restatement** of the subsidiaries' statements into the currency of the parent company is necessary. After restatement, the parent's and subsidiaries' statements can be consolidated in the usual way.

STOP ▶ REVIEW ▶ APPLY

LO4-1 What are eliminating entries, and where do they appear?

LO4-2 What is the value of consolidated financial statements?

LO4-3 Merchant Corporation's summary of significant accounting policies contained the following statement: "Principles Applied in Consolidation: Majority-owned subsidiaries are consolidated, except for leasing and finance companies and those subsidiaries not considered to be material." What accounting rule does this practice violate, and why?

LO4-4 The following item appeared on Merchant's consolidated balance sheet: "Minority Interest—$50,000." How did this item arise, and where would you expect to find it on the consolidated balance sheet?

(continued)

LO4-5 The following item also appeared on Merchant's consolidated balance sheet: "Goodwill from Consolidation—$70,000." How would this item arise, and where would you expect to find it on the consolidated balance sheet?

LO4-6 Why should intercompany receivables, payables, sales, and purchases be eliminated in consolidated financial statements?

LO4-7 Subsidiary Corporation, a wholly owned subsidiary, has total sales of $500,000, $100,000 of which were made to Parent Corporation. Parent Corporation has total sales of $1,000,000. What is the amount of sales on the consolidated income statement?

LO4-8 What step is necessary before consolidating the financial statements of foreign subsidiaries and their parent company?

Consolidation Calculations S Company has total stockholders' equity of $50,000. Fill in the dollar amounts for each of the following investments by P Company in S's common stock:

	Goodwill	*Minority Interest*
1. P Company pays $50,000 for 100% of S Company's common stock, and S Company's net assets are fairly valued at $50,000.	______	______
2. P Company pays $60,000 for 100% of S Company's common stock, and S Company's net assets are fairly valued at $50,000.	______	______
3. P Company pays $60,000 for 100% of S Company's common stock, and S Company's net assets are fairly valued at $60,000.	______	______
4. P Company pays $40,000 for 80% of S Company's common stock, and S Company's net assets are fairly valued at $50,000.	______	______
5. P Company pays $50,000 for 80% of S Company's common stock, and S Company's net assets are fairly valued at $62,500.	______	______

SOLUTION

	Goodwill	*Minority Interest*
1.	0	0
2.	$10,000	0
3.	0	0
4.	0	$10,000
5.	0	$12,500

Investments in Debt Securities

LO5 Explain the financial reporting implications of debt investments.

As noted in previous chapters, debt securities are considered financial instruments because they are claims that will be paid in cash. When a company purchases debt securities, it records them at cost plus any commissions and fees. Like investments in equity securities, short-term investments in debt securities are valued at fair value at the end of the accounting period and are accounted for as trading securities or available-for-sale securities. However, the accounting treatment is different if they qualify as held-to-maturity securities.

Study Note

Any brokerage costs or other costs involved in acquiring securities are part of the cost of the securities.

Held-to-Maturity Securities

As we noted earlier, held-to-maturity securities are debt securities that management intends to hold to their maturity date. Such securities are recorded at cost and are valued on the balance sheet at cost adjusted for the effects of interest. For example, suppose that on December 1, 2010, Espinosa Company pays $48,500 for U.S. Treasury bills, which are short-term debt of the federal government. The bills will mature in 120 days at $50,000. Espinosa would make the following entry:

A	=	L	+	SE
+48,500				
−48,500				

2010			
Dec. 1	Short-Term Investments	48,500	
	Cash		48,500
	Purchase of U.S. Treasury bills that mature in 120 days		

At Espinosa's year end on December 31, the entry to accrue the interest income earned to date would be as follows:

A	=	L	+	SE
+375				+375

2010			
Dec. 31	Short-Term Investments	375	
	Interest Income		375
	Accrual of interest on U.S. Treasury bills $1,500 × 30/120 = $375		

On December 31, the U.S. Treasury bills would be shown on the balance sheet as a short-term investment at their amortized cost of $48,875 ($48,500 + $375). When Espinosa receives the maturity value on March 31, 2011, the entry is as follows:

A	=	L	+	SE
+50,000				+1,125
−48,875				

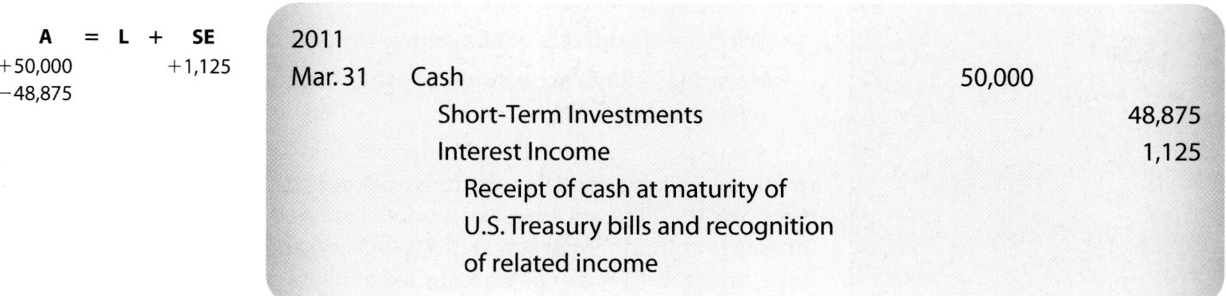

2011			
Mar. 31	Cash	50,000	
	Short-Term Investments		48,875
	Interest Income		1,125
	Receipt of cash at maturity of U.S. Treasury bills and recognition of related income		

Long-Term Investments in Bonds

Like all investments, investments in bonds are recorded at cost, which, in this case, is the price of the bonds plus the broker's commission. When bonds are purchased between interest payment dates, the purchaser must also pay an amount equal to the interest that has accrued on the bonds since the last interest payment date. Then, on the next interest payment date, the purchaser receives an interest payment for the whole period. The payment for accrued interest should be recorded as a debit to Interest Income, which will be offset by a credit to Interest Income when the semiannual interest is received.

Subsequent accounting for a corporation's long-term bond investments depends on the classification of the bonds. If the company plans to hold the bonds until they are paid off on their maturity date, they are considered held-to-maturity securities. Except in industries like insurance and banking, it is unusual for companies to buy the bonds of other companies with the express purpose of holding them until they mature, which can be in 10 to 30 years. Thus, most long-term bond investments are classified as available-for-sale securities, meaning that the company plans to sell them at some point before their maturity date. Such bonds are accounted for at fair value, much as equity or stock investments are; fair value is usually the market value. When bonds are intended to be held to maturity, they are accounted for not at fair value but at cost, adjusted for the amortization of their discount or premium. The procedure is similar to accounting for long-term bond liabilities, except that separate accounts for discounts and premiums are not used.

> **Study Note**
> The fair value of bonds is closely related to interest rates. An increase in interest rates lowers the fair value of bonds, and vice versa.

STOP ▶ REVIEW ▶ APPLY

LO5-1 **What are held-to-maturity securities, and at what value are they shown on the balance sheet?**

LO5-2 **Are most long-term investments in bonds classified as held-to-maturity securities or as available-for-sale securities? Explain your answer.**

A LOOK BACK AT ▶ eBay, Inc.

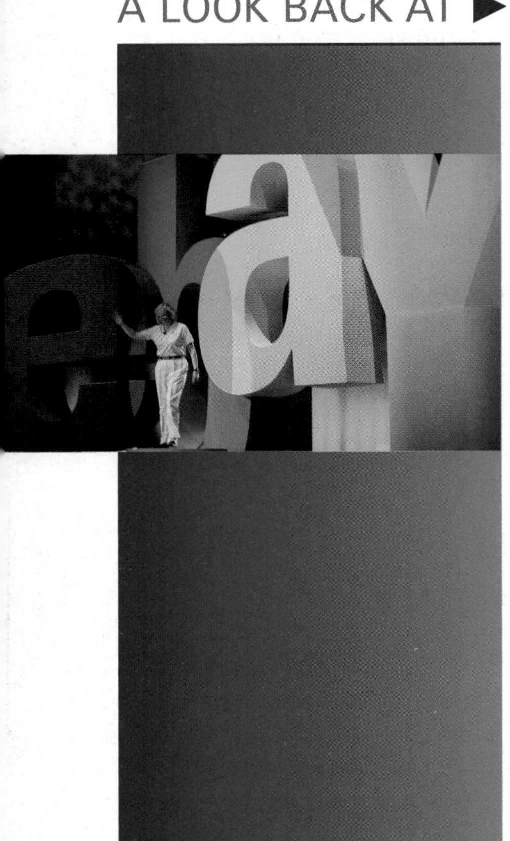

As shown in the Financial Highlights at the beginning of the chapter, short- and long-term investments and goodwill from acquisitions constitute a large portion of the total assets on **eBay's** balance sheet. The company's investments also have important effects on its income statement and statement of cash flows. To fully evaluate eBay's performance, users of its financial statements must address the following questions:

- **What are the effects of eBay's investments on its financial performance?**
- **How does eBay's acquisition of other companies affect its financial performance?**

As we pointed out in this chapter, eBay classifies both short- and long-term investments as available-for-sale securities and reports them at fair value on its balance sheet. It reports the difference between unrealized gains and losses in other comprehensive income (a component of stockholders' equity) and subjects its equity investments to an impairment test, which can be recorded as a loss on the income statement if a decline in an investment's value is deemed permanent.

In the case of eBay, the company had unrealized losses in 2007 of only $175,000 but had impairments of $1.4 billion. Because a majority of eBay's investments are debt securities, interest income is a significant component—almost 25 percent—of the company's income from operations. The investing section of its statement of cash flows reveals that in 2007, eBay spent about $271 million on investments.

In 2007, eBay made acquisitions totaling more than $864 million. It uses the equity method to account for investments over 20 percent and the purchase method to account for acquisitions. For instance, its purchase of StubHub, the on-line ticket company, for $283 million in cash resulted in goodwill of $221 million or almost 80 percent of the acquisition price.[17] In total, goodwill from all eBay's acquisitions represents 41 percent of its assets.

In short, it is not possible to fully evaluate eBay's performance without understanding the effect that investments and acquisitions have on that performance.

CHAPTER REVIEW

REVIEW of Learning Objectives

LO1 Identify and explain the management issues related to investments.

Investments are recorded on the date on which the transaction occurs, at which time there is either a transfer of funds or a definite obligation to pay. Investments are recorded at cost, or purchase price, including any commissions or fees. After the purchase, the balance sheet value of investments is adjusted to reflect subsequent conditions, including an option for fair value.

Investments are classified as short term or long term; as trading, available-for-sale, or held-to-maturity securities; and as noninfluential and noncontrolling, influential but noncontrolling, or controlling investments. These classifications play an important role in accounting for investments. Noninfluential and noncontrolling investments represent less than 20 percent ownership of a company; influential but noncontrolling investments represent 20 percent to 50 percent ownership; and controlling investments represent more than 50 percent ownership.

A company should disclose its accounting policies for investments and related details in the notes to its financial statements.

Managers and other employees must avoid using their knowledge of their company's planned investment transactions for personal gain.

LO2 Explain the financial reporting implications of short-term investments.

Short-term investments in stocks are classified as trading securities or available-for-sale securities. Trading securities are debt or equity securities that are bought and held principally for the purpose of being sold in the near term. They are classified as current assets on the balance sheet and are valued at fair value. Unrealized gains or losses on trading securities appear on the income statement.

Available-for-sale securities are debt or equity securities that do not meet the criteria for either trading or held-to-maturity securities. They are accounted for in the same way as trading securities with two exceptions: (1) an unrealized gain or loss is reported as a special item in the stockholders' equity section of the balance sheet; (2) if a decline in the value of a security is considered permanent, it is charged as a loss on the income statement.

LO3 Explain the financial reporting implications of long-term investments in stock and the cost-adjusted-to-market and equity methods used to account for them.

The cost-adjusted-to-market method is used to account for noninfluential and noncontrolling investments in stock. With this method, investments are initially recorded at cost and are then adjusted to market value by using an allowance account. The equity method is used to account for influential but noncontrolling investments. With this method, the investment is initially recorded at cost and is then adjusted for the investor's share of the company's net income or loss and subsequent dividends.

Consolidated financial statements are required when an investing company has legal and effective control over another company. Control exists when the parent company owns more than 50 percent of the voting stock of the subsidiary company.

LO4 Explain the financial reporting implications of consolidated financial statements.

Consolidated financial statements are useful to investors and others because they treat the parent company and its subsidiaries as an integrated economic unit. When a consolidated balance sheet is prepared at the date of acquisition, a work sheet entry is made to eliminate the investment from the parent company's financial statements and the stockholders' equity section of the subsidiary's financial statements. The assets and liabilities of the two companies are combined. If the parent owns less than 100 percent of the subsidiary, minority interest equal to the percentage of the subsidiary owned by minority stockholders multiplied by the subsidiary's net assets appears on the consolidated balance sheet. If the cost of the parent's investment in the subsidiary is greater than the subsidiary's book value, an amount equal to the excess of cost over book value is allocated to undervalued subsidiary assets and to goodwill. If the cost of the parent's investment in the subsidiary is less than book value, the excess of book value over cost should be used to reduce the book value of the subsidiary's long-term assets (other than long-term marketable securities).

When consolidated income statements are prepared, intercompany sales, purchases, interest income, interest expense, and other income and expenses from intercompany transactions must be eliminated to avoid double counting of these items.

The financial statements of foreign subsidiaries must be restated in terms of the parent company's reporting currency before consolidated financial statements can be prepared.

LO5 Explain the financial reporting implications of debt investments.

Held-to-maturity securities are debt securities that management intends to hold to their maturity date; they are valued on the balance sheet at cost adjusted for the effects of interest. Long-term investments in bonds fall into two categories: available-for-sale securities, which are recorded at cost and subsequently accounted for at fair value, and held-to-maturity securities.

REVIEW of Concepts and Terminology

The following concepts and terms were introduced in this chapter:

Available-for-sale securities: Debt or equity securities that do not meet the criteria for trading or held-to-maturity securities. **(LO1)**

Consolidated financial statements: Financial statements that reflect the combined operations of a parent company and its subsidiaries. **(LO3)**

Control: An investing company's ability to decide the operating and financial policies of another firm because it owns more than 50 percent of that firm's voting stock. **(LO1)**

Cost-adjusted-to-market method: A method of accounting for available-for-sale securities at cost adjusted for changes in the securities' market value. **(LO3)**

Eliminations: Entries made on consolidation work sheets to eliminate transactions between parent and subsidiary companies. **(LO4)**

Equity method: A method of accounting for influential but noncontrolling long-term investments in which the investment is initially recorded at cost and is then adjusted for the investor's share of the company's net income or loss and for dividends. **(LO3)**

Fair value: The exchange price associated with an actual or potential business transaction between market participants. **(LO1)**

Goodwill: The excess of the purchase price of a business over the fair market value of its net assets. Also called *goodwill from consolidation* **(LO4)**

Held-to-maturity securities: Debt securities that management intends to hold until their maturity date. **(LO1)**

Insider trading: Making use of inside information for personal gain. **(LO1)**

Marketable securities: Investments with a maturity of more than 90 days but that are intended to be held only until cash is needed to pay current obligations. Also called *short-term investments.* **(LO1)**

Minority interest: An amount recorded on a consolidated balance sheet that represents the holdings of owners of less than 50 percent of a subsidiary's voting stock. **(LO4)**

Multinational or transnational corporations: Companies that expand by establishing or buying foreign subsidiaries. **(LO4)**

Parent company: A company that has a controlling interest in another firm. **(LO3)**

Purchase method: A method of accounting for controlling investments in which similar accounts from the parent's and subsidiaries' statements are combined. **(LO4)**

Reporting currency: The currency in which consolidated financial statements are presented. **(LO4)**

Restatement: The stating of one currency in terms of another. **(LO4)**

Short-term investments: Investments that have a maturity of more than 90 days but that management intends to hold only until cash is needed to pay current obligations. Also called *marketable securities.* **(LO1)**

Significant influence: An investing company's ability to affect the operating and financial policies of the firm in which it has invested, even though it holds 50 percent or less of the voting stock. **(LO1)**

Subsidiary: A firm in which another company owns a controlling interest. **(LO3)**

Trading securities: Debt or equity securities bought and held principally for the purpose of being sold in the near term. **(LO1)**

REVIEW Problem

LO4 Consolidated Balance Sheet: Less than 100 Percent Ownership

In a cash transaction on June 30, 2010, Lapa Company purchased 90 percent of the outstanding stock of Poklader Company for $381,600. Directly after the acquisition, the balance sheets of the two companies were as follows:

	A	B	C	D	E
1				Lapa	Pokladek
2			Assets	Company	Company
3	Cash			$ 200,000	$ 24,000
4	Accounts receivable			325,000	120,000
5	Inventory			500,000	260,000
6	Investment in Pokladek Company			381,600	—
7	Plant and equipment (net)			750,000	440,000
8	Other assets			25,000	80,000
9	Total assets			$2,181,600	$924,000
10					
11			Liabilities and Stockholders' Equity		
12	Accounts payable			$ 400,000	$200,000
13	Long-term debt			500,000	300,000
14	Common stock			1,000,000	400,000
15	Retained earnings			281,600	24,000
16	Total liabilities and stockholders' equity			$2,181,600	$924,000
17					

The following information is also available:

1. Poklader Company's other assets represent a long-term investment in Lapa Company's long-term debt. Poklader purchased the debt for an amount equal to Lapa's carrying value of the debt.
2. Lapa Company owes Poklader Company $50,000 for services rendered.

Required

Prepare a work sheet for a consolidated balance sheet as of the acquisition date.

Answer to Review Problem

Lapa and Pokladek Companies
Work Sheet for Consolidated Balance Sheet
June 30, 2010

Accounts	Balance Sheet: Lapa Company	Balance Sheet: Pokladek Company	Eliminations: Debit		Eliminations: Credit		Consolidated Balance Sheet
Cash	200,000	24,000					224,000
Accounts receivable	325,000	120,000			(3)	50,000	395,000
Inventory	500,000	260,000					760,000
Investment in Pokladek Company	381,600	—			(1)	381,600	—
Plant and equipment (net)	750,000	440,000					1,190,000
Other assets	25,000	80,000			(2)	80,000	25,000
Total assets	2,181,600	924,000					2,594,000
Accounts payable	400,000	200,000	(3)	50,000			550,000
Long-term debt	500,000	300,000	(2)	80,000			720,000
Common stock	1,000,000	400,000	(1)	400,000			1,000,000
Retained earnings	281,600	24,000	(1)	24,000			281,600
Minority interest	—	—			(1)	42,400	42,400
Total liabilities and stockholders' equity	2,181,600	924,000		554,000		554,000	2,594,000

(1) Elimination of intercompany investment. Minority interest equals 10 percent of Pokladek Company's stockholders' equity [10% x ($400,000 + $24,000) = $42,400].
(2) Elimination of intercompany long-term debt.
(3) Elimination of intercompany receivables and payables.

CHAPTER ASSIGNMENTS

BUILDING Your Basic Knowledge and Skills

Short Exercises

LO2 **Trading Securities**

SE 1. Market Corporation began investing in trading securities in 2009. At the end of 2009, it had the following trading portfolio:

Security	Cost	Market Value
IBM (10,000 shares)	$440,000	$660,000
GAP (5,000 shares)	200,000	150,000
Totals	$640,000	$810,000

Prepare the necessary year-end adjusting entry on December 31 and the entry for the sale of all the GAP shares on the following March 23 for $190,000.

LO3 **Cost-Adjusted-to-Market Method**

SE 2. On December 31, 2009, the market value of Logan Tech Company's portfolio of long-term available-for-sale securities was $320,000. The cost of these securities was $285,000. Prepare the entry to adjust the portfolio to market at year end, assuming that the company did not have any long-term investments prior to 2009.

LO3 **Cost-Adjusted-to-Market Method**

SE 3. Refer to your answer to **SE 2**. Assume that on December 31, 2010, the cost of Logan Tech Company's portfolio of long-term available-for-sale securities was $285,000 and that its market value was $245,000. Prepare the entry to record the 2010 year-end adjustment.

LO3 **Equity Method**

SE 4. Perk Company owns 30 percent of Storm Company. In 2009, Storm Company earned $120,000 and paid $80,000 in dividends. Prepare entries in journal form for Perk Company's records on December 31 to reflect this information. Assume that the dividends are received on December 31.

LO3 **Methods of Accounting for Long-Term Investments**

SE 5. For each of the investments listed below, tell which of the following methods should be used for external financial reporting: (a) cost-adjusted-to-market method, (b) equity method, (c) consolidation of parent and subsidiary financial statements.

1. 49 percent investment in Ramir Corporation
2. 51 percent investment in Fur Corporation
3. 5 percent investment in Baker Corporation

LO4 **Purchase of 100 Percent at Book Value**

SE 6. Omega Corporation buys 100 percent ownership of Family Season Corporation for $200,000. At the time of the purchase, Family Season's stockholders' equity consisted of $40,000 in common stock and $160,000 in retained earnings. Omega's stockholders' equity consisted of $400,000 in common stock and $800,000 in retained earnings. After the purchase, what would be the amount, if any, of the following accounts on the consolidated balance sheet: goodwill, minority interest, common stock, and retained earnings?

LO4 **Purchase of Less than 100 Percent at Book Value**

SE 7. Assume the same facts as in **SE 6** except that Omega purchased 80 percent of Family Season Corporation for $160,000. After the purchase, what would be the amount, if any, of the following accounts on the consolidated balance sheet: goodwill, minority interest, common stock, and retained earnings?

LO4 **Purchase of 100 Percent at More than Book Value**

SE 8. Assume the same facts as in **SE 6** except that the purchase of 100 percent of Family Season Corporation was for $240,000. After the purchase, what would be the amount, if any, of the following accounts on the consolidated balance sheet: goodwill, minority interest, common stock, and retained earnings? Assume that the fair value of Family Season's net assets equals their book value.

LO4

Intercompany Transactions

SE 9. X Company owns 100 percent of Y Company. The following are accounts from the balance sheets and income statements of both companies:

	X Company	Y Company
Accounts receivable	$ 230,000	$150,000
Accounts payable	180,000	90,000
Sales	1,200,000	890,000
Cost of goods sold	710,000	540,000

What would be the combined amount of each of the above accounts on the consolidated financial statements assuming the following additional information? (1) Y Company sold to X Company merchandise at cost in the amount of $270,000; (2) X Company sold all the merchandise it bought from Y Company to customers, but it still owes Y Company $60,000 for the merchandise.

LO5

Held-to-Maturity Securities

SE 10. On May 31, Fournier Company invested $98,000 in U.S. Treasury bills. The bills mature in 120 days at $100,000. Prepare entries to record the purchase on May 31; the adjustment to accrue interest on June 30, which is the end of the fiscal year; and the receipt of cash at the maturity date of September 28.

Exercises

LO1 LO2 LO3

Discussion Questions

E 1. Develop brief answers to each of the following questions:

1. Where in the financial statements are investment transactions reported?
2. What would cause an Allowance to Adjust Short-Term Investments to Market account that has a negative (credit) balance at the beginning of the year to have a positive (debit) balance at the end of the year?
3. When a company uses the equity method to record its proportionate share of the income and dividends of a company in which it has invested, what are the cash flow effects?

LO4 LO5

Discussion Questions

E 2. Develop brief answers to each of the following questions:

1. Under what conditions would a company have both minority interest and goodwill in a consolidation?
2. Why must the financial statements of foreign subsidiaries be restated?
3. What is the logic behind treating held-to-maturity securities different from any other investment?

LO2

Trading Securities

E 3. Owen Corporation, which has begun investing in trading securities, engaged in the following transactions:

Jan. 6 Purchased 7,000 shares of Google stock, $60 per share.
Feb. 15 Purchased 9,000 shares of Starbucks, $44 per share.

At year end on June 30, Google was trading at $80 per share, and Starbucks was trading at $36 per share.

Record the entries for the purchases. Then record the necessary year-end adjusting entry. (Include a schedule of the trading portfolio cost and market in the explanation.) Also record the entry for the sale of all the Starbucks shares on August 20 for $32 per share. Is the last entry affected by the June 30 adjustment?

LO3 **Long-Term Investments**

E 4. Canalle Corporation has the following portfolio of long-term available-for-sale securities at year end, December 31, 2010:

Company	Percentage of Voting Stock Held	Cost	Year-End Market Value
K Corporation	4	$160,000	$190,000
L Corporation	12	750,000	550,000
M Corporation	5	60,000	110,000
Total		$970,000	$850,000

Both the Unrealized Loss on Long-Term Investments account and the Allowance to Adjust Long-Term Investments to Market account currently have a balance of $80,000 from the last accounting period. Prepare T accounts with a beginning balance for each of these accounts. Record the effects of the above information on the accounts and determine the ending balances.

LO3 **Long-Term Investments: Cost-Adjusted-to-Market and Equity Methods**

E 5. On January 1, Caviar Corporation purchased, as long-term investments, 8 percent of the voting stock of Union Corporation for $500,000 and 45 percent of the voting stock of Boss Corporation for $4 million. During the year, Union Corporation had earnings of $200,000 and paid dividends of $80,000. Boss Corporation had earnings of $600,000 and paid dividends of $400,000. The market value did not change for either investment during the year. Which of these investments should be accounted for using the cost-adjusted-to-market method? Which should be accounted for using the equity method? At what amount should each investment be carried on the balance sheet at year end? Give a reason for each choice.

LO3 **Long-Term Investments: Equity Method**

E 6. On January 1, 2010, Huang Corporation acquired 40 percent of the voting stock of Lee Corporation, an amount sufficient to exercise significant influence over Lee Corporation's activities, for $2,400,000 in cash. On December 31, Huang determined that Lee paid dividends of $400,000 but incurred a net loss of $200,000 for 2010. Prepare entries in T account form to reflect this information.

LO3 **Methods of Accounting for Long-Term Investments**

E 7. Teague Corporation has the following long-term investments:

1. 60 percent of the common stock of Oho Corporation
2. 13 percent of the common stock of Salt, Inc.
3. 50 percent of the nonvoting preferred stock of Kluz Corporation
4. 100 percent of the common stock of its financing subsidiary, LP, Inc.

5. 35 percent of the common stock of the French company Merli
6. 70 percent of the common stock of the Canadian company Ontario Cannery

For each of these investments, tell which of the following methods should be used for external financial reporting, and why:

a. Cost-adjusted-to-market method
b. Equity method
c. Consolidation of parent and subsidiary financial statements

LO4 **Elimination Entry for a Purchase at Book Value**

E 8. R&M Manufacturing Company purchased 100 percent of the common stock of Bonn Manufacturing Company for $1,200,000. Bonn's stockholders' equity included common stock of $800,000 and retained earnings of $400,000. Prepare the eliminating entry in journal form that would appear on the work sheet for consolidating the balance sheets of these two entities as of the acquisition date.

LO4 **Elimination Entry and Minority Interest**

E 9. The stockholders' equity section of Veritas Corporation's balance sheet appeared as follows on December 31:

Common stock, $10 par value, 40,000 shares	
authorized and issued	$400,000
Retained earnings	48,000
Total stockholders' equity	$448,000

Midas Manufacturing Company owns 80 percent of Veritas's voting stock and paid $11.20 per share. In journal form, prepare the entry (including minority interest) to eliminate Midas' investment and Veritas's stockholders' equity that would appear on the work sheet used in preparing the consolidated balance sheet for the two firms.

LO4 **Consolidated Balance Sheet with Goodwill**

E 10. On September 1, 2010, A Company purchased 100 percent of the voting stock of B Company for $480,000 in cash. The separate condensed balance sheets immediately after the purchase were as follows:

	A Company	B Company
Other assets	$1,103,000	$544,500
Investment in B Company	480,000	—
Total assets	$1,583,000	$544,500
Liabilities	$ 435,500	$ 94,500
Common stock	500,000	150,000
Retained earnings	647,500	300,000
Total liabilities and stockholders' equity	$1,583,000	$544,500

Prepare a work sheet for preparing the consolidated balance sheet immediately after A Company acquired control of B Company. Assume that any excess cost of A Company's investment in the subsidiary over book value is attributable to goodwill from consolidation.

LO4

Preparation of Consolidated Income Statement

E 11. Lowell Company has owned 100 percent of Rich Company since 2009. The income statements of these two companies for the year ended December 31, 2010, follow.

	Lowell Company	Rich Company
Net sales	$3,000,000	$1,200,000
Cost of goods sold	1,500,000	800,000
Gross margin	$1,500,000	$ 400,000
Less: Selling expenses	$ 500,000	$ 100,000
General and administrative expenses	600,000	200,000
Total operating expenses	$1,100,000	$ 300,000
Income from operations	$ 400,000	$ 100,000
Other income	120,000	—
Net income	$ 520,000	$ 100,000

The following is additional information: (1) Rich Company purchased $560,000 of inventory from Lowell Company, which it had sold to Rich customers by the end of the year. (2) Rich Company leased its building from Lowell Company for $120,000 per year. Prepare a consolidated income statement work sheet for the two companies for the year ended December 31, 2010. Ignore income taxes.

LO5

Held-to-Maturity Securities

E 12. Jolanta Company experiences heavy sales in the summer and early fall, after which time it has excess cash to invest until the next spring. On November 1, 2009, the company invested $388,000 in U.S. Treasury bills. The bills mature in 180 days at $400,000. Prepare entries to record the purchase on November 1; the adjustment to accrue interest on December 31, which is the end of the fiscal year; and the receipt of cash at the maturity date of April 30.

Problems

LO1 LO2

Accounting for Investments

P 1. Karas Gas Corporation is a successful oil and gas exploration business in the southwestern United States. At the beginning of 2010, the company made investments in three companies that perform services in the oil and gas industry. The details of each of these investments follow.

Karas Gas purchased 200,000 shares of Shore Service Corporation at a cost of $16 per share. Shore has 3 million shares outstanding and during 2010 paid dividends of $.80 per share on earnings of $1.60 per share. At the end of the year, Shore's shares were selling for $24 per share.

Karas Gas also purchased 4 million shares of Speed Drilling Company at $8 per share. Speed has 20 million shares outstanding. In 2010, Speed paid a dividend of $.40 per share on earnings of $.80 per share. During the year, the president of Karas Gas was appointed to Speed's board of directors. At the end of the year, Speed's stock was selling for $12 per share.

In another action, Karas Gas purchased 2 million shares of Tom Oil Field Supplies Company's 10 million outstanding shares at $12 per share. The president of Karas Gas sought membership on Tom's board of directors but was rebuffed when a majority of shareholders stated they did not want to be associated with Karas Gas. Tom paid a dividend of $.80 per share and reported a net income of only $.40 per share for the year. By the end of the year, its stock price had dropped to $4 per share.

Required

1. For each investment, make entries in journal form for (a) initial investment, (b) receipt of cash dividend, and (c) recognition of income (if appropriate).
2. What adjusting entry (if any) is required at the end of the year?
3. Assuming that Karas Gas sells its investment in Tom after the first of the year for $6 per share, what journal entry would be made?
4. Assuming no other transactions occur and that the market value of Karas Gas's investment in Shore exceeds cost by $4,800,000 at the end of the second year, what adjusting entry (if any) would be required?
5. **User insight ▶** What principal factors were considered in determining how to account for Karas Gas's investments? Should they be shown on the balance sheet as short-term or long-term investments? What factors affect this decision?

Long-Term Investments: Equity Method

P 2. Basic Company owns 40 percent of the voting stock of Oslo Company. The investment account for this company on Basic's balance sheet had a balance of $600,000 on January 1, 2010. During 2010, the Oslo Company reported the following quarterly earnings and dividends paid:

Quarter	Earnings	Dividends Paid
1	$ 80,000	$ 40,000
2	60,000	40,000
3	160,000	40,000
4	(40,000)	40,000
	$260,000	$160,000

Basic Company exercises a significant influence over Oslo's operations and therefore uses the equity method to account for its investment.

Required

1. Prepare a T account for Basic's investment in Oslo. Enter the beginning balance, the relevant entries for the year in total, and the ending balance.
2. **User insight ▶** What is the effect and placement of the entries in requirement **1** on Basic Company's earnings as reported on the income statement?
3. **User insight ▶** What is the effect and placement of the entries in requirement **1** on the statement of cash flows?
4. **User insight ▶** How would the effects on the statements differ if Basic's ownership represented only a 10 percent share of Oslo?

Consolidated Balance Sheet: Cost Exceeding Book Value

P 3. The balance sheets of Sail and Ivan Companies as of December 31, 2010, appear at the top of the next page.

Assume that Sail Company purchased 100 percent of Ivan's common stock for $700,000 immediately prior to December 31, 2010. Also assume that $50,000 of the excess of cost over book value is attributable to the increased value of Ivan Company's property, plant, and equipment. Sail considers the rest of the excess to be goodwill.

Required

1. Prepare a work sheet for preparing a consolidated balance sheet as of the acquisition date.

	Sail Company	Ivan Company
Assets		
Cash	$ 200,000	$ 60,000
Accounts receivable	275,000	600,000
Investment in Ivan Company	700,000	—
Property, plant, and equipment (net)	685,000	450,000
Total assets	$1,860,000	$1,110,000
Liabilities and Stockholders' Equity		
Accounts payable	$ 475,000	$ 535,000
Common stock, $20 par value	925,000	500,000
Retained earnings	460,000	75,000
Total liabilities and stockholders' equity	$1,860,000	$1,110,000

User insight ▶ 2. If you were reading Sail's consolidated balance sheet, what account would indicate that Sail paid more than fair value for Ivan and where would you find it on the balance sheet? Also, would you expect the amount of this account to change from year-to-year? What would cause it to change?

Consolidated Balance Sheet: Less than 100 Percent Ownership

P 4. In a cash transaction, Gil Company purchased 70 percent of the outstanding stock of Cat Company for $296,800 cash on June 30, 2010. Immediately after the acquisition, the separate balance sheets of the companies appeared as shown below.

	Gil Company	Cat Company
Assets		
Cash	$ 160,000	$ 24,000
Accounts receivable	260,000	120,000
Inventory	400,000	260,000
Investment in Cat Company	296,800	—
Property, plant, and equipment (net)	600,000	440,000
Other assets	20,000	80,000
Total assets	$1,736,800	$924,000
Liabilities and Stockholders' Equity		
Accounts payable	$ 320,000	$200,000
Long-term debt	400,000	300,000
Common stock, $10 par value	800,000	400,000
Retained earnings	216,800	24,000
Total liabilities and stockholders' equity	$1,736,800	$924,000

Additional information: (a) Cat Company's other assets represent a long-term investment in Gil Company's long-term debt. The debt was purchased for an amount equal to Gil's carrying value of the debt. (b) Gil Company owes Cat Company $40,000 for services rendered.

Required

1. Prepare a work sheet for preparing a consolidated balance sheet as of the acquisition date.

User insight ▶ 2. If you were reading Gil's consolidated balance sheet, what account would indicate that Gil owned less than 100 percent of Cat and where would you find it on the balance sheet?

Alternate Problems

LO3

Long-Term Investments: Equity Method

P 5. Snow Corporation owns 35 percent of the voting stock of Nivella Corporation. The Investment account on Snow's books as of January 1, 2010, was $360,000. During 2010, Nivella reported the following quarterly earnings and dividends:

Quarter	Earnings	Dividends Paid
1	$ 80,000	$ 50,000
2	120,000	50,000
3	60,000	50,000
4	(40,000)	50,000
	$220,000	$200,000

Because of the percentage of voting shares Snow owns, it can exercise significant influence over the operations of Nivella Corporation. Therefore, Snow Corporation must account for the investment using the equity method.

Required

1. Prepare a T account for Snow Corporation's investment in Nivella, and enter the beginning balance, the relevant entries for the year in total, and the ending balance.

User insight ▶ 2. What is the effect and placement of the entries in requirement **1** on Snow Corporation's earnings as reported on the income statement?

User insight ▶ 3. What is the effect and placement of the entries in requirement **1** on the statement of cash flows?

User insight ▶ 4. How would the effects on the statements differ if Snow's ownership represented only a 15 percent share of Nivella?

Consolidated Balance Sheet: Cost Exceeding Book Value

P 6. The balance sheets of Ola and Jake Companies as of December 31, 2010, appear at the top of the next page.

Assume that Ola Company purchased 100 percent of Jake's common stock for $350,000 immediately prior to December 31, 2010. Also assume that $80,000 of the excess of cost over book value is attributable to the increased value of Jake Company's property, plant, and equipment. The rest of the excess is considered by Ola Company to be goodwill.

Required

1. Prepare a work sheet for preparing a consolidated balance sheet as of the acquisition date.

User insight ▶ 2. If you were reading Ola's consolidated balance sheet, what account would indicate that Ola paid more than fair value for Jake and where would you find it on the balance sheet? Also, would you expect the amount of this account to change from year-to-year? What would cause it to change?

	Ola Company	Jake Company
Assets		
Cash	$ 60,000	$ 40,000
Accounts receivable	100,000	30,000
Investment in Jake Company	350,000	—
Property, plant, and equipment (net)	100,000	180,000
Total assets	$610,000	$250,000
Liabilities and Stockholders' Equity		
Accounts payable	$110,000	$ 30,000
Common stock, $20 par value	400,000	200,000
Retained earnings	100,000	20,000
Total liabilities and stockholders' equity	$610,000	$250,000

ENHANCING Your Knowledge, Skills, and Critical Thinking

Conceptual Understanding Cases

LO2 LO3 **Understanding Investment Accounting**

C 1. Dell Computer Corporation has significant investment activities. The following items are from Dell's 2007 financial statements (in millions):[18]

Short-term investments	$ 752
Long-term investments	2,147
Investment income	275
Purchase of investments	8,343
Sales of investments	10,320
Change in unrealized gains (losses) on long-term investments, net	31

Dell states that all debt and equities securities are classified as available-for-sale and are subject to an annual impairment test.

1. Where would you find each of the above items in Dell Computer's financial statements?
2. What value (cost or fair value) would you expect the first two items on Dell's balance sheet to represent?
3. What are impairments, and how do they differ from unrealized losses on long-term investments?

LO4 **Goodwill and Minority Interest**

C 2. DreamWorks Animation makes well-known animated films like *Shrek 2*. Two items on the company's 2006 balance sheet are as follows:[19]

Goodwill	$34,216
Minority interest	2,941

1. What is the difference between goodwill and minority interest and where do these items appear on the balance sheet?
2. The amount of goodwill did not change from 2005 to 2006. Assuming no new acquisitions or sales, what would cause the amount of goodwill to change from year to year? Would it increase or decrease?

Interpreting Financial Reports

Effects of Consolidating Finance Subsidiaries

C 3. American Stores Corporation is one of the largest owners of discount appliance stores in the United States. It owns Bi-Lo Superstores and several other discount chains. It has a wholly owned finance subsidiary handle its accounts receivable. Condensed balance sheets for American Stores and its finance subsidiary are shown below (in millions). The fiscal year ends January 31, 2010.

	American Stores Corporation	Finance Subsidiary
Assets		
Current assets (except accounts receivable)	$ 866	$ 1
Accounts receivable (net)	293	869
Property, equipment, and other assets	933	—
Investment in finance subsidiary	143	—
Total assets	$2,235	$870
Liabilities and Stockholders' Equity		
Current liabilities	$ 717	$ 10
Long-term liabilities	859	717
Stockholders' equity	659	143
Total liabilities and stockholders' equity	$2,235	$870

Total sales to customers were $4 billion. The FASB requires all majority-owned subsidiaries to be consolidated in the parent company's financial statements. American Stores' management believes it is misleading to consolidate the finance subsidiary because it distorts the real operations of the company.

1. Prepare a consolidated balance sheet for American Stores Corporation and its finance subsidiary.
2. Demonstrate the effects of consolidating by computing the following ratios for American Stores before and after the consolidation in **1**: receivable turnover, days' sales uncollected, and debt to equity ratio (use year-end balances).
3. What are some of the other ratios that will be affected by consolidating the financial statements? Does consolidation assist investors and creditors in assessing the risk of investing in American Stores' securities or lending the company money? Relate your answer to your calculations in **2**.
4. What do you think of management's view that it is misleading to consolidate the finance subsidiary?

Decision Analysis Using Excel

Accounting for Short-Term Investments

C 4. Malam Christmas Tree Company's business—the growing and selling of Christmas trees—is seasonal. By January 1, after its heavy selling season, the company has cash on hand that will not be needed for several months. It has minimal expenses from January to October and heavy expenses during the harvest and shipping months of November and December. The company's management follows the practice of investing the idle cash in marketable securities, which can be sold when funds are needed for operations. The company's fiscal year ends on June 30.

On January 10 of the current year, Malam has cash of $597,300 on hand. It keeps $20,000 on hand for operating expenses and invests the rest as follows:

$100,000 three-month Treasury bills	$ 97,800
5,000 shares of Ford Motor Co. ($10 per share)	50,000
5,000 shares of McDonald's ($25 per share)	125,000
4,350 shares of IBM ($70 per share)	304,500
Total short-term investments	$577,300

On February 10 and May 10, Malam receives quarterly cash dividends from each company in which it has invested: $.10 per share from Ford Motor Co., $.14 per share from McDonald's, and $.20 per share from IBM. The Treasury bills are redeemed at face value on April 10. On June 1, management sells 1,000 shares of McDonald's at $28 per share.

On June 30, the market values of the investments are as follows:

Ford Motor Co.	$11 per share
McDonald's	$23 per share
IBM	$65 per share

Malam receives another quarterly dividend from each company on August 10. It sells all its remaining shares on November 1 at the following prices:

Ford Motor Co.	$ 9 per share
McDonald's	$22 per share
IBM	$80 per share

1. Record the investment transactions that occurred on January 10, February 10, April 10, May 10, and June 1. The Treasury bills are accounted for as held-to-maturity securities, and the stocks are trading securities. Prepare the required adjusting entry on June 30 and record the investment transactions on August 10 and November 1.
2. Explain how the short-term investments would be shown on the balance sheet on June 30.
3. After November 1, what is the balance of Allowance to Adjust Short-Term Investments to Market, and what will happen to this account next June?
4. What is your assessment of Malam Christmas Tree Company's strategy with regard to idle cash?

Annual Report Case: CVS Caremark Corporation

Major Acquisition

C 5. Refer to Note 2 of the **CVS** annual report in the Supplement to Chapter 1. The company finalized a major acquisition in 2007 for the purchase of Caremark Rx, Inc. What is the purchase price of Caremark? Is CVS paying more than the fair value for the net assets of Caremark? If so, how much more is it paying and what does the excess represent?

Comparison Case: CVS Versus Southwest

LO2

Investments in Derivatives

C 6. Refer to the annual report of **CVS** and the financial statements of **Southwest Airlines Co**. in the Supplement to Chapter 1. Refer to comprehensive income (loss) in each company's statement of shareholders' equity. Which item for each company refers to derivatives (a type of investment involving future contracts)? What causes either an unrealized gain or loss to occur? In the case of Southwest, find the accounting policy with regard to financial derivatives instruments in Note 1 to the financial statements. What problem does Southwest's management face in determining the fair market value of its derivatives? How does management solve the problem?

Ethical Dilemma Case

LO1

Insider Trading

C 7. Refer to the discussion about insider trading in this chapter to answer the following questions:

1. What does *insider trading* mean?
2. Why do you think insider trading is illegal in the United States and in Germany?
3. Why do you think insider trading is permissible in some other countries?
4. Can you think of any reasons why insider trading should be permitted in the United States?

Internet Case

LO3 LO4

Comparison of Two Recent Acquisitions

C 8. Mergers and acquisitions are in the news almost every day. Go to the website for **MSNBC** and scan recent headlines to locate two articles related to one company purchasing or making an offer to purchase another company. Read the articles and summarize the nature of the actual or proposed acquisition. What are the companies' names? What industry are they in? What is the dollar amount of the acquisition? How will the acquisition be paid for—in cash, stock, or a combination of cash and stock? In what ways are the acquisitions similar? How do they differ? Be prepared to present your findings in class.

Group Activity Case

LO1 LO2 LO3

Identification of Investments and Resulting Gains and Losses

C 9. **Microsoft**, one of the most successful businesses in the history of commerce, has accumulated a large investment portfolio, which in a recent year consisted of the following (in millions):[20]

Cash and cash equivalents	$ 6,111
Short-term investments-available-for-sale	17,300
Long-term investments—equity securities	10,117
Total investments	$33,528

In addition, during the year Microsoft had net realized gains on investments of \$65 million, \$408 million of impairments, unrealized losses of \$108 million, and unrealized gains of \$1,907 million.

Divide into at least seven groups to discuss each of the four types of investments and the three types of gains or losses. Each group should discuss the nature of each gain or loss and the nature of the investment that gave rise to it. Discuss where each investment and gain or loss would appear in the financial statements. Be prepared to present your group's findings in class.

Business Communication Case

LO1 Presentation on Investment Classification and Valuation

C 10. The classification and valuation of investments can be confusing for someone not familiar with classifying investments. Suppose you have been asked to make a short (five-minute) presentation that explains this classification scheme. Develop a one-page outline with talking points that explains the three types of short-term and long-term investments and how they are valued at year end. Then briefly cover how accounting for long-term investments depends on the level and percentage of ownership. Be prepared to give your presentation in class or to a small group.

APPENDIX A Accounting for Unincorporated Businesses

Throughout the book, we have focused on accounting for the corporate form of business. In this appendix, our focus is on accounting for sole proprietorships and partnerships.

Accounting for Sole Proprietorships

A *sole proprietorship* is a business owned by one person. For the individual, this business form can be a convenient way of separating business activities from personal interests. Legally, however, the proprietorship is the same economic unit as the individual. The sole proprietor receives all the profits or losses and is liable for all the obligations of the business. Proprietorships represent the largest number of businesses in the United States, but typically they are the smallest in size. The life of a proprietorship ends when the owner wishes it to or at the owner's death or incapacity.

When someone invests in his or her own company, the amount of the investment is recorded in that person's Capital account. For example, the entry to record the initial investment of $10,000 by Hyun Hooper in her new mail-order business would be a debit to the Cash account for $10,000 and a credit to the Hyun Hooper, Capital account for $10,000.

During the period, Hooper will probably withdraw assets from the business for personal living expenses. Because there is no legal separation between the owner and the sole proprietorship, it is not necessary to make a formal declaration of a withdrawal, as would be required in the case of corporate dividends. The withdrawal of $500 by Hooper is recorded as a debit to the Hyun Hooper, Withdrawals account for $500 and a credit to the Cash account for $500.

Revenue and expense accounts for sole proprietorships are closed out to Income Summary in the same way as they are for corporations. Income Summary, however, is closed to the Capital account instead of to Retained Earnings. For example, the closing entries that follow assume a net income of $1,000 and withdrawals of $500:

Income Summary	1,000	
Hyun Hooper, Capital		1,000
To close Income Summary in a sole proprietorship		
Hyun Hooper, Capital	500	
Hyun Hooper, Withdrawals		500
To close Withdrawals		

Accounting for Partnerships

The Uniform Partnership Act, which has been adopted by a majority of the states, defines a *partnership* as "an association of two or more persons to carry on as co-owners of a business for profit." Normally, partnerships are formed when owners of small businesses wish to combine capital or managerial talents for some common business purpose. Partnerships are treated as separate entities in accounting, but legally there is no economic separation between them and their owners. They differ in many ways from the other forms of business. The following are some of their important characteristics:

Voluntary Association A partnership is a voluntary association of individuals rather than a legal entity in itself. Therefore, a partner is responsible under the law for his or her partners' actions within the scope of the business. A partner also has unlimited liability for the debts of the partnership. Because of these potential liabilities, a partner must be allowed to choose the people who join the partnership.

Partnership Agreement A partnership is easy to form. Two or more people simply agree to be partners in a business enterprise. This agreement is known as a *partnership agreement*. The partnership agreement does not have to be in writing. However, it is good business practice to have a written document that clearly states the details of the partnership, including the name, location, and purpose of the business; the partners' names and their respective duties; the investments of each partner; the method of distributing income and losses; and procedures for the admission and withdrawal of partners, the withdrawal of assets allowed each partner, and the liquidation (termination) of the business.

Limited Life Because a partnership is formed by an agreement between partners, it has a *limited life*. It may be dissolved when a new partner is admitted; when a partner withdraws, goes bankrupt, is incapacitated (to the point that he or she cannot perform as obligated), retires, or dies; or when the terms of the partnership agreement are met (e.g., when the project for which the partnership was formed is completed). The partnership agreement can be written to cover each of these situations, thus allowing the partnership to continue legally.

Mutual Agency Each partner is an agent of the partnership within the scope of the business. Because of this *mutual agency*, any partner can bind the partnership to a business agreement as long as he or she acts within the scope of the company's normal operations. For example, a partner in a used-car business can bind the partnership through the purchase or sale of used cars. But this partner cannot bind the partnership to a contract for buying men's clothing or any other goods that are not related to the used-car business.

Unlimited Liability Each partner has personal *unlimited liability* for all the debts of the partnership. If a partnership cannot pay its debts, creditors must first satisfy their claims from the assets of the business. If these assets are not enough to pay all debts, the creditors can seek payment from the personal assets of each partner. If a partner's personal assets are used up before the debts are paid, the creditors can claim additional assets from the remaining partners who are able to pay. Each partner, then, can be required by law to pay all the debts of the partnership.

Co-Ownership of Partnership Property When individuals invest property in a partnership, they give up the right to their separate use of the property. The property becomes an asset of the partnership and is owned jointly by the partners.

Participation in Partnership Income Each partner has the right to share in the company's income and the responsibility to share in its losses. The partnership agreement should state the method of distributing income and losses to each partner. If the agreement describes how income should be shared but does not mention losses, losses are distributed in the same way as income. If the agreement does not describe the method of income and loss distribution, the partners must by law share income and losses equally.

Accounting for Partners' Equity

The owners' equity of a partnership is called *partners' equity.* In accounting for partners' equity, it is necessary to maintain separate Capital and Withdrawals accounts for each partner and to divide the income and losses of the company among the partners. In the partners' equity section of the balance sheet, the balance of each partner's Capital account is listed separately:

Liabilities and Partners' Equity		
Total liabilities		$28,000
Partners' equity		
Desmond, capital	$25,000	
Frank, capital	34,000	
Total partners' equity		59,000
Total liabilities and partners' equity		$87,000

Each partner invests cash, other assets, or both in the partnership according to the partnership agreement. Noncash assets should be valued at their fair market value on the date they are transferred to the partnership. The assets invested by a partner are debited to the proper account, and the total amount is credited to the partner's Capital account.

To show how partners' investments are recorded, let's assume that Jack Haddock and Pilar Villamer have agreed to combine their capital and equipment in a partnership to operate a jewelry store. According to their partnership agreement, Haddock will invest $28,000 cash and $47,000 of equipment, and the partnership will assume a note payable on the equipment of $10,000. The entry to record one partner's initial investment is as follows:

Date	Account	Debit	Credit
July 1	Cash	28,000	
	Equipment	47,000	
	Note Payable		10,000
	Jack Haddock, Capital		65,000
	Initial investment of Jack Haddock in Haddock and Villamer		

Distribution of Partnership Income and Losses

A partnership's income and losses can be distributed according to whatever method the partners specify in the partnership agreement. Income in this form of business normally has three components: return to the partners for the use of their capital (called *interest on partners' capital*), compensation for services the partners have rendered (partners' salaries), and other income for any special contributions individual partners may make to the partnership or for risks they may take. The breakdown of total income into its three components helps clarify how much each partner has contributed to the firm.

Distributing income and losses among partners can be accomplished by using stated ratios or capital balance ratios or by paying the partners salaries and interest on their capital and sharing the remaining income according to stated ratios. *Salaries* and *interest* here are not *salaries expense* or *interest expense* in the ordinary sense of the terms. They do not affect the amount of reported net income. Instead, they refer to ways of determining each partner's share of net income or loss based on the time the partner spends on the business and the money he or she invests in it.

Stated Ratios One method of distributing income and losses is to give each partner a stated ratio of the total income or loss. If each partner is making an equal contribution to the firm, each can assume the same share of income and losses. It is important to understand that an equal contribution to the firm does not necessarily mean an equal capital investment in the firm. One partner may be devoting more time and talent to the firm, whereas another may have made a larger capital investment. And if the partners contribute unequally to the firm, unequal stated ratios can be appropriate. Let's assume that Haddock and Villamer had a net income last year of $140,000 and that the stated ratio for Haddock is 60 percent and for Villamer, it is 40 percent. The computation of each partner's share of the income and the journal entry to show the distribution based on these ratios are as follows:

Haddock ($140,000 × .60)	$ 84,000
Villamer ($140,000 × .40)	56,000
Net income	$140,000

June 30	Income Summary	140,000	
	Jack Haddock, Capital		84,000
	Pilar Villamer, Capital		56,000
	Distribution of income for the year to the partners' Capital accounts		

Capital Balance Ratios If invested capital produces the most income for the partnership, then income and losses may be distributed according to *capital balance*. One way of distributing income and losses here is to use a ratio based on each partner's capital balance at the beginning of the year.

For example, suppose that at the start of the fiscal year, July 1, 2010, Jack Haddock's Capital account showed a $65,000 balance and Pilar Villamer's Capital account showed a $60,000 balance. The total partners' equity in the firm, then, was $125,000. Each partner's capital balance at the beginning of the year divided by the total partners' equity at the beginning of the year is that partner's beginning capital balance ratio:

	Beginning Capital Balance	*Beginning Capital Balance Ratio*
Jack Haddock	$ 65,000	65 ÷ 125 = .52 = 52%
Pilar Villamer	60,000	60 ÷ 125 = .48 = 48%
	$125,000	

The income that each partner should receive when distribution is based on beginning capital balance ratios is figured by multiplying the total income by each partner's capital ratio. If we assume that income for the year was $140,000, Jack

Haddock's share of that income was $72,800, and Pilar Villamer's share was $67,200:

Jack Haddock	$140,000 × .52 =	$ 72,800
Pilar Villamer	$140,000 × .48 =	67,200
		$140,000

Salaries, Interest, and Stated Ratios Partners generally do not contribute equally to a firm. To make up for unequal contributions, a partnership agreement can allow for partners' salaries, interest on partners' capital balances, or a combination of both in the distribution of income. Again, salaries and interest of this kind are not deducted as expenses before the partnership income is determined. They represent a method of arriving at an equitable distribution of income or loss.

Salaries allow for differences in the services that partners provide the business. However, they do not take into account differences in invested capital. To allow for capital differences, each partner can receive, in addition to salary, a stated interest on his or her invested capital. Suppose that Jack Haddock and Pilar Villamer agree to annual salaries of $8,000 and $7,000, respectively, as well as 10 percent interest on their beginning capital balances, and to share any remaining income equally. The calculations for Haddock and Villamer, assuming income of $140,000, appear below.

	Income of Partner		Income
	Haddock	Villamer	Distributed
Total income for distribution			$140,000
Distribution of salaries			
Haddock	$ 8,000		
Villamer		$ 7,000	(15,000)
Remaining income after salaries			$125,000
Distribution of interest			
Haddock ($65,000 × .10)	6,500		
Villamer ($60,000 × .10)		6,000	(12,500)
Remaining income after salaries and interest			$112,500
Equal distribution of remaining income			
Haddock ($112,500 × .50)	56,250		
Villamer ($112,500 × .50)		56,250	(112,500)
Remaining income			—
Income of partners	$70,750	$69,250	$140,000

If the partnership agreement allows for the distribution of salaries or interest or both, the amounts must be allocated to the partners even if profits are not enough to cover the salaries and interest. In fact, even if the company has a loss, these allocations must nonetheless be made. After the allocation of salaries and interest, the negative balance, or loss, must be distributed according to the stated ratio in the partnership agreement or equally if the agreement does not mention a ratio.

For example, let's assume that Haddock and Villamer agreed to the following conditions, with much higher annual salaries, for the distribution of income and losses:

	Salaries	*Interest*	*Beginning Capital Balance*
Haddock	$70,000	10% of beginning	$65,000
Villamer	60,000	capital balances	60,000

The computations for the distribution of the income and loss, again assuming income of $140,000, are as follows:

	Income of Partner		**Income**
	Haddock	**Villamer**	**Distributed**
Total income for distribution			$140,000
Distribution of salaries			
Haddock	$70,000		
Villamer		$60,000	(130,000)
Remaining income after salaries			$ 10,000
Distribution of interest			
Haddock ($65,000 × .10)	6,500		
Villamer ($60,000 × .10)		6,000	(12,500)
Remaining income after salaries and interest			($ 2,500)
Equal distribution of negative balance*			
Haddock ($2,500 × .50)	(1,250)		
Villamer ($2,500 × .50)		(1,250)	2,500
Remaining income			—
Income of partners	$75,250	$64,750	$140,000

*Notice that the negative balance is distributed equally because the partnership agreement does not indicate how income and losses should be distributed after salaries and interest are paid.

Dissolution of a Partnership

Dissolution of a partnership occurs whenever there is a change in the original association of partners. When a partnership is dissolved, the partners lose their authority to continue the business as a going concern. This does not mean that the business operation necessarily is ended or interrupted, but it does mean—from a legal and accounting standpoint—that the separate entity ceases to exist. The remaining partners can act for the partnership in finishing the affairs of the business or in forming a new partnership that will be a new accounting entity. The dissolution of a partnership takes place through, among other events, the admission of a new partner, the withdrawal of a partner, or the death of a partner.

Admission of a New Partner The admission of a new partner dissolves the old partnership because a new association has been formed. Dissolving the old partnership and creating a new one requires the consent of all the original partners and the ratification of a new partnership agreement. An individual can be admitted to a partnership in one of two ways: by purchasing an interest in the partnership from one or more of the original partners, or by investing assets in the partnership.

Purchasing an Interest from a Partner When a person purchases an interest in a partnership from an original partner, the transaction is a personal one between these two people. However, the interest purchased must be transferred from the Capital account of the selling partner to the Capital account of the new partner.

Suppose that Jack Haddock decides to sell his interest of $70,000 in Haddock and Villamer to Richard Davis for $100,000 on August 31, and that Pilar Villamer agrees to the sale. The entry to record the sale on the partnership books looks like this:

Aug. 31	Jack Haddock, Capital	70,000	
	Richard Davis, Capital		70,000
	Transfer of Jack Haddock's equity to Richard Davis		

Notice that the entry records the book value of the equity, not the amount Davis pays. The amount Davis pays is a personal matter between Davis and Haddock.

Investing Assets in a Partnership When a new partner is admitted through an investment in the partnership, both the assets and the partners' equity in the firm increase. This is because the assets the new partner invests become partnership assets, and as partnership assets increase, partners' equity increases.

For example, assume that Richard Davis wants to invest $75,000 for a one-third interest in the partnership of Haddock and Villamer. The Capital accounts of Jack Haddock and Pilar Villamer are $70,000 and $80,000, respectively. The assets of the firm are valued correctly. So, the partners agree to sell Davis a one-third interest in the firm for $75,000. Davis's $75,000 investment equals a one-third interest in the firm after the investment is added to the previously existing capital of the partnership:

Jack Haddock, Capital	$ 70,000
Pilar Villamer, Capital	80,000
Davis's investment	75,000
Total capital after Davis's investment	$225,000
One-third interest = $225,000 ÷ 3 =	$ 75,000

The entry to record Davis's investment is as follows:

Aug. 31	Cash	75,000	
	Richard Davis, Capital		75,000
	Admission of Richard Davis for a one-third interest in the company		

Bonus to the Old Partners A partnership is sometimes so profitable or otherwise advantageous that a new investor is willing to pay more than the actual dollar interest he or she receives in the partnership. Suppose an individual pays $100,000 for an $80,000 interest in a partnership. The $20,000 excess of the payment over the interest purchased is a *bonus* to the original partners. The bonus must be distributed to the original partners according to the partnership agreement. When the agreement does not cover the distribution of bonuses, it should be distributed to the original partners in accordance with the method of distributing income and losses.

Assume that Haddock and Villamer's firm has operated for several years and that the partners' capital balances and the stated ratios for distribution of income and loss are as follows:

Partners	*Capital Balances*	*Stated Ratios*
Haddock	$160,000	55%
Villamer	140,000	45%
	$300,000	100%

Richard Davis wants to join the firm. He offers to invest $100,000 on December 1 for a one-fifth interest in the business and income. The original partners agree to the offer. This is the computation of the bonus to the original partners:

Partners' equity in the original partnership		$300,000
Cash investment by Richard Davis		100,000
Partners' equity in the new partnership		$400,000
Partners' equity assigned to Richard Davis ($400,000 × 1/5)		$ 80,000
Bonus to the original partners		
Investment by Richard Davis	$100,000	
Less equity assigned to Richard Davis	80,000	$ 20,000
Distribution of bonus to original partners		
Jack Haddock ($20,000 × .55)	$ 11,000	
Pilar Villamer ($20,000 × .45)	9,000	$ 20,000

This is the entry that records Davis's admission to the partnership:

Dec. 1	Cash	100,000	
	Jack Haddock, Capital		11,000
	Pilar Villamer, Capital		9,000
	Richard Davis, Capital		80,000
	Investment by Richard Davis for a one-fifth interest in the firm, and the bonus distributed to the original partners		

Bonus to the New Partner There are several reasons why a partnership might want a new partner. A partnership in financial trouble might need additional cash. Or the partners might want to expand the firm's markets and need more capital for this purpose than they themselves can provide. Also, the partners might know a person who would bring a unique talent to the firm. Under these conditions, a new partner may be admitted to the partnership with the understanding that part of the original partners' capital will be transferred (credited) to the new partner's Capital account as a bonus.

Withdrawal of a Partner Generally, a partner has the right to withdraw from a partnership in accord with legal requirements. However, to avoid disputes when a partner does decide to withdraw or retire from the firm, the partnership agreement should describe the procedures that are to be followed. The agreement should specify (1) whether an audit will be performed, (2) how the assets will be reappraised, (3) how a bonus will be determined, and (4) by what method the withdrawing partner will be paid.

A partner who wants to withdraw from a partnership can do so in one of several ways. The partner can sell his or her interest to another partner or to an outsider with the consent of the remaining partners, or the partner can withdraw assets equal to his or her capital balance, less than his or her capital balance (in this case, the remaining partners receive a bonus), or greater than his or her capital balance (in this case, the withdrawing partner receives a bonus). Bonuses upon withdrawal of a partner are allocated in much the same way as bonuses that arise when a new partner is admitted.

Death of a Partner When a partner dies, the partnership is dissolved because the original association has changed. The partnership agreement should state the actions to be taken. Normally, the books are closed, and financial statements are prepared. These actions are necessary to determine the capital balance of each partner on the date of the death. The agreement also may indicate whether an audit should be conducted, assets appraised, and a bonus recorded, as well as the procedures for settling with the deceased partner's heirs. The remaining partners may purchase the deceased's equity, sell it to outsiders, or deliver certain business assets to the estate. If the firm intends to continue, a new partnership must be formed.

Liquidation of a Partnership

Liquidation of a partnership is the process of ending the business—of selling enough assets to pay the partnership's liabilities and distributing any remaining assets among the partners. Liquidation is a special form of dissolution. When a partnership is liquidated, the business will not continue. As the assets of the business are sold, any gain or loss should be distributed to the partners according to the stated ratios. As cash becomes available, it must be applied first to outside creditors, then to loans from partners, and finally to the partners' capital balances. Any deficits in partners' capital accounts must be made up from personal assets.

Problems

Partnership Formation and Distribution of Income

P 1. In January 2010, Ed Rivers and Bob Bascomb agreed to produce and sell chocolate candies. Rivers contributed $240,000 in cash to the business. Bascomb contributed the building and equipment, valued at $220,000 and $140,000, respectively. The partnership had an income of $84,000 during 2010 but was less successful during 2011, when income was only $40,000.

Required

1. Prepare the journal entry to record the investment of both partners in the partnership.
2. Determine the share of income for each partner in 2010 and 2011 under each of the following conditions: (a) The partners agreed to share income equally. (b) The partners failed to agree on an income-sharing arrangement. (c) The partners agreed to share income according to the ratio of their original investments. (d) The partners agreed to share income by allowing interest of 10 percent on their original investments and dividing the remainder equally. (e) The partners agreed to share income by allowing salaries of $40,000 for Rivers and $28,000 for Bascomb, and dividing the remainder equally. (f) The partners agreed to share income by paying salaries of $40,000 to Rivers and $28,000 to Bascomb, allowing interest of 9 percent on their original investments, and dividing the remainder equally.

Admission and Withdrawal of a Partner

P 2. Margaret, Tracy, and Lou are partners in Woodwork Company. Their capital balances as of July 31, 2010, are as follows:

MARGARET, CAPITAL	TRACY, CAPITAL	LOU, CAPITAL
45,000	15,000	30,000

Each partner has agreed to admit Vonice to the partnership.

Required

Prepare the entries to record Vonice's admission to or Margaret's withdrawal from the partnership under each of the following conditions: (a) Vonice pays Margaret $12,500 for 20 percent of Margaret's interest in the partnership. (b) Vonice invests $20,000 cash in the partnership and receives an interest equal to her investment. (c) Vonice invests $30,000 cash in the partnership for a 20 percent interest in the business. A bonus is to be recorded for the original partners on the basis of their capital balances. (d) Vonice invests $30,000 cash in the partnership for a 40 percent interest in the business. The original partners give Vonice a bonus according to the ratio of their capital balances on July 31, 2010. (e) Margaret withdraws from the partnership, taking $52,500. The excess of withdrawn assets over Margaret's partnership interest is distributed according to the balances of the Capital accounts. (f) Margaret withdraws by selling her interest directly to Vonice for $60,000.

APPENDIX

B Present Value Tables

TABLE 1 Present Value of $1 to Be Received at the End of a Given Number of Time Periods

Periods	1%	2%	3%	4%	5%	6%	7%	8%	9%	10%	12%
1	0.990	0.980	0.971	0.962	0.952	0.943	0.935	0.926	0.917	0.909	0.893
2	0.980	0.961	0.943	0.925	0.907	0.890	0.873	0.857	0.842	0.826	0.797
3	0.971	0.942	0.915	0.889	0.864	0.840	0.816	0.794	0.772	0.751	0.712
4	0.961	0.924	0.888	0.855	0.823	0.792	0.763	0.735	0.708	0.683	0.636
5	0.951	0.906	0.883	0.822	0.784	0.747	0.713	0.681	0.650	0.621	0.567
6	0.942	0.888	0.837	0.790	0.746	0.705	0.666	0.630	0.596	0.564	0.507
7	0.933	0.871	0.813	0.760	0.711	0.665	0.623	0.583	0.547	0.513	0.452
8	0.923	0.853	0.789	0.731	0.677	0.627	0.582	0.540	0.502	0.467	0.404
9	0.914	0.837	0.766	0.703	0.645	0.592	0.544	0.500	0.460	0.424	0.361
10	0.905	0.820	0.744	0.676	0.614	0.558	0.508	0.463	0.422	0.386	0.322
11	0.896	0.804	0.722	0.650	0.585	0.527	0.475	0.429	0.388	0.350	0.287
12	0.887	0.788	0.701	0.625	0.557	0.497	0.444	0.397	0.356	0.319	0.257
13	0.879	0.773	0.681	0.601	0.530	0.469	0.415	0.368	0.326	0.290	0.229
14	0.870	0.758	0.661	0.577	0.505	0.442	0.388	0.340	0.299	0.263	0.205
15	0.861	0.743	0.642	0.555	0.481	0.417	0.362	0.315	0.275	0.239	0.183
16	0.853	0.728	0.623	0.534	0.458	0.394	0.339	0.292	0.252	0.218	0.163
17	0.844	0.714	0.605	0.513	0.436	0.371	0.317	0.270	0.231	0.198	0.146
18	0.836	0.700	0.587	0.494	0.416	0.350	0.296	0.250	0.212	0.180	0.130
19	0.828	0.686	0.570	0.475	0.396	0.331	0.277	0.232	0.194	0.164	0.116
20	0.820	0.673	0.554	0.456	0.377	0.312	0.258	0.215	0.178	0.149	0.104
21	0.811	0.660	0.538	0.439	0.359	0.294	0.242	0.199	0.164	0.135	0.093
22	0.803	0.647	0.522	0.422	0.342	0.278	0.226	0.184	0.150	0.123	0.083
23	0.795	0.634	0.507	0.406	0.326	0.262	0.211	0.170	0.138	0.112	0.074
24	0.788	0.622	0.492	0.390	0.310	0.247	0.197	0.158	0.126	0.102	0.066
25	0.780	0.610	0.478	0.375	0.295	0.233	0.184	0.146	0.116	0.092	0.059
26	0.772	0.598	0.464	0.361	0.281	0.220	0.172	0.135	0.106	0.084	0.053
27	0.764	0.586	0.450	0.347	0.268	0.207	0.161	0.125	0.098	0.076	0.047
28	0.757	0.574	0.437	0.333	0.255	0.196	0.150	0.116	0.090	0.069	0.042
29	0.749	0.563	0.424	0.321	0.243	0.185	0.141	0.107	0.082	0.063	0.037
30	0.742	0.552	0.412	0.308	0.231	0.174	0.131	0.099	0.075	0.057	0.033
40	0.672	0.453	0.307	0.208	0.142	0.097	0.067	0.046	0.032	0.022	0.011
50	0.608	0.372	0.228	0.141	0.087	0.054	0.034	0.021	0.013	0.009	0.003

Table 1 is used to compute the value today of a single amount of cash to be received sometime in the future. To use Table 1, you must first know (1) the time period in years until funds will be received, (2) the stated annual rate of interest, and (3) the dollar amount to be received at the end of the time period.

Example—Table 1. What is the present value of \$30,000 to be received 25 years from now, assuming a 14 percent interest rate? From Table 1, the required multiplier is .038, and the answer is

$$\$30,000 \times .038 = \$1,140$$

The factor values for Table 1 are

$$\text{PV Factor} = (1 + r)^{-n}$$

14%	15%	16%	18%	20%	25%	30%	35%	40%	45%	50%	Periods
0.877	0.870	0.862	0.847	0.833	0.800	0.769	0.741	0.714	0.690	0.667	1
0.769	0.756	0.743	0.718	0.694	0.640	0.592	0.549	0.510	0.476	0.444	2
0.675	0.658	0.641	0.609	0.579	0.512	0.455	0.406	0.364	0.328	0.296	3
0.592	0.572	0.552	0.516	0.482	0.410	0.350	0.301	0.260	0.226	0.198	4
0.519	0.497	0.476	0.437	0.402	0.328	0.269	0.223	0.186	0.156	0.132	5
0.456	0.432	0.410	0.370	0.335	0.262	0.207	0.165	0.133	0.108	0.088	6
0.400	0.376	0.354	0.314	0.279	0.210	0.159	0.122	0.095	0.074	0.059	7
0.351	0.327	0.305	0.266	0.233	0.168	0.123	0.091	0.068	0.051	0.039	8
0.308	0.284	0.263	0.225	0.194	0.134	0.094	0.067	0.048	0.035	0.026	9
0.270	0.247	0.227	0.191	0.162	0.107	0.073	0.050	0.035	0.024	0.017	10
0.237	0.215	0.195	0.162	0.135	0.086	0.056	0.037	0.025	0.017	0.012	11
0.208	0.187	0.168	0.137	0.112	0.069	0.043	0.027	0.018	0.012	0.008	12
0.182	0.163	0.145	0.116	0.093	0.055	0.033	0.020	0.013	0.008	0.005	13
0.160	0.141	0.125	0.099	0.078	0.044	0.025	0.015	0.009	0.006	0.003	14
0.140	0.123	0.108	0.084	0.065	0.035	0.020	0.011	0.006	0.004	0.002	15
0.123	0.107	0.093	0.071	0.054	0.028	0.015	0.008	0.005	0.003	0.002	16
0.108	0.093	0.080	0.060	0.045	0.023	0.012	0.006	0.003	0.002	0.001	17
0.095	0.081	0.069	0.051	0.038	0.018	0.009	0.005	0.002	0.001	0.001	18
0.083	0.070	0.060	0.043	0.031	0.014	0.007	0.003	0.002	0.001		19
0.073	0.061	0.051	0.037	0.026	0.012	0.005	0.002	0.001	0.001		20
0.064	0.053	0.044	0.031	0.022	0.009	0.004	0.002	0.001			21
0.056	0.046	0.038	0.026	0.018	0.007	0.003	0.001	0.001			22
0.049	0.040	0.033	0.022	0.015	0.006	0.002	0.001				23
0.043	0.035	0.028	0.019	0.013	0.005	0.002	0.001				24
0.038	0.030	0.024	0.016	0.010	0.004	0.001	0.001				25
0.033	0.026	0.021	0.014	0.009	0.003	0.001					26
0.029	0.023	0.018	0.011	0.007	0.002	0.001					27
0.026	0.020	0.016	0.010	0.006	0.002	0.001					28
0.022	0.017	0.014	0.008	0.005	0.002						29
0.020	0.015	0.012	0.007	0.004	0.001						30
0.005	0.004	0.003	0.001	0.001							40
0.001	0.001	0.001									50

TABLE 2 Present Value of $1 Received Each Period for a Given Number of Time Periods

Periods	1%	2%	3%	4%	5%	6%	7%	8%	9%	10%	12%
1	0.990	0.980	0.971	0.962	0.952	0.943	0.935	0.926	0.917	0.909	0.893
2	1.970	1.942	1.913	1.886	1.859	1.833	1.808	1.783	1.759	1.736	1.690
3	2.941	2.884	2.829	2.775	2.723	2.673	2.624	2.577	2.531	2.487	2.402
4	3.902	3.808	3.717	3.630	3.546	3.465	3.387	3.312	3.240	3.170	3.037
5	4.853	4.713	4.580	4.452	4.329	4.212	4.100	3.993	3.890	3.791	3.605
6	5.795	5.601	5.417	5.242	5.076	4.917	4.767	4.623	4.486	4.355	4.111
7	6.728	6.472	6.230	6.002	5.786	5.582	5.389	5.206	5.033	4.868	4.564
8	7.652	7.325	7.020	6.733	6.463	6.210	5.971	5.747	5.535	5.335	4.968
9	8.566	8.162	7.786	7.435	7.108	6.802	6.515	6.247	5.995	5.759	5.328
10	9.471	8.983	8.530	8.111	7.722	7.360	7.024	6.710	6.418	6.145	5.650
11	10.368	9.787	9.253	8.760	8.306	7.887	7.499	7.139	6.805	6.495	5.938
12	11.255	10.575	9.954	9.385	8.863	8.384	7.943	7.536	7.161	6.814	6.194
13	12.134	11.348	10.635	9.986	9.394	8.853	8.358	7.904	7.487	7.103	6.424
14	13.004	12.106	11.296	10.563	9.899	9.295	8.745	8.244	7.786	7.367	6.628
15	13.865	12.849	11.938	11.118	10.380	9.712	9.108	8.559	8.061	7.606	6.811
16	14.718	13.578	12.561	11.652	10.838	10.106	9.447	8.851	8.313	7.824	6.974
17	15.562	14.292	13.166	12.166	11.274	10.477	9.763	9.122	8.544	8.022	7.120
18	16.398	14.992	13.754	12.659	11.690	10.828	10.059	9.372	8.756	8.201	7.250
19	17.226	15.678	14.324	13.134	12.085	11.158	10.336	9.604	8.950	8.365	7.366
20	18.046	16.351	14.878	13.590	12.462	11.470	10.594	9.818	9.129	8.514	7.469
21	18.857	17.011	15.415	14.029	12.821	11.764	10.836	10.017	9.292	8.649	7.562
22	19.660	17.658	15.937	14.451	13.163	12.042	11.061	10.201	9.442	8.772	7.645
23	20.456	18.292	16.444	14.857	13.489	12.303	11.272	10.371	9.580	8.883	7.718
24	21.243	18.914	16.936	15.247	13.799	12.550	11.469	10.529	9.707	8.985	7.784
25	22.023	19.523	17.413	15.622	14.094	12.783	11.654	10.675	9.823	9.077	7.843
26	22.795	20.121	17.877	15.983	14.375	13.003	11.826	10.810	9.929	9.161	7.896
27	23.560	20.707	18.327	16.330	14.643	13.211	11.987	10.935	10.027	9.237	7.943
28	24.316	21.281	18.764	16.663	14.898	13.406	12.137	11.051	10.116	9.307	7.984
29	25.066	21.844	19.189	16.984	15.141	13.591	12.278	11.158	10.198	9.370	8.022
30	25.808	22.396	19.600	17.292	15.373	13.765	12.409	11.258	10.274	9.427	8.055
40	32.835	27.355	23.115	19.793	17.159	15.046	13.332	11.925	10.757	9.779	8.244
50	39.196	31.424	25.730	21.482	18.256	15.762	13.801	12.234	10.962	9.915	8.305

Table 2 is used to compute the present value of a *series* of *equal* annual cash flows.

Example—Table 2. Arthur Howard won a contest on January 1, 2010, in which the prize was $30,000, payable in 15 annual installments of $2,000 each December 31, beginning in 2010. Assuming a 9 percent interest rate, what is the present value of Howard's prize on January 1, 2010? From Table 2, the required multiplier is 8.061, and the answer is

$$\$2,000 \times 8.061 = \$16,122$$

The factor values for Table 2 are

$$\text{PVa Factor} = 1 - \frac{(1 + r)^{-n}}{r}$$

14%	15%	16%	18%	20%	25%	30%	35%	40%	45%	50%	Periods
0.877	0.870	0.862	0.847	0.833	0.800	0.769	0.741	0.714	0.690	0.667	1
1.647	1.626	1.605	1.566	1.528	1.440	1.361	1.289	1.224	1.165	1.111	2
2.322	2.283	2.246	2.174	2.106	1.952	1.816	1.696	1.589	1.493	1.407	3
2.914	2.855	2.798	2.690	2.589	2.362	2.166	1.997	1.849	1.720	1.605	4
3.433	3.352	3.274	3.127	2.991	2.689	2.436	2.220	2.035	1.876	1.737	5
3.889	3.784	3.685	3.498	3.326	2.951	2.643	2.385	2.168	1.983	1.824	6
4.288	4.160	4.039	3.812	3.605	3.161	2.802	2.508	2.263	2.057	1.883	7
4.639	4.487	4.344	4.078	3.837	3.329	2.925	2.598	2.331	2.109	1.922	8
4.946	4.772	4.607	4.303	4.031	3.463	3.019	2.665	2.379	2.144	1.948	9
5.216	5.019	4.833	4.494	4.192	3.571	3.092	2.715	2.414	2.168	1.965	10
5.453	5.234	5.029	4.656	4.327	3.656	3.147	2.752	2.438	2.185	1.977	11
5.660	5.421	5.197	4.793	4.439	3.725	3.190	2.779	2.456	2.197	1.985	12
5.842	5.583	5.342	4.910	4.533	3.780	3.223	2.799	2.469	2.204	1.990	13
6.002	5.724	5.468	5.008	4.611	3.824	3.249	2.814	2.478	2.210	1.993	14
6.142	5.847	5.575	5.092	4.675	3.859	3.268	2.825	2.484	2.214	1.995	15
6.265	5.954	5.669	5.162	4.730	3.887	3.283	2.834	2.489	2.216	1.997	16
6.373	6.047	5.749	5.222	4.775	3.910	3.295	2.840	2.492	2.218	1.998	17
6.467	6.128	5.818	5.273	4.812	3.928	3.304	2.844	2.494	2.219	1.999	18
6.550	6.198	5.877	5.316	4.844	3.942	3.311	2.848	2.496	2.220	1.999	19
6.623	6.259	5.929	5.353	4.870	3.954	3.316	2.850	2.497	2.221	1.999	20
6.687	6.312	5.973	5.384	4.891	3.963	3.320	2.852	2.498	2.221	2.000	21
6.743	6.359	6.011	5.410	4.909	3.970	3.323	2.853	2.498	2.222	2.000	22
6.792	6.399	6.044	5.432	4.925	3.976	3.325	2.854	2.499	2.222	2.000	23
6.835	6.434	6.073	5.451	4.973	3.981	3.327	2.855	2.499	2.222	2.000	24
6.873	6.464	6.097	5.467	4.948	3.985	3.329	2.856	2.499	2.222	2.000	25
6.906	6.491	6.118	5.480	4.956	3.988	3.330	2.856	2.500	2.222	2.000	26
6.935	6.514	6.136	5.492	4.964	3.990	3.331	2.856	2.500	2.222	2.000	27
6.961	6.534	6.152	5.502	4.970	3.992	3.331	2.857	2.500	2.222	2.000	28
6.983	6.551	6.166	5.510	4.975	3.994	3.332	2.857	2.500	2.222	2.000	29
7.003	6.566	6.177	5.517	4.979	3.995	3.332	2.857	2.500	2.222	2.000	30
7.105	6.642	6.234	5.548	4.997	3.999	3.333	2.857	2.500	2.222	2.000	40
7.133	6.661	6.246	5.554	4.999	4.000	3.333	2.857	2.500	2.222	2.000	50

Table 2 is the columnar sum of Table 1. Table 2 applies to *ordinary annuities,* in which the first cash flow occurs one time period beyond the date for which the present value is computed.

An *annuity due* is a series of equal cash flows for N time periods, but the first payment occurs immediately. The present value of the first payment equals the face value of the cash flow; Table 2 then is used to measure the present value of N − 1 remaining cash flows.

Example—Table 2. Determine the present value on January 1, 2010, of 20 lease payments; each payment of $10,000 is due on January 1, beginning in 2010. Assume an interest rate of 8 percent.

Present Value = Immediate Payment + Present Value of 19 Subsequent Payments at 8%
= $10,000 + ($10,000 × 9.604) = $106,040

ANSWERS TO STOP, REVIEW, AND APPLY QUESTIONS

Chapter 1

1-1. Accounting is considered an information system because it measures business data, processes the data into useful information, and communicates the information to decision makers in the form of financial statements.

1-2. Accounting information enables decision makers to make reasoned choices among alternative uses of scarce resources. It helps management achieve the goals of liquidity and profitability by supplying information that can be used in managing financing, investing, and operating activities.

1-3. Management accounting refers to all types of accounting information developed for the internal use of management. Financial accounting refers to accounting information developed for communication to those outside the organization as well as to management.

1-4. Accounting includes the design of an information system to meet users' needs. Bookkeeping is simply an accounting process, a means of recording financial transactions and keeping financial records. Management information systems are broader in scope than accounting; they process and communicate all information—financial and nonfinancial—within a business. The accounting information system is an extremely important part of a management information system because it manages the flow of financial data to all parts of a business and to interested parties outside the business.

1-5. Financial statements can be inadvertently misstated because of ignorance of accepted accounting practices, incorrect estimates, or failure to recognize that a transaction has occurred. They can also be intentionally misstated to deceive readers; when this is the case, the misstatement is called *fraudulent financial reporting.*

2-1. Three groups of decision makers use accounting information: those who manage a business; those outside a business who have a direct financial interest in the business; and those who have an indirect financial interest in the business. These categories apply to not-for-profit and governmental organizations as well as to profit-oriented ventures.

2-2. The management functions involved in achieving an adequate return for a business's owners include financing the business, investing the business's resources, producing goods and services, marketing goods and services, managing employees, and providing information to decision makers.

2-3. Investors are interested in reviewing a company's financial statements because they provide information about the company's past performance and its potential for future profits. Creditors are interested in reviewing financial statements because they indicate whether the company will have the cash to pay interest charges and debt when it is due.

2-4. People and organizations with an indirect interest in accounting information about a business include tax authorities, regulatory agencies, and other groups, such as labor unions, economic planners, financial analysts, and consumers' groups. Tax authorities use accounting information to determine tax liabilities, and regulatory agencies use it to determine compliance with laws. Economic planners use accounting information to determine economic policy, and other groups use it to support policies related to their economic interests.

2-5. Accounting information plays a critical role in achieving many of society's goals. It is used to determine taxes on businesses, the price of public commodities (gas, water, and electricity), and a business's economic impact on a community. It is used by tax authorities at the federal (IRS), state, and local levels; regulatory agencies, such as the SEC; the Federal Reserve Board and other governmental planners; and citizens' groups, including labor unions and consumer groups.

3-1. Financial accounting uses money measures to gauge the impact of business transactions on a separate business entity.

3-2. The sale is a business transaction. The price you pay is a money measure. CVS is a separate entity.

4-1. A sole proprietorship is a business owned by one person. A partnership is similar to a proprietorship in most respects, but it has more than one owner. A corporation is an economic unit that is legally separate from its owners. Accounting treats all three forms as separate economic units.

4-2. The stockholders, whose ownership of the corporation is represented by shares of stock, elect a board of directors. The board determines corporate policy, declares dividends, and appoints management. Management executes corporate policy and carries out the day-to-day operations of the firm.

4-3. The audit committee of a board of directors is made up of independent directors who have financial expertise. The committee is responsible for engaging the corporation's independent auditors, reviewing their work, and seeing that the firm has systems to safeguard its resources and ensure the reliability of its accounting records.

5-1. Assets are the economic resources of a business that are expected to benefit future operations.

5-2. Liabilities and stockholders' equity are similar in that they represent claims against the assets of a business. They differ in that liabilities are amounts owed to creditors and stockholders' equity represents the owners' interest in the company.

5-3. Revenues, which result from sales of products or services, increase retained earnings. Expenses and dividends decrease retained earnings. Expenses are the cost of operating the business, and dividends are distributions to stockholders of assets generated by past earnings.

5-4. The sale of an asset for cash is an example of a transaction that both increases and decreases assets. The collection of an account receivable is another example. In both cases, the Cash account increases, and Accounts Receivable decreases.

6-1. The statement of retained earnings shows changes in the Retained Earnings account over an accounting period. Two factors may account for changes in retained earnings: net income (loss) and dividend distributions.

6-2. The balance sheet is called the *statement of financial position* because it presents a company's financial position—its economic resources and the claims against those resources—at a specific date.

6-3. The purpose of the balance sheet is to show a company's financial position at a certain point in time. The purpose of the income statement is to show a business's income or loss over a period of time.

6-4. **a.** June 30, 2010
b. For the Year Ended June 30, 2010

6-5. The income statement measures profitability. The statement of cash flows measures liquidity.

7-1. GAAP (generally accepted accounting principles) are "the conventions, rules, and procedures necessary to define accepted accounting practice at a particular time." They are important to readers of financial statements because they provide the basis for understanding and interpreting those statements.

7-2. By using the phrase in *all material respects*, independent auditors are acknowledging that accounting is not an exact science and that the application of GAAP to the preparation of financial statements requires judgment and estimates. Although an auditor's report does not preclude minor or immaterial errors in the financial statements, a favorable report does imply that on the whole, the statements are a fair representation and are in compliance with GAAP.

7-3. The PCAOB (Public Company Accounting Oversight Board) is a governmental body established by the Sarbanes-Oxley Act of 2002 to regulate the accounting profession. Because it sets standards that must be followed in the audits of public companies, it has a major impact on financial reporting.

7-4. The Financial Accounting Standards Board (FASB) has the most influence on GAAP because it develops and issues rules on accounting practice, which are called *Statements of Financial Accounting Standards.*

7-5. International financial reporting standards (IFRS) are becoming more important because in addition to being used by companies in Europe and other parts of the world, the SEC has ruled that foreign companies registered in the United States may also use them. In addition, U.S. companies may be allowed to use IFRS in the future.

7-6. Codes of ethics are important in the accounting profession because they outline the responsibilities of accountants to anyone who relies on financial statements. Accountants who violate their codes of ethics can be disciplined or even suspended from practice.

Chapter 2

1-1. The three issues that underlie most major accounting decisions are recognition (deciding when a transaction should be recorded), valuation (deciding what value should be placed on the transaction), and classification (deciding how the components of the transaction should be categorized).

1-2. The transaction should not be recorded as a sale because no transfer of ownership has occurred.

1-3. Original cost is a practical valuation guideline for accountants because it is based on the exchange price, a price that can be verified.

1-4. The distinction between an asset and an expense is important because an asset represents a cost that will benefit the firm in the future, whereas an expense will immediately affect the firm's earnings.

1-5. Recognition, valuation, and classification are related to the ethics of financial reporting because fraudulent financial statements usually result from a violation of the generally accepted accounting principles that govern these issues.

2-1. The double-entry system is so called because it is based on the principle of duality, which means that every economic event has two aspects that balance each other. In the double-entry system, each transaction is recorded by at least one debit and one credit, and the total amount of the debits must equal the total amount of the credits.

2-2. Debits and credits are neither good nor bad. They simply indicate whether a transaction increases or decreases a particular account.

2-3. An account is the basic storage unit for accounting data. An account's normal balance is its usual balance and is the side (debit or credit) that increases the account.

2-4. A T account is a form of account shaped like a T that is used to analyze the effects of transactions.

2-5. **a.** Increases in assets are recorded by debits; decreases are recorded by credits.
b. Increases in liabilities are recorded by credits; decreases are recorded by debits.
c. Increases in stockholders' equity are recorded by credits; decreases are recorded by debits.

2-6. Accountants use separate accounts for revenues and expenses rather than entering them in Retained Earnings because these accounts will be used in the income statement. This enables users of the income statement to assess the company's earnings.

3-1. The total debits to cash exceed the total credits by $500. Thus, the Cash account has a total balance of $500 available for the business to use.

3-2. Decreases in stockholders' equity are shown by debits. Because expenses decrease stockholders' equity, increases in expenses are shown by debits. By debiting an expense, you are increasing the total decreases in stockholders' equity.

3-3. The steps in analyzing a business transaction are (1) state the transaction, (2) analyze it to determine which accounts are affected, (3) apply the rules of double-entry accounting by using T accounts to show how the transaction affects the accounting equation, (4) show the transaction in journal form, and (5) provide an explanation of the transaction.

3-4. The normal balance of Accounts Payable is a credit balance. A debit balance in Accounts Payable would occur if the company overpaid for goods or services.

4-1. The trial balance is a listing of all the accounts with their balances shown in either the debit or credit column. It is used to see if the accounts are in balance.

4-2. Even when the debit and credit balances in a trial balance are equal, errors can be present; transactions may not have been analyzed correctly or recorded in the proper accounts.

5-1. The timing of cash flows is important because it affects a company's ability to maintain adequate liquidity.

5-2. There is delay in collecting the cash from a sale when a company offers to accept payment later. This action results in an accounts receivable.

6-1.
- **c.** Occurrence of the transaction
- **a.** Analysis of the transaction
- **d.** Recording of an entry in the journal
- **b.** Posting of debits and credits from the journal to the ledger
- **e.** Preparation of the trial balance

6-2. A debit is written first. The names of accounts credited are set off by indentation; explanations of transactions are also indented.

6-3. The journal is where transactions are first entered in the accounting records. Later, the debit and credit portions of each transaction are transferred to the appropriate accounts in the ledger, where each account is kept on a separate page or card.

6-4.
- **a.** Chart of accounts—ledger
- **b.** Book of original entry—journal
- **c.** Post Ref. column—both
- **d.** Journalizing—journal
- **e.** Posting—both
- **f.** Footings—ledger

Chapter 3

1-1. Because *profit* means different things to different people, accountants use the term *net income* instead. Net income refers to the net increase in stockholders' equity produced by business operations. It equals revenues minus expenses when revenues exceed expenses.

1-2. To measure net income accurately, revenues and expenses must be assigned to the accounting period in which they occur. However, not all transactions can be easily assigned to specific periods. It is therefore necessary to make an assumption about periodicity—that is, although the lifetime of a business is uncertain, it is nonetheless useful to estimate a company's net income in terms of accounting periods.

1-3. The continuity assumption holds that unless there is evidence to the contrary, a business will continue to operate indefinitely. Thus, assets can be recorded and retained on the balance sheet at their historical cost rather than being revalued periodically to reflect their current values.

1-4. What is the most significant concept in accounting is a matter of opinion, but if one grants that income determination is one of accounting's most important functions, then the matching rule is one of the most important concepts. The rule states that revenues must be assigned to the period in which they are earned, which is when the goods or services are delivered to the buyer, and expenses must be assigned to the period in which they are incurred. To measure business income accurately over a given period, the accountant must match the revenues earned with the expenses incurred to produce those revenues.

2-1. The following conditions must be met before revenue can be recognized:
1. Persuasive evidence of an arrangement exists.
2. A product or service has been delivered.
3. The seller's price to the buyer is fixed or is determinable.
4. Collectibility is reasonably assured.

2-2. Under the cash basis of accounting, revenues and expenses are recorded as cash is received and paid out. Accrual accounting applies the matching rule: revenues are recorded when they are earned, and expenses are recorded when they are incurred.

2-3. Accrual accounting is accomplished (1) by recording revenues when they are earned, (2) by recording expenses when they are incurred, and (3) by making end-of-period adjustments to the accounts.

2-4. Adjusting entries are necessary to bring all account balances up to date at the end of an accounting period. This can mean recognizing a payment received in advance as earned revenue or a cost paid in advance as an expense, or recognizing a revenue or expense that has not yet been recorded.

2-5. Adjustments are needed to measure income and financial position fairly. Equally important, they make financial statements comparable from one period to the next. In addition, the cumulative effect of adjusting entries can be significant. If no adjustments were made, the matching rule would not be followed, a company's accounts would basically revert to a cash system, and there would not be a good determination of the company's earnings.

3-1. Adjusting entries are required (1) when recorded costs must be allocated between two or more accounting periods (e.g., allocating the costs of prepaid insurance between the periods that the policies cover); (2) when there are unrecorded expenses (e.g., recording wages that employees earned in the current accounting period but after the last pay period); (3) when recorded, unearned revenues must be allocated between two or more accounting periods (e.g., allocating between periods fees collected in advance for services to be rendered in future periods); and (4) when there are unrecorded, earned revenues (e.g., recording fees earned but not yet collected or billed to customers).

3-2. Certain business expenditures benefit more than one accounting period. These expenditures usually are debited to an asset account. Therefore, "some assets are expenses that have not expired." At the end of the accounting period, such asset accounts are reduced by the amount that was used during the period; the amount that has expired is transferred to expense accounts. For example, the part of prepaid rent used up during the period is credited to Prepaid Rent and debited to Rent Expense.

3-3. All of these assets must be allocated to expenses over time; this means they require adjusting entries at the end of the accounting period.

3-4. Accumulated Depreciation is a contra account associated with a long-term asset. The Accumulated Depreciation account reflects the total depreciation allocated as an expense to date on that asset. Depreciation expense represents the estimated portion of the asset that has become an expense during the current accounting period.

3-5. A contra account represents a deduction from an associated account. For example, the contra account Accumulated Depreciation–Office Equipment is associated with the Office Equipment account.

3-6. Contra accounts are used to record depreciation for two reasons. First, depreciation is an estimate, and the use of a contra account is recognition of this. Second, the use of the contra account preserves the original cost of the asset in the accounts. In combination with the asset account, it indicates how much of the asset's cost has been expensed and how much of the balance is left to be depreciated.

3-7. Unearned revenue arises when revenue is received in advance of the delivery of goods or services. The advance payments that a publishing company receives for magazine subscriptions are an example.

3-8. Unearned revenue appears as a liability on the balance sheet.

3-9. Accrued revenues are unrecorded revenues. Services have been performed or goods have been delivered, but the transactions have not been recorded. Interest that has been earned but not received is an example. At the end of the accounting period, the accountant makes an adjusting entry debiting Interest Receivable and crediting Interest Income. Interest Receivable is the asset account. (An adjusting entry for accrued revenue always debits an asset account and credits a revenue account.)

3-10. An accrued expense is an expense that has been incurred but not recorded. Accrued expenses require adjusting entries, which increase a related liability. Examples of accrued expenses include wages expense, income taxes expense, and interest expense.

4-1. The income statement is usually prepared first because the net income figure is needed to complete the statement of retained earnings.

4-2. The ending balance for Retained Earnings does not appear on the adjusted trial balance because all the current period's income statement accounts and dividends are in the adjusted trial balance. The balances of all these accounts have to be transferred to the statement of retained earnings to arrive at the ending balance. (Recall that the statement of retained earnings is prepared after the income statement and before the balance sheet.)

5-1. First, closing entries clear revenue, expense, and dividend accounts of their balances and transfer them to Retained Earnings. Second, they summarize a period's revenues and expenses.

5-2. Adjusting entries apply accrual accounting to transactions that span accounting periods. Closing entries assist in getting the account balances ready for the next period and for the preparation of financial statements.

5-3. Insurance Expense, Commission Revenue, Dividends, and Supplies Expense will not show a balance after the closing entries have been prepared and posted.

5-4. The post-closing trial balance is a check on the balance of the accounts after the closing entries have been prepared and posted.

6-1. Adjusting entries never affect a company's cash flows because they never involve the Cash account.

6-2. The cash paid for expenses in an accounting period often differs from the amount of expenses on the income statement because of the timing of the incurrence of the expenses and payment for them.

6-3. The cash received for services in an accounting period often differs from the amount of revenue on the income statement because of the timing of the provision of the services and the receipt of cash for them.

Chapter 4

1-1. According to the Financial Accounting Standards Board, the objective of financial reporting is to provide financial information that is useful for decision making. To be useful, information about financial reporting must assess cash flow prospects and stewardship, including information about business resources, claims against them, and changes in them.

1-2. Qualitative characteristics are standards for judging accounting information. The two most important characteristics are *relevance* (the information has a direct bearing on a decision) and *faithful representation* (the financial reporting for an entity must be a reliable depiction of what it purports to represent. To be faithful, financial information must be complete, neutral, and free from material error. Qualitative characteristics that complement the quality of information are *comparability* (enables users to identify similarities and differences between two sets of economic phenomena), *verifiability* (helps assure users that information faithfully represents what it purports to depict), *timeliness* (allows users to receive information in time to influence a decision), and *understandability* (enables users to comprehend the meaning of the information they receive.

1-3. Management is responsible for the preparation of financial statements. To ensure that the statements are reliable, the chief executive officers and chief financial officers of publicly traded companies must certify that, to their knowledge, the quarterly and annual statements that their companies file with the SEC are accurate and complete.

2-1. Accounting conventions are rules of thumb that accountants use in making estimates and applying the rules for recognition and allocation. These conventions help users interpret financial information.

2-2. Consistency helps users evaluate a company's performance over time and to compare it with the performance of other companies. Full disclosure means that the financial statements are transparent and include any information that is relevant to understanding them. Materiality dictates that items and events that are important enough to affect decisions must be accounted for properly. Conservatism states that when faced with a choice between two equally acceptable accounting procedures, the accountant should choose the one that is least likely to overstate assets and income. Cost-benefit holds that the benefits to be gained from accounting information should be greater than the costs of producing it.

3-1. The purpose of classified financial statements is to facilitate the analysis and evaluation of a company's financial position by dividing the major categories of accounts into useful subcategories.

3-2. Four common categories of assets on a classified balance sheet are current assets; investments; property, plant, and equipment; and intangible assets. Some companies group investments and intangibles into a category called *other assets.*

3-3. An asset is classified as current if a firm can reasonably expect to convert it to cash, sell it, or consume it within one year or within the firm's normal operating cycle, whichever is longer. Assets of a firm whose normal operating cycle exceeds one year are considered current if they will be converted to cash, sold, or consumed during that cycle. Two examples of such assets are the aging inventories of wine companies and the installment receivables of retail appliance companies.

3-4. Current assets should be listed in order of their liquidity—that is, the ease with which they can be converted to cash.

3-5. If management's intent is to use the investment as a temporary haven for idle cash, the investment is short term and is classified as a current asset. If the intent is to hold the security for more than a year, it is classified as an investment.

3-6. An intangible asset is a long-term asset with no physical substance whose value stems from the rights or privileges it extends to its owner. Examples of such assets are patents, copyrights, goodwill, franchises, and trademarks.

3-7. The two major categories of liabilities are current liabilities and long-term liabilities.

3-8. The equity section of the balance sheet for a sole proprietorship or partnership simply lists the balance of the owner's or partners' capital. The stockholders' equity section of a corporation's balance sheet separates contributed capital from retained earnings.

4-1. The primary difference between the operations of a merchandising business and those of a service business is that a merchandising business earns its revenues by buying products and selling them to customers rather than by performing a service. The buying and selling of merchandise adds several steps to the income statement. In a service business, net income is the difference between revenues and expenses when revenues exceed expenses. A merchandising business, in contrast, has cost of goods sold, which is deducted from net sales to arrive at gross margin. Net income or loss is the difference between gross margin and all other items affecting net income. Among these other items are operating expenses, other revenues and expenses, and income taxes.

4-2. Gross margin is the difference between net sales and cost of goods sold. It is important because if a merchandising or manufacturing company is going to earn a net income, its gross margin must exceed total operating expenses, the excess of other expenses over other revenues, and income taxes.

4-3. Other revenues and expenses are not related to a company's operating activities. In a multistep income statement, these items are separated from operating revenues and expenses to isolate them from income from operations.

4-4. Earnings per share is the net income earned on each share of common stock. It is computed by dividing net income by the average number of common shares outstanding, and it appears directly after net income on the income statement.

4-5. A multistep income statement classifies accounts into major components before arriving at income before income taxes. Its major advantage is the detail it provides on various income-producing aspects of a business. A single-step income statement simply groups all accounts other than income taxes as revenues or expenses and determines the difference, which is income before income taxes. Its advantage is simplicity.

5-1. Liquidity is a company's ability to pay its bills when they are due and to meet unexpected needs for cash. Two measures of liquidity are working capital and the current ratio.

5-2. The current ratio is computed by dividing current assets by current liabilities. Many believe it is a good indicator of a company's ability to pay its debts on time.

5-3. The goals of liquidity and profitability are equally important. Both goals must be met if a business is to survive.

5-4. Five measures of profitability are profit margin, asset turnover, return on assets, the debt to equity ratio, and return on equity.

5-5. If profit margin is multiplied by asset turnover, the result is return on assets.

Chapter 5

1-1. The transactions that make up the operating cycle of a merchandising business are (1) purchases of merchandise inventory for cash or on credit, (2) payment for purchases made on credit, (3) sales of merchandise inventory for cash or on credit, and (4) collection of cash from credit sales. When merchandise is sold for cash, the cash is collected immediately; when it is sold on credit, the company must wait a period of time before receiving the cash. A merchandising business must manage the operating cycle carefully because it affects the company's cash flow, or liquidity.

1-2. The financing period is the amount of time from the purchase of inventory until it is sold and payment is collected, less the amount of time creditors give the company to pay for the inventory. It consists of the days' inventory on hand plus the days' receivable less the days' payable.

1-3. Under the perpetual inventory system, continuous records are kept of the quality and, usually, the cost of individual items as they are bought and sold. Under the periodic inventory system, the inventory not yet sold is counted periodically, usually at the end of the accounting period.

1-4. An exchange gain or loss occurs when a company engages in a transaction in a foreign currency and the rate at which a dollar can be exchanged for the foreign currency changes between the date of sale and the date of payment.

1-5. Internal controls are needed to protect a company's assets from theft and embezzlement. Management is responsible for establishing an environment, accounting systems, and control procedures that will provide this protection.

2-1. A trade discount is a deduction (usually 30 percent or more) off a list or catalogue price; trade discounts are not entered in the accounting records. A sales discount is a discount given to a buyer for early payment of a credit sale; sales discounts are entered in the accounting records.

2-2. Sales Discounts is a contra-revenue account; it is deducted from sales on the income statement. Its normal balance is a debit balance.

2-3. It is impossible to tell which supplier is quoting the better deal without knowing what Supplier A will charge for shipping. If the transportation costs for all 50 items from Supplier A exceed $50, Supplier B is offering the better deal, but if they are less than $50, Supplier A is offering the better deal. A customer that accepted Supplier B's offer would pay approximately $1 per unit ($21 − $20, or 5 percent of the unit cost) for transportation.

2-4. Freight-in is not an operating expense. It is part of the cost of purchasing merchandise and is therefore usually included in the cost of goods sold.

3-1. The Cost of Goods Sold account is used in the perpetual inventory system. It is needed to record the transfer of the cost of merchandise from the Merchandise Inventory account at the time of a sale (or back to the Merchandise Inventory account in the case of a return). The Cost of Goods Sold account is not used in the periodic inventory system until the income statement is prepared.

3-2. The perpetual inventory system gives management up-to-date information, but it is more time-consuming and costly than the periodic inventory system. Thus, management must weigh the benefits against the costs. Companies that sell high-value items tend to use the perpetual inventory system. Companies that sell a high volume of lower-value items have generally used the periodic system. However, because of the computer's ability to keep track of large numbers of transactions at low cost, use of the perpetual system has increased significantly.

3-3. The Sales Returns and Allowances account helps management maintain control. It is a readily available measure of unsatisfactory products and dissatisfied customers.

4-1. The two main components of goods available for sale are beginning inventory and net cost of purchases during the period. The ending inventory is deducted from the goods available for sale to determine cost of goods sold.

4-2. Under the periodic inventory system, the amount of inventory at the end of the year is determined by a physical count of the merchandise.

4-3. The two dozen hammers (item **b**) are the only ones that should be debited to Purchases because they are the only ones bought for resale.

4-4. Under the periodic inventory system, the cost of inventory purchased during an accounting period is accumulated in a Purchases account. At the end of the period, a physical inventory is taken, and the cost of the merchandise is deducted from the cost of goods available for sale to arrive at cost of goods sold. Under the perpetual inventory system, the cost of each item is recorded in the Merchandise Inventory account when it is purchased. As merchandise is sold, its cost is transferred from the Merchandise Inventory account to the Cost of Goods Sold account. Thus, at any time, the balance of Merchandise Inventory equals the cost of goods on hand, and Cost of Goods Sold equals the total cost of goods sold to that point. The Purchases account is not used in a perpetual inventory system.

5-1. In addition to preventing and detecting fraud, internal control protects a firm's assets, ensures the accuracy and reliability of its accounting data, promotes efficient operations, and encourages adherence to management's policies.

5-2. The five components of internal control are the control environment, risk assessment, information and communication, control activities, and monitoring.

5-3. Examples of control activities include having managers authorize certain transactions and activities; establishing accountability for assets by recording all transactions; using documents that are designed to ensure the proper recording of transactions; restricting physical access to assets; having someone other than those responsible for the firm's accounting records and assets periodically check the records against the assets; separating employees' functional responsibilities; and using sound personnel practices.

5-4. The separation of duties is necessary to sound internal control because without it, a person responsible for multiple tasks—such as keeping records, overseeing a department, and managing assets—would be able to misappropriate assets without detection. The separation of duties assumes that two or more employees will not work together to overcome the controls.

5-5. In a small business in which the complete separation of duties is impossible, many other steps can be taken to improve the control of cash. Three examples are using banking facilities as much as possible, depositing all cash receipts promptly, and bonding employees who have access to cash.

6-1. The primary weakness in this system is that the sales clerks have access to both the cash (asset) and the cash register tape (record). The separation of duties has not been applied, increasing the likelihood of fraud. The cash register tape should be locked in the cash register and removed by the employee in the cashier's office who counts the cash.

6-2. A movie theater controls cash receipts by having a ticket seller give a ticket to each person who pays for admission. Another employee, who has no access to cash, collects the ticket. This person tears the ticket to prevent its being used again. At the end of the day, the total ticket stubs multiplied by the ticket price should equal the cash in the ticket seller's drawer. In effect, the custody of the assets (cash) is separated from the records (tickets).

Chapter 6

1-1. A merchandising company has only one type of inventory, whereas a manufacturing company has three types: raw materials, work in process, and finished goods ready for sale. A manufacturing company's costs of work in process and finished goods include the costs of raw materials, direct labor, and the overhead that supports production.

1-2. The primary objective of inventory accounting is to determine income properly by matching costs of the period against revenues for the period.

1-3. The level of inventory is important because management must balance the need to have enough inventory on hand to satisfy customers against the costs of carrying and storing the inventory. Two common and related measures of inventory level are inventory turnover and days' inventory on hand.

1-4. Inventory is particularly vulnerable to fraudulent financial reporting because the manipulation of the ending inventory will cause a dollar for dollar difference in reported net income. In other words, a company can overstate its income by overstating its ending inventory.

1-5. If inventory is overstated at the end of 2008, (a) the 2008 net income will be overstated, (b) the 2008 year-end balance sheet value will also be overstated, (c) the 2009 net income will be understated, and (d) there will be no effect on the 2009 year-end balance sheet value.

2-1. The cost of inventory should include the invoice price less applicable discounts plus applicable expenditures, such as freight-in, insurance, taxes, and tariffs.

2-2. Goods flow refers to the *actual* flow of goods in a firm's operations; cost flow refers to the association of costs with their *assumed* flow in operations.

2-3. Although the company has an order for the goods, the 130 units should be included in inventory because title has not passed to the customer.

2-4. In the phrase *lower of cost or market, market* refers to current replacement cost.

2-5. A company must disclose its method of inventory accounting because the method can affect both the value of inventory on the balance sheet and the amount of earnings on the income statement. This information helps users of the financial statements evaluate the company and compare its performance with the performance of other companies.

3-1. The quantities of ending inventory are the same under FIFO and LIFO. These methods affect the pricing of the inventory, not the quantities.

3-2. **a.** The earliest costs are assigned to inventory under the LIFO method.
b. The latest costs are assigned to inventory under the FIFO method.
c. The average costs are assigned to inventory under the average-cost method.

3-3. Both LIFO and FIFO have advantages and disadvantages from management's point of view. LIFO comes closest to matching replacement costs against revenues and thus is more realistic in that inventory must be replaced in an ongoing business. In addition, in periods of rising prices, reported income tends to be lower under LIFO, and thus income taxes may be lower. On the other hand, the inventory figure on the balance sheet may be unrealistic, and the reported lower earnings may adversely affect the market price of the company's stock and potential dividends. FIFO has the opposite effect; its advantages are thus similar to the disadvantages of LIFO. It results in a more realistic balance sheet valuation, and in periods of rising prices, it results in a higher net income (as well as higher taxes).

4-1. In periods of steadily rising prices, (a) FIFO will give the highest ending inventory cost, (b) LIFO will give the lowest ending inventory cost, (c) FIFO will give the highest net income, and (d) LIFO will give the lowest net income.

4-2. The IRS must approve changes in the inventory valuation method used in computing taxable income, except for a change to LIFO, which simply has to be reported. If the company uses LIFO for computing taxable income, it must use LIFO in its accounting records.

5-1. A perpetual inventory system is more expensive to maintain because detailed records must be kept as transactions occur. Also, a company may need to purchase special equipment to assist in its perpetual recordkeeping efforts.

5-2. A physical inventory should be taken periodically under the perpetual inventory system to compare the actual inventory on hand with the inventory records. This procedure will reveal any loss of inventory by theft or other means.

6-1. The retail method does not measure inventories at retail value on the balance sheet. It is a method of pricing inventory at estimated cost by deducting sales from beginning inventory and purchases, both priced at retail, to obtain an estimate of ending inventory at retail. The ending inventory at retail is then reduced by the ratio of cost to retail price.

6-2. The gross profit method of estimating inventory is used when inventory cannot be measured directly, as when inventory is lost or destroyed by theft or fire. Insurance companies often use this method to verify loss claims. It is also used instead of the retail method when records of the retail prices of beginning inventory and purchases are not kept. It may be used for interim reports but is not acceptable for valuing inventory in the annual financial statements.

Chapter 7

1-1. Cash consists of currency and coins on hand, checks and money orders from customers, and deposits in checking and savings accounts. A compensating balance is the minimum amount a bank requires a company to keep in its bank account as part of a credit-granting agreement.

1-2. By extending credit even when it expects that some accounts receivable will not be paid, a company expects to increase sales and make a greater profit overall. The function of a credit department is to decide whether to extend credit to customers.

1-3. **a.** Installment accounts receivable from regular customers are usually considered part of the normal operating cycle, and they are included in accounts receivable on the balance sheet.

b. Debit balances in customers' accounts are included in accounts receivable.

c. Receivables from employees should normally appear in an asset account separate from accounts receivable; whether such a receivable should be a current or other asset depends on the prospects for its collection.

d. Credit balances in customers' accounts are recorded as current liabilities.

e. Receivables from officers of the company should normally appear in an asset account separate from accounts receivable; whether such a receivable should be a current or other asset depends on the prospects for its collection.

1-4. The receivable turnover ratio shows how many times, on average, a company turns its accounts receivable into cash during an accounting period. By using this ratio to determine the days' sales uncollected, it is possible to ascertain how long, on average, the company will have to wait to receive cash from a credit sale.

1-5. A factor is an entity that provides financing by buying or receiving a transfer of a company's accounts receivable in exchange for cash. *Factoring with recourse* means that if the factor is unable to collect the accounts receivable from the customers, the company from which the factor purchased the receivables is liable. *Factoring without recourse* means that the factor shoulders the risk of nonpayment by customers. When factoring without recourse, the factor receives a higher fee than when factoring with recourse.

1-6. Accounting for receivables requires a company to estimate the amount of losses it will have from uncollectible accounts. Because these amounts can only be estimated, they can be easily manipulated to overstate or understate earnings.

2-1. Cash equivalents are investments that have a term to maturity of 90 days or less. For example, certificates of deposit and time deposits are considered cash equivalents if they mature in 90 days or less. Although such investments quickly revert to cash and are treated as cash on the balance sheet, they are not as readily available to pay debts as cash is.

2-2. An imprest system is an effective control over cash because a fund is established at a fixed amount, and the total of funds on hand plus receipts for expenditures must always equal the fixed amount. If they do not, the person responsible for the fund is held accountable.

2-3. A bank reconciliation is the process of accounting for the difference between the balance on a company's bank statement and the balance in its Cash account. These two amounts are reconciled to arrive at the correct cash balance.

3-1. The direct charge-off method violates the matching rule because it does not recognize the loss at the time of the sale.

3-2. According to GAAP, losses on uncollectible accounts occur at the time sales on credit are made. Because the exact amount of the loss is not known at that time, it must be estimated.

3-3. The more optimistic management is about the collection of accounts receivable, the smaller the estimate will be for uncollectible accounts expense. Thus, an optimistic view of collection of accounts receivable results in a higher net income than a pessimistic view does.

3-4. The percentage of net sales method of estimating uncollectible accounts is called an *income statement approach* because the estimate is based on net sales, an income statement account. The accounts receivable aging method is called a *balance sheet approach* because the estimate is based on an evaluation of accounts receivable, a balance sheet account.

3-5. The reasoning behind the percentage of net sales method is that a certain proportion of *net sales* will be uncollectible. The accounts receivable aging method is based on the premise that a certain proportion of *accounts receivable* will uncollectible.

3-6. **a.** The collectible value of Accounts Receivable is \$161,500 (\$176,000 − \$14,500).

b. The collectible value of Accounts Receivable will remain the same, \$161,500 (\$176,000 − \$14,500), because the \$450 account is deducted from both Accounts Receivable and Allowance for Uncollectible Accounts.

4-1. A promissory note is an unconditional promise to pay a definite sum of money on demand or at a future date.

4-2. The person who signs a promissory note and therefore promises to pay is the maker. The person to whom payment should be made is the payee.

4-3. Interest is the cost of borrowing money or the return on lending money. The interest rate is a percentage of the amount borrowed or lent used in determining the amount of interest.

4-4. **a.** November 16

b. November 14

c. May 24

Chapter 8

1-1. Examples of current liabilities are accounts payable, notes payable, wages payable, interest payable, income taxes payable, and unearned revenue.

1-2. Two measures of liquidity used to evaluate a firm's ability to pay its current liabilities are payables turnover and days' payable.

1-3. Payables turnover shows how many times, on average, a company pays its accounts payable in an accounting period. When used to determine days' payable, it shows how many days, on average, a company takes to pay its accounts payable.

1-4. The timing of liability recognition is important because it affects income measurement and financial position. When a liability for an expense is not recorded, income for a period is overstated and liabilities are understated.

1-5. A liability is current if the obligation will be satisfied within one year or within the normal operating cycle, whichever is longer.

1-6. The portion of a line of credit currently borrowed should be shown as a liability in the financial statements. Because Manly has not used any of its line of credit, it does not have to record it as a liability or disclose it in the notes to its financial statements.

2-1. A line of credit allows a company to borrow funds from a bank up to a specified amount to finance current operations. Commercial paper is a means of borrowing funds through unsecured loans that are sold to the public, usually through professionally managed investment firms. Details of both methods of borrowing funds are disclosed in a note to the financial statements.

2-2. When a portion of long-term debt must be paid within one year, it is classified as a current liability.

2-3. Three types of employer-related payroll liabilities are those for employee compensation, for employee payroll withholdings, and for employer payroll taxes.

2-4. Both the employee and the employer pay social security and Medicare taxes.

2-5. Unearned revenues are classified as liabilities because they represent obligations to perform services or deliver goods for which payment has been received in advance.

2-6. An estimated liability is a definite obligation; it is the amount of the liability that must be estimated.

2-7. Income taxes payable are considered estimated liabilities because the amount often cannot be determined until after the end of a company's fiscal year.

2-8. When the estimated amount of discount coupons that will be redeemed is recorded as a contra-sales account, it is treated as any sales discount would be—as a deduction from sales on the income statement. If it is recorded as a promotional expense, it is included in operating expenses, which are also deducted from gross margin on the income statement. In both cases, a current liability is created.

2-9. A company incurs a liability for a product warranty at the time it sells a warranted product.

3-1. A contingent liability is a potential liability; it depends on a future event arising out of a past transaction. It differs from a commitment in that a commitment is a legal obligation that does not meet the requirements for recognition as a liability and so is not recorded.

3-2. Contingent liabilities may arise from lawsuits, income tax disputes, and failure to follow government regulations. In each of these cases, a potential liability exists because if the ruling goes against the company, a liability will arise. Contingent liabilities also exist in the case of discounted notes receivable and loan guarantees because if the debtor does not pay, the company will be liable.

3-3. Leases and purchase agreements are examples of commitments.

4-1. The three approaches to measuring fair value are the market approach, the income approach, and the cost approach.

4-2. The time value of money refers to the costs or benefits derived from holding or not holding money over time.

4-3. Simple interest is the interest for one or more periods when the amount on which the interest is calculated stays the same from period to period. Compound interest is the interest for two or more periods when after each period, the interest earned in that period is added to the amount on which interest is computed in future periods.

4-4. An ordinary annuity is a series of equal payments made at the end of equal periods of time, with compound interest on these payments.

4-5. The key variable that relates present value to future value is time. Present value is the amount that must be invested today at a given rate of interest to produce a given future value.

4-6. Before using the present value tables to compute present value when a compounding period is less than one year, it is necessary to (1) divide the annual interest rate by the number of compounding periods in the year, and (2) multiply the number of periods in one year by the number of years.

5-1. Business decisions very often involve the use of money over time, and any use of money over time has an interest cost, either stated or implied, associated with it. Present value will tell how much future cash payments or receipts are worth today. Thus present value is an important factor in making business decisions.

5-2. Valuing an asset, computing a deferred payment, and accumulating a fund for loan repayment are a few examples of the many ways in which present value is used in financial reporting. Other applications include imputing interest on a noninterest-bearing note, valuing a bond, recording a lease, determining a pension liability, and analyzing the purchase price of a business or asset.

5-3. Businesses can make use of present value any time they are considering alternatives that require an outlay of money and affect future cash flows, such as the purchase of an asset, investing in the development of a new product, or acquiring another company.

Chapter 9

1-1. Long-term assets have a useful life of more than one year, are used in the operation of a business, and are not intended for resale to customers.

1-2. Land is different from other long-term assets because it has an unlimited life and is therefore not depreciated.

1-3. *Depreciation* refers to the periodic allocation of an asset's cost over its useful life. It does not refer to an asset's physical deterioration or decrease in market value over time. *Depletion* and *amortization* refer to the allocation of the cost of natural resources and intangible assets, respectively, over the accounting periods they benefit.

1-4. Asset impairment occurs when a long-term asset loses some or all of its potential to generate revenue. It requires reducing the carrying value of the asset to its fair value, an amount equal to the present value of the expected cash flows. The reduction of carrying value to fair value is recorded as a loss.

1-5. The cash flows (or savings) that a long-term asset is expected to generate are important considerations in the decision to acquire the asset. The cash flows must be sufficient to pay for the asset and provide a satisfactory return. In deciding how to finance the acquisition of a long-term asset, useful life is a consideration because the length of the financing should correspond to the period in which the asset is expected to produce cash flows.

1-6. Free cash flow is the amount of cash that remains after deducting the funds a company must commit to continue operating at its planned level. Its components are net cash flows from operating activities minus dividends minus purchases of plant assets plus sales of plant assets. A positive free cash flow means that a company has met all its cash commitments and has cash available to reduce debt or to expand operations. A negative free cash flow means that it must raise funds from investors or creditors to continue at its planned level.

1-7. In accounting for each of a company's long-term assets, the following questions must be addressed: (1) How is the cost of the long-term asset determined? (2) How should the expired portion of the cost of the long-term asset be allocated against revenues over time? (3) How should subsequent expenditures, such as repairs and additions, be treated? (4) How should disposal of the long-term asset be recorded?

2-1. Capital expenditures are expenditures for the purchase or expansion of long-term assets and are recorded in the asset accounts. Revenue expenditures are expenditures for repairs, maintenance, fuel, and other items necessary to maintain and operate long-term assets; they are recorded in the expense accounts. The distinction is important because capital expenditures are allocated as expenses over time through depreciation, whereas revenue expenditures are expenses in the period in which they occur.

2-2. An addition is an enlargement of an existing facility. A betterment is an improvement of an existing facility that does not add to the physical layout. An extraordinary repair does not add to or better an existing facility, but it significantly extends its estimated useful life or increases its residual value.

2-3. When an addition to a building is charged as a repair expense, income in the current period will be understated, and income in future periods income will be overstated.

2-4. In general, the cost of a long-term asset includes all expenditures reasonable and necessary to get it in place and ready for use.

2-5. Expenditures (a), (c), (d), (e), and (g) should be charged to the computer system's asset account.

2-6. The entry is incorrect. The dock should have been recorded at a cost of $40,000 because that was the amount involved in acquiring the asset. No gain or savings from choosing one alternative over another should be recorded.

3-1. It is useful to think of a plant asset as a bundle of service units because it aids in allocating the cost of the asset over its useful life.

3-2. Obsolescence often shortens the estimated useful life of technical equipment. In this case, if the equipment became obsolete in less than 12 years, the firm would have to depreciate it over the shorter period.

3-3. The company should continue depreciating the building because depreciation is an allocation of cost, not a valuation process.

3-4. Like certain other plant assets, parking lots may seem to last forever, but in reality they eventually have to be replaced or need repairs so massive that they are equivalent to replacement. Parking lots should therefore be depreciated.

3-5. Depreciation is not a valuation process; it is a process of allocating the cost of a plant asset to the periods in which the asset benefits the business.

3-6. The straight-line method is based on the assumption that depreciation depends only on the passage of time, whereas the production method is based on the assumption that depreciation is solely the result of use.

3-7. The principal argument supporting an accelerated depreciation method is that some plant assets provide more and better service in their early years.

3-8. The theory underlying group depreciation is that a group of similar assets will have similar useful lives and residual values. Thus, a depreciation rate applied to the group will approximate depreciation in total rather than for each item individually.

3-9. In revising a depreciation rate, the remaining depreciable cost of the asset should be spread over the remaining years of the asset's revised useful life.

4-1. Depreciation should be computed for the part of a year that precedes the sale of a plant asset because the company has benefited from the use of the long-term asset up to the date of the sale. Under the matching rule, the depreciation for the partial year must be classified as an expense of the period.

4-2. If a plant asset is discarded before the end of its useful life, the amount of loss is equal to its carrying value (cost less accumulated depreciation).

4-3. When an asset is sold for cash, the gain or loss is determined by deducting the carrying value (cost less accumulated depreciation) from the amount of cash received. If the result is positive, a gain results. If it is negative, a loss results.

5-1. Annual depletion differs from depletion expense when not all of the natural resource is sold in the year it is extracted. The part not sold is considered inventory.

5-2. A mining company can depreciate its plant assets over a period less than the assets' useful lives when the assets are so closely associated with the natural resource that they cannot be used after the resource is depleted.

5-3. Successful efforts accounting treats each exploration of oil and gas resources separately. If an exploration is successful, its cost is recorded as an asset; if it is not, its cost is recorded as an expense. The full-costing method records the costs of all explorations, both successful and unsuccessful, as assets.

6-1. Accounts receivable are not classified as intangible assets because of their short-term nature.

6-2. To appear on the balance sheet, intangible assets must be purchased. For example, the cost of developing a patent do not appear on the balance sheet, but if a firm purchases the right to a patent, the purchase cost does appear on the balance sheet.

6-3. The FASB requires that research and development costs be charged as revenue expenditures in the period in which they are incurred.

6-4. Before a technologically feasible software program has been developed, accounting for the costs of development is similar to accounting for research and development costs—that is, costs are expensed as incurred. After a feasible and working software program has been developed, however, the development costs are capitalized and amortized over a reasonable length of time.

6-5. A company should record goodwill only when it acquires a controlling interest in another business. Goodwill can remain on the balance sheet indefinitely. However, it is subject to an annual impairment review. If it is deemed impaired, it is reduced to fair value, and an impairment charge is reported on the income statement.

Chapter 10

1-1. Among the advantages of issuing long-term debt are that common stockholders do not relinquish any control over the company, interest on debt is tax-deductible, and financial leverage may increase a company's earnings. Disadvantages of long-term debt are that interest and principal must be repaid on schedule and financial leverage can work against a company if the earnings from its investments do not exceed its interest payments.

1-2. Interest coverage is important because it is an indicator of how much cushion a company has in making its interest payments. Default on interest payments can throw a company into bankruptcy.

1-3. The two components of a uniform monthly mortgage payment are interest on the debt (principal) and a reduction in the debt.

1-4. A capital lease is, in effect, an installment purchase or sale. The lessee in such a lease should treat it as a purchase made by incurring long-term debt. Thus, both an asset and a liability should be recorded. The income statement would contain deductions for interest expense and depreciation expense.

1-5. A pension plan is a contract that requires a company to pay benefits to its employees after they retire. A pension fund is a fund established by the contributions of an employer and often of employees from which benefits are paid to retirees.

1-6. Under a defined contribution plan, each year's contribution is fixed, but the benefits vary depending on how much the funds earn. Under a defined benefit plan, the benefits are fixed, but the annual contributions vary depending on assumptions about how much the funds will earn.

1-7. Other postretirement benefits include health care and other nonpension benefits provided to retired employees. Because employees earn these benefits during their employment, the FASB holds that in accordance with the matching rule, the benefits should be estimated and accrued during the time employees are working.

2-1. A bond issue is the total amount of bonds issued at one time. A bond certificate is a document that attests to a company's debt to a bondholder. A bond indenture is a contract that defines the rights of the bondholders. A bond indenture generally specifies the maturity date of the bonds, interest payment dates, interest rate, and call features and other restrictions.

2-2. The proceeds from the sale of $500,000 in bonds at 95 would be $475,000; at 100, $500,000; and at 102, $510,000.

2-3. If the face interest rate is less than the market interest rate, one would expect to pay less than par value for the bonds. In a competitive marketplace, investors are unwilling to pay par value for a fixed series of payments when the same funds could earn a higher rate of interest if invested elsewhere.

2-4. **a.** When a bond is issued for more than face value, the amount above face value is a premium. When a bond is sold below face value, the amount below face value is a discount.

b. Secured bonds give the bondholders a pledge of certain corporate assets as a guarantee of payment; unsecured (debenture) bonds do not.

c. When all the bonds of a bond issue mature on the same date, they are term bonds. When the bonds of an issue mature at different times, they are serial bonds.

d. A callable bond enables the issuer to buy back the bond at a specified price. A convertible bond allows the buyer to convert the bond into a specified number of shares of common stock.

e. A company that issues registered bonds maintains a list of the names and addresses of bondholders and pays them interest by check. Holders of coupon bonds must present a coupon at a bank to collect interest.

3-1. When bonds are sold at a discount, the market rate of interest is higher than the face interest rate because as the market interest rate goes up, the price of the bonds goes down.

3-2. When bonds are issued at a premium, the bonds are shown on the balance sheet at the total of the face value plus the premium.

3-3. Bond issue costs increase the discount on a bond issue because they reduce the proceeds from the issue, thereby increasing the difference between the face amount and the total proceeds.

4-1. The value of bonds depends on the series of equal interest payments and the face value, which will be paid at maturity.

4-2. The value of a bond can be determined by adding the present value of the series of equal interest payments to the present value of the single payment of the face value at maturity.

5-1. The total interest cost of a bond issue includes an addition for the amount of a bond discount or a subtraction for the amount of a bond premium.

5-2. The straight-line method is usually acceptable in cases where the difference in interest expense between the straight-line method and the effective-interest method is immaterial.

5-3. The amortization of a bond discount increases interest expense to an amount greater than interest paid because the amount received (borrowed) by the company at issuance is less than the amount that must be paid at maturity. The difference must be added to the total interest cost over the life of the bond. A bond premium has the opposite effect because when the bond matures, the company will pay an amount that is less than the amount it received at issuance.

5-4. Under the effective interest method, the amount of interest expense changes from period to period because the carrying value, on which the interest expense is computed, changes each period by the amount of the discount or premium amortized in the previous period.

6-1. When bond interest rates drop, a company may want to call its bonds and reissue debt at a lower rate. A company may also call its bonds if it has earned enough money to pay off the debt, if the reason for the debt no longer exists, or if it wants to restructure its debt to equity ratio.

6-2. Convertible bonds are advantageous to the issuing corporation because they usually carry a lower interest rate than bonds that are not convertible. In addition, if the market price of the corporation's common stock increases, bondholders will likely convert their bonds to common stock. This allows the corporation to raise equity capital and to avoid paying off the bonds. Despite their lower interest rate, convertible bonds are advantageous to the holder because of the potential gain if the stock price increases. Even if the stock price does not go up, the investor has earned a return and will be paid the face value of the bond at maturity.

7-1. A company collects an amount equal to the accrued interest from the buyer when it issues bonds between interest dates because on the next interest payment date, the holder will receive the full interest payment. This procedure reduces bookkeeping costs.

7-2. In making the year-end accrual for interest on bonds, interest payable and amortization of the premium or discount must be calculated. Together, the two calculations determine the interest expense.

Chapter 11

1-1. Advantages of the corporate form of business include the following:

Separate legal entity. A corporation can buy and sell property, sue other parties, enter into contracts, hire and fire employees, and be taxed.

Limited liability. Creditors can satisfy their claims only against a corporation's assets, not against those of a corporation's owners. Thus, the liability of stockholders is limited to the amount of their investments.

Ease of capital generation. It is fairly easy for a corporation to raise money because its stock is widely available at a relatively low price.

Ease of transfer of ownership. A stockholder can normally buy and sell shares of stock without affecting the corporation's activities and without the approval of other owners.

Lack of mutual agency. A stockholder cannot bind the corporation to a contract.

Continuous existence. Because a corporation is a separate legal entity, an owner's death, incapacity, or withdrawal has no effect on its existence.

Centralized authority and responsibility. The authority and responsibility for operating the corporation are delegated to one person, usually the president, who is accountable to the board and ultimately to the stockholders.

Professional management. Because management and ownership are separate, the corporation can hire the best talent available to operate the business.

1-2. Disadvantages of the corporate form of business include the following:

Government regulation. Corporations must meet the requirements of the laws of the states in which they are chartered. Publicly traded corporations must also file reports with the SEC and with the stock exchanges on which they are listed. Meeting these requirements is costly.

Taxation. Because a corporation is a separate legal entity, its earnings are subject to federal and state income taxes. In addition, stockholders must pay income tax on any dividends they receive. Thus, the earnings of a corporation are taxed twice.

Limited liability. Particularly for small corporations, limited liability can restrict the amount creditors are willing to lend.

Separation of ownership and control. The separation of ownership and control is a disadvantage when a firm's management makes bad decisions.

1-3. The three dates important in paying dividends are the declaration date, which is the date on which the board of directors formally declares that a dividend is going to be paid; the record date, which is the date on which ownership of stock, and thus the right to receive dividends, is determined; and the date of payment, which is the date on which the dividend is paid to the stockholders of record.

1-4. Dividends yield is computed by dividing the dividends per share by the market price per share. Investors use this ratio to evaluate the amount of dividends they receive.

1-5. Management can improve a company's return on equity by increasing earnings or by reducing stockholders' equity (e.g., by issuing debt rather than stock or by buying back the company's own stock on the open market).

1-6. The price/earnings (P/E) ratio is a measure of investors' confidence in a company's future; it is calculated by dividing the market price per share by earnings per share. Usually, the higher a company's P/E ratio, the more confidence the market has in its future earnings.

1-7. A stock option plan gives employees the right to purchase their company's stock under specified terms. Companies adopt stock option plans to motivate employees, as well as to compensate them.

2-1. Common stock is called *residual equity* because if a corporation is liquidated, the claims of creditors and preferred stockholders are paid before those of common stockholders.

2-2. Preferred stock differs from common stock in that it usually has preference over common stock in terms of receiving dividends and in terms of claims to assets when a corporation is liquidated.

2-3. Authorized shares are the maximum number of shares a corporation is allowed to issue. Issued shares are those that a corporation has sold or otherwise transferred to stockholders. Outstanding shares are the number of shares issued and that are in the hands of stockholders.

2-4. Treasury stock—shares that the issuing firm has repurchased—account for the difference between issued shares and outstanding shares.

3-1. Preferred stock's preference as to dividends means that common stockholders cannot receive dividends until after preferred stockholders have received their dividends. Preference as to assets means that in the event of a liquidation, the claims of preferred stockholders to corporate assets have precedence over the claims of common stockholders.

3-2. Cumulative preferred stock is preferred stock on which any unpaid dividends accumulated over time must be paid in full before common stock dividends can be paid. Dividends in arrears are dividends on cumulative preferred stock that have not been paid in the period in which they are due. They should be reported either in the body of the financial statements or in a note.

3-3. Convertible preferred stock can be converted to common stock at the option of the preferred stockholder. When preferred stock is callable, the corporation can redeem or retire the stock by paying a specified price to the stockholder.

4-1. *Par value* is the amount per share recorded in a company's capital stock account; it represents a company's legal capital. *No-par value* refers to capital stock that has no par value. Most states require no-par stock to have a *stated value,* which serves the same purpose as par value.

4-2. The total of par value and additional paid-in capital is more relevant to the analyst than either figure by itself because it represents stockholders' total investments in the company.

4-3. When stock is issued for noncash assets, the transaction is usually recorded at the stock's fair market value. If the stock's fair market value cannot be determined, the fair market value of the assets or services received is used to record the transaction.

5-1. Treasury stock is capital stock, either common or preferred, that the issuing company has reacquired and has not reissued or retired.

5-2. A company might buy back its own stock to have stock available to distribute to employees through stock option plans, to maintain a favorable market for the stock, to increase its earnings per share or stock price per share, to have additional shares of stock available for purchasing other companies, or to prevent takeover attempts.

5-3. The cost of treasury stock is deducted from total contributed capital and retained earnings in the stockholders' equity section of the balance sheet.

Chapter 12

1-1. Quality of earnings refers to the substance of earnings and their sustainability into future accounting periods. Gains and losses on transactions, write-downs and restructurings, and nonoperating items are components of the income statement that affect quality of earnings.

1-2. The reader of financial statements is interested in a company's choice of accounting methods and estimates because of their effect on the company's quality of earnings. For example, by shortening the period over which it depreciates long-term assets, a company can increase its quality of earnings.

1-3. A write-down is a reduction in the value of an asset below its carrying value on the balance sheet. A restructuring is the estimated cost of a change in a company's operations; it usually involves the closing of facilities and layoff of personnel. Both write-downs and restructurings reduce current operating income and boost future income by shifting future costs to the current accounting period. Both appear in the operating (top) portion of a corporate income statement.

1-4. Cash flows relate to quality of earnings in that if earnings have underlying cash flows, they are considered more sustainable and of higher quality. Thus, a company with low earnings and high cash flows has higher quality earnings than a company with high earnings and low cash flows.

2-1. Accounting income and taxable income should not be treated alike because they serve different purposes. The purpose of accounting income is to give some indication (however imperfect) of a business's financial status; the sole purpose of taxable income is to provide a basis for collecting government revenues. Income tax allocation is necessary because of differences between accounting and taxable income caused by the timing of revenues and expenses.

2-2. Deferred income taxes represent the difference between income tax expense and income tax payable. If the former is greater than the latter, a deferred income tax liability exists.

2-3. On the income statement, *net of taxes* means that income taxes have been allocated among the various components of the statement so that each item, such as a gain or loss, is shown at an amount that is net of any tax consequences.

3-1. Earnings per share are disclosed on the income statement and usually appear immediately below the net income figure. They are broken down into income from continuing operations, income before extraordinary items, and net income. If a company reports a gain or loss from discontinued operations or extraordinary items, earnings per share figures are presented for those as well. If a company has potentially dilutive securities, diluted earnings per share must be shown.

3-2. A company has a simple capital structure when it has issued no preferred stocks, bonds, or stock options that can be converted to common stock. A company that has issued securities or stock options that can be converted to common stock has a complex capital structure.

3-3. Diluted earnings per share differ from basic earnings per share in that they take into account the effect of all potentially dilutive securities on earnings per share.

4-1. Comprehensive income consists of items from sources other than stockholders that account for the change in stockholders' equity during an accounting period. Comprehensive income includes net income, changes in unrealized investment gains and losses, gains and losses from foreign currency translation, and other items affecting equity.

4-2. The statement of stockholders' equity summarizes changes in the components of the stockholders' equity section of the balance sheet that occurred during an accounting period. The stockholders' equity section of the balance sheet lists the items of contributed capital and retained earnings on the balance sheet date.

4-3. A company has a deficit in retained earnings when its dividends and subsequent losses exceed its accumulated profits from operations.

5-1. Accounting for a stock dividend and accounting for a cash dividend differ in that in accounting for a cash dividend, dividends payable is credited, and in accounting for a stock dividend, common stock distributable and additional paid-in capital are credited for the amount of the stock dividend measured at market value.

5-2. A stock dividend is a proportional distribution of newly issued shares of stock to stockholders. A stock split divides the shares already owned by stockholders into additional shares according to a predetermined ratio. Both increase the number of shares outstanding.

5-3. A stock dividend results in a transfer of ownership interest from retained earnings to contributed capital. A stock split changes the number and par value of the common stock; it does not change the dollar amount in retained earnings or contributed capital.

6-1. When a corporation has no preferred stock, the book value per share is determined by dividing stockholders' equity by the number of common shares outstanding.

6-2. Book value per share is based on total assets minus total liabilities. Because assets are usually recorded at historical cost, one would not expect book value per share to equal market value per share.

Chapter 13

1-1. In the statement of cash flows, cash includes both cash and cash equivalents. Cash equivalents are short-term (ninety days or less), highly liquid investments, such as money market accounts, commercial paper, and U.S. Treasury bills.

1-2. The primary purpose of the statement of cash flows is to provide information about a company's cash receipts and cash payments during an accounting period. A secondary purpose is to provide information about a company's operating, investing, and financing activities during the period.

1-3. Cash flows are classified under operating, investing, and financing activities. Cash flows related to operating activities include cash receipts from customers for goods and services and from interest and dividends on investments; cash payments for wages, goods, and services; interest paid on debt; and taxes paid. Cash flows related to investing activities include cash received from the sale of long-term assets and marketable securities and the collection of loans, and cash expended for purchases of long-term assets and marketable securities and the making of loans. Cash flows related to financing activities include proceeds from issues of stock, long-term debt, and short-term borrowings; repayment of loans; the purchase of treasury stock; and payments made to owners, including cash dividends.

1-4. Significant noncash investing and financing transactions do not affect current cash flows, but they will affect cash flows in the future. They are therefore disclosed in a separate schedule on the statement of cash flows.

1-5. Analysts consider cash flows from operations an important indicator of the cash flows that underlie earnings, or the quality of earnings. Thus, a company may try to make its cash flows from operating activities look better by placing items that belong in the operating section of the statement of cash flows in the investing or financing sections.

2-1. Cash-generating efficiency is a company's ability to generate cash from current or continuing operations.

2-2. Three ratios that measure cash-generating efficiency are cash flow yield, cash flows to sales, and cash flows to assets.

2-3. Free cash flow is the cash that remains after deducting the funds a company must commit to continue operating at its planned level.

2-4. If free cash flow is positive, it means that the company has met all its planned cash commitments and has cash available to reduce debt or to expand. A negative free cash flow means that the company will have to sell investments, borrow money, or issue stock in the short term to continue at its planned level.

3-1. The direct method adjusts each item on the income statement from an accrual basis to a cash basis. The indirect method does not require the adjustment of each item on the income statement; it lists only the adjustments necessary to convert net income to cash flows from operations.

3-2. A company can have a positive cash flow from operations despite a net loss if it has (1) large amounts of noncash expenses, such as depreciation and amortization; (2) large reductions in accounts receivable, inventories, or other prepaid assets; or (3) large increases in accounts payable, accrued liabilities, or income taxes payable. A positive cash flow occurs if the amount of any one of these items or their combined amount is greater than the net loss.

3-3. Depreciation is deducted from net income on the income statement, but it does not require a cash outlay and so does not affect cash flows in the current period. Thus, to arrive at cash flows from operating activities on the statement of cash flows, depreciation must be added back to net income.

3-4. The cash from the sale of an asset, which includes the amount of a gain, is included in the investing activities section of the statement of cash flows. The gain is also included in net income in the operating activities section. It is deducted in this section to prevent double counting.

3-5. Changes in current assets and current liabilities represent amounts by which the accrual accounting numbers for net income differ from the actual cash received or paid.

Thus, adjustments are necessary to convert the accrual-based net income to cash flows from operating activities.

3-6. When the indirect method is used to determine net cash flows from operating activities, (a) an increase in accounts receivable should be subtracted from net income, (b) a decrease in inventory should be added, (c) an increase in accounts payable should be added, (d) a decrease in wages payable should be subtracted, (e) depreciation expense should be added, and (f) amortization of patents should be added.

4-1. The two major categories of assets that relate to the investing activities section of the statement of cash flows are investments and plant assets.

4-2. A building that cost $50,000, that had accumulated depreciation of $32,000, and that is sold at a loss of $5,000 would result in an increase in cash flow of $13,000 (carrying value of $18,000 less the loss of $5,000). The transaction should be shown as the sale of a building for $13,000 in the investing activities section of the statement of cash flows. If the indirect method is used, the $5,000 loss should be added to net income to determine net cash flows from operating activities.

4-3. The transaction should be disclosed on the schedule of noncash investing and financing transactions that accompanies the statement of cash flows, as follows: Issue of mortgage for buildings and land, $234,000.

5-1. The major categories of liabilities and stockholders' equity that relate to the financing activities section of the statement of cash flows are long-term liabilities, stock issues and repurchases (treasury stock), and cash dividends.

5-2. The conversion of bonds to common stock does not involve cash and does not appear in the financing section of the statement of cash flows. It should, however, be listed in the schedule of noncash investing and financing transactions that accompanies the statement of cash flows.

Chapter 14

1-1. Both investors and creditors use financial performance evaluation in choosing investments that will provide a return commensurate with the risk involved. Each group, however, evaluates a different type of risk. Investors evaluate the risk that dividends and stock price will not meet the required rate of return. Creditors evaluate the risk that a debtor will default on a loan.

1-2. The degree of risk involved in making a loan or investment depends on how easy it is to predict a company's future liquidity or profitability. In return for taking a greater risk, a creditor may demand a higher interest rate, and an investor may look for a higher return.

1-3. Three commonly used standards of comparison for evaluating financial statements are rule-of-thumb measures, a company's past performance, and industry norms. Rule-of-thumb measures are the weakest approach because they do not take into consideration a company's individual characteristics. Comparison of a company's financial measures or ratios over time can be effective, but this standard must be used with care. Industry norms are useful in showing how a company compares with other companies in the same industry.

1-4. A financial analyst might compare Steelco's ratios with those of other steel companies to determine how Steelco ranks in the industry. If Steelco has characteristics that make it different from other steel companies, this comparison would not be valid.

1-5. The major sources of information about public corporations are reports published by the company, reports filed with the SEC, business periodicals, and credit and investment advisory services. Much of this information is available on the Internet.

1-6. A corporation's compensation committee, which is made up of independent directors appointed by the board of directors, is charged with determining how top executives will be paid. The common components of executive compensation are salary, bonuses, and stock options.

2-1. Both horizontal and trend analyses focus on a company's performance over time. However, horizontal analysis focuses on performance from one year to the next, whereas trend analysis has a long-term perspective. Thus, an investor would want to see both types of analyses.

2-2. The statement means that net income in 1990 was set equal to 100 and that net income in 2000 and 2001 was recomputed, or indexed, in reference to net income in 1990. That is, net income in 2000 was 240 percent of net income in 1990 and increased to 260 percent of that figure in 2001.

2-3. Horizontal analysis is a year-to-year analysis of the components of various financial statements. Vertical analysis is concerned with the relationship of items within a single financial statement.

2-4. The purpose of ratio analysis is to identify meaningful relationships between components of the financial statements.

3-1. Although these two companies have the same net income, without more information, it is impossible to conclude that they are equally successful. For example, if one of them had twice as many assets as the other, its return on assets (a measure of profitability) would be only half of the other company's.

3-2. Because Circo Company has a return on assets of 12 percent and a debt to equity ratio of .5, one would expect its return on equity to be more than 12 percent because of its ability to use financial leverage.

3-3. With a profit margin of less than 1 percent, a supermarket would have to maintain a high asset turnover to achieve a satisfactory return on assets.

3-4. The amount of net cash flows from operating activities is common to all cash flow adequacy ratios. These ratios are most closely related to the liquidity and long-term solvency ratios.

3-5. The ratios most relevant to determining the financing period are days' sales uncollected, days' inventory on hand, and days' payable. The longer a company's financing period (Days' Sales Uncollected + Days' Inventory on Hand − Days' Payable), the greater its financing or interest costs will be. Thus, determining the financing period is especially important in periods of high interest rates.

3-6. To determine whether investors are equally confident about the future of Companies J and Q, one would compare the companies' price/earnings (P/E) ratios. The P/E ratio is computed by dividing a company's market price by its earnings per share. A high P/E ratio indicates that investors have a high degree of confidence in a company's future earnings and therefore are willing to accept a lower rate of return.

Chapter 15

1-1. Investments are generally recorded on the date they are made and are valued at cost, which includes any commissions.

1-2. Trading securities are debt or equity securities bought and held principally for the purpose of being sold in the near term. Available-for-sale securities are debt or equity securities that may be sold at any time. Held-to-maturity securities are debt securities that a company intends to hold until their maturity date.

1-3. In accounting for equity investments, the level and percentage of ownership are important because they are factors in determining how the investments should be treated.

1-4. Disclosure of investments is important because it describes how the investments are classified and the methods used to account for them.

1-5. Insider trading is the unethical and illegal practice of using inside information (information not available to the public) for personal gain.

2-1. Trading securities are valued at fair value on the balance sheet date.

2-2. Unrealized gains and losses on trading securities are the differences between the securities' costs and current market values. They are reported on the income statement.

2-3. Accounting for available-for-sale securities differs from accounting for trading securities in two ways: (1) an unrealized gain or loss is reported as a special item in the stockholders' equity section of the balance sheet, not as a gain or loss on the income statement; (2) if a decline in the value of a security is considered permanent, it is charged as a loss on the income statement.

3-1. **a.** Less than 20 percent ownership constitutes a noninfluential and noncontrolling investment; the cost-adjusted-to-market method should be used.

b. A 20 to 50 percent ownership constitutes an influential but noncontrolling investment; the equity method should be used.

c. More than 50 percent ownership constitutes a controlling investment; consolidated financial statements should be prepared.

3-2. A parent-subsidiary relationship exists when a company (the parent) owns more than 50 percent of the voting stock of another company (the subsidiary).

3-3. Although information about American Home Products Corporation's subsidiaries may be helpful in assessing the corporation's performance, stockholders would be interested primarily in its consolidated financial statements because they give an overview of the entire economic entity.

3-4. Under the equity method, the parent company increases or decreases its investment in subsidiaries according to its share of their earnings and dividends. The equity method is required when the parent—in this case, Merchant Corporation—has significant influence over a subsidiary.

4-1. Eliminating entries prevent duplication of accounts in the records of a parent and its subsidiaries and reflect the financial position and operations of the consolidated entity. They are not entered in the accounting records; they appear only on the worksheets used in preparing consolidated financial statements.

4-2. Consolidated statements are valuable because they show the parent and all its subsidiaries as a single operating entity.

4-3. The practice violates the rule that *all* majority-owned subsidiaries must be consolidated.

4-4. Minority interest represents the holdings of owners of less than 50 percent of a subsidiary's voting stock. Minority interest appears on the consolidated balance sheet between long-term liabilities and stockholders' equity or as a separate item in the stockholders' equity section.

4-5. Goodwill from consolidation arises if a parent company (Merchant, in this case) pays more for an investment in a subsidiary than the fair value of the subsidiary's net assets. Goodwill from consolidation is shown on the balance sheet as a separate intangible asset.

4-6. To avoid double counting and overstating accounts, intercompany receivables, payables, sales, and purchases must be eliminated from consolidated financial statements. Only transactions with outside parties should be presented.

4-7. The amount of sales on the consolidated income statement is $1,400,000, or the sales of both companies minus the intercompany sales ($500,000 + $1,000,0000 – $100,000).

4-8. Before consolidating the financial statements of foreign subsidiaries and their parent company, the foreign subsidiaries' financial statements must be translated into the parent company's currency.

5-1. Held-to-maturity securities are debt securities that management intends to hold until their maturity date. They are valued on the balance sheet at cost adjusted for the effects of interest.

5-2. Most long-term bond investments are classified as available-for-sale securities because companies generally do not expect to hold them until their maturity date.

ENDNOTES

Chapter 1

1. *Statement of Financial Accounting Concepts No. 1*, "Objectives of Financial Reporting by Business Enterprises" (Norwalk, Conn.: Financial Accounting Standards Board, 1978), par. 9.
2. Ibid.
3. CVS Caremark Corporation, *Annual Report*, 2007.
4. John D. Stoll, "GM Sees a Cash Burn in 2007," *The Wall Street Journal*, January 12–14, 2007.
5. Rajan, "The Choice of Performance Measures in Annual Bonus Contracts," *The Accounting Review*, April 1997.
6. National Commission on Fraudulent Financial Reporting, *Report of the National Commission on Fraudulent Financial Reporting* (Washington, D.C.: 1987), p. 2.
7. Target Corporation, *Annual Report*, 2007.
8. "Gallup: Accounting Reputation in Recovery," telberg.com, August 22, 2005.
9. Robert Johnson, "The New CFO," *Crain's Chicago Business*, July 19, 2004.
10. Curtis C. Venschoor, "Corporate Performance Is Closely Tied to a Strong Ethical Commitment," *Journal of Business and Society*, Winter 1990; Verschoor, "Does Superior Governance Still Lead to Better Financial Performance?" *Strategic Finance*, October 2004.
11. *Accounting Principles Board Statement No. 4*, "Basic Concepts and Accounting Principles Underlying Financial Statements of Business Enterprises" (New York: AICPA, 1970), par. 138.
12. John D. McKinnon, "US-EU Deal Paves Way for Accounting- Rule Shift," *The Wall Street Journal*, May 1, 2007.
13. *Statement Number 1C*, "Standards of Ethical Conduct for Management Accountants" (Montvale, N.J.: Institute of Management Accountants, 1983; revised 1997).
14. CVS Caremark Corporation, *Annual Report*, 2007.
15. Costco Wholesale Corporation, *Annual Report*, 2006.
16. Southwest Airlines Co., *Annual Report*, 1996.
17. Queen Sook Kim, "Lechters Inc. Files for Chapter 11, Arranges Financing," *The Wall Street Journal*, May 22, 2001.
18. RIM Limited, *Annual Report*, 2007.
19. John D. Stoll, "GM Sees a Cash Burn in 2007," *The Wall Street Journal*, January 12–14, par. 9.

Chapter 2

1. Jeremy Herron, "Boeing Stock Soars on China Order," *The Seattle Times*, April 12, 2006.
2. The Boeing Company, *Annual Report*, 2006.
3. *Statement of Financial Accounting Standards No. 157*, "Fair Value Measurements" (Norwalk, Conn.: Financial Accounting Standards Board, 2007).
4. Intel Corporation, *Annual Report*, 2006.
5. Gary McWilliams, "EDS Accounting Change Cuts Past Earnings by $2.24 Billion," *The Wall Street Journal*, October 28, 2003.
6. The Boeing Company, *Annual Report*, 2006.
7. Ibid.
8. Ibid.
9. Mellon Bank, *Annual Report*, 2006.
10. Nike, Inc., *Annual Report*, 2006.

Chapter 3

1. Netflix, Inc., *Annual Report*, 2007.
2. Ibid.
3. "Microsoft Settles with SEC," CBSNews.com, June 5, 2002.
4. Christopher Lawton and Don Clark, "Dell to Restate 4 Years of Results," *The Wall Street Journal*, August 17, 2007.
5. Securities and Exchange Commission, *Staff Accounting Bulletin No. 10*, 1999.
6. Ken Brown, "Wall Street Plays Numbers Games with Savings, Despite Reforms," *The Wall Street Journal*, July 22, 2003.
7. Netflix, Inc., *Annual Report*, 2007.
8. Ibid.
9. Lyric Opera of Chicago, *Annual Report*, 2007.
10. The Walt Disney Company, *Annual Report*, 2006.

Chapter 4

1. Dell Computer Corporation, Presentation, February 28, 2008.
2. *Financial Accounting Series No. 1570-100*, "Conceptual Framework for Financial Reporting: The Objective of Financial Reporting and Qualitative Characteristics and Constraints of Decision-Useful Financial Reporting Information" (Norwalk, Conn.: Financial Accounting Standards Board, May 29, 2008), p. 1.
3. *Statement of Financial Accounting Concepts No. 2*, "Qualitative Characteristics of Accounting Information" (Norwalk, Conn.: Financial Accounting Standards Board, 1980), par. 20.
4. *Financial Accounting Series No. 1570-100*, "Conceptual Framework for Financial Reporting: The Objective of Financial Reporting and Qualitative Characteristics and Constraints of Decision-Useful Financial Reporting Information" (Norwalk, Conn.: Financial Accounting Standards Board, May 29, 2008), chapters 1 and 2.
5. Dell Computer Corporation, Form 10-K, 2008.
6. "Ex-Chief of WorldCom Is Found Guilty in $11 Billion Fraud," *The New York Times*, March 16, 2005.
7. *Accounting Principles Board Opinion No. 20*, "Accounting Changes" (New York: AICPA, 1971), par. 17.
8. www.fasb.org, July 12, 2008.
9. Securities and Exchange Commission, *Staff Accounting Bulletin No. 99*, 1999.
10. Ray J. Groves, "Here's the Annual Report. Got a Few Hours?" *The Wall Street Journal Europe*, August 26–27, 1994.
11. Roger Lowenstein, "Investors Will Fish for Footnotes in 'Abbreviated' Annual Reports," *The Wall Street Journal*, September 14, 1995.
12. Securities and Exchange Commission, "Rules and Regulations." *Federal Register*, vol. 73, no. 3, January 4, 2008.
13. Belverd E. Needles, Jr., Mark Frigo, and Marian Powers, "Performance Measures and Executive Compensation: Practices of High-Performance Companies," *Studies in Financial and Managerial Accounting* (London: JAI Elsevier Science Ltd.), forthcoming, vol. 18, 2008.
14. Albertson's Inc., *Annual Report*, 2004; Great Atlantic & Pacific Tea Company, *Annual Report*, 2004.

Chapter 5

1. Costco Wholesale Corporation, *Annual Report*, 2007.
2. Helen Shaw, "Former NBC Treasurer Arrested," CFO.com, January 25, 2007.
3. Costco Wholesale Corporation, *Annual Report*, 2007.
4. Jathon Sapsford, "As Cash Fades, America Becomes a Plastic Nation," The Wall Street Journal, July 23, 2004.
5. "US eCommerce: 2005 to 2010," Forester Research, 2007.
6. Joel Millman, "Here's What Happens to Many Lovely Gifts After Santa Rides Off," *The Wall Street Journal*, December 26, 2001.
7. Matthew Rose, "Magazine Revenue at Newsstands Falls in Worst Year Ever," *The Wall Street Journal*, May 15, 2001.
8. American Institute of Certified Public Accountants, *Professional Standards*, vol. 1 (New York: AICPA June 1, 1999), Sec. AU 322.07.
9. KPMG Peat Marwick, "1998 Fraud Survey," 1998.
10. Elizabeth Woyke, "Attention Shoplifters," *Business Week*, September 11, 2006.
11. Costco Wholesale Corporation, *Annual Report*, 2007.
12. Ibid.
13. Amy Merrick, "Starbucks Accuses Employee, Husband of Embezzling $3.7 Million from Firm," *The Wall Street Journal*, November 20, 2000.
14. Sid R. Ewer, "A Roundtrip Ticket to Trouble," *Strategic Finance*, April 2004.

Chapter 6

1. Toyota Motor Corporation, *Annual Report*, 2007.
2. Ibid.
3. Gary McWilliams, "Whirlwind on the Web," *BusinessWeek*, April 7, 1997.
4. Karen Lundebaard, "Bumpy Ride," *The Wall Street Journal*, May 21, 2001.
5. American Institute of Certified Public Accountants, *Accounting Trends & Techniques* (New York: AICPA, 2007).
6. Toyota Motor Corporation, *Annual Report*, 2007.
7. "Cisco's Numbers Confound Some," *International Herald Tribune*, April 19, 2001.
8. "Kmart Posts $67 Million Loss Due to Markdowns," *The Wall Street Journal*, November 10, 2000.
9. Ernst & Young, *U.S. GAAP vs. IFRS: The Basics*, 2007.
10. American Institute of Certified Public Accountants, *Accounting Trends & Techniques* (New York: AICPA, 2007).
11. "SEC Case Judge Rules Crazy Eddie Principals Must Pay $72.7 Million," *The Wall Street Journal*, May 11, 2000.
12. American Institute of Certified Public Accountants, *Accounting Trends & Techniques* (New York: AICPA, 2007).
13. Exxon Mobil Corporation, *Annual Report*, 2006.
14. Ibid.
15. Yamaha Motor Company, Ltd., *Annual Report*, 2007; Pioneer Corporation, *Annual Report*, 2007.

Chapter 7

1. Nike, Inc., *Annual Report*, 2007.
2. Peter Coy and Michael Arndt, "Up a Creek with Lots of Cash," *BusinessWeek*, November 12, 2001.
3. "So Much for Detroit's Cash Cushion," *BusinessWeek*, November 5, 2001.
4. Jesse Drucker, "Sprint Expects Loss of Subscribers," *The Wall Street Journal*, September 24, 2002.
5. Michael Selz, "Big Customers' Late Bills Choke Small Suppliers," *The Wall Street Journal*, June 22, 1994.
6. Deborah Solomon and Damian Paletta, "U.S. Drafts Sweeping Plans to Fight Crisis as Turmoil Worsens in Credit Markets," *The Wall Street Journal*, September 19, 2008.
7. Circuit City Stores, Inc., *Annual Report*, 2004.
8. Heather Timmons, "Do Household's Numbers Add Up?" *BusinessWeek*, December 10, 2001.
9. Steve Daniels, "Bank One Reserves Feed Earnings," *Crain's Chicago Business*, December 15, 2003.
10. Jonathon Weil, "Accounting Scheme Was Straightforward but Hard to Detect," *The Wall Street Journal*, March 20, 2003.
11. Nike, Inc., *Annual Report*, 2007.
12. Ibid.
13. American Institute of Certified Public Accountants, *Accounting Trends & Techniques* (New York: AICPA, 2007).
14. Tom Lauricella, Shefali Anand, and Valerie Bauerlein, "A $34 Billion Cash Fund to Close Up," *The Wall Street Journal*, December 11, 2007.
15. Jathon Sapsford, "As Cash Fades, America Becomes a Plastic Nation," *The Wall Street Journal*, July 23, 2004.
16. American Institute of Certified Public Accountants, *Accounting Trends & Techniques* (New York: AICPA, 2007).
17. "Bad Loans Rattle Telecom Vendors," *BusinessWeek*, February 19, 2001.
18. Scott Thurm, "Better Debt Bolsters Bottom Lines," *The Wall Street Journal*, August 18, 2003.
19. Nike, Inc., *Annual Report*, 2007.
20. Information based on promotional brochures of Mitsubishi Corp.
21. Elizabeth McDonald, "Unhatched Chickens," *Forbes*, February 19, 2001.
22. Fosters Group Limited, *Annual Report*, 2007; Heineken N.V., *Annual Report*, 2007.
23. Rhonda L. Rundle and Paul Davies, "Hospitals Administer Antidote for Bad Debt," *The Wall Street Journal*, May 4, 2004.

Chapter 8

1. Microsoft, *Annual Report*, 2007.
2. Pamela L. Moore, "How Zerox Ran Short of Black Ink," *BusinessWeek*, October 30, 2000.
3. Mark Heinzel, Deborah Solomon, and Joanne S. Lublin, "Nortel Board Fires CEO and Others," *The Wall Street Journal*, April 29, 2004.
4. Hershey Foods Corporation, *Annual Report*, 2006.
5. Goodyear Tire & Rubber Company, *Annual Report*, 2006.
6. Andersen Enterprise Group, cited in Crain's *Chicago Business*, July 5, 1999.
7. Promomagazine.com, July 6, 2005.
8. Scott McCartney, "Your Free Flight to Mars Is Hobbling the Airline Industry," *The Wall Street Journal*, February 4, 2004.
9. Hershey Foods Corporation, *Annual Report*, 2007.
10. *Statement of Financial Accounting Standards No. 5*, "Accounting for Contingencies" (Norwalk, Conn.: Financial Accounting Standards Board, 1975).
11. American Institute of Certified Public Accountants, *Accounting Trends & Techniques* (New York: AICPA, 2007).
12. Microsoft, *Annual Report*, 2007.
13. American Institute of Certified Public Accountants, *Accounting Trends & Techniques* (New York: AICPA, 2007).

14. *Statement of Financial Accounting Standards No. 157*, "Fair Value Measures" (Norwalk, Conn.: Financial Accounting Standards Board, 1975).
15. "Clarifications on Fair Value Accounting," U.S. Security and Exchange Commission, *Release 2008-234*, October 1, 2008.
16. WorldCom (MCI), *Annual Report*, 2004.
17. Advertisement, *Chicago Tribune*, December 2007.
18. Sun Microsystems Inc., *Annual Report*, 2007; Cisco Systems, Inc., *Annual Report*, 2007.
19. General Motors Corporation, *Annual Report*, 2006.
20. Advertisement, *Chicago Tribune*, 2000.

Chapter 9

1. Apple Computer, Inc., *Annual Report*, 2007.
2. *Statement of Financial Accounting Standards No. 144*, "Accounting for the Impairment or Disposal of Long-Lived Assets" (Norwalk, Conn.: Financial Accounting Standards Board, 2001).
3. Sharon Young, "Large Telecom Firms, After WorldCom Moves, Consider Writedowns, *The Wall Street Journal*, March 18, 2003.
4. Edward J. Riedl, "An Examination of Long-Lived Asset Impairments," *The Accounting Review*, vol. 79, No. 3, pp. 823–252.
5. *Statement of Financial Accounting Standards No. 34*, "Capitalization of Interest Cost" (Norwalk, Conn.: Financial Accounting Standards Board, 1979).
6. American Institute of Certified Public Accountants, *Accounting Trends & Techniques* (New York: AICPA, 2007).
7. Ibid.
8. Jonathan Weil, "Oil Reserves Can Sure Be Slick," *The Wall Street Journal*, March 11, 2004.
9. *Statement of Financial Accounting Standards No. 25*, "Suspension of Certain Accounting Requirements for Oil and Gas Producing Companies" (Norwalk, Conn.: Financial Accounting Standards Board, 1979).
10. *Statement of Financial Accounting Standards No. 142*, "Goodwill and Other Intangible Assets" (Norwalk, Conn.: Financial Accounting Standards Board, 2001), par. 11–17.
11. "The Top 100 Brands," *BusinessWeek Online*, 2007.
12. The New York Times Company, *Annual Report*, 2006.
13. General Motors Corporation, *Annual Report*, 2006.
14. Abbott Laboratories, *Annual Report*, 2006.
15. *Statement of Financial Accounting Standards No. 2*, "Accounting for Research and Development Costs" (Norwalk, Conn.: Financial Accounting Standards Board, 1974), par. 12.
16. *Statement of Financial Accounting Standards No. 86*, "Accounting for the Costs of Computer Software to Be Sold, Leased, or Otherwise Marketed" (Norwalk, Conn.: Financial Accounting Standards Board, 1985).
17. General Mills, Inc., *Annual Report*, 2007; H. J. Heinz Company, *Annual Report*, 2007; Cisco Systems, *Annual Report*, 2007.
18. *Statement of Financial Accounting Standards No. 142*, "Goodwill and Other Intangible Assets" (Norwalk, Conn.: Financial Accounting Standards Board, 2001), par. 11–17.
19. Southwest Airlines Co., *Annual Report*, 2002.
20. Costco Wholesale Corporation, *Annual Report*, 2007.
21. IBM Corporation, *Annual Report*, 2007.
22. Hilton Hotels Corporation, *Annual Report*, 2006; Marriott International, Inc., *Annual Report*, 2006.
23. "Stock Gives Case the Funds He Needs to Buy New Technology," *BusinessWeek*, April 15, 1996.
24. Polaroid Corporation, *Annual Report*, 1997.

Chapter 10

1. McDonald's Corporation, *Annual Report*, 2007.
2. Ibid.
3. Lee Hawkins, Jr., "S&P Cuts Rating on GM and Ford to Junk Status," *The Wall Street Journal*, May 6, 2005.
4. David Reilly and Silvia Ascarelli, "History Is Made (Again) in Convertibles Boom," *The Wall Street Journal*, July 9, 2003.
5. *Statement of Financial Accounting Standards No. 13*, "Accounting for Leases" (Norwalk, Conn.: Financial Accounting Standards Board, 1976), par. 10.
6. *Statement of Financial Accounting Standards No. 158*, "Employers' Accounting for Defined Benefit Pension and Other Postretirement Plans" (Norwalk, Conn.: Financial Accounting Standards Board, 2007).
7. General Motors Corporation, Form 10-K, 2007.
8. Deborah Soloman, "After Pension Fund Debacle, San Diego Is Mired in Probes," *The Wall Street Journal*, October 10, 2005.
9. Mary Williams Walsh, "$58 Billion Shortfall for New Jersey Retiree Care," *The New York Times*, July 25, 2007.
10. *Statement of Financial Accounting Standards No. 106*, "Employers' Accounting for Postretirement Benefits Other Than Pensions" (Norwalk, Conn.: Financial Accounting Standards Board, 1990).
11. General Motors Corporation, *Annual Report*, 2007.
12. Adapted from quotations in *The Wall Street Journal Online*, December 18, 2007.
13. Bill Barnhart, "Bond Bellwether," *Chicago Tribune*, December 4, 1996.
14. Accounting Principles Board, *Opinion No. 21*, "Interest on Receivables and Payables" (New York: AICPA, 1971), par. 15.
15. Continental Airlines, *Annual Report*, 2007.
16. Tom Sullivan and Sonia Ryst, "Kodak $1 Billion Issue Draws Crowds," *The Wall Street Journal*, October 8, 2003.
17. *The Wall Street Journal Online*, December 19, 2007.
18. "How Borrowing Yields Dividends at Many Firms," *The Wall Street Journal*, March 27, 2007.
19. Amazon.com, *Annual Report*, 2007.
20. Stanley Ziemba, "TWA, American Revise O'Hare Gate Agreement," *The Wall Street Journal*, May 13, 1992.
21. Ibid.
22. Sony Corporation, *Annual Report*, 2007; Panasonic, *Annual Report*, 2007.

Chapter 11

1. Google, Inc., Form S-1 (Registration Statement), 2004; *Annual Report*, 2007.
2. Microsoft Corporation, *Annual Report*, 2007.
3. Deborah Solomon, "AT&T Slashes Dividends 83%, Cuts Forecasts," *The Wall Street Journal*, December 21, 2002.
4. Abbott Laboratories, *Annual Report*, 2004.
5. Google, Inc., Form S-1 (Registration Statement), 2004.
6. Microsoft Corporation, *Annual Report*, 2007.
7. American Institute of Certified Public Accountants, *Accounting Trends & Techniques* (New York: AICPA, 2006).

8. *Statement of Accounting Standards No. 123*, "Stock-Based Payments" (Norwalk, Conn.: Financial Accounting Standards Board, 1995; amended 2004).
9. Google, Inc., Form S-1 (Registration Statement), 2004, p. 136.
10. David Henry, "How the Options Mess Got So Ugly and Expensive," *BusinessWeek*, September 11, 2006.
11. Joseph Weber, "One Share, Many Votes," *BusinessWeek*, March 29, 2004; "A Class (B) Act, *BusinessWeek*, May 28, 2007.
12. Michael Rapoport and Jonathan Weil, "More Truth-in-Labeling for Accounting Carries Liabilities," *The Wall Street Journal*, August 23, 2003.
13. "The FASB's Basic Ownership Approach and a Reclassification of Preferred Stock as a Liability," www.CFO.com, July 18, 2008.
14. American Institute of Certified Public Accountants, *Accounting Trends & Techniques* (New York: AICPA, 2006).
15. David Henry, "The Dirty Little Secret About Buybacks," *BusinessWeek*, January 23, 2006; Peter A. McKay and Justin Lahart, "Boom in Buybacks Helps Lift Stocks to Record Heights," *The Wall Street Journal*, July 18, 2007.
16. Marissa Marr, "DreamWorks Shares Rise 38% on First Day," *The Wall Street Journal*, October 10, 2004; *Yahoo Finance*, December 26, 2007.
17. Tom Herman, "Preferreds' Rich Yields Blind Some Investors to Risks," *The Wall Street Journal*, March 24, 1992.
18. IBM Corporation, *Annual Report*, 2006.
19. Stanley Ziemba, "USAir Defers Dividends on Preferred Stock," *Chicago Tribune*, September 30, 1994.
20. Susan Carey, "US Airways to Redeem Preferred Owned by Berkshire Hathaway," *The Wall Street Journal*, February 4, 1998.

Chapter 12

1. Motorola, Inc., *Annual Report*, 2007.
2. Cited in *The Week in Review* (Deloitte Haskins & Sells), February 28, 1985.
3. "Up to the Minute, Down to the Wire," *Twentieth Century Mutual Funds Newsletter*, 1996.
4. "After Charge for Licensing, McDonald's Posts a Record Loss," *The New York Times*, July 25, 2007; Christina Cheddar Berk, "Campbell's Profit Jumps 31 Percent," *The Wall Street Journal*, November 22, 2005.
5. American Institute of Certified Public Accountants, *Accounting Trends & Techniques* (New York: AICPA, 2007).
6. Elizabeth MacDonald, "Pro Forma Puff Jobs," *Forbes*, December 9, 2002.
7. Gary M. Entwistle, Glenn D. Felham, and Chima Mbagwu, "Financial Reporting Regulation and the Reporting of Pro Forma Earnings," *Accounting Horizons*, March 2006.
8. *Statement of Financial Accounting Standards No. 145*, "Recission and Amendments of Various Statements" (Norwalk, Conn.: Financial Accounting Standards Board, 2002).
9. Jesse Drucker, "Motorola's Profit: Special Again?" *The Wall Street Journal*, October 15, 2002.
10. *Statement of Accounting Standards No. 109*, "Accounting for Income Taxes" (Norwalk, Conn.: Financial Accounting Standards Board, 1992).
11. American Institute of Certified Public Accountants, *Accounting Trends & Techniques* (New York: AICPA, 2007).
12. *Accounting Principles Board, Opinion No. 15*, "Earnings per Share" (New York: AICPA, 1969), par. 12.
13. *Statement of Financial Accounting Standards No. 128*, "Earnings per Share and the Disclosure of Information About Capital Structure" (Norwalk, Conn.: Financial Accounting Standards Board, 1997).
14. *Statement of Financial Accounting Standards No. 130*, "Reporting Comprehensive Income" (Norwalk, Conn.: Financial Accounting Standards Board, 1997).
15. American Institute of Certified Public Accountants, *Accounting Trends & Techniques* (New York: AICPA, 2007).
16. American Institute of Certified Public Accountants, *Accounting Research Bulletin No. 43* (New York: AICPA, 1953), chap. 7, sec. B, par. 10.
17. Ibid., par. 13.
18. Nike, *Annual Report*, 2007.
19. Robert O'Brien, "Tech's Chill Fails to Stem Stock Splits," *The Wall Street Journal*, June 8, 2000.
20. *YahooFinance.com*, 2007.
21. "Technology Firms Post Strong Earnings but Stock Prices Decline Sharply," *The Wall Street Journal*, January 21, 1988; Donald R. Seace, "Industrials Plunge 57.2 Points—Technology Stocks' Woes Cited," *The Wall Street Journal*, January 21, 1988.
22. Rebecca Buckman, "Microsoft Posts Hefty 18% Revenue Rise," *The Wall Street Journal*, January 18, 2002; William M. Bulkeley, "IBM Reports 13% Decline in Net Income," *The Wall Street Journal*, January 18, 2002.

Chapter 13

1. Amazon.com, *Form 10-K*, 2007.
2. Ian McDonald, "Cash Dilemma: How to Spend It," *The Wall Street Journal*, May 24, 2006; Ian McDonald, "Companies Are Rolling in Cash. Too Bad," *The Wall Street Journal*, August 20, 2006.
3. "Deadweight on the Markets," *BusinessWeek*, February 19, 2001.
4. "Free Cash Flow Standouts," *Upside Newsletter*, October 3, 2005.
5. Amazon.com, Inc., *Form 10-K*, 2007.
6. Gary Slutsker, "Look at the Birdie and Say: "Cash Flow,'" *Forbes*, October 25, 1993.
7. Jonathan Clements, "Yacktman Fund Is Bloodied but Unbowed," *The Wall Street Journal*, November 8, 1993.
8. Jeffery Laderman, "Earnings, Schmearnings—Look at the Cash," *BusinessWeek*, July 24, 1989.
9. Amazon.com, Inc., *Form 10-K*, 2007.
10. American Institute of Certified Public Accountants, *Accounting Trends & Techniques* (New York: AICPA, 2006).
11. Martin Peers and Robin Sidel, "WorldCom Causes Analysts to Evaluate EBITDA's Role," *The Wall Street Journal*, July 15, 2002.
12. Richard Passov, "How Much Cash Does Your Company Need?" *Harvard Business Review*, November 2003.
13. "Cash Flow Shortfall in Quarter May Lead to Default on Loan," *The Wall Street Journal*, September 4, 2001.
14. Enron Corporation, *Press Release*, October 16, 2001.
15. Sony Corporation, *Annual Report*, 2007; Panasonic, *Annual Report*, 2007.

16. Chip Meyers, "The Last Laugh," *Business 2.0*, September 2002.
17. Dean Foust, "So Much Cash, So Few Dividends," *Business-Week*, January 20, 2003.

Chapter 14

1. Starbucks Corporation, *Annual Report*, 2007 (profit margin computed).
2. Craig Schneider, "Stock Options, Meet Pro Forma," *CFO.com*, October 31, 2005.
3. David Henry, "The Numbers Game," *BusinessWeek*, May 14, 2001.
4. *Statement of Financial Accounting Standards No. 131*, "Segment Disclosures" (Norwalk, Conn.: Financial Accounting Standards Board, 1997).
5. Starbucks Corporation, *Annual Report*, 2007.
6. Starbucks Corporation, *Proxy*, 2007.
7. Starbucks Corporation, *Proxy*, 2008; Walgreens, Inc., *Proxy*, 2008; Target, *Proxy*, 2008.
8. Starbucks Corporation, *Annual Report*, 2007.
9. Lee Hawkins Jr., "S&P Cuts Rating on GM and Ford to Junk Status," *The Wall Street Journal*, May 6, 2005.
10. H. J. Heinz Company, *Annual Report*, 2007.
11. Jesse Drucker, "Performance Bonus Out of Reach? Move the Target," *The Wall Street Journal*, April 29, 2003.
12. Pfizer, Inc., *Annual Report*, 2006; Roche Group, *Annual Report*, 2006.

Chapter 15

1. eBay, Inc., *Annual Report*, 2007.
2. *Statement of Financial Accounting Standards No. 157*, "Fair Value Measurements" (Norwalk, Conn.: Financial Accounting Standards Board, 2007); *Statement of Financial Accounting Standards No. 159*, "The Fair Value Option for Financial Assets and Financial Liabilities" (Norwalk, Conn.: Financial Accounting Standards Board, 2007).
3. *Statement of Financial Accounting Standards No. 115*, "Accounting for Certain Investments in Debt and Equity Securities" (Norwalk, Conn.: Financial Accounting Standards Board, 1993).
4. Holman W. Jenkins, Jr., "Mark to Meltdown," *The Wall Street Journal*, March 3, 2008.
5. eBay, Inc., *Annual Report*, 2007.
6. Jalal Soroosh and Jack T. Ciesielski, "Accounting for Special Purpose Entities Revised," FASB Interpretation (46R), *The CPA Journal*, July 2004.
7. Greg Steinmetz and Cacilie Rohwedder, "SAP Insider Probe Points to Reforms Needed in Germany," *The Wall Street Journal*, May 8, 1997.
8. Kathryn Kranhold and Deborah Solomon, "GE Restates Several Years of Earnings," *The Wall Street Journal*, May 9, 2005.
9. eBay, Inc., *Annual Report*, 2007.
10. *Statement of Financial Accounting Standards No. 115*, "Accounting for Certain Investments in Debt and Equity Securities" (Norwalk, Conn.: Financial Accounting Standards Board, 1993).
11. eBay, Inc., *Annual Report*, 2007.
12. *Statement of Financial Accounting Standards No. 94*, "Consolidation of All Majority-Owned Subsidiaries" (Norwalk, Conn.: Financial Accounting Standards Board, 1987).
13. eBay, Inc., *Annual Report*, 2007.
14. *Statement of Financial Accounting Standards No. 160*, "Noncontrolling Interest in Consolidated Financial Statements" (Norwalk, Conn.: Financial Accounting Standards Board, 2007).
15. Accounting Principles Board, Opinion No. 16, "Business Combinations" (New York: AICPA, 1970).
16. eBay, Inc., *Annual Report*, 2007.
17. Ibid.
18. Dell Computer Corporation, *Annual Report*, 2007.
19. DreamWorks Animation, *SEC Form 10Q*, 2006.
20. Microsoft Corporation, *Annual Report*, 2007.

COMPANY NAME INDEX

SUBJECT INDEX

Note: **Boldface** type indicates key terms.

Chapter 1 Check Figures

P 1. No check figure
P 2. Total assets, Set C: $1,900; Total liabilities and stockholders' equity, Set A: $2,700; Total liabilities and stockholders' equity, Set B: $26,000
P 3. Total assets: $122,800
P 4. Total assets: $28,300
P 5. No check figure
P 6. Total assets, Set A: $6,690; Total liabilities and stockholders' equity, Set B: $30,000; Total liabilities and stockholders' equity, Set C: $580
P 7. Total assets: $168,450
P 8. Total assets: $22,500

Chapter 2 Check Figures

P 1. Total assets: $72,790
P 2. No check figure
P 3. Trial balance: $17,200
P 4. Trial balance: $10,540
P 5. Trial balance: $30,900
P 6. Total assets: $28,940
P 7. Trial balance: $18,800
P 8. Trial balance: $24,005

Chapter 3 Check Figures

P 1. No check figure
P 2. No check figure
P 3. Adjusted trial balance: $111,412
P 4. Adjusted trial balance: $33,735
P 5. Adjusted trial balance: $678,759
P 6. No check figure
P 7. No check figure
P 8. Adjusted trial balance: $128,778

Supplement to Chapter 3 Check Figures

P 1. Total assets: $627,800
P 2. Adjusted trial balance, May 31: $10,338
Adjusted trial balance, June 30: $10,908
P 3. Net income: $78,622
P 4. Net income: $25,196

Chapter 4 Check Figures

P 1. No check figure
P 2. Income from operations: 2011: $34,320; 2010: $84,748
P 3. Total assets: $597,600
P 4. No check figure
P 5. Net income: $36,130; Total assets: $541,900
P 6. No check figure
P 7. Income from operations: 2010: $66,426; 2009: $110,628
P 8. No check figure

Chapter 5 Check Figures

P 1. Net income: $5,522
P 2. No check figure
P 3. Net income: $2,435
P 4. No check figure
P 5. No check figure
P 6. Net income: $13,435
P 7. No check figure
P 8. Net income: $18,941
P 9. No check figure

Chapter 6 Check Figures

P 1. 1. Cost of goods available for sale: $5,280,000
P 2. 2. Cost of goods sold: April, $19,000; May, $43,760
P 3. 1. Cost of goods sold: April, $19,320; May, $44,237
P 4. 3. Estimated inventory shortage: At cost, $12,104; At retail, $17,800
P 5. 1. Estimated loss of inventory in fire: $326,513.5
P 6. 1. Cost of goods available for sale: $78,990
P 7. 1. Cost of goods sold: March, $9,157; April, $21,319
P 8. 2. Cost of goods sold: March, $9,000; April, $21,080

Chapter 7 Check Figures

P 1. 1. Adjusted book balance: $55,485.60
P 2. 2. Uncollectible accounts expense: percentage of net sales method, $49,930; accounts receivable aging method, $54,200
P 3. 4. Amount of uncollectible accounts expense: $72,713
P 4. 2. Total accrued interest income as of June 30: $964.11
P 5. 1. Adjusted book balance: $148,464.28
P 6. 2. Uncollectible accounts expense: percentage of net sales method, $8,976; accounts receivable aging method, $7,850
P 7. 4. Amount of uncollectible accounts expense: $9,091

Chapter 8 Check Figures

P 1. No check figure
P 2. December 31 Interest Expense: $852.16
P 3. 1.b. Estimated Product Warranty Liability: $10,080
P 4. Total current liabilities: $20,152.10
P 5. PV of liability: $375,500; Cost of buyout: $158,500
P 6. June 30 Interest Expense: $276.16
P 7. 1.b. Estimated Product Warranty Liability: $5,400
P 8. Initial deposit: $55,125; Purchase price: $199,650